CHILD DEVELOPMENT

Fourteenth Edition

JOHN W. SANTROCK
University of Texas at Dallas

Mc Graw Hill Education

CHILD DEVELOPMENT, FOURTEENTH EDITION

Published by McGraw-Hill Education, 2 Penn Plaza, New York, NY 10121. Copyright © 2014 by
McGraw-Hill Education. All rights reserved. Printed in the United States of America. Previous editions
© 2011, 2009, and 2007. No part of this publication may be reproduced or distributed in any form or
by any means, or stored in a database or retrieval system, without the prior written consent of
McGraw-Hill Education, including, but not limited to, in any network or other electronic storage or
transmission, or broadcast for distance learning.

Some ancillaries, including electronic and print components, may not be available to customers outside the
United States.

This book is printed on acid-free paper.

9 10 11 12 13 14 QVS/QVS 23 22 21 20 19

ISBN 978-0-07-803533-3
MHID 0-07-803533-3

Senior Vice President, Products & Markets: *Kurt L. Strand*
Vice President, General Manager, Products & Markets: *Michael Ryan*
Vice President, Content Production & Technology Services: *Kimberly Meriwether David*
Managing Director: *William Glass*
Director: *Mike Sugarman*
Senior Brand Manager: *Allison McNamara*
Senior Director of Development: *Dawn Groundwater*
Digital Development Editor: *Sarah Colwell*
Marketing Manager: *Ann Helgerson*
Director, Content Production: *Terri Schiesl*
Content Project Manager: *Sheila M. Frank*
Buyer: *Nichole Birkenholz*
Design: *Trevor Goodman*
Lead Content Licensing Specialist: *Carrie K. Burger*
Compositor: *Aptara®, Inc.*
Typeface: *9.5/12 Minion Pro*
Printer: *Quad/Graphics*

All credits appearing on page or at the end of the book are considered to be an extension of the
copyright page.

Library of Congress Cataloging-in-Publication Data
Santrock, John W.
    Child development / John W. Santrock. — Fourteenth edition.
        pages cm
    Includes bibliographical references and index.
    ISBN 978-0-07-803533-3—ISBN 0-07-803533-3 (hard copy : alk. paper)
    1. Child development. 2. Child psychology. I. Title.
    RJ131.S264 2014
    618.92—dc23

                                                            2013013636

The Internet addresses listed in the text were accurate at the time of publication. The inclusion of a website
does not indicate an endorsement by the authors or McGraw-Hill Education, and McGraw-Hill Education
does not guarantee the accuracy of the information presented at these sites.

www.mhhe.com

With special appreciation to
my wife, Mary Jo; my children, Tracy and Jennifer;
and my grandchildren, Jordan, Alex, and Luke

about the **author**

John W. Santrock

John Santrock received his Ph.D. from the University of Minnesota in 1973. He taught at the University of Charleston and the University of Georgia before joining the program in Psychology and Human Development at the University of Texas at Dallas, where he currently teaches a number of undergraduate courses.

John Santrock (center) teaching an undergraduate psychology course.

John has been a member of the editorial boards of *Child Development* and *Developmental Psychology*. His research on father custody is widely cited and used in expert witness testimony to promote flexibility and alternative considerations in custody disputes. John also has authored these exceptional McGraw-Hill texts: *Psychology* (7th edition), *Children* (12th edition), *Adolescence* (14th edition), *Life-Span Development* (14th edition), and *Educational Psychology* (5th edition).

For many years John was involved in tennis as a player, a teaching professional, and a coach of professional tennis players. At the University of Miami (Florida), the tennis team on which he played still holds the NCAA Division I record for most consecutive wins (137) in any sport. His wife, Mary Jo, has a master's degree in special education and has worked as a teacher and a Realtor. He has two daughters—Tracy, who is a Realtor, and Jennifer, who is a medical sales specialist. He has one granddaughter, Jordan, age 21, currently an undergraduate student at Southern Methodist University, and two grandsons, Alex, age 8, and Luke, age 7. In the last decade, John also has spent time painting expressionist art.

brief contents

contents

SECTION 4   SOCIOEMOTIONAL DEVELOPMENT   278

expert consultants

Child development has become an enormous, complex field, and no single author, or even several authors, can possibly keep up with all of the rapidly changing content in the many different areas of child development. To solve this problem, author John Santrock sought the input of leading experts about content in a number of areas of child development. The experts provided detailed evaluations and recommendations in their area(s) of expertise.

The following individuals are among those who served as expert consultants for one or more of the previous thirteen editions of this text:

Claire Kopp, *University of California—Los Angeles*

Ross Thompson, *University of California—Davis*

Joan Grusec, *University of Toronto*

Hill Goldsmith, *University of Wisconsin*

Deanna Kuhn, *Columbia University*

Robert J. Sternberg, *University of Oklahoma*

Dante Cicchetti, *University of Minnesota*

Susan Harter, *University of Denver*

Scott Johnson, *University of California—Los Angeles*

Diane Hughes, *New York University*

Kirby Deater-Deckhard, *Virginia Tech University*

Tiffany Field, *University of Miami (Florida)*

Herb Pick, *University of Minnesota*

Cynthia Garcia Coll, *Brown University*

Robert Siegler, *Carnegie Mellon University*

Mary Gauvain, *University of California—Riverside*

Steven Ceci, *Cornell University*

Celia Brownell, *University of Pittsburgh*

Michael Lamb, *University of London*

Carolyn Saarni, *Sonoma State University*

Jeffrey Lachman, *Tulane University*

W. Andrew Collins, *University of Minnesota*

Catherine McBride-Chang, *The Chinese University of Hong Kong*

Daniel Hart, *Rutgers University*

Janet Spence, *University of Texas—Austin*

Lawrence Walker, *University of British Columbia*

Dale Schunk, *University of North Carolina—Greensboro*

Following are the biographies of the expert consultants for the fourteenth edition of this text, who (like the expert consultants for the previous editions) literally represent a Who's Who in the field of child development.

Rachel Keen Dr. Rachel Keen is widely recognized as one of the world's leading experts on children's motor and perceptual development. Formerly Rachel Keen Clifton, she currently is a professor of psychology at the University of Virginia and previously held that position at the University of Massachusetts–Amherst. Dr. Keen obtained her Ph.D. at the Institute of Child Development at the University of Minnesota. She is a former president of the International Society on Infant Studies and recently received the Distinguished Scientist Award from the Society for Research in Child Development. Dr. Keen has been awarded research grants from the National Institutes of Health, the National Science Foundation, and the March of Dimes. She held a Research Science Award from the National Institute of Mental Health for 20 years. Dr. Keen has served on the editorial boards of *Developmental Psychology, Child Development, Infant Behavior and Development,* and the *Journal of Experimental Child Psychology.* She also is a former editor of the *Monographs of the Society for Child Development.*

". . . the coverage of materials and writing style remain at the same high level as in previous editions of this text. . . . Every textbook author must be highly selective, but John Santrock has done an excellent job of using classical studies to lay the groundwork and recent research to keep the presentation cutting-edge. Strengths include

Santrock's careful reading and assessment of the literature, a clear and friendly writing style, openness to new ideas and ways of presenting material, use of good figures to illustrate points, and the 'connections' feature to help students relate material across chapters. . . . the framework is strong. Ideas flow from one section to the other, and are as fully developed as is possible for an undergraduate text. The learning goal sections will help students to come away from the text and retain the material." —**Rachel Keen**

Michael Lewis Dr. Michael Lewis is widely recognized as one of the world's leading experts on children's socioemotional development. He currently is University Distinguished Professor of Pediatrics and Psychiatry, and Director of the Institute for the Study of Child Development at Robert Wood Johnson Medical School. Dr. Lewis also is Professor of Psychology, Education, and Biomedical Engineering at Rutgers University and serves on the Executive Committee of the Cognitive Science Center. He has written and edited more than 35 books including *Social Cognition and the Acquisition of Self,* (1979), *Children's Emotions and Moods,* (1983), and his *Handbook of Emotions* (1993; 2000; 2008) which was awarded the 1995 Choice Magazine's Outstanding Academic Book Award, *Shame, The Exposed Self* (1992), and *Altering*

Fate: Why The Past Does Not Predict The Future (1997). Dr. Lewis recently edited *The Cambridge Handbook of Environment in Human Development* (2012) and is currently working on the third edition of the *Handbook of Developmental Psychopathology.* His most recent book, *The Development of Emotional Life,* is scheduled to be published in 2014 by Guilford Press. In addition, Dr. Lewis has had published over more than 350 articles and chapters published in professional journals and scholarly texts. Among his honors, Dr. Lewis is a Fellow of the New York Academy of Sciences, American Psychological Association, and the American Association of the Advancement of Science, as well as the Japan Society for the Promotion of Science. In 2009, Dr. Lewis received the 2009 Urie Bronfenbrenner Award for Lifetime Contribution to Developmental Psychology in the Service of Science and Society from the American Psychological Association, and in 2012 The New York Zero-to-Three Network honored Dr. Lewis with the Hedi Levenback Pioneer Award.

"I have finished reviewing the new edition of John Santrock's textbook, Child Development. *This volume promises to be as excellent as the last . . . The edition has gone out of its way to present a highly readable text while at the same time presents up to date research findings in a style to capture undergraduate students' interest and attention."* —**Michael Lewis**

 Debbie Laible Dr. Debbie Laible is a leading expert on children's emotional and moral development. She is currently an associate professor of psychology at Lehigh University. Dr. Laible obtained her Ph.D. in developmental psychology at the University of Nebraska–Lincoln. Her research interests focus broadly on children's social, emotional, and moral development. She has published numerous articles on attachment, mother–child emotional reminiscing, prosocial behavior, and children's socioemotional development. Dr. Laible is currently the associate editor of *Developmental Psychology* and has served or is serving on the editorial boards of *Child Development* and the *Journal of Youth and Adolescence.*

"There is no doubt that this chapter (Emotional Development) covers most of the important modern research. . . Actually, I think the strength of this text is that it has one of the most up-to-date coverages of research that I have ever seen in a text. John Santrock has managed to get his hands on research that is not even published yet. Thus, I have no doubt the text covers the most important ideas and thinking in developmental psychology. I also think the text is really approachable to students. . . . John Santrock does a lot to make sure he connects students to ideas. Thus, I really like some of the features of the text (such as making connections across chapters and the 'Reflect: Your Own Personal Journey of Life.' The book also handles diversity well and has a nice applied focus to it." —**Debbie Laible**

 David Moore Dr. David Moore is a leading expert on biological and environmental influences on children's development as well as perceptual and cognitive development in infancy. He obtained his undergraduate degree in psychology at Tufts University and his Ph.D. in developmental and biological psychology at Harvard University. Following post-doctoral work at the City University of New York, he joined the faculties of Pitzer College and Claremont Graduate University, where he currently is a professor of psychology. His book, *The Dependent Gene,* was widely adopted for use in undergraduate education, was translated into Japanese, and was nominated for the Cognitive Development Society's Best Authored Volume award. Dr. Moore's empirical research has focused on infants' reactions to infant-directed speech, the development of spatial cognition, and infants' rudimentary perception of numerical quantities. His theoretical writings have explored the contributions of genetic, environmental, and epigenetic factors to human development. His most recent contribution in this area is "Genetics, Behavior Genetics, and Epigenetics" which appeared in the *Oxford Handbook of Developmental Psychology* (2013), and he is writing a book on behavioral epigenetics for Oxford University Press. Dr. Moore serves on the editorial board of *Child Development Perspectives.*

"I am pleased to report that I think the chapter (Biological Beginnings) was engaging, thorough, well written, and current. . . . John Santrock has done an excellent job treating some sophisticated and controversial ideas in our field, presenting them to students in comprehensible and balanced ways. . . . I was impressed with the described 'connections' theme and with the 'learning system' that highlights various connections for readers. This approach should help students form an elaborated understanding of the ideas presented and help them avoid the feeling that they are learning a collection of isolated facts. I also believe the book's focus on research, real-life applications, and diversity will continue to attract the interest of professors hoping to really engage their students, because my students, too, are looking for textbooks with this kind of orientation." —**David Moore**

 Nancy Hazen Dr. Nancy Hazen is an expert on parenting and family relationships. She currently holds the position of Professor of Human Development and Family Sciences at the University of Texas at Austin. Dr. Hazen received her Ph.D. from the Institute of Child Development at the University of Minnesota. Her research focuses on the role of parenting and family relationships in the development of children's social competence, with a particular focus on attachment, peer relationships and the role of fathers. Dr. Hazen also studies the development children's emotional regulation and its link to internalizing and externalizing symptoms later in development. She teaches graduate and undergraduate classes in child development, peer relationships, and family relationships. Dr. Hazen serves on the editorial board of *Infancy* and is the President of the Society for Research in Human Development.

"These chapters (Families and Peers) present a clear and thorough overview of key theories and research in the area of family and peer relationships. The research is up-to-date. . . In this edition, John Santrock does a nice job of making connections between different topics and between later and earlier periods of development, which is always a challenge in a topically arranged textbook. . . . John Santrock also meets the challenge of achieving both breadth and depth by including a few in-depth descriptions of key studies or programs of research within each chapter. These more detailed descriptions of research are presented in an interesting and straightforward fashion. . . . Another strength of these chapters is that they highlight the relevance of research and theory of family and peer relationships to students' everyday lives." —**Nancy Hazen**

Joan Grusec Dr. Joan Grusec is one of the world's leading experts on family processes and socioemotional development. She obtained her Ph.D. at Stanford University and currently is professor of psychology at the University of Toronto. Dr. Grusec's longstanding research interests have focused on the influence of parenting and children's socialization, determinants of parenting practices, and emotional development. She has edited or co-edited a number of highly respected books in the field of child development, served as the associate editor of *Developmental Psychology,* and published a number of significant research studies on children's development. Among the chapters Dr. Grusec has contributed are "Socialization Processes" in the *Handbook of Child Psychology* (2006), "Socialization Processes in the Family: Social and Emotional Development" in the *Annual Review of Psychology* (2011), and "Social Development and Social Relationships in Middle Childhood" (with others) in the *Handbook of Psychology* (2nd ed., Vol. 6) (2013).

"It was a pleasure to read this chapter (Families). *It was pitched at just the right level that is easy to comprehend, and it is engagingly written. John Santrock also has a nice grasp of the literature—particularly impressive because this is such a small portion of the book. . . . The strengths of the chapter include its up-to-date coverage of the research literature. It is a very thorough survey of the evidence."* **—Joan Grusec**

John Columbo Dr. John Columbo is a leading expert on infant cognitive development. He obtained his Ph.D. in Psychology at the State University of New York at Buffalo. Dr. Columbo held faculty positions at Canisius College, Niagara University, and Youngstown State University before moving to the University of Kansas in the early 1980s. He currently is the Director of the Schiefelbusch Institute for Life Span Studies at the University of Kansas. His research interests focus on the developmental cognitive neuroscience of attention and learning, with a special focus on early individual differences in these areas and how they relate to the typical and atypical development of cognitive and intellectual functioning. Dr. Columbo is the author/editor of five books, more than 75 peer-reviewed articles, and 21 book chapters. He also has served on five different editorial boards for journals in developmental psychology, including two terms as an associate editor for *Child Development.*

". . . the level of updating and number of topics addressed in the Preface is impressive. John Santrock has done a really nice job in updating and covering important aspects of the science of child development. . . . Clearly, the author cares about students and about students' learning of content. He has put an enormous amount of work into this piece." **—John Columbo**

Catherine McBride-Chang Dr. Catherine McBride-Chang is a leading expert on children's language development. She currently is a professor and director of the Developmental Center at the University of Hong Kong. Dr. McBride-Chang obtained her Ph.D. in developmental psychology at the University of Southern California and was a post-doctoral fellow at Florida State University. Her research especially focuses on literacy development across cultures. She is the author of more than 100 peer-reviewed articles and two books. Dr. McBride-Chang also is an associate editor of *Developmental Psychology* and *Journal of Research on Reading.* She serves on the editorial boards of six other journals and is a Fellow in the American Psychological Association.

"This text provides a nice overview of the basics of language and literacy acquisition. Compared to most textbooks I have seen, this chapter (Language Development) *provides a relatively strong foundation on certain elements of literacy, particularly reading and writing. . . . Thus, I especially appreciate John Santrock's consideration of reading and writing in relation to language development through adolescence.* **—Catherine McBride-Chang**

Susan Harter Dr. Susan Harter is widely recognized as one of the pioneers and leading experts in children's and adolescents' development of the self and identity. She has served as a Professor of Psychology and Head of the Developmental Psychology Program (both graduate and postdoctoral components) at the University of Denver. After obtaining her bachelor's degree at Oberlin College, she received her Ph.D. from Yale University, which consisted of a joint degree in developmental and child-clinical psychology. Then Dr. Harter became the first female faculty member in Yale's psychology department, accepting a joint faculty appointment in the psychology department and the Yale Child Study Center, where she served as Chief Psychologist.

Dr. Harter joined the psychology faculty at the University of Denver in 1974. At the University of Denver she received the John Evans Professorship Award, the highest scholarly honor the University can bestow upon a faculty member for national and international recognition in one's chosen field of research. In two separate peer-reviewed publications she has been named as one of the 50 most influential developmental psychologists both in the United States and internationally.

She has published numerous scholarly articles and chapters, and has summarized much of her recent work in *The Construction of the Self: Developmental and Sociocultural Foundations* (2012). Her most recent interests include a detailed analysis of self-development over childhood and adolescence, self-processes in the classroom, the societal trend to unrealistically enhance the self-esteem and self-concepts of youth, cross-cultural approaches to the self, and a search for the authenticity of the self.

Making Connections . . . From My Classroom to *Child Development* to You

Having taught two or more undergraduate courses in developmental psychology—child development, adolescence, and life-span development—every year across four decades, I'm always looking for ways to improve my course and *Child Development*. Just as McGraw-Hill looks to those who teach the child development course for input, each year I ask the students in my undergraduate developmental courses to tell me what they like about the course and the text, and what they think could be improved. What have my students told me lately about my course and text? Students have said that highlighting connections among the different aspects of children's development would help them to better understand the concepts. As I thought about this, it became clear that a connections theme would provide a systematic, integrative approach to the course material. I have recently used this theme to shape my current goals for my course, which, in turn, influence the main goals of this text, as follows:

1. **Connecting with today's students** Helping students learn about child development more effectively
2. **Connecting research to what we know about children's development** Providing students with the best and most recent *theory and research* in the world today about each of the periods of child development
3. **Connecting topical and developmental processes** Guiding students in making *developmental connections* across different points in child development
4. **Connecting development to real life** Helping students understand ways to *apply* content about child development to the real world and improve people's lives, and to motivate students to think deeply about *their own personal journey through life* and better understand who they were, are, and will be

Connecting with Today's Students

My students often report that development courses are challenging because of the amount of material covered. To help today's students focus on the key ideas, the Learning Goals system I developed for *Child Development* provides extensive learning connections throughout the chapters. The learning system connects the chapter-opening outline, learning goals for the chapter, mini-chapter maps that open each main section of the chapter, *Review, Connect, and Reflect* at the end of each main section, and the chapter summary at the end of each chapter.

The learning system keeps the key ideas in front of the student from the beginning to the end of the chapter. The main headings of each chapter correspond to the learning goals, which are presented in the chapter-opening spread. Mini-chapter maps that link up with the learning goals are presented at the beginning of each major section in the chapter.

Then, at the end of each main section of a chapter, the learning goal is repeated in *Review, Connect, and Reflect,* which prompts students to review the key topics in the section, connect these topics to existing knowledge, and relate what they learned to their own personal journey through life. *Reach Your Learning Goals,* at the end of the chapter, guides students through the bulleted chapter review, connecting with the chapter outline/learning goals at the beginning of the chapter and the *Review, Connect, and Reflect* material at the end of each major section.

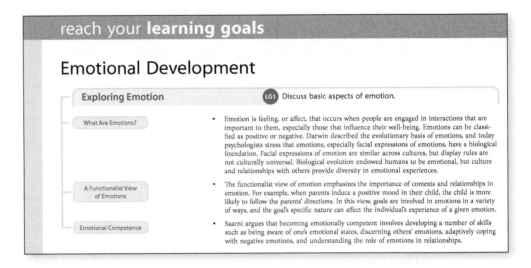

reach your **learning goals**

Emotional Development

Exploring Emotion	**LG1** Discuss basic aspects of emotion.

What Are Emotions?

- Emotion is feeling, or affect, that occurs when people are engaged in interactions that are important to them, especially those that influence their well-being. Emotions can be classified as positive or negative. Darwin described the evolutionary basis of emotions, and today psychologists stress that emotions, especially facial expressions of emotions, have a biological foundation. Facial expressions of emotion are similar across cultures, but display rules are not culturally universal. Biological evolution endowed humans to be emotional, but culture and relationships with others provide diversity in emotional experiences.

A Functionalist View of Emotions

- The functionalist view of emotion emphasizes the importance of contexts and relationships in emotion. For example, when parents induce a positive mood in their child, the child is more likely to follow the parents' directions. In this view, goals are involved in emotions in a variety of ways, and the goal's specific nature can affect the individual's experience of a given emotion.

Emotional Competence

- Saarni argues that becoming emotionally competent involves developing a number of skills such as being aware of one's emotional states, discerning others' emotions, adaptively coping with negative emotions, and understanding the role of emotions in relationships.

Connecting Research to What We Know About Children's Development

Over the years, it has been important for me to include the most up-to-date research available. I continue this tradition in this fourteenth edition by looking closely at specific areas of research, involving experts in related fields, and updating research throughout. **Connecting Through Research** describes a study or program to illustrate how research

connecting through research

(continued)

system. The researcher computes a baseline high-amplitude sucking rate in a one-minute silent period. Following the baseline, presentation of a sound is made contingent on the rate of amplitude sucking. Initially babies suck frequently so that the sound occurs often. Gradually, they lose interest in hearing the same sound so they begin to suck less often. Then the researcher changes the sound that is being presented. If the babies renew their vigorous sucking, the inference is that they have discriminated the sound change and are sucking more because they want to hear the interesting new sound (Menn & Stoel-Gammon, 2009).

The Orienting Response

A technique that can be used to determine whether an infant can see or hear is the *orienting response*, which involves turning one's head toward a sight or sound. Also, a startle response can be used as an indicator of an infant's reaction to a noise (Bendersky & Sullivan, 2007).

Equipment

Technology can facilitate the use of most methods for investigating the infant's perceptual abilities. Videotape equipment allows researchers to investigate elusive behaviors. High-speed computers make it possible to perform complex data analysis in minutes. Other equipment records respiration, heart rate, body movement, visual fixation, and sucking behavior, which provide clues to what the infant is perceiving. For example, some researchers use equipment that detects whether a change in infants' respiration follows a change in the pitch of a sound. If so, it suggests that the infants heard the pitch change.

Eye Tracking

The most important recent advance in measuring infant perception is the development of sophisticated eye-tracking equipment (Franchak & others, 2011; Morgante, Zolfaghari, & Johnson, 2012; Navab & others, 2012). Figure 5.8 shows an infant wearing an eye-tracking headgear in a recent study on visually guided motor behavior and social interaction.

One of the main reasons that infant perception researchers are so enthusiastic about the recent availability of sophisticated eye-tracking equipment is that looking time is among the most important measures of infant perceptual and cognitive development (Aslin, 2012). The new

FIGURE 5.8
AN INFANT WEARING EYE-TRACKING HEADGEAR. Using the ultralight, wireless, head-mounted eye-tracking equipment shown here, researchers can record where infants are looking while they freely locomote. (Source: Courtesy of Dr. Karen Adolph's laboratory, New York University.)

eye-tracking equipment allows for much greater precision than human observation in assessing various aspects of infant looking and gaze (Oakes, 2012). Among the areas of infant perception in which eye-tracking equipment is being used are memory, joint attention, and face processing (Falck-Ytter & others, 2012). Further, eye-tracking equipment is improving our understanding of atypically developing infants, such as those with autism (Sasson & Elison, 2012), and infants at risk for atypical developmental outcomes, including infants at risk for developing autism and preterm infants (Bedford & others, 2012).

In recent research on infants (14 months old), children (4 to 8 years old), and adults (20 to 22 years old) in a room filled with colorful toys and objects using eye-tracking headgear, the infants only centered their gaze on the objects about one-fourth of the time (Adolph, 2011; Franchak & Adolph, 2010). Adults fixated on objects about one-third of the time, 4- to 8-year-old children about 60 percent of the time. Thus, in a majority of instances, infants rather remarkably navigated their environment by merely glancing at the objects rather than centering their vision on the objects.

Another recent eye-tracking study shed light on the effectiveness of TV programs and DVDs that claim to educate infants (Kirkorian, Anderson, & Keen, 2012). In this study, 1-year-olds, 4-year-olds, and adults watched *Sesame Street* and the eye-tracking equipment recorded precisely what they looked at on the screen. The 1-year-olds were far less likely to consistently look at the same part of the screen than their older counterparts, suggesting that the 1-year-olds showed little understanding of the *Sesame Street* video but instead were more likely to be attracted by what was salient than by what was relevant.

Scientists have had to be very creative when assessing the development of infants, discovering ways to "interview" them even though they cannot yet talk. Other segments of the population, such as adults who have suffered from a stroke, have trouble communicating verbally. What kinds of methods or equipment do you think researchers might use to evaluate their perceptual abilities?

in child development is conducted and how it influences our understanding of the discipline. Topics range from "Do Children Conceived Through In Vitro Fertilization Show Significantly Different Outcomes in Adolescence?" (Chapter 2) to "How Can We Study Newborns' Perception?" (Chapter 5) to "How Does Theory of Mind Differ in Children with Autism?" (Chapter 7).

The tradition of obtaining detailed, extensive input from leading experts in different areas of child development also continues in this edition. Biographies and photographs of the leading experts in the field of child development appear on pages xii to xiv and the chapter-by-chapter highlights of new research content will be described shortly. Finally, the research discussions have been updated in every period and topic. I expended every effort to make this edition of *Child Development* as up-to-date as possible. To that end, there are more than 1,200 citations from 2011, 2012, and 2013 in this new edition of the text.

Connecting Topical and Developmental Processes

Too often we forget or fail to notice the many connections from one point in child development to another. I have substantially increased these connections made in the text narrative and have created several features to help students connect topics across the processes and periods of child development:

1. ***Developmental Connections***, which appears multiple times in the margins of each chapter, points students to where the topic is discussed in a previous, current, or subsequent chapter. This feature highlights links across development *and* connections among biological, cognitive, and socioemotional processes. The key developmental processes are typically discussed in isolation from each other, and so students often fail to see their connections. Included in ***Developmental Connections*** is a brief description of the backward or forward connection. For example, consider the rapidly increasing interest in the field of developmental cognitive neuroscience that focuses on connections among development, cognitive processes, and the brain. This topic is initially presented in Chapter 1, "Introduction," and then highlighted again in various chapters, especially Chapter 4, "Physical Development and Health."

2. A *Connect* question now appears in self-reviews—***Review, Connect, and Reflect***—at the end of each main section in a chapter so students can practice making connections among topics. For example, in Chapter 9, students are asked to connect what they learned in Chapter 5 about the effect of culture on motor development to what they just read in Chapter 8 about how different cultures have different concepts of intelligence.

Connecting Development to Real Life

In addition to helping students make research and developmental connections, *Child Development* shows the important connections among the concepts discussed and the real world. In recent years, students in my development course have increasingly told me that they want more of this type of information. In this edition, real-life connections are explicitly made in the chapter-opening vignette, in ***Caring Connections, Connecting with Diversity,*** and ***Connecting with Careers.***

Each chapter begins with a story designed to increase students' interest and motivation to read the chapter. ***Caring Connections*** provides applied information about parenting, education, or health and well-being in relation to topics ranging from "From Waterbirth to Music Therapy" (Chapter 3), to "Parents, Coaches, and Children's Sports" (Chapter 5), to "Guiding Children's Creativity" (Chapter 8). As will be seen later in the summary of chapter-by-chapter changes, I created a number of new ***Caring Connections*** interludes for this edition, as well as significantly updated and expanded applied topics in many areas of child development.

developmental **connection**

Biological Processes

Can specific genes be linked to specific environmental experiences? Chapter 2, p. 69

developmental **connection**

Research Methods

How does a correlational study differ from an experimental study? Chapter 1, p. 32

Connect

- In this section you learned that different cultures have different concepts of intelligence, and in Chapter 5 you learned about culture's effect on motor development. What do these findings have in common?

Child Development puts a strong emphasis on diversity. For a number of editions, this text has benefited from the involvement of one or more leading experts on diversity to ensure that it provides students with current, accurate, sensitive information related to diversity in children's development.

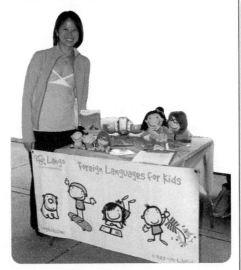

connecting with careers

Helen Schwe, Developmental Psychologist and Toy Designer

Helen Schwe obtained a Ph.D. from Stanford University in developmental psychology, but she now spends her days talking with computer engineers and designing "smart" toys for children. Smart toys are designed to improve children's problem-solving and symbolic thinking skills.

When she was a graduate student, Schwe worked part-time for Hasbro toys, testing its children's software on preschoolers. Her first job after graduate school was with Zowie Entertainment, which was subsequently bought by LEGO. According to Schwe, "Even in a toy's most primitive stage of development, . . . you see children's creativity in responding to challenges, their satisfaction when a problem is solved or simply their delight when they are having fun" (Schlegel, 2000, p. 50). In addition to conducting experiments and focus groups at different stages of a toy's development, Schwe also assesses the age appropriateness of a toy. Most of her current work focuses on 3- to 5-year-old children. (Source: Schlegel, 2000, pp. 50–51)

For more information about what researchers do, see page 42 in the Careers in Child Development appendix following Chapter 1.

Helen Schwe, a developmental psychologist, with some of the toys she designed for her current work on teaching foreign languages to children.

Diversity is discussed in every chapter, and Chapter 17, "Culture and Diversity," includes extensive material on the subject with substantial research updates in this edition of *Child Development*. Further, a feature called **Connecting with Diversity** appears throughout the text, focusing on a diversity topic related to the material at that point in the chapter. Topics range from "The Increased Diversity of Adopted Children and Adoptive Parents" (Chapter 2) to "Cultural Variations in Guiding Infants' Motor Development" (Chapter 5) to "The Contexts of Ethnic Identity Development" (Chapter 11).

Connecting with Careers profiles careers ranging from genetic counselor (Chapter 2) to toy designer (Chapter 7) to supervisor of gifted and talented education (Chapter 8), all of which require knowledge of child development. The careers highlighted extend from the Careers Appendix in Chapter 1, which provides a comprehensive overview of careers to show students where knowledge of child development could lead them.

Finally, part of applying knowledge of child development to the real world is understanding its impact on oneself. Accordingly, one of the goals of my child development course and this text is to motivate students to think deeply about their own journey through life. In reflecting about ways to encourage students to make personal connections to content in the text, I have added a **Reflect: Your Own Personal Journey of Life** prompt in the end-of-section review. This question asks students to reflect on some aspect of the discussion in the section they have just read and connect it to their own life. For example, in Chapter 1, related to a discussion of the early-later experience issue in development, students are asked,

> *Can you identify an early experience that you believe contributed in important ways to your development?*
>
> *Can you identify a recent or current (later) experience that you think had (is having) a strong influence on your development?*

Chapter-by-Chapter Changes

Following are the main chapter-by-chapter changes that were made in this new edition of *Child Development*.

Chapter 1: Introduction

- Substantial updating of citations, including many 2012 and 2013 references
- Expanded information about ethnic minority children, including concern about the discrimination and prejudice they experience (Benner & Graham, 2013; Tobler & others, 2013)
- Updated statistics on the increasing percentage of U.S. children and adolescents under 18 years of age living in poverty, especially in African American and Latino families (U.S. Census Bureau, 2012)
- New discussion of the recently created large-scale two-generation intervention, *Ascend,* by the Aspen Institute that is designed to help children escape from poverty through three avenues: education, economic support, and social capital (Aspen Institute, 2012)
- New section on cohort effects (Schaie, 2012)
- New material on cohort effects involving Millennial children, adolescents, and their parents, and how their experiences differ from those of earlier generations
- Inclusion of recent research and commentary on Millennials involving ethnic diversity and technology based on a recent national survey by the Pew Research Center (2010)
- New Figure 1.14 showing neuroimages of the brains of two adolescents (one a non-drinker, the other a heavy drinker) while they are engaging in a memory task
- Updated and expanded discussion of the leading journals in the field of child development
- Expanded coverage of cultural and ethnic bias, including reasons for studying Latino and Asian American adolescents and their families' acculturation level, generational status, and biculturalism (Gauvain, 2013; Schwartz & others, 2013)

Chapter 2: Biological Beginnings

- Updated coverage based on detailed reviews by leading experts David Moore and Kirby Deater-Deckard
- New discussion of the genome-wide association study that is increasingly used to identify genetic variations in individuals who have a disease, compared with those who don't (National Human Genome Research Institute, 2012)
- New coverage of some conditions for which genome-wide association studies recently have been conducted, including childhood obesity (Early Growth Genetics Consortium & others, 2012) and cardiovascular disease (Luisis, 2012)
- New discussion of linkage analysis in gene identification and discovery, including its use in the study of genetic influences on attention deficit hyperactivity disorder (Caylak, 2012), autism (O'Roak & others, 2012), and depression (Cohen-Woods, Craig, & McGuffin, 2012)
- New description of the recent interest in next-generation sequencing in determining genetic influences on disease and health (Rabbani & others, 2012)
- New coverage of the Thousand Genomes Project, the most detailed study of human genetic variation to date (Shibata & others, 2012)
- Expanded and updated material on modifications in DNA expression as a result of stress, radiation, and temperature (Georgakilas, 2011)
- Description of a recent study that found exposure to radiation changes the rate of DNA synthesis (Lee & others, 2011)
- Updated discussion of gene-gene interaction to include recent studies of immune system functioning (Reijmerink & others, 2011), asthma (Su & others, 2012), cancer (Bushel & others, 2012), and cardiovascular disease (Xiao & others, 2012)

- Updated material on noninvasive prenatal diagnosis (NIPD) (Chiu & Lo, 2012; Geaghan, 2012)
- New information about being able to determine the sex of the fetus at an earlier point in pregnancy through new noninvasive procedures (Kolialexi, 2012)
- Discussion of a recent meta-analysis indicating that a baby's sex can be determined as early as 7 weeks into pregnancy (Devaney & others, 2011)
- Coverage of recent reviews regarding child and adolescent outcomes for individuals conceived using new reproductive technologies (Golombok, 2011a, b; Golombok & Tasker, 2010)
- New material indicating that many U.S. adoptions now involve other family members (aunts/uncles/grandparents): 30 percent of U.S. adoptions are made by relatives and slightly more than 50 percent of U.S. adoptions involve the foster care system (Ledesma, 2012)
- Addition of information about epigenetic mechanisms involving the actual molecular modification of the DNA strand as a result of environmental inputs in ways that alter gene functioning (Feil & Fraga, 2012)
- Updated coverage of the concept of $G \times E$, which involves the interaction of a specific measured variation in the DNA sequence and a specific measured aspect of the environment (Bihagi & others, 2012; Petersen & others, 2012; Zannas & others, 2012)
- Description of recent research indicating that variations in dopamine-related genes interact with supportive or unsupportive environments to influence children's development (Bakermans-Kranenburg & van IJzendoorn, 2011)

Chapter 3: Prenatal Development and Birth

- Expanded and updated commentary about transport of drugs across the placenta (Menezes, Malek, & Keelan, 2011)
- Description of a recent study that found cigarette smoke weakened and increased oxidative stress in the fetal membranes from which the placenta develops (Menon & others, 2011)
- New discussion of the increasing inclusion of exercise in prenatal care programs
- Coverage of a recent study indicating that the risk of exercise-related injury during pregnancy was low (Vladutiu, Evenson, & Marshall, 2011)
- Description of a recent experimental study that found a three-month aerobic exercise program improved pregnant women's health-related quality of life (Montoya Arizabaleta & others, 2010)
- Inclusion of recent research indicating that exercise during pregnancy improved mothers' perception of their health (Barakat & others, 2011)
- Coverage of a recent experimental study of the effects of a CenteringPregnancy Plus program on high-stress pregnant women (Ickovics & others, 2011)
- Discussion of a recent research review indicating a link between prenatal home visits and improved prenatal care use but less evidence for their influence on newborns' birth weights (Issel & others, 2011)
- Inclusion of information from a recent research review indicating that high amounts of caffeine consumption by pregnant women does not increase the risk of miscarriage, congenital malformations, or growth retardation (Brent, Christian, & Diener, 2011)
- Coverage of recent research that found deficiencies in the brain pathways involved in the working memory of children with FASD (Diwadkar & others, 2012)
- Discussion of a recent meta-analysis linking maternal smoking during pregnancy to a modest increase in risk for childhood non-Hodgkin lymphoma (Antonopoulos & others, 2011)
- Information about a recent study that found environmental tobacco smoke exposure during pregnancy was linked to diminished ovarian functioning in female offspring (Kilic & others, 2012)

- Update on the most consistent negative outcomes of cocaine use during pregnancy (Gouin & others, 2011)
- Coverage of a recent research review that concluded cocaine quickly crosses the placenta to reach the fetus (De Giovanni & Marchetti, 2012)
- Description of recent research on the negative effects of cocaine exposure prenatally on children's attention and externalizing problems (Minnes & others, 2010; Richardson & others, 2011)
- New information from research on a link between prenatal cocaine exposure and elevated blood pressure at 9 years of age (Shankaran & others, 2010)
- Discussion of prenatal methamphetamine exposure and decreased brain activation, especially in the frontal lobes, in 7- to 15-year-olds (Roussotte, 2011)
- Coverage of a recent study that found prenatal meth exposure was associated with smaller head circumference, neonatal intensive care unit (NICU) admission, and referral to child protective services (Shah & others, 2012)
- Update on guidelines for eating certain types of fish during pregnancy (American Pregnancy Association, 2013; Mayo Clinic, 2013)
- Description of recent research on more than 30,000 offspring involving the time during prenatal development when maternal exposure to stress was most likely to increase the risk of preterm birth (Class & others, 2011)
- Coverage of recent research reviews that link maternal depression to preterm birth (Dunkel Schetter, 2011) and reduced empathy in childhood (Davalos, Yadon, & Tregellas, 2012)
- Description of a recent study that revealed paternal smoking around the time of the child's conception was linked to an increased risk of the child developing leukemia (Milne & others, 2012)
- Coverage of a recent research review indicating an increased risk of spontaneous abortion, autism, and schizophrenic disorders in offspring if the father is 40 years of age and older (Reproductive Endocrinology and Infertility Committee & others, 2012)
- Description of a recent study revealing that children born to fathers who are 40 years of age and older had increased risk of developing autism because of an increase in random gene mutations in the older fathers (Kong & others, 2012)
- Inclusion of recent research that found group prenatal care provided pregnant women with a broad network of social support (McNeil & others, 2012)
- Discussion of a recent study indicating that low Apgar scores are linked with development of ADHD in childhood (Li & others, 2011)
- Update on the dramatic 60 percent increase in cesarean deliveries in the United States from 1996 to 2009 and their effects on subsequent pregnancies (Hamilton, Martin, & Ventura, 2012; Solheim & others, 2011)
- New material on the recent increase in home births to non-Latino White women (Macdorman, Declercq, & Menacker, 2011)
- Discussion of a recent study that found waterbirth was linked with a shorter second stage of labor (Cortes, Basra, & Kelleher, 2011)
- Discussion of a recent study that revealed yoga and massage therapy sessions resulted in decreased levels of depression, anxiety, and back and leg pain (Field & others, 2012)
- Coverage of a recent research review that concluded practicing yoga during pregnancy is associated with a number of positive outcomes for mothers and a reduction in the incidence of low birth weight infants (Babbar, Parks-Savage, & Chauhan, 2012)
- Description of a recent research review that found positive outcomes for midwife-led care compared with physician-led care in low-risk women (Sutcliffe & others, 2012)
- Discussion of the results of two recent research reviews that indicated massage therapy reduces pain during labor (Jones & others, 2012; Smith, Levett, & others, 2012)
- Updated coverage of the percentage of infants born preterm in the United States, including the overall rate and ethnic variations in 2009 (National Center for Health Statistics, 2011)

- Updated data on the percentage of U.S. infants born with low birth weight (Hamilton, Martin, & Ventura, 2012)
- Description of recent research that found low birth weight was associated with childhood autism (Lampl & others, 2012)
- Description of a recent research review that concluded kangaroo care reduced the risk of mortality in low birth weight infants (Conde-Aguedelo, Belizan, & Diaz-Rossello, 2011)
- Coverage of a recent study that revealed the mechanisms responsible for weight gain in massaged preterm infants (Field, Diego, & Hernandez-Reif, 2010)
- New coverage of fathers having elevated depressive symptoms when their wives have postpartum depression (Letourneau & others, 2012; Ramchandani & others, 2011)

Chapter 4: Physical Development and Health

- Description of a recent study that found puberty is occurring earlier for boys, although the study has been criticized (Herman-Giddens & others, 2012)
- New discussion of the genetic and environmental contributions to puberty (Dvornyk & Waqar-ul-Haq, 2012)
- Inclusion of recent information on a longitudinal study of the sequence of pubertal events in boys and girls (Susman & others, 2010)
- Description of recent research that indicated severity of childhood sexual abuse was associated with early onset of menarche (Boynton-Jarrett & others, 2012)
- Coverage of a recent study that found a link between early maturation and substance abuse as well as early sexual intercourse (Gaudineau & others, 2010)
- Description of a recent study linking pubertal timing with subsequent engagement in delinquency (Negriff, Susman, & Trickett, 2011)
- Coverage of a recent study that found a linear increase in having a positive body image for both boys and girls as they moved from the beginning to the end of adolescence (Holsen, Carlson Jones, & Skogbrott Birkeland, 2012)
- Inclusion of changes in the coverage of the development of the brain based on leading expert consultant Martha Ann Bell's comments
- New section on the increasingly popular neuroconstructivist view to introduce the material on the development of the brain (Diamond, 2013; Peltzer-Karpf, 2012; Westerman, Thomas, & Karmiloff-Smith, 2011)
- Discussion of important research on the development of the brain in infancy conducted by Martha Ann Bell and her colleagues (Bell & Cuevas, 2012, 2013; Bell & Diaz, 2012; Morasch, Raj, & Bell, 2013) and John Richards and his colleagues (2009, 2010; Richards, Reynolds, & Courage, 2010; Sanchez, Richards, & Almli, 2012)
- Update on the role of myelination in providing energy for neurons (Harris & Attwell, 2012)
- New discussion of a recent study of adolescents from Mexican backgrounds that found those with stronger family obligation values showed decreased activation in the brain's regions involving reward sensitivity, which was linked to less real-life risk-taking behavior, and increased activation in the brain's regions involving cognitive control, which was associated with better decision-making skills (Telzer & others, 2013)
- Description of a recent research review of sleep patterns in infancy (Galland & others, 2012)
- Inclusion of information about a recent study that revealed by 6 months of age, a majority of infants slept through the night, awakening their mothers only once or twice a week (Weinraub & others, 2012)
- Discussion of a recent study that revealed nighttime wakings at 12 months of age predicted a lower level of sleep efficiency at 4 years of age (Tikotzky & Shaashua, 2012)
- New material on the most common sleep problem in infancy (The Hospital for Sick Children & others, 2010)

- Coverage of a recent study linking maternal emotional availability with fewer infant sleep problems (Teti & others, 2010)

- Discussion of a recent study indicating that paternal involvement in infant care was related to fewer infant sleep problems (Tikotzky, Sadeh, & Glickman-Gavrieli, 2010)

- Description of recent research on early life risk factors that are linked to infant sleep duration (Nevarez & others, 2010)

- Updated information about infant-parent bed sharing and an increasing trend of recommending that this not occur until the infant is at least 6 months old (Byard, 2012a, b; Weber & others, 2012)

- Coverage of a recent study indicating that infant-parent bed sharing was linked with higher rates of infant sleep problems, such as disordered breathing (Kelmanson, 2010)

- Updated and expanded coverage of SIDS, including the role of brain stem functioning and the neurotransmitter serotonin (Broadbent & others, 2012)

- New material on recent research indicating that as many as 10 to 15 percent of SIDS cases are linked to heart arrhythmias with gene mutations being involved in the arrhythmias (Brion & others, 2012; Van Norstrand & others, 2012)

- Discussion of a two recent research reviews linking breast feeding to a lower incidence of SIDS (Hauck & others, 2011; Zotter & Pichler, 2012)

- Description of a study linking sleep problems in early childhood with subsequent attention problems that in some cases persist into early adolescence (O'Callaghan & others, 2010)

- Coverage of a recent study indicating that having trouble sleeping in childhood was related to alcohol use problems in adolescence and early adulthood (Wong & others, 2010)

- Inclusion of a recent analysis indicating that chronic child sleep disorders that deprive children of adequate sleep may be lead to impaired brain development (Jan & others, 2010)

- New content on a comparison of U.S. and Asian adolescents' sleep patterns (Gradisar, Gardner, & Dohnt, 2011)

- New coverage of Mona El-Sheikh's (2013) recommendations for improving children's sleep environment

- Description of a recent study on delaying school start time for ninth- to twelfth-grade students and the resulting improvements in sleep, alertness, mood, and health (Owens, Belon, & Moss, 2010).

- New commentary about the intense search for possible genetic links to childhood cancers (Spector & others, 2013)

- Updated discussion of childhood cancer, including improving survival rates for some childhood cancers (National Cancer Institute, 2011; Wayne, 2011)

- Description of a recent study that found parental smoking was a risk factor for higher blood pressure in children (Simonetti & others, 2011)

- Coverage of a recent study that found the most frequently consumed vegetable by 2- and 3-year-olds was French fries or other fried potatoes (Fox & others, 2010)

- Inclusion of recent research that found low maternal sensitivity when infants were 15 and 24 months of age was linked to a higher risk of obesity in adolescence (Anderson & others, 2012)

- Updated data on the increasing percentage of U.S. women who breast feed their babies in the hospital and when the infant is six months old (Centers for Disease Control and Prevention, 2012b)

- Inclusion of the reconfirmation by the American Academy of Pediatrics Section on Breastfeeding (2012) of its recommendation of exclusive breast feeding in the first six months, followed by continued breast feeding as complementary foods are introduced, and further breast feeding for one year or longer as mutually desired by the mother and infant

- Coverage of recent data on the increasing percentage of 2- to 5-year-old obese children in the United States, including trends from 1976–1980 through 2007–2010 (Ogden & others, 2012)

- Discussion of a recent study indicating that preschool children who were overweight had a significant risk of being overweight/obese at 11 years of age (Shankaran & others, 2011)

- New discussion of a recent literacy intervention program with Spanish-speaking families in the Los Angeles WIC program that increased literacy resources and activities in homes, which in turn led to a higher level of school readiness in children (Whaley & others, 2011)

- Description of recent data on the percentage of U.S. 6- to 11-year-olds that are overweight or obese, which in 2009–2010 was significantly higher than the percentage of 2- to 5-year–olds who were overweight (Ogden & others, 2012)

- Updated data on trends in adolescent obesity from 1999–2000 to 2009–2010 with an increase in boys but not in girls during this time frame (Ogden & others, 2012)

- Description of a longitudinal study that found general and abdominal obesity increased in Chinese children from 1993 to 2009 (Liang & others, 2012)

- Coverage of recent intervention studies that indicate modifying parents' eating habits and increasing children's exercise can help overweight and obese children to lose weight (Brotman & others, 2012; Collins & others, 2011)

- Inclusion of recent research that found both peers and family members teased overweight children more than normal weight children (McCormack & others, 2011)

- Description of a recent study that found having two overweight/obese parents significantly increased the likelihood that children would be overweight/obese (Xu & others, 2011)

- Inclusion of information about a recent successful behavior modification program that increased overweight and obese children's exercise and reduced their TV viewing time (Goldfield, 2011)

- Inclusion of recent research on 9-year-olds that focused on the connection between physical activity level and risk for metabolic disease (Parrett & others, 2011)

- Description of recent research showing links between aerobic exercise and cognitive skills in children and adolescents (J. R. Best, 2010; Davis & others, 2011; Monti, Hillman, & Cohen, 2012)

- Inclusion of a recent experimental study that found positive effects of aerobic training on the insulin resistance and body fat levels of overweight/obese elementary school children (Davis & others, 2012)

- Updated date on gender and ethnic variations in adolescents' exercise patterns (Eaton & others, 2012)

- New coverage of the percentage of adolescents who participate in physical education classes at school (Eaton & others, 2012)

- New discussion of links between screen-based activity and physical exercise in adolescents, including recent research indicating that adolescents who combine low physical activity and high screen-based activity are nearly twice as likely to be overweight (Sisson & others, 2010)

- Discussion of a recent research review that found a higher level of screen time at 4 to 6 years of age was linked with a lower level of activity and being overweight from preschool to adolescence (te Velde & others, 2012)

- Coverage of a recent research review that found a higher level of screen-based sedentary behavior was associated with a number of adolescent problems, ranging from sleep disorders to depression (Costigan & others, 2012)

- Description of a recent study of young adolescents that found regular exercise was associated with higher academic achievement (Hashim, Freddy, & Rosmatunisah, 2012)

- Discussion of a recent study of depressed adolescents with low levels of exercise that revealed a 12-week exercise intervention lowered their depression (Dopp & others, 2012)

- New section on the role of peers in adolescent exercise, including a recent research review that indicated peer friend/support, friendship quality and acceptance, and peer victimization were associated with adolescents' physical activity (Fitzgerald, Fitzgerald, and Aherne, 2012)
- Description of a recent study that found a daily morning running program for three weeks improved adolescents' sleep quality, mood, and concentration (Kalak & others, 2012)

Chapter 5: Motor, Sensory, and Perceptual Development

- Inclusion of a number of chapter changes and updates based on leading expert Karen Adolph's feedback
- Updated discussion of infant reflexes arguing that reflexes are not exclusively inborn, genetic mechanisms but rather that infants can deliberately control such movements (Adolph & Berger, 2013)
- New coverage of recent research indicating that alternating leg movements occur during the fetal period and at birth (Adolph & Robinson, 2013)
- Description of a recent study by Karen Adolph and her colleagues (2012) that found 12- to 19-month-olds took 2,368 steps and fell 17 times an hour during free play, documenting the extensiveness of locomotor experience
- New discussion of the research of Karen Adolph and her colleagues (Adolph, 2011; Adolph & Berger, 2013; Adolph & Robinson, 2013) on the experimental conditions and outcomes involved when environmental features and experimental manipulation of body properties are instituted
- Added commentary about the traditional practice in many sub-Saharan villages of engaging babies in exercise (Super & Harkness, 2010)
- New examples of restricting movement in infants in some rural cultures, such as the use of sandbags in some rural Chinese provinces (Adolph, Karasik, & Tamis-LeMonda, 2010)
- Coverage of a recent study linking sports participation to a lower incidence of being overweight or obese (Antonogeorgos & others, 2011)
- New coverage of Rachel Keen's (2011) research suggesting that tool use is an excellent context for studying problem solving in children less than 3 years old because motor behavior can indicate how the infant tries to reach a goal
- Inclusion of recent research indicating that training infants to use sticky mittens resulted in advances in their reaching behavior (Libertus & Needham, 2011)
- New content on toddlers' and preschool children's tower-building that involves both planning and the development of motor skills, including new Figure 5.5 (Chen & others, 2010)
- A number of changes in the discussion of perceptual development based on feedback from leading experts Scott Johnson and Rachel Keen
- Revised, updated coverage of high-amplitude sucking as a measure of infant perceptual development
- Much expanded and updated coverage of the dramatic increase in the use of sophisticated eye-tracking equipment in the study of infant perception (Aslin, 2012; Oakes, 2012)
- Description of a recent eye-tracking study in which 1-year-old infants showed less efficient looking at an educational video than their older counterparts (Kirkorian, Anderson, & Keen, 2012)
- Description of a recent study indicating that imagining the various paths that a dropped ball might take improves preschoolers' ability to predict where it would land (Joh & others, 2011)
- Coverage of a recent study indicating that instructions to follow the path of a ball to the bottom of a tube improved 3-year-olds' ability to not succumb to a gravity bias (Bascandziev & Harris, 2011)

- Coverage of a recent fMRI study that confirmed the fetus can hear at 33 to 34 months into the prenatal period by assessing fetal brain responses to auditory stimuli (Jardri & others, 2012)
- Discussion of a recent study that found 7-month-old infants can process simultaneous pitches when they hear voices but are more likely to encode the higher-pitched voice (Marie & Trainor, 2012)
- New section on hearing problems in children that focuses on cochlear implants and otitis media
- New coverage of the longitudinal research of Daphne Maurer and her colleagues (Lewis & Maurer, 2009; Maurer, Mondloch, & Leis, 2007) on infants whose cataracts were removed at different points in development that illustrates how deprivation and experience influence visual development
- Added commentary suggesting that most perception is intermodal perception (Bahrick, 2010)

Chapter 6: Cognitive Developmental Approaches

- Expanded conclusions about the themes of the current field of infant cognitive development to emphasize the substantial increase in interest in cognitive developmental neuroscience and links between brain processes and cognitive processes (Diamond, 2013; Morasch & others, 2013; Peltzer-Karpf, 2012)
- Description of a recent fMRI study identifying brain locations that were linked to 9- and 10-year-olds' conservation success in comparison with non-conserving 5- and 6-year-olds (Houde & others, 2011)
- Expanded and updated coverage of the importance of perspective taking and ego development in explaining the imaginary audience and personal fable (Lapsley & Hill, 2010)
- New coverage of Daniel Lapsley and his colleagues' (Hill, Duggan, & Lapsley, 2012; Lapsley & Stey, 2012) view that the separation-individuation process, rather than cognitive developmental changes, is responsible for adolescent invulnerability
- Inclusion of recent research on the importance of distinguishing between two types of invulnerability (danger and psychological), which have different outcomes (Lapsley & Hill, 2010)
- Expanded and updated coverage of Barbara Rogoff's research, including recent work on the inadequate opportunities for children to participate in valued family and community activities in middle-SES European-heritage communities (Rogoff, Correa-Chavez, & Silva, 2011; Rogoff, Morelli, & Chavajay, 2010; Rogoff & others, 2011)

Chapter 7: Information Processing

- Discussion of a recent study indicating that processing speed was linked to oral reading fluency in children (Jacobson & others, 2011)
- Coverage of a recent study that found infants visually attend to events that are of intermediate complexity and are more likely to look away from events that are overly simple or complex (Kidd, Piantadosi, & Aslin, 2012)
- Discussion of a recent study that found responding to joint attention at 1 month of age was linked to self-regulation skills at 3 years of age (Van Hecke & others, 2012)
- Coverage of a recent research study linking television watching and video game playing to children's attention problems (Swing & others, 2010)
- Description of a recent study indicating that joint attention enhanced the long-term memory of 9-month-old infants (Kopp & Lindenberger, 2012)
- New material on using computer exercises to improve children's attention, including a Web site (www.teach-the-brain.org/learn/attention/index.htm) about how to use the games with children (Jaeggi, Berman, & Jonides, 2009; Steiner & others, 2011; Tang & Posner, 2009)

- Discussion of a recent study that revealed a region of the prefrontal cortex was activated when 5-month-old infants engaged in joint attention with another person (Grossmann & Johnson, 2010)

- Expanded coverage of attention in adolescence including new material on the importance of controlling attention and being able to reduce distractions that can interfere with learning (Bjorklund, 2012; Gillig & Sanders, 2011)

- Discussion of a recent study that found a computerized working memory program improved 9- to 11-year-olds' reading performance (Loosli & others, 2012)

- Description of a recent study that found assessment of working memory in kindergarten was a key process in predicting match achievement at the end of the first grade (Monette, Bigras, & Guay, 2011)

- New commentary suggesting that one of the reasons memory improves with age in childhood is the increasing use of effective strategies in middle and late childhood (Schneider, 2011)

- Revised definition of concepts and addition of *concepts* to the list of key terms

- Addition of recent commentary about learning by infant researcher Alison Gopnik (2010) on the importance of putting things into the right categories

- Updated and expanded discussion of the increasing interest in executive function, including the importance of its early development in the preschool years (Carlson & White, 2013; Carlson, Zelazo, & Faja, 2013)

- New Figure 7.11 that includes a photograph of a research setting in Stephanie Carlson's study of executive function in young children

- New description of Ann Masten and her colleagues' (Herbers & others, 2011; Masten, 2013; Masten & others, 2008) research that has found executive function and parenting skills are linked to school success in homeless children

- New coverage of Adele Diamond's (2013; Diamond & Lee, 2011) view on the key dimensions of executive function in 4- to 11-year-old children and interventions that have been shown to improve executive function

- Coverage of a 30-year longitudinal study that found children who were better at inhibitory control showed a number of positive aspects of development as adults (Moffitt, 2012; Moffitt & others, 2011)

- Expanded coverage of mindfulness and recent proposals for using mindfulness training, as well as other aspects of reflective science such as yoga, to improve children's cognitive and socioemotional skills (Roeser & Zelazo, 2012; Zelazo & Lyons, 2012)

- New discussion of the debate about how much benefit is derived from placing various cognitive processes under the broader concept of executive function

- New discussion of the importance of executive function in adolescent cognitive development, including Deanna Kuhn's (2009) view that executive function represents the key cognitive changes at this point in development

- New commentary on debate regarding whether infants have a theory of mind (Rakoczy, 2012)

- Expanded coverage of cognitive factors other than theory of mind that might be involved in autism, including eye gaze, face processing, memory, and language impairment (Boucher, Mays, & Bigham, 2012)

- Description of a recent study that found children improve their selection of effective strategies in solving problems from the third grade to the seventh grade (Lemaire & Lecacheur, 2011)

- New discussion of recent research indicating that adolescents make riskier decisions in stressful than non-stressful situations, but that the extent to which they make risky decisions in stressful contexts is associated with the type of risk taker they are (impulsive, calculated, or conservative) (Johnson, Dariotis, & Wang, 2012)

- Expanded coverage of the dual process model of decision making to include material on the importance of adolescents quickly getting the gist of a dangerous situation, which can cue personal values that will reduce the likelihood that adolescents engage in risky decision making (Chick & Reyna, 2012)

- Inclusion of information about how adolescents who have a higher trait level of inhibition (self-control) and find themselves in risky situations are less likely to engage in risky decision making (Chick & Reyna, 2012)
- Expanded description of what metacognition involves (Dimmitt & McCormick, 2012)
- Discussion of a recent study that found young adolescents increasingly use metacognitive skills from 12 to 14 years of age, and use them more effectively in math and history classes than other subjects (van der Stel & Veenman, 2010)
- Description of a recent study with college students indicating that metacognition is a key factor in the ability to engage effectively in critical thinking (Magno, 2010)

Chapter 8: Intelligence

- Substantial updating of research with addition of a number of 2011, 2012, and 2013 research citations
- New coverage of the link between lower intelligence in childhood and illness, chronic disease, and how long people will live (Deary & Batty, 2011)
- Description of a recent study of predicting academic performance based on measures of general mental abilities and emotional intelligence (Song & others, 2010)
- Discussion of a recent study that revealed the frontoparietal network is responsible for cognitive control and connectivity to brain regions outside the network (Cole & others, 2012)
- Description of a recent research review that concluded more than 1,000 genes may influence an individual's intelligence (Davies & others, 2011)
- New information from a recent research review about the environment's role in intelligence that is reflected in the 12- to 18-point IQ gain children make when they are adopted from lower-SES to middle-SES homes (Nisbett & others, 2012)
- Coverage of a recent analysis of the Abcedarian early childhood intervention when the children had reached 30 years of age, which found benefits for years of education attained but no gains regarding social adjustment and criminal activity (Campbell & others, 2012)
- Discussion of a recent study that revealed an accelerated Flynn effect for children whose mothers have more education and for children from higher-income families (Ang, Rodgers, & Wanstrom, 2010)
- Updated information about the reduction in the IQ gap between African American and non-Latino Whites (Nisbett & others, 2012)
- Expanded and updated coverage of ethnic comparisons of children's intelligence, including consistent ordering of children from different ethnic groups on intelligence tests (Suzuki, Short, & Lee, 2011)
- Description of the decreasing gap in intelligence between non-Latino White and African American children in the last three decades (Nisbett, 2009).
- Coverage of a longitudinal study indicating that information-processing skills in infancy and early childhood were linked to general intelligence at 11 years of age (Rose & others, 2012)
- Replacement of the label *mental retardation* with the currently used term of *intellectual disability* (Hodapp & others, 2011)
- New estimate of the percentage of children who are categorized as being gifted (Ford, 2012)
- New commentary about the underrepresentation of African American, Latino, and Native American children in gifted programs and the reasons for the underrepresentation (Ford, 2012)
- Expanded discussion of children's creative thinking, including recent research indicating a decline in creative thinking by U.S. schoolchildren and increased interest in teaching creative thinking in Chinese schools (Kim, 2010; Plucker, 2010)

- New description of noncognitive factors, such as motivation, creativity, and optimism, involved in giftedness (Reis & Renzulli, 2011)

Chapter 9: Language Development

- New description of the increasing emphasis on the development of pointing in infancy as a key aspect of joint attention and an important index of the social aspects of language (Begus & Southgate, 2012; Goldin-Meadow & Alibali, 2013)
- Updated information about developmental aspects of the pointing gesture in the first two years of life (Colonessi & others, 2010)
- Description of a recent study that revealed 6-month-old infants comprehend names of parts of their body, such as "feet" and "hands" (Tincoff & Jusczyk, 2012)
- New material on Kathy Hirsh-Pasek, Roberta Golinkoff, and Justin Harris' (Harris, Golinkoff, & Hirsch-Pasek, 2012; Hirsh-Pasek & Golinkoff, 2013) six principles for optimal word learning in young children
- New material on strategies for using books with preschoolers (Galinsky, 2010)
- Inclusion of information indicating that a computer-based program emphasizing phonics improved first-grade students' reading skills (Savage & others, 2009)
- New coverage of the important role that metacognitive strategies—especially those involving planning, drafting, revising, and editing—play in improving writing during the elementary school years (Dimmitt & McCormick, 2012; Harris & others, 2009; McCormick, Dimmitt, & Sullivan, 2013)
- Coverage of recent research indicating that bilingual children have a lower vocabulary in each language than monolingual children (Bialystok, 2011)
- Updated and revised discussion of English language learners (EELs), including recent research indicating that ELL children who are taught using a dual-language approach (home language and English) have a higher level of achievement (Genesee & Lindholm-Leary, 2012)
- Discussion of a recent research review that concluded the earlier and more frequently that adults read to children, the better their literacy and language skills were (Dunst, Simkus, & Hamby, 2012). In this study, the average age of children when adults began reading to them was 22 months
- Increased emphasis on how important it is for children's optimal development that parents and teachers provide children with many opportunities to talk and be talked with (Hirsh-Pasek & Golinkoff, 2013)

Chapter 10: Emotional Development

- Discussion of a recent study that revealed newborns of depressed mothers showed less vocal distress at the cries of another infant, reflecting emotional and physiological dysregulation (Jones, 2012)
- Description of a recent study that found mothers' emotional reactions (anxiety and anger) increased the risk of subsequent attachment insecurity (Leerkes, Parade, & Gudmundson, 2011)
- Inclusion of recent research indicating a link between problems in infant soothability at 6 months of age and insecure attachment at 12 months of age (Mills-Koonce, Propper, & Barnett, 2012)
- Discussion of a recent study that found emotionally reactive infants who also showed a high level of emotional regulation were more likely to have primary caregivers who engaged in positive parenting (Ursache & others, 2013)
- Coverage of a recent study that found fathers' emotion coaching was related to children's social competence (Baker, Fenning, & Crnic, 2011)
- Discussion of research indicating that mothers' knowledge about what distresses and comforts their children predicts children's coping, empathy, and prosocial behavior (Vinik, Almas, & Grusec, 2011)

- Discussion of a recent study that found parents' elicitation of talk about emotion with toddlers was associated with toddlers' sharing and helping (Brownell & others, 2012)

- New description of recent research by Cybelle Raver and her colleagues (Raver & others, 2012; Zhai, Raver, & Jones, 2012) on links between increased caregiver emotional expression, self-regulation, and reduced behavior problems in Head Start families

- Updated coverage of how various aspects of disasters and traumatic events affect children (McDermott & Cobham, 2012; Salloum & Overstreet, 2012)

- New material on dose/response effects in the study of how disasters and traumatic events affect children's adjustment and adaptation (Masten, 2013)

- Coverage of a recent study linking behavioral inhibition at 3 years of age with shyness at age 7 (Volbrecht & Goldsmith, 2010)

- Description of recent research that found being fearful in situations that are relatively low in threat at 24 months of age was related to higher levels of anxiety in kindergarten (Buss, 2011)

- Inclusion of recent research indicating that children with a lower level of cortisol regulation or mothers who were more likely to endorse non-supportive emotional reactions engaged in more maladaptive play behavior (Davis & Buss, 2012)

- Discussion of a recent longitudinal study linking shyness/inhibition in infancy/childhood to social anxiety at 21 years of age (Bohlin & Hagekull, 2009)

- Discussion of a recent study that revealed U.S. infants showed more temperamental fearfulness while Finnish infants engaged in more positive affect, especially effortful control (Gaias & others, 2012)

- New commentary suggesting that too often the biological foundations of temperament are interpreted as meaning that temperament doesn't develop and change; however, key dimensions (such as adaptability and soothability) of the self-regulatory aspect of temperament do develop and change as neurobiological and experiential processes develop and change (Easterbrooks & others, 2013)

- Addition of information about research indicating that decreases in infants' negative emotionality are related to higher levels of parents' sensitivity, involvement, and responsivity (Bates, 2012a, b; Penela & others, 2012)

- Inclusion of information from a recent study that linked maternal sensitivity to subsequent secure attachment during infancy (Leerkes, 2011)

- Coverage of a longitudinal study that found changes in attachment security/insecurity from infancy to adulthood were linked to stresses and supports in socioemotional contexts (Van Ryzin, Carlson, & Sroufe, 2011)

- New description of the developmental cascade model that is increasingly being used to study connections across domains over time that influence developmental pathways and outcomes (Cicchetti, 2013; Masten, 2013)

- Coverage of a recent study that found infants who were insecurely attached to both their mother and father had more externalizing problems in the elementary school years than their counterparts who were securely attached to at least one parent (Kochanska & Kim, 2012)

- New commentary noting that some researchers have not found support for gene-environment interactions related to infant attachment (Luijk & others, 2011; Roisman & Fraley, 2012)

- New main section on attachment in middle and late childhood

- New discussion of research by Kathryn Kerns and her colleagues (Brumariu, Kerns, & Siebert, 2012; Kerns & Siebert, 2012; Kerns, Siener, & Brumariu, 2011) that focuses on the role of secure attachment in internalizing symptoms, anxiety, depression, and emotion regulation

- Description of a recent research review that revealed a strong link between levels or patterns of oxytocin and aspects of mother-infant attachment (Galbally & others, 2011)

- Discussion of recent research indicating that fathers with a college-level education engaged in more stimulating physical activities with their infants and that fathers in a conflicting couple relationship participated in less caregiving and physical play with their infants (Cabrera, Hofferth, & Chae, 2011)

- Coverage of a recent study that revealed infants who showed a higher level of externalizing, disruptive problems at 1 year of age had fathers who displayed a low level of engagement with their infants as early as the third month of life (Ramchandani & others, 2013)

- Description of a recent study that found depressed fathers focused more on their own needs than their infants' needs and used more negative and critical speech when interacting with their infants (Sethna, Murray, & Ramchandani, 2012)

- Inclusion of recent research that found high-quality child care during the infant/ toddler years was linked to better memory skills at the end of the preschool years (Li & others, 2013)

- Coverage of recent research linking early higher quality of child care with higher cognitive-academic achievement and lower externalizing behavior at 15 years of age (Vandell & others, 2010)

- Description of a recent study using the NICHD SECCYD data indicating that the worst socioemotional outcomes for children occurred when both home and child care settings conferred risk (Watamura & others, 2011)

Chapter 11: The Self and Identity

- Revised and updated content on the development of the self based on comments from leading expert consultant Susan Harter

- Inclusion of a definition of the self

- Expanded and updated discussion of young children's optimistic self-conception to consider some young children's negative self-evaluations, especially when they experience stress and adverse family conditions (Goodvin & others, 2008; Thompson, 2011)

- Expanded and updated material on the increasing belief that young children are more socially sensitive than was previously envisioned and that this means parents and teachers can help young children to better understand people's internal cognitive and emotional states (Thompson, 2013c, d)

- Description of the current debate about Ross Thompson's (2013b, c) view that young children are more socially sensitive and Susan Harter's (2012) view that they are more egocentric

- Expanded discussion of the increase in social comparison in adolescence, including information about the looking glass self

- Description of recent research on young children's understanding of joint commitments (Grafenhain & others, 2009)

- New discussion of the role of executive function and children's perspective taking (Galinsky, 2010)

- Discussion of a recent study that focused on the positive aspects of perspective taking skills in children who are emotionally reactive (Bengtsson & Arvidsson, 2011)

- New section on understanding others in adolescence

- New section on perspective taking in adolescence, including recent research on gender differences (Smith, Rose, & Schwartz-Mette, 2010), developmental changes in perceiving social justice (Rubenstein, 2012), and relational aggression (Batanova & Loukas, 2011)

- New discussion of developmental changes in perceiving others' traits in adolescence

- New section on social cognitive monitoring in adolescence

- New information indicating that the foundations of self-esteem in middle and late childhood occur through the quality of relationships with parents in infancy and early childhood (Thompson, 2011, 2013a, b, c, d)

- Coverage of a recent study that found adolescents with low self-esteem had lower life-satisfaction at 30 years of age (Birkeland & others, 2012)

- Inclusion of a definition of identity
- New discussion based on a recent research review indicating that adolescents who have a mature identity are better adjusted and are characterized by more positive personality traits, such as conscientiousness and emotional stability (Meeus, 2011)
- Coverage of a recent study indicating that individuals from 12 to 20 years of age increasingly pursue in-depth exploration of their identity (Klimstra & others, 2010)
- Added commentary about the results of the recent meta-analysis by Jane Kroger and her colleagues (2010) indicating that mastery of identity development by early adulthood is far more elusive than Erikson (1968) envisioned
- Coverage of a recent research review indicating that identity is more stable in adults than adolescents (Meeus, 2011)
- Description of a recent meta-analysis that found links between secure attachment and identity achievement (Arseth & others, 2009)
- New section on identity and peer/romantic relationships (Galliher & Kerpelman, 2012)
- Description of recent research that found an open, active exploration of identity with close friends was linked to the positive quality of the friendship (Deamen & others, 2012)
- Inclusion of recent research indicating that friends were often a safe haven for exploring identity in adolescence, providing a potential testing ground for trying out self-disclosures with others (McLean & Jennings, 2012)
- New material on how adolescents and emerging adults in a romantic relationship are in the process of constructing their identities, with each partner providing the other with a context for identity exploration (Pittman & others, 2012)
- Revised and updated information about diversity, especially ethnic identity and immigration, based on feedback from leading expert Diane Hughes
- Extensive updating and expansion of the discussion of cultural and ethnic identity, including recent cross-cultural comparisons of identity development between North American and East Asian countries (Cheng & Berman, 2013; Schwartz & others, 2013)
- New coverage of findings by Seth Schwartz and his colleagues (2013) suggesting that individuals who have grown up as a member of an ethnic minority group or immigrated from another country are more likely to include cultural dimensions in their identity than are non-Latino Whites in the United States who have grown up in the majority culture
- Discussion of recent research indicating that Latino high school and college students were more likely to say that cultural identity was an important dimension of their overall self-concept than were non-Latino White students (Urdan, 2009, 2012)
- Inclusion of a definition of bicultural identity
- Coverage of a recent study of 14- to 21-year-olds' responses to the label "White" (Marks, Patton, & Garcia Coll, 2011)
- Coverage of a recent study that found a positive ethnic identity helped to buffer the negative effects of discrimination experienced by Mexican American adolescents (Umana-Taylor & others, 2012)

Chapter 12: Gender

- New discussion of greater acceptance of masculine girls who are described as tomboys than feminine boys who are described as sissies (Pasterski, Golombok, & Hines, 2011)
- New material on gender segregation in adolescence involving "hanging out" (Mehta & Strough, 2010)
- New section on the influence of schools and teachers on children's gender development
- Coverage of a recent gender stereotyping study of 6- to 10-year-olds who reported that math is mainly for boys (Cvencek, Meltzoff, & Greenwald, 2011)
- Description of a recent research review that focused on girls' negative attitudes about math and the negative expectations that parents and teachers have for girls' math competence (Gunderson & others, 2012)

- Substantial updating and expansion of same-sex education, including its dramatic increase in recent years (NASSPE, 2012).
- Inclusion of two recent research reviews, both of which concluded there have been no benefits of same-sex education for low-income youth of color (Goodkind, 2012; Halpern, Beninger, & Straight, 2011)
- New discussion of possible benefits of same-sex education exclusively for African American males and discussion of the successful Urban Prep Academy for Young Men in Chicago that opened in 2010 in which 100 percent of the school's first graduates enrolled in college (Mitchell & Stewart, 2013)
- Expanded and updated coverage of media influences on gender (Near, 2013)
- Description of recent research that found male teachers perceived boys more positively and viewed them as more educationally competent than did female teachers (Mullola & others, 2012)
- Coverage of a recent study of how gender is displayed in MTV music videos (Wallis, 2011)
- Inclusion of information about a recent meta-analysis that revealed no gender differences in math for adolescents (Lindberg & others, 2010)
- Updated data on the continuing gender gap in reading and writing among U.S. students (National Assessment of Educational Progress, 2012)
- Updated material on gender differences in high school dropout rates (National Center for Education Statistics, 2011)
- Update on the increasing gender difference involving more women than men attending college after high school (Women in Academia, 2011)
- Coverage of a recent large-scale study linking girls' positive attitudes about school to their higher grades and boys' negative attitudes toward school to their lower grades (Orr, 2011)
- Updated and expanded discussion of gender differences in emotion (Hertenstein & Keltner, 2011)
- Revised and updated discussion of gender differences in relationships, including information from recent research reviews indicating that girls are more people oriented and boys are more object oriented (Galambos, Berenbaum, & McHale, 2009; Perry & Pauletti, 2011)
- Discussion of a recent meta-analysis of children's emotional expression that found a small overall gender difference with girls showing more positive and internalizing emotions; however, this gender difference became more pronounced with age, increasing during middle and late childhood and adolescence (Chaplin & Aldao, 2013)
- Coverage of a recent research review indicating that gender differences in adolescence are small (Perry & Pauletti, 2011)
- Inclusion of information about a recent study that indicated hyper-gender behavior in boys and girls was linked to a lower level of school engagement and school attachment (Ueno & McWilliams, 2010)

Chapter 13: Moral Development

- Substantial updates based on feedback from leading experts Darcia Narváez and Daniel Lapsley
- Updated and expanded coverage of criticisms of Piaget's view of young children's moral development based on research indicating that young children often show a non-egocentric awareness of others' intentions and know when someone violates a moral prohibition (Thompson, 2012)
- Updated and expanded coverage of the personality domain and domain theory, including expanded examples of domains, in the opening material explaining moral development
- Expanded information about the domain theory of moral development and the distinction between moral, social conventional, and personal domains (Smetana, 2011a, b, 2013a, b; Smetana & others, 2012)

- Description of recent research indicating that 2½- to 4-year-old children distinguished hypothetical moral from conventional transgressions on many criteria but only older preschoolers did so when rating whether someone deserved punishment (Smetana & others, 2012)

- Description of a recent study of children's unwillingness to donate any money after watching a UNICEF film on children suffering from poverty until an adult gently probed their intentions, which supports the situational nature of moral behavior (van IJzendoorn & others, 2010)

- Coverage of a recent study of 5- to 13-year-olds that found with increasing age children attributed more positive emotions to people who sacrifice their own desires to help others who are needy and become more discriminating about the contexts that call for altruistic action (Weller & Lagattuta, 2013)

- Coverage of a recent study that revealed links between a higher level of multicultural experience and a lower level of closed mindedness, a growth mindset, and higher moral judgment (Narváez & Hill, 2010)

- Expanded discussion of moral identity with an emphasis on Darcia Narváez's (2010a) recent view that moral metacognition, especially through self-monitoring and self-reflection, is linked to moral maturity

- Description of a recent study that found adolescents' moral motivation was related to the quality of their relationship with their parents (Malti & Buchmann, 2010)

- Coverage of a recent study that linked authoritative parenting to an increase in adolescents' moral identity (Hardy & others, 2010)

- Discussion of two recent studies that revealed an important role of early secure attachment in children's and adolescents' future outcomes (Kochanska & others, 2010a, b)

- Discussion of recent research by Gustavo Carlo and his colleagues (2010) that illustrated the importance of considering the multidimensional aspects of prosocial behavior

- Coverage of a recent study of parenting techniques and adolescent moral development in which parental induction, as well as expression of disappointed expectations, was considered more appropriate by adolescents (Patrick & Gibbs, 2012). In this study, parental induction was linked to a higher level of adolescents' moral identity

- Inclusion of recent research showing that 3-year-olds were less likely to offer assistance to an adult they previously had observed being harmful to another person (Vaish, Carpenter, & Tomasello, 2010)

- Discussion of a recent study that found mothers', but not fathers', authoritative parenting was associated with adolescents' engagement in prosocial behavior one year later (Padilla-Walker & others, 2012)

- New discussion of a recent study that found adolescents' volunteering activity in the community was linked to a higher level of identity status and identity achievement (Crocetti, Jahromi, & Meeus, 2012)

- Description of a recent study that revealed adolescents' volunteer activities provided opportunities to explore and reason about moral issues (van Goethem, 2012)

- New material on the current efforts to get U.S. students involved in service learning that is mainly coordinated by the Corporation for National and Community Service

- Inclusion of a recent research study revealing that forgiveness varied when encountering a transgressing peer based on whether the peer was liked or disliked (Peets, Hodges, & Salmivalli, 2012)

- Description of a recent study that found expressing gratitude was linked to a lower level of depressive symptoms in adolescents (Lambert, Fincham, & Stillman, 2012)

- Coverage of a recent study of Chinese adolescents that found those who had a higher level of gratitude were less likely to engage in suicide ideation and suicide attempts (Li & others, 2012)

- Discussion of a four-year longitudinal study that found the most grateful adolescents had a stronger sense of meaning of life, were more satisfied with their life, were happier and more helpful, and had a lower level of negative emotions and were less depressed than the least grateful adolescents (Bono, 2012)

- New commentary about how we still do not have adequate research information about how youth perceive prosocial norms and the influence of school policies and peers on adolescents' prosocial behavior (Siu, Shek, & Law, 2012)
- Discussion of recent research on the role of parental monitoring and support during adolescence in reducing criminal behavior in emerging adulthood (Johnson & others, 2011)
- Coverage of a recent study that found for both African American and non-Latino White adolescents, low parental control predicted delinquency indirectly through its link to deviant peer affiliation (Deutsch & others, 2012)
- Description of recent research that revealed authoritative parenting increased youths' perception of the legitimacy of parental authority and that youths' perception of parental legitimacy was associated with a lower level of future delinquency (Trinkner & others, 2012)
- Inclusion of recent research on the role of engaged parenting and mothers' social network support in reducing delinquency in low-income families (Ghazarian & Roche, 2010)
- Discussion of a recent meta-analysis of five programs for reducing the recidivism of juvenile offenders, revealing that family treatment was the only one that was effective (Schwalbe & others, 2012)
- Description of a recent study that found repeated poverty was a high risk factor for delinquency (Najman & others, 2010)
- New description of a recent study that found poor academic performance and reduced attachment to school at age 15 predicted a higher level of criminal activity at 17 to 19 years of age (Savolainen & others, 2012)
- Discussion of recent research suggesting that school connectedness served as a protective factor against the development of conduct problems in young adolescents (Loukas, Roalson, & Herrera, 2010)
- Updated coverage of outcomes for the Fast Track delinquency intervention study through age 19 that found the program was successful in reducing juvenile arrest rates (Conduct Problems Prevention Research Group, 2010b; Miller & others, 2011)
- New coverage of distinctions between religion, religiousness, and spirituality based on a recent analysis by Pamela King and her colleagues (King, Carr, & Boiter, 2011; King, Ramos, & Clardy, 2012)
- Update of college freshmen's religious activities and preference (Pryor & others, 2010)
- Coverage of a recent meta-analysis that found adolescents' spirituality/religiosity was positively linked to their well-being, self-esteem, and three of the Big Five factors of personality (conscientiousness, openness, and agreeableness); in this meta-analysis, spirituality/religion was negatively associated with risk behavior and depression (Yonker, Schnabelrauch, & DeHaan, 2012)
- Inclusion of a recent study that found parents' religiousness during youths' adolescence was positively linked to youths' own religiousness during adolescence (Spilman & others, 2012)
- Discussion of recent research linking church engagement with a lower level of depression in adolescents (Kang & Romo, 2011)

Chapter 14: Families

- Inclusion of new information about the concept of transactions reflecting reciprocal socialization (Sameroff, 2009)
- New section on parental roles and the timing of parenthood that includes content on trends in the age at which adults have children and differences in parenting between younger and older parents (Carl, 2012; Lauer & Lauer, 2012)

- Expanded and updated discussion of the effects of punishment on children's development, including longitudinal studies that have linked early physical punishment to later aggression (Gershoff & others, 2012; Lansford & others, 2011), and cross-cultural studies that have found in countries in which physical punishment is considered normal and necessary for handling children's transgressions, the effects of punishment are less harmful (Lansford & others, 2005; Lansford & Deater-Deckard, 2012)

- Expanded and updated coverage of family-related factors that can contribute to child maltreatment (Cicchetti, 2013; Laslett & others, 2012; Turner & others, 2012)

- Discussion of research indicating links between early childhood maltreatment and subsequent problems in emotional development (Kim-Spoon, Cicchetti, & Rogosch, 2013)

- Coverage of a recent study that revealed a significant increase in suicide attempts before age 18 when repeated child maltreatment occurred (Jonson-Reid, Kohl, & Drake, 2012)

- Description of recent research studies that linked child maltreatment to risk for various diseases and physical health problems, sexual problems, and depression as adults (Lacelle & others, 2012; Nanni, Uher, & Danese, 2012)

- Discussion of a 30-year study that found middle-aged adults who had experienced child maltreatment had an increased risk of diabetes, lung disease, malnutrition, and visual problems (Widom & others, 2012)

- Coverage of a recent study linking fathers' play with young children to an increase in supportive coparenting (Jia & Schoppe-Sullivan, 2011)

- Inclusion of recent research studies on the transition to parenthood that involve negative changes in relationships for both married and cohabiting women with their partners, and violated expectations (Biehle & Mickelson, 2012; Mortensen & others, 2012)

- Description of recent research on factors linked to new mothers' low marital satisfaction (Dew & Wilcox, 2011)

- New section on managing and guiding infants' behavior (Holden, Vittrup, & Rosen, 2011)

- New material on the percentage of parents who use various management and corrective methods in dealing with infants' undesirable behaviors, including new Figure 14.2 (Vittrup, Holden, & Buck, 2006)

- Discussion of recent research focused on parent-adolescent relationships of Asian American parents and their adolescents (Russell, Crockett, & Chao, 2010)

- Inclusion of recent research on more than 36,000 eighth- and tenth-graders revealing that a higher level of parental monitoring was associated with lower alcohol and marijuana use, with the effects strongest among female adolescents and adolescents with the highest risk-taking profile (Dever & others, 2013)

- Expanded and updated discussion of the increasing interest in adolescents' management of their parents' access to information, including recent research findings (Metzger & others, 2013; Rote & others, 2012; Smetana, 2011a, b)

- New coverage of a recent study of U.S. and Chinese adolescents that found adolescents' disclosure to parents was linked to a higher level of academic competence over time (Cheung, Pomerantz, & Dong, 2013)

- New material on parent-adolescent conflict in immigrant families, such as Latinos and Asian Americans, that focuses on core cultural values with the conflict not always appearing openly but as underlying internal feelings (Fuligni, 2012; Juang & Umana-Taylor, 2012)

- New discussion of a study that found a higher level of parent-adolescent conflict was related to peer-reported aggression and juvenile delinquency (Ehrlich, Dykas, & Cassidy, 2012)

- Discussion of a recent study that found regardless of where they were born, Mexican-origin adolescent girls living in the United States had age expectations for autonomy at an earlier age than their parents preferred (Bamaca-Colbert & others, 2012)

- Inclusion of recent research on adolescents' perceptions of their parents' promotion of more psychological autonomy and less psychological control, and links to adolescent adjustment (Sher-Censor, Parke, & Coltrane, 2011)
- Description of a recent analysis that concluded the most consistent outcomes of secure attachment in adolescence involve positive peer relations and the development of emotion regulation capacities (Allen & Miga, 2010)
- Inclusion of recent research on the effects of sibling conflict about issues of equality and fairness, as well as invasion of one's personal domain, on subsequent well-being (Campione-Barr, Bassett-Greer, & Kruse, 2013)
- Added commentary about effects of parental work on adolescents not being only a maternal employment issue, but often involving the father as well (Parke & Clarke-Stewart, 2011)
- Coverage of a recent study that found adolescent girls from divorced families displayed lower levels of romantic competence, but that their mothers' coherent account of their own romantic experiences alleviated the negative link of divorce to daughters' romantic behavior (Shulman & others, 2012)
- Coverage of a recent study that found parental conflict during children's kindergarten years was linked to higher levels of emotional insecurity later in childhood, which in turn were associated with adjustment problems in adolescence such as depression and anxiety (Cummings & others, 2012)
- Expanded and updated coverage of the relationship between divorced parents and its link to visitations by the noncustodial parent (Fabricius & others, 2010)
- Added comment about father involvement dropping off more than mother involvement following a divorce, especially for fathers of girls
- Coverage of a recent study indicating that an intervention aimed at improving the mother-child relationship was linked to improvements in the coping skills of children in divorced families (Velez & others, 2011)
- Inclusion of information about joint custody working best for children when the divorced parents can get along with each other (Parke & Clarke-Stewart, 2011)
- Revised discussion of remarried families in terms of some of these families being more adult-focused, while others are more child-focused (Anderson & Greene, 2011)
- Coverage of recent information about child and adolescent outcomes for individuals conceived by new reproductive technologies, which are increasingly used by gay and lesbian adults (Golombok, 2011a, b; Golombok & Tasker, 2010)
- Discussion of recent research linking the transmission of divorce across generations, although this transmission has decreased in recent years (Wolfinger, 2011)

Chapter 15: Peers

- Coverage of a recent study that found children who were associated with prosocial peers at age 9 had a higher level of self-control at age 10 and children who were associated with deviant peers at age 9 had a lower level of self-control at age 10 (Meldrum & Hay, 2012)
- Description of recent research with 4-year-old children that found gender was a strong influence on the young children's selection of playmates (Martin & others, 2013)
- New research that indicated low parental control was associated with higher delinquency in adolescence through its link to deviant peer affiliation (Deutsch & others, 2012)
- Description of a recent meta-analysis that revealed the link between mother and peer attachment was much stronger than the association of father and peer attachment (Gorrese & Ruggieri, 2012)
- Coverage of a recent analysis indicating that one of the most consistent outcomes of attachment research in adolescence is that secure attachment to parents is linked to positive peer relations (Allen & Miga, 2010)

- New discussion of social knowledge and peer relations, including a recent study linking adolescents' social intelligence with their peer popularity (Meijs & others, 2010)
- New description of the role that play can have as an important context for the development of language and communication skills (Hirsh-Pasek & Golinkoff, 2013)
- New discussion of concerns expressed by Kathy Hirsh-Pasek, Roberta Golinkoff, and Dorothy Singer (Hirsh-Pasek & others, 2009; Singer, Golinkoff, & Hirsh-Pasek, 2006) about the decline of play in young children's lives causing them to miss out on the many positive cognitive and socioemotional outcomes that result from play
- Coverage of a recent study that found having supportive friends was linked to lower levels of bullying and victimization (Kendrick, Jutengren, & Stattin, 2012)
- New content on bullies' perceptions of their parents (Espelage & Holt, 2012)
- Discussion of recent research showing a higher level of depression and suicide in children who are the victims of bullying (Fisher & others, 2012; Lemstra & others, 2012)
- Description of a recent longitudinal study of more than 6,000 children that found a link between bullying/victimization and suicide ideation (Winsper & others, 2012)
- Coverage of a recent study indicating that victims of peer bullying were more likely to develop borderline personality symptoms (Wolke & others, 2012)
- Discussion of a recent study that asked former victims of bullying what had made the bullying stop (Frisen, Hasselblad, & Holmqvist, 2012)
- Description of a recent study linking bullying and moral disengagement (Obermann, 2011)
- Coverage of a recent study of developmental changes in the importance placed on peer popularity (LaFontana & Cillessen, 2010)
- Inclusion of information about a recent study linking preschool children's aggression in peer interaction to their self-regulation skills (Olson & others, 2011)
- New section on other-sex friendships that includes information about girls reporting more other-sex friendships than boys did
- Inclusion of information on parents likely monitoring their daughters' other-sex friendships more than their sons and recent research indicating that a higher level of parental monitoring led to fewer other-sex friendships, which in turn was associated with a lower level of subsequent alcohol use for girls but not boys (Poulin & Denault, 2012)
- Updated and expanded coverage of the positive outcomes of positive friendship relationships in adolescence (Kendrick, Jutengren, & Stattin, 2012; Tucker & others, 2012; Way & Silverman, 2012)
- Discussion of a study of young adolescents' friendships and depression (Brendgen & others, 2010)
- Description of research indicating benefits of mixed-age friendships for some young adolescents who don't have friends in their grade (Bowker & Spencer, 2010)
- Coverage of a recent study that found some adolescents who identified with certain crowds had more internalizing behavior problems while others who identified with other crowds had more externalizing problems (Doornwaard & others, 2012)
- Coverage of a recent meta-analysis that found a number of gender differences in adolescent girls' and boys' friendships (Gorrese & Ruggieri, 2012)
- Description of recent research that indicated adolescents with a more intense romantic involvement were more likely to engage in delinquency than their counterparts with a lower level of romantic involvement (Cui & others, 2012)
- Coverage of a recent study that revealed young adolescents who had negative relationships with their parents turned to romantic relationships for intimacy and support, which in turn provided the opportunity for early sexual initiation (de Graaf & others, 2012)
- New content on a longitudinal study that found links between adolescents' personality traits, beliefs about marriage, and romantic relationships in early adulthood (Masarik & others, 2012)

- Description of recent research on the negative outcomes of adolescent girls having an older romantic partner (Haydon & Halpern, 2010)
- Coverage of a recent study that found romantic activity was associated with depression in early adolescent girls (Starr & others, 2012)
- New section on parent-adolescent relationships and adolescents' and emerging adults' dating and romantic relationships
- Description of recent research linking the mother's marital satisfaction with the adolescent's romantic competence (Shulman, Davila, & Shachar-Shapira, 2011)
- Discussion of a recent study that found parental divorce influenced the timing of the adolescent's first romantic relationship but only when the divorce occurred in early adolescence (Ivanova, Veenstra, & Mills, 2012)
- Inclusion of recent information from a longitudinal study indicating that better-quality parent-adolescent and dating relationships in adolescence were linked to better-quality romantic relationships in emerging adulthood (Madsen & Collins, 2011)

Chapter 16: Schools and Achievement

- Description of a recent study that found Early Head Start had a protective effect on the risks children might experience in parenting, language development, and self-control (Ayoub, Vallotton, & Mastergeorge, 2011)
- New discussion of Robert Crosnoe's (2011) recent book, *Fitting In, Standing Out,* that emphasizes how the conformity demands of complex peer cultures in high school undermine students' academic achievement
- Updated and expanded discussion of high school dropout rates, including recent data for 2011 and revised Figure 16.3 (National Center for Education Statistics, 2012).
- New discussion of the controversy in determining accurate school dropout rates
- Updated data on the percentage of students who receive special education services and the areas in which they receive those services (Condition of Education, 2012)
- Discussion of recent research indicating that mindfulness training can be effective in improving the attention of adolescents who have ADHD, at least in the short term (van de Weijer-Bergsma & others, 2012)
- New description of some developmental outcomes of children with ADHD, including increased risks for dropping out of school, adolescent pregnancy, substance abuse problems, and engaging in antisocial behavior (Chang, Lichtenstein, & Larsson, 2012; Von Polier, Vloet, & Herpertz-Dahlman, 2012)
- Expanded discussion of the possible misdiagnosis, including details of a recent experimental study that found clinicians overdiagnosed ADHD symptoms, especially in boys (Bruchmiller, Margraf, & Schneider, 2012)
- Coverage of a recent study indicating delayed development in the frontal lobes of children with ADHD, likely due to delayed or decreased myelination (Nagel & others, 2011)
- Description of a recent study that linked cigarette smoking during pregnancy to ADHD in children (Sciberras, Ukoumunne, & Efron, 2011)
- New coverage of executive function deficits in children with ADHD and their links to brain functioning (Jacobson & others, 2011; Rinsky & Hinshaw, 2011)
- New material on deficits in theory of mind in children with ADHD (Buhler & others, 2011; Shuai, Chan, & Wang, 2011)
- Inclusion of recent estimates indicating that in 2008 1 in 88 children had an autistic spectrum disorder, a dramatic increase since 2002 estimates (Centers for Disease Control & Prevention, 2012c)
- New discussion of the role that connectivity between different brain regions might play in the development of autism (Just & others, 2012; Philip & others, 2012)
- Coverage of a recent study of 34 high school classrooms that revealed students who perceived their classrooms as allowing and encouraging autonomy in the first several

weeks of the semester were more engaged in their classrooms throughout the course (Hafen & others, 2012)

- New section on sustained attention, effort, and task persistence exploring the influence of these important processes on adolescent achievement

- Description of a recent study in which task persistence in early adolescence predicted career success in middle age (Andersson & Bergman, 2011)

- New Figure 16.10 that shows a module used in Carol Dweck's recent research on brainology

- Updated information about recent research conducted by Carol Dweck and her colleagues (Dweck, 2012; Good, Rattan, & Dweck, 2012; Job, Dweck, & Walton, 2010; Miller & others, 2012) examining how a growth mindset can prevent negative stereotypes from undermining achievement and how willpower is a virtually unlimited mindset that predicts how long people will work and resist temptations during stressful circumstances

- Discussion of a recent study showing positive developmental outcomes for adolescents with high self-efficacy parents (Steca & others, 2011)

- Expanded material on goal-setting, including the importance of setting personal goals (Wigfield & Cambria, 2010)

- Description of a study demonstrating the importance of intentional self-regulation and extracurricular activities in supporting positive developmental outcomes for young adolescents from low-income backgrounds (Urban, Lewin-Bizan, & Lerner, 2010)

- New coverage of the work done by Barry Zimmerman and his colleagues (Zimmerman, 2002; Zimmerman & Kitsantas, 1997; Zimmerman & Labuhn, 2012) in creating a three-phase model of self-regulation in achievement

- New discussion of the importance of delaying gratification in reaching goals, especially long-term goals (Cheng, Shein, & Chiou, 2012; Schlam & others, 2013)

- Coverage of a large-scale longitudinal study that focused on the importance of academic resources at home, especially in support of African American or low-SES students' achievement (Xia, 2010)

- Inclusion of recent international comparisons of 15-year-olds' reading, math, and science achievement in 65 countries, including new Figure 16.11 (OECD, 2010)

- New discussion of the importance of parental involvement in children's learning, describing the research of Eva Pomerantz and her colleagues (Cheung & Pomerantz, 2012; Pomerantz, Cheung, & Qin, 2012; Pomerantz, Kim, & Cheung, 2012) that especially focuses on comparisons of U.S. and Chinese children and their parents

Chapter 17: Culture and Diversity

- Updated data on the percentage of U.S. children and adolescents living in poverty (U.S. Census Bureau, 2012)

- Discussion of a recent study linking early and persistent poverty to lower cognitive functioning in 5-year-old children (Schoon & others, 2011)

- Inclusion of recent research on outcomes among 9- to 19-year-old African American boys who had experienced the New Hope antipoverty program (McLoyd & others, 2011)

- New discussion of the New Hope Project's work-based, anti-poverty intervention that had positive effects on adolescents' future orientation (Purtell & McLoyd, 2013)

- Description of a recent study that found neighborhood affluence, but not family wealth, was linked to adolescent problems (Lund & Dearing, 2013)

- Updated and expanded introduction to immigration and adolescent development that describes the complexity of immigration (Crosnoe & Fuligni, 2012)

- New coverage of two models of immigration—immigrant risk model and immigrant paradox model—and the conclusion that research supports both models to some degree (Crosnoe & Fuligni, 2012)

- Expanded and updated coverage of the stressful and difficult experiences that children in many immigrant families face, including children in undocumented families (Yoshikawa, 2012)

- Coverage of a recent study that found Mexican American adolescents spent less time with their family and identified less with family values after immigrating to the United States (Updegraff & others, 2012)

- Description of how ethnic/immigrant families often focus on issues associated with promoting children's ethnic pride, knowledge of their ethnic group, and discrimination (Rogers & others, 2012; Simpkins & others, 2012)

- Inclusion of recent research indicating that parents' education before migrating was strongly linked to their children's academic achievement (Pong & Landale, 2012)

- Expanded and updated material on immigrant families and their bicultural orientation, including recent research by Ross Parke and his colleagues (2011) on immigrant Mexican American families

- New discussion of immigrant adolescents as cultural brokers for their parents (Villanueva & Buriel, 2010)

- Discussion of a recent study of the outcomes of discrimination directed toward Latino and Asian American adolescents (Huynh & Fuligni, 2010)

- Discussion of a recent study that found African American adolescents' perceived racial discrimination was linked to their higher level of delinquency (Martin & others, 2011)

- Expanded and updated introduction to media use including the recent creation of the term *screen time* that encompasses the wide range of media/computer/communication/information devices that adolescents now use (De Decker & others, 2012)

- Description of a new study of 8- to 12-year-old girls that found a higher level of media multitasking was linked to negative social well-being while a higher level of face-to-face communication was associated with a higher level of social well-being, such as social success, feeling normal, and having fewer friends whom parents perceived as a bad influence (Pea & others, 2012)

- Substantial updating of media use based on a 2009 national survey of more than 2,000 U.S. adolescents, including comparisons with other previous national surveys to show trends in adolescent media use (Rideout, Foehr, & Roberts, 2010)

- New Figure 17.7 illustrating the dramatic recent increase in adolescent media use

- Description of a new study of 8- to 12-year-old girls that found a higher level of media multitasking was linked to negative social well-being while a higher level of face-to-face communication was associated with a higher level of social well-being, such as social success, feeling normal, and having fewer friends whom parents perceived as a bad influence (Pea & others, 2012)

- Updated and expanded discussion that focuses on the increasing concern about the extensive time young children spend in media and screen time (De Decker & others, 2012)

- Description of recent research indicating that 22 percent of 5- to 8-year-olds use computers daily (Common Sense Media, 2011)

- Much expanded coverage of video game use, including research that substantiates the negative effects of playing violent video games (DeWall, Anderson, & Bushman, 2013) but that also indicates positive child outcomes for prosocial skills after playing prosocial video games (Gentile & others, 2009), improved visuospatial skills (Schmidt & Vandewater, 2008), and weight loss for overweight adolescents following video game playing that requires exercise (Bond, Richards, & Calvert, 2013)

- New commentary that most studies of video game playing by adolescents have focused on possible negative rather than positive outcomes (Adachi & Willoughby, 2013)

- Description of a recent experimental research study that found overweight adolescents lost more weight following a 10-week competitive condition that involved playing the Nintendo Wii EA Sports Active video (Staiano, Abraham, & Calvert, 2012).

- New coverage of a research review on children's and adolescents' TV viewing and creativity concluding that overall there is a negative association between TV viewing and creativity but that there is an exception when children and adolescents watch educational TV content designed to teach creativity through the use of imaginative characters (Calvert & Valkenberg, 2011)
- Inclusion of a recent recommendation that for children 2 to 4 years of age, screen time should be limited to no more than one hour per day (Tremblay & others, 2012)
- Coverage of a recent study linking 3- to 5-year-olds' sleep problems to watching TV after 7 p.m. and watching violent TV shows (Garrison, Liekwig, & Christakis, 2011)
- Description of a recent national survey of trends in adolescents' use of social media, including dramatic increases in social networking and text messaging, and declines in tweeting and blogging (Lenhart & others, 2010)
- Updated coverage of social networking, with Facebook surpassing Google as the most visited Web site in 2010
- New commentary about text messaging now being the main way that adolescents prefer to connect with their friends (Lenhart & others, 2010)
- Inclusion of recent research on links between children's cyber aggression and negative effects on peer relations (Schoffstall & Cohen, 2011)
- Description of a recent study of parenting predictors of adolescent media use (Padilla-Walker & Coyne, 2011)

Resources

The resources listed here may accompany *Child Development*, 14th edition. Please contact your McGraw-Hill representative for details concerning policies, prices, and availability.

Online Learning Center at www.mhhe.com/santrockcd14e. The book's website contains an Instructor's Manual, Test Bank files, PowerPoint slides, Image Gallery, and other valuable materials to help you design and enhance your course. Ask your local McGraw-Hill representative for your password.

Instructor's Manual. Authored by Ralph Carlini, University of Massachusetts-Dartmouth, each chapter of the Instructor's Manual is introduced by a Total Teaching Package Outline. This fully integrated tool helps instructors more easily locate and choose among the many resources available for the course by linking each element of the Instructor's Manual to a particular teaching topic within the chapter. These elements include chapter outlines, suggested lecture topics, classroom activities and demonstrations, suggested student research projects, essay questions, critical thinking questions, and implications for guidance.

Test Bank and Computerized Test Bank. Developed by Diane Powers-Willard, Iowa Central Community College, this comprehensive Test Bank includes more than 1,500 multiple-choice and approximately 75 essay questions. Organized by chapter, the questions are designed to test factual, applied, and conceptual understanding. All test questions are compatible with EZ Test, McGraw-Hill's Computerized Test Bank program.

PowerPoint Presentations. Created by Len Mendola, Adelphia University, these presentations cover the key points of each chapter and include charts and graphs from the text. They can be used as is or modified to meet your specific needs.

McGraw-Hill's Visual Assets Database for Lifespan Development (VAD 2.0) at www.mhhe.com/vad. This online database of videos has been created specifically for instructors to use in the classroom. Customize classroom presentations by downloading the videos to your computer and showing the videos on their own or insert them into your course cartridge or PowerPoint presentations. All of the videos are available with or without captions. Ask your McGraw-Hill representative for access information.

ACKNOWLEDGMENTS

I very much appreciate the support and guidance provided to me by many people at McGraw-Hill. Mike Sugarman, Publisher, has brought a wealth of publishing knowledge and vision to bear on improving my texts. Allison McNamara, Brand Manager, deserves thanks for her work on this book. Also, Senior Development Editor Cara Labell and Development Editors Vicki Malinee and Elisa Adams have done an excellent job of editing the manuscript and handling the page-by-page changes to this new edition. Sarah Kiefer, Editorial Coordinator, has done a very competent job of obtaining reviewers and handling many editorial chores. Ann Helgerson, Marketing Manager, has contributed in numerous positive ways to this book. Janet Tilden did a superb job as the book's copy editor. Jennifer Blankenship provided me with excellent choices for selecting photos. And Sheila Frank did a terrific job coordinating the book's production.

I also want to thank my wife, Mary Jo, our children, Tracy and Jennifer, and our grandchildren, Jordan, Alex, and Luke, for their wonderful contributions to my life and for helping me to better understand the marvels and mysteries of children's development.

Reviewers

I owe a special debt of gratitude to previous and current reviewers who provided detailed feedback about the book. They have made this edition of *Child Development* a far better book than would have otherwise been possible.

Expert Consultants

Child development has become an enormous, complex field, and no single author can possibly be an expert in all areas of the field. To solve this problem, beginning with the sixth edition I have sought the input of leading experts in many different areas of child development. This tradition continues in the fourteenth edition. The experts have provided me with detailed recommendations of new research to include. The panel of experts is literally a *Who's Who* in the field of child development. Their biographies appear on pages xii–xiv.

Previous Edition Reviewers

Kristine Anthis, *Southern Connecticut State University;* **Brein K. Ashdown,** *St. Louis University;* **Ruth L. Ault,** *Davidson College;* **Mary Ballard,** *Appalachian State University;* **William H. Barber,** *Midwestern State University;* **Marjorie M. Battaglia,** *George Mason University;* **Jann Belcher,** *Utah Valley State College;* **Wayne Benenson,** *Illinois State University;* **Michael Bergmire,** *Jefferson College;* **David Bernhardt,** *Carleton University;* **Kathryn Norcross Black,** *Purdue University;* **Elain Blakemore,** *Indiana University;* **Susan Bland,** *Niagara County Community College;* **Bryan Bolea,** Grand Valley State University; **Amy Booth,** *Northwestern University;* **Marc Bornstein,** *National Institute of Child Health and Human Development;* **Teresa Bossert-Braasch,** *McHenry County College;* **Megan E. Bradley,** *Frostburg State University;* **Albert Bramante,** *Union County College;* **Jo Ann Burnside,** *Richard J Daley College;* **Catherine Caldwell-Harris,** *Boston University;* **Maureen Callahan,** *Webster University;* **Victoria Candelora,** *Brevard Community College;* **Gustavo Carlo,** *University of Nebraska;* **D. Bruce Carter,** *Syracuse University;* **Elaine Cassel,** *Marymount University, Lord Fairfax Community College;* **Lisa Caya,** *University of Wisconsin—LaCrosse;* **Steven Ceci,** *Cornell University;* **Theodore Chandler,** *Kent State University;* **Dante Cicchetti,** *University of Rochester;* **Audrey E. Clark,** *California State University, Northridge;* **Debra E. Clark,** *SUNY—Cortland;* **Robert Cohen,** *The University of Memphis;* **John D. Coie,** *Duke University;* **Cynthia Garcia Coll,** *Wellesley College;* **W. Andrew Collins,** *University of Minnesota;* **Robert C. Coon,** *Louisiana State University;* **Roger W. Coulson,** *Iowa State University;* **William Curry,** *Wesleyan College;* **Fred Danner,** University of Kentucky; **Darlene DeMarie,** *University of South Florida;* **Marlene DeVoe,** *Saint Cloud State University;* **Denise M. DeZolt,** *Kent State University;* **K. Laurie Dickson,** *Northern Arizona University;* **Daniel D. DiSalvi,** *Kean College;* **Ruth Doyle,**

Casper College; **Diane C. Draper,** *Iowa State University;* **Sean Duffy,** *Rutgers University;* **Jerry Dusek,** *Syracuse University;* **Beverly Brown Dupré,** *Southern University at New Orleans;* **Glen Elder, Jr.,** *University of North Carolina;* **Claire Etaugh,** *Bradley University;* **Karen Falcone,** *San Joaquin Delta College;* **Dennis T. Farrell,** *Luzerne County Community College;* **Saul Feinman,** *University of Wyoming;* **Gary Feng,** *Duke University;* **Tiffany Field,** *University of Miami;* **Oney Fitzpatrick, Jr.,** *Lamar University;* **Jane Goins Flanagan,** *Lamar University;* **Kate Fogarty,** *University of Florida—Gainesville;* **L. Sidney Fox,** *California State University—Long Beach;* **Janet Frick,** *University of Georgia;* **Douglas Frye,** *University of Virginia;* **Dale Fryxell,** *Chamainde University;* **Janet A. Fuller,** *Mansfield University;* **Irma Galejs,** *Iowa State University;* **Mary Gauvain,** *University of California, Riverside;* **Eugene Geist,** *Ohio University;* **John Gibbs,** *Ohio State University;* **Colleen Gift,** *Highland Community College;* **Margaret S. Gill,** *Kutztown University;* **Beverly Goldfield,** *Rhode Island College;* **Hill Goldsmith,** *University of Wisconsin— Madison;* **Cynthia Graber,** *Columbia University;* **Stephen B. Graves,** *University of South Florida;* **Donald E. Guenther,** *Kent State University;* **Julia Guttmann,** *Iowa Wesleyan College;* **Renee Ha,** *University of Washington;* **Robert A. Haaf,** *University of Toledo;* **Craig Hart,** *Brigham Young University;* **Susan Harter,** *University of Denver;* **Robin Harwood,** *Texas Tech University;* **Elizabeth Hasson,** *Westchester University;* **Rebecca Heikkinen,** *Kent State University;* **Joyce Hemphill,** *University of Wisconsin;* **Shirley-Anne Hensch,** *University of Wisconsin;* **Stanley Henson,** *Arkansas Technical University;* **Alice Honig,** *Syracuse University;* **Cynthia Hudley,** *University of California—Santa Barbara;* **Diane Hughes,** *New York University;* **Stephen Hupp,** *Southern Illinois University—Edwardsville;* **Vera John-Steiner,** *University of New Mexico;* **Helen L. Johnson,** *Queens College;* **Kathy E. Johnson,** *Indiana University— Purdue University, Indianapolis;* **Seth Kalichman,** *Loyola University;* **Kenneth Kallio,** *SUNY— Geneseo;* **Maria Kalpidou,** *Assumption College;* **Daniel W. Kee,** *California State University—Fullerton;* **Christy Kimpo,** *University of Washington;* **Melvyn B. King,** *SUNY— Cortland;* **Claire Kopp,** *UCLA;* **Deanna Kuhn,** *Columbia University;* **John Kulig,** *Northern Illinois University;* **Janice Kupersmidt,** *University of North Carolina;* **Michael Lamb,** *National Institute of Child Health and Human Development;* **Daniel K. Lapsley,** *University of Notre Dame;* **Michael Lewis,** *Rutgers University;* **David B. Liberman,** *University of Houston;* **Robert Lickliter,** *Florida International University;* **Hsin-Hui Lin,** *University of Houston—Victoria;* **Marianna Footo Linz,** *Marshall University;* **Gretchen S. Lovas,** *Susquehanna University;* **Pamela Ludemann,** *Framingham State College;* **Kevin MacDonald,** *California State University— Long Beach;* **Virginia A. Marchman,** *University of Texas at Dallas;* **Saramma T. Mathew,** *Troy State University;* **Barbara McCombs,** *University of Denver;* **Dottie McCrossen,** *University of Ottawa;* **Sheryll Mennicke,** *Concordia College, St. Paul;* **Carolyn Meyer,** *Lake Sumter Community College;* **Dalton Miller-Jones,** *NE Foundation for Children;* **Marilyn Moore,** *Illinois State University;* **Carrie Mori,** *Boise State University;* **Brad Morris,** *Grand Valley State University;* **Winnie Mucherah,** *Ball State University;* **John P. Murray,** *Kansas State University;* **Dara Musher-Eizenman,** *Bowling Green State University;* **José E. Nanes,** *University of Minnesota;* **Sherry J. Neal,** *Oklahoma City Community College;* **Larry Nucci,** *University of Illinois at Chicago;* **Daniel J. O'Neill,** *Briston Community College;* **Randall E. Osborne,** *Southwest Texas State University;* **Margaret Owen,** *University of Texas at Dallas;* **Robert Pasnak,** *George Mason University;* **Barbara Aldis Patton,** *University of Houston—Victoria;* **Judy Payne,** *Murray State University;* **Elizabeth Pemberton,** *University of Delaware;* **Herb Pick,** *University of Minnesota;* **Kathy Lee Pillow,** *Arkansas State University, Beebe;* **Nan Ratner,** *University of Maryland;* **Brenda Reimer,** *Southern Missouri State University;* **John Reiser,** *Vanderbilt University;* **Cynthia Rickert,** *Dominican College;* **Cosby Steele Rogers,** *Virginia Polytechnic Institute and State University;* **Kimberly A. Gordon Rouse,** *Ohio State University;* **Jaynati Roy,** *Southern Connecticut State University;* **Kenneth Rubin,** *University of Maryland;* **Donna Ruiz,** *University of Cincinnati;* **Alan Russell,** *Flinders University;* **Carolyn Saarni,** *Sonoma State University;* **Douglas B. Sawin,** *University of Texas, Austin;* **Krista Schoenfeld,** *Colby Community College;* **Ed Scholwinski,** *Southwest Texas State University;* **Dale Schunk,** *Purdue University;* **Bill M. Seay,** *Louisiana State University;* **Matthew J. Sharps,** *California State University, Fresno;* **Marilyn Shea,** *University of Maine, Farmington;* **Susan Shonk,** *SUNY—College of Brockport;* **Susan Siaw,** *California Polytechnic Institute—Pomona;* **Robert Siegler,** *Carnegie Mellon University;* **Evelyn D. Silva,** *Cosumnes River College;* **Mildred D. Similton,** *Pfeiffer University;* **Dorothy Justus Sluss,** *Virginia Polytechnic Institute and State University;* **Janet Spence,**

University of Texas—Austin; **Melanie Spence,** University of Texas—Dallas; **Richard Sprott,** California State University, East Bay; **Robert J. Sternberg,** Tufts University; **Mark S. Strauss,** University of Pittsburgh; **Margaret Szewczyk,** University of Chicago; **Ross Thompson,** University of California—Davis; **Donna J. Tyler Thompson,** Midland College; **Marion K. Underwood,** University of Texas—Dallas; **Margot Underwood,** College of DuPage; **Cherie Valeithian,** Kent State University; **Jaan Valsiner,** Clark University; **Robin Yaure,** Pennsylvania State—Mont Alto; **Kourtney Valliancourt**, New Mexico State University; **Elizabeth Vera,** Loyola University—Chicago; **Lawrence Walker,** University of British Columbia; **Kimberlee L. Whaley,** Ohio State University; **Belinda M. Wholeben,** Northern Illinois University; **Frederic Wynn,** County College of Morris.

CHILD
DEVELOPMENT

chapter 1

INTRODUCTION

chapter outline

1 Caring for Children

Learning Goal 1 Identify five areas in which children's lives need to be improved, and explain the roles of resilience and social policy in children's development.

Improving the Lives of Children

Resilience, Social Policy, and Children's Development

2 Developmental Processes, Periods, and Issues

Learning Goal 2 Discuss the most important processes, periods, and issues in development.

Biological, Cognitive, and Socioemotional Processes

Periods of Development

Age and Cohort Effects

Issues in Development

3 The Science of Child Development

Learning Goal 3 Summarize why research is important in child development, the main theories of child development, and research methods, designs, and challenges.

The Importance of Research

Theories of Child Development

Research Methods for Collecting Data

Research Designs

Challenges in Child Development Research

In every child who is born, under no matter what circumstances, and of no matter what parents, the potentiality of the human race is born again.

—JAMES AGEE
American Writer, 20th Century

The Nature of Child Development

Examining the shape of childhood allows us to understand it better. Every childhood is distinct, the first chapter of a new biography in the world. This book is about children's development, its universal features, its individual variations, its nature at the beginning of the twenty-first century. *Child Development* is about the rhythm and meaning of children's lives, about turning mystery into understanding, and about weaving together a portrait of who each of us was, is, and will be. In Section 1, you will read one chapter: "Introduction" (Chapter 1).

If I had my child to raise over again

If I had my child to raise over again,

I'd finger paint more, and point the finger less.

I'd do less correcting, and more connecting.

I'd take my eyes off my watch, and watch more with my eyes.

I would care to know less, and know to care more.

I'd take more hikes and fly more kites.

I'd stop playing serious, and seriously play.

I would run through more fields, and gaze at more stars.

I'd do more hugging, and less tugging.

I would be firm less often, and affirm much more.

I'd build self-esteem first, and the house later.

I'd teach less about the love of power,

And more about the power of love.

—Diane Loomans

Ted Kaczynski sprinted through high school, not bothering with his junior year and making only passing efforts at social contact. Off to Harvard at age 16, Kaczynski was a loner during his college years. One of his roommates at Harvard said that he avoided people by quickly shuffling by them and slamming the door behind him. After obtaining his Ph.D. in mathematics at the University of Michigan, Kaczynski became a professor at the University of California at Berkeley. His colleagues there remember him as hiding from social circumstances— no friends, no allies, no networking.

After several years at Berkeley, Kaczynski resigned and moved to a rural area of Montana, where he lived as a hermit in a crude shack for 25 years. Town residents described him as a bearded eccentric. Kaczynski traced his own difficulties to growing up as a genius in a kid's body and sticking out like a sore thumb in his surroundings as a child. In 1996, he was arrested and charged as the notorious Unabomber, America's most wanted killer. Over the course of 17 years, Kaczynski had sent 16 mail bombs that left 23 people wounded or maimed and 3 people dead. In 1998, he pleaded guilty to the offenses and was sentenced to life in prison.

A decade before Kaczynski mailed his first bomb, Alice Walker spent her days battling racism in Mississippi. She had recently won her first writing fellowship, but rather than use the money to follow her dream of moving to Senegal, Africa, she put herself into the heart and heat of the civil rights movement. Walker had grown up knowing the brutal effects of poverty and racism. Born in 1944, she was the eighth child of Georgia sharecroppers who earned $300 a year. When Walker was 8, her brother accidentally shot her in the left eye with a BB gun. Since her parents had no car, it took them a week to get her to a hospital. By the time she received medical care, she was blind in that eye, and it had developed a disfiguring layer of scar tissue. Despite the counts against her, Walker overcame pain and anger and went on to win a Pulitzer Prize for her book *The Color Purple*. She became not only a novelist but also an essayist, a poet, a short-story writer, and a social activist.

What leads one individual, so full of promise, to commit brutal acts of violence and another to turn poverty and trauma into a rich literary harvest? If you have ever wondered why people turn out the way they do, you have asked yourself the central question we will explore in this book.

Ted Kaczynski, the convicted Unabomber, traced his difficulties to growing up as a genius in a kid's body and not fitting in when he was a child.

Ted Kaczynski, about age 15–16.

Alice Walker won the Pulitzer Prize for her book *The Color Purple*. Like the characters in her book, Walker overcame pain and anger to triumph and celebrate the human spirit.

Alice Walker, about age 8.

preview

Why study children? Perhaps you are or will be a parent or teacher, and responsibility for children is or will be a part of your everyday life. The more you learn about children and the way researchers study them, the better you can guide them. Perhaps you hope to gain an understanding of your own history—as an infant, as a child, and as an adolescent. Perhaps you accidentally came across the course description and found it intriguing. Whatever your reasons, you will discover that the study of child development is provocative, intriguing, and informative. In this first chapter, we will explore historical views and the modern study of child development, consider why caring for children is so important, examine the nature of development, and outline how science helps us to understand it.

Caring for Children   LG1 Identify five areas in which children's lives need to be improved, and explain the roles of resilience and social policy in children's development.

> Improving the Lives of Children

> Resilience, Social Policy, and Children's Development

> Children are the legacy we leave for the time we will not live to see.
>
> —ARISTOTLE
> *Greek Philosopher, 4th Century* B.C.

What do we mean when we speak of an individual's development? **Development** is the pattern of change that begins at conception and continues through the life span. Most development involves growth, although it also includes decline. Anywhere you turn today, the development of children captures public attention.

Caring for children is an important theme of this text. To understand why caring for children is so important, we will explore why it is beneficial to study children's development, identify some areas in which children's lives need to be improved, and explore the roles of resilience and social policy in children's development.

IMPROVING THE LIVES OF CHILDREN

If you were to pick up a newspaper or magazine in any U.S. town or city, you might see headlines like these: "Political Leanings May Be Written in the Genes," "Mother Accused of Tossing Children into Bay," "Gender Gap Widens," and "FDA Warns About ADHD Drug." Researchers are examining these and many other topics of contemporary concern. The roles that health and well-being, parenting, education, and sociocultural contexts play in child development, as well as how social policy is related to these issues, are a particular focus of this textbook.

> We reach backward to our parents and forward to our children to a future we will never see, but about which we need to care.
>
> —CARL JUNG
> *Swiss Psychoanalyst, 20th Century*

development The pattern of movement or change that begins at conception and continues through the life span.

Health and Well-Being Does a pregnant woman endanger her fetus if she has a few beers a week? How does a poor diet affect a child's ability to learn? Are children exercising less today than in the past? What roles do parents and peers play in whether adolescents abuse drugs? Throughout this text, we will discuss many questions like these regarding health and well-being.

Health professionals today recognize the power of lifestyles and psychological states in children's health and well-being (Burns & others, 2013; Graham, Holt-Hale, & Parker, 2013). In every chapter of this book, issues of health and well-being are integrated into our discussion.

Clinical psychologists are among the health professionals who help people improve their well-being. In *Connecting with Careers,* you can read about clinical psychologist Luis Vargas, who helps adolescents with problems. A Careers Appendix that follows Chapter 1 describes the education and training required to become a clinical psychologist or to pursue other careers in child development.

connecting with careers

Luis Vargas, Clinical Child Psychologist

Luis Vargas is Director of the Clinical Child Psychology Internship Program and a professor in child and adolescent psychiatry at the University of New Mexico School of Medicine. He obtained an undergraduate degree in psychology from Trinity University in Texas and a Ph.D. in clinical psychology at the University of Nebraska–Lincoln.

Vargas' work includes assessing and treating children, adolescents, and their families, especially when a child or adolescent has a serious mental disorder. Vargas also trains mental health professionals to provide culturally responsive and developmentally appropriate mental health services. In addition, he is interested in cultural and assessment issues with children, adolescents, and their families.

Vargas' clinical work is heavily influenced by contextual and ecological theories of development (which we will discuss later in this chapter). His first undergraduate course in human development, and subsequent courses in development, contributed to his decision to pursue a career in clinical child psychology.

Following this chapter you can read about many careers in child development, including more about the field of child clinical psychology. Also, at appropriate places throughout the book we will provide profiles of individuals in various child development careers.

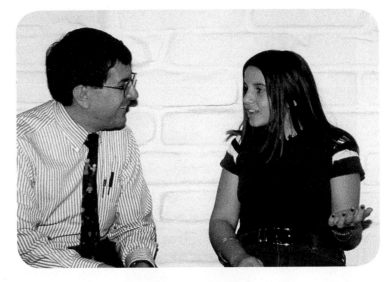

Luis Vargas (*left*) conducting a child therapy session.

For more information about what clinical psychologists do, see page 43 in the Careers in Child Development appendix that directly follows this chapter.

Parenting   Can two gay men raise a healthy family? Are children harmed if both parents work outside the home? Does spanking have negative consequences for a child's development? How damaging is divorce to children's development? Controversial answers to questions like these reflect pressures on the contemporary family (Grusec & others, 2013; Patterson, 2013). We'll examine these questions and others that provide a context for understanding factors that influence parents' lives and their effectiveness in raising their children. How parents, as well as other adults, can make a positive difference in children's lives is another major theme of this book.

You might be a parent someday or might already be one. You should take seriously the importance of rearing your children, because they are the future of our society. Good parenting takes considerable time. If you plan to become a parent, commit yourself day after day, week after week, month after month, and year after year to providing your children with a warm, supportive, safe, and stimulating environment that will make them feel secure and allow them to reach their full potential as human beings. The poster on this page that states "Children learn to love when they are loved" reflects this theme.

Understanding the nature of children's development can help you become a better parent (Grusec & others, 2013). Many parents learn parenting practices from their parents. Unfortunately, when parenting practices and child-care strategies are passed from one generation to the next, both desirable and undesirable ones are usually perpetuated. This book and your instructor's lectures in this course can help you become more knowledgeable about children's development and sort through which practices in your own upbringing you should continue with your own children and which you should abandon.

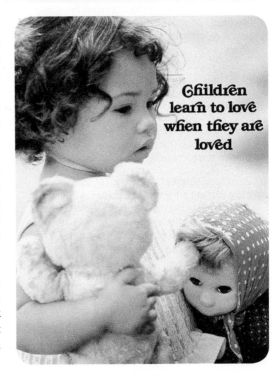

Children learn to love when they are loved

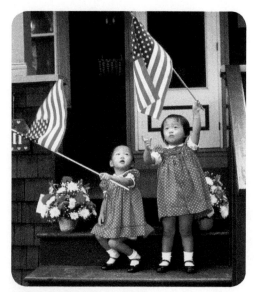

These two Korean-born children on the day they became U.S. citizens represent the dramatic increase in the percentage of ethnic minority children in the United States.

Inderjeet Poolust, 5, from India celebrates being one of 27 schoolchildren who recently became U.S. citizens at an induction ceremony in Queens, New York.

context The settings, influenced by historical, economic, social, and cultural factors, in which development occurs.

culture The behavior patterns, beliefs, and all other products of a group that are passed on from generation to generation.

cross-cultural studies Comparisons of one culture with one or more other cultures. These provide information about the degree to which children's development is similar, or universal, across cultures, and the degree to which it is culture-specific.

ethnicity A characteristic based on cultural heritage, nationality, race, religion, and language.

socioeconomic status (SES) Categorization based on a person's occupational, educational, and economic characteristics.

gender The characteristics of people as males and females.

Education   There is widespread agreement that something needs to be done to improve the education of our nation's children (Eccles & Roeser, 2013; McCombs, 2013; Reynolds & Miller, 2013). Among the questions involved in improving schools are the following: Are U.S. schools teaching children to be immoral? Are schools failing to teach students how to read and write and calculate adequately? Should there be more accountability in schools, with adequacy of student learning and teaching assessed by formal tests? Should schools challenge students more? Should schools focus only on developing children's knowledge and cognitive skills, or should they pay more attention to the whole child and consider the child's socioemotional and physical development as well? In this text, we will examine such questions about the state of education in the United States and consider recent research on solutions to educational problems (Miller & Reynolds, 2013).

Sociocultural Contexts and Diversity   Health and well-being, parenting, and education—like development itself—are all shaped by their sociocultural context (Bennett, 2012; Gauvain, 2013). The term **context** refers to the settings in which development occurs. These settings are influenced by historical, economic, social, and cultural factors (Spring, 2013). Four contexts that we pay special attention to in this text are culture, ethnicity, socioeconomic status, and gender.

  Culture encompasses the behavior patterns, beliefs, and all other products of a specific group of people that are passed on from generation to generation. Culture results from the interaction of people over many years (Gauvain, 2013). A cultural group can be as large as the United States or as small as an isolated Appalachian town. Whatever its size, the group's culture influences the behavior of its members. **Cross-cultural studies** compare aspects of two or more cultures. The comparison provides information about the degree to which development is similar, or universal, across cultures, or is instead culture-specific (Mistry, Contreras, & Dutta, 2013; Zhang & Sternberg, 2013).

  Ethnicity (the word *ethnic* comes from the Greek word for "nation") is rooted in cultural heritage, nationality, race, religion, and language. African Americans, Latinos, Asian Americans, Native Americans, Polish Americans, and Italian Americans are a few examples of ethnic groups. Diversity exists within each ethnic group (Trejos-Castillo, Bedore, & Trevino, 2013). Contrary to stereotypes, not all African Americans live in low-income circumstances; not all Latinos are Catholics; not all Asian Americans are high school math whizzes. A special concern is the discrimination and prejudice experienced by ethnic minority children (Benner & Graham, 2013; Tobler & others, 2013).

  Socioeconomic status (SES) refers to a person's position within society based on occupational, educational, and economic characteristics. Socioeconomic status implies certain inequalities. Generally, members of a society have (1) occupations that vary in prestige, with some individuals having more access than others to higher-status occupations; (2) different levels of educational attainment, with some individuals having more access than others to better education; (3) different economic resources; and (4) different levels of power to influence a community's institutions. These differences in the ability to control resources and to participate in society's rewards produce unequal opportunities (Doob, 2013; Purtell & McLoyd, 2013).

  Gender is another key dimension of children's development. **Gender** refers to the characteristics of people as males and females. Few aspects of our development are more central to our identity and social relationships than gender (Hyde & Else-Quest, 2013; Leaper, 2013; Matlin, 2012). How you view yourself, your relationships with other people, your life, and your goals are shaped to a great extent by whether you are male or female and how your culture defines the proper roles of males and females (Eagly, 2013; Patterson, 2013).

  In the United States, the sociocultural context has become increasingly diverse in recent years (Leong & others, 2013). The U.S. population includes a greater variety of cultures and ethnic groups than ever before. This changing demographic tapestry promises not only the richness that diversity produces but also difficult challenges in extending the American dream to all individuals (Schaefer, 2013; Spring, 2013). We will discuss sociocultural contexts and diversity in each chapter. In addition, *Connecting with Diversity*, which highlights an issue related to diversity, appears in every chapter. The *Connecting with*

connecting with diversity

Gender, Families, and Children's Development

Around the world, the experiences of female children and adolescents continue to be quite different from those of males (Mistry, Contreras, & Dutta, 2013; UNICEF, 2012). For example, one analysis found that a higher percentage of girls than boys around the world have never had any education (UNICEF, 2004) (see Figure 1.1). The countries with the fewest females being educated are in Africa, where girls and women in some areas receive no education at all. Canada, the United States, and Russia have the highest percentages of educated women. In developing countries, 67 percent of women over the age of 25 (compared with 50 percent of men) have never been to school. At the beginning of the twenty-first century, 80 million more boys than girls were in primary and secondary educational settings around the world (United Nations, 2002).

A special cross-cultural concern is the educational and psychological conditions of females around the world (UNICEF, 2012). Inadequate educational opportunities, violence, and mental health issues are just some of the problems faced by many females.

In many countries, adolescent females have less freedom to pursue a variety of careers and engage in various leisure acts than males (Helgeson, 2009; UNICEF, 2012). Gender differences in sexual expression are widespread, especially in India, Southeast Asia, Latin America, and Arab countries, where there are far more restrictions on the sexual activity of adolescent females than males. In certain areas around the world, these gender differences do appear to be narrowing over time. In some

countries, educational and career opportunities for women are expanding, and in some parts of the world control over adolescent girls' romantic and sexual relationships is weakening. However, in many countries females still experience considerable discrimination, and much work is needed to bridge the gap between the rights of males and females.

Consider Dhaka, Bangladesh, where sewers overflow, garbage rots in the streets, and children are undernourished. Nearly two-thirds of the young women in Bangladesh get married before they are 18. Doly Akter, age 17, who lives in a slum in Dhaka, recently created an organization supported by UNICEF in which girls go door-to-door to monitor the hygiene habits of households in their neighborhood. The girls' monitoring has led to improved hygiene and health in the families. Also, the organization Doly formed has managed to stop several child marriages by meeting with parents and convincing them that early marriage is not in their daughter's best interests. When talking with parents in their neighborhoods, the girls in the organization emphasize how staying in school will improve their daughter's future. Doly says the girls in her organization are far more aware of their rights than their mothers were (UNICEF, 2007).

What health and well-being, parenting, and educational problems and interventions have affected the development of females worldwide?

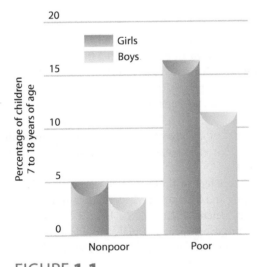

FIGURE 1.1

PERCENTAGE OF CHILDREN 7 TO 18 YEARS OF AGE AROUND THE WORLD WHO HAVE NEVER BEEN TO SCHOOL OF ANY KIND. When UNICEF (2004) surveyed the education that children around the world are receiving, it found that far more girls than boys receive no formal schooling at all.

Doly Akter

developmental **connection**

Peers

Peers especially play an important role in gender development during childhood. Chapter 12, p. 342

Ah! What would the world be to us
If the children were no more?
We should dread the desert
behind us
Worse than the dark before.

—**HENRY WADSWORTH LONGFELLOW**
American Poet, 19th Century

developmental **connection**

Socioeconomic Status

An increasing number of studies show that positive outcomes can be achieved by intervening in the lives of children experiencing poverty conditions. Chapter 17, p. 490

social policy A government's course of action designed to promote the welfare of its citizens.

Diversity interlude on the previous page focuses on gender, families, and children's development around the world.

RESILIENCE, SOCIAL POLICY, AND CHILDREN'S DEVELOPMENT

Some children develop confidence in their abilities despite negative stereotypes about their gender or their ethnic group, and some children triumph over poverty or other adversities. They show *resilience*. Think back to the chapter-opening story about Alice Walker. In spite of racism, poverty, low socioeconomic status, and a disfiguring eye injury, she went on to become a successful author and champion for equality.

Are there certain characteristics that make children like Alice Walker resilient? Are there other characteristics that make children lash out against society, like Ted Kaczynski, who became a killer despite his intelligence and education? After analyzing research on this topic, Ann Masten (2006, 2007, 2009, 2011, 2013) concluded that a number of individual factors, such as good intellectual functioning, influence resiliency. In addition, as Figure 1.2 shows, their families and resources outside the children's families tend to show certain features. For example, resilient children are likely to have a close relationship to a caring parent figure and bonds to caring adults outside the family.

Should governments also take action to improve the contexts of children's development and aid their resilience? **Social policy** is a government's course of action designed to promote the welfare of its citizens. The shape and scope of social policy related to children are tied to the political system. The values held by citizens and elected officials, the nation's economic strengths and weaknesses, and partisan politics all influence the policy agenda.

Out of concern that policy makers are doing too little to protect the well-being of children, researchers increasingly are undertaking studies that they hope will lead to wise and effective decision making about social policy (Cross & others, 2012; Fisher & others, 2013). Children who grow up in poverty represent a special concern (Purtell & McLoyd, 2013). In 2011, 21.9 percent of U.S. children and adolescents were living in families with household incomes below the poverty line, with African American and Latino families with children and adolescents having especially high rates of poverty (more than 30 percent) (U.S. Census Bureau, 2012). This is an increase from 2001 (16.2 percent) but slightly down from a peak of 22.7 percent in 1993. As indicated in Figure 1.3, one study found that a higher percentage of U.S. children in poor families than in middle-income families were exposed to family turmoil, separation from a parent, violence, crowding, excessive noise, and poor housing (Evans & English, 2002). One study also revealed that the more years children spent living in poverty, the higher were their physiological indices of stress (Evans & Kim, 2007).

The U.S. figure of 21.9 percent of children living in poverty is much higher than those from other industrialized nations. For example, Canada has a child poverty rate of 9 percent and Sweden has a rate of 2 percent.

What can we do to lessen the effect of these stressors on children and those who care for them? Strategies for improving the lives of children include improving social policy for families (Doob, 2013; Duncan & others, 2012). In the United States, the national government, state governments, and city governments all play a role in influencing the well-being of children. When families fail or seriously endanger a child's well-being, governments often step in to help.

At the national and state levels, policymakers for decades have debated whether helping poor parents ends up helping their children as well. Researchers are providing some answers by examining the effects of specific policies (Chase-Lansdale, 2012; Duncan, 2012; Duncan & others, 2012). For example, the Minnesota Family Investment Program (MFIP) was designed in the 1990s primarily to influence the behavior of adults—specifically, to move adults off the welfare rolls and into paid employment. A key element of the program was that it guaranteed that adults participating in the program would receive more income if they worked than if they did not. When the adults' income rose, how did that affect their children?

Source	Characteristic
Individual	Good intellectual functioning Appealing, sociable, easygoing disposition Self-confidence, high self-esteem Talents Faith
Family	Close relationship to caring parent figure Authoritative parenting: warmth, structure, high expectations Socioeconomic advantages Connections to extended supportive family networks
Extrafamilial Context	Bonds to caring adults outside the family Connections to positive organizations Attending effective schools

FIGURE **1.2**

CHARACTERISTICS OF RESILIENT CHILDREN AND THEIR CONTEXTS

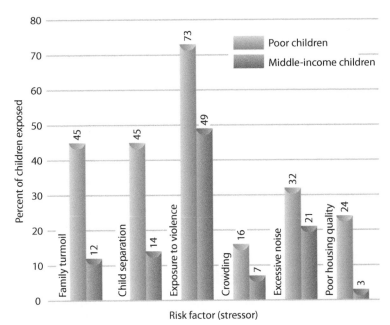

FIGURE **1.3**

EXPOSURE TO SIX STRESSORS AMONG POOR AND MIDDLE-INCOME CHILDREN. One study analyzed the exposure to six stressors among poor children and middle-income children (Evans & English, 2002). Poor children were much more likely to face each of these stressors.

A study of the effects of MFIP found that increases in the incomes of working poor parents were linked with benefits for their children (Gennetian & Miller, 2002). The children's achievement in school improved, and their behavior problems decreased. A current MFIP study is examining the influence of specific services on low-income families at risk for child maltreatment and other negative outcomes for children (Minnesota Family Investment Program, 2009).

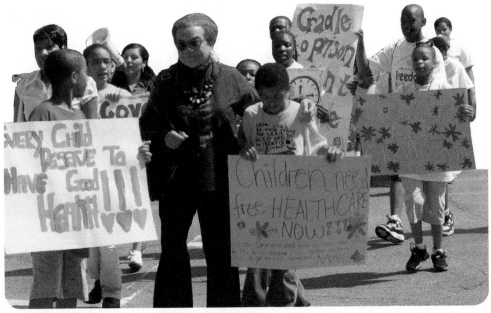

Marian Wright Edelman, president of the Children's Defense Fund (shown here interacting with young children), has been a tireless advocate of children's rights and has been instrumental in calling attention to the needs of children. *What are some of these needs?*

A recent large-scale effort to help children escape from poverty is the *Ascend* two-generation education intervention being conducted by the Aspen Institute (2012). The focus of the intervention emphasizes education (increasing postsecondary education for mothers and improving the quality of their children's early childhood education), economic support (housing, transportation, financial education, health insurance, and food assistance), and social capital (peer support including friends and neighbors; participation in community and faith-based organizations; school and work contacts).

Developmental psychologists and other researchers have examined the effects of many other government policies. They are seeking ways to help families living in poverty improve their well-being, and they have offered many suggestions for improving government policies (Duncan & others, 2012; Lerner & others, 2013; Purtell & McLoyd, 2013).

Review *Connect* Reflect

LG1 Identify five areas in which children's lives need to be improved, and explain the roles of resilience and social policy in children's development.

Review

- What are several aspects of children's development that need to be improved?
- What characterizes resilience in children's development? What is social policy, and how can it influence children's lives?

Connect

- How is the concept of resilience related to the story you read at the beginning of this chapter?

Reflect *Your Own Personal Journey of Life*

- Imagine what your development as a child would have been like in a culture that offered choices that were fewer or distinctively different from your own. How might your development have been different if your family had been significantly richer or poorer than it was as you were growing up?

Developmental Processes, Periods, and Issues

LG2 Discuss the most important processes, periods, and issues in development.

| Biological, Cognitive, and Socioemotional Processes | Periods of Development | Age and Cohort Effects | Issues in Development |

Each of us develops in certain ways like *all* other individuals, like *some* other individuals, and like *no* other individuals. Most of the time, our attention is directed to a person's uniqueness, but psychologists who study development are drawn to both our shared characteristics and those that make us unique. As humans, we all have traveled some common paths. Each of us—Leonardo da Vinci, Joan of Arc, George Washington, Martin Luther King, Jr., and you—walked at about the age of 1, engaged in fantasy play as a young child, and became more independent as a youth. What shapes this common path of human development, and what are its milestones?

BIOLOGICAL, COGNITIVE, AND SOCIOEMOTIONAL PROCESSES

The pattern of human development is created by the interplay of three key processes. They are biological, cognitive, and socioemotional in nature.

Biological Processes   **Biological processes** produce changes in an individual's body. Genes inherited from parents, the development of the brain, height and weight gains, acquisition of motor skills, and the hormonal changes of puberty all reflect the role of biological processes in development.

Cognitive Processes   **Cognitive processes** refer to changes in an individual's thought, intelligence, and language. The tasks of watching a mobile swinging above a crib, putting together a two-word sentence, memorizing a poem, solving a math problem, and imagining what it would be like to be a movie star all involve cognitive processes.

Socioemotional Processes   **Socioemotional processes** involve changes in an individual's relationships with other people, changes in emotions, and changes in personality. An infant's smile in response to her mother's touch, a child's attack on a playmate, another's development of assertiveness, and an adolescent's joy at the senior prom all reflect socioemotional development.

Connecting Biological, Cognitive, and Socioemotional Processes   Biological, cognitive, and socioemotional processes are inextricably intertwined (Diamond, 2013). Consider a baby smiling in response to a parent's touch. This response depends on biological processes (the physical nature of touch and responsiveness to it), cognitive processes (the ability to understand intentional acts), and socioemotional processes (the act of smiling often reflects a positive emotional feeling, and smiling helps to connect us in positive ways with other human beings). Nowhere is the connection across biological, cognitive, and socioemotional processes more obvious than in two rapidly emerging fields:

- *developmental cognitive neuroscience,* which explores links between development, cognitive processes, and the brain (Diamond, 2013; Johnson & de Haan, 2012; Zelazo, 2013)

- *developmental social neuroscience,* which examines connections between development, socioemotional processes, and the brain (Bell & Diaz, 2012; Blakemore & Mills, 2014)

In many instances, biological, cognitive, and socioemotional processes are bidirectional. For example, biological processes can influence cognitive processes and vice versa. Thus, although usually we will study the different processes of development (biological, cognitive, and socioemotional) separately rather than together, keep in mind that we are talking about the development of an integrated individual with a mind and body that are interdependent (see Figure 1.4).

In many places throughout this book we will call attention to connections between biological, cognitive, and socioemotional processes. A feature titled ***Developmental Connection*** appears multiple times in each chapter to highlight these as well as other content connections earlier or later in the text.

In Developmental Connection, you will see a backward-connecting arrow indicating chapter(s) where the topic has been discussed previously, or a forward-connecting arrow indicating chapter(s) where the topic will appear again. Included in the Developmental Connection feature is a brief description of the backward or forward connection.

FIGURE 1.4

CHANGES IN DEVELOPMENT ARE THE RESULT OF BIOLOGICAL, COGNITIVE, AND SOCIOEMOTIONAL PROCESSES. The processes interact as individuals develop.

developmental **connection**

Biological Processes

Can specific genes be linked to specific environmental experiences? Chapter 2, p. 69

biological processes Changes in an individual's body.

cognitive processes Changes in an individual's thinking, intelligence, and language skills.

socioemotional processes Changes in an individual's interpersonal relationships, emotions, and personality.

PEANUTS © United Features Syndicate, Inc.

"This is the path to adulthood. You're here."

prenatal period The time from conception to birth.

infancy The developmental period that extends from birth to about 18 to 24 months.

early childhood The developmental period that extends from the end of infancy to about 5 or 6 years of age, sometimes called the preschool years.

middle and late childhood The developmental period that extends from about 6 to 11 years of age, sometimes called the elementary school years.

adolescence The developmental period of transition from childhood to early adulthood, entered at approximately 10 to 12 years of age and ending at 18 or 19 years of age.

cohort effects Effects due to a person's time of birth, era, or generation but not to actual age.

Millennials The generation born after 1980, the first to come of age and enter emerging adulthood in the new millennium.

PERIODS OF DEVELOPMENT

For purposes of organization and understanding, a child's development is commonly described in terms of periods that correspond to approximate age ranges. The most widely used classification of developmental periods describes a child's development in terms of the following sequence: the prenatal period, infancy, early childhood, middle and late childhood, and adolescence.

The **prenatal period** is the time from conception to birth, roughly a nine-month period. During this amazing time, a single cell grows into an organism, complete with a brain and behavioral capabilities.

Infancy is the developmental period that extends from birth to about 18 to 24 months of age. Infancy is a time of extreme dependence on adults. Many psychological activities are just beginning—the abilities to speak, to coordinate sensations and physical actions, to think with symbols, and to imitate and learn from others.

Early childhood is the developmental period that extends from the end of infancy to about 5 or 6 years of age; sometimes this period is called the preschool years. During this time, young children learn to become more self-sufficient and to care for themselves, they develop school readiness skills (following instructions, identifying letters), and they spend many hours in play and with peers. First grade typically marks the end of this period.

Middle and late childhood is the developmental period that extends between about 6 and 11 years of age; sometimes this period is referred to as the elementary school years. Children master the fundamental skills of reading, writing, and arithmetic, and they are formally exposed to the larger world and its culture. Achievement becomes a more central theme of the child's world, and self-control increases.

Adolescence is the developmental period of transition from childhood to early adulthood, entered at approximately 10 to 12 years of age and ending at about 18 to 19 years of age. Adolescence begins with rapid physical changes—dramatic gains in height and weight; changes in body contour; and the development of sexual characteristics such as enlargement of the breasts, growth of pubic and facial hair, and deepening of the voice. The pursuit of independence and an identity are prominent features of this period of development. More and more time is spent outside the family. Thought becomes more abstract, idealistic, and logical.

Today, developmentalists do not believe that change ends with adolescence (Antonucci & others, 2013; Dixon & others, 2013). They describe development as a lifelong process. However, the purpose of this text is to describe the changes in development that take place from conception through adolescence. All of these periods of development are produced by the interplay of biological, cognitive, and socioemotional processes (see Figure 1.5).

AGE AND COHORT EFFECTS

A *cohort* is a group of people who are born at a similar point in history and share similar experiences as a result, such as living through the Vietnam War or growing up in the same city around the same time. These shared experiences may produce a range of differences between cohorts (Schaie, 2012). For example, adults who grew up during the Great Depression and World War II are likely to differ from their counterparts who grew up during the booming 1990s in their educational opportunities and economic status, in how they were raised, their attitudes and experiences related to gender, and their exposure to technology. In research on development, **cohort effects** are due to a person's time of birth, era, or generation but not to actual age.

In recent years, generations have been given labels by the popular culture. The most recent label is **Millennials,** referring to the generation born after 1980—the first to come of age and enter emerging adulthood in the new millennium. Thus, today's children and many of their parents are Millennials. Two characteristics of Millennials stand out: (1) their ethnic diversity, and (2) their connection to technology (Pew Research Center, 2010).

As their ethnic diversity has increased over prior generations, many Millennial adolescents and emerging adults are more tolerant and open-minded than their counterparts

Periods of Development

Prenatal period   Infancy   Early childhood   Middle and late childhood   Adolescence

Biological Processes

Cognitive Processes   Socioemotional Processes

Processes of Development

FIGURE **1.5**

PROCESSES AND PERIODS OF DEVELOPMENT. Development moves through the prenatal, infancy, early childhood, middle and late childhood, and adolescence periods. These periods of development are the result of biological, cognitive, and socioemotional processes.

in previous generations. One survey indicated that 60 percent of today's adolescents say their friends include someone from diverse ethnic groups (Teenage Research Unlimited, 2004).

Another major cohort change involving Millennials is the dramatic increase in their use of media and technology (Gross, 2013; Roblyer & Doering, 2013). According to one analysis,

> They are history's first "always connected" generation. Steeped in digital technology and social media, they treat their multi-tasking hand-held gadgets almost like a body part—for better or worse. More than 8-in-10 say they sleep with a cell phone glowing by the bed, poised to disgorge texts, phone calls, e-mails, songs, news, videos, games, and wake-up jingles. But sometimes convenience yields to temptation. Nearly two-thirds admit to texting while driving (Pew Research Center, 2010, p. 1).

We will have much more to say about technology in childhood and adolescence in Chapter 17, "Culture and Diversity."

ISSUES IN DEVELOPMENT

Was Ted Kaczynski born a killer, or did his life turn him into one? Kaczynski himself thought that his childhood was the root of his troubles. He grew up as a genius in a boy's body and never fit in with other children. Did his early experiences determine his later life? Is your own journey through life marked out ahead of time, or can your experiences change your path? Are experiences that occur early in your journey more important than later ones? Is your journey like taking an elevator up a skyscraper with distinct stops along the way, or more like a cruise down a river with smoother ebbs and flows? These questions point to three issues about the nature of development: the roles played by nature and nurture, continuity and discontinuity, and early and later experiences.

Continuity

Discontinuity

FIGURE **1.6**

CONTINUITY AND DISCONTINUITY IN DEVELOPMENT. Is human development more like that of a seedling gradually growing into a giant oak or more like that of a caterpillar suddenly becoming a butterfly?

nature-nurture issue Debate about whether development is primarily influenced by nature or nurture. The "nature" proponents claim biological inheritance is the most important influence on development; the "nurture" proponents claim that environmental experiences are the most influential factors.

continuity-discontinuity issue Question about whether development involves gradual, cumulative change (continuity) or distinct stages (discontinuity).

early-later experience issue Controversy regarding the degree to which early experiences (especially during infancy) or later experiences are the key determinants of children's development.

Nature and Nurture The **nature-nurture issue** involves the debate about whether development is primarily influenced by nature or by nurture. *Nature* refers to an organism's biological inheritance, *nurture* to its environmental experiences. Almost no one today argues that development can be explained by nature alone or by nurture alone. But some ("nature" proponents) claim that the most important influence on development is biological inheritance, and others ("nurture" proponents) claim that environmental experiences are the most important influence.

According to the nature proponents, just as a sunflower grows in an orderly way—unless it is defeated by an unfriendly environment—so does a person. The range of environments can be vast, but evolutionary and genetic foundations produce commonalities in growth and development (Buss, 2012; Durrant & Ellis, 2013). We walk before we talk, speak one word before two words, grow rapidly in infancy and less so in early childhood, and experience a rush of sexual hormones in puberty. Extreme environments—those that are psychologically barren or hostile—can stunt development, but nature proponents emphasize the influence of tendencies that are genetically wired into humans (Mader, 2012; Maxson, 2013).

By contrast, other psychologists emphasize the importance of nurture, or environmental experiences, to development (Dweck, 2013; Grusec & others, 2013). Experiences run the gamut from the individual's biological environment (nutrition, medical care, drugs, and physical accidents) to the social environment (family, peers, schools, community, media, and culture). For example, a child's diet can affect how tall the child grows and even how effectively the child can think and solve problems. Despite their genetic wiring, a child born and raised in a poor village in Bangladesh and a child in the suburbs of Denver are likely to have different skills, different ways of thinking about the world, and different ways of relating to people.

Continuity and Discontinuity Think about your own development for a moment. Did you become the person you are gradually, like the seedling that slowly, cumulatively grows into a giant oak? Or did you experience sudden, distinct changes, like the caterpillar that changes into a butterfly (see Figure 1.6)?

The **continuity-discontinuity issue** focuses on the extent to which development involves gradual, cumulative change (continuity) or distinct stages (discontinuity). For the most part, developmentalists who emphasize nurture usually describe development as a gradual, continuous process, like the seedling's growth into an oak. Those who emphasize nature often describe development as a series of distinct stages, like the change from caterpillar to butterfly.

Consider continuity first. As the oak grows from seedling to giant oak, it becomes more oak—its development is continuous. Similarly, a child's first word, though seemingly an abrupt, discontinuous event, is actually the result of weeks and months of growth and practice. Puberty, another seemingly abrupt, discontinuous occurrence, is actually a gradual process occurring over several years.

Viewed in terms of discontinuity, each person is described as passing through a sequence of stages in which change is qualitatively rather than quantitatively different. As the caterpillar changes to a butterfly, it does not become more caterpillar but a different kind of organism—its development is discontinuous. Similarly, at some point a child moves from not being able to think abstractly about the world to being able to do so. This change is a qualitative, discontinuous change in development, not a quantitative, continuous change.

Early and Later Experience The **early-later experience issue** focuses on the degree to which early experiences (especially in infancy) or later experiences are the key determinants of the child's development. That is, if infants experience harmful circumstances, can those experiences be overcome by later, positive ones? Or are the early experiences so critical—possibly because they are the infant's first, prototypical experiences—that they cannot be overridden by a later, better environment? To those who emphasize early experiences, life is an unbroken trail on which a psychological quality can be traced back to its origin (Kagan, 1992, 2000, 2013). In contrast, to those who emphasize later experiences, development is like a river, continually ebbing and flowing.

The early-later experience issue has a long history and continues to be hotly debated among developmentalists (Kagan, 2013; Dixon & others, 2013; Easterbrooks & others, 2013). Plato was sure that infants who were rocked frequently became better athletes. Nineteenth-century New England ministers told parents in Sunday afternoon sermons that the way they handled their infants would determine their children's later character. Some developmentalists argue that unless infants and young children experience warm, nurturing care, their development will never quite be optimal (Cassidy & others, 2011).

In contrast, later-experience advocates argue that children are malleable throughout development and that later sensitive caregiving is just as important as earlier sensitive caregiving. A number of developmentalists stress that too little attention has been given to later experiences in development (Schaie, 2012). They accept that early experiences are important contributors to development but assert that they are no more important than later experiences. Jerome Kagan (2000, 2010, 2013) points out that even children who show the qualities of an inhibited temperament, which is linked to heredity, have the capacity to change their behavior. In his research, almost one-third of a group of children who had an inhibited temperament at 2 years of age were not unusually shy or fearful when they were 4 years of age (Kagan & Snidman, 1991).

People in Western cultures, especially those influenced by Freudian theory, have tended to support the idea that early experiences are more important than later experiences (Lamb & Sternberg, 1992). The majority of people in the world do not share this belief. For example, people in many Asian countries believe that experiences occurring after about 6 or 7 years of age are more important to development than are earlier experiences. This stance stems from the long-standing belief in Eastern cultures that children's reasoning skills begin to develop in important ways during middle childhood.

What is the nature of the early and later experience issue?

Evaluating the Developmental Issues   Most developmentalists recognize that it is unwise to take an extreme position on the issues of nature and nurture, continuity and discontinuity, and early and later experiences. Development is not all nature or all nurture, not all continuity or all discontinuity, and not all early or later experiences. Nature and nurture, continuity and discontinuity, and early and later experiences all play a part in development through the human life span. Along with this consensus, there is still spirited debate about how strongly development is influenced by each of these factors (Durrant & Ellis, 2013; Grusec & others, 2013). Are girls less likely to do well in math mostly because of inherited characteristics or because of society's expectations and because of how girls are raised? Can enriched experiences during adolescence remove deficits resulting from poverty, neglect, and poor schooling during childhood? The answers to these questions have a bearing on social policy decisions about children and adolescents, and consequently on each of our lives.

Review *Connect* Reflect

 Discuss the most important processes, periods, and issues in development.

Review

- What are biological, cognitive, and socioemotional processes?
- What are the main periods of development?
- What are cohort effects?
- What are three important issues in development?

Connect

- Based on what you read earlier in this chapter, what do you think Ted Kaczynski would say about the early-later experience issue?

Reflect *Your Own Personal Journey of Life*

- Can you identify an early experience that you believe contributed in important ways to your development? Can you identify a recent or current (later) experience that you think had (or is having) a strong influence on your development?

The Science of Child Development

 LG3 Summarize why research is important in child development, the main theories of child development, and research methods, designs, and challenges.

The Importance of Research	Theories of Child Development	Research Methods for Collecting Data	Research Designs	Challenges in Child Development Research

Science refines everyday thinking.

—**ALBERT EINSTEIN**
German-born American Physicist, 20th Century

Some people have difficulty thinking of child development as a science like physics, chemistry, and biology. Can a discipline that studies how parents nurture children, how peers interact, the ways in which children's thinking develops over time, and whether watching TV hour after hour is linked with being overweight, be equated with disciplines that study the molecular structure of a compound and how gravity works? Is child development really a science?

THE IMPORTANCE OF RESEARCH

The answer to the last question is "yes." Science is defined not by *what* it investigates, but by *how* it investigates. Whether you're studying photosynthesis, butterflies, Saturn's moons, or children's development, it is the way you study that makes the approach scientific or not. How can we determine, for example, whether special care can repair the harm inflicted by child neglect or whether mentoring can improve children's achievement in school?

Scientific research provides the best answers to such questions. *Scientific research* is objective, systematic, and testable. It reduces the likelihood that information will be based on personal beliefs, opinions, and feelings (Smith & Davis, 2013; Stanovich, 2013). In conducting research, child development researchers use the **scientific method**, a four-step process: (1) conceptualize a process or problem to be studied, (2) collect research information (data), (3) analyze data, and (4) draw conclusions.

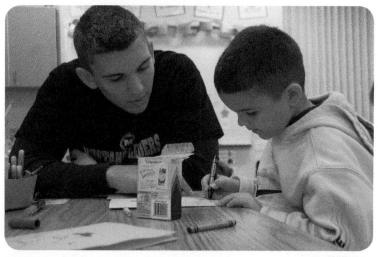

A high school senior mentors a kindergarten child as part of the Book Buddy mentoring program. *If a researcher wanted to study the effects of the mentoring program on children's academic achievement by following the scientific method, what steps would the researcher take in setting up the study?*

THEORIES OF CHILD DEVELOPMENT

Theorizing is part of the scientific study of children's development. In the scientific method just described, theories often guide the conceptualization of a process or problem to be studied. A **theory** is an interrelated, coherent set of ideas that helps to explain and to make predictions. For example, a theory on mentoring might attempt to explain and predict why sustained support, guidance, and concrete experience make a difference in the lives of children from impoverished backgrounds. The theory might focus on children's opportunities to model the behavior and strategies of mentors, or it might focus on the effects of individual attention, which might be missing in the children's lives. A **hypothesis** is a specific, testable assumption or prediction. A hypothesis is often written as an *if-then* statement. In our example, a sample hypothesis might be: If children from impoverished backgrounds are given individual attention by mentors, then the children will spend more time studying and earn higher grades. Testing a hypothesis can inform researchers whether a theory is likely to be accurate.

Wide-ranging theories make understanding children's development a challenging undertaking. This section outlines key aspects of five theoretical orientations to development: psychoanalytic, cognitive, behavioral and social cognitive, ethological, and ecological. Each contributes an important piece to the puzzle of understanding children's development. Although the theories disagree about certain aspects of development, many of their ideas are

scientific method An approach that can be used to obtain accurate information by carrying out four steps: (1) conceptualize the problem, (2) collect data, (3) draw conclusions, and (4) revise research conclusions and theory.

theory An interrelated, coherent set of ideas that helps to explain and make predictions.

hypotheses Specific assumptions and predictions that can be tested to determine their accuracy.

Oral Stage	Anal Stage	Phallic Stage	Latency Stage	Genital Stage
Infant's pleasure centers on the mouth.	Child's pleasure focuses on the anus.	Child's pleasure focuses on the genitals.	Child represses sexual interest and develops social and intellectual skills.	A time of sexual reawakening; source of sexual pleasure becomes someone outside the family.
Birth to 1½ Years	1½ to 3 Years	3 to 6 Years	6 Years to Puberty	Puberty Onward

FIGURE **1.7**
FREUDIAN STAGES.

complementary rather than contradictory. Together they let us see the total landscape of children's development in all its richness.

Psychoanalytic Theories **Psychoanalytic theories** describe development as primarily unconscious (beyond awareness) and heavily colored by emotion. Psychoanalytic theorists emphasize that behavior is merely a surface characteristic and that a true understanding of development requires analyzing the symbolic meanings of behavior and the deep inner workings of the mind. Psychoanalytic theorists also stress that early experiences with parents extensively shape development. These characteristics are highlighted in the psychoanalytic theory of Sigmund Freud (1856–1939).

Freud's Theory As Freud listened to, probed, and analyzed his patients, he became convinced that their problems were the result of experiences early in life. He thought that as children grow up, their focus of pleasure and sexual impulses shifts from the mouth to the anus and eventually to the genitals. As a result, we go through five stages of psychosexual development: oral, anal, phallic, latency, and genital (see Figure 1.7). Our adult personality, Freud (1917) claimed, is determined by the way we resolve conflicts between sources of pleasure at each stage and the demands of reality.

Freud's theory has been significantly revised by a number of psychoanalytic theorists. Many of today's psychoanalytic theorists maintain that Freud overemphasized sexual instincts; they place more emphasis on cultural experiences as determinants of an individual's development. Unconscious thought remains a central theme, but thought plays a greater role than Freud envisioned. Next, we will outline the ideas of an important revisionist of Freud's ideas—Erik Erikson.

Erikson's Psychosocial Theory Erik Erikson (1902–1994) recognized Freud's contributions but believed that Freud misjudged some important dimensions of human development. For one thing, Erikson (1950, 1968) said we develop in psychosocial stages, rather than in psychosexual stages as Freud maintained. According to Freud, the primary motivation for human behavior is sexual in nature; according to Erikson, it is social and reflects a desire to affiliate with other people. According to Freud, our basic personality is shaped in the first five years of life; according to Erikson, developmental change occurs throughout the life span. Thus, in terms of the early-versus-later-experience issue described earlier in the chapter, Freud viewed early experience as far more important than later experiences, whereas Erikson emphasized the importance of both early and later experiences.

In **Erikson's theory,** eight stages of development unfold as we go through life (see Figure 1.8 on page 20). At each stage, a unique developmental task confronts individuals with a crisis that must be resolved. According to Erikson, this crisis is not a catastrophe but a turning point marked by both increased vulnerability and enhanced potential. The more successfully an individual resolves the crises, the healthier development will be.

Trust versus mistrust is Erikson's first psychosocial stage, which is experienced in the first year of life. Trust in infancy sets the stage for a lifelong expectation that the world will be a good and pleasant place to live.

Autonomy versus shame and doubt is Erikson's second stage. This stage occurs in late infancy and toddlerhood (1 to 3 years). After gaining trust in their caregivers, infants begin

Sigmund Freud, the pioneering architect of psychoanalytic theory. *What are some characteristics of Freud's theory?*

psychoanalytic theories Theories that describe development as primarily unconscious and heavily colored by emotion. Behavior is merely a surface characteristic, and the symbolic workings of the mind have to be analyzed to understand behavior. Early experiences with parents are emphasized.

Erikson's theory Description of eight stages of human development. Each stage consists of a unique developmental task that confronts individuals with a crisis that must be resolved.

Erikson's Stages	Developmental Period
Integrity versus despair	Late adulthood (60s onward)
Generativity versus stagnation	Middle adulthood (40s, 50s)
Intimacy versus isolation	Early adulthood (20s, 30s)
Identity versus identity confusion	Adolescence (10 to 20 years)
Industry versus inferiority	Middle and late childhood (elementary school years, 6 years to puberty)
Initiative versus guilt	Early childhood (preschool years, 3 to 5 years)
Autonomy versus shame and doubt	Infancy (1 to 3 years)
Trust versus mistrust	Infancy (first year)

FIGURE **1.8**
ERIKSON'S EIGHT LIFE-SPAN STAGES

One's children's children's children.
Look back to us as we look to you; we are related by our imaginations. If we are able to touch, it is because we have imagined each other's existence, our dreams running back and forth along a cable from age to age.

—Roger Rosenblatt
American Writer, 20th Century

Erik Erikson with his wife, Joan, an artist. Erikson generated one of the most important developmental theories of the twentieth century. *Which stage of Erikson's theory are you in? Does Erikson's description of this stage characterize you?*

to discover that their behavior is their own. They start to assert their sense of independence or autonomy. They realize their will. If infants and toddlers are restrained too much or punished too harshly, they are likely to develop a sense of shame and doubt.

Initiative versus guilt, Erikson's third stage of development, occurs during the preschool years. As preschool children encounter a widening social world, they face new challenges that require active, purposeful, responsible behavior. Feelings of guilt may arise, though, if the child is irresponsible and is made to feel too anxious.

Industry versus inferiority is Erikson's fourth developmental stage, occurring approximately in the elementary school years. Children now need to direct their energy toward mastering knowledge and intellectual skills. The negative outcome is that the child may develop a sense of inferiority—feeling incompetent and unproductive.

During the adolescent years, individuals confront the tasks of finding out who they are, what they are all about, and where they are going in life. This is Erikson's fifth developmental stage, *identity versus identity confusion*. If adolescents explore roles in a healthy manner and arrive at a positive path to follow in life, then they achieve a positive identity; if not, identity confusion reigns.

Intimacy versus isolation is Erikson's sixth developmental stage, which individuals experience during the early adulthood years. At this time, individuals face the developmental task of forming intimate relationships. If young adults form healthy friendships and an intimate relationship with another, intimacy will be achieved; if not, isolation will result.

Generativity versus stagnation, Erikson's seventh developmental stage, occurs during middle adulthood. By generativity Erikson means primarily a concern for helping the younger generation to develop and lead useful lives. The feeling of having done nothing to help the next generation is stagnation.

Integrity versus despair is Erikson's eighth and final stage of development, which individuals experience in late adulthood. During this stage, a person reflects on the past. If the person's life review reveals a life well spent, integrity will be achieved; if not, the retrospective glances likely will yield doubt or gloom—the despair Erikson described.

We will discuss Erikson's theory again in the chapters on socioemotional development. In *Caring Connections,* you can read about some effective strategies for improving the lives of children based on Erikson's view.

Evaluating Psychoanalytic Theories   Contributions of psychoanalytic theories include an emphasis on a developmental framework, family relationships, and unconscious aspects of the mind. Criticisms include a lack of scientific support, too much emphasis on sexual underpinnings (Freud's theory), too much credit given to the unconscious mind, and an image of children that is too negative (Freud's theory).

Cognitive Theories   Whereas psychoanalytic theories stress the importance of the unconscious, cognitive theories emphasize conscious thoughts. Three important cognitive theories are Piaget's cognitive developmental theory, Vygotsky's sociocultural cognitive theory, and information-processing theory.

caring *connections*

Strategies for Parenting, Educating, and Interacting with Children Based on Erikson's Theory

Parents, child care specialists, teachers, counselors, youth workers, and other adults can adopt positive strategies for interacting with children based on Erikson's theory. These strategies include the following:

1. ***Nurture infants and develop their trust, then encourage and monitor toddlers' autonomy.*** Because infants depend on others to meet their needs, it is critical for caregivers to consistently provide positive, attentive care for infants. Infants who experience consistently positive care feel safe and secure, sensing that people are reliable and loving, which leads them to develop trust in the world. Caregivers who neglect or abuse infants are likely to raise infants who develop a sense of mistrust in their world. After having developed a sense of trust in their world, children moving from infancy into the toddler years should be given the freedom to explore it. Toddlers whose caregivers are too restrictive or harsh are likely to develop shame and doubt, sensing that they can't adequately do things on their own. As toddlers gain more independence, caregivers need to monitor their exploration and curiosity because there are many things that can harm them, such as running into the street or touching a hot stove.

2. ***Encourage initiative in young children.*** Children should be given a great deal of freedom to explore their world. They should be allowed to choose some of the activities they engage in. If their requests for doing certain activities are reasonable, the requests should be honored. Children need to be provided exciting materials that will stimulate their imagination. Young children at this stage love to play. It not only benefits their socioemotional development but also serves as an important medium for their cognitive growth. Criticism should be kept to a minimum so that children will not develop high levels of guilt and anxiety. Young children are going to make lots of mistakes and have lots of spills. They need good models far more than harsh critics. Their activities and environment should be structured for success rather than failure by giving them developmentally appropriate tasks. For example, young children get frustrated when they have to sit for long periods of time and do academic paper-and-pencil tasks.

3. ***Promote industry in elementary school children.*** It was Erikson's hope that teachers could provide an atmosphere in which children would become passionate about learning. In Erikson's words, teachers should mildly but firmly coerce children into the adventure of finding out that they can learn to accomplish things that they themselves would never have thought they could do. In elementary school, children thirst to know. Most arrive at elementary school steeped in curiosity and fueled by a motivation to master tasks. In Erikson's view, it is important for teachers to nourish this motivation for mastery and curiosity. Teachers need to challenge students without overwhelming them; be firm in requiring students to be productive, but not be overly critical; and especially be tolerant of honest mistakes and make sure that every student has opportunities for many successes.

What are some applications of Erikson's theory for effective parenting?

4. ***Stimulate identity exploration in adolescence.*** It is important to recognize that the adolescent's identity is multidimensional. Aspects include vocational goals; intellectual achievement; and interests in hobbies, sports, music, and other areas. Adolescents can be asked to write essays about such dimensions, exploring who they are and what they want to do with their lives. They should be encouraged to think independently and to freely express their views, which stimulates their self-exploration. Adolescents can also be encouraged to listen to debates on political and ideological issues, which stimulates them to examine different perspectives. Another good strategy is to encourage adolescents to talk with a school counselor about career options as well as other aspects of their identity. Teachers can invite people in different careers to come into the classroom and talk with their students about their work, regardless of students' grade levels.

In the strategies above, identify what Erikson called the "vulnerability" and the "potential" that adults need to take into account in trying to help children accomplish the tasks of each developmental stage.

Sensorimotor Stage	**Preoperational Stage**	**Concrete Operational Stage**	**Formal Operational Stage**
The infant constructs an understanding of the world by coordinating sensory experiences with physical actions. An infant progresses from reflexive, instinctual action at birth to the beginning of symbolic thought toward the end of the stage.	The child begins to represent the world with words and images. These words and images reflect increased symbolic thinking and go beyond the connection of sensory information and physical action.	The child can now reason logically about concrete events and classify objects into different sets.	The adolescent reasons in more abstract, idealistic, and logical ways.
Birth to 2 Years of Age	**2 to 7 Years of Age**	**7 to 11 Years of Age**	**11 Years of Age Through Adulthood**

FIGURE **1.9**

PIAGET'S FOUR STAGES OF COGNITIVE DEVELOPMENT

developmental **connection**

Cognitive Theory

We owe to Piaget the entire field of children's cognitive development, but a number of criticisms of his theory have been made. Chapter 6, p. 183

Piaget's theory Theory stating that children actively construct their understanding of the world and go through four stages of cognitive development: sensorimotor, preoperational, concrete operational, and formal operational.

Piaget's Cognitive Developmental Theory **Piaget's theory** states that children actively construct their understanding of the world and go through four stages of cognitive development. Two processes underlie the four stages of development in Piaget's theory: organization and adaptation. To make sense of our world, we organize our experiences. For example, we separate important ideas from less important ideas, and we connect one idea to another. In addition to organizing our observations and experiences, we *adapt,* adjusting to new environmental demands.

Piaget (1954) also held that we go through four stages in understanding the world (see Figure 1.9). Each stage is age-related and consists of a distinct way of thinking, a *different* way of understanding the world. Thus, according to Piaget, the child's cognition is *qualitatively* different in one stage compared with another. What are Piaget's four stages of cognitive development like?

The *sensorimotor stage,* which lasts from birth to about 2 years of age, is the first Piagetian stage. In this stage, infants construct an understanding of the world by coordinating sensory experiences (such as seeing and hearing) with physical, motoric actions—hence the term *sensorimotor.*

The *preoperational stage,* which lasts from approximately 2 to 7 years of age, is Piaget's second stage. In this stage, children begin to go beyond simply connecting sensory information with physical action and represent the world with words, images, and drawings. However, according to Piaget, preschool children still lack the ability to perform what he calls *operations,* which are internalized mental actions that allow children to do mentally what they previously could only do physically. For example, if you imagine putting two sticks together to see whether they would be as long as another stick, without actually moving the sticks, you are performing a concrete operation.

The *concrete operational stage,* which lasts from approximately 7 to 11 years of age, is the third Piagetian stage. In this stage, children can perform operations that involve objects, and they can reason logically as long as reasoning can be applied to specific or concrete examples.

For instance, concrete operational thinkers cannot imagine the steps necessary to complete an algebraic equation, which is too abstract for thinking at this stage of development.

The *formal operational stage,* which appears between the ages of 11 and 15 and continues through adulthood, is Piaget's fourth and final stage. In this stage, individuals move beyond concrete experiences and think in abstract and more logical terms. As part of thinking more abstractly, adolescents develop images of ideal circumstances. They might think about what an ideal parent is like and compare their parents to this ideal standard. They begin to entertain possibilities for the future and are fascinated with what they can be. In solving problems, they become more systematic, developing hypotheses about why something is happening the way it is and then testing these hypotheses.

The preceding discussion is a brief introduction to Piaget's theory. It is provided here, along with other theories, to give you a broad understanding. In Chapter 6, "Cognitive Developmental Approaches," we will return to Piaget and examine his theory in more depth.

Vygotsky's Sociocultural Cognitive Theory

Like Piaget, the Russian developmentalist Lev Vygotsky (1896–1934) argued that children actively construct their knowledge. However, Vygotsky (1962) gave social interaction and culture far more important roles in cognitive development than Piaget did. **Vygotsky's theory** is a sociocultural cognitive theory that emphasizes how culture and social interaction guide cognitive development.

Vygotsky portrayed the child's development as inseparable from social and cultural activities (Mahn & John-Steiner, 2013). He argued that development of

Jean Piaget, the famous Swiss developmental psychologist, changed the way we think about the development of children's minds. *What are some key ideas in Piaget's theory?*

memory, attention, and reasoning involves learning to use the inventions of society, such as language, mathematical systems, and memory strategies. Thus, in one culture, children might learn to count with the help of a computer; in another, they might learn by using beads. According to Vygotsky, children's social interaction with more-skilled adults and peers is indispensable to their cognitive development. Through this interaction, they learn to use the tools that will help them adapt and be successful in their culture. For example, if you regularly help children learn how to read, you not only advance their reading skills but also communicate to them that reading is an important activity in their culture.

Vygotsky's theory has stimulated considerable interest in the view that knowledge is *situated* and *collaborative* (Gauvain, 2013). In this view, knowledge is not generated from within the individual but rather is constructed through interaction with other people and objects in the culture, such as books. This suggests that knowledge can best be advanced through interaction with others in cooperative activities.

Vygotsky's theory, like Piaget's, remained virtually unknown to American psychologists until the 1960s, but eventually both approaches became influential among educators as well as psychologists. We will further examine Vygotsky's theory in Chapter 6.

Information-Processing Theory

Early computers may be the best candidates for the title of "founding fathers" of information-processing theory. Although many factors stimulated the growth of this theory, none was more important than the computer. Psychologists began to wonder if the logical operations carried out by computers might tell us something about how the human mind works. They drew analogies between a computer's hardware and the brain and between computer software and cognition.

This line of thinking helped to generate **information-processing theory,** which emphasizes that individuals manipulate information, monitor it, and strategize about it. Unlike Piaget's theory but like Vygotsky's theory, information-processing theory does not

- - - - - - - - - - - →

developmental **connection**

Education

Applications of Vygotsky's theory to children's education have been made in recent years. Chapter 6, pp. 187–189

There is considerable interest today in Lev Vygotsky's sociocultural cognitive theory of child development. *What were Vygotsky's basic ideas about children's development?*

Vygotsky's theory A sociocultural cognitive theory that emphasizes how culture and social interaction guide cognitive development.

information-processing theory Emphasizes that individuals manipulate information, monitor it, and strategize about it. Central to this theory are the processes of memory and thinking.

describe development as happening in stages. Instead, according to this theory, individuals develop a gradually increasing capacity for processing information, which allows them to acquire increasingly complex knowledge and skills (Bjorklund, 2013; Gelman, 2013; Zelazo, 2013).

Robert Siegler (2006, 2013), a leading expert on children's information processing, states that thinking is information processing. In other words, when individuals perceive, encode, represent, store, and retrieve information, they are thinking. Siegler emphasizes that an important aspect of development is learning good strategies for processing information. For example, becoming a better reader might involve learning to monitor the key themes of the material being read.

Evaluating the Cognitive Theories   Contributions of cognitive theories include a positive view of development and an emphasis on the active construction of understanding. Criticisms include skepticism about the pureness of Piaget's stages and assertions that too little attention is paid to individual variations.

Behavioral and Social Cognitive Theories   At about the same time that Freud was interpreting patients' unconscious minds through their recollections of early childhood experiences, Ivan Pavlov and John B. Watson were conducting detailed observations of behavior in controlled laboratory settings. Their work provided the foundations of *behaviorism*, which essentially holds that we can study scientifically only what can be directly observed and measured. Out of the behavioral tradition grew the belief that development is observable behavior that can be learned through experience with the environment (Chance, 2014; Miltenberger, 2012). In terms of the continuity-discontinuity issue discussed earlier in this chapter, the behavioral and social cognitive theories emphasize continuity in development and argue that development does not occur in stages. The three versions of the behavioral approach that we will explore are Pavlov's classical conditioning, Skinner's operant conditioning, and Bandura's social cognitive theory.

Pavlov's Classical Conditioning   In the early 1900s, the Russian physiologist Ivan Pavlov (1927) knew that dogs salivate when they taste food. He became curious when he observed that dogs also salivate in response to various sights and sounds before eating their food. For example, when an individual paired the ringing of a bell with the food, the bell ringing subsequently elicited salivation from the dogs when it was presented by itself. With this experiment, Pavlov discovered the principle of *classical conditioning*, in which a neutral stimulus (in our example, hearing a bell ring) acquires the ability to produce a response originally produced by another stimulus (in our example, tasting food).

In the early twentieth century, John Watson and Rosalie Rayner (1920) demonstrated that classical conditioning occurs in human beings. He showed an infant named Albert a white rat to see if he was afraid of it. He was not. As Albert played with the rat, a loud noise was sounded behind his head. As you might imagine, the noise caused little Albert to cry. After several pairings of the loud noise and the white rat, Albert began to cry at the sight of the rat even when the noise was not sounded. Albert had been classically conditioned to fear the rat. Similarly, many of our fears may result from classical conditioning: fear of the dentist may be learned from a painful experience, fear of driving from being in an automobile accident, fear of heights from falling off a high chair when we were infants, and fear of dogs from being bitten.

Skinner's Operant Conditioning   Classical conditioning may explain how we develop many involuntary responses such as fears, but B. F. Skinner argued that a second type of conditioning accounts for the development of other types of behavior. According to Skinner (1938), through *operant conditioning* the consequences of a behavior produce changes in the probability of the behavior's occurrence. A behavior followed by a rewarding stimulus is more likely to recur, whereas a behavior followed by a punishing stimulus is less likely to recur. For example, when a person smiles at a child after the child has done something, the child is more likely to engage in the activity than if the person gives the child a nasty look.

social cognitive theory The view of psychologists who emphasize behavior, environment, and cognition as the key factors in development.

In 1920, Watson and Rosalie Rayner conditioned 11-month-old Albert to fear a white rat by pairing the rat with a loud noise. When little Albert was subsequently presented with other stimuli similar to the white rat, such as the rabbit shown here with little Albert, he was afraid of them, too. This illustrates the principle of stimulus generalization in classical conditioning.

B. F. Skinner was a tinkerer who liked to make new gadgets. The younger of his two daughters, Deborah, was raised in Skinner's enclosed Air-Crib, which he invented because he wanted to control her environment completely. The Air-Crib was sound-proofed and temperature-controlled. Debbie, shown here as a child with her parents, is currently a successful artist, is married, and lives in London. *What do you think about Skinner's Air-Crib?*

According to Skinner, such rewards and punishments shape development. For example, Skinner's approach argues that shy people learned to be shy as a result of experiences they had while growing up. It follows that modifications in an environment can help a shy person become more socially oriented. Also, for Skinner the key aspect of development is behavior, not thoughts and feelings. He emphasized that development consists of the pattern of behavioral changes that are brought about by rewards and punishments.

Bandura's Social Cognitive Theory   Some psychologists agree with the behaviorists' notion that development is learned and is influenced strongly by environmental interactions. However, unlike Skinner, they argue that cognition is also important in understanding development. **Social cognitive theory** holds that behavior, environment, and cognition are the key factors in development.

American psychologist Albert Bandura (1925–) is the leading architect of social cognitive theory. Bandura (2001, 2007, 2009, 2010a, b, 2012) emphasizes that cognitive processes have important links with the environment and behavior. His early research program focused heavily on *observational learning* (also called *imitation* or *modeling*), which is learning that occurs through observing what others do. For example, a young boy might observe his father yelling in anger and treating other people with hostility; with his peers, the young boy later acts very aggressively, showing the same characteristics his father displayed. A girl might adopt the dominant and sarcastic style of her teacher, saying to her younger brother, "You are so slow. How can you do this work so slowly?" Social cognitive theorists stress that people acquire a wide range of behaviors, thoughts, and feelings through observing others' behavior and that these observations form an important part of children's development.

What is *cognitive* about observational learning, in Bandura's view? He proposes that people cognitively represent the behavior of others and then sometimes adopt this behavior themselves.

Bandura's (2009, 2010a, b, 2012) most recent model of learning and development includes three elements: behavior, the person/cognition, and the environment. An individual's confidence that he or she can control his or her success is an example of a person factor; strategies

Albert Bandura has been one of the leading architects of social cognitive theory. *How does Bandura's theory differ from Skinner's?*

developmental **connection**

Theories

Bandura emphasizes that self-efficacy is a key person/cognitive factor in children's achievement. Chapter 16, p. 473

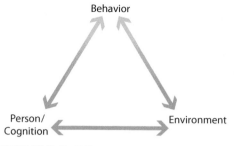

FIGURE **1.10**

BANDURA'S SOCIAL COGNITIVE MODEL. The arrows illustrate how relations between behavior, person/cognition, and environment are reciprocal rather than unidirectional.

- - - - - - - - - - - - →

developmental **connection**

Attachment

Human babies go through a series of phases in developing an attachment to a caregiver. Chapter 10, p. 300

ethology Stresses that behavior is strongly influenced by biology, is tied to evolution, and is characterized by critical or sensitive periods.

are an example of a cognitive factor. As shown in Figure 1.10, behavior, person/cognition, and environmental factors operate interactively. Behavior can influence person factors and vice versa. Cognitive activities can influence the environment. The environment can change the person's cognition, and so on.

Evaluating the Behavioral and Social Cognitive Theories   Contributions of the behavioral and social cognitive theories include an emphasis on scientific research and environmental determinants of behavior, and in Bandura's social cognitive theory reciprocal links between the environment, behavior, and person/cognitive factors. Criticisms include too little emphasis on cognition in Skinner's view and giving inadequate attention to developmental changes and biological foundations.

Behavioral and social cognitive theories emphasize the importance of environmental experiences in human development. Next we turn our attention to a theory that underscores the importance of the biological foundations of development—ethological theory.

Ethological Theory   American developmental psychologists began to pay attention to the biological bases of development during the mid-twentieth century thanks to the work of European zoologists who pioneered the field of ethology. **Ethology** stresses that behavior is strongly influenced by biology, is tied to evolution, and is characterized by critical or sensitive periods. These are specific time frames during which, according to ethologists, the presence or absence of certain experiences has a long-lasting influence on individuals.

European zoologist Konrad Lorenz (1903–1989) helped bring ethology to prominence. In his best-known experiment, Lorenz (1965) studied the behavior of greylag geese, which will follow their mothers as soon as they hatch.

In a remarkable set of experiments, Lorenz separated the eggs laid by one goose into two groups. One group he returned to the goose to be hatched by her. The other group was hatched in an incubator. The goslings in the first group performed as predicted. They followed their mother as soon as they hatched. However, those in the second group, which saw Lorenz when they first hatched, followed him everywhere, as though he were their mother. Lorenz marked the goslings and then placed both groups under a box. Mother goose and "mother" Lorenz stood aside as the box lifted. Each group of goslings went directly to its "mother." Lorenz called this process imprinting—rapid, innate learning within a limited, critical period of time that involves attachment to the first moving object seen.

At first, ethological research and theory had little or nothing to say about the nature of social relationships across the *human* life span, and the theory stimulated few studies involving people. Ethologists' viewpoint that normal development requires that certain behaviors emerge during a *critical period*, a fixed time period very early in development, seemed to be overstated. However, John Bowlby's work (1969, 1989) illustrated an important application of ethological theory to human development. Bowlby argued that attachment to a caregiver during the first year of life has important consequences throughout the life span.

Konrad Lorenz, a pioneering student of animal behavior, is followed through the water by three imprinted greylag geese. Describe Lorenz's experiment with the geese. *Do you think his experiment would have the same results with human babies?* Explain.

In his view, if this attachment is positive and secure, the infant will likely develop positively in childhood and adulthood. If the attachment is negative and insecure, children's development will likely be less than optimal. Thus, in this view the first year of life is a *sensitive period* for the development of social relationships. In Chapter 10, "Emotional Development," we will explore the concept of infant attachment in greater detail.

Contributions of ethological theory include a focus on the biological and evolutionary basis of development, and the use of careful observations in naturalistic settings. Critics assert that too much emphasis is placed on biological foundations and that the critical and sensitive period concepts might be too rigid.

Another theory that emphasizes the biological aspects of human development—evolutionary psychology—will be presented in Chapter 2, "Biological Beginnings," along with views on the role of heredity in development.

Ecological Theory Whereas ethological theory stresses biological factors, ecological theory emphasizes environmental factors. One ecological theory that has important implications for understanding children's development was created by Urie Bronfenbrenner (1917–2005).

Bronfenbrenner's ecological theory (1986, 2000, 2004; Bronfenbrenner & Morris, 1998, 2006) holds that development reflects the influence of several environmental systems. The theory identifies five environmental systems (see Figure 1.11):

- *Microsystem:* The setting in which the individual lives. These contexts include the person's family, peers, school, neighborhood, and work. It is within the microsystem that the most direct interactions with social agents take place—with parents, peers, and teachers, for example.

- *Mesosystem:* Relations between microsystems or connections between contexts. Examples are the relationships between family experiences and school experiences, school experiences and church experiences, and family experiences and peer experiences. For example, children whose parents have rejected them may have difficulty developing positive relationships with teachers.

- *Exosystem:* Links between a social setting in which the individual does not have an active role and the individual's immediate context. For example, a husband's or child's experience at home may be influenced by a mother's experiences at work. The mother might receive a promotion that requires more travel, which might increase conflict with the husband and change patterns of interaction with the child.

- *Macrosystem:* The culture in which individuals live. Remember from earlier in this chapter that *culture* refers to the behavior patterns, beliefs, and all other products of a group of people that are passed from generation to generation. Remember also that cross-cultural studies—comparisons of one culture with one or more other cultures—provide information about the generality of development (Mistry, Contreras, & Dutta, 2013).

- *Chronosystem:* The patterning of environmental events and transitions over the life course, as well as sociohistorical circumstances (Schaie, 2012). For example, divorce is one transition. Researchers have found that the negative effects of divorce on children often peak in the first year after the divorce (Hetherington, 1993, 2006). By two years

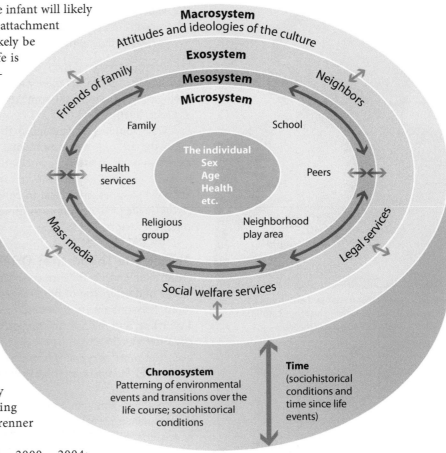

FIGURE 1.11

BRONFENBRENNER'S ECOLOGICAL THEORY OF DEVELOPMENT. Bronfenbrenner's ecological theory consists of five environmental systems: microsystem, mesosystem, exosystem, macrosystem, and chronosystem.

Bronfenbrenner's ecological theory An environmental systems theory that focuses on five environmental systems: microsystem, mesosystem, exosystem, macrosystem, and chronosystem.

Urie Bronfenbrenner developed ecological theory, a perspective that is receiving increased attention. *What is the nature of ecological theory?*

eclectic theoretical orientation An orientation that does not follow any one theoretical approach but rather selects from each theory whatever is considered its best aspects.

after the divorce, family interaction is less chaotic and more stable. As an example of sociohistorical circumstances, consider how career opportunities for women have increased during the last 30 years.

Bronfenbrenner (2000, 2004; Bronfenbrenner & Morris, 1998, 2006) has added biological influences to his theory and now describes it as a bioecological theory. Nonetheless, ecological, environmental contexts still predominate in Bronfenbrenner's theory (Gauvain & Parke, 2010).

Contributions of ecological theory include a systematic examination of macro and micro dimensions of environmental systems, and attention to connections between environmental systems. A further contribution of Bronfenbrenner's theory is its emphasis on a range of social contexts beyond the family, such as neighborhood, religious organization, school, and workplace, as influential in children's development (Gauvain, 2013). Criticisms include giving inadequate attention to biological factors, as well as placing too little emphasis on cognitive factors.

An Eclectic Theoretical Orientation No single theory described in this chapter can explain entirely the rich complexity of children's development, but each has contributed to our understanding of development. Psychoanalytic theory best explains the unconscious mind. Erikson's theory best describes the changes that occur in adult development. Piaget's, Vygotsky's, and the information-processing views provide the most complete description of cognitive development. The behavioral and social cognitive and ecological theories have been the most adept at examining the environmental determinants of development. The ethological theories have highlighted biology's role and the importance of sensitive periods in development.

In short, although theories are helpful guides, relying on a single theory to explain development is probably a mistake. This book instead takes an **eclectic theoretical orientation,** which does not follow any one theoretical approach but rather selects from each theory whatever is considered its best features. In this way, you can view the study of development as it actually exists—with different theorists making different assumptions, stressing different empirical problems, and using different strategies to discover information. Figure 1.12

THEORY	ISSUES		
	Nature and nurture	**Early and later experience**	**Continuity and discontinuity**
Psychoanalytic	Freud's biological determinism interacting with early family experiences; Erikson's more balanced biological/cultural interaction perspective	Early experiences in the family very important influences	Emphasis on discontinuity between stages
Cognitive	Piaget's emphasis on interaction and adaptation; environment provides the setting for cognitive structures to develop. Vygotsky's theory involves interaction of nature and nurture with strong emphasis on culture. The information-processing approach has not addressed this issue extensively; mainly emphasizes biological/environment interaction.	Childhood experiences important influences	Discontinuity between stages in Piaget's theory; no stages in Vygotsky's theory or the information-processing approach
Behavioral and Social Cognitive	Environment viewed as the main influence on development	Experiences important at all points in development	Continuity with no stages
Ethological	Strong biological view	Early experience very important, which can contribute to change early in development; after early critical or sensitive period has passed, stability likely to occur	Discontinuity because of early critical or sensitive period; no stages
Ecological	Strong environmental view	Experiences involving the five environmental systems important at all points in development	No stages but little attention to the issue

FIGURE **1.12**
A COMPARISON OF THEORIES AND ISSUES IN CHILD DEVELOPMENT

compares the main theoretical perspectives in terms of how they view important issues in children's development.

RESEARCH METHODS FOR COLLECTING DATA

If they follow an eclectic orientation, how do scholars and researchers determine that one feature of a theory is somehow better than another? The scientific method discussed earlier in this chapter provides the guide. Recall that the steps in the scientific method involve conceptualizing the problem, collecting data, drawing conclusions, and revising research conclusions and theories. Through scientific research, the features of theories can be tested and refined.

Whether we are interested in studying attachment in infants, the cognitive skills of children, or peer relations among adolescents, we can choose from several ways of collecting data. Here we outline the measures most often used, looking at the advantages and disadvantages of each.

Observation Scientific observation requires an important set of skills (Gravetter & Forzano, 2012). Unless we are trained observers and practice our skills regularly, we might not know what to look for, we might not remember what we saw, we might not realize that what we are looking for is changing from one moment to the next, and we might not communicate our observations effectively.

For observations to be effective, they have to be systematic. We have to have some idea of what we are looking for. We have to know whom we are observing, when and where we will observe, how the observations will be made, and how they will be recorded.

Where should we make our observations? We have two choices: the laboratory and the everyday world.

When we observe scientifically, we often need to control certain factors that determine behavior but are not the focus of our inquiry (Rosnow & Rosenthal, 2013). For this reason, some research in life-span development is conducted in a **laboratory,** a controlled setting from which many of the complex factors of the "real world" have been removed. For example, suppose you want to observe how children react when they see other people behave aggressively. If you observe children in their homes or schools, you have no control over how much aggression the children observe, what kind of aggression they see, which people they see acting

What are some important strategies in conducting observational research with children?

laboratory A controlled setting from which many of the complex factors of the "real world" have been removed.

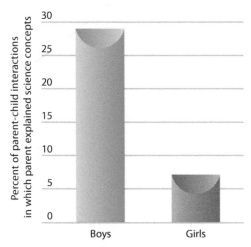

FIGURE **1.13**

PARENTS' EXPLANATIONS OF SCIENCE TO SONS AND DAUGHTERS AT A SCIENCE MUSEUM. In a naturalistic observation study at a children's science museum, parents were more than three times more likely to explain science to boys than to girls (Crowley & others, 2001). The gender difference occurred regardless of whether the father, the mother, or both parents were with the child, although the gender difference was greatest for fathers' science explanations to sons and daughters.

naturalistic observation Behavioral observation that takes place in real-world settings.

standardized test A test with uniform procedures for administration and scoring. Many standardized tests allow a person's performance to be compared with the performance of other individuals.

aggressively, or how other people treat the children. In contrast, if you observe the children in a laboratory, you can control these and other factors and therefore have more confidence about how to interpret your observations.

Laboratory research does have some drawbacks, however, including the following:

- It is almost impossible to conduct research without letting participants know they are being studied.
- The laboratory setting is unnatural and therefore can cause the participants to behave unnaturally.
- People who are willing to come to a university laboratory may not fairly represent groups from diverse cultural backgrounds.
- People who are unfamiliar with university settings and with the idea of "helping science" may be intimidated by the laboratory setting.
- Some aspects of children's development are difficult, if not impossible, to examine in the laboratory.
- Laboratory studies of certain types of stress may even be unethical.

Naturalistic observation provides insights that we sometimes cannot achieve in the laboratory (Graziano & Raulin, 2013). **Naturalistic observation** means observing behavior in real-world settings, making no effort to manipulate or control the situation. Child development researchers conduct naturalistic observations in homes, child-care centers, schools, neighborhoods, malls, and other contexts.

Naturalistic observation was used in one study that focused on conversations in a children's science museum (Crowley & others, 2001). Parents of boys were more than three times as likely as parents of girls to engage their children in explanatory talk while visiting exhibits at the science museum, suggesting a gender bias that encourages boys more than girls to be interested in science (see Figure 1.13). In another study, Mexican American parents who had completed high school used more explanations with their children when visiting a science museum than Mexican American parents who had not completed high school (Tenenbaum & others, 2002).

Survey and Interview   Sometimes the best and quickest way to get information about people is to ask them for it. One technique is to interview them directly. A related method is the survey (sometimes referred to as a questionnaire), which is especially useful when information from many people is needed (Leedy & Ormrod, 2013). A standard set of questions is used to obtain people's self-reported attitudes or beliefs about a particular topic. In a good survey, the questions are clear and unbiased, allowing respondents to answer unambiguously.

Surveys and interviews can be used to study a wide range of topics, from religious beliefs to sexual habits to attitudes about gun control to beliefs about how to improve schools. Surveys and interviews today are conducted in person, over the telephone, and on the Internet.

One problem with surveys and interviews is the tendency for participants to answer questions in a way that they think is socially acceptable or desirable rather than telling what they truly think or feel (Creswell, 2008). For example, on a survey or in an interview some individuals might say that they do not take drugs even though they do.

Standardized Test   A **standardized test** has uniform procedures for administration and scoring. Many standardized tests allow a person's performance to be compared with the performance of other individuals, thus providing information about individual differences among people (Watson, 2012). One example is the Stanford-Binet intelligence test, which is described in Chapter 8, "Intelligence." Your score on the Stanford-Binet test shows how your performance compares with that of thousands of other people who have taken the test.

Standardized tests have three key weaknesses. First, they do not always predict behavior in non-test situations. Second, standardized tests are based on the belief that a person's behavior is consistent and stable, yet personality and intelligence—two primary targets of standardized testing—can vary with the situation. For example, individuals may perform poorly on a standardized intelligence test in an office setting but score much higher at home, where they are less anxious. This criticism is especially relevant for members of minority groups, some of whom have been inaccurately classified as intellectually disabled on the basis of their scores on intelligence tests. A third weakness of standardized tests is that many psychological tests developed in Western cultures might not be appropriate in other cultures (Hall, 2010). The experiences of people in differing cultures may lead them to interpret and respond to questions differently.

Case Study   A **case study** is an in-depth look at a single individual. Case studies are performed mainly by mental health professionals when, for either practical or ethical reasons, the unique aspects of an individual's life cannot be duplicated and tested in other ways. A case study provides information about one person's fears, hopes, fantasies, traumatic experiences, upbringing, family relationships, health, or anything that helps the psychologist understand the person's mind and behavior. In later chapters, we discuss vivid case studies, such as that of Michael Rehbein, who had much of the left side of his brain removed at 7 years of age to end severe epileptic seizures.

Case histories provide dramatic, in-depth portrayals of people's lives, but remember that we must be cautious when generalizing from this information (Yin, 2012). The subject of a case study is unique, with a genetic makeup and personal history that no one else shares. In addition, case studies involve judgments of unknown reliability. Psychologists who conduct case studies rarely check to see if other psychologists agree with their observations.

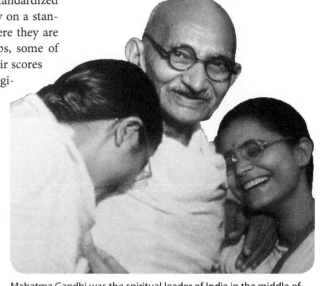

Mahatma Gandhi was the spiritual leader of India in the middle of the twentieth century. Erik Erikson conducted an extensive case study of his life to determine what contributed to his identity development. *What are some limitations of the case study approach?*

Physiological Measures   Researchers are increasingly using physiological measures when they study children's development (Bauer & Dunn, 2013). For example, as puberty unfolds, the blood levels of certain hormones increase. To determine the nature of these hormonal changes, researchers take blood samples from willing adolescents (Susman & Dorn, 2013).

Another physiological measure that is increasingly used to study children and adolescents is neuroimaging, especially *functional magnetic resonance imaging* (fMRI), in which electromagnetic waves are used to construct images of an individual's brain tissue and biochemical activity (Fletcher & Rapp, 2013). Figure 1.14 compares the brain images of two adolescents—one a non-drinker and the other a heavy drinker—while engaged in a memory task. We will have much more to say about neuroimaging and other physiological measures at various points in this book.

case study An in-depth look at a single individual.

FIGURE **1.14**

BRAIN IMAGING OF 15-YEAR-OLD ADOLESCENTS. The two brain images indicate how alcohol can influence the functioning of an adolescent's brain. Notice the pink and red coloring (which indicates effective brain functioning involving memory) in the brain of the 15-year-old non-drinker while engaging in a memory task and the lack of those colors in the brain of the 15-year-old under the influence of alcohol.

RESEARCH DESIGNS

Suppose you want to find out whether the children of permissive parents are more likely than other children to be rude and unruly. The data-collection method that researchers choose often depends on the goal of their research. The goal may be simply to describe a phenomenon, or it may be to describe relationships between phenomena, or to determine the causes or effects of a phenomenon.

Perhaps you decide that you need to observe both permissive and strict parents with their children and compare them. How would you do that? In addition to choosing a method for collecting data, you would need to select a research design. There are three main types of research designs: descriptive, correlational, and experimental.

Descriptive Research   All of the data-collection methods that we have discussed can be used in **descriptive research,** which aims to observe and record behavior. For example, a researcher might observe the extent to which people behave altruistically or aggressively toward each other. By itself, descriptive research cannot prove what causes a specific phenomenon, but it can yield important information about people's behavior (Leedy & Ormrod, 2013).

Correlational Research   In contrast with descriptive research, correlational research goes beyond describing phenomena and provides information that helps predict how people will behave. In **correlational research,** the goal is to describe the strength of the relationship between two or more events or characteristics. The more strongly the two events are correlated (or related or associated), the more effectively we can predict one event from the other (Rossi, 2013).

For example, to determine whether children of permissive parents have less self-control than other children, you would need to carefully record observations of parents' permissiveness and their children's self-control. The data could then be analyzed statistically to yield a numerical measure, called a **correlation coefficient,** a number based on a statistical analysis that is used to describe the degree of association between two variables. The correlation coefficient ranges from −1.00 to +1.00. A negative number means an inverse relation. For example, researchers often find a negative correlation between permissive parenting and children's self-control. By contrast, they often find a positive correlation between parental monitoring of children and children's self-control.

The higher the correlation coefficient (whether positive or negative), the stronger the association between the two variables. A correlation of 0 means that there is no association between the variables. A correlation of −.40 is stronger than a correlation of +.20 because we disregard whether the correlation is positive or negative in determining the strength of the correlation.

A caution is in order, however. Correlation does not equal causation (Graziano & Raulin, 2013). The correlational finding just mentioned does not mean that permissive parenting necessarily causes low self-control in children. It might mean that a child's lack of self-control caused the parents to simply give up trying to control the child. It might also mean that other factors, such as heredity or poverty, caused the correlation between permissive parenting and low self-control in children. Figure 1.15 illustrates these possible interpretations of correlational data.

descriptive research Research that involves observing and recording behavior.

correlational research Research in which the goal is to describe the strength of the relationship between two or more events or characteristics.

correlation coefficient A number based on statistical analysis that is used to describe the degree of association between two variables.

Observed Correlation: As permissive parenting increases, children's self-control decreases.

Possible explanations for this observed correlation

Permissive parenting   causes   →   Children's lack of self-control

Children's lack of self-control   causes   →   Permissive parenting

A third factor such as genetic tendencies or poverty   causes both   →   Permissive parenting and children's lack of self-control

An observed correlation between two events cannot be used to conclude that one event causes the second event. Other possibilities are that the second event causes the first event or that a third event causes the correlation between the first two events.

FIGURE **1.15**
POSSIBLE EXPLANATIONS OF CORRELATIONAL DATA

Throughout this book you will read about numerous correlational research studies. Keep in mind how easy (and misleading) it can be to assume causality when two events or characteristics merely are correlated (Caldwell, 2013).

Experimental Research   To study causality, researchers turn to experimental research. An **experiment** is a carefully regulated procedure in which one or more factors believed to influence the behavior being studied are manipulated while all other factors are held constant. If the behavior under study changes when a factor is manipulated, we say that the manipulated factor has caused the behavior to change. In other words, the experiment has demonstrated cause and effect. The cause is the factor that was manipulated. The effect is the behavior that changed because of the manipulation. Nonexperimental research methods (descriptive and correlational research) cannot establish cause and effect because they do not involve manipulating factors in a controlled way (Leedy & Ormrod, 2013).

Independent and Dependent Variables   Experiments include two types of changeable factors, or variables: independent and dependent. An independent variable is a manipulated, influential, experimental factor. It is a potential cause. The label *independent* is used because this variable can be manipulated independently of other factors to determine its effect. One experiment may include several independent variables.

A dependent variable is a factor that can change in an experiment, in response to changes in the independent variable. As researchers manipulate the independent variable, they measure the dependent variable for any resulting effect.

For example, suppose that you conducted a study to determine whether aerobic exercise by pregnant women changes the breathing and sleeping patterns of their newborn babies. You might require one group of pregnant women to engage in a certain amount of exercise each week; the amount of exercise is thus the independent variable. When the infants are born, you would observe and measure their breathing and sleeping patterns. These patterns are the dependent variable, the factor that changes as the result of your manipulation.

Experimental and Control Groups   Experiments can involve one or more experimental groups and one or more control groups. An experimental group is a group whose experience is manipulated. A control group is a comparison group that is as much like the experimental group as possible and that is treated in every way like the experimental group except for the manipulated factor (independent variable). The control group serves as a baseline against which the effects of the manipulated condition can be compared.

Random assignment is an important principle for deciding whether each participant will be placed in the experimental group or in the control group. Random assignment means that researchers assign participants to experimental and control groups by chance. It reduces the likelihood that the experiment's results will be due to any preexisting differences between groups (Kirk, 2013). In the example of the effects of aerobic exercise by pregnant women on the breathing and sleeping patterns of their newborns, you would randomly assign half of the pregnant women to engage in aerobic exercise over a period of weeks (the experimental group) and the other half to not exercise over the same number of weeks (the control group). Figure 1.16 illustrates the nature of experimental research.

Time Span of Research   Researchers in child development have a special concern with studies that focus on the relationship between age and some other variable. To do this, they study individuals of different ages and compare them, or they study the same individuals as they age over time.

Cross-Sectional Approach   The **cross-sectional approach** is a research strategy in which individuals of different ages are compared at one time. A typical cross-sectional study might include a group of 5-year-olds, 8-year-olds, and 11-year-olds. The groups can be compared with respect to a variety of dependent variables: IQ, memory, peer relations, attachment to parents, hormonal changes, and so on. All of this can be accomplished in a short time. In some studies,

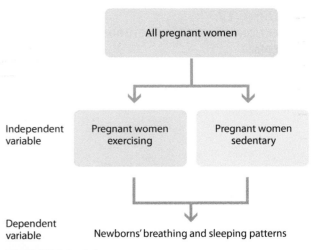

Independent variable

Dependent variable

FIGURE **1.16**

PRINCIPLES OF EXPERIMENTAL RESEARCH. Imagine that you decide to conduct an experimental study of the effects of aerobic exercise by pregnant women on their newborns' breathing and sleeping patterns. You would randomly assign pregnant women to experimental and control groups. The experimental-group women would engage in aerobic exercise over a specified number of sessions and weeks. The control group would not. Then, when the infants are born, you would assess their breathing and sleeping patterns. If the breathing and sleeping patterns of newborns whose mothers were in the experimental group were more positive than those of the control group, you would conclude that aerobic exercise caused the positive effects.

experiment A carefully regulated procedure in which one or more of the factors believed to influence the behavior being studied are manipulated while all other factors are held constant.

cross-sectional approach A research strategy in which individuals of different ages are compared at the same point in time.

FIGURE **1.17**
CONNECTIONS OF RESEARCH METHODS TO THEORIES

Research Method	Theory
Observation	• All theories emphasize some form of observation. • Behavioral and social cognitive theories place the strongest emphasis on laboratory observation. • Ethological theory places the strongest emphasis on naturalistic observation.
Interview/survey	• Psychoanalytic and cognitive studies (Piaget, Vygotsky) often use interviews. • Behavioral, social cognitive, and ethological theories are the least likely to use surveys or interviews.
Standardized test	• None of the theories discussed emphasize the use of this method.
Correlational research	• All of the theories use this research method, although psychoanalytic theories are the least likely to use it.
Experimental research	• The behavioral and social cognitive theories and the information-processing theories are the most likely to use the experimental method. • Psychoanalytic theories are the least likely to use it.
Cross-sectional/ longitudinal methods	• No theory described uses these methods more than any other.

data are collected in a single day. Even in large-scale cross-sectional studies with hundreds of participants, data collection does not usually take longer than several months to complete.

The main advantage of the cross-sectional study is that researchers don't have to wait for children to grow older. Despite its efficiency, the cross-sectional approach has its drawbacks. It gives no information about how individual children change or about the stability of their characteristics. It can obscure the increases and decreases of development—the hills and valleys of growth and development.

Longitudinal Approach   The **longitudinal approach** is a research strategy in which the same individuals are studied over a period of time, usually several years or more. For example, if a study of self-esteem were conducted longitudinally, the same children might be assessed three times—such as at 5, 8, and 11 years of age. Some longitudinal studies take place over shorter time frames, even just a year or so.

Longitudinal studies provide a wealth of information about important issues such as stability and change in development and the influence of early experience on later development, but they are not without problems (Reznick, 2013). They are expensive and time-consuming. Also, the longer the study lasts, the greater the number of participants who drop out. For example, children's families may move, get sick, lose interest, and so forth. Those who remain in the study may be dissimilar to those who drop out, biasing the results. Those individuals who remain in a longitudinal study over a number of years may be more compulsive and conformity-oriented than average, for example, or they might lead more stable lives.

Earlier in the chapter we described *cohort effects,* which are effects due to a person's time of birth, era, or generation rather than to actual age. Cohort effects are important in research on children, adolescents, and their parents because they can powerfully affect the dependent measures in a study ostensibly concerned with age (Schaie, 2012). Cross-sectional studies can show how different cohorts respond, but they can confuse age changes and cohort effects. Longitudinal studies are effective in studying age changes but only within one cohort.

Theories are often linked with a particular research method or methods. Therefore, methods that researchers use are associated with their particular theoretical approaches. Figure 1.17 illustrates connections between research methods and theories.

So far we have discussed many aspects of scientific research in child development, but where can you read about this research firsthand? Read *Connecting Through Research* to find out.

longitudinal approach A research strategy in which the same individuals are studied over a period of time, usually several years.

connecting through research

Where Is Child Development Research Published?

Regardless of whether you pursue a career in child development, psychology, or some related scientific field, you can benefit by learning about the journal process. As a student you might be required to look up original research in journals. As a parent, teacher, or nurse you might want to consult journals to obtain information that will help you understand and work more effectively with people. And as an inquiring person, you might look up information in journals after you have heard or read something that piqued your curiosity.

A journal publishes scholarly and academic information, usually in a specific domain such as physics, math, sociology, or our current interest, child development. Scholars in these fields publish most of their research in journals, which are the source of core information in virtually every academic discipline.

An increasing number of journals publish information about child development. Among the leading journals in child development are *Child Development, Developmental Psychology, Developmental Science, Development and Psychopathology, Pediatrics, Pediatric Nursing, Infant Behavior and Development, Journal of Research on Adolescence, Human Development, Social Development, Cognitive Development,* and many others. Also, a number of journals that do not focus solely on development include articles on various aspects of human development. These journals include *Journal of Educational Psychology, Sex Roles, Journal of Cross-Cultural Research, Journal of Marriage and the Family, Exceptional Children,* and *Journal of Consulting and Clinical Psychology.*

Every journal has a board of experts who evaluate articles submitted for publication. Each submitted paper is accepted or rejected on the basis of factors such as its contribution to the field, methodological excellence, and clarity of writing. Some of the most prestigious journals reject as many as 80 to 90 percent of the articles submitted.

Journal articles are usually written for other professionals in the specialized field of the journal's focus; therefore, they often contain technical language and terms specific to the discipline that are difficult for

Research journals are the core of information in virtually every academic discipline. Those shown here are among the increasing number of research journals that publish information about child development. *What are the main parts of a research article that presents findings from original research?*

nonprofessionals to understand. They usually consist of the following elements: abstract, introduction, method, results, discussion, and references. The *abstract* is a brief summary that appears at the beginning of the article. The abstract lets readers quickly determine whether the article is relevant to their interests. The *introduction* introduces the problem or issue that is being studied. It includes a concise review of research relevant to the topic, theoretical ties, and one or more hypotheses to be tested. The *method* section consists of a clear description of the subjects evaluated in the study, the measures used, and the procedures that were followed. The method section should be sufficiently clear and detailed so that reading it could allow another researcher to repeat or replicate the study. The *results* section reports the analysis of the data collected. In most cases, the results section includes statistical analyses that are difficult for nonprofessionals to understand. The *discussion* section describes the author's conclusions, inferences, and interpretation of what was found. Statements are usually made about whether the hypotheses presented in the introduction were supported, limitations of the study, and suggestions for future research. The last part of the journal article, called *references,* includes bibliographic information for each source cited in the article. The references section is often a good resource for finding other articles relevant to a topic that interests you.

Where do you find journals such as those we have described? Your college or university library likely has some of them, and some public libraries also carry journals. Online resources such as PsycINFO, which can facilitate the search for journal articles, are available to students on many campuses.

The research published in the journals mentioned above shapes our lives. It not only informs the work of other child development researchers, but it also informs the practices of law and policy makers, physicians, educators, parents, and many others. In fact, much of what you will find that is new in this edition of this textbook comes directly from research that can be found in the journals mentioned above.

CHALLENGES IN CHILD DEVELOPMENT RESEARCH

The scientific foundation of research in child development helps to minimize the effect of research bias and maximize the objectivity of the results. Still, subtle challenges remain for each researcher to resolve. One is to ensure that research is conducted in an ethical way; another is to recognize, and try to overcome, deeply buried personal biases.

Conducting Ethical Research   The explosion in technology has forced society to grapple with looming ethical questions that were unimaginable only a few decades ago. The same line of research that enables previously sterile couples to have children might someday let prospective parents "call up and order" the characteristics they prefer in their children or tip the balance of males and females in the world. For example, should embryos left over from procedures for increasing fertility be saved or discarded? Should people with inheritable fatal diseases (such as Huntington's disease) be discouraged from having their own biological children?

Researchers also face ethical questions both new and old. They have a responsibility to anticipate the personal problems their research might cause and to at least inform the participants of the possible fallout. Safeguarding the rights of research participants is a challenge because the potential harm is not always obvious (Graziano & Raulin, 2013).

Ethics in research may affect you personally if you ever serve as a participant in a study. In that event, you need to know your rights as a participant and the responsibilities of researchers to assure that these rights are safeguarded.

If you ever become a researcher in child development yourself, you will need an even deeper understanding of ethics. Even if you only carry out experimental projects in psychology courses, you must consider the rights of the participants in those projects.

Today, proposed research at colleges and universities must pass the scrutiny of a research ethics committee before the research can be initiated. In addition, the American Psychological Association (APA) has developed ethics guidelines for its members. The APA code of ethics instructs psychologists to protect their participants from mental and physical harm. The participants' best interests need to be kept foremost in the researcher's mind. APA's guidelines address four important issues: informed consent, confidentiality, debriefing, and deception.

- *Informed consent*. All participants must know what their participation will involve and what risks might develop. For example, participants in a study on dating should be told beforehand that a questionnaire might stimulate thoughts about issues in their relationship that they had not considered. Participants also should be informed that in some instances a discussion of the issues might improve their relationship, but in others it might worsen the relationship and even end it. Even after informed consent is given, participants must retain the right to withdraw from the study at any time and for any reason.

- *Confidentiality*. Researchers are responsible for keeping all of the data they gather on individuals completely confidential and, when possible, completely anonymous.

- *Debriefing*. After the study has been completed, participants should be informed of its purpose and the methods that were used. In most cases, the experimenter also can inform participants in a general manner beforehand about the purpose of the research without leading participants to behave in a way they think that the experimenter is expecting. When preliminary information about the study is likely to affect the results, participants can at least be debriefed after the study has been completed.

- *Deception*. This is an ethical issue that researchers debate extensively. In some circumstances, telling the participants beforehand what the research study is about substantially alters the participants' behavior and invalidates the researcher's data. In all cases of deception, however, the psychologist must ensure that the deception will not harm the participants and that the participants will be told the complete nature of the study (debriefed) as soon as possible after the study is completed.

connecting with careers

Pam Reid, Educational and Developmental Psychologist

When she was a child, Pam Reid liked to play with chemistry sets. Reid majored in chemistry during college and wanted to become a doctor. However, when some of her friends signed up for a psychology class as an elective, she also decided to take the course. She was intrigued by learning about how people think, behave, and develop—so much so that she changed her major to psychology. Reid went on to obtain her Ph.D. in psychology (American Psychological Association, 2003, p. 16).

For many years Reid was a professor of education and psychology at the University of Michigan, where she also was a research scientist at the Institute for Research on Women and Gender, focusing on how children and adolescents develop social skills, with a special interest in the development of African American girls (Reid & Zalk, 2001). In 2004, Reid became provost and executive vice-president at Roosevelt University and then President of the University of Saint Joseph in 2008.

Pam Reid (*center*) with students at the University of Saint Joseph in Hartford, Connecticut, where she is the president of the university.

For more information about what professors, researchers, and educational psychologists do, see pages 42–43 in the Careers in Child Development appendix immediately following this chapter.

Minimizing Bias Studies of children's development are most useful when they are conducted without bias or prejudice toward any particular group of people. Of special concern is bias based on gender and bias based on culture or ethnicity.

Gender Bias For most of its existence, our society has had a strong gender bias, a preconceived notion about the abilities of males and females that prevented individuals from pursuing their own interests and achieving their full potential (Matlin, 2012). Gender bias also has had a less obvious effect within the field of child development. For example, it is not unusual for conclusions to be drawn about females' attitudes and behaviors from research conducted with males as the only participants.

Furthermore, when researchers find gender differences, their reports sometimes magnify those differences (Hyde & Else-Quest, 2013). For example, a researcher might report that 74 percent of the boys in a study had high achievement expectations versus only 67 percent of the girls and go on to talk about the differences in some detail. In reality, this might be a rather small difference. It also might disappear if the study was repeated, or the study might have methodological problems that don't allow such strong interpretations.

Pam Reid is a leading researcher who studies gender and ethnic bias in development. To read about Pam's interests, see *Connecting with Careers*.

Cultural and Ethnic Bias The realization that research on children's development needs to include more children from diverse ethnic groups has also been building (Benner & Graham, 2013; Trejos-Castillo, Bedore, & Trevino, 2013). Historically, children from ethnic minority groups (African American, Latino, Asian American, and Native American) were excluded from most research in the United States and simply thought of as variations from the norm or average. If minority children were included in samples and their scores didn't fit the norm, they were viewed as confounds or "noise" in data and discounted. Given the fact that children from diverse ethnic groups were excluded from research on child development for so long, we might reasonably conclude that children's real lives are perhaps more varied than research data have indicated in the past.

developmental **connection**

Culture and Ethnicity

What characterizes an adolescent's ethnic identity? Chapter 11, p. 331

Look at these two photographs, one (*left*) of all non-Latino white boys, the other (*right*) of boys and girls from diverse ethnic backgrounds. Consider a topic in child development, such as independence seeking, cultural values, parenting education, or health care. *If you were conducting research on this topic, might the results of the study be different depending on whether the participants in your study were the children in the photo on the left or the photo on the right?*

Researchers also have tended to overgeneralize about ethnic groups. **Ethnic gloss** is using an ethnic label such as *African American* or *Latino* in a superficial way that portrays an ethnic group as being more homogeneous than it really is (Trimble, 1988). For example, a researcher might describe a research sample like this: "The participants were 60 Latinos." A more complete description of the Latino group might be something like this: "The 60 Latino participants were Mexican Americans from low-income neighborhoods in the southwestern area of Los Angeles. Thirty-six were from homes in which Spanish is the dominant language spoken, 24 from homes in which English is the main language spoken. Thirty were born in the United States, 30 in Mexico. Twenty-eight described themselves as Mexican American, 14 as Mexican, 9 as American, 6 as Chicano, and 3 as Latino." Ethnic gloss can cause researchers to obtain samples of ethnic groups that are not representative of the group's diversity, which can lead to overgeneralization and stereotyping.

Research on ethnic minority children and their families has not been given adequate attention, especially in light of their significant rate of growth within the U.S. population (Crosnoe & Fuligni, 2012; Tobler & others, 2013). Until recently, ethnic minority families were combined in the category "minority," which masks important differences among ethnic groups as well as diversity within an ethnic group. At present and in the foreseeable future, the growth of minority families in the United States will be mainly due to the immigration of Latino and Asian families. Researchers need to take into account families' acculturation level and the generational status of both parents and adolescents (Gauvain, 2013). More attention needs to be given to biculturalism because many immigrant children and adolescents identify with two or more ethnic groups (Schwartz & others, 2012).

ethnic gloss Use of an ethnic label such as *African American* or *Latino* in a superficial way that portrays an ethnic group as being more homogeneous than it really is.

Review *Connect* Reflect

LG3 Summarize why research is important in child development, the main theories of child development, and research methods, designs, and challenges.

Review

- What is scientific research, what is it based on, and why is scientific research on child development important?
- What are the main theories of child development?
- What are the main research methods for collecting data about children's development?
- What types of research designs do child development researchers use?
- What are some research challenges in studying children's development?

Connect

- Which of the research methods for collecting data would be appropriate or inappropriate for studying Erikson's stage of trust versus mistrust? Why?

Reflect *Your Own Personal Journey of Life*

- Which of the theories of child development do you think best explains your own development? Why?

Introduction

Caring for Children

 Identify five areas in which children's lives need to be improved, and explain the roles of resilience and social policy in children's development.

Improving the Lives of Children

Resilience, Social Policy, and Children's Development

- Health and well-being is an important area in which children's lives can be improved. Today, many children in the United States and around the world need improved health care. We now recognize the importance of lifestyles and psychological states in promoting health and well-being. Parenting is an important influence on children's development. One-parent families, working parents, and child care are among the family issues that influence children's well-being. Education can also contribute to children's health and well-being. There is widespread concern that the education of children needs to be more effective, and there are many views in contemporary education about ways to improve schools.

- Some children triumph over adversity—they are resilient. Researchers have found that resilient children are likely to have a close relationship with a parent figure and to form bonds with caring people outside the family. Social policy is a government's course of action designed to promote the welfare of its citizens. The poor conditions of life for a significant percentage of U.S. children, and the lack of attention to prevention of these poor conditions, point to the need for revised social policies.

Developmental Processes, Periods, and Issues

 Discuss the most important processes, periods, and issues in development.

Biological, Cognitive, and Socioemotional Processes

Periods of Development

Age and Cohort Effects

Issues in Development

- Three key processes of development are biological, cognitive, and socioemotional. Biological processes (such as genes inherited from parents) involve changes in an individual's body. Cognitive processes (such as thinking) consist of changes in an individual's thought, intelligence, and language. Socioemotional processes (such as the advent of smiling) include changes in an individual's relationships with others, in emotions, and in personality.

- Childhood's five main developmental periods are (1) prenatal, from conception to birth, (2) infancy, from birth to 18 to 24 months, (3) early childhood, from the end of infancy to about 5 or 6 years of age, (4) middle and late childhood, from about 6 to 11 years of age, and (5) adolescence, which begins at about 10 or 12 and ends at about 18 or 19 years of age.

- Cohort effects are due to a person's time of birth, era, or generation but not to actual age. Two characteristics of today's children and many of their parents—the generation labeled Millennials—that stand out are their ethnic diversity and their connection to technology.

- The nature-nurture issue focuses on the extent to which development is mainly influenced by nature (biological inheritance) or nurture (environmental experience). Some developmentalists describe development as continuous (gradual, cumulative change), while others describe it as discontinuous (a sequence of distinct stages). The early-later experience issue focuses on whether early experiences (especially in infancy) are more important in development than later experiences. Most developmentalists recognize that extreme positions on the nature-nurture, continuity-discontinuity, and early-later experience issues are not supported by research. Despite this consensus, they continue to debate the degree to which each issue influences children's development.

The Science of Child Development

Summarize why research is important in child development, the main theories of child development, and research methods, designs, and challenges.

The Importance of Research

- Scientific research is objective, systematic, and testable. Scientific research is based on the scientific method, which includes the following steps: (1) conceptualize the problem, (2) collect data, (3) draw conclusions, and (4) revise theory. Scientific research on child development reduces the likelihood that the information gathered is based on personal beliefs, opinions, and feelings.

Theories of Child Development

- Psychoanalytic theories describe development as primarily unconscious and as heavily colored by emotion. The two main psychoanalytic theories in developmental psychology are Freud's and Erikson's. Freud also proposed that individuals go through five psychosexual stages—oral, anal, phallic, latency, and genital. Erikson's theory emphasizes eight psychosocial stages of development. The three main cognitive theories are Piaget's cognitive developmental theory, Vygotsky's sociocultural theory, and information-processing theory. Cognitive theories emphasize conscious thoughts. In Piaget's theory, children go through four cognitive stages: sensorimotor, preoperational, concrete operational, and formal operational. Vygotsky's sociocultural cognitive theory emphasizes how culture and social interaction guide cognitive development. The information-processing theory emphasizes that individuals manipulate information, monitor it, and strategize about it. Three versions of the behavioral and social cognitive theories are Pavlov's classical conditioning, Skinner's operant conditioning, and Bandura's social cognitive theory. Ethology stresses that behavior is strongly influenced by biology, is tied to evolution, and is characterized by critical or sensitive periods. Ecological theory is Bronfenbrenner's environmental systems view of development. It consists of five environmental systems: microsystem, mesosystem, exosystem, macrosystem, and chronosystem. An eclectic theoretical orientation does not follow any one theoretical approach but rather selects from each theory whatever is considered the best in it.

Research Methods for Collecting Data

- Research methods for collecting data about child development include observation (in a laboratory or a naturalistic setting), survey (questionnaire) or interview, standardized test, case study, and physiological measures.

Research Designs

- Descriptive research aims to observe and record behavior. In correlational research, the goal is to describe the strength of the relationship between two or more events or characteristics. Experimental research involves conducting an experiment that can determine cause and effect. An independent variable is the manipulated, influential, experimental factor. A dependent variable is a factor that can change in an experiment, in response to changes in the independent variable. Experiments can involve one or more experimental groups and control groups. In random assignment, researchers assign participants to experimental and control groups by chance. When researchers decide about the time span of their research, they can conduct cross-sectional or longitudinal studies.

Challenges in Child Development Research

- Researchers' ethical responsibilities include seeking participants' informed consent, ensuring their confidentiality, debriefing them about the purpose and potential personal consequences of participating, and avoiding unnecessary deception of participants. Researchers need to guard against gender, cultural, and ethnic bias in research. Every effort should be made to make research equitable for both females and males. Individuals from varied ethnic backgrounds need to be included as participants in child research, and overgeneralization about diverse members within a group must be avoided.

key terms

development 6
context 8
culture 8
cross-cultural studies 8
ethnicity 8
socioeconomic status (SES) 8
gender 8
social policy 10
biological processes 13
cognitive processes 13
socioemotional processes 13
prenatal period 14

infancy 14
early childhood 14
middle and late childhood 14
adolescence 14
cohort effects 14
Millennials 14
nature-nurture issue 16
continuity-discontinuity issue 16
early-later experience issue 16
scientific method 18
theory 18
hypothesis 18

psychoanalytic theories 19
Erikson's theory 19
Piaget's theory 22
Vygotsky's theory 23
information-processing
    theory 23
social cognitive theory 24
ethology 26
Bronfenbrenner's ecological
    theory 27
eclectic theoretical
    orientation 28

laboratory 29
naturalistic observation 30
standardized test 30
case study 31
descriptive research 32
correlational research 32
correlation coefficient 32
experiment 33
cross-sectional
    approach 33
longitudinal approach 34
ethnic gloss 38

key people

Ann Masten 10
Jerome Kagan 17
Sigmund Freud 10
Erik Erikson 19

Jean Piaget 22
Lev Vygotsky 23
Robert Siegler 24
Ivan Pavlov 24

John Watson 24
Rosalie Rayner 24
B. F. Skinner 24
Albert Bandura 25

Konrad Lorenz 26
Urie Bronfenbrenner 27

appendix

Careers in Child Development

Each of us wants to find a rewarding career and enjoy the work we do. The field of child development offers an amazing breadth of career options that can provide extremely satisfying work.

If you decide to pursue a career in child development, what career options are available to you? There are many. College and university professors teach courses in areas of child development, education, family development, nursing, and medicine. Teachers impart knowledge, understanding, and skills to children and adolescents. Counselors, clinical psychologists, nurses, and physicians help parents and children of all ages to cope more effectively with their lives and well-being. Various professionals work with families to improve the quality of family functioning.

Although an advanced degree is not absolutely necessary in some areas of child development, you usually can expand your opportunities (and income) considerably by obtaining a graduate degree. Many careers in child development pay reasonably well. For example, psychologists earn well above the median salary in the United States. Also, by working in the field of child development you can guide people in improving their lives, understand yourself and others better, possibly advance the state of knowledge in the field, and have an enjoyable time while you are doing these things.

If you are considering a career in child development, would you prefer to work with infants, children, adolescents, parents or a combination of these? As you go through this term, try to spend some time with children of different ages. Observe their behavior. Talk with them about their lives. Think about whether you would like to work with children of this age in your life's work.

Another important way to explore careers is to talk with people who work in various jobs. For example, if you have some interest in becoming a school counselor, call a school, ask to speak with a counselor, and set up an appointment to discuss the counselor's career and work.

Something else that should benefit you is to work in one or more jobs related to your career interests while you are in college. Many colleges and universities have internships or work experiences for students who major in fields such as child development. In some instances, these jobs earn course credit or pay; in others, they are strictly on a volunteer basis. Take advantage of these opportunities. They can provide you with valuable experiences to help you decide whether

this is the right career for you, and they can help you get into graduate school if you decide that you want to go.

In the upcoming sections, we will profile careers in four areas: education and research; clinical and counseling; medical, nursing, and physical development; and families and relationships. We have provided page numbers after some entries telling you where within the text you can find *Connecting with Careers,* the career profiles of people who hold some of these positions. These are not the only career options in child development, but they should provide you with an idea of the range of opportunities available and information about some of the main career avenues you might pursue. In profiling these careers, we will address the amount of education required, the type of training involved, and the nature of the work.

Education and Research

Numerous career opportunities in child development involve education or research. These positions range from college professor to child-care director to school psychologist.

College/University Professor

Courses in child development are taught in many programs and schools in colleges and universities, including psychology, education, nursing, child and family studies, social work, and medicine. The work that college professors do includes teaching courses at the undergraduate or graduate level (or both), conducting research in a specific area, advising students and/or directing their research, and serving on college or university committees. Some college instructors do not conduct research as part of their job but instead focus mainly on teaching. Research is most likely to be part of the job description at universities with master's and Ph.D. programs. A Ph.D. or master's degree almost always is required to teach in some area of child development in a college or university. Obtaining a doctoral degree usually takes four to six years of graduate work. A master's degree requires approximately two years of graduate work. The training involves taking graduate courses, learning to conduct research, and attending and presenting papers at professional meetings. Many graduate students work as teaching or research assistants for professors in an apprenticeship relationship that helps them to become competent teachers and researchers.

If you are interested in becoming a college or university professor, you might want to make an appointment with your instructor in this class on child development to learn more about his or her profession and work. **Read a profile of a professor on p. 495.**

Researcher

Some individuals in the field of child development work in research positions. In most instances, they have either a master's degree or Ph.D. in some area of child development. The researchers might work at a university, perhaps in a university professor's research program, in government at agencies such as the National Institute of Mental Health, or in private industry. Individuals who have full-time research positions in child development generate innovative research ideas, plan studies, carry out the research by collecting data, analyze the data, and then interpret it. Then they will usually attempt to publish the research in a scientific journal. A researcher often works in a collaborative manner with other researchers on a project and may present the research at scientific meetings. One researcher might spend much of his or her time in a laboratory while another researcher might work out in the field, such as in schools, hospitals, and so on.

Elementary School Teacher

The work of an elementary or secondary school teacher involves teaching in one or more subject areas, preparing the curriculum, giving tests, assigning grades, monitoring students' progress, conducting parent-teacher conferences, and attending in-service workshops. Becoming an elementary or secondary school teacher requires a minimum of an undergraduate degree. The training involves taking a wide range of courses with a major or concentration in education as well as completing a supervised practice-teaching internship. **Read a profile of an elementary school teacher on p. 188.**

Exceptional Children (Special Education) Teacher

A teacher of exceptional children spends concentrated time with individual children who have a disability or are gifted. Among the students a teacher of exceptional children might work with are children with learning disabilities, ADHD (attention deficit hyperactivity disorder), intellectual disability, or a physical disability such as cerebral palsy. Some of this work will usually be done outside of the student's regular classroom, and some of it will be carried out when the student is in the regular classroom. A teacher of exceptional children works closely with the student's regular classroom teacher and parents to create the best educational program for the student. Becoming a teacher of exceptional children requires a minimum of an undergraduate degree. The training consists of taking a wide range of courses in education and a concentration of courses in educating children with disabilities or children who are gifted. Teachers of exceptional children often continue their education after obtaining their undergraduate degree and attain a master's degree.

Early Childhood Educator

Early childhood educators work on college faculties and have a minimum of a master's degree in their field. In graduate school, they take courses in early childhood education and receive supervisory training in child-care or early childhood programs. Early childhood educators usually teach in community colleges that award an associate's degree in early childhood education.

Preschool/Kindergarten Teacher

Preschool teachers teach mainly 4-year-old children, and kindergarten teachers primarily teach 5-year-old children. They usually have an undergraduate degree in education, specializing in early childhood education. State certification to become a preschool or kindergarten teacher usually is required.

Family and Consumer Science Educator

Family and consumer science educators may specialize in early childhood education or instruct middle and high school students on topics such as nutrition, interpersonal relationships, human sexuality, parenting, and human development. Hundreds of colleges and universities throughout the United States offer two- and four-year degree programs in family and consumer science. These programs usually include an internship requirement. Additional education courses may be needed to obtain a teaching certificate. Some family and consumer educators go on to graduate school for further training, which provides a background for possible jobs in college teaching or research.

Educational Psychologist

An educational psychologist most often teaches in a college or university and conducts research in areas of educational psychology such as learning, motivation, classroom management, and assessment. Most educational psychologists have a doctorate in education, which takes four to six years of graduate work. They help to train students who will take various positions in education, including educational psychology, school psychology, and teaching.

School Psychologist

School psychologists focus on improving the psychological and intellectual well-being of elementary and secondary school students. They may work in a centralized office in a school district or in one or more schools. They give psychological tests, interview students and their parents, consult with teachers, and may provide counseling to students and their families.

School psychologists usually have a master's or doctoral degree in school psychology. In graduate school, they take courses in counseling, assessment, learning, and other areas of education and psychology.

Clinical and Counseling

A wide variety of clinical and counseling jobs are linked with child development. These range from child clinical psychologist to adolescent drug counselor.

Clinical Psychologist

Clinical psychologists seek to help people with psychological problems. They work in a variety of settings, including colleges and universities, clinics, medical schools, and private practice. Some clinical psychologists only conduct psychotherapy, others do psychological assessment and psychotherapy, and some also do research. Clinical psychologists may specialize in a particular age group, such as children (child clinical psychologist).

Clinical psychologists have either a Ph.D. (which involves clinical and research training) or a Psy.D. degree (which only involves clinical training). This graduate training usually takes five to seven years and includes courses in clinical psychology and a one-year supervised internship in an accredited setting toward the end of the training. In most cases, they must pass a test to become licensed in a state and to call themselves clinical psychologists. **Read a profile of a clinical child psychologist on p. 7.**

Psychiatrist

Like clinical psychologists, psychiatrists might specialize in working with children (child psychiatry) or adolescents (adolescent psychiatry). Psychiatrists might work in medical schools in teaching and research roles, in a medical clinic, or in private practice. In addition to administering drugs to help improve the lives of people with psychological problems, psychiatrists also may conduct psychotherapy. Psychiatrists obtain a medical degree and then do a residency in psychiatry. Medical school takes approximately four years, and the psychiatry residency another three to four years. Unlike psychologists (who do not go to medical school) in most states, psychiatrists can administer drugs to clients.

Counseling Psychologist

Counseling psychologists work in the same settings as clinical psychologists, and may do psychotherapy, teach, or conduct research. In many instances, however, counseling psychologists do not work with individuals who have a severe mental disorder. A counseling psychologist might specialize in working with children, adolescents, and/or families.

Counseling psychologists go through much of the same training as clinical psychologists, although they are enrolled in a graduate program in counseling rather than clinical psychology. Counseling psychologists have either a master's degree or a doctoral degree. They also must go through a licensing procedure. One type of master's degree in counseling leads to the designation of licensed professional counselor.

School Counselor

School counselors help to identify students' abilities and interests, guide students in developing academic plans, and explore career options with students. They may help students cope with adjustment problems. They may work with students individually, in small groups, or even in a classroom. They often consult with parents, teachers, and school administrators when trying to help students with their problems.

High school counselors advise students on choosing a major, satisfying admissions requirements for college, taking entrance exams, applying for financial aid, and pursuing appropriate vocational and technical training. Elementary school counselors are mainly involved in counseling students about social and personal problems. They may observe children in the classroom and at play as part of their work. School counselors usually have a master's degree in counseling.

Social Worker

Social workers often are involved in helping children and adults with social or economic problems. They may investigate, evaluate, and attempt to rectify reported cases of abuse, neglect, endangerment, or domestic disputes. They can intervene in families if necessary and provide counseling and referral services to children and families.

Social workers have a minimum of an undergraduate degree from a school of social work that includes coursework in various areas of sociology and psychology. Some social workers also have a master's or doctoral degree. They often work for publicly funded agencies at the city, state, or national level, although increasingly they work in the private sector in areas such as drug rehabilitation and family counseling.

In some cases, social workers specialize in a certain area, as is true of a medical social worker, who has a master's degree in social work (MSW). This involves graduate coursework and supervised clinical experiences in medical settings. A medical social worker might coordinate a variety of support services provided to people with severe or long-term disabilities. Family care social workers often work with families who need support services.

connecting with careers

Katherine Duchen Smith, Nurse and Child-Care Health Consultant

Katherine Duchen Smith has a master's degree in nursing and works as a child-care health consultant. She lives in Fort Collins, Colorado, and in 2004 was appointed public relations chair of the National Association of Pediatric Nurse Practitioners (NAPNAP), which has more than 6,000 members.

Smith provides health consultation and educational services to child-care centers, private schools, and hospitals. She also teaches in the Regis University Family Nurse Practitioner Program. Smith developed an interest in outreach and public-relations activities during her five-year term as a board member for the Fort Collins Poudre Valley Hospital System. Later, she became the organization's outreach consultant.

As child-care health consultants, nurses might provide telephone consultation and link children, families, or staff with primary care providers. In underserved areas, they might also be asked to administer immunizations, help chronically ill children access specialty care, or develop a comprehensive health promotion or injury prevention program for caregivers and families.

Katherine Duchen Smith (*left*), nurse and child-care health consultant, at a child-care center where she is a consultant.

Drug Counselor

Drug counselors provide counseling to children and adults with drug abuse problems. They may work on an individual basis with a substance abuser or conduct group therapy sessions. They may work in private practice, with a state or federal government agency, with a company, or in a hospital setting. Some drug counselors specialize in working with adolescents or families. Most states provide a certification procedure for obtaining a license to practice drug counseling.

At a minimum, drug counselors go through an associate's or certificate program. Many have an undergraduate degree in substance-abuse counseling, and some have master's and doctoral degrees.

Medical, Nursing, and Physical Development

This third main area of careers in child development includes a wide range of careers in the medical and nursing areas, as well as jobs that focus on improving some aspect of the child's physical development.

Obstetrician/Gynecologist

An obstetrician/gynecologist prescribes prenatal and postnatal care and performs deliveries in maternity cases. The individual also treats diseases and injuries of the female reproductive system. Obstetricians may work in private practice, in a medical clinic, in a hospital, or in a medical school. Becoming an obstetrician/ gynecologist requires a medical degree plus three to five years of residency in obstetrics/ gynecology.

Pediatrician

A pediatrician monitors infants' and children's health, works to prevent disease or injury, helps children attain optimal health, and treats children with health problems. Pediatricians may work in private practice, in a medical clinic, in a hospital, or in a medical school. As medical doctors, they can administer drugs to children and may counsel parents and children on ways to improve children's health. Many pediatricians on the faculties of medical schools also teach and conduct research on children's health and diseases. Pediatricians have attained a medical degree and completed a three- to five-year residency in pediatrics.

Neonatal Nurse

A neonatal nurse is involved in the delivery of care to newborn infants. The neonatal nurse may work to improve the health and well-being of infants born under normal circumstances or be involved in the delivery of care to premature and critically ill neonates.

A minimum of an undergraduate degree in nursing with a specialization in the newborn is required. This training involves coursework in nursing and the biological sciences, as well as supervisory clinical experiences.

Nurse-Midwife

A nurse-midwife formulates and provides comprehensive care to selected maternity patients, cares for the expectant mother as she prepares to give birth and guides her through the birth process, and cares for the postpartum patient. The nurse-midwife also may provide care to the newborn, counsel parents on the infant's development and parenting, and provide guidance about health practices. Becoming a nurse-midwife generally requires an undergraduate degree from a school of nursing. A nurse-midwife most often works in a hospital setting. **Read the profile of a perinatal nurse on p. 90.**

Pediatric Nurse

Pediatric nurses have a degree in nursing that takes from two to five years to complete. Some also may obtain a master's or doctoral degree in pediatric nursing. Pediatric nurses take courses in biological sciences, nursing care, and pediatrics, usually in a school of nursing. They also undergo supervised clinical experiences in medical settings. They monitor infants' and children's health, work to prevent disease or injury, and help children attain optimal health. They may work in hospitals, schools of nursing, or with pediatricians in private practice or at a medical clinic. **Read a profile of a pediatric nurse on p. 44.**

Audiologist

An audiologist has a minimum of an undergraduate degree in hearing science. This includes courses and supervisory training. Audiologists assess and identify the presence and severity of hearing loss as well as problems in balance. Some audiologists also go on to obtain a master's and/or doctoral degree. They may work in a medical clinic, with a physician in private practice, in a hospital, or in a medical school.

Speech Therapist

Speech therapists are health-care professionals who are trained to identify, assess, and treat speech and language problems. They may work with physicians, psychologists, social workers, and other health-care professionals as a team to help individuals with physical or psychological problems that include speech and language problems. Speech pathologists have a minimum of an undergraduate degree in speech and hearing science or communication disorders. They may work in private practice, in hospitals and medical schools, or in government agencies with individuals of any age. Some specialize in working with children or with a particular type of speech disorder. **Read a profile of a speech pathologist on p. 260.**

Genetic Counselor

Genetic counselors work as members of a health care team, providing information and support to families who have members with birth defects or genetic disorders and to families who may be at risk for a variety of inherited conditions. They identify families at risk and provide supportive counseling. They serve as educators and resource people for other health care professionals and the public. Almost half work in university medical centers and another one-fourth work in private hospital settings.

Most genetic counselors enter the field after majoring in undergraduate school in such disciplines as biology, genetics, psychology, nursing, public health, and social work. They have specialized graduate degrees and experience in medical genetics and counseling. **Read a profile of a genetic counselor on p. 60.**

Families and Relationships

A number of careers involve working with families and relationship problems. These range from being a child welfare worker to a marriage and family therapist.

Child Welfare Worker

A child welfare worker is employed by the child protective services unit of each state. The child welfare worker protects the child's rights, evaluates any maltreatment the child might experience, and may have the child removed from the home if necessary. A child social worker has a minimum of an undergraduate degree in social work.

Child Life Specialist

Child life specialists work with children and their families when the child needs to be hospitalized. They monitor the child patient's activities, seek to reduce the child's stress, help the child cope effectively, and assist the child in enjoying the hospital experience as much as possible. Child life specialists may provide parent education and develop individualized treatment plans based on an assessment of the child's development, temperament, medical plan, and available social supports.

Child life specialists have an undergraduate degree. As undergraduates, they take courses in child development and education and usually take additional courses in a child life program.

Marriage and Family Therapist

The work of marriage and family therapists is based on the principle that many individuals who have psychological problems benefit when psychotherapy is provided in the context of a marital or family relationship. Marriage and family therapists may provide marital therapy, couples therapy to individuals in a relationship who are not married, and family therapy to two or more members of a family.

Marriage and family therapists have a master's or doctoral degree. They go through a training program in graduate school similar to that of a clinical psychologist but with a focus on marital and family relationships. To practice marital and family therapy in most states, it is necessary to go through a licensing procedure.

These are only a handful of careers that require knowledge of developmental psychology. *Connecting with Careers* throughout this text highlight additional careers, including toy designer (p. 214), infant assessment specialist (p. 241), supervisor of gifted and talented education (p. 246), English Language Learner (ELL) teacher (p. 267), child-care director (p. 307), health psychologist (p. 380), and director of children's services (p. 456). *What other careers can you think of that require knowledge of children's development?*

What endless questions vex the thought, of whence and whither, when and how.

—**SIR RICHARD BURTON**
British Explorer, 19th Century

Biological Processes, Physical Development, and Perceptual Development

The rhythm and meaning of life involve beginnings, with questions raised about how, from so simple a beginning, complex forms develop, grow, and mature. What was this organism, what is this organism, and what will this organism be? In Section 2, you will read four chapters: "Biological Beginnings" (Chapter 2), "Prenatal Development and Birth" (Chapter 3), "Physical Development and Health" (Chapter 4), and "Motor, Sensory, and Perceptual Development" (Chapter 5).

chapter 2

BIOLOGICAL BEGINNINGS

chapter **outline**

1 The Evolutionary Perspective

Learning Goal 1 Discuss the evolutionary perspective on child development.

Natural Selection and Adaptive Behavior
Evolutionary Psychology

2 Genetic Foundations of Development

Learning Goal 2 Describe what genes are and how they influence children's development.

The Collaborative Gene
Genes and Chromosomes
Genetic Principles
Chromosomal and Gene-Linked Abnormalities

3 Reproductive Challenges and Choices

Learning Goal 3 Identify some important reproductive challenges and choices.

Prenatal Diagnostic Tests
Infertility and Reproductive Technology
Adoption

4 Heredity and Environment Interaction: The Nature-Nurture Debate

Learning Goal 4 Explain some of the ways that heredity and environment interact to produce individual differences in development.

Behavior Genetics
Heredity-Environment Correlations
Shared and Nonshared Environmental Experiences
The Epigenetic View and Gene × Environment (G × E) Interaction
Conclusions About Heredity-Environment Interaction

Jim Springer and Jim Lewis are identical twins. They were separated at 4 weeks of age and did not see each other again until they were 39 years old. Both worked as part-time deputy sheriffs, vacationed in Florida, drove Chevrolets, had dogs named Toy, and married and divorced women named Betty. One twin named his son James Allan, and the other named his son James Alan. Both liked math but not spelling, enjoyed carpentry and mechanical drawing, chewed their fingernails down to the nubs, had almost identical drinking and smoking habits, had hemorrhoids, put on 10 pounds at about the same point in development, first suffered headaches at the age of 18, and had similar sleep patterns.

Jim and Jim do have some differences. One wears his hair over his forehead; the other slicks it back and has sideburns. One expresses himself best orally; the other is more proficient in writing. But, for the most part, their profiles are remarkably similar.

Jim Springer (*left*) and Jim Lewis (*right*).

Another pair of identical twins, Daphne and Barbara, are called the "giggle sisters" because, after being reunited, they were always making each other laugh. A thorough search of their adoptive families' histories revealed no gigglers. The giggle sisters ignored stress, avoided conflict and controversy whenever possible, and showed no interest in politics.

Jim and Jim and the giggle sisters were part of the Minnesota Study of Twins Reared Apart, directed by Thomas Bouchard and his colleagues. The study brings identical twins (identical genetically because they come from the same fertilized egg) and fraternal twins (who come from different fertilized eggs) from all over the world to Minneapolis to investigate their lives. There the twins complete personality and intelligence tests, and they provide detailed medical histories, including information about diet and smoking, exercise habits, chest X-rays, heart stress tests, and EEGs. The twins are asked more than 15,000 questions about their family and childhood, personal interests, vocational orientation, values, and aesthetic judgments (Bouchard & others, 1990).

When genetically identical twins who were separated as infants show such striking similarities in their tastes and habits and choices, can we conclude that their genes must have caused the development of those tastes and habits and choices? Other possible causes need to be considered. The twins shared not only the same genes but also some experiences. Some of the separated twins lived together for several months prior to their adoption; some of the twins had been reunited prior to testing (in some cases, many years earlier); adoption agencies often place twins in similar homes; and even strangers who spend several hours together and start comparing their lives are likely to come up with some coincidental similarities (Joseph, 2006). The Minnesota study of identical twins points to both the importance of the genetic basis of human development and the need for further research on genetic and environmental factors (Lykken, 2001).

preview

The examples of Jim and Jim and the giggle sisters stimulate us to think about our genetic heritage and the biological foundations of our existence. However, organisms are not like billiard balls, moved by simple external forces to predictable positions on life's table. Environmental experiences and biological foundations work together to make us who we are. Our coverage of life's biological beginnings focuses on evolution, genetic foundations, challenges and choices regarding reproduction, and the interaction of heredity and environment.

The Evolutionary Perspective [LG1] Discuss the evolutionary perspective on child development.

- Natural Selection and Adaptive Behavior
- Evolutionary Psychology

In evolutionary time, humans are relative newcomers to Earth. As our earliest ancestors left the forest to feed on the savannahs and then to form hunting societies on the open plains, their minds and behaviors changed, and they eventually established humans as the dominant species on Earth. How did this evolution come about?

NATURAL SELECTION AND ADAPTIVE BEHAVIOR

Natural selection is the evolutionary process by which those individuals of a species that are best adapted are the ones that survive and reproduce. To understand what this means, let's return to the middle of the nineteenth century, when the British naturalist Charles Darwin was traveling around the world, observing many different species of animals in their natural surroundings. Darwin, who published his observations and thoughts in *On the Origin of Species* (1859), noted that most organisms reproduce at rates that would cause enormous increases in the population of most species and yet populations remain nearly constant. He reasoned that an intense, constant struggle for food, water, and resources must occur among the many young born each generation, because many of the young do not survive. Those that do survive and reproduce pass on their characteristics to the next generation. Darwin argued that these survivors are better *adapted* to their world than are the nonsurvivors (Simon, Dickey, & Reese, 2013). The best-adapted individuals survive to leave the most offspring. Over the course of many generations, organisms with the characteristics needed for survival make up an increasing percentage of the population. Over many, many generations, this could produce a gradual modification of the whole population (Brooker & others, 2014). If environmental conditions change, however, other characteristics might become favored by natural selection, moving the species in a different direction (Mader & Windelspecht, 2013).

All organisms must adapt to particular places, climates, food sources, and ways of life (Hoefnagels, 2013). An eagle's claws are a physical adaptation that facilitates predation. *Adaptive behavior* is behavior that promotes an organism's survival in the natural habitat. For example, attachment between a caregiver and a baby ensures the infant's closeness to a caregiver for feeding and protection from danger, thus increasing the infant's chances of survival.

EVOLUTIONARY PSYCHOLOGY

Although Darwin introduced the theory of evolution by natural selection in 1859, his ideas only recently have become a popular framework for explaining behavior. Psychology's newest approach, **evolutionary psychology,** emphasizes the importance of adaptation, reproduction, and "survival of the fittest" in shaping behavior. "Fit" in this sense refers to the ability to bear offspring that survive long enough to bear offspring of their own. In this view, natural selection favors behaviors that increase reproductive success—the ability to pass genes to the next generation (Cosmides, 2013; Durrant & Ellis, 2013).

There are one hundred and ninety-three living species of monkeys and apes. One hundred and ninety-two of them are covered with hair. The exception is the naked ape, self-named Homo sapiens.

—DESMOND MORRIS
British Zoologist, 20th Century

evolutionary psychology Branch of psychology that emphasizes the importance of adaptation, reproduction, and "survival of the fittest" in shaping behavior.

David Buss (1995, 2004, 2008, 2012) has been especially influential in stimulating new interest in how evolution can explain human behavior. He reasons that just as evolution has contributed to our physical features such as body shape and height, it also pervasively influences how we make decisions, how aggressive we are, our fears, and our mating patterns. For example, assume that our ancestors were hunters and gatherers on the plains and that men did most of the hunting and women stayed close to home gathering seeds and plants for food. If you have to travel some distance from your home to find and slay a fleeing animal, you need certain physical traits along with the capacity for certain types of spatial thinking. Men born with these traits would be more likely than men without them to survive, to bring home lots of food, and to be considered attractive mates—and thus to reproduce and pass on these characteristics to their children. In other words, if these assumptions were correct, potentially these traits would provide a reproductive advantage for males. Over many generations, men with good spatial thinking skills might become more numerous in the population. Critics point out that this scenario might or might not have actually happened.

Evolutionary Developmental Psychology Recently, interest has grown in using the concepts of evolutionary psychology to understand human development (Belsky, 2013; Bjorklund, 2007, 2012, 2013; Narvaez & others, 2013). Here we discuss some ideas proposed by evolutionary developmental psychologists (Bjorklund & Pellegrini, 2002).

An extended childhood period might have evolved because humans require time to develop a large brain and learn the complexity of human societies. Humans take longer to become reproductively mature than any other mammal (see Figure 2.1). During this extended childhood period, they develop a large brain and have the experiences needed to become competent adults in a complex society.

How does the attachment of this Vietnamese baby to its mother reflect the evolutionary process of adaptive behavior?

Many of our evolved psychological mechanisms are domain-specific— that is, the mechanisms apply only to a specific aspect of a person's psychological makeup. According to evolutionary psychology, the mind is not a general-purpose device that can be applied equally to a vast array of problems. Instead, as our ancestors dealt with certain recurring problems such as hunting and finding shelter, specialized modules evolved that process information related to those problems. For example, such specialized modules might include a module for physical knowledge for tracking animals, a module for mathematical knowledge for trading, and a module for language.

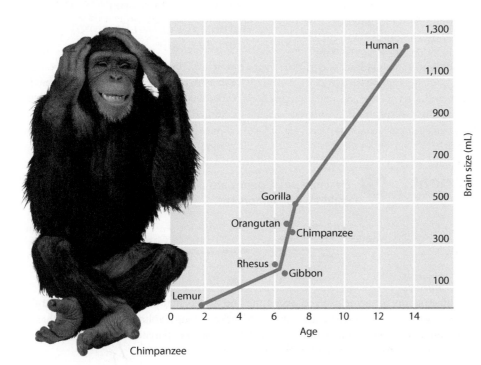

FIGURE **2.1**

THE BRAIN SIZES OF VARIOUS PRIMATES AND HUMANS IN RELATION TO THE LENGTH OF THE CHILDHOOD PERIOD. Compared with other primates, humans have both a larger brain and a longer childhood period. *What conclusions can you draw from the relationship indicated by this graph?*

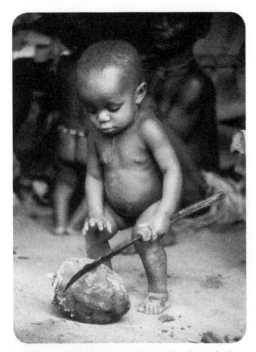

Children in all cultures are interested in the tools that adults in their cultures use. For example, this 11-month-old boy from the Efe culture in the Democratic Republic of the Congo in Africa is trying to cut a papaya with an apopau (a smaller version of a machete). *Might the infant's behavior be evolutionary-based or be due to both biological and environmental conditions?*

Evolved mechanisms are not always adaptive in contemporary society. Some behaviors that were adaptive for our prehistoric ancestors may not serve us well today. For example, the food-scarce environment of our ancestors likely led to humans' propensity to gorge when food is available and to crave high-caloric foods, a trait that might lead to an epidemic of obesity when food is plentiful.

Evaluating Evolutionary Psychology   Although the popular press gives a lot of attention to the ideas of evolutionary psychology, it remains just one theoretical approach among many. Like the theories described in Chapter 1, it has limitations, weaknesses, and critics (Hyde & Else-Quest, 2013; Matlin, 2012). Albert Bandura (1998), whose social cognitive theory was described in Chapter 1, acknowledges the important influence of evolution on human adaptation. However, he rejects what he calls "one-sided evolutionism," which sees social behavior as strictly the product of evolved biology. An alternative is a bidirectional view, in which environmental and biological conditions influence each other. In this view, evolutionary pressures created changes in biological structures that allowed the use of tools, which enabled our ancestors to manipulate the environment, constructing new environmental conditions. In turn, environmental innovations produced new selection pressures that led to the evolution of specialized biological systems for consciousness, thought, and language.

In other words, evolution gave us biological potentialities, but it does not dictate behavior. People have used their biological capacities to produce diverse cultures—aggressive and peace-loving, egalitarian and autocratic. As American scientist Stephen Jay Gould (1981) concluded, in most domains of human functioning, biology allows a broad range of cultural possibilities.

The "big picture" idea of natural selection leading to the development of human traits and behaviors is difficult to refute or test because evolution is on a time scale that does not lend itself to empirical study. Thus, studying specific genes in humans and other species—and their links to traits and behaviors—may be the best approach for testing ideas coming out of the evolutionary psychology perspective.

Review Connect Reflect

 LG1 Discuss the evolutionary perspective on child development.

Review

- How can natural selection and adaptive behavior be defined?
- What is evolutionary psychology? What are some basic ideas about human development proposed by evolutionary psychologists? How might evolutionary influences have different effects at different points in the life span? How can evolutionary psychology be evaluated?

Connect

- In Chapter 1, you learned about how different developmental processes interact. How was that principle reinforced by the information in this section?

Reflect *Your Own Personal Journey of Life*

- Which do you think is more persuasive in explaining your development: the views of evolutionary psychologists or those of their critics? Why?

Genetic Foundations of Development

 LG2 Describe what genes are and how they influence children's development.

The Collaborative Gene	Genes and Chromosomes	Genetic Principles	Chromosomal and Gene-Linked Abnormalities

Genetic influences on behavior evolved over time and across many species. The many traits and characteristics that are genetically influenced have a long evolutionary history that is retained in our DNA. Our DNA is not just inherited from our parents; it includes what we inherited as a species from other species that were our ancestors.

How are characteristics that suit a species for survival transmitted from one generation to the next? Darwin did not know the answer to this question because genes and the principles of genetics had not yet been discovered. Each of us carries a human "genetic code" that we inherited from our parents. Because a fertilized egg carries this human code, a fertilized human egg cannot grow into an egret, eagle, or elephant.

THE COLLABORATIVE GENE

Each of us began life as a single cell weighing about one twenty-millionth of an ounce! This tiny piece of matter housed our entire genetic code—information that helps us grow from that single cell to a person made of trillions of cells, each containing a replica of the original code. That code is carried by our genes. What are genes and what do they do? For the answer, we need to look into our cells.

The nucleus of each human cell contains **chromosomes,** which are threadlike structures made up of deoxyribonucleic acid, or DNA. **DNA** is a complex molecule that has a double helix shape (like a spiral staircase) and contains genetic information. **Genes,** the units of hereditary information, are short segments of DNA, as you can see in Figure 2.2. They help cells to reproduce themselves and to assemble proteins. Proteins, in turn, are the building blocks of cells as well as the regulators that direct the body's processes (Belk & Maier, 2013; Tortora, Funke, & Case, 2013).

Each gene has its own location, its own designated place on a particular chromosome. Today, there is a great deal of enthusiasm about efforts to discover the specific locations of genes that are linked to certain functions and developmental outcomes (Plomin, 2012; Raven & others, 2014). An important step in this direction is the Human Genome Project's efforts to map the human genome—the complete set of developmental information for creating proteins that initiate the making of a human organism (Hughes & Rozen, 2012).

Among the major approaches to gene identification and discovery that are being used today are the genome-wide association method, linkage analysis, next-generation sequencing, and the 1,000 Genomes Project:

- Completion of the Human Genome Project has led to use of the *genome-wide association method* to identify genetic variations linked to a particular disorder, such as autism spectrum disorders, cancer, and cardiovascular disease (National Human Genome Research Institute, 2012). To conduct a genome-wide association study, researchers obtain DNA from individuals who have the disorder and from others who don't have it. Then each participant's complete set of DNA, or genome, is purified from the blood or cells and scanned on machines to determine markers of genetic variation. If the genetic variations occur more frequently in people who have the disorder, the variations point to the region in the human genome where the disorder-causing problem exists. Genome-wide association studies have recently been conducted for child obesity (Early Growth Genetics Consortium & others, 2012), cardiovascular disease (Yu & others, 2013), and depression (Hek & others, 2013).

- *Linkage analysis,* in which the goal is to discover the location of a gene(s) in relation to a marker gene (whose position is already known), is often used in the search for a disease gene(s) (Lyon & Wang, 2013). Genes transmitted to offspring tend to be in close proximity to each other so that the gene(s) involved in the disease are usually located near the marker gene. Gene linkage studies are now being conducted on a wide variety of disorders and health, including attention deficit hyperactivity disorder (Caylak, 2012), autism spectrum disorders (O'Roak & others, 2012), and depression (Cohen-Woods, Craig, & McGuffin, 2012).

- *Next-generation sequencing* is a term that is now used to describe the vast increase in genetic data generated at a much reduced cost and in a much shorter period of time. Next-generation sequencing has considerably increased knowledge about genetic influences on development in recent years (Hastie & others, 2013; Jia & others, 2013).

- The human genome varies between individuals in small but very important ways. To understand these variations will require examination of the whole genomes of many individuals. A current project that began in 2008, the 1,000 Genomes Project, is the most detailed study of human genetic variation to date, with the goal of determining the genomic sequences of at least 1,000 individuals from different ethnic groups

FIGURE **2.2**

CELLS, CHROMOSOMES, DNA, AND GENES.
(*Top*) The body contains trillions of cells. Each cell contains a central structure, the nucleus. (*Middle*) Chromosomes are threadlike structures located in the nucleus of the cell. Chromosomes are composed of DNA. (*Bottom*) DNA has the structure of a spiral staircase. A gene is a segment of DNA.

chromosomes Threadlike structures that come in 23 pairs, with one member of each pair coming from each parent. Chromosomes contain the genetic substance DNA.

DNA A complex molecule that contains genetic information.

genes Units of hereditary information composed of DNA. Genes help cells to reproduce themselves and manufacture the proteins that maintain life.

(*Left*) A positive result from the Human Genome Project. Shortly after Andrew Gobea was born , his cells were genetically altered to prevent his immune system from failing. (*Right*) A healthy Andrew Gobea later in Infancy.

around the world (Shibata & others, 2012). Compiling complete descriptions of the genetic variations of many people will make it possible for researchers to conduct studies of genetic variations in disease in a more detailed manner.

One of the big surprises of the Human Genome Project was an early report indicating that humans have only about 30,000 genes (U.S. Department of Energy, 2001). More recently, the number of human genes was revised further downward to approximately 20,500 (Science Daily, 2008). Scientists had thought that humans had as many as 100,000 or more genes. They had also maintained that each gene programmed just one protein. In fact, humans have far more proteins than they have genes, so there cannot be a one-to-one correspondence between genes and proteins (Commoner, 2002). Each gene is not translated, in automaton-like fashion, into one and only one protein. A gene does not act independently, as developmental psychologist David Moore (2001) emphasized by titling his book *The Dependent Gene*.

Rather than being a group of independent genes, the human genome consists of many genes that collaborate both with each other and with nongenetic factors inside and outside the body. The collaboration operates at many points (Moore, 2013). For example, the cellular machinery mixes, matches, and links small pieces of DNA to reproduce the genes—and that machinery is influenced by what is going on around it (Moore, 2013).

Whether a gene is turned "on," working to assemble proteins, is also a matter of collaboration. The activity of genes (genetic expression) is affected by their environment (Gottlieb, 2007). For example, hormones that circulate in the blood make their way into the cell where they can turn genes "on" and "off." And the flow of hormones can be affected by environmental conditions such as light, day length, nutrition, and behavior. Numerous studies have shown that external events outside of the original cell and the person, as well as events inside the cell, can excite or inhibit gene expression (Gottlieb, Wahlsten, & Lickliter, 2006; Moore, 2013). Recent research has documented that factors such as stress, radiation, and temperature can influence gene expression (Georgakilas, 2011). For example, one study revealed that an increase in the concentration of stress hormones such as cortisol produced a fivefold increase in DNA damage (Flint & others, 2007). A recent study also found that exposure to radiation changed the rate of DNA synthesis in cells (Lee & others, 2011).

In short, a single gene is rarely the source of a protein's genetic information, much less of an inherited trait (Gottlieb, 2007; Moore, 2013).

GENES AND CHROMOSOMES

Genes are not only collaborative, they are enduring. How do the genes manage to get passed from generation to generation and end up in all of the trillion cells in the body? Three processes explain the heart of the story: mitosis, meiosis, and fertilization.

mitosis Cellular reproduction in which the cell's nucleus duplicates itself with two new cells being formed, each containing the same DNA as the parent cell, arranged in the same 23 pairs of chromosomes.

meiosis A specialized form of cell division that forms eggs and sperm (also known as gametes).

fertilization A stage in reproduction during which an egg and a sperm fuse to create a single cell, called a zygote.

zygote A single cell formed through fertilization.

Calvin and Hobbes   by Bill Watterson

FIGURE 2.3

A SINGLE SPERM PENETRATING AN EGG AT THE POINT OF FERTILIZATION

Mitosis, Meiosis, and Fertilization   Every cell in your body, except the sperm and egg, has 46 chromosomes arranged in 23 pairs. These cells reproduce through a process called **mitosis.** During mitosis, the cell's nucleus—including the chromosomes—duplicates itself and the cell divides. Two new cells are formed, each containing the same DNA as the original cell, arranged in the same 23 pairs of chromosomes.

However, a different type of cell division—**meiosis**—forms eggs and sperm (which also are called *gametes*). During meiosis, a cell of the testes (in men) or ovaries (in women) duplicates its chromosomes but then divides twice, thus forming four cells, each of which has only half of the genetic material of the parent cell (Johnson, 2012). By the end of meiosis, each egg or sperm has 23 unpaired chromosomes.

During **fertilization,** an egg and a sperm fuse to create a single cell, called a **zygote** (see Figure 2.3). In the zygote, the 23 unpaired chromosomes from the egg and the 23 unpaired chromosomes from the sperm combine to form one set of 23 paired chromosomes—one chromosome of each pair from the mother's egg and the other from the father's sperm. In this manner, each parent contributes half of the offspring's genetic material.

Figure 2.4 shows 23 paired chromosomes of a male and a female. The members of each pair of chromosomes are both similar and different: Each chromosome in the pair contains varying forms of the same genes, at the same location on the chromosome. A gene that influences hair color, for example, is located on both members of one pair of chromosomes, in the same location on each. However, one of those chromosomes might carry a gene associated with blond hair; the other chromosome in the pair might carry a gene associated with brown hair.

Do you notice any obvious differences between the chromosomes of the male and the chromosomes of the female in Figure 2.4? The difference lies in the 23rd pair. Ordinarily, in females this pair consists of two chromosomes called X chromosomes; in males the 23rd pair consists of an X and a Y chromosome. The presence of a Y chromosome is one factor that makes a person male rather than female.

Sources of Variability   Combining the genes of two parents in their offspring increases genetic variability in the population, which is valuable for a species because it provides more characteristics for natural selection to operate on (Starr & others, 2013). In fact, the human genetic process creates several important sources of variability.

First, the chromosomes in the zygote are not exact copies of those in the mother's ovaries and the father's testes. During the formation of the sperm and egg in meiosis, the members of each pair of chromosomes are separated, but which chromosome in the pair goes to the gamete is a matter of chance. In addition, before the pairs separate, pieces of the two chromosomes in each pair are exchanged, creating a new combination of genes on each chromosome (Mader, 2014). Thus, when chromosomes from the mother's egg and the father's sperm are brought together in the zygote, the result is a truly unique combination of genes.

If each zygote is unique, how do identical twins like those discussed in the opening of the chapter exist? *Identical twins* (also called monozygotic twins) develop from a single zygote that splits into two genetically identical replicas, each of which becomes a person. *Fraternal twins* (called dizygotic twins) develop when two eggs are each fertilized by a different sperm, creating two zygotes that are genetically no more similar than ordinary siblings.

(a)

(b)

FIGURE 2.4

THE GENETIC DIFFERENCE BETWEEN MALES AND FEMALES. Set (*a*) shows the chromosome structure of a male, and set (*b*) shows the chromosome structure of a female. The last pair of 23 pairs of chromosomes is in the bottom right box of each set. Notice that the Y chromosome of the male is smaller than the X chromosome of the female. To obtain this kind of chromosomal picture, a cell is removed from a person's body, usually from the inside of the mouth. The chromosomes are stained by chemical treatment, magnified extensively, and then photographed.

Another source of variability comes from DNA (Starr & others, 2013). Chance events, a mistake by cellular machinery, or damage from an environmental agent such as radiation may produce a *mutated gene,* which is a permanently altered segment of DNA.

Even when their genes are identical, however, people vary. The difference between genotypes and phenotypes helps us to understand this source of variability. All of a person's genetic material makes up his or her **genotype.** However, not all of the genetic material is apparent in our observed and measurable characteristics. A **phenotype** consists of observable characteristics. Phenotypes include physical characteristics (such as height, weight, and hair color) and psychological characteristics (such as personality and intelligence).

For each genotype, a range of phenotypes can be expressed, providing another source of variability (Rende, 2013). An individual can inherit the genetic potential to grow very large, for example, but good nutrition, among other things, will be essential for achieving that potential.

GENETIC PRINCIPLES

What determines how a genotype is expressed to create a particular phenotype? Much is unknown about the answer to this question (Moore, 2013). However, a number of genetic principles have been discovered, among them those of dominant-recessive genes, sex-linked genes, genetic imprinting, and polygenically determined characteristics.

Dominant-Recessive Genes Principle   In some cases, one gene of a pair always exerts its effects; it is *dominant,* overriding the potential influence of the other gene, called the recessive gene. This is the *dominant-recessive genes principle.* A recessive gene exerts its influence only if the two genes of a pair are both recessive. If you inherit a recessive gene for a trait from each of your parents, you will show the trait. If you inherit a recessive gene from only one parent, you may never know you carry the gene. Brown hair, farsightedness, and dimples rule over blond hair, nearsightedness, and freckles in the world of dominant-recessive genes.

Can two brown-haired parents have a blond-haired child? Yes, they can. Suppose that each parent has a dominant gene for brown hair and a recessive gene for blond hair. Since dominant genes override recessive genes, the parents have brown hair, but both are carriers of blondness and pass on their recessive genes for blond hair. With no dominant gene to override them, the recessive genes can make the child's hair blond.

Sex-Linked Genes   Most mutated genes are recessive. When a mutated gene is carried on the X chromosome, the result is called *X-linked inheritance.* The implications for males may be very different from those for females (McClelland, Bowles, & Koopman, 2012). Remember that males have only one X chromosome. Thus, if there is an absent or altered, disease-relevant gene on the X chromosome, males have no "backup" copy to counter the harmful gene and therefore may develop an X-linked disease. However, females have a second X chromosome, which is likely to be unchanged. As a result, they are not likely to have the X-linked disease. Thus, most individuals who have X-linked diseases are males. Females who have one abnormal copy of the gene on the X chromosome are known as "carriers," and they usually do not show any signs of the X-linked disease. Hemophilia and fragile X syndrome, which we discuss later in the chapter, are examples of X-linked inherited diseases (Bartel, Weinstein, & Schaffer, 2012).

Genetic Imprinting   *Genetic imprinting* occurs when genes have differing effects depending on whether they are inherited from the mother or the father (Lambertini & others, 2012). A chemical process "silences" one member of the gene pair. For example, as a result of imprinting, only the maternally derived copy of a gene might be active, while the paternally derived copy of the same gene is silenced—or vice versa. Only a small percentage of human genes appears to undergo imprinting, but it is a normal and important aspect of development. When imprinting goes awry, development is disturbed, as in the case of Beckwith-Wiedemann syndrome, a growth disorder, and Wilms tumor, a type of cancer (Royer-Pokora, 2012).

Polygenic Inheritance   Genetic transmission is usually more complex than the simple examples we have examined thus far (Lewis, 2012). Few characteristics reflect the influence of

genotype A person's genetic heritage; the actual genetic material present in each cell.

phenotype The way an individual's genotype is expressed in observed and measurable characteristics.

Name	Description	Treatment	Incidence
Down syndrome	An extra chromosome causes mild to severe intellectual disability and physical abnormalities.	Surgery, early intervention, infant stimulation, and special learning programs	1 in 1,900 births at age 20 1 in 300 births at age 35 1 in 30 births at age 45
Klinefelter syndrome (XXY)	An extra X chromosome causes physical abnormalities.	Hormone therapy can be effective	1 in 600 male births
Fragile X syndrome	An abnormality in the X chromosome can cause intellectual disability, learning disabilities, or short attention span.	Special education, speech and language therapy	More common in males than in females
Turner syndrome (XO)	A missing X chromosome in females can cause intellectual disability and sexual underdevelopment.	Hormone therapy in childhood and puberty	1 in 2,500 female births
XYY syndrome	An extra Y chromosome can cause above-average height.	No special treatment required	1 in 1,000 male births

FIGURE 2.5

SOME CHROMOSOMAL ABNORMALITIES. The treatments for these abnormalities do not necessarily erase the problem but may improve the individual's adaptive behavior and quality of life.

only a single gene or pair of genes. Most are determined by the interaction of many different genes; they are said to be *polygenically determined*. Even simple characteristics such as height, for example, reflect the interaction of many genes, as well as the influence of the environment.

The term *gene-gene interaction* is increasingly used to describe studies that focus on the interdependence of two or more genes in influencing characteristics, behavior, diseases, and development (Baye & others, 2011). For example, recent studies have documented gene-gene interaction in children's immune system functioning (Reijmerink & others, 2011), asthma (Su & others, 2012), cancer (Bushel & others, 2010), and cardiovascular disease (Xiao & others, 2012).

developmental **connection**

Conditions, Diseases, and Disorders

Intellectual disability can be classified in several ways. Chapter 8, p. 243

CHROMOSOMAL AND GENE-LINKED ABNORMALITIES

Abnormalities characterize the genetic process in some indviduals. Some of these abnormalities involve whole chromosomes that do not separate properly during meiosis. Other abnormalities are produced by harmful genes.

Chromosomal Abnormalities Sometimes a gamete is formed in which the male's sperm and/or the female's ovum do not have their normal set of 23 chromosomes. The most notable examples involve Down syndrome and abnormalities of the sex chromosomes (see Figure 2.5).

Down Syndrome An individual with **Down syndrome** has a round face, a flattened skull, an extra fold of skin over the eyelids, a protruding tongue, short limbs, and disabilities involving motor and intellectual development. The syndrome is caused by the presence of an extra copy of chromosome 21. It is not known why the extra chromosome is present, but the health of the male sperm or female ovum may be involved.

Down syndrome appears approximately once in every 700 live births. Women between the ages of 16 and 34 are less likely to give birth to a child with Down syndrome than are younger or older women. African American children are rarely born with Down syndrome.

Sex-Linked Chromosomal Abnormalities Recall that a newborn normally has either an X and a Y chromosome, or two X chromosomes. Human embryos must possess at least one X chromosome to be viable. The most common sex-linked chromosomal abnormalities involve

These athletes, several of whom have Down syndrome, are participating in a Special Olympics competition. Notice the distinctive facial features of the individuals with Down syndrome, such as a round face and a flattened skull. *What causes Down syndrome?*

Down syndrome A chromosomally transmitted form of intellectual disability, caused by the presence of an extra copy of chromosome 21.

A boy with fragile X syndrome.

the presence of an extra chromosome (either an X or Y) or the absence of one X chromosome in females.

Klinefelter syndrome is a chromosomal disorder in which males have an extra X chromosome, making them XXY instead of XY (Aksglaede & others, 2013). Males with this disorder have undeveloped testes, and they usually have enlarged breasts and become tall. A recent study revealed significant impairment in language, academic, attentional, and motor abilities in boys with the syndrome (Ross & others, 2012). Klinefelter syndrome occurs approximately once in every 800 live male births.

Fragile X syndrome is a genetic disorder that results from an abnormality in the X chromosome, which becomes constricted and often breaks. The physical appearance of children with fragile X syndrome often appears normal, although these children typically have prominent ears, a long face, a high-arched palate, and soft skin. Mental deficiency often is an outcome, but it may take the form of intellectual disability, a learning disability, or a short attention span. One study revealed that boys with fragile X syndrome were characterized by cognitive deficits in inhibition, memory, and planning (Hooper & others, 2008). This disorder occurs more frequently in males than in females, possibly because the second X chromosome in females negates the effects of the abnormal X chromosome (Fung & others, 2012).

Turner syndrome is a chromosomal disorder in females in which either an X chromosome is missing, making the person XO instead of XX, or part of one X chromosome is deleted. Females with Turner syndrome are short in stature and have a webbed neck (Kaur & Phadke, 2012). They might be infertile and have difficulty in mathematics, but their verbal ability often is quite good. Turner syndrome occurs in approximately 1 of every 2,500 live female births (Kim & others, 2011).

XYY syndrome is a chromosomal disorder in which the male has an extra Y chromosome (Stochholm & others, 2012). Early interest in this syndrome focused on the belief that the extra Y chromosome found in some males contributed to aggression and violence. However, researchers subsequently found that XYY males are no more likely to commit crimes than are XY males (Witkin & others, 1976).

Gene-Linked Abnormalities Abnormalities can be produced not only by an abnormal number of chromosomes but also by harmful genes (Johnson, 2012). More than 7,000 such genetic disorders have been identified, although most of them are rare.

Phenylketonuria (PKU) is a genetic disorder in which the individual cannot properly metabolize phenylalanine, an amino acid. It results from a recessive gene and occurs about once in every 10,000 to 20,000 live births. Today, phenylketonuria is easily detected, and it is treated by a diet that prevents an excess accumulation of phenylalanine (Giovannini & others, 2012). If phenylketonuria is left untreated, however, excess phenylalanine builds up in the child, producing intellectual disability and hyperactivity. Phenylketonuria accounts for approximately 1 percent of institutionalized individuals who are intellectually disabled, and it occurs primarily in non-Latino Whites.

The story of phenylketonuria has important implications for the nature-nurture issue. Although phenylketonuria is a genetic disorder (nature), how or whether a gene's influence in phenylketonuria is played out depends on environmental influences because the disorder can be treated (nurture) using an environmental manipulation (Mehari & others, 2012). That is, the presence of a genetic defect *does not* inevitably lead to the development of the disorder *if* the individual develops in the right environment (one free of phenylalanine). This is one example of the important principle of heredity-environment interaction. Under one environmental condition (phenylalanine in the diet), intellectual disability results, but when other nutrients replace phenylalanine, intelligence develops in the normal range. The same genotype has different outcomes depending on the environment (in this case, the nutritional environment).

Sickle-cell anemia, which occurs most often in African Americans, is a genetic disorder that impairs the functioning of the body's red blood cells. Red blood cells carry oxygen to the body's other cells and are usually shaped like a disk. In sickle-cell anemia, a recessive gene causes the red blood cell to become a hook-shaped "sickle" that cannot carry oxygen properly and dies quickly. As a result, the body's cells do not receive adequate oxygen, causing anemia and early death (Dworkis & others, 2011; Eckman & Embury, 2011). About 1 in 400 African American babies is affected by sickle-cell anemia. One in 10 African Americans is a carrier,

Klinefelter syndrome A chromosomal disorder in which males have an extra X chromosome, making them XXY instead of XY.

fragile X syndrome A genetic disorder involving an abnormality in the X chromosome, which becomes constricted and often breaks.

Turner syndrome A chromosome disorder in females in which either an X chromosome is missing, making the person XO instead of XX, or the second X chromosome is partially deleted.

XYY syndrome A chromosomal disorder in which males have an extra Y chromosome.

phenylketonuria (PKU) A genetic disorder in which an individual cannot properly metabolize an amino acid. PKU is now easily detected but, if left untreated, results in intellectual disability and hyperactivity.

sickle-cell anemia A genetic disorder that affects the red blood cells and occurs most often in people of African descent.

Name	Description	Treatment	Incidence
Cystic fibrosis	Glandular dysfunction that interferes with mucus production; breathing and digestion are hampered, resulting in a shortened life span.	Physical and oxygen therapy, synthetic enzymes, and antibiotics; most individuals live to middle age.	1 in 2,000 births
Diabetes	Body does not produce enough insulin, which causes abnormal metabolism of sugar.	Early onset can be fatal unless treated with insulin.	1 in 2,500 births
Hemophilia	Delayed blood clotting causes internal and external bleeding.	Blood transfusions/injections can reduce or prevent damage due to internal bleeding.	1 in 10,000 males
Huntington disease	Central nervous system deteriorates, producing problems in muscle coordination and mental deterioration.	Does not usually appear until age 35 or older; death likely 10 to 20 years after symptoms appear.	1 in 20,000 births
Phenyketonuria (PKU)	Metabolic disorder that, left untreated, causes intellectual disability.	Special diet can result in average intelligence and normal life span.	1 in 10,000 to 1 in 20,000 births
Sickle-cell anemia	Blood disorder that limits the body's oxygen supply; it can cause joint swelling, as well as heart and kidney failure.	Penicillin, medication for pain, antibiotics, and blood transfusions.	1 in 400 African American children (lower among other groups)
Spina bifida	Neural tube disorder that causes brain and spine abnormalities.	Corrective surgery at birth, orthopedic devices, and physical/medical therapy.	2 in 1,000 births
Tay-Sachs disease	Deceleration of mental and physical development caused by an accumulation of lipids in the nervous system.	Medication and special diet are used, but death is likely by 5 years of age.	1 in 30 American Jews is a carrier.

FIGURE **2.6**
SOME GENE-LINKED ABNORMALITIES

as is 1 in 20 Latin Americans. A National Institutes of Health (2008) panel concluded that the only FDA-approved drug (hydroxyurea) to treat sickle-cell anemia in adolescents and adults is not widely used. Research is currently being conducted in a study named Baby HUG to determine whether the drug works with babies (Alvarez & others, 2012).

Other diseases that result from genetic abnormalities include cystic fibrosis, some forms of diabetes, hemophilia, spina bifida, and Tay-Sachs disease (Tabara, Kohara, & Miki, 2012; Wu & others, 2012). Figure 2.6 provides further information about these diseases. Someday, scientists may identify why these and other genetic abnormalities occur and discover how to cure them.

Dealing with Genetic Abnormalities Every individual carries DNA variations that might predispose the person to serious physical disease or mental disorder. But not all individuals who carry a genetic disorder develop the disorder. Other genes or developmental events sometimes compensate for genetic abnormalities (Gottlieb, 2007; Lickliter, 2013). For example, recall the example of phenylketonuria from the previous section: Even though individuals might carry the genetic disorder associated with phenylketonuria, the phenotype does not develop when phenylalanine is replaced by other nutrients in their diet.

Thus, genes are not destiny, but genes that are missing, nonfunctional, or mutated can be associated with disorders (Hensen & others, 2011; Jentarra & others, 2011). Identifying such genetic flaws could enable doctors to predict an individual's risks, recommend healthy practices, and prescribe the safest and most effective drugs (Devers & others, 2013; McDermott, Downing, & Stratton, 2011). A decade or two from now, parents of a newborn baby may be able to leave the hospital with a full genome analysis of their offspring that identifies disease risks.

However, this knowledge might bring important costs as well as benefits. Who would have access to a person's genetic profile? An individual's ability to land and hold jobs or obtain insurance might be threatened if it is known that a person is considered at risk for

During a physical examination for a college football tryout, Jerry Hubbard, 32, learned that he carried the gene for sickle-cell anemia. Daughter Sara is healthy, but daughter Avery (in the print dress) has sickle-cell anemia. *If you were a genetic counselor, would you recommend that this family have more children?* Explain.

connecting with careers

Holly Ishmael, Genetic Counselor

Holly Ishmael is a genetic counselor at Children's Mercy Hospital in Kansas City. She obtained an undergraduate degree in psychology and a master's degree in genetic counseling from Sarah Lawrence College.

Genetic counselors like Ishmael work as members of a health care team, providing information and support to families with birth defects or genetic disorders. They identify families at risk by analyzing inheritance patterns, and they explore options with each family. Some genetic counselors, like Ishmael, become specialists in prenatal and pediatric genetics; others specialize in cancer genetics or psychiatric genetic disorders.

Ishmael says, "Genetic counseling is a perfect combination for people who want to do something science-oriented, but need human contact and don't want to spend all of their time in a lab or have their nose in a book" (Rizzo, 1999, p. 3).

Genetic counselors have specialized graduate degrees in the areas of medical genetics and counseling. They enter graduate school with undergraduate backgrounds from a variety of disciplines, including biology, genetics, psychology, public health, and social work. There are approximately 30 graduate genetic counseling programs in the United States. If you are interested in this profession, you can

Holly Ishmael (*left*) in a genetic counseling session.

obtain further information from the National Society of Genetic Counselors at www.nsgc.org.

For more information about what genetic counselors do, see page 45 in the Careers in Child Development appendix immediately preceding this chapter.

some disease. For example, should an airline pilot or a neurosurgeon who is predisposed to develop a disorder that makes one's hands shake be required to leave that job early?

Genetic counselors, usually physicians or biologists who are well versed in the field of medical genetics, understand the kinds of problems just described, the odds of encountering them, and helpful strategies for offsetting some of their effects (Kingsmore & others, 2013; Zaccaro & Freda, 2013). A research review found that many individuals who receive genetic counseling find it difficult to quantify risk and tend to overestimate risk (Sivell & others, 2008). To read about the career and work of a genetic counselor, see the *Connecting with Careers* profile.

Review *Connect* Reflect

 LG2 Describe what genes are and how they influence children's development.

Review

- What are genes?
- How are genes passed on?
- What basic principles describe how genes interact?
- What are some chromosomal and gene-linked abnormalities?

Connect

- Explain how environment interacts with genes in gene-linked abnormalities.

Reflect *Your Own Personal Journey of Life*

- Would you want to be able to access a full genome analysis of yourself or your offspring? Why or why not?

| Prenatal Diagnostic Tests | Infertility and Reproductive Biology | Adoption |

The facts and principles we have discussed regarding meiosis, genetics, and genetic abnormalities are a small part of the recent explosion of knowledge about human biology. This knowledge not only helps us understand human development but also opens up many new choices to prospective parents—choices that can also raise ethical questions.

PRENATAL DIAGNOSTIC TESTS

One choice open to prospective mothers is the extent to which they should undergo prenatal testing. A number of tests can indicate whether a fetus is developing normally; these include ultrasound sonography, fetal MRI, chorionic villus sampling, amniocentesis, maternal blood screening, and noninvasive prenatal diagnosis (NIPD). There has been a dramatic increase in research on the use of less invasive techniques, such as fetal MRI and NIPD, which pose lower risks to the fetus than more invasive techniques such as chorionic villus sampling and amniocentesis.

A 6-month-old infant poses with the ultrasound sonography record taken four months into the baby's prenatal development. *What is ultrasound sonography?*

Ultrasound Sonography An ultrasound test is often conducted seven weeks into a pregnancy and at various times later in pregnancy. *Ultrasound sonography* is a prenatal medical procedure in which high-frequency sound waves are directed into the pregnant woman's abdomen (Chitty & others, 2013). The echo from the sounds is transformed into a visual representation of the fetus's inner structures. This technique can detect many structural abnormalities in the fetus, including microencephaly, a form of intellectual disability involving an abnormally small brain; it can also determine the number of fetuses and give clues to the baby's sex (Masselli & others, 2011). This test poses virtually no risk to the woman or the fetus.

Fetal MRI The development of brain-imaging techniques has led to increasing use of *fetal MRI* to diagnose fetal malformations (To, 2012) (see Figure 2.7). MRI, which stands for magnetic resonance imaging, uses a powerful magnet and radio images to generate detailed images of the body's organs and structure. Currently, ultrasound is still the first choice in fetal screening, but fetal MRI can provide more detailed images than ultrasound. In many instances, ultrasound will indicate a possible abnormality and then fetal MRI will be used to obtain a clearer, more detailed image (Koeblinger & others, 2013). Among the fetal malformations that fetal MRI may be able to detect better than ultrasound sonography are certain abnormalities of the central nervous system, chest, gastrointestinal tract, genital/urinary system, and placenta (Sethi & others, 2013; Sorensen & others, 2013).

Chorionic Villus Sampling At some point between 9.5 and 12.5 weeks of pregnancy, chorionic villus sampling may be used to detect genetic defects and chromosomal abnormalities, such as the ones discussed in the previous section (Bauland & others, 2012). Diagnosis takes approximately 10 days. *Chorionic villus sampling* (CVS) is a prenatal medical procedure in which a small sample of the placenta (the vascular organ that links the fetus to the mother's uterus) is removed (Akolekar & others, 2011). There is a small risk of limb deformity when CVS is used.

FIGURE **2.7**

A FETAL MRI, WHICH IS INCREASINGLY BEING USED IN PRENATAL DIAGNOSIS OF FETAL MALFORMATIONS

Amniocentesis Between the 14th and 20th weeks of pregnancy, amniocentesis may be performed. *Amniocentesis* is a prenatal medical procedure in which a sample of amniotic fluid is withdrawn by syringe and tested for chromosomal or metabolic disorders (Athanasiadis & others,

- - - - - - - - - ➤

developmental **connection**

Biological Processes

Discover what the development of the fetus is like at the time chorionic villus sampling and amniocentesis can be used. Chapter 3, p. 77

2011). The amniotic fluid is found within the amnion, a thin sac in which the embryo is suspended. Ultrasound sonography is often used during amniocentesis so that the syringe can be placed precisely. The later amniocentesis is performed, the better its diagnostic potential. The earlier it is performed, the more useful it is in deciding how to handle a pregnancy. It may take two weeks for enough cells to grow so that amniocentesis test results can be obtained. Amniocentesis brings a small risk of miscarriage—about 1 woman in every 200 to 300 miscarries after amniocentesis.

Both amniocentesis and chorionic villus sampling provide valuable information about the presence of birth defects, but they also raise difficult issues for parents about whether an abortion should be obtained if birth defects are present (Quadrelli & others, 2007). Chorionic villus sampling allows a decision to be made sooner, at a time when abortion is safer and less traumatic. Although earlier reports indicated that chorionic villus sampling brings a slightly higher risk of pregnancy loss than amniocentesis, a subsequent U.S. study of more than 40,000 pregnancies found that loss rates for CVS decreased from 1998 to 2003 and that the risk of pregnancy loss was no greater for CVS than for amniocentesis (Caughey, Hopkins, & Norton, 2006).

Maternal Blood Screening   During the 16th to 18th weeks of pregnancy, maternal blood screening may be performed. *Maternal blood screening* identifies pregnancies that have an elevated risk for birth defects such as spina bifida (a defect in the spinal cord) and Down syndrome (Ballard, 2011). The current blood test is called the *triple screen* because it measures three substances in the mother's blood. After an abnormal triple screen result, the next step is usually an ultrasound examination. If an ultrasound does not explain the abnormal triple screen results, amniocentesis is typically used.

Noninvasive Prenatal Diagnosis (NIPD)   *Noninvasive prenatal diagnosis* (*NIPD*) is increasingly being explored as an alternative to procedures such as chorionic villus sampling and amniocentesis (Avent, 2012; Peterson & others, 2013). At this point, NIPD has mainly focused on brain imaging techniques, the isolation and examination of fetal cells circulating in the mother's blood, and analysis of cell-free fetal DNA in maternal plasma (Geaghan, 2012; Papasavva & others, 2013).

Researchers already have used NIPD to successfully test for genes inherited from a father that cause cystic fibrosis and Huntington's disease. They also are exploring the potential for using NIPD very early in fetal development to diagnose a baby's sex and detect Down syndrome (Fernandez-Martinez & others, 2012; Mercy & others, 2013).

Fetal Sex Determination   Chorionic villus sampling has often been used to determine the sex of the fetus at some point between 11 and 13 weeks of gestation. Recently, though, some noninvasive techniques have been able to detect the sex of the fetus at an earlier point (Kolialexi, 2012; Moise & others, 2013). A recent meta-analysis of studies confirmed that a baby's sex can be detected as early as 7 weeks into pregnancy (Devaney & others, 2011). Being able to detect an offspring's sex as well as the presence of various diseases and defects at such an early stage raises ethical concerns about couples' motivation to terminate a pregnancy (Lewis & others, 2012).

INFERTILITY AND REPRODUCTIVE TECHNOLOGY

Recent advances in biological knowledge have also opened up many choices for infertile people (Beall & Decherney, 2012; Ming & others, 2012). Approximately 10 to 15 percent of couples in the United States experience infertility, which is defined as the inability to conceive a child after 12 months of regular intercourse without contraception. The cause of infertility can rest with the woman or the man (Reindollar & Goldman, 2012). The woman may not be ovulating (releasing eggs to be fertilized), she may be producing abnormal ova, her fallopian tubes by which ova normally reach the womb may be blocked, or she may have a disease that prevents implantation of the embryo into the uterus.

A technician using a micro-needle to inject human sperm into a human egg cell as part of an in vitro fertilization procedure. The injected sperm fertilizes the egg, and the resulting zygote is then grown in the laboratory until it reaches an early stage of embryonic development. Then it is implanted in the uterus.

The man may produce too few sperm, the sperm may lack motility (the ability to move adequately), or he may have a blocked passageway (Kini & others, 2010).

In the United States, more than 2 million couples seek help for infertility every year. In some cases of infertility, surgery may correct the cause; in others, hormone-based drugs may improve the probability of having a child. Of the 2 million couples who seek help for infertility every year, about 40,000 try high-tech assisted reproduction. By far the most common technique used is *in vitro fertilization* (IVF), in which eggs and sperm are combined in a laboratory dish. If any eggs are successfully fertilized, one or more of the resulting fertilized eggs is transferred into the woman's uterus. A national study in the United States by the Centers for Disease Control and Prevention (2006) found the success rate for IVF depends on the mother's age (see Figure 2.8).

The creation of families by means of the new reproductive technologies raises important questions about the physical and psychological consequences for children (Steel & Sutcliff, 2010). One result of fertility treatments is an increase in multiple births (Jones, 2007). Twenty-five to 30 percent of pregnancies achieved by fertility treatments—including in vitro fertilization—now result in multiple births. A recent *meta-analysis* (a statistical technique that combines the results of multiple studies to determine the strength of the effect) revealed that twins conceived through in vitro fertilization have a slightly increased risk of low birth weight (McDonald & others, 2010), and another meta-analysis found that in vitro fertilization singletons have a significant risk of low birth weight (McDonald & others, 2009). To read about a study that addresses longer-term consequences of in vitro fertilization, see *Connecting Through Research*.

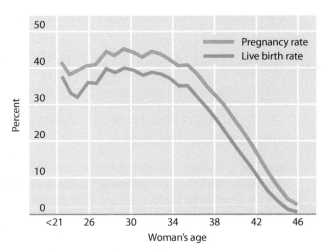

FIGURE **2.8**

SUCCESS RATES OF IN VITRO FERTILIZATION VARY ACCORDING TO THE WOMAN'S AGE

connecting through research

Do Children Conceived Through In Vitro Fertilization Show Significantly Different Developmental Outcomes in Adolescence?

A longitudinal study examined 34 in vitro fertilization families, 49 adoptive families, and 38 families with a naturally conceived child (Golombok, MacCallum, & Goodman, 2001). Each type of family included a similar portion of boys and girls. Also, the age of the young adolescents did not differ according to family type (mean age of 11 years, 11 months).

Children's socioemotional development was assessed by (1) interviewing the mother and obtaining detailed descriptions of any problems the child might have; (2) administering a Strengths and Difficulties questionnaire to the child's mother and teacher; and (3) administering the Social Adjustment Inventory for Children and Adolescents, which examines functioning in school, peer relationships, and self-esteem.

No significant differences between the children from the in vitro fertilization, adoptive, and naturally conceiving families were found. The results from the Social Adjustment Inventory for Children and Adolescents are shown in Figure 2.9. Recent reviews by leading researchers conclude that the children and adolescents conceived through new reproductive technologies—such as in vitro fertilization—are as well adjusted as their counterparts conceived by natural means (Golombok, 2011a, b; Golombok & Tasker, 2010).

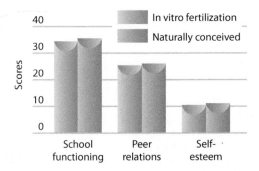

FIGURE **2.9**

SOCIOEMOTIONAL FUNCTIONING OF CHILDREN CONCEIVED THROUGH IN VITRO FERTILIZATION. This graph shows the results of a study that compared the socioemotional functioning of young adolescents who had either been conceived through in vitro fertilization (IVF) or naturally conceived (Golombok, MacCallum, & Goodman, 2001). For each type of family, the study included a similar portion of boys and girls and children of similar age (mean age of 11 years, 11 months). Although the means for the naturally conceived group were slightly higher, this is likely due to chance; there were no significant differences between the groups.

The Increased Diversity of Adopted Children and Adoptive Parents

A number of changes have characterized adoptive children and adoptive parents in the last three to four decades (Brodzinsky & Pinderhughes, 2002). In the first half of the twentieth century, most U.S. adopted children were healthy, non-Latino White infants who were adopted at birth or soon after; however, in recent decades as abortion became legal and contraception increased, fewer of these infants became available for adoption. Increasingly, U.S. couples adopted a much wider diversity of children—from other countries, from other ethnic groups, children with physical and/or mental problems, and children who had been neglected or abused.

Changes also have characterized adoptive parents in the last three to four decades (Brodzinsky & Pinderhughes, 2002). In the first half of the twentieth century, most adoptive parents were married couples from non-Latino White middle or upper socioeconomic status backgrounds who did not have any type of disability. However, in recent decades, increased diversity has characterized adoptive parents. Many adoption agencies today have no income requirements for adoptive parents and now permit adoption by adults from a wide range of backgrounds, including single adults, gay male and lesbian adults, and older adults. Further, many adoptions involve other family members (aunts/uncles/grandparents); currently, 30 percent of U.S. adoptions are made by relatives (Ledesma, 2012). And slightly more than 50 percent of U.S. adoptions occur through the foster care system; recently, more than 100,000 children in the U.S. foster care system were waiting for someone to adopt them (Ledesma, 2012).

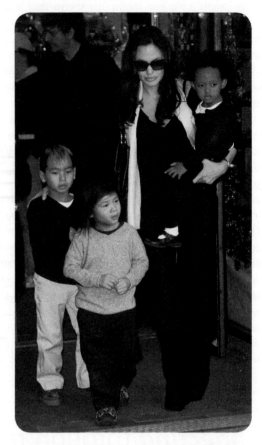

An increasing number of Hollywood celebrities are adopting children from developing countries. Actress Angelina Jolie (*above*) carries her adopted daughter Zahara with adopted sons Maddox and Pax walking beside them.

Many fertile adults adopt children, but many more adoptive parents are infertile. Based on what you read prior to this interlude, why might an infertile couple or individual decide to adopt rather than undergo reproductive technology procedures?

ADOPTION

Although surgery and fertility drugs can sometimes solve the infertility problem, another choice is to adopt a child (Baldwin, 2011; Scott, Roberts, & Glennen, 2011). Adoption is the social and legal process by which a parent-child relationship is established between persons unrelated at birth. As discussed in *Connecting with Diversity,* an increase in diversity has characterized the adoption of children in the United States in recent years.

How do adopted children fare after they are adopted? Children who are adopted very early in their lives are more likely to have positive outcomes than children adopted later in life (Bernard & Dozier, 2008). In one study, the later adoption occurred, the more problems the adoptees had. Infant adoptees had the fewest adjustment difficulties; those adopted after they were 10 years of age had the most problems (Sharma, McGue, & Benson, 1996). A recent Danish study indicated that being adopted was not a risk for juvenile delinquency if the individual was adopted at 12 months of age or earlier (Laubjerg & Petersson, 2011). However, those adopted after 12 months of age had 3 to 4 times higher risk of becoming a juvenile delinquent than their nonadopted counterparts.

A majority of adopted children and adolescents (including those adopted at older ages, transracially, and across national borders) adjust effectively, and their parents report considerable

caring *connections*

Parenting Adopted Children

Many of the keys to effectively parenting adopted children are no different from those for effectively parenting biological children: Be supportive and caring, be involved and monitor the child's behavior and whereabouts, be a good communicator, and help the child learn to develop self-control. However, parents of adopted children face some unique circumstances (Fontenot, 2007; Von Korff & Grotevant, 2011). They need to recognize the differences involved in adoptive family life, communicate about these differences, show respect for the birth family, and support the child's search for self and identity.

Following are some of the problems parents face when their adopted children are at different points in development and some recommendations for how to handle these problems (Brodzinsky & Pinderhughes, 2002):

- **Infancy.** Researchers have found few differences in the attachment that adopted and nonadopted infants form with their parents. However, attachment can become problematic if parents have unresolved fertility issues or the child does not meet the parents' expectations. Counselors can help prospective adoptive parents develop realistic expectations.
- **Early childhood.** Because many children begin to ask where they came from when they are about 4 to 6 years old, this is a natural time to begin to talk in simple ways to children about their adoption status (Warshak, 2007). Some parents (although not as many as in the past) decide not to tell their children about the adoption. This secrecy may create psychological risks for the child if he or she later finds out about the adoption.
- **Middle and late childhood.** During the elementary school years, children begin to show more interest in their origins and may ask

What are some strategies for parenting adopted children at different points in their development?

questions related to where they came from, what their parents looked like, and why their parents placed them for adoption. As they grow older, children may develop mixed feelings about being adopted and question their adoptive parents' explanations. It is important for adoptive parents to recognize that this ambivalence is normal. Also, problems may arise from the desire of adoptive parents to make life too perfect for the adoptive child and to present a perfect image of themselves to the child. The result too often is that adopted children feel that they cannot release any angry feelings or openly discuss problems.

- **Adolescence.** Adolescents are likely to develop more abstract and logical thinking processes, to focus their attention on their bodies, and to search for an identity. These characteristics provide the foundation for adopted adolescents to reflect on their adoption status in more complex ways, such as focusing on physical differences between themselves and their adoptive parents. As they explore their identity, adopted adolescents may have difficulty incorporating their adopted status into their identity in positive ways. It is important for adoptive parents to understand the complexity of the adopted adolescent's identity exploration and be patient with the adolescent's lengthy identity search.

According to the information presented in this box and in the text that precedes it, how can mental health professionals help adopting parents and adopted children?

satisfaction with their decision to adopt (Brodzinsky & Pinderhughes, 2002; Castle & others, 2010). A research review of 88 studies also revealed no difference in the self-esteem of adopted and nonadopted children and adolescents, as well as no differences between transracial and same-race adoptees (Juffer & van IJzendoorn, 2007).

Also keep in mind that changes in adoption practice over the last several decades make it difficult to generalize about the average adopted child or average adoptive parent. To read more about adoption, see the *Caring Connections* interlude in which we discuss effective parenting strategies with adopted children.

Review *Connect* Reflect

LG3 Identify some important reproductive challenges and choices.

Review

- What are some common prenatal diagnostic tests?
- What are some techniques that help infertile people to have children?
- How does adoption affect children's development?

Connect

- In Chapter 1, you learned about different methods for collecting data. How would you characterize the methods used in prenatal diagnostic testing?

Reflect *Your Own Personal Journey of Life*

- If you were an adult who could not have children, would you want to adopt a child? Why or why not?

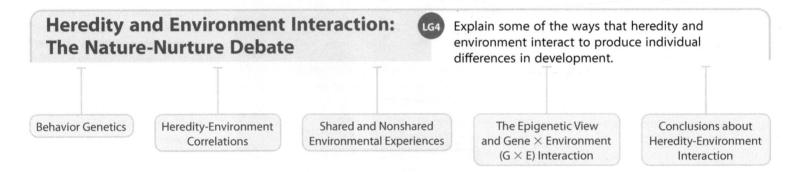

Heredity and Environment Interaction: The Nature-Nurture Debate

LG4 Explain some of the ways that heredity and environment interact to produce individual differences in development.

| Behavior Genetics | Heredity-Environment Correlations | Shared and Nonshared Environmental Experiences | The Epigenetic View and Gene × Environment (G × E) Interaction | Conclusions about Heredity-Environment Interaction |

Is it possible to untangle the influence of heredity from that of environment and discover the role of each in producing individual differences in development? When heredity and environment interact, how does heredity influence the environment, and vice versa?

BEHAVIOR GENETICS

Behavior genetics is the field that seeks to discover the influence of heredity and environment on individual differences in human traits and development (Kaplan, 2012; Maxson, 2013). Note that behavior genetics does not identify the extent to which genetics or the environment affects an individual's traits. Instead, behavior geneticists try to figure out what is responsible for the differences among people—that is, to what extent people vary because of differences in genes, environment, or a combination of these factors (Wang & others, 2012). To study the influence of heredity on behavior, behavior geneticists often use either twins or adoption situations (Kubarych & others, 2012).

In the most common **twin study,** the behavioral similarity of identical twins (who are genetically identical) is compared with the behavioral similarity of fraternal twins. Recall that although fraternal twins share the same womb, they are no more genetically alike than non-twin siblings. Thus, by comparing groups of identical and fraternal twins, behavior geneticists capitalize on the basic knowledge that identical twins are more similar genetically than are fraternal twins (Bell & Saffery, 2012; Chang & others, 2013; Wichers & others, 2013). For example, one study found that conduct problems were more prevalent in identical twins than fraternal twins; the researchers concluded that the study demonstrated an important role for heredity in conduct problems (Scourfield & others, 2004).

However, several issues complicate interpretation of twin studies. For example, perhaps the environments of identical twins are more similar than the environments of fraternal twins.

behavior genetics The field that seeks to discover the influence of heredity and environment on individual differences in human traits and development.

twin study A study in which the behavioral similarity of identical twins is compared with the behavioral similarity of fraternal twins.

adoption study A study in which investigators seek to discover whether, in behavior and psychological characteristics, adopted children are more like their adoptive parents, who provided a home environment, or more like their biological parents, who contributed their heredity. Another form of the adoption study is one that compares adoptive and biological siblings.

Adults might stress the similarities of identical twins more than those of fraternal twins, and identical twins might perceive themselves as a "set" and play together more than fraternal twins do. If so, the influence of the environment on the observed similarities between identical and fraternal twins might be very significant.

In an **adoption study,** investigators seek to discover whether the behavior and psychological characteristics of adopted children are more like those of their adoptive parents, who have provided a home environment, or more like those of their biological parents, who have contributed their heredity (Kendler & others, 2012). Another form of the adoption study compares adoptive and biological siblings.

HEREDITY-ENVIRONMENT CORRELATIONS

The difficulties that researchers encounter when they interpret the results of twin studies and adoption studies reflect the complexities of heredity-environment interaction. Some of these interactions are heredity-environment correlations, which means that individuals' genes may influence the types of environments to which they are exposed. In a sense, individuals "inherit" environments that may be related or linked to genetic "propensities." Behavior geneticist Sandra Scarr (1993) described three ways that heredity and environment are correlated (see Figure 2.10):

Twin studies compare identical twins with fraternal twins. Identical twins develop from a single fertilized egg that splits into two genetically identical organisms. Fraternal twins develop from separate eggs, making them genetically no more similar than nontwin siblings. *What is the nature of the twin study method?*

- **Passive genotype-environment correlations** occur because biological parents, who are genetically related to the child, provide a rearing environment for the child. For example, the parents might have a genetic predisposition to be intelligent and read skillfully. Because they read well and enjoy reading, they provide their children with books to read. The likely outcome is that their children, given their own inherited predispositions from their parents and their book-filled environment, will become skilled readers.

- **Evocative genotype-environment correlations** occur because a child's genetically influenced characteristics elicit certain types of environments. For example, active, smiling children receive more social stimulation than passive, quiet children do. Cooperative, attentive children evoke more pleasant and instructional responses from the adults around them than uncooperative, distractible children do.

- **Active (niche-picking) genotype-environment correlations** occur when children seek out environments that they find compatible and stimulating. Niche-picking refers to finding a setting that is suited to one's genetically influenced abilities. Children select from their surrounding environment some aspect that they respond

passive genotype-environment correlations Correlations that exist when the natural parents, who are genetically related to the child, provide a rearing environment for the child.

evocative genotype-environment correlations Correlations that exist when the child's genetically influenced characteristics elicit certain types of environments.

active (niche-picking) genotype-environment correlations Correlations that exist when children seek out environments they find compatible and stimulating.

Heredity-Environment Correlation	Description	Examples
Passive	Children inherit genetic tendencies from their parents, and parents also provide an environment that matches their own genetic tendencies.	Musically inclined parents usually have musically inclined children and are likely to provide an environment rich in music for their children.
Evocative	The child's genetic tendencies elicit stimulation from the environment that supports a particular trait. Thus, genes evoke environmental support.	A happy, outgoing child elicits smiles and friendly responses from others.
Active (niche-picking)	Children actively seek out "niches" in their environment that reflect their own interests and talents and are thus in accord with their genotype.	Libraries, sports fields, and a store with musical instruments are examples of environmental niches children might seek out if they have intellectual interests in books, talent in sports, or musical talents, respectively.

FIGURE **2.10**
EXPLORING HEREDITY-ENVIRONMENT CORRELATIONS

Tennis stars Venus and Serena Williams. *What might be some shared and nonshared environmental experiences they had while they were growing up that contributed to their tennis stardom?*

to, learn about, or ignore. Their active selections of environments are related to their particular genotype. For example, outgoing children tend to seek out social contexts in which to interact with people, whereas shy children don't. Children who are musically inclined are likely to select musical environments in which they can successfully perform their skills. How these "tendencies" come about will be discussed shortly under the topic of the epigenetic view.

Scarr observes that the relative importance of the three genotype-environment correlations changes as children develop from infancy through adolescence. In infancy, much of the environment that children experience is provided by adults. Thus, passive genotype-environment correlations are more common in the lives of infants and young children than they are for older children and adolescents who can extend their experiences beyond the family's influence and create their environments to a greater degree.

SHARED AND NONSHARED ENVIRONMENTAL EXPERIENCES

Behavior geneticists have argued that to understand the environment's role in differences between people, we should distinguish between shared and nonshared environments. That is, we should consider experiences that children share in common with other children living in the same home, and experiences that are not shared (Burt, McGue, & Iacono, 2010; Klahr & others, 2011).

Shared environmental experiences are siblings' common experiences, such as their parents' personalities or intellectual orientation, the family's socioeconomic status, and the neighborhood in which they live. By contrast, **nonshared environmental experiences** are a child's unique experiences, both within the family and outside the family, that are not shared with a sibling. Even experiences occurring within the family can be part of the "nonshared environment." For example, parents often interact differently with each sibling, and siblings interact differently with parents. Siblings often have different peer groups, different friends, and different teachers at school, all of which contribute to nonshared environments.

Behavior geneticist Robert Plomin (2004) has found that shared environment accounts for little of the variation in children's personality or interests. In other words, even though two children live under the same roof with the same parents, their personalities are often very different. Further, Plomin argues that heredity influences the nonshared environments of siblings through the heredity-environment correlations we described earlier. For example, a child who has inherited a genetic tendency to be athletic is likely to spend more time in environments related to sports, and a child who has inherited a tendency to be musically inclined is more likely to spend time in environments related to music.

What are the implications of Plomin's interpretation of the role of shared and nonshared environments in development? In the *Nurture Assumption,* Judith Harris (1998) argued that what parents do does not make a difference in their children's and adolescents' behavior. Yell at them. Hug them. Read to them. Ignore them. Harris says it won't influence how they turn out. She argues based on data like Plomin's indicating that genes and peers have far greater influence than parents do in children's and adolescents' development.

Genes and peers do matter, but Harris' descriptions of peer influences do not take into account the complexity of peer contexts and developmental trajectories (Hartup, 2009). In addition, Harris is wrong in saying that parents don't matter. For example, in the early childhood years parents play an important role in selecting children's peers and indirectly influencing children's development. Volumes of parenting literature with many research studies document the importance of parents in children's development (Grusec, 2011; Parke & Clarke-Stewart, 2011; Russell, 2011).

Despite the strong criticism of her views, Harris (2009) published a revised and updated edition of her earlier book, restating her claim that parents matter far less than most people think. We discuss parents' important roles throughout this book.

shared environmental experiences Siblings' common environmental experiences, such as their parents' personalities and intellectual orientation, the family's socioeconomic status, and the neighborhood in which they live.

nonshared environmental experiences The child's own unique experiences, both within the family and outside the family, that are not shared by another sibling.

THE EPIGENETIC VIEW AND GENE × ENVIRONMENT (G × E) INTERACTION

Critics argue that the concept of heredity-environment correlation gives heredity too much of a one-sided influence in determining development because it does not consider the role of prior environmental influences in shaping the correlation itself (Gottlieb, 2007). However, earlier in this chapter we discussed how genes are collaborative, not determining an individual's traits in an independent manner but rather interacting with the environment.

The Epigenetic View In line with the concept of a collaborative gene, Gilbert Gottlieb (2007) emphasizes the **epigenetic view,** which states that development is the result of an ongoing, bidirectional interchange between heredity and the environment. Figure 2.11 compares the heredity-environment correlation and epigenetic views of development.

Let's look at an example that reflects the epigenetic view. A baby inherits genes from both parents at conception. During prenatal development, toxins, nutrition, and stress can influence some genes to stop functioning while others become stronger or weaker. During infancy, environmental experiences such as toxins, nutrition, stress, learning, and encouragement continue to modify genetic activity and the activity of the nervous system that directly underlies behavior. Heredity and environment operate together—or collaborate—to produce a person's intelligence, temperament, height, weight, ability to pitch a baseball, ability to read, and so on (Gottlieb, 2007; Lickliter, 2013; Meaney, 2010; Moore, 2013).

Gene × Environment Interaction (G × E) An increasing number of studies are exploring how the interaction between heredity and environment influences development, including interactions that involve specific DNA sequences (Bihagi & others, 2012). The epigenetic mechanisms involve the actual molecular modification of the DNA strand as result of environmental inputs in ways that alter genetic functioning (Feil & Fraga, 2012).

One study found that individuals who have a short version of a genotype labeled 5-HTTLPR (a gene involving the neurotransmitter serotonin) have an elevated risk of developing depression only if they *also* have stressful lives (Caspi & others, 2003). Thus, the specific gene did not directly cause depression to develop; rather, the gene interacted with a stressful environment in a way that allowed the researchers to predict whether individuals would develop depression. Recent studies also have found support for the interaction between the 5-HTTLPR gene and stress levels in predicting depression in adolescents and older adults (Miller & others, 2013; Petersen & others, 2012; Zannas & others, 2012).

Other research involving interaction between genes and environmental experience has focused on attachment, parenting, and supportive child rearing environments (Berry & others, 2012). In one study, adults who experienced parental loss as young children were more likely to have unresolved attachment as adults only when they had the short version of the 5-HTTLPR gene (Caspers & others, 2009). The long version of the serotonin transporter gene apparently provided some protection and ability to cope better with parental loss. Other recent research has found that variations in dopamine-related genes interact with supportive or unsupportive rearing environments to influence children's development (Bakermans-Kranenburg & van IJzendoorn, 2011). The type of research just described is referred to as **gene × environment (G × E) interaction**—the interaction of a specific, measured variation in DNA and a specific, measured aspect of the environment (Alexander & others, 2012; Karg & Sen, 2012; Oppenheimer & others, 2013).

CONCLUSIONS ABOUT HEREDITY-ENVIRONMENT INTERACTION

If an attractive, popular, intelligent girl is elected president of her senior class in high school, is her success due to heredity or to environment? Of course, the answer is both.

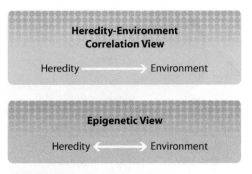

FIGURE **2.11**
COMPARISON OF THE HEREDITY-ENVIRONMENT CORRELATION AND EPIGENETIC VIEWS

developmental **connection**

Biological Processes

A recent study revealed links between infant attachment, responsive parenting, and the short/long version of the 5-HTTLPR gene. Chapter 10, p. 303

epigenetic view Theory that development is the result of an ongoing, bidirectional interchange between heredity and environment.

gene × environment (G × E) interaction The interaction of a specific, measured variation in the DNA and a specific, measured aspect of the environment.

To what extent are this young girl's piano skills likely due to heredity, environment, or both? Explain.

developmental **connection**

Nature vs. Nurture

The nature and nurture issue is one of the main issues in the study of children's development. Chapter 1, p. 16

The relative contributions of heredity and environment are not additive. That is, we can't say that such-and-such a percentage of nature and such-and-such a percentage of experience make us who we are. Nor is it accurate to say that full genetic expression happens once, around conception or birth, after which we carry our genetic legacy into the world to see how far it takes us. Genes produce proteins throughout the life span, in many different environments. Or they don't produce these proteins, depending in part on how harsh or nourishing those environments are.

The emerging view is that complex behaviors are influenced by genes in a way that gives people a propensity for a particular developmental trajectory (Maxson, 2013; Plomin, 2012). However, the actual development requires more: an environment. And that environment is complex, just like the mixture of genes we inherit (Grusec & others, 2013; Moore, 2013; Mistry, Conteras, & Dutta, 2013). Environmental influences range from the things we lump together under "nurture" (such as parenting, family dynamics, schooling, and neighborhood quality) to biological encounters (such as viruses, birth complications, and even biological events in cells).

Imagine for a moment that there is a cluster of genes somehow associated with youth violence (this example is hypothetical because we don't know of any such combination). The adolescent who carries this genetic mixture might experience a world of loving parents, regular nutritious meals, lots of books, and a series of masterful teachers. Or the adolescent's world might include parental neglect, a neighborhood in which gunshots and crime are everyday occurrences, and inadequate schooling. In which of these environments are the adolescent's genes likely to manufacture the biological underpinnings of criminality?

If heredity and environment interact to determine the course of development, is that all there is to answering the question of what causes development? Are children completely at the mercy of their genes and environment as they develop? Genetic heritage and environmental experiences are pervasive influences on development (Dodge & Rutter, 2011; Gregory, Ball, & Button, 2011). But children's development is not solely the outcome of their heredity and environment; children also can author a unique developmental path by changing their environment. As one psychologist recently concluded:

> In reality, we are both the creatures and creators of our worlds. We are . . . the products of our genes and environments. Nevertheless, . . . the stream of causation that shapes the future runs through our present choices . . . Mind matters . . . Our hopes, goals, and expectations influence our future. (Myers, 2010, p. 168)

Review Connect Reflect

LG4 Explain some of the ways that heredity and environment interact to produce individual differences in development.

Review

- What is behavior genetics?
- What are three types of heredity-environment correlations?
- What is meant by the concepts of shared and nonshared environmental experiences?
- What is the epigenetic view of development? What characterizes gene × environment (G × E) interaction?
- What conclusions can be reached about heredity-environment interaction?

Connect

- Of passive, evocative, and active genotype-environment correlations, which is the best explanation for the similarities discovered between the twins discussed in the story that opened this chapter?

Reflect *Your Own Personal Journey of Life*

- Imagine that someone tells you that he or she has analyzed your genetic background and environmental experiences and reached the conclusion that the environment you grew up in as a child definitely had little influence on your intelligence. What would you say about this analysis?

Biological Beginnings

The Evolutionary Perspective

 Discuss the evolutionary perspective on child development.

Natural Selection and Adaptive Behavior

Evolutionary Psychology

- Natural selection is the process by which those individuals of a species that are best adapted to the environment survive and reproduce. Darwin proposed that natural selection fuels evolution. In evolutionary theory, adaptive behavior is behavior that promotes the organism's survival in a natural habitat.

- Evolutionary psychology holds that adaptation, reproduction, and "survival of the fittest" are important in shaping behavior. Ideas proposed by evolutionary developmental psychology include the view that an extended childhood period is needed to develop a large brain and learn the complexity of human social communities. Like other theoretical approaches to development, evolutionary psychology has limitations. Bandura rejects "one-sided evolutionism" and argues for a bidirectional link between biology and environment. Biology allows for a broad range of cultural possibilities.

Genetic Foundations of Development

LG2 Describe what genes are and how they influence children's development.

The Collaborative Gene

Genes and Chromosomes

Genetic Principles

Chromosome and Gene-Linked Abnormalities

- Short segments of DNA constitute genes, the units of hereditary information that direct cells to reproduce and manufacture proteins. Genes act collaboratively, not independently.

- Genes are passed on to new cells when chromosomes are duplicated during the process of mitosis and meiosis, which are two ways in which new cells are formed. When an egg and a sperm unite in the fertilization process, the resulting zygote contains the genes from the chromosomes in the father's sperm and the mother's egg. Despite this transmission of genes from generation to generation, variability is created in several ways, including through the exchange of chromosomal segments during meiosis, through mutations, and through environmental influences.

- Genetic principles include those involving dominant-recessive genes, sex-linked genes, genetic imprinting, and polygenic inheritance.

- Chromosome abnormalities produce Down syndrome, which is caused by the presence of an extra copy of chromosome 21. Other sex-linked chromosomal abnormalities include Klinefelter syndrome, fragile X syndrome, Turner syndrome, and XYY syndrome. Gene-linked abnormalities involve absent or harmful genes. Gene-linked disorders include phenylketonuria (PKU) and sickle-cell anemia. Genetic counseling offers couples information about their risk of having a child with inherited abnormalities.

Reproductive Challenges and Choices

 Identify some important reproductive challenges and choices.

Prenatal Diagnostic Tests

Infertility and Reproductive Technology

Adoption

- Ultrasound sonography, fetal MRI, chorionic villus sampling, amniocentesis, and maternal blood screening are used to determine whether a fetus is developing normally. Noninvasive prenatal diagnosis is increasingly being explored. Sex determination of the fetus is occurring much earlier than in the past.

- Approximately 10 to 15 percent of U.S. couples have infertility problems, some of which can be corrected through surgery or fertility drugs. An additional option is in vitro fertilization.

- The vast majority of adopted children adapt effectively. When adoption occurs very early in development, the outcomes for the child are improved. Because of the dramatic changes that occurred in adoption in recent decades, it is difficult to generalize about the average adopted child or average adoptive family.

Heredity and Environment Interaction: The Nature-Nurture Debate

 LG4 Explain some of the ways that heredity and environment interact to produce individual differences in development.

Behavior Genetics

Heredity-Environment Correlations

Shared and Nonshared Environmental Experiences

The Epigenetic View and Gene × Environment (G × E) Interaction

Conclusions About Heredity-Environment Interaction

- Behavior genetics is the field concerned with the influence of heredity and environment on individual differences in human traits and development. Methods used by behavior geneticists include twin studies and adoption studies.

- In Scarr's view of heredity-environment correlations, heredity directs the types of environments that children experience. She describes three genotype-environment correlations: passive, evocative, and active (niche-picking). Scarr argues that the relative importance of these three genotype-environment correlations changes as children develop.

- Shared environmental experiences refer to siblings' common experiences, such as their parents' personalities and intellectual orientation, the family's socioeconomic status, and the neighborhood in which they live. Nonshared environmental experiences involve the child's unique experiences, both within a family and outside a family, that are not shared with a sibling. Many behavior geneticists argue that differences in the development of siblings are due to nonshared environmental experiences (and heredity) rather than shared environmental experiences.

- The epigenetic view emphasizes that development is the result of an ongoing, bidirectional interchange between heredity and environment. Gene × environment interaction involves the interaction of a specific, measured variation in the DNA and a specific, measured aspect of the environment. An increasing number of G × E studies are being conducted.

- Behaviors are influenced by genes in a way that gives people a propensity for a particular developmental trajectory. However, actual development also requires an environment, and that environment is complex. The interaction of heredity and environment is extensive. Much remains to be discovered about the specific ways that heredity and environment interact to influence development. Although heredity and environment are pervasive influences on development, humans can author a unique developmental path by changing their environment.

---

key terms

evolutionary psychology 50
chromosomes 53
DNA 53
genes 53
mitosis 54
meiosis 54
fertilization 54
zygote 54
genotype 56

phenotype 56
Down syndrome 57
Klinefelter syndrome 58
fragile X syndrome 58
Turner syndrome 58
XYY syndrome 58
phenylketonuria (PKU) 58
sickle-cell anemia 58
behavior genetics 66

twin study 66
adoption study 66
passive genotype-environment
  correlations 67
evocative genotype-environment
  correlations 67
active (niche-picking)
  genotype-environment
  correlations 67

shared environmental
  experiences 68
nonshared environmental
  experiences 68
epigenetic view 69
gene × environment (G × E)
  interaction 69

---

key people

Thomas Bouchard 49
Charles Darwin 50
David Buss 51

Albert Bandura 52
Stephen Jay Gould 52
David Moore 54

Sandra Scarr 67
Robert Plomin 68
Judith Harris 68

Gilbert Gottlieb 69

chapter 3

PRENATAL DEVELOPMENT AND BIRTH

chapter **outline**

Alex, also known as "Mr. Littles."

Diana and Roger married when he was 38 and she was 34. Both worked full-time and were excited when Diana became pregnant. Two months later, Diana began to have some unusual pains and bleeding. Just two months into her pregnancy she had lost the baby. Diana thought deeply about possible reasons she had been unable to carry the baby to full term. At about the time she became pregnant, the federal government had begun to warn that eating certain types of fish with a high mercury content during pregnancy on a regular basis might cause a miscarriage. Now she eliminated these fish from her diet.

Six months later, Diana became pregnant again. She and Roger read about pregnancy and signed up for birth preparation classes. Each Friday night for eight weeks they practiced relaxation techniques during simulated contractions. They talked about what kind of parents they wanted to be and discussed how their lives would change after the baby was born. When they found out that their offspring was going to be a boy, they gave him a nickname: Mr. Littles.

This time, Diana's pregnancy went well and Alex was born. During the birth, however, Diana's heart rate dropped precipitously, and she was given a stimulant to raise it. Apparently the stimulant also increased Alex's heart rate and breathing to a dangerous point, and he was placed in a neonatal intensive care unit (NICU).

Several times a day, Diana and Roger visited Alex in the NICU. A number of babies in the NICU who had a very low birth weight had been in intensive care for weeks, and some of these babies were not doing well. Fortunately, Alex was in better health. After several days in the NICU, his parents were permitted to take home a very healthy Alex.

preview

This chapter chronicles the truly remarkable developments from conception through birth. We will look at normal development as well as hazards to normal development (such as mercury, mentioned in the preceding story). We will outline the birth process and describe the tests used to assess the newborn. We will examine the physical, emotional, and psychological adjustments that a mother goes through during the time following birth—the postpartum period. And we will end the chapter by comparing theories on parent-infant bonding.

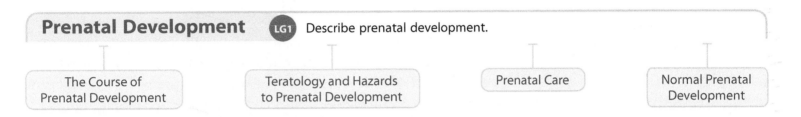

Prenatal Development **LG1** Describe prenatal development.

- The Course of Prenatal Development
- Teratology and Hazards to Prenatal Development
- Prenatal Care
- Normal Prenatal Development

Imagine how Alex ("Mr. Littles") came to be. Out of thousands of eggs and millions of sperm, one egg and one sperm united to produce him. Had the union of sperm and egg come a day or even an hour earlier or later, he might have been very different—maybe even of the opposite sex. *Conception* occurs when a single sperm cell from the male unites with an ovum (egg) in the female's fallopian tube in a process called fertilization. Over the next few months, the genetic code discussed in Chapter 2 directs a series of changes in the fertilized egg, but many events and hazards will influence how that egg develops and becomes tiny Alex.

THE COURSE OF PRENATAL DEVELOPMENT

Typical prenatal development begins with fertilization and ends with birth, lasting between 266 and 280 days (from 38 to 40 weeks). It can be divided into three periods: germinal, embryonic, and fetal.

The Germinal Period The **germinal period** is the period of prenatal development that takes place in the first two weeks after conception. It includes the creation of the fertilized egg, called a zygote, followed by cell division and attachment of the zygote to the uterine wall.

Rapid cell division by the zygote continues throughout the germinal period (recall from Chapter 2 that this cell division occurs through a process called *mitosis*). By approximately one week after conception, the differentiation of these cells—their specialization for different tasks—has already begun. At this stage, the group of cells, now called the **blastocyst,** consists of an inner mass of cells that will eventually develop into the embryo, and the **trophoblast,** an outer layer of cells that later provides nutrition and support for the embryo. *Implantation,* the attachment of the zygote to the uterine wall, takes place about 11 to 15 days after conception. Figure 3.1 illustrates some of the most significant developments during the germinal period.

The Embryonic Period The **embryonic period** is the period of prenatal development that occurs from two to eight weeks after conception. During the embryonic period, the rate of cell differentiation intensifies, support systems for cells form, and organs appear.

This period begins as the blastocyst attaches to the uterine wall. The mass of cells is now called an *embryo,* and three layers of cells form. The embryo's *endoderm* is the inner layer of cells, which will develop into the digestive and respiratory systems. The *mesoderm* is the

The history of man for nine months preceding his birth would, probably, be far more interesting, and contain events of greater moment than all three score and ten years that follow it.

—SAMUEL TAYLOR COLERIDGE
English Poet and Essayist, 19th Century

germinal period The period of prenatal development that takes place in the first two weeks after conception. It includes the creation of the zygote, continued cell division, and the attachment of the zygote to the uterine wall.

blastocyst The inner layer of cells that develops during the germinal period. These cells later develop into the embryo.

trophoblast The outer layer of cells that develops in the germinal period. These cells provide nutrition and support for the embryo.

embryonic period The period of prenatal development that occurs two to eight weeks after conception. During the embryonic period, the rate of cell differentiation intensifies, support systems for the cells form, and organs appear.

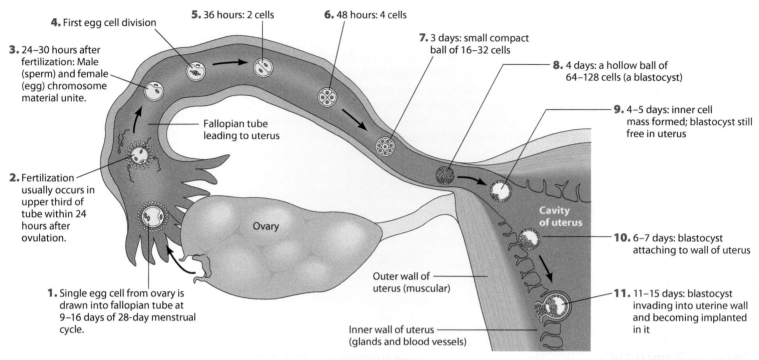

FIGURE **3.1**

SIGNIFICANT DEVELOPMENTS IN THE GERMINAL PERIOD. Just one week after conception, cells of the blastocyst have already begun specializing. The germination period ends when the blastocyst attaches to the uterine wall. *Which of the steps shown in the drawing occur in the laboratory when IVF (described in Chapter 2) is used?*

middle layer, which will become the circulatory system, bones, muscles, excretory system, and reproductive system. The *ectoderm* is the outermost layer, which will become the nervous system and brain, sensory receptors (ears, nose, and eyes, for example), and skin parts (hair and nails, for example). Every body part eventually develops from these three layers. The endoderm primarily produces internal body parts, the mesoderm primarily produces parts that surround the internal areas, and the ectoderm primarily produces surface parts.

As the embryo's three layers form, life-support systems for the embryo develop rapidly. These life-support systems include the amnion, the umbilical cord (both of which develop from the fertilized egg, not the mother's body), and the placenta. The **amnion** is like a bag or an envelope and contains a clear fluid in which the developing embryo floats. The amniotic fluid provides an environment that is temperature and humidity controlled as well as shock-proof. The **umbilical cord,** which contains two arteries and one vein, connects the baby to the placenta. The **placenta** consists of a disk-shaped group of tissues in which small blood vessels from the mother and the offspring intertwine but do not join.

Figure 3.2 illustrates the placenta, the umbilical cord, and the blood flow in the expectant mother and developing organism. Very small molecules—oxygen, water, salt, food from the mother's blood, as well as carbon dioxide and digestive wastes from the offspring's blood—pass back and forth between the mother and embryo or fetus (Woolett, 2011). Virtually any drug or chemical substance the pregnant woman ingests can cross the placenta to some degree, unless it is metabolized or altered during passage, or is too large (Hutson & others, 2013; Iqbal & others, 2012). A recent study revealed that cigarette smoke weakened and increased the oxidative stress of fetal membranes, from which the placenta develops (Menon & others, 2011). Large molecules that cannot pass through the placental wall include red blood cells and harmful substances, such as most bacteria, maternal wastes, and hormones. The complex mechanisms that govern the transfer of substances across the placental barrier are still not entirely understood (Matlow & others, 2013; Saunders, Liddelow, & Dziegielewska, 2012; Yuen & others, 2013).

By the time most women know they are pregnant, the major organs of the developing offspring have begun to form. **Organogenesis** is the name given to the process of organ

amnion Prenatal life-support system that is a bag or envelope containing a clear fluid in which the developing embryo floats.

umbilical cord A life-support system that contains two arteries and one vein and connects the baby to the placenta.

placenta A life-support system that consists of a disk-shaped group of tissues in which small blood vessels from the mother and offspring intertwine.

organogenesis Organ formation that takes place during the first two months of prenatal development.

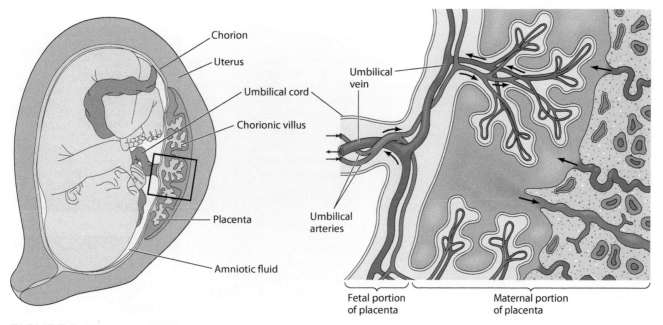

FIGURE **3.2**

THE PLACENTA AND THE UMBILICAL CORD. The area bound by the square in the right half of the illustration is enlarged. Arrows indicate the direction of blood flow. Maternal blood flows through the uterine arteries to the spaces housing the placenta, and it returns through the uterine veins to the maternal circulation. Fetal blood flows through the umbilical arteries into the capillaries of the placenta and returns through the umbilical vein to the fetal circulation. The exchange of materials takes place across the layer separating the maternal and fetal blood supplies, so the bloods never come into contact. *What is known about how the placental barrier works and its importance?*

formation during the first two months of prenatal development. While they are being formed, the organs are especially vulnerable to environmental changes (Wei & others, 2013). In the third week after conception, the neural tube that eventually becomes the spinal cord forms. At about 21 days, eyes begin to appear, and at 24 days the cells for the heart begin to differentiate. During the fourth week, the urogenital system becomes apparent and arm and leg buds emerge. Four chambers of the heart take shape, and blood vessels appear. From the fifth to the eighth week, arms and legs differentiate further; at this time, the face starts to form but still is not very recognizable. The intestinal tract develops and the facial structures fuse. At eight weeks, the developing organism weighs about 1/30 ounce and is just over 1 inch long.

The Fetal Period   The **fetal period,** lasting about seven months, is the prenatal period between two months after conception and birth in typical pregnancies. Growth and development continue their dramatic course during this time.

Three months after conception, the fetus is about 3 inches long and weighs about 3 ounces. It has become active, moving its arms and legs, opening and closing its mouth, and moving its head. The face, forehead, eyelids, nose, and chin are distinguishable, as are the upper arms, lower arms, hands, and lower limbs. In most cases, the genitals can be identified as male or female. By the end of the fourth month of pregnancy, the fetus has grown to 6 inches in length and weighs 4 to 7 ounces. At this time, a growth spurt occurs in the body's lower parts. For the first time, the mother can feel arm and leg movements.

By the end of the fifth month, the fetus is about 12 inches long and weighs close to a pound. Structures of the skin have formed—toenails and fingernails, for example. The fetus is more active, showing a preference for a particular position in the womb. By the end of the sixth month, the fetus is about 14 inches long and has gained another half pound to a pound. The eyes and eyelids are completely formed, and a fine layer of hair covers the head. A grasping reflex is present and irregular breathing movements occur.

As early as six months of pregnancy (about 24 to 25 weeks after conception), the fetus for the first time has a chance of surviving outside of the womb—that is, it is *viable.* Infants who are born early, or between 24 and 37 weeks of pregnancy, usually need help breathing

fetal period The period from two months after conception until birth, lasting about seven months in typical pregnancies.

First trimester (first 3 months)

Conception to 4 weeks

- Is less than $1/10$ inch long
- Beginning development of spinal cord, nervous system, gastrointestinal system, heart, and lungs
- Amniotic sac envelops the preliminary tissues of entire body
- Is called a "zygote"

8 weeks

- Is just over 1 inch long
- Face is forming with rudimentary eyes, ears, mouth, and tooth buds
- Arms and legs are moving
- Brain is forming
- Fetal heartbeat is detectable with ultrasound
- Is called an "embryo"

12 weeks

- Is about 3 inches long and weighs about 1 ounce
- Can move arms, legs, fingers, and toes
- Fingerprints are present
- Can smile, frown, suck, and swallow
- Sex is distinguishable
- Can urinate
- Is called a "fetus"

Second trimester (middle 3 months)

16 weeks

- Is about 6 inches long and weighs about 4 to 7 ounces
- Heartbeat is strong
- Skin is thin, transparent
- Downy hair (lanugo) covers body
- Fingernails and toenails are forming
- Has coordinated movements; is able to roll over in amniotic fluid

20 weeks

- Is about 12 inches long and weighs close to 1 pound
- Heartbeat is audible with ordinary stethoscope
- Sucks thumb
- Hiccups
- Hair, eyelashes, eyebrows are present

24 weeks

- Is about 14 inches long and weighs 1 to 1½ pounds
- Skin is wrinkled and covered with protective coating (vernix caseosa)
- Eyes are open
- Waste matter is collected in bowel
- Has strong grip

Third trimester (last 3 months)

28 weeks

- Is about 16 inches long and weighs about 3 pounds
- Is adding body fat
- Is very active
- Rudimentary breathing movements are present

32 weeks

- Is 16½ to 18 inches long and weighs 4 to 5 pounds
- Has periods of sleep and wakefulness
- Responds to sounds
- May assume the birth position
- Bones of head are soft and flexible
- Iron is being stored in liver

36 to 38 weeks

- Is 19 to 20 inches long and weighs 6 to 7½ pounds
- Skin is less wrinkled
- Vernix caseosa is thick
- Lanugo is mostly gone
- Is less active
- Is gaining immunities from mother

FIGURE **3.3**

THE THREE TRIMESTERS OF PRENATAL DEVELOPMENT. Both the germinal and embryonic periods occur during the first trimester. The end of the first trimester as well as the second and third trimesters are part of the fetal period.

neurons Nerve cells, which handle information processing at the cellular level in the brain.

teratogen From the Greek word *tera,* meaning "monster," this term refers to any agent that causes a birth defect. Teratology is the field of study that investigates the causes of birth defects.

because their lungs are not yet fully mature. By the end of the seventh month, the fetus is about 16 inches long and weighs about 3 pounds.

During the last two months of prenatal development, fatty tissues develop and the functioning of various organ systems—heart and kidneys, for example—steps up. During the eighth and ninth months, the fetus grows longer and gains substantial weight—about another 4 pounds. At birth, the average American baby weighs 7½ pounds and is about 20 inches long.

Figure 3.3 gives an overview of the main events during prenatal development. Notice that instead of describing development in terms of germinal, embryonic, and fetal periods, Figure 3.3 divides prenatal development into equal periods of three months, called *trimesters.* Remember that the three trimesters are not the same as the three prenatal periods we have discussed. The germinal and embryonic periods occur in the first trimester. The fetal period begins toward the end of the first trimester and continues through the second and third trimesters. Viability (the possibility of surviving outside the womb) occurs at the very end of the second trimester.

The Brain   One of the most remarkable aspects of the prenatal period is the development of the brain (Nelson, 2012). By the time babies are born, they have approximately 100 billion **neurons,** or nerve cells, which handle information processing at the cellular level in the brain. During prenatal development, neurons spend time moving to the right locations and are starting to become connected. The basic architecture of the human brain is assembled during the first two trimesters of prenatal development. In typical development, the third trimester of prenatal development and the first two years of postnatal life are characterized by connectivity and functioning of neurons (Moulson & Nelson, 2008).

As the human embryo develops inside its mother's womb, the nervous system begins forming as a long, hollow tube located on the embryo's back. This pear-shaped *neural tube,* which forms at about 18 to 24 days after conception, develops out of the ectoderm. The tube closes at the top and bottom at about 24 days after conception. Figure 3.4 shows that the nervous system still has a tubular appearance six weeks after conception.

Two birth defects related to a failure of the neural tube to close are anencephaly and spina bifida. The highest regions of the brain fail to develop when fetuses have anencephaly or when the head end of the neural tube fails to close. Such infants die in the womb, during childbirth, or shortly after birth (Jin & others, 2013). Spina bifida results in varying degrees of paralysis of the lower limbs. Individuals with spina bifida usually need assistive devices such as crutches, braces, or wheelchairs. A strategy that can help to prevent neural tube defects is for women to take adequate amounts of the B vitamin folic acid, a topic we will discuss later in this chapter (Collins & others, 2011). And both maternal diabetes and obesity place the fetus at risk for developing neural tube defects (McGuire, Dyson, & Renfrew, 2010).

In a normal pregnancy, once the neural tube has closed, a massive proliferation of new immature neurons begins to takes place at about the fifth prenatal week and continues throughout the remainder of the prenatal period. The generation of new neurons is called *neurogenesis* (Kronenberg & others, 2010). At the peak of neurogenesis, it is estimated that as many as 200,000 neurons are being generated every minute.

At approximately 6 to 24 weeks after conception, *neuronal migration* occurs (Nelson, 2012). This involves cells moving outward from their point of origin to their appropriate locations and creating the different levels, structures, and regions of the brain (Cozzi & others, 2010). Once a cell has migrated to its target destination, it must mature and develop a more complex structure.

At about the 23rd prenatal week, connections between neurons begin to occur, a process that continues postnatally (Kostovic, Judas, & Sedmak, 2011). We will have much more to say about the structure of neurons, their connectivity, and the development of the infant brain in Chapter 4.

TERATOLOGY AND HAZARDS TO PRENATAL DEVELOPMENT

For Alex, the baby discussed at the opening of this chapter, the course of prenatal development went smoothly. His mother's womb protected him as he developed. Despite this protection, the environment can affect the embryo or fetus in many well-documented ways.

General Principles   A **teratogen** is any agent that can potentially cause a birth defect or negatively alter cognitive and behavioral outcomes. (The word comes from the Greek word *tera,* meaning "monster.") So many teratogens exist that practically every fetus is exposed to at least some teratogens. For this reason, it is difficult to determine which teratogen causes which problem. In addition, it may take a long time for the effects of a teratogen to show up. Only about half of all potential effects appear at birth.

Yelyi Nordone, 12, of New York City, recently cast her line out into the pond during Camp Spifida at Camp Victory, near Millville, Pennsylvania. Camp Spifida is a week-long residential camp for children with spina bifida.

- - - - - - - - - - ->

developmental **connection**

Brain Development

At birth, the brain's weight is approximately 25 percent of its adult weight. Chapter 4, p. 113

FIGURE **3.4**

EARLY FORMATION OF THE NERVOUS SYSTEM. The photograph shows the primitive, tubular appearance of the nervous system at six weeks in the human embryo.

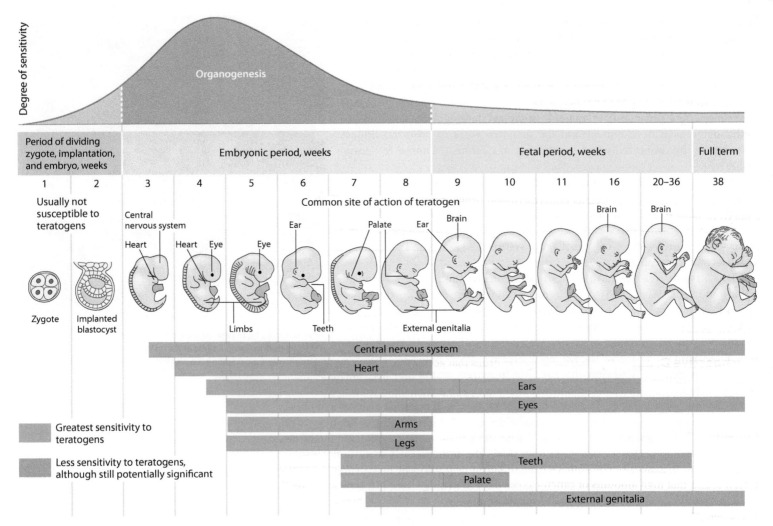

Degree of sensitivity

Organogenesis

Period of dividing zygote, implantation, and embryo, weeks		Embryonic period, weeks						Fetal period, weeks					Full term
1	2	3	4	5	6	7	8	9	10	11	16	20–36	38

Usually not susceptible to teratogens

Common site of action of teratogen

Central nervous system · Heart · Eye · Ear · Palate · Brain · Limbs · Teeth · External genitalia · Brain

Zygote · Implanted blastocyst

		Central nervous system											
			Heart										
				Ears									
			Eyes										
			Arms										
			Legs										
				Teeth									
				Palate									
			External genitalia										

Greatest sensitivity to teratogens

Less sensitivity to teratogens, although still potentially significant

FIGURE 3.5

TERATOGENS AND THE TIMING OF THEIR EFFECTS ON PRENATAL DEVELOPMENT. The danger of structural defects caused by teratogens is greatest early in embryonic development. The period of organogenesis (red color) lasts for about six weeks. Later assaults by teratogens (blue-green color) mainly occur in the fetal period and instead of causing structural damage are more likely to stunt growth or cause problems of organ function.

The field of study that investigates the causes of birth defects is called *teratology* (Hyoun & others, 2012). Some exposures to teratogens do not cause physical birth defects but can alter the developing brain and influence cognitive and behavioral functioning, in which case the field of study is called *behavioral teratology*.

The dose, genetic susceptibility, and the time of exposure to a particular teratogen influence both the severity of the damage to an embryo or fetus and the type of defect:

- *Dose*. The dose effect is rather obvious—the greater the dose of an agent, such as a drug, the greater the effect.
- *Genetic susceptibility*. The type or severity of abnormalities caused by a teratogen is linked to the genotype of the pregnant woman and the genotype of the embryo or fetus (Charlet & others, 2012). For example, how a mother metabolizes a particular drug can influence the degree to which the drug effects are transmitted to the embryo or fetus. The extent to which an embryo or fetus is vulnerable to a teratogen may also depend on its genotype (Dufour-Rainfray & others, 2011). Also, for unknown reasons, male fetuses are far more likely to be affected by teratogens than female fetuses.
- *Time of exposure*. Teratogen exposure does more damage when it occurs at some points in development than at others. Damage during the germinal period may even prevent implantation. In general, the embryonic period is more vulnerable than the fetal period (Levine & O'Connor, 2012).

Figure 3.5 summarizes additional information about the effects of time of exposure to a teratogen. The probability of a structural defect is greatest early in the embryonic period, when organs are being formed (Holmes, 2011). Each body structure has its own critical period of formation. Recall from Chapter 1 that a critical period is a fixed time period very early in development during which certain experiences or events can have a long-lasting effect on development. The critical period for the nervous system (week 3) is earlier than for arms and legs (weeks 4 and 5).

After organogenesis is complete, teratogens are less likely to cause anatomical defects. Instead, exposure during the fetal period is more likely to stunt growth or to create problems in the way organs function. To examine some key teratogens and their effects, let's begin with drugs.

Prescription and Nonprescription Drugs   Many U.S. women are given prescriptions for drugs while they are pregnant—especially antibiotics, analgesics, and asthma medications. Prescription as well as nonprescription drugs, however, may have effects on the embryo or fetus that the women never imagine.

Prescription drugs that can function as teratogens include antibiotics, such as streptomycin and tetracycline; some antidepressants; certain hormones, such as progestin and synthetic estrogen; and Accutane (which often is prescribed for acne) (Koren & Nordeng, 2012).

Nonprescription drugs that can be harmful include diet pills and high dosages of aspirin. However, recent research indicated that low doses of aspirin pose no harm for the fetus but that high doses can contribute to maternal and fetal bleeding (Bennett, Bagot, & Arya, 2012).

Psychoactive Drugs   *Psychoactive drugs* are drugs that act on the nervous system to alter states of consciousness, modify perceptions, and change moods. Examples include caffeine, alcohol, and nicotine, as well as illicit drugs such as cocaine, methamphetamine, marijuana, and heroin.

Caffeine   People often consume caffeine when they drink coffee, tea, or colas, or when they eat chocolate. Although the U.S. Food and Drug Administration recommends that pregnant women either not consume caffeine or consume it only sparingly, a recent research review found that high amounts of caffeine consumption by pregnant women do not increase the risk of miscarriage, congenital malformations, or growth retardation (Brent, Christian, & Diener, 2011).

Alcohol   Heavy drinking by pregnant women can be devastating to their offspring (Brocardo, Gil-Mohapel, & Christie, 2011; Frost, Gist, & Adriano, 2011). **Fetal alcohol spectrum disorders (FASD)** are a cluster of abnormalities and problems that appear in the offspring of mothers who drink alcohol heavily during pregnancy. The abnormalities include facial deformities and defective limbs, face, and heart (Arnold & others, 2013; Paintner, Williams, & Burd, 2012). Some children with FASD have these body malformations, but others don't. Most children with FASD have learning problems, and many are below average in intelligence with some having an intellectual disability (Paintner, Williams, & Burd, 2012). A recent study revealed that children with FASD have deficiencies in the brain pathways involved in working memory (Diwadkar & others, 2012). Although women who drink heavily during pregnancy are at a higher risk of having a child with FASD, not all pregnant heavy drinkers have children with FASD.

What are some guidelines for alcohol use during pregnancy? Even drinking just one or two servings of beer or wine or one serving of hard liquor a few days a week may have negative effects on the fetus, although it is generally agreed that this level of alcohol use will not cause fetal alcohol spectrum disorders (Valenzuela & others, 2012). The U.S. Surgeon General recommends that no alcohol be consumed during pregnancy. And research suggests that it may not be wise to consume alcohol at the time of conception. One study revealed that intakes of alcohol by both men and women during the weeks of conception increased the risk of early pregnancy loss (Henriksen & others, 2004).

Nicotine   Cigarette smoking by pregnant women can also adversely influence prenatal development, birth, and postnatal development. Preterm births and low birth weights, fetal and neonatal deaths, and respiratory problems and sudden infant death syndrome (SIDS, also known as crib death) are all more common among the offspring of mothers

Fetal alcohol spectrum disorders (FASD) are characterized by a number of physical abnormalities and learning problems. Notice the wide-set eyes, flat cheekbones, and thin upper lip in this child with FASD.

fetal alcohol spectrum disorders (FASD) A cluster of abnormalities and problems that appear in the offspring of mothers who drink alcohol heavily during pregnancy.

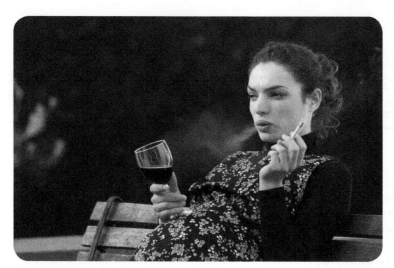

What are some links between expectant mothers' drinking and cigarette smoking and outcomes for their offspring?

who smoked during pregnancy (Brown & others, 2013; Burstyn & others, 2012). Researchers also have found that maternal smoking during pregnancy is a risk factor for the development of attention deficit hyperactivity disorder in children (Abbott & Winzer-Serhan, 2012; Sagiv & others, 2013). Researchers also have documented that environmental tobacco smoke is linked to an increased risk of low birth weight in offspring (Leonardo-Bee & others, 2008) and to diminished ovarian functioning in female offspring (Kilic & others, 2012). Further, a recent study revealed that environmental tobacco smoke was associated with 114 deregulations, especially those involving immune functioning, in the fetal cells of offspring (Votavova & others, 2012). And a recent meta-analysis indicated that maternal smoking during pregnancy was linked to a modest increase in risk for childhood non-Hodgkin lymphoma (Antonopoulos & others, 2011).

Cocaine   Does cocaine use during pregnancy harm the developing embryo and fetus? A recent research review concluded that cocaine quickly crosses the placenta to reach the fetus (De Giovanni & Marchetti, 2012). The most consistent finding is that cocaine exposure during prenatal development is associated with reduced birth weight, length, and head circumference (Gouin & others, 2011). Also, in other studies, prenatal cocaine exposure has been linked to lower arousal, less effective self-regulation, higher excitability, and lower quality of reflexes at 1 month of age (Ackerman, Riggins, & Black, 2010; Lester & others, 2002); to impaired motor development in the second year of life (Richardson, Goldschmidt, & Willford, 2008); to slower growth rate through 10 years of age (Richardson, Goldschmidt, & Willford, 2008); to elevated blood pressure at 9 years of age (Shankaran & others, 2010); to impaired language development and information processing (Beeghly & others, 2006), including attention deficits (especially impulsivity) (Accornero & others, 2006; Richardson & others, 2011); to learning disabilities at age 7 (Morrow & others, 2006); to increased likelihood of being in a special education program that involves support services (Levine & others, 2008); and to increased behavioral problems, especially externalizing problems such as high rates of aggression and delinquency (Minnes & others, 2010; Richardson & others, 2011).

Some researchers argue that these findings should be interpreted cautiously. Why? Because other factors in the lives of pregnant women who use cocaine (such as poverty, malnutrition, and other substance abuse) often cannot be ruled out as possible contributors to the problems found in their children (Hurt & others, 2005; Messiah & others, 2011). For example, cocaine users are more likely than nonusers to smoke cigarettes, use marijuana, drink alcohol, and take amphetamines. Despite these cautions, the weight of research evidence indicates that children born to mothers who use cocaine are likely to have neurological and cognitive deficits (Cain, Bornick, & Whiteman, 2013; Field, 2007; Mayer & Zhang, 2009; Richardson & others, 2011). Cocaine use by pregnant women is never recommended.

This baby was exposed to cocaine prenatally. *What are some of the possible effects on development of being exposed to cocaine prenatally?*

Methamphetamine   Methamphetamine, like cocaine, is a stimulant, speeding up an individual's nervous system. Babies born to mothers who use methamphetamine, or "meth," during pregnancy are at risk for a number of problems, including high infant mortality, low birth weight, and developmental and behavioral problems (Piper & others, 2011). A recent study revealed that prenatal meth exposure was associated with smaller head circumference, increased rates of neonatal intensive care unit (NICU) admission, and referral to child protective services (Shah & others, 2012). And another study found that prenatal exposure to meth was linked to less brain activation in a number of areas, especially the frontal lobes, in 7- to 15-year-olds (Roussotte & others, 2011).

Marijuana   An increasing number of studies find that marijuana use by pregnant women also has negative outcomes for offspring. For example, researchers found that prenatal marijuana exposure was related to lower intelligence in children (Goldschmidt & others, 2008). Another study indicated that prenatal exposure to marijuana was linked to marijuana use at 14 years of age (Day, Goldschmidt, & Thomas, 2006). In sum, marijuana use is not recommended for pregnant women.

Heroin   It is well documented that infants whose mothers are addicted to heroin show several behavioral difficulties at birth (Ortigosa Gomez & others, 2011). The difficulties include withdrawal symptoms, such as tremors, irritability, abnormal crying, disturbed sleep, and impaired motor control. Many still show behavioral problems at their first birthday, and attention deficits may appear later in development. The most common treatment for heroin addiction, methadone, is associated with very severe withdrawal symptoms in newborns (Blandthorn, Forster, & Love, 2011).

Incompatible Blood Types   Incompatibility between the mother's and father's blood types poses another risk to prenatal development. Blood types are created by differences in the surface structure of red blood cells. One type of difference in the surface of red blood cells creates the familiar blood groups—A, B, O, and AB. A second difference creates what is called Rh-positive and Rh-negative blood. If a surface marker, called the *Rh-factor,* is present in an individual's red blood cells, the person is said to be Rh-positive; if the Rh-marker is not present, the person is said to be Rh-negative. If a pregnant woman is Rh-negative and her partner is Rh-positive, the fetus may be Rh-positive. If the fetus' blood is Rh-positive and the mother's is Rh-negative, the mother's immune system may produce antibodies that will attack the fetus. This can result in any number of problems, including miscarriage or stillbirth, anemia, jaundice, heart defects, brain damage, or death soon after birth (Li & others, 2010).

Generally, the first Rh-positive baby of an Rh-negative mother is not at risk, but with each subsequent pregnancy the risk increases. A vaccine (RhoGAM) may be given to the mother within three days of the first child's birth to prevent her body from making antibodies that will attack any future Rh-positive fetuses in subsequent pregnancies. Also, babies affected by Rh incompatibility can be given blood transfusions before or immediately after birth (Flegal, 2007).

Environmental Hazards   Many aspects of our modern industrial world can endanger the embryo or fetus. Some specific hazards to the embryo or fetus include radiation, toxic wastes, and other chemical pollutants (Wiesel & others, 2011).

X-ray radiation can affect the developing embryo or fetus, especially in the first several weeks after conception, when women do not yet know they are pregnant. Women and their physicians should weigh the risks against the benefits of an X-ray when an actual or potential pregnancy is involved (Rajaraman & others, 2011). However, a routine diagnostic X-ray of a body area other than the abdomen, with the woman's abdomen protected by a lead apron, is generally considered safe (Brent, 2009, 2011).

Environmental pollutants and toxic wastes are also sources of danger to unborn children. Among the dangerous pollutants are carbon monoxide, mercury, and lead, as well as certain fertilizers and pesticides.

Maternal Diseases   Maternal diseases and infections can produce defects in offspring by crossing the placental barrier, or they can cause damage during birth. Rubella (German measles) is one disease that can cause prenatal defects. Women who plan to have children should have a blood test before they become pregnant to determine whether they are immune to the disease (Rasmussen, 2012).

Syphilis (a sexually transmitted infection) is more damaging later in prenatal development—four months or more after conception. Damage includes eye lesions, which can cause blindness, and skin lesions.

Another infection that has received widespread attention is genital herpes. Newborns contract this virus when they are delivered through the birth canal of a mother who has genital herpes (Nigro & others, 2011). About one-third of babies delivered through an infected birth canal die; another one-fourth become brain damaged. If an active case of genital herpes is detected in a pregnant woman close to her delivery date, a cesarean section can be performed (in which the infant is delivered through an incision in the mother's abdomen) to keep the virus from infecting the newborn (Patel & others, 2011).

An explosion at the Chernobyl nuclear power plant in the Ukraine produced radioactive contamination that spread to surrounding areas. Thousands of infants were born with health problems and deformities as a result of the nuclear contamination, including this boy whose arm did not form. *Other than radioactive contamination, what are some other types of environmental hazards to prenatal development?*

Because the fetus depends entirely on its mother for nutrition, it is important for the pregnant woman to have good nutritional habits. In Kenya, this government clinic provides pregnant women with information about how their diet can influence the health of their fetus and offspring. *What might the information about diet be like?*

AIDS is a sexually transmitted infection that is caused by the human immunodeficiency virus (HIV), which destroys the body's immune system. A mother can infect her offspring with HIV/AIDS in three ways: (1) during gestation across the placenta, (2) during delivery through contact with maternal blood or fluids, and (3) postpartum (after birth) through breast feeding. The transmission of AIDS through breast feeding is especially a problem in many developing countries (UNICEF, 2012). Babies born to HIV-infected mothers can be (1) infected and symptomatic (show HIV symptoms), (2) infected but asymptomatic (not show HIV symptoms), or (3) not infected at all. An infant who is infected and asymptomatic may still develop HIV symptoms until 15 months of age.

The more widespread disease of diabetes, characterized by high levels of sugar in the blood, also affects offspring (Desai, Beall, & Ross, 2013; El Hajj & others). A large-scale study revealed that twice as many women and five times as many adolescents giving birth had diabetes in 2005 as in 1999 (Lawrence & others, 2008).

A research review indicated that newborns with physical defects are more likely to have diabetic mothers (Eriksson, 2009). Women who have gestational diabetes also may deliver very large infants (weighing 10 pounds or more), and these infants are at risk for diabetes themselves (Gluck & others, 2009).

Other Parental Factors   So far we have discussed a number of drugs, environmental hazards, maternal diseases, and incompatible blood types that can harm the embryo or fetus. Here we will explore other characteristics of the mother and father that can affect prenatal and child development, including nutrition, age, and emotional states and stress.

Maternal Diet and Nutrition   A developing embryo or fetus depends completely on its mother for nutrition, which comes from the mother's blood. The nutritional status of the embryo or fetus is determined by the mother's total caloric intake and by her intake of proteins, vitamins, and minerals. Children born to malnourished mothers are more likely than other children to be malformed.

Being overweight before and during pregnancy can also put the embryo or fetus at risk, and an increasing number of pregnant women in the United States are overweight (Marengo, Farag, & Canfield, 2013). Maternal obesity adversely affects pregnancy outcomes through elevated rates of hypertension, diabetes, respiratory complications, and infections in the mother (Nodine & Hastings-Tolsma, 2012). Management of obesity that includes weight loss and increased exercise prior to pregnancy is likely to benefit the mother and the baby (Vesco & others, 2012).

One aspect of maternal nutrition that is important for normal prenatal development is consumption of folic acid, a B-complex vitamin (Waddell, 2012). A study of more than 34,000 women indicated that taking folic acid either alone or as part of a multivitamin for at least one year prior to conceiving was linked with a 70 percent lower risk of delivering at 20 to 28 weeks and a 50 percent lower risk of delivering at 28 to 32 weeks (Bukowski & others, 2008). Another recent study revealed that toddlers of mothers who did not use folic acid supplements in the first trimester of pregnancy had more behavior problems (Roza & others, 2010). Also, as indicated earlier in the chapter, a lack of folic acid is related to neural tube defects in offspring, such as spina bifida (a defect in the spinal cord) (Stern & others, 2011). The U.S. Department of Health and Human Services (2009) recommends that pregnant women consume a minimum of 400 micrograms of folic acid per day (about twice the amount the average woman gets in one day). Orange juice and spinach are examples of foods rich in folic acid.

Eating fish is often recommended as part of a healthy diet, but pollution has made many types of fish a risky choice for pregnant women. Some fish contain high levels of mercury, which is released into the air both naturally and by industrial pollution (Wells, 2011). When mercury falls into the water it can become toxic and accumulate in large fish, such as shark, swordfish, king mackerel, and some species of large tuna (American Pregnancy Association, 2013; Mayo Clinic, 2013). Mercury is easily transferred across the

- - - - - - - - - - ▶

developmental **connection**

Nutrition and Weight

What are some key factors that influence whether children become obese? Chapter 4, p. 130

placenta, and the embryo's developing brain and nervous system are highly sensitive to the metal. Researchers have found that prenatal mercury exposure is linked to adverse outcomes, including miscarriage, preterm birth, and lower intelligence (Triche & Hossain, 2007).

Maternal Age When possible harmful effects on the fetus and infant are considered, two maternal ages are of special interest: adolescence and 35 years and older (Malizia, Hacker, & Penzias, 2009; Rudang & others, 2012). The mortality rate of infants born to adolescent mothers is double that of infants born to mothers in their twenties. Adequate prenatal care decreases the probability that a child born to an adolescent girl will have physical problems. However, among women in all age groups adolescents are the least likely to obtain prenatal care from clinics and health services.

What are some of the risks for infants born to adolescent mothers?

Maternal age is also linked to the risk that a child will have Down syndrome (Allen & others, 2009; Ghosh & others, 2010). As discussed in Chapter 2, an individual with *Down syndrome* has distinctive facial characteristics, short limbs, and retardation of motor and mental abilities. A baby with Down syndrome rarely is born to a mother 16 to 34 years of age. However, when the mother reaches 40 years of age, the probability is slightly over 1 in 100 that a baby born to her will have Down syndrome, and by age 50 it is almost 1 in 10. When mothers are 35 years and older, risks also increase for low birth weight, preterm delivery, and fetal death (Koo & others, 2012).

We still have much to learn about the role of the mother's age in pregnancy and childbirth. As women remain active, exercise regularly, and are careful about their nutrition, their reproductive systems may remain healthier at older ages than was thought possible in the past.

Emotional States and Stress When a pregnant woman experiences intense fears, anxieties, and other emotions or negative mood states, physiological changes occur that may affect her fetus (Breedlove & Fryzelka, 2011). A mother's stress may also influence the fetus indirectly by increasing the likelihood that the mother will engage in unhealthy behaviors such as taking drugs and receiving poor prenatal care.

High maternal anxiety and stress during pregnancy can have long-term consequences for the offspring (Howerton & Bayle, 2012). A research review indicated that pregnant women with high levels of stress are at increased risk for having a child with emotional or cognitive problems, attention deficit hyperactivity disorder (ADHD), and language delay (Taige & others, 2007). A recent study of more than 30,000 offspring revealed that across the nine months of pregnancy, their risk of being born preterm was highest when maternal exposure to stress occurred during the fifth and sixth months of pregnancy (Class & others, 2011).

How do pregnant women's emotional states and stress affect prenatal development and birth?

Might maternal depression also have an adverse effect on birth outcomes? A recent research review concluded that maternal depression during pregnancy is linked to preterm birth (Dunkel Schetter, 2011). Another recent research review indicated that untreated prenatal maternal depression is associated with negative outcomes for offspring, including reduced empathy in childhood (Davalos, Yadon, & Tregellas, 2012).

Paternal Factors So far, we have discussed how characteristics of the mother—such as drug use, disease, diet and nutrition, age, and emotional states—can influence prenatal development and the development of the child. Might there also be some paternal risk factors? Indeed, there are several. Men's exposure to lead, radiation, certain pesticides, and petrochemicals may cause abnormalities in sperm that lead to miscarriage or diseases such as childhood cancer (Cordier, 2008). The father's smoking during the mother's pregnancy also can cause problems for the offspring. In one study, heavy paternal smoking was associated with the risk of early pregnancy loss (Venners & others, 2004). This negative outcome may be related to exposure to secondhand smoke. And in a recent study, paternal smoking around the time of the child's conception was linked to an increased risk of the child developing leukemia (Milne & others, 2012). Also, a recent research review concluded that there is an increased risk of spontaneous abortion, autism, and schizophrenic disorders when the father is 40 years of age and older (Reproductive Endocrinology and Infertility Committee & others, 2011). And in another study, children born to fathers who were 40 years of age or older had increased risk of developing autism because of an increase in random gene mutation in the older fathers (Kong & others, 2012).

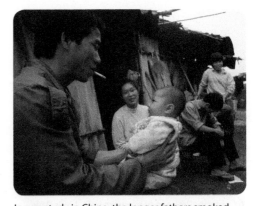

In one study in China, the longer fathers smoked, the greater the risk that their children would develop cancer (Ji & others, 1997). What are some other paternal factors that can influence the development of the fetus and the child?

PRENATAL CARE

Although prenatal care varies enormously, it usually involves a defined schedule of visits for medical care, which typically includes screening for manageable conditions and treatable diseases that can affect the baby or the mother (London & others, 2011). In addition to medical care, prenatal programs often include comprehensive educational, social, and nutritional services (Ickovics & others, 2011).

Exercise increasingly is recommended as part of a comprehensive prenatal care program (Field, 2012; Field & others, 2013). Exercise during pregnancy helps prevent constipation, conditions the body, and is associated with a more positive mental state (Robledo-Colonia & others, 2012; Ruchat & others, 2012). A recent experimental study found that pregnant women who completed a 3-month supervised aerobic exercise program showed improved health-related quality of life, including better physical functioning and reduced bodily pain, than their counterparts who did not participate in the program (Montoya Arizabaleta & others, 2010). Another recent study revealed that exercise during pregnancy improved mothers' perception of their health (Barakat & others, 2011). However, it is important to remember not to overdo it. A recent study of almost 1,500 pregnant women found that the incidence of exercise-related injuries was low (Vladutiu, Evenson, & Marshall, 2010). Pregnant women should always consult their physician before starting any exercise program (Olson & others, 2009).

Does prenatal care matter? Information about pregnancy, labor, delivery, and caring for the newborn can be especially valuable for first-time mothers (Davidson & others, 2012; Gabbe & others, 2012). A recent study revealed that group prenatal care provided pregnant women with a broad network of social support (McNeil & others, 2012).

Prenatal care is also very important for women in poverty and immigrant women because it links them with other social services (Lyberg & others, 2012). An innovative program that is rapidly expanding in the United States is CenteringPregnancy (Ickovics & others, 2011; Steming, 2008). This program is relationship-centered and provides complete prenatal care in a group setting. CenteringPregnancy replaces traditional 15-minute physician visits with 90-minute peer group support sessions and self-examination led by a physician or certified nurse-midwife. Groups of up to 10 women (and often their partners) meet regularly beginning at 12 to 16 weeks of pregnancy. The sessions emphasize empowering women to

How might a woman's exercise in pregnancy benefit her health?

A CenteringPregnancy program in St. Louis Park, Minnesota. This rapidly expanding program alters routine prenatal care by bringing women out of exam rooms and into relationship-oriented groups.

play an active role in experiencing a positive pregnancy. A recent study revealed that participants in CenteringPregnancy groups made more prenatal visits, had higher breast feeding rates, and were more satisfied with their prenatal care than women in individual care (Klima & others, 2009). In another recent study, high-stress women were randomly assigned to a CenteringPregnancy Plus group, group prenatal care, or standard individual care from 18 weeks gestation to birth (Ickovics & others, 2011). The most stressed women in the CenteringPregnancy Plus group showed increased self-esteem and decreased stress and social conflict in their third trimester of pregnancy; their levels of social conflict and depression also were lower at one year postpartum.

Some prenatal programs for parents focus on home visitation (Issel & others, 2011; Lee & others, 2009). A recent research review concluded that prenatal home visits were linked to improved use of prenatal care, although there was less evidence that they improve newborns' birth weight (Issel & others, 2011). Research evaluations indicate that the most successful home visitation program is the Nurse Family Partnership created by David Olds and his colleagues (2004, 2007; Zielinski, Eckenrode, & Olds, 2009). The Nurse Family Partnership involves home visits by trained nurses beginning in the second or third trimester of prenatal development. The extensive program consists of approximately 50 home visits from the prenatal period through 2 years of age. The home visits focus on the mother's health, access to health care, parenting, and improvement of the mother's life by providing her with guidance in education, work, and relationships. Research revealed that the Nurse Family Partnership has numerous positive outcomes including fewer subsequent pregnancies, better work circumstances, and greater stability in relationship partners for the mother and improved academic success and social development for the child (Olds & others, 2004, 2007).

NORMAL PRENATAL DEVELOPMENT

Much of our discussion so far in this chapter has focused on what can go wrong with prenatal development. Prospective parents should take steps to avoid the vulnerabilities to fetal development that we have described. But it is important to keep in mind that most of the time prenatal development does not go awry and development occurs along the positive path that we described at the beginning of the chapter.

Review *Connect* Reflect

 Describe prenatal development.

Review

- What is the course of prenatal development?
- What is teratology, and what are some of the main hazards to prenatal development?
- What are some good prenatal care strategies?
- Why is it important to take a positive approach to prenatal development?

Connect

- In Chapter 2, we discussed chromosomal and gene-linked abnormalities that can affect prenatal development. How are the symptoms of the related conditions or risks similar to or different from those caused by teratogens or other hazards?

Reflect *Your Own Personal Journey of Life*

- If you are a woman, imagine that you have just found out that you are pregnant. What health-enhancing strategies will you follow during the prenatal period? For men, imagine that you are the partner of a woman who has just found out she is pregnant. What will be your role in increasing the likelihood that the prenatal period will go smoothly?

There was a star danced, and under that I was born.

—WILLIAM SHAKESPEARE
English Playwright, 17th Century

After the long journey of prenatal development, birth takes place. During birth the baby is on a threshold between two worlds. *What is the fetus/newborn transition like?*

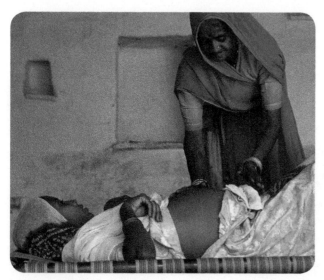

In India, a midwife checks on the size, position, and heartbeat of a fetus. Midwives deliver babies in many cultures around the world. *What are some cultural variations in prenatal care?*

afterbirth The third stage of birth, when the placenta, umbilical cord, and other membranes are detached and expelled.

Nature writes the basic script for how birth occurs, but parents make important choices about conditions surrounding birth. We look first at the sequence of physical steps that take place when a child is born.

THE BIRTH PROCESS

The birth process occurs in stages, takes place in different contexts, and in most cases involves one or more attendants.

Stages of Birth The birth process occurs in three stages. The first stage is the longest of the three. Uterine contractions are 15 to 20 minutes apart at the beginning and last up to a minute each. These contractions cause the woman's cervix to stretch and open. As the first stage progresses, the contractions come closer together, appearing every two to five minutes. Their intensity increases. By the end of the first birth stage, contractions dilate the cervix to an opening of about 10 centimeters (4 inches), so that the baby can move from the uterus into the birth canal. For a woman having her first child, the first stage lasts an average of 6 to 12 hours; for subsequent children, this stage typically is much shorter.

The second birth stage begins when the baby's head starts to move through the cervix and the birth canal. It terminates when the baby emerges completely from the mother's body. With each contraction, the mother bears down hard to push the baby out of her body. By the time the baby's head is out of the mother's body, the contractions come almost every minute and last for about a minute each. This stage typically lasts approximately 45 minutes to an hour.

Afterbirth is the third stage, at which time the placenta, umbilical cord, and other membranes are detached and expelled. This final stage is the shortest of the three birth stages, lasting only minutes.

Childbirth Setting and Attendants In the United States, 99 percent of births take place in hospitals (Martin & others, 2005). However, a 5 percent increase in home births occurred in 2005 and 2006 (Macdorman, Declercq, & Menacker, 2011). This increase in home births occurred mainly for non-Latino White women, especially those who were older and married. For non-Latino White women, two-thirds of their home births were attended by a midwife.

The people who help a mother during birth vary across cultures. In U.S. hospitals, it has become the norm for fathers or birth coaches to be with the mother throughout labor and delivery. In the East African Nigoni culture, by contrast, men are completely excluded from the childbirth process. When a woman is ready to give birth, female relatives move into the woman's hut and the husband leaves, taking his belongings (clothes, tools, weapons, and so on) with him. He is not permitted to return until after the baby is born. In some cultures, childbirth is an open, community affair. For example, in the Pukapukan culture in the Pacific Islands, women give birth in a shelter that is open for villagers to observe.

Midwives Midwifery is practiced in most countries throughout the world (Jesse & Kilpatrick, 2013). In Holland, more than 40 percent of babies are delivered by midwives rather than doctors. However, in 2003, 91 percent of U.S. births were attended by physicians, and only 8 percent of women who delivered a baby were attended by a *midwife* (Martin & others, 2005). Nonetheless, the 8 percent figure in 2003 represents a substantial increase from less than 1 percent of U.S. women attended by a midwife in 1975 (Martin & others, 2005). Ninety-five percent of the midwives who delivered babies in the United States in 2003 were certified nurse-midwives. A recent research review concluded that for low-risk women, midwife-led care was characterized by a reduction in procedures during labor and increased satisfaction with care (Sutcliffe & others, 2012). Also, in this study no adverse outcomes were found for midwife-led care compared with physician-led care.

Doulas   In some countries, a doula attends a childbearing woman. Doula is a Greek word that means "a woman who helps." A **doula** is a caregiver who provides continuous physical, emotional, and educational support for the mother before, during, and after childbirth. Doulas remain with the parents throughout labor, assessing and responding to the mother's needs. Researchers have found positive effects when a doula is present at the birth of a child (Akhavan & Lundgren, 2012; Torres, 2013).

In the United States, most doulas work as independent providers hired by the expectant parents. Doulas typically function as part of a "birthing team," serving as an adjunct to the midwife or the hospital's obstetric staff.

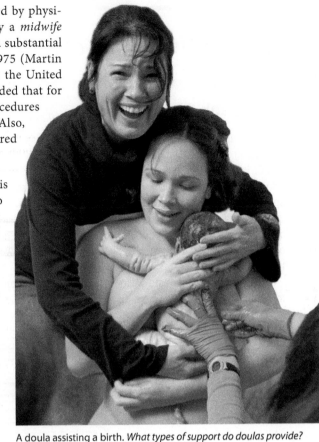
A doula assisting a birth. *What types of support do doulas provide?*

Methods of Childbirth   U.S. hospitals often allow the mother and her obstetrician a range of options regarding the method of delivery. Key choices involve the use of medication, whether to use any of a number of nonmedicated techniques to reduce pain, and when to have a cesarean delivery.

Medication   Three basic kinds of drugs that are used for labor are analgesia, anesthesia, and oxytocin/pitocin.

Analgesia is used to relieve pain. Analgesics include tranquilizers, barbiturates, and narcotics (such as Demerol).

Anesthesia is used in late first-stage labor and during delivery to block sensation in an area of the body or to block consciousness. Researchers are continuing to explore safer drug mixtures for use at lower doses to improve the effectiveness and safety of epidural anesthesia (Samhan & others, 2013).

Predicting how a drug will affect an individual woman and her fetus is difficult (Davidson & others, 2012). A particular drug might have only a minimal effect on one fetus yet have a much stronger effect on another. The drug's dosage also is a factor.

An instructor conducting a Lamaze class. *What characterizes the Lamaze method?*

connecting with careers

Linda Pugh, Perinatal Nurse

Perinatal nurses work with childbearing women to support health and well-being during the childbearing experience. Linda Pugh, Ph.D., R.N.C., is a perinatal nurse on the faculty at The Johns Hopkins University School of Nursing. She is certified as an inpatient obstetric nurse and specializes in the care of women during labor and delivery. She teaches undergraduate and graduate students, educates professional nurses, and conducts research. In addition, Pugh consults with hospitals and organizations about women's health issues and topics we discuss in this chapter.

Her research interests include nursing interventions with low-income breast feeding women, discovering ways to prevent and ameliorate fatigue during childbearing, and using breathing exercises during labor.

Linda Pugh (*right*) with a new mother and baby.

---

doula A caregiver who provides continuous physical, emotional, and educational support for the mother before, during, and after childbirth.

natural childbirth This method attempts to reduce the mother's pain by decreasing her fear through education about childbirth and relaxation techniques during delivery.

prepared childbirth Developed by French obstetrician Ferdinand Lamaze, this childbirth strategy is similar to natural childbirth but includes a special breathing technique to control pushing in the final stages of labor and a more detailed anatomy and physiology course.

breech position The baby's position in the uterus that causes the buttocks to be the first part to emerge from the vagina.

cesarean delivery Removal of the baby from the mother's uterus through an incision made in her abdomen.

Natural and Prepared Childbirth   For a brief time not long ago, the idea of avoiding all medication during childbirth gained favor in the United States. Instead, many women chose to reduce the pain of childbirth through techniques known as natural childbirth and prepared childbirth. Today, at least some medication is used in the typical childbirth, but elements of natural childbirth and prepared childbirth remain popular (Oates & Abraham, 2010).

Natural childbirth is the method that aims to reduce the mother's pain by decreasing her fear through education about childbirth and by teaching her and her partner to use breathing methods and relaxation techniques during delivery.

French obstetrician Ferdinand Lamaze developed a method similar to natural childbirth that is known as **prepared childbirth,** or the Lamaze method. It includes a special breathing technique to control pushing in the final stages of labor, as well as more detailed education about anatomy and physiology. The Lamaze method has become very popular in the United States. The pregnant woman's partner usually serves as a coach who attends childbirth classes with her and helps her with her breathing and relaxation during delivery.

In sum, proponents of current prepared childbirth methods conclude that when information and support are provided, women *know* how to give birth. To read about one nurse whose research focuses on fatigue during childbearing and breathing exercises during labor, see the *Connecting with Careers* profile on Linda Pugh. And to read about the increased variety of techniques now being used to reduce stress and control pain during labor, see *Caring Connections*.

Cesarean Delivery   Normally, the baby's head comes through the vagina first. But if the baby is in a **breech position,** the baby's buttocks are the first part to emerge from the vagina. In 1 of every 25 deliveries, the baby's head is still in the uterus when the rest of the body is out. Breech births can cause respiratory problems. As a result, if the baby is in a breech position, a surgical procedure known as a cesarean section, or a cesarean delivery, is usually performed. In a **cesarean delivery,** the baby is removed from the mother's uterus through an incision made in her abdomen (Lee, El-Sayed, & Gould, 2008).

From Waterbirth to Music Therapy

The effort to reduce stress and control pain during labor has recently led to an increase in the use of some older and some newer non-medicated techniques (Dhany, Mitchell, & Foy, 2012; Kalder & others, 2011; Simkin & Bolding, 2004). These include waterbirth, massage, acupuncture, hypnosis, and music therapy.

Waterbirth

Waterbirth involves giving birth in a tub of warm water. Some women go through labor in the water and get out for delivery; others remain in the water for delivery. The rationale for waterbirth is that the baby has been in an amniotic sac for many months and that delivery in a similar environment is likely to be less stressful for the baby and the mother (Dahlen & others, 2013; Meyer, Weible, & Woeber, 2010). Mothers get into the warm water when contractions become closer together and more intense. Getting into the water too soon can cause labor to slow or stop. Reviews of research have indicated mixed results for waterbirths (Cluett & Burns, 2009; Field, 2007). A recent study did find that waterbirth was linked with a shorter second stage of labor (Cortes, Basra, & Kelleher, 2011). Waterbirth has been practiced more often in European countries such as Switzerland and Sweden in recent decades than in the United States but is increasingly being included in U.S. birth plans.

Massage

Massage is increasingly used prior to and during delivery (Field & Hernandez, 2013). Two recent research reviews concluded that massage therapy reduces pain during labor (Jones & others, 2012; Smith & others, 2012). One study revealed that massage therapy reduced pain during labor and delivery and alleviated prenatal depression in both parents while improving their relationship (Field, Figueiredo, & others, 2008).

Yoga

A recent research review concluded that practicing yoga during pregnancy was associated with a number of positive outcomes for mothers and a reduction in the incidence of low birth weight infants (Babbar & others, 2012). Also, a recent study found that yoga and massage therapy sessions during pregnancy were associated with decreased levels of depression, anxiety, and back and leg pain (Babbar & others, 2012; Field & others, 2012).

Acupuncture

Acupuncture, the insertion of very fine needles into specific locations in the body, is used as a standard procedure to reduce the pain of childbirth in China, although it only recently has begun to be used in the United States for this purpose. Recent research studies indicate that acupuncture can have positive effects on labor and delivery (Borup & others, 2009; Citkovitz, Schnyer, & Hoskins, 2011).

Hypnosis

Hypnosis, the induction of a psychological state of altered attention and awareness in which the individual is unusually responsive to suggestions, is also increasingly being used during childbirth (Wilcox, 2010). Some studies have indicated positive effects of hypnosis for reducing pain during childbirth (Abasi & others, 2009; Barabasz & Perez, 2007).

Music Therapy

Music therapy during childbirth, which involves the use of music to reduce stress and manage pain, is becoming more prevalent (Liu, Chang, & Chen, 2010). More research is needed to determine its effectiveness (Laopaiboon & others, 2009).

What characterizes the use of waterbirth in delivering a baby?

What are some reasons that childbirth methods such as these might be chosen instead of the use of medication?

Score	0	1	2
Heart rate	Absent	Slow—less than 100 beats per minute	Fast—100–140 beats per minute
Respiratory effort	No breathing for more than one minute	Irregular and slow	Good breathing with normal crying
Muscle tone	Limp and flaccid	Weak, inactive, but some flexion of extremities	Strong, active motion
Body color	Blue and pale	Body pink, but extremities blue	Entire body pink
Reflex irritability	No response	Grimace	Coughing, sneezing and crying

FIGURE **3.6**

THE APGAR SCALE.
A newborn's score on the Apgar Scale indicates whether the baby has urgent medical problems. *What are some trends in the Apgar scores of U.S. babies?*

The benefits and risks of cesarean sections continue to be debated (Gibbons & others, 2013; O'Neill & others, 2013). Some critics believe that too many babies are delivered by cesarean section in the United States (Arikan & others, 2012). More cesarean sections are performed in the United States than in any other country in the world. In 2009, 33 percent of babies in the U.S. were cesarean deliveries, a 60 percent increase since 1996 (Hamilton, Martin, & Ventura, 2012; Solheim & others, 2011).

ASSESSING THE NEWBORN

Almost immediately after birth, after the baby and its parents have been introduced, a newborn is taken to be weighed, cleaned up, and tested for signs of developmental problems that might require urgent attention (Miyakoshi & others, 2013; Therrells & others, 2010). The **Apgar Scale** is widely used to assess the health of newborns at one and five minutes after birth. The Apgar Scale evaluates infants' heart rate, respiratory effort, muscle tone, body color, and reflex irritability. An obstetrician or a nurse does the evaluation and gives the newborn a score, or reading, of 0, 1, or 2 on each of these five health signs (see Figure 3.6). A total score of 7 to 10 indicates that the newborn's condition is good. A score of 5 indicates there may be developmental difficulties. A score of 3 or below signals an emergency and indicates that the baby might not survive.

The Apgar Scale is especially good at assessing the newborn's ability to cope with the stress of delivery and the new environment (Reynolds, 2010; Shehata & others, 2011). It also identifies high-risk infants who need resuscitation.

A recent study revealed that compared to children with a high Apgar score (9 to 10), the risk of developing attention deficit hyperactivity disorder (ADHD) in childhood was 75 percent higher for newborns with a low Apgar score (1 to 4) and 63 percent higher for those with an Apgar score of 5 to 6 (Li & others, 2011). For a more thorough assessment of the newborn, the Brazelton Neonatal Behavioral Assessment Scale or the Neonatal Intensive Care Unit Network Neurobehavioral Scale may be used.

The **Brazelton Neonatal Behavioral Assessment Scale (NBAS)** is typically performed within 24 to 36 hours after birth. It is also used as a sensitive index of neurological competence up to one month after birth for typical infants and as a measure in many studies of infant development (Costa & Figueiredo, 2011; Hernandez-Martinez & others, 2011). The NBAS assesses the newborn's neurological development, reflexes, and reactions to people and objects. Sixteen reflexes, such as sneezing, blinking, and rooting, are assessed, along with reactions to animate stimuli (such as a face and voice) and inanimate stimuli (such as

Apgar Scale A widely used method to assess the health of newborns at one and five minutes after birth. The Apgar Scale evaluates infants' heart rate, respiratory effort, muscle tone, body color, and reflex irritability.

Brazelton Neonatal Behavioral Assessment Scale (NBAS) A measure that is used in the first month of life to assess the newborn's neurological development, reflexes, and reactions to people and objects.

a rattle). (We will have more to say about reflexes in Chapter 5 when we discuss motor development in infancy.)

An "offspring" of the NBAS, the **Neonatal Intensive Care Unit Network Neurobehavioral Scale (NNNS)** provides another assessment of the newborn's behavior, neurological and stress responses, and regulatory capacities (Brazelton, 2004; Lester & others, 2011). Whereas the NBAS was developed to assess normal, healthy, full-term infants, T. Berry Brazelton, along with Barry Lester and Edward Tronick, developed the NNNS to assess "at-risk" infants (Lester, Tronick, & Brazelton, 2004). The NNNS is especially useful for evaluating preterm infants (although it may not be appropriate for those of less than 30 weeks' gestational age) and substance-exposed infants (Boukydis & Lester, 2008). A recent NNNS assessment (at one month of age) of preterm infants who were exposed to substance abuse prenatally revealed that the NNNS predicted certain developmental outcomes, such as neurological difficulties, IQ, and reduced school readiness at 4.5 years of age (Liu & others, 2010).

PRETERM AND LOW BIRTH WEIGHT INFANTS

Conditions that pose threats for newborns have been given different labels. We will examine these conditions and discuss interventions that can improve outcomes of preterm infants.

Preterm and Small for Date Infants   Three related conditions pose threats to many newborns: low birth weight, preterm delivery, and being small for date. **Low birth weight infants** weigh less than 5½ pounds at birth. *Very low birth weight* newborns weigh under 3½ pounds, and *extremely low birth weight* newborns weigh under 2 pounds. **Preterm infants** are those born three weeks or more before the pregnancy has reached its full term—in other words, before the completion of 37 weeks of gestation (the time between fertilization and birth). **Small for date infants** (also called *small for gestational age infants*) are those whose birth weight is below normal when the length of the pregnancy is considered. They weigh less than 90 percent of all babies of the same gestational age. Small for date infants may be preterm or full term. One study found that small for date infants had more than a fourfold increased risk of death (Regev & others, 2003).

In 2009, 12.2 percent of U.S. infants were born preterm—a 35 percent increase since the 1980s but a 0.6 percent decrease since 2006 (Hamilton, Martin, & Ventura, 2012; National Center for Health Statistics, 2011). The increase in preterm birth since the 1980s is likely due to several factors, including the increasing number of births to women 35 years and older, increasing rates of multiple births, increased management of maternal and fetal conditions (for example, inducing labor preterm if medical technology indicates it will increase the likelihood of survival), increased substance abuse (tobacco, alcohol), and increased stress (Goldenberg & Culhane, 2007). Ethnic variations characterize preterm birth (Lhila & Long, 2011). For example, in 2006, the likelihood of being born preterm was 12.8 percent for all U.S. infants, but the rate was 18.5 percent for African American infants (National Center for Health Statistics, 2009).

Recently, there has been considerable interest in exploring the role that progestin might play in reducing preterm births (Likis & others, 2013; O'Brien & Lewis, 2009). Research reviews indicate that progestin is most effective in reducing preterm births when it is administered to women with a history of a previous spontaneous birth at less than 37 weeks (da Fonseca, Bittar, & others, 2009), to women who have a short cervical length of 15 mm or less (da Fonseca, Celik, & others, 2009), and to women pregnant with a singleton rather than twins (Norman & others, 2009; Rode & others, 2009).

The incidence of low birth weight varies considerably from country to country. To read about cross-cultural variations in low birth weight, see *Connecting with Diversity*.

Consequences of Preterm Birth and Low Birth Weight   Although most preterm and low birth weight infants are healthy, as a group they experience higher rates of illness and developmental problems than infants of normal birth weight (Minde & Zelkowitz, 2008). For preterm birth, the terms *extremely preterm* and *very preterm* are increasingly used. *Extremely*

A "kilogram kid," weighing less than 2.3 pounds at birth. *What are some long-term outcomes for weighing so little at birth?*

Neonatal Intensive Care Unit Network Neurobehavioral Scale (NNNS) An "offspring" of the NBAS, the NNNS provides an assessment of the "at-risk" newborn's behavior, neurological and stress responses, and regulatory capacities.

low birth weight infant Infant that weighs less than 5½ pounds at birth.

preterm infants Those born before the completion of 37 weeks of gestation (the time between fertilization and birth).

small for date infants Also called small for gestational age infants, these infants have birth weights that are below normal when the length of pregnancy is considered. Small for date infants may be preterm or full term.

Cross-Cultural Variations in the Incidence and Causes of Low Birth Weight

In some countries, such as India and Sudan, where poverty is rampant and the health and nutrition of mothers are poor, the percentage of low birth weight babies reaches as high as 31 percent (see Figure 3.7). In the United States, there has been an increase in low birth weight infants in the last two decades. The U.S. low birth weight rate of 8.1 percent in 2011 is considerably higher than that of many other developed countries (Centers for Disease Control and Prevention, 2012; Hoyert, 2012). For example, only 4 percent of the infants born in Sweden, Finland, Norway, and Korea are low birth weight, and only 5 percent of those born in New Zealand, Australia, and France are low birth weight.

In both developed and developing countries, adolescents who give birth when their bodies have not fully matured are at risk for having low birth weight babies (Malamitsi-Puchner & Boutsikou, 2006). In the United States, the increase in the number of low birth weight infants has been attributed to drug use, poor nutrition, multiple births, reproductive technologies, and improved technology and prenatal care that result in more high-risk babies surviving (Chen & others, 2007). Nonetheless, poverty continues to be a major factor in preterm birth in the United States. Women living in poverty are more likely to be obese, have diabetes and hypertension, smoke cigarettes, and use illicit drugs, and they are less likely to receive regular prenatal care (Goldenberg & Nagahawatte, 2008).

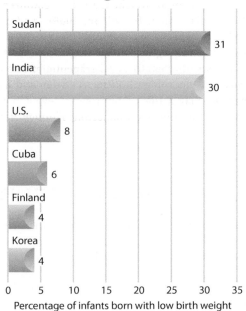

FIGURE **3.7**

PERCENTAGE OF INFANTS BORN WITH LOW BIRTH WEIGHT IN SELECTED COUNTRIES

In the last sentence above, we learned that women living in poverty are less likely to receive regular prenatal care. What did you learn earlier in the chapter about the benefits of regular prenatal care? Aside from women living in poverty, which other demographic group is not likely to receive adequate prenatal care?

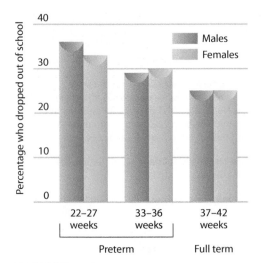

FIGURE **3.8**

PERCENTAGE OF PRETERM AND FULL-TERM BIRTH INFANTS WHO DROPPED OUT OF SCHOOL

preterm infants are those born before the 28th week of pregnancy, and *very preterm infants* are those born before 33 weeks of gestational age. Figure 3.8 shows the results of a recent Norwegian study indicating that the earlier preterm infants are born, the more likely they are to drop out of school (Swamy, Ostbye, & Skjaerven, 2008).

The number and severity of these problems increase when infants are born very early and as their birth weight decreases (Baron & others, 2011; Wariki & others, 2013). Survival rates for infants who are born very early and very small have risen, but with this improved survival rate have come increased rates of severe brain damage (Casey, 2008). Children born at low birth weights are more likely than their normal birth weight counterparts to develop a learning disability, attention deficit hyperactivity disorder, or breathing problem such as asthma (Anderson & others, 2011). And a recent study found that low birth weight was associated with childhood autism (Lampl & others, 2012). Approximately 50 percent of all low birth weight children are enrolled in special education programs.

Nurturing Low Birth Weight and Preterm Infants Two increasingly used interventions in the neonatal intensive care unit (NICU) are kangaroo care and massage therapy. **Kangaroo care** involves skin-to-skin contact in which the baby, wearing only a diaper, is held upright against the parent's bare chest, much as a baby kangaroo is carried inside its mother's pouch. Kangaroo care is typically practiced for two to three hours per day, skin-to-skin, over an extended time in early infancy (Ahmed & others, 2011).

Why use kangaroo care with preterm infants? Preterm infants often have difficulty coordinating their breathing and heart rate, and the close physical contact with the parent provided by kangaroo care can help to stabilize the preterm infant's heartbeat, temperature, and breathing (Cong, Ludington-Hoe, & Walsh, 2011; Kaffashi & others, 2013). Preterm infants who experience kangaroo care also gain more weight than their counterparts who are not given this care (Gathwala, Singh, & Balhara, 2008). And a recent research review concluded that kangaroo care decreased the risk of mortality in low birth weight infants (Conde-Aguedelo, Belizan, & Diaz-Rossello, 2011).

Many adults will attest to the therapeutic effects of receiving a massage. In fact, many will pay a premium to receive one at a spa on a regular basis. But can massage play a role in improving developmental outcomes for preterm infants? To find out, see *Connecting Through Research*.

A new mother practicing kangaroo care. *What is kangaroo care?*

kangaroo care Treatment for preterm infants that involves skin-to-skin contact.

connecting through research

How Does Massage Therapy Affect the Mood and Behavior of Babies?

Throughout history and in many cultures, caregivers have massaged infants. In Africa and Asia, infants are routinely massaged by parents or other family members for several months after birth. In the United States, interest in using touch and massage to improve the growth, health, and well-being of infants has been stimulated by the research of Tiffany Field (2001, 2007; Diego, Field, & Hernandez-Reif, 2008; Field, Diego, & Hernandez-Reif, 2008, 2010; Field & Hernandez-Reif, 2013; Field & others, 2006; Hernandez-Reif, Diego, & Field, 2007), director of the Touch Research Institute at the University of Miami School of Medicine.

In a recent study, preterm infants in a neonatal intensive care unit (NICU) were randomly assigned to a massage therapy group or a control group (Hernandez-Reif, Diego, & Field, 2007). For five consecutive days, the preterm infants in the massage group were given three 15-minute moderate pressure massages. Behavioral observations of the following stress behaviors were made on the first and last days of the study: crying, grimacing, yawning, sneezing, jerky arm and leg movements, startles, and finger flaring. The various stress behaviors were summarized in a composite stress behavior index. As indicated in Figure 3.9, massage had a stress-reducing effect on the preterm

FIGURE **3.9**

PRETERM INFANTS SHOW REDUCED STRESS BEHAVIORS AND ACTIVITY AFTER FIVE DAYS OF MASSAGE THERAPY (HERNANDEZ-REIF, DIEGO, & FIELD, 2007)

Shown here is Tiffany Field massaging a newborn infant. *What types of infants has massage therapy been shown to help?*

(continued)

(continued)

infants, which is especially important because they encounter numerous stressors while they are hospitalized.

In a research review of massage therapy with preterm infants, Field and her colleagues (2004) concluded that the most consistent findings involve two positive results: (1) increased weight gain and (2) discharge from the hospital three to six days earlier. A recent study revealed that the mechanisms responsible for increased weight gain as a result of massage therapy were stimulation of the vagus nerve (one of 12 cranial nerves leading to the brain) and in turn the release of insulin (a food absorption hormone) (Field, Diego, & Hernandez-Reif, 2010).

Infants are not the only ones who may benefit from massage therapy (Field, 2007; Field & Hernandez-Reif, 2013). In other studies, Field and her colleagues have demonstrated the benefits of massage therapy with women in reducing labor pain (Field, Hernandez-Reif, Taylor, & others, 1997), with children who have asthma (Field, Henteleff, & others, 1998), with autistic children's attentiveness (Field, Lasko, & others, 1997), and with adolescents who have attention deficit hyperactivity disorder (Field, Quintino, & others, 1998).

Review *Connect* Reflect

 LG2 Discuss the birth process.

Review

- What are the three main stages of birth? What are some different birth strategies? What is the transition from fetus to newborn like for the infant?
- What are three measures of neonatal health and responsiveness?
- What are the outcomes for children if they are born preterm or with a low birth weight?

Connect

- What correlations have been found between birth weight and country of birth, and what might the causes be?

Reflect *Your Own Personal Journey of Life*

- If you are a female who would like to have a baby, which birth strategy do you prefer? Why? If you are a male, how involved would you want to be in helping your partner through the birth of your baby? Explain.

The Postpartum Period

 LG3 Explain the changes that take place in the postpartum period.

Physical Adjustments   Emotional and Psychological Adjustments   Bonding

postpartum period The period after childbirth when the mother adjusts, both physically and psychologically, to the process of childbirth. This period lasts about six weeks or until her body has completed its adjustment and returned to a near prepregnant state.

The weeks after childbirth present challenges for many new parents and their offspring. This is the **postpartum period,** the period after childbirth or delivery that lasts for about six weeks or until the mother's body has completed its adjustment and has returned to a nearly prepregnant state. It is a time when the woman adjusts, both physically and psychologically, to the process of childbearing.

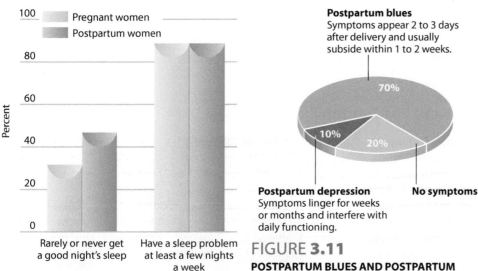

FIGURE **3.10**

SLEEP DEPRIVATION IN PREGNANT AND POSTPARTUM WOMEN

Postpartum blues
Symptoms appear 2 to 3 days after delivery and usually subside within 1 to 2 weeks.

Postpartum depression
Symptoms linger for weeks or months and interfere with daily functioning.

No symptoms

FIGURE **3.11**

POSTPARTUM BLUES AND POSTPARTUM DEPRESSION AMONG U.S. WOMEN. Some health professionals refer to the postpartum period as the "fourth trimester." Although the time span of the postpartum period does not necessarily cover three months, the term "fourth trimester" suggests continuity and the importance of the first several months after birth for the mother.

The postpartum period involves a great deal of adjustment and adaptation. The adjustments needed are physical, emotional, and psychological.

PHYSICAL ADJUSTMENTS

A woman's body makes numerous physical adjustments in the first days and weeks after childbirth (Mattson & Smith, 2011). She may have a great deal of energy or feel exhausted and let down. These changes are normal, but fatigue can undermine the new mother's sense of well-being and confidence in her ability to cope with a new baby and a new family life (Runquist, 2007).

A concern is the loss of sleep that the primary caregiver experiences in the postpartum period (Montgomery-Downs & others, 2010). In the 2007 Sleep in America survey, a substantial percentage of women reported loss of sleep during pregnancy and in the postpartum period (National Sleep Foundation, 2007) (see Figure 3.10). The loss of sleep can contribute to stress, marital conflict, and impaired decision making (Meerlo, Sgoifo, & Suchecki, 2008).

After delivery, a mother's body undergoes sudden and dramatic changes in hormone production. When the placenta is delivered, estrogen and progesterone levels drop steeply and remain low until the ovaries start producing hormones again.

EMOTIONAL AND PSYCHOLOGICAL ADJUSTMENTS

Emotional fluctuations are common for mothers in the postpartum period. For some women, emotional fluctuations decrease within several weeks after the delivery, but other women experience more long-lasting mood swings.

As shown in Figure 3.11, about 70 percent of new mothers in the United States have what are called the postpartum blues. About two to three days after birth, they begin to feel depressed, anxious, and upset. These feelings may come and go for several months after the birth, often peaking about three to five days after birth. Even without treatment, these feelings usually go away after one or two weeks.

However, some women develop **postpartum depression,** which involves a major depressive episode that typically occurs about four weeks after delivery. Women with postpartum depression have such strong feelings of sadness, anxiety, or despair that for

postpartum depression Characteristic of women who have such strong feelings of sadness, anxiety, or despair that they have trouble coping with daily tasks during the postpartum period.

Diane Sanford, Clinical Psychologist and Postpartum Expert

Diane Sanford has a doctorate in clinical psychology, and for many years she had a private practice that focused on marital and family relationships. But after she began collaborating with a psychiatrist whose clients included women with postpartum depression, Dr. Sanford, together with a women's health nurse, founded Women's Healthcare Partnership in St. Louis, Missouri, which specializes in women's adjustment during the postpartum period. Subsequently, they added a marriage and family relationships counselor and a social worker to their staff, and then later hired nurse educators, a dietician, and a fitness expert as consultants (Clay, 2001).

For more information about what clinical psychologists do, see page 43 in the Careers in Child Development appendix following Chapter 1.

Diane Sanford holding an infant of one of the mothers who comes to her for help in coping with postpartum issues.

The postpartum period is a time of considerable adjustment and adaptation for both the mother and the father. Fathers can provide an important support system for mothers, especially in helping mothers care for young infants. *What kinds of tasks might the father of a newborn do to support the mother?*

bonding The formation of a close connection, especially a physical bond, between parents and their newborn in the period shortly after birth.

at least a two-week period they have trouble coping with their daily tasks. Without treatment, postpartum depression may become worse and last for many months (Nolen-Hoeksema, 2011; Stuart, 2012). Unfortunately, many women with postpartum depression don't seek help. For example, one study found that 15 percent of the women reported postpartum depression symptoms but less than half sought help (McGarry & others, 2009). Estimates indicate that 10 to 14 percent of new mothers experience postpartum depression.

Several antidepressant drugs are effective in treating postpartum depression and appear to be safe for breast feeding women (Logsdon, Wisner, & Hanusa, 2009). Psychotherapy, especially cognitive therapy, also is an effective treatment of postpartum depression for many women (Miller & Larusso, 2011). And engaging in regular exercise may help in reducing postpartum depression (Daley, Macarthur, & Winter, 2007).

Can a mother's postpartum depression affect the way she interacts with her infant? A recent research review concluded that the interaction difficulties of depressed mothers and their infants occur across cultures and socioeconomic status groups, and encompass less sensitivity of the mothers and less responsiveness on the part of their infants (Field, 2010). Several caregiving activities also are compromised, including feeding (especially breast feeding), sleep routines, and safety practices. To read about one individual who specializes in helping women adjust during the postpartum period, see *Connecting with Careers.*

Fathers also undergo considerable adjustment during the postpartum period, even when they work away from home all day. When the mother experiences postpartum depression, many fathers also develop depressed feelings (Letourneau & others, 2012; Ramchandani & others, 2011). Many fathers feel that the baby comes first and gets all of the mother's attention; some feel that they have been replaced by the baby.

The father's support and caring can play a role in whether the mother develops postpartum depression (Dietz & others, 2009; Persson & others, 2011). A recent study revealed that higher support by fathers was related to lower rates of postpartum depression in women (Smith & Howard, 2008).

BONDING

A special component of the parent-infant relationship is **bonding,** the formation of a connection, especially a physical bond between parents and the newborn in the period shortly after birth. Sometimes hospitals seem determined to deter bonding. Drugs given to the mother to make her delivery less painful can make the mother drowsy, interfering with her ability to respond to and stimulate the newborn. Mothers and newborns are often separated shortly after delivery, and preterm infants are isolated from their mothers even more than full-term infants.

Do these practices do any harm? Some physicians believe that during the period shortly after birth, the parents and newborn need to form an emotional attachment as a foundation for optimal development in the years to come (Kennell, 2006; Kennell & McGrath, 1999). Is there evidence that close contact between mothers and infants in the first several days after birth is critical for optimal development later in life? Although some research supports this bonding hypothesis (Klaus & Kennell, 1976), a body of research challenges the significance of the first few days of life as a critical period (Bakeman & Brown, 1980; Rode & others, 1981). Indeed, the extreme form of the bonding hypothesis—that the newborn must have close contact with the mother in the first few days of life to develop optimally—simply is not true.

Nonetheless, the weakness of the bonding hypothesis should not be used as an excuse to keep motivated mothers from interacting with their newborns. Such contact brings pleasure to many mothers. In some mother-infant pairs—including preterm infants, adolescent mothers, and mothers from disadvantaged circumstances—early close contact may establish a climate for improved interaction after the mother and infant leave the hospital.

Many hospitals now offer a *rooming-in* arrangement, in which the baby remains in the mother's room most of the time during its hospital stay. However, if parents choose not to use this rooming-in arrangement, the weight of the research suggests that this decision will not harm the infant emotionally (Lamb, 1994).

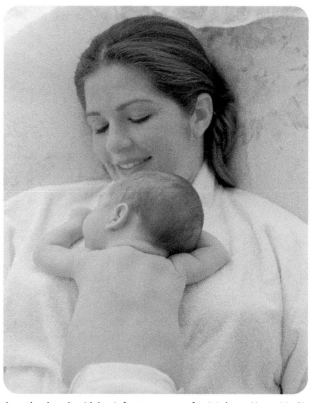

A mother bonds with her infant moments after it is born. *How critical is bonding for the development of social competence later in childhood?*

developmental **connection**

Theories

Lorenz demonstrated the importance of bonding in graylag geese, but the first few days of life are unlikely to be a critical period for bonding in human infants. Chapter 1, p. 26

Review *Connect* Reflect

 Explain the changes that take place in the postpartum period.

Review

- What does the postpartum period involve? What physical adjustments does the woman's body make during this period?
- What emotional and psychological adjustments characterize the postpartum period?
- Is bonding critical for optimal development?

Connect

- How can exercise help pregnant women before delivery and women with postpartum depression after giving birth?

Reflect *Your Own Personal Journey of Life*

- If you are a female who plans to have children, what can you do to adjust effectively in the postpartum period? If you are the partner of a new mother, what can you do to help during the postpartum period?

Prenatal Development and Birth

Prenatal Development

LG1 Describe prenatal development.

The Course of Prenatal Development

- Prenatal development is divided into three periods: germinal (conception until 10 to 14 days later), which ends when the zygote (a fertilized egg) attaches to the uterine wall; embryonic (two to eight weeks after conception), during which the embryo differentiates into three layers, life-support systems develop, and organ systems form (organogenesis); and fetal (two months after conception until about nine months, or when the infant is born), a time when organ systems have matured to the point at which life can be sustained outside of the womb. Neurogenesis is the formation of new neurons. The nervous system begins with the formation of a neural tube at 18 to 24 days after conception, and by the time babies are born they have approximately 100 billion neurons, or nerve cells. Proliferation and migration are two processes that characterize brain development in the prenatal period. The basic architecture of the brain is formed in the first two trimesters of prenatal development.

Teratology and Hazards to Prenatal Development

- Teratology is the field that investigates the causes of congenital (birth) defects. Any agent that causes birth defects is called a teratogen. The dose, genetic susceptibility, and time of exposure influence the severity of the damage to an unborn child and the type of defect that occurs. Prescription drugs that can be harmful include antibiotics, some antidepressants, certain hormones, and Accutane. Nonprescription drugs that can be harmful include diet pills and aspirin. Legal psychoactive drugs that are potentially harmful to prenatal development include caffeine, alcohol, and nicotine. Fetal alcohol spectrum disorders are a cluster of abnormalities that appear in offspring of mothers who drink heavily during pregnancy. Even when pregnant women drink moderately (one to two drinks a few days a week), negative effects on their offspring have been found. Cigarette smoking by pregnant women has serious adverse effects on prenatal and child development (such as low birth weight). Illegal psychoactive drugs that are potentially harmful to offspring include methamphetamine, marijuana, cocaine, and heroin. Incompatibility of the mother's and the father's blood types can also be harmful to the fetus. Environmental hazards include radiation, environmental pollutants, and toxic wastes. Syphilis, rubella (German measles), genital herpes, and AIDS are infectious diseases that can harm the fetus. Other parental factors include maternal diet and nutrition, age, emotional states and stress, and paternal factors. A developing fetus depends entirely on its mother for nutrition. Maternal age can negatively affect the offspring's development if the mother is an adolescent or over 35. High stress in the mother is linked with less than optimal prenatal and birth outcomes. Paternal factors that can adversely affect prenatal development include exposure to lead, radiation, certain pesticides, and petrochemicals.

Prenatal Care

- Prenatal care varies extensively but usually involves medical care services with a defined schedule of visits.

Normal Prenatal Development

- It is important to remember that, although things can and do go wrong during pregnancy, most of the time pregnancy and prenatal development go well.

Birth

LG2 Discuss the birth process.

The Birth Process

- Childbirth occurs in three stages. The first stage, which lasts about 6 to 12 hours for a woman having her first child, is the longest stage. The cervix dilates to about 10 centimeters (4 inches) at the end of the first stage. The second stage begins when the baby's head starts to move through the cervix and ends with the baby's complete emergence. The third stage involves the delivery of the placenta after birth. Childbirth strategies involve the childbirth setting and attendants. In many countries, a doula attends a childbearing woman. Methods of delivery include medicated, natural or prepared, and cesarean. Being born involves considerable stress for the baby, but the baby is well prepared and adapted to handle the stress.

Assessing the Newborn

- For many years, the Apgar Scale has been used to assess the health of newborn babies. The Brazelton Neonatal Behavioral Assessment Scale (NBAS) examines the newborn's neurological development, reflexes, and reactions to people. Recently, the Neonatal Intensive Care Unit Network Neurobehavioral Scale (NNNS) was created to assess at-risk infants.

Preterm and Low Birth Weight Infants

- Low birth weight infants weigh less than 5½ pounds, and they may be preterm (born before the completion of 37 weeks of gestation) or small for date (also called small for gestational age), which refers to infants whose birth weight is below normal when the length of pregnancy is considered. Small for date infants may be preterm or full term. Although most low birth weight and preterm infants are normal and healthy, as a group they experience more illness and developmental problems than infants of normal birth weight. Kangaroo care and massage therapy have been shown to benefit preterm infants.

The Postpartum Period

LG3 Explain the changes that take place in the postpartum period.

Physical Adjustments

- The postpartum period is the period after childbirth or delivery. The period lasts for about six weeks or until the woman's body has completed its adjustment. Physical adjustments in the postpartum period include fatigue, involution (the process by which the uterus returns to its prepregnant size five or six weeks after birth), and hormonal changes.

Emotional and Psychological Adjustments

- Emotional fluctuations on the part of the mother are common in this period, and they can vary greatly from one mother to the next. Postpartum depression characterizes women who have such strong feelings of sadness, anxiety, or despair that they have trouble coping with daily tasks in the postpartum period. Postpartum depression occurs in about 10 to 14 percent of new mothers. The father also goes through a postpartum adjustment.

Bonding

- Bonding is the formation of a close connection, especially a physical bond, between parents and the newborn shortly after birth. Early bonding has not been found to be critical in the development of a competent infant.

key terms

germinal period 75
blastocyst 75
trophoblast 75
embryonic period 75
amnion 76
umbilical cord 76
placenta 76
organogenesis 76
fetal period 77

neurons 78
teratogen 78
fetal alcohol spectrum disorders (FASD) 81
afterbirth 88
doula 89
natural childbirth 89
prepared childbirth 89
breech position 90

cesarean delivery 90
Apgar Scale 92
Brazelton Neonatal Behavioral Assessment Scale (NBAS) 92
Neonatal Intensive Care Unit Network Neurobehavioral Scale (NNNS) 93
low birth weight infants 93

preterm infants 93
small for date infants 93
kangaroo care 95
postpartum period 96
postpartum depression 97
bonding 98

key people

David Olds 86

Ferdinand Lamaze 89

T. Berry Brazelton 93

Tiffany Field 95

chapter 4

PHYSICAL DEVELOPMENT AND HEALTH

chapter **outline**

1 Body Growth and Change

Learning Goal 1 Discuss developmental changes in the body.

Patterns of Growth
Infancy and Childhood
Adolescence

2 The Brain

Learning Goal 2 Describe how the brain changes.

The Neuroconstructivist View
Brain Physiology
Infancy
Childhood
Adolescence

3 Sleep

Learning Goal 3 Summarize how sleep patterns change as children and adolescents develop.

Infancy
Childhood
Adolescence

4 Health

Learning Goal 4 Characterize children's health.

Illness and Injuries Among Children
Nutrition and Eating Behavior
Exercise

Angie, an elementary-school-aged girl, provided the following comments about losing weight:

When I was eight years old, I weighed 125 pounds. My clothes were the size that large teenage girls wear. I hated my body and my classmates teased me all the time. I was so overweight and out of shape that when I took a P.E. class my face would get red and I had trouble breathing. I was jealous of the kids who played sports and weren't overweight like I was.

I'm nine years old now and I've lost 30 pounds. I'm much happier and proud of myself. How did I lose the weight? My mom said she had finally decided enough was enough. She took me to a pediatrician who specializes in helping children lose weight and keep it off. The pediatrician counseled my mom about my eating and exercise habits, then had us join a group that he had created for overweight children and their parents. My mom and I go to the group once a week and we've now been participating in the program for six months. I no longer eat fast food meals and my mom is cooking more healthy meals. Now that I've lost weight, exercise is not as hard for me and I don't get teased by the kids at school. My mom's pretty happy too because she's lost 15 pounds herself since we've been in the counseling program.

Not all overweight children are as successful as Angie at reducing their weight. Indeed, being overweight in childhood has become a major national concern in the United States (Schiff, 2013). Later in the chapter, we will explore the causes and consequences of being overweight in childhood.

preview

Think about how much you changed physically as you grew up. You came into this life as a small being but grew very rapidly in infancy, more slowly in childhood, and once again more rapidly during puberty. In this chapter, we will explore changes in body growth, the brain, and sleep. We also will examine aspects of children's health.

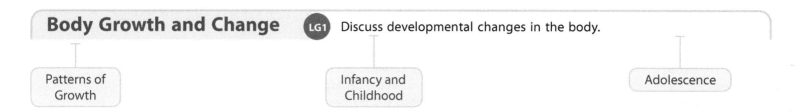

Body Growth and Change (LG1) Discuss developmental changes in the body.

- Patterns of Growth
- Infancy and Childhood
- Adolescence

In the journey of childhood, we go through many bodily changes. Let's begin by studying some basic patterns of growth and then turn to the bodily changes that occur from infancy through adolescence.

PATTERNS OF GROWTH

During prenatal development and early infancy, the head constitutes an extraordinarily large portion of the total body (see Figure 4.1). Gradually, the body's proportions change. Why? Growth is not random. Instead, it generally follows two patterns: the cephalocaudal pattern and the proximodistal pattern.

The **cephalocaudal pattern** is the sequence in which the fastest growth always occurs at the top—the head. Physical growth in size, weight, and feature differentiation gradually works its way down from the top to the bottom—for example, from neck to shoulders, to middle trunk, and so on. This same pattern occurs in the head area; the top parts of the head—the eyes and brain—grow faster than the lower parts, such as the jaw.

cephalocaudal pattern The sequence in which the fastest growth occurs at the top of the body—the head—with physical growth in size, weight, and feature differentiation gradually working from top to bottom.

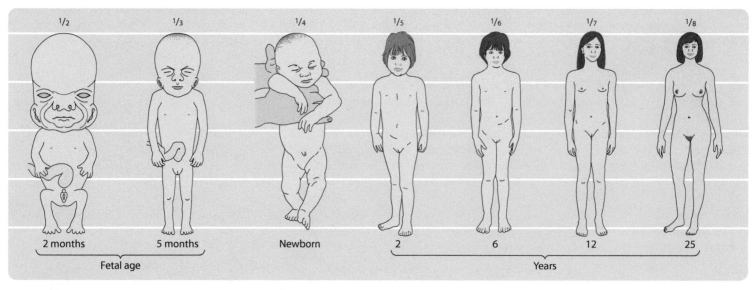

| 1/2 | 1/3 | 1/4 | 1/5 | 1/6 | 1/7 | 1/8 |

| 2 months | 5 months | Newborn | 2 | 6 | 12 | 25 |

Fetal age | Years

FIGURE **4.1**

CHANGES IN PROPORTIONS OF THE HUMAN BODY DURING GROWTH. As individuals develop from infancy through adulthood, one of the most noticeable physical changes is that the head becomes smaller in relation to the rest of the body. The fractions listed refer to head size as a proportion of total body length at different ages.

Sensory and motor development also generally proceed according to the cephalocaudal principle. For example, infants see objects before they can control their torso, and they can use their hands long before they can crawl or walk. However, one study found that infants reached for toys with their feet prior to using their hands (Galloway & Thelen, 2004). On average, infants first touched the toy with their feet when they were 12 weeks old and with their hands when they were 16 weeks old. We will have much more to say about sensory and motor development in Chapter 5.

The **proximodistal pattern** is the growth sequence that starts at the center of the body and moves toward the extremities. For example, muscle control of the trunk and arms matures before control of the hands and fingers. Further, infants use their whole hand as a unit before they can control several fingers.

- - - - - - - - - - →

developmental **connection**

Dynamic Systems Theory

Sensory and motor development are coupled in many aspects of children's acquisition of skills. Chapter 5, p. 161

INFANCY AND CHILDHOOD

Height and weight increase rapidly in infancy (Lampl, 2008). Growth takes a slower course during the childhood years.

Infancy   The average North American newborn is 20 inches long and weighs 7½ pounds. Ninety-five percent of full-term newborns are 18 to 22 inches long and weigh between 5½ and 10 pounds.

In the first several days of life, most newborns lose 5 to 7 percent of their body weight. Once infants adjust to sucking, swallowing, and digesting, they grow rapidly, gaining an average of 5 to 6 ounces per week during the first month. They have doubled their birth weight by the age of 4 months and have nearly tripled it by their first birthday. Infants grow about one inch per month during the first year, reaching approximately 1½ times their birth length by their first birthday.

In the second year of life, infants' rate of growth slows considerably (Burns & others, 2013). By 2 years of age, infants weigh approximately 26 to 32 pounds, having gained a quarter to half a pound per month during the second year; at age 2 they have reached about one-fifth of their adult weight. The average 2-year-old is 32 to 35 inches tall, which is nearly one-half of adult height.

Early Childhood   As the preschool child grows older, the percentage of increase in height and weight decreases with each additional year (McMahon & Stryjewski, 2012). Girls are only slightly smaller and lighter than boys during these years. Both boys and girls slim down as the trunks of their bodies lengthen. Although their heads are still somewhat large for their bodies, by the end of the preschool years most children have lost their top-heavy look. Body fat declines slowly but steadily during the preschool years. Girls have more fatty tissue than boys; boys have more muscle tissue.

Growth patterns vary individually (Florin & Ludwig, 2011). Much of the variation is due to heredity, but environmental experiences are involved to some extent. A review of the height and weight of children around the world concluded that two important contributors to height differences are ethnic origin and nutrition (Meredith, 1978). Also, urban, middle-socioeconomic-status, and firstborn children were taller than rural, lower-socioeconomic-status, and later-born children. The children whose mothers smoked during pregnancy were half an inch shorter than the children whose mothers did not smoke during pregnancy. In the United States, African American children are taller than White children.

Why are some children unusually short? The culprits are congenital factors (genetic or prenatal problems), growth hormone deficiency, a physical problem that develops in childhood, or an emotional difficulty (Wit, Kiess, & Mullis, 2011). When congenital growth problems are the cause of unusual shortness, often the child can be treated with hormones (Collett-Solberg, 2011). Usually this treatment is directed at the pituitary, the body's master gland, located at the base of the brain. This gland secretes growth-related hormones. Physical problems during childhood that can stunt growth include malnutrition and chronic infections. However, if the problems are properly treated, normal growth usually is attained.

The bodies of 5-year-olds and 2-year-olds have different proportions. Notice how the 5-year-old not only is taller and weighs more, but also has a longer trunk and legs than the 2-year-old. *What might be some other physical differences between 2- and 5-year-olds?*

proximodistal pattern The sequence in which growth starts at the center of the body and moves toward the extremities.

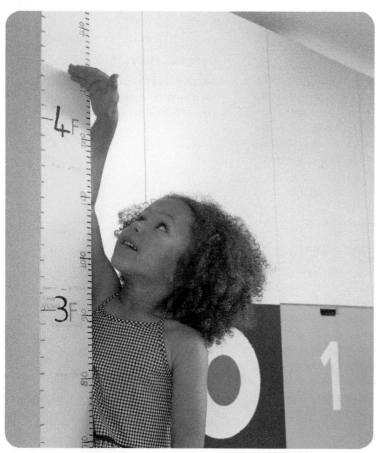

What characterizes physical growth during middle and late childhood?

Middle and Late Childhood   The period of middle and late childhood—from about 6 to 11 years of age—involves slow, consistent growth. This is a period of calm before the rapid growth spurt of adolescence.

During the elementary school years, children grow an average of 2 to 3 inches a year. At the age of 8 the average girl and the average boy are 4 feet 2 inches tall. During the middle and late childhood years, children gain about 5 to 7 pounds a year. The average 8-year-old girl and the average 8-year-old boy weigh 56 pounds (National Center for Health Statistics, 2000). The weight increase is due mainly to increases in the size of the skeletal and muscular systems, as well as the size of some body organs. Muscle mass and strength gradually increase as "baby fat" decreases in middle and late childhood.

The loose movements of early childhood give way to improved muscle tone in middle and late childhood. Children also double their strength capacity during these years. The increase in muscular strength is due to heredity and to exercise. Because they have more muscle cells, boys tend to be stronger than girls.

Changes in proportions are among the most pronounced physical changes in middle and late childhood. Head circumference, waist circumference, and leg length decrease in relation to body height (Burns & others, 2013). A less noticeable physical change is that bones continue to harden during middle and late childhood; still, they yield to pressure and pull more than mature bones.

ADOLESCENCE

After slowing through childhood, growth surges during puberty. **Puberty** is a period of rapid physical maturation involving hormonal and bodily changes that occur primarily in early adolescence. The features and proportions of the body change as the individual becomes capable of reproducing. We will begin our exploration of puberty by describing its determinants and then examine important physical changes and psychological accompaniments of puberty.

Determinants of Puberty   Puberty is not the same as adolescence. For virtually everyone, puberty has ended long before adolescence is over. Puberty is often thought of as the most important marker for the beginning of adolescence.

There are wide variations in the onset and progression of puberty (Dorn & Biro, 2011). Puberty might begin as early as 10 years of age or as late as 13½ for boys. It might end as early as 13 years or as late as 17 years.

puberty A period of rapid physical maturation involving hormonal and bodily changes that take place primarily in early adolescence.

In fact, over the years the timing of puberty has changed. Imagine a 3-year-old girl with fully developed breasts or a boy just slightly older with a deep male voice. That is what toddlers would be like by the year 2250 if the age at which puberty arrives were to continue decreasing as it did for much of the twentieth century. For example, in Norway, **menarche**—a girl's first menstruation—now occurs at just over 13 years of age, compared with 17 years of age in the 1840s (Petersen, 1979). In the United States, where children mature up to a year earlier than in European countries, the average age of menarche dropped an average of two to four months per decade for much of the twentieth century, to about 12½ years today. Some researchers have found evidence that the age of puberty is still dropping for American girls; others suggest that the evidence is inconclusive or that the decline in age is slowing down (Herman-Giddens, 2007). A recent study also found that puberty is continuing to occur earlier for boys, although critics say the study sample is skewed toward including more early maturing boys because parents likely brought their sons to see the participating physicians because of health concerns (Herman-Giddens & others, 2012). The earlier onset of puberty is likely the result of improved health and nutrition (Herman-Giddens, 2007; Herman-Giddens & others, 2012).

The normal range for the onset and progression of puberty is wide enough that, given two boys of the same chronological age, one might complete the pubertal sequence before the other one has begun it. For girls, the age range of menarche is even wider. It is considered within a normal range when it occurs between the ages of 9 and 15.

Precocious puberty is the term used to describe the very early onset and rapid progression of puberty. Judith Blakemore and her colleagues (2009) described the following characteristics of precocious puberty. Precocious puberty is usually diagnosed when pubertal onset occurs before 8 years of age in girls and before 9 years of age in boys. Precocious puberty occurs approximately 10 times more often in girls than in boys. When precocious puberty takes place, it typically is treated by reducing gonadotropic secretions, which temporarily stops pubertal change (Sultan & others, 2012). The reasons for this treatment is that children who experience precocious puberty are ultimately likely to have short stature, early sexual capability, and the potential for engaging in age-inappropriate behavior (Blakemore, Berenbaum, & Liben, 2009).

Heredity and Environmental Influences   Puberty is not an environmental accident. It does not take place at 2 or 3 years of age, and it does not occur in the twenties. Programmed into the genes of every human being is a timing for the emergence of puberty. Recently, scientists have begun to conduct molecular genetic studies in an attempt to identify specific genes that are linked to the onset and progression of puberty (Dvornyk & Waqar-ul-Haq, 2012).

Environmental factors, such as family influences and stress, can also influence its onset and duration (Arim & others, 2011). Experiences that are linked to earlier pubertal onset include adoption, father absence, low socioeconomic status, family conflict, maternal harshness, child maltreatment, and early substance use (Deardorff & others, 2011; Ellis & others, 2011). In many cases, puberty comes months earlier in these situations, and this earlier onset of puberty is likely explained by high rates of conflict and stress in these social contexts. One study revealed that maternal harshness in early childhood was linked to early maturation as well as sexual risk taking in adolescence (Belsky & others, 2010). Another study found that early onset of menarche was associated with severe child sexual abuse (Boynton-Jarrett & others, 2013).

Hormones   Behind the first whisker in boys and the widening of hips in girls is a flood of hormones. **Hormones** are powerful chemical substances secreted by the endocrine glands and carried through the body by the bloodstream. In the case of puberty, the secretion of key hormones is controlled by the interaction of the hypothalamus, the pituitary gland, and the gonads (sex glands). The *hypothalamus* is a structure in the brain best known for monitoring eating, drinking, and sex. The *pituitary gland* is an important endocrine gland that controls growth and regulates other glands. The *gonads* are the sex glands—the testes in males, the ovaries in females.

The key hormonal changes involve two classes of hormones that have significantly different concentrations in males and females (Susman & Dorn, 2013). **Androgens** are the main class of male sex hormones. **Estrogens** are the main class of female sex hormones.

Testosterone is an androgen that is a key hormone in the development of puberty in boys (Colvin & Abdullatif, 2012). As the testosterone level rises during puberty, external genitals enlarge, height increases, and the voice changes. **Estradiol** is an estrogen that plays

menarche A girl's first menstruation.

precocious puberty Very early onset and rapid progression of puberty.

hormones Powerful chemical substances secreted by the endocrine glands and carried through the body by the bloodstream.

androgens The main class of male sex hormones.

estrogens The main class of female sex hormones.

testosterone An androgen that is a key hormone in boys' pubertal development.

estradiol An estrogen that is a key hormone in girls' pubertal development.

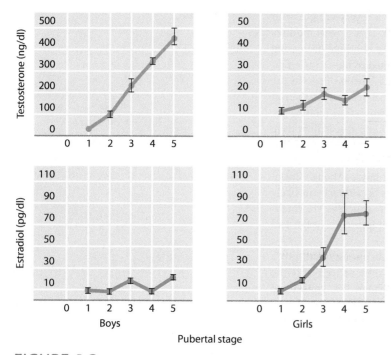

FIGURE **4.2**

HORMONE LEVELS BY SEX AND PUBERTAL STAGE FOR TESTOSTERONE AND ESTRADIOL. The five stages range from the early beginning of puberty (stage 1) to the most advanced stage of puberty (stage 5). Notice the significant increase in testosterone in boys and the significant increase in estradiol in girls.

an important role in female pubertal development. As the estradiol level rises, breast development, uterine development, and skeletal changes occur. In one study, testosterone levels increased eighteen-fold in boys but only twofold in girls across puberty; estradiol levels increased eightfold in girls but only twofold in boys across puberty (Nottleman & others, 1987) (see Figure 4.2).

Are there links between concentrations of hormones and adolescent behavior? Findings are inconsistent (Vermeersch & others, 2008). In any event, hormonal factors alone are not responsible for adolescent behavior (Graber, 2008). For example, one study found that social factors accounted for two to four times as much variance as hormonal factors in young adolescent girls' depression and anger (Brooks-Gunn & Warren, 1989). Hormones do not act independently; hormonal activity is influenced by many environmental factors, including parent-adolescent relationships. Stress, eating patterns, sexual activity, and depression can also activate or suppress various aspects of the hormone system (Susman & Dorn, 2013).

Growth Spurt   Puberty ushers in the most rapid increases in growth since infancy. As indicated in Figure 4.3, the growth spurt associated with puberty occurs approximately two years earlier for girls than for boys. The mean beginning of the growth spurt in the United States today is 9 years of age for girls and 11 years of age for boys. Pubertal change peaks at an average of 11.5 years for girls and 13.5 years for boys. During their growth spurt, girls increase in height about 3.5 inches per year, boys about 4 inches.

Boys and girls who are shorter or taller than their peers before adolescence are likely to remain so during adolescence. At the beginning of adolescence, girls tend to be as tall as or taller than boys their age, but by the end of the middle school years most boys have caught up, or, in many cases, even surpassed girls in height. And although height in elementary school is a good predictor of height later in adolescence, as much as 30 percent of the height of individuals in late adolescence is unexplained by height in the elementary school years.

Sexual Maturation   Think back to the onset of your puberty. Of the striking changes that were taking place in your body, what was the first change that occurred? Researchers have found that male pubertal characteristics develop in this order: increase in penis and testicle size, appearance of straight pubic hair, minor voice change, first ejaculation (which usually

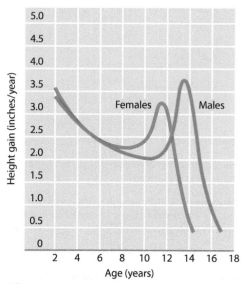

FIGURE **4.3**

PUBERTAL GROWTH SPURT. On average, the peak of the growth spurt that characterizes pubertal change occurs two years earlier for girls (11½) than for boys (13½).

occurs through masturbation or a wet dream), appearance of curly pubic hair, onset of maximum body growth, growth of hair in armpits, more detectable voice changes, and growth of facial hair. Three of the most noticeable areas of sexual maturation in boys are penis elongation, testes development, and growth of facial hair. The normal range and average age of development in boys and girls for these sexual characteristics, along with height spurt, is shown in Figure 4.4.

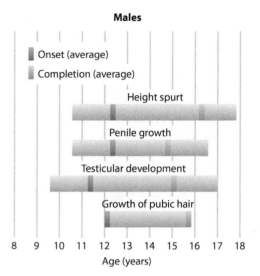

What is the order of appearance of physical changes in females? First, on average the breasts enlarge and then pubic hair appears. These are two of the most noticeable aspects of female pubertal development. A recent longitudinal study revealed that on average, girls' breast development preceded their pubic hair development by about 2 months (Susman & others, 2010). Later, hair appears in the armpits. As these changes occur, the female grows in height, and her hips become wider than her shoulders. Her first menstruation (menarche) occurs rather late in the pubertal cycle; it is considered normal if it occurs between the ages of 9 and 15. Initially, her menstrual cycles may be highly irregular. For the first several years, she might not ovulate during every menstrual cycle. Some girls do not become fertile until two years after their periods begin. Pubertal females do not experience voice changes comparable to those in pubertal males. By the end of puberty, the female's breasts have become more fully rounded.

Psychological Dimensions of Puberty A host of psychological changes accompany an adolescent's pubertal development. Two of the most pronounced psychological changes involve body image and early and late maturation.

Body Image One psychological aspect of physical change in puberty is certain: Adolescents are preoccupied with their bodies and develop images of what their bodies are like (Park & Epstein, 2013; Williams, Wyatt, & Winters, 2013). Preoccupation with body image is strong throughout adolescence, but it is especially acute during early adolescence, a time when adolescents are more dissatisfied with their bodies than in late adolescence. Nonetheless, when the entirety of adolescence was considered, not just puberty, a recent study found that both boys' and girls' body images became more positive as they moved from the beginning to the end of adolescence (Holsen, Carlson Jones, & Skogbrott Birkeland, 2012).

Gender differences characterize adolescents' perceptions of their bodies. In general, girls are less happy with their bodies and have more negative body images than boys throughout puberty (Benowitz-Fredericks & others, 2012). As pubertal change proceeds, girls often become more dissatisfied with their bodies, probably because their body fat increases. In contrast, boys become more satisfied as they move through puberty, probably because their muscle mass increases.

Although we have described gender differences in the body images of adolescents, emphasizing that girls tend to have more negative body images than boys, keep in mind that there is considerable variation, with many adolescent girls having positive body images and many adolescent boys having negative body images. Further, a recent research review revealed an increase in body satisfaction for non-Latino White adolescent girls but not for African American adolescent girls (Grabe & Hyde, 2006).

Early and Late Maturation Did you enter puberty early, late, or on time? When adolescents mature earlier or later than their peers, they often perceive themselves differently and their maturational timing is linked to their socioemotional development and whether they develop problems (Negriff, Susman, & Trickett, 2011). In the Berkeley Longitudinal Study conducted some years ago, early-maturing boys perceived themselves more positively and had more successful peer relations than did late-maturing boys (Jones, 1965). The findings for early-maturing

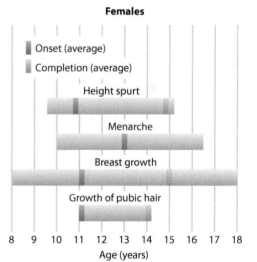

FIGURE 4.4

NORMAL RANGE AND AVERAGE DEVELOPMENT OF SEXUAL CHARACTERISTICS IN MALES AND FEMALES

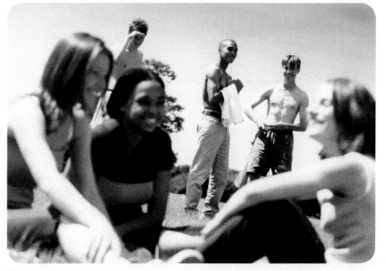

What gender differences characterize adolescents' body image? What might explain the differences?

How does early and late maturation influence adolescent development?

girls were similar but not as strong as for boys. When the late-maturing boys were in their thirties, however, they had developed a more positive identity than the early-maturing boys had (Peskin, 1967). Perhaps the late-maturing boys had more time to explore life's options, or perhaps the early-maturing boys continued to focus on their physical status instead of paying attention to career development and achievement.

An increasing number of researchers have found that early maturation increases girls' vulnerability to a number of problems (Sontag-Padilla & others, 2012; Susman & Dorn, 2013; Negriff, Susman, & Trickett, 2011). Early-maturing girls are more likely to smoke, drink, be depressed, have an eating disorder, engage in delinquency, struggle for earlier independence from their parents, and have older friends; and their bodies are likely to elicit responses from males that lead to earlier dating and earlier sexual experiences (de Rose & others, 2011; Negriff, Susman, & Trickett, 2011). And early-maturing girls are more likely to drop out of high school and to cohabit and marry earlier (Cavanagh, 2009). Apparently as a result of their social and cognitive immaturity, combined with early physical development, early-maturing girls are easily lured into problem behaviors, not recognizing the possible long-term effects of these on their development. Two recent studies document the negative outcomes of early pubertal timing in girls:

- Early-maturing girls were more likely to engage in substance abuse and early sexual intercourse (Gaudineau & others, 2010).
- A study of 9- to 13-year-old girls found that early pubertal timing at time 1 was linked to a higher level of sexual activity at time 2, which in turn was related to higher delinquency at time 3 (Negriff, Susman, & Trickett, 2011).

Review Connect Reflect

LG1 Discuss developmental changes in the body.

Review

- What are cephalocaudal and proximodistal patterns?
- How do height and weight change in infancy and childhood?
- What changes characterize puberty?

Connect

- Describe the influence of nature and nurture on the relationship between hormones and puberty.

Reflect *Your Own Personal Journey of Life*

- Did you experience puberty early, late, or on time? How do you think this affected your social relationships and development?

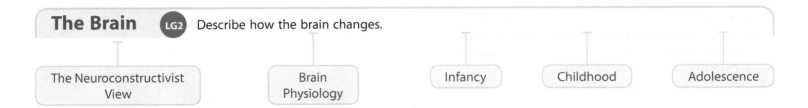

The Brain **LG2** Describe how the brain changes.

| The Neuroconstructivist View | Brain Physiology | Infancy | Childhood | Adolescence |

neuroconstructivist view Theory of brain development emphasizing the following points: (a) biological processes and environmental conditions influence the brain's development, (b) the brain has plasticity and is context dependent, and (c) the development of the brain and the child's cognitive development are closely linked.

In every physical change we have described so far, the brain is involved in some way. Structures of the brain help to regulate not only behavior but also metabolism, the release of hormones, and other aspects of the body's physiology.

We described the amazing growth of the brain from conception to birth in Chapter 3. In this section, we initially will explore the neuroconstructivist view, describe basic structures and function of the brain, and then examine developmental changes in the brain from infancy through adolescence.

THE NEUROCONSTRUCTIVIST VIEW

Until recently, little was known for certain about how the brain changes as children develop. Not long ago, scientists thought that our genes determined how our brains were "wired" and that the cells in the brain responsible for processing information just maturationally unfolded with little or no input from environmental experiences. Whatever brain your heredity dealt you, you were essentially stuck with it. This view, however, turned out to be wrong. Instead, the brain has plasticity, and its development depends on context (Diamond, 2013; Nelson, 2012).

In the increasingly popular **neuroconstructivist view,** (a) biological processes (genes, for example) and environmental conditions (enriched or impoverished, for example) influence the brain's development, (b) the brain has plasticity and is context dependent, and (c) development of the brain is closely linked with the child's cognitive development. These factors constrain or advance the child's construction of cognitive skills (Diamond, 2013; Peltzer-Karpf, 2012; Westermann, Thomas, & Karmiloff-Smith, 2011). The neuroconstructivist view emphasizes the importance of considering interactions between experience and gene expression in the brain's development, much in the same way the epigenetic view proposes (see Chapter 2, "Biological Beginnings").

BRAIN PHYSIOLOGY

The brain includes a number of major structures. The key components of these structures are *neurons,* the nerve cells that handle information processing, which we initially described in Chapter 3.

Structure and Function   Looked at from above, the brain has two halves, or hemispheres (see Figure 4.5). The top portion of the brain, farthest from the spinal cord, is known as the forebrain. Its outer layer of cells, the cerebral cortex, covers it like a cap. The cerebral cortex is responsible for about 80 percent of the brain's volume and is critically important in perception, thinking, language, and other functions.

Each hemisphere of the cortex has four major areas, called lobes. Although the lobes usually work together, each has a somewhat different primary function (see Figure 4.6):

- *Frontal lobes* are involved in voluntary movement, thinking, personality, and intentionality or purpose.
- *Occipital lobes* function in vision.
- *Temporal lobes* facilitate hearing, language processing, and memory.
- *Parietal lobes* help to register spatial location, direct attention, and maintain motor control.

Deeper in the brain, beneath the cortex, lie other key structures. These include the hypothalamus and the pituitary gland as well as the *amygdala,* which plays an important role in emotions, and the *hippocampus,* which is especially active in memory and emotion.

Neurons   How do neurons work? As we indicated, these nerve cells process information. Figure 4.7 shows some important parts of the neuron, including the *axon* and *dendrites*. Basically, an axon sends electrical signals away from the central part of the neuron. At the end of the axon are terminal buttons, which release chemicals called *neurotransmitters* into *synapses,* which are tiny gaps between neurons' fibers. Chemical interactions in synapses connect axons and dendrites, allowing information to pass from neuron to neuron (Emes & Grant, 2013). Think of the synapse as a river that blocks a road. A grocery truck arrives at one bank of the river, crosses by ferry, and continues its journey to market. Similarly, a message in the brain is "ferried" across the synapse by a neurotransmitter, which pours out information contained in chemicals when it reaches the other side of the river.

developmental **connection**

Nature and Nurture

In the epigenetic view, development is an ongoing, bidirectional interchange between heredity and the environment. Chapter 2, p. 69

FIGURE 4.5
THE HUMAN BRAIN'S HEMISPHERES. The two halves (hemispheres) of the human brain are clearly seen in this photograph.

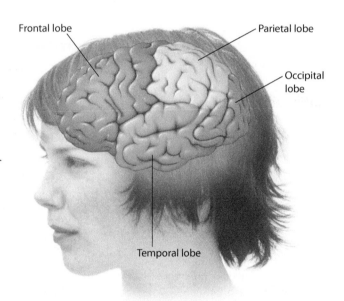

Frontal lobe

Parietal lobe

Occipital lobe

Temporal lobe

FIGURE 4.6
THE BRAIN'S FOUR LOBES. Shown here are the locations of the brain's four lobes: frontal, occipital, temporal, and parietal.

developmental **connection**

Intelligence

Are some regions of the brain linked with children's intelligence more than others? Chapter 8, p. 235

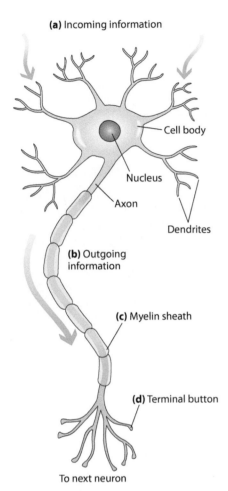

(a) Incoming information

Cell body

Nucleus

Axon

Dendrites

(b) Outgoing information

(c) Myelin sheath

(d) Terminal button

To next neuron

FIGURE **4.7**

THE NEURON. (*a*) The dendrites receive information from other neurons, muscles, or glands. (*b*) Axons transmit information away from the cell body. (*c*) A myelin sheath covers most axons and speeds information transmission. (*d*) As the axon ends, it branches out into terminal buttons.

developmental **connection**

Gender

How large are gender differences in the brain? Chapter 12, p. 347

developmental **connection**

Brain Development

How does the brain change from conception to birth? Chapter 3, p. 79

lateralization Specialization of function in one hemisphere of the cerebral cortex or the other.

myelination The process of encasing axons with a myelin sheath that increases the speed of processing information.

Most axons are covered by a myelin sheath, which is a layer of fat cells. The sheath helps impulses travel faster along the axon, increasing the speed with which information travels from neuron to neuron (Buttermore, Thaxton, & Bhat, 2013). The myelin sheath developed as the brain evolved. As brain size increased, it became necessary for information to travel faster over longer distances in the nervous system. We can compare the myelin sheath's development to the evolution of freeways as cities grew. A freeway is a shielded road, and it keeps fast-moving, long-distance traffic from getting snarled by slow local traffic.

Which neurons get which information? Clusters of neurons known as *neural circuits* work together to handle particular types of information (Homae & others, 2011). The brain is organized in many neural circuits (Rueda & Posner, 2013; Short & others, 2013). For example, one neural circuit is important in attention and working memory (the type of memory that holds information for a brief time and serves as a "mental workbench" as we perform a task) (Krimer & Goldman-Rakic, 2001). This neural circuit uses the neurotransmitter dopamine and lies in the prefrontal cortex and midbrain areas of the brain (D'Ardenne & others, 2012).

To some extent, the type of information handled by neurons depends on whether they are in the left or right hemisphere of the cortex (Griffiths & others, 2013). Speech and grammar, for example, depend on activity in the left hemisphere in most people; humor and the use of metaphors depend on activity in the right hemisphere (McGettigan & others, 2012). This specialization of function in one hemisphere of the cerebral cortex or the other is called **lateralization.** However, most neuroscientists agree that complex functions such as reading or performing music involve both hemispheres (Ibrahim & Eviatar, 2013). Labeling people as "left-brained" because they are logical thinkers and "right-brained" because they are creative thinkers does not correspond to the way the brain's hemispheres work. Complex thinking in normal people is the outcome of communication between both hemispheres of the brain (Liegeois & others, 2008). For example, a recent meta-analysis revealed no hemispheric specialization in creative thinking (Mihov, Denzler, & Forster, 2010).

INFANCY

As we saw in Chapter 3, brain development occurs extensively during the prenatal period. The brain's development is also substantial during infancy and later on (Diamond, 2013; Markant & Thomas, 2013; Zelazo, 2013).

Because the brain is still developing so rapidly in infancy, the infant's head should be protected from falls or other injuries and the baby should never be shaken. *Shaken baby syndrome,* which includes brain swelling and hemorrhaging, affects hundreds of babies in the United States each year (Swaiman & others, 2012). A recent analysis found that fathers were the most frequent perpetrators of shaken baby syndrome, followed by child care providers and by a boyfriend of the victim's mother (National Center on Shaken Baby Syndrome, 2011).

Studying the brain's development in infancy is not as easy as it might seem. Even the latest brain-imaging technologies (described in Chapter 1) cannot make out fine details in adult brains and cannot be used with babies (Nelson, 2012). Positron-emission tomography (PET) scans pose a radiation risk to babies, and infants wriggle too much to allow technicians to capture accurate images using magnetic resonance imaging (MRI). However, researchers have been successful in using the electroencephalogram (EEG), a measure of the brain's electrical activity, to learn about the brain's development in infancy (Bell & Cuevas, 2012, 2013). Among the researchers who are making strides in finding out more about the brain's development in infancy are Martha Ann Bell and her colleagues (Bell & Cuevas, 2012, 2013; Bell & Diaz, 2012; Morasch, Raj, & Bell, 2013), Charles Nelson and his colleagues (Nelson, 2007, 2012, 2013a, b; Righi & Nelson, 2013), and John Richards and his colleagues (Richards, 2009, 2010; Richards, Reynolds, & Courage, 2010; Sanchez, Richards, & Almi, 2012) (see Figure 4.8).

As an infant walks, talks, runs, shakes a rattle, smiles, and frowns, changes in its brain are occurring. Consider that the infant began life as a single cell and nine months later was born with a brain and nervous system that contained approximately 100 billion nerve cells, or neurons. What determines how those neurons are connected to communicate with each other?

Early Experience and the Brain Children who grow up in a deprived environment may also have depressed brain activity (Zeanah, Fox, & Nelson, 2012). As shown in Figure 4.9, a child who grew up in the unresponsive and unstimulating environment of a Romanian orphanage showed considerably depressed brain activity compared with a normal child.

Are the effects of deprived environments irreversible? There is reason to think the answer is no (Bryck & Fisher, 2012; Sharma, Classen, & Cohen, 2013). The brain demonstrates both flexibility and resilience. Consider 14-year-old Michael Rehbein. At age 7, he began to experience uncontrollable seizures—as many as 400 a day. Doctors said the only solution was to remove the left hemisphere of his brain where the seizures were occurring. Recovery was slow, but his right hemisphere began to reorganize and take over functions that normally occur in the brain's left hemisphere, including speech (see Figure 4.10). One study of 10 children who had experienced an arterial stroke perinatally (during or around birth) revealed that in 8 of the 10 the right hemisphere was dominant in processing language (Guzzetta & others, 2008).

Neuroscientists believe that what wires the brain—or rewires it, in the case of Michael Rehbein—is repeated experience. Each time a baby tries to touch an attractive object or gazes intently at a face, tiny bursts of electricity shoot through the brain, knitting together neurons into circuits. The results are some of the behavioral milestones we discuss in this chapter.

In sum, the infant's brain is waiting for experiences to determine how connections are made (Mai & others, 2012). Before birth, it appears that genes mainly direct basic wiring patterns. Neurons grow and travel to distant places awaiting further instructions (Nelson, 2012). After birth, the inflowing stream of sights, sounds, smells, touches, language, and eye contact help shape the brain's neural connections (Diamond, 2013; Lamb, 2013; Narvaez & others, 2013).

Changing Neurons At birth, the newborn's brain is about 25 percent of its adult weight. By the second birthday, the brain is about 75 percent of its adult weight. Two key developments during these first two years involve the myelin sheath (the layer of fat cells that speeds up the electrical impulse along the axon) and connections between dendrites.

Myelination, the process of encasing axons with a myelin sheath, begins prenatally and continues

FIGURE **4.8**

MEASURING THE ACTIVITY OF AN INFANT'S BRAIN. By attaching up to 128 electrodes to a baby's scalp to measure the brain's activity, Charles Nelson (2003, 2012) has found that even newborns produce distinctive brain waves that reveal they can distinguish their mother's voice from another woman's, even while they are asleep. *Why is it so difficult to measure infants' brain activity?*

(a)   (b)

FIGURE **4.9**

EARLY DEPRIVATION AND BRAIN ACTIVITY. These two photographs are PET (positron emission tomography) scans (which use radioactive tracers to image and analyze blood flow and metabolic activity in the body's organs) of the brains of (*a*) a normal child and (*b*) an institutionalized Romanian orphan who experienced substantial deprivation since birth. In PET scans, the highest to lowest brain activity is reflected in the colors of red, yellow, green, blue, and black, respectively. As can be seen, red and yellow show up to a much greater degree in the PET scan of the normal child than the deprived Romanian orphan.

(b)

(a)

FIGURE 4.10

PLASTICITY IN THE BRAIN'S HEMISPHERES.
(a) Michael Rehbein at 14 years of age. (b) Michael's right hemisphere (*right*) has reorganized to take over the language functions normally carried out by corresponding areas in the left hemisphere of an intact brain (*left*). However, the right hemisphere is not as efficient as the left, and more areas of the brain are recruited to process speech.

after birth (see Figure 4.11). The myelin sheath insulates axons and helps electrical signals travel faster down the axon (Markant & Thomas, 2013; Nelson, 2012). As we indicated earlier, myelination increases the speed at which information is processed. It also is involved in providing energy to neurons and in communication (Harris & Attwell, 2012). Myelination for visual pathways occurs rapidly after birth and is completed during the first six months. Auditory myelination is not completed until 4 or 5 years of age. Some aspects of myelination continue even into adolescence. Indeed, the most extensive changes in myelination in the frontal lobes occur during adolescence (Giedd, 2012).

Dramatic increases in dendrites and synapses (the tiny gaps between neurons across which neurotransmitters carry information) also characterize the development of the brain in the first two years of life (see Figure 4.12). Nearly twice as many of these connections are made as will ever be used (Huttenlocher & others, 1991; Huttenlocher & Dabholkar, 1997). The connections that are used become strengthened and survive; the unused ones are replaced by other pathways or disappear. That is, connections are "pruned" (Campbell & others, 2012). Figure 4.13 vividly illustrates the growth and later pruning of synapses in the visual, auditory, and prefrontal cortex areas of the brain (Huttenlocher & Dabholkar, 1997).

Myelin Sheath   Axon

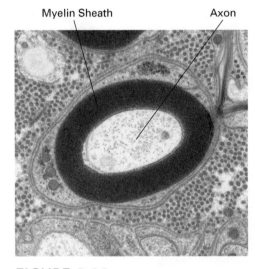

FIGURE 4.11

MYELINATED NERVE FIBER. The myelin sheath, shown in brown, encases the axon (white). This image was produced by an electron microscope that magnified the nerve fiber 12,000 times. *What role does myelination play in the brain's development?*

FIGURE 4.12

THE DEVELOPMENT OF DENDRITIC

SPREADING. Note the increase in connectedness between neurons over the course of the first two years of life.
The Postnatal Development of the Human Cerebral Cortex, Volumes I–VIII by Jesse LeRoy Conel, Cambridge, Mass.: Harvard University Press, Copyright © 1939, 1941, 1947, 1951, 1955, 1959, 1963, 1967 by the President and Fellows of Harvard College. Copyright © renewed 1967, 1969, 1975, 1979, 1983, 1987, 1991.

At birth   1 month   3 months   15 months   24 months

As shown in Figure 4.13, "blooming and pruning" vary considerably by brain region in humans. For example, the peak synaptic overproduction in the area concerned with vision occurs about the fourth postnatal month, followed by a gradual pruning until the middle to end of the preschool years (Huttenlocher & Dabholkar, 1997). In areas of the brain involved in hearing and language, a similar, though somewhat later, course is detected. However, in the prefrontal cortex (the area of the brain where higher-level thinking and self-regulation occur), the peak of overproduction occurs at just after 3 years of age. Both heredity and environment are thought to influence synaptic overproduction and subsequent pruning.

Changing Structures At birth, the hemispheres already have started to specialize: Newborns show greater electrical activity in the left hemisphere than in the right hemisphere when they are making or listening to speech sounds (Imada & others, 2007).

In general, some areas of the brain, such as the primary motor areas, develop earlier than others, such as the primary sensory areas. The frontal lobes are immature in the newborn. However, as neurons in the frontal lobes become myelinated and interconnected during the first year of life, infants develop an ability to regulate their physiological states, such as sleep, and gain more control over their reflexes. Cognitive skills that require deliberate thinking do not emerge until later in the first year (Bell & Cuevas, 2013).

CHILDHOOD

The brain and other parts of the nervous system continue developing through childhood and adolescence. These changes enable children to plan their actions, to attend to stimuli more effectively, and to make considerable strides in language development (Diamond, 2013).

During early childhood, the brain and head grow more rapidly than any other part of the body. Figure 4.14 shows how the growth curve for the head and brain advances more rapidly than the growth curve for height and weight. Some of the brain's increase in size is due to myelination and some is due to an increase in the number and size of dendrites. Some developmentalists conclude that myelination is important in the maturation of a number of abilities in children (Fair & Schlaggar, 2008). For example, myelination in the areas of the brain related to hand-eye coordination is not complete until about 4 years of age. A functional magnetic resonance imaging (fMRI) study of children (mean age, 4 years) found that those who were characterized by developmental delay of motor and cognitive milestones had significantly reduced levels of myelination (Pujol & others, 2004). Myelination in the areas of the brain related to focusing attention is not complete until middle or late childhood.

The brain in early childhood is not growing as rapidly as it did in infancy. However, the anatomical changes in the child's brain between the ages of 3 and 15 are dramatic. By repeatedly obtaining brain scans of the same children for up to four years, scientists have found that children's brains experience rapid, distinct bursts of growth (Gogtay & Thompson, 2010; Thompson & others, 2000). The amount of brain material in some areas can nearly double in as little as one year, followed by a drastic loss of tissue as unneeded cells are purged and the brain continues to reorganize itself. The overall size of the brain does not increase dramatically from 3 to 15. What does dramatically change are local patterns within the brain (Gogtay & Thompson, 2010; Thompson & others, 2000). From 3 to 6 years of age, the most rapid growth occurs in the frontal lobe areas involved in planning and organizing new actions and in maintaining attention to tasks (Diamond, 2013). From age 6 through puberty, the most dramatic growth takes place in the temporal and parietal lobes, especially in areas that play major roles in language and spatial relations.

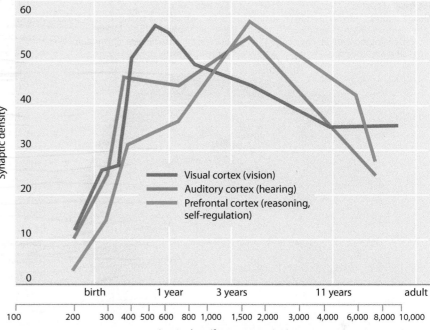

FIGURE **4.13**

SYNAPTIC DENSITY IN THE HUMAN BRAIN FROM INFANCY TO ADULTHOOD. The graph shows the dramatic increase and then pruning in synaptic density for three regions of the brain: visual cortex, auditory cortex, and prefrontal cortex. Synaptic density is believed to be an important indication of the extent of connectivity between neurons.

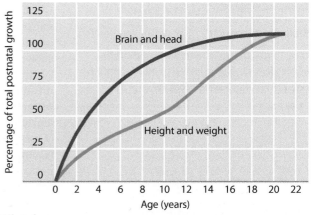

FIGURE **4.14**

GROWTH CURVES FOR THE HEAD AND BRAIN AND FOR HEIGHT AND WEIGHT. The more rapid growth of the brain and head can easily be seen. Height and weight advance more gradually over the first two decades of life.

Prefrontal cortex
This "judgment" region reins in intense emotions but doesn't finish developing until at least emerging adulthood.

Corpus callosum
These nerve fibers connect the brain's two hemispheres; they thicken in adolescence to process information more effectively.

Amygdala
The seat of emotions such as anger; this area develops quickly before other regions that help to control it.

FIGURE 4.15
CHANGES IN THE ADOLESCENT BRAIN

- - - - - - - - ➤

developmental **connection**

Brain Development

How might developmental changes in the adolescent's brain be linked to adolescents' decision-making skills? Chapter 7, p. 218

corpus callosum Brain area where fibers connect the brain's left and right hemispheres.

prefrontal cortex The highest level of the frontal lobes that is involved in reasoning, decision making, and self-control.

amygdala The seat of emotions in the brain.

Developmental neuroscientist Mark Johnson and his colleagues (2009) proposed that the prefrontal cortex likely orchestrates the functions of many other brain regions during development. As part of this neural leadership and organizational role, the prefrontal cortex may provide an advantage to neural connections and networks that include the prefrontal cortex. In the view of these researchers, the prefrontal cortex likely coordinates the best neural connections for solving a problem.

Links between the changing brain and children's cognitive development involve activation of brain areas, with some areas increasing in activation while others decrease. One shift in activation that occurs as children develop in middle and late childhood is from diffuse, larger areas to more focal, smaller areas (Durston & others, 2006). This shift is characterized by synaptic pruning in which areas of the brain not being used lose synaptic connections and those being used show an increase in connections. In a recent study, researchers found less diffusion and more focal activation in the prefrontal cortex (the highest level of the frontal lobes) from 7 to 30 years of age (Durston & others, 2006). The activation change was accompanied by increased efficiency in cognitive performance, especially in *cognitive control*, which involves flexible and effective control in a number of areas. These areas include controlling attention, reducing interfering thoughts, inhibiting motor actions, and being flexible in switching between competing choices (Carlson, Zelazo, & Faja, 2013; Diamond, 2013).

ADOLESCENCE

Along with the rest of the body, the brain is changing during adolescence, but the study of adolescent brain development is in its infancy (Blakemore & Mills, 2014; Giedd & others, 2012). As advances in technology take place, significant strides will also likely be made in charting developmental changes in the adolescent brain. What do we know now?

Earlier we indicated that connections between neurons become "pruned" as children and adolescents develop. The pruning means that the connections which are used strengthen and survive, while the unused ones are replaced by other pathways or disappear. As a result of this pruning, by the end of adolescence individuals have "fewer, more selective, more effective neuronal connections than they did as children" (Kuhn, 2009, p. 153). And this pruning indicates that the activities adolescents choose to engage in and not to engage in influence which neural connections will be strengthened and which will disappear.

Using fMRI brain scans, scientists have recently discovered that adolescents' brains undergo significant structural changes (Chein & others, 2011; Lenroot & Giedd, 2011). The **corpus callosum,** where fibers connect the brain's left and right hemispheres, thickens in adolescence; this improves adolescents' ability to process information. We just described advances in the development of the **prefrontal cortex**—the highest level of the frontal lobes involved in reasoning, decision making, and self-control. The prefrontal cortex doesn't finish maturing until the emerging adult years (approximately 18 to 25 years of age) or later, but the **amygdala**—the seat of emotions such as anger—matures earlier than the prefrontal cortex (Casey, Duhoux, & Malter Cohen, 2010). Figure 4.15 shows the locations of the corpus callosum, prefrontal cortex, and amygdala. A recent study of 137 early adolescents revealed a positive link between the volume of the amygdala and the duration of adolescents' aggressive behavior during interactions with parents (Whittle & others, 2008).

Many of the changes in the adolescent brain that have been described involve the rapidly emerging field of *developmental social neuroscience,* which involves connections between development, the brain, and socioemotional processes (Blakemore & Mills, 2014; Salley, Miller, & Bell, 2013). For example, consider leading researcher Charles Nelson's (2003) view that although adolescents are capable of very strong emotions, their prefrontal cortex hasn't developed to the point at which they can control these passions. It is as if their brain doesn't have the brakes to slow down their emotions. Or consider this interpretation of the development of emotion and cognition in adolescents: "early activation of strong 'turbo-charged' feelings with a relatively un-skilled set of 'driving skills' or cognitive abilities to modulate strong emotions and motivations" (Dahl, 2004, p. 18).

Of course, a major issue in adolescent brain development is which comes first: biological changes in the brain or experiences that stimulate these changes (Lerner, Boyd, & Du, 2009). Consider a study in which the prefrontal cortex thickened and more brain connections formed when adolescents resisted peer pressure (Paus & others, 2007). A recent study also found that adolescents from Mexican backgrounds with greater family obligation values showed decreased activation in the brain's regions (ventral striatum) involving reward sensitivity, which was linked to less real-life risk-taking behavior, and increased activation in the brain's regions (prefrontal cortex) involving cognitive control, which was associated with better decision-making skills (Telzer & others, 2013).

Scientists have yet to determine whether the brain changes come first or whether they result from experiences with peers, parents, and others. Once again, we encounter the nature/nurture issue that is so prominent in examining development (Giedd & others, 2012).

developmental **connection**

Brain Development

Developmental social neuroscience is a recently emerging field that focuses on connections between development, socio-emotional factors, and neuroscience. Chapter 1, p. 13

Review *Connect* Reflect

LG2 Describe how the brain changes.

Review

- What are some key features of the neuroconstructivist view?
- What is the nature of brain physiology?
- How does the brain change in infancy?
- What characterizes the development of the brain in childhood?
- How does the brain change in adolescence, and how might this change be linked to adolescents' behavior?

Connect

- Both infancy and adolescence are times of significant change in the brain. Compare and contrast these changes.

Reflect *Your Own Personal Journey of Life*

- A parent tells you that his or her child is "left-brained" and that this aspect of the brain explains why the child does well in school. Is the parent likely to be providing an accurate explanation or probably off-base? Explain.

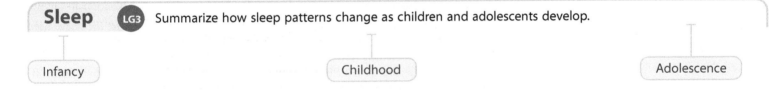

Sleep **LG3** Summarize how sleep patterns change as children and adolescents develop.

Infancy   Childhood   Adolescence

Sleep restores, replenishes, and rebuilds our brains and bodies. Some neuroscientists believe that sleep gives neurons that have been used while we are awake a chance to shut down and repair themselves (National Institute of Neurological Disorders and Stroke, 2013). How do sleeping patterns change during the childhood years?

INFANCY

When we were infants, sleep consumed more of our time than it does now. Newborns sleep 16 to 17 hours a day, although some sleep more and others less—the range is from a low of about 10 hours to a high of about 21 hours per day. A recent research review concluded that infants 0 to 2 years of age slept an average of 12.8 hours out of the 24, within a range of

> Sleep that knits up the ravelled sleave of care . . . Balm of hurt minds, nature's second course. Chief nourisher in life's feast.
>
> —**WILLIAM SHAKESPEARE**
> *English playwright, 17th century*

FIGURE **4.16**

DEVELOPMENTAL CHANGES IN REM AND NON-REM SLEEP

9.7 to 15.9 hours (Galland & others, 2012). A recent study also revealed that by 6 months of age the majority of infants slept through the night, awakening their mothers only once or twice a week (Weinraub & others, 2012).

Although total sleep remains somewhat consistent for young infants, their sleep during the day does not always follow a rhythmic pattern. An infant might change from sleeping several long bouts of 7 or 8 hours to three or four shorter sessions only several hours in duration. By about 1 month of age, most infants have begun to sleep longer at night. By 6 months of age, they usually have moved closer to adult-like sleep patterns, spending their longest span of sleep at night and their longest span of waking during the day (Sadeh, 2008).

The most common infant sleep-related problem reported by parents is night-time waking (The Hospital for Sick Children & others, 2010). Surveys indicate that 20 to 30 percent of infants have difficulty going to sleep at night and staying asleep (Sadeh, 2008). A recent study revealed that the mother's emotional availability at bedtime was linked to fewer infant sleep problems, supporting the premise that parents' emotional availability to infants in sleep contexts increases feelings of safety and security, and consequently promotes better-regulated infant sleep (Teti & others, 2010). Further, a recent study found that a higher involvement of fathers in overall infant care was related to fewer infant sleep problems (Tikotzky, Sadeh, & Glickman-Gavrieli, 2010). However, infant nighttime waking problems have consistently been linked to excessive parental involvement in sleep-related interactions with their infant (Sadeh, 2008). And a recent study revealed that maternal depression during pregnancy, early introduction of solid foods, infant TV viewing, and child care attendance were related to shorter duration of infant sleep (Nevarez & others, 2010). Also, a recent study found that nighttime wakings at 1 year of age predicted lower sleep efficiency at 4 years of age (Tikotzky & Shaashua, 2012).

REM Sleep In REM sleep, the eyes flutter beneath closed lids; in non-REM sleep, this type of eye movement does not occur and sleep is quieter. Figure 4.16 shows developmental changes in the average number of total hours spent in REM and non-REM sleep. By the time they reach adulthood, individuals spend about one-fifth of their night in REM sleep, and REM sleep usually appears about one hour after non-REM sleep. However, about half of an infant's sleep is REM sleep, and infants often begin their sleep cycle with REM sleep rather than non-REM sleep (Sadeh, 2008). A much greater amount of time is taken up by REM sleep in infancy than at any other point in the life span. By the time infants reach 3 months of age, the percentage of time they spend in REM sleep falls to about 40 percent, and REM sleep no longer begins their sleep cycle.

Why do infants spend so much time in REM sleep? Researchers are not certain. The large amount of REM sleep may provide infants with added self-stimulation, since they spend less time awake than do older children. REM sleep also might promote the brain's development in infancy (Graven, 2006).

When adults are awakened during REM sleep, they frequently report that they have been dreaming, but when they are awakened during non-REM sleep they are much less likely to report having been dreaming (Cartwright & others, 2006). Since infants spend more time than adults in REM sleep, can we conclude that they dream a lot? We don't know whether infants dream or not, because they don't have any way of reporting dreams.

Shared Sleeping Some child experts stress that there are benefits to shared sleeping (as when an infant sleeps in the same bed with its mother). They state that it can promote breast feeding, lets the mother respond more quickly to the baby's cries, and allows her to detect breathing pauses in the baby that might be dangerous (Pelayo & others, 2006). Sharing a bed with a mother is common practice in many countries, such as Guatemala and China, whereas in others, such as the United States and Great Britain, most newborns sleep in a crib, either in the same room as the parents or in a separate room.

Shared sleeping remains a controversial issue, with some experts recommending it and others arguing against it, although recently the recommendation trend has been to avoid infant-parent bed sharing, especially until the infant is at least six months of age (Byard, 2012a, b; Weber & others, 2012). The American Academy of Pediatrics Task Force on Infant Positioning and SIDS (AAPTFIPS) (2000) recommends against shared sleeping. Its members argue that in some instances bed sharing might lead to sudden infant death syndrome (SIDS), as could be the case if a sleeping mother rolls over on her baby. Recent studies have found that bed sharing is linked with a greater incidence of SIDS, especially when parents smoke (Byard 2012a, b). And a recent study of 2-month-old infants revealed that they had more sleep problems such as disordered breathing when they shared the bed with parents (Kelmanson, 2010).

SIDS   **Sudden infant death syndrome (SIDS)** is a condition that occurs when infants stop breathing, usually during the night, and die suddenly without an apparent cause. SIDS remains the highest cause of infant death in the United States, with nearly 3,000 infant deaths attributed to it annually (Montagna & Chokroverty, 2011). Risk of SIDS is highest at 2 to 4 months of age (National Institute of Child Health and Development, 2013).

Since 1992, The American Academy of Pediatrics (AAP) has recommended that infants be placed to sleep on their backs to reduce the risk of SIDS, and the frequency of prone (on the stomach) sleeping among U.S. infants has dropped dramatically (AAPTFIPS, 2000). Researchers have found that SIDS does indeed decrease when infants sleep on their backs rather than their stomachs or sides (Darrah & Bartlett, 2013). Among the reasons given for prone sleeping being a high-risk factor for SIDS are that it impairs the infant's arousal from sleep and restricts the infant's ability to swallow effectively (Moon & Fu, 2012).

In addition to sleeping in a prone position, researchers have found that the following are risk factors for SIDS:

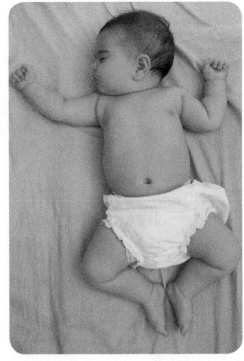

Is this a good sleep position for infants? Why or why not?

- SIDS occurs more often in infants with abnormal brain stem functioning involving the neurotransmitter serotonin (Broadbrent & others, 2012; Duncan & others, 2010).

- Heart arrhythmias are estimated to occur in as many as 15 percent of SIDS cases, and two recent studies found that gene mutations were linked to the occurrence of these arrhythmias (Brion & others, 2012; Van Norstrand & others, 2012).

- Six percent of infants with sleep apnea, a temporary cessation of breathing in which the airway is completely blocked, usually for 10 seconds or longer, die of SIDS (Ednick & others, 2010; McNamara & Sullivan, 2000).

- Low birth weight infants are 5 to 10 times more likely to die of SIDS than are their normal-weight counterparts (Horne & others, 2002).

- Infants whose siblings have died of SIDS are two to four times as likely to die of it (Lenoir, Mallet, & Calenda, 2000).

- African American and Eskimo infants are four to six times as likely as all others to die of SIDS (Ige & Shelton, 2004; Kitsantas & Gaffney, 2010).

- SIDS is more common in lower socioeconomic groups (Mitchell & others, 2000).

- Two recent reviews concluded that breast feeding is linked to a lower incidence of SIDS (Hauck & others, 2011; Zotter & Pichler, 2012).

- SIDS is more common in infants who are passively exposed to cigarette smoke (Dietz & others, 2010).

- SIDS is more common when infants and parents share the same bed (Senter & others, 2010).

- SIDS is more common if infants sleep in soft bedding (Moon & Fu, 2012).

- SIDS is more likely to occur in infants who do not use a pacifier when they go to sleep than in those who do use a pacifier (Jenik & Vain, 2010).

- SIDS is less common when infants sleep in a bedroom with a fan. A recent study revealed that sleeping in a bedroom with a fan lowers the risk of SIDS by 70 percent (Coleman-Phox, Odouli, & Li, 2008).

CHILDHOOD

A good night's sleep is an important aspect of a child's development (El-Sheikh, 2013; El-Sheikh & others, 2013). Experts recommend that young children get 11 to 13 hours of sleep each night and that first- to fifth-graders get 10 to 11 hours of sleep each night (National

sudden infant death syndrome (SIDS) A condition that occurs when an infant stops breathing, usually during the night, and suddenly dies without an apparent cause.

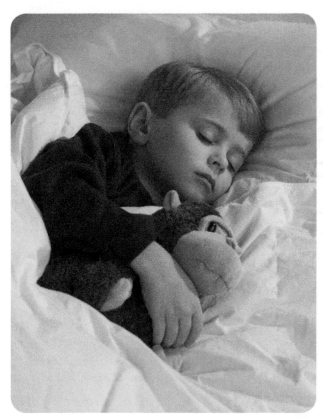

What are some links between children's sleep patterns and other aspects of development?

Sleep Foundation, 2013). Most young children sleep through the night and have one daytime nap. Not only is the amount of sleep children get important, but so is uninterrupted sleep (Moore, 2012). However, it sometimes is difficult to get young children to go to sleep as they drag out their bedtime routine.

To improve sleep, Mona El-Sheikh (2013) recommends ensuring that children have a bedroom that is cool, dark, and comfortable; consistent bed times and wake times; and positive family relationships. Also, helping the child slow down before bedtime often contributes to less resistance in going to bed. Reading the child a story, playing quietly with the child in the bath, and letting the child sit on the caregiver's lap while listening to music are quieting activities.

Children can experience a number of sleep problems (El-Sheikh, 2011). One estimate indicates that more than 40 percent of children experience a sleep problem at some point in their development (Boyle & Cropley, 2004). The following research studies indicate links between children's sleep problems and negative developmental outcomes:

- Children who had trouble sleeping in childhood were more likely to have alcohol use problems in adolescence and early adulthood (Wong & others, 2010).

- Sleep problems in early childhood were a subsequent indicator of attention problems that in some cases persisted into early adolescence (O'Callaghan & others, 2010).

- A recent analysis concluded that chronic sleep disorders that deprive children of adequate sleep may result in impaired brain development (Jan & others, 2010).

- Emotional security in parent and marital relationships when children were in the third grade predicted fewer sleep problems when they reached the fifth grade (Keller & El-Sheikh, 2010).

ADOLESCENCE

There has recently been a surge of interest in adolescent sleep patterns (Mak & others, 2012; Short & others, 2012). This interest focuses on the belief that many adolescents are not getting enough sleep, that there are physiological underpinnings to the desire of adolescents, especially older ones, to stay up later at night and sleep longer in the morning, and that these findings have implications for understanding the times of day when adolescents learn most effectively in school (Hansen & others, 2005). For example, a recent national survey found that 8 percent of middle school students and 14 percent of high school students are late for school or miss school because they oversleep (National Sleep Foundation, 2006). Also in this survey, 6 percent of middle school students and 28 percent of high school students fall asleep in U.S. schools on any given day. Studies recently have confirmed that adolescents in other countries also are not getting adequate sleep (Leger & others, 2012; Short & others, 2012). In one recent study, Asian adolescents had later bedtimes and were getting less sleep than U.S. adolescents (Gradisar, Gardner, & Duhnt, 2011).

Getting too little sleep in adolescence is linked to a number of problems, including delinquency (Clinkinbeard & others, 2011), sleep disturbances in emerging and early adulthood (Dregan & Armstrong, 2010), and less effective attention (Beebe, Rose, & Amin, 2010). A longitudinal study in which adolescents completed daily diaries for 14-day periods in ninth, tenth, and twelfth grades found that regardless of how much students studied each day, when the students sacrificed sleep time to study more than usual, they had difficulty understanding what was taught in class and were more likely to struggle with class assignments the next day (Gillen-O'Neel, Huynh, & Fuligni, 2012).

Mary Carskadon (2002, 2004, 2005, 2006, 2011) has conducted a number of research studies on adolescent sleep patterns. She has found that adolescents sleep an average of 9 hours and 25 minutes when given the opportunity to sleep as long as they like. Most adolescents get considerably less sleep than this, especially during the week. This creates a sleep debt, which adolescents often try to make up on the weekend. Carskadon also found that older adolescents are often more sleepy during the day than are younger adolescents and concluded that this was not because of factors such as academic work and social pressures. Rather, her research suggests that adolescents' biological clocks undergo a hormonal phase shift as they get older. This pushes the time of wakefulness to an hour later than when they were young adolescents. Carskadon found that this shift was caused by a delay in the nightly presence of the hormone *melatonin,* which is produced by the brain's pineal gland in preparing the body for sleep. Melatonin is secreted at about 9:30 p.m. in younger adolescents but is produced approximately an hour later in older adolescents, which delays the onset of sleep.

Carskadon determined that early school starting times can result in grogginess and lack of attention in class and poor performance on tests. Based on this research, some schools are now starting later (Cassoff & others, 2013). For example, school officials in Edina, Minnesota, made the decision to start classes at 8:30 a.m. instead of 7:25 a.m. Discipline problems and the number of students who report an illness or depression have dropped. Test scores in Edina have improved for high school students but not for middle school students, which supports Carskadon's idea that older adolescents are more affected by earlier school start times than younger adolescents are. Also, a recent study found that just a 30-minute delay in school start time was linked to improvements in adolescents' sleep, alertness, mood, and health (Owens, Belon, & Moss, 2010).

In Mary Carskadon's sleep laboratory at Brown University, an adolescent girl's brain activity is being monitored. Carskadon (2005) says that in the morning, sleep-deprived adolescents'"brains are telling them it's nighttime . . . and the rest of the world is saying it's time to go to school" (p. 19).

Review *Connect* Reflect

LG3 Summarize how sleep patterns change as children and adolescents develop.

Review

- How can sleep be characterized in infancy?
- What changes occur in sleep during childhood?
- How does adolescence affect sleep?

Connect

- In this section, you learned that exposure to cigarette smoke can affect an infant's risk for SIDS. In Chapter 3, what did you learn about cigarette smoke's effect on fetal development?

Reflect *Your Own Personal Journey of Life*

- Did your sleep patterns start to change when you became an adolescent? Have they changed since you went through puberty? If so, how?

Health   **LG4**   Characterize children's health.

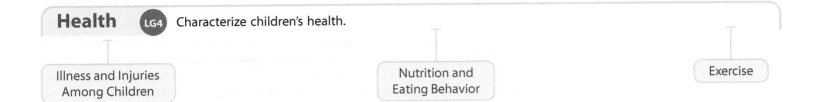

| Illness and Injuries Among Children | Nutrition and Eating Behavior | Exercise |

What are the major threats to children's health today? We will look first at the major illnesses and injuries experienced by children and adolescents before turning to less obvious threats to healthy development: poor nutrition and eating habits, and lack of exercise. The formation of healthy habits in childhood, such as eating foods low in fat and cholesterol and engaging in regular exercise, not only has immediate benefits but also contributes to the delay or prevention of premature

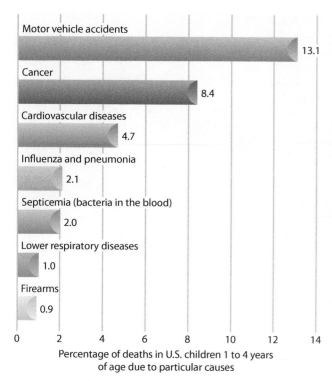

Motor vehicle accidents — 13.1

Cancer — 8.4

Cardiovascular diseases — 4.7

Influenza and pneumonia — 2.1

Septicemia (bacteria in the blood) — 2.0

Lower respiratory diseases — 1.0

Firearms — 0.9

0   2   4   6   8   10   12   14

Percentage of deaths in U.S. children 1 to 4 years
of age due to particular causes

FIGURE **4.17**

**MAIN CAUSES OF DEATH IN CHILDREN 1 THROUGH 4
YEARS OF AGE.** These figures show the percentage of deaths in
U.S. children 1 to 4 years of age due to particular causes in 2002
(National Vital Statistics Reports, 2004).

disability and mortality in adulthood from heart disease, stroke, diabetes, and cancer. And adolescence is a critical juncture in the adoption of many health-enhancing behaviors, such as regular exercise, and health-compromising behaviors, such as smoking (Catalano & others, 2012; Phillips & Edwards, 2013).

ILLNESS AND INJURIES AMONG CHILDREN

In this section, we first examine broad patterns in the causes of illness and death among children and adolescents. Then we turn to the difficulties faced by poor children in the United States and around the world.

Early Childhood Young children's active and exploratory nature, coupled with being unaware of danger in many instances, often puts them in situations in which they are at risk for injuries. Most of the cuts, bumps, and bruises sustained by young children are minor, but some accidental injuries can produce serious impairment or even death. In the United States, motor vehicle accidents are the leading cause of death in young children, followed by cancer and cardiovascular disease (National Vital Statistics Report, 2004) (see Figure 4.17). In addition to motor vehicle accidents, other accidental deaths in children involve drowning, falls, burns, and poisoning (Conde, 2012; Gielen & others, 2012).

An increasing number of studies reach the conclusion that children are at risk for health problems when they live in homes in which a parent smokes (Been & others, 2013; Hwang & others, 2012). Children exposed to tobacco smoke in the home are more likely to develop wheezing symptoms and asthma than children in nonsmoking homes (Yi & others, 2012). A recent study found that parental smoking was a risk factor for higher blood pressure in children (Simonetti & others, 2011). And another recent study revealed that exposure to secondhand smoke was related to young children's sleep problems, including sleep-disordered breathing (Yolton & others, 2010).

An estimated 3 million U.S. children under 6 years of age are thought to be at risk for lead poisoning (Moya, Bearer, & Etzel, 2004). The negative effects of high lead levels in children's blood include lower intelligence, lower achievement, attention deficit hyperactivity disorder, and elevated blood pressure (Burke & Miller, 2011). Children in poverty face a higher risk for lead poisoning than children living in higher socioeconomic conditions (Vivier & others, 2011).

Middle and Late Childhood For the most part, middle and late childhood is a time of excellent health (Van Dyck, 2007). Disease and death are less prevalent in this period than in early childhood and adolescence.

The most common cause of severe injury and death in middle and late childhood is motor vehicle accidents, either as a pedestrian or as a passenger (Frisbie, Hummer, & McKinnon, 2009). Using safety-belt restraints is important in reducing the severity of motor vehicle injuries.

Most accidents occur in or near the child's home or school. The most effective strategy for preventing injury is to educate the child about the hazards of risk taking and improper use of equipment (Snowdon & others, 2008). Appropriate safety helmets, protective eye and mouth shields, and protective padding are recommended for children who engage in active sports.

Cancer Children not only are vulnerable to injuries, they also may develop life-threatening diseases. Cancer is the second leading cause of death in children 5 to 14 years of age. Three percent of all children's deaths in this age period are due to cancer. Currently, 1 in every 330 children in the United States develops cancer before the age of 19. Moreover, the incidence of cancer in children is increasing (National Cancer Institute, 2011).

Childhood cancers have a different profile from adult cancers. Cancers in adults attack mainly the lungs, colon, breast, prostate, and pancreas. In children, cancers mainly attack the white blood cells (leukemia), brain, bone, lymphatic system, muscles, kidneys, and nervous system. Researchers are intensely searching for possible genetic links to childhood cancers (Crespi, 2011; Spector & others, 2013).

The most common cancer in children is leukemia, a cancer of the tissues that make blood cells (Kelly & others, 2013). In leukemia, the bone marrow makes an abundance of white blood cells that don't function properly. They crowd out normal cells, making the child susceptible to bruising and infection.

Because of advancements in cancer treatment, children with cancer are surviving longer (Sung & others, 2013). Approximately 80 percent of children with acute lymphoblastic leukemia are cured with current chemotherapy treatment (Wayne, 2011).

Cardiovascular Disease   Cardiovascular disease is uncommon in children. Nonetheless, environmental experiences and behavior in the childhood years can sow the seeds for cardio-vascular disease in adulthood. Many elementary-school-aged children already possess one or more of the risk factors for cardiovascular disease, such as hypertension and obesity (Malatesta-Muncher & Mitsnefes, 2012; Peters & others, 2012). A national study found that an increasing percentage of U.S. children and adolescents had elevated blood pressure from 1988 to 2006 (Ostchega & others, 2009). In this study, children who were obese were more likely to have elevated blood pressure. Further, one study revealed that high blood pressure goes undiagnosed in 75 percent of children with the disease (Hansen, Gunn, & Kaelber, 2007).

Health, Illness, and Poverty Among the World's Children   An estimated 7 per-cent of U.S. children receive no health care, and the vast majority of these children live in poverty. One approach to children's health aims to treat not only medical problems of the individual child but also the conditions of the entire family. In fact, some programs seek to identify children who are at risk for problems and then try to alter the risk factors in an effort to prevent illness and disease.

Poverty in the United States is dwarfed by poverty in developing countries around the world. Each year UNICEF produces a report entitled *The State of the World's Children*. In recent years, the following factors that are especially influenced by poverty are linked to the under-5 mortality rate: the nutritional health and health knowledge of mothers, levels of immunization, dehydration, availability of maternal and child health services, income and food availability in the family, availability of clean water and safe sanitation, and the overall safety of the child's environment.

Devastating effects on the health of young children occur in countries where poverty rates are high (UNICEF, 2012). The poor are the majority in nearly one of every five nations in the world (UNICEF, 2012). They often experience hunger, malnutrition, illness, inadequate access to health care, unsafe water, and a lack of protection from harm (Horton, 2006).

What are some of the main causes of death in young children around the world?

In the last decade, there has been a dramatic increase in the number of young children who have died because HIV/AIDS was transmitted to them by their parents (UNICEF, 2012). Deaths in young children due to HIV/AIDS occur most frequently in countries with high rates of poverty and low levels of education. For example, uneducated people are four times more likely to believe that there is no way to avoid AIDS and three times more likely to be unaware that the virus can be transmitted from mother to child (UNICEF, 2006).

Many of the deaths of young children around the world can be prevented by a reduction in poverty and improvements in nutrition, sanitation, education, and health services (UNICEF, 2012).

NUTRITION AND EATING BEHAVIOR

Poverty influences health in part through its effects on nutrition. However, it is not just children living in low-income families who have health-related nutrition problems; across the spectrum of income levels, recent decades have seen a dramatic increase in the percent of U.S. children who are overweight.

Infancy   From birth to 1 year of age, human infants nearly triple their weight and increase their length by 50 percent. What do they need to sustain this growth?

Nutritional Needs and Eating Behavior   Individual differences among infants in terms of their nutrient reserves, body composition, growth rates, and activity patterns make it difficult to define actual nutrient needs (Schiff, 2013). However, because parents need guidelines, nutritionists recommend that infants consume approximately 50 calories per day for each pound they weigh—more than twice an adult's requirement per pound.

A national study of more than 3,000 randomly selected 4- to 24-month-olds documented that many U.S. parents aren't feeding their babies enough fruits and vegetables, but are feeding them too much junk food (Fox & others, 2004). Up to one-third of the babies ate no vegetables and fruit but frequently ate French fries, and almost half of the 7- to 8-month-old babies were fed desserts, sweets, or sweetened drinks. By 15 months, French fries were the most common vegetable the babies ate.

Such poor dietary patterns early in development can result in more infants being overweight (Black & others, 2009; Thorisdottir, Gunnarsdottir, & Thorisdottir, 2013). The Centers for Disease Control and Prevention (2013) has a category of obesity for adults but does not have an obesity category for infants, children, and adolescents because of the stigma the label may bring. Rather, they have categories for being overweight or at risk for being overweight in childhood and adolescence. Children are considered overweight if they are above the 95th percentile in weight for their age and gender; they are labeled at risk for being overweight if they are between the 85th and 95th percentiles.

One analysis revealed that in 1980, 3.4 percent of U.S. babies less than 6 months old were overweight, a percentage that increased to 5.9 percent in 2001 (Kim & others, 2006). As shown in Figure 4.18, as younger infants become older infants, an even greater percentage are overweight. Also in this study, in addition to the 5.9 percent of infants less than 6 months old who were overweight in 2001, another 11 percent were categorized as at risk for being overweight.

In addition to consuming too many French fries, sweetened drinks, and desserts, are there other factors that might explain this increase in overweight U.S. infants? A mother's weight gain during pregnancy and a mother's own high weight before pregnancy may be factors (Rios-Castillo & others, 2013). One important factor seems to be whether an infant is breast-fed or bottle-fed. Breast-fed infants have lower rates of weight gain than bottle-fed infants by school age, and it is estimated that breast feeding reduces the risk of obesity by approximately 20 percent (Li & others, 2007).

Breast Versus Bottle Feeding   For the first four to six months of life, human milk or an alternative formula is the baby's source of nutrients and energy. For years, debate has focused on whether breast feeding is better for the infant than bottle feeding. The growing consensus is that breast feeding is better for the baby's

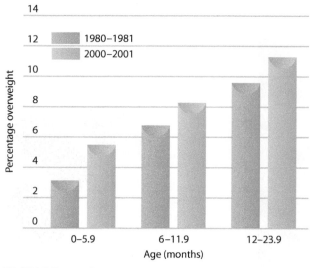

FIGURE **4.18**

PERCENTAGE OF OVERWEIGHT U.S. INFANTS IN 1980–1981 AND 2000–2001. *Note:* Infants above the 95th percentile for their age and gender on a weight-for-height index were categorized as overweight.

health (McKinney & Murray, 2013; Vasquez & Berg, 2012). Since the 1970s, breast feeding by U.S. mothers has soared (see Figure 4.19) (Centers for Disease Control and Prevention, 2012). In 2009, 77 percent of U.S. mothers breast-fed their newborns and 44 percent breast-fed their 6-month-olds. The American Academy of Pediatrics Section on Breastfeeding (2012) recently reconfirmed its recommendation of exclusive breast feeding in the first six months followed by continued breast feeding as complementary foods are introduced, and further breast feeding for one year or longer as mutually desired by the mother and infant.

What are some of the benefits of breast feeding? The following conclusions are based on the current status of research:

Evaluation of Outcomes for Child

- *Gastrointestinal infections.* Breast-fed infants have fewer gastrointestinal infections (Garofalo, 2010).

- *Lower respiratory tract infections.* Breast-fed infants have fewer infections of the lower respiratory tract (Prameela, 2012).

- *Allergies.* A recent research review by the American Academy of Pediatrics indicated that there is no evidence that breast feeding reduces the risk of allergies in children (Greer & others, 2008). The research review also concluded that modest evidence exists for feeding hyperallergenic formulas to susceptible babies if they are not solely breast-fed.

- *Asthma.* The recent research review by the American Academy of Pediatrics concluded that exclusive breast feeding for three months protects against wheezing in babies, but whether it prevents asthma in older children is unclear (Greer & others, 2008).

- *Otitis media.* Breast-fed infants are less likely to develop this middle ear infection (Rovers, de Kok, & Schilder, 2006).

- *Atopic dermatitis.* Breast-fed babies are less likely to have this chronic inflammation of the skin (Snijders & others, 2007). The recent research review by the American Academy of Pediatrics also concluded that for infants with a family history of allergies, breast feeding exclusively for at least four months is linked to a lower risk of skin rashes (Greer & others, 2008).

- *Overweight and obesity.* Research indicates that breast-fed infants are less likely to become overweight or obese in childhood, adolescence, and adulthood (Khuc & others, 2013; Scott, Ng, & Cobiac, 2012).

- *Diabetes.* Breast-fed infants are less likely to develop type 1 diabetes in childhood (Ping & Hagopian, 2006) and type 2 diabetes in adulthood (Villegas & others, 2008).

- *SIDS.* Breast-fed infants are less likely to experience SIDS (Zotter & Pichler, 2012).

In recent large-scale research reviews, no conclusive evidence for the benefits of breast feeding was found for children's cognitive development and cardiovascular health (Agency for Healthcare Research and Quality, 2007; Ip & others, 2009).

Evaluation of Outcomes for Mother

- *Breast cancer.* Consistent evidence indicates a lower incidence of breast cancer in women who breast feed their infants (Akbari & others, 2011; Shema & others, 2007).

- *Ovarian cancer.* Evidence also reveals a reduction in ovarian cancer in women who breast feed their infants (Jordan & others, 2008; Stuebe & Schwartz, 2010).

- *Type 2 diabetes.* Some evidence suggests a small reduction in type 2 diabetes in women who breast feed their infants (Ip & others, 2009; Stuebe & Schwartz, 2010).

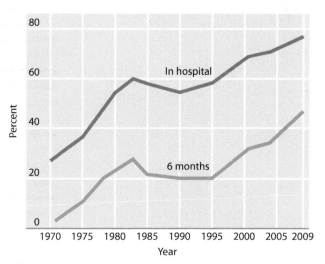

FIGURE **4.19**

TRENDS IN BREAST FEEDING IN THE UNITED STATES, 1970–2009

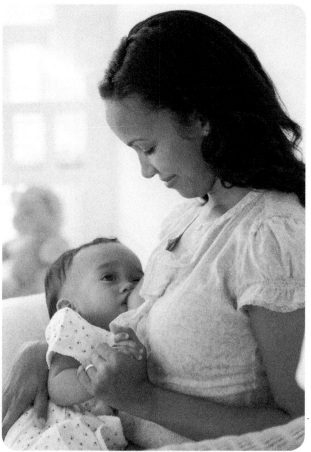

Human milk or an alternative formula is a baby's source of nutrients for the first four to six months. The growing consensus is that breast feeding is better for the baby's health, although controversy still swirls about the issue of breast feeding versus bottle feeding. *Why is breast feeding strongly recommended by pediatricians?*

In recent large-scale research reviews, no conclusive evidence could be found for maternal benefits of breast feeding with regard to return to prepregnancy weight, osteoporosis, and postpartum depression (Agency for Healthcare Research and Quality, 2007; Ip & others, 2009). However, a recent study revealed that women who breast-fed their infants had a lower incidence of metabolic syndrome (a disorder characterized by obesity, hypertension, and insulin resistance) in midlife (Ram & others, 2008).

Many health professionals have argued that breast feeding facilitates the development of an attachment bond between the mother and infant (Britton, Britton, & Gronwaldt, 2006; Wittig & Spatz, 2008). However, a research review found that the positive role of breast feeding on the mother-infant relationship is not supported by research (Jansen, de Weerth, & Riksen-Walraven, 2008). The review concluded that recommending breast feeding should not be based on its role in improving the mother-infant relationship but rather on its positive effects on infant and maternal health.

The AAP Work Group on Breastfeeding strongly endorses breast feeding throughout the first year of life (AAPWGB, 1997). Are there circumstances when mothers should not breast feed? Yes, a mother should not breast feed (1) when she is infected with HIV or some other infectious disease that can be transmitted through her milk, (2) if she has active tuberculosis, or (3) if she is taking any drug that may not be safe for the infant (Goga & others, 2012).

Some women cannot breast feed their infants because of physical difficulties; others feel guilty if they terminate breast feeding early. Mothers may also worry that they are depriving their infants of important emotional and psychological benefits if they bottle feed rather than breast feed. Some researchers have found, however, that there are no psychological differences between breast-fed and bottle-fed infants (Ferguson, Harwood, & Shannon, 1987; Young, 1990).

A further issue in interpreting the benefits of breast feeding was underscored in recent large-scale research reviews (Agency for Healthcare Research and Quality, 2007; Ip & others, 2009). While highlighting a number of breast feeding benefits for children and mothers, the report issued a caution about breast feeding research: None of the findings imply causality. Breast versus bottle feeding studies are correlational rather than experimental, and women who breast feed are wealthier, older, more educated, and likely more health-conscious than their bottle-feeding counterparts, which could explain why breast-fed children are healthier.

Malnutrition in Infancy   Early weaning of infants from breast milk to inadequate sources of nutrients, such as unsuitable and unsanitary cow's milk formula, can cause protein deficiency and malnutrition in infants (UNICEF, 2012). Something that looks like milk but is not, usually a form of tapioca or rice, is also often substituted for breast milk. In many of the world's developing countries, mothers used to breast feed their infants for at least two years. To become more modern, they stopped breast feeding much earlier and replaced it with bottle feeding. Comparisons of breast-fed and bottle-fed infants in countries such as Afghanistan, Haiti, Ghana, and Chile document that the mortality rate of bottle-fed infants is as much as five times that of breast-fed infants (Grant, 1997). However, in the *Connecting with Diversity* interlude, you can read about a recent concern regarding breast feeding.

Two life-threatening conditions that can result from malnutrition are marasmus and kwashiorkor. **Marasmus** is caused by a severe protein-calorie deficiency and results in a wasting away of body tissues in the infant's first year. The infant becomes grossly underweight and his or her muscles atrophy. **Kwashiorkor,** caused by severe protein deficiency, usually appears between 1 and 3 years of age. Children with kwashiorkor sometimes appear to be well fed even though they are not because the disease can cause the child's abdomen and feet to swell with water. Kwashiorkor causes a child's vital organs to collect the nutrients that are present and deprive other parts of the body of them. The child's hair becomes thin, brittle, and colorless, and the child's behavior often becomes listless.

Even if it is not fatal, severe and lengthy malnutrition is detrimental to physical, cognitive, and socioemotional development (Schiff, 2013). A study of Indian children documented the negative influence of chronic malnutrition on children's cognitive development. Children who

developmental **connection**

Research Methods

How does a correlational study differ from an experimental study? Chapter 1, p. 32

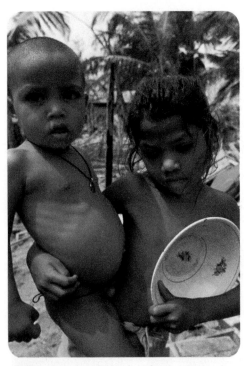

This Bangladeshi child has kwashiorkor. Notice the telltale sign of kwashiorkor—a greatly expanded abdomen. *What are some other characteristics of kwashiorkor?*

marasmus Severe malnutrition caused by an insufficient protein-calorie intake, resulting in a shrunken, elderly appearance.

kwashiorkor Severe malnutrition caused by a protein-deficient diet, causing the feet and abdomen to swell with water.

The Stories of Latonya and Ramona: Breast and Bottle Feeding in Africa

Latonya is a newborn baby in Ghana. During her first days of life, she has been kept apart from her mother and bottle-fed. Manufacturers of infant formula provide free or subsidized milk powder to the hospital where she was born. Her mother has been persuaded to bottle feed rather than breast feed Latonya. When her mother bottle feeds Latonya, she overdilutes the milk formula with unclean water. Latonya's feeding bottles have not been sterilized. Latonya becomes very sick, and she dies before her first birthday.

Ramona was born in Nigeria, where her family takes part in a "baby-friendly" program. In this program, babies are not separated from their mothers when they are born, and the mothers are encouraged to breast feed them. The mothers are told of the perils that bottle feeding can bring because of unsafe water and unsterilized bottles. They also are informed about the advantages of breast milk, which include its nutritious and hygienic qualities, its ability to immunize babies against common illnesses, and its role in reducing the mother's risk of breast and ovarian cancer. Ramona's mother is breast feeding her. At 1 year of age, Ramona is very healthy.

For many years, maternity units in hospitals favored bottle feeding and did not give mothers adequate information about the benefits of breast feeding. In recent years, the World Health Organization and UNICEF have tried to reverse the trend toward bottle feeding of infants in many impoverished countries. They instituted the "baby-friendly" program in many countries. They also persuaded the International Association of Infant Formula Manufacturers to stop marketing their baby formulas to hospitals in countries where the governments support the baby-friendly initiatives (Grant, 1997). For the hospitals themselves, costs actually were reduced as infant formula, feeding bottles, and separate nurseries became unnecessary. For example, baby-friendly Jose Fabella Memorial Hospital in the Philippines reported saving 8 percent of its annual budget.

The advantages of breast feeding in impoverished countries are substantial. However, these advantages must be balanced against the risk of passing HIV to babies through breast milk if the mothers have the virus; the majority of mothers don't know that they are infected (Goga & others, 2012). In some areas of Africa, more than 30 percent of mothers have the human immunodeficiency virus (HIV).

(*Top*) An HIV-infected mother breast feeding her baby in Nairobi, Africa. (*Bottom*) A Rwandan mother bottle feeding her baby. *What are some concerns about breast versus bottle feeding in impoverished African countries?*

In what ways does education play a role in the health decisions discussed in this interlude?

Improving the Nutrition of Infants and Young Children Living in Low-Income Families

Poor nutrition is a special concern in the lives of infants from low-income families. To address this problem in the United States, the WIC (Women, Infants, and Children) program provides federal grants to states for healthy supplemental foods, health care referrals, and nutrition education for women from low-income families beginning in pregnancy, and to infants and young children up to 5 years of age who are at nutritional risk (Hillier & others, 2012; Kong & others, 2013; Marshall & others, 2013; Whaley & others, 2012; WIC New York, 2011). WIC serves approximately 7,500,000 participants in the United States.

Positive influences on infants' and young children's nutrition and health have been found for participants in WIC (Black & others, 2012; Davis, Lazariu, & Sekhobo, 2010; Sekhobo & others, 2010). A recent study revealed that a WIC program that introduced peer counseling services for pregnant women increased breast feeding initiation by 27 percent (Olson & others, 2010a, b). Another recent study found that entry during the first trimester of pregnancy to the WIC program in Rhode Island reduced maternal cigarette smoking (Brodsky, Viner-Brown, & Handler, 2009). And a recent multiple-year literacy intervention with Spanish-speaking families in the WIC program in Los Angeles increased literacy resources and activities at home, which in turn led to a higher level of school readiness in children (Whaley & others, 2011).

Participants in the WIC program. *What characterizes the WIC program?*

Why would the WIC program provide lactation counseling as part of its services?

had a history of chronic malnutrition performed more poorly on tests of attention and memory than their counterparts who were not malnourished (Kar, Rao, & Chandramouli, 2008).

Another study linked the diets of rural Guatemalan infants with their social development at the time they entered elementary school (Barrett, Radke-Yarrow, & Klein, 1982). Children whose mothers had been given nutritional supplements during pregnancy, and who themselves had been given more nutritious, high-calorie foods in their first two years of life, were more active, more involved, more helpful with their peers, less anxious, and happier than their counterparts who had not been given nutritional supplements. Also, a recent study found that two food-assisted maternal and child health nutrition programs (both emphasizing food provision, communication about behavior change, and preventive health services) helped to reduce the impact of economic hardship on stunting of children's growth in Haiti (Donegan & others, 2010). To read further about improving infants' and young children's nutrition, as well as other aspects of their lives, see *Caring Connections.*

Adequate early nutrition is an important aspect of healthy development (Hurley & others, 2013; Schiff, 2013). In addition to sound nutrition, children need a nurturing, supportive environment (Lumeng & others, 2012). Caregivers who are not sensitive to developmental changes in infants' nutritional needs, neglectful caregivers, and conditions of poverty can contribute to the development of eating problems in infants (Black & Lozoff, 2008). A recent study found that low maternal sensitivity when infants were 15 and 24 months of age was linked to a higher risk of obesity in adolescence (Anderson & others, 2012).

One individual who has stood out as an advocate of caring for children is T. Berry Brazelton, who is featured in the *Connecting with Careers* profile.

T. Berry Brazelton, Pediatrician

T. Berry Brazelton is America's best-known pediatrician as a result of his numerous books, television appearances, and newspaper and magazine articles about parenting and children's health. He takes a family-centered approach to child development issues and communicates with parents in easy-to-understand ways.

Dr. Brazelton founded the Child Development Unit at Boston Children's Hospital and created the Brazelton Neonatal Behavioral Assessment Scale, a widely used measure of the newborn's health and well-being (described in Chapter 3). He also has conducted a number of research studies on infants and children and has been president of the Society for Research in Child Development, a leading research organization.

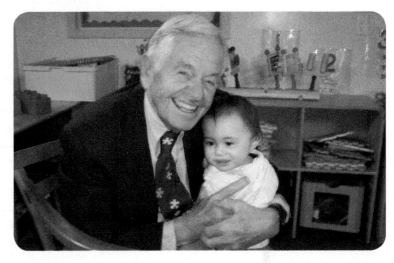

T. Berry Brazelton, pediatrician, with a young child.

For more information about what pediatricians do, see page 44 in the Careers in Child Development appendix following Chapter 1.

Childhood Poor nutrition in childhood can lead to a number of problems and occurs more frequently in low-income than in higher-income families. A special concern is the increasing epidemic of overweight children.

Eating Behavior and Parental Feeding Styles For most children in the United States, insufficient food is not the key problem. Instead, unhealthy eating habits and being overweight threaten their present and future health. A recent study of 2- and 3-year-olds found that French fries and other fried potatoes were the vegetable they were most likely to consume (Fox, Levitt, & Nelson, 2010).

Children's eating behavior is strongly influenced by their caregivers' behavior (Black & Hurley, 2007; Hurley & others, 2013; Mitchell & others, 2013). Children's eating behavior improves when caregivers eat with children on a predictable schedule, model eating healthy food, make mealtimes pleasant occasions, and engage in certain feeding styles. Distractions from television, family arguments, and competing activities should be minimized so children can focus on eating. A sensitive/responsive caregiver feeding style is recommended, in which the caregiver is nurturant, provides clear information about what is expected, and responds appropriately to children's cues (Black & Hurley, 2007). Forceful and restrictive caregiver behaviors are not recommended. For example, a restrictive feeding style is linked to children being overweight (Black & Lozoff, 2008).

Overweight Children Being overweight has become a serious health problem in early childhood (Thompson, Manore, & Vaughan, 2013). A national study revealed that 45 percent of children's meals exceed recommendations for saturated and trans fat, which can raise cholesterol levels and increase the risk of heart disease (Center for Science in the Public Interest, 2008). This study also found that one-third of children's daily caloric intake comes from restaurants, twice the percentage consumed away from home in the 1980s. Further, 93 percent of almost 1,500 possible choices at 13 major fast food chains exceeded 430 calories—one-third of what the National Institute of Medicine recommends that 4- to 8-year-old children consume in a day. Nearly every combination of children's meals at KFC, Taco Bell, Sonic, Jack in the Box, and Chick-fil-A were too high in calories.

The percentages of young children who are overweight or at risk of becoming overweight in the United States have increased dramatically in recent decades, and these percentages are likely to grow unless changes occur in children's lifestyles (Summerbell & others, 2012). In 2009–2010, 12.1 percent of U.S. 2- to 5-year-olds were classified as obese compared with 5 percent in 1976–1980 and 10.4 percent in 2007–2008 (Ogden & others, 2012). That figure is significantly higher for 6- to 11-year-old U.S. children—in 2009–2010, 18 percent of U.S. 6- to 11-year-olds were classified as obese (Ogden & others, 2012).

Girls are more likely than boys to be overweight, and this gender difference occurs in many countries (Sweeting, 2008). In a large-scale U.S. study, African American and Latino children were more likely to be overweight or obese than non-Latino White children (Benson, Baer, & Kaelber, 2009).

It is not just in the United States that children are becoming more overweight. For example, a study found that general and abdominal obesity in Chinese children increased significantly from 1993 to 2009 (Liang & others, 2012).

The risk that overweight young children will continue to be overweight when they are older was documented in a study in which 80 percent of the children who were at risk for being overweight at age 3 were also at risk for being overweight or were overweight at age 12 (Nader & others, 2006). A recent study revealed that preschool children who were overweight were at significant risk for being overweight/obese at age 12 (Shankaran & others, 2011).

Being overweight in childhood also is linked to being overweight in adulthood. One study revealed that girls who were overweight in childhood were 11 to 30 times more likely to be obese in adulthood than girls who were not overweight in childhood (Thompson & others, 2007).

The increase in overweight children in recent decades is cause for great concern because being overweight raises the risk for many medical and psychological problems (Anspaugh & Ezell, 2013). Diabetes, hypertension (high blood pressure), and elevated blood cholesterol levels are common in children who are overweight (Pulgaron, 2013; Riley & Bluhm, 2012). Once considered rare, hypertension in children has become increasingly common in overweight children (Lytle, 2012). Social and psychological consequences of being overweight in childhood include low self-esteem, depression, and some exclusion of obese children from peer groups (Gomes & others, 2011). In one study, obese children were perceived as less attractive, more tired, and more socially withdrawn than non-obese peers (Zeller, Reiter-Purtill, & Ramey, 2008). In a recent study, overweight children reported being teased more by their peers and family members than did normal weight children (McCormack & others, 2011).

Both heredity and environment influence whether children will become overweight. Genetic analysis indicates that heredity is an important factor in children becoming overweight (Morandi & others, 2012; Xia & Grant, 2013). Overweight parents tend to have overweight children, even if they are not living in the same household (Schiff, 2013). One study found that the greatest risk factor for being overweight at 9 years of age was having a parent who was overweight (Agras & others, 2004). And a recent study revealed that having two overweight/obese parents significantly increased the likelihood of a child being overweight/obese (Xu & others, 2011).

Environmental factors that influence whether children become overweight or not include the greater availability of food (especially food high in fat content), energy-saving devices, declining physical activity, parents' eating habits and monitoring of children's eating habits, the context in which a child eats, and heavy screen time (watching TV, playing video games, texting, and so on) (Costigan & others, 2013; Mitchell & others, 2013; Mitchell, Pate, & Blair, 2012). A recent behavior modification study of overweight and obese children made watching TV contingent on their engagement in exercise (Goldfield, 2011). The intervention markedly increased their exercise and reduced their TV viewing time.

Parents play an important role in preventing children from becoming overweight (Barr-Anderson & others, 2013; Rodenburg & others, 2012). Recent research studies indicate intervention programs that emphasize getting parents to engage in healthier lifestyles themselves, as well as feeding their children healthier food and getting them to exercise more, can produce weight reduction in overweight and obese children (Brotman & others, 2012).

connecting with careers

Barbara Deloin, Pediatric Nurse

Barbara Deloin is a pediatric nurse in Denver, Colorado. She practices nursing in the Pediatric Oral Feeding Clinic and is involved in research as part of an irritable infant study for the Children's Hospital in Denver. She also is on the faculty of nursing at the Colorado Health Sciences Center. Deloin previously worked in San Diego where she was coordinator of the Child Health Program for the County of San Diego.

Her research interests focus on children with special health-care needs, especially high-risk infants and children, and promoting positive parent-child experiences. Deloin was elected president of the National Association of Pediatric Nurse Associates and Practitioners for the 2000–2001 term.

For more information about what pediatric nurses do, see page 44 in the Careers in Child Development appendix following Chapter 1.

Barbara Deloin working with a child with special health care needs.

For example, a recent study found that combining a child-centered activity program with a parent-centered dietary modification program was successful in helping overweight children lose pounds over a two-year period (Collins & others, 2011). Some intervention programs with overweight children are conducted through schools and often focus on teaching children and parents about developing a healthy diet, exercising more, and reducing screen time (Summerbell & others, 2012; Zask & others, 2012). A promising strategy is to provide students with healthier foods to eat at school. Several states now have laws that require healthier foods to be sold in vending machines at schools. In one intervention, reducing soft drink consumption at schools was linked with a subsequent reduction in the number of 7- to 11-year-old children who were overweight (James & others, 2004).

In sum, healthy eating and an active rather than sedentary lifestyle play important roles in children's development (Kotte, Winkler, & Takken, 2013; Wang & others, 2013). Pediatric nurses can influence the health of children by providing advice to parents about

What are some concerns about overweight children?

ways to improve their children's eating habits and activity levels. To read about the work of one pediatric nurse, see the *Connecting with Careers* profile of Barbara Deloin.

EXERCISE

Exercise can make significant contributions to not only children's physical development but also their cognitive development (Wuest & Fisette, 2012; Davis & others, 2011). We explore developmental aspects of children's exercise and the roles of parents, schools, and screen-based activity.

Early Childhood   Routine physical activity should be a daily occurrence for young children. Guidelines recommend that preschool children engage in two hours of physical activity per day, divided into one hour of structured activity and one hour of unstructured free play (National Association for Sport and Physical Education, 2002). The child's life should be centered around activities, not meals.

Following are descriptions of three recent research studies that examine young children's exercise and activities:

- Observations of 3- to 5-year-old children during outdoor play at preschools revealed that the preschool children were mainly sedentary even when participating in outdoor play (Brown & others, 2009). In this study, throughout the day the preschoolers were sedentary 89 percent of the time, engaged in light activity 8 percent of the time, and participated in moderate to vigorous physical activity only 3 percent of the time.
- Preschool children's physical activity was enhanced by family members engaging in sports together and by parents' perception that it was safe for their children to play outside (Beets & Foley, 2008).
- Incorporation of a "move and learn" physical activity curriculum increased the activity level of 3- to 5-year-old children in a half-day preschool program (Trost, Fees, & Dzewaltowski, 2008).
- A recent research review concluded that a higher level of screen time (watching TV, using a computer) at 4 to 6 years of age was linked to a lower activity level and being overweight from preschool through adolescence (te Velde & others, 2012).

To find out how much activity most preschool students are currently getting, see *Connecting Through Research*.

Middle and Late Childhood   An increasing number of studies document the importance of exercise in children's physical development (Morano & others, 2012). One study found that 45 minutes of moderate physical activity and 15 minutes of vigorous physical activity daily were related to decreased odds that the children were overweight (Wittmeier, Mollard, & Kriellaars, 2008). And a recent study of 9-year-olds revealed that a higher level of physical activity was linked to a lower level of metabolic disease risk based on measures such as cholesterol, waist circumference, and insulin (Parrett & others, 2011). Also, a recent experimental study found that 13 weeks of aerobic training had significant benefits for insulin resistance and body fat levels of overweight/obese elementary children, regardless of gender or ethnicity (Davis & others, 2012).

A recent research review concluded that aerobic exercise also increasingly is linked to children's cognitive skills (Best, 2010). Researchers have found that aerobic exercise benefits

What are some positive outcomes when young children exercise regularly?

Are Preschool Children Getting Enough Physical Activity?

One study examined the activity level of 281 3- to 5-year-olds in nine preschools (Pate & others, 2004). Each child wore an accelerometer (a small activity monitor) for four to five hours a day. Height and weight assessments of the children were made to calculate each child's body mass index (BMI).

Recently developed guidelines recommend that preschool children engage in two hours of physical activity per day, divided into one hour of structured activity and one hour of unstructured free play (National Association for Sport and Physical Education, 2002). In this study, the young children participated in an average of 7.7 minutes per hour of moderate to vigorous activity, usually in a block of time when they were outside. Over the course of eight hours of a preschool day, these children would get approximately one hour of moderate and vigorous physical activity, only about 50 percent of the amount recommended. The researchers concluded that young children are unlikely to engage in another hour per day of moderate and vigorous physical activity outside their eight hours spent in preschool and thus are not getting adequate opportunities for physical activity.

Gender and age differences characterized the preschool children's physical activity. Boys were more likely to engage in moderate or vigorous physical activity than girls. Children who were 4 or 5 years old were more likely to be sedentary than 3-year-old children.

The young children's physical activity also varied according to the particular preschool they attended. The extent to which they participated in moderate and vigorous physical activity ranged from 4.4 to 10.2 minutes per hour across the nine preschools. Thus, the policies and practices of particular preschools influence the extent to which children engage in physical activity. The researchers concluded that young children need more vigorous play and organized activities. Unfortunately, there is a trend toward reducing time for physical activity, especially eliminating recess, in U.S. elementary schools that is trickling down to kindergarten and preschool programs. This decrease is part of a larger trend that involves narrowing early childhood programs to focus on academic learning and moving away from more comprehensive programs that focus on the whole child (Hyson, Copple, & Jones, 2006).

children's attention, memory, effortful and goal-directed thinking and behavior, and creativity (Davis & Cooper, 2011; Davis & others, 2007, 2011; Monti, Hillman, & Cohen, 2012).

Adolescence Gender and ethnic differences in exercise participation rates are noteworthy, and they reflect the trend of decreasing exercise from early through late adolescence. One study revealed that 40 percent of female and 57 percent of male adolescents met U.S. guidelines for physical activity (Butcher & others, 2008). A recent national study also found that adolescent boys were much more likely to engage in 60 minutes or more of vigorous exercise per day than were girls (Eaton & others, 2012). Also, as indicated in Figure 4.20, in the National Youth Risk Survey, non-Latino White boys exercised the most, African American girls the least (Eaton & others, 2012).

Exercise is linked to a number of positive outcomes in adolescence, including weight regulation as well as lower levels of blood pressure and type 2 diabetes (Goldfield & others, 2012; So & others, 2013). Consider also these recent studies that found positive effects of exercise on a range of adolescent outcomes:

- Adolescents who engaged in higher levels of exercise had lower levels of alcohol, cigarette, and marijuana use (Teery-McElrath, O'Malley, & Johnston, 2011).
- A daily morning running program for three weeks improved the sleep quality, mood, and concentration of adolescents (Kalak & others, 2012).
  - Engaging in a 12-week exercise intervention lowered the depression of adolescents who were depressed and not regular exercisers (Dopp & others, 2012).

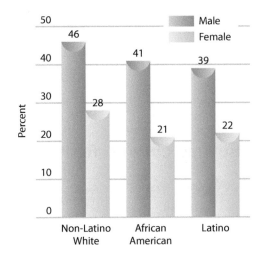

FIGURE **4.20**

EXERCISE RATES OF U.S. HIGH SCHOOL STUDENTS IN 2011: GENDER AND ETHNICITY.
Note: Data are for high school students who were physically active doing any kind of physical activity that increased their heart rate and made them breathe hard some of the time for a total of at least 60 minutes a day on five or more of the seven days preceding the survey. (Source: After Eaton & others, 2012, Table 91).

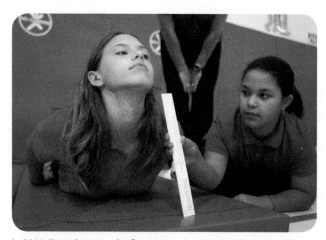

In 2007, Texas became the first state to test students' physical fitness. The student shown here is performing the trunk lift. Other assessments include aerobic exercise, muscle strength, and body fat. Assessments will be done annually.

- Participating in regular exercise was associated with higher academic achievement in young adolescents (Hashim, Freddy, & Rosmatunisah, 2012).

Parents, Peers, Schools, and the Media   Parents play important roles in children's and adolescents' exercise habits (Davis & others, 2013; Loprinzi & others, 2012). Growing up with parents who regularly exercise provides positive models of exercise for children and adolescents.

A recent research review concluded that peers play an important role in children's and adolescents' physical activity (Fitzgerald, Fitzgerald, & Aherne, 2012). In this review, peer/friend support of exercise, better friendship quality and acceptance, and not having experienced peer victimization were linked to adolescents' physical activity.

Some of the blame for inactivity also falls on the nation's schools, many of which fail to provide daily physical education classes (Fung & others, 2012). A recent national survey revealed that only about 50 percent of U.S. ninth- through twelfth-graders participated in physical education classes on one or more days in an average school week and only 31.5 percent did so on five days (Eaton & others, 2012).

Screen-based activity (watching television, using computers, talking on the phone, texting, and instant messaging for long hours) is linked to lower levels of physical fitness in children and adolescents (Mitchell, Pate, & Blair, 2012). A recent study revealed that children and adolescents who engaged in the highest amount of daily screen-based activity (TV/video/video games in this study) were less likely to exercise daily (Sisson & others, 2010). In this study, children and adolescents who engaged in low physical activity and high screen-based activity were almost twice as likely to be overweight as their more active, less sedentary counterparts (Sisson & others, 2010). A recent research review concluded that screen-based activity is linked to a number of adolescent health problems (Costigan & others, 2013). In this review, screen-based sedentary behavior was associated with being overweight, sleep problems, lower levels of physical activity/fitness and well-being, and a higher level of depression.

Here are some ways to get children and adolescents to exercise more:

- Improve physical fitness classes in schools.
- Offer more physical activity programs run by volunteers at school facilities.
- Have children plan community and school exercise activities that interest them.
- Encourage families to focus on physical activity, and challenge parents to exercise more.

Review Connect Reflect

 Characterize children's health

Review

- What are the key health problems facing children?
- What are some important aspects of children's nutrition and eating behavior?
- What role does exercise play in children's development?

Connect

- Nutrition was discussed earlier in the chapter as well. What did you learn about nutrition's effect on growth?

Reflect *Your Own Personal Journey of Life*

- What were your eating habits like as a child? In what ways are they similar to or different from your current eating habits? Do you think your early eating habits predicted whether you would have weight problems in adulthood?

Physical Development and Health

Body Growth and Change

LG1 Discuss developmental changes in the body.

Patterns of Growth

- Human growth follows cephalocaudal and proximodistal patterns. In a cephalocaudal pattern, the fastest growth occurs at the top—the head. Physical growth in size, weight, and feature differentiation occurs gradually and moves from the top to the bottom. In a proximodistal pattern, growth begins at the center of the body and then moves toward the extremities.

Infancy and Childhood

- Height and weight increase rapidly in infancy and then take a slower course during childhood. The average North American newborn is 20 inches long and weighs 7½ pounds. Infants grow about 1 inch per month during their first year. In early childhood, girls are only slightly smaller and lighter than boys. Growth is slow and consistent in middle and late childhood, and head circumference, waist circumference, and leg length decrease in relation to body height.

Adolescence

- Puberty is a rapid maturation involving hormonal and body changes that occur primarily in early adolescence. Puberty began to occur at younger ages during the twentieth century. There are wide individual variations in the age at which puberty begins. Heredity plays an important role in determining the onset of puberty. Key hormones involved in puberty are testosterone and estradiol. Rising testosterone levels in boys cause voice changes, enlargement of external genitals, and increased height. In girls, increased levels of estradiol influence breast and uterine development and skeletal change. Key physical changes of puberty include a growth spurt as well as sexual maturation. The growth spurt occurs an average of two years earlier for girls than for boys. Adolescents are preoccupied with their bodies and develop images of their bodies. Adolescent girls have more negative body images than adolescent boys. Early maturation favors boys during adolescence, but in adulthood late-maturing boys have a more successful identity. Early-maturing girls are vulnerable to a number of problems including eating disorders, smoking, and depression.

The Brain

LG2 Describe how the brain changes.

The Neuroconstructivist View

- The old view was that genes determined how a child's brain is wired and that environmental experiences play little or no role in the brain's development. However, in the neuroconstructivist view, (a) biological processes and environmental conditions influence the brain's development, (b) the brain has plasticity and is context dependent, and (c) the development of the brain and the child's cognitive development are closely linked,

Brain Physiology

- Each hemisphere of the brain's cerebral cortex has four lobes (frontal, occipital, temporal, and parietal) with somewhat different primary functions. Neurons are nerve cells in the brain that process information. Communication between neurons occurs through the release of neurotransmitters at gaps called synapses. Communication is speeded by the myelin sheath that covers most axons. Clusters of neurons, known as neural circuits, work together to handle particular types of information. Specialization of functioning occurs in the brain's hemispheres, as in speech and grammar, but for the most part both hemispheres are involved in most complex functions, such as reading or performing music.

Infancy

- Researchers have found that experience influences the brain's development. Early experiences are very important in brain development, and growing up in deprived environments can harm the brain. Myelination continues throughout the childhood years and even into adolescence for some brain areas such as the frontal lobes. Dramatic increases in dendritic and synaptic connections occur in infancy. These connections are overproduced and later pruned.

Childhood

- During early childhood, the brain and head grow more rapidly than any other part of the body. Rapid, distinct bursts of growth occur in different areas of the brain between 3 and 15 years of age. One shift in brain activation in middle and late childhood is from diffuse, larger areas to more focal, smaller areas, especially in cognitive control.

Adolescence

- In adolescence, the corpus callosum thickens, and this improves information processing. Also, the amygdala, which is involved in emotions such as anger, develops earlier than the prefrontal cortex, which functions in reasoning and self-regulation. This gap in development may help to explain the increase in risk-taking behavior that characterizes adolescence.

Sleep

LG3 Summarize how sleep patterns change as children and adolescents develop.

Infancy

- The typical newborn sleeps 16 to 17 hours a day. By 6 months of age, most infants have sleep patterns similar to those of adults. REM sleep occurs more in infancy than in childhood and adulthood. Sleeping arrangements vary across cultures, and there is controversy about shared sleeping. SIDS is a special concern in early infancy.

Childhood

- Most young children sleep through the night and have one daytime nap. It is recommended that preschool children sleep 11 to 13 hours each night and 5- to 12-year-old children 10 to 12 hours each night. Among sleep problems that may develop are narcolepsy, insomnia, and nightmares. Sleep problems in childhood are linked to negative outcomes in other areas of children's development.

Adolescence

- Many adolescents stay up later than when they were children and are getting less sleep than they need. Research suggests that as adolescents get older, the hormone melatonin is released later at night, shifting the adolescent's biological clock. Inadequate sleep is linked to an unhealthy diet, low exercise level, depression, and ineffective stress management.

Health

LG4 Characterize children's health.

Illness and Injuries Among Children

- Motor vehicle accidents are the number one cause of death in childhood. Parental smoking is a major danger for young children. For the most part, middle and late childhood is a time of excellent health. Caregivers play an important role in preventing childhood injuries. Two diseases of special concern in childhood are cancer and cardiovascular disease. A special concern also is the health of children living in poverty here and abroad. Improvements are needed in sanitation, nutrition, education, and health services in addition to a reduction in poverty. In low-income countries, there has been a dramatic increase in the number of children who have died from HIV/AIDS that was transmitted to them by their parents.

Nutrition and Eating Behavior

- The importance of adequate energy intake consumed in a loving and supportive environment during infancy cannot be overstated. Breast feeding is increasingly recommended over bottle feeding. Marasmus and kwashiorkor are diseases caused by severe malnutrition. Concerns about nutrition in childhood focus especially focus on content in diet and overweight/obese children. The percentage of overweight/obese children has increased dramatically in recent decades but has begun to level off. Being overweight increases a child's risk of developing many medical and psychological problems. Parents play an important role in helping children avoid weight problems.

Exercise

- Most children and adolescents are not getting nearly enough exercise. Boys and girls become less active as they reach and progress through adolescence. Parents, schools, and screen-based activity play important roles in whether children and adolescents are physically fit or unfit.

key terms

cephalocaudal pattern 104
proximodistal pattern 105
puberty 106
menarche 107
precocious puberty 107

hormones 107
androgens 107
estrogens 107
testosterone 107
estradiol 107

neuroconstructivist view 110
lateralization 112
myelination 112
corpus callosum 116
prefrontal cortex 116

amygdala 116
sudden infant death syndrome
 (SIDS) 119
marasmus 126
kwashiorkor 126

key people

Martha Ann Bell 112
Charles Nelson 112

John Richards 112

Mona El-Sheikh 120

Mark Johnson 116

chapter 5

MOTOR, SENSORY, AND PERCEPTUAL DEVELOPMENT

chapter outline

In 1950, the newly born Steveland Morris was placed in an incubator in which he was given too much oxygen. The result was permanent blindness. In 1962, as 12-year-old singer and musician Stevie Wonder, he began a career that has included such hits as "My Cherie Amour" and "Signed, Sealed, Delivered." In the twenty-first century, his music is still perceived by some as "wondrous."

At age 12, Andrea Bocelli lost his sight in a soccer mishap. Today, in his forties and after a brief career as a lawyer, Andrea has taken the music world by storm with his magnificent, classically trained voice.

Although Bocelli's and Stevie Wonder's accomplishments are great, imagine how very difficult it must have been for them as children to do many of the things we take for granted in sighted children. Yet children who lose one channel of sensation—such as vision—often compensate for the loss by enhancing their sensory skills in another area, such as hearing or touch. For example, researchers have found that blind individuals are more accurate at locating a sound source and have greater sensitivity to touch than sighted individuals do (Lewald, 2012; Proulx & others, 2013). In one study, blind children were more skillful than blindfolded sighted children at using hearing to detect walls (Ashmead & others, 1998). In this study, acoustic information was most useful when the blind children were within one meter of a wall—at which point, sound pressure increases.

Two "sensations": Stevie Wonder (*left*) and Andrea Bocelli (*right*). *How have they adapted to life without sight?*

preview

Think about what is required for children to find their way around their environment, to play sports, or to create art. These activities require both active perception and precisely timed motor actions. Neither innate, automatic movements nor simple sensations are enough to let children do the things they do every day. How do children develop perceptual and motor abilities? In this chapter, we will focus first on the development of motor skills, then on sensory and perceptual development, and finally on the coupling of perceptual-motor skills.

A baby is the most complicated object made by unskilled labor.

—ANONYMOUS

Motor Development LG1 Describe how motor skills develop.

| The Dynamic Systems View | Reflexes | Gross Motor Skills | Fine Motor Skills |

Esther Thelen is shown conducting an experiment to discover how infants learn to control their arms to reach and grasp for objects. A computer device is used to monitor the infant's arm movements and to track muscle patterns. Thelen's research is conducted from a dynamic systems perspective. *What is the nature of this perspective?*

dynamic systems theory A theory, proposed by Esther Thelen, that seeks to explain how motor behaviors are assembled for perceiving and acting.

reflexes Built-in reactions to stimuli.

rooting reflex A newborn's built-in reaction that occurs when the infant's cheek is stroked or the side of the mouth is touched. In response, the infant turns its head toward the side that was touched, in an apparent effort to find something to suck.

sucking reflex A newborn's built-in reaction of automatically sucking an object placed in its mouth. The sucking reflex enables the infant to get nourishment before it has associated a nipple with food.

Moro reflex A neonatal startle response that occurs in reaction to a sudden, intense noise or movement. When startled, the newborn arches its back, throws its head back, and flings out its arms and legs. Then the newborn rapidly closes its arms and legs to the center of the body.

Most adults are capable of coordinated, purposive actions requiring considerable skill, including driving a car, playing golf, and typing accurately on a computer keyboard. Some adults have extraordinary motor skills, such as those involved in winning an Olympic pole vault competition, performing heart surgery, painting a masterpiece, or in the case of Stevie Wonder, being extraordinarily talented at playing the piano. Look all you want at a newborn infant, and you will observe nothing even remotely approaching these skilled actions. How, then, do the motor behaviors of adults come about?

THE DYNAMIC SYSTEMS VIEW

Arnold Gesell (1934) thought his painstaking observations had revealed how people develop their motor skills. He had discovered that infants and children develop rolling, sitting, standing, and other motor skills in a fixed order and within specific time frames. These observations, said Gesell, show that motor development comes about through the unfolding of a genetic plan, or *maturation*.

Later studies, however, have demonstrated that the sequence of developmental milestones is not as fixed as Gesell indicated and not due as much to heredity as Gesell argued (Adolph & Berger 2013; Adolph & Robinson, 2013). In the last two decades, the study of motor development experienced a renaissance as psychologists developed new insights about *how* motor skills develop (Thelen & Smith, 1998, 2006). One increasingly influential theory is dynamic systems theory, proposed by Esther Thelen (1941–2004).

According to **dynamic systems theory,** infants assemble motor skills for perceiving and acting. Notice that perception and action are coupled, according to this theory (Thelen & Smith, 2006). To develop motor skills, infants must perceive something in the environment that motivates them to act and then use their perceptions to fine-tune their movements. Motor skills represent solutions to the infant's goals (Clearfield & others, 2009).

How is a motor skill developed, according to this theory? When infants are motivated to do something, they might create a new motor behavior. The new behavior is the result of many converging factors: the development of the nervous system, the body's physical properties and its possibilities for movement, the goal the child is motivated to reach, and the environmental support for the skill (von Hofsten, 2008). For example, babies learn to walk only when maturation of the nervous system allows them to control certain leg muscles, when their legs have grown enough to support their weight, and when they want to move.

Mastering a motor skill requires the infant's active efforts to coordinate several components of the skill. Infants explore and select possible solutions to the demands of a new task; they assemble adaptive patterns by modifying their current movement patterns. The first step occurs when the infant is motivated by a new challenge—such as the desire to cross a room—and gets into the "ballpark" of the task demands by taking a couple of stumbling steps. Then, the infant "tunes" these movements to make them smoother and more effective. The tuning is achieved through repeated cycles of action and perception of the consequences of that action. According to the dynamic systems view, even universal milestones, such as crawling, reaching, and walking, are learned through this process of adaptation: infants modulate their movement patterns to fit a new task by exploring and selecting possible configurations (Adolph & Berger, 2011, 2013; Spencer & others, 2009).

To see how dynamic systems theory explains motor behavior, imagine that you offer a new toy to a baby named Gabriel (Thelen & others, 1993). There is no exact program that can tell Gabriel ahead of time how to move his arm and hand and fingers to grasp the toy. Gabriel must adapt to his goal—grasping the toy—and the context. From his sitting position, he must make split-second adjustments to extend his arm, holding his body steady so that his arm and torso don't plow into the toy. Muscles in his arm and shoulder contract and stretch in a host of combinations, exerting a variety of forces. He improvises a way to reach out with one arm and wrap his fingers around the toy.

Thus, according to dynamic systems theory, motor development is not a passive process in which genes dictate the unfolding of a sequence of skills over time. Rather, the infant actively puts together a skill to achieve a goal within the constraints set by the infant's body and environment. Nature and nurture, the infant and the environment, are all working together as part of an ever-changing system.

As we examine the course of motor development, we will describe how dynamic systems theory applies to some specific skills. First, though, let's see how the story of motor development begins with reflexes.

How might dynamic systems theory explain the development of learning to walk?

REFLEXES

The newborn is not completely helpless. Among other things, it has some basic reflexes. For example, the newborn automatically holds its breath and contracts its throat to keep water out. **Reflexes** are built-in reactions to stimuli; they govern the newborn's movements, which are automatic and beyond the newborn's control. Reflexes are genetically carried survival mechanisms. They allow infants to respond adaptively to their environment before they have had an opportunity to learn.

The rooting and sucking reflexes are important examples. Both have survival value for newborn mammals, who must find a mother's breast to obtain nourishment. The **rooting reflex** occurs when the infant's cheek is stroked or the side of the mouth is touched. In response, the infant turns its head toward the side that was touched in an apparent effort to find something to suck. The **sucking reflex** occurs when newborns automatically suck an object placed in their mouth. This reflex enables newborns to get nourishment before they have associated a nipple with food; sucking also serves as a self-soothing or self-regulating mechanism.

Another example is the **Moro reflex,** which occurs in response to a sudden, intense noise or movement. When startled, the newborn arches its back, throws back its head, and flings out its arms and legs. Then the newborn rapidly closes its arms and legs. The Moro reflex is believed to be a way of grabbing for support while falling; it would have had survival value for our primate ancestors.

Some reflexes—coughing, sneezing, blinking, shivering, and yawning, for example—persist throughout life. They are as important for the adult as they are for the infant. Other reflexes, though, disappear several months following birth, as the infant's brain matures, and voluntary control over many behaviors develops (Pedroso, 2008). The rooting and Moro reflexes, for example, tend to disappear when the infant is 3 to 4 months old.

The movements of some reflexes eventually become incorporated into more complex, voluntary actions. One important example is the **grasping reflex,** which occurs when something touches the infant's palms. The infant responds by grasping tightly. By the end of the third month, the grasping reflex diminishes, and the infant shows a more voluntary grasp. As its motor development becomes smoother, the infant will grasp objects, carefully manipulate them, and explore their qualities. An overview of the reflexes we have discussed, along with others, is given in Figure 5.1.

Although reflexes are automatic and inborn, differences in reflexive behavior are soon apparent. For example, the sucking capabilities of newborns vary considerably. Some newborns

developmental **connection**

Nature and Nurture

The epigenetic view states that development is an ongoing, bidirectional interchange between heredity and environment. Chapter 2, p. 69

Moro reflex

The Moro reflex usually disappears around the age of 3 months.

grasping reflex A neonatal reflex that occurs when something touches the infant's palms. The infant responds by grasping tightly.

Reflex	Stimulation	Infant's Response	Developmental Pattern
Blinking	Flash of light, puff of air	Closes both eyes	Permanent
Babinski	Sole of foot stroked	Fans out toes, twists foot in	Disappears after 9 months to 1 year
Grasping	Palms touched	Grasps tightly	Weakens after 3 months, disappears after 1 year
Moro (startle)	Sudden stimulation, such as hearing loud noise or being dropped	Startles, arches back, throws head back, flings out arms and legs and then rapidly closes them to center of body	Disappears after 3 to 4 months
Rooting	Cheek stroked or side of mouth touched	Turns head, opens mouth, begins sucking	Disappears after 3 to 4 months
Stepping	Infant held above surface and feet lowered to touch surface	Moves feet as if to walk	Disappears after 3 to 4 months
Sucking	Object touching mouth	Sucks automatically	Disappears after 3 to 4 months
Swimming	Infant put face down in water	Makes coordinated swimming movements	Disappears after 6 to 7 months
Tonic neck	Infant placed on back	Forms fists with both hands and usually turns head to the right (sometimes called the "fencer's pose" because the infant looks like it is assuming a fencer's position)	Disappears after 2 months

FIGURE 5.1

INFANT REFLEXES. This chart describes some of the infant's reflexes.

are efficient at forcefully sucking and obtaining milk; others are not as adept and get tired before they are full. Most infants take several weeks to establish a sucking style that is coordinated with the way the mother is holding the infant, the way milk is coming out of the bottle or breast, and the infant's temperament (Blass, 2008).

The old view of reflexes is that they were exclusively genetic, built-in mechanisms that govern the infant's movements. The new perspective on infant reflexes is that they are not automatic or completely beyond the infant's control. For example, infants can control such movements as alternating their legs to make a mobile jiggle or change their sucking rate to listen to a recording (Adolph & Berger, 2013).

Pediatrician T. Berry Brazelton (1956) observed how infants' sucking changed as they grew older. Over 85 percent of the infants engaged in considerable sucking behavior unrelated to feeding. They sucked their fingers, their fists, and pacifiers. By the age of 1 year, most had stopped the sucking behavior, but as many as 40 percent of children continued to suck their thumbs after starting school (Kessen, Haith, & Salapatek, 1970). Most developmentalists do not attach a great deal of significance to this behavior.

GROSS MOTOR SKILLS

Ask any parents about their baby, and sooner or later you are likely to hear about motor milestones, such as "Cassandra just learned to crawl," "Jesse is finally sitting alone," or "Angela took her first step last week." Parents proudly announce such milestones as their children transform themselves from babies unable to lift their heads to toddlers who grab things off the grocery store shelf, chase a cat, and participate actively in the family's social life (Thelen, 2000). These milestones are examples of **gross motor skills,** which are skills that involve large-muscle activities, such as moving one's arms and walking.

The Development of Posture How do gross motor skills develop? As a foundation, these skills require postural control (Adolph & Robinson, 2013). For example, to track moving objects, you must be able to control your head in order to stabilize your gaze; before you can walk, you must be able to balance on one leg.

gross motor skills Motor skills that involve large-muscle activities, such as moving one's arms and walking.

Posture is more than just holding still and straight. Posture is a dynamic process that is linked with sensory information in the skin, joints, and muscles, which tell us where we are in space; in vestibular organs in the inner ear that regulate balance and equilibrium; and in vision and hearing (Thelen & Smith, 2006).

Newborn infants cannot voluntarily control their posture. Within a few weeks, though, they can hold their heads erect, and soon they can lift their heads while prone. By 2 months of age, babies can sit while supported on a lap or an infant seat, but they cannot sit independently until they are 6 or 7 months of age. Standing also develops gradually during the first year of life. By about 8 to 9 months of age, infants usually learn to pull themselves up and hold on to a chair, and they often can stand alone by about 10 to 12 months of age.

Learning to Walk   Locomotion and postural control are closely linked, especially in walking upright (Adolph & Berger, 2011; Adolph & Robinson, 2011). To walk upright, the baby must be able both to balance on one leg as the other is swung forward and to shift the weight from one leg to the other.

Even young infants can make the alternating leg movements that are needed for walking. The neural pathways that control leg alternation are in place from a very early age, even at birth or before. Indeed, researchers have found that alternating leg movements occur during the fetal period and at birth (Adolph & Robinson, 2013).

When infants learn to walk, they typically take small steps because of their limited balance control and strength. However, one study revealed that infants occasionally take a few large steps that even exceed their leg length, and these large steps indicate increased balance and strength (Badaly & Adolph, 2008).

In learning to locomote, infants learn what kinds of places and surfaces are safe for locomotion (Adolph & Berger, 2011, 2013). Karen Adolph (1997) investigated how experienced and inexperienced crawling infants and walking infants go down steep slopes (see Figure 5.2). Newly crawling infants, who averaged about 8½ months in age, rather indiscriminately went down the steep slopes, often falling in the process (with their mothers next to the slope to catch them). After weeks of practice, the crawling babies became more adept at judging which slopes were too steep to crawl down and which ones they could navigate safely. New walkers also could not judge the safety of the slopes, but experienced walkers accurately matched their skills with the steepness of the slopes. They rarely fell downhill, either refusing to go down the steep slopes or going down backward in a cautious manner. Experienced walkers perceptually assessed the situation—looking, swaying, touching, and thinking before they moved down the slope. With experience, both the crawlers and the walkers learned to avoid the risky slopes where they would fall, integrating perceptual information with the development of a new motor behavior. In a recent study, Adolph and her colleagues (2012) observed 12- to 19-month-olds during free play. Locomotor experience was extensive, with the infants averaging 2,368 steps and 17 falls per hour.

What are some developmental changes in posture during infancy?

Newly crawling infant

Experienced walker

FIGURE **5.2**

THE ROLE OF EXPERIENCE IN CRAWLING AND WALKING INFANTS' JUDGMENTS OF WHETHER TO GO DOWN A SLOPE. Karen Adolph (1997) found that locomotor experience rather than age was the primary predictor of adaptive responding on slopes of varying steepness. Newly crawling and walking infants could not judge the safety of the various slopes. With experience, they learned to avoid slopes where they would fall. When expert crawlers began to walk, they again made mistakes and fell, even though they had judged the same slope accurately when crawling. Adolph referred to this as the *specificity of learning* because it does not transfer across crawling and walking.

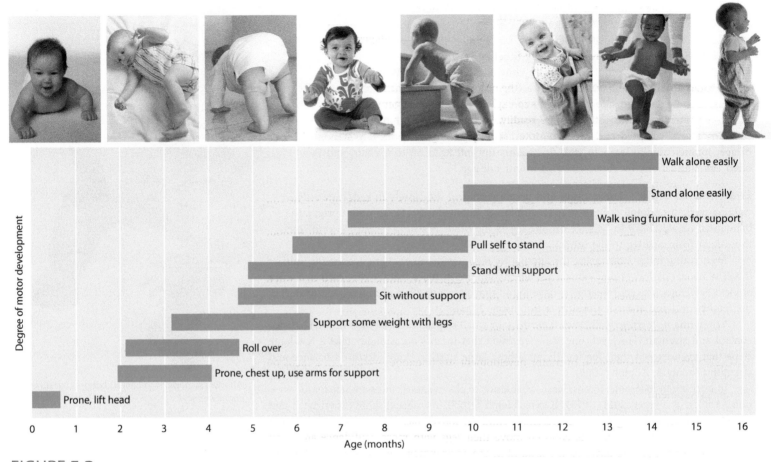

FIGURE **5.3**

MILESTONES IN GROSS MOTOR DEVELOPMENT

An important conclusion from Karen Adolph's (1997) study involves the *specificity of learning*—the idea that infants who have experience with one mode of locomotion (crawling, for example) don't seem to appreciate the dangers inherent in another mode of locomotion—risky walkways when they are making the transition to walking. Also in Adolph's (1997) research, we again see the importance of perceptual-motor coupling in the development of motor skills.

Practice is especially important in learning to walk (Adolph, 2011). However, practice does not involve exact repetition. Infants and toddlers accumulate an immense number of experiences with balance and locomotion. For example, the average toddler traverses almost 40 football fields a day and has 15 falls per hour (Adolph, 2011). From the perspective of Karen Adolph and her colleagues (2003, p. 495):

> Thousands of daily walking steps, each step slightly different from the last because of variations in the terrain and the continually varying bio-mechanical constraints on the body, may help infants to identify the relevant combination of strength and balance required to improve their walking skills.

The First Year: Motor Development Milestones and Variations   Figure 5.3 summarizes important accomplishments in gross motor skills during the first year, culminating in the ability to walk easily. The timing of these milestones, especially the later ones, may vary by as much as two to four months, and experiences can modify the onset of these accomplishments (Eaton, 2008). For example, since 1992, when pediatricians began recommending that parents place their babies on their backs when they sleep, fewer babies crawled, and those who did crawled later (Davis & others, 1998). Also, some infants do not follow the standard sequence of motor accomplishments. For example, many American infants never crawl on their belly or on their hands and knees. They may discover an idiosyncratic form of locomotion before walking, such as rolling, or they might never locomote until they get upright (Adolph & Joh, 2009). In the African Mali tribe, most infants do not crawl (Bril, 1999).

According to Karen Adolph and Sarah Berger (2005), "The old-fashioned view that growth and motor development reflect merely the age-related output of maturation is, at best, incomplete. Rather, infants acquire new skills with the help of their caregivers in a real-world environment of objects, surfaces, and planes."

Development in the Second Year The motor accomplishments of the first year bring increasing independence, allowing infants to explore their environment more extensively and to initiate interaction with others more readily. In the second year of life, toddlers become more motorically skilled and mobile. Motor activity during the second year is vital to the child's competent development, and few restrictions, except for safety, should be placed on their adventures.

By 13 to 18 months, toddlers can pull a toy attached to a string and use their hands and legs to climb up a number of steps. By 18 to 24 months, toddlers can walk quickly or run stiffly for a short distance, balance on their feet in a squatting position while playing with objects on the floor, walk backward without losing their balance, stand and kick a ball without falling, stand and throw a ball, and jump in place.

Can parents give their babies a head start on becoming physically fit and physically talented through structured exercise classes? Most infancy experts recommend against structured exercise classes for babies. But there are other ways of guiding infants' motor development. Caregivers in some cultures do handle babies vigorously, and this might advance motor development, as we discuss in *Connecting with Diversity*.

Childhood Our exploration of motor development in childhood begins with a focus on developmental changes in gross motor skills, and then we examine the role of sports in children's development.

Developmental Changes The preschool child no longer has to make an effort to stay upright and to move around. As children move their legs with more confidence and carry themselves more purposefully, moving around in the environment becomes more automatic.

At 3 years of age, children enjoy simple movements, such as hopping, jumping, and running back and forth, just for the sheer delight of performing these activities. They take considerable pride in showing how they can run across a room and jump all of 6 inches. The run-and-jump will win no Olympic gold medals, but for the 3-year-old the activity is a source of pride.

At 4 years of age, children are still enjoying the same kind of activities, but they have become more adventurous. They scramble over low jungle gyms as they display their athletic prowess. Although they have been able to climb stairs with one foot on each step for some time, they are just beginning to be able to come down the same way.

At 5 years of age, children are even more adventuresome than they were at 4. It is not unusual for self-assured 5-year-olds to perform hair-raising stunts on practically any climbing object. They run hard and enjoy races with each other and their parents.

During middle and late childhood, children's motor development becomes much smoother and more coordinated than it was in early childhood. For example, only one child in a thousand can hit a tennis ball over the net at the age of 3, yet by the age of 10 or 11 most children can learn to play the sport. Running, climbing, skipping rope, swimming, bicycle riding, and skating are just a few of the many physical skills elementary school children can master. And, when mastered, these physical skills are a source of great pleasure and a sense of accomplishment. A recent study of 9-year-olds revealed that those who were more physically fit had a better mastery of motor skills (Haga, 2008). In gross motor skills involving large-muscle activity, boys usually outperform girls.

As children move through the elementary school years, they gain greater control over their bodies and can sit and pay attention for longer periods of time. However, elementary school children are far from being physically mature, and they need to be active. Elementary school children become more fatigued by long periods of sitting than by running, jumping, or bicycling (Wuest & Fisette, 2012). Physical action is essential for these children to refine their developing skills, such as batting a ball, skipping rope, or balancing on a beam. Children benefit from exercise breaks periodically during the school day on the order of 15 minutes

The experiences of the first three years are almost entirely lost to us, and when we attempt to enter into a small child's world, we come as foreigners who have forgotten the landscape and no longer speak the native tongue.

—SELMA FRAIBERG
Developmentalist and Child Advocate, 20th Century

developmental **connection**

Exercise

Children's engagement in aerobic exercise in linked to advances in a number of aspects of cognitive development. Chapter 4, p. 132

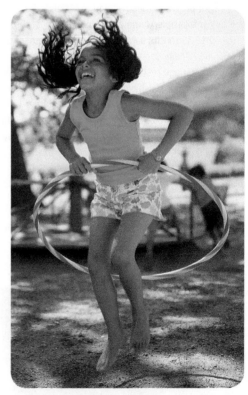

What are some developmental changes in children's motor development in early childhood and middle and late childhood?

Cultural Variations in Guiding Infants' Motor Development

Mothers in developing countries tend to stimulate their infants' motor skills more than mothers in more modern countries (Hopkins, 1991). In many African, Indian, and Caribbean cultures, mothers massage and stretch their infants during daily baths (Adolph, Karasik, & Tamis-LeMonda, 2010). Jamaican and Mali mothers regularly massage their infants and stretch their arms and legs (Adolph, Karasik, & Tamis-LeMonda, 2010). Mothers in the Gusii culture of Kenya also encourage vigorous movement in their babies (Hopkins & Westra, 1988).

And in sub-Saharan Africa, traditional practices in many villages involve mothers and siblings engaging babies in exercises, such as frequent exercise for trunk and pelvic muscles (Super & Harkness, 2010).

Do these cultural variations make a difference in the development of motor skills? When caregivers provide babies with physical guidance by physically handling them in special ways (such as stroking, massaging, or stretching) or by giving them opportunities for exercise, the infants often reach motor milestones earlier than infants whose caregivers have not provided these activities (Adolph, Karasik, & Tamis-LeMonda, 2010). For example, Jamaican mothers expect their infants to sit and walk alone 2 to 3 months earlier than English mothers do (Hopkins & Westra, 1990).

Many forms of restricted movement—such as Chinese sandbags, orphanage restrictions, and failure of caregivers to encourage movement in Budapest—have been found to produce substantial delays in motor development (Adolph, Karasik, & Tamis-LeMonda, 2010). In some rural Chinese provinces, babies are placed in a bag of fine sand, which acts as a diaper and is changed once a day. The baby is left alone, face up, and is

(*Left*) In the Algonquin culture in Quebec, Canada, babies are strapped to a cradle board for much of their infancy. (*Right*) In Jamaica, mothers massage and stretch their infants' arms and legs. *To what extent do cultural variations in the activity infants engage in influence the time at which they reach motor milestones?*

visited only when being fed by the mother (Xie & Young, 1999). Some studies of swaddling show slight delays in motor development, but other studies show no delays. Cultures that do swaddle infants usually do so early in the infant's development when the infant is not mobile; when the infant becomes more mobile, swaddling decreases.

Nonetheless, even when infants' motor activity is restricted, many infants still reach the milestones of motor development at a normal age. For example, Algonquin infants in Quebec, Canada, spend much of their first year strapped to a cradle board. Despite their inactivity, these infants still sit up, crawl, and walk within an age range similar to that of infants in cultures where they have had much greater opportunity for activity.

To help babies with their motor development, is stroking, massaging, or stretching their arms and legs a better or worse strategy than engaging them in a structured exercise class?

every two hours (Keen, 2005). In sum, elementary school children should be engaged in active, rather than passive, activities (Davis & others, 2012; Fung & others, 2012).

Sports Organized sports are one way of encouraging children to be active and to develop their motor skills. Schools and community agencies offer programs for children that involve baseball, soccer, football, basketball, swimming, gymnastics, and other sports. For children who participate in them, these programs may play a central role in their lives.

Participation in sports can have both positive and negative consequences for children (Myer & others, 2011). Participation can provide exercise, opportunities to learn how to compete, self-esteem, persistence, and a setting for developing peer relations and friendships (Theokas, 2009). Further, participating in sports reduces the likelihood that children will become obese (Drake & others, 2012). A recent study revealed that 10- to 12-year-old girls who

Parents, Coaches, and Children's Sports

Most sports psychologists stress that it is important for parents to show an interest in their children's sports participation. Most children want their parents to watch them perform in sports. Many children whose parents do not come to watch them play in sporting events feel that their parents do not adequately support them. However, some children become extremely nervous when their parents watch them perform, or they get embarrassed when their parents cheer too loudly or make a fuss. If children request that their parents not watch them perform, parents should respect their children's wishes (Schreiber, 1990).

Parents should compliment their children for their sports performance, and if they don't become overinvolved, they can help their children build their physical skills and help them emotionally—discussing with them how to deal with a difficult coach, how to cope with a tough loss, and how to put in perspective a poorly played game. The following guidelines provided by the Women's Sports Foundation (2001) in its booklet *Parents' Guide to Girls' Sports* can benefit both parents and coaches of all children in sports:

The Dos

- Make sports fun; the more children enjoy sports, the more they will want to play.
- Remember that it is okay for children to make mistakes; it means they are trying.
- Allow children to ask questions about the sport and discuss the sport in a calm, supportive manner.
- Show respect for the child's sports participation.
- Be positive and convince the child that he or she is making a good effort.
- Be a positive role model for the child in sports.

The Don'ts

- Yell or scream at the child.
- Condemn the child for poor play or continue to bring up failures long after they happen.
- Point out the child's errors in front of others.
- Expect the child to learn something immediately.
- Expect the child to become a pro.
- Ridicule or make fun of the child.
- Compare the child to siblings or to more talented children.
- Make sports all work and no fun.

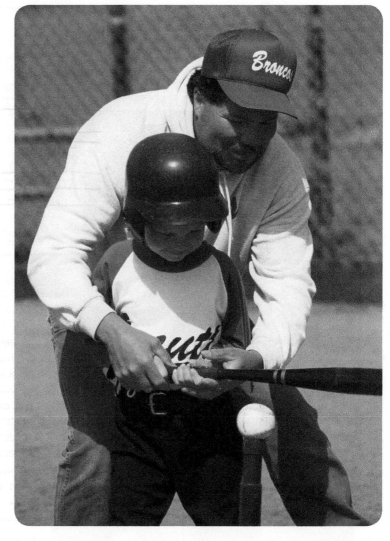

What are some guidelines that can benefit parents and coaches of children in sports?

What are some of the potentially positive and negative aspects of children's participation in sports?

participated in more than 3 hours a week in extracurricular sports activities were 59 percent less likely to be overweight or obese than their nonparticipating counterparts (Antonogeorgos & others, 2011). However, sports also can bring pressure to achieve and win, physical injuries, a distraction from academic work, and unrealistic expectations for success as an athlete (Lerch, Cordes, & Baumeister, 2011; Pakzad-Vaezi & Singhal, 2012). The *Caring Connections* interlude examines the roles of parents and coaches in children's sports.

FINE MOTOR SKILLS

Whereas gross motor skills involve large-muscle activity, **fine motor skills** involve finely tuned movements. Grasping a toy, using a spoon, buttoning a shirt, or doing anything that requires finger dexterity demonstrates fine motor skills.

Infancy Infants have hardly any control over fine motor skills at birth, but they do have many components of what will become finely coordinated arm, hand, and finger movements. The onset of reaching and grasping marks a significant achievement in infants' ability to interact with their surroundings (Greif & Needham, 2012; Savelsbergh, van der Kamp, & van Wersmerskerken, 2013). During the first two years of life, infants refine how they reach and grasp (Libertus & Needham, 2011). Initially, infants reach by moving their shoulders and elbows crudely, swinging toward an object. Later, when infants reach for an object they move their wrists, rotate their hands, and coordinate their thumb and forefinger. Infants do not have to see their own hands in order to reach for an object (Clifton & others, 1993). Cues from muscles, tendons, and joints, not sight of the limb, guide reaching by 4-month-old infants.

A young girl using a pincer grip to pick up puzzle pieces.

Infants refine their ability to grasp objects by developing two types of grasps. Initially, infants grip with the whole hand, which is called the *palmer grasp*. Later, toward the end of the first year, infants also grasp small objects with their thumb and forefinger, which is called the *pincer grip*. Their grasping system is very flexible. They vary their grip on an object depending on its size, shape, and texture, as well as the size of their own hands relative to the object's size. Infants grip small objects with their thumb and forefinger (and sometimes their middle finger too), whereas they grip large objects with all of the fingers of one hand or both hands.

Perceptual-motor coupling is necessary for the infant to coordinate grasping (Needham, 2011). Which perceptual system the infant is most likely to use to coordinate grasping varies with age. Four-month-old infants rely greatly on touch to determine how they will grip an object; 8-month-olds are more likely to use vision as a guide (Newell & others, 1989). This developmental change is efficient because vision lets infants preshape their hands as they reach for an object.

Experience plays a role in reaching and grasping. In one study, 3-month-old infants participated in play sessions wearing "sticky mittens . . . mittens with palms that stuck to the edges of toys and allowed the infants to pick up the toys" (Needham, Barrett, & Peterman, 2002, p. 279) (see Figure 5.4). Infants who participated in sessions with the mittens grasped and manipulated objects earlier in their development than a control group of infants who did not receive the "mitten" experience. The experienced infants looked at the objects longer, swatted at them more during visual contact, and were more likely to mouth the objects. In a recent study, 5-month-old infants whose parents trained them to use the sticky mittens for 10 minutes a day over a two-week period showed advances in their reaching behavior at the end of the two weeks (Libertus & Needham, 2011).

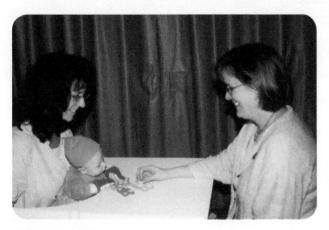

FIGURE **5.4**

INFANTS' USE OF "STICKY MITTENS" TO EXPLORE OBJECTS. Amy Needham and her colleagues (2002) found that "sticky mittens" enhanced young infants' object exploration skills.

fine motor skills Motor skills that involve more finely tuned movements, such as finger dexterity.

Just as infants need to exercise their gross motor skills, they also need to exercise their fine motor skills (Needham & Libertus, 2011; Libertus & Needham, 2011). Especially when they can manage a pincer grip, infants delight in picking up small objects. Many develop the pincer grip and begin to crawl at about the same time, and infants at this time pick up virtually everything in sight, especially on the floor, and put the objects in their mouth. Thus, parents need to be vigilant in regularly monitoring what objects are within the infant's reach (Keen, 2005).

Around 18 to 24 months of age, toddlers begin to build towers with blocks (see Figure 5.5). Initially, they can only balance two- to three-block towers, but soon the tower increases to four, five, and even more blocks. To build a tower, toddlers must engage in the cognitive activity of planning, in this case a plan that involves a number of sequential movements in picking up and stacking blocks in a precise way (Keen, 2011). Also, they need to have developed the motor skill to release blocks smoothly so the tower won't topple. In a recent study, substantial individual differences in the tower building of 18- to 21-month-olds occurred (Chen & others, 2010). In this study, toddlers who built higher towers at this age continued to be more advanced in tower building at 3 years of age.

Rachel Keen (2011) emphasizes that tool use is an excellent context for studying problem solving in infants because tool use provides information about how infants plan to reach a goal. Researchers in this area have studied infants' intentional actions that range from picking up a spoon in different orientations to retrieving rakes placed inside tubes.

Childhood As children get older, their fine motor skills improve (Keen, 2011). At 3 years of age, children have had the ability to pick up the tiniest objects between their thumb and forefinger for some time, but they are still somewhat clumsy at it. Many 3-year-olds can build surprisingly high block towers, each block placed with intense concentration but often not in a completely straight line. When 3-year-olds play with a form board or a simple puzzle, they are rather rough in placing the pieces. When they try to position a piece in a hole, they often try to force the piece or pat it vigorously.

By 4 years of age, children's fine motor coordination is much more precise. Sometimes 4-year-old children have trouble building high towers with blocks because, in their desire to place each of the blocks perfectly, they upset those already stacked. By age 5, children's fine motor coordination has improved further. Hand, arm, and fingers all move together under better command of the eye. Mere towers no longer interest the 5-year-old, who now wants to build a house or a church, complete with steeple. (Adults may still need to be told what each finished project is meant to be.)

Increased myelination of the central nervous system is reflected in the improvement of fine motor skills during middle and late childhood. Recall from Chapter 4 that myelination involves the covering of the axon with a myelin sheath, a process that increases the speed with which information travels from neuron to neuron. By middle childhood, children can use their hands adroitly as tools. Six-year-olds can hammer, paste, tie shoes, and fasten clothes. By 7 years of age, children's hands have become steadier. At this age, children prefer a pencil to a crayon for printing, and reversal of letters is less common. Printing becomes smaller. At 8 to 10 years of age, children can use their hands independently with more ease and precision; children can now write rather than print words. Letter size becomes smaller and more even. At 10 to 12 years of age, children begin to show manipulative skills similar to the abilities of adults. The complex, intricate, and rapid movements needed to produce fine-quality crafts or to play a difficult piece on a musical instrument can be mastered. Girls usually outperform boys in fine motor skills.

FIGURE **5.5**

TOWER-BUILDING TODDLERS. This 18-month-old is building a block tower in the study by Chen & others (2010). Note the kinematic sensors on the toddler's wrists for obtaining data on speed, location, and timing of movement.

Review *Connect* Reflect

 Describe how motor skills develop.

Review

- What is the dynamic systems view of motor development?
- What are some reflexes of infants?
- How do gross motor skills develop?
- How do fine motor skills develop?

Connect

- In this section, you learned how infants explore their environment as they develop gross and fine motor skills. How does this experience affect infants' neural connections (discussed in Chapter 4)?

Reflect *Your Own Personal Journey of Life*

- If and when you become a parent, how would you evaluate the benefits and drawbacks of allowing your 7-year-old to play for a soccer team in a competitive league in your town or city?

Sensory and Perceptual Development

LG2 Outline the course of sensory and perceptual development.

| What Are Sensation and Perception? | The Ecological View | Visual Perception | Other Senses | Intermodal Perception | Nature, Nurture, and Perceptual Development |

How do sensations and perceptions develop? Can a newborn see? If so, what can it perceive? What about the other senses—hearing, smell, taste, and touch? What are they like in the newborn, and how do they develop? Can an infant put together information from two modalities, such as sight and sound? What roles do nature and nurture play in perceptual development? These are among the intriguing questions that we will explore in this section.

WHAT ARE SENSATION AND PERCEPTION?

How does a newborn know that her mother's skin is soft rather than rough? How does a 5-year-old know what color his hair is? Infants and children "know" these things as a result of information that comes through the senses. Without vision, hearing, touch, taste, and smell, we would be isolated from the world; we would live in dark silence, a tasteless, colorless, feelingless void.

Sensation occurs when information interacts with sensory *receptors*—the eyes, ears, tongue, nostrils, and skin. The sensation of hearing occurs when waves of pulsating air are collected by the outer ear and transmitted through the bones of the inner ear to the auditory nerve. The sensation of vision occurs as rays of light contact the eyes, become focused on the retina, and are transmitted by the optic nerve to the visual centers of the brain.

Perception is the interpretation of what is sensed. The air waves that contact the ears might be interpreted as noise or as musical sounds, for example. The physical energy transmitted to the retina of the eye might be interpreted as a particular color, pattern, or shape, depending on how it is perceived.

THE ECOLOGICAL VIEW

In recent decades, much of the research on perceptual development in infancy has been guided by the ecological view of Eleanor and James J. Gibson (E. Gibson, 1969, 1989, 2001; J. Gibson, 1966, 1979). They argue that we do not have to take bits and pieces of data from sensations and build up representations of the world in our minds. Instead, our perceptual system can select from the rich information that the environment itself provides.

How would you use the Gibsons' ecological theory of perception and the concept of affordance to explain the role that perception is playing in this baby's activity?

According to the Gibsons' **ecological view,** we directly perceive information that exists in the world around us. The view is called *ecological* "because it connects perceptual capabilities to information available in the world of the perceiver" (Kellman & Arterberry, 2006, p. 112). Thus, perception brings us into contact with the environment so that we can interact with and adapt to it. Perception is designed for action. Perception gives people such information as when to duck, when to turn their bodies to get through a narrow passageway, and when to put their hands up to catch something.

In the Gibsons' view, objects have **affordances,** which are opportunities for interaction offered by objects that fit within our capabilities to perform activities. A pot may afford you something to cook with, and it may afford a toddler something to bang. Adults typically know when a chair is appropriate for sitting, when a surface is safe for walking, or when an object is within reach. We directly and accurately perceive these affordances by sensing information from the environment—the light or sound reflecting from the surfaces of the world—and from our own bodies through muscle receptors, joint receptors, and skin receptors, for example (Ziemer, Plumert, & Pick, 2012).

As we described earlier in the section on motor development, infants who were just learning to crawl or just learning to walk were less cautious when confronted with a steep slope than experienced crawlers or walkers were (Adolph, 1997). The more experienced crawlers

sensation Reaction that occurs when information contacts sensory receptors—the eyes, ears, tongue, nostrils, and skin.

perception The interpretation of sensation.

ecological view The view, proposed by the Gibsons, that people directly perceive information in the world around them. Perception brings people in contact with the environment so that they can interact with and adapt to it.

affordances Opportunities for interaction offered by objects that are necessary to perform activities.

and walkers perceived that a slope *affords* the possibility for not only faster locomotion but also for falling. Again, infants coupled perception and action to make a decision about what to do in their environment. Through perceptual development, children become more efficient at discovering and using affordances.

In Karen Adolph's (2011) research, slopes, gaps, apertures, and dropoffs, coupled with experimental manipulation of infants' body properties (slippery Teflon shoes or floors, for example), are used to examine infants' success in connecting their motor decisions to actual affordances for action. Using such observational measures as checklist diaries, telephone diaries, step-counters, and video tracking, she and her colleagues (Adolph, 2011; Adolph & Berger, 2011, 2013; Adolph, Joh, & Eppler, 2010; Adolph & Robinson, 2013; Franchak & Adolph, 2010) collected information about infants' everyday locomotor experiences. They have discovered that the extent of infants' experiences have good predictive power in explaining developmental changes beyond their body dimensions and chronological age. And they have found that experience with surfaces varying in friction and rigidity allows only narrow transfer to situations with the same visual context.

Studying the infant's perception has not been an easy task. For instance, if newborns have limited communication abilities and are unable to tell us what they are seeing, hearing, smelling, and so on, how can we study their perception? *Connecting Through Research* describes some of the ingenious ways researchers study infants' perception.

visual preference method A method developed by Fantz to determine whether infants can distinguish one stimulus from another by measuring the length of time they attend to different stimuli.

habituation Decreased responsiveness to a stimulus after repeated presentations of the stimulus.

dishabituation The recovery of a habituated response after a change in stimulation.

connecting through research

How Can We Study Newborns' Perception?

The creature has poor motor coordination and can move itself only with great difficulty. Although it cries when uncomfortable, it uses few other vocalizations. In fact, it sleeps most of the time, about 16 to 17 hours a day. You are curious about this creature and want to know more about what it can do. You think to yourself, "I wonder if it can see. How could I find out?"

You obviously have a communication problem with the creature. You must devise a way that will allow the creature to "tell" you that it can see. While examining the creature one day, you make an interesting discovery. When you move an object horizontally in front of the creature, its eyes follow the object's movement.

The creature's head movement suggests that it has at least some vision. In case you haven't already guessed, the creature you have been reading about is the human infant, and the role you played is that of a researcher interested in devising techniques to learn about the infant's visual perception. After years of work, scientists have developed research methods and tools sophisticated enough to examine the subtle abilities of infants and to interpret their complex actions (Bendersky & Sullivan, 2007).

Visual Preference Method

Robert Fantz (1963) was a pioneer in the study of infants' perception. Fantz made an important discovery that advanced the ability of researchers to investigate infants' visual perception: Infants look at different things for different lengths of time. Fantz placed infants in a "looking chamber," which had two visual displays on the ceiling above the infant's head. An experimenter viewed the infant's eyes by looking through a peephole. If the

infant was fixating on one of the displays, the experimenter could see the display's reflection in the infant's eyes. This allowed the experimenter to determine how long the infant looked at each display. Fantz (1963) found that infants only 2 days old look longer at patterned stimuli, such as faces and concentric circles, than at red, white, or yellow discs. Infants 2 to 3 weeks old preferred to look at patterns—a face, a piece of printed matter, or a bull's-eye—longer than at red, yellow, or white discs (see Figure 5.6). Fantz's research method—studying whether infants can distinguish one stimulus from another by measuring the length of time they attend to different stimuli—is referred to as the **visual preference method.**

Habituation and Dishabituation

Another way that researchers have studied infants' perception is to present a stimulus (such as a sight or a sound) a number of times. If the infant decreases its response to the stimulus after several presentations, this indicates that the infant is no longer interested in looking at the stimulus. If the researcher now presents a new stimulus, the infant's response will recover, indicating that the infant could discriminate between the old and new stimuli (Colombo & others, 2010; Colombo, Brez, & Curtindale, 2013).

Habituation is the name given to decreased responsiveness to a stimulus after repeated presentations of the stimulus. **Dishabituation** is the recovery of a habituated response after a change in stimulation. Newborn infants can habituate to repeated sights, sounds, smells, or touches (Rovee-Collier, 2004). Among the measures researchers use in habituation studies are sucking behavior (sucking stops when the young

(continued)

connecting through research

(continued)

FIGURE **5.6**

FANTZ'S EXPERIMENT ON INFANTS' VISUAL PERCEPTION. (*a*) Infants 2 to 3 weeks old preferred to look at some stimuli more than others. In Fantz's experiment, infants preferred to look at patterns rather than at color or brightness. For example, they looked longer at a face, a piece of printed matter, or a bull's-eye than at red, yellow, or white discs. (*b*) Fantz used a "looking chamber" to study infants' perception of stimuli.

(a)

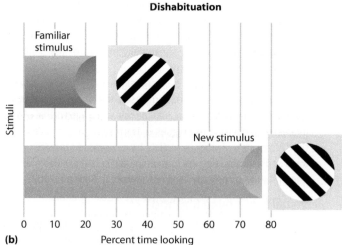

(b)

infant attends to a novel object), heart and respiration rates, and the length of time the infant looks at an object. Figure 5.7 shows the results of one study of habituation and dishabituation with newborns (Slater, Morison, & Somers, 1988).

High-Amplitude Sucking

To assess an infant's attention to sound, researchers often use a method called *high-amplitude sucking*. In this method, infants are given a nonnutritive nipple to suck, and the nipple is connected to a sound-generating

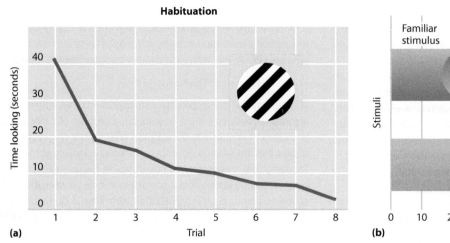

FIGURE **5.7**

HABITUATION AND DISHABITUATION. In the first part of one study, 7-hour-old newborns were shown the stimulus in (*a*). As indicated, the newborns looked at it an average of 41 seconds when it was first presented to them (Slater, Morison, & Somers, 1988). Over seven more presentations of the stimulus, they looked at it less and less. In the second part of the study, infants were presented with both the familiar stimulus to which they had just become habituated (*a*) and a new stimulus (shown in *b*, which was rotated 90 degrees). The newborns looked at the new stimulus three times as much as the familiar stimulus.

(continued)

system. The researcher computes a baseline high-amplitude sucking rate in a one-minute silent period. Following the baseline, presentation of a sound is made contingent on the rate of amplitude sucking. Initially babies suck frequently so that the sound occurs often. Gradually, they lose interest in hearing the same sound so they begin to suck less often. Then the researcher changes the sound that is being presented. If the babies renew their vigorous sucking, the inference is that they have discriminated the sound change and are sucking more because they want to hear the interesting new sound (Menn & Stoel-Gammon, 2009).

The Orienting Response

A technique that can be used to determine whether an infant can see or hear is the *orienting response*, which involves turning one's head toward a sight or sound. Also, a startle response can be used as an indicator of an infant's reaction to a noise (Bendersky & Sullivan, 2007).

Equipment

Technology can facilitate the use of most methods for investigating the infant's perceptual abilities. Videotape equipment allows researchers to investigate elusive behaviors. High-speed computers make it possible to perform complex data analysis in minutes. Other equipment records respiration, heart rate, body movement, visual fixation, and sucking behavior, which provide clues to what the infant is perceiving. For example, some researchers use equipment that detects whether a change in infants' respiration follows a change in the pitch of a sound. If so, it suggests that the infants heard the pitch change.

Eye Tracking

The most important recent advance in measuring infant perception is the development of sophisticated eye-tracking equipment (Franchak & others, 2011; Morgante, Zolfaghari, & Johnson, 2012; Navab & others, 2012). Figure 5.8 shows an infant wearing an eye-tracking headgear in a recent study on visually guided motor behavior and social interaction.

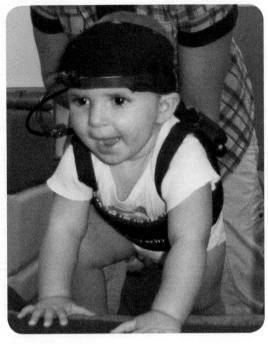

FIGURE **5.8**

AN INFANT WEARING EYE-TRACKING HEADGEAR.
Using the ultralight, wireless, head-mounted eye-tracking equipment shown here, researchers can record where infants are looking while they freely locomote. (Source: Courtesy of Dr. Karen Adolph's laboratory, New York University.)

One of the main reasons that infant perception researchers are so enthusiastic about the recent availability of sophisticated eye-tracking equipment is that looking time is among the most important measures of infant perceptual and cognitive development (Aslin, 2012). The new eye-tracking equipment allows for much greater precision than human observation in assessing various aspects of infant looking and gaze (Oakes, 2012). Among the areas of infant perception in which eye-tracking equipment is being used are memory, joint attention, and face processing (Falck-Ytter & others, 2012). Further, eye-tracking equipment is improving our understanding of atypically developing infants, such as those with autism (Sasson & Elison, 2013), and infants at risk for atypical developmental outcomes, including infants at risk for developing autism and preterm infants (Bedford & others, 2012).

In recent research on infants (14 months old), children (4 to 8 years old), and adults (20 to 22 years old) in a room filled with colorful toys and objects using eye-tracking headgear, the infants only centered their gaze on the objects about one-fourth of the time (Adolph, 2011; Franchak & Adolph, 2010). Adults fixated on objects about one-third of the time, 4- to 8-year-old children about 60 percent of the time. Thus, in a majority of instances, infants rather remarkably navigated their environment by merely glancing at the objects rather than centering their vision on the objects.

Another recent eye-tracking study shed light on the effectiveness of TV programs and DVDs that claim to educate infants (Kirkorian, Anderson, & Keen, 2012). In this study, 1-year-olds, 4-year-olds, and adults watched *Sesame Street* and the eye-tracking equipment recorded precisely what they looked at on the screen. The 1-year-olds were far less likely to consistently look at the same part of the screen than their older counterparts, suggesting that the 1-year-olds showed little understanding of the *Sesame Street* video but instead were more likely to be attracted by what was salient than by what was relevant.

FIGURE **5.9**

VISUAL ACUITY DURING THE FIRST MONTHS OF LIFE. The four photographs represent a computer estimation of what a picture of a face looks like to a 1-month-old, 2-month-old, 3-month-old, and 1-year-old (which approximates the visual acuity of an adult).

VISUAL PERCEPTION

What do newborns see? How does visual perception develop in infancy? How does visual perception develop in childhood?

Infancy Some important changes in visual perception with age can be traced to differences in how the eye itself functions over time. For example, changes in eye function influence how clearly we can see an object, whether we can differentiate its colors, at what distance, and in what light.

Visual Acuity Psychologist William James (1890/1950) called the newborn's perceptual world a "blooming, buzzing confusion." More than a century later, we can safely say that he was wrong (Atkinson & Braddick, 2013; Schmuckler, 2013). Even the newborn perceives a world with some order. That world, however, is far different from the one perceived by the toddler or the adult.

Just how well can infants see? At birth, the nerves and muscles and lens of the eye are still developing. As a result, newborns cannot see small things that are far away. The newborn's vision is estimated to be 20/240 on the well-known Snellen chart used for eye examinations, which means that a newborn can see at 20 feet only as much as a normal adult can see at 240 feet (Aslin & Lathrop, 2008). In other words, an object 20 feet away is only as clear to the newborn as it would be if it were 240 feet away from an adult with normal vision (20/20). By 6 months of age, though, on *average* vision is 20/40 (Aslin & Lathrop, 2008).

Face Perception Infants show an interest in human faces soon after birth (Lee & others, 2013). Figure 5.9 shows a computer estimation of what a picture of a face looks like to an infant at different ages from a distance of about 6 inches. Infants spend more time looking at their mother's face than a stranger's face as early as 12 hours after being born (Bushnell, 2003). By 3 months of age, infants match voices to faces, distinguish between male and female faces, and discriminate between faces of their own ethnic group and those of other ethnic groups (Kelly & others, 2007, 2009; Liu & others, 2011).

As infants develop, they change the way they gather information from the visual world, including human faces (Lee & others, 2013). A recent study recorded eye movements of 3-, 6-, and 9-month-old infants as they viewed clips from an animated film—*A Charlie Brown Christmas* (Frank, Vul, & Johnson, 2009). From 3 to 9 months of age, infants gradually began focusing their attention more on the faces of the characters in the animated film and less on salient background stimuli.

Pattern Perception As we discussed in the *Connecting Through Research* interlude, young infants can perceive certain patterns. With the help of his "looking chamber," Robert Fantz (1963) revealed that even 2- to 3-week-old infants prefer to look at patterned displays rather than nonpatterned displays. For example, they prefer to look at a normal human face rather than one with scrambled features, and they prefer to look at a bull's-eye target or black-and-white stripes rather than a plain circle.

Color Vision The infant's color vision also improves over time (Kellman & Arterberry, 2006). By 8 weeks, and possibly as early as 4 weeks, infants can discriminate between some

developmental **connection**

Research Methods

The still-face paradigm has been used to study face-to-face interaction between infants and caregivers. Chapter 10, p. 298

colors (Kelly, Borchert, & Teller, 1997). By 4 months of age, they have color preferences that mirror those of adults in some cases, preferring saturated colors such as royal blue over pale blue, for example (Bornstein, 1975). A recent study of 4- to 5-month-olds found that they looked longest at reddish hues and shortest at greenish hues (Franklin & others, 2010). In part, these changes in vision reflect maturation. Experience, however, is also necessary for vision to develop normally. For example, one study found that experience is necessary for normal color vision to develop (Sugita, 2004).

Perceptual Constancy   Some perceptual accomplishments are especially intriguing because they indicate that the infant's perception goes beyond the information provided by the senses (Johnson, 2012, 2013; Slater & others, 2010, 2011). This is the case in *perceptual constancy*, in which sensory stimulation is changing but perception of the physical world remains constant. If infants did not develop perceptual constancy, each time they saw an object at a different distance or in a different orientation, they would perceive it as a different object. Thus, the development of perceptual constancy allows infants to perceive their world as stable. Two types of perceptual constancy are size constancy and shape constancy.

Size constancy is the recognition that an object remains the same even though the retinal image of the object changes as you move toward or away from the object (Kavsek & Granrud, 2012). The farther away from us an object is, the smaller is its image on our eyes. Thus, the size of an object on the retina is not sufficient to tell us its actual size. For example, you perceive a bicycle standing right in front of you as smaller than the car parked across the street, even though the bicycle casts a larger image on your eyes than the car does. When you move away from the bicycle, you do not perceive it to be shrinking even though its image on your retinas shrinks; you perceive its size as constant.

But what about babies? Do they have size constancy? Researchers have found that babies as young as 3 months of age show size constancy (Bower, 1966; Day & McKenzie, 1973). However, at 3 months of age, this ability is not full-blown. It continues to develop until 10 or 11 years of age (Kellman & Banks, 1998).

Shape constancy is the recognition that an object remains the same shape even though its orientation to us changes. Look around the room you are in right now. You likely see objects of varying shapes, such as tables and chairs. If you get up and walk around the room, you will see these objects from different sides and angles. Even though your retinal image of the objects changes as you walk and look, you will still perceive the objects as the same shape.

Do babies have shape constancy? As with size constancy, researchers have found that babies as young as 3 months of age have shape constancy (Bower, 1966; Day & McKenzie, 1973). Three-month-old infants, however, do not have shape constancy for irregularly shaped objects, such as tilted planes (Cook & Birch, 1984).

Perception of Occluded Objects   Look around the context where you are now. You likely see that some objects are partly occluded by other objects that are in front of them—possibly a desk behind a chair, some books behind a computer, or a car parked behind a tree. Do infants perceive an object as complete when it is occluded by an object in front of it?

In the first two months of postnatal development, infants don't perceive occluded objects as complete, instead only perceiving what is visible (Johnson, 2012, 2013). Beginning at about 2 months of age, infants develop the ability to perceive that occluded objects are whole (Slater, Field, & Hernandez-Reif, 2007). How does perceptual completion develop? In Scott Johnson's research (2004, 2010, 2011, 2012, 2013), learning, experience, and self-directed exploration via eye movements play key roles in the development of perceptual completion in young infants.

Many objects that are occluded appear and disappear behind closer objects, as when you are walking down the street and see cars appear and disappear behind buildings as they move or you move. Can infants predictively track briefly occluded moving objects? They develop the ability to track briefly occluded moving objects at about 3 to 5 months of age (Bertenthal, 2008). One study explored 5- to 9-month-old infants' ability to track moving objects that disappeared gradually behind an occluded partition, disappeared abruptly, or imploded (shrank quickly in size) (Bertenthal, Longo, & Kenny, 2007) (see Figure 5.10). In this study, the infants were more likely to accurately predict the path of the moving object when it disappeared gradually than when it disappeared abruptly or imploded.

(a) Gradual occlusion

(b) Abrupt occlusion

(c) Implosion

FIGURE **5.10**

INFANTS' PREDICTIVE TRACKING OF A BRIEFLY OCCLUDED MOVING BALL. The top drawing shows a visual scene that infants experienced. At the beginning of each event, a multicolored ball bounded up and down with an accompanying bouncing sound, and then rolled across the floor until it disappeared behind the partition. The bottom drawing shows the three stimulus events the 5- to 9-month-old infants experienced: occlusion, disappearance, and implosion. (*a*) *Gradual Occlusion:* The ball gradually disappears behind the right side of the occluding partition located in the center of the display. (*b*) *Abrupt Disappearance:* The ball abruptly disappears when it reaches the location of the white circle and then abruptly reappears 2 seconds later at the location of the second white circle on the other side of the occluding partition. (*c*) *Implosion:* The rolling ball quickly decreases in size as it approaches the occluding partition and rapidly increases in size as it reappears on the other side of the occluding partition.

size constancy Recognition that an object remains the same even though the retinal image of the object changes.

shape constancy Recognition that an object remains the same even though its orientation to the viewer changes.

FIGURE **5.11**

EXAMINING INFANTS' DEPTH PERCEPTION ON THE VISUAL CLIFF.
Eleanor Gibson and Richard Walk (1960) found that most infants would not crawl out on the glass, which, according to Gibson and Walk, indicated that they had depth perception. However, critics point out that the visual cliff is a better indication of the infant's social referencing and fear of heights than the infant's perception of depth.

Depth Perception   Might infants be able to perceive depth? To investigate this question, Eleanor Gibson and Richard Walk (1960) constructed in their laboratory a miniature cliff with a dropoff covered by glass. They placed infants on the edge of this visual cliff and had their mothers coax them to crawl onto the glass (see Figure 5.11). Most infants would not crawl out on the glass, choosing instead to remain on the shallow side, an indication that they could perceive depth, according to Gibson and Walk. However, critics point out that the visual cliff likely is a better test of social referencing and fear of heights than depth perception.

The 6- to 12-month-old infants in the visual cliff experiment had extensive visual experience. Do younger infants without this experience still perceive depth? Since younger infants do not crawl, this question is difficult to answer. Two- to 4-month-old infants show differences in heart rate when they are placed directly on the deep side of the visual cliff instead of on the shallow side (Campos, Langer, & Krowitz, 1970). However, these differences might mean that young infants respond to differences in some visual characteristics of the deep and shallow cliffs, with no actual knowledge of depth (Adolph & Kretch, 2012). Although researchers do not know exactly how early in life infants can perceive depth, we do know that infants develop the ability to use binocular cues to discern depth by about 3 to 4 months of age.

Childhood   Perceptual development continues in childhood (Lee & others, 2011b; Vida & Maurer, 2012). Children become increasingly efficient at detecting the boundaries between colors (such as red and orange) at 3 to 4 years of age (Gibson, 1969). When they are about 4 or 5 years old, most children's eye muscles are developed enough for them to move their eyes efficiently across a series of letters. Many preschool children are farsighted, unable to see close up as well as they can see far away. By the time they enter first grade, though, most children can focus their eyes and sustain their attention effectively on close-up objects.

After infancy, children's visual expectations about the physical world continue to develop (Keen, 2011). In one study, 2- to 4½-year-old children were given a task in which the goal was to find a toy ball that had been dropped through an opaque tube (Hood, 1995). As shown in Figure 5.12, if the ball is dropped into the tube at the top right, it will land in the box at the bottom left. However, in this task, most of the 2-year-olds, and even some of the 4-year-olds, persisted in searching in the box immediately beneath the dropping point. For them, gravity ruled, and they had failed to perceive the end location of the curved tube.

In a recent study 3-year-olds were presented with the same task shown in Figure 5.12 (Joh, Jaswal, & Keen, 2011). In the group that was told to imagine the various paths the ball might take, the young children were more accurate in predicting where the ball would land. In another recent study, 3-year-olds improved their performance on the ball-dropping task shown in Figure 5.12 when they were instructed to follow the tube with their eyes to the bottom (Bascandziev & Harris, 2011). Thus, in these two studies, 3-year-olds were able to overcome the gravity bias and their impulsive tendencies when they were given verbal instructions from a knowledgeable adult (Keen, 2011).

How do children learn to deal with situations like that in Figure 5.12, and how do they come to understand other laws of the physical world? These questions are addressed by research on children's cognitive development, which we will discuss in Chapters 6 and 7.

FIGURE **5.12**

VISUAL EXPECTATIONS ABOUT THE PHYSICAL WORLD. When young children see a ball dropped into the tube, many of them will search for it immediately below the dropping point. *How might verbal instructions from a knowledgeable adult help younger children overcome a gravity bias?*

OTHER SENSES

Other sensory systems besides vision also develop during infancy. We will explore development in hearing, touch and pain, smell, and taste.

Hearing   During the last two months of pregnancy, as the fetus nestles in its mother's womb, it can hear sounds such as the mother's voice, music, and so on (Kisilevsky & Hains, 2011; Kisilevsky & others, 2009). Two psychologists wanted to find out if a fetus that heard

(a)   (b)

FIGURE **5.13**

HEARING IN THE WOMB. (*a*) Pregnant mothers read *The Cat in the Hat* to their fetuses during the last few months of pregnancy. (*b*) When they were born, the babies preferred listening to a recording of their mothers reading *The Cat in the Hat*—as evidenced by the way they sucked on a nipple—rather than another story, *The King, the Mice and the Cheese*.

Dr. Seuss' classic story *The Cat in the Hat* while still in the mother's womb would prefer hearing the story after birth (DeCasper & Spence, 1986). During the last months of pregnancy, 16 women read *The Cat in the Hat* to their fetuses. Then shortly after they were born, the mothers read either *The Cat in the Hat* or a story with a different rhyme and pace, *The King, the Mice and the Cheese* (which was not read to them during prenatal development). The infants sucked on a nipple in a different way when the mothers read the two stories, suggesting that the infants recognized the pattern and tone of *The Cat in the Hat* (see Figure 5.13). This study illustrates not only that a fetus can hear but also that it has a remarkable ability to learn even before birth. A recent fMRI study assessed fetal brain response to auditory stimuli, confirming that the fetus can hear at 33 to 34 weeks gestation (Jardri & others, 2012).

The fetus can also recognize the mother's voice, as one study demonstrated (Kisilevsky & others, 2004). Sixty third-trimester fetuses (mean gestational age, 38.4 weeks) were exposed to a tape recording either of their mother or of a female stranger reading a passage. The sounds of the tape were delivered through a loudspeaker held just above the mother's abdomen. Fetal heart rate increased in response to the mother's voice but decreased in response to the stranger's voice.

What kind of changes in hearing take place during infancy? They involve perception of a sound's loudness, pitch, and localization:

- *Loudness.* Immediately after birth, infants cannot hear soft sounds quite as well as adults can; a stimulus must be louder to be heard by a newborn than by an adult (Trehub & others, 1991). For example, an adult can hear a whisper from about 4 to 5 feet away, but a newborn requires that sounds be closer to a normal conversational level to be heard at that distance.

- *Pitch.* Infants are also less sensitive to the pitch of a sound than adults are. *Pitch* is the perception of the frequency of a sound. A soprano voice sounds high-pitched, a bass voice low-pitched. Infants are less sensitive to low-pitched sounds and are more likely to hear high-pitched sounds (Aslin, Jusczyk, & Pisoni, 1998). By 2 years of age, infants have considerably improved their ability to distinguish between sounds with different pitches. A recent study revealed that by 7 months of age, infants can process simultaneous pitches when they hear voices but they are more likely to encode the higher-pitched voice (Marie & Trainor, 2012).

- *Localization.* Even newborns can determine the general location from which a sound is coming, but by 6 months of age, they are more proficient at *localizing* sounds or detecting their origins. Their ability to localize sounds continues to improve during the second year (Burnham & Mattock, 2010).

developmental **connection**

Biological Processes

Prenatal development is divided into three periods: germinal (first 2 weeks after conception), embryonic (2 to 8 weeks after conception), and fetal (begins at 2 months after conception and lasts for 7 months on average). Chapter 3, p. 75

Cochlear implants—small, electronic devices that directly stimulate the auditory nerve—are now done routinely for congenitally deaf children, even as early as 12 months of age. Many of the hearing-impaired children who have early cochlear implant surgery show good progress in learning speech and in understanding others' speech, which allows them to function effectively in a hearing world (Asp, Eskilsson, & Berninger, 2011; Hassepass & others, 2013; Radulescu & others, 2013).

Otitis media is a middle-ear infection that can impair hearing temporarily. If it continues too long, it can interfere with language development and socialization (Grossman, Silverman, & Miron, 2013). As many as one-third of all U.S. children from have three or more episodes between birth and age 3. In some cases, the infection can develop into a more chronic condition in which the middle ear becomes filled with fluid, and this can seriously impair hearing. Treatments for otitis media include antibiotics and placement of a tube in the inner ear to drain fluid (Khodaverdi & others, 2013; Wald, 2011).

Touch and Pain   Do newborns respond to touch? Can they feel pain?

Newborns do respond to touch. A touch to the cheek produces a turning of the head; a touch to the lips produces sucking movements.

Newborns can also feel pain (Gunnar & Quevado, 2007). If and when you have a son and consider whether he should be circumcised, the issue of an infant's pain perception probably will become important to you. Circumcision is usually performed on young boys about the third day after birth. Will your young son experience pain if he is circumcised when he is 3 days old? An investigation by Megan Gunnar and her colleagues (1987) found that newborn infant males cried intensely during circumcision. Circumcised infants also display amazing resiliency. Within several minutes after the surgery, they can nurse and interact in a normal manner with their mothers. And, if allowed to, the newly circumcised newborn drifts into a deep sleep, which seems to serve as a coping mechanism.

For many years, doctors performed operations on newborns without anesthesia. This practice was accepted because of the dangers of anesthesia and because of the supposition that newborns did not feel pain. As researchers demonstrated that newborns can feel pain, the practice of operating on newborns without anesthesia was challenged. Anesthesia now is used in some circumcisions (Taddio, 2008).

Smell   Newborns can differentiate odors (Doty & Shah, 2008). The expressions on their faces seem to indicate that they like the way vanilla and strawberry smell but do not like the way rotten eggs and fish smell (Steiner, 1979). In one investigation, 6-day-old infants who were breast fed showed a clear preference for smelling their mother's breast pad rather than a clean breast pad (MacFarlane, 1975) (see Figure 5.14). However, when they were 2 days old, they did not show this preference, indicating that they require several days of experience to recognize this odor.

Taste   Sensitivity to taste is present even before birth (Doty & Shah, 2008). Human newborns learn tastes prenatally through the amniotic fluid and in breast milk after birth (Beauchamp & Mennella, 2009; Mennella, 2009). In one study, even at only 2 hours of age, babies made different facial expressions when they tasted sweet, sour, and bitter solutions (Rosenstein & Oster, 1988) (see Figure 5.15). At about 4 months of age, infants begin to prefer salty tastes, which as newborns they had found to be aversive (Harris, Thomas, & Booth, 1990).

INTERMODAL PERCEPTION

Imagine yourself playing basketball or tennis. You are experiencing many visual inputs: the ball coming and going, other players moving around, and so on. However, you are experiencing many auditory inputs as well: the sound of the ball bouncing or being hit, the grunts and groans of the players, and so on. There is a good correspondence between much of the visual and auditory information: When you see the ball bounce, you hear a bouncing sound; when a player stretches to hit a ball,

FIGURE 5.14

NEWBORNS' PREFERENCE FOR THE SMELL OF THEIR MOTHER'S BREAST PAD. In the experiment by MacFarlane (1975), 6-day-old infants preferred to smell their mother's breast pad rather than a clean one that had never been used, but 2-day-old infants did not show this preference, indicating that this odor preference requires several days of experience to develop.

(a)　　　　　　　　　(b)　　　　　　　　　(c)

FIGURE **5.15**
NEWBORNS' FACIAL RESPONSES TO BASIC TASTES. Facial expression elicited by (*a*) a sweet solution, (*b*) a sour solution, and (*c*) a bitter solution.

you hear a groan. When you look at and listen to what is going on, you do not experience just the sounds or just the sights—you put all these things together. You experience a unitary episode. This is **intermodal perception,** which involves integrating information from two or more sensory modalities, such as vision and hearing (Bremner & others, 2011). Most perception is intermodal (Bahrick, 2010).

Early, exploratory forms of intermodal perception exist even in newborns (Bahrick & Hollich, 2008). For example, newborns turn their eyes and their head toward the sound of a voice or rattle when the sound is maintained for several seconds (Clifton & others, 1981), but the newborn can localize a sound and look at an object only in a crude way (Bechtold, Bushnell, & Salapatek, 1979). These early forms of intermodal perception become sharpened with experience in the first year of life (Kirkham & others, 2012). In one study, infants as young as 3 months old looked more at their mother when they also heard her voice and longer at their father when they also heard his voice (Spelke & Owsley, 1979). Thus, even young infants can coordinate visual-auditory information involving people.

Can young infants put vision and sound together as precisely as adults do? In the first six months, infants have difficulty connecting sensory input from different modes, but in the second half of the first year they show an increased ability to make this connection mentally.

The important ability to connect information about vision with information about touch also is evident early in infancy. Coordination of vision and touch has been demonstrated in 2- to 3-month-olds (Streri, 1993).

Thus, babies are born into the world with some innate abilities to perceive relations among sensory modalities, but their intermodal abilities improve considerably through experience (Bahrick, 2010). As with all aspects of development, in perceptual development, nature and nurture interact and cooperate (Johnson, 2012, 2013; Maurer & Lewis, 2013).

NATURE, NURTURE, AND PERCEPTUAL DEVELOPMENT

Now that we have discussed many aspects of perceptual development, let's explore one of developmental psychology's key issues as it relates to perceptual development: the nature-nurture issue. There has been a long-standing interest in how strongly infants' perception is influenced by nature or nurture (Aslin, 2009; Johnson, 2012, 2013; Slater & others, 2011). In the field of perceptual development, nature proponents are referred to as *nativists* and those who emphasize learning and experience are called *empiricists*.

In the nativist view, the ability to perceive the world in a competent, organized way is inborn or innate. At the beginning of our discussion of perceptual development, we examined the ecological view of the Gibsons because it has played such a pivotal role in guiding research in perceptual development. The Gibsons' ecological view leans toward a nativist explanation of perceptual development because it holds that perception is direct and evolved over time to

What is intermodal perception? Which two senses is this infant using to integrate information about the blocks?

intermodal perception The ability to relate and integrate information about two or more sensory modalities, such as vision and hearing.

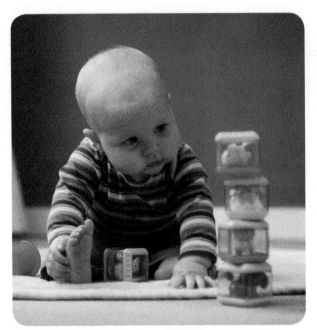

What roles do nature and nurture play in the infant's perceptual development?

allow the detection of size and shape constancy, a three-dimensional world, intermodal perception, and so on early in infancy. However, the Gibsons' view is not entirely nativist because they emphasized that "perceptual development involves distinctive features that are detected at different ages" (Slater & others, 2011). Further, the Gibsons argued that a key question in infant perception is what information is available in the environment and how infants learn to generate, differentiate, and discriminate the information—certainly not a nativist view.

The Gibsons' ecological view is quite different from Piaget's constructivist view, which reflects an empiricist approach to explaining perceptual development. According to Piaget, much of perceptual development in infancy must await the development of a sequence of cognitive stages for infants to construct more complex perceptual tasks. Thus, in Piaget's view, the ability to perceive size and shape constancy, a three-dimensional world, intermodal perception, and so on develops later in infancy than the Gibsons envision.

Today, it is clear that an extreme empiricist position on perceptual development is unwarranted. Much of early perception develops from innate (nature) foundations and the basic foundation of many perceptual abilities can be detected in newborns, whereas other abilities unfold maturationally (Arterberry, 2008). However, as infants develop, environmental experiences (nurture) refine or calibrate many perceptual functions and may be the driving force behind some functions (Amso & Johnson, 2010).

The longitudinal research of Daphne Maurer and her colleagues (Lewis & Maurer, 2005, 2009; Maurer & Lewis, 2013; Maurer & others, 1999) has focused on infants born with cataracts—a thickening of the lens of the eye that causes vision to become cloudy, opaque, and distorted, severely restricting infants' ability to experience their visual world. Studying infants whose cataracts were removed at different points in development, they discovered that those whose cataracts were removed and new lenses placed in their eyes in the first several months after birth showed a normal pattern of visual development. However, the longer the delay in removing the cataracts, the more their visual development was impaired. In their research, Maurer and her colleagues (2007) have found that experiencing patterned visual input early in infancy is important for holistic and detailed face processing after infancy. Maurer's research program illustrates how deprivation and experience influence visual development, particularly during an early sensitive period in which visual input is necessary for normal visual development (Maurer & Lewis, 2013).

Thus, the accumulation of experience with and knowledge about their perceptual world contributes to infants' ability to form coherent perceptions of people and things (Johnson, 2012, 2013). A full portrait of perceptual development includes the influence of nature, nurture, and a developing sensitivity to information (Arterberry, 2008; Maurer & Lewis, 2013).

- - - - - - - - →

developmental **connection**

Cognitive Development

Piaget's theory states that children construct their understanding of the world and go through four stages of cognitive development. Chapter 1, p. 22; Chapter 6, p. 169

← - - - - - - - -

Review *Connect* Reflect

LG2 Outline the course of sensory and perceptual development.

Review

- What are sensation and perception?
- What is the ecological view of perception? What are some research methods used to study infant perception?
- How does vision develop?
- How do the senses other than vision develop?
- What is intermodal perception, and how does it develop?
- What roles do nature and nurture play in perceptual development?

Connect

- One of the topics we discussed in this section was vision. What did you learn about development, vision loss, and the other senses in the story that opened the chapter?

Reflect *Your Own Personal Journey of Life*

- Imagine that you are the parent of a 1-year-old infant. What would you do to effectively stimulate the sensory development of your very young child?

Perceptual-Motor Coupling **LG3** Discuss perceptual-motor coupling.

As we come to the end of this chapter, we return to the important theme of perceptual-motor coupling. The distinction between perceiving and doing has been a time-honored tradition in psychology. However, a number of experts on perceptual and motor development question whether this distinction makes sense (Adolph & Berger, 2013; Keen, 2011; Thelen & Smith, 2006). The main thrust of research in Esther Thelen's dynamic systems approach is to explore how people assemble motor behaviors for perceiving and acting. The main theme of the ecological approach of Eleanor and James J. Gibson is to discover how perception guides action. Action can guide perception, and perception can guide action. Only by moving one's eyes, head, hands, and arms and by moving from one location to another can an individual fully experience his or her environment and learn how to adapt to it. Perception and action are coupled (Keen, 2011).

Babies, for example, continually coordinate their movements with perceptual information to learn how to maintain balance, reach for objects in space, and move across various surfaces and terrains (Adolph & Robinson, 2013; Thelen & Smith, 2006). They are motivated to move by what they perceive. Consider the sight of an attractive toy across the room. In this situation, infants must perceive the current state of their bodies and learn how to use their limbs to reach the toy. Although their movements at first are awkward and uncoordinated, babies soon learn to select patterns that are appropriate for reaching their goals.

How are perception and action coupled in infants' development?

Equally important is the other part of the perception-action coupling. That is, action educates perception (Adolph & Berger, 2013; Thelen & Smith, 2006). For example, watching an object while exploring it manually helps infants to discriminate its texture, size, and hardness. Locomoting in the environment teaches babies about how objects and people look from different perspectives, or whether surfaces will support their weight.

How do infants develop new perceptual-motor couplings? Recall from our discussion earlier in this chapter that in the traditional view of Gesell, infants' perceptual-motor development is prescribed by a genetic plan to follow a fixed and sequential progression of stages in development. The genetic determination view has been replaced by the dynamic systems view that infants learn new perceptual-motor couplings by assembling skills for perceiving and acting. New perceptual-motor coupling is not passively accomplished; rather, the infant actively develops a skill to achieve a goal within the constraints set by the infant's body and the environment.

Children perceive in order to move and move in order to perceive. Perceptual and motor development do not occur in isolation from each other but instead are coupled (Adolph & Berger, 2013; Keen, 2011).

Review *Connect* Reflect

 LG3 Discuss perceptual-motor coupling.

Review

- How are perception and motor actions coupled in development?

Connect

- In this section, you learned that perceptual and motor development do not occur in isolation from each other but instead are coupled. How is this distinction similar to the distinction psychologists make when speaking of nature and nurture when describing development?

Reflect *Your Own Personal Journey of Life*

- Think about your development as a child. Describe two examples, not given in the text, in which your perception guided your action. Then describe two examples, not given in the text, in which your action guided your perception.

Motor, Sensory, and Perceptual Development

Motor Development Describe how motor skills develop.

The Dynamic Systems View

- Thelen's dynamic systems theory describes the development of motor skills as the assembling of behaviors for perceiving and acting. Perception and action are coupled. According to this theory, the development of motor skills depends on the development of the nervous system, the body's physical properties and its movement possibilities, the goal the child is motivated to reach, and environmental support for the skill. In the dynamic systems view, motor development is far more complex than the result of a genetic blueprint; the infant or child actively puts together a skill in order to achieve a goal within constraints set by the body and the environment.

Reflexes

- Reflexes—built-in reactions to stimuli—govern the newborn's movements. They include the sucking, rooting, and Moro reflexes, all of which typically disappear after three to four months. Some reflexes, such as blinking and yawning, persist throughout life; components of other reflexes are incorporated into voluntary actions.

Gross Motor Skills

- Gross motor skills involve large-muscle activities. Key skills developed during infancy include control of posture and walking. Gross motor skills improve dramatically during the childhood years. Boys usually outperform girls in gross motor skills involving large-muscle activity.

Fine Motor Skills

- Fine motor skills involve finely tuned movements. The onset of reaching and grasping marks a significant accomplishment. Fine motor skills continue to develop through the childhood years and by 4 years of age are much more precise. Children can use their hands as tools by middle childhood, and at 10 to 12 years of age start to show manipulative fine motor skills similar to those of adults.

Sensory and Perceptual Development LG2 Outline the course of sensory and perceptual development.

What Are Sensation and Perception?

- Sensation occurs when information interacts with sensory receptors. Perception is the interpretation of sensation.

The Ecological View

- The Gibsons' ecological view states that people directly perceive information that exists in the world. Perception brings people in contact with the environment so that they can interact with and adapt to it. Affordances are opportunities for interaction offered by objects that are necessary to perform activities. Researchers have developed a number of methods to assess infants' perception, including the visual preference method (which Fantz used to determine young infants' interest in looking at patterned over nonpatterned displays), habituation and dishabituation, high-amplitude sucking, and tracking.

Visual Perception

- The infant's visual acuity increases dramatically in the first year of life. Infants show an interest in human faces soon after birth, and young infants systematically scan faces. Possibly by 4 weeks of age, infants can discriminate some colors. By 3 months of age, infants show size and shape constancy. At approximately 2 months of age, infants develop the ability to perceive that occluded objects are complete. In Gibson and Walk's classic study, infants as young as 6 months of age had depth perception. After infancy, children's visual expectations continue to develop, and further color differentiation occurs from 3 to 4 years of age. A number of children experience vision problems.

Other Senses	• The fetus can hear several weeks prior to birth. Developmental changes in the perception of loudness, pitch, and localization of sound occur during infancy. Newborns can respond to touch and feel pain. Newborns can differentiate between odors, and sensitivity to taste may be present before birth.

• The fetus can hear several weeks prior to birth. Developmental changes in the perception of loudness, pitch, and localization of sound occur during infancy. Newborns can respond to touch and feel pain. Newborns can differentiate between odors, and sensitivity to taste may be present before birth.

Intermodal Perception

• Intermodal perception is the ability to relate and integrate information from two or more sensory modalities. Crude, exploratory forms of intermodal perception are present in newborns and become sharpened over the first year of life.

Nature, Nurture, and Perceptual Devleopment

• With regard to the study of perception, nature advocates are referred to as nativists and nurture proponents are called empiricists. The Gibsons' ecological view that has guided much of perceptual development research leans toward a nativist approach but still allows for developmental changes in distinctive features. Piaget's constructivist view leans toward an empiricist approach, emphasizing that many perceptual accomplishments must await the development of cognitive stages in infancy. A strong empiricist approach is unwarranted. A full account of perceptual development includes the roles of nature, nurture, and increasing sensitivity to information.

Perceptual-Motor Coupling

 LG3 Discuss perceptual-motor coupling.

• Perception and action are coupled—individuals perceive in order to move and move in order to perceive. New perceptual-motor couplings do not occur as the result of genetic predetermination but rather because the infant actively assembles skills for perceiving and acting.

key terms

dynamic systems theory 140
reflexes 140
rooting reflex 140
sucking reflex 140
Moro reflex 140

grasping reflex 141
gross motor skills 142
fine motor skills 148
sensation 150
perception 150

ecological view 150
affordances 150
visual preference
    method 151
habituation 151

dishabituation 151
size constancy 155
shape constancy 155
intermodal perception 159

key people

Esther Thelen 140
T. Berry Brazelton 142
Karen Adolph 145

Rachel Keen 149
Eleanor and James J. Gibson 150
Robert Fantz 151

William James 154
Scott Johnson 155
Richard Walk 156

Megan Gunnar 156
Daphne Maurer 160

Learning is an ornament in prosperity, a refuge in adversity.

—**ARISTOTLE**
Greek Philosopher, 4th Century B.C.

Cognition and Language

Children thirst to know and understand. In their effort to know and understand, they construct their own ideas about the world around them. They are remarkable for their curiosity and their intelligence. In Section 3, you will read four chapters: "Cognitive Developmental Approaches" (Chapter 6), "Information Processing" (Chapter 7), "Intelligence" (Chapter 8), and "Language Development" (Chapter 9).

chapter 6

COGNITIVE DEVELOPMENTAL APPROACHES

chapter outline

1 Piaget's Theory of Cognitive Development

Learning Goal 1 Discuss the key processes and four stages in Piaget's theory.

Processes of Development
Sensorimotor Stage
Preoperational Stage
Concrete Operational Stage
Formal Operational Stage

2 Applying and Evaluating Piaget's Theory

Learning Goal 2 Apply Piaget's theory to education and evaluate his theory.

Piaget and Education
Evaluating Piaget's Theory

3 Vygotsky's Theory of Cognitive Development

Learning Goal 3 Identify the main concepts in Vygotsky's theory and compare it with Piaget's theory.

The Zone of Proximal Development
Scaffolding
Language and Thought
Teaching Strategies
Evaluating Vygotsky's Theory

Jean Piaget, the famous Swiss psychologist, was a meticulous observer of his three children—Laurent, Lucienne, and Jacqueline. His books on cognitive development are filled with these observations. Here are a few of Piaget's observations of his children in infancy (Piaget, 1952):

- At 21 days of age, "Laurent found his thumb after three attempts: prolonged sucking begins each time. But, once he has been placed on his back, he does not know how to coordinate the movement of the arms with that of the mouth and his hands draw back even when his lips are seeking them" (p. 27).

- During the third month, thumb sucking becomes less important to Laurent because of new visual and auditory interests. But, when he cries, his thumb goes to the rescue.

- Toward the end of Lucienne's fourth month, while she is lying in her crib, Piaget hangs a doll above her feet. Lucienne thrusts her feet at the doll and makes it move. "Afterward, she looks at her motionless foot for a second, then recommences. There is no visual control of her foot, for the movements are the same when Lucienne only looks at the doll or when I place the doll over her head. On the other hand, the tactile control of the foot is apparent: after the first shakes, Lucienne makes slow foot movements as though to grasp and explore" (p. 159).

- At 11 months, "Jacqueline is seated and shakes a little bell. She then pauses abruptly in order to delicately place the bell in front of her right foot; then she kicks hard. Unable to recapture it, she grasps a ball which she then places at the same spot in order to give it another kick" (p. 225).

- At 1 year, 2 months, "Jacqueline holds in her hands an object which is new to her: a round, flat box which she turns all over, shakes, (and) rubs against the bassinet. . . . She lets it go and tries to pick it up. But she only succeeds in touching it with her index finger, without grasping it. She nevertheless makes an attempt and presses on the edge. The box then tilts up and falls again" (p. 273). Jacqueline shows an interest in this result and studies the fallen box.

For Piaget, these observations reflect important changes in the infant's cognitive development. Later in the chapter, you will learn that Piaget argued that infants go through six substages of development and that the behaviors you have just read about characterize those substages.

preview

Cognitive developmental approaches place a special emphasis on how children actively construct their thinking. They also focus heavily on how thinking changes from one point in development to another. In this chapter, we will highlight the cognitive developmental approaches of Jean Piaget and Lev Vygotsky.

Piaget's Theory of Cognitive Development

LG1 Discuss the key processes and four stages in Piaget's theory.

| Processes of Development | Sensorimotor Stage | Preoperational Stage | Concrete Operational Stage | Formal Operational Stage |

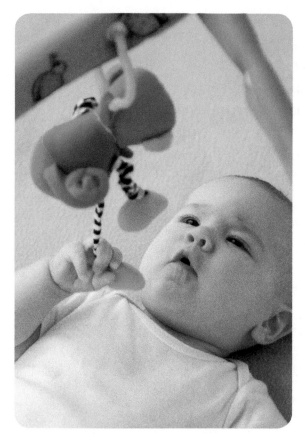

In Piaget's view, what is a scheme? What schemes might this young infant be displaying?

schemes In Piaget's theory, actions or mental representations that organize knowledge.

assimilation Piagetian concept of the incorporation of new information into existing knowledge.

accommodation Piagetian concept of adjusting schemes to fit new information and experiences.

Poet Nora Perry asked, "Who knows the thoughts of a child?" As much as anyone, Piaget knew. Through careful observations of his own three children—Laurent, Lucienne, and Jacqueline—and observations and interviews with other children, Piaget changed perceptions of the way children think about the world.

Piaget's theory is a general, unifying story of how biology and experience sculpt cognitive development. Piaget thought that, just as our physical bodies have structures that enable us to adapt to the world, we build mental structures that help us to adapt to the world. *Adaptation* involves adjusting to new environmental demands. Piaget stressed that children actively construct their own cognitive worlds; information is not just poured into their minds from the environment. He sought to discover how children at different points in their development think about the world and how systematic changes in their thinking occur.

PROCESSES OF DEVELOPMENT

What processes do children use as they construct their knowledge of the world? Piaget stressed that the following processes are especially important in this regard: schemes, assimilation, accommodation, organization, and equilibration.

Schemes   Piaget (1954) said that as the child seeks to construct an understanding of the world, the developing brain creates **schemes.** These are actions or mental representations that organize knowledge. In Piaget's theory, behavioral schemes (physical activities) characterize infancy, and mental schemes (cognitive activities) develop in childhood (Lamb, Bornstein, & Teti, 2002). A baby's schemes are structured by simple actions that can be performed on objects, such as sucking, looking, and grasping. Older children have schemes that include strategies and plans for solving problems. For example, a 5-year-old might have a scheme that involves the strategy of classifying objects by size, shape, or color. By the time we have reached adulthood, we have constructed an enormous number of diverse schemes, ranging from driving a car to balancing a budget to achieving fairness.

Assimilation and Accommodation   To explain how children use and adapt their schemes, Piaget proposed two concepts: assimilation and accommodation. Recall that **assimilation** occurs when children incorporate new information into their existing schemes. **Accommodation** occurs when children adjust their schemes to fit new information and experiences.

Think about a toddler who has learned the word *car* to identify the family's car. The toddler might call all moving vehicles on roads "cars," including motorcycles and trucks; the child has assimilated these objects into his or her existing scheme. But the child soon learns that motorcycles and trucks are not cars and then fine-tunes the category to exclude motorcycles and trucks, accommodating the scheme.

Assimilation and accommodation operate even in very young infants. Newborns reflexively suck everything that touches their lips; they assimilate all sorts of objects into their sucking scheme. By sucking different objects, they learn about their taste, texture, shape, and so on. After several months of experience, though, they construct their understanding of the world differently. Some objects, such as fingers and the mother's breast, can be sucked, and others, such as fuzzy blankets, should not be sucked. In other words, babies accommodate their sucking scheme.

How might assimilation and accommodation be involved in infants' sucking?

Organization To make sense out of their world, said Piaget, children cognitively organize their experiences. **Organization** in Piaget's theory is the grouping of isolated behaviors and thoughts into a higher-order system. Continual refinement of this organization is an inherent part of development. A boy who has only a vague idea about how to use a hammer may also have a vague idea about how to use other tools. After learning how to use each one, he relates these uses, grouping items into categories and organizing his knowledge.

Equilibration and Stages of Development **Equilibration** is a mechanism that Piaget proposed to explain how children shift from one stage of thought to the next. The shift occurs as children experience cognitive conflict, or disequilibrium, in trying to understand the world. Eventually, they resolve the conflict and reach a balance, or equilibrium, of thought. Piaget argued that there is considerable movement between states of cognitive equilibrium and disequilibrium as assimilation and accommodation work in concert to produce cognitive change. For example, if a child believes that the amount of a liquid changes simply because the liquid is poured into a container with a different shape—for instance, from a container that is short and wide into a container that is tall and narrow—she might be puzzled by such issues as where the "extra" liquid came from and whether there is actually more liquid to drink. The child will eventually resolve these puzzles as her thought becomes more advanced. In the everyday world, the child is constantly faced with such counterexamples and inconsistencies.

Assimilation and accommodation always take the child to a higher ground. For Piaget, the motivation for change is an internal search for equilibrium. As old schemes are adjusted and new schemes are developed, the child organizes and reorganizes the old and new schemes. Eventually, the organization is fundamentally different from the old organization; it is a new way of thinking, a new stage. The result of these processes, according to Piaget, is that individuals go through four stages of development. A different way of understanding the world makes one stage more advanced than another. Cognition is *qualitatively* different in one stage compared with another. In other words, the way children reason at one stage is different from the way they reason at another stage.

Each of Piaget's stages is age-related and consists of distinct ways of thinking. Piaget identified four stages of cognitive development: sensorimotor, preoperational, concrete operational, and formal operational (see Figure 6.1).

SENSORIMOTOR STAGE

The **sensorimotor stage** lasts from birth to about 2 years of age. In this stage, infants construct an understanding of the world by coordinating sensory experiences (such as seeing and hearing) with physical, motoric actions—hence the term "sensorimotor." At the beginning of this stage, newborns have little more than reflexive patterns with which to work. At the end of the sensorimotor stage, 2-year-olds can produce complex sensorimotor patterns and use primitive symbols. We first will summarize Piaget's descriptions of how infants develop. Later we will consider criticisms of his views.

Substages Piaget divided the sensorimotor stage into six substages: (1) simple reflexes; (2) first habits and primary circular reactions; (3) secondary circular reactions; (4) coordination

> We are born capable of learning.
>
> —JEAN-JACQUES ROUSSEAU
> *Swiss-Born French Philosopher, 18th Century*

organization Piaget's concept of grouping isolated behaviors into a higher-order, more smoothly functioning cognitive system; the grouping or arranging of items into categories.

equilibration A mechanism that Piaget proposed to explain how children shift from one stage of thought to the next. The shift occurs as children experience cognitive conflict, or disequilibrium, in trying to understand the world. Eventually, they resolve the conflict and reach a balance, or equilibrium, of thought.

sensorimotor stage The first of Piaget's stages, which lasts from birth to about 2 years of age, when infants construct an understanding of the world by coordinating sensory experiences (such as seeing and hearing) with motoric actions.

Sensorimotor Stage

Infants gain knowledge of the world from the physical actions they perform on it. Infants coordinate sensory experiences with these physical actions. An infant progresses from reflexive, instinctual action at birth to the beginning of symbolic thought toward the end of the stage.

Birth to 2 Years of Age

Preoperational Stage

The child begins to use mental representations to understand the world. Symbolic thinking, reflected in the use of words and images, is used in this mental representation, which goes beyond the connection of sensory information with physical action. However, there are some constraints on the child's thinking at this stage, such as egocentrism and centration.

2 to 7 Years of Age

Concrete Operational Stage

The child can now reason logically about concrete events, understands the concept of conservation, organizes objects into hierarchical classes (classification), and places objects in ordered series (seriation).

7 to 11 Years of Age

Formal Operational Stage

The adolescent reasons in more abstract, idealistic, and logical (hypothetical-deductive) ways.

11 Years of Age Through Adulthood

FIGURE **6.1**
PIAGET'S FOUR STAGES OF COGNITIVE DEVELOPMENT

of secondary circular reactions; (5) tertiary circular reactions, novelty, and curiosity; and (6) internalization of schemes (see Figure 6.2).

- *Simple reflexes,* the first sensorimotor substage, corresponds to the first month after birth. In this substage, sensation and action are coordinated primarily through reflexive behaviors, such as the rooting and sucking reflexes. Soon the infant produces behaviors that resemble reflexes in the absence of the usual stimulus for the reflex. For example, a newborn will suck a nipple or bottle only when it is placed directly in the baby's mouth or touched to the lips. But soon the infant might suck when a bottle or nipple is only nearby. The infant is initiating action and is actively structuring experiences in the first month of life.

- *First habits and primary circular reactions* is the second sensorimotor substage, which develops between 1 and 4 months of age. In this substage, the infant coordinates sensation and two types of schemes: habits and primary circular reactions.

- A *habit* is a scheme based on a reflex that has become completely separated from its eliciting stimulus. For example, infants in substage 1 suck when bottles are put to their lips or when they see a bottle. Infants in substage 2 might suck even when no bottle is present. A *circular reaction* is a repetitive action.

- A *primary circular reaction* is a scheme based on the attempt to reproduce an event that initially occurred by chance. For example, suppose an infant accidentally sucks his fingers when they are placed near his mouth. Later, he searches for his fingers to suck them again, but the fingers do not cooperate because the infant cannot coordinate visual and manual actions.

  Habits and circular reactions are stereotyped—that is, the infant repeats them the same way each time. During this substage, the infant's own body remains the infant's center of attention. There is no outward pull by environmental events.

Substage	Age	Description	Example
1 **Simple reflexes**	Birth to 1 month	Coordination of sensation and action through reflexive behaviors.	Rooting, sucking, and grasping reflexes; newborns suck reflexively when their lips are touched.
2 **First habits and primary circular reactions**	1 to 4 months	Coordination of sensation and two types of schemes: habits (reflex) and primary circular reactions (reproduction of an event that initially occurred by chance). Main focus is still on the infant's body.	Repeating a body sensation first experienced by chance (sucking thumb, for example); then infants might accommodate actions by sucking their thumb differently from how they suck on a nipple.
3 **Secondary circular reactions**	4 to 8 months	Infants become more object-oriented, moving beyond self-preoccupation; repeat actions that bring interesting or pleasurable results.	An infant coos to make a person stay near; as the person starts to leave, the infant coos again.
4 **Coordination of secondary circular reactions**	8 to 12 months	Coordination of vision and touch—hand-eye coordination; coordination of schemes and intentionality.	Infant manipulates a stick in order to bring an attractive toy within reach.
5 **Tertiary circular reactions, novelty, and curiosity**	12 to 18 months	Infants become intrigued by the many properties of objects and by the many things they can make happen to objects; they experiment with new behavior.	A block can be made to fall, spin, hit another object, and slide across the ground.
6 **Internalization of schemes**	18 to 24 months	Infants develop the ability to use primitive symbols and form enduring mental representations.	An infant who has never thrown a temper tantrum before sees a playmate throw a tantrum; the infant retains a memory of the event, then throws one himself the next day.

FIGURE 6.2
PIAGET'S SIX SUBSTAGES OF SENSORIMOTOR DEVELOPMENT

- *Secondary circular reactions* is the third sensorimotor substage, which develops between 4 and 8 months of age. In this substage, the infant becomes more object-oriented, moving beyond preoccupation with the self. By chance, an infant might shake a rattle. The infant repeats this action for the sake of its fascination.

  The infant also imitates some simple actions, such as the baby talk or burbling of adults, and some physical gestures. However, the baby imitates only actions that he or she is already able to produce. Although directed toward objects in the world, the infant's schemes are not intentional or goal-directed.

- *Coordination of secondary circular reactions* is Piaget's fourth sensorimotor substage, which develops between 8 and 12 months of age. To progress into this substage, the infant must coordinate vision and touch, hand and eye. Actions become more outwardly directed. Significant changes during this substage involve the coordination of schemes and intentionality. Infants readily combine and recombine previously learned schemes in a coordinated way. They might look at an object and grasp it simultaneously, or they might visually inspect a toy, such as a rattle, and finger it simultaneously, exploring it tactilely. Actions are even more outwardly directed than before. Related to this coordination is the second achievement—the presence of intentionality. For example, infants might manipulate a stick in order to bring a desired toy within reach, or they might knock over one block to reach and play with another one.

- *Tertiary circular reactions, novelty, and curiosity* is Piaget's fifth sensorimotor substage, which develops between 12 and 18 months of age. In this substage, infants become intrigued by the many properties of objects and by the many things that they can make happen to objects. A block can be made to fall, spin, hit another object, and slide across the ground. *Tertiary circular reactions* are schemes in which the infant purposely explores new possibilities with objects, continually doing new things to them and exploring the results. Piaget says that this stage marks the starting point for human curiosity and interest in novelty.

- *Internalization of schemes* is Piaget's sixth and final sensorimotor substage, which develops between 18 and 24 months of age. In this substage, the infant develops the ability to use primitive symbols. For Piaget, a *symbol* is an internalized sensory image or word that represents an event. Primitive symbols permit the infant to think about concrete

This 17-month-old is in Piaget's stage of tertiary circular reactions. *What might the infant do that suggests she is in this stage?*

FIGURE **6.3**

OBJECT PERMANENCE. Piaget argued that object permanence is one of infancy's landmark cognitive accomplishments. For this 5-month-old boy, "out of sight" is literally out of mind. The infant looks at the toy monkey (*top*), but when his view of the toy is blocked (*bottom*), he does not search for it. Several months later, he will search for the hidden toy monkey, reflecting the presence of object permanence.

object permanence The Piagetian term for one of an infant's most important accomplishments: understanding that objects and events continue to exist even when they cannot directly be seen, heard, or touched.

A-not-B error Also called AB̄ error, this occurs when infants make the mistake of selecting the familiar hiding place (A) to locate an object, rather than looking in the new hiding place (B), as they progress into substage 4 in Piaget's sensorimotor stage.

events without directly acting them out or perceiving them. Moreover, symbols allow the infant to manipulate and transform the represented events in simple ways. In a favorite Piagetian example, Piaget's young daughter saw a matchbox being opened and closed. Later, she mimicked the event by opening and closing her mouth. This was an obvious expression of her image of the event.

Object Permanence   Imagine how chaotic and unpredictable your life would be if you could not distinguish between yourself and your world. This is what the life of a newborn must be like, according to Piaget. There is no differentiation between the self and world; objects have no separate, permanent existence.

By the end of the sensorimotor period, children understand that objects are both separate from the self and permanent. **Object permanence** is the understanding that objects and events continue to exist even when they cannot be seen, heard, or touched. Acquiring the sense of object permanence is one of the infant's most important accomplishments. According to Piaget, infants develop object permanence in a series of substages that correspond to the six substages of sensorimotor development.

How can anyone know whether an infant has developed a sense of object permanence? The principal way that object permanence is studied is by watching an infant's reaction when an interesting object disappears (see Figure 6.3). If infants search for the object, it is assumed that they believe it continues to exist.

Object permanence is just one of the basic concepts about the physical world developed by babies. To Piaget, children—even infants—are much like little scientists, examining the world to see how it works. But how can adult scientists determine what these "baby scientists" are finding out about the world and at what age they're finding it out? To answer this question, read the *Connecting Through Research* interlude that follows.

Evaluating Piaget's Sensorimotor Stage   Piaget opened up a new way of looking at infants with his view that their main task is to coordinate their sensory impressions with their motor activity. However, the infant's cognitive world is not as neatly packaged as Piaget portrayed it, and some of Piaget's explanations for the cause of cognitive changes in development are debated. In the past several decades, sophisticated experimental techniques have been devised to study infants, and there have been a large number of research studies on infant development. Much of the new research suggests that Piaget's view of sensorimotor development needs to be modified (Baillargeon & others, 2012; Diamond, 2013; Johnson, 2012, 2013; Meltzoff & Williamson, 2013).

The A-not-B Error   One modification concerns Piaget's claim that certain processes are crucial in transitions from one stage to the next. The data do not always support his explanations. For example, in Piaget's theory, an important feature in the progression into substage 4, *coordination of secondary circular reactions,* is an infant's inclination to search for a hidden object in a familiar location rather than to look for the object in a new location. For example, if a toy is hidden twice, initially at location A and subsequently at location B, 8- to 12-month-old infants search correctly at location A initially. But when the toy is subsequently hidden at location B, they make the mistake of continuing to search for it at location A. **A-not-B error** (also called AB̄ error) is the term used to describe this common mistake. Older infants are less likely to make the A-not-B error because their concept of object permanence is more complete.

Researchers have found, however, that the A-not-B error does not show up consistently (Sophian, 1985). The evidence indicates that A-not-B errors are sensitive to the delay between hiding the object at B and the infant's attempt to find it (Diamond, 1985). Thus, the A-not-B error might be due to a failure in memory. Another explanation is that infants tend to repeat a previous motor behavior (Clearfield & others, 2006).

Perceptual Development and Expectations   A number of theorists, such as Eleanor Gibson (2001) and Elizabeth Spelke (2011), argue that infants' perceptual abilities are highly developed very early in life. Spelke concludes that young infants interpret the world as having predictable occurrences. For example, in Chapter 4 we discussed research that demonstrated the presence of intermodal perception—the ability to coordinate information from two or more sensory modalities, such as vision and hearing—by 3½ months of age, much earlier than Piaget would have predicted (Spelke & Owsley, 1979).

connecting through research

How Do Researchers Determine Infants' Understanding of Object Permanence and Causality?

Two accomplishments of infants that Piaget examined were the development of object permanence and the child's understanding of causality. Let's examine two research studies that address these topics.

In both studies, Renée Baillargeon and her colleagues used a research method that involves *violation of expectations*. In this method, infants see an event happen as it normally would. Then, the event is changed in a way that violates what the infant expects to see. When infants look longer at the event that violates their expectations, it indicates they are surprised by it.

In one study focused on object permanence, researchers showed infants a toy car that moved down an inclined track, disappeared behind a screen, and then reemerged at the other end, still on the track (Baillargeon & DeVoe, 1991) (see Figure 6.4a). After this sequence was repeated several times, something different occurred: A toy mouse was placed *behind* the tracks but was hidden by the screen while the car rolled by (b). This was the "possible" event. Then, the researchers created an "impossible event": The toy mouse was placed *on* the tracks but was secretly removed after the screen was lowered so that the car seemed to go through the mouse (c). In this study, infants as young as 3½ months of age looked longer at the impossible event than at the possible event, indicating that they were surprised by it. Their surprise suggested that not only did they remember that the toy mouse still existed (object permanence), but they also recalled its location.

Another study focused on infants' understanding of causality (Kotovsky & Baillargeon, 1994). In this research, a cylinder rolls down a ramp and hits a toy bug at the bottom of the ramp. By 5½ and 6½ months of age, after infants have seen how far the bug will be pushed by a medium-sized cylinder, their reactions indicate that they understand that the bug will roll farther if it is hit by a large cylinder than if it is hit by a small cylinder. Thus, by the middle of the first year of life infants understand that the size of a moving object determines how far it will move a stationary object that it collides with.

In Baillargeon's (2008; Baillargeon & others, 2012; Luo & Baillargeon, 2010) view, infants have a pre-adapted, innate bias called the *principle of persistence* that explains their assumption that objects don't change their properties—including how solid they are, their location, their color, and their form—unless some external factor (a person who moves the object, for example) obviously intervenes. Shortly, we will revisit the extent to which nature and nurture are at work in the changes that take place in the infant's cognitive development.

The research findings discussed in this interlude and other research indicate that infants develop object permanence and causal reasoning much earlier than Piaget proposed (Baillargeon, 2014; Baillargeon & others, 2012). Indeed, as you will see in the next section, a major theme of infant cognitive development today is that infants are more cognitively competent than Piaget envisioned.

(a) Practice (No toy mouse)

(b) Possible event (Toy mouse behind the track)

(c) Impossible event (Toy mouse on the track)

FIGURE **6.4**

USING THE VIOLATION OF EXPECTATIONS METHOD TO STUDY OBJECT PERMANENCE IN INFANTS. If infants looked longer at (c) than at (b), researchers reasoned that the impossible event in (c) violated the infants' expectations and that they remembered that the toy mouse existed.

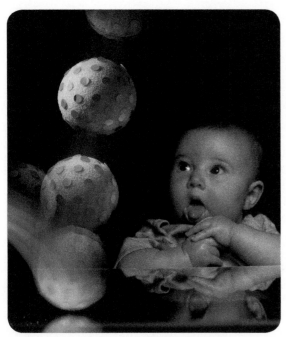

A 4-month-old in Elizabeth Spelke's infant perception laboratory is tested to determine if she knows that an object in motion will not stop in midair. Spelke concluded that at 4 months babies don't expect objects like these balls to obey gravitational constraints, but that they do expect objects to be solid and continuous. Research by Spelke, Renée Baillargeon, and others suggests that infants develop an ability to understand how the world works earlier than Piaget envisioned. However, critics such as Andrew Meltzoff fault their research and conclude there is still controversy about how early some infant cognitive accomplishments occur.

developmental **connection**

Theories

Eleanor Gibson was a pioneer in crafting the ecological perception view of development. Chapter 5, p. 150

core knowledge approach States that infants are born with domain-specific innate knowledge systems, such as those involving space, number sense, object permanence, and language.

Research also suggests that infants develop the ability to understand how the world works at a very early age (Scott & Baillargeon, 2013). For example, by the time they are 3 to 4 months of age, infants develop expectations about future events. What kinds of expectations do infants form? Experiments by Spelke (1991, 2000; Spelke & Hespos, 2001) have addressed these questions. She placed babies before a puppet stage and showed them a series of actions that are unexpected if you know how the physical world works—for example, one ball seemed to roll through a solid barrier, another seemed to leap between two platforms, and a third appeared to hang in midair (Spelke, 1979). Spelke measured and compared the babies' looking times for unexpected and expected actions. She concluded that, by 4 months of age, even though infants do not yet have the ability to talk about objects, move and manipulate objects, or even see objects with high resolution, they expect objects to be solid and continuous. However, at 4 months of age, infants do not expect an object to obey gravitational constraints (Spelke & others, 1992). Similarly, research by Renée Baillargeon and her colleagues (Baillargeon, 2008, 2014; Baillargeon & others, 2012) documents that infants as young as 3 to 4 months expect objects to be *substantial* (in the sense that other objects cannot move through them) and *permanent* (in the sense that objects continue to exist when they are hidden).

However, some critics, such as Andrew Meltzoff (2008; Moore & Meltzoff, 2008), argue that Spelke's and Baillargeon's research relies on how long infants look at unexpected events and thus assesses infants' *perceptual expectations* about where and when objects will reappear rather than tapping their *knowledge* about where the objects are when they are out of sight. Meltzoff points out that whether infants act on their perception is an important aspect of assessing object permanence but it does not appear that young infants can act on the information. Thus, Meltzoff (2008) concludes, it is still unclear whether longer looking time is a valid measure of object permanence and how early infants develop object permanence.

By 6 to 8 months, infants have learned to perceive gravity and support—that an object hanging on the end of a table should fall, that ball bearings will travel farther when rolled down a longer rather than a shorter ramp, and that cup handles will not fall when attached to a cup (Slater, Field, & Hernandez-Reif, 2007). As infants develop, their experiences and actions on objects help them to understand physical laws (Bremner, 2010).

The Nature-Nurture Issue   In considering the big issue of whether nature or nurture plays the more important role in infant development, Elizabeth Spelke (Hyde & Spelke, 2012; Kinzler, Dupoux, & Spelke, 2012; Spelke, 2000, 2011; Spelke, Bernier, & Snedeker, 2013) comes down clearly on the side of nature. Spelke endorses a **core knowledge approach,** which states that infants are born with domain-specific innate knowledge systems. Among these domain-specific knowledge systems are those involving space, number sense, object permanence, and language (which we will discuss later in this chapter). Strongly influenced by evolution, the core knowledge domains are theorized to be prewired to allow infants to make sense of their world. After all, Spelke asks, how could infants possibly grasp the complex world in which they live if they didn't come into the world equipped with core sets of knowledge? In this approach, the innate core knowledge domains form a foundation on which more mature cognitive functioning and learning develop. Proponents of the core knowledge approach argue that Piaget greatly underestimated the cognitive abilities of infants, especially young infants (Hyde & Spelke, 2011; Kinzler, Dupoux, & Spelke, 2012).

An intriguing domain of core knowledge that has been investigated in young infants is whether they have a sense of number. Spelke concludes that they do. Using the violations of expectations method discussed in the *Connecting Through Research* interlude, Karen Wynn (1992) conducted an early experiment on infants' sense of number (see Figure 6.5). Five-month-old infants were shown one or two Mickey Mouse dolls on a puppet stage. Then the experimenter hid the doll(s) behind a screen and visibly removed or added one. Next, when the screen was lifted, the infants looked longer when they saw the incorrect number of dolls. Spelke and her colleagues (Hyde & Spelke, 2009, 2011; Lipton & Spelke, 2004; Spelke & Kinzler, 2007; Xu, Spelke, & Goddard, 2005) have found that infants can distinguish between different numbers of objects, actions, and sounds.

Not everyone agrees with Spelke's conclusions about young infants' math skills (Cohen, 2002). One criticism is that infants in the number experiments are merely responding to changes in the display that violated their expectations.

Original event

1. Object placed in case
2. Screen comes up
3. Second object added
4. Hand leaves empty

(a)

Test events

Possible outcome
5. Screen drops... revealing 2 objects

(b)

Impossible outcome
5. Screen drops... revealing 1 object

(c)

FIGURE 6.5

INFANTS' NUMBER SENSE. Shown here is one of the sequences in Karen Wynn's (1992) study of 5-month-old infants' number sense. The experimenter was hidden behind the display and manipulated the objects through a trap door in the wall of the display. Five-month-old infants who saw the impossible event (only one Mickey Mouse doll) looked longer at the event than their 5-month-old counterparts who saw the possible event (two dolls). Reprinted by permission from Macmillan Publishers Ltd: NATURE, 358, pp. 749–750, "Addition and Subtraction by Human Infants" by Karen Wynn. Copyright © 1992.

In criticizing the core knowledge approach, British developmental psychologist Mark Johnston (2008) says that the infants Spelke assesses in her research already have accumulated hundreds, and in some cases even thousands, of hours of experience in grasping what the world is about, which gives considerable room for the environment's role in the development of infant cognition (Highfield, 2008). According to Johnston (2008), infants likely come into the world with "soft biases to perceive and attend to different aspects of the environment, and to learn about the world in particular ways." Although debate about the cause and course of infant cognitive development continues, most developmentalists today agree that Piaget underestimated the early cognitive accomplishments of infants and that both nature and nurture are involved in infants' cognitive development (Baillargeon, 2014; Diamond, 2013; Meltzoff & Williamson, 2013).

Conclusions In sum, many researchers conclude that Piaget wasn't specific enough about how infants learn about their world and that infants, especially young infants, are more competent than Piaget thought (Bauer, 2013; Johnson, 2013; Rakison & Lawson, 2013). As researchers have examined the specific ways that infants learn, the field of infant cognition has become very specialized. Many researchers are at work on different questions, with no general theory emerging that can connect all of the different findings (Nelson, 1999). Their theories often are local theories, focused on specific research questions, rather than grand theories like Piaget's (Kuhn, 1998). If there is a unifying theme, it is that investigators in infant development seek to understand more precisely how developmental changes in cognition take place and to explore the big issue of nature and nurture (Aslin, 2009). As they seek to identify more precisely the contributions of nature and nurture to infant development, researchers face the difficult task of determining whether the course of acquiring information, which is very rapid in some domains, is better accounted for by an innate set of biases (that is, core knowledge) or by the extensive input of environmental experiences to which the infant is exposed (Aslin, 2009, 2012). Recall from Chapter 1 that exploring connections between brain, cognition, and development involves the recently emerging field of *developmental cognitive neuroscience* (Bauer, 2013; Diamond, 2013; Morasch & others, 2013).

developmental **connection**

Nature vs. Nurture

The nature-nurture issue involves the debate about whether development is primarily influenced by nature (biological inheritance) or nurture (environmental experiences). Chapter 1, p. 16; Chapter 2, p. 69

What revisions in Piaget's theory of sensorimotor development do contemporary researchers conclude need to be made? What characterizes the nature-nurture controversy in infant cognitive development?

PREOPERATIONAL STAGE

The cognitive world of the preschool child is creative, free, and fanciful. The imaginations of preschool children work overtime, and their mental grasp of the world improves. Piaget described the preschool child's cognition as *preoperational*. What did he mean?

Because Piaget called this stage preoperational, it might sound unimportant. Not so. Preoperational thought is anything but a convenient waiting period for the next stage, concrete operational thought. However, the label *preoperational* emphasizes that the child does not yet perform **operations,** which are internalized actions that allow children to do mentally what they could formerly do only physically. Operations are reversible mental actions. Mentally adding and subtracting numbers are examples of operations. *Preoperational thought* is the beginning of the ability to reconstruct in thought what has been established in behavior.

The **preoperational stage,** which lasts from approximately 2 to 7 years of age, is the second Piagetian stage. In this stage, children begin to represent the world with words, images, and drawings. Symbolic thought goes beyond simple connections of sensory information and physical action. Stable concepts are formed, mental reasoning emerges, egocentrism is present, and magical beliefs are constructed. Preoperational thought can be divided into substages: the symbolic function substage and the intuitive thought substage.

The Symbolic Function Substage

The **symbolic function substage** is the first substage of preoperational thought, occurring roughly between the ages of 2 and 4. In this substage, the young child gains the ability to mentally represent an object that is not present. This ability vastly expands the child's mental world (Deloache, 2011; Mandler & Deloache, 2013). Young children use scribble designs to represent people, houses, cars, clouds, and so on; they begin to use language and engage in pretend play. However, although young children make distinct progress during this substage, their thought still has several important limitations, two of which are egocentrism and animism.

Egocentrism is the inability to distinguish between one's own perspective and someone else's perspective. The following telephone conversation between 4-year-old Mary, who is at home, and her father, who is at work, typifies Mary's egocentric thought:

> *Father:* Mary, is Mommy there?
> *Mary:* (Silently nods)
> *Father:* Mary, may I speak to Mommy?
> *Mary:* (Nods again silently)

Mary's response is egocentric in that she fails to consider her father's perspective before replying. A nonegocentric thinker would have responded verbally.

Piaget and Barbel Inhelder (1969) initially studied young children's egocentrism by devising the three-mountains task (see Figure 6.6). The child walks around the model of the mountains

---

operations Internalized actions that allow children to do mentally what before they had done only physically. Operations also are reversible mental actions.

preoperational stage The second Piagetian developmental stage, which lasts from about 2 to 7 years of age, when children begin to represent the world with words, images, and drawings.

symbolic function substage The first substage of preoperational thought, occurring roughly between the ages of 2 and 4. In this substage, the young child gains the ability to represent mentally an object that is not present.

egocentrism An important feature of preoperational thought: the inability to distinguish between one's own and someone else's perspective.

animism A facet of preoperational thought: the belief that inanimate objects have lifelike qualities and are capable of action.

intuitive thought substage The second substage of preoperational thought, occurring between approximately 4 and 7 years of age, when children begin to use primitive reasoning.

centration Focusing attention on one characteristic to the exclusion of all others.

conservation The realization that altering an object's or substance's appearance does not change its basic properties.

Model of Mountains

A
Child seated here

Photo 1 (View from A) Photo 2 (View from B) Photo 3 (View from C) Photo 4 (View from D)

FIGURE 6.6

THE THREE-MOUNTAINS TASK. The mountain model on the far left shows the child's perspective from view A, where he or she is sitting. The four squares represent photos showing the mountains from four different viewpoints of the model—A, B, C, and D. The experimenter asks the child to identify the photo in which the mountains look as they would from position B. To identify the photo correctly, the child has to take the perspective of a person sitting at spot B. Invariably, a child who thinks in a preoperational way cannot perform this task. When asked what a view of the mountains looks like from position B, the child selects Photo 1, taken from location A (the child's own view at the time) instead of Photo 2, the correct view.

and becomes familiar with what the mountains look like from different perspectives, and she can see that there are different objects on the mountains. The child is then seated on one side of the table on which the mountains are placed. The experimenter moves a doll to different locations around the table, at each location asking the child to select from a series of photos the one photo that most accurately reflects the view the doll is seeing. Children in the preoperational stage often pick their own view rather than the doll's view. Preschool children frequently show perspective skills on some tasks but not others.

Animism, another limitation of preoperational thought, is the belief that inanimate objects have lifelike qualities and are capable of action (Gelman & Opfer, 2004; Opfer & Gelman, 2011). A young child might show animism by saying, "That tree pushed the leaf off, and it fell down" or "The sidewalk made me mad; it made me fall down." A young child who uses animism fails to distinguish the appropriate occasions for using human and nonhuman perspectives.

Possibly because young children are not very concerned about reality, their drawings are fanciful and inventive. Suns are blue, skies are yellow, and cars float on clouds in their symbolic, imaginative world. One 3½-year-old looked at a scribble he had just drawn and described it as a pelican kissing a seal (see Figure 6.7a). The symbolism is simple but strong, like abstractions found in some modern art. Twentieth-century Spanish artist Pablo Picasso commented, "I used to draw like Raphael but it has taken me a lifetime to draw like young children." In the elementary school years, a child's drawings become more realistic, neat, and precise (see Figure 6.7b). Suns are yellow, skies are blue, and cars travel on roads (Winner, 1986).

The Intuitive Thought Substage

The **intuitive thought substage** is the second substage of preoperational thought, occurring between approximately 4 and 7 years of age. In this substage, children begin to use primitive reasoning and want to know the answers to all sorts of questions. Consider 4-year-old Tommy, who is at the beginning of the intuitive thought substage. Although he is starting to develop his own ideas about the world he lives in, his ideas are still simple, and he is not very good at thinking things out. He has difficulty understanding events that he knows are taking place but which he cannot see. His fantasized thoughts bear little resemblance to reality. He cannot yet answer the question "What if?" in any reliable way. For example, he has only a vague idea of what would happen if a car were to hit him. He also has difficulty negotiating traffic because he cannot do the mental calculations necessary to estimate whether an approaching car will hit him when he crosses the road.

By the age of 5, children have just about exhausted the adults around them with "why" questions. The child's questions signal the emergence of interest in reasoning and in figuring out why things are the way they are. Following are some samples of the questions children ask during the questioning period of 4 to 6 years of age (Elkind, 1976):

"What makes you grow up?"

"What makes you stop growing?"

"Why does a lady have to be married to have a baby?"

"Who was the mother when everybody was a baby?"

"Why do leaves fall?"

"Why does the sun shine?"

Piaget called this substage *intuitive* because young children seem so sure about their knowledge and understanding yet are unaware of how they know what they know. That is, they know something but know it without the use of rational thinking.

Centration and the Limitations of Preoperational Thought

One limitation of preoperational thought is **centration,** a centering of attention on one characteristic to the exclusion of all others. Centration is most clearly evidenced in young children's lack of **conservation,** the awareness that altering an object's or a substance's appearance does not change its basic properties. For example, to adults, it is obvious that a certain amount of liquid stays the same, regardless of a container's shape. But this is not at all obvious to young children. Instead, they are struck by the height of the liquid in the container; they focus on that characteristic to the exclusion of others.

(a)

"Pelican" "More eyes" "Nose" "Eyes" "Seal"

(b)

FIGURE **6.7**

THE SYMBOLIC DRAWINGS OF YOUNG CHILDREN. (*a*) A 3½-year-old's symbolic drawing. Halfway into this drawing, the 3½-year-old artist said it was "a pelican kissing a seal." (*b*) This 11-year-old's drawing is neater and more realistic but also less inventive.

"I still don't have all the answers, but I'm beginning to ask the right questions."

FIGURE 6.8

PIAGET'S CONSERVATION TASK. The beaker test is a well-known Piagetian task to determine whether a child can think operationally—that is, whether he or she can mentally reverse actions and show conservation of the substance. (*a*) Two identical beakers are presented to the child. Next, the experimenter pours the liquid from B into C, which is taller and thinner than A or B. (*b*) The child is asked if these beakers (A and C) have the same amount of liquid. The preoperational child says "no." When asked to point to the beaker that has more liquid, the preoperational child points to the tall, thin beaker.

The situation that Piaget devised to study conservation is his most famous task. In the conservation task, a child is presented with two identical beakers, each filled to the same level with liquid (see Figure 6.8). The child is asked if these beakers have the same amount of liquid, and she usually says "yes." Then the liquid from one beaker is poured into a third beaker, which is taller and thinner than the first two. The child is then asked if the amount of liquid in the tall, thin beaker is equal to that which remains in one of the original beakers. Children who are less than 7 or 8 years old usually say "no" and justify their answers in terms of the differing height or width of the beakers. Older children usually answer "yes" and justify their answers appropriately ("If you poured the water back, the amount would still be the same").

In Piaget's theory, failing the conservation-of-liquid task is a sign that children are at the preoperational stage of cognitive development. The preoperational child fails to show conservation not only of liquid but also of number, matter, length, volume, and area. Figure 6.9 portrays several of these dimensions of conservation.

Children often vary in their performance on different conservation tasks. Thus, a child might be able to conserve volume but not number. Recently, researchers have discovered links between children's number conservation and the brain's development (Poirel & others, 2012). A recent fMRI brain imaging study of conservation of number revealed that advances in a network in the parietal and frontal lobes were linked to 9- and 10-year-olds' conservation success when compared to non-conserving 5- and 6-year-olds (Houde & others, 2011).

Some developmentalists do not believe Piaget was entirely correct in his estimate of when children's conservation skills emerge. For example, Rochel Gelman (1969) showed that when the child's attention to relevant aspects of the conservation task is improved, the child is more likely to conserve. Gelman has also demonstrated that attentional training on one dimension, such as number, improves the preschool child's performance on another dimension, such as mass. Thus, Gelman suggests that conservation appears earlier than Piaget thought and that attention is especially important in explaining conservation.

CONCRETE OPERATIONAL STAGE

concrete operational stage Piaget's third stage, which lasts from approximately 7 to 11 years of age, when children can perform concrete operations, and logical reasoning replaces intuitive reasoning as long as the reasoning can be applied to specific or concrete examples.

horizontal décalage Piaget's concept that similar abilities do not appear at the same time within a stage of development.

The **concrete operational stage,** which lasts approximately from 7 to 11 years of age, is the third Piagetian stage. In this stage, logical reasoning replaces intuitive reasoning as long as the reasoning can be applied to specific or concrete examples. For instance, concrete operational thinkers cannot imagine the steps necessary to complete an algebraic equation, which is too abstract for thinking at this stage of development. Children at this stage can perform *concrete operations,* which are reversible mental actions on real, concrete objects.

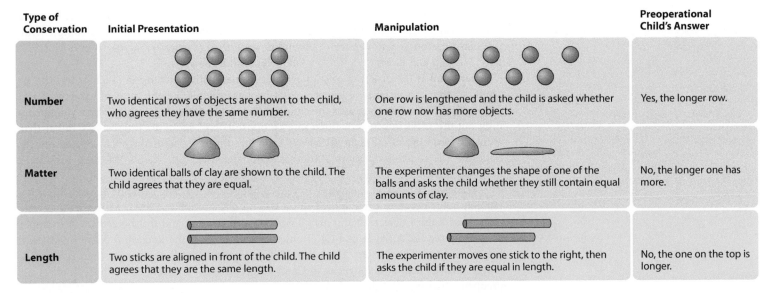

Type of Conservation	Initial Presentation	Manipulation	Preoperational Child's Answer
Number	Two identical rows of objects are shown to the child, who agrees they have the same number.	One row is lengthened and the child is asked whether one row now has more objects.	Yes, the longer row.
Matter	Two identical balls of clay are shown to the child. The child agrees that they are equal.	The experimenter changes the shape of one of the balls and asks the child whether they still contain equal amounts of clay.	No, the longer one has more.
Length	Two sticks are aligned in front of the child. The child agrees that they are the same length.	The experimenter moves one stick to the right, then asks the child if they are equal in length.	No, the one on the top is longer.

FIGURE **6.9**

SOME DIMENSIONS OF CONSERVATION: NUMBER, MATTER, AND LENGTH. *What characteristics of preoperational thought do children demonstrate when they fail these conservation tasks?*

Conservation   The conservation tasks demonstrate a child's ability to perform concrete operations. In the test of reversibility of thought involving conservation of matter (shown in Figure 6.9), a child is presented with two identical balls of clay. An experimenter rolls one ball into a long, thin shape; the other remains in its original ball shape. The child is then asked if there is more clay in the ball or in the long, thin piece of clay. By the time children reach the age 7 or 8, most answer that the amount of clay is the same. To answer this problem correctly, children have to imagine the clay ball rolling back into a ball after it has been changed into a long, thin shape; they need to mentally reverse the action on the ball.

Concrete operations allow children to coordinate several characteristics rather than focus on a single property of an object. In the clay example, a preoperational child is likely to focus on height or width, while a concrete operational child coordinates information about both dimensions. Conservation involves recognizing that the length, number, mass, quantity, area, weight, and volume of objects and substances are not changed by transformations that merely alter their appearance.

Children do not conserve all quantities or conserve on all tasks simultaneously. The order of their mastery is number, length, liquid quantity, mass, weight, and volume. **Horizontal décalage** is Piaget's concept that similar abilities do not appear at the same time within a stage of development. During the concrete operational stage, conservation of number usually appears first and conservation of volume last. Also, an 8-year-old child may know that a long stick of clay can be rolled back into a ball but not understand that the ball and the stick weigh the same. At about 9 years of age, the child recognizes that they weigh the same, and eventually, at about 11 to 12 years of age, the child understands that the clay's volume is unchanged by rearranging it. Children initially master tasks in which the dimensions are more salient and visible, only later mastering those not as visually apparent, such as volume.

Classification   Many of the concrete operations identified by Piaget involve the ways children reason about the properties of objects. One important skill that characterizes children in the concrete operational stage is the ability to classify things and to consider their relationships. Specifically, concrete operational children can understand (1) the interrelationships among sets and subsets, (2) seriation, and (3) transitivity.

The ability of the concrete operational child to divide things into sets and subsets and understand their relationships is illustrated by a family tree of four generations (Furth & Wachs, 1975) (see Figure 6.10). This family tree suggests that the grandfather (A) has three children (B, C, and D), each of whom has two children (E through J), and that one of these

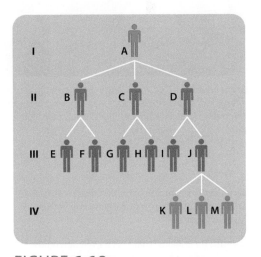

FIGURE **6.10**

CLASSIFICATION: AN IMPORTANT ABILITY IN CONCRETE OPERATIONAL THOUGHT. A family tree of four generations (*I to IV*): The preoperational child has trouble classifying the members of the four generations; the concrete operational child can classify the members vertically, horizontally, and obliquely (up and down and across). For example, the concrete operational child understands that a family member can be a son, a brother, and a father, all at the same time.

children (J) has three children (K, L, and M). The concrete operational child understands that person J can, at the same time, be father, brother, and grandson. A child who comprehends this classification system can move up and down a level (vertically), across a level (horizontally), and up and down and across (obliquely) within the system.

Seriation is the ordering of stimuli along a quantitative dimension (such as length). To see if children can serialize, a teacher might haphazardly place eight sticks of varying lengths on a table. The teacher then asks the children to order the sticks by length. Many young children put the sticks into two or three small groups of "big" sticks or "little" sticks, rather than a correct ordering of all eight sticks. Or they line up the tops of the sticks but ignore the bottoms. The concrete operational thinker simultaneously understands that each stick must be longer than the one that precedes it and shorter than the one that follows it.

Transitivity involves the ability to reason about and logically combine relationships. If a relation holds between a first object and a second object, and also holds between the second object and a third object, then it also holds between the first and third objects. For example, consider three sticks (A, B, and C) of differing lengths. A is the longest, B is intermediate in length, and C is the shortest. Does the child understand that if A is longer than B, and B is longer than C, then A is longer than C? In Piaget's theory, concrete operational thinkers do; preoperational thinkers do not.

Might adolescents' ability to reason hypothetically and to evaluate what is ideal versus what is real lead them to engage in demonstrations, such as this protest related to the need to improve ethnic relations? What other causes might be attractive to adolescents' newfound cognitive abilities of hypothetical-deductive reasoning and idealistic thinking?

seriation The concrete operation that involves ordering stimuli along a quantitative dimension (such as length).

transitivity Principle that says if a relation holds between a first object and a second object, and holds between the second object and a third object, then it holds between the first object and the third object. Piaget argued that an understanding of transitivity is characteristic of concrete operational thought.

formal operational stage Piaget's fourth and final stage, which occurs between the ages of 11 and 15, when individuals move beyond concrete experiences and think in more abstract and logical ways.

FORMAL OPERATIONAL STAGE

So far we have studied the first three of Piaget's stages of cognitive development: sensorimotor, preoperational, and concrete operational. What are the characteristics of the fourth stage?

The **formal operational stage,** which appears between 11 and 15 years of age, is the fourth and final Piagetian stage. In this stage, individuals move beyond concrete experiences and think in abstract and more logical ways. As part of thinking more abstractly, adolescents develop images of ideal circumstances. They might think about what an ideal parent is like and compare their parents to their ideal standards. They begin to entertain possibilities for the future and are fascinated with what they might become. In solving problems, formal operational thinkers are more systematic and use logical reasoning.

Abstract, Idealistic, and Logical Thinking The abstract quality of the adolescent's thought at the formal operational level is evident in the adolescent's verbal problem-solving ability. The concrete operational thinker needs to see the concrete elements A, B, and C to be able to make the logical inference that if A = B and B = C, then A = C. The formal operational thinker can solve this problem merely through verbal presentation.

Another indication of the abstract quality of adolescents' thought is their increased tendency to think about thought itself. One adolescent commented, "I began thinking about why I was thinking about what I was. Then I began thinking about why I was thinking about what I was thinking about what I was." If this sounds abstract, it is, and it characterizes the adolescent's enhanced focus on thought and its abstract qualities.

Accompanying the abstract thought of adolescence is thought full of idealism and possibilities. While children frequently think in concrete ways, or in terms of what is real and limited, adolescents begin to engage in extended speculation about ideal characteristics—qualities they desire in themselves and in others. Such thoughts often lead adolescents to compare themselves with others in regard to ideal standards. And the thoughts of adolescents are often fantasy flights into future possibilities. It is not unusual for the adolescent to become impatient with these newfound ideal standards and to become perplexed over which of many ideal standards to adopt.

As adolescents are learning to think more abstractly and idealistically, they are also learning to think more logically. Children are likely to solve problems in a trial-and-error fashion. Adolescents begin to think more as a scientist thinks, devising plans to solve problems and systematically testing solutions. They use **hypothetical-deductive reasoning,** which means that they develop hypotheses, or best guesses, and systematically deduce, or conclude, which is the best path to follow in solving the problem.

Assimilation (incorporating new information into existing knowledge) dominates the initial development of formal operational thought, and these thinkers perceive the world subjectively and idealistically. Later in adolescence, as intellectual balance is restored, these individuals accommodate to the cognitive upheaval that has occurred (they adjust to the new information).

Some of Piaget's ideas on formal operational thought are being challenged (Blakemore & Mills, 2014; Diamond, Casey, & Munakata, 2011; Kuhn, 2009, 2011). There is much more individual variation in formal operational thought than Piaget envisioned. Only about one in three young adolescents is a formal operational thinker. Many American adults never become formal operational thinkers, and neither do many adults in other cultures.

Adolescent Egocentrism   In addition to thinking more logically, abstractly, and idealistically—characteristics of Piaget's formal operational thought stage—in what other ways do adolescents change cognitively? David Elkind (1978) described how adolescent egocentrism governs the way that adolescents think about social matters. **Adolescent egocentrism** is the heightened self-consciousness of adolescents, which is reflected in their belief that others are as interested in them as they are themselves, and in their sense of personal uniqueness and invincibility. Elkind argued that adolescent egocentrism can be dissected into two types of social thinking—imaginary audience and personal fable.

The **imaginary audience** refers to the aspect of adolescent egocentrism that involves feeling one is the center of everyone's attention and sensing that one is on stage. An adolescent boy might think that others are as aware of a few hairs that are out of place as he is. An adolescent girl walks into her classroom and thinks that all eyes are riveted on her complexion. Adolescents especially sense that they are "on stage" in early adolescence, believing they are the main actors and all others are the audience.

According to Elkind, the **personal fable** is the part of adolescent egocentrism that involves an adolescent's sense of personal uniqueness and invincibility. Adolescents' sense of personal uniqueness makes them feel that no one can understand how they really feel. For example, an adolescent girl thinks that her mother cannot possibly sense the hurt she feels because her boyfriend has broken up with her. As part of their effort to retain a sense of personal uniqueness, adolescents might craft stories about themselves that are filled with fantasy, immersing themselves in a world that is far removed from reality. Personal fables frequently show up in adolescent diaries.

Recent research studies, however, suggest that, rather than perceiving themselves to be invulnerable, many adolescents portray themselves as vulnerable (Reyna & Rivers, 2008). For example, in a recent study, 12- to 18-year-olds were asked about their chance of dying in the next year and prior to age 20 (Fischhoff & others, 2010). The adolescents greatly overestimated their chance of dying.

Some researchers have questioned the view that invulnerability is a unitary concept and argued rather that it consists of two dimensions (Duggan & others, 2000; Lapsley & Hill, 2010):

- *Danger invulnerability,* which involves adolescents' sense of indestructibility and tendency to take on physical risks (driving recklessly at high speeds, for example)
- *Psychological invulnerability,* which captures an adolescent's felt invulnerability related to personal or psychological distress (getting one's feelings hurt, for example)

A recent study revealed that adolescents who scored high on a danger invulnerability scale were more likely to engage in juvenile delinquency, substance abuse, or be depressed (Lapsley & Hill, 2010). In this study, adolescents who scored high on psychological invulnerability were less likely to be depressed, had higher self-esteem, and engaged in better interpersonal relationships. In terms of psychological invulnerability, adolescents often benefit from the normal developmental challenges of exploring identity options, making new friends, asking someone to go out on a date, and learning a new skill. All of these important adolescent tasks involve risk and failure as an option, but if successful result in enhanced self-image.

Many adolescent girls spend long hours in front of the mirror, depleting cans of hairspray, tubes of lipstick, and jars of cosmetics. *How might this behavior be related to changes in adolescent cognitive and physical development?*

I check my look in the mirror.
I wanna change my clothes,
my hair, my face.

—**Bruce Springsteen**
Contemporary American Rock Star

hypothetical-deductive reasoning Piaget's formal operational concept that adolescents have the cognitive ability to develop hypotheses about ways to solve problems and can systematically deduce which is the best path to follow in solving the problem.

adolescent egocentrism The heightened self-consciousness of adolescents, which is reflected in adolescents' beliefs that others are as interested in them as they are in themselves, and in adolescents' sense of personal uniqueness and invulnerability.

imaginary audience The aspect of adolescent egocentrism that involves attention-getting behavior motivated by a desire to be noticed, visible, and "onstage."

personal fable The part of adolescent egocentrism that involves an adolescent's sense of uniqueness and invincibility.

In the view of Daniel Lapsley and his colleagues (Hill, Duggan, & Lapsley, 2012; Lapsley & Stey, 2012), the separation-individuation process—which involves adolescents separating from their parents and developing independence and identity—is responsible for the findings just discussed, rather than cognitive developmental changes. With respect to personal fables, they argue that invulnerability and personal uniqueness are forms of adolescent narcissism.

Review Connect Reflect

LG1 Discuss the key processes and four stages in Piaget's theory.

Review

- What are the key processes in Piaget's theory of cognitive development?
- What are the main characteristics of the sensorimotor stage? What revisions of Piaget's sensorimotor stage have been proposed?
- What are the main characteristics of the preoperational stage?
- What are the main characteristics of the concrete operational stage?
- What are the main characteristics of the formal operational stage? How has Piaget's formal operational stage been criticized?

Connect

- How does Piaget's sensorimotor stage relate to what you learned about perceptual-motor coupling in Chapter 5?

Reflect *Your Own Personal Journey of Life*

- Do you consider yourself to be a formal operational thinker? Do you still sometimes feel like a concrete operational thinker? Give examples.

Applying and Evaluating Piaget's Theory

LG2 Apply Piaget's theory to education and evaluate his theory.

Piaget and Education

Evaluating Piaget's Theory

What are some applications of Piaget's theory to education? What are the main contributions and criticisms of Piaget's theory?

PIAGET AND EDUCATION

Piaget was not an educator, but he provided a sound conceptual framework for viewing learning and education. Following are some ideas in Piaget's theory that can be applied to teaching children (Elkind, 1976; Heuwinkel, 1996):

1. *Take a constructivist approach.* Piaget emphasized that children learn best when they are active and seek solutions for themselves. Piaget opposed teaching methods that treat children as passive receptacles. The educational implication of Piaget's view is that, in all subjects, students learn best by making discoveries, reflecting on them, and discussing them, rather than by blindly imitating the teacher or doing things by rote.

2. *Facilitate rather than direct learning.* Effective teachers design situations that allow students to learn by doing. These situations promote students' thinking and discovery. Teachers listen, watch, and question students, to help them gain better understanding.

3. *Consider the child's knowledge and level of thinking.* Students do not come to class with empty minds. They have concepts of space, time, quantity, and causality. These ideas differ from the ideas of adults. Teachers need to interpret what a student is saying and respond in a way that is not too far from the student's level. Also, Piaget suggested that it is important to examine children's mistakes in thinking, not just what they get correct, to help guide them to a higher level of understanding.

4. *Promote the student's intellectual health.* When Piaget came to lecture in the United States, he was asked, "What can I do to get my child to a higher cognitive stage sooner?" He

was asked this question so often here compared with other countries that he called it the American question. For Piaget, children's learning should occur naturally. Children should not be pushed and pressured into achieving too much too early in their development, before they are maturationally ready. Some parents spend long hours every day holding up large flash cards with words on them to improve their baby's vocabulary. In the Piagetian view, this is not the best way for infants to learn. It places too much emphasis on speeding up intellectual development, involves passive learning, and will not lead to positive outcomes.

5. *Turn the classroom into a setting of exploration and discovery.* What do actual classrooms look like when the teachers adopt Piaget's views? Several first- and second-grade math classrooms provide some good examples (Kamii, 1985, 1989). The teachers emphasize students' own exploration and discovery. The classrooms are less structured than what we think of as a typical classroom. Workbooks and predetermined assignments are not used. Rather, the teachers observe the students' interests and natural participation in activities to determine what the course of learning will be. For example, a math lesson might be constructed around counting the day's lunch money or dividing supplies among students. Games are often used in the classroom to stimulate mathematical thinking.

What are some educational strategies that can be derived from Piaget's theory?

EVALUATING PIAGET'S THEORY

What were Piaget's main contributions? Has his theory withstood the test of time?

Contributions Piaget was a giant in the field of developmental psychology, the founder of the present field of children's cognitive development. Psychologists owe him for a long list of masterful concepts of enduring power and fascination: assimilation, accommodation, object permanence, egocentrism, conservation, and others (Miller, 2011). Psychologists also owe him for the current vision of children as active, constructive thinkers. And they are indebted to him for creating a theory that generated a huge volume of research on children's cognitive development.

Piaget also was a genius when it came to observing children. His careful observations demonstrated inventive ways to discover how children act on and adapt to their world. Piaget showed us some important things to look for in cognitive development, such as the shift from preoperational to concrete operational thinking. He also showed us how children need to make their experiences fit their schemes (cognitive frameworks) yet simultaneously adapt their schemes to experience. Piaget also revealed how cognitive change is likely to occur if the context is structured to allow gradual movement to the next higher level. Concepts do not emerge suddenly, full-blown, but instead develop through a series of partial accomplishments that lead to increasingly comprehensive understanding (Rakison & Lawson, 2013).

Criticisms Piaget's theory has not gone unchallenged. Questions are raised about estimates of children's competence at different developmental levels, stages, the training of children to reason at higher levels, and culture and education.

Estimates of Children's Competence Some cognitive abilities emerge earlier than Piaget thought (Baillargeon, 2014; Bauer, 2013). For example, as previously noted, some aspects of object permanence emerge earlier than he proposed. Even 2-year-olds are nonegocentric in some contexts. When they realize that another person will not see an object, they investigate whether the person is blindfolded or looking in a different direction. Some understanding of the conservation of number has been demonstrated as early as age 3, although Piaget did not think it emerged until 7. Young children are not as uniformly "pre" this and "pre" that (precausal, preoperational) as Piaget thought.

Cognitive abilities also can emerge later than Piaget thought (Brynes, 2012). Many adolescents still think in concrete operational ways or are just beginning to master formal

Jean Piaget, the main architect of the field of cognitive development.

operations. Even many adults are not formal operational thinkers. In sum, recent theoretical revisions highlight more cognitive competencies of infants and young children and more cognitive shortcomings of adolescents and adults.

Stages   Piaget conceived of stages as unitary structures of thought. Thus, his theory assumes developmental synchrony—that is, various aspects of a stage should emerge at the same time. However, some concrete operational concepts do not appear in synchrony. For example, children do not learn to conserve at the same time that they learn to cross-classify. Thus, most contemporary developmentalists agree that children's cognitive development is not as stage-like as Piaget thought (Kuhn, 2009).

Effects of Training   Some children who are at one cognitive stage (such as preoperational) can be trained to reason at a higher cognitive stage (such as concrete operational). This poses a problem for Piaget's theory. He argued that such training is only superficial and ineffective, unless the child is at a maturational transition point between the stages (Gelman & Williams, 1998).

neo-Piagetians Developmentalists who have elaborated on Piaget's theory, believing that children's cognitive development is more specific in many respects than Piaget thought and giving more emphasis to how children use memory, attention, and strategies to process information.

Culture and Education   Culture and education exert stronger influences on children's development than Piaget reasoned (Gauvain, 2013). For example, the age at which children acquire conservation skills is related to how much practice their culture provides in these skills. Among Wolof children in the West African nation of Senegal, only 50 percent of the 10- to 13-year-olds understood the principle of conservation (Greenfield, 1966). Comparable studies among cultures in central Australia, New Guinea (an island north of Australia), the Amazon jungle region of Brazil, and rural Sardinia (an island off the coast of Italy) yielded similar results (Dasen, 1977). An outstanding teacher and instruction in the logic of math and science can promote the development of concrete and formal operational thought.

An outstanding teacher and education in the logic of science and mathematics are important cultural experiences that promote the development of operational thought. *Might Piaget have underestimated the roles of culture and schooling in children's cognitive development?*

The Neo-Piagetian Approach   **Neo-Piagetians** argue that Piaget got some things right but that his theory needs considerable revision. They give more emphasis to how children use attention, memory, and strategies to process information (Case, 1987, 1999; Morra & others, 2007). They especially believe that a more accurate portrayal of children's thinking requires attention to children's strategies, the speed at which children process information, the particular task involved, and the division of problems into smaller, more precise steps (Demetriou, 2001). In Chapter 7 we will discuss these aspects of children's thought.

Review *Connect* Reflect

 Apply Piaget's theory to education and evaluate his theory.

Review

- How can Piaget's theory be applied to educating children?
- What are some key contributions and criticisms of Piaget's theory?

Connect

- In this section, you learned that culture exerts a strong influence on cognitive development. In Chapter 5, what did we learn about the influence of different cultural practices on infants' motor skills?

Reflect *Your Own Personal Journey of Life*

- How might thinking in formal operational ways rather than concrete operational ways help you to develop better study skills?

| The Zone of Proximal Development | Scaffolding | Language and Thought | Teaching Strategies | Evaluating Vygotsky's Theory |

Piaget's theory is a major developmental theory. Another developmental theory that focuses on children's cognition is Vygotsky's theory. Like Piaget, Lev Vygotsky (1962) emphasized that children actively construct their knowledge and understanding. In Piaget's theory, children develop ways of thinking and understanding by their actions and interactions with the physical world. In Vygtosky's theory, children are more often described as social creatures than in Piaget's theory. They develop their ways of thinking and understanding primarily through social interaction (Mahn & John-Steiner, 2013). Their cognitive development depends on the tools provided by society, and their minds are shaped by the cultural context in which they live (Goncu & Gauvain, 2012).

We briefly described Vygotsky's theory in Chapter 1. Here we take a closer look at his ideas about how children learn and his view of the role of language in cognitive development.

THE ZONE OF PROXIMAL DEVELOPMENT

Vygotsky's belief in the importance of social influences, especially instruction, on children's cognitive development is reflected in his concept of the zone of proximal development. **Zone of proximal development (ZPD)** is Vygotsky's term for the range of tasks that are too difficult for the child to master alone but that can be learned with guidance and assistance of adults or more-skilled children. Thus, the lower limit of the ZPD is the level of skill reached by the child working independently. The upper limit is the level of additional responsibility the child can accept with the assistance of an able instructor (see Figure 6.11). The ZPD captures the child's cognitive skills that are in the process of maturing and can be accomplished only with the assistance of a more-skilled person (Daniels, 2011; Petrick-Steward, 2012). Vygotsky (1962) called these the "buds" or "flowers" of development, to distinguish them from the "fruits" of development, which the child already can accomplish independently.

Vygotsky's concept of the zone of proximal development—that children learn by interacting with more experienced adults and peers, who help them think beyond the "zone" in which they would be able to perform without assistance—has been applied primarily to academic learning. Barbara Rogoff (1990, 2003; Rogoff, Correa-Chavez, & Silva, 2011; Rogoff, Morelli, & Chavajay, 2010; Rogoff & others, 2007, 2011) argues that many of Vygotsky's ideas, including the zone of proximal development, are important in understanding children's development beyond the classroom in everyday interactions with adults and peers. To read further about Rogoff's ideas, see *Connecting with Diversity*.

SCAFFOLDING

Closely linked to the idea of the ZPD is the concept of scaffolding. **Scaffolding** means changing the level of support. Over the course of a teaching session, a more-skilled person (a teacher or advanced peer) adjusts the amount of guidance to fit the child's current performance (Mahn & John-Steiner, 2013). When the student is learning a new task, the skilled person may use direct instruction. As the student's competence increases, less guidance is given.

Dialogue is an important tool of scaffolding in the zone of proximal development (Tappan, 1998). Vygotsky viewed children as having rich but unsystematic, disorganized, and spontaneous concepts. In a dialogue, these concepts meet with the skilled helper's more systematic, logical, and rational concepts. As a result, the child's concepts become more systematic, logical, and rational. For example, a dialogue might take place between

Upper limit

Level of additional responsibility child can accept with assistance of an able instructor

Zone of proximal development (ZPD)

Lower limit

Level of problem solving reached on these tasks by child working alone

FIGURE **6.11**

VYGOTSKY'S ZONE OF PROXIMAL DEVELOPMENT. Vygotsky's zone of proximal development has a lower limit and an upper limit. Tasks in the ZPD are too difficult for the child to perform alone. They require assistance from an adult or a more-skilled child. As children experience the verbal instruction or demonstration, they organize the information in their existing mental structures so that they can eventually perform the skill or task alone.

zone of proximal development (ZPD) Vygotsky's term for tasks that are too difficult for children to master alone but can be mastered with assistance from adults or more-skilled children.

scaffolding In cognitive development, Vygotsky used this term to describe the practice of changing the level of support provided over the course of a teaching session, with the more-skilled person adjusting guidance to fit the child's current performance level.

connecting with diversity

Guided Participation and Cultural Contexts

According to Rogoff, children serve a sort of apprenticeship in thinking through *guided participation* in social and cultural activities. Guided participation may occur, for example, when adults and children share activities.

Parents can broaden or limit children's opportunities through their decisions about how much and when to expose children to books, television, and child care. They may give children opportunities to learn about cultural traditions and practices through their routines and play. For example, in the Zambian culture of Chewa, children play numerous games, such as "hide-and-seek, guessing games, complex sand drawing games, imaginative games representing local work and family routines, skill games like jacks and a rule game requiring considerable strategic planning and numerical calculations, and constructing models of wire or clay" (Rogoff, 2003, p. 297). In addition, through observational learning, or as Rogoff calls it, learning by "osmosis," children adopt values, skills, and mannerisms by simply watching and listening to peers and adults.

Guided participation is widely used around the world, but cultures may differ in the goals of development—what content is to be learned— and the means for providing guided participation (Rogoff & others, 2007). Around the world, caregivers and children arrange children's activities and revise children's responsibilities as they gain skill and knowledge. With guidance, children participate in cultural activities that socialize them into skilled activities. For example, Mayan mothers in Guatemala help their daughters learn to weave through guided participation. Throughout the world, learning occurs, not just by studying or by attending classes, but also through interaction with knowledgeable people.

In recent work, Rogoff and her colleagues (2011; Rogoff, Correa-Chavez, & Silva, 2011) have studied cultural variations in children's attention and learning. They highlight two contrasting approaches: (1) Participation of children in a wide variety of family and community activities, which characterizes many Indigenous-heritage

At about 7 years of age, Mayan girls in Guatemala are assisted in beginning to learn to weave a simple belt, with the loom already set up for them. The young girl shown here is American developmental psychologist Barbara Rogoff's daughter, being taught to weave by a Mayan woman. *What are some other ways that children learn through guided participation?*

communities in North and South America; and (2) Separation of children from the variety of family and community activities and creating activities for them in specialized settings, such as school, which is prevalent in middle SES European-heritage communities. Rogoff and her colleagues (2011; Rogoff, Correa-Chavez, & Silva, 2011) conclude that in the United States, children's out-of-school time provides limited opportunities to learn by observing and participating in a variety of valued family and community activities. In their view, including children in meaningful family and community activities would help them to better understand valued work and other activities in their culture.

How does Rogoff's concept of guided participation relate to Vygotsky's concept of the zone of proximal development?

---

developmental **connection**

Parenting

Scaffolding also is an effective strategy for parents to adopt in interacting with their infants. Chapter 14, p. 392

a teacher and a child when the teacher uses scaffolding to help a child understand a concept like "transportation."

LANGUAGE AND THOUGHT

The use of dialogue as a tool for scaffolding is only one example of the important role of language in a child's development. According to Vygotsky, children use speech not only for social communication, but also to help them solve tasks. Vygotsky (1962) further concluded that young children use language to plan, guide, and monitor their behavior. This use of language for self-regulation is called *private speech*. For Piaget private speech is egocentric and immature, but for Vygotsky it is an important tool of thought during the early childhood years (Wertsch, 2007).

Vygotsky said that language and thought initially develop independently of each other and then merge. He emphasized that all mental functions have external, or social, origins.

Children must use language to communicate with others before they can focus inward on their own thoughts. Children also must communicate externally and use language for a long period of time before they can make the transition from external to internal speech. This transition period occurs between 3 and 7 years of age and involves talking to oneself. After a while, the self-talk becomes second nature to children, and they can act without verbalizing. When this occurs, children have internalized their egocentric speech in the form of *inner speech,* which becomes their thoughts.

Vygotsky reasoned that children who use a lot of private speech are more socially competent than those who don't. He argued that private speech represents an early transition in becoming more socially communicative. For Vygotsky, when young children talk to themselves, they are using language to govern their behavior and guide themselves. For example, a child working on a puzzle might say to herself, "Which pieces should I put together first? I'll try those green ones first. Now I need some blue ones. No, that blue one doesn't fit there. I'll try it over here."

Piaget stressed that self-talk is egocentric and reflects immaturity. However, researchers have found support for Vygotsky's view that private speech plays a positive role in children's development (Winsler, Carlton, & Barry, 2000). Researchers have found that children use private speech more when tasks are difficult, when they have made a mistake, and when they are not sure how to proceed (Berk, 1994). They also have revealed that children who use private speech are more attentive and improve their performance more than children who do not use private speech (Berk & Spuhl, 1995).

Lev Vygotsky (1896–1934), shown here with his daughter, believed that children's cognitive development is advanced through social interaction with skilled individuals embedded in a sociocultural backdrop.

TEACHING STRATEGIES

Vygotsky's theory has been embraced by many teachers and has been successfully applied to education (Daniels, 2011; Costley, 2012; Gauvain, 2013; Shayer & Adhami, 2010). Here are some ways Vygotsky's theory can be incorporated in classrooms:

1. *Assess the child's ZPD.* Like Piaget, Vygotsky did not think that formal, standardized tests are the best way to assess children's learning. Rather, Vygotsky argued that assessment should focus on determining the child's zone of proximal development. The skilled helper presents the child with tasks of varying difficulty to determine the best level at which to begin instruction.

2. *Use the child's ZPD in teaching.* Teaching should begin toward the zone's upper limit, so that the child can reach the goal with help and move to a higher level of skill and knowledge. Offer just enough assistance. You might ask, "What can I do to help you?" Or simply observe the child's intentions and attempts and provide support when needed. When the child hesitates, offer encouragement. And encourage the child to practice the skill. You may watch and appreciate the child's practice or offer support when the child forgets what to do.

3. *Use more-skilled peers as teachers.* Remember that it is not just adults who are important in helping children learn. Children also benefit from the support and guidance of more-skilled children (Mahn & John-Steiner, 2013).

4. *Monitor and encourage children's use of private speech.* Be aware of the developmental change from externally talking to oneself when solving a problem during the preschool years to privately talking to oneself in the early elementary school years. In the elementary school years, encourage children to internalize and self-regulate their talk to themselves.

5. *Place instruction in a meaningful context.* Educators today are moving away from abstract presentations of material, instead providing students with opportunities to experience learning in real-world settings. For example, instead of just memorizing math formulas, students work on math problems with real-world implications.

6. *Transform the classroom with Vygotskian ideas.* What does a Vygotskian classroom look like? The Kamehameha Elementary Education Program

- - - - - - - - - - - ▶

developmental **connection**

Language

In thinking about links between language and cognition, we might ask: (1) Is language necessary for cognition? and (2) Is cognition necessary for language? Chapter 9, p. 274

How can Vygotsky's ideas be applied to educating children?

Donene Polson, Elementary School Teacher

Donene Polson teaches at Washington Elementary School in Salt Lake City, Utah. Washington is an innovative school that emphasizes the importance of people learning together as part of a community of learners. Children as well as adults plan learning activities. Throughout the school day, children work in small groups.

Polson says that she loves working in a school in which students, teachers, and parents work together as a community to help children learn. Before the school year begins, Polson meets with parents at the family's home to prepare for the upcoming year, get acquainted, and establish schedules to determine when parents can contribute to classroom instruction. At monthly parent-teacher meetings, Polson and the parents plan the curriculum and discuss how children's learning is progressing. They brainstorm about resources in the community that can be used effectively to promote children's learning.

For more information about what elementary school teachers do, see page 42 in the Careers in Child Development appendix following Chapter 1.

(KEEP) is based on Vygotsky's theory (Tharp, 1994). The ZPD is the key element of instruction in this program and many of the learning activities take place in small groups. All children spend at least 20 minutes each morning in a setting called "Center One." In this context, scaffolding is used to improve children's literary skills. The instructor asks questions, responds to students' queries, and builds on the ideas that students generate. Thousands of children from low-income families have attended KEEP public schools—in Hawaii, on an Arizona Navajo Indian reservation, and in Los Angeles. Compared with a control group of non-KEEP children, the KEEP children participated more actively in classroom discussion, were more attentive in class, and had higher levels of reading achievement (Tharp & Gallimore, 1988).

To read about the work of a teacher who applies Vygotsky's theory to her teaching, see the *Connecting with Careers* profile. The *Caring Connections* interlude further explores the implications of Vygotsky's theory for children's education.

EVALUATING VYGOTSKY'S THEORY

Even though their theories were proposed at about the same time, most of the world learned about Vygotsky's theory later than they learned about Piaget's theory, so Vygotsky's theory has not yet been evaluated as thoroughly. Vygotsky's view of the importance of sociocultural influences on children's development fits with the current belief that it is important to evaluate the contextual factors in learning (Deater-Deckard, 2013; Gauvain, 2013).

We already have mentioned several distinctions between Vygotsky's and Piaget's theories, such as Vygotsky's emphasis on the importance of inner speech in development and Piaget's view that such speech is immature. Although both theories are constructivist, Vygotsky's is a **social constructivist approach,** which emphasizes the social contexts of learning and the construction of knowledge through social interaction (O'Donnell, 2012).

In moving from Piaget to Vygotsky, the conceptual shift is from the individual to collaboration, social interaction, and sociocultural activity (Mahn & John-Steiner, 2013). The end point of cognitive development for Piaget is formal operational thought. For Vygotsky, the endpoint can differ, depending on which skills are considered to be the most important in a particular culture. For Piaget, children construct knowledge by transforming, organizing, and reorganizing previous knowledge. For Vygotsky, children construct knowledge through social interaction (Gauvain, 2013). The implication of Piaget's theory for teaching is that children

- - - - - - - - - >
developmental **connection**

Education and Achievement

Whether to adopt a direct instruction or constructivist approach is a major issue in educating children. Chapter 16, p. 451

social constructivist approach An emphasis on the social contexts of learning and the construction of knowledge through social interaction. Vygotsky's theory reflects this approach.

caring *connections*

Tools of the Mind

Tools of the Mind is an early childhood education curriculum that emphasizes children's development of self-regulation and the cognitive foundations of literacy (Diamond, 2013; Hyson, Copple, & Jones, 2006). The curriculum was created by Elena Bodrova and Deborah Leong (2007) and has been implemented in more than 200 classrooms. Most of the children in the Tools of the Mind programs are at risk because of their living circumstances, which in many instances involve poverty and other difficult conditions such as being homeless and having parents with drug problems.

Tools of the Mind is grounded in Vygotsky's (1962) theory, with special attention given to cultural tools and developing self-regulation, the zone of proximal development, scaffolding, private speech, shared activity, and play as important activity. In a Tools of the Mind classroom, dramatic play has a central role. Teachers guide children in creating themes that are based on the children's interests, such as treasure hunt, store, hospital, and restaurant. Teachers also incorporate field trips, visitor presentations, videos, and books in the development of children's play. They help children develop a play plan, which increases the maturity of their play. Play plans describe what the children expect to do during the play period, including the imaginary context, roles, and props to be used. The play plans increase the quality of their play and self-regulation.

Scaffolding writing is another important theme in the Tools of the Mind classroom. Teachers guide children in planning their own message by drawing a line to stand for each word the child says. Children then repeat the message, pointing to each line as they say the word. Next, the child writes on the lines, trying to represent each word with some letters or symbols. Figure 6.12 shows how the scaffolding writing process improved a 5-year-old child's writing over the course of two months.

Research assessments of children's writing in Tools of the Mind classrooms revealed that they have more advanced writing skills than children in other early childhood programs (Bodrova & Leong, 2007) (see Figure 6.12). For example, they write more complex messages, use more words, spell more accurately, show better letter recognition, and have a better understanding of the concept of a sentence.

One study assessed the effects of the Tools of the Mind curriculum on at-risk preschool children (Diamond & others, 2007). The results indicated that the Tools of the Mind curriculum improved the self-regulatory and cognitive control skills (such as resisting distractions and temptations) of the at-risk children. Other research on the Tools of the Mind curriculum also has found that it improves young children's cognitive skills (Barnett & others, 2006; Saifer, 2007).

Earlier in this section of the chapter, we outlined strategies for incorporating Vygotsky's theory into teaching. Revisit that list and explain how the Tools of the Mind curriculum uses those strategies.

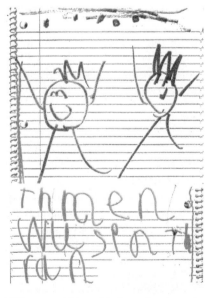

(a) Five-year-old Aaron's independent journal writing prior to the scaffolded writing technique.

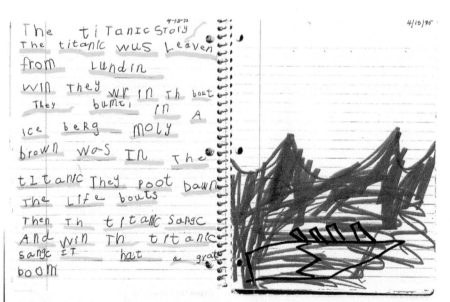

(b) Aaron's journal two months after using the scaffolded writing technique.

FIGURE **6.12**

WRITING PROGRESS OF A 5-YEAR-OLD BOY OVER TWO MONTHS USING THE SCAFFOLDING WRITING PROCESS IN TOOLS OF THE MIND

	Vygotsky	Piaget
Sociocultural Context	Strong emphasis	Little emphasis
Constructivism	Social constructivist	Cognitive constructivist
Stages	No general stages of development proposed	Strong emphasis on stages (sensorimotor, preoperational, concrete operational, and formal operational)
Key Processes	Zone of proximal development, language, dialogue, tools of the culture	Schema, assimilation, accommodation, operations, conservation, classification
Role of Language	A major role; language plays a powerful role in shaping thought	Language has a minimal role; cognition primarily directs language
View on Education	Education plays a central role, helping children learn the tools of the culture	Education merely refines the child's cognitive skills that have already emerged
Teaching Implications	Teacher is a facilitator and guide, not a director; establish many opportunities for children to learn with the teacher and more-skilled peers	Also views teacher as a facilitator and guide, not a director; provide support for children to explore their world and discover knowledge

FIGURE **6.13**
COMPARISON OF VYGOTSKY'S AND PIAGET'S THEORIES

need support to explore their world and discover knowledge. The main implication of Vygotsky's theory for teaching is that students need many opportunities to learn with their teachers and more-skilled peers. In both Piaget's and Vygotsky's theories, teachers serve as facilitators and guides, rather than as directors and molders of learning. Figure 6.13 compares Vygotsky's and Piaget's theories.

Criticisms of Vygotsky's theory also have surfaced (Karpov, 2006). Some critics point out that Vygotsky was not specific enough about age-related changes (Gauvain, 2008). Another criticism asserts that Vygotsky does not adequately describe how changes in socioemotional capabilities contribute to cognitive development (Gauvain, 2008). Yet another criticism is that he overemphasized the role of language in thinking. Also, his emphasis on collaboration and guidance has potential pitfalls. Might facilitators be too helpful in some cases, as when a parent becomes overbearing and controlling? Further, some children might become lazy and expect help when they might have learned more by doing something on their own.

Review *Connect* Reflect

 LG3 Identify the main concepts in Vygotsky's theory and compare it with Piaget's theory.

Review

- What is the zone of proximal development?
- What is scaffolding?
- How did Vygotsky view language and thought?
- How can Vygotsky's theory be applied to education?
- What are some similarities and differences between Vygotsky's and Piaget's theories?
- What are some criticisms of Vygotsky's theory?

Connect

- Compare the strategies that were laid out in the section for using Piaget's theories in teaching to those for applying Vygotsky's theories in teaching. What are the similarities? Differences?

Reflect *Your Own Personal Journey of Life*

- Which theory—Piaget's or Vygotsky's—do you think is more effective in explaining your own cognitive development as a child?

Cognitive Developmental Approaches

Piaget's Theory of Cognitive Development LG1 Discuss the key processes and four stages in Piaget's theory.

Processes of Development

- According to Piaget's theory, children construct their own cognitive worlds, building mental structures to adapt to their world. Schemes are actions or mental representations that organize knowledge. Behavioral schemes (physical activities) characterize infancy, and mental schemes (cognitive activities) develop in childhood. Adaptation involves assimilation and accommodation. Assimilation occurs when children incorporate new information into their existing schemes. Accommodation refers to children's adjustment of their schemes to fit new information and experiences. Through organization, children group isolated behaviors into a higher-order, more smoothly functioning cognitive system. Equilibration is a mechanism Piaget proposed to explain how children shift from one cognitive stage to the next. As children experience cognitive conflict in trying to understand the world, they seek equilibrium. The result is equilibration, which brings the child to a new stage of thought. According to Piaget, there are four qualitatively different stages of thought: sensorimotor, preoperational, concrete operational, and formal operational.

Sensorimotor Stage

- In sensorimotor thought, the first of Piaget's four stages, the infant organizes and coordinates sensory experiences (such as seeing and hearing) with physical movements. This stage lasts from birth to about 2 years of age and is nonsymbolic throughout, according to Piaget. Sensorimotor thought has six substages: simple reflexes; first habits and primary circular reactions; secondary circular reactions; coordination of secondary circular reactions; tertiary circular reactions, novelty, and curiosity; and internalization of schemes. One key aspect of this stage is object permanence, the ability to understand that objects continue to exist even though the infant is no longer observing them. Another aspect involves infants' understanding of cause and effect. In the past two decades, revisions of Piaget's view have been proposed based on research. For example, researchers have found that a stable and differentiated perceptual world is established earlier than Piaget envisioned. However, controversy surrounds the question of when object permanence emerges. The nature-nurture issue is a key aspect of infant cognitive development. Spelke's core knowledge approach is a strong naturist view. Most developmentalists conclude that nature and nurture are both important in infant cognitive development.

Preoperational Stage

- Preoperational thought is the beginning of the ability to reconstruct at the level of thought what has been established in behavior. It involves a transition from a primitive to a more sophisticated use of symbols. In preoperational thought, the child does not yet think in an operational way. The symbolic function substage occurs roughly from 2 to 4 years of age and is characterized by symbolic thought, egocentrism, and animism. The intuitive thought substage stretches from about 4 to 7 years of age. It is called intuitive because children seem sure about their knowledge yet are unaware of how they know what they know. The preoperational child lacks conservation and asks a barrage of questions.

Concrete Operational Stage

- Concrete operational thought occurs roughly from 7 to 11 years of age. During this stage, children can perform concrete operations, think logically about concrete objects, classify things, and reason about relationships among classes of things. Concrete thought is not as abstract as formal operational thought.

Formal Operational Stage

- Formal operational thought appears between 11 and 15 years of age. Formal operational thought is more abstract, idealistic, and logical than concrete operational thought. Piaget maintains that adolescents become capable of engaging in hypothetical-deductive reasoning. But Piaget did not give adequate attention to individual variation in adolescent thinking. Many young adolescents do not think in hypothetical-deductive ways but rather are consolidating their concrete operational thinking. In addition, according to Elkind, adolescents develop a special kind of egocentrism that involves an imaginary audience and a personal fable about being unique and invulnerable. However, recent research questions the accuracy of the invulnerability aspect of the personal fable.

Applying and Evaluating Piaget's Theory Apply Piaget's theory to education and evaluate his theory.

- Piaget and Education

- Evaluating Piaget's Theory

- Piaget was not an educator, but his constructivist views have been applied to teaching. These applications include an emphasis on facilitating rather than directing learning, considering the child's level of knowledge, using ongoing assessment, promoting the student's intellectual health, and turning the classroom into a setting for exploration and discovery.

- We owe to Piaget the field of cognitive development. He was a genius at observing children, and he gave us a number of masterful concepts such as assimilation, accommodation, object permanence, and egocentrism. Critics question his estimates of competence at different developmental levels, his stage concept, and other ideas. Neo-Piagetians, who emphasize the importance of information processing, stress that children's cognition is more specific than Piaget thought.

Vygotsky's Theory of Cognitive Development Identify the main concepts in Vygotsky's theory and compare it with Piaget's theory.

- The Zone of Proximal Development

- Scaffolding

- Language and Thought

- Teaching Strategies

- Evaluating Vygotsky's Theory

- Zone of proximal development (ZPD) is Vygotsky's term for the range of tasks that are too difficult for children to master alone but can be learned with the guidance and assistance of adults or more-skilled peers.

- Scaffolding is a teaching technique in which a more-skilled person adjusts the level of guidance to fit the child's current performance level. Dialogue is an important aspect of scaffolding.

- Vygotsky stressed that language plays a key role in cognition. Language and thought initially develop independently, but then children internalize their egocentric speech in the form of inner speech, which becomes their thoughts. This transition to inner speech occurs between 3 and 7 years of age.

- Applications of Vygotsky's ideas to education include using the child's ZPD and scaffolding, using more-skilled peers as teachers, monitoring and encouraging children's use of private speech, and accurately assessing the ZPD. These practices can transform the classroom and establish a meaningful context for instruction.

- Like Piaget, Vygotsky emphasized that children actively construct their understanding of the world. Unlike Piaget, he did not propose stages of cognitive development, and he emphasized that children construct knowledge through social interaction. According to Vygotsky's theory, children depend on tools provided by the culture, which determines which skills they will develop. Vygotsky's view contrasts with Piaget's view that young children's private speech is immature and egocentric. Critics of Vygotsky's theory assert that it lacks specificity about age-related changes and overemphasizes the role of language in thinking.

key terms

key people

INFORMATION PROCESSING

chapter outline

Laura Bickford is a master teacher who chairs the English Department at Nordoff High School in Ojai, California. She recently spoke about how she encourages her students to think:

I believe the call to teach is a call to teach students how to think. In encouraging critical thinking, literature itself does a good bit of work for us but we still have to be guides. We have to ask good questions. We have to show students the value in asking their own questions, in having discussions and conversations. In addition to reading and discussing literature, the best way to move students to think critically is to have them write. We write all the time in a variety of modes: journals, formal essays, letters, factual reports, news articles, speeches, or other formal oral presentations. We have to show students where they merely scratch the surface in their thinking and writing. I call these moments "hits and runs." When I see this "hit and run" effort, I draw a window on the paper. I tell them it is a "window of opportunity" to go deeper, elaborate, and clarify. Many students don't do this kind of thinking until they are prodded to do so.

I also ask them to keep reading logs so they can observe their own thinking as it happens. In addition, I ask students to comment on their own learning by way of grading themselves. This year a student gave me one of the most insightful lines about her growth as a reader I have ever seen from a student. She wrote, "I no longer think in a monotone when I'm reading." I don't know if she grasps the magnitude of that thought or how it came to be that she made that change. It is magic when students see themselves growing like this.

Laura Bickford (standing), working with students who are writing papers.

preview

What do children notice in the environment? What do they remember? And how do they think about it? These questions illustrate the information-processing approach. Using this approach, researchers usually do not describe children as being in one stage of cognitive development or another. But they do describe and analyze how information processing, attention, memory, thinking, and metacognition change over time.

The Information-Processing Approach **LG1** Explain the information-processing approach.

| The Information-Processing Approach to Development | Cognitive Resources: Capacity and Speed of Processing Information | Mechanisms of Change | Comparisons with Piaget's Theory |

What are some of the basic ideas in the information-processing approach? How is it similar to and different from the cognitive developmental approaches we described in Chapter 6?

THE INFORMATION-PROCESSING APPROACH TO DEVELOPMENT

The information-processing approach shares a basic characteristic with the theories of cognitive development that were discussed in Chapter 6. Like those theories, the information-processing approach rejected the behavioral perspective that dominated psychology during the first half of the twentieth century. As we discussed in Chapter 1, the behaviorists argued that to explain behavior it is important to examine associations between stimuli and behavior. In contrast, the theories of Piaget and Vygotsky (described in Chapter 6) and the information-processing approach focus on how children think.

The **information-processing approach** analyzes how children manipulate information, monitor it, and create strategies for handling it (Siegler, 2006, 2012, 2013). A computer metaphor can illustrate how the information-processing approach can be applied to development. A computer's information processing is *limited* by its hardware and software. The hardware limitations include the amount of data the computer can process—its capacity—and speed. The software limits the kind of data that can be used as input and the ways that data can be manipulated; word processing programs will not handle music, for example. Similarly, children's information processing may be limited by capacity and speed as well as by their ability to manipulate information—in other words, their ability to apply appropriate strategies to acquire and use knowledge. In the information-processing approach, children's cognitive development results from their ability to overcome processing limitations by increasingly executing basic operations, expanding information-processing capacity, and acquiring new knowledge and strategies.

> The mind is an enchanting thing.
>
> —**Marianne Moore**
> *American Poet, 20th Century*

COGNITIVE RESOURCES: CAPACITY AND SPEED OF PROCESSING INFORMATION

Developmental changes in information processing are likely to be influenced by increases in both capacity and speed of processing (Frye, 2004). These two characteristics are often referred to as *cognitive resources*, which are proposed to have an important influence on memory and problem solving.

Both biology and experience contribute to growth in cognitive resources (Bjorklund, 2013; Kuhn, 2013). Think about how much faster you can process information in your native language than a second language. The changes in the brain we described in Chapter 4 provide

information-processing approach An approach that focuses on the ways children process information about their world—how they manipulate information, monitor it, and create strategies to deal with it.

How does speed of processing information change during the childhood and adolescent years?

a biological foundation for increased cognitive resources (Zelazo, 2013). Important biological developments occur both in brain structures, such as changes in the frontal lobes, and at the level of neurons, such as the blooming and pruning of connections between neurons. Also, as we discussed in Chapter 4, myelination (the process in which the axon is covered with a myelin sheath) increases the speed of electrical impulses in the brain. Myelination continues throughout childhood and adolescence (Steinberg, 2013).

Most information-processing psychologists argue that an increase in capacity also improves processing of information (Halford & Andrews, 2011; Kuhn, 2013). For example, as children's information-processing capacity increases, they likely can hold in mind several dimensions of a topic or problem simultaneously, whereas younger children are more prone to focus on only one dimension.

What is the role of processing speed? How quickly children can process information often influences what they can do with that information (Robinson-Riegler & Robinson-Riegler, 2012). A recent study of 9- to 14-year-olds revealed that faster processing speed was linked to a higher level of oral reading fluency (Jacobson & others, 2011). And if an adolescent is trying to add up mentally the cost of items he or she is buying at the grocery store, the adolescent needs to be able to compute the sum before he or she has forgotten the price of the individual items. Children's speed in processing information is linked with their competence in thinking (Bjorklund, 2012). For example, the speed with which children can articulate a series of words affects how many words they can remember. Generally, fast processing is linked with good performance on cognitive tasks. However, some compensation for slower processing speed can be achieved by creating effective strategies.

Researchers have devised a number of ways to assess processing speed. For example, it can be assessed through a *reaction-time task* in which individuals are asked to push a button as soon as they see a stimulus such as a light. Or individuals might be asked to match letters or match numbers with symbols on a computer screen.

encoding The mechanism by which information gets into memory.

automaticity The ability to process information with little or no effort.

There is abundant evidence that the speed with which such tasks are completed improves dramatically across the childhood years (Kail, 2007; Kuhn, 2013). For example, a study of 8- to 13-year-old children revealed that processing speed increased with age, and furthermore, that the developmental change in processing speed preceded an increase in working memory capacity (Kail, 2007).

MECHANISMS OF CHANGE

Robert Siegler (1998, 2012, 2013) argues that mechanisms of change are especially important in the advances children make in cognitive development. According to Siegler, three mechanisms work together to create changes in children's cognitive skills: encoding, automaticity, and strategy construction.

Encoding is the process by which information gets into memory. Changes in children's cognitive skills depend on increased skill at encoding relevant information and ignoring irrelevant information. For example, to a 4-year-old, an *s* in cursive writing is a shape very different from an *s* that is printed. But a 10-year-old has learned to encode the relevant fact that both are the letter *s* and to ignore the irrelevant differences in their shape.

Automaticity refers to the ability to process information with little or no effort. Practice allows children to encode increasing amounts of information automatically. For example, once children have learned to read well, they do not think about each letter in a word as a letter; instead, they encode whole words. Once a task is automatic, it does not require conscious effort. As a result, as information processing becomes more automatic, we can complete tasks

What are some important mechanisms of change in the development of children's information processing?

more quickly and handle more than one task at a time. If you did not encode words automatically but instead read this page by focusing your attention on each letter in each word, imagine how long it would take you to read it.

Strategy construction is the creation of new procedures for processing information. For example, children's reading benefits when they develop the strategy of stopping periodically to take stock of what they have read so far (Dimmitt & McCormick, 2012).

In addition, Siegler (2006, 2012, 2013) argues that children's information processing is characterized by *self-modification*. That is, children learn to use what they have learned in previous circumstances to adapt their responses to a new situation. Part of this self-modification draws on **metacognition,** which means knowing about knowing (Flavell, 2004; McCormick, Dimmitt, & Sullivan, 2013). One example of metacognition is what children know about the best ways to remember what they have read. Do they know that they will remember what they have read better if they can relate it to their own lives in some way? Thus, in Siegler's application of the information-processing approach to development, children play an active role in their cognitive development.

COMPARISONS WITH PIAGET'S THEORY

How does the information-processing approach compare with Piaget's theory? According to Piaget (as discussed in Chapter 6), children actively construct their knowledge and understanding of the world. Their thinking develops in distinct stages. At each stage, children develop qualitatively different types of mental structures (or schemes) that allow them to think about the world in new ways.

Like Piaget's theory, some versions of the information-processing approach are constructivist; they see children as directing their own cognitive development. And like Piaget, information-processing psychologists identify cognitive capabilities and limitations at various points in development (Siegler, 2013; Zelazo, 2013). They describe ways in which individuals do and do not understand important concepts at different points in life and try to explain how more advanced understanding grows out of a less advanced version (Rakison & Lawson, 2013). They emphasize the impact that existing understanding has on the ability to acquire a new understanding of something.

Unlike Piaget, however, developmentalists who take an information-processing approach do not see development as occurring abruptly in distinct stages with a brief transition period from one stage to the next. Instead, according to the information-processing approach, individuals develop a gradually increasing capacity to process information, which allows them to acquire increasingly complex knowledge and skills (Kuhn, 2013). Compared with Piaget's theory, the information-processing approach also focuses on more precise analysis of change and on the contributions made by ongoing cognitive activity—such as encoding and strategies—to that change.

developmental **connection**

Cognitive Theory

Piaget theorized that cognitive development occurs in four stages: sensorimotor, preoperational, concrete operational, and formal operational. Chapter 6, p. 170

developmental **connection**

Theories

In Skinner's behavioral view, it is external rewards and punishment that determine behavior, not thoughts. Chapter 1, p. 24

strategy construction Creation of new procedures for processing information.

metacognition Cognition about cognition, or "knowing about knowing."

Review *Connect* Reflect

LG1 Explain the information-processing approach.

Review

- What is the information-processing approach to development?
- How do capacity and processing speed change developmentally?
- What are three important mechanisms of change involved in information processing?
- How can the information-processing approach be compared to Piaget's theory?

Connect

- In this section, we learned that changes in the brain are linked to advances in information processing. What did you learn about changes in brain structure and the cognitive abilities of infants, children, and adolescents in Chapter 4?

Reflect *Your Own Personal Journey of Life*

- In terms of your ability to learn, think about your early childhood, elementary, and middle school years. Describe a task on which you were faster in processing information in elementary school than in preschool, and then describe a task on which you were faster in processing information in middle school than in elementary school.

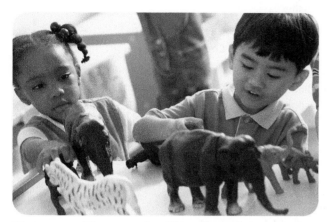

What are some different ways that children allocate their attention?

The world holds a lot of information to perceive. Right now, you are perceiving the letters and words that make up this sentence. Now look around you and pick out something to look at other than this book. After that, curl up the toes on your right foot. In each of these circumstances, you engaged in the process of paying attention. What is attention, and what effect does it have on processing information? How does attention change with age?

WHAT IS ATTENTION?

Attention is the focusing of mental resources. Attention improves cognitive processing for many tasks, from grabbing a toy to hitting a baseball or adding numbers. At any one time, though, children, like adults, can pay attention to only a limited amount of information. A recent study examined 7- and 8-month-old infants' visual attention to sequences of events that varied in complexity (Kidd, Piantadosi, & Aslin, 2012). The infants tended to look away from events that were overly simple or complex, preferring instead to attend to events of intermediate complexity.

Children allocate their attention in different ways (Colombo, Brez, & Curtindale, 2013; Fisher & others, 2013; Rueda & Posner, 2013). Psychologists have labeled these types of allocation as selective attention, divided attention, sustained attention, and executive attention.

- **Selective attention** is focusing on a specific aspect of experience that is relevant while ignoring others that are irrelevant (Stevens & Bavelier, 2012). Focusing on one voice among many in a crowded room or a noisy restaurant is an example of selective attention. When you switched your attention to the toes on your right foot, you were engaging in selective attention.

- **Divided attention** involves concentrating on more than one activity at the same time. If you are listening to music or a television program while you are reading this, you are engaging in divided attention.

- **Sustained attention** is the ability to maintain attention to a selected stimulus for a prolonged period of time. Sustained attention is also called *focused attention* and *vigilance*.

- **Executive attention** involves planning actions, allocating attention to goals, detecting and compensating for errors, monitoring progress on tasks, and dealing with novel or difficult circumstances.

INFANCY

How effectively can infants attend to something? Even newborns can detect a contour and fixate on it. Older infants scan patterns more thoroughly. By 4 months, infants can selectively attend to an object.

Orienting/Investigative Process   Attention in the first year of life is dominated by an *orienting/investigative process* (Colombo, Brez, & Curtindale, 2013). This process involves directing attention to potentially important locations in the environment (that is, *where*) and recognizing objects and their features (such as color and form) (that is, *what*) (Richards, 2011). From 3 to 9 months of age, infants can deploy their attention more flexibly and quickly.

Another important type of attention is *sustained attention*, also referred to as *focused attention* (Martin, Razza, & Brooks-Gunn, 2012). New stimuli typically elicit an orienting

---

developmental **connection**

Brain Development

Orienting attention to an object or event involves the parietal lobes in the cerebral cortex. Chapter 4, p. 111

---

attention Concentrating and focusing mental resources.

selective attention Focusing on a specific aspect of experience that is relevant while ignoring others that are irrelevant.

divided attention Concentrating on more than one activity at the same time.

sustained attention The ability to maintain attention to a selected stimulus for a prolonged period of time. Sustained attention is also called *focused attention* and *vigilance*.

executive attention Involves planning actions, allocating attention to goals, detecting and compensating for errors, monitoring progress on tasks, and dealing with novel or difficult circumstances.

response followed by sustained attention. It is sustained attention that allows infants to learn about and remember characteristics of a stimulus as it becomes familiar. Researchers have found that infants as young as 3 months of age can engage in 5 to 10 seconds of sustained attention. From this age through the second year, the length of sustained attention increases (Courage & Richards, 2008).

Habituation and Dishabituation   Closely linked with attention are the processes of habituation and dishabituation that we discussed in Chapter 5 (Kavsek, 2009, 2013). Recall that if a stimulus—a sight or sound—is presented to infants several times in a row, they usually pay less attention to it each time. This suggests they are bored with it. This is the process of *habituation*—decreased responsiveness to a stimulus after repeated presentations of the stimulus. *Dishabituation* is the recovery of a habituated response after a change in stimulation.

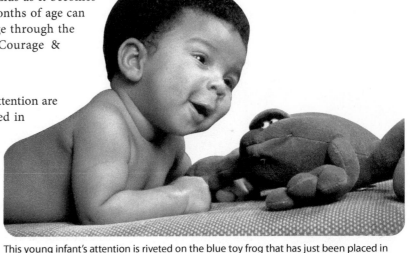

This young infant's attention is riveted on the blue toy frog that has just been placed in front of him. The young infant's attention to the toy frog will be strongly regulated by the processes of habituation and dishabituation. *What characterizes these processes?*

Infants' attention is so strongly governed by novelty and habituation that when an object becomes familiar, attention becomes shorter, making infants more vulnerable to distraction (Colombo, Brez, & Curtindale, 2013). Researchers study habituation to determine the extent to which infants can see, hear, smell, taste, and experience touch (Slater, Field, & Hernandez-Reif, 2007).

Parents can use knowledge of habituation and dishabituation to improve interaction with their infant. If parents keep repeating the same form of stimulation, the infant will stop responding. It is important for parents to do novel things and to repeat them often until the infant stops responding. Wise parents sense when the infant shows interest and know that many repetitions of the stimulus may be necessary for the infant to process the information. The parents stop or change their behavior when the infant redirects attention (Rosenblith, 1992).

developmental **connection**

Research Methods

Among the measures researchers use in habituation studies are sucking behavior, heart and respiration rates, and how long an infant looks at an object. Chapter 5, p. 151

Joint Attention   Another aspect of attention that is an important infant development is **joint attention,** in which individuals focus on the same object or event. Joint attention requires (1) an ability to track another's behavior, such as following someone's gaze; (2) one person directing another's attention; and (3) reciprocal interaction. Early in infancy, joint attention usually involves a caregiver pointing or using words to direct an infant's attention (Rossano, Carpenter, & Tomasello, 2012). Emerging forms of joint attention occur at about 7 to 8 months, but it is not until toward the end of the first year that joint attention skills are frequently observed (Liszkowski, 2007). In a study conducted by Rechele Brooks and Andrew Meltzoff (2005), at 10 to 11 months of age infants first began engaging in "gaze following," which involves looking where another person has just looked (see Figure 7.1). And by their first birthday, infants have begun to direct adults to objects that capture their interest (Heimann & others, 2006).

FIGURE **7.1**

GAZE FOLLOWING IN INFANCY. Researcher Rechele Brooks and colleague Andrew Meltzoff (2005) found that infants begin to engage in a behavior called "gaze following" at 10 to 11 months of age. *Why might gaze following be an important accomplishment for an infant?*

joint attention Individuals focusing on the same object or event; requires the ability to track another's behavior, one person directing another's attention, and reciprocal interaction.

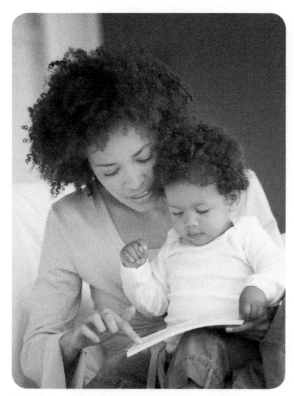

A mother and her infant daughter engaging in joint attention. *What about this photograph tells you that joint attention is occurring? Why is joint attention an important aspect of infant development?*

Joint attention plays important roles in many aspects of infant development and considerably increases infants' ability to learn from other people (Carpenter, 2011; Mateus & others, 2013). Nowhere is this more apparent than in observations of interchanges between caregivers and infants as infants are learning language (Tomasello, 2011). When caregivers and infants frequently engage in joint attention, infants say their first word earlier and develop a larger vocabulary (Flom & Pick, 2003). Later in the chapter in our discussion of language, we further discuss joint attention as an early predictor of language development in older infants and toddlers (Tomasello, 2011). A recent study also revealed that the extent to which 9-month-old infants engaged in joint attention was linked to their long-term memory (a one-week delay), possibly because joint attention enhances the relevance of attended items (Kopp & Lindenberger, 2012). Another recent study of 5-month-old infants found that a region of the prefrontal cortex was activated when they engaged in joint attention with another person (Grossmann & Johnson, 2010).

Joint attention skills in infancy also are associated with the development of self-regulation later in childhood. For example, a recent study revealed that responding to joint attention at 12 months of age was linked to self-regulation skills at 3 years of age that involved delaying gratification for an attractive object (Van Hecke & others, 2012).

CHILDHOOD

The child's ability to pay attention improves significantly during the preschool years (Bell & Cuevas, 2013; Rueda & Posner, 2013). The toddler wanders around, shifts attention from one activity to another, and seems to spend little time focused on any one object or event. In contrast, the preschool child might watch television for a half-hour at a time. In one study in which 99 families were observed in their homes for 4,672 hours, visual attention to television dramatically increased during the preschool years (Anderson & others, 1985). However, a recent research study revealed that television watching and video game playing were both linked to attention problems in children (Swing & others, 2010).

Young children especially make advances in two aspects of attention—executive attention and sustained attention. Mary Rothbart and Maria Gartstein (2008, p. 332) described why advances in executive and sustained attention are so important in early childhood:

> The development of the . . . executive attention system supports the rapid increases in effortful control in the toddler and preschool years. Increases in attention are due, in part, to advances in comprehension and language development. As children are better able to understand their environment, this increased appreciation of their surroundings helps them to sustain attention for longer periods of time.

In Central European countries such as Hungary, kindergarten children participate in exercises designed to improve their attention (Mills & Mills, 2000; Posner & Rothbart, 2007). For example, in one eye-contact exercise, the teacher sits in the center of a circle of children, and each child is required to catch the teacher's eye before being permitted to leave the group. In other exercises created to improve attention, teachers have children participate in stop-go activities during which they have to listen for a specific signal, such as a drumbeat or an exact number of rhythmic beats, before stopping the activity. Computer exercises also recently have been developed to improve children's attention (Jaeggi, Berman, & Jonides, 2009; Rueda & Posner, 2013; Stevens & Bavelier, 2012; Tang & Posner, 2009; Steiner & others, 2011). For example, one study revealed that five days of computer exercises that involved learning how to use a joystick, applying working memory, and resolving conflict improved the attention of 4- to 6-year-old children (Rueda & others, 2005). In one of the computer games young children have to move a joystick to keep a cat on the grass and out of the mud, and in another they help a cat find a

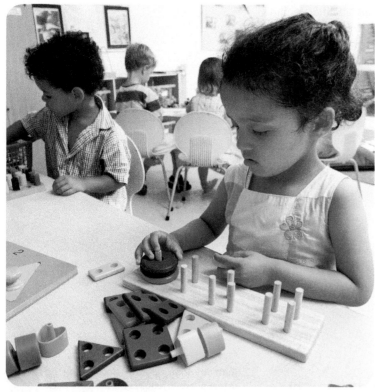

What are some advances in children's attention as they go through early childhood and middle and late childhood?

duck in a pond. Although these games are not commercially available, further information about computer exercises for improving children's attention is available at www.teach-the-brain.org/learn/attention/index.

Control over attention shows important changes during middle and late childhood (Posner & Rothbart, 2007; Wendelken & others, 2011). External stimuli are likely to determine the target of the preschooler's attention; what is salient, or obvious, grabs the preschooler's attention. For example, suppose a flashy, attractive clown presents the directions for solving a problem. Preschool children are likely to pay attention to the clown and ignore the directions, because they are influenced strongly by the salient features of the environment. After the age of 6 or 7, children pay more attention to features relevant to performing a task or solving a problem, such as the directions. Thus, instead of being controlled by the most striking stimuli in their environment, older children can direct their attention to more important stimuli. This change reflects a shift to *cognitive control* of attention, so that children act less impulsively and reflect more. Recall from Chapter 4 that the increase in cognitive control during the elementary school years is linked to changes in the brain, especially more focal activation in the prefrontal cortex (Diamond, 2013).

Preschool children's ability to control and sustain their attention is related to school readiness (Rothbart, 2011). For example, a study of more than 1,000 children revealed that their ability to sustain their attention at 54 months of age was linked to their school readiness (which included achievement and language skills) (NICHD Early Child Care Research Network, 2005). And in one study, children whose parents and teachers rated them as having fewer attention problems at 4½ years of age had a higher level of social skills in peer relations in the first and third grades (NICHD Early Child Care Research Network, 2009).

ADOLESCENCE

Adolescents typically have better attentional skills than children do, although there are wide individual differences in how effectively adolescents deploy their attention. Sustained and executive attention are very important aspects of adolescent cognitive development. As adolescents are required to engage in larger, increasingly complex tasks that require longer time frames to complete, their ability to sustain attention is critical for succeeding on the tasks. An increase in executive attention supports the rapid increase in effortful control required to effectively engage in these complex academic tasks (Rothbart & Gartstein, 2008).

One trend involving divided attention is adolescents' multitasking, which in some cases involves dividing attention not just between two activities, but even among three or more (Bauerlein, 2008). A major influence on the increase in multitasking is availability of multiple electronic media. Many adolescents have a range of electronic media at their disposal. It is not unusual for adolescents to simultaneously divide their attention among working on homework, engaging in an instant messaging conversation, surfing the Web, and listening to music on an iPod. And a national survey revealed that 50 percent of adolescents made and answered phone calls while driving, and 13 percent (approximately 1.7 million) wrote and/or read text messages while driving (Allstate Foundation, 2005).

Is this multitasking beneficial or distracting? Multitasking expands the information adolescents attend to and forces the brain to share processing resources, which can distract the adolescent's attention from what might be most important at the moment (Begley & Interlandi, 2008). And, if the key task is at all complex and challenging, such as trying to figure out how to solve a homework problem, multitasking considerably reduces attention to the key task (Myers, 2008).

Controlling attention is a key aspect of learning and thinking in adolescence and emerging adulthood (Bjorklund, 2012; Rueda & Posner, 2013). Distractions that can interfere with attention in adolescence and emerging adulthood come from the external environment (other students talking while the student is trying to listen to a lecture or when the student switches on a computer screen to Facebook during a lecture and looks at a new friend request, for example) or intrusive distractions from competing thoughts in the individual's mind. Self-oriented thoughts, such as worrying, self-doubt, and intense emotions, may especially interfere with focusing attention on thinking tasks (Gillig & Sanders, 2011; Walsh, 2011).

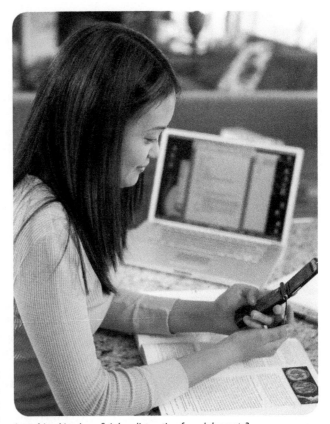

Is multitasking beneficial or distracting for adolescents?

developmental **connection**

Brain Development

One shift in activation of some areas of the brain more than others in middle and late childhood is from diffuse, large areas to more focused, smaller areas, which especially involves more focal activation in the prefrontal cortex. Chapter 4, p. 116

developmental **connection**

Media

A recent study revealed that when media multitasking was taken into account, 11- to 14-year-olds spent nearly 12 hours a day using media (Rideout, Foehr, & Roberts, 2010). Chapter 17, p. 500

Review

- What is attention? What are four ways in which children can allocate attention?
- How does attention develop in infancy?
- How does attention develop in childhood?
- What are some characteristics of attention in adolescence?

Connect

- In this section, you learned about joint attention. How might a child's ability to engage in joint attention be important in the successful implementation of a zone of proximal development teaching strategy?

Reflect *Your Own Personal Journey of Life*

- Imagine that you are an elementary school teacher. Devise some strategies to help children pay attention in class.

Memory **LG3** Describe what memory is and how it changes.

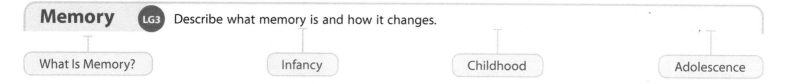

What Is Memory?   Infancy   Childhood   Adolescence

Twentieth-century American playwright Tennessee Williams once commented that life is all memory except for that one present moment that goes by so quickly that you can hardly catch it going. But just what do we do when we remember something, and how does our ability to remember develop?

WHAT IS MEMORY?

Memory is the retention of information over time. Without memory you would not be able to connect what happened to you yesterday with what is going on in your life today. Human memory is truly remarkable when you consider how much information we put into our memories and how much we must retrieve to perform all of life's activities.

Processes and Types of Memory   Researchers study how information is initially placed or encoded into memory, how it is retained or stored after being encoded, and how it is found or retrieved for a certain purpose later (see Figure 7.2). Encoding, storage, and retrieval are the basic processes required for memory. Failures can occur in any of these processes. Some part of an event might not be encoded, the mental representation of the event might not be stored, or even if the memory exists, you might not be able to retrieve it.

memory Retention of information over time.

short-term memory Limited-capacity memory system in which information is usually retained for up to 30 seconds, assuming there is no rehearsal of the information. Using rehearsal, individuals can keep the information in short-term memory longer.

long-term memory A relatively permanent and unlimited type of memory.

working memory A mental "workbench" where individuals manipulate and assemble information when making decisions, solving problems, and comprehending written and spoken language.

schema theory States that when people reconstruct information, they fit it into information that already exists in their minds.

schemas Mental frameworks that organize concepts and information.

Encoding

Getting information into memory

Storage

Retaining information over time

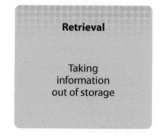

Retrieval

Taking information out of storage

FIGURE **7.2**

PROCESSING INFORMATION IN MEMORY. As you read about the many aspects of memory in this chapter, think about the organization of memory in terms of these three main activities.

Examining the storage process led psychologists to classify memories based on their permanence. **Short-term memory** is a memory system with a limited capacity in which information is usually retained for up to 15 to 30 seconds unless strategies are used to retain it longer. **Long-term memory** is a relatively permanent and unlimited type of memory. People are usually referring to long-term memory when they talk about "memory." When you remember the type of games you enjoyed playing as a child or the details of your first date, you are drawing on your long-term memory. But when you remember the word you just read a few seconds ago, you are using short-term memory.

When psychologists first analyzed short-term memory, they described it as if it were a passive storehouse with shelves to store information until it is moved to long-term memory. But we do many things with the information stored in short-term memory. For example, the words in this sentence are part of your short-term memory, and you are manipulating them to form a meaningful whole.

The concept of working memory acknowledges the importance of our manipulations of the information in short-term memory (Myatchin & Lagae, 2013). **Working memory** is a kind of mental "workbench" where individuals manipulate and assemble information when they make decisions, solve problems, and comprehend written and spoken language (Baddeley, 1990, 2001, 2007, 2010, 2012). Many psychologists prefer the term *working memory* over *short-term memory* to describe how memory works.

Figure 7.3 shows Alan Baddeley's model of working memory. Notice that it includes two short-term stores—one for speech and one for visual and spatial information—as well as a central executive. It is the job of the central executive to monitor and control the system—determining what information is stored, relating information from long-term memory to the information in the short-term stores, and moving information into long-term memory.

Working memory is linked to many aspects of children's development (Camos & Barrouillet, 2011; Baddeley, 2012). For example, children who have better working memory are more advanced in reading comprehension, math skills, and problem solving than their counterparts with less effective working memory (Dyck & Piek, 2010; Kroesbergen, van 't Noordende, & Kolkman, 2013; Nevo & Breznitz, 2013).

The following four recent studies illustrate the importance of working memory in children's cognitive development:

- Working memory and attention control predicted growth in emergent literacy and number skills in young children in low-income families (Welsh & others, 2010).

- Working memory capacity at 9 to 10 years of age predicted foreign language comprehension two years later at 11 to 12 years of age (Andersson, 2010).

- A computerized working memory intervention with 9- to 11-year-old children improved their reading performance (Loosli & others, 2012).

- Assessment of working memory in kindergarten was a key process in predicting math achievement at the end of the first grade (Monette, Bigras, & Guay, 2011).

Constructing Memories

Memory is not like a tape recorder or a camera or even like computer memory; we don't store and retrieve bits of data in computer-like fashion. Children and adults construct and reconstruct their memories (Bauer, 2013; De Brigard, Szpunar, & Schacter, 2013).

Schema Theory   According to **schema theory,** people mold memories to fit information that already exists in their minds. This process is guided by **schemas,** which are mental frameworks that organize concepts and information. Suppose a football fan and a visitor from a country

"Can we hurry up and get to the test? My short-term memory is better than my long-term memory."
© Wm Hoest Enterprises, Inc. Reprinted courtesy of Bunny Hoest.

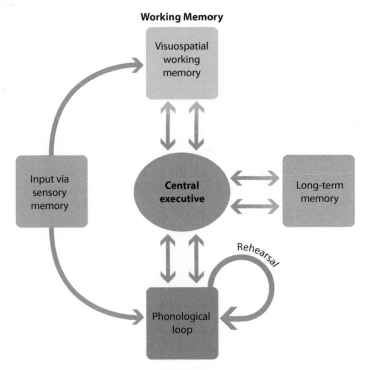

FIGURE **7.3**

WORKING MEMORY. In Baddeley's working memory model, working memory is like a mental workbench where a great deal of information processing is carried out. Working memory consists of three main components: the phonological loop and visuospatial working memory serve as assistants, helping the central executive do its work. Input from sensory memory goes to the phonological loop, where information about speech is stored and rehearsal takes place, and visuospatial working memory, where visual and spatial information, including imagery, are stored. Working memory is a limited-capacity system, and information is stored there for only a brief time. Working memory interacts with long-term memory, using information from long-term memory in its work and transmitting information to long-term memory for longer storage.

------------->

developmental **connection**

Gender

Gender schema theory emphasizes children's gender schemas that organize the world in terms of male and female. Chapter 12, p. 344

where the sport isn't played are eating at a restaurant and overhear a conversation about last night's game. Because the visitor doesn't have a schema for information about football, he or she is more likely than the fan to mishear what is said. Perhaps the visitor will interpret the conversation in terms of a schema for another sport, constructing a false memory of the conversation.

Schemas influence the way we encode, make inferences about, and retrieve information. We reconstruct the past rather than take an exact photograph of it, and the mind can distort an event as it encodes and stores impressions of it. Often when we retrieve information, we fill in the gaps with fragmented memories.

Fuzzy Trace Theory Another variation of how individuals reconstruct their memories has been proposed by Charles Brainerd and Valerie Reyna (2004; Holliday, Brainerd, & Reyna, 2011; Reyna & Brainerd, 1995). **Fuzzy trace theory** states that when individuals encode information, they create two types of memory representations: (1) a *verbatim memory trace*, which consists of precise details; and (2) a *fuzzy trace*, or *gist*, which is the central idea of the information. For example, consider a child who is presented with information about a pet store that has 10 birds, 6 cats, 8 dogs, and 7 rabbits. Then the child is asked two types of questions: (1) verbatim questions, such as "How many cats are in the pet store, 6 or 8?" and (2) gist questions, such as "Are there more cats or more dogs in the pet store?" Researchers have found that preschool children tend to remember verbatim information more than gist information, but elementary-school-aged children are more likely to remember gist information (Brainerd & Gordon, 1994). The increased use of gist by elementary-school-aged children accounts for their improved memory because fuzzy traces are less likely to be forgotten than verbatim traces (Reyna & Rivers, 2008).

Content Knowledge and Expertise Our ability to remember new information about a subject depends considerably on what we already know about it (Staszewski, 2013). Much of the research on the role of knowledge in memory has compared experts and novices (Ericsson & others, 2006). *Experts* have acquired extensive knowledge about a particular content area; this knowledge influences what they notice and how they organize, represent, and interpret information. This in turn affects their ability to remember, reason, and solve problems. When individuals have expertise about a particular subject, their memory also tends to be good regarding material related to that subject (Gobet & Charness, 2006).

For example, one study found that 10- and 11-year-olds who were experienced chess players ("experts") were able to remember more information about chess pieces than college students who were not chess players ("novices") (Chi, 1978) (see Figure 7.4). In contrast, when the college students were presented with other stimuli, they were able to remember them better than the children were. Thus, the children's expertise in chess gave them superior memories, but only in chess.

There are developmental changes in expertise. Older children usually have more expertise about a subject than younger children do, which can contribute to their better memory for the subject.

In their study of memory, researchers have not extensively examined the roles that sociocultural factors might play. In *Connecting with Diversity*, we will explore culture's role in children's memory.

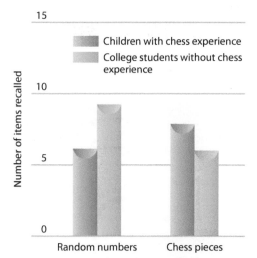

FIGURE 7.4

MEMORY FOR NUMBERS AND CHESS PIECES. Notice that when 10- and 11-year-old children and college students were asked to remember a string of random numbers that had been presented to them, the college students fared better. However, the 10- and 11-year-olds who had experience playing chess ("experts") had better memory for the location of chess pieces on a chess board than college students with no chess experience ("novices") (Chi, 1978).

fuzzy trace theory States that memory is best understood by considering two types of memory representations: (1) verbatim memory trace; and (2) fuzzy trace, or gist. According to this theory, older children's better memory is attributed to the fuzzy traces created by extracting the gist of information.

INFANCY

Popular child-rearing expert Penelope Leach (1990) told parents that 6- to 8-month-old babies cannot hold in their mind a picture of their mother or father. Child development researchers, however, have revealed that infants as young as 3 months of age show a limited type of memory (Courage, Howe, & Squires, 2004).

Culture and Children's Memory

A culture sensitizes its members to certain objects, events, and strategies, which in turn can influence the nature of memory (Bauer & Fivush, 2013; Fivush, 2009). In schema theory, a child's background, which is encoded in schemas, is revealed in the way the child reconstructs a story. This effect of cultural background on memory is called the *cultural-specificity hypothesis*. It states that cultural experiences determine what is relevant in a person's life and thus what the person is likely to remember. For example, imagine a child living on a remote island in the Pacific Ocean whose parents make their livelihood by fishing. The child's memory about how weather affects fishing is likely to be highly developed. By contrast, a Pacific Islander child might be hard-pressed to encode and recall the details of a major league baseball team.

Cultures may vary in the strategies that children use to remember information, and these cultural variations are usually due to schooling (Cole & Packer, 2011). Children who have experienced schooling are more likely to cluster items together in meaningful ways, which helps them to remember the items. Schooling provides children with specialized information-processing tasks, such as committing large amounts of information to memory in a short time frame and using logical reasoning, that may generate specialized memory strategies. However, there is no evidence that

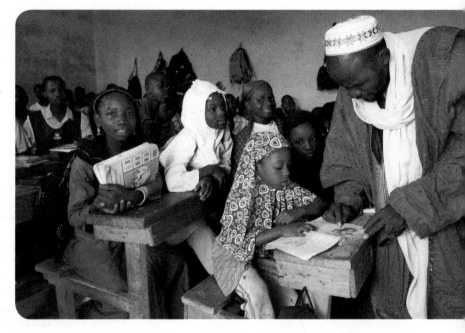

Students in class at a school in Mali, Africa. *How might their schooling influence their memory?*

schooling increases memory capacity per se; rather, it influences the strategies for remembering (Cole & Packer, 2011).

Scripts are schemas for an event. In one study, adolescents in the United States and Mexico remembered according to script-based knowledge (Harris, Schoen, & Hensley, 1992). In line with common practices in their respective cultures, adolescents in the United States remembered information about a dating script better when no chaperone was present on a date, whereas adolescents in Mexico remembered the information better when a chaperone was present.

American children, especially American girls, describe autobiographical narratives

that are longer, more detailed, more specific, and more 'personal' (both in terms of mention of self, and mention of internal states), than narratives

by children from China and Korea. The pattern is consistent with expectations derived from the finding that in their conversations about past events, American mothers and their children are more elaborative and more focused on autonomous themes . . . and that Korean mothers and their children have less frequent and less detailed conversations about the past. . . . (Bauer, 2006, p. 411)

Possibly the more elaborated content of American children's narratives contributes to the earlier first memories researchers have found in American adults (Han, Leichtman, & Wang, 1998).

How might guided participation, which is used in many different cultures (as discussed in Chapter 6), support the influence of culture on memory?

First Memories   Carolyn Rovee-Collier (1987, 2007; Rovee-Collier & Barr, 2010) has conducted research demonstrating that infants can remember perceptual-motor information. In a characteristic experiment, she places a baby in a crib underneath an elaborate mobile and ties one end of a ribbon to the baby's ankle and the other end to the mobile. The baby kicks and makes the mobile move (see Figure 7.5). Weeks later, the baby is returned to the crib, but its foot is not tied to the mobile. The baby kicks, apparently trying to make the mobile move. However, if the mobile's makeup is changed even slightly, the baby doesn't kick. If the mobile is then restored to being exactly as it was when the baby's ankle was originally tied to it, the baby will begin kicking again. According to Rovee-Collier, even by 2½ months the baby's memory is incredibly detailed.

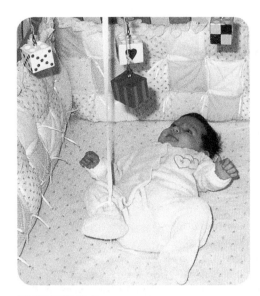

FIGURE **7.5**

THE TECHNIQUE USED IN ROVEE-COLLIER'S INVESTIGATION OF INFANT MEMORY. In Rovee-Collier's experiment, infants as young as 2½ months of age retained information from the experience of being conditioned. *What did infants recall in Rovee-Collier's experiment?*

Age Group	Length of Delay
6-month-olds	24 hours
9-month-olds	1 month
10–11-month-olds	3 months
13–14-month-olds	4–6 months
20-month-olds	12 months

FIGURE **7.6**

AGE-RELATED CHANGES IN THE LENGTH OF TIME OVER WHICH MEMORY OCCURS.
Source: Bauer (2009).

implicit memory Memory without conscious recollection; memory of skills and routine procedures that are performed automatically.

explicit memory Conscious memory of facts and experiences.

How well can infants remember? Some researchers such as Rovee-Collier have concluded that infants as young as 2 to 6 months of age can remember some experiences through 1½ to 2 years of age (Rovee-Collier & Barr, 2010). However, critics such as Jean Mandler (2000), a leading expert on infant cognition, argue that the infants in Rovee-Collier's experiments are displaying only implicit memory. **Implicit memory** refers to memory without conscious recollection—memories of skills and routine procedures that are performed automatically, such as riding a bicycle. In contrast, **explicit memory** refers to the conscious memory of facts and experiences.

When people think about memory, they are usually referring to explicit memory. Most researchers find that babies do not show explicit memory until the second half of the first year (Bauer, 2013). Then, explicit memory improves substantially during the second year of life (Ghetti & Bauer, 2012). In a longitudinal study, infants were assessed several times during their second year (Bauer & others, 2000). Older infants showed more accurate memory and required fewer prompts to demonstrate their memory than younger infants did. Figure 7.6 summarizes how long researchers have found infants of different ages can remember information (Bauer, 2009). As indicated in Figure 7.6, researchers have documented that 6-month-olds can remember information for 24 hours, but by 20 months of age infants can remember information they encountered 12 months earlier.

What changes in the brain are linked to infants' memory development? From about 6 to 12 months of age, the maturation of the hippocampus and the surrounding cerebral cortex, especially the frontal lobes, makes the emergence of explicit memory possible (Bauer, 2013; Nelson, 2012) (see Figure 7.7). Explicit memory continues to improve in the second year, as these brain structures further mature and connections between them increase. Less is known about the areas of the brain involved in implicit memory in infancy.

Cerebral cortex (tan-colored area with wrinkles and folds)

Frontal lobe

Hippocampus

FIGURE **7.7**

KEY BRAIN STRUCTURES INVOLVED IN EXPLICIT MEMORY DEVELOPMENT IN INFANCY

Infantile Amnesia Let's examine another aspect of memory. Do you remember your third birthday party? Probably not. Most adults can remember little, if anything, from the first three years of their life (Riggins, 2012). This is called *infantile,* or *childhood, amnesia.* The few reported adult memories of life at age 2 or 3 are at best very sketchy (Howe, Courage,

& Rooksby, 2009). Elementary school children also do not remember much about their early childhood years (Lie & Newcombe, 1999).

What is the cause of infantile amnesia? One reason older children and adults have difficulty recalling events from their infant and early child years is that during these early years the prefrontal lobes of the brain are immature; this area of the brain is believed to play an important role in storing memories of events (Boyer & Diamond, 1992).

In sum, most of young infants' conscious memories appear to be rather fragile and short-lived, although their implicit memory of perceptual-motor actions can be substantial (Bauer, 2013; Mandler, 2004). By the end of the second year, long-term memory is more substantial and reliable (Ghetti & Bauer, 2012).

CHILDHOOD

Children's memory improves considerably after infancy (Bauer & Fivush, 2013; Bjorklund, 2013). Sometimes the long-term memories of preschoolers seem erratic, but young children can remember a great deal of information if they are given appropriate cues and prompts.

One reason children remember less than adults is that they are far less expert in most areas, but their growing knowledge is one likely source of their memory improvement. For example, a child's ability to recount what she has seen on a trip to the library depends greatly on what she already knows about libraries, such as where books on certain topics are located, how to check out books, and so on. If a child knows little about libraries, she will have a much more difficult time recounting what she saw there.

Fuzzy trace theory suggests another way in which memory develops during childhood. Recall from our earlier discussion that young children tend to encode, store, and retrieve verbatim traces, whereas elementary-school-aged children begin to use gist more. The increased use of gist likely produces more enduring memory traces of information. Other sources of improvement in children's memory include changes in memory span and their use of strategies.

Memory Span   Unlike long-term memory, short-term memory has a very limited capacity. One method of assessing that capacity is the *memory-span task*. You simply hear a short list of stimuli—usually digits—presented at a rapid pace (one per second, for example). Then you are asked to repeat the digits.

Research with the memory-span task suggests that short-term memory increases during childhood (Schneider, 2011). For example, in one investigation, memory span increased from about two digits in 2-year-old children to about five digits in 7-year-old children. Between 7 and 12 years of age, memory span increased by only one and a half digits (Dempster, 1981) (see Figure 7.8). Keep in mind, though, that individuals have different memory spans.

Why does memory span change with age? Speed of processing information is important, especially the speed with which memory items can be identified. For example, one study tested children on their speed at repeating words presented orally (Case, Kurland, & Goldberg, 1982). Speed of repetition was a powerful predictor of memory span. Indeed, when the speed of repetition was controlled, the 6-year-olds' memory spans were equal to those of young adults. Rehearsal of information is also important; older children rehearse the digits more than younger children. And children are more effective in using strategies to remember in middle childhood than in early childhood (Schneider, 2011).

Strategies   Learning to use effective strategies is a key aspect of improving memory (MacArthur, 2012; McCormick, Dimmitt, & Sullivan, 2013). Rehearsal is just one of the strategies that can sometimes aid memory, although rehearsal is a better strategy for short-term memory than long-term memory. Following are some strategies that benefit children's long-term retention of information.

Organization   If children organize information when they encode it, their memory benefits. Consider this demonstration: Recall the 12 months of the year as quickly as you can. How long did it take you? What was the order of your recall? You probably answered something like "a few seconds" and "in chronological order." Now try to remember the months of the year in alphabetical order. Did you make any errors? How long did it take you? It should be obvious that your memory for the months of the year is organized in a particular way.

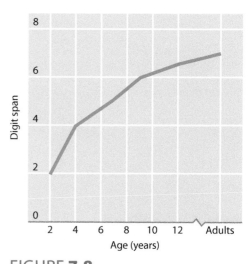

FIGURE **7.8**

DEVELOPMENTAL CHANGES IN MEMORY SPAN. In one study, memory span increased by about three digits from 2 years of age to 7 years of age (Dempster, 1981). By 12 years of age, memory span had increased on average another one and a half digits.

Frank and Ernest

FRANK & ERNEST © Thaves/Dist. by United Features Syndicate, Inc.

Organizing is a strategy that older children (and adults) typically use, and it helps them to remember information. Preschool children usually don't use strategies like organization; in middle and late childhood they are more likely to use organization when they need to remember something (Flavell, Miller, & Miller, 2002).

Elaboration   Another important strategy is elaboration, which involves engaging in more extensive processing of information. When individuals engage in elaboration, their memory benefits. Thinking of examples is a good way to elaborate information. For example, self-reference is an effective way to elaborate information. Thinking about personal associations with information makes the information more meaningful and helps children to remember it.

The use of elaboration changes developmentally (Pressley, 2003; Schneider, 2011). Adolescents are more likely than children to use elaboration spontaneously. Elementary-school-aged children can be taught to use elaboration strategies on a learning task, but they will be less likely than adolescents to use the strategies on other learning tasks in the future. Nonetheless, verbal elaboration can be an effective strategy even for young elementary-school-aged children.

Imagery   Creating mental images is another strategy for improving memory. However, using imagery to remember verbal information works better for older children than for younger children (Schneider, 2004, 2011). Using mental imagery can help young school-children to remember pictures (Schneider, 2004, 2011).

Teaching Strategies   So far we have described several important strategies adults can adopt when guiding children to remember information more effectively over the long term. These strategies include guiding children to organize information, elaborate the information, and develop images of the information. Another good strategy is to encourage children to understand the material that needs to be remembered rather than rotely memorizing it. Two other strategies adults can use to guide children's retention of memory were recently proposed:

- Repeat with variation on the instructional information and link early and often. These are memory development research expert Patricia Bauer's (2009) recommendations to improve children's consolidation and reconsolidation of the information they are learning. Variations on a lesson theme increase the number of associations in memory storage, and linking expands the network of associations in memory storage; both strategies expand the routes for retrieving information from storage.

- Embed memory-relevant language when instructing children. Teachers vary considerably in how much they use memory-relevant language that encourages students to remember information. In recent research that involved extensive observations of a number of first-grade teachers in the classroom, Peter Ornstein & his colleagues (Ornstein, Coffman, & Grammer, 2007, 2009; Ornstein & others, 2010) found that in the time segments observed, the teachers rarely used strategy suggestions or metacognitive (thinking about thinking) questions. In this research, when lower-achieving students were placed in classrooms in which teachers were categorized as "high-mnemonic teachers" who frequently embedded memory-relevant information in their teaching, their achievement increased (Ornstein, Coffman, & Grammer, 2007).

What are some good teaching strategies for guiding children's long-term memory?

Reconstructive Memory and Children as Eyewitnesses Children's memories, like those of adults, are constructive and reconstructive. Children have schemas for all sorts of information, and these schemas affect how they encode, store, and retrieve memories. If a teacher tells her class a story about two men and two women who were involved in a train crash in France, students won't remember every detail of the story and will reconstruct the story, putting their own individual stamp on it. One student might reconstruct the story by saying the characters died in a plane crash, another might describe three men and three women, another might say the crash was in Germany, and so on.

Reconstruction and distortion are nowhere more apparent than in clashing testimony given by eyewitnesses at trials. A special concern is susceptibility to suggestion and how this can alter memory (Bruck & Ceci, 2012; Budd, Connell, & Clark, 2013; Lamb & Malloy, 2013). Consider a study of individuals who had visited Disneyland (Pickrell & Loftus, 2001). Four groups of participants read ads and answered questionnaires about a trip to Disneyland. One group saw an ad that mentioned no cartoon characters; the second read the same ad and saw a 4-foot-tall cardboard figure of Bugs Bunny; the third read a fake ad for Disneyland with Bugs Bunny on it; and the fourth saw the same fake ad along with cardboard Bugs. Participants were asked whether they had ever met Bugs Bunny at Disneyland. Less than 10 percent of those in the first two groups reported having met Bugs Bunny at Disneyland, but approximately 30 to 40 percent of the third and fourth groups remembered meeting Bugs there. People were persuaded they had met Bugs Bunny at Disneyland, even though Bugs is a Warner Brothers character who would never appear at a Disney theme park.

The following conclusions about children as eyewitnesses indicate that a number of factors can influence the accuracy of a young child's memory (Bruck & Ceci, 1999):

- *There are age differences in children's susceptibility to suggestion.* Preschoolers are the most suggestible age group in comparison with older children and adults (Ceci, Papierno, & Kulkofsky, 2007). For example, preschool children are more susceptible to believing misleading or incorrect information given after an event (Ghetti & Alexander, 2004). Despite these age differences, there is still concern about the reaction of older children when they are subjected to suggestive interviews (La Rooy, Brown, & Lamb, 2013; Poole & Lindsay, 1996).

- *There are individual differences in susceptibility.* Some preschoolers are highly resistant to interviewers' suggestions, whereas others immediately succumb to the slightest suggestion (Bruck & Ceci, 2012; Kuehnle & Connell, 2013).

- *Interviewing techniques can produce substantial distortions in children's reports about highly salient events.* Children are suggestible not just about peripheral details but also about the central aspects of an event (Malloy & others, 2012). When children do accurately recall information about an event, the interviewer often has a neutral tone, there is limited use of misleading questions, and there is an absence of any motivation for the child to make a false report (Bruck & Ceci, 2012).

In sum, whether a young child's eyewitness testimony is accurate may depend on a number of factors such as the type, number, and intensity of the suggestive techniques the child has experienced (Bruck & Ceci, 2012; Spencer & Lamb, 2013).

ADOLESCENCE

There has been little research on memory changes in adolescence. As you saw in Figure 7.8, memory span (which is a measure of short-term memory) increases during adolescence. There also is evidence that working memory increases during adolescence. In one study, the performances of individuals from 6 to 57 years of age were examined on both verbal and visuospatial working memory tasks (Swanson, 1999). As shown in Figure 7.9, working memory increased substantially from 8 through 24 years of age no matter what the task. Thus, the adolescent years are likely to be an important developmental period for improvement in working memory. Note that working memory continues to improve through the transition to adulthood and beyond.

Four-year-old Jennifer Royal was the only eyewitness to one of her playmates being shot to death. She was allowed to testify in open court, and the clarity of her statements helped to convict the gunman. *What are some issues involved in whether young children should be allowed to testify in court?*

Verbal tasks

Semantic Association
1.33 | 1.70 | 1.86 | 2.24 | 2.60

Digit/Sentence
1.75 | 2.34 | 2.94 | 2.98 | 3.71

Visuospatial tasks

Mapping/Directions
3.13 | 3.60 | 4.09 | 3.92 | 4.64

Visual Matrix
1.67 | 2.06 | 2.51 | 2.68 | 3.47

Age 8 | Age 10 | Age 13 | Age 16 | Age 24

FIGURE **7.9**

DEVELOPMENTAL CHANGES IN WORKING MEMORY. *Note:* The scores shown here are the means for each age group, and the age also represents a mean age. Higher scores reflect superior working memory performance.

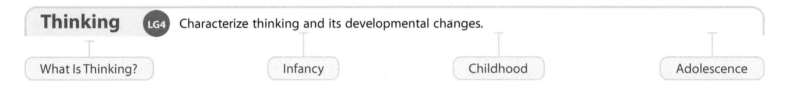

Review *Connect* Reflect

(LG3) Describe what memory is and how it changes.

Review

- What is memory? What are some important processes and types of memory?
- How does memory develop in infancy?
- How does memory change in childhood?
- How does memory change in adolescence?

Connect

- In this section, we learned about *schemas* as they relate to memory. How is this concept similar to or different from the concept of *schemes*, as related to Piaget's theory of development discussed in Chapter 6?

Reflect *Your Own Personal Journey of Life*

- What is your earliest memory? Why do you think you can remember this particular situation?

Thinking (LG4) Characterize thinking and its developmental changes.

What Is Thinking? | Infancy | Childhood | Adolescence

Attention and memory are often steps toward another level of information processing—thinking. What is thinking? How does it change developmentally? What is children's scientific thinking like, and how do they solve problems? Let's explore these questions.

WHAT IS THINKING?

Thinking involves manipulating and transforming information in memory; it is the job of the central executive in Baddeley's model of working memory shown in Figure 7.3. We think in order to reason, reflect, evaluate ideas, solve problems, and make decisions. Let's explore how thinking changes developmentally, beginning with infancy.

INFANCY

Interest in thinking during infancy has especially focused on concept formation and categorization (Gelman, 2013; Rakison & Lawson, 2013). **Concepts** are cognitive groupings of similar objects, events, people, or ideas. Without concepts, you would see each object and event as unique; you would not be able to make any generalizations.

Do infants have concepts? Yes, they do, although we do not know just how early concept formation begins (Quinn & others, 2013).

"For God's sake, think! Why is he being so nice to you?"
Copyright © The New Yorker Collection, 1998, Sam Gross from cartoonbank.com. All rights reserved.

thinking Transforming and manipulating information in memory. Individuals think in order to reason, reflect, evaluate ideas, solve problems, and make decisions.

concepts Cognitive groupings of similar objects, events, people, or ideas.

Using habituation experiments like those described in Chapter 5, some researchers have found that infants as young as 3 to 4 months of age can group together objects with similar appearances, such as animals (Quinn & others, 2013). This research capitalizes on the knowledge that infants are more likely to look at a novel object than a familiar object.

Jean Mandler (2004, 2010) argues that these early categorizations are best described as *perceptual categorization*. That is, the categorizations are based on similar perceptual features of objects, such as size, color, and movement, as well as parts of objects, such as legs for animals. Mandler (2004) concludes that it is not until about 7 to 9 months of age that infants form *conceptual* categories rather than just making perceptual discriminations between different categories. In one study of 9- to 11-month-olds, infants classified birds as animals and airplanes as vehicles even though the objects were perceptually similar—airplanes and birds with their wings spread (Mandler & McDonough, 1993) (see Figure 7.10).

Further advances in categorization occur in the second year of life (Booth & Ware, 2010). Many infants' "first concepts are broad and global in nature, such as 'animal' or 'indoor thing.' Gradually, over the first two years these broad concepts become more differentiated into concepts such as 'land animal,' then 'dog,' or to 'furniture,' then 'chair'" (Mandler, 2009, p. 1). Also in the second year, infants often categorize objects on the basis of their shape (Landau, Smith, & Jones, 1998).

Learning to put things into the correct categories—what makes something one kind of thing rather than another kind of thing, such as what makes a bird a bird, or a fish a fish—is an important aspect of learning. As infant development researcher Alison Gopnik (2010, p. 159) pointed out, "If you can sort the world into the right categories—put things in the right boxes—then you've got a big advance on understanding the world."

Do some very young children develop an intense, passionate interest in a particular category of objects or activities? One study confirmed that they do (DeLoache, Simcock, & Macari, 2007). A striking finding was the large gender difference in categories, with an intense interest in particular categories stronger for boys than girls. Categorization of boys' intense interests focused on vehicles, trains, machines, dinosaurs, and balls; girls' intense interests were more likely to involve dress-ups and books/reading. When your author's grandson Alex was 18 to 24 months old, he already had developed an intense, passionate interest in the category of vehicles. For example, at this age, he categorized vehicles into such subcategories as cars, trucks, earth-moving equipment, and buses. In addition to common classifications of cars into police cars, jeeps, taxis, and such, and trucks into fire trucks, dump trucks, and the like, his categorical knowledge of earth-moving equipment included bulldozers and excavators, and he categorized buses into school buses, London buses, and funky Malta buses (retro buses on the island of Malta). Later, at 2 to 3 years of age, Alex developed an intense, passionate interest in categorizing dinosaurs.

In sum, the infant's advances in processing information—through attention, memory, imitation, and concept formation—is much richer, more gradual and less stage-like, and occurs earlier than was envisioned by earlier theorists, such as Piaget (Bauer, 2013; Diamond, 2013; Meltzoff & Williamson, 2013; Quinn & others, 2013). As leading infant researcher Jean Mandler (2004) concluded, "The human infant shows a remarkable degree of learning power and complexity in what is being learned and in the way it is represented" (p. 304).

FIGURE **7.10**

CATEGORIZATION IN 9- TO 11-MONTH-OLDS. These are the stimuli used in the study that indicated 9- to 11-month-old infants categorized birds as animals and airplanes as vehicles even though the objects were perceptually similar (Mandler & McDonough, 1993).

> Infants are creating concepts and organizing their world into conceptual domains that will form the backbone of their thought throughout life.
>
> —**JEAN MANDLER**
> *Contemporary Psychologist, University of California–San Diego*

The author's grandson Alex at 2 years of age showing his intense, passionate interest in the category of vehicles while playing with a London taxi and a funky Malta bus.

CHILDHOOD

To explore thinking in childhood, we will examine four important types of thinking: executive function, critical thinking, scientific thinking, and problem solving.

Executive Function   Recently, interest has increased regarding the development of children's **executive function,** an umbrella-like concept that encompasses a number of

executive function An umbrella-like concept that consists of a number of higher-level cognitive processes linked to the development of the brain's prefrontal cortex. Executive function involves managing one's thoughts to engage in goal-directed behavior and to exercise self-control.

MINDS AT WORK

developmental **connection**

The Brain

The prefrontal cortex is the location in the brain where much of executive function occurs. Chapter 4, p. 116

◄ — — — — — — — — — — —

FIGURE **7.11**

STUDYING EXECUTIVE FUNCTION IN YOUNG CHILDREN.
Researcher Stephanie Carlson has conducted a number of research studies on young children's executive function. In one study, young children were read either *Planet Opposite*—a fantasy book in which everything is turned upside down—or *Fun Town*—a reality-oriented fiction book (Carlson & White, 2011). After being read one of the books, the young children completed the Less Is More Task, in which they were shown two trays of candy—one with 5 pieces, the other with 2—and told that the tray they pick will be given to the stuffed animal seated at the table. This task is difficult for 3-year-olds who tend to pick up the tray that they themselves want (and so ending up losing the tray to the stuffed animal). Sixty percent of the 3-year-olds who heard the *Planet Opposite* story selected the smaller number of candies (hence keeping the five pieces of candy), compared with only 20 percent of their counterparts who heard the more straightforward story. The results indicated that learning about a topsy-turvy imaginary world likely helped the young children become more flexible in their thinking.

higher-level cognitive processes linked to the development of the brain's prefrontal cortex. Executive function involves managing one's thoughts to engage in goal-directed behavior and to exercise self-control (Carlson, Zelazo, & Faja, 2013; Liew, 2012; Zhou, Chen, & Main, 2012). Earlier in this chapter, we described the recent interest in *executive attention,* which comes under the umbrella of executive function.

In early childhood, executive function especially involves developmental advances in cognitive inhibition (such as inhibiting a strong tendency that is incorrect), cognitive flexibility (such as shifting attention to another item or topic), goal-setting (such as sharing a toy or mastering a skill like catching a ball), and delay of gratification (the ability to forego an immediate pleasure or reward for a more desirable one later) (Beck & others, 2011; Bell & Cuevas, 2013; Carlson & White, 2011). During early childhood, the relatively stimulus-driven toddler is transformed into a child capable of flexible, goal-directed problem solving that characterizes executive function (Zelazo & Muller, 2011). Figure 7.11 describes a research study on young children's executive function (Carlson & White, 2011).

Researchers have discovered that advances in executive function in the preschool years are linked with school readiness (Ursache, Blair, & Raver, 2012). Parents and teachers play important roles in the development of executive function. Ann Masten and her colleagues (Herbers & others, 2011; Masten, 2013; Masten & others, 2008) have found that executive function and parenting skills are linked to homeless children's success in school. Masten believes that executive function and good parenting skills are related. In her words, "When we see kids with good executive function, we often see adults around them that are good self-regulators. . . . Parents model, they support, and they scaffold these skills" (Masten, 2012, p. 11).

How might executive function change during the middle and late childhood years and be linked to children's success in school? Adele Diamond and Kathleen Lee (2011) recently highlighted the following dimensions of executive function that they conclude are the most important for 4- to 11-year-old children's cognitive development and school success:

- *Self-control/inhibition.* Children need to develop self-control that will allow them to concentrate and persist on learning tasks, to inhibit their tendencies to repeat incorrect responses, and to resist the impulse to do something now that they would regret later.
- *Working memory.* Children need an effective working memory to process the masses of information they will encounter as they go through school and beyond.
- *Flexibility.* Children need to be flexible in their thinking to consider different strategies and perspectives.

Some researchers have found that executive function is a better predictor of school readiness than general IQ (Blair & Razza, 2007). A number of diverse activities have been found to increase children's executive function, such as computerized training that uses games to improve working memory (CogMed, 2013), aerobic exercise (Chang & others, 2012), mindfulness (the Tools of the Mind program discussed in Chapter 6, for example) (Bodrova, Leong, & Akhutina, 2011), and some types of school curricula (the Montessori curriculum, for example) (Diamond, 2013; Diamond & Lee, 2011).

Further, a longitudinal study of an important dimension of executive function—inhibitory control—found that 3- to 11-year-old children who had better inhibitory control (able to wait their turn, not easily distracted, more persistent, and less impulsive) were more likely to still be in school, less likely to engage in risk-taking behavior, and less likely to be taking drugs in adolescence (Moffitt & others, 2011). Thirty years after they were initially assessed, the children with better inhibitory control had better physical and mental health (they were less likely to be overweight, for example), had better earnings in their career, were more law-abiding, and were happier (Moffitt, 2012; Moffitt & others, 2011).

Some critics argue that not much benefit is derived from placing various cognitive processes under the broader concept of executive function. Although we have described a number of components of executive function here—working memory, cognitive inhibition, cognitive flexibility, and so on—a consensus has not been reached on what the components are, how they are connected, and how they develop. That said, the concept of executive function is not likely to go away any time soon, and further research, especially meta-analyses, should provide a clearer picture of executive function and how it develops (Luszcz, 2013).

Critical Thinking Executive function also involves the ability to think critically in effective ways. Currently, there is considerable interest among psychologists and educators in critical thinking (Sternberg & Sternberg, 2013). **Critical thinking** involves thinking reflectively and productively, and evaluating evidence. If you think critically, you will do the following things:

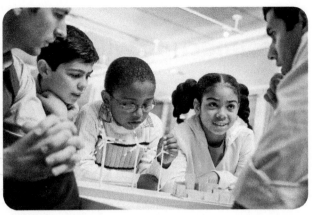

What are some good strategies for guiding students to think critically?

- Ask not only what happened but how and why.
- Examine supposed "facts" to determine whether there is evidence to support them.
- Argue in a reasoned way rather than through emotions.
- Recognize that there is sometimes more than one good answer or explanation.
- Compare various answers and judge which is the best answer.
- Evaluate what other people say rather than immediately accepting it as the truth.
- Ask questions and speculate beyond what is known to create new ideas and new information.

In the view of critics such as Jacqueline and Martin Brooks (1993, 2001), few schools teach students to think critically. Schools push students to give a single correct answer rather than encouraging them to come up with new ideas and rethink conclusions. Too often teachers ask students to recite, define, describe, state, and list rather than to analyze, infer, connect, synthesize, criticize, create, evaluate, think, and rethink. As a result, many schools graduate students who think superficially, staying on the surface of problems rather than becoming deeply engaged in meaningful thinking.

One way to encourage students to think critically is to present them with controversial topics or both sides of an issue to discuss (Osborne, 2010). Some teachers shy away from having students debate issues because arguments supposedly are not "polite" or "nice" (Winn, 2004). But debates can motivate students to delve more deeply into a topic and examine issues, especially if teachers refrain from stating their own views so that students feel free to explore multiple perspectives.

According to Ellen Langer (2005), **mindfulness**—being alert, mentally present, and cognitively flexible while going through life's everyday activities and tasks—is an important aspect of thinking critically. Mindful children and adults maintain an active awareness of the circumstances in their life and are motivated to find the best solutions to tasks. Mindful individuals create new ideas, are open to new information, and can operate from more than one perspective. By contrast, mindless individuals are entrapped in old ideas, engage in automatic behavior, and operate from a single perspective.

Recently, Robert Roeser and Philip Zelazo have emphasized that mindfulness is an important mental process that children can engage in to improve a number of cognitive and socioemotional skills, such as executive function, focused attention, emotion regulation, and empathy (Roeser & Zelazo, 2012). It has been proposed that mindfulness training could be implemented in schools, using age-appropriate activities that increase children's reflection on moment-to-moment experiences to improve self-regulation (Zelazo & Lyons, 2012).

In addition to mindfulness, techniques such as yoga, meditation, and tai chi have been recently proposed as candidates for improving children's cognitive and socioemotional development. Together these activities are being grouped under the topic of *reflective science,* a cross-disciplinary term that involves the study of how various types of mental and physical training might enhance children's development (Roeser & Zelazo, 2012).

To read about one developmental psychologist who used her training in cognitive development to pursue a career in an applied area, see the *Connecting with Careers* profile.

developmental **connection**

Exercise

Recent research indicates that more physically fit children have better thinking skills, including those involving executive function, than less physically fit children. Chapter 4, pp. 132–133

critical thinking Thinking reflectively and productively, and evaluating the evidence.

mindfulness Being alert, mentally present, and cognitively flexible while going through life's everyday activities and tasks.

connecting with careers

Helen Schwe, Developmental Psychologist and Toy Designer

Helen Schwe obtained a Ph.D. from Stanford University in developmental psychology, but she now spends her days talking with computer engineers and designing "smart" toys for children. Smart toys are designed to improve children's problem-solving and symbolic thinking skills.

When she was a graduate student, Schwe worked part-time for Hasbro toys, testing its children's software on preschoolers. Her first job after graduate school was with Zowie Entertainment, which was subsequently bought by LEGO. According to Schwe, "Even in a toy's most primitive stage of development, . . . you see children's creativity in responding to challenges, their satisfaction when a problem is solved or simply their delight when they are having fun" (Schlegel, 2000, p. 50). In addition to conducting experiments and focus groups at different stages of a toy's development, Schwe also assesses the age appropriateness of a toy. Most of her current work focuses on 3- to 5-year-old children. (Source: Schlegel, 2000, pp. 50–51)

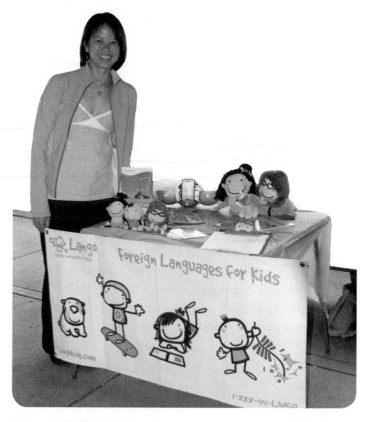

For more information about what researchers do, see page 42 in the Careers in Child Development appendix following Chapter 1.

Helen Schwe, a developmental psychologist, with some of the toys she designed for her current work on teaching foreign languages to children.

Scientific Thinking   Some aspects of thinking are specific to a particular domain, such as mathematics, science, or reading. We will explore reading in Chapter 9, "Language Development." Here we will examine scientific thinking by children.

Like scientists, children ask fundamental questions about reality and seek answers to questions that seem utterly trivial or unanswerable to other people (such as "Why is the sky blue?"). Do children generate hypotheses, perform experiments, and reach conclusions about their data in ways resembling those of scientists?

Scientific reasoning often is aimed at identifying causal relations. Like scientists, children place a great deal of emphasis on causal mechanisms. Their understanding of how events are caused weighs more heavily in their causal inferences than even such strong influences as whether the cause happened immediately before the effect.

There also are important differences between the reasoning of children and the reasoning of scientists (Kuhn, 2011, 2013). Children are more influenced by happenstance events than by an overall pattern (Kuhn, 2011). Often, children maintain their old theories regardless of the evidence (Kuhn, Schauble, & Garcia-Mila, 1992).

Children might go through mental gymnastics trying to reconcile seemingly contradictory new information with their existing beliefs. For example, after learning about the solar system, children sometimes conclude that there are two earths, the seemingly flat world in which they live and the round ball floating in space that their teacher described.

Children also have difficulty designing experiments that can distinguish among alternative causes. Instead, they tend to bias the experiments in favor of whatever hypothesis they began with. Sometimes they see the results as supporting their original hypothesis even when the results directly contradict it. Thus, although there are important similarities between children and scientists, in their basic curiosity and in the kinds of questions they ask, there are also important differences in the degree to which they can separate theory from evidence and in their ability to design conclusive experiments (Lehrer & Schauble, 2006).

Too often, the skills scientists use, such as careful observation, graphing, self-regulatory thinking, and knowing when and how to apply one's knowledge to solve problems, are not routinely taught in schools (Zembal-Saul, McNeill, & Hershberger, 2013). Children hold many concepts that are incompatible with science and reality. Good teachers perceive and understand a child's underlying scientific concepts, then use the concepts as a scaffold for learning. Effective science teaching helps children distinguish between fruitful errors and misconceptions, and detect plainly wrong ideas that need to be replaced with more accurate conceptions (Herrell, Jordan, & Eby, 2013).

It is important for teachers to initially scaffold students' science learning, extensively monitor their progress, and ensure that they are learning science content (McNeill & Krajcik, 2013). Thus, in pursuing science investigations, students need to learn inquiry skills and science content (Lehrer & Schauble, 2006).

Solving Problems   Children face many problems, both in school and out of school. *Problem solving* involves finding an appropriate way to attain a goal. Let's examine two ways children solve problems—by applying rules and by using analogies—and then consider some ways to help children learn effective strategies for solving problems.

Using Rules to Solve Problems   During early childhood, the relatively stimulus-driven toddler is transformed into a child capable of flexible, goal-directed problem solving (Zelazo & Muller, 2011). One element in this change is children's developing ability to form representations of reality.

For example, because they lack a concept of perspectives, 3- to 4-year-olds cannot understand that a single stimulus can be redescribed in a different, incompatible way (Perner & others, 2002). Consider a problem in which children must sort stimuli using the rule of *color* (van Bers & others, 2011). In the course of the color sorting, a child may describe a red rabbit as a *red one* to solve the problem. However, in a subsequent task, the child may need to discover a rule that describes the rabbit as just a *rabbit* to solve the problem. If 3- to 4-year-olds fail to understand that it is possible to provide multiple descriptions of the same stimulus, they persist in describing the stimulus as a red rabbit. In other words, the 3- to 4-year-olds show representational inflexibility. Researchers have found that at about 4 years of age, children acquire the concept of perspectives, which allows them to appreciate that a single thing can be described in different ways (Frye, 1999).

With age, children also learn better rules to apply to problems (Williamson, Jaswal, & Meltzoff, 2010). Figure 7.12 provides an example; it shows the balance scale problem that has been used to examine children's use of rules in solving problems. The scale includes a fulcrum and an arm that can rotate around it. The arm can tip left or right or remain level, depending on how weights (metal disks with holes in the center) are arranged on the pegs in each side

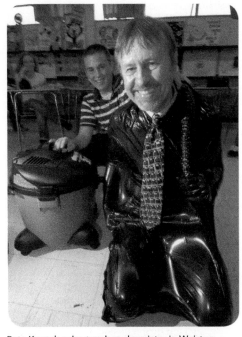

Pete Karpyk, who teaches chemistry in Weirton, West Virginia, uses an extensive array of activities that bring science to life for students. Here he has shrink-wrapped himself to demonstrate the effects of air pressure. He has some students give chemistry demonstrations at elementary schools and has discovered that in some cases students who don't do well on tests excel when they teach children. He also adapts his teaching based on feedback from former students and incorporates questions from their college chemistry tests as bonus questions on the tests he gives his high school students. (Source: Wong Briggs, 2005. p. 6D).

Rule I. If the weight is the same on both sides, predict that the scale will balance. If the weight differs, predict that the side with more weight will go down.

Rule II. If the weight is greater on one side, say that that side will go down. If the weights on the two sides are equal, choose the side on which the weight is farther from the fulcrum.

Balance scale apparatus

Rule III. Act as in Rule II, except that if one side has more weight and the weight on the other side is farther from the fulcrum, then guess.

Rule IV. Proceed as in Rule III, unless one side has more weight and the other more distance. In that case, calculate torques by multiplying weight times distance on each side. Then predict that the side with the greater torque will go down.

FIGURE 7.12

THE TYPE OF BALANCE SCALE USED BY SIEGLER (1976). Weights could be placed on pegs on each side of the fulcrum; the torque (the weight on each side times the distance of that weight from the fulcrum) determined which side would go down.

of the fulcrum. The child's task is to look at the configuration of weights on the pegs in each problem and then predict whether the left side will go down, the right side will go down, or the arm will balance.

Robert Siegler (1976) hypothesized that children would use one of the four rules listed in Figure 7.12. He reasoned that presenting problems on which different rules would generate different outcomes would allow assessment of each child's rules. Through a child's pattern of correct answers and errors on a set of such problems, that child's underlying rule could be inferred.

What were the results? Almost all 5-year-olds used Rule I, in which the child considers only the weight on the scales. Almost all 9-year-olds used either Rule II, which takes both weight and distance into account, or Rule III, which calls for guessing if the weight and distance dimensions would give conflicting information. Both 13-year-olds and 17-year-olds generally used Rule III.

In other words, the older children performed better at solving the problems because they used a better rule. But even 5-year-old children can be trained to use Rule III if they are taught to pay attention to differences in distance. As children learn more about what is relevant to a problem and learn to encode the relevant information, they are better at using rules in problem solving.

Interestingly, despite the 17-year-olds' having studied balance scales in their physics course, almost none of them used the only rule that generated consistently correct answers, Rule IV. Discussions with their teachers revealed why: The balance scale the students had studied was a pan balance, on which small pans could be hung from various locations along the arm, rather than an arm balance, with pegs extending upward. Retesting the high school students showed that most could consistently solve the problems when the familiar pan balance was used. This example illustrates a set of lessons that frequently emerge from studies of problem solving—learning is often quite narrow, generalization beyond one's existing knowledge is difficult, and even analogies that seem straightforward are often missed.

Using Analogies to Solve Problems   An *analogy* involves correspondence in some respects between things that are dissimilar. Even very young children can draw reasonable analogies under some circumstances and use them to solve problems (Morrison, Doumas, & Richland, 2011). Under other circumstances, even college students fail to draw seemingly obvious analogies (as in the high school students' difficulty in extrapolating from the familiar pan balance to the unfamiliar arm balance).

In one effort to discover developmental changes in young children's analogical problem solving, Judy DeLoache (1989) created a situation in which 2½- and 3-year-olds were shown a small toy hidden within a scale model of a room. The child was then asked to find the toy in a real room that was a bigger version of the scale model. If the toy was hidden under the armchair in the scale model, it was also hidden under the armchair in the real room. Considerable development occurred between 2½ and 3 years of age on this task. Thirty-month-old children rarely could solve the problem, but most 36-month-old children could.

Why was the task so difficult for the 2½-year-olds? Their problem was not an inability to understand that a symbol can represent another situation. Shown line drawings or photographs of the larger room, 2½-year-olds had no difficulty finding the object. Instead, the difficulty seemed to come from the toddlers' simultaneously viewing the scale model as a symbol of the larger room and as an object in itself. When children were allowed to play with the scale model before using it as a symbol, their performance worsened, presumably because playing with it made them think of it more as an object in itself. Conversely, when the scale model was placed in a glass case, where the children could not handle it at all, more children used it successfully to find the object hidden in the larger room. The general lesson is that young children can use a variety of tools to draw analogies, but they easily can forget that an object is being used as a symbol of something else and instead treat it as an object in its own right (DeLoache, 2011).

Using Strategies to Solve Problems   Good thinkers routinely use strategies and effective planning to solve problems (Bjorklund, 2013; McCormick, Dimmitt, & Sullivan, 2013). A

Judy DeLoache has conducted research that focuses on young children's developing cognitive abilities. She has demonstrated that children's symbolic representation between 2½ and 3 years of age enables them to find a toy in a real room that is a much bigger version of the scale model.

Helping Children Learn Strategies

In Michael Pressley's view (Pressley, 2003, 2007; Pressley & Hilden, 2006), the key to education is helping students learn a rich repertoire of strategies for solving problems. Pressley argues that when children are given instruction about effective strategies, they often can apply strategies that they had not used on their own. Pressley emphasizes that children benefit when the teacher (1) models the appropriate strategy, (2) verbalizes the steps in the strategy, and (3) guides the children to practice the strategy and supports their practice with feedback. "Practice" means that children use the strategy over and over until they perform it automatically. To execute strategies effectively, they need to have the strategies in long-term memory, and extensive practice makes this possible.

Just having children learn a new strategy is usually not enough for them to continue to use it and to transfer the strategy to new situations. Children need to be motivated to learn and to use the strategies. For effective maintenance and transfer, children should be encouraged to monitor the effectiveness of the new strategy by comparing their performance on tests and other assessments.

Let's examine an example of effective strategy instruction. Good readers extract the main ideas from text and summarize them. In contrast, novice readers (for example, most children) usually don't store the main ideas of what they read. One intervention based on what is known about the summarizing strategies of good readers consisted of instructing children to (1) skim over trivial information, (2) ignore redundant information, (3) replace less inclusive terms with more inclusive ones, (4) use a more inclusive action term to combine a series of events, (5) choose a topic sentence, and (6) create a topic sentence if none is given (Brown & Day, 1983). Instructing elementary school students to use these summarizing strategies improves their reading performance (Rinehart, Stahl, & Erickson, 1986).

Pressley and his colleagues (Pressley & Harris, 2006; Pressley & Hilden, 2006; Pressley & others, 2001, 2003, 2004, 2007) have spent considerable time in recent years observing the use of strategy instruction

What are some effective ways that teachers can help students learn to develop a rich repertoire of strategies for solving problems?

by teachers and strategy use by students in elementary and secondary school classrooms. They conclude that teachers' use of strategy instruction is far less complete and intense than what is needed for students to learn how to use strategies effectively. They argue that education needs to be restructured so that students are provided with more opportunities to become competent strategic learners.

How do the research findings of Peter Ornstein and his colleagues regarding teachers' use of strategy suggestions or metacognitive questions in the classroom (mentioned earlier in this chapter) compare with the findings of Pressley and his colleagues about teaching strategies?

recent study revealed that children's selection of effective strategies in solving problems improves from the third grade to the seventh grade (Lemaire & Lecacheur, 2011).

Do children use one strategy or multiple strategies in problem solving? They often use more than one strategy (Pressley, 2007). Most children benefit from generating a variety of alternative strategies and experimenting with different approaches to a problem, discovering what works well, when, and where. This is especially true for children from the middle elementary school grades on, although some cognitive psychologists stress that even young children should be encouraged to practice varying strategies (Siegler, 2012, 2013). To read further about guiding children to learn effective strategies, see the *Caring Connections* interlude.

ADOLESCENCE

In Deanna Kuhn's (2009) view, during the later years of childhood and continuing in adolescence, individuals approach cognitive levels that may or may not be achieved, in contrast with the largely universal cognitive levels that young children attain. By adolescence, considerable variation in cognitive functioning is present across individuals. This variability supports the argument that adolescents are producers of their own development to a greater extent than are children.

Kuhn (2009) further argues that the most important cognitive change in adolescence is improvement in *executive function*, which we discussed earlier in this chapter. Our coverage of executive function in adolescence focuses on monitoring and managing cognitive resources, critical thinking, and decision making.

Monitoring and Managing Cognitive Resources
It is increasingly thought that executive function strengthens during adolescence (Kuhn, 2009). This executive function

> assumes a role of monitoring and managing the deployment of cognitive resources as a function of task demands. As a result, cognitive development and learning itself become more effective. . . . Emergence and strengthening of this executive (functioning) is arguably the single most important and consequential intellectual development to occur in the second decade of life (Kuhn & Franklin, 2006, p. 987).

Critical Thinking
Adolescence is an important transitional period in the development of critical thinking (Keating, 1990). Among the cognitive changes that allow improvement in critical thinking during this period are the following:

- Increased speed, automaticity, and capacity of information processing, which free cognitive resources for other purposes
- Greater breadth of content knowledge in a variety of domains
- Increased ability to construct new combinations of knowledge
- A greater range and more spontaneous use of strategies and procedures for obtaining and applying knowledge, such as planning, considering the alternatives, and cognitive monitoring

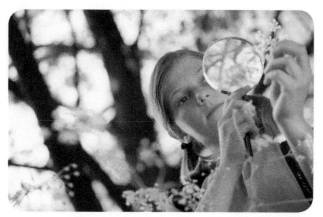

What are some cognitive changes that allow adolescents to think more critically than children?

Although adolescence is an important period in the development of critical-thinking skills, if a solid basis of fundamental skills (such as literacy and math skills) was not developed during childhood, critical-thinking skills are unlikely to develop adequately in adolescence. In one study of fifth-, eighth-, and eleventh-graders, critical thinking increased with age but still occurred only in 43 percent of eleventh-graders. Many adolescents showed self-serving biases in their thinking.

Decision Making
Adolescence is a time of increased decision making—which friends to choose, which person to date, whether to have sex, buy a car, go to college, and so on (Stanovich, West, & Toplak, 2012; Steinberg, 2012, 2013). How competent are adolescents at making decisions? In some reviews, older adolescents are described as more competent than younger adolescents, who in turn are more competent than children (Keating, 2004). Compared with children, young adolescents are more likely to generate different options, examine a situation from a variety of perspectives, anticipate the consequences of decisions, and consider the credibility of sources.

However, older adolescents' (as well as adults') decision-making skills are far from perfect, and having the capacity to make competent decisions does not guarantee they will be made in everyday life, where breadth of experience often comes into play (Kuhn, 2009). As an example, driver-training courses improve adolescents' cognitive and motor skills to levels equal to, or sometimes superior to, those of adults. However, driver training has not been effective in reducing adolescents' high rate of traffic accidents, although researchers have found that implementing a graduated driver licensing (GDR) program can reduce crash and fatality rates for adolescent drivers (Keating, 2007). GDR components include a learner's holding period, practice-driving certification, night-driving restriction, and passenger restriction.

Most people make better decisions when they are calm rather than emotionally aroused, which often is especially true for adolescents (Steinberg, 2012, 2013). Recall from our

How do emotions and social contexts influence adolescents' decision making?

discussion of brain development in Chapter 4 that adolescents have a tendency to be emotionally intense (Giedd & others, 2012). Thus, the same adolescent who makes a wise decision when calm may make an unwise decision when emotionally aroused. In the heat of the moment, then, adolescents' emotions may especially overwhelm their decision-making ability.

The social context plays a key role in adolescent decision making (Steinberg, 2011). For example, adolescents' willingness to make risky decisions is more likely to occur in contexts where alcohol, drugs, and other temptations are readily available (Reyna & Rivers, 2008). Recent research reveals that the presence of peers in risk-taking situations increases the likelihood that adolescents will make risky decisions (Albert & Steinberg, 2011a, b). In one study of risk taking involving a simulated driving task, the presence of peers increased an adolescent's decision to engage in risky driving by 50 percent but had no effect on adults (Gardner & Steinberg, 2005). One view is that the presence of peers activates the brain's reward system, especially its dopamine pathways (Albert & Steinberg, 2011a, b).

It also is important to consider how the stress level of situations and individual differences in risk taking can influence adolescents' decisions. Few research studies have examined how trait-like tendencies might influence the types of decisions adolescents make when faced with stressful and risky situations. A recent study found that adolescents took more risks in stressful than in non-stressful situations (Johnson, Dariotis, & Wang, 2012). However, risk taking in the stressful conditions was associated with the type of risk taker the adolescent was. In the stressful condition, impulsive risk takers were less accurate and planful; calculated risk takers took fewer risks; and conservative risk takers engaged in low risk taking in both the non-stressful and stressful conditions.

Adolescents need more opportunities to practice and discuss realistic decision making. Many real-world decisions on matters such as sex, drugs, and daredevil driving occur in an atmosphere of stress that includes time constraints and emotional involvement. One strategy for improving adolescent decision making in such circumstances is to provide more opportunities for them to engage in role playing and group problem solving. Another strategy is for parents to involve adolescents in appropriate decision-making activities.

To better understand adolescent decision making, Valerie Reyna and her colleagues (Reyna & Brainerd, 2011; Reyna & Farley, 2006; Reyna & others, 2010, 2011) have proposed the **dual-process model,** which states that decision making is influenced by two cognitive systems—one analytical and one experiential—that compete with each other. The dual-process model emphasizes that it is the experiential system—monitoring and managing actual experiences—that benefits adolescents' decision making, not the analytical system. In this view, adolescents don't benefit from engaging in reflective, detailed, higher-level cognitive analysis about a decision, especially in high-risk,

dual-process model States that decision making is influenced by two systems, one analytical and one experiential, that compete with each other. In this model, it is the experiential system—monitoring and managing actual experiences—that benefits adolescent decision making.

real-world contexts. In such contexts, adolescents just need to know that there are some circumstances that are so dangerous that they need to be avoided at all costs.

In the experiential system, in risky situations, it is important for an adolescent to quickly get the *gist*, or meaning, of what is happening and glean that the situation is a dangerous context, which can cue personal values that will protect the adolescent from making a risky decision (Chick & Reyna, 2012). Further, adolescents who have a higher level of trait inhibition (self-control that helps them to manage their impulses effectively) and find themselves in risky contexts are less likely to engage in risk-taking behavior than their adolescent counterparts with a lower level of trait inhibition (Chick & Reyna, 2012).

However, some experts on adolescent cognition argue that in many cases adolescents benefit from both analytical and experiential systems (Kuhn, 2009).

Review Connect Reflect

LG4 Characterize thinking and its developmental changes.

Review

- What is thinking?
- How does thinking develop in infancy?
- What characterizes children's development of executive function, critical thinking, scientific thinking, and problem solving?
- What are some important aspects of thinking in adolescence?

Connect

- In this section, you learned about a study that found a difference between boys' and girls' interests in particular categories of objects or activities. Why do researchers need to be cautious about making conclusions regarding gender-linked aspects of their findings?

Reflect *Your Own Personal Journey of Life*

- How good was your decision making in adolescence? What factors do you think contributed to whether you made good decisions during adolescence?

Metacognition **LG5** Define metacognition and summarize its developmental changes.

What Is Metacognition?

The Child's Theory of Mind

Metacognition in Childhood

Metacognition in Adolescence

Cognitive developmentalist John Flavell is a pioneer in providing insights about children's thinking. Among his many contributions are establishing the field of metacognition and conducting numerous studies in this area, including metamemory and theory of mind studies.

As discussed earlier in this chapter, *metacognition* is cognition about cognition, or "knowing about knowing" (Flavell, 2004). It is a function of the central executive in Baddeley's model (see Figure 7.3).

WHAT IS METACOGNITION?

Metacognition can take many forms. It includes thinking about and knowing when and where to use particular strategies for learning or for solving problems. Conceptualization of metacognition includes several dimensions of executive function, such as planning (deciding on how much time to focus on the task, for example), evaluation (monitoring progress toward task completion, for example), and self-regulation (modifying strategies as work on the task progresses, for example) (Dimmitt & McCormick, 2012).

Metacognition helps children to perform many cognitive tasks more effectively (Flavell, 2004; McCormick, Dimmitt, & Sullivan, 2013). In one study, students were taught metacognitive skills to help them solve math problems (Cardelle-Elawar, 1992). In each of 30 daily lessons involving math story problems, a teacher guided low-achieving students to recognize when they did not know the meaning of a word, did not have all of the information necessary to solve a problem, did not know how to subdivide the problem into specific steps, or did not know how to carry out a computation. After the 30 daily lessons, the students who were given this metacognitive training had better math achievement and attitudes toward math.

Metacognition can take many forms. It includes knowledge about when and where to use particular strategies for learning or for solving problems. **Metamemory,** individuals' knowledge about memory, is an especially important form of metacognition. Metamemory includes general knowledge about memory, such as knowing that recognition tests (such as multiple-choice questions) are easier than recall tests (such as essay questions). It also encompasses knowledge about one's own memory, such as knowing whether you have studied enough for an upcoming test.

THE CHILD'S THEORY OF MIND

Even young children are curious about the nature of the human mind (Apperly, 2012; Gelman, 2013). They have a **theory of mind,** which refers to awareness of one's own mental processes and the mental processes of others. Studies of theory of mind view the child as "a thinker who is trying to explain, predict, and understand people's thoughts, feelings, and utterances" (Harris, 2006, p. 847).

Developmental Changes   Although whether infants have a theory of mind continues to be questioned by some (Rakoczy, 2012), the consensus is that some changes occur quite early in development, as we see next. From 18 months to 3 years of age, children begin to understand three mental states:

- *Perceptions.* By 2 years of age, children recognize that another person will see what's in front of her own eyes instead of what's in front of the child's eyes (Lempers, Flavell, & Flavell, 1977), and by 3 years of age, they realize that looking leads to knowing what's inside a container (Pratt & Bryant, 1990).

- *Emotions.* The child can distinguish between positive (for example, happy) and negative (for example, sad) emotions. A child might say, "Tommy feels bad."

- *Desires.* All humans have some sort of desires. But when do children begin to recognize that someone else's desires may differ from their own? Toddlers recognize that if people want something, they will try to get it. For instance, a child might say, "I want my mommy."

Two- to 3-year-olds understand the way that desires are related to actions and to simple emotions. For example, they understand that people will search for what they want and that if they obtain it, they are likely to feel happy, but if they don't get it they will keep searching for it and are likely to feel sad or angry (Wellman & Woolley, 1990). Children also refer to desires earlier and more frequently than they refer to cognitive states such as thinking and knowing (Bartsch & Wellman, 1995).

One of the landmark developments in understanding others' desires is recognizing that someone else may have different desires from one's own (Doherty, 2009; Wellman, 2011). Eighteen-month-olds understand that their own food preferences may not match the preferences of others—they will give an adult the food to which she says "Yummy!" even if the food is something that the infants detest (Repacholi & Gopnik, 1997). As they get older, they can verbalize that they themselves do not like something but an adult might (Flavell & others, 1992).

Between the ages of 3 and 5, children come to understand that the mind can represent objects and events accurately or inaccurately (Low & Simpson, 2012). The realization that people can have *false beliefs*—beliefs that are not true—develops in a majority of children by the time they are 5 years old (Wellman, Cross, & Watson, 2001) (see Figure 7.13). This awareness is often described as a pivotal milestone in understanding the mind—recognizing that beliefs are not just mapped directly into the mind from the surrounding world, but also that different people can have different, and sometimes incorrect, beliefs (Gelman, 2009). In a classic false-belief task, young children were shown a Band-Aids box and asked what was inside (Jenkins & Astington, 1996). To the children's surprise, the box actually contained pencils. When asked what a child who had never seen the box would think was inside, 3-year-olds typically responded, "Pencils." However, the 4- and 5-year-olds, grinning at the anticipation of the false beliefs of other children who had not seen what was inside the box, were more likely to say "Band-Aids."

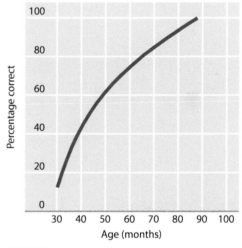

FIGURE **7.13**

DEVELOPMENTAL CHANGES IN FALSE-BELIEF PERFORMANCE. False-belief recognition dramatically increases from 2½ years of age through the middle of the elementary school years. In a summary of the results of many studies, 2½-year-olds gave incorrect responses about 80 percent of the time (Wellman, Cross, & Watson, 2001). At 3 years, 8 months, they were correct about 50 percent of the time, and after that, gave increasingly correct responses.

metamemory Knowledge about memory.

theory of mind Awareness of one's own mental processes and the mental processes of others.

FIGURE 7.14

THE SALLY AND ANNE FALSE-BELIEF TASK. In the false-belief task, the skit above in which Sally has a basket and Anne has a box is shown to children. Sally places a toy in her basket and then leaves. While Sally is gone and can't watch, Anne removes the toy from Sally's basket and places it in her box. Sally then comes back and the children are asked where they think Sally will look for her toy. Children are said to "pass" the false-belief task if they understand that Sally looks in her basket first before realizing the toy isn't there.

In a similar task, children are told a story about Sally and Anne: Sally places a toy in a basket and then leaves the room (see Figure 7.14). In her absence, Anne takes the toy from the basket and places it in a box. Children are asked where Sally will look for the toy when she returns. The major finding is that 3-year-olds tend to fail false-belief tasks, saying that Sally will look in the box (even though Sally could not know that the toy has been moved to this new location). Four-year-olds and older children tend to pass the task, correctly saying that Sally will have a "false belief"—she will think the object is in the basket, even though that belief is now false. The conclusion from these studies is that children younger than 4 years old do not understand that it is possible to have a false belief.

It is only beyond the preschool years—at approximately 5 to 7 years of age—that children have a deepening appreciation of the mind itself rather than just an understanding of mental states (Wellman, 2011). For example, they begin to recognize that people's behaviors do not necessarily reflect their thoughts and feelings (Flavell, Green, & Flavell, 1993). Not until middle and late childhood do children see the mind as an active constructor of knowledge or a processing center (Flavell, Green, & Flavell, 1998) and move from understanding that beliefs can be false to realizing that the same event can be open to multiple interpretations (Carpendale & Chandler, 1996). For example, in one study, children saw an ambiguous line drawing (for example, a drawing that could be seen as either a duck or a rabbit); one puppet told the child she believed the drawing was a duck while another puppet told the child he believed the drawing was a rabbit (see Figure 7.15). Before the age of 7, children said that there was one right answer, and it was not okay for both puppets to have different opinions.

While most research on children's theory of mind focuses on children around or before their preschool years, at 7 years of age and beyond there are important developments in the ability to understand the beliefs and thoughts of others. Although understanding that people may have different interpretations is important, it is also necessary to recognize that some interpretations and beliefs may still be evaluated on the basis of the merits of arguments and evidence (Kuhn, Cheney, & Weinstock, 2000). In early adolescence, children begin to understand that people can have ambivalent feelings (Flavell & Miller, 1998). They start to recognize that the same person can feel both happy and sad about the same event. They also engage in more recursive thinking: thinking about what other people are thinking about.

Individual Differences   As in other developmental research, there are individual differences in the ages when children reach certain milestones in their theory of mind. For example, children who talk with their parents about feelings frequently as 2-year-olds show better performance on theory of mind tasks (Ruffman, Slade, & Crowe, 2002), as do children who frequently engage in pretend play (Harris, 2000).

Executive function, which describes several functions (such as inhibition and planning) that are important for flexible, future-oriented behavior, also may be connected to theory of mind development (Carroll & others, 2012; Muller & others, 2012). For example, in one executive function task, children are asked to say the word "night" when they see a picture of a sun, and the word "day" when they see a picture of a moon and stars. Children who perform better at executive function tasks seem also to have a better understanding of theory of mind (Sabbagh & others, 2006).

Another individual difference in understanding the mind involves autism (Doherty, 2009). To learn how theory of mind differs in children with autism, see *Connecting Through Research*.

METACOGNITION IN CHILDHOOD

By 5 or 6 years of age, children usually know that familiar items are easier to learn than unfamiliar ones, that short lists are easier to remember than long ones, that recognition is easier than recall, and that forgetting becomes more likely over time (Lyon & Flavell, 1993).

FIGURE 7.15
AMBIGUOUS LINE DRAWING

How Does Theory of Mind Differ in Children with Autism?

Approximately 1 in 150 children is estimated to have some sort of autism spectrum disorder (National Autism Association, 2010). Autism can usually be diagnosed by the age of 3 years, and sometimes earlier. Children with autism show a number of behaviors different from children their age, including deficits in social interaction and communication as well as repetitive behaviors or interests. They often show indifference toward others, in many instances preferring to be alone and showing more interest in objects than people. It now is accepted that autism is linked to genetic and brain abnormalities (Deeley & Murphy, 2009; Glessner & others, 2009). Children and adults with autism have difficulty in social interactions. These deficits are generally greater than deficits in children the same mental age with intellectual disability (Baron-Cohen, 2009, 2011). Researchers have found that children with autism have difficulty in developing a theory of mind, especially in understanding others' beliefs and emotions (Bertoglio & Hendren, 2009; Peterson & others, 2009). Although children with autism tend to do poorly when reasoning on false-belief tasks (Peterson, 2005), they can perform much better on reasoning tasks requiring an understanding of physical causality. Recently, it has been emphasized that children with autism might have difficulty in understanding others' beliefs and emotions not solely because of theory of mind deficits but also due to other aspects of cognition such as problems in focusing attention, eye gaze, face recognition, memory, language impairment, or some general intellectual impairment (Boucher, 2012a, b; Boucher, Mayes, & Bigham, 2012).

In relation to theory of mind, however, it is important to consider the effects of individual variations in the abilities of children with autism (Harris, 2006). Children with autism are not a homogeneous group, and some have less severe social and communication problems than others. Thus, it is not surprising that children who have less severe forms of autism do better than those who have more severe forms of the disorder on some theory of mind tasks. For example, higher-functioning children

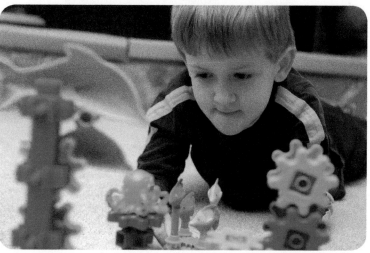

A young boy with autism. *What are some characteristics of children who are autistic? What are some deficits in their theory of mind?*

with autism show reasonable progress in understanding others' desires (Harris, 2006). A further important consideration in thinking about autism and theory of mind is that children with autism might have difficulty in understanding others' beliefs and emotions not solely due to theory of mind deficits but to other aspects of cognition such as problems in focusing attention or some general intellectual impairment (Renner, Grofer Klinger, & Klinger, 2006). Some recent theories of autism suggest that weaknesses in executive function may be related to the problems experienced by those with autism in performing theory of mind tasks. Other theories have pointed out that typically developing individuals process information by extracting the big picture, whereas those with autism process information in a very detailed, almost obsessive way. It may be that in autism, a number of different but related deficits lead to social cognitive deficits (Rajendran & Mitchell, 2007).

However, in other ways young children's metamemory is limited. They don't understand that related items are easier to remember than unrelated ones or that remembering the gist of a story is easier than remembering information verbatim (Kreutzer & Flavell, 1975). By fifth grade, students understand that gist recall is easier than verbatim recall.

Preschool children also have an inflated opinion of their memory abilities. For example, in one study, a majority of preschool children predicted that they would be able to recall all 10 items on a list of 10 items. When tested, none of the young children managed this feat (Flavell, Friedrichs, & Hoyt, 1970). As they move through the elementary school years, children give more realistic evaluations of their memory skills (Schneider & Pressley, 1997).

How does metacognition change in childhood and adolescence?

Preschool children also have little appreciation for the importance of cues to memory, such as "It helps when you can think of an example of it." By 7 or 8 years of age, children better appreciate the importance of cueing for memory. In general, children's understanding of their memory abilities and their skill in evaluating their performance on memory tasks is relatively poor at the beginning of the elementary school years but improves considerably by 11 to 12 years of age (Bjorklund, 2012).

METACOGNITION IN ADOLESCENCE

Important changes in metacognition take place during adolescence (Kuhn, 2008, 2009). Compared with when they were children, adolescents have an increased capacity to monitor and manage cognitive resources to effectively meet the demands of a learning task. This increased metacognitive ability results in cognitive functioning and learning becoming more effective.

A recent longitudinal study revealed that from 12 to 14 years of age, young adolescents increasingly used metacognitive skills and used them more effectively in math and history classes (van der Stel & Veenman, 2010). For example, 14-year-olds monitored their own text comprehension more frequently and did so more effectively than their younger counterparts. Another recent study documented the importance of metacognitive skills, such as planning, strategies, and monitoring, in college students' ability to think critically (Magno, 2010).

An important aspect of cognitive functioning and learning is determining how much attention will be allocated to an available resource. Evidence is accumulating that adolescents have a better understanding of how to effectively deploy their attention to different aspects of a task than children do (Kuhn, 2009). Further, adolescents have a better meta-level understanding of strategies—that is, knowing the best strategy to use and when to use it in performing a learning task.

Keep in mind, though, that there is considerable individual variation in adolescents' metacognition. Indeed, some experts argue that individual variation in metacognition becomes much more pronounced in adolescence than in childhood (Kuhn, 2009). Thus, some adolescents are quite good at using metacognition to improve their learning, while others are far less so.

Review *Connect* Reflect

 Define metacognition and summarize its developmental changes.

Review

- What is metacognition?
- What is theory of mind? How does children's theory of mind change developmentally?
- How does metacognition change during childhood?

Connect

- Compare the classic false-belief task study you learned about in this section with what you learned about A-not-B error studies in Chapter 6. What is similar and what is different about these studies and what they are assessing?

Reflect *Your Own Personal Journey of Life*

- Do you remember your teachers ever instructing you in ways to improve your use of metacognition—that is, your "knowing about knowing" and "thinking about thinking," when you were in elementary and secondary school? To help you to think further about this question, connect the discussion of metacognition that you just read with the discussion of strategies earlier in the chapter.

Information Processing

The Information-Processing Approach **LG1** Explain the information-processing approach.

The Information-
Processing Approach
to Development

- The information-processing approach analyzes how individuals manipulate information, monitor it, and create strategies for handling it. Attention, memory, and thinking are involved in effective information processing. The computer has served as a model for how humans process information. In the information-processing approach, children's cognitive development results from their ability to overcome processing limitations by increasingly executing basic operations, expanding information-processing capacity, and acquiring new knowledge and strategies.

Cognitive Resources:
Capacity and Speed of
Processing Information

- Capacity and speed of processing information, often referred to as cognitive resources, increase across childhood and adolescence. Changes in the brain serve as biological foundations for developmental changes in cognitive resources. In terms of capacity, the increase is reflected in older children being able to hold in mind several dimensions of a topic simultaneously. A reaction-time task has often been used to assess speed of processing. Processing speed continues to improve in early adolescence.

Mechanisms of Change

- According to Siegler, three important mechanisms of change are encoding (how information gets into memory), automaticity (ability to process information with little or no effort), and strategy construction (creation of new procedures for processing information). Children's information processing is characterized by self-modification, and an important aspect of this self-modification involves metacognition—that is, knowing about knowing.

Comparisons with
Piaget's Theory

- Unlike Piaget's theory, the information-processing approach does not portray development as occurring in distinct stages. Instead, this approach holds that individuals develop a gradually increasing capacity for processing information, which allows them to develop increasingly complex knowledge and skills. Like Piaget's theory, some versions of the information-processing approach are constructivist—they see children directing their own cognitive development.

Attention   **LG2** Define attention and outline its developmental changes.

What Is Attention?

- Attention is the focusing of mental resources. Four ways that children can allocate their attention are selective attention (focusing on a specific aspect of experience that is relevant while ignoring others that are irrelevant); divided attention (concentrating on more than one activity at the same time); sustained attention (maintaining attention to a selected stimulus for a prolonged period of time, also referred to as focused attention and vigilance); and executive attention (planning actions, allocating attention to goals, detecting errors and compensating for them, monitoring progress on tasks, and dealing with novel or difficult tasks).

Infancy

- Even newborns can fixate on a contour, but as infants get older they can scan a pattern more thoroughly. Attention in the first year of life is dominated by the orienting/investigative process. Attention in infancy is often studied through habituation and dishabituation. Habituation can provide a measure of an infant's maturity and well-being. Joint attention increases an infant's ability to learn from others.

Childhood

- Salient stimuli tend to capture the attention of the preschooler. After 6 or 7 years of age, there is a shift to more cognitive control of attention. Young children especially make advances in executive and sustained attention. Selective attention also improves through childhood. Children's attentional skills are increasingly being found to predict later cognitive competencies, such as school readiness.

| Adolescence | • Adolescents typically have better attentional skills than children do, although there are wide individual differences in how effectively adolescents deploy their attention. Sustained attention and executive attention are especially important as adolescents are required to work on increasingly complex tasks that take longer to complete. Multitasking is an example of divided attention, and it can harm adolescents' attention when they are engaging in a challenging task. |

Memory

LG3 Describe what memory is and how it changes.

What Is Memory?

• Memory is the retention of information over time. Psychologists study the processes of memory: how information is initially placed or encoded into memory, how it is retained or stored, and how it is found or retrieved for a certain purpose later. Short-term memory involves retaining information for up to 30 seconds, assuming there is no rehearsal of the information. Long-term memory is a relatively permanent and unlimited type of memory. Working memory is a kind of "mental workbench" where individuals manipulate and assemble information when they make decisions, solve problems, and comprehend written and spoken language. Many contemporary psychologists prefer the term *working memory* over *short-term memory*. Working memory is linked to children's reading comprehension and problem solving. People construct and reconstruct their memories. Schema theory states that people mold memories to fit the information that already exists in their minds. Fuzzy trace theory states that memory is best understood by considering two types of memory representation: (1) verbatim memory trace, and (2) fuzzy trace, or gist. According to this theory, older children's better memory is attributed to the fuzzy traces created by extracting the gist of information. Children's ability to remember new information about a subject depends on what they already know about it. The contribution of content knowledge is especially relevant in the memory of experts. Experts have a number of characteristics that can explain why they solve problems better than novices do.

Infancy

• Infants as young as 2 to 3 months of age display implicit memory, which is memory without conscious recollection, as in memory of perceptual-motor skills. However, many experts stress that explicit memory, which is the conscious memory of facts and experiences, does not emerge until the second half of the first year of life. Older children and adults remember little if anything from the first three years of their lives.

Childhood

• Young children can remember a great deal of information if they are given appropriate cues and prompts. One method of assessing short-term memory is with a memory-span task, on which there are substantial developmental changes through the childhood years. Children's memory improves in the elementary school years as they begin to use gist more, acquire more content knowledge and expertise, develop large memory spans, and use more effective strategies. Organization, elaboration, and imagery are important memory strategies. Current research focuses on how accurate children's long-term memories are and the implications of this accuracy for children as eyewitnesses.

Adolescence

• Short-term memory, as assessed in memory span, increases during adolescence. Working memory also increases in adolescence.

Thinking

LG4 Characterize thinking and its developmental changes.

What Is Thinking?

• Thinking involves manipulating and transforming information in memory. We can think about the past, reality, and fantasy. Thinking helps us reason, reflect, evaluate, solve problems, and make decisions.

Infancy

• Studies of thinking in infancy focus on concept formation and categorization. Concepts refer to cognitive groupings of similar objects, events, people, or ideas. Infants form concepts early in their development, with perceptual categorization appearing as early as 3 months of age. Mandler argues that it is not until about 7 to 9 months of age that infants form conceptual categories. Infants' first concepts are broad. Over the first two years of life, these broad concepts gradually become more differentiated.

Childhood	• Advances in executive function, an umbrella-like concept that consists of a number of higher-level cognitive processes linked to the development of the prefrontal cortex, occur in childhood. Executive function involves managing one's thoughts to engage in goal-directed behavior and to exercise self-control. Critical thinking involves thinking reflectively and productively, and evaluating the evidence. Mindfulness is an important aspect of critical thinking. A lack of emphasis on critical thinking in schools is a special concern. Children and scientists think alike in some ways but not in others. Problem solving relies on the use of strategies, rules, and analogies. Even young children can use analogies to solve problems in some circumstances.
Adolescence	• Key changes in information processing during adolescence especially focus on executive function. These changes include monitoring and managing cognitive resources, engaging in critical thinking, and making decisions. It is increasingly thought that executive function strengthens during adolescence. Adolescence is an important transitional period in critical thinking because of cognitive changes such as increased speed, automaticity, and capacity of information processing; more breadth of content knowledge; increased ability to construct new combinations of knowledge; and increased use of spontaneous strategies.

Metacognition

LG5 Define metacognition and summarize its developmental changes.

What Is Metacognition?

The Child's Theory of Mind

Metacognition in Childhood

Metacognition in Adolescence

• Metacognition is cognition about cognition, or knowing about knowing.

• Theory of mind refers to a child's awareness of his or her own mental processes and the mental processes of others. Young children are curious about the human mind, and this has been studied under the topic of theory of mind. A number of developmental changes characterize children's theory of mind. For example, by 5 years of age most children realize that people can have false beliefs—beliefs that are untrue. Individual variations also are involved in theory of mind. For example, autistic children have difficulty in developing a theory of mind.

• Metamemory improves in middle and late childhood. As children progress through the elementary school years, they make more realistic judgments about their memory skills and increasingly understand the importance of memory cues.

• Adolescents have an increased capacity to monitor and manage resources to effectively meet the demands of a learning task, although there is considerable individual variation in metacognition during adolescence.

key terms

information-processing
   approach 195
encoding 196
automaticity 196
strategy construction 197
metacognition 197
attention 198
selective attention 198

divided attention 198
sustained attention 198
executive attention 198
joint attention 199
memory 202
short-term memory 202
long-term memory 202
working memory 202

schema theory 202
schemas 202
fuzzy trace theory 204
implicit memory 206
explicit memory 206
thinking 210
concepts 210
executive function 211

critical thinking 213
mindfulness 213
dual-process model 219
metamemory 221
theory of mind 221

key people

Robert Siegler 196
Mary Rothbart 200
Maria Gartstein 200
Alan Baddeley 203

Charles Brainerd 204
Valerie Reyna 204
Carolyn Rovee-Collier 205
Jean Mandler 206

Stephanie Carlson 212
Jacqueline and Martin Brooks 213
Ellen Langer 213
Robert Roeser 213

Philip Zelazo 213
Judy DeLoache 216
Valerie Reyna 219
Michael Pressley 217

chapter 8

INTELLIGENCE

chapter **outline**

Shiffy Landa, a first-grade teacher at H. F. Epstein Hebrew Academy in St. Louis, Missouri, uses the multiple-intelligences approach of Howard Gardner (1983, 1993) in her classroom. Gardner argues that there is not just one general type of intelligence but at least eight specific types.

Landa (2000, pp. 6–8) believes that the multiple-intelligences approach is the best way to reach children because they have many different kinds of abilities. In Landa's words,

> My role as a teacher is quite different from the way it was just a few years ago. No longer do I stand in front of the room and lecture to my students. I consider my role to be one of a facilitator rather than a frontal teacher. The desks in my room are not all neatly lined up in straight rows . . . students are busily working in centers in cooperative learning groups, which gives them the opportunity to develop their interpersonal intelligences.

Landa explains that students use their "body-kinesthetic intelligence to form the shapes of the letters as they learn to write. . . . They also use this intelligence to move the sounds of the vowels that they are learning, blending them together with letters, as they begin to read."

Landa believes that "intrapersonal intelligence is an intelligence that often is neglected in the traditional classroom." In her classroom, students "complete their own evaluation sheets after they have concluded their work at the centers. They evaluate their work and create their own portfolios," in which they keep their work so they can see their progress.

As she was implementing the multiple-intelligences approach in her classroom, Landa recognized that she needed to educate parents about it. She created a parent education class called The Parent-Teacher Connection, which meets periodically to view videos, talk about multiple intelligences, and discuss how the multiple intelligences are being introduced in the classroom. She also sends a weekly newsletter to parents, informing them about the week's multiple-intelligences activities and students' progress.

preview

Shiffy Landa's classroom techniques build on Howard Gardner's multiple-intelligences theory, one of the theories of intelligence that we will explore in this chapter. You will see that there is spirited debate about whether people have a general intelligence or a number of specific intelligences. The concept of intelligence also has generated other controversies, including whether intelligence is more strongly influenced by heredity or by environment, whether there is cultural bias in intelligence testing, and whether intelligence tests are misused. We will explore these controversies in this chapter, and we will trace the development of intelligence from infancy through adolescence. Finally, we will look at the extremes of intelligence and creativity.

The Concept of Intelligence **LG1** Explain the concept of intelligence.

| What Is Intelligence? | Intelligence Tests | Theories of Multiple Intelligences | The Neuroscience of Intelligence | The Influence of Heredity and Environment | Group Comparisons |

Intelligence is one of our most prized attributes. However, even the most intelligent people do not agree on how to define it and how to measure it.

WHAT IS INTELLIGENCE?

What does the term *intelligence* mean to psychologists? Some experts describe intelligence as the ability to solve problems. Others describe it as the capacity to adapt and learn from experience. Still others argue that intelligence includes characteristics such as creativity and interpersonal skills.

The problem with intelligence is that, unlike height, weight, and age, intelligence cannot be directly measured. We can't peel back a person's scalp and see how much intelligence he or she has. We can evaluate intelligence only *indirectly* by studying and comparing the intelligent acts that people perform.

The primary components of intelligence are similar to the cognitive processes of memory and thinking that we discussed in Chapter 7. The differences in how these cognitive processes are described, and how we will discuss intelligence, lie in the concepts of individual differences and assessment (Deary, 2012; Reynolds & Livingston, 2012). *Individual differences* are the stable, consistent ways in which people differ from one another. Individual differences in intelligence generally have been measured by intelligence tests designed to tell us whether a person can reason better than others who have taken the test.

We will use as our definition of **intelligence** the ability to solve problems and to adapt and learn from experiences. But even this broad definition doesn't satisfy everyone. As you will see shortly, Howard Gardner proposes that musical skills should be considered part of intelligence. Also, a definition of intelligence based on a theory such as Vygotsky's, which we discussed in Chapter 6, would have to include the ability to use the tools of the culture with help from more-skilled individuals. Because intelligence is such an abstract, broad concept, it is not surprising that there are different ways to define it.

INTELLIGENCE TESTS

The two main intelligence tests that are administered to children on an individual basis today are the Stanford-Binet test and the Wechsler scales. As you will see next, an early version of the Binet was the first intelligence test to be devised.

---

developmental **connection**

Information Processing

The information-processing approach emphasizes how children manipulate, monitor, and create strategies for handling information. Chapter 7, p. 195

intelligence The ability to solve problems and to adapt to and learn from experiences.

The Binet Tests In 1904, the French Ministry of Education asked psychologist Alfred Binet to devise a method of identifying children who were unable to learn in school. School officials wanted to reduce crowding by placing in special schools students who would not benefit from regular classroom teaching. Binet and his student Theophile Simon developed an intelligence test to meet this request. The test is called the 1905 Scale. It consisted of 30 questions, ranging from the ability to touch one's ear to the abilities to draw designs from memory and define abstract concepts.

Binet developed the concept of **mental age (MA)**, an individual's level of mental development relative to others. In 1912, William Stern created the concept of **intelligence quotient (IQ)**, which refers to a person's mental age divided by chronological age (CA), multiplied by 100. That is, $IQ = MA/CA \times 100$.

If mental age is the same as chronological age, then the person's IQ is 100. If mental age is above chronological age, then IQ is more than 100. For example, a 6-year-old with a mental age of 8 would have an IQ of 133. If mental age is below chronological age, then IQ is less than 100. For example, a 6-year-old with a mental age of 5 would have an IQ of 83.

The Binet test has been revised many times to incorporate advances in the understanding of intelligence and intelligence testing (MacIntosh, 2011). These revisions are called the *Stanford-Binet tests* (because the revisions were made at Stanford University). By administering the test to large numbers of people of different ages from different backgrounds, researchers have found that scores on a Stanford-Binet test approximate a normal distribution (see Figure 8.1). A **normal distribution** is symmetrical, with a majority of the scores falling in the middle of the possible range of scores and few scores appearing toward the extremes of the range.

The current Stanford-Binet test is administered individually to people aged 2 through adult. It includes a variety of items, some of which require verbal responses, others nonverbal responses. For example, items that reflect a typical 6-year-old's level of performance on the test include the verbal ability to define at least six words, such as *orange* and *envelope*, as well as the nonverbal ability to trace a path through a maze. Items that reflect an average adult's level of performance include defining such words as *disproportionate* and *regard*, explaining a proverb, and comparing idleness and laziness.

The fourth edition of the Stanford-Binet was published in 1985. One important addition to this version was the analysis of the individual's responses in terms of four functions: verbal reasoning, quantitative reasoning, abstract visual reasoning, and short-term memory. A general composite score is still obtained to reflect overall intelligence. The Stanford-Binet continues to be one of the most widely used tests to assess students' intelligence (Neukrug & Fawcett, 2010).

Alfred Binet constructed the first intelligence test after being asked to create a measure to determine which children could benefit from instruction in France's schools and which could not.

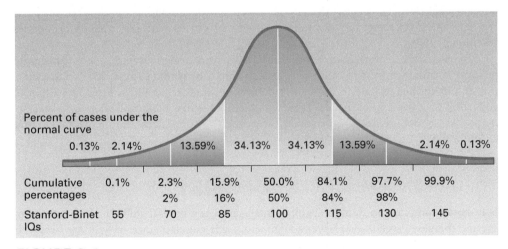

FIGURE **8.1**

THE NORMAL CURVE AND STANDARD-BINET IQ SCORES. The distribution of IQ scores approximates a normal curve. Most of the population falls in the middle range of scores. Notice that extremely high and extremely low scores are very rare. Slightly more than two-thirds of the scores fall between 84 and 116. Only about 1 in 50 individuals has an IQ above 132, and only about 1 in 50 individuals has an IQ below 68.

mental age (MA) An individual's level of mental development relative to others.

intelligence quotient (IQ) An individual's mental age divided by chronological age and multiplied by 100; devised in 1912 by William Stern.

normal distribution A symmetrical distribution with a majority of the cases falling in the middle of the possible range of scores and few scores appearing toward the extremes of the range.

Verbal Subscales

Similarities

A child must think logically and abstractly to answer a number of questions about how things might be similar.

Example: "In what way are a lion and a tiger alike?"

Comprehension

This subscale is designed to measure an individual's judgment and common sense.

Example: "What is the advantage of keeping money in a bank?"

Nonverbal Subscales

Block Design

A child must assemble a set of multicolored blocks to match designs that the examiner shows.
Visual-motor coordination, perceptual organization, and the ability to visualize spatially are assessed.

Example: "Use the four blocks on the left to make the pattern on the right."

FIGURE **8.2**

SAMPLE SUBSCALES OF THE WECHSLER INTELLIGENCE SCALE FOR CHILDREN–FOURTH EDITION (WISC-IV).

Simulated items similar to those in the *Wechsler Intelligence Scale for Children*–Fourth Edition (*WISC-IV*). Copyright © 2003 by NCS Pearson, Inc. Reproduced with permission. All rights reserved. *"Wechsler Intelligence Scale for Children"* and *"WISC"* are trademarks, in the US and/or other countries, of Pearson Education, Inc. or its affiliates.

triarchic theory of intelligence Sternberg's theory that intelligence comes in three forms: analytical, creative, and practical.

"How are her scores?"
© Edward Koren/The New Yorker Collection/
www.cartoonbank.com

The Wechsler Scales   Another set of tests widely used to assess students' intelligence is called the *Wechsler scales,* developed by psychologist David Wechsler. They include the Wechsler Preschool and Primary Scale of Intelligence–Third Edition (WPPSI-III) to test children from 2 years 6 months to 7 years 3 months of age; the Wechsler Intelligence Scale for Children–Fourth Edition (WISC-IV) for children and adolescents 6 to 16 years of age; and the Wechsler Adult Intelligence Scale–Third Edition (WAIS-III).

The Wechsler scales not only provide an overall IQ score and scores on a number of subtests but also yield several composite indexes (for example, the Verbal Comprehension Index, the Working Memory Index, and the Processing Speed Index). The subtest and composite scores allow the examiner to quickly determine the areas in which the child is strong or weak. Three of the Wechsler subscales are shown in Figure 8.2.

Intelligence tests such as the Stanford-Binet and Wechsler are given on an individual basis. A psychologist approaches an individual assessment of intelligence as a structured interaction between the examiner and the child. This provides the psychologist with an opportunity to sample the child's behavior. During the testing, the examiner observes the ease with which rapport is established, the child's enthusiasm and interest, whether anxiety interferes with the child's performance, and the child's degree of tolerance for frustration.

The Use and Misuse of Intelligence Tests   Intelligence tests have real-world applications as predictors of longevity, school success, and work success (Deary, 2012; Reynolds & Livingston, 2012). Researchers have found that lower intelligence in childhood is linked to illness, chronic disease, and how long people will live (Deary & Batty, 2011). Also, scores on tests of general intelligence are substantially correlated with school grades and achievement test performance, both at the time of the test and years later (Brody, 2007). IQ in the sixth grade correlates about .60 with the number of years of education the individual will eventually obtain (Jencks, 1979). Intelligence tests also are moderately correlated with work performance (Lubinski, 2000).

Despite the links between IQ and academic achievement and occupational success, it is important to keep in mind that many other factors contribute to success in school and work. These include the motivation to succeed, physical and mental health, and social skills (Sternberg, 2012).

The single number provided by many IQ tests can easily lead to false expectations about an individual (Rosnow & Rosenthal, 1996). Sweeping generalizations are too often made on the basis of an IQ score. IQ scores are misused and can become self-fulfilling prophecies (Weinstein, 2004).

To be effective, information about a child's performance on an intelligence test should be used in conjunction with other information about the child (Urbina, 2011). For example, an intelligence test alone should not determine whether a child is placed in a special education or gifted class. The child's developmental history, medical background, performance in school, social competencies, and family experiences should be taken into account, too.

THEORIES OF MULTIPLE INTELLIGENCES

Is it more appropriate to think of a child's intelligence as a general ability or as a number of specific abilities? Psychologists have thought about this question since early in the twentieth century and continue to debate the issue.

Sternberg's Triarchic Theory   According to Robert J. Sternberg's (1986, 2004, 2010, 2012a, 2013a, c) **triarchic theory of intelligence,** intelligence comes in three forms: analytical, creative, and practical. *Analytical intelligence* involves the ability to analyze, judge, evaluate, compare, and contrast. *Creative intelligence* consists of the ability to create, design, invent, originate, and imagine. *Practical intelligence* focuses on the ability to use, apply, implement, and put into practice.

Sternberg (2013a, c) says that students with different triarchic patterns look different in school. Students with high analytic ability tend to be favored in conventional schools. They often do well in classes in which the teacher lectures and gives objective tests. These students typically get good grades, do well on traditional IQ tests and the SAT, and later gain admission to competitive colleges.

Students high in creative intelligence often are not in the top rung of their class. Creatively intelligent students might not conform to teachers' expectations about how assignments should be done. They give unique answers, for which they might get reprimanded or marked down.

Like students high in creative intelligence, students who are practically intelligent often do not relate well to the demands of school. However, these students frequently do well outside the classroom's walls. Their social skills and common sense may allow them to become successful managers or entrepreneurs, despite undistinguished school records.

Sternberg (2012b, 2013b) argues that wisdom is linked to both practical and academic intelligence. In his view, academic intelligence is a necessary but in many cases insufficient requirement for wisdom. Practical knowledge about the realities of life also is needed for wisdom. For Sternberg, balance between self-interest, the interests of others, and contexts produces a common good. Thus, wise individuals don't just look out for themselves—they also need to consider others' needs and perspectives, as well as the particular context involved. Sternberg assesses wisdom by presenting problems that require solutions highlighting various intrapersonal, interpersonal, and contextual interests. He also emphasizes that such aspects of wisdom should be taught in schools (Sternberg, 2013b).

Robert J. Sternberg, who developed the triarchic theory of intelligence.

Gardner's Eight Frames of Mind

As we indicated in the introduction to this chapter, Howard Gardner (1983, 1993, 2002) says there are many specific types of intelligence, or frames of mind. They are described here along with examples of the occupations in which they are reflected as strengths (Campbell, Campbell, & Dickinson, 2004):

- *Verbal skills:* The ability to think in words and to use language to express meaning.
  Occupations: Authors, journalists, speakers.
- *Mathematical skills:* The ability to carry out mathematical operations.
  Occupations: Scientists, engineers, accountants.
- *Spatial skills:* The ability to think three-dimensionally.
  Occupations: Architects, artists, sailors.
- *Bodily-kinesthetic skills:* The ability to manipulate objects and be physically adept.
  Occupations: Surgeons, craftspeople, dancers, athletes.
- *Musical skills:* A sensitivity to pitch, melody, rhythm, and tone.
  Occupations: Composers, musicians, and music therapists.
- *Intrapersonal skills:* The ability to understand oneself and effectively direct one's life.
  Occupations: Theologians, psychologists.
- *Interpersonal skills:* The ability to understand and effectively interact with others.
  Occupations: Teachers, mental health professionals.
- *Naturalist skills:* The ability to observe patterns in nature and understand natural and human-made systems.
  Occupations: Farmers, botanists, ecologists, landscapers.

"You're wise, but you lack tree smarts."
© Donald Reilly/The New Yorker Collection/
www.cartoonbank.com

Recently, Gardner has considered adding a ninth type of intelligence to his list of multiple intelligences—*existentialist*, which involves exploring and finding meaning in life, especially regarding questions about life, death, and existence.

Gardner argues that each form of intelligence can be destroyed by a different pattern of brain damage, that each involves unique cognitive skills, and that each shows up in unique ways in both the gifted and idiot savants (individuals who have an intellectual disability but have an exceptional talent in a particular domain, such as drawing, music, or numerical computation).

Children in the Key School form "pods" in which they pursue activities of special interest to them. Every day, each child can choose from activities that draw on Gardner's eight intelligences. The school has pods that range from gardening to architecture to gliding to dancing.

What characterizes emotional intelligence?

emotional intelligence The ability to perceive and express emotion accurately and adaptively, to understand emotion and emotional knowledge, to use feelings to facilitate thought, and to manage emotions in oneself and others.

Let's look at a school that used Gardner's multiple intelligences as a foundation of its instruction. The Key School, a K–6 elementary school in Indianapolis, immerses students in activities involving a range of skills that closely correlate with Gardner's eight intelligences (Goleman, Kaufman, & Ray, 1993). Each day every student is exposed to materials designed to stimulate a range of human abilities, including art, music, language skills, math skills, and physical games. In addition, students devote attention to understanding themselves and others.

The Key School's goal is to allow students to discover their natural curiosity and talent, then let them explore these domains. Gardner underscores that if teachers give students opportunities to use their bodies, imaginations, and different senses, almost every student finds that he or she is good at something. Even students who are not outstanding in any single area will still find that they have relative strengths.

Emotional Intelligence   Both Gardner's and Sternberg's theories include one or more categories related to the ability to understand oneself and others and to get along in the world. In Gardner's theory, the categories are called interpersonal intelligence and intrapersonal intelligence; in Sternberg's theory, practical intelligence. Other theorists who emphasize interpersonal, intrapersonal, and practical aspects of intelligence focus on what is called *emotional intelligence,* which was popularized by Daniel Goleman (1995) in his book *Emotional Intelligence.*

The concept of emotional intelligence was initially developed by Peter Salovey and John Mayer (1990). They conceptualize **emotional intelligence** as the ability to perceive and express emotion accurately and adaptively (such as taking the perspective of others), to understand emotion and emotional knowledge (such as understanding the roles that emotions play in friendship and other relationships), to use feelings to facilitate thought (such as being in a positive mood, which is linked to creative thinking), and to manage emotions in oneself and others (such as being able to control one's anger).

There continues to be considerable interest in the concept of emotional intelligence (Gorgens-Eckermans & Brand, 2012; Killgore & others, 2012; Lomas & others, 2012). A recent study of college students revealed that both a test of general mental abilities and an assessment of emotional intelligence were linked to academic performance, although the general mental abilities test was a better predictor (Song & others, 2010). In this study, emotional intelligence was associated with the quality of peer relations.

Critics argue that emotional intelligence broadens the concept of intelligence too far to be useful and has not been adequately assessed and researched (Davidson & Kemp, 2011; Fiori & Antonakis, 2012).

Do People Have One or Many Intelligences?   Figure 8.3 provides a comparison of Sternberg's, Gardner's, and Salovey/Mayer's views of intelligence. Notice that Sternberg's view is unique in emphasizing creative intelligence and that Gardner's includes a number of types of intelligence that are not addressed by the other views. These theories of multiple intelligence have much to offer. They have stimulated us to think more broadly about what makes up people's intelligence and competence (Sternberg, 2012a, b, 2013a, c), and they have motivated educators to develop programs that instruct students in different domains.

Theories of multiple intelligences have critics who conclude that the research base to support these theories has not yet been developed (Jensen, 2008). In particular, some argue that Gardner's classification seems arbitrary. For example, if musical skills represent a type of intelligence, why don't we also refer to chess intelligence, prizefighter intelligence, and so on?

A number of psychologists still support the concept of *g* (general intelligence) (Irwing & others, 2012; Lynn, 2012; Penke & others, 2012). For example, one expert on intelligence, Nathan Brody (2007), argues that people who excel at one type of intellectual task are likely to excel at other intellectual tasks. Thus, individuals who do well at memorizing lists of digits are also likely to be good at solving verbal problems and spatial layout problems. This general intelligence includes abstract reasoning or thinking, the capacity to acquire knowledge, and problem-solving ability (Carroll, 1993).

Advocates of the concept of general intelligence point to its success in predicting school and job performance (Deary, 2012). For example, scores on tests of general intelligence are substantially correlated with school grades and achievement test performance, both at the time of the test and years later (Strenze, 2007). And intelligence tests are moderately correlated with job performance (Lubinski, 2000). Individuals with higher scores on tests designed to measure general intelligence tend to get higher-paying, more prestigious jobs (Strenze, 2007). However, general IQ tests predict only about one-fourth of the variation in job success, with most variation being attributable to other factors such as motivation and education (Wagner & Sternberg, 1986).

Some experts who argue for the existence of general intelligence conclude that individuals also have specific intellectual abilities (Brody, 2007). In sum, controversy still characterizes whether it is more accurate to conceptualize intelligence as a general ability, specific abilities, or both (Roberts & Lipnevich, 2012; Sternberg, 2013a, c). Sternberg (2012) actually accepts that there is a *g* for the kinds of analytical tasks that traditional IQ tests assess but thinks that the range of tasks those tests measure is far too narrow.

THE NEUROSCIENCE OF INTELLIGENCE

In the current era of extensive research on the brain, interest in the neuroscience underpinnings of intelligence has increased (Deary, 2012; Haier, 2011). Among the questions asked about the brain's role in intelligence are the following: Is having a big brain linked to higher intelligence? Is intelligence located in certain brain regions? Is intelligence related to how fast the brain processes information?

Are individuals with a big brain more intelligent than those with a smaller brain? Recent research using MRI scans to assess total brain volume indicates a moderate correlation (about .3 to .4) between brain size and intelligence (Luders & others, 2009).

Might intelligence be linked to specific regions of the brain? Early consensus was that the frontal lobes are the likely location of intelligence. However, researchers recently have found that intelligence is distributed more widely across brain regions (Lee & others, 2012; Sepulcre & others, 2012). The most prominent finding from brain imaging studies is that a distributed neural network involving the frontal and parietal lobes is related to higher intelligence (Deary, Penke, & Johnson, 2010) (see Figure 8.4). A recent study revealed that the frontoparietal network is responsible for cognitive control and connectivity to brain regions outside the network (Cole & others, 2012). Albert Einstein's total brain size was average, but a region of his brain's parietal lobe that is very active in processing math and spatial information was 15 percent larger than average (Witelson, Kigar, & Harvey, 1999). Other brain regions that have been linked to higher intelligence (although at a lower level of significance than the frontal/parietal lobe network) include the temporal and occipital lobes as well as the cerebellum (Luders & others, 2009).

Examining the neuroscience of intelligence has also led to study of the role that neurological speed might play in intelligence (Waiter & others, 2009). Research results have not been consistent for this possible link, although one recent study did find that speed of neurological functioning was faster for intellectually gifted children than for children with average intelligence (Liu & others, 2007).

As the technology to study the brain's functioning continues to advance in coming decades, we are likely to see more specific conclusions about the brain's

Gardner	Sternberg	Salovey/Mayer
Verbal Mathematical	Analytical	
Spatial Movement Musical	Creative	
Interpersonal Intrapersonal	Practical	Emotional
Naturalistic		

FIGURE **8.3**

COMPARING STERNBERG'S, GARDNER'S, AND SALOVEY/MAYER'S INTELLIGENCES

developmental **connection**

Brain Development

The frontal lobes continue to develop through the adolescent and emerging adult years. Chapter 4, p. 116

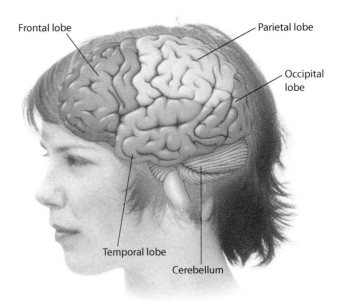

FIGURE **8.4**

INTELLIGENCE AND THE BRAIN. Researchers have found that a higher level of intelligence is linked to a distributed neural network in the frontal and parietal lobes. To a lesser extent than the frontal/parietal network, the temporal and occipital lobes, as well as the cerebellum, also have been found to have links to intelligence. The current consensus is that intelligence is likely to be distributed across brain regions rather than being localized in a specific region such as the frontal lobes.

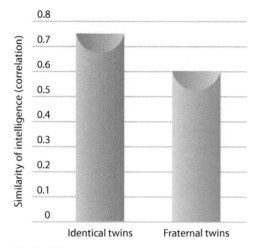

FIGURE 8.5

CORRELATION BETWEEN INTELLIGENCE TEST SCORES AND TWIN STATUS. The graph represents a summary of research findings that have compared the intelligence test scores of identical and fraternal twins. An approximate .15 difference has been found, with a higher correlation for identical twins (.75) and a lower correlation for fraternal twins (.60).

heritability The fraction of the variance in a population that is attributed to genetics.

role in intelligence (Haier, 2011). As this research proceeds, keep in mind that both heredity and environment likely contribute to links between the brain and intelligence, including the connections we discussed between brain size and intelligence.

THE INFLUENCE OF HEREDITY AND ENVIRONMENT

We have seen that intelligence is a slippery concept with competing definitions, tests, and theories. It is not surprising, therefore, that attempts to understand the concept of intelligence are filled with controversy. One of the most controversial areas in the study of intelligence centers on the extent to which intelligence is influenced by genetics and the extent to which it is influenced by environment (Mandelman & Grigorenko, 2011; Nickerson, 2011). In Chapter 2, we indicated how difficult it is to tease apart these influences, but that has not kept psychologists from trying to unravel them.

Genetic Influences   To what degree do our genes make us smart? A research review found that the difference in the average correlations for identical and fraternal twins was not very high—only .15 (Grigorenko, 2000) (see Figure 8.5).

Have scientists been able to pinpoint specific genes that are linked to intelligence? A recent research review concluded that there may be more than 1,000 genes that affect intelligence, each possibly having a small influence on an individual's intelligence (Davies & others, 2011). However, researchers have not been able to identify the specific genes that contribute to intelligence (Deary, 2012).

Adoption studies are also used in attempts to analyze the relative importance of heredity and environment in intelligence (Plomin, DeFries, & Fulker, 2007). In most *adoption studies*, researchers determine whether the behavior of adopted children is more like that of their biological parents or their adoptive parents. In two studies, the educational levels attained by biological parents were better predictors of children's IQ scores than were the IQs of the children's adoptive parents (Petrill & Deater-Deckard, 2004; Scarr & Weinberg, 1983). But studies of adoption also document the influence of environments. A recent research analysis by Richard Nisbett and his colleagues (2012) revealed a 12 to 18 point increase in IQ when children were adopted from low-income into middle- and upper-income homes.

How strong is the effect of heredity on intelligence? The concept of heritability attempts to tease apart the effects of heredity and environment in a population. **Heritability** is the fraction of the variance within a population that is attributed to genetics. The heritability index is computed using correlational techniques. Thus, the highest degree of heritabilty is 1.00, and correlations of .70 and above suggest a strong genetic influence. A committee of respected researchers convened by the American Psychological Association concluded that by late adolescence, the heritability of intelligence is about .75, which reflects a strong genetic influence (Neisser & others, 1996).

A key point to keep in mind about heritability is that it refers to a specific group (population), *not* to individuals. Researchers use the concept of heritability to try to describe why people differ. Heritability says nothing about why a single individual has a certain intelligence. Nor does heritability say anything about differences *between* groups.

Most research on heredity and environment does not include environments that differ radically. Thus, it is not surprising that many genetic studies show environment to be a fairly weak influence on intelligence.

The heritability index has a number of flaws (Daley & Onwuegbuzi, 2011). It is only as good as the data that are entered into its analysis and the interpretations made from it. The data are virtually all from traditional IQ tests, which some experts believe are not always the best indicator of intelligence (Davis & others, 2011; Sternberg, 2013a, c). Also, the heritability index assumes that we can treat genetic and environmental influences as factors that can be separated, with each part contributing a distinct amount of influence. As we discussed in Chapter 2, genes and the environment always work together. Genes always exist in an environment, and the environment shapes their activity.

Environmental Influences   Most experts today agree that the environment also plays an important role in intelligence (Hunt, 2011a, b; Sternberg, 2013a, c). This means that improving children's environments can raise their intelligence (Barnett & others, 2011). One argument for the importance of environment in intelligence involves the increasing scores on IQ tests

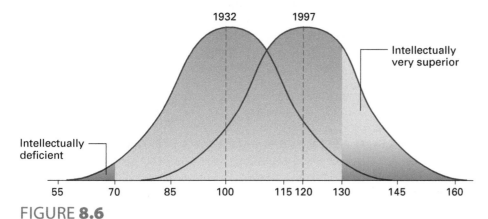

FIGURE **8.6**

THE INCREASE IN IQ SCORES FROM 1932 TO 1997. As measured by the Stanford-Binet intelligence test, American children seem to be getting smarter. Scores of a group tested in 1932 fell along a bell-shaped curve with half below 100 and half above. Studies show that if children took that same test today, half would score above 120 on the 1932 scale. Very few of them would score in the "intellectually deficient" range on the left side, and about one-fourth would rank in the "very superior" range.

around the world. Scores on these tests have been increasing so fast that a high percentage of people regarded as having average intelligence in the early 1900s would be considered below average in intelligence today (Flynn, 1999, 2007, 2011, 2013) (see Figure 8.6). If a representative sample of today's children took the Stanford-Binet test used in 1932, about one-fourth would be defined as very superior, a label usually accorded to less than 3 percent of the population. Because the increase has taken place in a relatively short period of time, it can't be due to heredity (Flynn & Rossi-Case, 2012). Rather, it might result from environmental factors such as increased exposure to information and education. One analysis indicated that the substantial increase in intelligence scores in recent years may be due to prenatal and early postnatal nutrition (Lynn, 2009). And another recent study revealed that children with more highly educated (especially college-educated) mothers and/or children born into higher-income families received higher scores on math achievement tests than children who had less-educated mothers and/or belonged to lower-income families (Ang, Rodgers, & Wanstrom, 2010). The worldwide increase in intelligence test scores over a short time frame is called the *Flynn effect* after the researcher who discovered it, James Flynn (1999, 2007, 2011, 2013).

Studies of schooling also reveal effects on intelligence (Barnett & others, 2011; Ceci & Gilstrap, 2000; Gustafsson, 2007). The biggest effects occurred when large groups of children were deprived of formal education for an extended period, resulting in lower intelligence. In one study, the intellectual functioning of ethnic Indian children in South Africa, whose schooling was delayed by four years because of the unavailability of teachers, was investigated (Ramphal, 1962). Compared with children in nearby villages who had teachers, the Indian children whose entry into school was delayed by four years experienced a drop of 5 IQ points for each year of delay.

Researchers increasingly are interested in manipulating the early environment of children who are at risk for impoverished intelligence (Bagnato & Macy, 2012; Phillips & Lowenstein, 2011). The emphasis is on prevention rather than remediation. Many low-income parents have difficulty providing an intellectually stimulating environment for their children. Programs that educate parents to be more sensitive caregivers and better teachers, as well as support services such as quality child-care programs, can enhance a child's intellectual development (Johnson & Brooks-Gunn, 2012; Squires & others, 2013).

What can we learn from research on the influence of early intervention on intelligence? To find out, see *Connecting Through Research.*

Revisiting the Nature vs. Nurture Issue In sum, there is a consensus among psychologists that both heredity and environment influence intelligence (Pleh, 2012; Sternberg, 2013a, c). This consensus reflects the nature versus nurture issue that was highlighted in

Students in an elementary school in South Africa. *How might schooling influence the development of children's intelligence?*

The highest-risk children often benefit the most cognitively when they experience early interventions.

—**CRAIG RAMEY**
Contemporary Psychologist, Georgetown University

developmental **connection**

Nature vs. Nurture

The epigenetic view emphasizes that development is an ongoing, bidirectional interchange between heredity and environment. Chapter 2, p. 69

connecting through research

The Abecedarian Project

In the Abecedarian Intervention program at the University of North Carolina at Chapel Hill, conducted by Craig Ramey and his colleagues (Campbell & others, 2012; Ramey & Campbell, 1984; Ramey & Ramey, 1998; Ramey, Ramey, & Lanzi, 2006), 111 young children from low-income, poorly educated families were randomly assigned to either an intervention group, which received full-time, year-round child care along with medical and social work services, or a control group, which received medical and social benefits but no child care. The child-care program included game-like learning activities aimed at improving language, motor, social, and cognitive skills.

The success of the program in improving IQ was evident by the time the children were 3 years of age. At that age, the experimental group showed normal IQs averaging 101, a 17-point advantage over the control group. Recent follow-up results suggest that the effects are long-lasting. More than a decade later at age 15, children from the intervention group maintained an IQ advantage of 5 points over the control-group children (97.7 to 92.6) (Campbell & others, 2001; Ramey, Ramey, & Lanzi, 2001). They also did better on standardized tests of reading and math and were less likely to be held back a year in school. Also, the greatest IQ gains were made by the children whose mothers had especially low IQs—below 70.

At age 15, these children showed a 10-point IQ advantage over a group of children whose mothers' IQs were below 70 but who had not experienced the child-care intervention. In a recent analysis of the Abcedarian intervention project, at age 30 the children who had experienced the early intervention had attained more years of education but the intervention had not led to any benefits involving social adjustment and criminal activity (Campbell & others, 2012).

The results of the Abecedarian Intervention program are not unprecedented. A review of the research on early interventions reached the following conclusions (Brooks-Gunn, 2003):

- High-quality center-based interventions are associated with increases in children's intelligence and school achievement.
- Early interventions are most successful with poor children and children whose parents have little education.
- The positive benefits continue through adolescence but are stronger in early childhood and at the beginning of elementary school.
- The programs that are continued into middle and late childhood have the best long-term results.

Chapter 1. Recall that the nature versus nurture issue focuses on the extent to which development is influenced by nature (heredity) and nurture (environment). Although psychologists agree that intelligence is the product of both nature and nurture, there is still disagreement about how strongly each factor influences intelligence (Deary, Penke, & Johnson, 2010; Sternberg, 2012; Wadsworth, Olson, & Defries, 2010).

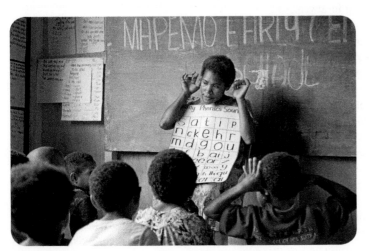

The intelligence of the Iatmul people of Papua New Guinea involves the ability to remember the names of many clans.

On the 680 Caroline Islands in the Pacific Ocean east of the Philippines, the intelligence of their inhabitants includes the ability to navigate by the stars. *Why might it be difficult to create a culture-fair intelligence test for the Iatmul children, Caroline Islands children, and U.S. children?*

Why Is It So Hard to Create Culture-Fair Tests?

Why is it so hard to create culture-fair tests? Most tests tend to reflect what the dominant culture thinks is important (Zhang & Sternberg, 2013). If tests have time limits, that will bias the test against groups that are not concerned with time. If languages differ, the same words might have different meanings for different language groups. Even pictures can produce bias because some cultures have less experience with drawings and photographs. Within the same culture, different groups could have different attitudes, values, and motivation, and this could affect their performance on intelligence tests (Barnett & others,

2011). Items that ask why buildings should be made of brick are biased against children with little or no experience with brick houses. Questions about railroads, furnaces, seasons of the year, distances between cities, and so on can be biased against groups who have less experience than others with these contexts. Because of such difficulties in creating culture-fair tests, Robert Sternberg (2012b; Zhang & Sternberg, 2013) concludes that there are no culture-fair tests, but only culture-reduced tests.

GROUP COMPARISONS

For decades, many controversies surrounding intelligence tests have grown from the tendency to compare one group with another. Many people keep asking whether their culture or ethnic group is more intelligent than others.

Cross-Cultural Comparisons   Cultures vary in the way they describe what it means to be intelligent (Ang, Dyne, & Tan, 2011; Zhang & Sternberg, 2013). People in Western cultures tend to view intelligence in terms of reasoning and thinking skills, whereas people in Eastern cultures see intelligence as a way for members of a community to successfully engage in social roles (Nisbett, 2003). One study found that Taiwanese-Chinese conceptions of intelligence emphasize understanding and relating to others, including knowing when to show and when not to show one's intelligence (Yang & Sternberg, 1997).

Cultural Bias in Testing   Many of the early intelligence tests were culturally biased, favoring people who were from urban rather than rural environments, of middle socioeconomic status rather than lower socioeconomic status, and White rather than African American (Miller-Jones, 1989; Provenzo, 2002). For example, one question on an early test asked what you should do if you find a 3-year-old child in the street. The correct answer was "call the police." But children from inner-city families who perceive the police as adversaries are unlikely to choose this answer. Also, members of minority groups who do not speak English or who speak nonstandard English are at a disadvantage in trying to understand questions framed in standard English (Suzuki, Short, & Lee, 2011).

Psychologists have developed **culture-fair tests,** which are intelligence tests that aim to avoid cultural bias. Two types of culture-fair tests have been developed. The first includes questions that are familiar to people from all socioeconomic and ethnic backgrounds. For example, a child might be asked how a bird and a dog are different, on the assumption that virtually all children are familiar with birds and dogs. The second type of culture-fair test contains no verbal questions. Figure 8.7 shows a sample question from Raven's Progressive Matrices tests. Even though tests such as Raven's Progressive Matrices are designed to be culture-fair, people with more education still score higher than those with less education (Greenfield, 2003). To read further about culture-fair tests, see the *Connecting with Diversity* interlude.

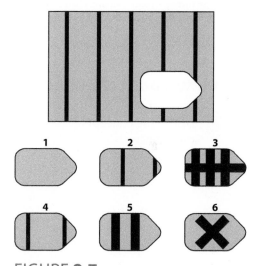

FIGURE **8.7**

SAMPLE ITEM FROM RAVEN'S PROGRESSIVE MATRICES TESTS. Individuals are presented with a matrix arrangement of symbols, such as the one at the top of this figure, and must then complete the matrix by selecting the appropriate missing symbol from a group of symbols, such as the ones at the bottom. Simulated items similar to those in *Raven's Progressive Matrices*. Copyright © 1998 by NCS Pearson, Inc. Reproduced by permission. All rights reserved. "Raven's Progressive Matrices" is a trademark, in the U.S. and/or other countries, of Pearson Education, Inc. or its affiliates.

culture-fair tests Intelligence tests that aim to avoid cultural bias.

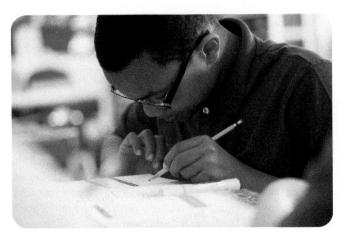

How might stereotype threat be involved in ethnic minority students' performance on standardized tests?

stereotype threat Anxiety that one's behavior might confirm a stereotype about one's group.

Ethnic Comparisons   Assessments of ethnic comparisons consistently indicate the following order from highest to lowest scores on intelligence tests: (1) Asian Americans, (2) non-Latino Whites, (3) Latinos, and (4) African Americans (Suzuki, Short, & Lee, 2011; Yeung, 2012). These are *average scores,* however. There is always considerable within-group variation on psychological tests, so that although African American children score lower than non-Latino White children overall on intelligence tests, many African American children score higher than non-Latino White children.

Further, a recent research review concluded that as African Americans have gained social, economic, and educational opportunities, the IQ gap between African American and non-Latino Whites has decreased considerably in recent years (Nisbett & others, 2012). In one analysis, IQ differences between non-Latino Whites and African American children have dropped about 6 points over the last three decades, from a difference of 15 points to 9 points (Nisbett, 2009).

One potential influence on intelligence test performance is **stereotype threat,** the anxiety that one's behavior might confirm a negative stereotype about one's group (Carr & Dweck, 2011; Halpern, Beninger, & Straight, 2011). For example, when African Americans take an intelligence test, they may experience anxiety about confirming the old stereotype that African Americans are "intellectually inferior." Some studies have confirmed the existence of stereotype threat (Carr & Steele, 2009; Kellow & Jones, 2008). For example, African American students do more poorly on standardized tests if they perceive that they are being evaluated. If they think the test doesn't count, they perform as well as White students (Aronson, 2002). However, critics argue that the extent to which stereotype threat explains the testing gap has been exaggerated (Sackett, Hardison, & Cullen, 2005).

Review *Connect* Reflect

LG1 Explain the concept of intelligence.

Review

- What is intelligence?
- What are the main individual tests of intelligence?
- What theories of multiple intelligences have been developed? Do people have one intelligence or many intelligences?
- What are some links between the brain and intelligence?
- What evidence indicates that heredity influences IQ scores? What evidence indicates that environment influences IQ scores?
- What is known about the intelligence of people from different cultures and ethnic groups?

Connect

- In this section you learned that different cultures have different concepts of intelligence, and in Chapter 5 you learned about culture's effect on motor development. What do these findings have in common?

Reflect *Your Own Personal Journey of Life*

- A CD-ROM is being sold to parents for testing their child's IQ. Several parents tell you that they purchased the CD-ROM and assessed their children's IQs. Why might you be skeptical about giving your children an IQ test and interpreting the results yourself?

The Development of Intelligence   Discuss the development of intelligence.

Tests of Infant Intelligence

Stability and Change in Intelligence Through Adolescence

How can the intelligence of infants be assessed? Is intelligence stable through childhood? These are some of the questions we will explore as we examine the development of intelligence.

Toosje Thyssen Van Beveren, Infant Assessment Specialist

Toosje Thyssen Van Beveren is a developmental psychologist at the University of Texas Medical Center in Dallas. She has a master's degree in child clinical psychology and a Ph.D. in human development. Currently, Van Beveren is involved in a 12-week program called New Connections, which is a comprehensive intervention for young children who were affected by substance abuse prenatally and for their caregivers.

In the New Connections program, Van Beveren assesses infants' developmental status and progress. She might refer the infants to a speech, physical, or occupational therapist and monitor the infants' services and progress. Van Beveren trains the program staff and encourages them to use the exercises she recommends. She also discusses the child's problems with the primary caregivers, suggests activities, and assists them in enrolling infants in appropriate programs.

During her graduate work at the University of Texas at Dallas, Van Beveren was author John Santrock's teaching assistant in his undergraduate course on life-span development for four years. As a teaching assistant, she attended classes, graded exams, counseled students, and occasionally gave lectures. Each semester, Van Beveren returns to give a lecture on prenatal development and infancy. She also teaches a number

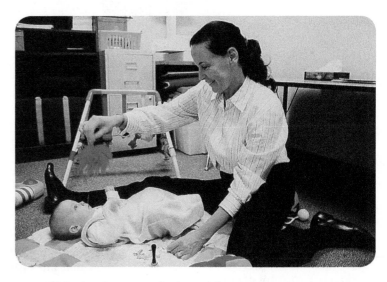

Toosje Thyssen Van Beveren conducting an infant assessment.

of courses in the psychology department at UT–Dallas, including the course "Child Development." In Van Beveren's words, "My days are busy and full. The work is often challenging. There are some disappointments, but mostly the work is enormously gratifying."

TESTS OF INFANT INTELLIGENCE

The infant-testing movement grew out of the tradition of IQ testing. However, tests that assess infants are necessarily less verbal than IQ tests for older children. Tests for infants contain far more items related to perceptual-motor development. They also include measures of social interaction. To read about the work of one infant assessment specialist, see *Connecting with Careers*.

The most important early contributor to the testing of infants was Arnold Gesell (1934). He developed a measure that helped sort out potentially normal babies from abnormal ones. This was especially useful to adoption agencies, which had large numbers of babies awaiting placement. Gesell's examination was used widely for many years and still is frequently employed by pediatricians to distinguish between normal and abnormal infants. The current version of the Gesell test has four categories of behavior: motor, language, adaptive, and personal-social. The **developmental quotient (DQ)** combines subscores in these categories to provide an overall score.

The widely used **Bayley Scales of Infant Development** were developed by Nancy Bayley (1969) to assess infant behavior and predict later development. The current version, Bayley-III, has five scales: cognitive, language, motor, socioemotional, and adaptive (Bayley, 2006). The first three scales are administered directly to the infant; the latter two are questionnaires given to the caregiver. The Bayley-III also is more appropriate for use in clinical settings than the two previous editions (Lennon & others, 2008).

How should a 6-month-old perform on the Bayley cognitive scale? The 6-month-old infant should be able to vocalize pleasure and displeasure, persistently search for objects that

developmental quotient (DQ) An overall developmental score that combines subscores on motor, language, adaptive, and personal-social domains in the Gesell assessment of infants.

Bayley Scales of Infant Development Initially created by Nancy Bayley, these scales are widely used in assessing infant development. The current version has five scales: cognitive, language, motor, socioemotional, and adaptive.

Items used in the Bayley Scales of Infant Development.

are just out of immediate reach, and approach a mirror that is placed in front of the infant by the examiner. By 12 months of age, the infant should be able to inhibit behavior when commanded to do so, imitate words the examiner says (such as *Mama*), and respond to simple requests (such as "Take a drink").

The explosion of interest in infant development has produced many new measures, especially tasks that evaluate the ways infants process information (Fagan, 2011). The Fagan Test of Infant Intelligence is increasingly being used (Fagan, 1992). This test focuses on the infant's ability to process information by encoding the attributes of objects, detecting similarities and differences between objects, forming mental representations, and retrieving these representations. For example, it estimates intelligence by comparing the amount of time babies look at a new object with the amount of time they spend looking at a familiar object.

Unlike the Gesell and Bayley scales, the Fagan test is correlated with measures of intelligence in older children. In fact, evidence is accumulating that measures of habituation and dishabituation are linked to intelligence in childhood, adolescence, and even adulthood. For example, one study revealed that selective attention to novelty at 6 to 12 months correlated positively with intelligence at 21 years of age (Fagan, Holland, & Wheeler, 2007). And a longitudinal study revealed that four information processing domains (attention, processing speed, memory, and representational competence) assessed in infancy and early childhood were linked to general intelligence scores on the Wechsler Intelligence Scale for Children–III assessed at 11 years of age (Rose & others, 2012).

It is important, however, not to go too far and think that connections between cognitive development in early infancy and later cognitive development are so strong that no discontinuity takes place. As we discussed in Chapters 6 and 7, some important changes in cognitive development occur after infancy.

developmental **connection**

Information Processing

Habituation and dishabituation are important aspects of attention in infancy. Chapter 7, p. 199

STABILITY AND CHANGE IN INTELLIGENCE THROUGH ADOLESCENCE

A recent longitudinal study examined the intelligence of 200 children from 12 months (using the Bayley scales) to 4 years of age (using the Stanford-Binet test) (Blaga & others, 2009). The results indicated considerable stability from late infancy through the preschool years.

An early study examined correlations between IQ at a number of different ages (Honzik, MacFarlane, & Allen, 1948). There was a strong relation between IQ scores obtained at the ages of 6, 8, and 9 and IQ scores obtained at the age of 10. For example, the correlation between IQ at the age of 8 and IQ at the age of 10 was .88. The correlation between IQ at the age of 9 and IQ at the age of 10 was .90. These figures show a very close relationship between IQ scores obtained in these years. The correlation between IQ in the preadolescent years and IQ at the age of 18 was slightly lower but was still statistically significant. For example, the correlation between IQ at the age of 10 and IQ at the age of 18 was .70.

What has been said so far about the stability of intelligence has been based on measures of groups of individuals. The stability of intelligence also can be evaluated through studies of individuals. Robert McCall and his associates (McCall, Appelbaum, & Hogarty, 1973) studied 140 children between the ages of 2½ and 17. They found that the average range of IQ scores was more than 28 points. The scores of one out of three children changed by as much as 40 points.

What can we conclude about stability and changes in intelligence during childhood? Intelligence test scores can fluctuate dramatically across the childhood years. Intelligence is not as stable as the original intelligence theorists envisioned. Children are adaptive beings. They have the capacity for intellectual change, but they do not become entirely new intelligent beings. In a sense, children's intelligence changes but remains connected with early points in development.

Review *Connect* Reflect

LG2 Discuss the development of intelligence.

Review

- How is intelligence assessed during infancy?
- How much does intelligence change through childhood and adolescence?

Connect

- In this section, you learned about research on the development of intelligence. Referring back to Chapter 1, identify which research methods and designs were used in these research studies and describe their pros and cons relative to their subject matter.

Reflect *Your Own Personal Journey of Life*

- As a parent, would you want to have your infant's intelligence tested? Why or why not?

The Extremes of Intelligence and Creativity

 LG3 Describe the characteristics of intellectual disability, giftedness, and creativity.

| Intellectual Disabilty | Giftedness | Creativity |

Intellectual disability and intellectual giftedness are the extremes of intelligence. Often intelligence tests are used to identify exceptional individuals. After discussing intellectual disability and giftedness, we'll explore how creativity differs from intelligence.

INTELLECTUAL DISABILITY

The most distinctive feature of intellectual disability (formerly called mental retardation) is inadequate intellectual functioning. Long before formal tests were developed to assess intelligence, individuals with an intellectual disability were identified by a lack of age-appropriate skills in learning and caring for themselves. Once intelligence tests were developed, they were used to identify the degree of intellectual disability. But of two individuals with an intellectual disability who have the same low IQ, one might be married, employed, and involved in the community and the other might require constant supervision in an institution. Such differences in social competence led psychologists to include deficits in adaptive behavior in their definition of intellectual disability.

Intellectual disability is a condition of limited mental ability in which the individual (1) has a low IQ, usually below 70 on a traditional intelligence test; (2) has difficulty adapting to everyday life; and (3) first exhibits these characteristics by age 18 (Hodapp & others, 2011). The age limit is included in the definition of intellectual disability because, for example, we don't usually think of a college student who suffers massive brain damage in a car accident, resulting in an IQ of 60, as having an "intellectual disability." The low IQ and low adaptiveness should be evident in childhood, not after normal functioning is interrupted by damage of some form. About 5 million Americans fit this definition of intellectual disability.

There are several ways to define degrees of intellectual disability (Hallahan, Kaufmann, & Pullen, 2012; Hodapp & others, 2011). Most school systems use the classifications shown in Figure 8.8, in which IQ scores categorize intellectual disability as mild, moderate, severe, or profound.

Note that a large majority of individuals diagnosed with an intellectual disability fit into the mild category. However, these categories are not perfect predictors of functioning. A different classification system is based on the degree of support required for a person with an intellectual disability to function at the highest level. These categories of support are intermittent (supports given as needed), limited (supports are intense over time), extensive (supports needed are regular, typically occurring every day), and pervasive (supports are constant, intense, and are needed in all settings).

Type of Intellectual Disability	IQ Range	Percentage
Mild	55–70	89
Moderate	40–54	6
Severe	25–39	4
Profound	Below 25	1

FIGURE **8.8**

CLASSIFICATION OF INTELLECTUAL DISABILITY BASED ON IQ

intellectual disability A condition of limited mental ability in which the individual (1) has a low IQ, usually below 70 on a traditional intelligence test; (2) has difficulty adapting to everyday life; and (3) has an onset of these characteristics by age 18.

This young boy has Down syndrome. *What causes a child to develop Down syndrome? In what major classification of intellectual disability does the condition fall?*

Some cases of intellectual disability have an organic cause. *Organic intellectual disability* describes a genetic disorder or a lower level of intellectual functioning caused by brain damage. Down syndrome is one form of organic intellectual disability, and it occurs when an extra chromosome is present. Other causes of organic intellectual disability include fragile X syndrome, an abnormality in the X chromosome that was discussed in Chapter 2, "Biological Beginnings"; prenatal malformation; metabolic disorders; and diseases that affect the brain. Most people who suffer from organic intellectual disability have IQs between 0 and 50.

When no evidence of organic brain damage can be found, cases are labeled *cultural-familial intellectual disability*. Individuals with this type of disability have IQs between 55 and 70. Psychologists suspect that this type of disability often results from growing up in a below-average intellectual environment. Children with this type of disability can be identified in schools, where they often fail, need tangible rewards (candy rather than praise), and are highly sensitive to what others expect of them. However, as adults, they are usually invisible, perhaps because adult settings don't tax their cognitive skills as heavily. It may also be that they increase their intelligence as they move toward adulthood.

GIFTEDNESS

There have always been people whose abilities and accomplishments have outshined others'—the whiz kid in class, the star athlete, the natural musician. People who are **gifted** have above-average intelligence (an IQ of 130 or higher) and/or superior talent for something. When it comes to programs for the gifted, most school systems select children who have intellectual superiority and academic aptitude, whereas children who are talented in the visual and performing arts (arts, drama, dance), who are skilled athletes, or who possess other special aptitudes tend to be overlooked (Grigorenko & others, 2012). Estimates vary but indicate that approximately 3 to 5 percent of U.S. students are gifted (National Association for Gifted Children, 2009). This percentage is likely conservative because it focuses more on children who are gifted intellectually and academically, often failing to include those who are gifted in creative thinking as well as the visual and performing arts (Ford, 2012).

What are the characteristics of children who are gifted? Despite speculation that giftedness is linked with having a mental disorder, no connection between giftedness and mental disorder has been found. Similarly, the idea that gifted children are maladjusted is a myth, as Lewis Terman (1925) found when he conducted an extensive study of 1,500 children whose Stanford-Binet IQs averaged 150. The children in Terman's study were socially well adjusted, and many went on to become successful doctors, lawyers, professors, and scientists. Studies support the conclusion that gifted people tend to be more mature than others, have fewer emotional problems than average, and grow up in a positive family climate (Davidson, 2000).

Noncognitive contributors to giftedness have received increasing attention in recent years (Reis & Renzulli, 2011). Creativity, motivation, optimism, and physical and mental energy are examples of noncognitive factors that can influence whether children display giftedness.

Ellen Winner (1996) described three criteria that characterize gifted children, whether in art, music, or academic domains:

At 2 years of age, art prodigy Alexandra Nechita colored in coloring books for hours and also took up pen and ink drawing. She had no interest in dolls or friends. By age 5 she was using watercolors. Once she started school, she would start painting as soon as she got home. At the age of 8, she saw the first public exhibit of her work. In succeeding years, working quickly and impulsively on canvases as large as 5 feet by 9 feet, she has completed hundreds of paintings, some of which sell for close to $100,000 apiece. As a teenager, she continues to paint—relentlessly and passionately. It is, she says, what she loves to do. *What are some characteristics of children who are gifted?*

1. *Precocity.* Gifted children are precocious. They begin to master an area earlier than their peers. Learning in their domain is more effortless for them than for ordinary children. In most instances, these gifted children are precocious because they have an inborn high ability in a particular domain or domains.

2. *Marching to their own drummer.* Gifted children learn in a qualitatively different way from ordinary children. One way that they march to a different drummer is that they need minimal help, or scaffolding, from adults to learn. In many instances, they resist any kind of explicit instruction. They often make discoveries on their own and solve problems in unique ways.

3. *A passion to master.* Gifted children are driven to understand the domain in which they have high ability. They display an intense, obsessive interest and an ability to focus. They motivate themselves, says Winner, and do not need to be "pushed" by their parents.

Nature vs. Nurture Is giftedness a product of heredity or environment? Likely both (Grigorenko & others, 2012). Individuals who are gifted recall that they had signs of high ability in a particular area at a very young age, prior to or at the beginning of formal training (Howe & others, 1995). This suggests the importance of innate ability in giftedness. However, researchers have also found that individuals with world-class status in the arts, mathematics, science, and sports all report strong family support and years of training and practice (Bloom, 1985). Deliberate practice is an important characteristic of individuals who become experts in a particular domain. For example, in one study, the best musicians engaged in twice as much deliberate practice over their lives as did the least successful ones (Ericsson, Krampe, & Tesch-Romer, 1993).

Developmental Changes and Domain-Specific Giftedness Can we predict from infancy who will be gifted as children, adolescents, and adults? John Colombo and his colleagues (2004, 2009) have found that measures of infant attention and habituation are not good predictors of high cognitive ability later in development. However, they have discovered a link between assessment with the Home Observation for Measure of the Environment at 18 months of age and high cognitive ability in the preschool years. The best predictor at 18 months of high cognitive ability in the preschool years was the provision of materials and a variety of experiences in the home. These findings illustrate the importance of the cognitive environment provided by parents in the development of children's giftedness.

A young Bill Gates, founder of Microsoft and now the world's richest person. Like many highly gifted students, Gates was not especially fond of school. He hacked a computer security system when he was 13 and as a high school student, he was allowed to take some college math classes. He dropped out of Harvard University and began developing a plan for what was to become Microsoft Corporation. *What are some ways that schools can enrich the education of such highly talented students as Gates to make it a more challenging, interesting, and meaningful experience?*

Individuals who are highly gifted are typically not gifted in many domains, and research on giftedness is increasingly focused on domain-specific developmental trajectories (Feldman & Morelock, 2011). During the childhood years, the domains in which individuals are gifted usually emerge. Thus, at some point in the childhood years, the child who will become a gifted artist or the child who will become a gifted mathematician begins to show expertise in that domain. Regarding domain-specific giftedness, software genius Bill Gates (1998), the founder of Microsoft and one of the world's richest persons, commented that when you are good at something you may have to resist the urge to think that you will be good at everything. Gates says that because he has been so successful at software development, people expect him to be brilliant about other domains in which he is far from being a genius.

Identifying an individual's domain-specific talent and providing the individual with individually appropriate and optional educational opportunities needs to be accomplished by adolescence at the latest (Keating, 2009). During adolescence, individuals who are talented become less reliant on parental support and increasingly pursue their own interests.

Some children who are gifted become gifted adults, but many gifted children do not become gifted and highly creative adults. In Terman's research on children with superior IQs, the children typically became experts in a well-established domain, such as medicine, law, or business. However, they did not become major creators (Winner, 2000). That is, they did not create a new domain or revolutionize an old domain.

Education of Children Who Are Gifted An increasing number of experts argue that the education of children who are gifted in the United States requires a significant overhaul (Olszewski-Kubilius & Thomson, 2013). Underchallenged gifted children can become disruptive, skip classes, and lose interest in achieving. Sometimes these children just disappear into the woodwork, becoming passive and apathetic toward school. It is extremely important for teachers to challenge children who are gifted to reach high expectations.

Ellen Winner (1996, 2006) argues that too often children who are gifted are socially isolated and underchallenged in the classroom. It is not unusual for them to be ostracized and labeled "nerds" or "geeks." A child who is truly gifted often is the only child in the classroom who does not have the opportunity to learn with students of like ability. Many eminent adults report that school was a negative experience for them, that they were bored and sometimes knew more than their teachers (Bloom, 1985). Winner argues that American education will benefit when standards are raised for all children. When some children are still underchallenged, she recommends

gifted Possession of above-average intelligence (an IQ of 130 or higher) and/or superior talent for something.

Sterling Jones, Supervisor of Gifted and Talented Education

Sterling Jones is program supervisor for gifted and talented children in the Detroit Public School System. Jones has been working for more than three decades with children who are gifted. He believes that students' mastery of skills mainly depends on the amount of time devoted to instruction and the length of time allowed for learning. Thus, he believes that many basic strategies for challenging children who are gifted to develop their skills can be applied to a wider range of students than once believed. He has rewritten several pamphlets for use by teachers and parents, including *How to Help Your Child Succeed* and *Gifted and Talented Education for Everyone*.

Jones holds undergraduate and graduate degrees from Wayne State University, and he taught English for a number of years before becoming involved in the program for gifted children. He also has written materials on African Americans, such as *Voices from the Black Experience*, that are used in the Detroit schools.

Sterling Jones with some of the children in the gifted program in the Detroit Public School System.

For more information about what teachers of exceptional children (special education) do, see page 42 in the Careers in Child Development appendix following Chapter 1.

Margaret (Peg) Cagle with some of the gifted seventh- and eighth-grade math students she teaches at Lawrence Middle School in Chatsworth, California. Cagle especially advocates challenging students who are gifted to take intellectual risks. To encourage collaboration, she often has students work together in groups of four, and frequently tutors students during lunch hour. As 13-year-old Madeline Lewis commented, "If you don't get it one way, she'll explain it another and talk to you about it and show you until you do get it." Cagle says it is important to be passionate about teaching math and to open up a world for students that shows them how beautiful learning math can be (Wong Briggs, 2007, p. 6D).

that they be allowed to attend advanced classes in their domain of exceptional ability. For example, some especially precocious middle school students should be allowed to take college classes in their area of expertise. Bill Gates, founder of Microsoft, took college math classes and hacked a computer security system at 13; Yo-Yo Ma, famous cellist, graduated from high school at 15 and attended Juilliard School of Music in New York City.

A final concern is that African American, Latino, and Native American children are underrepresented in gifted programs (Ford, 2012). Much of the underrepresentation involves the lower test scores for these children compared to non-Latino White and Asian American children, which may be due to test bias and fewer opportunities to develop language skills such as vocabulary and comprehension (Ford, 2012).

A number of individuals work in various capacities in school systems with children who are gifted. To read about the work of Sterling Jones, specialist in gifted and talented education, see *Connecting with Careers*.

CREATIVITY

We brought up the term "creative" on several occasions in our discussion of intelligence and giftedness. What does it mean to be creative? **Creativity** is the ability to think about something in novel and unusual ways and come up with unique solutions to problems.

Intelligence and creativity are not the same thing (Sternberg & Sternberg, 2012). Most creative people are quite intelligent, but the reverse is not necessarily true. Many highly intelligent people (as measured by high scores on conventional tests of intelligence) are not very creative (Sternberg, 2013a, b). Many highly intelligent people produce large numbers of products that are not necessarily novel.

Why don't IQ scores predict creativity? Creativity requires divergent thinking (Guilford, 1967). **Divergent thinking** produces many answers to the same question. In contrast, conventional intelligence tests require **convergent thinking.** For example, a typical question on a conventional intelligence test is, "How many quarters will you get in return for 60 dimes?" There is only one correct answer to this question. In contrast, a question such as "What image comes to mind when you hear the phrase 'sitting alone in a dark room'?" has many possible answers; it calls for divergent thinking.

Just as in being gifted, children show creativity in some domains more than others (Feldman & Morelock, 2011). For example, a child who shows creativity in mathematics might not be as creative in art.

A special concern is that children's creative thinking appears to be declining. A study of approximately 300,000 U.S. children and adults found that creativity scores rose until 1990, but since then have been steadily declining (Kim, 2010). Among the likely causes of the creativity decline are the number of hours U.S. children watch TV and play video games instead of engaging in creative activities, as well as the lack of emphasis on creative thinking skills in schools (Gregorson, Kaufman, & Snyder, 2013; Kaufman & Sternberg, 2012, 2013). Some countries, though, are placing increasing emphasis on creative thinking in schools. For example, creative thinking historically was discouraged in Chinese schools. However, Chinese educators are now encouraging teachers to spend more classroom time on creative activities (Plucker, 2010). To read about some strategies for helping children become more creative, see *Caring Connections.*

creativity The ability to think in novel and unusual ways and come up with unique solutions to problems.

divergent thinking Thinking that produces many answers to the same question; characteristic of creativity.

convergent thinking Thinking that produces one correct answer; characteristic of the kind of thinking required on conventional intelligence tests.

brainstorming A technique in which children are encouraged to come up with creative ideas in a group, play off one another's ideas, and say practically whatever comes to mind.

caring *connections*

Guiding Children's Creativity

An important goal of teachers is to help children become more creative (Hennessey, 2011; Kaufman & Sternberg, 2013). What are the best strategies for accomplishing this goal? We examine some of these strategies next.

Encourage Creative Thinking on a Group and Individual Basis

Brainstorming is a technique in which children are encouraged to come up with creative ideas in a group, play off each other's ideas, and say practically whatever comes to mind that seems relevant to a particular issue. Participants are usually told to hold off from criticizing others' ideas at least until the end of the brainstorming session.

Provide Environments That Stimulate Creativity

Some environments nourish creativity, while others inhibit it. Parents and teachers who encourage creativity often rely on children's natural curiosity (Fairweather & Cramond, 2011). They provide exercises and activities that stimulate children to find insightful solutions to problems, rather than ask a lot of questions that require rote answers (Baer & Kaufman, 2013). Teachers also encourage creativity by taking students on field trips to locations where creativity is valued. Howard Gardner (1993) emphasizes that science, discovery, and children's museums offer rich opportunities to stimulate creativity.

What are some good strategies teachers can use to guide children in thinking more creatively?

Don't Overcontrol Students

Teresa Amabile (1993) says that telling children exactly how to do things leaves them feeling that originality is a mistake and exploration is a waste of time. If, instead of dictating which activities they should engage in, you

(continued)

Intelligence

| The Concept of Intelligence | **LG1** Explain the concept of intelligence. |

What Is Intelligence?

- Intelligence consists of the ability to solve problems and to adapt and learn from experiences. A key aspect of intelligence focuses on its individual variations. Traditionally, intelligence has been measured by tests designed to compare people's performance on cognitive tasks.

Intelligence Tests

- Alfred Binet developed the first intelligence test and created the concept of mental age. William Stern developed the concept of IQ for use with the Binet test. Revisions of the Binet test are called the Stanford-Binet. The test scores on the Stanford-Binet approximate a normal distribution. The Wechsler scales, created by David Wechsler, are the other main intelligence assessment tool. These tests provide an overall IQ, scores on a number of subtests, and several composite indexes. When used by a judicious examiner, tests can be valuable tools for determining individual differences in intelligence. Test scores should be only one type of information used to evaluate an individual. IQ scores can produce unfortunate stereotypes and false expectations.

Theories of Multiple Intelligences

- Sternberg's triarchic theory states that there are three main types of intelligence: analytical, creative, and practical. Sternberg created the Sternberg Triarchic Abilities Test to assess these three types of intelligence and has described applications of triarchic theory to children's education. Gardner maintains that there are eight types of intelligence, or frames of mind: verbal skills, mathematical skills, spatial skills, bodily-kinesthetic skills, musical skills, interpersonal skills, intrapersonal skills, and naturalist skills. The Key School applies Gardner's view to educating children by immersing students in activities that closely correlate with Gardner's eight frames of mind. Emotional intelligence is the ability to perceive and express emotion accurately and adaptively, to understand emotion and emotional knowledge, to use feelings to facilitate thought, and to manage emotions in oneself and others. The multiple-intelligences approaches have broadened the definition of intelligence and motivated educators to develop programs that instruct students in different domains. Critics maintain that Gardner's multiple-intelligence classification seems arbitrary. Critics also say that there is insufficient research to support the concept of multiple intelligences.

The Neuroscience of Intelligence

- Interest in discovering links between the brain and intelligence has been stimulated by advances in brain imaging. A moderate correlation has been found between overall brain size and intelligence. Recent research has revealed a link between a distributed neural network in the frontal and parietal lobes and intelligence. Research on a connection between neural processing speed and intelligence has produced inconsistent findings.

The Influence of Heredity and Environment

- Genetic similarity might explain why identical twins show stronger correlations on intelligence tests than fraternal twins do. Some studies indicate that the IQs of adopted children are more similar to the IQs of their biological parents than to those of their adoptive parents. Many studies show that intelligence has a reasonably strong heritability component, but environmental influences also are important. Intelligence test scores have risen considerably around the world in recent decades—called the Flynn effect—and this supports the role of environment in intelligence. Researchers have found that being deprived of formal education lowers IQ scores. Ramey's research revealed the positive effects of educational child care on intelligence.

Group Comparisons

- Cultures vary in the way they define intelligence. Early intelligence tests favored White, middle-socioeconomic-status, urban individuals. Tests may be biased against certain groups that are not familiar with a standard form of English, with the content tested, or with the testing situation. Tests are likely to reflect the values and experience of the dominant culture. In the United States, children from African American and Latino families score below children from White families on standardized intelligence tests.

The Development of Intelligence

 LG2 Discuss the development of intelligence.

Tests of Infant Intelligence

- A test developed by Gesell was an important early contributor to the developmental testing of infants. Tests designed to assess infant intelligence include the widely used Bayley scales. The Fagan Test of Infant Intelligence, which assesses how effectively infants process information, is increasingly being used. Infant information-processing tasks that involve attention—especially habituation and dishabituation—are related to standardized scores of intelligence in childhood.

Stability and Change in Intelligence Through Adolescence

- Intelligence is not as stable across childhood and adolescence as the original theorists believed. Many children's scores on intelligence tests fluctuate considerably.

The Extremes of Intelligence and Creativity

 LG3 Describe the characteristics of intellectual disability, giftedness, and creativity.

Intellectual Disability

- Intellectual disability is a condition of limited mental ability in which the individual (1) has a low IQ, usually below 70; (2) has difficulty adapting to everyday life; and (3) has an onset of these characteristics by age 18. Most affected individuals have an IQ in the 55 to 70 range (mild intellectual disability). Intellectual disability can have an organic cause (called organic intellectual disability) or be social and cultural in origin (called cultural-familial intellectual disability).

Giftedness

- Individuals who are gifted have above-average intelligence (an IQ of 130 or higher) and/or superior talent for something. Three characteristics of gifted children are precocity, marching to their own drummer, and a passion to master their domain. Giftedness is likely a consequence of both heredity and environment. Developmental changes characterize giftedness, and increasingly the domain-specific aspect of giftedness is emphasized. Concerns exist about the education of children who are gifted.

Creativity

- Creativity is the ability to think about something in novel and unusual ways and come up with unique solutions to problems. Although most creative people are intelligent, individuals with high IQs are not necessarily creative. Creative people tend to be divergent thinkers; traditional intelligence tests measure convergent thinking. Parents and teachers can use a number of strategies to increase children's creative thinking.

key terms

intelligence 230
mental age (MA) 231
intelligence quotient (IQ) 231
normal distribution 231
triarchic theory of intelligence 232

emotional intelligence 234
heritability 236
culture-fair tests 239
stereotype threat 240
developmental quotient (DQ) 241

Bayley Scales of Infant
   Development 241
intellectual disability 243
gifted 245
creativity 247

divergent thinking 247
convergent thinking 247
brainstorming 247

key people

Alfred Binet 231
Theophile Simon 231
David Wechsler 232
Robert J. Sternberg 232

Howard Gardner 230
Daniel Goleman 234
Peter Salovey 234
John Mayer 234

James Flynn 237
Craig Ramey 238
Arnold Gesell 241
Nancy Bayley 241

Robert McCall 242
Lewis Terman 244
Ellen Winner 244
John Colombo 245

LANGUAGE DEVELOPMENT

chapter outline

Helen Keller.

Astunning portrayal of a child isolated from the mainstream of language is the case of Helen Keller (1880–1968). At 18 months of age, Helen was an intelligent toddler in the process of learning to say her first words. Then she developed an illness that left her both deaf and blind, suffering the double affliction of sudden darkness and silence. For the next five years, she lived in a world she learned to fear because she could not see or hear.

Even with her fears, Helen spontaneously invented a number of gestures to reflect her wants and needs. For example, when she wanted ice cream, she turned toward the freezer and shivered. When she wanted bread and butter, she imitated the motions of cutting and spreading. But this homemade language system severely limited her ability to communicate with the surrounding community, which did not understand her idiosyncratic gestures.

Alexander Graham Bell, the famous inventor of the telephone, suggested to her parents that they hire a tutor named Anne Sullivan to help Helen overcome her fears. By using sign language, Anne was able to teach Helen to communicate. Anne realized that language learning needs to occur naturally, so she did not force Helen to memorize words out of context as in the drill methods that were in vogue at the time. Sullivan's success depended not only on the child's natural ability to organize language according to form and meaning but also on introducing language in the context of communicating about objects, events, and feelings about others. Helen Keller eventually graduated from Radcliffe with honors, became a very successful educator, and crafted books about her life and experiences. She had this to say about language:

> Whatever the process, the result is wonderful. Gradually from naming an object we advance step by step until we have traversed the vast distance between our first stammered syllable and the sweep of thought in a line of Shakespeare.

preview

In this chapter, we will tell the remarkable story of language and how it develops. The questions we will explore include these: What is language? What is the developmental course of language? What does biology contribute to language? How does experience influence language? How are language and cognition linked?

What Is Language? **LG1** Define language and describe its rule systems.

> Defining Language

> Language's Rule Systems

Language allows us to communicate with others. *What are some important characteristics of language?*

In 1799, a nude boy was observed running through the woods in France. The boy was captured when he was 11 years old. He was called the Wild Boy of Aveyron and was believed to have lived in the woods alone for six years (Lane, 1976). When found, he made no effort to communicate. He never learned to communicate effectively. Sadly, a modern-day wild child named Genie was discovered in Los Angeles in 1970. Despite intensive intervention, Genie acquired only a limited form of spoken language. Both cases—the Wild Boy of Aveyron and Genie—raise questions about the biological and environmental determinants of language—topics that we will examine later in the chapter. First, though, we need to define language.

DEFINING LANGUAGE

Language is a form of communication—whether spoken, written, or signed—that is based on a system of symbols. Language consists of the words used by a community and the rules for varying and combining them.

Think how important language is in our everyday lives. It is difficult to imagine what Helen Keller's life would have been like if she had never learned language. We need language to communicate with others—to speak, listen, read, and write. Our language enables us to describe past events in detail and to plan for the future. Language lets us pass down information from one generation to the next and create a rich cultural heritage.

All human languages have some common characteristics (Berko Gleason, 2009). These include infinite generativity and organizational rules. **Infinite generativity** is the ability to produce an endless number of meaningful sentences using a finite set of words and rules. When we say "rules," we mean that language is orderly and that rules describe the way language works. Let's further explore what these rules involve.

LANGUAGE'S RULE SYSTEMS

When nineteenth-century American writer Ralph Waldo Emerson said, "The world was built in order and the atoms march in tune," he must have had language in mind. Language is highly ordered and organized (de Villiers & de Villiers, 2013). The organization involves five systems of rules: phonology, morphology, syntax, semantics, and pragmatics.

Phonology Every language is made up of basic sounds. **Phonology** is the sound system of a language, including the sounds that are used and how they may be combined (Kuhl & Damasio, 2012). For example, English has the sounds *sp*, *ba*, and *ar*, but the sound sequences *zx* and *qp* do not occur. A *phoneme* is the basic unit of sound in a language; it is the smallest unit of sound that affects meaning. A good example of a phoneme in English is /k/, the sound represented by the letter *k* in the word *ski* and the letter *c* in the word *cat*. The /k/ sound is slightly different in these two words, and in some languages such as Arabic these two sounds are separate phonemes. However, this variation is not distinguished in English, and the /k/ sound is therefore a single phoneme.

> Words not only affect us temporarily; they change us, they socialize us, and they unsocialize us.
>
> —**DAVID RIESMAN**
> *American Social Scientist, 20th Century*

language A form of communication, whether spoken, written, or signed, that is based on a system of symbols.

infinite generativity The ability to produce an endless number of meaningful sentences using a finite set of words and rules.

phonology The sound system of a language, which includes the sounds used and rules about how they may be combined.

Morphology Morphology is the rule system that governs how words are formed in a language. A *morpheme* is a minimal unit of meaning; it is a word or a part of a word that cannot be broken into smaller meaningful parts. Every word in the English language is made up of one or more morphemes. Some words consist of a single morpheme (for example, *help*), whereas others are made up of more than one morpheme (for example, *helper*, which has two morphemes, *help* and *er*, with the morpheme *-er* meaning "one who"—in this case "one who helps"). Thus, not all morphemes are words by themselves; for example, *-pre*, *-tion*, and *-ing* are morphemes.

Just as the rules that govern phonology describe the sound sequences that can occur in a language, the rules of morphology describe the way meaningful units (morphemes) can be combined in words (Brown, 2013). Morphemes have many jobs in grammar, such as marking tense (for example, she *walks* versus she *walked*) and number (*she* walks versus *they* walk) (Booij, 2013).

Syntax Syntax involves the way words are combined to form acceptable phrases and sentences. The term *syntax* is often used interchangeably with the term *grammar*. If someone says to you, "Bob slugged Tom" or "Bob was slugged by Tom," you know who did the slugging and who was slugged in each case because you have a syntactic understanding of these sentence structures. You also understand that the sentence, "You didn't stay, did you?" is a grammatical sentence but that "You didn't stay, didn't you?" is unacceptable and ambiguous.

If you learn another language, English syntax will not get you very far. For example, in English an adjective usually precedes a noun (as in *blue sky*), whereas in Spanish the adjective usually follows the noun (*cielo azul*). Despite the differences in their syntactic structures, however, the world's languages have much in common (de Villiers & de Villiers, 2013; O'Grady, 2013). For example, consider the following short sentences:

> The cat killed the mouse.
> The farmer chased the cat.

In many languages, it is possible to combine these sentences into more complex sentences. For example:

> The farmer chased the cat that killed the mouse.
> The mouse the cat killed ate the cheese.

However, no language we know of permits sentences like the following one:

> The mouse the cat the farmer chased killed ate the cheese.

Can you make sense of this sentence? If you can, you probably can do it only after wrestling with it for several minutes. You likely could not understand it at all if someone uttered it during a conversation. It appears that language users cannot process subjects and objects arranged in too complex a fashion in a sentence. That is good news for language learners, because it means that all syntactic systems have some common ground. Such findings are also considered important by researchers who are interested in the universal properties of syntax (Culicover, 2013; Whaley, 2013).

Semantics Semantics refers to the meaning of words and sentences. Every word has a set of semantic features, or required attributes related to meaning. *Girl* and *woman*, for example, share many semantic features but differ semantically in regard to age.

morphology The rule system that governs how words are formed in a language.

syntax The ways words are combined to form acceptable phrases and sentences.

semantics The meaning of words and sentences.

FRANK & ERNEST © Thaves. Distr. by United Features Syndicate, Inc.

Rule System	Description	Examples
Phonology	The sound system of a language. A phoneme is the smallest sound unit in a language.	The word *chat* has three phonemes or sounds: /ch/ /ã/ /t/. An example of a phonological rule in the English language is while the phoneme /r/ can follow the phonemes /t/ or /d/ in an English consonant cluster (such as *track* or *drab*), the phoneme /l/ cannot follow these letters.
Morphology	The system of meaningful units involved in word formation.	The smallest sound units that have a meaning are called morphemes, or meaning units. The word *girl* is one morpheme, or meaning unit; it cannot be broken down any further and still have meaning. When the suffix *s* is added, the word becomes *girls* and has two morphemes because the *s* changed the meaning of the word, indicating that there is more than one girl.
Syntax	The system that involves the way words are combined to form acceptable phrases and sentences.	Word order is very important in determining meaning in the English language. For example, the sentence "Sebastian pushed the bike" has a different meaning than "The bike pushed Sebastian."
Semantics	The system that involves the meaning of words and sentences.	Knowing the meaning of individual words—that is, vocabulary. For example, semantics includes knowing the meaning of such words as *orange*, *transportation*, and *intelligent*.
Pragmatics	The system of using appropriate conversation and knowledge of how to effectively use language in context.	An example is using polite language in appropriate situations, such as being mannerly when talking with one's teacher. Taking turns in a conversation involves pragmatics.

FIGURE 9.1
THE RULE SYSTEMS OF LANGUAGE

Words have semantic restrictions on how they can be used in sentences. The sentence *The bicycle talked the boy into buying a candy bar* is syntactically correct but semantically incorrect. The sentence violates our semantic knowledge that bicycles don't talk.

Pragmatics   A final set of language rules involves **pragmatics,** the appropriate use of language in different contexts. Pragmatics covers a lot of territory (Elbourne, 2012). When you take turns speaking in a discussion or use a question to convey a command ("Why is it so noisy in here?" "What is this, Grand Central Station?"), you are demonstrating knowledge of pragmatics. You also apply the pragmatics of English when you use polite language in appropriate situations (for example, when talking to your teacher) or tell stories that are interesting, jokes that are funny, and lies that convince. In each of these cases, you are demonstrating that you understand the rules of your culture for adjusting language to suit the context.

Pragmatic rules can be complex and differ from one culture to another (Bryant, 2012). If you were to study the Japanese language, you would come face-to-face with countless pragmatic rules about conversing with individuals of various social levels and with various relationships to you. Some of these pragmatic rules concern the ways of saying *thank you*. Indeed, the pragmatics of saying *thank you* are complex even in our own culture. Preschoolers' use of the phrase *thank you* varies with sex, socioeconomic status, and the age of the individual they are addressing.

At this point, we have discussed five important rule systems involved in language. An overview of these rule systems is presented in Figure 9.1.

pragmatics The appropriate use of language in different contexts.

Review *Connect* Reflect

 LG1 Define language and describe its rule systems.

Review
- What is language?
- What are language's five main rule systems?

Connect
- Describe how the use of dialogue in scaffolding, discussed in Chapter 6, is reflected in the story about Helen Keller and Anne Sullivan at the beginning of this chapter.

Reflect *Your Own Personal Journey of Life*
- How good are your family members and friends at the pragmatics of language? Describe an example in which someone showed pragmatic skills and another in which another person did not.

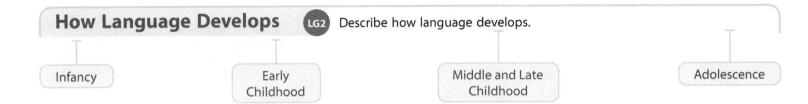
According to a historian of ancient cultures, a thirteenth-century emperor of Germany, Frederick II, had a cruel idea. He wanted to know what language children would speak if no one talked to them. He selected several newborns and threatened their caregivers with death if they ever talked to the infants. Frederick never found out what language the children would speak because they all died. As we move forward in the twenty-first century, we are still curious about infants' development of language, although our experiments and observations are, to say the least, far more humane than the evil Frederick's.

INFANCY

Whatever language they learn, infants all over the world follow a similar path in language development. What are some key milestones in this development?

Babbling and Other Vocalizations Long before infants speak recognizable words, they produce a number of vocalizations (Parish-Morris, Golinkoff, & Hirsh-Pasek, 2013; Ramsdell & others, 2012). The functions of these early vocalizations are to practice making sounds, to communicate, and to attract attention. Babies' sounds go through the following sequence during the first year:

1. *Crying.* Babies cry even at birth. Crying can signal distress, but as we will discuss in Chapter 10, different types of cries signal different things.

2. *Cooing.* Babies first coo at about 1 to 2 months. These are gurgling sounds that are made in the back of the throat and usually express pleasure during interaction with the caregiver.

3. *Babbling.* In the middle of the first year babies babble—that is, they produce strings of consonant-vowel combinations, such as *ba, ba, ba, ba.*

When deaf infants are born to deaf parents who use sign language, they babble with their hands and fingers at about the same age that hearing children babble vocally (Bloom, 1998). Such similarities in timing and structure between manual and vocal babbling indicate that a unified language capacity underlies signed and spoken language.

Gestures Infants start using gestures, such as showing and pointing, at about 8 to 12 months of age. They may wave bye-bye, nod to mean "yes," show an empty cup to ask for more milk, and point to a dog to draw attention to it. Some early gestures are symbolic, as when an infant smacks her lips to indicate food or drink. Pointing is considered by language experts to be an important index of the social aspects of language, and it follows this developmental sequence: from pointing without checking on adult gaze to pointing while looking back and forth between an object and the adult (Goldin-Meadow & Alibali, 2013).

Lack of pointing is a significant indicator of problems in the infant's communication system (Goldin-Meadow & Alibali, 2013). Pointing is a key aspect of the development of joint attention and an important index of the social aspects of language (Begus & Southgate, 2012). Failure to engage in pointing also characterizes many autistic children. The ability to use the pointing gesture effectively improves in the second year of life as advances in other aspects of language communication occur (Colonnesi & others, 2010).

A recent study found that parents of high socioeconomic status (SES) were more likely to use gestures when communicating with their 14-month-old infants (Rowe & Goldin-Meadow, 2009). Further, the infants' use of gestures at 14 months of age in high-SES families was linked to a larger vocabulary at 54 months of age.

- - - - - - - - - ➤

developmental **connection**

Emotional Development

Three basic cries that infants display are the basic cry, anger cry, and pain cry. Chapter 10, p. 286

Long before infants speak recognizable words, they communicate by producing a number of vocalizations and gestures. *At approximately what ages do infants begin to produce different types of vocalizations and gestures?*

FIGURE **9.2**

FROM UNIVERSAL LINGUIST TO LANGUAGE-SPECIFIC LISTENER. In Patricia Kuhl's research laboratory, babies listen to tape-recorded voices that repeat syllables. When the sounds of the syllables change, the babies quickly learn to look at the bear. Using this technique, Kuhl has demonstrated that babies are universal linguists until about 6 months of age, but in the next six months become language-specific listeners. *Does Kuhl's research give support to the view that either "nature" or "nurture" is the source of language acquisition?*

Recognizing Language Sounds   Long before they begin to learn words, infants can make fine distinctions among the sounds of the language. In Patricia Kuhl's (1993, 2000, 2007, 2009, 2011, 2012) research, phonemes from languages all over the world are piped through a speaker for infants to hear (see Figure 9.2). A box with a toy bear in it is placed where the infant can see it. A string of identical syllables is played; then the syllables are changed (for example, *ba ba ba ba*, and then *pa pa pa pa*). If the infant turns its head when the syllables change, the box lights up and the bear dances and drums, rewarding the infant for noticing the change.

Kuhl's (2007, 2009, 2011, 2012) research has demonstrated that from birth to about 6 months of age, infants are "citizens of the world": they recognize when sounds change most of the time, no matter what language the syllables come from. But over the next six months, infants get even better at perceiving the changes in sounds from their "own" language, the one their parents speak, and gradually lose the ability to recognize differences that are not important in their own language.

Infants must fish out individual words from the nonstop stream of sound that makes up ordinary speech (Harris, Golinkoff, & Hirsh-Pasek, 2012). To do so, they must find the boundaries between words, which is very difficult for infants because adults don't pause between words when they speak. Still, infants begin to detect word boundaries by 8 months of age. For example, in one study, 8-month-old infants listened to recorded stories that contained unusual words, such as *hornbill* and *python* (Jusczyk & Hohne, 1997). Two weeks later, the researchers tested the infants with two lists of words, one made up of words in the stories, the other of new, unusual words that did not appear in the stories. The infants listened to the familiar words for a second longer, on average, than the new words.

First Words   Infants understand words before they can produce or speak them. For example, many infants recognize their name when someone says it as early as 5 months of age. However, the infant's first spoken word, a milestone eagerly anticipated by every parent, usually doesn't occur until 10 to 15 months of age and at an average of about 13 months. Yet long before babies say their first words, they have been communicating with their parents, often by gesturing and using their own special sounds. The appearance of first words is a continuation of this communication process (Berko Gleason, 2009).

A child's first words include those that name important people (*dada*), familiar animals (*kitty*), vehicles (*car*), toys (*ball*), food (*milk*), body parts (*eye*), clothes (*hat*), household items (*clock*), and greeting terms (*bye*). These were the first words of babies 50 years ago. They are the first words of babies today. Children often express various intentions with their single words, so that "cookie" might mean "That's a cookie" or "I want a cookie."

As indicated earlier, children understand their first words earlier than they speak them. On average, infants understand about 50 words at age 13 months, but they can't say this many words until about 18 months (Menyuk, Liebergott, & Schultz, 1995). Thus, in infancy *receptive vocabulary* (words the child understands) considerably exceeds *spoken vocabulary* (words the child uses). A recent study revealed that 6-month-olds understand words that refer to body parts, such as "hand" and "feet," but of course, they cannot yet speak these words (Tincoff & Jusczyk, 2012).

The infant's spoken vocabulary increases rapidly once the first word is spoken (Parish-Morris, Golinkoff, & Hirsh-Pasek, 2013; Wagner & Hoff, 2013). The average 18-month-old can

What characterizes the infant's early word learning?

FIGURE **9.3**
VARIATION IN LANGUAGE MILESTONES

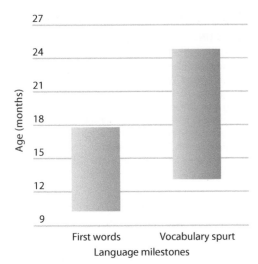

What is a difference in the way children learn Chinese Mandarin and English?

Around the world, most young children learn to speak in two-word utterances, at about 18 to 24 months of age. *What implications does this have for the biological basis of language?*

telegraphic speech The use of short, precise words without grammatical markers such as articles, auxiliary verbs, and other connectives.

speak about 50 words, but by the age of 2 years a child can speak about 200 words. This rapid increase in vocabulary that begins at approximately 18 months is called the *vocabulary spurt* (Bloom, Lifter, & Broughton, 1985).

Like the timing of a child's first word, the timing of the vocabulary spurt varies. Figure 9.3 shows the range for these two language milestones in 14 children. On average, these children said their first word at 13 months and had a vocabulary spurt at 19 months. However, the ages for the first word of individual children varied from 10 to 17 months and for their vocabulary spurt from 13 to 25 months.

Cross-linguistic differences occur in word learning. Children learning Mandarin Chinese, Korean, and Japanese acquire more verbs earlier in their development than do children learning English. This cross-linguistic difference reflects the greater use of verbs in these Asian languages.

Children sometimes overextend or underextend the meanings of the words they use (Woodward & Markman, 1998). Overextension is the tendency to apply a word to objects that are inappropriate for the word's meaning. For example, children at first may say "dada" not only for "father" but also for other men, strangers, or boys. Children may overextend word meanings because they don't know the appropriate word or can't recall it. With time, overextensions decrease and eventually disappear. Underextension is the tendency to apply a word too narrowly; it occurs when children fail to use a word to name a relevant event or object. For example, a child might use the word *boy* to describe a 5-year-old neighbor but not apply the word to a male infant or to a 9-year-old male. The most common explanation of underextension is that children have heard a name used only in reference to a small, unrepresentative sample.

Two-Word Utterances   By the time children are 18 to 24 months of age, they usually utter two-word messages (Tomasello, 2011). To convey meaning with just two words, the child relies heavily on gesture, tone, and context. The wealth of meaning children can communicate with a two-word utterance includes the following (Slobin, 1972):

- Identification: "See doggie."
- Location: "Book there."
- Repetition: "More milk."
- Possession: "My candy."
- Attribution: "Big car."
- Agent-action: "Mama walk."
- Question: "Where ball?"

These examples are from children whose first language is English, German, Russian, Finnish, Turkish, or Samoan.

Notice that the two-word utterances omit many parts of speech and are remarkably succinct. In fact, in every language, a child's first combinations of words have this economical quality; they are telegraphic. **Telegraphic speech** is the use of short and precise words without grammatical markers such as articles, auxiliary verbs, and other connectives. Telegraphic speech is not limited to two words. "Mommy give ice cream" and "Mommy give Tommy ice cream" also are examples of telegraphic speech.

We have discussed a number of language milestones in infancy. Figure 9.4 summarizes the ages at which infants typically reach these milestones.

EARLY CHILDHOOD

Toddlers move rather quickly from producing two-word utterances to creating three-, four-, and five-word combinations. Between 2 and 3 years of age they begin the transition from saying simple sentences that express a single proposition to saying complex sentences (Bloom, 1998).

Young children's understanding sometimes goes far beyond their speech. One 3-year-old, laughing with delight as an abrupt summer breeze stirred his hair and tickled his skin, commented, "I got breezed!" Many of the oddities of young children's language sound like mistakes to adult listeners. However, from the children's point of view, they are not mistakes. They represent the way young children perceive and understand their world. As children go through their early childhood years, their grasp of the rule systems that govern language increases.

As young children learn the special features of their own language, there are extensive regularities in how they acquire that particular language (Berko Gleason, 2009; de Villiers & de Villiers, 2013). For example, all children learn the prepositions *on* and *in* before other prepositions. Children learning other languages, such as Russian or Chinese, also acquire the particular features of those languages in a consistent order.

However, some children develop language problems, including speech and hearing problems. To read about the work of one individual who helps children who have speech/language and hearing problems, see *Connecting with Careers*.

Understanding Phonology and Morphology   During the preschool years, most children gradually become more sensitive to the sounds of spoken words and become increasingly capable of producing all the sounds of their language. By the time children are 3 years of age, they can produce all the vowel sounds and most of the consonant sounds (Menn & Stoel-Gammon, 2009).

Young children can even produce complex consonant clusters such as *str-* and *-mpt*. They notice rhymes, enjoy poems, make up silly names for things by substituting one sound for another (such as bubblegum, bubblebum, bubbleyum), and clap along with each syllable in a phrase.

By the time children move beyond two-word utterances, they demonstrate a knowledge of morphology rules (Park & others, 2012). Children begin using the plural and possessive forms of nouns (such as *dogs* and *dog's*). They put appropriate endings on verbs (such as *-s* when the subject is third-person singular and *-ed* for the past tense). They use prepositions (such as *in* and *on*), articles (such as *a* and *the*), and various forms of the verb *to be* (such as "I was going to the store"). Some of the best evidence for changes in children's use of morphological rules occurs in their overgeneralization of the rules, as when a preschool child says "foots" instead of "feet," or "goed" instead of "went."

In a classic experiment that was designed to study children's knowledge of morphological rules, such as how to make a plural, Jean Berko (1958) presented preschool children and first-grade children with cards such as the one shown in Figure 9.5. Children were asked to look at the card while the experimenter read aloud the words on the card. Then the children were asked to supply the missing word. This might sound easy, but Berko was interested in the children's ability to apply the appropriate morphological rule—in this case, to say "wugs" with the *z* sound that indicates the plural.

Although the children's answers were not perfect, they were much better than they could have been by chance. What makes Berko's study impressive is that most of the words were made up for the experiment. Thus, the children could not base their responses on remembering past instances of hearing the words. Since they could make the plurals or past tenses of words they had never heard before, this was proof that they knew the morphological rules.

Changes in Syntax and Semantics   Preschool children also learn and apply rules of syntax (Gertner & Fisher, 2012). They show a growing mastery of complex rules for how words should be ordered.

Consider *wh-* questions, such as "Where is Daddy going?" or "What is that boy doing?" To ask these questions properly, the child must know two important differences between *wh-* questions and affirmative statements (for instance, "Daddy is going to work" and "That boy is waiting on the school bus"). First, a *wh-* word must be added at the beginning of the sentence. Second, the auxiliary verb must be inverted—that is, exchanged with the subject of the sentence. Young children learn quite early where to put the *wh-* word, but they take much longer to learn the auxiliary-inversion rule. Thus, preschool children might ask, "Where Daddy is going?" and "What that boy is doing?"

Gains in semantics also characterize early childhood. Vocabulary development is dramatic (Crain & Zhou, 2012). Some experts have concluded that between 18 months and 6 years of age, young children learn approximately one new word every waking hour (Carey, 1977; Gelman & Kalish, 2006)! By the time they enter first grade, it is estimated that children know

Typical Age	Language Milestones
Birth	Crying
2 to 4 months	Cooing begins
5 months	Understands first word
6 months	Babbling begins
7 to 11 months	Change from universal linguist to language-specific listener
8 to 12 months	Uses gestures, such as showing and pointing Comprehension of words appears
13 months	First word spoken
18 months	Vocabulary spurt starts
18 to 24 months	Uses two-word utterances Rapid expansion of understanding of words

FIGURE 9.4

SOME LANGUAGE MILESTONES IN INFANCY. Despite great variations in the language input received by infants, around the world they follow a similar path in learning to speak.

connecting with careers

Sharla Peltier, Speech Pathologist

A speech pathologist is a health professional who works with individuals who have a communication disorder. Sharla Peltier is a speech pathologist in Manitoulin, Ontario, Canada. Peltier works with Native American children in the First Nations Schools. She conducts screening for speech/language and hearing problems and assesses infants as young as 6 months of age as well as school-aged children. She works closely with community health nurses to identify hearing problems.

Diagnosing problems is only about half of what Peltier does in her work. She especially enjoys treating speech/language and hearing problems. She conducts parent training sessions to help parents understand and help with their children's language problems. As part of this training, she guides parents in improving their communication skills with their children.

For more information about what speech therapists do, see page 45 in the Careers in Child Development appendix following Chapter 1.

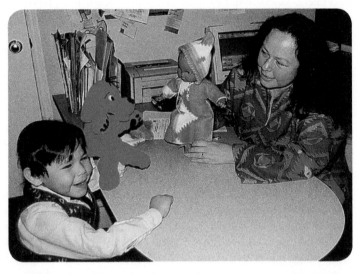

Speech therapist Sharla Peltier helping a young child improve her language and communication skills.

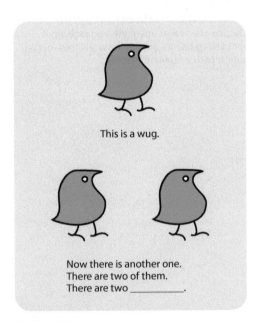

This is a wug.

Now there is another one.
There are two of them.
There are two _____.

FIGURE **9.5**

STIMULI IN BERKO'S STUDY OF YOUNG CHILDREN'S UNDERSTANDING OF MORPHOLOGICAL RULES. In Jean Berko's (1958) study, young children were presented cards, such as this one with a "wug" on it. Then the children were asked to supply the missing word; in supplying the missing word, they had to say it correctly too. "Wugs" is the correct response here.

about 14,000 words (Clark, 1993). Children who enter elementary school with a small vocabulary are at risk for developing reading problems (Berninger, 2006).

Why can children learn so many new words so quickly? One possible explanation is **fast mapping,** which involves children's ability to make an initial connection between a word and its referent after only limited exposure to the word (Woodward, Markman, & Fitzimmons, 1994). Researchers have found that exposure to words on multiple occasions over several days results in more successful word learning than the same number of exposures in a single day (Childers & Tomasello, 2002).

Language researchers have proposed that young children may use a number of working hypotheses to accomplish their fast mapping (Pan & Uccelli, 2009). One working hypothesis children use is to give a novel label to a novel object. Parents can be especially helpful in aiding children's learning of novel labels for novel objects. As a mother looks at a picture book with her young child, she knows that the child understands the referent for *car* but not *bus,* so she says, "That's a bus, not a car. A bus is bigger than a car." Another working hypothesis children use is that a word refers to a whole object rather than parts of an object, such as labeling a tiger a *tiger* instead of a *tail* or *paw.* Sometimes children's initial mappings are incorrect. In such cases, they benefit from hearing the words mature speakers use to test and revise their word-referent connections (Gershkoff-Stowe & Hahn, 2007).

What are some important aspects of how word learning optimally occurs? Kathy Hirsh-Pasek and Roberta Golinkoff (Harris, Golinkoff, & Hirsh-Pasek, 2012; Hirsh-Pasek & Golinkoff, 2013) emphasize six key principles in young children's vocabulary development:

1. *Children learn the words they hear most often.* They learn the words that they encounter when interacting with parents, teachers, siblings, and peers, and also from books. They especially benefit from encountering words that they do not know.

2. *Children learn words for things and events that interest them.* Parents and teachers can direct young children to experience words in contexts that interest the children; playful peer interactions are especially helpful in this regard.

3. *Children learn words best in responsive and interactive contexts rather than in passive contexts.* Children who experience turn-taking opportunities, joint focusing experiences, and positive, sensitive socializing contexts with adults encounter the scaffolding necessary for optimal word learning. They learn words less effectively when they are passive learners.

4. *Children learn words best in contexts that are meaningful.* Young children learn new words more effectively when new words are encountered in integrated contexts rather than as isolated facts.

5. *Children learn words best when they access clear information about word meaning.* Children whose parents and teachers are sensitive to words the children might not understand and provide support and elaboration with hints about word meaning learn words better than children whose parents and teachers quickly state a new word and don't monitor whether children understand its meaning.

How do children's language abilities develop during early childhood?

6. *Children learn words best when grammar and vocabulary are considered.* Children who experience a large number of words and diversity in verbal stimulation develop a richer vocabulary and better understanding of grammar. In many cases, vocabulary and grammar development are connected.

How parents talk to their children is linked with the children's vocabulary growth and the family's socioeconomic status. To read about how family environment affects children's language development, see *Connecting Through Research.*

Advances in Pragmatics Changes in pragmatics also characterize young children's language development (Bryant, 2012). A 6-year-old is simply a much better conversationalist than a 2-year-old is. What are some of the improvements in pragmatics during the preschool years?

Young children begin to engage in extended discourse (Akhtar & Herold, 2008). For example, they learn culturally specific rules of conversation and politeness, and increasingly adapt their speech in different settings. Their developing linguistic skills and improving ability to understand the perspective of others contribute to their use of more competent narratives.

As children get older, they become increasingly able to talk about things that are not here (Grandma's house, for example) and not now (what happened to them yesterday or might happen tomorrow, for example). A preschool child can tell you what she wants for lunch tomorrow, something that would not have been possible at the two-word stage of language development.

At about 4 years of age, children develop a remarkable sensitivity to the needs of others in conversation. One way in which they show such sensitivity is through their use of the articles *the* and *an* (or *a*). When adults tell a story or describe an event, they generally use *an* (or *a*) when they first refer to an animal or an object, and then use *the* when referring to it later. (For example, "Two boys were walking through the jungle when *a* fierce lion appeared. *The* lion lunged at one boy while the other ran for cover.") Even 3-year-olds follow part of this rule; they consistently use the word *the* when referring to previously mentioned things. However, the use of the word *a* when something is initially mentioned develops more slowly. Although 5-year-old children follow this rule on some occasions, they fail to follow it on others.

At around 4 to 5 years of age, children learn to change their speech style to suit the situation. For example, even 4-year-old children speak to a 2-year-old differently from the way they speak to a same-aged peer; they use shorter sentences with the 2-year-old. They also speak to an adult differently from the way they speak to a same-aged peer, using more polite and formal language with the adult (Shatz & Gelman, 1973).

Early Literacy Concern about U.S. children's reading and writing skills has led to a careful examination of preschool and kindergarten children's educational experiences, in the hope that a positive orientation toward reading and writing can be developed early in life (Giorgis & others, 2013). What should a literacy program for preschool children be like? Instruction

> Children pick up words as pigeons peas.
>
> —**JOHN RAY**
> *English Naturalist, 17th Century*

What are some advances in pragmatics that characterize children's development in early childhood?

fast mapping A process that helps to explain how young children learn the connection between a word and its referent so quickly.

How Does Family Environment Affect Young Children's Language Development?

What characteristics of families influence children's language development? Socioeconomic status has been linked with how much parents talk to their children and with young children's vocabulary. Betty Hart and Todd Risley (1995) observed the language environments of children whose parents were professionals and children whose parents were on welfare. Compared with the professional parents, the parents on welfare talked much less to their young children, talked less about past events, and provided less elaboration. As indicated in Figure 9.6, the children of the professional parents had a much larger vocabulary at 36 months of age than the children whose parents were on welfare.

Other research has explored the relationship between how much mothers speak to their infants and the infants' vocabularies. For example, in one study by Janellen Huttenlocher and her colleagues (1991), infants whose mothers spoke to them more often had markedly higher vocabularies. By age 2, vocabulary differences were substantial. However, a study of 1- to 3-year-old children living in low-income families found that the sheer amount of maternal talk was not the best predictor of a child's vocabulary growth (Pan & others, 2005). Rather, it was maternal language and literacy skills and mothers' use of diverse vocabulary that best predicted children's vocabulary development.

One study revealed that maternal sensitivity (warm response to the child's bids for attention and anticipation of her child's emotional needs, for example), regardless of socioeconomic status and ethnicity, was positively linked with growth in young children's receptive and expressive language development from 18 to 36 months of age (Pungello & others, 2009). In this study, negative intrusive parenting (physically restraining the child or dominating interaction with the child with unnecessary verbal direction, for example) was related to a slower rate of growth of receptive language.

These research studies and others (NICHD Early Child Care Research Network, 2005) demonstrate the important effect that early speech input and poverty can have on the development of a child's language skills. Children in low-income families are more likely to have less-educated parents, receive inadequate nutrition, live in low-income communities, and attend substandard schools than children in middle- and high-income families (Row, Burns, & Griffin, 1998). However, living in a low-income family should not be used as the sole identifier in predicting whether children will have difficulties in language development, such as a low vocabulary and reading problems. If children growing up in low-income families experience effective instruction and support, they can develop effective language skills (Barbarin & Aikens, 2009).

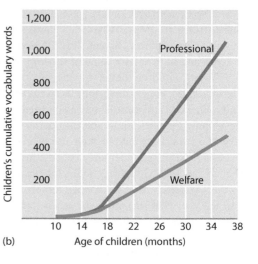

(a) Age of children (months)   (b) Age of children (months)

FIGURE **9.6**

LANGUAGE INPUT IN PROFESSIONAL AND WELFARE FAMILIES AND YOUNG CHILDREN'S VOCABULARY DEVELOPMENT. (*a*) In this study (Hart & Risley, 1995), parents who were professionals talked with their young children more than parents from welfare families. (*b*) All of the children learned to talk, but children whose parents were professionals developed vocabularies that were twice as large as those of children from welfare families. Thus, by the time children go to preschool, they already have experienced considerable differences in language input in their families and developed different levels of vocabulary that are linked to their socioeconomic context. *Does this study indicate that poverty caused deficiencies in vocabulary development?*

should be built on what children already know about oral language, reading, and writing. Further, early precursors of literacy and academic success include language skills, phonological and syntactic knowledge, letter identification, and conceptual knowledge about print and its conventions and functions (Gunning, 2013). Parents and teachers need to provide a supportive environment to help children develop literacy skills (Tamis-LeMonda & Song, 2013). One study revealed that children whose mothers had more education had more advanced emergent literacy skills than children whose mothers had less education (Korat, 2009). Another study found that literacy experiences (such as how often the child was read to), the quality of the mother's engagement with her child (such as attempts to cognitively stimulate the child), and provision of learning materials (such as age-appropriate learning materials and books) were important home literacy experiences in low-income families that were linked to the children's language development in positive ways (Rodriquez & others, 2009).

What are some strategies for using books effectively with preschool children? Ellen Galinsky (2010) recently emphasized these strategies:

- *Use books to initiate conversation with young children.* Ask them to put themselves in the book characters' places and imagine what they might be thinking or feeling.
- *Use what and why questions.* Ask young children what they think is going to happen next in a story and then see if it occurs.
- *Encourage children to ask questions about stories.*
- *Choose some books that play with language.* Creative books on the alphabet, including those with rhymes, often interest young children.

The following longitudinal studies indicate the importance of early language skills to children's school readiness:

- Phonological awareness, letter name and sound knowledge, and naming speed in kindergarten were linked to reading success in the first and second grade (Schattschneider & others, 2004).
- Children's early home environment influenced their early language skills, which in turn predicted their readiness for school (Forget-Dubois & others, 2009).

What are some effective strategies for supporting young children's literacy skills?

So far, our discussion of early literacy has focused on U.S. children. However, the extent to which phonological awareness supports learning to read effectively varies across language to some extent (McBride-Chang, 2004). One study of second-grade students from Beijing, Hong Kong, Korea, and the United States revealed that phonological awareness may be more important for early reading development in English and Korean than it is in Chinese (McBride-Chang & others, 2005). Further, rates of dyslexia differ across countries and are linked with the spelling and phonetic rules that characterize the language (McCardle & others, 2011). English is one of the more difficult languages to learn because of its irregular spellings and pronunciations. In countries where English is spoken, the rate of dyslexia is higher than it is in countries where the alphabet script is more phonetically pronounced.

MIDDLE AND LATE CHILDHOOD

Children gain new skills as they enter school that make it possible for them to learn to read and write, or to advance the reading and writing skills they have developed in early childhood. These new skills include increasingly using language to talk about things that are not physically present, learning what a word is, and learning how to recognize and talk about sounds (Berko Gleason, 2005). They have to learn the alphabetic principle, that the letters of the alphabet represent sounds of the language. As children develop during middle and late childhood, changes in their vocabulary and grammar also take place (Vukelich, Christie, & Enz, 2008).

Vocabulary, Grammar, and Metalinguistic Awareness During middle and late childhood, changes occur in the way children's mental vocabulary is organized. When asked to say the first word that comes to mind when they hear a word, young children typically provide a word that often follows the word in a sentence. For example, when asked to respond to *dog* the young child may say "barks," or to the word *eat* say "lunch." At about 7 years of age, children begin to respond with a word that is the same part of speech as the stimulus word. For example, a child may now respond to the word *dog* with "cat" or "horse." To *eat*, they now might say "drink." This is evidence that at age 7 children have begun to categorize their vocabulary by parts of speech (Berko Gleason, 2003).

The process of categorizing becomes easier as children increase their vocabulary (Clark, 2012). Children's vocabulary increases from an average of about 14,000 words at 6 years of age to an average of about 40,000 words by 11 years of age.

Stage	Age Range/Grade Level	Descripton
0	Birth to first grade	Children master several prerequisites for reading. Many learn the left-to-right progression and order of reading, how to identify letters of the alphabet, and how to write their names. Some learn to read words that appear on signs. As a result of TV shows like *Sesame Street* and attending preschool and kindergarten programs, many young children today develop greater knowledge about reading earlier than in the past.
1	First and second grades	Many children learn to read at this time. In doing so, they acquire the ability to sound out words (that is, translate letters into sounds and blend sounds into words). They also complete their learning of letter names and sounds.
2	Second and third grades	Children become more fluent at retrieving individual words and other reading skills. However, at this stage reading is still not used much for learning. The demands of reading are so taxing for children at this stage that they have few resources left over to process the content.
3	Fourth through eighth grades	In fourth through eighth grade, children become increasingly able to obtain new information from print. In other words, they read to learn. They still have difficulty understanding information presented from multiple perspectives within the same story. When children don't learn to read, a downward spiral unfolds that leads to serious difficulties in many academic subjects.
4	High school	Many students become fully competent readers. They develop the ability to understand material told from many perspectives. This allows them to engage in sometimes more sophisticated discussions of literature, history, economics, and politics.

FIGURE **9.7**

A MODEL OF DEVELOPMENTAL STAGES IN READING

developmental **connection**

Information Processing

Metacognition is cognition about cognition or knowing about knowing. Chapter 7, p. 220

This teacher is helping a student sound out words. Researchers have found that phonics instruction is a key aspect of teaching students to read, especially beginning readers and students with weak reading skills.

metalinguistic awareness Knowledge about language.

Children make similar advances in grammar (Behrens, 2012). During the elementary school years, children's improvement in logical reasoning and analytical skills helps them to understand constructions such as the appropriate use of comparatives (shorter, deeper) and subjunctives ("If you were president …"). During the elementary school years, children become increasingly able to understand and use complex grammar, such as the following sentence: "The boy who kissed his mother wore a hat." They also learn to use language to produce connected discourse. They become able to relate sentences to one another to produce descriptions, definitions, and narratives that make sense. Children must be able to do these things orally before they can be expected to deal with them in written assignments.

These advances in vocabulary and grammar during the elementary school years are accompanied by the development of **metalinguistic awareness,** which is knowledge about language, such as understanding what a preposition is or being able to discuss the sounds of a language. Metalinguistic awareness allows children "to think about their language, understand what words are, and even define them" (Berko Gleason, 2009, p. 4). This awareness improves considerably during the elementary school years (Pan & Uccelli, 2009). Defining words becomes a regular part of classroom discourse, and children increase their knowledge of syntax as they study and talk about the components of sentences such as subjects and verbs (Crain, 2012).

Children also make progress in understanding how to use language in culturally appropriate ways—pragmatics (Bryant, 2012). By the time they enter adolescence, most children know the rules for the use of language in everyday contexts—that is, what is appropriate to say and what is inappropriate to say.

Reading   One model identifies five stages in the development of reading skills (Chall, 1979) (see Figure 9.7). The age boundaries are approximate and do not apply to every child, but the stages convey a sense of the developmental changes involved in learning to read.

Before learning to read, children learn to use language to talk about things that are not present; they learn what a word is; and they learn how to recognize sounds and talk about them (Berko Gleason, 2003). If they develop a large vocabulary, their path to reading is eased. Children who begin elementary school with a small vocabulary are at risk when it comes to learning to read (Berko Gleason, 2003).

Vocabulary development plays an important role in reading comprehension (Vacca & others, 2012). For example, one study revealed that a good vocabulary was linked with reading comprehension in second-grade students (Berninger & Abbott, 2005). Having a good vocabulary helps readers access word meaning effortlessly.

Analyses by Rich Mayer (2008) focused on the cognitive processes a child needs to go through in order to read a printed word. In his view, the three processes are (1) being aware of sound units in words, which consists of recognizing phonemes; (2) decoding words, which involves converting printed words into sounds; and (3) accessing word meaning, which consists of finding a mental representation of a word's meaning.

What are the most effective ways to teach children how to read? Education and language experts continue to debate how children should be taught to read. Currently, debate focuses on the phonics approach versus the whole-language approach (Fox, 2012; Reutzel & Cooter, 2013; Vacca & others, 2012).

The **phonics approach** emphasizes that reading instruction should focus on teaching basic rules for translating written symbols into sounds. Early reading instruction should involve simplified materials. Only after children have learned the correspondence rules that relate spoken phonemes to the alphabet letters that represent them should they be given complex reading materials, such as books and poems (Fox, 2012).

By contrast, the **whole-language approach** stresses that reading instruction should parallel children's natural language learning. Reading materials should be whole and meaningful. That is, children should be given material in its complete form, such as stories and poems, so that they learn to understand language's communicative function. Reading should be connected with listening and writing skills. Although there are variations in whole-language programs, most share the premise that reading should be integrated with other skills and subjects, such as science and social studies, and that it should focus on real-world material. Thus, a class might read newspapers, magazines, or books, and then write about and discuss them. In some whole-language classes, beginning readers are taught to recognize whole words or even entire sentences, and to use the context of what they are reading to guess at unfamiliar words.

Which approach is better? Research suggests that children can benefit from both approaches, but instruction in phonics needs to be emphasized (Fox & Alexander, 2011; Reutzel & Cooter, 2012, 2013). An increasing number of experts in the field of reading now conclude that direct instruction in phonics is a key aspect of learning to read (Cunningham, 2013; Dow & Baer, 2013). A recent study revealed that a computer-based phonics program improved first-grade students' reading skills (Savage & others, 2009).

Beyond the phonics/whole language issue in learning to read, becoming a good reader includes learning to read fluently (Gunning, 2013; Kamil, 2012). Many beginning or poor readers do not recognize words automatically. Their processing capacity is consumed by the demands of word recognition, so they have less capacity to devote to comprehension of groupings of words as phrases or sentences. As their processing of words and passages becomes more automatic, it is said that their reading becomes more *fluent* (Fox, 2012). Metacognitive strategies, such as learning to monitor one's reading progress, getting the gist of what is being read, and summarizing also are important in becoming a good reader (Dimmitt & McCormick, 2012; McCormick, Dimmitt, & Sullivan, 2013).

Reading, like other important skills, takes time and effort. In a national assessment, children in the fourth grade had higher scores on a national reading test when they read 11 or more pages daily for school and homework (National Assessment of Educational Progress, 2000) (see Figure 9.8). Teachers who required students to read a great deal on a daily basis had students who were more proficient at reading than teachers who required little reading by their students.

Writing Children's writing emerges out of their early scribbles, which appear at around 2 to 3 years of age. In early childhood, children's motor skills usually develop to the point that they can begin printing letters. Most 4-year-olds can print their first name. Five-year-olds can reproduce letters and copy several short words. They gradually learn to distinguish the distinctive characteristics of letters, such as whether the lines are curved or straight, open or closed. During the early elementary grades, many children continue to reverse letters such as *b* and *d* and *p* and *q* (Temple & others, 1993). At this age, if other aspects of the child's development are normal, letter reversals do not predict literacy problems.

As they begin to write, children often invent spellings. Usually they base these spellings on the sounds of words they hear (Cunningham, 2013). Parents and teachers should encourage children's early writing but not be overly concerned about letter formation or spelling.

Like becoming a good reader, becoming a good writer takes many years and lots of practice (Temple, Nathan, & Temple, 2013). Children should be given many writing opportunities in the elementary and secondary school years (Tompkins, 2013). As their language and cognitive

developmental **connection**

Conditions, Diseases, and Disorders

Dyslexia is a severe impairment in the ability to read and spell; dysgraphia is a severe impairment in handwriting ability. Chapter 16, p. 465

Children most at risk for reading difficulties in the first grade are those who began school with less verbal skill, less phonological awareness, less letter knowledge, and less familiarity with the basic purposes and mechanisms of reading.

—CATHERINE SNOW
Harvard University

phonics approach An approach emphasizing that reading instruction should focus on teaching the basic rules for translating written symbols into sounds.

whole-language approach An approach stressing that reading instruction should parallel children's natural language learning. Reading materials should be whole and meaningful.

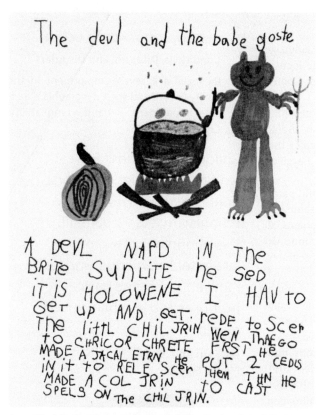

The devl and the babe goste

A DEVL NAPD IN THE
BRITE SUNLITE he SED
IT IS HOLOWENE I HAV TO
GET UP AND GET reDE to SceP
The littL CHILJRIN WEN ThAE GO
to CHRICOR CHRETE FRST He
MADE A JACAL ETRN He PUT 2 CEDLS
IN it to RELE SceP THEM THN He
MADE A COL JRIN to CAST
SPELS ON The CHIL JRIN.

Anna Mudd is the 6-year-old author of "The Devl and the Babe Goste." Anna has been writing stories for at least two years. Her story includes poetic images, sophisticated syntax, and vocabulary that reflect advances in language development.

FIGURE **9.8**

THE RELATION OF READING ACHIEVEMENT TO NUMBER OF PAGES READ DAILY. In the analysis of reading in the fourth grade in the National Assessment of Educational Progress (2000), reading more pages daily in school and as part of homework assignments was related to higher scores on a reading test in which scores ranged from 0 to 500.

skills improve with good instruction, so will their writing skills. For example, developing a more sophisticated understanding of syntax and grammar serves as an underpinning for better writing (Irvin, Buehl, & Klemp, 2007).

So do cognitive skills such as organization and logical reasoning. As they go through elementary, middle, and high school, students develop increasingly sophisticated methods of organizing their ideas. In early elementary school, they narrate and describe or write short poems. In late elementary and middle school, they move to projects such as book reports that combine narration with more reflection and analysis. In high school, they become more skilled at forms of exposition that do not depend on narrative structure (Conley, 2008). A recent meta-analysis (use of statistical techniques to combine the results of studies) revealed that the following interventions were the most effective in improving fourth- through twelfth-grade students' writing quality: (1) strategy instruction, (2) summarization, (3) peer assistance, and (4) setting goals (Graham & Perin, 2007).

Major concerns about students' writing competence are increasingly being voiced (Soter, 2013). One study revealed that 70 to 75 percent of U.S. students in grades 4 through 12 are low-achieving writers (Persky, Dane, & Jin, 2003). College instructors report that 50 percent of high school graduates are not prepared for college-level writing (Achieve, Inc., 2005).

The metacognitive strategies needed to be a competent writer are linked with those required to be a competent reader because the writing process involves competent reading and rereading during composition and revision (Dimmitt & McCormick, 2012; McCormick, Dimmitt, & Sullivan, 2013). Further, researchers have found that strategy instruction in planning, drafting, revising, and editing improves older elementary school children's metacognitive awareness and writing competence (Harris & others, 2009).

As with reading, teachers play a critical role in students' development of writing skills (Rijlaarsdam & others, 2012). Classroom observations made by Michael Pressley and his colleagues (2007) indicate that students become good writers when teachers spend considerable time on writing instruction and are passionate about teaching students to write. Their observations also indicate that classrooms with students who receive high scores on writing assessments have walls that overflow with examples of effective writing, whereas it is much harder to find such examples on the walls of classrooms that have many students who receive low scores on writing assessments.

Bilingualism and Second-Language Learning   Are there sensitive periods in learning a second language? That is, if individuals want to learn a second language, how important is the age at which they begin to learn it? For many years, it was claimed that if individuals did not learn a second language prior to puberty, they would never reach native-language-learners' proficiency in the second language (Johnson & Newport, 1991). However, recent research indicates a more complex conclusion: Sensitive periods likely vary across different language systems (Thomas & Johnson, 2008). Thus, for late language learners, such as adolescents and adults, new vocabulary is easier to learn than new sounds or new grammar (Neville, 2006). For example, children's ability to pronounce words with a native-like accent in a second language typically decreases with age, with an especially sharp drop occurring after the age of about 10 to 12. Also, adults tend to learn a second language faster than children, but their final level of second-language attainment is not as high as children's. And the way children and adults learn a second language differs somewhat. Compared with adults, children are less sensitive to feedback, less

PEANUTS © United Features Syndicate, Inc.

likely to use explicit strategies, and more likely to learn a second language from a large amount of input (Thomas & Johnson, 2008).

Some aspects of children's ability to learn a second language are transferred more easily to the second language than others (Pena & Bedore, 2009). Children who are fluent in two languages perform better than their single-language counterparts on tests of control of attention, concept formation, analytical reasoning, inhibition, cognitive flexibility, cognitive complexity, and cognitive monitoring (Bialystok, 2001, 2007, 2011; Bialystok & Craik, 2010; Genesee & Lindholm-Leary, 2012). They also are more conscious of the structure of spoken and written language and better at noticing errors of grammar and meaning, skills that benefit their reading ability (Bialystok, 1997; Kuo & Anderson, 2012). However, recent research indicates that bilingual children have a smaller vocabulary in each language than monolingual children (Bialystok, 2011).

Students in the United States are far behind their counterparts in many developed countries in learning a second language. For example, schools in Russia have 10 grades, called *forms,* that correspond roughly to the 12 grades in American schools. Children begin school at age 7 in Russia and begin learning English in the third form. Because of this emphasis on teaching English, most Russian citizens under the age of 40 today are able to speak at least some English. The United States is the only technologically advanced Western nation that does not require foreign language study in high school, even for students in rigorous academic programs.

In the United States, many immigrant children go from being monolingual in their home language to bilingual in that language and in English, only to end up monolingual speakers of English. This is called subtractive bilingualism, and it can have negative effects on children if they become ashamed of their home language.

A current controversy related to English Language Learners (ELLs) involves the most effective way of teaching children whose primary language is not English and who are enrolled in U.S. schools (Oller & Jarmulowicz, 2010; Gonzalez, 2009). To read about the work of one teacher of ELLs, see the *Connecting with Careers* profile of Salvador Tamayo, and for a discussion of the debate about teaching ELLs, read the *Connecting with Diversity* interlude that follows.

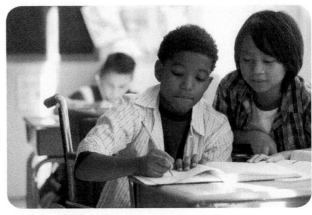

Beverly Gallagher, a third-grade teacher in Princeton, New Jersey, works with students to stimulate their interest in writing. She created the Imagine the Possibilities program, which brings nationally known poets and authors to her school. She phones each student's parents periodically to describe their child's progress and new interests. She invites students from higher grades to work with small groups in her class so that she can spend more one-on-one time with students. Each of her students keeps a writer's notebook to record thoughts, inspirations, and special words that intrigue them. Students get special opportunities to sit in an author's chair, where they read their writing to the class. (*Source: USA Today,* 2000)

developmental **connection**

Cognitive Theory

According to Piaget, at 11 to 15 years of age a new stage—formal operational thought—emerges that is characterized by thinking that is more abstract, idealistic, and logical. Chapter 6, p. 180

connecting with careers

Salvador Tamayo, Teacher of English Language Learners

Salvador Tamayo teaches English Language Learners (ELLs) in the fifth grade at Indian Knoll Elementary School in West Chicago. In 2000, he received a National Educator Award from the Milken Family Foundation for his ELL work at Turner Elementary School in West Chicago. Tamayo is especially adept at integrating technology into his ELL classes. He and his students created several award-winning Web sites about the West Chicago City Museum, the local Latino community, and the history of West Chicago. His students also developed an "I Want to Be an American Citizen" Web site to assist family and community members in preparing for the U.S. Citizenship Test. Tamayo also teaches a class in ELL instruction at Wheaton College.

For more information about what elementary school teachers do, see page 42 in the Careers in Child Development appendix following Chapter 1.

Salvador Tamayo working with English Language Learners.

English Language Learners

What is the best way to teach English Language Learners? ELLs have been taught in one of two main ways: (1) instruction in English only, or (2) a *dual-language* (formerly called *bilingual*) approach that involves instruction in their home language and English (Genesee & Lindholm-Leary, 2012). In a dual-language approach, instruction is given in both the ELL child's home language and English for varying amounts of time at certain grade levels. One of the arguments in favor of the dual-language approach is the research discussed earlier demonstrating that bilingual children have more advanced information-processing skills than monolingual children (Genesee & Lindholm-Leary, 2012).

If a dual-language strategy is used, too often it has been thought that immigrant children need only one or two years of this type of instruction. However, in general it takes immigrant children approximately three to five years to develop speaking proficiency and seven years to develop reading proficiency in English (Hakuta, Butler, & Witt, 2001). Also, immigrant children vary in their ability to learn English (Horowitz, 2013). Children who come from lower socioeconomic backgrounds have more difficulty than those from higher socioeconomic backgrounds (Hakuta, 2001). Thus, especially for immigrant children from low socioeconomic backgrounds, more years of dual-language instruction may be needed than they currently are receiving.

What have researchers found regarding outcomes of ELL programs? Drawing conclusions about the effectiveness of ELL programs is difficult because of variations across programs in the number of years they are in effect, type of instruction, quality of schooling other than ELL instruction, teachers, children, and other factors. Further, no effective experiments that compare ELL instruction with English-only education in the United States have been conducted (Snow & Kang, 2006). Some experts have concluded that the quality of instruction is more important in determining outcomes than the language in which it is delivered (Lesaux & Siegel, 2003).

Nonetheless, other experts, such as Kenji Hakuta (2001, 2005), support the combined home language and English approach because

A first- and second-grade English-Cantonese teacher instructing ELL students in Chinese in Oakland, California. *What have researchers found about the effectiveness of ELL instruction?*

(1) children have difficulty learning a subject when it is taught in a language they do not understand; and (2) when both languages are integrated in the classroom, children learn the second language more readily and participate more actively. In support of Hakuta's view, most large-scale studies have found that the academic achievement of ELLs is higher in dual-language programs than English-only programs (Genesee & Lindholm-Leary, 2012).

You learned that immigrant children who come from lower-socioeconomic-status (SES) backgrounds typically have a more difficult time learning English. What did you learn about SES and vocabulary development in the Connecting Through Research *interlude earlier in this chapter? What research questions are suggested by comparing these findings?*

ADOLESCENCE

Language development during adolescence includes increased sophistication in the use of words (Berman, 2010). With an increase in abstract thinking, adolescents are much better than children at analyzing the function a word performs in a sentence.

Adolescents also develop more subtle abilities with words. They make strides in understanding **metaphor,** which is an implied comparison between unlike things. For example, individuals "draw a line in the sand" to indicate a nonnegotiable position; a political campaign is said to be "a marathon, not a sprint"; a person's faith is "shattered." And adolescents become better able to understand and to use **satire,** which is the use of irony, derision, or wit to expose folly or wickedness. Caricatures are an example of satire. More advanced logical thinking also allows adolescents, from about 15 to 20 years of age, to understand complex literary works.

metaphor An implied comparison between two unlike things.

satire The use of irony, derision, or wit to expose folly or wickedness.

dialect A variety of language that is distinguished by its vocabulary, grammar, or pronunciation.

Most adolescents are also much better readers and writers than children are. As indicated in Figure 9.7, many adolescents increase their understanding of material told from different perspectives, which allows them to engage in more sophisticated discussions of various topics. In terms of writing, they are better at organizing ideas before they write, at distinguishing between general and specific points as they write, at stringing together sentences that make sense, and at organizing their writing into an introduction, body, and concluding remarks.

Everyday speech changes during adolescence, and "part of being a successful teenager is being able to talk like one" (Berko Gleason, 2005, p. 9). Young adolescents often speak a **dialect** with their peers that is characterized by jargon and slang (Cave, 2002). A dialect is a variety of language that is distinguished by its vocabulary, grammar, or pronunciation. For example, when meeting a friend, instead of saying hello, a young adolescent might say, "Hey, dude, 'sup?" Nicknames that are satirical and derisive ("Stilt," "Refrigerator," "Spaz") also characterize the dialect of young adolescents. Such labels might be used to show that one belongs to the group and to reduce the seriousness of a situation (Cave, 2002).

What are some changes in language development in adolescence?

Review *Connect* Reflect

LG2 Describe how language develops.

Review

- What are some key milestones of language development during infancy?
- How do language skills change during early childhood?
- How does language develop in middle and late childhood?
- How does language develop in adolescence?

Connect

- Which of the teaching strategies inspired by Vygotsky's theory (discussed in Chapter 6)

would you say is related to the whole-language approach discussed in this section?

Reflect *Your Own Personal Journey of Life*

- How many languages can you speak and read? If and when you have children, do you want them to learn more than one language while they are young? Explain.

Biological and Environmental Influences

 LG3 Discuss the biological and environmental contributions to language development.

Biological Influences | Environmental Influences | An Interactionist View of Language

We have described how language develops, but we have not explained what makes this amazing development possible. Everyone who uses language in some way "knows" its rules and has the ability to create an infinite number of words and sentences. Where does this knowledge come from? Is it the product of biology? Or is language learned and influenced by experiences?

BIOLOGICAL INFLUENCES

Some language scholars view the remarkable similarities in how children acquire language all over the world, despite the vast variation in language input they receive, as strong evidence that language has a biological basis. What role did evolution play in the biological foundations of language?

Evolution and the Brain's Role in Language   The ability to speak and understand language requires a certain vocal apparatus as well as a nervous system with certain capabilities. The nervous system and vocal apparatus of humanity's predecessors changed over hundreds of

In the wild, chimps communicate through calls, gestures, and expressions, which evolutionary psychologists believe might be the roots of true language.

Broca's area An area of the brain's left frontal lobe that is involved in speech production and grammatical processing.

Wernicke's area An area of the brain's left hemisphere that is involved in language comprehension.

aphasia A disorder resulting from brain damage to Broca's area or Wernicke's area that involves a loss or impairment of the ability to use or comprehend words.

language acquisition device (LAD) Chomsky's term that describes a biological endowment enabling children to detect the features and rules of language, including phonology, syntax, and semantics.

Broca's area   Wernicke's area

FIGURE **9.9**

BROCA'S AREA AND WERNICKE'S AREA. Broca's area is located in the frontal lobe of the brain's left hemisphere, and it is involved in the control of speech. Wernicke's area is a portion of the left hemisphere's temporal lobe that is involved in understanding language. *How does the role of these areas of the brain relate to lateralization, which was discussed in Chapter 4?*

thousands or millions of years. With advances in the nervous system and vocal structures, Homo sapiens went beyond the grunting and shrieking of other animals to develop speech. Although estimates vary, many experts believe that humans acquired language about 100,000 years ago, which in evolutionary time represents a very recent acquisition. It gave humans an enormous edge over other animals and increased the chances of human survival (Arbib, 2012).

There is evidence that particular regions of the brain are predisposed to be used for language (Lee & others, 2012). Two regions involved in language were first discovered in studies of brain-damaged individuals: **Broca's area,** an area in the left frontal lobe of the brain involved in speech production and grammatical processing, and **Wernicke's area,** a region of the brain's left hemisphere involved in language comprehension (see Figure 9.9). Damage to either of these areas produces types of **aphasia,** which is a loss or impairment of language processing. Individuals with damage to Broca's area have difficulty producing words correctly; individuals with damage to Wernicke's area have poor comprehension and often produce fluent but incomprehensible speech.

Chomsky's Language Acquisition Device (LAD)   Linguist Noam Chomsky (1957) proposed that humans are biologically prewired to learn language at a certain time and in a certain way. He said that children are born into the world with a **language acquisition device (LAD),** a biological endowment that enables the child to detect certain features and rules of language, including phonology, syntax, and semantics. Children are prepared by nature with the ability to detect the sounds of language, for example, and follow rules such as how to form plurals and ask questions.

Chomsky's LAD is a theoretical construct, not a physical part of the brain. Is there evidence for the existence of a LAD? Supporters of the LAD concept cite the uniformity of language milestones across languages and cultures, evidence that children create language even in the absence of well-formed input, and biological substrates of language. But as we will see, critics argue that even if infants have something like a LAD, it cannot explain the whole story of language acquisition.

ENVIRONMENTAL INFLUENCES

Decades ago, behaviorists opposed Chomsky's hypothesis and argued that language represents nothing more than chains of responses acquired through reinforcement (Skinner, 1957). A baby happens to babble "Ma-ma"; Mama rewards the baby with hugs and smiles; the baby says "Mama" more and more. Bit by bit, said the behaviorists, the baby's language is built up. According to behaviorists, language is a complex, learned skill, much like playing the piano or dancing.

The behavioral view of language learning has several problems. First, it does not explain how people create novel sentences—sentences that people have never heard or spoken before. Second, children learn the syntax of their native language even if they are not reinforced for doing so. Social psychologist Roger Brown (1973) spent long hours observing parents and their young children. He found that parents did not directly or explicitly reward or correct the syntax of most children's utterances. That is, parents did not say "good," "correct," "right," "wrong," and so on. Also, parents did not offer direct corrections such as "You should say two shoes, not two shoe." However, as we will see shortly, many parents do expand on their young children's grammatically incorrect utterances and recast many of those that have grammatical errors (Clark, 2009).

The behavioral view is no longer considered a viable explanation of how children acquire language. But a great deal of research describes ways in which children's environmental experiences influence their language skills (Berko Gleason & Ratner, 2009). Many language experts argue that a child's experiences, the particular language to be learned, and the context in which learning takes place can strongly influence language acquisition (Goldfield & Snow, 2009).

Language is not learned in a social vacuum. Most children are bathed in language from a very early age (Kuhl, 2011, 2012). The Wild Boy of Aveyron, who never learned to communicate effectively, had lived in social isolation for years. The support and involvement of caregivers and teachers greatly facilitate a child's language learning (Giorgis & Glazer, 2013; Hirsh-Pasek & Golinkoff, 2013; Tamis-LeMonda & Song, 2013). For example, one study found that when mothers immediately smiled and touched their 8-month-old infants after they babbled, the infants subsequently made more complex speech-like sounds than when mothers responded to their infants in a random manner (Goldstein, King, & West, 2003) (see Figure 9.10).

Michael Tomasello (2008, 2009, 2011; Tomasello & Hamann, 2012; Tomasello & Vaish, 2013) stresses that young children are intensely interested in their social world and that early in their development they can understand the intentions of other people. His interaction view of language emphasizes that children learn language in specific contexts. For example, when a toddler and a father are jointly focused on a book, the father might say, "See the birdie." In this case, even a toddler understands that the father intends to name something and knows to look in the direction of the pointing. Through this kind of joint attention, early in their development children are able to use their social skills to acquire language (Carpenter, 2011; Tomasello, 2011).

One intriguing component of the young child's linguistic environment is **child-directed speech,** language spoken in a higher pitch than normal with simple words and sentences (Naoi & others, 2012). It is hard to use child-directed speech when not in the presence of a baby. As soon as you start talking to a baby, though, you shift into child-directed speech. Much of this is automatic and something most parents are not aware they are doing. As mentioned previously in this chapter, even 4-year-olds speak in simpler ways to 2-year-olds than to their 4-year-old friends. Child-directed speech has the important function of capturing the infant's attention and maintaining communication (Jaswal & Fernald, 2007).

Adults often use strategies other than child-directed speech to enhance the child's acquisition of language, including recasting, expanding, and labeling:

- **Recasting** is rephrasing something the child has said, perhaps turning it into a question or restating the child's immature utterance in the form of a fully grammatical sentence. For example, if the child says, "The dog was barking," the adult can respond by asking, "When was the dog barking?" Effective recasting lets the child indicate an interest and then elaborates on that interest.

- **Expanding** is restating, in a linguistically sophisticated form, what a child has said. For example, a child says, "Doggie eat," and the parent replies, "Yes, the doggie is eating."

- **Labeling** is identifying the names of objects. Young children are continually being asked to identify the names of objects. Roger Brown (1958) called this "the original word game" and claimed that much of a child's early vocabulary is motivated by this adult pressure to identify the words associated with objects.

Parents use these strategies naturally and in meaningful conversations. Parents do not (and should not) use any deliberate method to teach their children to talk, even for children who are slow in learning language. Children usually benefit when parents guide their children's discovery of language rather than overloading them with language; "following in order to lead" helps a child learn language. If children are not ready to take in some information, they are likely to tell you (perhaps by turning away). Thus, giving the child more information is not always better.

Infants, toddlers, and young children benefit when adults read books to and with them (shared reading) (Hirsh-Pasek & Golinkoff, 2013). A recent analysis found that the earlier children were read to and the more often they were read to, the better were their literacy and language skills (Dunst, Simkus, & Hamby, 2012). In this analysis, the average age of children when adults began reading to them was 22 months of age. Storybook reading especially benefits children when parents extend the meaning of the text by discussing the text with children and encouraging them to ask and answer questions (Barbarin & Aikens, 2009; Whitehurst & Lonigan, 1998).

MIT linguist Noam Chomsky. *What is Chomsky's view of language?*

FIGURE **9.10**

SOCIAL INTERACTION AND BABBLING. One study focused on two groups of mothers and their 8-month-old infants (Goldstein, King, & West, 2003). One group of mothers was instructed to smile and touch their infants immediately after the babies cooed and babbled; the other group was also told to smile and touch their infants but in a random manner, unconnected to sounds the infants made. The infants whose mothers immediately responded in positive ways to their babbling subsequently made more complex, speechlike sounds, such as "da" and "gu." The research setting for this study, which underscores how important caregivers are in the early development of language, is shown here.

child-directed speech Language spoken in a higher pitch than normal, with simple words and sentences.

recasting Rephrasing a statement that a child has said, perhaps turning it into a question, or restating a child's immature utterance in the form of a fully grammatical utterance.

expanding Restating, in a linguistically sophisticated form, what a child has said.

labeling Identifying the names of objects.

What is shared reading and how might it benefit infants and toddlers?

In one study, a majority of U.S. mothers in low-income families reported that they were reading to their infants and toddlers with some regularity (Raikes & others, 2006). In this study, non-Latino White, more highly educated mothers who were parenting a first-born child were more likely to read books to their infants and toddlers than were African American and Latino mothers who were parenting later-born children. Reading daily to children at 14 to 24 months of age was positively related to the children's language and cognitive development at 36 months of age. To read further about ways that parents can facilitate children's language development, see *Caring Connections*.

Our discussion of environmental influences on language development has mainly focused on parents. However, children interact with many other people who can influence their language development, including teachers and peers. A recent study of more than 1,800 4-year-olds focused on ways in which peers might influence children's language development (Mashburn & others, 2009). In this study, peers' expressive language abilities were positively linked with young children's receptive and expressive language development.

AN INTERACTIONIST VIEW OF LANGUAGE

If language acquisition depended only on biology, then Genie and the Wild Boy of Aveyron (discussed earlier in the chapter) should have talked without difficulty. A child's experiences influence language acquisition. But we have seen that language does have strong biological foundations (Shafer & Garrido-Nag, 2010). No matter how much you converse with a dog, it won't learn to talk. In contrast, children are biologically prepared to learn language. Children all over the world acquire language milestones at about the same time and in about the same order. However, there are cultural variations in the type of support given to children's language development. For example, caregivers in the Kaluli culture prompt young children to use a loud voice and particular morphemes that direct the speech act performed (calling out) and to refer to names, kinship relations, and places where there has been a shared past experience that indicates a closeness to the person being addressed (Ochs & Schieffelin, 2008; Schieffelin, 2005).

An interactionist view emphasizes that both biology and experience contribute to language development (Wagner & Hoff, 2013). This interaction of biology and experience can be seen in

> The linguistics problems children have to solve are always embedded in personal and interpersonal contexts.
>
> —LOIS BLOOM
> *Contemporary Psychologist, Columbia University*

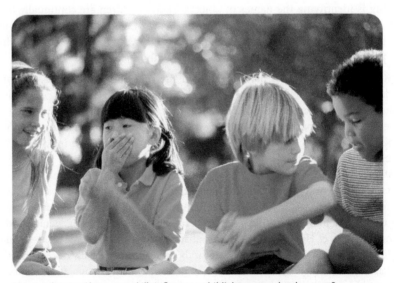

How might peers' language skills influence a child's language development?

How Parents Can Facilitate Infants' and Toddlers' Language Development

Linguist Naomi Baron (1992) in *Growing Up with Language,* and more recently Ellen Galinsky (2010) in *Mind in the Making,* provided ideas to help parents facilitate their infants' and toddlers' language development. A summary of their ideas follow:

- *Be an active conversational partner.* Talk to your baby from the time it is born. Initiate conversation with the baby. If the baby is in a day-long child-care program, ensure that the baby receives adequate language stimulation from adults.
- *Talk in a slowed-down pace and don't worry about how you sound to other adults when you talk to your baby.* Talking in a slowed-down pace will help your baby detect words in the sea of sounds they experience. Babies enjoy and attend to the high-pitched sound of child-directed speech.
- *Use parent-look and parent-gesture, and name what you are looking at.* When you want your child to pay attention to something, look at it and point to it. Then name it—for example, by saying "Look, Alex, there's an airplane."
- *When you talk with infants and toddlers, be simple, concrete, and repetitive.* Don't try to talk to them in abstract, high-level ways and think you have to say something new or different all of the time. Using familiar words often will help them remember the words.
- *Play games.* Use word games like peek-a-boo and pat-a-cake to help infants learn words.
- *Remember to listen.* Since toddlers' speech is often slow and laborious, parents are often tempted to supply words and thoughts for them. Be patient and let toddlers express themselves, no matter how painstaking the process is or how great a hurry you are in.
- *Expand and elaborate language abilities and horizons with infants and toddlers.* Ask questions that encourage answers other than "Yes" and "No." Actively repeat, expand, and recast the utterances. Your toddler might say, "Dada." You could follow with, "Where's Dada?", and then you might continue, "Let's go find him."
- *Adjust to your child's idiosyncrasies instead of working against them.* Many toddlers have difficulty pronouncing words and making themselves understood. Whenever possible, make toddlers feel that they are being understood.

It is a good idea for parents to begin talking to their babies at the start. The best language teaching occurs when the talking is begun before the infant becomes capable of intelligible speech. *What are some other guidelines for parents to follow in helping their infants and toddlers develop their language skills?*

- *Resist making normative comparisons.* Be aware of the ages at which your child reaches specific milestones (such as the first word, first 50 words), but do not measure this development rigidly against that of other children. Such comparisons can bring about unnecessary anxiety.

Based on what you read earlier in this section of the chapter, would parents be wise to combine these strategies here with deliberate methods to teach their children to talk?

the variations in the acquisition of language. Children vary in their ability to acquire language, and this variation cannot be readily explained by differences in environmental input alone. However, virtually every child benefits enormously from opportunities to talk and be talked with. Children whose parents and teachers provide them with a rich verbal environment show many positive outcomes (Gunning, 2013; Tamis-LeMonda & Song, 2013). Parents and teachers who pay attention to what children are trying to say, expand children's utterances, read to them, and label things in the environment, are providing valuable, if unintentional, benefits (Hirsh-Pasek & Golinkoff, 2013).

LG3 Discuss the biological and environmental contributions to language development.

Review

- What are the biological foundations of language?
- What are the behavioral and environmental aspects of language?
- How does an interactionist view describe language?

Connect

- In this section, you learned about two areas in the left hemisphere of the brain that are involved in speech production and recognition. Related to this, what did you learn in Chapter 2 about hemisphere specialization in infants?

Reflect *Your Own Personal Journey of Life*

- If and when you become a parent, how should you respond to your child's grammatical mistakes when conversing with the child? Will you allow the mistakes to continue and assume that your young child will grow out of them, or will you closely monitor your young child's grammar and correct mistakes whenever you hear them? Explain.

Language and Cognition

LG4 Evaluate how language and cognition are linked.

Wendy Verougstraete as a child (*left*) and as an adult (*right*).

As a teenager, Wendy Verougstraete felt that she was on the road to becoming a professional author. "You are looking at a professional author," she said. "My books will be filled with drama, action, and excitement. And everyone will want to read them. I am going to write books, page after page, stack after stack."

Overhearing her remarks, you might have been impressed not only by Wendy's optimism and determination, but also by her expressive verbal skills. In fact, at a young age Wendy showed a flair for writing and telling stories. Wendy has a rich vocabulary, creates lyrics for love songs, and enjoys telling stories. You probably would not be able to immediately guess that she has an IQ of only 49 and cannot tie her shoes, cross the street by herself, read or print words beyond the first-grade level, or do even simple arithmetic.

Wendy Verougstraete has Williams syndrome, a genetic birth disorder that was first described in 1961 and affects about 1 in 20,000 births (Mervis & Becerra, 2007; Morris, 2010). Williams syndrome stems from a genetic deletion on chromosome 7 (Musolino & Landau, 2012). The most noticeable features of the syndrome include a unique combination of expressive verbal skills with an extremely low IQ and limited visuospatial skills and motor control (O'Hearn & Luna, 2009). Children with Williams syndrome are natural-born storytellers who provide highly expressive narratives (Mervis & John, 2010). Figure 9.11 shows the great disparity in the verbal and motor skills of one person with Williams syndrome. Individuals with Williams syndrome often have good musical skills and interpersonal skills (Asada & Itakura, 2012; Lincoln & others, 2007). One study indicated that children with Williams syndrome in the United States and Japan were more sociable than normally developing children in their respective countries, reflecting a genetic predisposition for sociability in children with Williams syndrome (Zitzer-Comfort & others, 2007). However, normally developing U.S. children were as sociable as Japanese children with Williams syndrome, reflecting different cultural expectations in the two countries. The syndrome also includes a number of physical characteristics as well, such as heart defects and a pixie-like facial appearance. Despite having excellent verbal skills and competent interpersonal skills, most individuals with Williams syndrome cannot live independent lives (American Academy of Pediatrics, 2001). For example, Wendy Verougstraete lives in a group home for adults who are have an intellectual disability.

The verbal abilities of individuals with Williams syndrome are very distinct from those shown by individuals with Down syndrome, a type of intellectual disability that we discussed in Chapters 2 and 8 (Dodd & Crosbie, 2011; Levy & Eilam, 2013). On vocabulary tests, children with Williams syndrome show a liking for unusual words. When asked to name as many animals as they can think of in one minute, Williams children come up with creatures like ibex, chihuahua, saber-toothed tiger, weasel, crane, and newt. Children with Down syndrome give simple examples like dog, cat, and mouse. When children with Williams syndrome tell stories, their voices come alive with drama and emotion, punctuating the dialogue with audience attention-grabbers like "gadzooks" or "lo and behold!" By contrast, children with Down syndrome tell very simple stories with little emotion.

Aside from being an interesting genetic disorder, Williams syndrome offers insights into the normal development of thinking and language (Carney, Brown, & Henry, 2013). In our society, verbal ability is generally associated with high intelligence. But Williams syndrome raises the possibility that thinking and language might not be so closely related. Williams disorder is due to a defective gene that seems to protect expressive verbal ability but not reading and many other cognitive skills (Carney, Brown, & Henry, 2013). Thus, cases like Wendy Verougstraete's cast some doubt on the general categorization of intelligence as verbal ability and prompt the question, "What is the relationship between thinking and language?"

Two basic and separate issues characterize connections between language and cognition. The first is whether cognition is necessary for language. Although some researchers have noted that certain aspects of language development typically follow mastery of selected cognitive skills in both normally developing children and children with an intellectual disability, it is not clear that language development depends on any specific aspect of cognitive abilities (Lenneberg, 1967). Some experts argue that it is more likely that language and cognitive development occur in parallel but dissociated fashions (Cromer, 1987). Thus, according to research and experts' judgments, cognition is not necessary for language development.

The second issue is whether language is necessary for (or important to) cognition. This issue is addressed by studies of deaf children. On a variety of thinking and problem-solving skills, deaf children perform at the same level as children of the same age who have no hearing problems. Some of the deaf children in these studies do not even have command of written or sign language (Furth, 1973). Thus, based on studies of deaf children, language is not necessary for cognitive development.

There is, however, evidence of links between the cognitive and language worlds of children (Oates & Grayson, 2004). Piaget's concept of object permanence has been the focus of some research that connects cognitive and language development. Piaget emphasized that children come to learn about the world first and then learn to label what they know. Infants may need a concept of object permanence before they start to use words for disappearance, such as "all gone" (Gopnik & Meltzoff, 1997).

One study explored whether four aspects of information-processing skills—memory, representational competence, processing speed, and attention—were related to infants' and young children's language development (Rose, Feldman, & Jankowski, 2009). In this study, memory and representational competence assessed at 12 months of age predicted language at 36 months of age independently of birth status, 12-month language, and 12-month scores on the Bayley Developmental Scales. The dimensions of memory that best predicted language development were recognition and recall but not short-term memory; the dimensions of representation competence that best predicted language development were cross-modal transfer (matching touch to vision) and object permanence. Other research has found that joint attention in infancy is linked to vocabulary development in childhood (Colombo & others, 2009a, b).

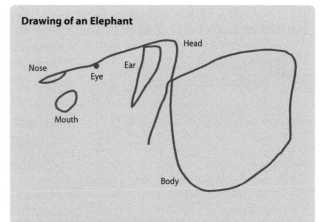

Drawing of an Elephant

Verbal Description of an Elephant

And what an elephant is, it is one of the animals. And what the elephant does, it lives in the jungle. It can also live in the zoo. And what it has, it has long gray ears, fan ears, ears that can blow in the wind. It has a long trunk that can pick up grass, or pick up hay.... If they're in a bad mood it can be terrible.... If the elephant gets mad it could stomp; it could charge. Sometimes elephants can charge. They have big long tusks. They can damage a car.... It could be dangerous. When they're in a pinch, when they're in a bad mood it can be terrible. You don't want an elephant as a pet. You want a cat or a dog or a bird....

FIGURE **9.11**

DISPARITY IN THE VERBAL AND MOTOR SKILLS OF AN INDIVIDUAL WITH WILLIAMS SYNDROME

Review

- What characterizes children with Williams syndrome? To what extent are language and cognition linked? Are they part of a single, automated cognitive system?

Connect

- In Chapter 8, you learned how Down syndrome is classified as intellectual disability.

In this section of Chapter 9, you learned that Williams syndrome is not classified as intellectual disability. Why not?

Reflect *Your Own Personal Journey of Life*

- Did you always think in words when you were growing up? Explain.

reach your **learning goals**

Language Development

What Is Language?

 LG1 Define language and describe its rule systems.

Defining Language

- Language is a form of communication, whether spoken, written, or signed, that is based on a system of symbols. Language consists of all the words used by a community and the rules for varying and combining them. Infinite generativity is the ability to produce an endless number of meaningful sentences using a finite set of words and rules.

Language's Rule Systems

- The five main rule systems of language are phonology, morphology, syntax, semantics, and pragmatics. Phonology is the sound system of a language, including the sounds used and the particular sound sequences that may occur in the language. Morphology refers to how words are formed. Syntax is the way words are combined to form acceptable phrases and sentences. Semantics involves the meaning of words and sentences. Pragmatics is the appropriate use of language in different contexts.

How Language Develops

LG2 Describe how language develops.

Infancy

- Among the milestones in infant language development are crying (birth), cooing (1 to 2 months), babbling (6 months), making the transition from universal linguist to language-specific listener (6 to 12 months), using gestures (8 to 12 months), recognition of their name (as early as 5 months), first word spoken (10 to 15 months), vocabulary spurt (18 months), rapid expansion of understanding words (18 to 24 months), and two-word utterances (18 to 24 months).

Early Childhood

- Advances in phonology, morphology, syntax, semantics, and pragmatics continue in early childhood. The transition to complex sentences begins at 2 or 3 years and continues through the elementary school years. Currently, there is considerable interest in the early literacy of children.

Middle and Late Childhood

- In middle and late childhood, children become more analytical and logical in their approach to words and grammar. One model proposes five stages in reading, ranging from birth/first grade to high school. Current debate involving how to teach children to read focuses on the phonics approach versus the whole-language approach. Researchers have found strong evidence that the phonics approach should be used in teaching children to read, especially in kindergarten and the first grade and with struggling readers, but that children also benefit from the whole-language approach. Children's writing emerges out of scribbling. Advances in children's language and cognitive development provide the underpinnings for improved writing. Strategy instruction is especially effective in improving children's writing. Children who are fluent in two languages have more advanced information-processing skills. Instruction for English language learners (ELLs) has taken one of two main forms: (1) instruction in English only, or (2) dual-language instruction in the child's home language and English. The majority of large-scale research studies have found a higher level of academic achievement when the dual-language approach is used.

Adolescence

- In adolescence, language changes include more effective use of words; improvements in the ability to understand metaphor, satire, and adult literary works; and improvements in writing. Young adolescents often speak a dialect with their peers, using jargon and slang.

Biological and Environmental Influences

 LG3 Discuss the biological and environmental contributions to language development.

Biological Influences

- In evolution, language clearly gave humans an enormous edge over other animals and increased their chance of survival. A substantial portion of language processing occurs in the brain's left hemisphere, with Broca's area and Wernicke's area being important left-hemisphere locations. Chomsky argues that children are born with the ability to detect basic features and rules of language. In other words, they are biologically equipped to learn language with a prewired language acquisition device (LAD).

Environmental Influences

- The behavioral view of language acquisition—that children acquire language as a result of reinforcement—is no longer supported. Adults help children acquire language through child-directed speech, recasting, expanding, and labeling. Environmental influences are demonstrated by differences in the language development of children as a consequence of being exposed to different language environments in the home. Parents should talk extensively with an infant, especially about what the baby is attending to.

An Interactionist View of Language

- An interactionist view emphasizes the contributions of both biology and experience in language.

Language and Cognition

 LG4 Evaluate how language and cognition are linked.

- Children with Williams syndrome have a unique combination of expressive verbal skills with an extremely low IQ and limited visuospatial skills and motor control. Study of these children offers insights into the normal development of thinking and language. Two basic and separate issues are these: (1) Is cognition necessary for language? (2) Is language necessary for cognition? At an extreme, the answer likely is no to these questions, but there is evidence of linkages between language and cognition. A recent study revealed that infants' information-processing skills were linked to the growth of language development in early childhood.

key terms

language 253
infinite generativity 253
phonology 253
morphology 254
syntax 254
semantics 254
pragmatics 255

telegraphic speech 258
fast mapping 261
metalinguistic
    awareness 264
phonics approach 265
whole-language approach 265
metaphor 268

satire 268
dialect 268
Broca's area 270
Wernicke's area 270
aphasia 270
language acquisition device
    (LAD) 270

child-directed speech 271
recasting 271
expanding 271
labeling 271

key people

Helen Keller 252
Patricia Kuhl 257
Jean Berko 259
Kathy Hirsh-Pasek 240

Roberta Golinkoff 240
Betty Hart 262
Todd Risley 262

Janellen Huttenlocher 262
Ellen Galinsky 263
Noam Chomsky 270

Roger Brown 270
Naomi Baron 273

I am what I hope and give.

—**ERIK ERIKSON**
European-Born American Psychotherapist, 20th Century

Socioemotional Development

As children develop, they need the meeting eyes of love. They split the universe into two halves: "me" and "not me." They juggle the need to curb their own will with becoming what they can will freely. They also want to fly but discover that first they have to learn to stand and walk and climb and dance. As they become adolescents, they try on one face after another, looking for a face of their own. In Section 4, you will read four chapters: "Emotional Development" (Chapter 10), "The Self and Identity" (Chapter 11), "Gender" (Chapter 12), and "Moral Development" (Chapter 13).

EMOTIONAL DEVELOPMENT

chapter **outline**

Today an increasing number of fathers are staying home to care for their children (Lamb & Lewis, 2013). Consider 17-month-old Darius. On weekdays, Darius' father, a writer, cares for him during the day while his mother works full-time as a landscape architect. Darius' father is doing a great job of caring for him. Darius' father keeps Darius nearby while he is writing and spends lots of time talking to him and playing with him. From their interactions, it is clear that they genuinely enjoy each other's company.

Last month, Darius began spending one day a week at a child-care center. His parents carefully selected the center after observing a number of centers and interviewing teachers and center directors. His parents placed him in the center one day a week so Darius could get some experience with peers and his father could have some time out from caregiving.

Darius' father looks to the future and imagines the Little League games Darius will play in and the many other activities he can enjoy with Darius. Remembering how little time his own father spent with him, he is dedicated to making sure that Darius has an involved, nurturing experience with his father.

When Darius' mother comes home in the evening, she spends considerable time with him. Darius has a secure attachment with both his mother and his father.

Many fathers are spending more time with their infants today than in the past.

preview

For many years, emotion was neglected in the study of children's development. Today, emotion is increasingly important in conceptualizations of development. Even infants show different emotional styles, display varying temperaments, and begin to form emotional bonds with their caregivers. In this chapter, we will study the roles of temperament and attachment in development. But first we will examine emotion itself, exploring the functions of emotions in children's lives and the development of emotion from infancy through middle and late childhood.

Exploring Emotion LG1 Discuss basic aspects of emotion.

What Are Emotions?

A Functionalist View of Emotions

Emotional Competence

Imagine your life without emotion. Emotion is the color and music of life, as well as the tie that binds people together. How do psychologists define and classify emotions, and why are they important to development?

WHAT ARE EMOTIONS?

For our purposes, we will define **emotion** as feeling, or affect, that occurs when people are in a state or an interaction that is important to them, especially one that influences their well-being. In many instances emotions involve people's communication with the world. Although emotion consists of more than communication, in infancy the communication aspect is at the forefront of emotion (Witherington & others, 2010).

Psychologists classify the broad range of emotions in many ways, but almost all classifications designate an emotion as either positive or negative (Christenfeld & Mandler, 2013; Izard, 2009). Positive emotions include enthusiasm, joy, and love. Negative emotions include anxiety, anger, guilt, and sadness.

Emotions are influenced by biological foundations and experience (Calkins, 2012; Kagan, 2013). In evolutionary theory, evolution endowed human beings with a biological foundation for emotion. The biological foundation of emotion involves the development of the nervous system. Emotions are linked with early-developing regions of the human nervous system, including structures of the limbic system and the brain stem (de Haan & Matheson, 2009; Easterbrooks & others, 2013). The capacity of infants to show distress, excitement, and rage reflects the early emergence of these biologically rooted emotional brain systems. Significant advances in emotional responding occur during infancy and childhood as a result of changes in neurobiological systems (including the frontal regions of the cerebral cortex) that can exert control over the more primitive limbic system (Cuevas & others, 2012). As children develop, maturation of the cerebral cortex allows a decrease in unpredictable mood swings and an increase in the self-regulation of emotion. However, such mood swings increase during adolescence, likely as a result of the earlier development of the limbic system, especially the amygdala (which is extensively involved in emotional processing), and the protracted development of the frontal cortex (which is heavily involved in reasoning and self-regulation) (Giedd & others, 2012; Steinberg, 2013).

Social relationships, in turn, provide the setting for the development of a rich variety of emotions (Duncombe & others, 2012; Thompson, 2013c, d). When toddlers hear their parents quarreling, they often react with distress and inhibit their play. Members of well-functioning families make each other laugh and may develop a light mood to defuse conflicts.

Blossoms are scattered
by the wind
And the wind cares nothing, but
The blossoms of the heart,
No wind can touch.

—Youshida Kenko
Buddhist Monk, 14th Century

developmental **connection**

Brain Development

The prefrontal cortex is not as well developed in adolescence as it is in adulthood. For adolescents, it is as if their brain doesn't have the brakes to slow down their emotions. Chapter 4, p. 116

emotion Feeling, or affect, that occurs when people are engaged in an interaction that is important to them, especially one that influences their well-being.

Cultural variations reveal the role of experience in emotion (Tamis-Lemonda & Song, 2013). For example, display rules—when, where, and how emotions should be expressed—are not culturally universal. Researchers have found that East Asian infants display less frequent and less intense positive and negative emotions than non-Latino White infants (Camras & others, 1998). Throughout childhood, East Asian parents encourage their children to show emotional reserve rather than emotional expressivity (Cole & Tan, 2007). Further, Japanese parents try to prevent their children from experiencing negative emotions, whereas non-Latino White mothers are more likely to respond after their children become distressed and then help them cope (Cole & Tan, 2007).

Caregivers play a role in the infant's neurobiological regulation of emotions (Thompson, 2013b, c, d; Ursache & others, 2013). For example, by soothing the infant when the infant cries and shows distress, caregivers help infants to modulate their emotion and reduce the level of stress hormones (Gunnar & Quevado, 2007).

In sum, biological evolution has endowed human beings to be emotional, but culture and relationships with others provide diversity in emotional experiences (Tamis-LeMonda & Song, 2013; Thompson, 2013c, d). As we see next, this emphasis on the role of relationships in emotion is at the core of the functionalist view of emotion.

How do Japanese mothers handle their infants' and children's emotional development differently from non-Latino White mothers?

A FUNCTIONALIST VIEW OF EMOTIONS

Many developmentalists today view emotions as the result of individuals' attempts to adapt to specific contextual demands (Saarni & others, 2006). Thus, a child's emotional responses cannot be separated from the situations in which they are evoked. In many instances, emotions are elicited in interpersonal contexts. For example, emotional expressions serve the important functions of signaling to others how one feels, regulating one's own behavior, and playing pivotal roles in social exchange.

One implication of the functionalist view is that emotions are *relational rather than strictly internal, intrapsychic phenomena* (Thompson, 2013c, d). Consider just some of the roles of emotion in parent-child relationships. The beginnings of an emotional bond between parents and an infant are based on affectively toned interchanges, as when an infant cries and the caregiver sensitively responds. By the end of the first year, a parent's facial expression—either smiling or fearful—influences whether an infant will explore an unfamiliar environment. Well-functioning families often include humor in their interactions, sometimes making each other laugh and creating a light mood state to defuse conflict. When a positive mood has been induced in a child, the child is more likely to comply with a parent's directions.

A second implication of the functionalist view is that emotions are *linked with an individual's goals in a variety of ways* (Saarni & others, 2006). Regardless of what the goal is, an individual who overcomes an obstacle to attain a goal experiences happiness. By contrast, a person who must relinquish a goal as unattainable experiences sadness. And a person who faces difficult obstacles in pursuing a goal often experiences frustration, which can become anger when the obstacles are perceived as unfair or intentionally put in the way to hinder the individual's goal attainment.

The specific nature of the goal can affect the experience of a given emotion. For example, the avoidance of threat is linked with fear, the desire to atone is related to guilt, and the wish to avoid the scrutiny of others is associated with shame.

EMOTIONAL COMPETENCE

In Chapter 8, we briefly described the concept of emotional intelligence. Here we will examine a closely related concept, emotional competence, that focuses on the adaptive nature of emotional experience. Carolyn Saarni (1999; Saarni & others, 2006) argues that becoming emotionally competent involves developing a number of skills in social contexts. Figure 10.1 describes these skills and provides examples of each one. As children acquire these emotional competence skills in a variety of contexts, they are more likely to effectively manage their emotions, become resilient in the face of stressful circumstances, and develop more positive relationships.

developmental **connection**

Intelligence

Emotional intelligence involves perceiving and expressing emotions accurately, understanding emotion and possessing emotional knowledge, using feelings to facilitate thought, and managing emotions effectively. Chapter 8, p. 234

FIGURE **10.1**
EMOTIONAL COMPETENCE SKILLS

Skill	Example
Awareness of one's emotional states	Being able to differentiate whether sad or anxious
Detecting others' emotions	Understanding when another person is sad rather than afraid
Using the vocabulary of emotion terms in socially and culturally appropriate ways	Appropriately describing a social situation in one's culture when a person is feeling distress
Empathic and sympathetic sensitivity to others' emotional experiences	Being sensitive to others when they are feeling distressed
Recognizing that inner emotional states do not have to correspond to outer expressions	Recognizing that one can feel very angry yet manage one's emotional expression so that it appears more neutral
Adaptively coping with negative emotions by using self-regulatory strategies that reduce the intensity or duration of such emotional states	Reducing anger by walking away from an aversive situation and engaging in an activity that takes one's mind off of the aversive situation
Awareness that the expression of emotions plays a major role in a relationship	Knowing that expressing anger toward a friend on a regular basis is likely to harm the friendship
Viewing oneself overall as feeling the way one wants to feel	Feeling like one can cope effectively with the stress in one's life and feeling that one is doing this successfully

Review *Connect* Reflect

 Discuss basic aspects of emotion.

Review

- How is emotion defined?
- What characterizes functionalism in emotion?
- What constitutes emotional competence, according to Saarni?

Connect

- How are the competence skills listed in Figure 10.1 related to the four aspects of emotional intelligence described in Chapter 8?

Reflect *Your Own Personal Journey of Life*

- Think back to your childhood and adolescent years. How would you describe your emotional competence as a child and adolescent, based on the descriptions in Figure 10.1?

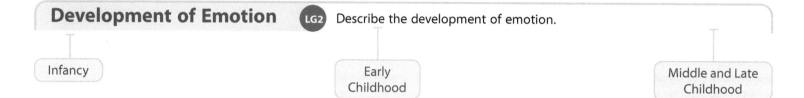

Development of Emotion — LG2 Describe the development of emotion.

Infancy — Early Childhood — Middle and Late Childhood

Does an older child's emotional life differ from a younger child's? Does a young child's emotional life differ from an infant's? Does an infant even have an emotional life? In this section, we will sketch an overview of the changes in emotion from infancy through middle childhood, looking not only at changes in emotional experience but also at the development of emotional competence.

INFANCY

What are some early developmental changes in emotions? What functions do infants' cries serve? When do infants begin to smile?

Early Emotions A leading expert on infant emotional development, Michael Lewis (2008, 2010) distinguishes between primary emotions and self-conscious emotions. **Primary emotions** are emotions that are present in humans and other animals; these emotions appear in the first six months of the human infant's development. Primary emotions include surprise, interest, joy, anger, sadness, fear, and disgust (see Figure 10.2 for infants' facial expressions of some of these early emotions). In Lewis' classification, **self-conscious emotions** require self-awareness that involves consciousness and a sense of "me." Self-conscious emotions include jealousy, empathy, embarrassment, pride, shame, and guilt. Lewis argues that these self-conscious emotions occur for the first time at some point in the second half of the first year through the second year. Some experts on emotion call self-conscious emotions such as embarrassment, shame, guilt, and pride *other-conscious emotions* because they involve the emotional reactions of others when they are generated (Saarni & others, 2006). For example, approval from parents is linked to toddlers beginning to show pride when they successfully complete a task.

Leading researchers such as Joseph Campos (2009) and Michael Lewis (2008) debate how early in the infant and toddler years the emotions that we have described first appear and their sequence. As an indication of the controversy regarding when certain emotions first are displayed by infants, consider jealousy. Some researchers argue that jealousy does not emerge until approximately 18 months of age (Lewis, 2008), whereas others emphasize that it is displayed much earlier (Draghi-Lorenz, Reddy, & Costall, 2001). Consider a research study in which 6-month-old infants observed their mothers giving attention either to a life-like baby doll (hugging or gently rocking it, for example) or to a book (Hart & Carrington, 2002). When mothers directed their attention to the doll, the infants were more likely to display negative emotions, such as anger and sadness, which may have indicated their jealousy (see Figure 10.3). However, their expressions of anger and sadness may have reflected frustration in not being able to have the novel doll to play with.

Debate about the onset of an emotion such as jealousy illustrates the complexity and difficulty of indexing early emotions. That said, some experts on infant socioemotional development, such as Jerome Kagan (2010), conclude that the structural immaturity of the infant brain make it unlikely that emotions requiring thought—such as guilt, pride, despair, shame, empathy, and jealousy—can be experienced in the first year. Thus, both Kagan (2010) and Campos (2009) argue that so-called "self-conscious" emotions don't occur until after the first year, which increasingly reflects the view of most developmental psychologists. Thus, in regard to the photograph in Figure 10.3, it is unlikely that the 6-month-old infant is experiencing jealousy.

Emotional Expression and Social Relationships

Emotional expressions are involved in infants' first relationships. The ability of infants to communicate emotions permits coordinated interactions with their caregivers and the beginning of an emotional bond between them (Thompson, 2013a, d). Not only do parents change their emotional expressions in response to infants' emotional expressions, but infants also modify their emotional expressions in response to their parents' emotional expressions. In other words, these interactions are mutually regulated (Bridgett & others, 2009). Because of this coordination, the interactions are described as *reciprocal,* or *synchronous,* when all is going well. Sensitive, responsive parents help their infants grow emotionally, whether the infants respond in distressed or happy ways (Thompsons, 2013a, b). A recent study revealed that parents' elicitation of talk about emotion with toddlers was associated with the toddlers' sharing and helping (Brownell & others, 2012).

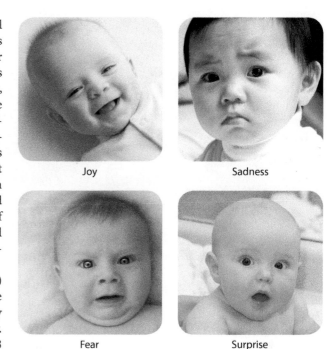

Joy   Sadness

Fear   Surprise

FIGURE **10.2**

EXPRESSION OF DIFFERENT EMOTIONS IN INFANTS

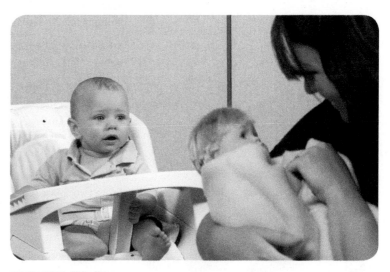

FIGURE **10.3**

IS THIS THE EARLY EXPRESSION OF JEALOUSY? In the study by Hart and Carrington (2002), the researchers concluded that the reactions of the 6-month-old infants who observed their mothers giving attention to a baby doll may indicate the early appearance of jealousy because of the negative emotions—such as anger and sadness—they displayed. However, experts on emotional development, such as Joseph Campos (2009) and Jerome Kagan (2010) argue that emotions such as jealousy don't appear during the first year. *Why do they conclude that jealousy does not occur in the first year?*

primary emotions Emotions that are present in humans and other animals, and emerge early in life; examples are joy, anger, sadness, fear, and disgust.

self-conscious emotions Emotions that require self-awareness, especially consciousness and a sense of "me"; examples include jealousy, empathy, and embarrassment.

What are some different types of cries?

He who binds himself to joy
Does the winged life destroy;
But he who kisses the joy as it flies;
Lives in eternity's sun rise.

—**William Blake**
English Poet, 19th Century

FIGURE **10.4**
A 6-MONTH-OLD'S STRONG SMILE. This strong smile reflects the Duchenne marker (eye constriction) and mouth opening.

basic cry A rhythmic pattern usually consisting of a cry, a briefer silence, a shorter inspiratory whistle that is higher pitched than the main cry, and then a brief rest before the next cry.

anger cry A cry similar to the basic cry but with more excess air forced through the vocal cords.

pain cry A sudden appearance of loud crying without preliminary moaning, and a long initial cry followed by an extended period of breath holding.

Crying and smiling are two emotional expressions that infants display when interacting with parents. These are babies' first forms of emotional communication.

Crying   Crying is the most important mechanism newborns have for communicating with their world. The first cry verifies that the baby's lungs have filled with air. Cries also may provide information about the health of the newborn's central nervous system. Newborns even tend to respond with cries and negative facial expressions when they hear other newborns cry (Dondi, Simion, & Caltran, 1999). However, a recent study revealed that newborns of depressed mothers showed less vocal distress when another infant cried, reflecting emotional and physiological dysregulation (Jones, 2012).

Babies have at least three types of cries:

- **Basic cry:** A rhythmic pattern that usually consists of a cry, followed by a briefer silence, then a shorter whistle that is somewhat higher in pitch than the main cry, then another brief rest before the next cry. Some infancy experts argue that hunger is one of the conditions that incite the basic cry.

- **Anger cry:** A variation of the basic cry in which more excess air is forced through the vocal cords.

- **Pain cry:** A sudden long, initial loud cry followed by breath holding; no preliminary moaning is present. The pain cry is stimulated by a high-intensity stimulus.

Most adults can determine whether an infant's cries signify anger or pain (Zeskind, Klein, & Marshall, 1992). Parents can distinguish the cries of their own baby better than those of another baby.

Smiling   Smiling is critical as a means of developing a new social skill and is a key social signal (Witherington & others, 2010). Two types of smiling can be distinguished in infants:

- **Reflexive smile:** A smile that does not occur in response to external stimuli and appears during the first month after birth, usually during sleep.

- **Social smile:** A smile that occurs in response to an external stimulus, typically a face in the case of the young infant. Social smiling occurs as early as 4 to 6 weeks of age in response to a caregiver's voice (Campos, 2005).

Daniel Messinger (2008) recently described the developmental course of infant smiling. From two to six months after birth, infants' social smiling increases considerably, both in self-initiated smiles and smiles in response to others' smiles. At 6 to 12 months of age, smiles that couple what is called the Duchenne marker (eye constriction) and mouth opening occur in the midst of highly enjoyable interactions and play with parents (see Figure 10.4). In the second year, smiling continues to occur in such positive circumstances with parents, and in many cases an increase in smiling occurs when interacting with peers. Also in the second year, toddlers become increasingly aware of the social meaning of smiles, especially in their relationship with parents.

Infants also engage in *anticipatory smiling,* in which they communicate preexisting positive emotion by smiling at an object and then turning their smile toward an adult. A recent study revealed that anticipatory smiling at 9 months of age was linked to parents' rating of the child's social competence at 2½ years of age (Parlade & others, 2009).

Fear   One of a baby's earliest emotions is fear, which typically first appears at about 6 months of age and peaks at about 18 months. However, abused and neglected infants can show fear as early as 3 months (Witherington & others, 2010). Researchers have found that infant fear is linked to guilt, empathy, and low aggression at 6 to 7 years of age (Rothbart, 2011).

The most frequent expression of an infant's fear involves **stranger anxiety,** in which an infant shows a fear and wariness of strangers. Stranger anxiety usually emerges gradually. It first appears at about 6 months of age in the form of wary reactions. By age 9 months, the fear of strangers is often more intense, and it continues to escalate through the infant's first birthday (Scher & Harel, 2008).

Not all infants show distress when they encounter a stranger. Besides individual variations, whether an infant shows stranger anxiety also depends on the social context and the characteristics of the stranger (Kagan, 2008).

Infants show less stranger anxiety when they are in familiar settings. For example, in one study, 10-month-olds showed little stranger anxiety when they met a stranger in their own home but much greater fear when they encountered a stranger in a research laboratory (Sroufe, Waters, & Matas, 1974). Also, infants show less stranger anxiety when they are sitting on their mothers' laps than when they are placed in an infant seat several feet away from their mothers (Bohlin & Hagekull, 1993). Thus, it appears that when infants feel secure, they are less likely to show stranger anxiety.

Who the stranger is and how the stranger behaves also influence stranger anxiety in infants. Infants are less fearful of child strangers than adult strangers. They also are less fearful of friendly, outgoing, smiling strangers than of passive, unsmiling strangers (Bretherton, Stolberg, & Kreye, 1981).

In addition to stranger anxiety, infants experience fear of being separated from their caregivers (Scher & Harel, 2008). The result is **separation protest**—crying when the caregiver leaves. Separation protest tends to peak at about 15 months among U.S. infants (Kagan, 2008). In fact, one study found that separation protest peaked at about 13 to 15 months in four different cultures (Kagan, Kearsley, & Zelazo, 1978). As indicated in Figure 10.5, the percentage of infants who engaged in separation protest varied across cultures, but the infants reached a peak of protest at about the same age—just before the middle of the second year of life.

Emotional Regulation and Coping   During the first year of life, the infant gradually develops an ability to inhibit, or minimize, the intensity and duration of emotional reactions (Calkins, 2012). From early in infancy, babies put their thumbs in their mouths to soothe themselves. But at first, infants mainly depend on caregivers to help them soothe their emotions, as when a caregiver rocks an infant to sleep, sings lullabies to the infant, gently strokes the infant, and so on.

The caregivers' actions influence the infant's neurobiological regulation of emotions (Thompson, 2013c, d). By soothing the infant, caregivers help infants to modulate their emotion and reduce the level of stress hormones (de Haan & Gunnar, 2009). Many developmentalists stress that it is a good strategy for a caregiver to soothe an infant before the infant gets into an intense, agitated, uncontrolled state (Thompson, 1994). A recent study found that emotionally reactive infants who also showed a high level of emotional regulation were more likely to have primary caregivers who engaged in positive parenting behavior during a parent-child interaction task (Ursache & others, 2013).

In the second year of life, when infants become aroused, they sometimes redirect their attention or distract themselves in order to reduce their arousal (Grolnick, Bridges, & Connell, 1996). By 2 years of age, toddlers can use language to define their feeling states and the context that is upsetting them (Kopp & Neufeld, 2002). A toddler might say, "Feel bad. Dog scare." This type of communication may help caregivers to assist the child in regulating emotion.

Contexts can influence emotional regulation (Easterbrooks & others, 2013). Infants are often affected by fatigue, hunger, time of day, which people are around them, and where they are. Infants must learn to adapt to different contexts that require emotional regulation. Further, new demands appear as the infant becomes older and parents modify their expectations. For example, a parent may take it in stride if a 6-month-old infant screams in a grocery store but may react very differently if a 2-year-old starts screaming.

To soothe or not to soothe—should a crying baby be given attention and soothed, or does this spoil the infant? Many years ago, the behaviorist John Watson (1928) argued that parents spend too much time responding to infant crying. As a consequence, he said, parents reward crying and increase its incidence. Some researchers have found that a caregiver's quick, soothing response to crying increased crying (Gewirtz, 1977). However, infancy experts Mary Ainsworth (1979) and John Bowlby (1989) stress that you can't respond too much to infant crying in the first year of life. They argue that a quick, comforting response to the infant's cries is an important ingredient in the development of a strong bond between the infant and caregiver.

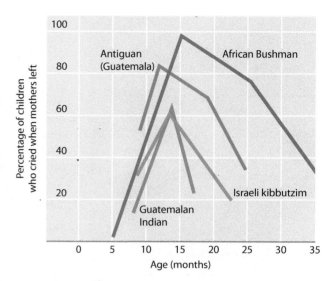

FIGURE **10.5**

SEPARATION PROTEST IN FOUR CULTURES. Note that separation protest peaked at about the same time in all four cultures in this study (13 to 15 months of age) (Kagan, Kearsley, & Zelazo, 1978). However, a higher percentage (100 percent) of infants in an African Bushman culture engaged in separation protest compared to only about 60 percent of infants in Guatemalan Indian and Israeli kibbutzim cultures. *What might explain the fact that separation protest peaks at about the same time in these cultures?*
Infancy: Its Place in Human Development by Jerome Kagan, Richard B. Kearsley, and Philip R. Zelazo, Cambridge, Mass.: Harvard University Press, Copyright © 1978 by the President and Fellows of Harvard College.

reflexive smile A smile that does not occur in response to external stimuli. It happens during the month after birth, usually during sleep.

social smile A smile in response to an external stimulus, which, early in development, typically is a face.

stranger anxiety An infant's fear of and wariness toward strangers; it tends to appear in the second half of the first year of life.

separation protest Occurs when infants experience a fear of being separated from a caregiver, which results in crying when the caregiver leaves.

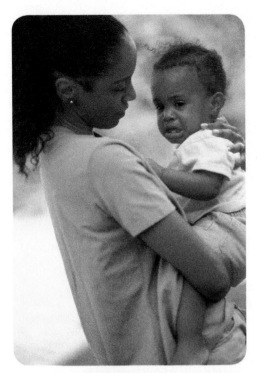

In one of Ainsworth's studies, infants whose mothers responded quickly when they cried at 3 months of age cried less later in the first year of life (Bell & Ainsworth, 1972).

Controversy still characterizes the question of whether or how parents should respond to an infant's cries. However, developmentalists increasingly argue that an infant cannot be spoiled in the first year of life, which suggests that parents should soothe a crying infant. This reaction should help infants develop a sense of trust and secure attachment to the caregiver. A recent study revealed that mothers' emotional reactions (anger and anxiety) to crying increased the risk of subsequent attachment insecurity (Leerkes, Parade, & Gudmundson, 2011). And another recent study found that problems in infant soothability at 6 months of age were linked to insecure attachment at 12 months of age (Mills-Koonce, Propper, & Barnett, 2012).

EARLY CHILDHOOD

The young child's growing awareness of self is linked to the ability to feel an expanding range of emotions. Young children, like adults, experience many emotions during the course of a day. At times, they also try to make sense of other people's emotional reactions and to control their own emotions. Parents and peers play important roles in children's emotional development.

Should a crying baby be given attention and soothed, or does this spoil the infant? Should the infant's age, the type of cry, and the circumstances be considered?

Expressing Emotions   Recall from our discussion of emotional development in infancy that there is controversy about how early in their development infants experience what Michael Lewis (2008, 2010) called *self-conscious emotions*. To experience self-conscious emotions such as pride, shame, embarrassment, and guilt, children must be able to refer to themselves and be aware of themselves as distinct from others (Lewis, 2008, 2010). Self-conscious emotions do not appear to develop until self-awareness appears at around 18 months of age.

During the early childhood years, emotions such as pride and guilt become more common. They are especially influenced by parents' responses to children's behavior. For example, a young child may experience shame when a parent says, "You should feel bad about biting your sister."

Understanding Emotions   Among the most important changes in emotional development in early childhood is an increased understanding of emotion (Bassett & others, 2012; Denham & others, 2012). During early childhood, young children increasingly understand that certain situations are likely to evoke particular emotions, that facial expressions indicate specific emotions, that emotions affect behavior, and that emotions can be used to influence others' emotions (Cole & others, 2009). A recent meta-analysis revealed that emotion knowledge (such as understanding emotional cues—for example, when a young child understands that a peer feels sad about being left out of a game) was positively related to 3- to 5-year-olds' social competence (such as offering an empathic response to the child left out of a game) and negatively related to their internalizing (high level of anxiety, for example) and externalizing problems (high level of aggressive behavior, for example) (Trentacosta & Fine, 2009). A recent study also found that young children's understanding of emotions was linked to their prosocial behavior (Ensor, Spencer, & Hughes, 2010).

Between 2 and 4 years of age, children considerably increase the number of terms they use to describe emotions. During this time, they are also learning about the causes and consequences of feelings (Denham & others, 2012).

When they are 4 to 5 years of age, children show an increased ability to reflect on emotions. They also begin to understand that the same event can elicit different feelings in different people. Moreover, they show a growing awareness that they need to manage their emotions to meet social standards. And, by 5 years of age, most children can accurately identify emotions that are produced by challenging circumstances and describe strategies they might call on to cope with everyday stress (Cole & others, 2009).

A child expressing the emotion of shame, which occurs when a child evaluates his or her actions as not living up to standards. *Why is shame called a self-conscious emotion?*

Regulating Emotions   Emotional regulation especially plays a key role in children's ability to manage the demands and conflicts they face in interacting with others (Eisenberg, 2010; Lewis, Todd, & Xu, 2011; Thompson, 2011a, b). Many researchers consider the growth of emotional regulation in children to be fundamental to the development of social competence (Perry & others, 2013; Thompson, 2013a, b). Emotional regulation can be conceptualized as an important component of self-regulation or of executive function. Recall from Chapter 5 that executive function is increasingly thought to be a key concept in describing the young child's higher-level cognitive functioning (Carlson & White, 2013). Let's explore the roles that parents and peers play in children's emotional regulation.

Parenting and Children's Emotional Development Parents can play an important role in helping young children regulate their emotions (Havighurst & others, 2013; Thompson, 2013c, d). Depending on how they talk with their children about emotion, parents can be described as taking an *emotion-coaching* or an *emotion-dismissing* approach (Gottman, 2013). The distinction between these approaches is most evident in the way the parent deals with the child's negative emotions (anger, frustration, sadness, and so on). *Emotion-coaching parents* monitor their children's emotions, view their children's negative emotions as opportunities for teaching, assist them in labeling emotions, and coach them in how to deal effectively with emotions. In contrast, *emotion-dismissing parents* view their role as to deny, ignore, or change negative emotions. Emotion-coaching parents interact with their children in a less rejecting manner, use more scaffolding and praise, and are more nurturant than are emotion-dismissing parents (Gottman & DeClaire, 1997). More- over, the children of emotion-coaching parents are better at soothing themselves when they get upset, more effective in regulating their negative affect, focus their attention better, and have fewer behavior problems than the children of emotion-dismissing parents. One study revealed that having emotion-dismissing parents was linked with children's poor emotional regu- lation (Lunkenheimer, Shields, & Cortina, 2007). And another recent study found that fathers' emotion coaching was related to children's social competence (Baker, Fenning, & Crnic, 2011).

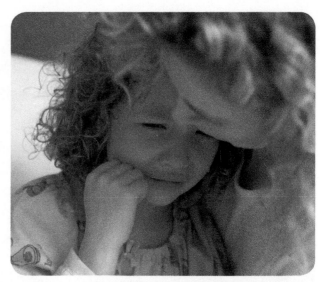

An emotion-coaching parent. *What are some differences between emotion-coaching and emotion-dismissing parents?*

Parents' knowledge of their children's emotional world can help them to guide their chil- dren's emotional development and show them how to cope effectively with problems. A recent study found that mothers' knowledge about what distresses and comforts their children pre- dicts the children's coping, empathy, and prosocial behavior (Vinik, Almas, & Grusec, 2011).

A problem that parents face is that young children typically don't want to talk about dif- ficult emotional topics, such as being distressed or engaging in negative behaviors. Among the strategies young children use to avoid these conversations is to not talk at all, change the topic, push away, or run away. In a recent study, Ross Thompson and his colleagues (2009) found that young children were more likely to openly discuss difficult emotional circumstances when they were securely attached to their mother and when their mother conversed with them in a way that validated and accepted the child's views. And Cybelle Raver and her colleagues (McCoy & Raver, 2011; Raver & others, 2011, 2012; Zhai, Raver, & Jones, 2012) are using interventions, such as increasing caregiver emotional expressiveness, to improve young chil- dren's emotional regulation and reduce behavior problems in Head Start families.

Regulation of Emotion and Peer Relations Emotions play a strong role in determining the success of a child's peer relationships (Howes, 2009). Specifically, the ability to modulate one's emotions is an important skill that benefits children in their relationships with peers. Moody and emotionally negative children are more likely to experience rejection by their peers, whereas emotionally positive children are more popular (Stocker & Dunn, 1990). Emotional regulation typically increases as children mature. A recent study revealed that 4-year-olds recognized and generated strategies for controlling their anger more than did 3-year-olds (Cole & others, 2009).

MIDDLE AND LATE CHILDHOOD

During middle and late childhood, many children show marked improvement in understanding and managing their emotions (Cunningham, Kliewer, & Garner, 2009). However, in some instances, as when they experience stressful circumstances, their coping abilities can be challenged.

Developmental Changes in Emotion Here are some important developmental changes in emotions during middle and late childhood (Denham, Bassett, & Wyatt, 2007; Denham & others, 2012; Kuebli, 1994; Thompson, 2013c, d):

- *Improved emotional understanding.* Children in elementary school develop an increased ability to understand complex emotions such as pride and shame. These emotions become

developmental **connection**

Peers

The combination of being rejected by peers and being aggressive often forecasts problems. Chapter 15, p. 430

What are some developmental changes in emotion in middle and late childhood?

less tied to the reactions of other people; they become more self-generated and integrated with a sense of personal responsibility.

- *Increased understanding that more than one emotion can be experienced in a particular situation.* A third-grader, for example, may realize that achieving something might involve both anxiety and joy.

- *Increased tendency to be aware of the events leading to emotional reactions.* A fourth-grader may become aware that her sadness today is influenced by her friend moving to another town last week.

- *Ability to suppress or conceal negative emotional reactions.* A fifth-grader has learned to tone down his anger better than he used to when one of his classmates irritates him.

- *The use of self-initiated strategies for redirecting feelings.* During the elementary school years, children become more reflective about their emotional lives and increasingly use strategies to control their emotions. They become more effective at cognitively managing their emotions, such as by soothing themselves after an upset.

- *A capacity for genuine empathy.* For example, a fourth-grader feels sympathy for a distressed person and experiences vicariously the sadness the distressed person is feeling.

Coping with Stress   An important aspect of children's maturation is learning how to cope with stress (Mash & Wolfe, 2013; Morris & others, 2013). As children get older, they are able to more accurately appraise a stressful situation and determine how much control they have over it. Older children generate more coping alternatives to stressful conditions and use more cognitive coping strategies (Saarni & others, 2006). For example, older children are better than younger children at intentionally shifting their thoughts to something that is less stressful. Older children are also better at reframing, or changing their perception of a stressful situation. For example, younger children may be very disappointed that their teacher did not say hello to them when they arrived at school. Older children may reframe this type of situation and think, "She may have been busy with other things and just forgot to say hello."

By 10 years of age, most children are able to use these cognitive strategies to cope with stress (Saarni & others, 2006). However, in families that have not been supportive and are characterized by turmoil or trauma, children may be so overwhelmed by stress that they do not use such strategies (Thabet & others, 2009).

Disasters can especially harm children's development and produce adjustment problems (McDermott & Cobham, 2012). Among the outcomes for children who experience disasters are acute stress reactions, depression, panic disorder, and post-traumatic stress disorder (Salloum & Overstreet, 2012). The likelihood that a child will face these problems following a disaster depends on factors such as the nature and severity of the disaster and the type of support available to the child.

Following are descriptions of recent studies exploring how various aspects of traumatic events and disasters affect children:

- In a study of mothers and their children aged 5 years and younger who were directly exposed to the 9/11 attacks in New York City, the mothers who developed post-traumatic stress disorder (PTSD) and depression were less likely to help their children regulate their emotions and behavior than mothers who were only depressed or only had PTSD (Chemtob & others, 2010). This outcome was linked to their children having anxiety, depression, aggression, and sleep problems.

- A study of the effects of the 2004 tsunami in Sri Lanka found that severe exposure to the tsunami combined with more exposure to other adversities, such as an ongoing war and family violence, was linked to poorer adjustment after the tsunami disaster (Catani & others, 2010).

- A research review revealed that children with disabilities are more likely than children without disabilities to live in poverty conditions, which increases their exposure to hazards and disasters (Peek & Stough, 2010). When a disaster occurs, children with disabilities have more difficulty escaping from the disaster.

In research on disasters/trauma, the term *dose-response effects* is often used. A widely supported finding in this research area is that the more severe the disaster/trauma (dose), the worse the adaptation and adjustment (response) following the disaster/trauma (Masten, 2013).

Recommendations for parents, teachers, and other adults caring for children who are involved in disasters and terrorist attacks include the following (Gurwitch & others, 2001, pp. 4–11):

- Reassure children (numerous times, if necessary) of their safety and security.
- Allow children to retell events, and be patient in listening to them.
- Encourage children to talk about any disturbing or confusing feelings, reassuring them that such feelings are normal after a stressful event.
- Protect children from reexposure to frightening situations and reminders of the trauma—for example, by limiting discussion of the event in front of the children.
- Help children make sense of what happened, keeping in mind that children may misunderstand what took place. For example, young children "may blame themselves, believe things happened that did not happen, believe that terrorists are in the school, etc. Gently help children develop a realistic understanding of the event" (p. 10).

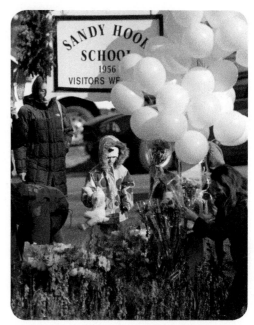

What are some effective strategies to help surviving children cope with traumatic events such as the attack by a gunman at Sandy Hook Elementary School in Connecticut in December 2012, when 26 people—20 of them children—were killed?

Review *Connect* Reflect

 Describe the development of emotion.

Review

- How does emotion develop in infancy?
- What characterizes emotional development in early childhood?
- What changes take place in emotion during middle and late childhood?

Connect

- In this section, you learned about how children develop the ability to recognize and react appropriately to the emotions of others. How is this ability related to children's theory of mind (discussed in Chapter 7)?

Reflect *Your Own Personal Journey of Life*

- Imagine that you are the parent of an 8-month-old baby and you are having difficulty getting enough sleep because the baby wakes up in the middle of the night crying. How would you deal with this situation?

Temperament Characterize variations in temperament and their significance.

Describing and Classifying Temperament	Biological Foundations and Experience	Goodness of Fit and Parenting

Do you get upset often? Does it take much to get you angry, or to make you laugh? Even at birth, babies seem to have different emotional styles. One infant is cheerful and happy much of the time; another baby seems to cry constantly. These tendencies reflect **temperament,** which involves individual differences in behavioral styles, emotions, and characteristic ways of responding. With regard to its link to emotion, temperament refers to individual differences in how quickly the emotion is shown, how strong it is, how long it lasts, and how quickly it fades away (Campos, 2009).

temperament Involves individual differences in behavioral styles, emotions, and characteristic ways of responding.

DESCRIBING AND CLASSIFYING TEMPERAMENT

How would you describe your temperament or the temperament of a friend? Researchers have described and classified the temperament of individuals in different ways. Here we will examine three of those ways.

Chess and Thomas' Classification   Psychiatrists Alexander Chess and Stella Thomas (Chess & Thomas, 1977; Thomas & Chess, 1991) identified three basic types, or clusters, of temperament:

- An **easy child** is generally in a positive mood, quickly establishes regular routines in infancy, and adapts easily to new experiences.
- A **difficult child** reacts negatively and cries frequently, engages in irregular daily routines, and is slow to accept change.
- A **slow-to-warm-up child** has a low activity level, is somewhat negative, and displays a low intensity of mood.

In their longitudinal investigation, Chess and Thomas found that 40 percent of the children they studied could be classified as easy, 10 percent as difficult, and 15 percent as slow to warm up. Notice that 35 percent did not fit any of the three patterns. Researchers have found that these three basic clusters of temperament are moderately stable across the childhood years. One study revealed that young children with a difficult temperament showed more problems when they experienced low-quality child care and fewer problems when they experienced high-quality child care than did young children with an easy temperament (Pluess & Belsky, 2009).

Kagan's Behavioral Inhibition   Another way of classifying temperament focuses on the differences between a shy, subdued, timid child and a sociable, extraverted, bold child (Clauss & Blackford, 2012). Jerome Kagan (2002, 2008, 2010, 2013) regards shyness with strangers (peers or adults) as one feature of a broad temperament category called *inhibition to the unfamiliar*. Inhibited children react to many aspects of unfamiliarity with initial avoidance, distress, or subdued affect, beginning at about 7 to 9 months of age.

"Oh, he's cute, all right, but he's got the temperament of a car alarm."
© Barbara Smaller/The New Yorker Collection/www. cartoonbank.com

What are some ways that developmentalists have classified infants' temperaments? Which classification makes the most sense to you based on your observations of infants?

Kagan has found that inhibition shows considerable stability from infancy through early childhood. One study classified toddlers into extremely inhibited, extremely uninhibited, and intermediate groups (Pfeifer & others, 2002). Follow-up assessments occurred at 4 and 7 years of age. Continuity was demonstrated for both inhibition and lack of inhibition, although a substantial number of the inhibited children moved into the intermediate groups at 7 years of age.

Rothbart and Bates' Classification   New classifications of temperament continue to be forged. Mary Rothbart and John Bates (2006) argue that three broad dimensions best represent what researchers have found to characterize the structure of temperament: extraversion/surgency, negative affectivity, and effortful control (self-regulation):

- *Extraversion/surgency* includes "positive anticipation, impulsivity, activity level, and sensation seeking" (Rothbart, 2004, p. 495). Kagan's uninhibited children fit into this category.
- *Negative affectivity* includes "fear, frustration, sadness, and discomfort" (Rothbart, 2004, p. 495). These children are easily distressed; they may fret and cry often. Kagan's inhibited children fit this category. Negative emotional reactivity or irritability reflect the core of Chess and Thomas' category of the difficult child (Bates & Pettit, 2007).

Why are some children inhibited?

- *Effortful control (self-regulation)* includes "attentional focusing and shifting, inhibitory control, perceptual sensitivity, and low-intensity pleasure" (Rothbart, 2004, p. 495). Infants who are high on effortful control show an ability to keep their arousal from getting too high and have strategies for soothing themselves. By contrast, children low on effortful control are often unable to control their arousal; they become easily agitated and intensely emotional (Rothbart & Sheese, 2007). A recent study of school-age children in the United States and China revealed that in both cultures low effortful control was linked to externalizing problems, such as lying, cheating, being disobedient, and being overly aggressive (Zhou, Lengua, & Wang, 2009).

In Rothbart's (2004, p. 497) view, "early theoretical models of temperament stressed the way we are moved by our positive and negative emotions or level of arousal, with our actions driven by these tendencies." The more recent emphasis on effortful control, however, emphasizes that individuals can engage in a more cognitive, flexible approach to stressful circumstances.

easy child A temperament style in which the child is generally in a positive mood, quickly establishes regular routines, and adapts easily to new experiences.

difficult child A temperament style in which the child tends to react negatively and cry frequently, engages in irregular daily routines, and is slow to accept new experiences.

slow-to-warm-up child A temperament style in which the child has a low activity level, is somewhat negative, and displays a low intensity of mood.

An important point about temperament classifications such as those devised by Chess and Thomas and by Rothbart and Bates is that children should not be pigeonholed as having only one temperament dimension, such as "difficult" or "negative affectivity." A good strategy when attempting to classify a child's temperament is to think of temperament as consisting of multiple dimensions (Bates, 2008, 2012a, b). For example, a child might be extraverted, show little emotional negativity, and have good self-regulation. Another child might be introverted, show little emotional negativity, and have a low level of self-regulation.

Rothbart and Maria Gartstein (2008, p. 323) recently described the following developmental changes in temperament during infancy. During early infancy, smiling and laughter are emerging as part of the positive affectivity dimension of temperament. Also, by 2 months of age, infants show anger and frustration when their actions don't produce an interesting outcome. During this time, infants often are susceptible to distress and overstimulation. From 4 to 12 months of age fear and irritability become more differentiated, with inhibition (fear) increasingly linked to new and unpredictable experiences. Not all temperament characteristics are in place by the first birthday. Positive emotionality becomes more stable later in infancy, and the characteristics of extraversion/surgency can be determined in the toddler period. Improved attention skills in the toddler and preschool years are related to an increase in effortful control, which serves as a foundation for improved self-regulation.

The developmental changes just described reflect normative capabilities of children, not individual differences in children. The development of these capabilities, such as effortful control, allows individual differences to emerge (Bates, 2008, 2012a, b). For example, although maturation of the brain's prefrontal lobes must occur for any child's attention to improve and the child to achieve effortful control, some children develop effortful control and others do not. And it is these individual differences in children that are at the heart of what temperament is (Bates, 2008, 2012a, b).

BIOLOGICAL FOUNDATIONS AND EXPERIENCE

How does a child acquire a certain temperament? Kagan (2002, 2010) argues that children inherit a physiology that biases them to have a particular type of temperament. However, through experience they may learn to modify their temperament to some degree. For example, children may inherit a physiology that biases them to be fearful and inhibited, but they can learn to reduce their fear and inhibition to some degree.

Biological Influences   Physiological characteristics have been linked with different temperaments (Diaz & Bell, 2012; Mize & Jones, 2012). In particular, an inhibited temperament is associated with a unique physiological pattern that includes high and stable heart rate, high level of the hormone cortisol, and high activity in the right frontal lobe of the brain (Kagan, 2003, 2010, 2013). This pattern may be tied to the excitability of the amygdala, a structure of the brain that plays an important role in fear and inhibition (Kagan, 2003, 2010, 2013). An inhibited temperament or negative affectivity may also be linked to low levels of the neurotransmitter serotonin, which may increase an individual's vulnerability to fear and frustration (Pauli-Pott & others, 2009).

What is heredity's role in the biological foundations of temperament? Twin and adoption studies suggest that heredity has a moderate influence on differences in temperament within a group of people (Plomin & others, 2009). The contemporary view is that temperament is a biologically based but evolving aspect of behavior; it evolves as the child's experiences are incorporated into a network of self-perceptions and behavioral preferences that characterize the child's personality (Easterbrooks & others, 2013).

Too often, though, the biological foundations of temperament are interpreted as meaning that temperament cannot develop or change. However, important self-regulatory dimensions of temperament such as adaptability, soothability, and persistence look very different in a 1-year-old and a 5-year-old (Easterbrooks & others, 2013). These temperament dimensions develop and change with the growth of the neurobiological foundations of self-regulation.

Gender, Culture, and Temperament   Gender may be an important factor shaping the context that influences the fate of temperament (Gaias & others, 2012). Parents might react differently to an infant's temperament depending on whether the baby is a boy or a

developmental **connection**

Research Methods

Twin and adoption studies have been used to sort out hereditary and environmental influences on development. Chapter 2, pp. 66–67 girl. For example, in one study, mothers were more responsive to the crying of irritable girls than to the crying of irritable boys (Crockenberg, 1986).

Similarly, the reaction to an infant's temperament may depend in part on culture (Chen & others, 2011; Fung, 2011). For example, an active temperament might be valued in some cultures (such as the United States) but not in other cultures (such as China). And behavioral inhibition is more highly valued in China than in North America (Chen & others, 1998). Also, a recent study revealed that U.S. infants showed more temperamental fearfulness while Finnish infants engaged in more positive affect, such as effortful control (Gaias & others, 2012).

An infant's temperament can vary across cultures. *What do parents need to know about a child's temperament?*

Developmental Connections Do young adults show the same behavioral style and characteristic emotional responses as they did when they were infants or young children? Activity level is an important dimension of temperament. Are children's activity levels linked to their personality in early adulthood? In one longitudinal study, children who were highly active at age 4 were likely to be very outgoing at age 23, which reflects continuity (Franz, 1996). From adolescence into early adulthood, most individuals show fewer emotional mood swings, become more responsible, and engage in less risk-taking behavior, which reflects discontinuity (Caspi, 1998).

Is temperament in childhood linked with adjustment in adulthood? Here is what we know based on the few longitudinal studies that have been conducted on this topic (Caspi, 1998). In one longitudinal study, children who had an easy temperament at 3 to 5 years of age were likely to be well adjusted as young adults (Chess & Thomas, 1977). In contrast, many children who had a difficult temperament at 3 to 5 years of age were not well adjusted as young adults. Also, other researchers have found that boys with a difficult temperament in childhood are less likely as adults to continue their formal education, whereas girls with a difficult temperament in childhood are more likely to experience marital conflict as adults (Wachs, 2000).

Inhibition is another temperament characteristic that has been studied extensively (Kagan, 2008, 2010, 2013). A recent study revealed that behavioral inhibition at 3 years of age was linked to shyness four years later (Volbrecht & Goldsmith, 2010). Another study found that 24-month-olds who were fearful in situations relatively low in threat displayed higher anxiety levels in kindergarten (Buss, 2011). And recent research indicated that shy children with poor cortisol regulation or mothers who were more likely to endorse non-supportive emotion reactions engaged in more maladaptive play behavior (Davis & Buss, 2012). Also, research indicates that individuals with an inhibited temperament in childhood are less likely as adults to be assertive or to experience social support, and more likely to delay entering a stable job track (Asendorph, 2008). In the Uppsala (Sweden) Longitudinal Study, shyness/inhibition in infancy/childhood was linked to social anxiety at 21 years of age (Bohlin & Hagekull, 2009).

Yet another aspect of temperament involves emotionality and the ability to control one's emotions. In one longitudinal study, when 3-year-old children showed good control of their emotions and were resilient in the face of stress, they were likely to continue to handle emotions effectively as adults (Block, 1993). By contrast, when 3-year-olds had low emotional control and were not very resilient, they were likely to show problems in these areas as young adults.

In sum, these studies reveal some continuity between certain aspects of temperament in childhood and adjustment in early adulthood. However, keep in mind that these connections between childhood temperament and adult adjustment are based on only a small number of studies; more research is needed to verify these linkages (Shiner & DeYoung, 2013; Wachs & Bates, 2010).

Developmental Contexts What accounts for the continuities and discontinuities between a child's temperament and an adult's personality? Physiological and hereditary factors likely are involved in continuity (Kagan, 2008, 2010, 2013). Theodore Wachs

developmental **connection**

Culture and Ethnicity

Cross-cultural studies seek to determine culture-universal and culture-specific aspects of development. Chapter 1, p. 8

Initial Temperament Trait: Inhibition		
	Child A	**Child B**
Intervening Context		
Caregivers	Caregivers (parents) who are sensitive and accepting, and who let the child set his or her own pace.	Caregivers who use inappropriate "low-level control" and attempt to force the child into new situations.
Physical Environment	Presence of "stimulus shelters" or "defensible spaces" that the children can retreat to when there is too much stimulation.	Child continually encounters noisy, chaotic environments that allow no escape from stimulation.
Peers	Peer groups with other inhibited children with common interests, so the child feels accepted.	Peer groups consist of athletic extroverts, so the child feels rejected.
Schools	School is "undermanned," so inhibited children are more likely to be tolerated and feel they can make a contribution.	School is "overmanned," so inhibited children are less likely to be tolerated and more likely to feel undervalued.
Personality Outcomes		
	As an adult, individual is closer to extraversion (outgoing, sociable) and is emotionally stable.	As an adult, individual is closer to introversion and has more emotional problems.

FIGURE **10.6**

TEMPERAMENT IN CHILDHOOD, PERSONALITY IN ADULTHOOD, AND INTERVENING CONTEXTS. Varying experiences with caregivers, the physical environment, peers, and schools may modify links between temperament in childhood and personality in adulthood. The example given here is for inhibition.

(1994, 2000) proposed ways that linkages between temperament in childhood and personality in adulthood might vary depending on the contexts in individuals' experience. Figure 10.6 summarizes how one characteristic might develop in different ways, depending on the context.

In short, many aspects of a child's environment can encourage or discourage the persistence of temperament characteristics (Bates, 2012a, b; Rothbart, 2011). One useful way of thinking about these relationships applies the concept of goodness of fit, which we examine next.

GOODNESS OF FIT AND PARENTING

Goodness of fit refers to the match between a child's temperament and the environmental demands the child must cope with. Suppose Jason is an active toddler who is made to sit still for long periods of time and Jack is a slow-to-warm-up toddler who is abruptly pushed into new situations on a regular basis. Both Jason and Jack face a lack of fit between their temperament and environmental demands. Lack of fit can produce adjustment problems (Rothbart, 2011).

Some temperament characteristics pose more parenting challenges than others, at least in modern Western societies (Rothbart, 2011). When children are prone to distress, as exhibited by frequent crying and irritability, their parents may eventually respond by ignoring the child's distress or trying to force the child to "behave." In one research study, though, extra support and training for mothers of distress-prone infants improved the quality of mother-infant interaction (van den Boom, 1989). The training led the mothers to alter their demands on the child, improving the fit between the child and the environment. Researchers also have found that decreases in infants' negative emotionality are linked to higher levels of parental sensitivity, involvement, and responsivity (Bates, 2012a, b; Penela & others, 2012).

What are some good strategies for parents to adopt when responding to their infant's temperament?

goodness of fit The match between a child's temperament and the environmental demands the child must cope with.

Many parents don't become believers in temperament's importance until the birth of their second child. They viewed their first child's behavior as a result of how they treated the child. But then they find that some strategies that worked with their first child are not as effective with the second child. Some problems experienced with the first child (such as those involved

Parenting and the Child's Temperament

What are the implications of temperamental variations for parenting? Although answers to this question necessarily are speculative, these conclusions regarding the best parenting strategies to use in relation to children's temperaments were reached by temperament experts Ann Sanson and Mary Rothbart (1995):

- *Attention to and respect for individuality.* One implication is that it is difficult to generate general prescriptions for "good parenting." A goal might be accomplished in one way with one child and in another way with another child, depending on the child's temperament. Parents need to be sensitive to the infant's signals and flexible in adjusting to his or her needs.
- *Structuring the child's environment.* Crowded, noisy environments can pose greater problems for some children (such as a "difficult child") than for others (such as an "easy child"). We might also expect that a fearful, withdrawing child would benefit from slower entry into new contexts.
- *The "difficult child" and packaged parenting programs.* Programs for parents often focus on dealing with children who have "difficult" temperaments, such as children who are irritable, display anger often, and don't follow directions well. Acknowledging that some children

are harder than others to parent is often helpful, and advice on how to handle particular difficult characteristics can be useful. However, whether a particular characteristic is difficult depends on its fit with the environment. To label a child "difficult" has the danger of becoming a self-fulfilling prophecy. If a child is identified as difficult, people may treat the child in a way that actually elicits difficult behavior. One recent study found that having access to experiences that encourage coping and build self-regulatory skills was beneficial to children with a difficult temperament (Bradley & Corwyn, 2008).

Too often, we pigeonhole children into categories without examining the context (Bates. 2012a, b; Rothbart, 2011). Nonetheless, caregivers need to take children's temperaments into account. Research does not yet allow for many highly specific recommendations, but in general, caregivers should (1) be sensitive to the individual characteristics of the child, (2) be flexible in responding to these characteristics, and (3) avoid applying negative labels to the child.

How does the advice to "structure the child's environment" reflect what you learned about the concept of "goodness of fit"?

in feeding, sleeping, and coping with strangers) do not exist with the second child, but new problems arise. Such experiences strongly suggest that children differ from each other very early in life, and that these differences have important implications for parent-child interaction (Kwak & others, 1999; Rothbart, 2011).

To read further about some positive strategies for parenting that take into account the child's temperament, see *Caring Connections.*

Review *Connect* Reflect

 LG3 Characterize variations in temperament and their significance.

Review

- How can temperament be described and classified?
- How is temperament influenced by biological foundations and experience?
- What is goodness of fit? What are some positive parenting strategies for dealing with a child's temperament?

Connect

- In this section, you learned that twin and adoption studies suggest that heredity has a moderate influence on differences in

temperament. In Chapter 2, what did you learn were the issues that complicate the interpretation of twin studies?

Reflect *Your Own Personal Journey of Life*

- Consider your own temperament. We described a number of temperament categories. Which one best describes your temperament? Has your temperament changed as you have gotten older? If your temperament has changed, what factors contributed to the changes?

Social Orientation/Understanding, Attachment, and Child Care

LG4 Explain the early development of social orientation/ understanding, attachment, and variations in child care.

Social Orientation/
Understanding

Attachment

Fathers and Mothers
as Caregivers

Child Care

So far, we have discussed how emotions and emotional competence change as children develop. We have also examined the role of emotional style; in effect, we have seen how emotions set the tone of our experiences in life. But emotions also write the lyrics because they are at the core of our interest in the social world and our relationships with others.

SOCIAL ORIENTATION/UNDERSTANDING

As socioemotional beings, infants show a strong interest in their social world and are motivated to orient to it and understand it (Thompson, 2006, 2013a). In earlier chapters, we described many of the biological and cognitive foundations that contribute to the infant's development of social orientation and understanding. We will call attention to relevant biological and cognitive factors as we explore social orientation; locomotion; intention, goal-directed behavior, and cooperation; and social referencing.

Social Orientation From early in their development, infants are captivated by their social world. As we discussed in our coverage of infant perception in Chapter 5, young infants stare intently at faces and are attuned to the sounds of human voices, especially their caregiver's (Lowe & others, 2012). Later, they become adept at interpreting the meaning of facial expressions.

Face-to-face play often begins to characterize caregiver-infant interactions when the infant is about 2 to 3 months of age. The focused social interaction of face-to-face play may include vocalizations, touch, and gestures (Leppanen & others, 2007). Such play is part of many mothers' motivation to create a positive emotional state in their infants (Thompson, 2013a, d).

In part because of such positive social interchanges between caregivers and infants, by 2 to 3 months of age infants respond to people differently from the way they respond to objects, showing more positive emotion toward people than inanimate objects such as puppets (Legerstee, 1997). At this age, most infants expect people to react positively when the infants initiate a behavior, such as a smile or a vocalization. This finding has been discovered using a method called the still-face paradigm, in which the caregiver alternates between engaging in face-to-face interaction with the infant and remaining still and unresponsive (Bigelow & Power, 2012; Lee & others, 2013). As early as 2 to 3 months of age, infants show more withdrawal, negative emotions, and self-directed behavior when their caregivers are still and unresponsive (Adamson & Frick, 2003). The frequency of face-to-face play decreases after 7 months of age as infants become more mobile (Thompson, 2006). A meta-analysis revealed that infants' higher positive affect and lower negative affect as displayed during the still-face paradigm were linked to secure attachment at 1 year of age (Mesman, van IJzendoorn, & Bakersman-Kranenburg, 2009).

Infants also learn about their social world through contexts other than face-to-face play with a caregiver (Easterbrooks & others, 2013). Even though infants as young as 6 months of age show an interest in each other, their interaction with peers increases considerably in the last half of the second year. Between 18 and 24 months of age, children markedly increase their imitative and reciprocal play, such as imitating nonverbal actions like jumping and running (Eckerman & Whitehead, 1999). One study involved presenting 1- and 2-year-olds with a simple cooperative task that consisted of pulling handles to activate an attractive musical toy (Brownell, Ramani, & Zerwas, 2006) (see Figure 10.7). Any coordinated actions of the 1-year-olds appeared to be mostly coincidental rather than cooperative, whereas the 2-year-olds' behavior was characterized more as active cooperation to reach a goal. As

developmental connection

Biological, Cognitive, and Socioemotional Processes

Discussing biological, cognitive, and social processes together reminds us of an important aspect of development: These processes are intricately intertwined (Diamond, 2013). Chapter 1, p. 13

A mother and her baby engaging in face-to-face play. *At what age does face-to-face play usually begin, and when does it typically start decreasing in frequency?*

increasing numbers of U.S. infants experience child care outside the home, they are spending more time in social play with peers (Lamb & Lewis, 2013). Later in the chapter, we will further discuss child care.

Locomotion   Recall from earlier in the chapter how important independence is for infants, especially in the second year of life. As infants develop the ability to crawl, walk, and run, they are able to explore and expand their social world. These newly developed self-produced locomotor skills allow the infant to independently initiate social interchanges on a more frequent basis (Laible & Thompson, 2007). Remember from Chapter 5 that acquisition of these gross motor skills is the result of a number of factors including the development of the nervous system, the goal the infant is motivated to reach, and environmental support for the skill (Adolph & Berger, 2013; Adolph & Robinson, 2013).

The infant's and toddler's push for independence also is likely paced by the development of locomotor skills. Locomotion is important for its motivational implications (Adolph & Berger, 2013). Once infants have the ability to move in goal-directed pursuits, the reward from these pursuits leads to further efforts to explore and develop skills.

FIGURE **10.7**

THE COOPERATION TASK. The cooperation task consisted of two handles on a box, atop which was an animated musical toy, surreptitiously activated by remote control when both handles were pulled. The handles were placed far enough apart that one child could not pull both handles. The experimenter demonstrated the task, saying, "Watch! If you pull the handles, the doggie will sing" (Brownell, Ramani, & Zerwas, 2006).

Intention, Goal-Directed Behavior, and Cooperation

Perceiving people as engaging in intentional and goal-directed behavior is an important social cognitive accomplishment, and this initially occurs toward the end of the first year (Thompson, 2013a, d). Joint attention and gaze following help the infant to understand that other people have intentions (Mateus & others, 2013). Recall from Chapter 7 that *joint attention* occurs when the caregiver and infant focus on the same object or event. We indicated that emerging aspects of joint attention occur at about 7 to 8 months, but at about 10 to 11 months of age joint attention intensifies and infants begin to follow the caregiver's gaze. By their first birthday, infants have begun to direct the caregiver's attention to objects that capture their interest (Heimann & others, 2006).

developmental **connection**

Dynamic Systems Theory

Dynamic systems theory is increasingly recognized as an important means of understanding children's development. Chapter 5, p. 140

Social Referencing   Another important social cognitive accomplishment in infancy is developing the ability to "read" the emotions of other people (Cornew & others, 2012). **Social referencing** is the term used to describe "reading" emotional cues in others to help determine how to act in a particular situation. The development of social referencing helps infants to interpret ambiguous situations more accurately, as when they encounter a stranger and need to know whether to fear the person (Pelaez, Virues-Ortega, & Gewirtz, 2012). By the end of the first year, a mother's facial expression—either smiling or fearful—influences whether an infant will explore an unfamiliar environment.

Infants become better at social referencing in the second year of life. At this age, they tend to "check" with their mother before they act; they look at her to see if she is happy, angry, or fearful. For example, in one study, 14- to 22-month-old infants were more likely to look at their mother's face as a source of information for how to act in a situation than were 6- to 9-month-old infants (Walden, 1991).

Infants' Social Sophistication and Insight   In sum, researchers are discovering that infants are more socially sophisticated and insightful at younger ages than was previously envisioned (Thompson, 2013a, d). This sophistication and insight is reflected in infants' perceptions of others' actions as intentionally motivated and goal-directed and their motivation to share and participate in that intentionality by their first birthday. The more advanced social cognitive skills of infants could be expected to influence their understanding and awareness of attachment to a caregiver.

social referencing "Reading" emotional cues in others to help determine how to act in a particular situation.

ATTACHMENT

What is attachment? **Attachment** is a close emotional bond between two people. Interest in attachment has especially focused on infants and their caregivers.

Theories of Attachment   There is no shortage of theories about why infants become attached to a caregiver. Three theorists discussed in Chapter 1—Freud, Erikson, and Bowlby—proposed influential views.

Freud reasoned that infants become attached to the person or object that provides oral satisfaction. For most infants, this is the mother, since she is most likely to feed the infant. Is feeding as important as Freud thought? A classic study by Harry Harlow (1958) reveals that the answer is no (see Figure 10.8).

Harlow removed infant monkeys from their mothers at birth; for six months they were reared by surrogate (substitute) "mothers." One surrogate mother was made of wire, the other of cloth. Half of the infant monkeys were fed by the wire mother, half by the cloth mother. Periodically, the amount of time the infant monkeys spent with either the wire or the cloth mother was computed. Regardless of which mother fed them, the infant monkeys spent far more time with the cloth mother. Even if the wire mother but not the cloth mother provided nourishment, the infant monkeys spent more time with the cloth mother. And when Harlow frightened the monkeys, those "raised" by the cloth mother ran to the mother and clung to it; those raised by the wire mother did not. Whether the mother provided comfort seemed to determine whether the monkeys associated the mother with security. This study clearly demonstrated that feeding is not the crucial element in the attachment process, and that contact comfort is important.

Physical comfort also plays a role in Erik Erikson's (1968) view of the infant's development. Recall Erikson's proposal that the first year of life represents the stage of trust versus mistrust. Physical comfort and sensitive care, according to Erikson (1968), are key to establishing a basic trust in infants. The infant's sense of trust, in turn, is the foundation for attachment and sets the stage for a lifelong expectation that the world will be a good and pleasant place to be.

The ethological perspective of British psychiatrist John Bowlby (1969, 1989) also stresses the importance of attachment in the first year of life and the responsiveness of the caregiver. Bowlby points out that both infants and their primary caregivers are biologically predisposed to form attachments. He argues that the newborn is biologically equipped to elicit attachment behavior. The baby cries, clings, coos, and smiles. Later, the infant crawls, walks, and follows the mother. The immediate result is to keep the primary caregiver nearby; the long-term effect is to increase the infant's chances of survival.

Attachment does not emerge suddenly but rather develops in a series of phases, moving from a baby's general preference for human beings to a partnership with primary caregivers. Following are four such phases based on Bowlby's conceptualization of attachment (Schaffer, 1996):

- *Phase 1: From birth to 2 months.* Infants instinctively orient to human figures. Strangers, siblings, and parents are equally likely to elicit smiling or crying from the infant.

- *Phase 2: From 2 to 7 months.* Attachment becomes focused on one figure, usually the primary caregiver, as the baby gradually learns to distinguish familiar from unfamiliar people.

- *Phase 3: From 7 to 24 months.* Specific attachments develop. With increased locomotor skills, babies actively seek contact with regular caregivers, such as the mother or father.

- *Phase 4: From 24 months on.* Children become aware of others' feelings, goals, and plans and begin to take these into account in directing their own actions. Researchers' recent findings that infants are more socially sophisticated and insightful than previously envisioned suggests that some of the characteristics of Bowlby's phase 4, such as understanding the goals and intentions of the attachment figure, appear to be developing in phase 3 as attachment security is taking shape (Thompson, 2008).

Bowlby argued that infants develop an *internal working model* of attachment: a simple mental model of the caregiver, their relationship, and the self as deserving of nurturant care. The infant's internal working model of attachment with the caregiver influences the infant's

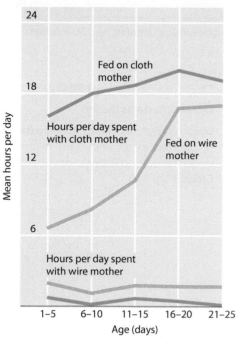

FIGURE **10.8**

CONTACT TIME WITH WIRE AND CLOTH SURROGATE MOTHERS. Regardless of whether the infant monkeys were fed by a wire or a cloth mother, they overwhelmingly preferred to spend contact time with the cloth mother. *How do these results compare with what Freud's theory and Erikson's theory would predict about human infants?*

attachment A close emotional bond between two people.

and later the child's subsequent responses to other people (Bretherton, 2012; Roisman & Groh, 2011). The internal model of attachment also has played a pivotal role in the discovery of links between attachment and subsequent emotion understanding, conscience development, and self-concept (Thompson, 2013a).

In sum, attachment emerges from the social cognitive advances that allow infants to develop expectations for the caregiver's behavior and to determine the affective quality of their relationship (Thompson, 2013a). These social cognitive advances include recognizing the caregiver's face, voice, and other features, as well as developing an internal working model of expecting the caregiver to provide pleasure in social interaction and relief from distress.

Individual Differences in Attachment   Although attachment to a caregiver intensifies midway through the first year, isn't it likely that the quality of babies' attachment experiences varies? Mary Ainsworth (1979) thought so. Ainsworth created the **Strange Situation,** an observational measure of infant attachment in which the infant experiences a series of introductions, separations, and reunions with the caregiver and an adult stranger in a prescribed order. In using the Strange Situation, researchers hope that their observations will provide information about the infant's motivation to be near the caregiver and the degree to which the caregiver's presence provides the infant with security and confidence.

Based on how babies respond in the Strange Situation, they are described as being securely attached or insecurely attached (in one of three ways) to the caregiver:

In Bowlby's model, what are the four phases of attachment?

- **Securely attached babies** use the caregiver as a secure base from which to explore the environment. When they are in the presence of their caregiver, securely attached infants explore the room and examine toys that have been placed in it. When the caregiver departs, securely attached infants might protest mildly, and when the caregiver returns these infants reestablish positive interaction with her, perhaps by smiling or climbing onto her lap. Subsequently, they often resume playing with the toys in the room.

- **Insecure avoidant babies** show insecurity by avoiding the mother. In the Strange Situation, these babies engage in little interaction with the caregiver, are not distressed when she leaves the room, usually do not reestablish contact with her on her return, and may even turn their back on her. If contact is established, the infant usually leans away or looks away.

- **Insecure resistant babies** often cling to the caregiver and then resist her by fighting against the closeness, perhaps by kicking or pushing away. In the Strange Situation, these babies often cling anxiously to the caregiver and don't explore the playroom. When the caregiver leaves, they often cry loudly and push away if she tries to comfort them on her return.

- **Insecure disorganized babies** are disorganized and disoriented. In the Strange Situation, these babies might appear dazed, confused, and fearful. To be classified as disorganized, babies must show strong patterns of avoidance and resistance or display certain specified behaviors, such as extreme fearfulness around the caregiver.

What is the nature of secure and insecure attachment?

Evaluating the Strange Situation   Does the Strange Situation capture important differences among infants? As a measure of attachment, it may be culturally biased. For example, German and Japanese babies often show patterns of attachment different from those of American infants. As illustrated in Figure 10.9, German infants are more likely to show an avoidant attachment pattern and Japanese infants are less likely to display this pattern than U.S. infants (van IJzendoorn & Kroonenberg, 1988). The avoidant pattern in German babies likely occurs because their caregivers encourage them to be independent (Grossmann & others, 1985). Also as shown in Figure 10.9, Japanese babies are more likely than American babies to be categorized as resistant. This may have more to do with the Strange Situation as a measure of attachment than with attachment insecurity itself. Japanese mothers rarely let anyone unfamiliar with their babies care for them. Thus, the Strange Situation might create considerably more stress for Japanese infants than for American infants, who are more accustomed to separation from their mothers (Miyake, Chen, & Campos, 1985). Even though there are cultural variations in attachment classification, the most frequent

Strange Situation Ainsworth's observational measure of infant attachment to a caregiver, which requires the infant to move through a series of introductions, separations, and reunions with the caregiver and an adult stranger in a prescribed order.

securely attached babies Babies who use the caregiver as a secure base from which to explore the environment.

insecure avoidant babies Babies who show insecurity by avoiding the mother.

insecure resistant babies Babies who might cling to the caregiver, then resist her by fighting against the closeness, perhaps by kicking or pushing away.

insecure disorganized babies Babies who show insecurity by being disorganized and disoriented.

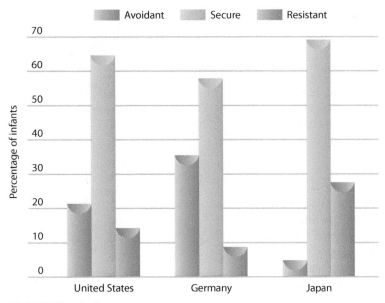

FIGURE **10.9**

CROSS-CULTURAL COMPARISON OF ATTACHMENT. In one study, infant attachment in three countries—the United States, Germany, and Japan—was measured in the Ainsworth Strange Situation (van IJzendoorn & Kroonenberg, 1988). The dominant attachment pattern in all three countries was secure attachment. However, German infants were more avoidant and Japanese infants were less avoidant and more resistant than U.S. infants. *What are some explanations for differences in how German, Japanese, and U.S. infants respond to the Strange Situation?*

classification in every culture studied so far is secure attachment (Thompson, 2006, 2012; van IJzendoorn & Kroonenberg, 1988).

Some critics stress that behavior in the Strange Situation—like other laboratory assessments—might not indicate what infants would do in a natural environment. But researchers have found that infants' behaviors in the Strange Situation are closely related to how they behave at home in response to separation and reunion with their mothers (Pederson & Moran, 1996). Thus, many infant researchers conclude that the Strange Situation continues to show merit as a measure of infant attachment.

Interpreting Differences in Attachment Do individual differences in attachment matter? Ainsworth observes that secure attachment in the first year of life provides an important foundation for psychological development later in life. The securely attached infant moves freely away from the mother but keeps track of where she is through periodic glances. The securely attached infant responds positively to being picked up by others and, when put back down, freely moves away to play. An insecurely attached infant, by contrast, avoids the mother or is ambivalent toward her, fears strangers, and is upset by minor, everyday separations.

If early attachment to a caregiver is important, it should influence a child's social behavior later in development. For some children, early attachments seem to foreshadow later functioning (Bretherton, 2012; Brisch, 2012). In the extensive longitudinal study conducted by Alan Sroufe and his colleagues (2005; Sroufe, Coffino, & Carlson, 2010), early secure attachment (assessed by the Strange Situation at 12 and 18 months) was linked with positive emotional health, high self-esteem, self-confidence, and socially competent interaction with peers, teachers, camp counselors, and romantic partners through adolescence. Another study found that attachment security at 24 and 36 months was linked to the child's enhanced social problem-solving at 54 months (Raikes & Thompson, 2009). And a meta-analysis revealed that disorganized attachment was more strongly linked to externalizing problems (aggression and hostility, for example) than were avoidant and resistant attachment (Fearon & others, 2010).

Few studies have assessed infants' attachment security to the mother and the father separately. However, a recent study revealed that infants who were insecurely attached to their mother and father ("double-insecure") at 15 months of age had more externalizing problems (out-of-control behavior, for example) in the elementary school years than their counterparts who were securely attached to at least one parent (Kochanska & Kim, 2013).

An important issue regarding attachment is whether infancy is a critical or sensitive period for development. Many, but not all, research studies reveal the power of infant attachment to predict subsequent development (Fraley, Roisman, & Haltigan, 2013; Roisman & Groh, 2011; Thompson, 2013a). In one longitudinal study, attachment classification in infancy did not predict attachment classification at 18 years of age (Lewis, Feiring, & Rosenthal, 2000). In this study, the best predictor of an insecure attachment classification at 18 was the occurrence of parental divorce in the intervening years.

Consistently positive caregiving over a number of years is likely an important factor in connecting early attachment with the child's functioning later in development. Indeed, researchers have found that early secure attachment and subsequent experiences, especially maternal care and life stresses, are linked with children's later behavior and adjustment (Thompson, 2013a). For example, a longitudinal study revealed that changes in attachment security/insecurity from infancy to adulthood were linked to stresses and supports in socioemotional contexts (Van Ryzin, Carlson, & Sroufe, 2011). These results suggest that attachment continuity may reflect stable social contexts as much as early working models. The study just described (Van Ryzin, Carlson, & Sroufe, 2011) reflects an increasingly accepted view of the development of attachment and its influence on development. That is, it is important to recognize that attachment security in infancy does not always by itself produce long-term positive outcomes, but rather is linked to later outcomes through connections with the way children and adolescents subsequently experience various social contexts as they develop.

The Van Ryzin, Carlson, and Sroufe (2011) study reflects a **developmental cascade model,** which involves connections across domains over time that influence developmental pathways and outcomes (Cicchetti, 2013; Masten, 2013). Developmental cascades can include connections between a wide range of biological, cognitive, and socioemotional processes (attachment, for example), and also can involve social contexts such as families, peers, schools, and culture. Further, links can produce positive or negative outcomes at different points in development, such as infancy, early childhood, middle and late childhood, adolescence, and adulthood.

Some developmentalists conclude that too much emphasis has been placed on the attachment bond in infancy (Newcombe, 2007). Jerome Kagan (1987, 2002), for example, points out that infants are highly resilient and adaptive; he argues that they are evolutionarily equipped to stay on a positive developmental course, even in the face of wide variations in parenting. Kagan and others stress that genetic characteristics and temperament play more important roles in a child's social competence than the attachment theorists, such as Bowlby and Ainsworth, are willing to acknowledge (Bakermans-Kranenburg & others, 2007). For example, if some infants inherit a low tolerance for stress, this—rather than an insecure attachment bond—may be responsible for an inability to get along with peers. One study found that infants with the short version of the serotonin transporter gene—5-HTTLPR—developed a disorganized attachment style only when their mothers were low in responsiveness to them (Spangler & others, 2009). This is an example of a finding involving gene-environment interaction. However, some researchers have not found support for gene-environment interactions related to infant attachment (Luijk & others, 2011; Roisman & Fraley, 2012).

developmental **connection**

Nature Versus Nurture

What is involved in gene-environment (G × E) interaction? Chapter 2, p. 69

Another criticism of attachment theory is that it ignores the diversity of socializing agents and contexts that exists in an infant's world. A culture's value system can influence the nature of attachment (Jin & others, 2012). Mothers' expectations for infants to be independent are high in northern Germany, whereas Japanese mothers are more strongly motivated to keep their infants close to them (Grossmann & others, 1985; Rothbaum & Trommsdorff, 2007). Not surprisingly, northern German infants tend to show less distress than Japanese infants when separated from their mothers. Also, in some cultures, infants show attachments to many people. Among the Hausa (who live in Nigeria), both grandmothers and siblings provide a significant amount of care for infants (Harkness & Super, 1995). Infants in agricultural societies tend to form attachments to older siblings, who are assigned a major responsibility for younger siblings' care. Researchers recognize the importance of competent, nurturant caregivers in an infant's development (Grusec & others, 2013). At issue, though, is whether or not secure attachment, especially to a single caregiver, is critical (Fraley, Roisman, & Haltigan, 2013; Thompson, 2013c, d).

Despite such criticisms, there is ample evidence that security of attachment is important to development (Bretherton, 2012; Crugnola & others, 2013; Sroufe, Coffino, & Carlson, 2010; Thompson, 2013c, d). Secure attachment in infancy is important because it reflects a positive parent-infant relationship and provides a foundation that supports healthy socioemotional development in the years that follow.

Caregiving Styles and Attachment   Is the style of caregiving linked with the quality of the infant's attachment? Securely attached babies have caregivers who are sensitive to their signals and are consistently available to respond to their infants' needs (Bigelow & others, 2010; Jin & others, 2012). These caregivers often let their babies have an active part in determining the onset and pacing of interaction in the first year of life. A recent study revealed that maternal sensitive responding was linked to infant attachment security (Finger & others, 2009). Another study found that maternal sensitivity—but not infants' temperament—when infants were 6 months old was linked to subsequent attachment security (Leerkes, 2011). Yet another study found that maternal sensitivity in parenting was related to secure attachment in infants in two different cultures: the United States and Colombia (Carbonell & others, 2002). Although maternal sensitivity is positively linked to the development of secure attachment in infancy, it is important to note that the link is not especially strong (Campos, 2009).

How do the caregivers of insecurely attached babies interact with them? Caregivers of avoidant babies tend to be unavailable or rejecting (Posada & Kaloustian, 2010). They often don't respond to their babies' signals and have little physical contact with them. When they do interact with their babies, they may behave in an angry and irritable way. Caregivers of

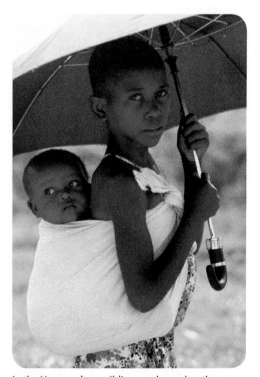

In the Hausa culture, siblings and grandmothers provide a significant amount of care for infants. *How might this practice affect attachment?*

developmental cascade model Involves connections across domains over time that influence developmental pathways and outcomes.

resistant babies tend to be inconsistent; sometimes they respond to their babies' needs, and sometimes they don't. In general, they tend not to be very affectionate with their babies and show little synchrony when interacting with them. Caregivers of disorganized babies often neglect or physically abuse them (Bohlin & others, 2012; Cicchetti, 2013). In some cases, these caregivers are depressed. In sum, caregivers' interactions with infants influence whether the infants are securely or insecurely attached to them (Stroufe, Coffino, & Carlson, 2010).

So far in our discussion of attachment, we have focused on the importance of secure attachment in infancy and the role of sensitive parenting in attachment (Berlin, 2012; Bretherton, 2012; Thompson, 2013a). The attachment process continues to be an important aspect of children's development in the childhood years. In middle and late childhood, attachment becomes more sophisticated and as children's social worlds expand to include peers, teachers, and others, they typically spend less time with parents.

Kathryn Kerns and her colleagues (Brumariu, Kerns, & Siebert, 2012; Kerns & Siebert, 2012; Kerns, Siener, & Brumariu, 2011; Siener & Kerns, 2012) have studied links between attachment to parents and various child outcomes in the middle and late childhood years. They have found that during this period of development, secure attachment is associated with a lower level of internalized symptoms, anxiety, and depression in children (Brumariu & Kerns, 2010). For example, a recent study revealed that children who were less securely attached to their mother reported having more anxiety (Brumariu, Kerns, & Seibert, 2012). Also in this study, secure attachment was linked to a higher level of children's emotional regulation and less difficulty in identifying emotions. In Chapter 14, "Families," you will read about the role of attachment in adolescent development.

Developmental Social Neuroscience and Attachment In Chapter 1, we described the emerging field of developmental social neuroscience that examines connections between socioemotional processes, development, and the brain (Pfeifer & Blakemore, 2012; Singer, 2012). Attachment is one of the main areas in which theory and research on developmental social neuroscience has focused. These connections of attachment and the brain involve the neuroanatomy of the brain, neurotransmitters, and hormones.

Theory and research on the role of the brain's regions in mother-infant attachment is just emerging (De Haan & Gunnar, 2009). A recent theoretical view proposed that the prefrontal cortex likely has an important role in maternal attachment behavior, as do the subcortical (areas of the brain lower than the cortex) regions of the amygdala (which is strongly involved in emotion) and the hypothalamus (Gonzalez, Atkinson, & Fleming, 2009). An ongoing fMRI longitudinal study is exploring the possibility that different attachment patterns can be distinguished by different patterns of brain activity (Strathearn, 2007, 2011).

Research on the role of hormones and neurotransmitters in attachment has emphasized the importance of two neuropeptide hormones—oxytocin and vasopressin—in the formation of the maternal-infant bond (Strathearn & others, 2012). Oxytocin, a mammalian hormone that also acts as a neurotransmitter in the brain, is released during breastfeeding and by contact and warmth (Ebstein & others, 2012). Oxytocin is especially thought to be a likely candidate in the formation of infant-mother attachment (Feldman, 2012). A recent research review concluded that strong links exist between levels or patterns of oxytocin and aspects of mother-infant attachment (Galbally & others, 2011).

The influence of these neuropeptides on the neurotransmitter dopamine in the nucleus accumbens (a collection of neurons in the forebrain that are involved in pleasure) likely is important in motivating approach to the attachment object (de Haan & Gunnar, 2009). Figure 10.10 shows the regions of the brain we have described that are likely to be important in infant-mother attachment.

FIGURE **10.10**

REGIONS OF THE BRAIN PROPOSED AS LIKELY IMPORTANT IN INFANT-MOTHER ATTACHMENT. This illustration shows the brain's left hemisphere. The corpus callosum is the large bundle of axons that connect the brain's two hemispheres.

FATHERS AND MOTHERS AS CAREGIVERS

Much of our discussion of attachment has focused on mothers as caregivers. Do mothers and fathers differ in their caregiving roles?

On average, mothers spend considerably more time in caregiving with infants and children than do fathers (Blakemore, Berenbaum, & Liben, 2009; Shwalb, Shwalb, & Lamb, 2013). Mothers especially are more likely to engage in the managerial role with their children, coordinating their activities, making sure their health care needs are fulfilled, and so on (Parke & Buriel, 2006).

However, an increasing number of U.S. fathers stay home full-time with their children (Lamb & Lewis, 2013). As indicated in Figure 10.11, there was a 300-plus percent increase in stay-at-home fathers in the United States from 1996 to 2006. A large portion of full-time fathers have career-focused wives who provide the main family income. A recent study revealed that the stay-at-home fathers were as satisfied with their marriage as traditional parents, although they indicated that they missed their daily life in the workplace (Rochlen & others, 2007). In this study, the stay-at-home fathers reported that they tended to be ostracized when they took their children to playgrounds and often were excluded from parent groups.

Can fathers take care of infants as competently as mothers can? Observations of fathers and their infants suggest that fathers have the ability to act as sensitively and responsively as mothers with their infants (Parke & Buriel, 2006; Parke & Clarke-Stewart, 2011; Shaw, 2013). A recent study found that infants who showed a higher level of externalizing, disruptive problems at 1 year of age had fathers who displayed a low level of engagement with their infants as early as the third month of life (Ramchandani & others, 2013). Another recent study revealed that fathers with a college-level education engaged in more stimulating physical activities with their infants and that fathers in a conflicting couple relationship participated in less caregiving and physical play with their infants (Cabrera, Hofferth, & Chae, 2011).

Consider the Aka pygmy culture in Africa, where fathers spend as much time interacting with their infants as do their mothers (Hewlett, 1991, 2000; Hewlett & MacFarlan, 2010). Remember, however, that although fathers can be active, nurturant, involved caregivers with their infants as Aka pygmy fathers do, in many cultures men have not chosen to follow this pattern (Lamb & Lewis, 2013). Also, if fathers have mental health problems, they may not interact as effectively with their infants. A recent study revealed that depressed fathers focused more on their own needs than their infants' needs and that they directed more negative and critical speech toward infants (Sethna, Murray, & Ramchandani, 2012).

Do fathers behave differently from mothers with their infants? Maternal interactions usually center on child-care activities—feeding, changing diapers, and bathing. Paternal interactions are more likely to include play (Lamb & Lewis, 2013; Parke & Clarke-Stewart, 2011). Fathers engage in more rough-and-tumble play. They bounce infants, throw them up in the air, tickle them, and so on. Mothers do play with infants, but their play is less physical and arousing than that of fathers.

In one study, fathers were interviewed about their caregiving responsibilities when their children were 6, 15, 24, and 36 months of age (NICHD Early Child Care Research Network, 2000). Some of the fathers were videotaped while playing with their children at 6 and 36 months. Fathers were more involved in caregiving—bathing, feeding, dressing the child, taking the child to child care, and so on—when they worked fewer hours and mothers worked more hours, when mothers and fathers were younger, when mothers reported greater marital intimacy, and when the children were boys.

Do children benefit when fathers are positively involved in their caregiving? One study of more than 7,000 children who were assessed from infancy to adulthood revealed that those whose fathers were extensively involved in their lives (such as engaging in various activities with them and showing a strong interest in their education) were more successful in school (Flouri & Buchanan, 2004).

CHILD CARE

Many U.S. children today experience multiple caregivers. Most do not have a parent staying home to care for them; instead, the children have some type of care provided by others—"child care." Many parents worry that child care will

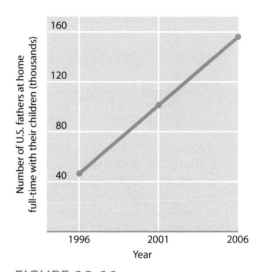

FIGURE **10.11**

THE INCREASE IN THE NUMBER OF U.S. FATHERS STAYING AT HOME FULL-TIME WITH THEIR CHILDREN

An Aka pygmy father with his infant son. In the Aka culture, fathers were observed to be holding or near their infants 47 percent of the time (Hewlett, 1991).

Child-Care Policies Around the World

Child-care policies around the world vary (O'Brien & Moss, 2010; Tolani & Brooks-Gunn, 2008). Europe led the way in creating new standards of parental leave: The European Union (EU) mandated a paid 14-week maternity leave in 1992. In most European countries today, working parents on leave receive from 70 to 100 percent of their prior wage, and paid leave averages about 16 weeks (Tolani & Brooks-Gunn, 2008). The United States currently allows workers up to 12 weeks of unpaid leave to care for a newborn.

Most countries restrict eligible benefits to women employed for a minimum time prior to childbirth. In Denmark, even unemployed mothers are eligible for extended parental leave related to childbirth. In Germany, child-rearing leave is available to almost all parents. The Nordic countries (Denmark, Norway, and Sweden) have extensive gender-equity family leave policies for childbirth that emphasize the contributions of both women and men (O'Brien & Moss, 2010; Tolani & Brooks-Gunn, 2008). For example, in Sweden, parents can take an 18-month job-protected parental leave with benefits allowed to be shared by parents and applied to full-time or part-time work.

In light of the data you saw in Figure 10.12, why might it be helpful if U.S. leave policies were more like those in Scandinavian countries?

How are child-care policies in many European countries, such as Sweden, different from those in the United States?

reduce their infants' emotional attachment to them, retard infants' cognitive development, fail to teach them how to control anger, and allow them to be unduly influenced by their peers. How extensive is the use of child care? Are the worries of these parents justified?

Parental Leave   Today far more young children are in child care than at any other time in history. About 2 million children in the United States currently receive formal, licensed child care, and uncounted millions of children are cared for by unlicensed babysitters. In part, these numbers reflect the fact that U.S. adults cannot receive paid leave from their jobs to care for their young children. However, as described in *Connecting with Diversity*, many countries provide extensive parental leave policies.

Variations in Child Care   Because the United States does not have a policy of paid leave for child care, child care in the United States has become a major national concern (Berlin, 2012; Lamb, 2013). Many factors influence the effects of child care, including the age of the child, the type of child care, how long the child is in child care, and the quality of the program.

The type of child care varies extensively (Coley & others, 2013; Lamb, 2013). Child care is provided in large centers with elaborate facilities and in private homes. Some child-care centers are commercial operations; others are nonprofit centers run by churches, civic groups, and employers. Some child-care providers are professionals; others are untrained adults who want to earn extra money. Figure 10.12 presents the primary care arrangement for children under 5 years of age with employed mothers (Clarke-Stewart & Miner, 2008).

In the United States, approximately 15 percent of children 5 years of age and younger attend more than one child-care arrangement. A recent study of 2- and 3-year-old children revealed

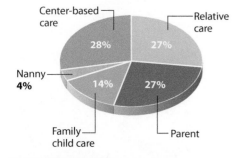

FIGURE **10.12**

PRIMARY CARE ARRANGEMENTS IN THE UNITED STATES FOR CHILDREN UNDER 5 YEARS OF AGE WITH EMPLOYED MOTHERS

Wanda Mitchell, Child-Care Director

Wanda Mitchell is the Center Director at the Hattie Daniels Day Care Center in Wilson, North Carolina. Her responsibilities include directing the operation of the center, which involves creating and maintaining an environment in which young children can learn effectively, and ensuring that the center meets state licensing requirements. Wanda obtained her undergraduate degree from North Carolina A & T University, majoring in Child Development. Prior to her current position, she was an education coordinator for Head Start and an instructor at Wilson Technical Community College. Describing her career, Wanda says, "I really enjoy working in my field. This is my passion. After graduating from college, my goal was to advance in my field."

For more information about what early childhood educators do, see page 43 in the Careers in Child Development appendix following Chapter 1.

Wanda Mitchell, child-care director, working with some of the children at her center.

that an increase in the number of child-care arrangements the children experienced was linked to an increase in behavioral problems and a decrease in prosocial behavior (Morrissey, 2009).

Use of different types of child care varies by ethnicity (Howes & Wishard Guerra, 2009). For example, Latino families are far less likely than non-Latino White and African American families to have children in child-care centers—11 percent, 20 percent, and 21 percent, respectively, in one study (Smith, 2002). Despite indicating a preference for center-based care, African American and Latino families often rely on family-based care, especially by grandmothers. However, there has been a substantial increase in the use of center-based care by African American mothers.

Child-care quality makes a difference. What constitutes a high-quality child-care program for infants? In high-quality child care (Clarke-Stewart & Miner, 2008, p. 273),

> caregivers encourage the children to be actively engaged in a variety of activities, have frequent, positive interactions that include smiling, touching, holding, and speaking at the child's eye level, respond properly to the child's questions or requests, and encourage children to talk about their experiences, feelings, and ideas.

High-quality child care also involves providing children with a safe environment, access to age-appropriate toys and participation in age-appropriate activities, and a low caregiver-to-child ratio that allows caregivers to spend considerable time with children on an individual basis.

Children are more likely to experience poor-quality child care if they come from families with few resources (psychological, social, and economic) (Cabrera, Hutchens, & Peters, 2006). Many researchers have examined the role of poverty in quality of child care (Lucas & others, 2008). One study found that extensive child care was harmful to low-income children only when the care was of low quality (Votruba-Drzal, Coley, & Chase-Lansdale, 2004). Even if the child was in child care more than 45 hours a week, high-quality care was linked with fewer internalizing problems (anxiety, for example) and externalizing problems (aggressive and destructive behaviors, for example). A recent study revealed that children from low-income families benefited in terms of school readiness and language development when their parents selected higher-quality child care (McCartney & others, 2007).

To read about one individual who provides quality child care to individuals from impoverished backgrounds, see the *Connecting with Careers* profile of Wanda Mitchell. Do children

> We have all the knowledge necessary to provide absolutely first-rate child care in the United States. What is missing is the commitment and the will.
>
> —EDWARD ZIGLER
> *Contemporary Developmental Psychologist, Yale University*

in low-income families get quality care at day care? For the answer to that question, as well as other information on the effects of child care on children's development, see *Connecting Through Research*.

What are some strategies parents can follow in regard to child care? Child-care expert Kathleen McCartney (2003, p. 4) offered this advice:

- Recognize that the quality of your parenting is a key factor in your child's development.
- Make decisions that will improve the likelihood you will be good parents. "For some this will mean working full-time"—for personal fulfillment, income, or both. "For others, this will mean working part-time or not working outside the home."
- Monitor your child's development. "Parents should observe for themselves whether their children seem to be having behavior problems." They need to talk with child-care providers and their pediatrician about their child's behavior.
- Take some time to find the best child care available. Observe different child-care facilities and be certain that you like what you see. Quality child care costs money, and not all parents can afford the child care they want. However, state subsidies and programs like Head Start are available for families in need.

connecting through research

How Does the Quality and Quantity of Child Care Affect Children?

In 1991, the National Institute of Child Health and Human Development (NICHD) began a comprehensive, longitudinal study of child-care experiences. Data were collected on a diverse sample of almost 1,400 children and their families at 10 locations across the United States over a period of seven years. Researchers used multiple methods (trained observers, interviews, questionnaires, and testing) and measured many facets of children's development, including physical health, cognitive development, and socioemotional development. Following are some of the results of what is now referred to as the NICHD Study of Early Child Care and Youth Development or NICHD SECCYD (NICHD Early Child Care Network, 2001, 2002, 2003, 2004, 2005, 2006, 2010).

- *Patterns of use.* Many families placed their infants in child care very soon after the child's birth, and there was considerable instability in the child-care arrangements. By 4 months of age, nearly three-fourths of the infants had entered some form of nonmaternal child care. Almost half of the infants were cared for by a relative when they first entered care; only 12 percent were enrolled in child-care centers. Socioeconomic factors were linked to the amount and type of care. For example, mothers with higher incomes and families that were more dependent on the mother's income placed their infants in child care at an earlier age. Mothers who believed that maternal employment has positive effects on children were more likely than other mothers to place their infant in nonmaternal care for more hours. Low-income families were more likely than more affluent families to use child care, but infants from low-income families who were in child care averaged as many hours as other income groups. In the preschool years, mothers who were single, those with more education, and families with higher incomes used more

What are some important findings from the National Longitudinal Study of Child Care conducted by the National Institute of Child Health and Human Development?

hours of center care than other families. Minority families and mothers with less education used more hours of care by relatives.

- *Quality of care.* Evaluations of quality of care were based on such characteristics as group size, child-adult ratio, physical environment, caregiver characteristics (such as formal education, specialized training, and child-care experience), and caregiver behavior (such as sensitivity to children). An alarming conclusion is that a majority of

(continued)

connecting through research

(continued)

the child care in the first three years of life was of unacceptably low quality. Positive caregiving by nonparents in child-care settings was infrequent—only 12 percent of the children studied experienced positive nonparental child care (such as positive talk, lack of detachment or flat affect, and language stimulation)! Further, infants from low-income families experienced lower-quality child care than infants from higher-income families. When quality of care was high, children performed better on cognitive and language tasks, were more cooperative with their mothers during play, showed more positive and skilled interaction with peers, and had fewer behavior problems. Caregiver training and good child-staff ratios were linked with higher cognitive and social competence when children were 54 months of age.

Higher-quality child care was also related to higher-quality mother-child interaction among the families that used nonmaternal care. Further, poor-quality care was related to an increase in insecure attachment to the mother among infants who were 15 months of age, but only when the mother was low in sensitivity and responsiveness. However, child-care quality was not linked to attachment security at 36 months of age. A recent study found that high-quality infant-toddler child care was linked to better memory skills at the end of the preschool years (Li & others, 2013). A recent study revealed that higher-quality child care from birth to 4½ years of age was linked to higher cognitive-academic achievement at 15 years of age (Vandell & others, 2010). In this study, higher quality of early child care also was related to youth reports of less externalizing behavior (lower rates of delinquency, for example).

- *Amount of child care.* The quantity of child care predicted some child outcomes. When children spent extensive amounts of time in child care beginning in infancy, they experienced less sensitive interactions with their mother, showed more behavior problems, and had higher rates of illness. Many of these comparisons involved children in child care for less than 30 hours a week versus those in child care for more than 45 hours a week. In general, though, when children spent 30 hours or more per week in child care, their development was less than optimal (Ramey, 2005).

- *Family and parenting influences.* The influence of families and parenting was not weakened by extensive child care. Parents played a significant role in helping children to regulate their emotions. Especially important parenting influences were being sensitive to children's needs, being involved with children, and cognitively stimulating them. Indeed, parental sensitivity has been the most consistent predictor of a secure attachment, with child-care experiences being relevant in many cases only when mothers engage in insensitive parenting (Friedman, Melhuish, & Hill, 2010). An important point about the extensive NICHD research is that findings show that family factors are considerably stronger and more consistent predictors of a wide variety of child outcomes than are child-care experiences (such as quality, quantity, type). The worst outcomes for children occur when both home and child care settings are of poor quality. For example, a recent study involving the NICHD SECCYD data revealed that worse socioemotional outcomes (more problem behavior, low level of prosocial behavior) for children occurred when they experienced both home and child care environments that conferred risk (Watamura & others, 2011).

This study reinforces the conclusions of other researchers cited earlier in this section of the chapter—it is not the *quantity* as much as the *quality* of child care a child receives that is important. What is also significant to note is the emphasis on the positive effect families and parents can have on children's child-care experiences.

Review *Connect* Reflect

 LG4 Explain the early development of social orientation/understanding, attachment, and variations in child care.

Review
- What characterizes the early development of social orientation and social understanding?
- How does attachment develop in infancy?
- How do mothers and fathers interact with infants?
- What is the nature of child care?

Connect
- In this section, you learned that maternal sensitive responding was linked (if not strongly) to security of infant attachment.

What did you learn about maternal sensitivity and children's language development in the *Connecting Through Research* interlude in Chapter 9?

Reflect *Your Own Personal Journey of Life*
- Imagine that a friend of yours is getting ready to put her baby in child care. What advice would you give to her? Do you think she should stay home with the baby? Why or why not? What type of child care would you recommend?

Emotional Development

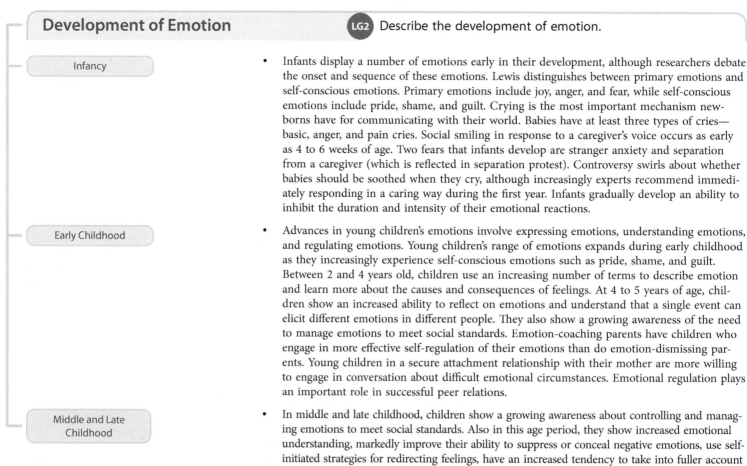

Exploring Emotion

LG1 Discuss basic aspects of emotion.

What Are Emotions?

- Emotion is feeling, or affect, that occurs when people are engaged in interactions that are important to them, especially those that influence their well-being. Emotions can be classified as positive or negative. Darwin described the evolutionary basis of emotions, and today psychologists stress that emotions, especially facial expressions of emotions, have a biological foundation. Facial expressions of emotion are similar across cultures, but display rules are not culturally universal. Biological evolution endowed humans to be emotional, but culture and relationships with others provide diversity in emotional experiences.

A Functionalist View of Emotions

- The functionalist view of emotion emphasizes the importance of contexts and relationships in emotion. For example, when parents induce a positive mood in their child, the child is more likely to follow the parents' directions. In this view, goals are involved in emotions in a variety of ways, and the goal's specific nature can affect the individual's experience of a given emotion.

Emotional Competence

- Saarni argues that becoming emotionally competent involves developing a number of skills such as being aware of one's emotional states, discerning others' emotions, adaptively coping with negative emotions, and understanding the role of emotions in relationships.

Development of Emotion

LG2 Describe the development of emotion.

Infancy

- Infants display a number of emotions early in their development, although researchers debate the onset and sequence of these emotions. Lewis distinguishes between primary emotions and self-conscious emotions. Primary emotions include joy, anger, and fear, while self-conscious emotions include pride, shame, and guilt. Crying is the most important mechanism newborns have for communicating with their world. Babies have at least three types of cries—basic, anger, and pain cries. Social smiling in response to a caregiver's voice occurs as early as 4 to 6 weeks of age. Two fears that infants develop are stranger anxiety and separation from a caregiver (which is reflected in separation protest). Controversy swirls about whether babies should be soothed when they cry, although increasingly experts recommend immediately responding in a caring way during the first year. Infants gradually develop an ability to inhibit the duration and intensity of their emotional reactions.

Early Childhood

- Advances in young children's emotions involve expressing emotions, understanding emotions, and regulating emotions. Young children's range of emotions expands during early childhood as they increasingly experience self-conscious emotions such as pride, shame, and guilt. Between 2 and 4 years old, children use an increasing number of terms to describe emotion and learn more about the causes and consequences of feelings. At 4 to 5 years of age, children show an increased ability to reflect on emotions and understand that a single event can elicit different emotions in different people. They also show a growing awareness of the need to manage emotions to meet social standards. Emotion-coaching parents have children who engage in more effective self-regulation of their emotions than do emotion-dismissing parents. Young children in a secure attachment relationship with their mother are more willing to engage in conversation about difficult emotional circumstances. Emotional regulation plays an important role in successful peer relations.

Middle and Late Childhood

- In middle and late childhood, children show a growing awareness about controlling and managing emotions to meet social standards. Also in this age period, they show increased emotional understanding, markedly improve their ability to suppress or conceal negative emotions, use self-initiated strategies for redirecting feelings, have an increased tendency to take into fuller account the events that lead to emotional reactions, and develop a capacity for genuine empathy.

Temperament

LG3 Characterize variations in temperament and their significance.

Describing and Classifying Temperament

- Temperament involves individual differences in behavioral styles, emotions, and characteristic ways of responding. Developmentalists are especially interested in the temperament of infants. Chess and Thomas classified infants as (1) easy, (2) difficult, or (3) slow to warm up. Kagan argues that inhibition to the unfamiliar is an important temperament category. Rothbart and Bates' view of temperament emphasizes the following classification: (1) extraversion/surgency, (2) negative affectivity, and (3) effortful control (self-regulation).

Biological Foundations and Experience

- Physiological characteristics are associated with different temperaments, and a moderate influence of heredity has been found in twin and adoption studies of the heritability of temperament. Children inherit a physiology that biases them to have a particular type of temperament, but through experience they learn to modify their temperament style to some degree. Very active young children are likely to become outgoing adults. In some cases, a difficult temperament is linked with adjustment problems in early adulthood. The link between childhood temperament and adult personality depends in part on context, which helps shape the reaction to a child and thus the child's experiences. For example, the reaction to a child's temperament depends in part on the child's gender and on the culture.

Goodness of Fit and Parenting

- Goodness of fit refers to the match between a child's temperament and the environmental demands the child must cope with. Goodness of fit can be an important aspect of a child's adjustment. Although research evidence is sketchy at this point, some general recommendations are that caregivers should (1) be sensitive to the individual characteristics of the child, (2) be flexible in responding to these characteristics, and (3) avoid negative labeling of the child.

Social Orientation/Understanding, Attachment, and Child Care

LG4 Explain the early development of social orientation/ understanding, attachment, and variations in child care.

Social Orientation/ Understanding

- Infants show a strong interest in their social world and are motivated to understand it. Infants orient to their social world early in their development. Face-to-face play with a caregiver begins to occur at 2 to 3 months of age. Newly developed self-produced locomotion skills significantly expand the infant's ability to initiate social interchanges and explore their social world more independently. Perceiving people as engaging in intentional and goal-directed behavior is an important social cognitive accomplishment, and this occurs toward the end of the first year. Social referencing increases in the second year of life.

Attachment

- Attachment is a close emotional bond between two people. In infancy, contact comfort and trust are important in the development of attachment. Bowlby's ethological theory stresses that the caregiver and the infant are biologically predisposed to form an attachment. Attachment develops in four phases during infancy. Securely attached babies use the caregiver, usually the mother, as a secure base from which to explore the environment. Three types of insecure attachment are avoidant, resistant, and disorganized. Ainsworth created the Strange Situation, an observational measure of attachment. Ainsworth points out that secure attachment in the first year of life provides an important foundation for psychological development later in life. The strength of the link between early attachment and later development has varied somewhat across studies. Some critics argue that attachment theorists have not given adequate attention to genetics and temperament. Other critics stress that they have not adequately taken into account the diversity of social agents and contexts. Cultural variations in attachment have been found, but in all cultures studied to date, secure attachment is the most common classification. Caregivers of secure babies are sensitive to the babies' signals and are consistently available to meet their needs. Caregivers of avoidant babies tend to be unavailable or rejecting. Caregivers of resistant babies tend to be inconsistently available to their babies and usually are not very affectionate. Secure attachment continues to be important in the childhood years.

  Caregivers of disorganized babies often neglect or physically abuse their babies. Increased interest has been directed toward the role of the brain in the development of attachment. The hormone oxytocin is a key candidate for influencing the development of maternal-infant attachment.

Fathers and Mothers as Caregivers

Child Care

- In recent years fathers have increased the amount of time they interact with infants, but mothers still spend considerably more time in caregiving with infants than do fathers. The mother's primary role when interacting with the infant is caregiving; the father's is playful interaction.

- More U.S. children are in child care now than at any earlier point in history. The quality of child care is uneven, and child care remains a controversial topic. Quality child care can be achieved and seems to have few adverse effects on children. In the NICHD child-care study, infants from low-income families were more likely to receive the lowest quality of care. Also, higher quality of child care was linked to a higher level of children's cognitive development and to fewer childhood problems.

key terms

emotion 282
primary emotions 285
self-conscious emotions 285
basic cry 286
anger cry 286
pain cry 286

reflexive smile 287
social smile 287
stranger anxiety 287
separation protest 287
temperament 291
easy child 293

difficult child 293
slow-to-warm-up child 293
goodness of fit 296
social referencing 299
attachment 300
Strange Situation 301

securely attached babies 301
insecure avoidant babies 301
insecure resistant babies 301
insecure disorganized babies 301
developmental cascade
    model 303

key people

Joseph Campos 285
Carolyn Saarni 283
Michael Lewis 285
John Watson 287
Ross Thompson 289
Cybelle Raver 289

Mary Ainsworth 287
John Bowlby 289
Daniel Messinger 286
Alexander Chess and Stella
    Thomas 292

Jerome Kagan 292
Mary Rothbart 293
Theodore Wachs 295
Harry Harlow 300
Erik Erikson 300

Alan Sroufe 302
Kathryn Kerns 304
Kathleen McCartney 308

chapter 11

THE SELF AND IDENTITY

chapter outline

Maxine Hong Kingston as a young girl and as an adult.

Maxine Hong Kingston's vivid portrayals of her Chinese ancestry and the struggles of Chinese immigrants have made her one of the world's leading Asian American writers. Kingston's parents were Chinese immigrants. Born in California in 1940, she spent many hours working with her parents and five brothers and sisters in the family's laundry. As a youth, Kingston was profoundly influenced by her parents' struggle to adapt to American culture and by their descriptions of their Chinese heritage.

Growing up as she did, Kingston felt the pull of two very different cultures. She was especially intrigued by stories about Chinese women who were perceived as either privileged or degraded.

Her first book was *The Woman Warrior: Memoirs of a Girlhood Among Ghosts* (Kingston, 1976). In *The Woman Warrior,* Kingston described her aunt, who gave birth to an illegitimate child. Because having a child outside of wedlock was taboo and perceived as a threat to the community's stability, the entire Chinese village condemned her, pushing her to kill herself and her child. From then on, even mentioning her name was forbidden. Kingston says she likes to guide people to find meaning in their lives, especially by exploring their cultural backgrounds.

preview

Maxine Hong Kingston's life and writings remind us of important aspects of each of our lives as we grew up: our efforts to understand ourselves and to develop an identity that reflects our cultural heritage. This chapter is about the self and identity. As we examine these topics, reflect on how well you understood yourself at different points in your life as you were growing up, and think about how you acquired the stamp of your identity.

Self-Understanding and Understanding Others Discuss the development of self-understanding and understanding others.

> Self-Understanding

> Understanding Others

The **self** consists of all of the characteristics of a person. Theorists and researchers who focus on the self usually argue that the self is the central aspect of the individual's personality and that the self lends an integrative dimension to our understanding of different personality characteristics (Harter, 2012; Rochat, 2013; Thompson, Winer, & Goodvin, 2011). Several aspects of the self have been studied more than others. These include self-understanding, self-esteem, and self-concept.

Recent research studies show that young children are more psychologically aware of themselves and others than used to be thought (Thompson, 2013b, c). This psychological awareness reflects young children's expanding psychological sophistication.

SELF-UNDERSTANDING

Self-understanding is a child's cognitive representation of the self—the substance and content of the child's self-conceptions. For example, an 11-year-old boy understands that he is a student, a boy, a football player, a family member, a video game lover, and a rock music fan. A 13-year-old girl understands that she is a middle school student, in the midst of puberty, a girl, a cheerleader, a student council member, and a movie fan. A child's self-understanding is based, in part, on the various roles and membership categories that define who children are (Harter, 2006, 2012). Though not the whole of personal identity, self-understanding provides its rational underpinnings.

Developmental Changes Children are not just given a self by their parents or culture; rather, they construct selves. As children develop, their self-understanding changes.

Infancy Studying the self in infancy is difficult mainly because infants cannot tell us how they experience themselves. Infants cannot verbally express their views of the self. They also cannot understand complex instructions from researchers.

A rudimentary form of self-recognition—being attentive and positive toward one's image in a mirror—appears as early as 3 months of age (Mascolo & Fischer, 2007; Pipp, Fischer, & Jennings, 1987). However, a central, more complete index of self-recognition—the ability to recognize one's physical features—does not emerge until the second year (Thompson, 2006).

One ingenious strategy to test infants' visual self-recognition is the use of a mirror technique, in which an infant's mother first puts a dot of rouge on the infant's nose without the infant's awareness. Then an observer watches to see how often the infant touches its nose. Next, the infant is placed in front of a mirror, and observers detect whether nose touching increases. Why does this matter? The idea is that increased nose touching indicates that the

> When I say "I,"
> I mean something
> absolutely unique,
> not to be confused
> with any other.
>
> **—UGO BETTI**
> *Italian Playwright, 20th Century*

self All of the characteristics of a person.

self-understanding A child's cognitive representation of the self—the substance and content of a child's self-conceptions.

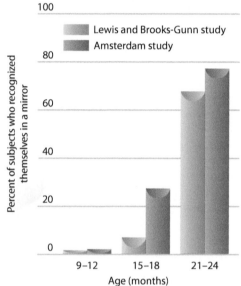

100

80

60

40

20

0

Percent of subjects who recognized themselves in a mirror

Lewis and Brooks-Gunn study

Amsterdam study

9–12   15–18   21–24

Age (months)

FIGURE 11.1

THE DEVELOPMENT OF SELF-RECOGNITION IN INFANCY. The graph shows the findings of two studies in which infants less than 1 year of age did not recognize themselves in the mirror. A slight increase in the percentage of infant self-recognition occurred around 15 to 18 months of age. By 2 years of age, a majority of children recognized themselves. *Why do researchers study whether infants recognize themselves in a mirror?*

The living self has one purpose only: to come into its own fullness of being, as a tree comes into full blossom, or a bird into spring beauty, or a tiger into lustre.

—D. H. Lawrence
English Author, 20th Century

infant recognizes the self in the mirror and is trying to touch or rub off the rouge because the rouge violates the infant's perception of what he or she looks like. Increased touching indicates that the infant realizes that it is the self in the mirror but that something is not right since the real self does not have a dot of rouge on it.

Figure 11.1 displays the results of two investigations that used the mirror technique. The researchers found that before infants were 1 year old, they did not recognize themselves in the mirror (Amsterdam, 1968; Lewis & Brooks-Gunn, 1979). Signs of self-recognition began to appear among some infants when they were 15 to 18 months old. By the time they were 2 years old, most children recognized themselves in the mirror. In sum, infants begin to develop a self-understanding called visual self-recognition at approximately 18 months of age (Hart & Karmel, 1996; Lewis & others, 1989).

Late in the second year and early in the third year, toddlers show other emerging forms of self-awareness that reflect a sense of "me" (Laible & Thompson, 2007). For example, they refer to themselves by saying "Me big"; they label internal experiences such as emotions; they monitor themselves, as when a toddler says, "Do it myself"; and they say that things are theirs (Bullock & Lutkenhaus, 1990; Fasig, 2000). A recent study revealed that it is not until the second year that infants develop a conscious awareness of their own bodies (Brownell & others, 2009). This developmental change in body awareness marks the beginning of children's representation of their own three-dimensional body shape and appearance, providing an early step in the development of their self-image and identity (Brownell, 2009).

Early Childhood   Because children can communicate verbally, research on self-understanding in childhood is not limited to visual self-recognition, as it is during infancy (Harter, 2012). Mainly through interviews, researchers have probed many aspects of children's self-understanding (Easterbrooks & others, 2013; Thompson, 2013b, c). Here are five main characteristics of self-understanding in young children:

- *Confusion of self, mind, and body.* Young children generally confuse self, mind, and body. Most young children conceive of the self as part of the body, which usually means the head. For them, the self can be described along many material dimensions, such as size, shape, and color.

- *Concrete descriptions.* Preschool children mainly think of themselves and define themselves in concrete terms. A young child might say, "I know my ABC's," "I can count," and "I live in a big house" (Harter, 2006). Although young children mainly describe themselves in terms of concrete, observable features and action tendencies, at about 4 to 5 years of age, as they hear others use psychological trait and emotion terms, they begin to include these in their own self-descriptions (Thompson, 2006). Thus, in a self-description, a 4-year-old might say, "I'm not scared. I'm always happy."

- *Physical descriptions.* Young children also distinguish themselves from others through many physical and material attributes. Says 4-year-old Sandra, "I'm different from Jennifer because I have brown hair and she has blond hair." Says 4-year-old Ralph, "I am different from Hank because I am taller, and I am different from my sister because I have a bicycle."

- *Active descriptions.* The *active dimension* is a central component of the self in early childhood. For example, preschool children often describe themselves in terms of activities such as play.

- *Unrealistic positive overestimations.* Self-evaluations during early childhood are often unrealistically positive and represent an overestimation of personal attributes (Harter, 2012). These unrealistic positive overestimations of the self occur because young children (1) have difficulty differentiating between their desired and actual competence, (2) cannot yet generate an ideal self that is distinguished from a real self, and (3) rarely engage in *social comparison*—exploring how they compare with others. This overestimation of one's attributes helps to protect young children against negative self-evaluations.

However, as in virtually all areas of children's development, there are individual variations in young children's self-conceptions, and there is increasing evidence that some children are vulnerable to negative self-attributions (Thompson, 2011). For example, one study revealed that insecurely attached preschool children whose mothers reported a high level of parenting stress and depressive symptoms had a lower self-concept than other young children in more positive family circumstances (Goodvin & others, 2008). This research indicates that young children's generally optimistic self-ascriptions do not buffer them from adverse, stressful family conditions.

Middle and Late Childhood   Children's self-evaluation becomes more complex during middle and late childhood. Five key changes characterize the increased complexity:

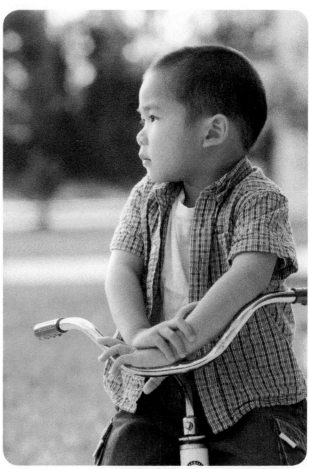

What characterizes young children's self-understanding?

- *Psychological characteristics and traits.* In middle and late childhood, especially from 8 to 11 years of age, children increasingly describe themselves with psychological characteristics and traits in contrast to the more concrete self-descriptions of younger children. Older children are more likely to describe themselves as *popular, nice, helpful, mean, smart,* and *dumb* (Harter, 2006, 2012). Older children also are less likely than younger children to overestimate their abilities or to cite only virtuous aspects of the self. Rather, they now have the cognitive capabilities to realize that they can be both *nice* and *mean, smart* as well as *dumb.*

- *Social descriptions.* In middle and late childhood, children begin to include *social aspects* such as references to social groups in their self-descriptions (Harter, 2006, 2012; Livesly & Bromley, 1973). For example, a child might describe herself as a Girl Scout, as a Catholic, or as someone who has two close friends.

- *Social comparison.* Children's self-understanding in middle and late childhood includes increasing reference to social comparison (Harter, 2006, 2012). At this point in development, children are more likely to distinguish themselves from others in comparative rather than in absolute terms. That is, elementary-school-age children are likely to think about what they can do in comparison with others. If they feel that they fall short of others, they are likely to evaluate themselves negatively.

- *Real self and ideal self.* In middle and late childhood, children begin to distinguish between their real and ideal selves (Harter, 2006, 2012). This involves differentiating their actual competencies from those they aspire to have and think are the most important. This discrepancy also can lead to negative self-evaluations.

- *Realistic.* In middle and late childhood, children's self-evaluations become more realistic (Harter, 2006, 2012). This may occur because of increased social comparison and perspective taking.

Adolescence   The development of self-understanding in adolescence is complex and involves a number of aspects of the self (Harter, 2006, 2012):

- *Abstract and idealistic.* Remember from our discussion of Piaget's theory of cognitive development in Chapter 6 that many adolescents begin to think in more *abstract* and *idealistic* ways. When asked to describe themselves, adolescents are more likely than children to use abstract and idealistic labels. Consider 14-year-old Laurie's abstract description of herself: "I am a human being. I am indecisive. I don't know who I am." Also consider her idealistic description of herself: "I am a naturally sensitive person who really cares about people's feelings. I think I'm pretty good looking." Not all adolescents describe themselves in idealistic ways, but most adolescents distinguish between the real self and the ideal self.

- *Self-consciousness.* Adolescents are more likely than children to be *self-conscious* about and *preoccupied* with their self-understanding. This self-consciousness and self-preoccupation reflect adolescent egocentrism, which we discussed in Chapter 6.

developmental **connection**

Cognitive Theory

In Piaget's fourth stage of cognitive development, thought becomes more abstract, idealistic, and logical. Chapter 6, p. 180

How does self-understanding change in adolescence?

Know thyself, for once we know ourselves, we may learn how to care for ourselves, but otherwise we never shall.

—Socrates
Greek Philosopher, 5th Century B.C.

What characterizes adolescents' possible selves?

developmental **connection**

Attention

Joint attention and gaze following help the infant to understand that other people have intentions. Chapter 10, p. 299

possible self What an individual might become, would like to become, and is afraid of becoming.

social cognition The processes involved in understanding the world around us, especially how we think and reason about other people.

• *Contradictions within the self.* As adolescents begin to differentiate their concept of the self into multiple roles in different relationship contexts, they sense potential contradictions between their differentiated selves (Harter, 2006, 2012). An adolescent might use this self-description: "I'm insensitive *and* understanding, ugly *and* attractive, bored *and* inquisitive, caring *and* uncaring, and introverted *and* fun-loving" (Harter, 1986). These contradictions characterize the self-descriptions of young adolescents more than older adolescents.

• *The fluctuating self.* The adolescent's self-understanding fluctuates across situations and across time (Harter, 2006, 2012). The adolescent's self continues to be characterized by instability until the adolescent constructs a more unified theory of self, usually not until late adolescence or emerging adulthood.

• *Real and ideal selves.* The adolescent's emerging ability to construct ideal selves in addition to actual ones can be perplexing and agonizing to the adolescent. In one view, an important aspect of the ideal or imagined self is the **possible self**—what individuals might become, what they would like to become, and what they are afraid of becoming (Markus & Kitayama, 2010, 2012). The attributes of future positive selves (getting into a good college, being admired, having a successful career) can direct future positive states. And the attributes of future negative selves (being unemployed, being lonely, not getting into a good college) can identify what is to be avoided.

• *Social comparison.* The tendency to compare themselves with others continues to increase during the adolescent years. However, when asked whether they engage in social comparison, most adolescents deny it because they are aware that it is somewhat socially undesirable to do so. That is, they think that acknowledging their social comparison motives will endanger their popularity. An individual's beliefs about how he or she is viewed by others is referred to as the *looking glass* self.

• *Self-integration.* In late adolescence and emerging adulthood, self-understanding becomes more *integrative* as the disparate parts of the self are more systematically pieced together (Harter, 2006, 2012). Older adolescents are more likely to detect inconsistencies in their earlier self-descriptions as they attempt to construct a general theory of self and an integrated sense of identity.

UNDERSTANDING OTHERS

Young children are more sophisticated at understanding not only themselves, but others, than used to be thought (Thompson, 2013b, c). The term **social cognition** refers to the processes involved in understanding the world around us, especially how we think and reason about other people. Developmental psychologists are increasingly studying how children develop this understanding of others (Mills, 2012; Rubin & others, 2013).

In Chapter 10, "Emotional Development," we described the development of social understanding in infancy. Recall that perceiving people as engaging in intentional and goal-directed behavior is an important social cognitive accomplishment, and this occurs toward the end of the first year. Social referencing, which involves "reading" emotional cues in others to help determine how to act in a particular situation, increases in the second year of life. Here we will describe further changes in social understanding that occur during the child and adolescent years.

Early Childhood Children also make advances in their understanding of others in early childhood (Mills, 2013). As you saw in Chapter 7, "Information Processing," young children's theory of mind includes understanding that other people have emotions and desires (Astington & Hughes, 2013; Wellman, 2011). And at about 4 to 5 years, children not only start describing themselves in terms of psychological traits but also begin to perceive others in terms of psychological traits. Thus, a 4-year-old might say, "My teacher is nice."

An important step in children's development is beginning to understand that people don't always give accurate reports of their beliefs (Gee & Heyman, 2007). Researchers have found that even 4-year-olds understand that people may make untrue statements to obtain what they want or to avoid trouble (Lee & others, 2002). For example, one recent study revealed that 4- and 5-year-olds were increasingly skeptical of another child's claim to be sick when the children were informed that the child was motivated to avoid having to go to camp (Gee & Heyman, 2007).

Both the extensive theory of mind research and the recent research on young children's social understanding underscore that young children are not always as egocentric as Piaget envisioned (Sokol, Snjezana, & Muller, 2010; Thompson, 2012). Piaget's concept of egocentrism has become so ingrained in people's thinking about young children that too often the current research on social awareness in infancy and early childhood has been overlooked. Research increasingly shows that young children are more socially sensitive and perceptive than previously envisioned, suggesting that parents and teachers can help them to better understand and interact in the social world by how they interact with them (Thompson 2013b, c). If young children are seeking to better understand various mental and emotional states (intentions, goals, feelings, desires) that they know underlie people's actions, then talking with them about these internal states can improve young children's understanding of them (Thompson, 2013b, c).

However, debate continues to characterize whether young children are socially sensitive or basically egocentric. Ross Thompson (2012, 2013b, c) comes down on the side of viewing young children as socially sensitive, while Susan Harter (2012) argues that there is still evidence to support the conclusion that young children are essentially egocentric.

Another important aspect of understanding others involves understanding joint commitments (Schneider & others, 2011). One study revealed that 3-year-olds, but not 2-year-olds, recognized when an adult is committed and when they themselves are committed to joint activity that involves obligation to a partner (Grafenhain & others, 2009).

Individual differences characterize young children's social understanding (Lewis & Carpendale, 2011). Some young children are better than others at understanding what people are feeling and what they desire, for example. To some degree, these individual differences are linked to conversations caregivers have with young children about other people's feelings and desires, and children's opportunities to observe others talking about people's feelings and desires. For example, a mother might say to a 3-year-old, "You should think about Raphael's feelings next time before you hit him."

To understand others, it is necessary to take their perspective. **Perspective taking** is the social cognitive process involved in assuming the perspective of others and understanding their thoughts and feelings. Executive functioning, discussed in Chapter 7, "Information Processing," is at work in perspective taking (Galinsky, 2010). Among the executive functions called on when children engage in perspective taking are cognition inhibition (controlling one's own thoughts to consider the perspective of others) and cognitive flexibility (seeing situations in different ways).

Middle and Late Childhood
In middle and late childhood, children show an increase in perspective taking. In Robert Selman's view (1980), at about 6 to 8 years of age, children begin to understand that others may have a different perspective because some people have more access to information than others do. Then, he says, in the next several years, children become aware that each individual is aware of the other's perspective and that putting oneself in another person's place is a way of judging the other person's intentions, purposes, and actions.

Perspective taking is thought to be especially important in determining whether children develop prosocial or antisocial attitudes and behavior. In terms of prosocial behavior, taking another's perspective improves children's likelihood of understanding and sympathizing with others when they are distressed or in need. A recent study revealed that in children characterized as being emotionally reactive, good perspective-taking skills were linked to being able to

developmental **connection**

Cognitive Theory

Theory of mind refers to awareness of one's own mental processes and the mental processes of others. Chapter 7, p. 221

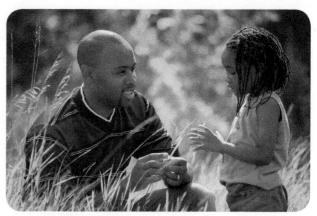

Young children are more psychologically aware of themselves and others than used to be thought. Some children are better than others at understanding people's feelings and desires—and, to some degree, these individual differences are influenced by conversations caregivers have with young children about feelings and desires.

perspective taking The social cognitive process involved in assuming the perspective of others and understanding their thoughts and feelings.

What are some changes in children's understanding of others in middle and late childhood?

regain a neutral emotional state after being emotionally aroused (Bengtsson & Arvidsson, 2011). In this study, children who made gains in perspective-taking skills reduced their emotional reactivity over a two-year period.

Earlier we indicated that even 4-year-old children show some skepticism of others' claims (Mills, Elashi, & Archacki, 2011). In middle and late childhood, children become increasingly skeptical of some sources of information about psychological traits. For example, in one study, 10- to 11-year-olds were more likely to reject other children's self-reports that they were *smart* and *honest* than were 6- to 7-year-olds (Heyman & Legare, 2005). Compared with the 6- to 7-year-olds, the more psychologically sophisticated 10- to 11-year-olds also showed a better understanding that others' self-reports are likely to focus on socially desirable tendencies.

Elementary-school-aged children also begin to understand others' motivations. For example, they understand that a desire to win a prize may tarnish someone's judgment (Mills & Keil, 2005).

Adolescence   Of course, becoming a competent adolescent involves not only understanding oneself but also understanding others. Among the aspects of understanding others that are important in adolescent development are perspective taking, perceiving others' traits, and social cognitive monitoring.

Perspective Taking   In Robert Selman's (1980) developmental theory, perspective taking begins with having an egocentric viewpoint in early childhood and ends with using in-depth perspective taking in adolescence. Only recently has research on perspective taking in adolescence taken hold. Following are the results of several recent research investigations on this topic:

- Among sixth- to eighth-graders, girls engaged in more social perspective taking than boys did (Smith, 2009; Smith & Rose, 2011), and girls also experienced more empathic distress, which involves taking on their friend's distress as their own, than did boys.

- Among ninth- to twelfth-graders, adolescents assumed a social perspective that was naïve to the disparities that exist between vulnerable and less vulnerable social groups in regard to racism and sexism (Rubenstein, 2012). In this study, twelfth-graders showed more sophisticated social justice understanding than ninth-graders did.

- A lower level of perspective taking was linked to increased relational aggression (harming someone by using strategies such as spreading vicious rumors) one year later in middle school students (Batanova & Loukas, 2011).

What are some important aspects of social understanding in adolescence?

Perceiving Others' Traits   One way to study how adolescents perceive others' traits is to ask them about the extent to which others' self-reports are accurate. In one comparison of 6- and 10-year-olds, the 10-year-olds were much more skeptical about others' self-reports of their intelligence and social skills than the 6-year-olds were (Heyman & Legare, 2005). In this study, the 10-year-olds understood that other people at times may distort the truth about their own traits to make a better impression on others.

As adolescence proceeds, teenagers develop a more sophisticated understanding of others. They come to understand that other people are complex and have public and private faces (Harter, 2006).

Social Cognitive Monitoring   In Chapter 7, you read that an important cognitive activity in metacognition is cognitive monitoring, which can also be very helpful in social situations (McCormick, Dimmitt, & Sullivan, 2013). As part of their increased awareness of themselves and others, adolescents monitor their social world more extensively than they did when they were children. Adolescents engage in a number of social cognitive monitoring activities on virtually a daily basis. An adolescent might think, "I would like to get to know this guy better, but he is not very open. Maybe I can talk to some other students about what he is like." Another adolescent might check incoming information about a club or a clique to determine whether it is consistent with her impressions of the club or clique. Yet another adolescent might question someone or paraphrase what the person has just said about her feelings to make sure that he has accurately understood them. Adolescents' ability to monitor their social cognition may be an important aspect of their social maturity (Flavell, 1979).

Review Connect Reflect

LG1 Discuss the development of self-understanding and understanding others.

Review

- What is self-understanding? How does self-understanding change from infancy through adolescence?
- How does the understanding of others develop?

Connect

- In this section, you learned that in middle and late childhood, children show an increase in perspective taking. Which disorder (discussed in Chapter 7) causes children to have difficulty understanding others' beliefs and emotions?

Reflect *Your Own Personal Journey of Life*

- If a psychologist had interviewed you at 10 and at 16 years of age, how would your self-understanding have differed?

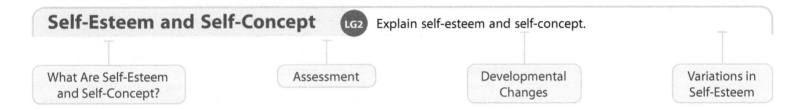

Self-Esteem and Self-Concept

LG2 Explain self-esteem and self-concept.

- What Are Self-Esteem and Self-Concept?
- Assessment
- Developmental Changes
- Variations in Self-Esteem

Self-conception involves more than self-understanding. Not only do children try to define and describe attributes of the self (self-understanding), but they also evaluate these attributes. These evaluations create self-esteem and self-concept, and they have far-reaching implications for children's development.

WHAT ARE SELF-ESTEEM AND SELF-CONCEPT?

Sometimes the terms *self-esteem* and *self-concept* are used interchangeably, or they are not precisely defined (Harter, 2006, 2012). Here we use **self-esteem** to refer to a person's self-worth or self-image, a global evaluation of the self. For example, a child might perceive that she is not merely a person but a good person. (To evaluate your self-esteem, see Figure 11.2.) We use the term **self-concept** to refer to domain-specific evaluations of the self. Children can make self-evaluations in many domains of their lives—academic, athletic, physical appearance, and so on. In sum, self-esteem refers to global self-evaluations, self-concept to more domain-specific evaluations. Having high self-esteem and a positive self-concept are important aspects of children's well-being (Baumeister, 2013; Campbell, 2012).

The foundations of self-esteem and self-concept emerge from the quality of parent-child interaction in infancy and early childhood. Thus, if children have low self-esteem in middle and late childhood, they may have experienced neglect or abuse in relationships with their

self-esteem The global evaluative dimension of the self; also called self-worth or self-image.

self-concept Domain-specific self-evaluations.

These items are from a widely used measure of self-esteem, the Rosenberg Scale of Self-Esteem. The items deal with your general feelings about yourself. Place a check mark in the column that best describes your feelings about yourself:
1 = strongly agree, 2 = agree, 3 = disagree, 4 = strongly disagree.

	1	2	3	4
1. I feel that I am a person of worth, at least on an equal plane with others.				
2. I feel that I have a number of good qualities.				
3. All in all, I am inclined to feel that I am a failure.				
4. I am able to do things as well as most other people.				
5. I feel I do not have much to be proud of.				
6. I take a positive attitude toward myself.				
7. On the whole, I am satisfied with myself.				
8. I wish I could have more respect for myself.				
9. I certainly feel useless at times.				
10. At times I think I am no good at all.				

To obtain your self-esteem score, reverse your scores for items 3, 5, 8, 9, and 10. (That is, on item 3 if you gave yourself a 1, instead give yourself a 4.) Add those scores to your scores for items 1, 2, 4, 6, and 7 for your overall self-esteem score. Scores can range from 10 to 40. If you scored below 20, consider contacting the counseling center at your college or university for help in improving your self-esteem.

FIGURE 11.2
EVALUATING SELF-ESTEEM

parents earlier in development. Children with high self-esteem are more likely to be securely attached to their parents and have parents who engage in sensitive caregiving (Thompson, 2011, 2013a, b, c, d).

For most children, high self-esteem and a positive self-concept are important aspects of their well-being (Campbell, 2012). However, for some children, self-esteem reflects perceptions that do not always match reality (Vohs & Baumeister, 2012). A child's self-esteem might reflect a belief about whether he or she is intelligent and attractive, for example, but that belief is not necessarily accurate. Thus, high self-esteem may refer to accurate, justified perceptions of one's worth as a person and one's successes and accomplishments, but it can also refer to an arrogant, grandiose, unwarranted sense of superiority over others. In the same manner, low self-esteem may reflect either an accurate perception of one's shortcomings or a distorted, even pathological insecurity and inferiority.

ASSESSMENT

Measuring self-esteem and self-concept hasn't always been easy (Dusek & McIntyre, 2003). An example of a useful measure developed to assess self-evaluations by children is Susan Harter's (1985) Self-Perception Profile for Children. It taps general self-worth plus self-concept for five specific domains: scholastic competence, athletic competence, social acceptance, physical appearance, and behavioral conduct.

The Self-Perception Profile for Children is designed to be used with third-grade through sixth-grade children. Harter also developed a separate scale for adolescents, the Self-Perception Profile for Adolescents (Harter, 1989). It assesses global self-worth and the five domains tested for children plus three additional domains—close friendship, romantic appeal, and job competence.

Harter's measures can separate self-evaluations in different domains of one's life. How are these specific self-evaluations related to self-esteem in general? Even children have both a general level of self-esteem and varying levels of self-conceptions in particular domains of their lives (Harter, 1998; Ward, 2004). For example, a child might have a moderately high level of general self-esteem but have varying self-conceptions in specific areas: high in athletic competence, high in social acceptance, high in physical appearance, high in behavioral conduct, but low in scholastic competence.

Self-esteem appears to have an especially strong tie with self-perception in one domain in particular: physical appearance. Researchers have found that among adolescents, global self-esteem is correlated more strongly with perceived physical appearance than with scholastic competence, social acceptance, behavioral conduct, or athletic competence (Harter, 1999, 2006; Maeda, 1999) (see Figure 11.3). Notice in Figure 11.3 that the link between perceived physical appearance and self-esteem has been made in many countries. This association between physical appearance and self-esteem is not confined to adolescence; it holds from early childhood through middle age (Harter, 1999, 2006).

DEVELOPMENTAL CHANGES

Researchers disagree about the extent to which self-esteem varies with age. One study found that self-esteem is high in childhood, declines in adolescence, and increases in adulthood until late adulthood, when it declines again (Robins & others, 2002) (see Figure 11.4). Some researchers argue that although there may be a decrease in self-esteem during adolescence, the drop is actually very slight and not nearly as pronounced as it is presented in the media (Harter, 2012; Hyde & Else-Quest, 2013).

Notice in Figure 11.4 that the self-esteem of males was higher than that of females through most of the life span. During adolescence, the self-esteem of girls declined more than that of boys. Another study revealed that male adolescents had higher self-esteem than did female adolescents. One explanation for this gender difference holds that the drop in self-esteem is driven by a negative body image and that girls tend to have more negative body images during pubertal change than boys do. Another explanation emphasizes the greater interest that adolescent girls take in social relationships and society's failure to reward that interest (Impett & others, 2008). But also note in Figure 11.4 that despite the drop in self-esteem among adolescent girls, their average self-esteem score (3.3) was still higher than the neutral point on the scale (3.0). How do adolescents rate different aspects of their self-images, such as their psychological self, social self, coping self, familial self, and sexual self? To find out, see *Connecting Through Research*.

Domain	Harter's U.S. samples	Other countries
Physical Appearance	.65	.62
Scholastic Competence	.48	.41
Social Acceptance	.46	.40
Behavioral Conduct	.45	.45
Athletic Competence	.33	.30

FIGURE 11.3

CORRELATIONS BETWEEN GLOBAL SELF-ESTEEM AND SELF-EVALUATIONS OF DOMAINS OF COMPETENCE. *Note:* The correlations shown are the average correlations computed across a number of studies. The other countries in this evaluation were England, Ireland, Australia, Canada, Germany, Italy, Greece, the Netherlands, and Japan. Recall from Chapter 1 that correlation coefficients can range from −1.00 to +1.00. The correlations between physical appearance and global self-esteem (.65 and .62) are moderately high.

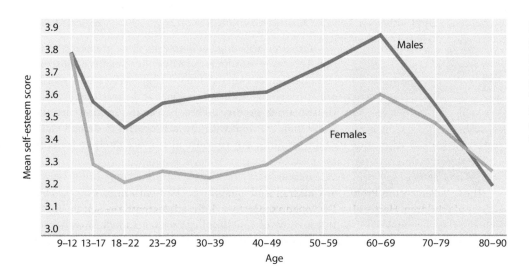

FIGURE 11.4

SELF-ESTEEM ACROSS THE LIFE SPAN. One large-scale study asked more than 300,000 individuals to rate the extent to which they have high self-esteem on a 5-point scale, with 5 being "Strongly Agree" and 1 being "Strongly Disagree." Self-esteem dropped in adolescence and late adulthood. Self-esteem of females was lower than self-esteem of males through most of the life span.

connecting through research

How Do Adolescents Rate Their Self-Images Across Five Different Areas?

One study examined the self-images of 675 adolescents (289 males and 386 females) ranging from 13 to 19 years of age in Naples, Italy (Bacchini & Magliulo, 2003). Self-image was assessed using the Offer Self-Image Questionnaire, which consists of 130 items grouped into 11 scales that define five different aspects of self-image:

- The psychological self (made up of scales that assess impulse control, emotional tone, and body image)
- The social self (consists of scales that evaluate social relationships, morals, and vocational and educational aspirations)
- The coping self (composed of scales that measure mastery of the world, psychological problems, and adjustment)
- The familial self (made up of only one scale that evaluates how adolescents feel about their parents)
- The sexual self (composed of only one scale that examines adolescents' feelings and attitudes about sexual matters)

The adolescents had positive self-images, with scores higher than a neutral score (3.5) on all 11 scales. For example, the adolescents' average body self-image score was 4.2. The aspect of their lives in which adolescents had the most positive self-image involved their educational and vocational aspirations (average score of 4.8). The lowest self-image score was for impulse control (average score of 3.9). These results support the view that adolescents have a more positive perception of themselves than is commonly believed.

Gender differences were found on a number of the self-image scales, with boys consistently having more positive self-images than did girls. Keep in mind, though, that as we indicated earlier, even though girls reported lower self-images than boys, their self-images still were mainly in the positive range.

VARIATIONS IN SELF-ESTEEM

Variations in self-esteem have been linked with many aspects of children's development. However, much of the research is *correlational* rather than *experimental*. Recall from Chapter 1 that correlation does not equal causation. Thus, if a correlational study finds an association between children's low self-esteem and low academic achievement, low academic achievement could cause the low self-esteem as much as low self-esteem might cause low academic achievement (Bowles, 1999). In fact, there are only moderate correlations between school performance and self-esteem, and these correlations do not suggest that high self-esteem produces better school performance (Baumeister & others, 2003). Efforts to increase students' self-esteem have not always led to improved school performance (Davies & Brember, 1999).

Children with high self-esteem show greater initiative, but this can produce positive or negative outcomes (Baumeister & others, 2003). High-self-esteem children are prone to both prosocial and antisocial actions (Bushman & others, 2009). For example, they are more likely than children with low self-esteem to defend victims against bullies, but they are also more likely to be bullies themselves.

Researchers have also found strong links between self-esteem and happiness (Baumeister & others, 2003). For example, the two were strongly related in an international study of 13,000 college students from 49 universities in 31 countries (Diener & Diener, 1995). It seems likely

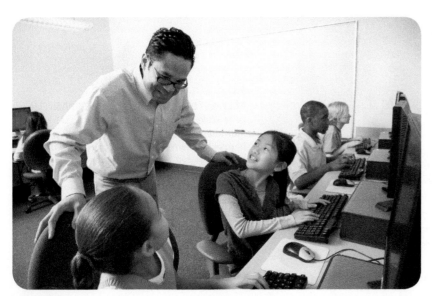

What are some issues involved in understanding children's self-esteem in school?

Increasing Children's Self-Esteem

A current concern is that too many of today's children and adolescents grow up receiving empty praise and as a consequence develop inflated self-esteem (Graham, 2005; Stipek, 2005). Too often they are given praise for performance that is mediocre or even poor. They may have difficulty handling competition and criticism. The title of a book, *Dumbing Down Our Kids: Why American Children Feel Good About Themselves But Can't Read, Write, or Add* (Sykes, 1995) vividly captures the theme that the academic problems of many U.S. children, adolescents, and college students stem from unmerited praise aimed at propping up their self-esteem. But it is possible to raise children's self-esteem by (1) identifying the domains of competence important to the child, (2) providing emotional support and social approval, (3) praising achievement, and (4) encouraging coping.

Harter (1999) argues that intervention must occur at the level of the causes of self-esteem if the individual's self-esteem

How can parents help children develop higher self-esteem?

is to improve significantly. Children have the highest self-esteem when they perform competently in domains that are important to them. Therefore, children should be encouraged to identify and to value areas in which they are competent.

Emotional support and social approval also powerfully influence children's self-esteem. Some children with low self-esteem come from conflicted families or experienced abuse or neglect—situations in which emotional support was unavailable. For some children, formal programs such as Big Brothers & Big Sisters can provide alternative sources of emotional support and social approval; for

others, support can come informally through the encouragement of a teacher, a coach, or another significant adult. Peer approval becomes increasingly important during adolescence, but adult as well as peer support continues to be an important influence on self-esteem through adolescence.

Achievement also can improve children's self-esteem. The straightforward teaching of real skills to children often results in increased achievement and enhanced self-esteem. When children know what tasks are necessary to achieve goals and have experience performing these or similar tasks, their self-esteem improves.

Self-esteem also is often increased when children face a problem and try to cope with it, rather than avoid it (Compas, 2004). If coping rather than avoidance prevails, children often face problems realistically, honestly, and nondefensively. This produces favorable self-evaluative thoughts, which lead to the self-generated approval that raises self-esteem. The converse is true of low self-esteem: unfavorable self-evaluations trigger denial, deception, and avoidance, which lead to self-generated disapproval.

Dumbing Down Our Kids *suggests that the academic problems of many U.S. children, adolescents, and college students stem from unmerited praise aimed at propping up their self-esteem. What did you learn earlier in the "Variations in Self-Esteem" section of this chapter about self-esteem and school performance?*

that high self-esteem increases happiness (Baumeister & others, 2003). Many studies have found that individuals with low self-esteem report that they feel more depressed than individuals with high self-esteem (Orth & others, 2009). Low self-esteem has also been linked to suicide attempts and to anorexia nervosa (Brockmeyer & others, 2012; Kleiman & Riskand, 2013). And one study found that low self-esteem in childhood was linked with depression in adolescence and early adulthood (Orth & others, 2008). A recent study also revealed that adolescents with low self-esteem had lower levels of life satisfaction at 30 years of age (Birkeland & others, 2012).

To explore ways that children's low self-esteem might be increased, see *Caring Connections.*

Review

- What are self-esteem and self-concept?
- What are two measures for assessing self-esteem and self-concept?
- How is self-esteem linked with age?
- What are some variations in self-esteem, and how are they linked to children's development? What role do parent-child relationships play in self-esteem?

Connect

- As discussed in the "Regulation of Emotion" section of Chapter 10, which parenting approach might help accomplish the fourth strategy for increasing children's self-esteem mentioned in the *Caring Connections* interlude on page 325?

Reflect *Your Own Personal Journey of Life*

- Review the characteristics of self-understanding in adolescence. Which of these characteristics do you associate most closely with your self-understanding as an adolescent?

Identity   LG3   Describe identity and its development.

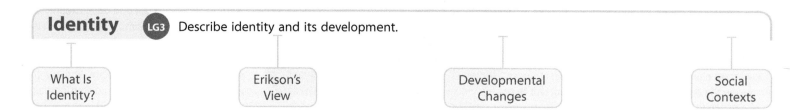

| What Is Identity? | Erikson's View | Developmental Changes | Social Contexts |

Who am I? What am I all about? What am I going to do with my life? What is different about me? How can I make it on my own? These questions reflect the search for an identity.

By far the most comprehensive and provocative theory of identity development is Erik Erikson's. In this section, you will explore his views on identity, contemporary research on how identity develops, and how social contexts influence that development.

WHAT IS IDENTITY?

Identity is who a person is, representing a synthesis and integration of self-understanding. Identity is a self-portrait composed of many pieces, including these:

- The career and work path the person wants to follow (vocational/career identity)
- Whether the person is conservative, liberal, or middle-of-the-road (political identity)
- The person's spiritual beliefs (religious identity)
- Whether the person is single, married, divorced, and so on (relationship identity)
- The extent to which the person is motivated to achieve and is intellectually oriented (achievement, intellectual identity)
- Whether the person is heterosexual, homosexual, bisexual, or transgendered (sexual identity)
- Which part of the world or country a person is from and how intensely the person identifies with his or her cultural heritage (cultural/ethnic identity)
- The kind of things a person likes to do, which can include sports, music, hobbies, and so on (interests)
- The individual's personality characteristics, such as being introverted or extraverted, anxious or calm, friendly or hostile, and so on (personality)
- The individual's body image (physical identity)

We put these pieces together to form a sense of ourselves continuing through time within a social world. Synthesizing the identity components can be a long and complex process, with many negations and affirmations of various roles and faces. Identity development takes place

"Who are you?" said the caterpillar. Alice replied rather shyly, "I—I hardly know, sir, just at present—at least I know who I was when I got up this morning, but I must have changed several times since then."

—**Lewis Carroll**
English Writer, 19th Century

identity Who a person is, representing a synthesis and integration of self-understanding.

in bits and pieces. Decisions are not made once and for all, but have to be made again and again. Identity development does not happen neatly, nor does it happen cataclysmically (Coté, 2009; Moshman, 2011).

ERIKSON'S VIEW

Questions about identity surface as common, virtually universal, concerns during adolescence. It was Erik Erikson (1950, 1968) who first understood how central such questions are to understanding adolescent development. That identity is now believed to be a key aspect of adolescent development is a result of Erikson's masterful thinking and analysis. Recall that his fifth developmental stage, which individuals experience during adolescence, is **identity versus identity confusion.** During this time, said Erikson, adolescents are faced with deciding who they are, what they are all about, and where they are going in life.

These questions about identity occur throughout life, but they become especially important for adolescents. Erikson points out that adolescents face an overwhelming number of choices. As they gradually come to realize that they will be responsible for themselves and their own lives, adolescents try to determine what those lives are going to be.

The search for an identity during adolescence is aided by a **psychosocial moratorium,** which is Erikson's term for the gap between childhood security and adult autonomy. During this period, society leaves adolescents relatively free of responsibilities and able to try out different identities. Adolescents in effect search their culture's identity files, experimenting with different roles and personalities. They may want to pursue one career one month (lawyer, for example) and another career the next month (doctor, actor, teacher, social worker, or astronaut, for example). They may dress neatly one day, sloppily the next. This experimentation is a deliberate effort on the part of adolescents to find out where they fit in the world.

Youth who successfully cope with these conflicting identities emerge with a new sense of self that is both refreshing and acceptable. Adolescents who do not successfully resolve this identity crisis suffer what Erikson calls *identity confusion.* The confusion takes one of two courses: individuals withdraw, isolating themselves from peers and family, or they immerse themselves in the world of peers and lose their identity in the crowd.

There are hundreds of roles for adolescents to try out, and probably just as many ways to pursue each role. Erikson stresses that, by late adolescence, vocational roles are central to identity development, especially in a highly technological society like the United States. Youth who have been well trained to enter a workforce that offers the potential of reasonably high self-esteem will experience the least stress during this phase of identity development.

A current concern about the development of identity in adolescence and emerging adulthood was voiced recently by William Damon (2008) in his book, *The Path to Purpose.* Damon acknowledges that successful identity development is a long-term process of extended exploration and reflection, and in some instances it can involve postponing decisions for a number of years. However, Damon feels that too many of today's youth aren't moving toward any identity resolution. In Damon's (2008, pp. 5, 7) words,

> Their delay is characterized more by indecision than by motivated reflection, more by confusion than by pursuit of clear goals, more by ambivalence than by determination. Directionless shift is not a constructive moratorium in either a developmental or a societal sense. Without a sense of direction, opportunities are lost, and doubt and self-absorption can set in. Maladaptive habits are established and adaptive ones not built. . . . What is too often missing is . . . the kind of wholehearted dedication to an activity or interest that stems from serious purpose, a purpose that can give meaning and direction to life.

In Damon's (2008, p. 47) view, too many youth are left to their own devices in dealing with some of life's biggest questions: "What is my calling? What can I contribute to the world? What am I here for?" Damon acknowledges that adults can't make youths' decisions for them, but he emphasizes that it is very important for parents, teachers, mentors, and other adults to provide guidance, feedback, and contexts that will improve the likelihood that youth will develop a positive identity. Youth need a cultural climate that inspires rather than demoralizes them and supports their chances of reaching their aspirations.

What are some important dimensions of identity?

Erik Erikson.

identity versus identity confusion Erikson's fifth developmental stage, which individuals experience during the adolescent years. At this time, adolescents examine who they are, what they are all about, and where they are going in life.

psychosocial moratorium Erikson's term for the gap between childhood security and adult autonomy that adolescents experience as part of their identity exploration.

		Has the person made a commitment?	
		Yes	**No**
Has the person explored meaningful alternatives regarding some identity question?	**Yes**	Identity Achievement	Identity Moratorium
	No	Identity Foreclosure	Identity Diffusion

FIGURE 11.5

MARCIA'S FOUR STATUSES OF IDENTITY

crisis A period of identity development during which the adolescent is choosing among meaningful alternatives.

commitment Personal investment in identity.

identity diffusion Marcia's term for the status of individuals who have not yet experienced a crisis (that is, they have not yet explored meaningful alternatives) or made any commitments.

identity foreclosure Marcia's term for the status of individuals who have made a commitment but have not experienced a crisis.

identity moratorium Marcia's term for the status of individuals who are in the midst of a crisis but whose commitments either are absent or are only vaguely defined.

identity achievement Marcia's term for the status of individuals who have undergone a crisis and made a commitment.

DEVELOPMENTAL CHANGES

Although questions about identity are particularly likely to emerge during adolescence, identity formation neither begins nor ends during these years (McLean & Syed, 2013; Schwartz & others, 2013; Syed, 2013). It begins with the appearance of attachment, the development of the sense of self, and the emergence of independence in infancy; the process reaches its final phase with a life review and integration in old age. What is important about identity development in adolescence, especially late adolescence, is that for the first time, physical development, cognitive development, and socioemotional development advance to the point at which the individual can begin to sort through and synthesize childhood identities and identifications to construct a viable path toward adult maturity.

Some decisions made during adolescence might seem trivial: whom to date, whether or not to break up, which major to study, whether to study or play, whether or not to be politically active, and so on. Over the years of adolescence, however, such decisions begin to form the core of what the individual is all about as a human being—what is called his or her identity.

A recent research review concluded that adolescents who have a mature identity show high levels of adjustment and a positive personality profile (Meeus, 2011). For example, adolescents who are highly committed in their identity development are characterized by higher levels of conscientiousness and emotional stability (Meeus, 2011).

A recent study found that as individuals matured from early adolescence to emerging adulthood, they increasingly pursued in-depth exploration of their identity (Klimstra & others, 2010). One way that researchers are examining identity changes in depth is to use a *narrative approach,* which involves asking individuals to tell their life stories and then evaluating the extent to which their stories are meaningful and integrated (McAdams, 2012; Syed, 2010, 2011, 2013). A recent study using the narrative identity approach revealed that from age 11 to 18, boys increasingly engaged in thinking about the meaningfulness of their lives, especially meaning related to the self as changing (McLean, Breen, & Fournier, 2010).

Identity Statuses How do individual adolescents go about the process of forming an identity? Eriksonian researcher James Marcia (1980, 1994) proposes that Erikson's theory of identity development contains four statuses of identity, or ways of resolving the identity crisis: identity diffusion, identity foreclosure, identity moratorium, and identity achievement. What determines an individual's identity status? Marcia classifies individuals based on the existence or extent of their crisis or commitment (see Figure 11.5). **Crisis** is defined as a period of identity development during which the individual is exploring alternatives. Most researchers use the term *exploration* rather than *crisis*. **Commitment** is personal investment in identity.

The four statuses of identity are as follows:

- **Identity diffusion** is the status of individuals who have not yet experienced a crisis or made any commitments. Not only are they undecided about occupational and ideological choices, they are also likely to show little interest in such matters.

- **Identity foreclosure** is the status of individuals who have made a commitment but not experienced a crisis. This occurs most often when parents hand down commitments to their adolescents, usually in an authoritarian way, before adolescents have had a chance to explore different approaches, ideologies, and vocations on their own.

- **Identity moratorium** is the status of individuals who are in the midst of a crisis but whose commitments are either absent or are only vaguely defined.

- **Identity achievement** is the status of individuals who have undergone a crisis and made a commitment.

To evaluate your identity in different areas of development, see Figure 11.6. Let's explore some examples of Marcia's identity statuses. Thirteen-year-old Mia has neither begun to explore her identity in any meaningful way nor made an identity commitment; she is identity diffused. Eighteen-year-old Oliver's parents want him to be a medical doctor, so he is planning on majoring in premedicine in college and has not explored other options; he is identity foreclosed. Nineteen-year-old Sasha is not quite sure what life paths she wants to follow, but she recently

Think deeply about your exploration and commitment in the areas listed here. For each area, check whether your identity status is diffused, foreclosed, moratorium, or achieved.

FIGURE **11.6**

EXPLORING YOUR IDENTITY. If you checked diffused or foreclosed for any areas, take some time to think about what you need to do to move into a moratorium identity status in those areas.

Identity Component	Identity Status			
	Diffused	Foreclosed	Moratorium	Achieved
Vocational (career)				
Political				
Religious				
Relationships				
Achievement				
Sexual				
Gender				
Ethnic/Cultural				
Interests				
Personality				
Physical				

went to the counseling center at her college to find out about different careers; she is in identity moratorium status. Twenty-one-year-old Marcelo extensively explored several career options in college, eventually getting his degree in science education, and is looking forward to his first year of teaching high school students; his status is identity achieved. These examples focused on the career dimension, but remember that identity has a number of dimensions.

In Marcia's terms, young adolescents are primarily in the identity statuses of diffusion, foreclosure, or moratorium. To move to the status of identity achievement, young adolescents need three things (Marcia, 1987, 1996): (1) they must be confident that they have parental support, (2) they must have an established sense of industry, and (3) they must be able to adopt a self-reflective stance toward the future.

The identity status approach has been sharply criticized by some researchers and theoreticians (Coté, 2009). They maintain that the identity status approach distorts and trivializes Erikson's notions of crisis and commitment. For example, Erikson's idea of commitment loses the meaning of investing oneself in certain lifelong projects and is interpreted simply as having made a firm decision or not. Others argue that the identity status approach is a valuable contribution to understanding identity (Marcia, 2002; Waterman, 1992).

Emerging Adulthood and Beyond   A consensus is developing that the key changes in identity are more likely to take place in emerging adulthood (18 to 25 years of age) or later than in adolescence (Schwartz & others, 2013; Syed, 2013). For example, Alan Waterman (1985, 1992) has found that from the years preceding high school through the last few years of college, the number of individuals who are identity achieved increases, whereas the number who are identity diffused decreases. College upperclassmen are more likely to be identity achieved than college freshmen or high school students. Many young adolescents, on the other hand, are identity diffused. These developmental changes are especially true for vocational choice. In terms of religious beliefs and political ideology, fewer college students reach the identity-achieved status; a substantial number are characterized by foreclosure and diffusion. Thus, the timing of identity development may depend on the particular dimension involved.

Why might college produce some key changes in identity? Increased complexity in the reasoning skills of college students combined with a wide range of new experiences that highlight contrasts between home and college and between themselves and others stimulates them to reach a higher level of integrating various dimensions of their identity (Phinney, 2008).

A recent meta-analysis of 124 studies revealed that identity moratorium status rose steadily to 19 years of age and then declined; identity achievement rose across late adolescence

As long as one keeps searching, the answers come.

—**JOAN BAEZ**
American Folk Singer, 20th Century

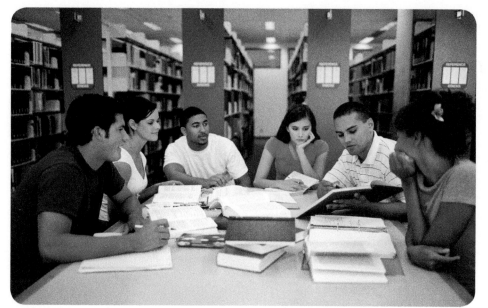

How does identity change in emerging adulthood?

and early adulthood; and foreclosure and diffusion statuses declined across the high school years but fluctuated in late adolescence and early adulthood (Kroger, Martinussen, & Marcia, 2010). A large portion of individuals were not identity achieved by early adulthood. This important finding—that significant numbers of older adolescents and emerging adults had not reached an identity achieved status—suggests that mastering identity development by the end of adolescence is more elusive for most individuals than Erikson (1968) envisioned.

A recent research review concluded that identity is more stable in adulthood than in adolescence (Meeus, 2011), but resolution of the identity issue during adolescence and emerging adulthood does not mean that identity will be stable through the remainder of life (McAdams, 2012). Many individuals who develop positive identities follow what are called "MAMA" cycles; that is, their identity status changes from *mora-torium* to *achievement* to *moratorium* to *achievement* (Marcia, 1994). These cycles may be repeated throughout life. Marcia (2002) points out that the first identity is just that—it is not, and should not be expected to be, the final product.

SOCIAL CONTEXTS

Social contexts play important roles in identity. Let's examine how family, culture, and ethnicity are linked to identity development.

Family Influences   Parents are important figures in the adolescent's development of identity (Cooper, 2011). It is during adolescence that the search for balance between the need for autonomy and the need for connectedness becomes especially important to identity. Developmentalists Catherine Cooper and Harold Grotevant (Cooper, 2011; Cooper & Grotevant, 1989; Grotevant & Cooper, 1985, 1998) have found that the presence of a family atmosphere that promotes both individuality and connectedness are important to the adolescent's identity development:

- **Individuality** consists of two dimensions: self-assertion—the ability to have and communicate a point of view, and separateness—the use of communication patterns to express how one is different from others.

- **Connectedness** also consists of two dimensions: mutuality, which involves sensitivity to and respect for others' views, and permeability, which involves openness to others' views.

In general, Cooper's research indicates that identity formation is enhanced by family relationships that are both individuated, which encourages adolescents to develop their own point of view, and connected, which provides a secure base from which to explore the widening social worlds of adolescence. When connectedness is strong and individuation weak, adolescents often have an identity-foreclosure status. When connectedness is weak, adolescents often reveal identity confusion.

Research interest also has increased regarding the role that attachment to parents might play in identity development. A meta-analysis found weak to moderate correlations between attachment to parents in adolescence and identity development (Arseth & others, 2009). In this study, though, securely attached adolescents were far more likely to be identity achieved than their counterparts who were identify diffused or identity foreclosed.

Peer/Romantic Relationships   Researchers have recently found that the capacity to explore one's identity during adolescence and emerging adulthood is linked to the quality of

---------->

developmental **connection**

Attachment

Even while adolescents seek autonomy, attachment to parents is important; secure attachment in adolescence is linked to a number of positive outcomes. Chapter 14, p. 408

individuality Consists of two dimensions: self-assertion, the ability to have and communicate a point of view; and separateness, the use of communication patterns to express how one is different from others.

connectedness Consists of two dimensions: mutuality, sensitivity to and respect for others' views; and permeability, openness to others' views.

ethnic identity An enduring aspect of the self that includes a sense of membership in an ethnic group, along with the attitudes and feelings related to that membership.

bicultural identity Identity formation that occurs when adolescents identify in some ways with their ethnic group and in other ways with the majority culture.

friendships and romantic relationships (Galliher & Kerpelman, 2012). For example, a recent study found that an open, active exploration of identity when adolescents are comfortable with close friends contributes to the positive quality of the friendship (Deamen & others, 2012). In another study, friends were often a safe context for exploring identity-related experiences, providing a means for testing how self-disclosing comments are viewed by others (McLean & Jennings, 2012).

In terms of links between identity and romantic relationships in adolescence and emerging adulthood, two individuals in a romantic relationship are both in the process of constructing their own identities and each person provides the other with a context for identity exploration (Pittman & others, 2012). The extent of their secure attachment with each other can influence how each partner constructs his or her own identity.

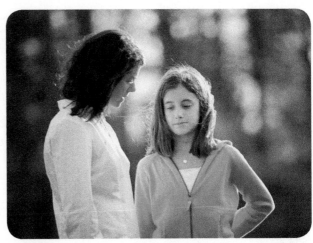

How is an adolescent's identity development influenced by parents?

Culture and Ethnicity Most research on identity development has been based on data obtained from adolescents and emerging adults in the United States and Canada, most of whom were non-Latino Whites (Schwartz & others, 2013). Many of these individuals have grown up with a cultural identity that emphasizes the individual. However, in many countries around the world, adolescents and emerging adults have grown up influenced by a collectivist emphasis on fitting in with the group and connecting with others. The collectivist emphasis is especially prevalent in East Asian countries such as China. Researchers have found that self-oriented identity exploration may not be the main process through which identity achievement is attained in East Asian countries (Schwartz & others, 2013). Rather, East Asian adolescents and emerging adults may develop their identity through identification with and imitation of others in the cultural group (Bosma & Kunnen, 2001). This emphasis on interdependence in East Asian cultures includes an expectation that adolescents and emerging adults will accept and embrace social and family roles (Berman & others, 2011). Thus, some patterns of identity development, such as the foreclosed status, may be more adaptive in East Asian countries than in North American countries (Cheng & Berman, 2013).

Seth Schwartz and his colleagues (2013) recently noted that while everyone identifies with a particular "culture," many individuals in cultural majority groups take their cultural identity for granted. Thus, many adolescents and emerging adults who are part of the cultural majority of non-Latino Whites in the United States are unlikely to spend much time thinking of themselves as "White American." However, for many adolescents and emerging adults who have grown up as members of an ethnic minority group in the United States or emigrated from another country, cultural dimensions likely are an important aspect of their identity. Researchers recently have found that at both the high school and college level, Latino students were more likely to indicate that their cultural identity was an important dimension of their overall self-concept than were non-Latino White students (Urdan, 2009, 2012).

Ethnic identity is an enduring aspect of the self that includes a sense of membership in an ethnic group, along with the attitudes and feelings related to that membership (Phinney, 2006). Throughout the world, ethnic minority groups have struggled to maintain their ethnic identities while blending in with the dominant culture (Erikson, 1968). Many adolescents develop a **bicultural identity.** That is, they identify in some ways with their ethnic group and in other ways with the majority culture (Cooper, 2011; Marks, Patton, & Garcia Coll, 2011; Phinney & Baldelomar, 2011). A study of Mexican American and Asian American college students found that they identified both with the American mainstream culture and with their culture of origin (Devos, 2006). A recent study explored bicultural identity in 14- to 21-year-olds (Marks, Patton, & Garcia Coll, 2011). Younger bicultural adolescents primarily responded to the label "White" with an inhibited response, suggesting hesitation in determining whether the label was "like me" or "not like me."

Many aspects of sociocultural contexts may influence ethnic identity (Phinney & Baldelomar, 2011; Syed & Azmitia, 2010). Ethnic identity tends to be stronger among members of minority groups than among members of mainstream groups.

One adolescent girl, 16-year-old Michelle Chin, made these comments about ethnic identity development: "My parents do not understand that teenagers need to find out who they are, which means a lot of experimenting, a lot of mood swings, a lot of emotions and awkwardness. Like any teenager, I am facing an identity crisis. I am still trying to figure out whether I am a Chinese American or an American with Asian eyes." *What are some other aspects of developing an ethnic identity in adolescence?*

Researcher Margaret Beale Spencer, shown here talking with adolescents, stresses that adolescence is often a critical juncture in the identity development of ethnic minority individuals. Most ethnic minority individuals consciously confront their ethnicity for the first time in adolescence.

What characterizes ethnic identity development in emerging adulthood?

For example, in one study, the exploration of ethnic identity was higher among ethnic minority college students than among White non-Latino college students (Phinney & Alipuria, 1990).

Time is another aspect of the sociocultural context that influences ethnic identity. The indicators of identity often differ for each succeeding generation of immigrants (Phinney, 2003; Phinney & Ong, 2007). First-generation immigrants are likely to be secure in their identities and unlikely to change much; they may or may not develop a new identity. The degree to which they begin to feel "American" appears to be related to whether or not they learn English, develop social networks beyond their ethnic group, and become culturally competent in their new country. Second-generation immigrants are more likely to think of themselves as "American," possibly because citizenship is granted at birth. Maxine Hong Kingston noted, "I have been in America all of my life; Chinese is a foreign culture to me" (Alegre & Welsch, 2003). For second-generation immigrants, ethnic identity is likely to be linked to retention of their ethnic language and social networks. In the third and later generations, the issues become more complex. Broad social factors may affect the extent to which members of this generation retain their ethnic identities. For example, media images may encourage members of an ethnic group to identify with their group or retain parts of its culture. Discrimination may force people to see themselves as cut off from the majority group and encourage them to seek support from their own ethnic culture.

Researchers also are increasingly finding that a positive ethnic identity is related to positive outcomes for ethnic minority adolescents (Neblett, Rivas-Drake, & Umaña-Taylor, 2011; Umaña Taylor & others, 2012). One study indicated that Navajo adolescents' positive ethnic heritage was linked to higher self-esteem, school connectedness, and social functioning (Jones & Galliher, 2007). Also, a study of Latino youth indicated that growth in identity exploration was linked with heightened self-esteem (Umaña-Taylor, Gonzales-Backen, & Guimond, 2009). And a recent study revealed that having a positive ethnic identity helped to buffer some of the negative effects of discrimination experienced by Mexican American adolescents (Umaña-Taylor & others, 2012).

To read about one individual who guides Latino adolescents in developing a positive identity, see the *Connecting with Careers* profile of Armando Ronquillo.

Jean Phinney (2006) described how ethnic identity may change in emerging adulthood, especially highlighting how certain experiences of ethnic minority individuals may shorten or lengthen emerging adulthood. For ethnic minority individuals who must take on family responsibilities and cannot go to college, identity formation may occur earlier. By contrast, especially for ethnic minority individuals who go to college, identity formation may take longer because of the complexity of exploring and understanding a bicultural identity. The cognitive challenges of higher education likely stimulate ethnic minority individuals to reflect on their identity and examine changes in the way they want to identify themselves. This increased reflection may focus on integrating parts of one's ethnic minority culture with elements of the mainstream non-Latino White culture. For example, some emerging adults have to come to grips with resolving a conflict between the family loyalty and interdependence emphasized in their ethnic minority culture and the values of independence and self-assertion emphasized by the mainstream non-Latino White culture (Arnett, 2006). One recent study of Mexican American and Asian American college students found that they identified both with the American mainstream culture and their culture of origin (Devos, 2006). To read further about ethnic identity development in adolescence, see *Connecting with Diversity*.

Armando Ronquillo, High School Counselor

Armando Ronquillo is a high school counselor and admissions advisor at Pueblo High School in a low-income area of Tucson, Arizona. More than 85 percent of the students have a Latino background. Ronquillo was named the top high school counselor in the state of Arizona for the year 2000.

Ronquillo especially works with Latino students to guide them in developing a positive identity. He talks with them about their Latino background and what it's like to have a bicultural identity—preserving important aspects of their Latino heritage while also pursuing the elements of success in the contemporary culture of the United States.

He believes that helping Latino youth to stay in school and getting them to think about the lifelong opportunities provided by a college education will benefit their identity development. Ronquillo also works with parents to help them understand that sending their child to college is doable and affordable.

Armando Ronquillo, counseling a Latina high school student about college.

For more information about what school counselors do, see page 43 in the Careers in Child Development appendix following Chapter 1.

The Contexts of Ethnic Identity Development

The environmental contexts of ethnic minority youth influence their identity development (Phinney & Baldelomar, 2011). In the United States, many ethnic minority youth live in low-SES urban settings where support for developing a positive identity is lacking. Many of these youth live in pockets of poverty; are exposed to drugs, gangs, and criminal activities; and interact with youth and adults who have dropped out of school or are unemployed. In such settings, support organizations and programs for youth can make an important contribution to identity development.

Individuals with a negative ethnic identity are likely to reexamine their identity as they go to college and/or enter the work world. What did you read earlier in this section of the chapter about why identity formation might take longer for ethnic minorities?

How do social contexts influence adolescents' ethnic identity?

Review

- What is identity?
- What is Erikson's view of identity?
- How do individuals develop their identity? What identity statuses can be used to classify individuals?
- How do the social contexts of family, peers/romantic relationships, culture, and ethnicity influence identity?

Connect

- Identity versus identity confusion is the fifth stage of Erikson's theory of development. What crisis should a child have resolved in the fourth stage to be able to successfully move on to confront the identity versus identity confusion crisis?

Reflect *Your Own Personal Journey of Life*

- How did your identity change as you developed through adolescence? How does your current identity differ from your identity as an adolescent? To guide your self-evaluation of your identity changes, revisit Figure 11.6 and reflect on what are likely some of the key aspects of your identity.

reach your **learning goals**

The Self and Identity

Self-Understanding and Understanding Others

 Discuss the development of self-understanding and understanding others.

Self-Understanding

- Self-understanding is a child's cognitive representation of the self—the substance and content of the child's self-conceptions. It provides the rational underpinnings for personal identity. Infants develop a rudimentary form of self-recognition as early as 3 months of age and a more complete form of self-understanding at approximately 18 months of age. Self-understanding in early childhood is characterized by confusion of self, mind, and body; concrete, physical, and active descriptions; and unrealistic positive overestimations. Self-understanding in middle and late childhood involves an increased use of psychological characteristics and traits, social descriptions, and social comparison; distinction between the real and ideal self; and increasingly realistic self-evaluations. Adolescents develop abstract and idealistic conceptions of themselves, become more self-conscious about their self-understanding, and engage in more social comparison than when they were children. Their self-understanding often fluctuates and they construct multiple selves, including possible selves.

Understanding Others

- Young children display more sophisticated self-understanding and understanding of others than was previously thought. Even 4-year-olds understand that people make statements that aren't true to obtain what they want or to avoid trouble. Children increase their perspective taking in middle and late childhood, and they become even more skeptical of others' claims. Three important aspects of understanding others in adolescence are perspective taking, perceiving others' traits, and social cognitive monitoring.

Self-Esteem and Self-Concept

 Explain self-esteem and self-concept.

What Are Self-Esteem and Self-Concept?

- Self-esteem, also referred to as self-worth or self-image, is the global, evaluative dimension of the self. Self-concept refers to domain-specific evaluations of the self.

| Assessment | | • Harter's Self-Perception Profile for Children is used with third-grade through sixth-grade children to assess general self-worth and self-concept in five skill domains. Harter's Self-Perception Profile for Adolescents assesses global self-worth in five skill domains, plus additional domains dealing with friendship, romance, and job competence. |

- Harter's Self-Perception Profile for Children is used with third-grade through sixth-grade children to assess general self-worth and self-concept in five skill domains. Harter's Self-Perception Profile for Adolescents assesses global self-worth in five skill domains, plus additional domains dealing with friendship, romance, and job competence.

Developmental Changes

- Some researchers have found that self-esteem drops in adolescence, more so for girls than boys, but there is controversy about how extensively self-esteem varies with age.

Variations in Self-Esteem

- Researchers have found only moderate correlations between self-esteem and school performance. Individuals with high self-esteem have greater initiative than those with low self-esteem, and this can produce positive or negative outcomes. Self-esteem is related to perceived physical appearance and happiness. Low self-esteem is linked with depression, suicide attempts, and anorexia nervosa.

Identity

LG3 Describe identity and its development.

What Is Identity?

- Identity development is complex and takes place in bits and pieces. At a bare minimum, identity involves commitment to a vocational direction, an ideological stance, and a sexual orientation. Synthesizing identity components can be a long, complex process.

Erikson's View

- Erikson argues that identity versus identity confusion is the fifth stage of the human life span, which individuals experience during adolescence. This stage involves entering a psychosocial moratorium between the security of childhood and the autonomy of adulthood. Personality and role experimentation are important aspects of identity development. In technological societies like those in North America, the vocational role is especially important.

Developmental Changes

- Identity development begins during infancy and continues through old age. James Marcia proposed four identity statuses—identity diffusion, foreclosure, moratorium, and achievement— that are based on crisis (exploration) and commitment. Some experts argue the main changes in identity occur in emerging adulthood rather than adolescence. Individuals often follow moratorium-achievement-moratorium-achievement (MAMA) cycles in their lives.

Social Contexts

- Parents are important figures in adolescents' identity development. Both individuality and connectedness in family relations are related to identity development. Peer and romantic relationships also provide social contexts that influence adolescents' identity development. Throughout the world, ethnic minority groups have struggled to maintain their identities while blending into the majority culture. A positive ethnic identity is linked to positive outcomes for ethnic minority adolescents.

key terms

self 315
self-understanding 315
possible self 318
social cognition 318
perspective taking 319
self-esteem 321

self-concept 321
identity 326
identity versus identity
    confusion 327
psychosocial moratorium 327
crisis 328

commitment 328
identity diffusion 328
identity foreclosure 328
identity moratorium 328
identity achievement 328
individuality 330

connectedness 330
ethnic identity 330
bicultural identity 330

key people

Susan Harter 319
Ross Thompson 319
Robert Selman 319

Erik Erikson 327
William Damon 327
James Marcia 328

Alan Waterman 329
Catherine Cooper 330
Harold Grotevant 330

Seth Schwartz 331
Jean Phinney 332

GENDER

chapter outline

Gender and emotion researcher Stephanie Shields (1998) analyzed how the movie *Jerry Maguire* reflects the role of gender in emotions and relationships. In brief, the movie is a "buddy" picture in which sports agent Jerry Maguire (played by Tom Cruise) is paired with two buddies: the too-short Arizona Cardinals wide receiver Rod Tidwell (played by Cuba Gooding, Jr.) and 6-year-old Ray, son of Jerry's love interest, accountant Dorothy Boyd (played by Renee Zellweger). Through his buddies, the thinking-but-not-feeling Jerry discovers the right path by connecting to Ray's emotional honesty and Rod's devotion to his family.

Images of nurturing and nurtured males are woven throughout the movie. In discovering a caring relationship with Ray, Jerry makes his first genuine move toward emotional maturity. The boy is the guide to the man. Chad, Ray's babysitter, provides another good example of appropriate caring by a male.

Males are shown crying in the movie. Jerry sheds tears while writing his mission statement, thinking about Dorothy's possible move to another city (which also means he would lose Ray), and witnessing the success of his lone client (Rod). Rod is brought to tears when he speaks of his family. Historically, weeping, more than any other form of emotional expression, has been associated with feminine emotion. However, it has increasingly taken on a more prominent role in the male's emotional makeup.

How are gender, emotion, and caring portrayed in the movie Jerry Maguire?

The movie *Jerry Maguire* reflects changes in gender roles as an increasing number of males show an interest in improving their social relationships and achieving emotional maturity. However, as we will see later in this chapter, experts on gender argue that females are more competent in their social relationships than males, and that large numbers of males still have considerable room for improvement in dealing with their emotions.

preview

We begin this chapter by examining what gender involves, then turn our attention to various influences on gender development—biological, social, and cognitive. Next, we explore gender stereotypes, similarities, and differences. Our final discussion focuses on how gender roles are classified.

What Is Gender? **LG1** Summarize what gender involves.

> To be meek, patient, tactful, modest, honorable, brave, is not to be either manly or womanly; it is to be humane.
>
> —JANE HARRISON
> *English Writer, 20th Century*

At what age do children know whether they are male or female?

Gender refers to the characteristics of people as males and females. **Gender identity** involves a sense of one's own gender, including knowledge, understanding, and acceptance of being male or female (Leaper, 2013; Perry, 2013). **Gender roles** are sets of expectations that prescribe how females or males should think, act, and feel. During the preschool years, most children increasingly act in ways that match their culture's gender roles. **Gender typing** refers to acquisition of a traditional masculine or feminine role. For example, fighting is more characteristic of a traditional masculine role and crying is more characteristic of a traditional feminine role.

One aspect of gender identity involves knowing whether you are a boy or a girl (Perry, 2013). Until recently, it was thought that this aspect of gender identity emerged at about 2½ years. However, a recent longitudinal study that explored the acquisition of gender labels in infancy and their implications for gender-typed play revealed that gender identity likely emerges before 2 years of age (Zosuls & others, 2009). In this study, infants began using gender labels on average at 19 months of age, with girls beginning to use gender labels earlier than boys. This gender difference became present at 17 months of age and increased at 21 months of age. Use of gender labels was linked to gender-typed play, indicating that knowledge of gender categories may affect gender typing earlier than 2 years of age.

One study revealed that sex-typed behavior (boys playing with cars and girls with jewelry, for example) increased during the preschool years and that children who engaged in the most sex-typed behavior during the preschool years were still doing so at 8 years of age (Golombok & others, 2008).

Review Connect Reflect

LG1 Summarize what gender involves.

Review

- What is gender? What are some components of gender?

Connect

- In Chapter 1, what did you learn about gender and research that you should keep in mind as you read more about research in the area of gender and development in the following sections of this chapter?

Reflect Your Own Personal Journey of Life

- As you begin this chapter, think about the role of gender in your life as you were growing up. What are some examples of how your behavior as a child reflected a masculine or feminine role?

Influences on Gender Development

 LG2 Discuss the main biological, social, and cognitive influences on gender.

| Biological Influences | Social Influences | Cognitive Influences |

How is gender influenced by biology? By children's social experiences? By cognitive factors?

BIOLOGICAL INFLUENCES

It was not until the 1920s that researchers confirmed the existence of human sex chromosomes, the genetic material that determines our sex. Humans normally have 46 chromosomes, arranged in pairs. A 23rd pair with two X-shaped chromosomes produces a female. A 23rd pair with an X chromosome and a Y chromosome produces a male.

Hormones In Chapter 4, we discussed the two classes of hormones that have the most influence on gender: estrogens and androgens. Estrogens and androgens occur in both females and males, but in very different concentrations.

Estrogens primarily influence the development of female physical sex characteristics and help regulate the menstrual cycle. Estrogens are a general class of hormones. An example of an important estrogen is estradiol. In females, estrogens are produced mainly by the ovaries.

Androgens primarily promote the development of male genitals and secondary sex characteristics. One important androgen is testosterone. Androgens are produced by the adrenal glands in males and females, and by the testes in males.

In the first few weeks of gestation, female and male embryos look alike. Male sex organs start to differ from female sex organs when a gene on the Y chromosome directs a small piece of tissue in the embryo to turn into testes. Once the tissue has turned into testes, they begin to secrete testosterone. Because females have no Y chromosome, the tissue turns into ovaries. To explore biological influences on gender, researchers have studied individuals who are exposed to unusual levels of sex hormones early in development (Hines, 2013). Here are four examples of problems that may occur as a result (Lippa, 2005, pp. 122–124, 136–137):

- *Congenital adrenal hyperplasia (CAH).* Some girls have this condition, which is caused by a genetic defect. Their adrenal glands enlarge, resulting in abnormally high levels of androgens. Although CAH girls are XX females, they vary in how much their genitals look like male or female genitals. Their genitals may be surgically altered to look more like those of a typical female. Although CAH girls usually grow up to think of themselves as girls and women, they are less content with being a female and show a stronger interest in being a male than non-CAH girls do (Berenbaum & Bailey, 2003; Ehrhardt & Baker, 1974; Hall & others, 2004). They like sports and enjoy playing with boys and boys' toys. CAH girls usually don't like typical girl activities such as playing with dolls and wearing makeup.
- *Androgen-insensitive males.* Because of a genetic error, a small number of XY males don't have androgen cells in their bodies. Their bodies look female, they develop a female gender identity, and they usually are sexually attracted to males.
- *Pelvic field defect.* A small number of newborns have a disorder called pelvic field defect, which in boys involves a missing penis. These XY boys have normal amounts of testosterone prenatally but usually have been castrated just after being born and raised as females. One study revealed that despite the efforts by parents to rear them as girls, most of the XY children insisted that they were boys (Reiner & Gearhart, 2004). Apparently, normal exposure to androgens prenatally had a stronger influence on their gender identity than being castrated and raised as girls.

developmental **connection**

Biological Processes

Hormones are powerful chemical substances secreted by the endocrine glands and carried through the body by the bloodstream. Chapter 4, p. 107

gender The characteristics of people as males and females.

gender identity The sense of being male or female, which most children acquire by the time they are 3 years old.

gender role A set of expectations that prescribes how females or males should think, act, and feel.

gender typing Acquisition of a traditional masculine or feminine role.

estrogens Hormones, the most important of which is estradiol, that influence the development of female physical sex characteristics and help regulate the menstrual cycle.

androgens Hormones, the most important of which is testosterone, that promote the development of male genitals and secondary sex characteristics.

developmental **connection**

Theories

Evolutionary psychology emphasizes the importance of adaptation, reproduction, and "survival of the fittest" in shaping behavior. Chapter 2, p. 50

"How is it gendered?"
© Edward Koren/The New Yorker Collection/
www.cartoonbank.com

social role theory A theory stating that gender differences result from the contrasting roles of women and men—social hierarchy and division of labor strongly influence gender differences in power, assertiveness, and nurture.

psychoanalytic theory of gender A theory that stems from Freud's view that preschool children develop erotic feelings toward the opposite-sex parent. Eventually these feelings cause anxiety, so that at 5 or 6 years of age, children renounce these feelings and identify with the same-sex parent, unconsciously adopting the same-sex parent's characteristics.

social cognitive theory of gender This theory emphasizes that children's gender development occurs through observation and imitation of gender behavior, and through rewards and punishments they experience for gender-appropriate and gender-inappropriate behavior.

- In an unusual and ultimately tragic case, one of two identical twin boys lost his penis during a botched circumcision. The twin who lost his penis, Bruce Reimer, was castrated, given female hormones, renamed "Brenda," and raised as a girl. Initially John Money (1975), the psychologist who handled the Reimer case, reported that the sex reassignment had produced positive outcomes, but later it became clear that "Brenda" had not adjusted well to life as a girl and was bullied and ostracized by classmates (Diamond & Sigmundson, 1997). As an adolescent, "Brenda" was told about the sex reassignment and decided to live as a male and take the name David. He underwent hormonal and surgical treatment, got married, and adopted his wife's children (Colapinto, 2000). In 2004, when David was 38 years old and his marriage was disintegrating, he committed suicide.

Although sex hormones alone do not determine behavior, researchers have found links between sex hormone levels and certain behaviors (Hines, 2013). The most established effects of testosterone on humans involve aggressive behavior and sexual behavior (Hyde & Else-Quest, 2013). Levels of testosterone are correlated with sexual behavior in boys during puberty (Udry & others, 1985). And a recent study revealed that higher fetal testosterone levels measured from amniotic fluid were linked to increased male-typical play, such as increased aggression, in 6- to 10-year-old boys and girls (Auyeung & others, 2009).

The Evolutionary Psychology View   In Chapter 2 we described the approach of evolutionary psychology, which emphasizes that adaptation during the evolution of humans produced psychological differences between males and females (Buss, 1995, 2008, 2012). Evolutionary psychologists argue that primarily because of their differing roles in reproduction, males and females faced different pressures in primeval environments when the human species was evolving. In particular, because having multiple sexual liaisons improves the likelihood that males will pass on their genes, natural selection favored males who adopted short-term mating strategies. These males competed with other males to acquire more resources in order to access females. Therefore, say evolutionary psychologists, males evolved dispositions that favor violence, competition, and risk taking.

In contrast, according to evolutionary psychologists, females' contributions to the gene pool were enhanced by securing resources for their offspring, which was promoted by obtaining long-term mates who could support a family. As a consequence, natural selection favored females who devoted effort to parenting and chose mates who could provide their offspring with resources and protection. Females developed preferences for successful, ambitious men who could provide these resources (Buss, 2012).

Critics of evolutionary psychology argue that its hypotheses are backed by speculations about prehistory, not evidence, and that in any event people are not locked into behavior that was adaptive in the evolutionary past. Critics also claim that the evolutionary view pays little attention to cultural and individual variations in gender differences (Brannon, 2012; Hyde & Else-Quest, 2013; Matlin, 2012).

SOCIAL INFLUENCES

Many social scientists do not locate the cause of psychological gender differences in biological dispositions. Rather, they argue that these differences are due to social experiences. Three theories that reflect this view have been influential—social role theory, psychoanalytic theory, and social cognitive theory.

Alice Eagly (2001, 2010, 2012) proposed **social role theory,** which states that gender differences result from the contrasting roles of women and men. In most cultures around the world, women have less power and status than men do and they control fewer resources (UNICEF, 2011). Compared with men, women perform more domestic work, spend fewer hours in paid employment, receive lower pay, and are more thinly represented in the highest levels of organizations. In Eagly's view, as women adapted to roles with less power and less status in society, they showed more cooperative, less dominant profiles than men. Thus, the social hierarchy and division of labor are important causes of gender differences in power, assertiveness, and nurture (Eagly, 2010).

Theory	Processes	Outcome
Psychoanalytic theory	Sexual attraction to opposite-sex parent at 3 to 5 years of age; anxiety about sexual attraction and subsequent identification with same-sex parent at 5 to 6 years of age	Gender behavior similar to that of same-sex parent
Social cognitive theory	Rewards and punishments of gender-appropriate and-inappropriate behavior by adults and peers; observation and imitation of models' masculine and feminine behavior	Gender behavior

FIGURE **12.1**
PARENTS INFLUENCE THEIR CHILDREN'S GENDER DEVELOPMENT BY ACTION AND EXAMPLE

The **psychoanalytic theory of gender** stems from Sigmund Freud's view that the preschool child develops erotic feelings toward the opposite-sex parent. Eventually, these feelings arouse anxiety, so that at 5 or 6 years of age, the child renounces these feelings and identifies with the same-sex parent, unconsciously adopting the same-sex parent's characteristics. However, developmentalists do not believe gender development proceeds as Freud proposed (Callan, 2001).

The social cognitive approach discussed in Chapter 1 provides an alternative explanation of how children develop gender-typed behavior (see Figure 12.1). According to the **social cognitive theory of gender,** children's gender development occurs through observation and imitation, and through the rewards and punishments children experience for gender-appropriate and gender-inappropriate behavior (Bussey & Bandura, 1999). Social cognitive theory emphasizes the importance of social contexts—such as parenting, peer relationships, schools, and the media—in gender development.

Parental Influences   Parents, by action and example, influence their children's and adolescents' gender development (Hilliard & Liben, 2012). As soon as the label *girl* or *boy* is assigned, virtually everyone, from parents to siblings to strangers, begins treating the infant in gender-specific ways (see Figure 12.2). Parents often use rewards and punishments to teach their daughters to be feminine ("Karen, you are such a good mommy with your dolls") and their sons to be masculine ("C'mon now, Keith, big boys don't cry").

developmental **connection**

Social Cognitive Theory

Social cognitive theory holds that behavior, environment, and person/cognitive factors are the key aspects of development. Chapter 1, p. 25

Mothers and fathers often interact differently with their children and adolescents. Mothers are more involved with their children and adolescents than are fathers, although fathers increase the time they spend in parenting when they have sons and are less likely to become divorced when they have sons (Galambos, Berenbaum, & McHale, 2009). Mothers' interactions with their children and adolescents often center on caregiving and teaching activities, while fathers' interactions often involve leisure activities (Galambos, Berenbaum, & McHale, 2009).

Mothers and fathers often interact differently with sons and daughters, and these gendered interactions that begin in infancy usually continue through childhood and adolescence. In reviewing research on this topic, Phyllis Bronstein (2006) recently provided these conclusions:

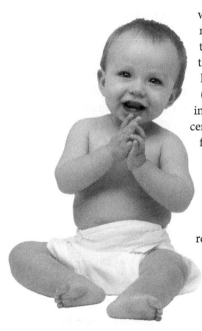

FIGURE **12.2**

EXPECTATIONS FOR BOYS AND GIRLS.
First imagine that this is a photograph of a baby girl. *What expectations would you have for her?* Then imagine that this is a photograph of a baby boy. *What expectations would you have for him?*

- *Mothers' socialization strategies.* In many cultures mothers socialize their daughters to be more obedient and responsible than their sons. They also place more restrictions on daughters' autonomy.
- *Fathers' socialization strategies.* Fathers show more attention to sons than daughters, engage in more activities with sons, and put forth more effort to promote sons' intellectual development.

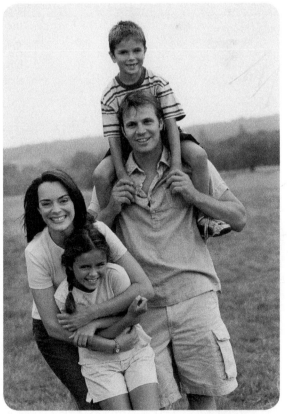

How do mothers and fathers interact differently with their children and adolescents?

What are some developmental changes that characterize the gender makeup of children's peer relations?

Thus, according to Bronstein (2006, pp. 269–270), "Despite an increased awareness in the United States and other Western cultures of the detrimental effects of gender stereotyping, many parents continue to foster behaviors and perceptions that are consonant with traditional gender role norms."

Peers   As children get older, peers become increasingly important. Peers extensively reward and punish gender behavior (Leaper, 2013; Leaper & Bigler, 2011). For example, when children play in ways that the culture says are sex-appropriate, they tend to be rewarded by their peers. Those who engage in activities that are considered sex-inappropriate tend to be criticized or abandoned by their peers. It is generally more accepted for girls to act more like boys than it is for boys to act more like girls; thus, use of the term *tomboy* to describe masculine girls is often thought of as less derogatory than the term *sissy* to describe feminine boys (Pasterski, Golombok, & Hines, 2011).

Children show a clear preference for being with and liking same-sex peers, and this tendency usually becomes stronger during the middle and late childhood years (Maccoby, 2002) (see Figure 12.3). What kind of socialization takes place in these same-sex play groups? In one study, researchers observed preschoolers over a period of six months (Martin & Fabes, 2001). The more time boys spent interacting with other boys, the more their activity level, rough-and-tumble play, and sex-typed choice of toys and games increased, and the less time boys spent near adults. By contrast, the more time preschool girls spent interacting with other girls, the more their activity level and aggression decreased, and the more their girl-type play activities and time spent near adults increased. After watching elementary school children repeatedly play in same-sex groups, two researchers characterized the playground as "gender school" (Luria & Herzog, 1985).

In adolescence, peer approval or disapproval is a powerful influence on gender attitudes and behavior (Mrug & McCay, 2013). Peer groups in adolescence are more likely to be a mix of boys and girls than they were in childhood. However, a recent study of 15- to 17-year-olds indicated that gender segregation characterizes some aspects of adolescents' social life (Mehta & Strough, 2010). In this study, 72 percent of peers said they were most likely to "hang out" with the same gender of adolescents as themselves.

Schools and Teachers   Some observers have expressed concerns that schools and teachers have biases against both boys and girls (Mullola & others, 2012). What evidence might indicate that the classroom is biased against boys? Here are some factors to consider (DeZolt & Hull, 2001):

- Compliance, following rules, and being neat and orderly are valued and reinforced in many classrooms. These are behaviors that usually characterize girls more than boys.

- A large majority of teachers are female, especially in the elementary school. This trend may make it more difficult for boys than for girls to identify with their teachers and model their teachers' behavior. A recent study revealed that male teachers perceived boys more positively and saw them as being more educationally competent than did female teachers (Mullola & others, 2012).

- Boys are more likely than girls to have a learning disability or ADHD and to drop out of school.

- Boys are more likely than girls to be criticized.

- School personnel tend to ignore the fact that many boys are clearly having academic problems, especially in the language arts.

- School personnel tend to stereotype boys' behavior as problematic.

What evidence suggests that the classroom is biased against girls? Consider the following (Sadker & Sadker, 2005):

- In a typical classroom, girls are more compliant, boys more rambunctious. Boys demand more attention, girls are more likely to quietly wait their turn. Teachers are more likely to scold and reprimand boys, as well as send boys to school authorities for disciplinary action. Educators worry that girls' tendency to be compliant and quiet comes at a cost: diminished assertiveness.

FIGURE **12.3**

DEVELOPMENTAL CHANGES IN PERCENTAGE OF TIME SPENT IN SAME-SEX AND MIXED-GROUP SETTINGS. Observations of children show that they are more likely to play in same-sex than mixed-sex groups. This tendency increases between 4 and 6 years of age.

- In many classrooms, teachers spend more time watching and interacting with boys, whereas girls work and play quietly on their own. Most teachers don't intentionally favor boys by spending more time with them, yet somehow the classroom frequently ends up with this type of gendered profile.
- Boys get more instruction than girls and more help when they have trouble with a question. Teachers often give boys more time to answer a question, provide more hints regarding the correct answer, and allow further tries if they give the wrong answer.
- Boys are more likely than girls to get lower grades and to be grade repeaters, yet girls are less likely to believe that they will be successful in college work.
- Girls and boys enter first grade with roughly equal levels of self-esteem. Yet by the middle school years, girls' self-esteem is lower than boys'.
- When elementary school children are asked to list what they want to do when they grow up, boys describe more career options than girls do.

Thus, there is evidence of gender bias against both males and females in schools. Many school personnel are not aware of their gender-biased attitudes. These attitudes are deeply entrenched in and supported by the general culture. Increasing awareness of gender bias in schools is clearly an important strategy for reducing such bias.

Might single-sex education be better for children than coed schooling? An argument in favor of single-sex education is that it eliminates distraction from the other sex and reduces sexual harassment. Single-sex public education has increased dramatically in recent years. In 2002, only 12 public schools provided same-sex education; in the 2011–2012 school year, 116 public schools were single-sex and an additional 390 provided some single-sex experiences (NASSPE, 2012).

The increase in single-sex education has especially been fueled by its inclusion in sections of the No Child Left Behind legislation that emphasize improving the educational experiences and academic achievement of low-income students of color. It appears that many of the public schools offering single-sex education have a high percentage of such youth (Klein, 2011). Two recent research reviews concluded that there have been no documented benefits of single-sex education for low-income students of color (Goodkind, 2013; Halpern & others, 2011). In one review, titled "The Pseudoscience of Single-Sex Schooling," Diane Halpern and her colleagues (2011) concluded that same-sex education is highly misguided, misconstrued, and unsupported by any valid scientific evidence. They emphasize that among the many arguments against same-sex education, the strongest is its reduction of opportunities for boys and girls to work together in a supervised, purposeful environment.

What are some changes in single-sex education in the United States? What does research say about whether same-sex education is beneficial?

There has been a special call for same-sex public education for one group of adolescents—African American boys—because of their historically poor academic achievement and high dropout rate from school (Mitchell & Stewart, 2013). In 2010, the Urban Prep Academy for Young Men became the first all-male, all African American public charter school. One hundred percent of its first graduating class enrolled in college, despite the school's location in a section of Chicago where poverty, gangs, and crime predominate. Because so few public schools are limited to African American boys, it is too early to tell whether this type of single-sex education can be effective across a wide range of participants.

Media Influences   The messages about gender roles carried by the mass media also are important influences on children's and adolescents' gender development (Adams, 2012; Silverman, 2012). Men are portrayed as more powerful than women on many TV shows. A recent study of MTV videos indicated that the scenarios depicted in the videos reinforced stereotypical notions of women as sexual objects and females as subordinate to males (Wallis, 2011). The media influence adolescents' body images, and some studies reveal gender differences in this area (Frechette, 2012; Hyde & Else-Quest, 2013; Pecot-Hebert, 2012). For example, one study of 10- to 17-year-olds found that girls were more likely than boys to perceive that the media influences their body images (Polce-Lynch & others, 2001). Another study revealed that the more time that adolescent girls and boys spent watching entertainment television, the more negative their body images were (Anderson & others, 2001). Adolescent boys are exposed to a highly muscular body ideal for males in media outlets, especially in advertisements that include professional athletes and in video games (Near, 2013).

connecting through research

How Do Young Children Use Gender Schemas to Make Judgments About Occupations?

In one study, researchers interviewed children 3 to 7 years old about 10 traditionally masculine occupations (airplane pilot, car mechanic) and feminine occupations (clothes designer, secretary), using questions such as the following (Levy, Sadovsky, & Troseth, 2000):

- *Example of a traditionally masculine occupation item:* An airplane pilot is a person who "flies airplanes for people." Who do you think would do the best job as an airplane pilot, a man or a woman?

- *Example of a traditionally feminine occupation item:* A clothes designer is a person "who draws up and makes clothes for people." Who do you think would do the best job as a clothes designer, a man or a woman?

As indicated in Figure 12.4, the children had well-developed gender schemas, in this case reflected in stereotypes of occupations. They "viewed men as more competent than women in masculine occupations, and rated women as more competent than men in feminine occupations" (p. 993). Also, "girls' ratings of women's competence at feminine occupations were substantially higher than their ratings of men's competence at masculine occupations. Conversely, boys' ratings of men's competence at masculine occupations were considerably greater than their ratings of women's competence at feminine occupations" (p. 1002). These findings demonstrate that most children as young as 3 to 4 years of age tend to have strong gender schemas regarding the perceived competencies of men and women in gender-typed occupations.

The researchers also asked the children to select from a list of emotions how they would feel if they grew up to have each of the 10 occupations. Girls said they would be happy with the feminine occupations and angry or

	Boy	Girl
"Masculine Occupations"		
Percentage who judged men more competent	87	70
Percentage who judged women more competent	13	30
"Feminine Occupations"		
Percentage who judged men more competent	35	8
Percentage who judged women more competent	64	92

FIGURE **12.4**

CHILDREN'S JUDGMENTS ABOUT THE COMPETENCE OF MEN AND WOMEN IN GENDER-STEREOTYPED OCCUPATIONS

disgusted with the masculine occupations. As expected, boys said they would be happy if they grew up to have the masculine occupations but angry and disgusted with the feminine occupations. However, the boys' emotions were more intense (more angry and disgusted) in desiring to avoid the feminine occupations than girls in wanting to avoid the masculine occupations. This finding supports other research that indicates gender roles tend to constrict boys more than girls (Hyde, 2007; Matlin, 2012).

Children in this study were at the height of gender stereotyping. Most older children, adolescents, and adults become more flexible about occupational roles (Leaper & Bigler, 2011). What does our understanding of this flexibility suggest about the role of education in reducing gender-based stereotypes?

COGNITIVE INFLUENCES

Observation, imitation, rewards, and punishment—these are the mechanisms by which gender develops, according to social cognitive theory. Interactions between the child and the social environment are the main keys to gender development in this view. Some critics argue that this explanation pays too little attention to the child's own mind and understanding by depicting the child as passively acquiring gender roles (Martin, Ruble, & Szkrybalo, 2002).

One influential cognitive theory is **gender schema theory,** which states that gender typing emerges as children gradually develop gender schemas of what is gender-appropriate and gender-inappropriate in their culture (Martin & Ruble, 2010; Miller & others, 2013). A *schema* is a cognitive structure, a network of associations that guide an individual's perceptions. A *gender schema* organizes the world in terms of female and male. Children are internally motivated to perceive the world and to act in accordance with their developing schemas. Bit by bit, children pick up what is gender-appropriate and gender-inappropriate in their culture, and develop gender schemas that shape how they perceive the world and what they remember (Conry-Murray, Kim, & Turiel, 2012). Children are motivated to act in ways that conform with these gender schemas. Thus, gender schemas fuel gender typing.

How do young children use gender schemas to make judgments about occupations? To find out, see the *Connecting Through Research* interlude.

gender schema theory According to this theory, gender typing emerges as children gradually develop schemas of what is gender-appropriate and gender-inappropriate in their culture.

In sum, cognitive factors contribute to the way children think and act as males and females. Through biological, social, and cognitive processes, children develop their gender attitudes and behaviors (Leaper, 2013).

Review Connect Reflect

LG2 Discuss the main biological, social, and cognitive influences on gender.

Review

- What are some ways that biology may influence gender?
- What are three social theories of gender, and how might social contexts influence gender development?
- What are two cognitive views of gender?

Connect

- In this section, you learned that in most cultures around the world, women have less power and status than men do and

they control fewer resources. How might this be related to what you read about gender and education in the *Connecting with Diversity* interlude in Chapter 1?

Reflect *Your Own Personal Journey of Life*

- How do you think your parents influenced your gender development? How do you think your peers influenced your gender development?

Gender Stereotypes, Similarities, and Differences

LG3 Describe gender stereotypes, similarities, and differences.

Gender Stereotyping

Gender Similarities and Differences

How pervasive is gender stereotyping? What are the real differences between boys and girls?

GENDER STEREOTYPING

Gender stereotypes are general impressions and beliefs about females and males. For example, men are powerful; women are weak. Men make good mechanics; women make good nurses. Men are good with numbers; women are good with words. Women are emotional; men are not. All of these are stereotypes. They are generalizations about a group that reflect widely held beliefs (Matlin, 2012). Researchers have found that boys' gender stereotypes are more rigid than girls' (Blakemore, Berenbaum, & Liben, 2009).

Traditional Masculinity and Femininity A classic study in the early 1970s assessed which traits and behaviors college students believed were characteristic of females and which they believed were characteristic of males (Broverman & others, 1972). The traits associated with males were labeled *instrumental:* They included characteristics such as being independent, aggressive, and power oriented. The traits associated with females were labeled *expressive:* They included characteristics such as being warm and sensitive.

Thus, the instrumental traits associated with males suited them for the traditional masculine role of going out into the world as the breadwinner. The expressive traits associated with females paralleled the traditional feminine role of being the sensitive, nurturing caregiver in the home. These roles and traits, however, are not just different; they also are unequal in terms of social status and power. The traditional feminine characteristics are childlike, suitable for someone who is dependent upon and subordinate to others. The traditional masculine characteristics equip a person to deal competently with the wider world and to wield authority.

Stereotyping and Culture How widespread is gender stereotyping? In a far-ranging study of college students in 30 countries, stereotyping of females and males was pervasive

If you are going to generalize about women, you will find yourself up to here in exceptions.

—DOLORES HITCHENS
American Mystery Writer, 20th Century

gender stereotypes Broad categories that reflect impressions and widely held beliefs about what behavior is appropriate for females and males.

(Williams & Best, 1982). Males were widely believed to be dominant, independent, aggressive, achievement oriented, and enduring. Females were widely believed to be nurturant, affiliative, less esteemed, and more helpful in times of distress.

Of course, in the decades since this study was conducted, traditional gender stereotypes and gender roles have been challenged in many societies, and social inequalities between men and women have diminished. Do gender stereotypes change when the relationship between men and women changes? In a subsequent study, women and men who lived in relatively wealthy, industrialized countries perceived themselves as more similar than did women and men who lived in less-developed countries (Williams & Best, 1989). In the more-developed countries, the women were more likely to attend college and to be gainfully employed. Thus, as sexual equality increases, gender stereotypes may diminish.

However, recent research continues to find that gender stereotyping is pervasive (Leaper, 2013). For example, one study found extensive differences in the stereotyping of females' and males' emotions (Durik & others, 2006). Females were stereotyped as expressing more fear, guilt, love, sadness, shame, surprise, and sympathy than their male counterparts. Males were stereotyped as expressing more anger and pride than their female counterparts. Researchers also have found that boys' gender stereotypes are more rigid than girls' (Blakemore, Berenbaum, & Liben, 2009).

Developmental Changes in Gender Stereotyping

Earlier we described how young children stereotype occupations as being "masculine" or "feminine." When do children begin to engage in gender stereotyping? One study examined the extent to which children and their mothers engage in gender stereotyping (Gelman, Taylor, & Nguyen, 2004). The researchers videotaped mothers and their 2-, 4-, and 6-year-old sons and daughters as they discussed a picture book with stereotyped (a boy playing football, for example) and nonstereotyped (a female race car driver, for example) gender activities. Children engaged in more gender stereotyping than did their mothers. However, mothers expressed gender concepts to their children by referencing categories of gender ("Why do you think only *men* can be firefighters?" for example), labeling gender ("That looks like a daddy," for example), and contrasting males and females ("Is that a girl job or a boy job?" for example). Gender stereotyping by children was present even in the 2-year-olds, but increased considerably by 4 years of age. This study demonstrated that even when adults don't explicitly engage in gender stereotyping when talking with children, they provide children with information about gender by categorizing gender, labeling gender, and contrasting males and females. Children use these cues to construct an understanding of gender and to guide their behavior (Leaper & Bigler, 2004).

Gender stereotyping continues to change during middle and late childhood and adolescence (Leaper & Bigler, 2011; Miller & others, 2013). By the time children enter elementary school, they have considerable knowledge about which activities are linked with being male or female. Until about 7 to 8 years of age, gender stereotyping is extensive because young children don't recognize individual variations in masculinity and femininity. By 5 years of age, both boys and girls stereotype boys as powerful and in more negative terms, such as mean, and girls in more positive terms, such as nice (Miller & Ruble, 2005). Across the elementary school years, children become more flexible in their gender attitudes (Trautner & others, 2005).

One study of 3- to 10-year-old U.S. children revealed that girls and older children used a higher percentage of gender stereotypes (Miller & others, 2009). In this study, appearance stereotypes were more prevalent on the part of girls while activity (sports, for example) and trait (aggressive, for example) stereotyping was more commonly engaged in by boys.

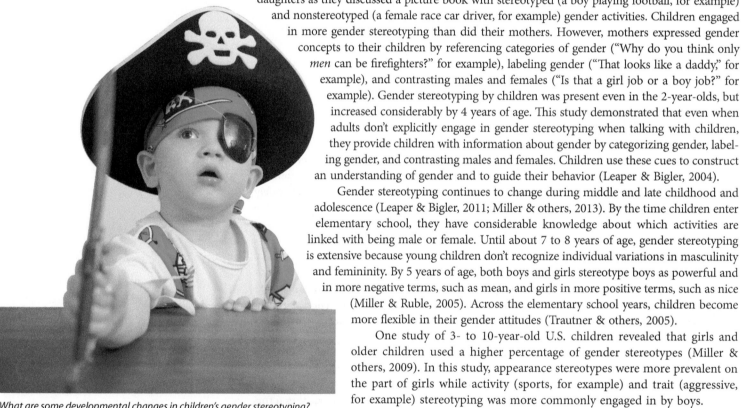

What are some developmental changes in children's gender stereotyping?

GENDER SIMILARITIES AND DIFFERENCES

What is the reality behind gender stereotypes? Let's examine some of the differences between the sexes, keeping in mind that (1) the differences are averages and do not apply to all females or all males; (2) even when gender differences occur, there often is considerable overlap between males and females; and (3) the differences may be due primarily to biological factors, sociocultural factors, or both.

Physical Similarities and Differences   We could devote pages to describing physical differences between the average man and woman. For example, women have about twice the body fat of men, with most of it concentrated around their breasts and hips. In males, fat is more likely to go to the abdomen. On average, males grow to be 10 percent taller than females. Androgens (the "male" hormones) promote the growth of long bones; estrogens (the "female" hormones) stop such growth at puberty.

Many physical differences between men and women are tied to health. From conception on, females have a longer life expectancy than males, and females are less likely than males to develop physical or mental disorders. Females are more resistant to infection, and their blood vessels are more elastic than males'. Males have higher levels of stress hormones, which cause faster clotting and higher blood pressure.

Does gender matter when it comes to brain structure and activity? Human brains are much more alike than different, whether the brain belongs to a male or a female (Hyde, 2007b). However, researchers have found some brain differences between females and males. Among the differences that have been discovered are the following:

- Female brains are approximately 10 percent smaller than male brains, but female brains have more folds; the larger folds (called *convolutions*) allow more surface brain tissue within the skulls of females than males (Giedd & others, 2012; Luders & others, 2004).

- One part of the hypothalamus involved in sexual behavior tends to be larger in men than in women (Swaab & others, 2001).

- Portions of the corpus callosum—the band of tissues through which the brain's two hemispheres communicate—may be larger in females than in males, although some studies have found this not to be the case (Bishop & Wahlsten, 1997; Driesen & Raz, 1995; LeVay, 1994).

- An area of the parietal lobe that functions in visuospatial skills tends to be larger in males than in females (Frederikse & others, 2000).

- The areas of the brain involved in emotional expression tend to show more metabolic activity in females than in males (Gur & others, 1995).

developmental **connection**

Brain Development

The human brain has two hemispheres (left and right). To some extent the type of information processed by neurons depends on whether they are in the left or right hemisphere of the brain. Chapter 4, p. 111

Although some differences in brain structure and function have been found, many of these differences are either small or inconsistently supported by research. Also, when sex differences in the brain have been revealed, in many cases they have not been directly linked to psychological differences (Blakemore, Berenbaum, & Liben, 2009). Although research on sex differences in the brain is still in its infancy, it is likely that there are far more similarities than differences in the brains of females and males. A further point is worth noting: Anatomical sex differences in the brain may be due to the biological origins of these differences, behavioral experiences (demonstrating the brain's ongoing plasticity), or a combination of these factors.

Cognitive Similarities and Differences   No gender differences in general intelligence have been revealed, but gender differences have been found in some cognitive areas (Blakemore, Berenbaum, & Liben, 2009; Halpern, 2012). Research has shown that girls and women generally have slightly better verbal skills than boys and men, although in some areas of verbal skill the differences are substantial (Blakemore, Berenbaum, & Liben, 2009). For example, in recent national assessments, girls were significantly better than boys in reading and writing (National Assessment of Educational Progress, 2005, 2007).

Are there gender differences in math aptitude? A recent very large-scale study of more than 7 million U.S. students in grades 2 through 11 revealed no differences in math scores for boys and girls (Hyde & others, 2008). And a meta-analysis found no gender differences in math for adolescents (Lindberg & others, 2010). In a recent study, however, 6- to 12-year-olds stated that math is mainly for boys (Cvencek, Meltzoff, & Greenwald, 2011).

One area of math that has been examined for possible gender differences is visuospatial skills, which include being able to rotate objects mentally and determine what they would look

"So according to the stereotype, you can put two and two together, but I can read the handwriting on the wall."
© 1994 Joel Pett. All Rights Reserved.

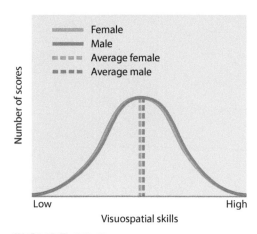

Female
Male
Average female
Average male

Number of scores

Low · Visuospatial skills · High

FIGURE **12.5**

VISUOSPATIAL SKILLS OF MALES AND FEMALES. Notice that, although an average male's visuospatial skills are higher than an average female's, scores for the two sexes almost entirely overlap. Not all males have better visuospatial skills than all females—the overlap indicates that, although the average male score is higher, many females outperform most males on such tasks.

like when rotated (Halpern, 2012). These types of skills are important in courses such as plane and solid geometry and geography. A research review revealed that boys have better visuospatial skills than girls (Halpern & others, 2007). For example, despite equal participation in the National Geography Bee, in most years all 10 finalists are boys (Liben, 1995). However, some experts argue that the gender difference in visuospatial skills is small (Hyde & Else-Quest, 2013) (see Figure 12.5).

Are there gender differences in reading and writing skills? There is strong evidence that females outperform males in reading and writing. In national studies, girls have shown higher reading achievement than have boys (National Assessment of Educational Progress, 2012). Girls also have consistently outperformed boys in writing skills in the National Assessment of Educational Progress in fourth-, eighth-, and twelfth-grade assessments.

Let's further explore gender difference related to schooling and achievement. In 2009, males were more likely to drop out of school than females (9 percent versus 7 percent) (National Center for Education Statistics, 2011). Boys predominate in the academic bottom half of high school classes. That is, although many boys perform at the average or advanced level, the bottom 50 percent academically is made up mainly of boys. Half a century ago in 1961, less than 40 percent of women who graduated from high school went on to attend college. Beginning in 1996, women were more likely to enroll in college than men. In 2009, almost 75 percent of women attended college after high school, compared with 66 percent of men (Women in Academia, 2011).

Piecing together the information about school dropouts, the percentage of males in the bottom half of their high school classes, and the percentage of males in college classes, we can conclude that currently females show greater overall academic interest and achievement than do males in the United States. Females are more likely to be engaged with academic material, to pay attention in class, to put forth more academic effort, and to participate more in class than boys are (DeZolt & Hull, 2001). A recent large-scale study revealed that girls had more positive attitudes about school than boys did (Orr, 2011). And further, girls' positive attitudes about school were linked to their higher grades; boys' negative attitudes about school were related to their lower grades.

Despite these positive characteristics of girls, increasing evidence of similarity in the math and science skills of girls and boys, and legislative efforts to attain gender equality in recent years, gender differences in science, technology, and math careers continue to favor males (Meece & Askew, 2012; Watt, 2008; Watt & Eccles, 2008). Toward the end of high school, girls are less likely to take high-level math courses and less likely to plan to enter the so-called "STEM" fields of science, technology, engineering, and math. A recent research review concluded that girls have more negative math attitudes and that parents' and teachers' expectancies for children's math competence are often gender-biased in favor of boys (Gunderson & others, 2012).

Socioemotional Similarities and Differences   Four areas of socioemotional development in which gender similarities and differences have been studied extensively are aggression, relationship communication, emotion, and prosocial behavior.

Aggression   One of the most consistent gender differences is that boys are more physically aggressive than girls (Brendgen, 2009; Hyde, 2014). The difference occurs in all cultures and appears very early in children's development. The physical aggression difference is especially pronounced when children are provoked. Both biological and environmental factors have been proposed to account for gender differences in aggression. Biological factors include heredity and hormones. Environmental factors include cultural expectations, adult and peer models, and social agents that reward aggression in boys and punish aggression in girls.

Although boys are consistently more physically aggressive than girls, might girls show at least as much verbal aggression (such as yelling) as boys? When verbal aggression is examined, gender differences

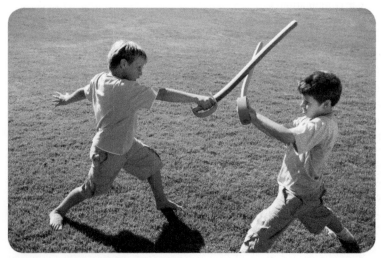

What are some gender differences in aggression?

often disappear, although verbal aggression sometimes is more pronounced in girls than boys (Eagly & Steffen, 1986).

Recently, increased interest has been shown in relational aggression, which involves harming someone by manipulating a relationship (Kawabata & others, 2012; Underwood, 2011). Relational aggression includes such behaviors as trying to make others dislike a certain individual by spreading malicious rumors about the person. Relational aggression increases in middle and late childhood (Dishion & Piehler, 2009). Mixed findings have characterized research on whether girls show more relational aggression than boys, but one consistency in findings is that relational aggression comprises a greater percentage of girls' overall aggression than is the case for boys (Putallaz & others, 2007). And a recent research review revealed that girls engage in more relational aggression than boys in adolescence but not in childhood (Smith, Rose, & Schwartz-Mette, 2010).

Relationship Communication   Are males and females so dramatically different that "men are from Mars" and "women are from Venus," as was proposed in a best-selling book a few years ago (Gray, 1992)? Perhaps the gender differences that fascinate people most involve how males and females communicate with each other.

In relationship communication, sociolinguist Deborah Tannen (1990) distinguishes between rapport talk and report talk:

- **Rapport talk** is the language of conversation and a way of establishing connections and negotiating relationships. Girls enjoy rapport talk and conversation that is relationship oriented more than boys do.
- **Report talk** is talk that gives information. Public speaking is an example of report talk. Males hold center stage through report talk with verbal performances such as storytelling, joking, and lecturing with information.

Tannen says that boys and girls grow up in different worlds of talk—parents, siblings, peers, teachers, and others talk to boys and girls differently. The play of boys and girls is also different. Boys tend to play in large groups that are hierarchically structured, and their groups usually have a leader who tells the others what to do and how to do it. Boys' games have winners and losers and often are the subject of arguments. And boys often boast of their skill and argue about who is best at what. In contrast, girls are more likely to play in small groups or pairs, and at the center of a girl's world is often a best friend. In girls' friendships and peer groups, intimacy is pervasive. Turn-taking is more characteristic of girls' games than of boys' games. And much of the time, girls simply like to sit and talk with each other, concerned more about being liked by others than jockeying for status in some obvious way.

In sum, Tannen concludes that females are more relationship oriented than males—and that this relationship orientation should be prized as a skill in our culture more than it currently is. Note, however, that some researchers criticize Tannen's ideas as being overly simplified and suggest that communication between males and females is more complex than Tannen indicates (Edwards & Hamilton, 2004). Further, some researchers have found similarities in males' and females' relationship communication strategies (Hyde, 2007a, b). In one study, in their talk men and women described and responded to relationship problems in ways that were more similar than different (MacGeorge, 2004).

Researchers have found that girls are more "people oriented" and boys are more "things oriented" (Galambos & others, 2009; Su, Rounds, & Armstrong, 2009). In a recent research review on gender and adolescent development, this conclusion was supported by findings that girls spend more time in relationships, while boys spend more time alone, playing video games, and playing sports; that girls work at part-time jobs that are people-oriented such as waitressing and baby-sitting, while boys are more likely to take part-time jobs that involve manual labor and using tools; and that girls are interested in careers that are more people-oriented, such as teaching and social work, while boys are more likely to be interested in object-oriented careers, such as mechanics and engineering (Perry & Pauletti, 2011). Also,

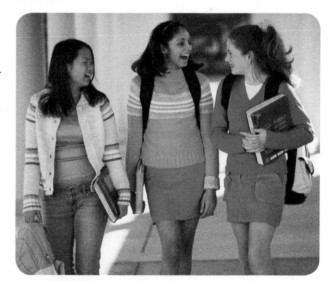

What conclusions can be reached about gender similarities/differences in relationship communication?

rapport talk The language of conversation and a way of establishing connections and negotiating relationships; more characteristic of females than of males.

report talk Talk that conveys information; more characteristic of males than females.

What gender differences characterize children's prosocial behavior?

in support of Tannen's view, researchers have found that adolescent girls engage in more self-disclosure (communication of intimate details about themselves) in close relationships and are better at actively listening in a conversation than are boys (Leaper & Friedman, 2007).

Emotion and Its Regulation   Gender differences occur in some aspects of emotion (Hertenstein & Keltner, 2011). Females express emotion more than do males, are better than males at decoding emotion, smile more, cry more, and are happier (Gross, Fredrickson, & Levenson, 1994; LaFrance, Hecht, & Paluck, 2003). Males report experiencing and expressing more anger than do females (Kring, 2000). A recent meta-analysis found that overall gender differences in children's emotional expression were small, with girls showing more positive emotion (sympathy, for example) and more internalized emotions (sadness and anxiety, for example) than boys (Chaplin & Aldao, 2013). In this analysis, the gender difference in positive emotions became more pronounced with age as girls more strongly expressed positive emotions than boys in middle and late childhood and in adolescence.

An important skill is to be able to regulate and control one's emotions and behavior (Thompson, 2013c, d). Boys usually show less emotional self-regulation than girls (Pascual & others, 2012). This low self-control can translate into behavior problems.

Prosocial Behavior   Are there gender differences in prosocial behavior? Females view themselves as more prosocial and empathic than males (Eisenberg, Spinrad, & Morris, 2013). Across childhood and adolescence, females engage in more prosocial behavior (Eisenberg, Spinrad, & Morris, 2013). The biggest gender difference occurs for kind and considerate behavior, with a smaller difference in sharing.

developmental **connection**

Moral Development

Prosocial behavior involves behavior intended to benefit other people. Chapter 13, p. 376

Gender Controversy   Controversy continues about the extent of gender differences and what might cause them (Blakemore, Berenbaum, & Liben, 2009; Leaper, 2013). As we saw earlier, evolutionary psychologists such as David Buss (2012) argue that gender differences are extensive and caused by the adaptive problems humans have faced across their evolutionary history. Alice Eagly (2010, 2012) also concludes that gender differences are substantial, but she reaches a very different conclusion about their cause. She emphasizes that gender differences are due to social conditions that have resulted in women having less power and controlling fewer resources than men.

By contrast, Janet Shibley Hyde (2007, 2014; Hyde & Else-Quest, 2013) concludes that gender differences have been greatly exaggerated, with this perspective being especially fueled by popular books such as John Gray's (1992) *Men Are from Mars, Women Are from Venus* and Deborah Tannen's (1990) *You Just Don't Understand.* She argues that the research indicates females and males are similar on most psychological factors. In a research review, Hyde (2005) summarized the results of 44 meta-analyses of gender differences and similarities. A *meta-analysis* is a statistical analysis that combines the results of many different studies. In most areas, including math ability and communication, gender differences either were nonexistent or small. Gender differences in physical aggression were moderate. The largest difference occurred in motor skills (favoring males), followed by sexuality (males masturbate more and are more likely to endorse sex in a casual, uncommitted relationship), and physical aggression (males are more physically aggressive than are females). A recent research review also concluded that gender differences in adolescence are quite small (Perry & Pauletti, 2011).

Hyde's summary of meta-analyses is still not likely to quiet the controversy about gender differences and similarities, but further research should continue to provide a basis for more accurate judgments about this topic.

At this point, we have discussed many aspects of gender stereotypes, similarities, differences, and controversies in children's development. The following *Caring Connections* interlude provides some recommendations for parents and teachers in regard to children's gender development.

Guiding Children's Gender Development

Boys

1. ***Encourage boys to be sensitive in relationships and engage in more prosocial behavior.*** An important socialization task is to help boys become more interested in having positive close relationships and become more caring. Fathers can play an especially important role for boys in this regard by being a model of a male who is sensitive and caring.

2. ***Encourage boys to be less physically aggressive.*** Too often, boys are encouraged to be tough and physically aggressive. A positive strategy is to encourage them to be self-assertive but not physically aggressive.

3. ***Encourage boys to handle their emotions more effectively.*** This involves helping boys not only to regulate their emotions, as in controlling their anger, but also to express their anxieties and concerns rather than keeping them bottled up.

4. ***Work with boys to improve their school performance.*** Girls get better grades, put forth more academic effort, and are less likely than boys to be assigned to special/remedial classes. Parents and teachers can help boys by emphasizing the importance of school and expecting better academic effort.

Girls

1. ***Encourage girls to be proud of their relationship skills and caring.*** The strong interest that girls show in relationships and caring should be supported by parents and teachers.

2. ***Encourage girls to develop their self-competencies.*** While guiding girls to retain their relationship strengths, adults also can help girls to develop their ambition and achievement.

3. ***Encourage girls to be more self-assertive.*** Girls tend to be more passive than boys and can benefit from being encouraged to be more self-assertive.

4. ***Encourage girls' achievement.*** This can involve encouraging girls to have higher academic expectations and exposing them to a wider range of career options.

Boys and Girls

1. ***Help children to reduce gender stereotyping and discrimination.*** Don't engage in gender stereotyping and discrimination yourself; otherwise, you will be providing a model of gender stereotyping and discrimination for children.

The second piece of advice for guiding boys' gender development is to encourage them to be less physically aggressive. Near the beginning of this chapter, what did you learn about hormones and boys' aggression?

Review *Connect* Reflect

 Describe gender stereotypes, similarities, and differences.

Review

- What are gender stereotypes? How extensive is gender stereotyping?
- What are some gender similarities and differences in the areas of biological, cognitive, and socioemotional development?

Connect

- In this section, you learned about the ways in which parents may purposefully or unwittingly engage in gender stereotyping of their children. In Chapter 10, you learned that parents have to deal with being gender stereotyped too. For instance, according to one study, what did some stay-at-home fathers report?

Reflect *Your Own Personal Journey of Life*

- How is your gender behavior and thinking similar to or different from your mother's and grandmothers' if you are a female? How is your gender behavior and thinking different from your father's and grandfathers' if you are a male?

Not long ago, it was accepted that boys should grow up to be masculine and girls to be feminine, that boys are made of "snips and snails and puppy dogs' tails" and girls are made of "sugar and spice and everything nice." Let's further explore gender classifications of boys and girls as "masculine" and "feminine."

WHAT IS GENDER-ROLE CLASSIFICATION?

In the past, a well-adjusted boy was expected to be independent, aggressive, and powerful. A well-adjusted girl was expected to be dependent, non-aggressive, and uninterested in power. The masculine characteristics were valued more highly by society than the feminine ones.

In the 1970s, as both females and males became dissatisfied with the burdens imposed by their stereotypic roles, alternatives to femininity and masculinity were proposed. Instead of describing masculinity and femininity as a continuum in which more of one means less of the other, it was proposed that individuals could have both masculine and feminine traits. This thinking led to the development of the concept of **androgyny,** the presence of masculine and feminine characteristics in the same person (Bem, 1977; Spence & Helmreich, 1978). For example, the androgynous boy might be assertive (masculine) and nurturant (feminine). The androgynous girl might be powerful (masculine) and sensitive to others' feelings (feminine). In one study, it was confirmed that societal changes are encouraging females to be more assertive (Spence & Buckner, 2000).

Measures have been developed to assess androgyny. One of the most widely used measures is the Bem Sex-Role Inventory. To find out whether your gender-role classification is masculine, feminine, or androgynous, see Figure 12.6.

Gender experts such as Sandra Bem argue that androgynous individuals are more flexible, competent, and mentally healthy than their masculine or feminine counterparts. To some degree, though, deciding which gender-role classification is best depends on the context involved (Woodhill & Samuels, 2004). For example, in close relationships, feminine and androgynous orientations might be more desirable because of the expressive nature of such relationships. However, masculine and androgynous orientations might be more desirable in traditional academic and work settings because of the achievement demands in these contexts. For example, one study found that masculine and androgynous individuals had higher expectations for being able to control the outcomes of their academic efforts than feminine or undifferentiated (neither masculine nor feminine) individuals (Choi, 2004).

MASCULINITY IN CHILDHOOD AND ADOLESCENCE

Concern about the ways boys traditionally have been brought up to behave has been called a "national crisis of boyhood" by William Pollack (1999) in his book *Real Boys.* Pollack says that although there has been considerable talk about the "sensitive male," little has been done to change what he calls the "boy code." He says that this code tells boys they should show little if any emotion as they are growing up. Too often boys are socialized to not show their feelings and to act tough, says Pollack. Boys learn the boy code in many different contexts—sandboxes, playgrounds, schoolrooms, camps, hangouts—and are taught the code by parents, peers, coaches, teachers, and other adults. Pollack, as well as many others, argues that boys would benefit from being socialized to express their anxieties and concerns rather than keep them

Examples of masculine items

Defends open beliefs
Forceful
Willing to take risks
Dominant
Aggressive

Examples of feminine items

Does not use harsh language
Affectionate
Loves children
Understanding
Gentle

Scoring: The items are scored on independent dimensions of masculinity and femininity as well as androgyny and undifferentiate classifications.

FIGURE 12.6

THE BEM SEX-ROLE INVENTORY. These items are from the Bem Sex-Role Inventory (BSRI). When taking the BSRI, an individual is asked to indicate on a 7-point scale how well each of the 60 characteristics describes herself or himself. The scale ranges from 1 (never or almost never true) to 7 (always or almost always true). The items are scored on independent dimensions of masculinity and femininity. Individuals who score high on the masculine items and low on the feminine items are categorized as masculine; those who score high on the feminine items and low on the masculine items are categorized as feminine; and those who score high on both the masculine and feminine items are categorized as androgynous.

androgyny The presence of masculine and feminine characteristics in the same person.

bottled up, as well as being guided in how to better regulate their aggression.

There also is a special concern about boys who adopt a strong masculine role in adolescence, because this is associated with problem behaviors. Joseph Pleck (1995) points out that what defines traditional masculinity in many Western cultures includes behaviors that do not have social approval but nonetheless validate the adolescent boy's masculinity. In the male adolescent culture, male adolescents perceive that they will be thought of as more masculine if they engage in premarital sex, drink alcohol, take drugs, and participate in illegal delinquent activities. A recent study revealed that both boys and girls who engaged in extreme gender-typed (hyper-gender) behaviors had lower levels of school engagement and school attachment (Ueno & McWilliams, 2010).

What are some concerns about adolescent males adopting a strong masculine role?

GENDER-ROLE TRANSCENDENCE

Some critics of androgyny say that there has been too much talk about gender and that androgyny is less of a panacea than originally envisioned. An alternative is *gender-role transcendence*, the view that when an individual's competence is at issue, it should be conceptualized on a personal basis rather than on the basis of masculinity, femininity, or androgyny (Pleck, 1983). That is, we should think about ourselves as people first, not as being masculine, feminine, or androgynous. Parents should rear their children to be competent boys and girls, not masculine, feminine, or androgynous, say the gender-role critics. They stress that such gender-role classification leads to too much stereotyping.

GENDER IN CONTEXT

The concept of gender-role classification involves categorization of a person in terms of personality traits. However, it may be helpful to think of personality in terms of person-situation interaction rather than traits alone (Cloninger, 2013). Thus, in our discussion of gender-role classification, we described how some gender roles might be more appropriate than others, depending on the context or setting involved.

To see the importance of considering gender in context, let's examine helping behavior and emotion. The stereotype is that females are better than males at helping. However, the difference depends on the situation. Females are more likely than males to volunteer their time to help children with personal problems and to engage in caregiving behavior (Taylor, 2002). However, in situations in which males feel a sense of competence, especially circumstances that involve danger, males are more likely than females to help (Eagly & Crowley, 1986). For example, a male is more likely than a female to stop and help a person who is stranded by the roadside with a flat tire.

"She is emotional; he is not"—that is the master emotional stereotype. However, like differences in helping behavior, emotional differences in males and females depend on the particular emotion involved and the context in which it is displayed (Shields, 1998). Males are more likely to show anger toward strangers, especially male strangers, when they feel they have been challenged. Males also are more likely to turn their anger into aggressive action. Emotional differences between females and males often show up in contexts that highlight social roles and relationships. For example, females are more likely than males to discuss emotions in terms of relationships, and they are more likely to express fear and sadness.

The importance of considering gender in context is nowhere more apparent than when examining what is culturally prescribed behavior for females and males in various countries around the world (Best, 2010; Matsumoto & Juang, 2013). To read further about cross-cultural variations in gender, see *Connecting with Diversity*.

developmental **connection**

Theories

Bronfenbrenner's ecological theory emphasizes the importance of contexts; in his theory, the macrosystem includes cross-cultural comparisons. Chapter 1, p. 27

Gender Roles Across Cultures

In recent decades, roles assumed by males and females in the United States have become increasingly similar—that is, more androgynous. In many countries, though, gender roles have remained more gender-specific (UNICEF, 2011). For example, in a number of Middle Eastern countries, the division of labor between males and females is dramatic: males are socialized to work in the public sphere, females in the private world of home and child rearing; a man's duty is to provide for his family, the woman's to care for her family and household. Any deviations from this traditional gender-role orientation receive severe disapproval.

Access to education for girls has improved somewhat around the world, but girls' education still lags behind boys' education. For example, according to a UNICEF (2003) analysis of education around the world, by age 18 girls have received, on average, 4.4 years less education than boys have. This lack of education reduces their chances of fully developing their potential. Noticeable exceptions to lower participation and completion rates in education for girls occur in Western nations, Japan, and the Philippines (Brown & Larson, 2002). In most countries, more men than women gain advanced training or advanced degrees (Fussell & Greene, 2002).

Although access to education for girls has improved, boys still receive approximately 4.4 years more education around the world than girls do. Shown here is a private school for boys in Africa.

Although most countries still have gender gaps that favor males, evidence of increasing gender equality is appearing (Brown & Larson, 2002). For example, among upper-socioeconomic-status families in India and Japan, fathers are assuming more child-rearing responsibilities (Stevenson & Zusho, 2002; Verma & Saraswathi, 2002). Rates of employment and career opportunities for women are expanding in many countries. Restrictions on adolescent girls' social relationships, especially sexual and romantic relationships, are decreasing in some countries.

Cultural and ethnic backgrounds also influence how boys and girls are socialized in the United States (Cheah & Yeung, 2011). One study revealed that Latino and Latina adolescents were socialized differently as they were growing up (Raffaelli & Ontai, 2004). Latinas experienced far greater restrictions than Latinos in curfews, interacting with members of the other sex, getting a driver's license, getting a job, and participating in after-school activities.

The last study mentioned above focused on adolescents. In Chapter 4, what did you learn about differences between adolescent girls' and boys' perceptions of their bodies?

Review *Connect* Reflect

 Identify how gender roles can be classified.

Review
- What is gender-role classification?
- What are some risks of masculinity in childhood and adolescence?
- What is gender-role transcendence?
- How can gender be conceptualized in terms of context?

Connect
- In this section, you learned about risks related to masculinity in childhood and adolescence. How might early or late maturation (discussed in Chapter 4) affect these risks?

Reflect *Your Own Personal Journey of Life*
- If and when you have a child, how attentive will you likely be to rearing your child to be masculine, feminine, or androgynous? Explain.

Gender

What Is Gender?

 Summarize what gender involves.

- Gender refers to the characteristics of people as males and females. Among the components of gender are gender identity, gender roles, and gender stereotyping. Recent research indicates that most children know whether they are a boy or a girl by 2 years of age.

Influences on Gender Development

 Discuss the main biological, social, and cognitive influences on gender.

Biological Influences

- The 23rd pair of chromosomes determines our sex. Ordinarily, females have two X chromosomes, and males have one X and one Y. Males and females also produce different concentrations of the hormones known as androgens and estrogens. Early hormonal production is linked with later gender development. In the evolutionary psychology view, evolutionary adaptations produced psychological sex differences that are especially present in sexual behavior and mating strategies. Chromosomes determine anatomical sex differences, but culture and society strongly influence gender.

Social Influences

- In social role theory, gender differences result from men's and women's contrasting roles; in most cultures, women have less power and status than men and control fewer resources. This gender hierarchy and sexual division of labor are important causes of sex-differentiated behavior. Psychoanalytic theory of gender emphasizes sexual attraction to the same-sex parent, anxiety about this attraction, and subsequent adoption of the same-sex parent's gender characteristics. Social cognitive theory emphasizes gender models and rewards and punishments for gender-appropriate and gender-inappropriate behavior. Peers are especially adept at rewarding gender-appropriate behavior. Schools and teachers, as well as the media, influence children's gender development.

Cognitive Influences

- Gender schema theories emphasize the role of cognition in gender development. In gender schema theory, gender typing emerges gradually as children develop gender schemas of what their culture considers to be gender-appropriate and gender-inappropriate.

Gender Stereotypes, Similarities, and Differences

 Describe gender stereotypes, similarities, and differences.

Gender Stereotyping

- Gender stereotypes are general impressions and beliefs about males and females. Gender stereotypes are widespread. Gender stereotyping changes developmentally; it is present even at 2 years of age but increases considerably in early childhood. In middle and late childhood, children become more flexible in their gender attitudes, but gender stereotyping may increase again in early adolescence. By late adolescence, gender attitudes are often more flexible.

Gender Similarities and Differences

- Physical and biological differences between males and females are substantial. Women have about twice the body fat of men, are less likely to develop physical or mental disorders, and have a longer life expectancy. Boys and girls show similar achievement in math, although boys have slightly better visuospatial skills. Girls perform better in writing and reading. Some experts, such as Hyde, argue that cognitive differences between males and females have been exaggerated. Males are more physically aggressive than females, while females are more likely to show stronger affiliative interests in adolescence, express their emotions openly and intensely, have better emotional control, and engage in more prosocial behavior. There is considerable controversy about how similar or different females and males are in a number of areas.

Gender-Role Classification **LG4** Identify how gender roles can be classified.

What Is Gender-Role Classification?

- In the past, the well-adjusted male was supposed to show masculine traits; the well-adjusted female, feminine traits. During the 1970s, alternatives to traditional gender roles were introduced. It was proposed that competent individuals could show both masculine and feminine traits. This thinking led to the development of the concept of androgyny, the presence of masculine and feminine traits in one individual. Gender-role measures often categorize individuals as masculine, feminine, androgynous, or undifferentiated. Most androgynous individuals are flexible and mentally healthy, although the particular context and the individual's culture also determine the adaptiveness of a gender-role orientation.

Masculinity in Childhood and Adolescence

- A special concern is that boys raised in a traditional manner are socialized to conceal their emotions. Researchers have found that problem behaviors often characterize highly masculine adolescents.

Gender-Role Transcendence

- One alternative to androgyny is gender-role transcendence, a theory that states that there has been too much emphasis on gender and that a better strategy is to think about competence in terms of individual characteristics rather than gender.

Gender in Context

- In thinking about gender, it is important to keep in mind the context in which gender behavior is displayed. In many countries, traditional gender roles remain dominant.

key terms

gender 339
gender identity 339
gender role 339
gender typing 339
estrogens 339

androgens 339
social role theory 340
psychoanalytic theory
   of gender 340

social cognitive theory of
   gender 340
gender schema theory 344
gender stereotypes 345

rapport talk 349
report talk 349
androgyny 352

key people

Alice Eagly 340
Sigmund Freud 341
Phyllis Bronstein 341

Diane Halpern 343
Janet Shibley Hyde 350
Deborah Tannen 349

David Buss 350
Sandra Bem 352

William Pollack 352
Joseph Pleck 353

chapter 13

MORAL DEVELOPMENT

chapter **outline**

1 Domains of Moral Development

Learning Goal 1 Discuss theory and research on the domains of moral development.

What Is Moral Development?
Moral Thought
Moral Behavior
Moral Feeling
Moral Personality
Social-Cognitive Domain Theory

2 Contexts of Moral Development

Learning Goal 2 Explain how parenting and schools influence moral development.
Parenting
Schools

3 Prosocial and Antisocial Behavior

Learning Goal 3 Describe the development of prosocial and antisocial behavior.

Prosocial Behavior
Antisocial Behavior

4 Religious and Spiritual Development

Learning Goal 4 Summarize the nature of children's and adolescents' religious and spiritual development.

Childhood
Adolescence

The mayor of the city says that this young woman is "everywhere." She recently persuaded the city's school committee to consider ending the practice of locking tardy students out of their classrooms. She also swayed a neighborhood group to support her proposal for a winter jobs program. According to one city councilman, "People are just impressed with the power of her arguments and the sophistication of the argument" (Silva, 2005, pp. B1, B4). She is Jewel E. Cash, and she is just 16 years old.

A junior at Boston Latin Academy, Jewel was raised in one of Boston's housing projects by her mother, a single parent. Today she belongs to the Boston Student Advisory Council, mentors children, volunteers at a women's shelter, manages and dances in two troupes, and volunteers with a neighborhood watch group—among other activities.

Jewel told an interviewer from the *Boston Globe:*

> I see a problem and I say, "How can I make a difference?" . . . I can't take on the world, even though I can try. . . . I'm moving forward but I want to make sure I'm bringing people with me (Silva, 2005, pp. B1, B4).

Jewel is far from typical, but her motivation to help others illustrates the positive side of moral development.

Jewel Cash, seated next to her mother, participating in a crimewatch meeting at a community center. She is an exemplar of positive teenage community involvement.

preview

Most people have strong opinions not only about moral and immoral behavior but also about how moral behavior should be fostered in children. We will begin our coverage of moral development by exploring its main domains and then examine some important contexts that influence moral development. Next, we discuss children's prosocial and antisocial behavior. The chapter concludes with an overview of children's religious and spiritual development.

Domains of Moral Development **LG1** Discuss theory and research on the domains of moral development.

- What Is Moral Development?
- Moral Thought
- Moral Behavior
- Moral Feeling
- Moral Personality
- Social-Cognitive Domain Theory

What is moral development? What are its main domains?

WHAT IS MORAL DEVELOPMENT?

Moral development involves changes in thoughts, feelings, and behaviors regarding standards of right and wrong. Moral development has an *intrapersonal* dimension, which regulates a person's activities when she or he is not engaged in social interaction, and an *interpersonal* dimension, which regulates social interactions and arbitrates conflict (Walker, 2006). To understand moral development, we need to consider five basic questions:

First, how do children and adolescents reason, *or think, about rules for ethical conduct?* For example, we might present them with a story in which someone has a conflict about whether or not to cheat in a specific situation, such as taking a test in school. Then they are asked to decide what is appropriate for the character to do and why. The focus is placed on the reasoning the children and adolescents use to justify their moral decisions.

Second, how do children and adolescents actually behave *in moral circumstances?* For example, with regard to cheating, we might observe whether they resist the temptation to cheat and the environmental circumstances that produced the resistance or cheating. We could conduct our study through a one-way mirror as they are taking a test. We might note whether they take out "cheat" notes, look at another student's answers, and so on.

Third, how do children and adolescents feel *about moral matters?* In the example of cheating, do they feel enough guilt to resist temptation? If they do cheat, do feelings of guilt after the transgression keep them from cheating the next time they face temptation?

Fourth, what comprises children's and adolescents' moral personality? Continuing with the example of cheating, do they have a moral identity and moral character that is so strong they resist the temptation to cheat?

Fifth, how is children's and adolescents' moral domain different from their social conventional and personal domains? In domain theory (discussed later in this chapter), cheating resides in the moral domain, along with lying, stealing, and harming another person. Behaviors such as cutting in a line or speaking out of turn are in the social conventional rather than the moral domain, and choosing friends is in the personal domain.

Keep in mind that although we have separated moral development into different domains, the components often are interrelated. For example, if the focus is on the child or adolescent's behavior, it is still important to evaluate his or her intentions (moral thought). Similarly, emotions accompany, and can distort, moral reasoning.

Let's now discuss the various domains of moral development. We begin with the cognitive domain.

moral development Changes in thoughts, feelings, and behaviors regarding standards of right and wrong.

How is this child's moral thinking likely to be different about stealing a cookie, depending on whether he is in Piaget's heteronomous or autonomous stage?

MORAL THOUGHT

How do individuals think about what is right and wrong? Are children able to evaluate moral questions in the same way that adults can? Piaget had some answers to these questions. So did Lawrence Kohlberg.

Piaget's Theory Interest in how children think about moral issues was stimulated by Jean Piaget (1932), who extensively observed and interviewed children from the ages of 4 through 12. Piaget watched children play marbles to learn how they used and thought about the game's rules. He also asked children about ethical issues—theft, lies, punishment, and justice, for example. Piaget concluded that children go through two distinct stages, separated by a transition period, in how they think about morality.

- From 4 to 7 years of age, children display **heteronomous morality,** the first stage of moral development in Piaget's theory. Children think of justice and rules as unchangeable properties of the world, removed from the control of people.
- From 7 to 10 years of age, children are in a transition showing some features of the first stage of moral reasoning and some aspects of the second stage, autonomous morality.
- From about 10 years of age and older, children show **autonomous morality,** Piaget's second stage of moral development. They become aware that rules and laws are created by people, and in judging an action, they consider the actor's intentions as well as the consequences.

Because young children are heteronomous moralists, they judge the rightness or goodness of behavior by considering its consequences, not the intentions of the actor. For example, to the heteronomous moralist, breaking twelve cups accidentally is worse than breaking one cup intentionally. As children develop into moral autonomists, intentions assume paramount importance.

The heteronomous thinker also believes that rules are unchangeable and are handed down by all-powerful authorities. When Piaget suggested to young children that they use new rules in a game of marbles, they resisted. By contrast, older children—moral autonomists—accept change and recognize that rules are merely convenient conventions, subject to change.

The heteronomous thinker also believes in **immanent justice,** the concept that if a rule is broken, punishment will be meted out immediately. The young child believes that a violation is connected automatically to its punishment. Thus, young children often look around worriedly after doing something wrong, expecting inevitable punishment. Immanent justice also implies that if something unfortunate happens to someone, the person must have transgressed earlier. Older children, who are moral autonomists, recognize that punishment occurs only if someone witnesses the wrongdoing and that, even then, punishment is not inevitable. They also realize that bad things can happen to innocent people.

How do these changes in moral reasoning occur? Piaget argued that, as children develop, they become more sophisticated in thinking about social matters, especially about the possibilities and conditions of cooperation. Piaget reasoned that this social understanding comes about through the mutual give-and-take of peer relations. In the peer group, where others have power and status similar to the child's, plans are negotiated and coordinated, and disagreements are reasoned about and eventually settled. Parent-child relations, in which parents have the power and children do not, are less likely to advance moral reasoning because rules are often handed down in an authoritarian way.

Recall from Chapter 6 Ross Thompson's view that young children are not as egocentric as Piaget envisioned. Thompson (2012) further elaborated on this view, arguing that recent research indicates that young children often show a non-egocentric awareness of others' goals, feelings, and desires and how such internal states are influenced by the actions of others. These ties between advances in moral understanding and theory of mind indicate that young children possess cognitive resources that allow them to be aware of others' intentions and to know when someone violates a moral prohibition. One study of 3-year-olds found that they were

developmental **connection**

Cognitive Theory

In which of Piaget's cognitive developmental stages is a 5-year-old heteronomous thinker likely to be? Chapter 6, p. 176

heteronomous morality The first stage of moral development in Piaget's theory, occurring from 4 to 7 years of age. Justice and rules are conceived of as unchangeable properties of the world, beyond the control of people.

autonomous morality The second stage of moral development in Piaget's theory, displayed by older children (about 10 years of age and older). The child becomes aware that rules and laws are created by people and that, in judging an action, one should consider the actor's intentions as well as the consequences.

immanent justice Piaget's concept of the childhood expectation that if a rule is broken, punishment will be meted out immediately.

less likely to offer assistance to an adult they had previously observed being harmful to another person (Vaish, Carpenter, & Tomasello, 2010).

However, because of limitations in their self-control skills, social understanding, and cognitive flexibility, young children's moral advancements often are inconsistent and vary across situations. They still have a long way to go before they have the capacity for developing a consistent moral character and making ethical judgments.

Lawrence Kohlberg.

Kohlberg's Theory   A second major perspective on moral development was proposed by Lawrence Kohlberg (1958, 1986). Piaget's cognitive stages of development serve as the underpinnings for Kohlberg's theory, but Kohlberg suggested that there are six stages of moral development. These stages, he argued, are universal. Development from one stage to another, said Kohlberg, is fostered by opportunities to take the perspective of others and to experience conflict between one's current stage of moral thinking and the reasoning of someone at a higher stage.

Kohlberg arrived at his view after 20 years of using a unique interview with children. In the interview, children are presented with a series of stories in which characters face moral dilemmas. The following is the most popular Kohlberg dilemma:

> In Europe a woman was near death from a special kind of cancer. There was one drug that the doctors thought might save her. It was a form of radium that a druggist in the same town had recently discovered. The drug was expensive to make, but the druggist was charging ten times what the drug cost him to make. He paid $200 for the radium and charged $2,000 for a small dose of the drug. The sick woman's husband, Heinz, went to everyone he knew to borrow the money, but he could only get together $1,000, which is half of what it cost. He told the druggist that his wife was dying and asked him to sell it cheaper or let him pay later. But the druggist said, "No, I discovered the drug, and I am going to make money from it." So Heinz got desperate and broke into the man's store to steal the drug for his wife. (Kohlberg, 1969, p. 379)

This story is one of 11 that Kohlberg devised to investigate the nature of moral thought. After reading the story, the interviewee answers a series of questions about the moral dilemma. Should Heinz have stolen the drug? Was stealing it right or wrong? Why? Is it a husband's duty to steal the drug for his wife if he can get it no other way? Would a good husband steal? Did the druggist have the right to charge that much when there was no law setting a limit on the price? Why or why not?

The Kohlberg Stages   Based on the answers interviewees gave for this and other moral dilemmas, Kohlberg described three levels of moral thinking, each of which is characterized by two stages (see Figure 13.1). A key concept in understanding progression through the levels and stages is that the person's morality gradually becomes more internal or mature. That is, their reasons for moral decisions or values begin to go beyond the external or superficial reasons they gave when they were younger. Let's further examine Kohlberg's stages.

- ***Kohlberg's Level 1: Preconventional Reasoning***   **Preconventional reasoning** is the lowest level of reasoning in Kohlberg's theory and consists of two stages: punishment and obedience orientation (stage 1) and individualism, instrumental purpose, and exchange (stage 2).

  Stage 1. Punishment and obedience orientation is the first Kohlberg stage of moral development. At this stage, moral thinking is often tied to punishment. For example, children and adolescents obey adults because adults tell them to obey.

  Stage 2. Individualism, instrumental purpose, and exchange is the second stage of Kohlberg's theory. At this stage, individuals pursue their own interests but also let others do the same. Thus, what is right involves an equal exchange. People are nice to others so that others will be nice to them in return.

- ***Kohlberg's Level 2: Conventional Reasoning***   **Conventional reasoning** is the second, or intermediate, level in Kohlberg's theory of moral development. Individuals abide by certain standards (internal), but they are the standards of others (external), such as parents or the laws of society. The conventional reasoning level consists of two stages: mutual interpersonal expectations, relationships, and interpersonal conformity (stage 3) and social systems morality (stage 4).

preconventional reasoning The lowest level in Kohlberg's theory. At this level, morality is often focused on reward and punishment. The two stages in preconventional reasoning are punishment and obedience orientation (stage 1) and individualism, instrumental purpose, and exchange (stage 2).

conventional reasoning The second, or intermediate, level in Kohlberg's theory of moral development. At this level, individuals abide by certain standards (internal), but they are the standards of others such as parents or the laws of society (external). The conventional level consists of two stages: mutual interpersonal expectations, relationships, and interpersonal conformity (stage 3) and social systems morality (stage 4).

LEVEL 1	LEVEL 2	LEVEL 3
Preconventional Level	**Conventional Level**	**Postconventional Level**
Stage 1 Punishment and Obedience Orientation	**Stage 3** Mutual Interpersonal Expectations, Relationships, and Interpersonal Conformity	**Stage 5** Social Contract or Utility and Individual Rights
Children obey because adults tell them to obey. People base their moral decisions on fear of punishment.	*Individuals value trust, caring, and loyalty to others as a basis for moral judgments.*	*Individuals reason that values, rights, and principles undergird or transcend the law.*
Stage 2 Individualism, Purpose, and Exchange	**Stage 4** Social System Morality	**Stage 6** Universal Ethical Principles
Individuals pursue their own interests but let others do the same. What is right involves equal exchange.	*Moral judgments are based on understanding and the social order, law, justice, and duty.*	*The person has developed moral judgments that are based on universal human rights. When faced with a dilemma between law and conscience, a personal, individualized conscience is followed.*

FIGURE **13.1**
KOHLBERG'S THREE LEVELS AND SIX STAGES OF MORAL DEVELOPMENT

Stage 3. Mutual interpersonal expectations, relationships, and interpersonal conformity is Kohlberg's third stage of moral development. At this stage, individuals value trust, caring, and loyalty to others as a basis of moral judgments. Children and adolescents often adopt their parents' moral standards at this stage, seeking to be thought of by their parents as a "good girl" or a "good boy."

Stage 4. Social systems morality is the fourth stage in Kohlberg's theory of moral development. At this stage, moral judgments are based on understanding the social order, law, justice, and duty. For example, adolescents may say that, for a community to work effectively, it needs to be protected by laws that are adhered to by its members.

• *Kohlberg's Level 3: Postconventional Reasoning* **Postconventional reasoning** is the third and highest level in Kohlberg's theory. At this level, morality is more internal. The postconventional level of morality consists of two stages: social contract or utility and individual rights (stage 5) and universal ethical principles (stage 6).

Stage 5. Social contract or utility and individual rights is the fifth Kohlberg stage. At this stage, individuals reason that values, rights, and principles undergird or transcend the law. A person evaluates the validity of actual laws and examines social systems in terms of the degree to which they preserve and protect fundamental human rights and values.

Stage 6. Universal ethical principles is the sixth and highest stage in Kohlberg's theory of moral development. At this stage, the person has developed a moral standard based on universal human rights. When faced with a conflict between law and conscience, the person will follow conscience, even though the decision might involve personal risk.

Kohlberg observed that these levels and stages occur in a sequence and are age related: Before age 9, most children use stage 1, preconventional reasoning based on external rewards and punishments, when they consider moral choices. By early adolescence, their moral reasoning is increasingly based on the application of standards set by others. Most adolescents reason at stage 3, with some signs of stages 2 and 4. By early adulthood, a small number of individuals reason in postconventional ways.

What evidence supports this model of moral development? A 20-year longitudinal investigation found that use of stages 1 and 2 decreased with age (Colby & others, 1983) (see Figure 13.2). Stage 4, which did not appear at all in the moral reasoning of 10-year-olds, was reflected in the moral thinking of 62 percent of the 36-year-olds. Stage 5 did not appear until age 20 to 22 and never characterized more than 10 percent of the individuals.

Thus, the moral stages appeared somewhat later than Kohlberg initially envisioned, and reasoning at the higher stages, especially stage 6, was rare. Although stage 6 has been removed

postconventional reasoning The third and highest level in Kohlberg's theory of moral development. At this level, morality is more internal. The postconventional level consists of two stages: social contract or utility and individual rights (stage 5) and universal ethical principles (stage 6).

from the Kohlberg moral judgment scoring manual, it still is considered to be theoretically important in the Kohlberg scheme of moral development.

Influences on the Kohlberg Stages   What factors influence movement through Kohlberg's stages? Although moral reasoning at each stage presupposes a certain level of cognitive development, Kohlberg argued that advances in children's cognitive development did not ensure development of moral reasoning. Instead, moral reasoning also reflects children's experiences in dealing with moral questions and moral conflict.

Several investigators have tried to advance individuals' levels of moral development by having a person present arguments that reflect moral thinking one stage above the individuals' established levels. This approach applies the concepts of equilibrium and conflict that Piaget used to explain cognitive development. By presenting arguments slightly beyond the children's level of moral reasoning, the researchers created a disequilibrium that motivated the children to restructure their moral thought. The upshot of studies using this approach is that virtually any plus-stage discussion, for any length of time, seems to promote more advanced moral reasoning (Walker, 1982).

Kohlberg emphasized that peer interaction and perspective taking are critical aspects of the social stimulation that challenges children to change their moral reasoning. Whereas adults characteristically impose rules and regulations on children, the give-and-take among peers gives children an opportunity to take the perspective of another person and to generate rules democratically. Kohlberg stressed that in principle, encounters with any peers can produce perspective-taking opportunities that may advance a child's moral reasoning. A recent research review of cross-cultural studies involving Kohlberg's theory revealed strong support for a link between perspective-taking skills and more advanced moral judgments (Gibbs & others, 2007).

Kohlberg's Critics   Kohlberg's theory has provoked debate, research, and criticism (Lapsley, 2013; Lapsley & Yeager, 2013; Nucci, 2013; Smetana, 2013a, b; Walker, 2013). First, let's examine the extent of the link between moral thought and moral behavior.

Moral Thought and Moral Behavior   Kohlberg's theory has been criticized for placing too much emphasis on moral thought and not enough emphasis on moral behavior (Walker, 2004). Moral reasons can sometimes be a shelter for immoral behavior. Corrupt CEOs and politicians endorse the loftiest of moral virtues in public until their own behavior is exposed. Whatever the latest public scandal, you will probably find that the culprits displayed virtuous thoughts but engaged in immoral behavior. No one wants a nation of cheaters and thieves who can reason at the postconventional level. The cheaters and thieves may know what is right yet still do what is wrong. Heinous actions can be cloaked in a mantle of moral virtue.

Culture and Moral Reasoning   Culture influences moral development more than Kohlberg thought (Tappan, 2013; Wainryb, 2013). Kohlberg emphasized that his stages of moral reasoning are universal, but some critics claim his theory is culturally biased (Miller, 2007, 2013). Both Kohlberg and his critics may be partially correct.

One review of 45 studies in 27 cultures around the world, mostly non-European, provided support for the

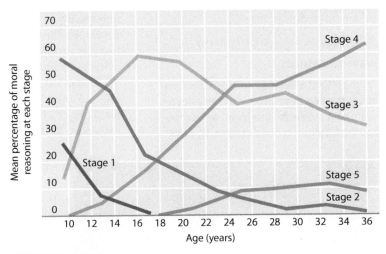

FIGURE **13.2**

AGE AND THE PERCENTAGE OF INDIVIDUALS AT EACH KOHLBERG STAGE. In one longitudinal study of males from 10 to 36 years of age, at age 10 most moral reasoning was at stage 2 (Colby & others, 1983). At 16 to 18 years of age, stage 3 became the most frequent type of moral reasoning, and it was not until the mid-twenties that stage 4 became the most frequent. Stage 5 did not appear until 20 to 22 years of age and it never characterized more than 10 percent of the individuals. In this study, the moral stages appeared somewhat later than Kohlberg envisioned, and stage 6 was absent.

Why did Piaget and Kohlberg think peer relations are so important in moral development?

developmental connection

Research Methods

Cross-cultural studies provide information about the degree to which children's development is universal, or similar, across cultures or is culture-specific. Chapter 17, p. 485

This 14-year-old boy in Nepal is thought to be the sixth holiest Buddhist in the world. In one study of 20 adolescent male Buddhist monks in Nepal, the issue of justice, a basic theme in Kohlberg's theory, was not a central focus in the monks' moral views (Huebner & Garrod, 1993). Also, the monks' concerns about prevention of suffering and the importance of compassion are not captured in Kohlberg's theory.

developmental connection

Gender

Janet Shibley Hyde concluded that many views and studies of gender exaggerate differences. Chapter 12, p. 350

justice perspective A moral perspective that focuses on the rights of the individual; individuals independently make moral decisions.

care perspective The moral perspective of Carol Gilligan, in which people are assessed in terms of their connectedness with others and the quality of their interpersonal communication, relationships with others, and concern for others.

universality of Kohlberg's first four stages (Snarey, 1987). Individuals in diverse cultures developed through these four stages in sequence as Kohlberg predicted. A more recent research study revealed support for the qualitative shift from stage 2 to stage 3 across cultures (Gibbs & others, 2007).

Stages 5 and 6, however, have not been found in all cultures (Gibbs & others, 2007; Snarey, 1987). Furthermore, Kohlberg's scoring system does not recognize the higher-level moral reasoning of certain cultures—thus, moral reasoning is more culture-specific than Kohlberg envisioned (Snarey, 1987).

In particular, researchers have heard moral judgments based on the principles of communal equity and collective happiness in Israel, the unity and sacredness of all life forms in India, and collective moral responsibility in New Guinea (Snarey, 1987). These examples of moral reasoning would not be scored at the highest level in Kohlberg's system because they are not based on principles of justice. Similar results occurred in a study that assessed the moral development of 20 adolescent male Buddhist monks in Nepal (Huebner & Garrod, 1993). Justice, a basic theme in Kohlberg's theory, was not of paramount importance in the monks' moral views, and their concerns about the prevention of suffering and the role of compassion are not captured by Kohlberg's theory.

In the view of John Gibbs (2010), most young adolescents around the world use the moral judgment of mutuality (stage 3) that makes intimate friendships possible. And by late adolescence, many individuals also are beginning to grasp the importance of agreed-upon standards and institutions for the common good (stage 4). A main exception, though, is the delayed moral judgment of adolescents who regularly engage in delinquency.

A recent study explored links between culture, mindset, and moral judgment (Narváez & Hill, 2010). In this study, a higher level of multicultural experience was linked to closed mindedness (being cognitively inflexible), a growth mindset (perceiving that one's qualities can change and improve through effort), and higher moral judgment.

In sum, although Kohlberg's approach does capture much of the moral reasoning voiced in various cultures around the world, his approach misses or misconstrues some important moral concepts in particular cultures (Gibbs, 2010). To read further about cultural variations in moral reasoning, see *Connecting with Diversity.*

Families and Moral Development   Kohlberg argued that family processes are essentially unimportant in children's moral development. As noted earlier, he argued that parent-child relationships usually provide children with little opportunity for give-and-take or perspective taking. Rather, Kohlberg said that such opportunities are more likely to be provided by children's peer relations.

Did Kohlberg underestimate the contribution of family relationships to moral development? A number of developmentalists stress that parents' moral values influence children's developing moral thoughts (Dunn, 2013; Grusec, 2013; Thompson, Meyer, & McGinley, 2013). Nonetheless, most developmentalists agree with Kohlberg, and Piaget, that peers play an important role in the development of moral reasoning.

Gender and the Care Perspective   The most publicized criticism of Kohlberg's theory has come from Carol Gilligan (1982, 1992, 1996), who argues that Kohlberg's theory reflects a gender bias. According to Gilligan, Kohlberg's theory is based on a male norm that puts abstract principles above relationships and concern for others and sees the individual as standing alone and independently making moral decisions. It puts justice at the heart of morality. In contrast to Kohlberg's **justice perspective,** which focuses on the rights of the individual, Gilligan argues for a **care perspective,** a moral perspective that views people in terms of their connectedness with others and emphasizes interpersonal communication, relationships with others, and concern for others. According to Gilligan, Kohlberg greatly underplayed the care perspective, perhaps because he was a male, because most of his

Moral Reasoning in the United States and India

Cultural meaning systems vary around the world, and these systems shape children's morality (Gibbs, 2010; Shiraev & Levy, 2010). Consider a comparison of American and Indian Hindu Brahman children (Shweder, Mahapatra, & Miller, 1987). Like people in many other non-Western societies, Indians view moral rules as part of the natural world order. This means that Indians do not distinguish between physical, moral, and social regulation, as Americans do. For example, in India, violations of food taboos and marital restrictions can be just as serious as acts intended to cause harm to others. In India, social rules are seen as inevitable, much like the law of gravity.

According to William Damon (1988), in places where culturally specific practices take on profound moral and religious significance, as in India, the moral development of children focuses extensively on their adherence to custom and convention. In contrast, Western moral doctrine tends to elevate abstract principles, such as justice and welfare, to a higher moral status than customs or conventions. As in India, socialization practices in many developing countries actively instill in children a great respect for their culture's traditional codes and practices.

How would you revise Kohlberg's stages of moral development to better accommodate other cultures? Or do you think this is impossible?

How might Asian Indian children and American children reason differently about moral issues?

research was with males rather than females, and because he used male responses as a model for his theory.

A meta-analysis (a statistical analysis that combines the results of many different studies) casts doubt on Gilligan's claim of substantial gender differences in moral judgment (Jaffee & Hyde, 2000). In this study, overall, only a small sex difference in care-based reasoning favored females, but this sex difference was greater in adolescence than childhood. When differences occurred, they were better explained by the nature of the dilemma than by gender (for example, both males and females tended to use care-based reasoning to deal with interpersonal dilemmas and justice reasoning to handle societal dilemmas). In sum, experts now conclude that there is no evidence to support Gilligan's claim that Kohlberg downplayed females' moral thinking (Hyde, 2007, 2014; Walker, 2006, 2013).

MORAL BEHAVIOR

What are the basic processes responsible for moral behavior? What is the nature of self-control and resistance to temptation? How does social cognitive theory view moral development?

Basic Processes The processes of reinforcement, punishment, and imitation have been invoked to explain how individuals learn certain responses and why their responses differ from those of other persons (Grusec, 2006). When individuals are reinforced for behavior that is consistent with laws and social conventions, they are likely to repeat that behavior. When

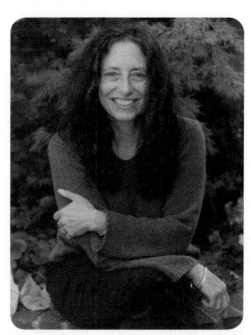

Carol Gilligan. *What is Gilligan's view of moral development?*

provided with models who behave morally, individuals are likely to adopt their actions. Finally, when individuals are punished for immoral behaviors, those behaviors can be eliminated, but at the expense of sanctioning punishment by its very use and of causing emotional side effects for the individual.

These general conclusions come with some important qualifiers. The effectiveness of reward and punishment depends on the consistency and timing with which they are administered. For example, it is generally more effective to reward moral behavior soon after the event occurs than to do so later. The effectiveness of modeling depends on the characteristics of the model and the cognitive skills of the observer. For example, if a parent models giving a donation to a charity, her child must be old enough to understand this behavior in order for it to have an impact on the child's moral development.

Behavior is situationally dependent. Thus, individuals do not consistently display moral behavior in different situations. How consistent is moral behavior? In a classic investigation of moral behavior, one of the most extensive ever conducted, Hugh Hartshorne and Mark May (1928–1930) observed the moral responses of 11,000 children who were given the opportunity to lie, cheat, and steal in a variety of circumstances—at home, at school, at social events, and in athletics. A completely honest or a completely dishonest child was difficult to find. Situation-specific behavior was the rule. Children were more likely to cheat when their friends put pressure on them to do so and when the chance of being caught was slim. However, other analyses suggest that although moral behavior is influenced by situational determinants, some children are more likely than others to cheat, lie, and steal (Burton, 1984).

In further support of the situational determinants of morality, a recent study found that very few 7-year-olds were willing to donate any money after watching a UNICEF film on children suffering from poverty (van IJzendoorn & others, 2010). However, after gentle probing by an adult, most children were willing to donate some of their money.

Social Cognitive Theory   The **social cognitive theory of morality** emphasizes a distinction between an individual's moral competence (the ability to perform moral behaviors) and moral performance (performing those behaviors in specific situations) (Mischel & Mischel, 1975). *Moral competencies* include what individuals are capable of doing, what they know, their skills, their awareness of moral rules and regulations, and their cognitive ability to construct behaviors. Moral competence is the outgrowth of cognitive-sensory processes. *Moral performance*, or behavior, however, is determined by motivation and the rewards and incentives to act in a specific moral way.

Albert Bandura (1991, 2002) also stresses that moral development is best understood by considering a combination of social and cognitive factors, especially those involving self-control. He proposes that in developing a moral self, individuals adopt standards of right and wrong that serve as guides and deterrents for conduct. In this self-regulatory process, people monitor their conduct and the conditions under which it occurs, judge it in relation to moral standards, and regulate their actions by the consequences they apply to themselves. They do things that provide them with satisfaction and a sense of self-worth. They refrain from behaving in ways that violate their moral standards because such conduct will bring self-condemnation. Self-sanctions keep conduct in line with internal standards (Bandura, 2002). Thus, in Bandura's view, self-regulation rather than abstract reasoning is the key to positive moral development.

MORAL FEELING

Think about how you feel when you do something you sense is wrong. Does it affect you emotionally? Maybe you get a twinge of guilt. And when you give someone a gift, you might feel joy. What role do emotions play in moral development, and how do these emotions develop?

Psychoanalytic Theory   According to Sigmund Freud, guilt and the desire to avoid feeling guilty are the foundation of moral behavior. In Freud's theory, the *superego* is the moral branch of personality. According to Freud, children fear losing their parents' love and

developmental **connection**

Social Cognitive Theory

What are the main themes of Bandura's social cognitive theory? Chapter 1, p. 25

social cognitive theory of morality The theory that distinguishes between moral competence—the ability to produce moral behaviors—and moral performance—use of those behaviors in specific situations.

empathy Reacting to another's feelings with an emotional response that is similar to the other's feelings.

being punished for their unacceptable sexual attraction to the opposite-sex parent. To reduce anxiety, avoid punishment, and maintain parental affection, children identify with the same-sex parent. Through this identification, children *internalize* the parents' standards of right and wrong, which reflect societal prohibitions, and hence develop the superego. In the psychoanalytic account of moral development, children conform to societal standards to avoid guilt. In this way, self-control replaces parental control.

Freud's claims regarding the formation of the ego ideal and conscience cannot be verified. However, researchers can examine the extent to which children feel guilty when they misbehave. Grazyna Kochanska and her colleagues (Kochanska & Askan, 2007; Kochanska & others, 2002, 2008, 2009) have conducted a number of studies that explore children's conscience development. In a recent research review of children's conscience, she concluded that young children are aware of right and wrong, have the capacity to show empathy toward others, experience guilt, indicate discomfort following a transgression, and are sensitive to violating rules (Kochanska & Aksan, 2007). In one study, Kochanska and her colleagues (2002) observed 106 preschool children in laboratory situations in which they were led to believe that they had damaged valuable objects. In these mishaps, the behavioral indicators of guilt that were coded by observers included avoiding gaze (looking away or down), body tension (squirming, backing away, hanging head down, covering face with hands), and distress (looking uncomfortable, crying). Girls expressed more guilt than boys did. Children with a more fearful temperament expressed more guilt. Children of mothers who used power-oriented discipline (such as spanking, slapping, and yelling) displayed less guilt.

Empathy   Positive feelings, such as empathy, contribute to the child's moral development (Eisenberg, Spinrad, & Sadovsky, 2013). Feeling **empathy** means reacting to another's feelings with an emotional response that is similar to the other's feelings. To empathize is not just to sympathize; it is to put oneself in another's place emotionally.

Although empathy is an emotional state, it has a cognitive component—the ability to discern another's inner psychological states, or what we have previously called *perspective taking* (Eisenberg & others, 2009). Infants have the capacity for some purely empathic responses, but for effective moral action, children must learn to identify a wide range of emotional states in others and to anticipate what kinds of action will improve another person's emotional state.

What are the milestones in children's development of empathy? According to an analysis by child developmentalist William Damon (1988), changes in empathy take place in early infancy, at 1 to 2 years of age, in early childhood, and at 10 to 12 years of age.

Global empathy is the young infant's empathic response in which clear boundaries between the feelings and needs of the self and those of another have not yet been established. For example, one 11-month-old infant fought off her own tears, sucked her thumb, and buried her head in her mother's lap after she had seen another child fall and hurt himself. Not all infants cry every time someone else is hurt, though. Many times, an infant will stare at another's pain with curiosity. Although global empathy is observed in some infants, it does not consistently characterize all infants' behavior.

When they are 1 to 2 years of age, infants may feel genuine concern for the distress of other people, but only when they reach early childhood can they respond appropriately to another person's distress. This ability depends on children's new awareness that people have different reactions to situations. By late childhood, they may begin to feel empathy for the unfortunate.

At about 10 to 12 years of age, individuals develop an empathy for people who live in unfortunate circumstances (Damon, 1988). Children's concerns are no longer limited to the feelings of specific persons in situations they directly observe. Instead, 10- to 12-year-olds expand their concerns to the general problems of people in unfortunate circumstances—those who are poor, handicapped, social outcasts, and so forth. This newfound sensitivity may lead older children to behave altruistically, and later may give a humanitarian flavor to adolescents' development of ideological and political views.

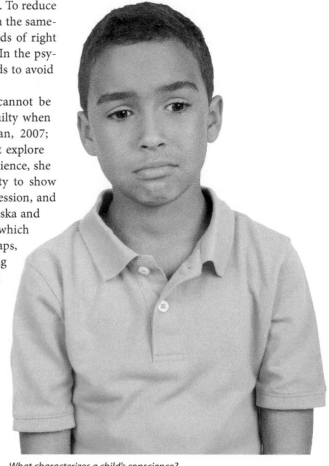

What characterizes a child's conscience?

developmental **connection**

Social Cognition

In Robert Selman's view, perspective taking is a key aspect of whether children develop prosocial or antisocial attitudes and behavior. Chapter 11, p. 320

What are some developmental changes in empathy?

FIGURE **13.3**

**DAMON'S DESCRIPTION OF
DEVELOPMENTAL CHANGES IN EMPATHY**

Age Period	Nature of Empathy
Early infancy	Characterized by global empathy, the young infant's empathic response does not distinguish between feelings and needs of self and others.
1 to 2 years of age	Undifferentiated feelings of discomfort at another's distress grow into more genuine feelings of concern, but infants cannot translate realization of other's unhappy feelings into effective action.
Early childhood	Children become aware that every person's perspective is unique and that someone else may have a different reaction to a situation. This awareness allows the child to respond more appropriately to another person's distress.
10 to 12 years of age	Children develop an emergent orientation of empathy for people who live in unfortunate circumstances—the poor, the handicapped, and the socially outcast. In adolescence, this newfound sensitivity may give a humanitarian flavor to the individual's ideological and political views.

Although every adolescent may be capable of responding with empathy, not all adolescents do so. Adolescents' empathic behavior varies considerably. For example, in older children and adolescents, empathic dysfunctions can contribute to antisocial behavior. Some delinquents convicted of violent crimes show a lack of feeling for their victims' distress. A 13-year-old boy convicted of violently mugging a number of older adults, when asked about the pain he had caused one blind woman, said, "What do I care? I'm not her" (Damon, 1988). To read further about Damon's description of the developmental changes in empathy from infancy through adolescence, see Figure 13.3.

The Contemporary Perspective on the Role of Emotion in Moral Development We have seen that classical psychoanalytic theory emphasizes the power of unconscious guilt in moral development but that other theorists, such as Damon, emphasize the role of empathy. Today, many child developmentalists conclude that both positive feelings—such as empathy, sympathy, admiration, and self-esteem—and negative feelings—such as anger, outrage, shame, and guilt—contribute to children's moral development (Eisenberg & others, 2009; Thompson, 2013c, d). When strongly experienced, these emotions influence children to act in accord with standards of right and wrong (Prinz, 2009).

MORAL PERSONALITY

So far we have examined three key dimensions of moral development: thoughts, behavior, and feelings. Recently, there has been a surge of interest in a fourth dimension: personality (Frimer & others, 2011; Walker, 2013). Three aspects of moral personality that have recently been emphasized are (1) moral identity, (2) moral character, and (3) moral exemplars.

Moral Identity A central aspect of the recent interest in the role of personality in moral development focuses on **moral identity.** Individuals have a moral identity when moral notions and commitments are central to their life. In this view, behaving in a manner that violates this moral commitment places the integrity of the self at risk (Aquino, McFerran, & Laven, 2011; Walker, 2013).

Recently, Darcia Narváez (2010b) concluded that a mature moral individual cares about morality and being a moral person. For these individuals, moral responsibility is central to their identity. Mature moral individuals engage in moral metacognition, including moral self-monitoring and moral self-reflection. Moral self-monitoring involves monitoring one's thoughts and actions related to moral situations, and engaging in self-control when it is needed. Moral self-reflection encompasses critical evaluations of one's self-judgments and efforts to minimize bias and self-deception.

Moral Character In James Rest's (1995) view, *moral character* involves having strong convictions, persisting, and overcoming distractions and obstacles. If individuals don't have moral character, they may wilt under pressure or fatigue, fail to follow through, or become

developmental **connection**

Identity

According to James Marcia, what are the four statuses of identity development? Chapter 11, p. 328

moral identity The aspect of personality that is present when individuals have moral notions and commitments that are central to their lives.

moral exemplars People who have lived extraordinary lives, having developed their personality, identity, character, and virtue to a level that reflects moral excellence and commitment.

social-cognitive domain theory Theory stating that there are different domains of social knowledge and reasoning, including moral, social conventional, and personal domains. These domains arise from children's and adolescents' attempts to understand and deal with different forms of social experience.

Rosa Parks (*left photo,* sitting in the front of a bus after the U.S. Supreme Court ruled that segregation was illegal on her city's bus system) and Andrei Sakharov (*right photo*) are moral exemplars. Parks (1913–2005), an African American seamstress in Montgomery, Alabama, became famous for her quiet, revolutionary act of not giving up her bus seat to a non-Latino White man in 1955. Her heroic act is cited by many historians as the beginning of the modern civil rights movement in the United States. Across the next four decades, Parks continued to work for progress in civil rights. Sakharov (1921–1989) was a Soviet physicist who spent several decades designing nuclear weapons for the Soviet Union and came to be known as the father of the Soviet hydrogen bomb. However, later in his life he became one of the Soviet Union's most outspoken critics and worked relentlessly to promote human rights and democracy.

distracted and discouraged, and fail to behave morally. Moral character presupposes that the person has set moral goals and that achieving those goals involves the commitment to act in accord with those goals.

Lawrence Walker (2002; Walker, 2013; Walker & Pitts, 1998) has studied moral character by examining people's conceptions of moral excellence. Among the moral virtues people emphasize are "honesty, truthfulness, and trustworthiness, as well as those of care, compassion, thoughtfulness, and considerateness. Other salient traits revolve around virtues of dependability, loyalty, and conscientiousness" (Walker, 2002, p. 74).

Moral Exemplars **Moral exemplars** are people who have lived exemplary lives. Moral exemplars have a moral personality, identity, character, and set of virtues that reflect moral excellence and commitment (Frimer & others, 2011; Walker, 2013).

In one study, three different exemplars of morality were examined—brave, caring, and just (Walker & Hennig, 2004). Different personality profiles emerged for the three exemplars. The brave exemplar was characterized by being dominant and extraverted, the caring exemplar by being nurturant and agreeable, and the just exemplar by being conscientious and open to experience. However, a number of traits characterized all three moral exemplars, considered by the researchers to reflect a possible core of moral functioning. This core included being honest and dependable.

SOCIAL-COGNITIVE DOMAIN THEORY

Judith Smetana (2011a, b; 2013a, b; Smetana & others, 2012) has proposed **social-cognitive domain theory,** which states that there are different domains of social knowledge and reasoning, including moral, social conventional, and personal domains. In social-cognitive domain theory, children's and adolescents' moral, social conventional, and personal knowledge and reasoning emerge from their attempts to understand and deal with different forms of social experience.

Social conventional reasoning focuses on conventional rules that have been established by social consensus in order to control behavior and maintain the social system. The rules themselves are arbitrary, such as raising your hand in class before speaking, using one staircase at school to go up and the other to go down, not cutting in front of someone standing in line to buy movie tickets, and stopping at a stop sign when driving. There are sanctions if we violate these conventions, although the rules can be changed by consensus.

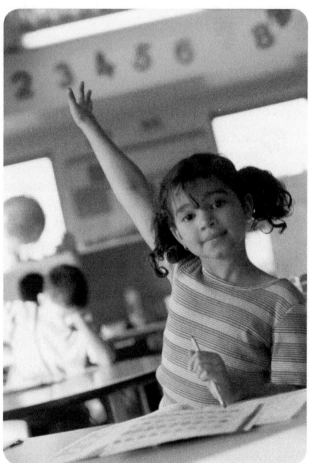

How does social conventional reasoning differ from moral reasoning? What are some examples of social conventional reasoning?

social conventional reasoning Focuses on conventional rules established by social consensus, as opposed to moral reasoning that stresses ethical issues.

In contrast, moral reasoning focuses on ethical issues and rules of morality. Unlike conventional rules, moral rules are not arbitrary. They are obligatory, widely accepted, and somewhat impersonal (Helwig & Turiel, 2011). Rules pertaining to lying, cheating, stealing, and physically harming another person are moral rules because violation of these rules affronts ethical standards that exist apart from social consensus and convention. Moral judgments involve concepts of justice, whereas social conventional judgments are concepts of social organization. Violating moral rules is usually more serious than violating conventional rules. In a recent study of 2½- to 4-year-olds, children distinguished moral from conventional transgressions on many criteria, but only older preschoolers did so when rating whether others deserved punishment (Smetana & others, 2012).

The social conventional approach is a serious challenge to Kohlberg's approach because Kohlberg argued that social conventions are a stopover on the road to higher moral sophistication. For social conventional reasoning advocates, social conventional reasoning is not lower than postconventional reasoning but rather something that needs to be disentangled from the moral thread (Helwig & Turiel, 2011; Smetana, 2011a, b, 2013a, b; Smetana & others, 2012).

Recently, a distinction also has been made between moral and conventional issues, which are viewed as legitimately subject to adult social regulation, and personal issues, which are more likely subject to the child's or adolescent's independent decision making and personal discretion (Helwig & Turiel, 2011; Smetana, 2011a, b). Personal issues include control over one's body, privacy, and choice of friends and activities. Thus, some actions belong to a *personal* domain not governed by moral strictures or social norms.

Review *Connect* Reflect

LG1 Discuss theory and research on the domains of moral development.

Review

- What is moral development?
- What are Piaget's and Kohlberg's theories of moral development? What are some criticisms of Kohlberg's theory? What is social conventional reasoning?
- What processes are involved in moral behavior? What is the social cognitive theory of moral development?
- How are moral feelings related to moral development?
- What characterizes moral personality?
- What characterizes the social-cognitive domain theory of moral development?

Connect

- In this section, you learned that, according to Piaget, children from 7 to 10 years of age

are in a transition period between the heteronomous morality and autonomous morality stages of development. Which stage of cognitive development (as discussed in Chapter 1) would these children be in, according to Piaget?

Reflect *Your Own Personal Journey of Life*

- Which of the five approaches—cognitive, psychoanalytic, behavioral/social cognitive, personality, and social-cognitive domain— do you think best describes the way you developed morally? Explain.

Contexts of Moral Development

LG2 Explain how parenting and schools influence moral development.

Parenting

Schools

What other contexts play a role in moral development? In particular, what are the roles of parents and schools?

PARENTING

Both Piaget and Kohlberg held that parents do not provide unique or essential inputs to children's moral development. Parents, in their view, are responsible for providing role-taking opportunities and cognitive challenges, but peers play the primary role in moral development. Research reveals that both parents and peers contribute to children's moral maturity (Walker, Hennig, & Krettenauer, 2000). A recent study found that adolescents' moral motivation was positively linked to the quality of their relationship with their parents (Malti & Buchmann, 2010). Another recent study revealed that dimensions of authoritative parenting (such as a combination of responsiveness, autonomy-granting, and demandingness) predicted an increase in adolescents' moral identity (Hardy & others, 2010).

In Ross Thompson's (2006, 2010) view, young children are moral apprentices, striving to understand what is moral. They can be assisted in this quest by adult mentors in the home who communicate lessons about morality in everyday experiences (Thompson, Meyer, & McGinley, 2013). Among the most important aspects of the relationship between parents and children that contribute to children's moral development are relational quality, parental discipline, and proactive strategies.

Relational Quality
Parent-child relationships introduce children to the mutual obligations of close relationships (Laible & Thompson, 2007; Thompson, 2013a, c, d; Thompson, Meyer, & McGinley, 2013). Parents' obligations include engaging in positive caregiving and guiding children to become competent human beings. Children's obligations include responding appropriately to parents' initiatives and maintaining a positive relationship with parents.

In terms of relationship quality, secure attachment may play an important role in children's and adolescents' moral development. A secure attachment can place children on a positive path for internalizing parents' socializing goals and family values. In a recent study, early secure attachment defused a maladaptive trajectory toward antisocial outcomes (Kochanska, Barry, & others, 2010). In another recent study, securely attached children's willing, cooperative stance was linked to positive future socialization outcomes such as a lower incidence of externalizing problems (high level of aggression, for example) (Kochanska, Woodard, & others, 2010).

Parental Discipline
Discipline techniques used by parents can be classified as love withdrawal, power assertion, and induction (Hoffman, 1970, 1988):

- **Love withdrawal** is a discipline technique in which a parent withholds attention or love from the child, as when the parent refuses to talk to the child or states a dislike for the child. For example, the parent might say, "I'm going to leave you if you do that again" or "I don't like you when you do that."

- **Power assertion** is a discipline technique in which a parent attempts to gain control over the child or the child's resources. Examples include spanking, threatening, or removing privileges.

- **Induction** is a discipline technique in which a parent uses reasoning and explains how the child's actions are likely to affect other people. Examples of induction include, "Don't hit him. He was only trying to help" and "Why are you yelling at her? She didn't mean to trip you."

In contrast to love withdrawal and power assertion, induction is more likely to produce a moderate level of arousal in children, a level that permits them to attend to the cognitive rationale parents offer. Furthermore, induction focuses the child's attention on the action's consequences for others, not on the child's own shortcomings. Thus, child developmentalists recommend induction over power assertion and love withdrawal in disciplining children. A recent study explored the role of inductive discipline in the moral development of adolescents (Patrick & Gibbs, 2012). In this study, adolescents considered parental induction and expression of disappointed expectations as more appropriate than power assertion and love withdrawal and responded with more positive emotion, as well as guilt, to parental induction than to the other parenting techniques. Further, parental induction was linked to a higher moral identity in this study.

> Both theory and empirical data support the conclusion that parents play an important role in children's moral development.
>
> —**Nancy Eisenberg**
> *Contemporary Psychologist, Arizona State University*

love withdrawal A discipline technique in which a parent withholds attention or love from the child in an effort to control the child's behavior.

power assertion A discipline technique in which a parent attempts to gain control over the child or the child's resources.

induction A discipline technique in which a parent uses reasoning and explains how the child's actions are likely to affect others.

How are parents' discipline techniques linked to children's moral development? What are some proactive strategies parents can use to avert potential misbehavior by children before it happens?

Parenting Recommendations for Raising a Moral Child

A research review (Eisenberg & Valiente, 2002, p. 134) concluded that, in general, children who behave morally tend to have parents who:

- "are warm and supportive rather than punitive;
- use inductive discipline;
- provide opportunities for the children to learn about others' perspectives and feelings;
- involve children in family decision making and in the process of thinking about moral decisions;
- model moral behaviors and thinking themselves, and provide opportunities for their children to do so;
- provide information about what behaviors are expected and why; and
- foster an internal rather than an external sense of morality."

Parents who show this configuration of behaviors likely foster concern and caring about others in their children, and create a positive parent-child relationship. In addition, parenting recommendations based on Ross Thompson's (2006, 2010; Thompson, Meyer, & McGinley, 2013) analysis of parent-child relations suggest that children's moral development is likely to benefit when there are mutual parent-child obligations involving warmth and responsibility, and when parents use proactive strategies.

One of the strategies above suggests modeling moral behaviors and thinking. According to the research cited in the Moral Exemplars section of this chapter, which two traits were common to moral exemplars?

What are some good strategies parents can adopt to foster their child's moral development?

Proactive Strategies   An important parenting strategy is to proactively avert potential misbehavior by children before it takes place (Thompson, 2009a; Thompson, Meyer, & McGinley, 2013). With younger children, being proactive means using diversion, such as distracting their attention or engaging them in alternative activities. With older children, being proactive may involve talking with them about values that the parents deem important. Transmitting these values can help older children and adolescents to resist the temptations that inevitably emerge in contexts such as peer relations and the media that can be outside the scope of direct parental monitoring.

To read further about strategies parents can adopt to promote their children's moral development, see *Caring Connections*.

SCHOOLS

No matter how parents treat their children at home, they may feel that they have little control over a great deal of their children's moral education. Children spend extensive time away from their parents at school, and the time spent in that environment can influence children's moral development (Berkowitz & others, 2013; Narvaez, 2013; Narváez & Lapsley, 2009; Nucci, 2013).

hidden curriculum The pervasive moral atmosphere that characterizes each school.

character education A direct moral education approach that involves teaching students a basic "moral literacy" to prevent them from engaging in immoral behavior or doing harm to themselves or others.

The Hidden Curriculum   More than 60 years ago, educator John Dewey (1933) recognized that even when schools do not have specific programs in moral education, they provide moral education through a "hidden curriculum." The **hidden curriculum** is conveyed by the moral atmosphere that is a part of every school. The moral atmosphere is created by school and classroom rules, the moral orientation of teachers and school administrators, and text materials. Teachers serve as models of ethical or unethical behavior. Classroom rules and peer relations at school transmit attitudes about cheating, lying, stealing, and consideration for others. And by creating and enforcing rules and regulations, the school administration infuses the school with a value system.

Character Education   Yet another approach to moral education is **character education,** a direct education approach that involves teaching students a basic "moral literacy" to prevent them from engaging in immoral behavior and doing harm to themselves or others (Narváez & Lapsley, 2009). The argument is that behaviors such as lying, stealing, and cheating are wrong, and students should be taught this throughout their education (Berkowitz, 2012; Berkowitz & others, 2013; Berkowitz, Battistich, & Bier, 2008).

Every school should have an explicit moral code that is clearly communicated to students. Any violations of the code should be met with sanctions. Instruction in specified moral concepts, such as cheating, can take the form of example and definition, class discussions and role playing, or rewarding students for proper behavior. More recently, an emphasis on the importance of encouraging students to develop a care perspective has been accepted as a relevant aspect of character education (Noddings, 2008). Rather than just instructing adolescents to refrain from engaging in morally deviant behavior, a care perspective advocates educating students in the importance of engaging in prosocial behaviors, such as considering others' feelings, being sensitive to others, and helping others through a semester-long course covering a number of moral issues. The hope is that students will develop more advanced notions of concepts such as cooperation, trust, responsibility, and community (Enright & others, 2008). Currently, 40 of 50 states have mandates to include character education in children's education (Nucci & Narváez, 2008).

Values Clarification   One approach to providing moral education is **values clarification,** which means helping people to clarify what their lives are for and what is worth working for. Unlike character education, which tells students what their values should be, values clarification encourages students to define their own values and understand the values of others (Williams & others, 2003).

Advocates of values clarification say it is value-free. However, critics argue that its content offends community standards and that the values-clarification exercises fail to stress right behavior.

Cognitive Moral Education   Another approach to moral education, **cognitive moral education,** is based on the belief that students should learn to value such things as democracy and justice as their moral reasoning develops. Kohlberg's theory has served as the foundation for a number of cognitive moral education programs. In a typical program, high school students meet in a semester-long course to discuss a number of moral issues. The instructor acts as a facilitator rather than as a director of the class. The hope is that students will develop more advanced notions of concepts such as cooperation, trust, responsibility, and community (Power & Higgins-D'Alessandro, 2008).

Service Learning   At the beginning of the chapter you read about 16-year-old Jewel Cash, who is strongly motivated to make a positive difference in her community. Jewel Cash has a sense of social responsibility that an increasing number of educational programs seek to promote in students through **service learning,** a form of education that promotes social responsibility through service to the community. In service learning, adolescents engage in activities such as tutoring, helping older adults, working in a hospital, assisting at a child-care center, or cleaning up a vacant lot to make a play area. Much of the effort to get students involved in service learning is orchestrated through the Corporation for

More than just about anything else, 12-year-old Katie Bell wanted a playground in her New Jersey town. She knew that other kids also wanted one, so she put together a group that generated fundraising ideas for the playground. They presented their ideas to the town council. Her group got more youth involved. They helped raise money by selling candy and sandwiches door-to-door. Katie says, "We learned to work as a community. This will be an important place for people to go and have picnics and make new friends." Katie's advice: "You won't get anywhere if you don't try."

values clarification Helping people clarify their sense of their purpose in life and what is worth working for. Students are encouraged to define their own values and understand others' values.

cognitive moral education Education based on the belief that students should learn to value things like democracy and justice as their moral reasoning develops; Kohlberg's theory has been the basis for many of the cognitive moral education approaches.

service learning A form of education that promotes social responsibility and service to the community.

Nina Vasan (*center*) founded ACS Teens, a nationwide group of adolescent volunteers who support the efforts of the American Cancer Society (ACS). Nina's organization has raised hundreds of thousands of dollars for cancer research, helped change state tobacco laws, and conducted a number of cancer control programs. She created a national letter-writing campaign to obtain volunteers, established a Web site and set up an e-mail network, started a newsletter, and arranged monthly phone calls to communicate ideas and plan projects.

In Nina's words, "I realized that teenagers like myself could make a big difference in the fight against cancer. I knew that the best way to help was to start a teen organization. . . . To be a beneficial part of the human race, it is essential and fundamental to give back to the community and others" (Vasan, 2002, p. 1).

Nina Vasan's work on behalf of cancer research involved pursuing an objective. She says that the success of her work involving cancer far outweighs the many honors she has been awarded (Damon, 2008).

National and Community Service. For program descriptions and opportunities to volunteer, go to www.nationalservice.gov.

An important goal of service learning is to help adolescents become less self-centered and more strongly motivated to help others (Hart, Adkins, & Donnelly, 2013; Schmidt, Shumow, & Kackar, 2012). Service learning takes education out into the community (Gaylord, Chyka, & Lawley, 2012; Rosenkranz, 2012). Adolescent volunteers tend to be extraverted, be committed to others, and have a high level of self-understanding (Eisenberg & others, 2009). Also, a recent study revealed that adolescent girls participated in service learning more than adolescent boys (Webster & Worrell, 2008).

Researchers have found that service learning benefits adolescents in a number of ways (Hart, Atkins, & Donnelly, 2013). Improvements in adolescent development attributed to service learning include higher grades in school, increased goal-setting, higher self-esteem, an improved sense of empowerment to make a difference for others, and an increased likelihood of serving as volunteers in the future. A study of more than 4,000 high school students revealed that those who worked directly with individuals in need were better adjusted academically, while those who worked for organizations had better civic outcomes (Schmidt, Shumow, & Kackar, 2007). And, in a recent study, 74 percent of African American and 70 percent of Latino adolescents said that service learning programs could have a "fairly or very big effect" on keeping students from dropping out of school (Bridgeland, Dilulio, & Wulsin, 2008).

Recently, interest has been shown in the role that civic engagement might play in adolescents' identity and moral development (Flanagan, Beyers, & Zukauskiene, 2012). A recent study found that compared with adolescents who have a diffused identity status, those who were identity achieved were more involved in volunteering in their community (Crocetti, Jahromi, & Meeus, 2012). In this study, adolescents' volunteer activity also was linked to their values, such as social responsibility, and the view that they, along with others, could make an impact on their community. Another recent study revealed that adolescents' volunteer activities provided opportunities to explore and reason about moral issues (van Goethem, 2012).

One analysis revealed that 26 percent of U.S. public high schools require students to participate in service learning (Metz & Youniss, 2005). The benefits of service learning, both for the volunteer and the recipient, suggest that more adolescents should be required to participate in such programs (Enfield & Collins, 2008; Nelson & Eckstein, 2008).

Cheating   A moral education concern is whether students cheat and how to handle the cheating if teachers discover it (Anderman & Anderman, 2010). Academic cheating can take many forms, including plagiarism, using "cheat sheets" during an exam, copying from a neighbor during a test, purchasing papers, and falsifying lab results. A 2008 survey of almost 30,000 high school students revealed that 64 percent of the students said they had cheated on a test in school during the past year and 36 percent of the students reported that they had plagiarized information from the Internet for an assignment in the past year (Josephson Institute of Ethics, 2008).

Why do students cheat? Among the reasons students give for cheating include pressure to get high grades, compressed schedules, poor teaching, and lack of interest (Stephens, 2008). In terms of poor teaching, "students are more likely to cheat when they perceive their teacher to be incompetent, unfair, and uncaring" (Stephens, 2008, p. 140).

The context affects whether or not students cheat (Vandehey, Diekhoff, & LaBeff, 2007). For example, students are more likely to cheat when they are not being closely monitored during a test, when they know their peers are cheating, when they know whether another student has been caught cheating, and when student scores are made public (Anderman & Anderman, 2010).

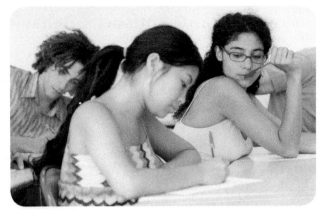

Why do students cheat? What are some strategies teachers can adopt to prevent cheating?

Among the strategies for decreasing academic cheating are preventive measures such as making sure students are aware of what constitutes cheating and what the consequences will be if they cheat; closely monitoring students' behavior while they are taking tests; and emphasizing the importance of being a moral, responsible individual who engages in academic integrity. In promoting academic integrity, many colleges have instituted an honor code policy that emphasizes self-responsibility, fairness, trust, and scholarship. However, few secondary schools have developed honor code policies. The Center for Academic Integrity (www.academicintegrity.org/) has made extensive materials available to help schools develop academic integrity policies.

An Integrative Approach   Darcia Narvaez (2006, 2010a, b, 2013) emphasizes an *integrative approach* to moral education that encompasses both the reflective moral thinking and commitment to justice advocated in Kohlberg's approach, and the process of developing a particular moral character emphasized in the character education approach. She highlights the Child Development Project as an excellent example of an integrative moral education approach. In the Child Development Project, students are given multiple opportunities to discuss other students' experiences, which encourages empathy and perspective taking, and they participate in exercises that encourage them to reflect on their own behaviors in terms of values such as fairness and social responsibility (Solomon & others, 2002). Adults coach students in ethical decision making and guide them in becoming more caring individuals. Students experience a caring community, not only in the classroom, but also in after-school activities and through parental involvement in the program. Research evaluations of the Child Development Project indicate that it is related to an improved sense of community, an increase in prosocial behavior, better interpersonal understanding, and enhanced social problem solving (Battistich, 2008).

Review Connect Reflect

 LG2 Explain how parenting and schools influence moral development.

Review

- How does parental discipline affect moral development? What are some effective parenting strategies for advancing children's moral development?
- What is the hidden curriculum? What are some contemporary approaches to moral education?

Connect

- In this section, you learned that secure attachment in infancy was linked to early development of conscience. What characterizes secure attachment (discussed in Chapter 10)?

Reflect *Your Own Personal Journey of Life*

- What type of discipline did your parents use with you? What effect do you think this approach has had on your moral development?

Prosocial
Behavior

Antisocial
Behavior

It is one of the beautiful compensations of this life that no one can sincerely try to help another without helping himself.

—CHARLES DUDLEY WARNER
American Essayist, 19th Century

Service learning encourages positive moral behavior. This behavior is not just moral behavior but behavior that is intended to benefit other people, and psychologists call it *prosocial behavior* (Carlo, 2013; Eisenberg, Spinrad, & Morris, 2013). Jewel Cash, whose story was introduced at the beginning of the chapter, is an exemplary model of someone committed to prosocial behavior. Of course, people have always engaged in antisocial behavior as well. In this section, we will take a closer look at prosocial and antisocial behavior, focusing on how each type of behavior develops.

PROSOCIAL BEHAVIOR

Caring about the welfare and rights of others, feeling concern and empathy for them, and acting in a way that benefits others are all components of prosocial behavior. The purest forms of prosocial behavior are motivated by **altruism,** an unselfish interest in helping another person (Grusec, Hastings, & Almas, 2011). As we see next, learning to share is an important aspect of prosocial behavior.

William Damon (1988) described a developmental sequence by which sharing develops in children. Most sharing during the first three years of life is done for nonempathic reasons, such as for the fun of the social play ritual or out of imitation. Then, at about 4 years of age, a combination of empathic awareness and adult encouragement produces a sense of obligation on the part of the child to share with others. Most 4-year-olds are not selfless saints, however. Children believe they have an obligation to share but do not necessarily think they should be as generous to others as they are to themselves. Neither do their actions always support their beliefs, especially when they covet an object. What is important developmentally is that the child has developed a belief that sharing is an obligatory part of a social relationship and involves a question of right and wrong. These early ideas about sharing set the stage for giant strides that children make in the years that follow.

By the start of the elementary school years, children begin to express more complicated notions of what is fair. Throughout history, varied definitions of fairness have been used as the basis for distributing goods and resolving conflicts. These definitions involve the principles of equality, merit, and benevolence: *Equality* means that everyone is treated the same; *merit* means giving extra rewards for hard work, skillful performance, or other laudatory behavior; *benevolence* means giving special consideration to individuals in a disadvantaged condition.

Equality is the first of these principles used regularly by elementary school children. It is common to hear 6-year-old children use the word *fair* as synonymous with *equal* or *same.* By the middle to late elementary school years, children also believe that equity means special treatment for those who deserve it—a belief that applies the principles of merit and benevolence.

Parental advice and prodding certainly foster standards of sharing, but the give-and-take of peer requests and arguments provide the most immediate stimulation of sharing. Parents can set examples that children carry into their interactions and communication with peers, but parents are not present during all of their children's peer exchanges. The day-to-day construction of fairness standards is often done by children in collaboration and negotiation with each other. A recent study found that authoritative parenting by mothers, but not fathers, contributed to adolescents' subsequent engagement in prosocial behavior one year later (Padilla-Walker & others, 2012). Other research also has found that mothers are more likely to influence adolescents' prosocial behavior than are fathers (Carlo & others, 2011).

How does prosocial behavior change through childhood and adolescence? Prosocial behavior occurs more often in adolescence than in childhood, although examples of caring

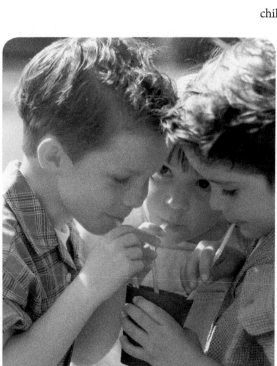

How does children's sharing change from the preschool to the elementary school years?

altruism An unselfish interest in helping another person.

for others and comforting someone in distress occur even during the preschool years (Eisenberg, Spinrad, & Sadovsky, 2006). A recent study of 5- to 13-year-olds found that with increasing age children attributed more positive emotions to people who sacrifice their own desires to help others who are needy and that they become more discriminating about contexts that call for altruistic action (Weller & Lagattuta, 2013).

Also, keep in mind the gender differences in prosocial behavior described in Chapter 12. Recall that females view themselves as more prosocial and empathic, and they also engage in more prosocial behavior than males (Eisenberg, Spinrad, & Morris, 2013).

Are there different types of prosocial behavior? In a recent study, Gustavo Carlo and his colleagues (2010, pp. 340–341) explored this topic and confirmed the presence of six types of prosocial behavior in young adolescents:

- altruism ("One of the best things about doing charity work is that it looks good.")
- public ("Helping others while I'm being watched is when I work best.")
- emotional ("I usually help others when they are very upset.")
- dire ("I tend to help people who are hurt badly.")
- anonymous ("I prefer to donate money without anyone knowing.")
- compliant ("I never wait to help others when they ask for it.")

In this study, adolescent girls reported more emotional, dire, compliant, and altruistic behavior than did boys, while boys engaged in more public prosocial behavior. Parental monitoring was positively related to emotional, dire, and compliant behavior but not to the other types of behavior. Compliant, anonymous, and altruistic prosocial behavior were positively related to religiosity.

Most research on prosocial behavior depicts the concept in a global and unidimensional manner. The study by Carlo & others (2010) illustrates the important point that in thinking about and studying prosocial behavior, it is important to consider multiple dimensions.

Two other aspects of prosocial behavior are forgiveness and gratitude. **Forgiveness** is an aspect of prosocial behavior that occurs when the injured person releases the injurer from possible behavioral retaliation. In one investigation, individuals from the fourth grade through college and adulthood were asked questions about forgiveness (Enright, Santos, & Al-Mabuk, 1989). The individuals were especially swayed by peer pressure in their willingness to forgive others. Also, a recent study revealed that when adolescents encountered hurtful experiences in school settings if they disliked the transgressor they had more hostile thoughts, feelings of anger, and avoidance/revenge tendencies than when they liked the transgressing peer (Peets, Hodges, & Salmivalli, 2013).

Gratitude is a feeling of thankfulness and appreciation, especially in response to someone doing something kind or helpful (Grant & Gino, 2010). Interest in studying adolescents' gratitude or lack thereof is increasing. Consider the following recent studies:

- Gratitude was linked to a number of positive aspects of development in young adolescents, including satisfaction with one's family, optimism, and prosocial behavior (Froh, Yurkewicz, & Kashdan, 2009).
- Adolescents' expression of gratitude was linked to having fewer depressive symptoms (Lambert, Fincham, & Stillman, 2012).
- Chinese adolescents who had a higher level of gratitude were less likely to engage in suicidal ideation and suicide attempts (Li & others, 2012).
- A longitudinal study assessed the gratitude of adolescents at 10 to 14 years of age (Bono, 2012). Four years later, the most grateful adolescents (top 20 percent) had a stronger sense of the meaning of life, were more satisfied with their life, were happier and more hopeful, and had a lower level of negative emotions and were less depressed than the least grateful students (bottom 20 percent).

Compared with antisocial behavior such as juvenile delinquency, less attention has been given to prosocial behavior in adolescence. We still do not have adequate research information about such topics as how youth perceive prosocial norms and how school policies and peers influence prosocial behavior (Siu, Shek, & Law, 2012).

forgiveness An aspect of prosocial behavior that occurs when an injured person releases the injurer from possible behavioral retaliation.

gratitude A feeling of thankfulness and appreciation, especially in response to someone doing something kind or helpful.

ANTISOCIAL BEHAVIOR

Most children and adolescents at one time or another act out or do things that are destructive or troublesome for themselves or others. If these behaviors occur often, psychiatrists diagnose them as conduct disorders. If these behaviors result in illegal acts by juveniles, society labels them delinquents. Both problems are much more common in males than in females.

What are some characteristics of conduct disorder?

Conduct Disorder   **Conduct disorder** refers to age-inappropriate actions and attitudes that violate family expectations, society's norms, and the personal or property rights of others. Children with conduct problems show a wide range of rule-violating behaviors, from swearing and temper tantrums to severe vandalism, theft, and assault (Burke, 2011; Farrington, 2009). Conduct disorder is much more common among boys than girls (McCabe & others, 2004).

An estimated 5 percent of children show serious conduct problems. These children are often described as showing an *externalizing,* or *undercontrolled,* pattern of behavior. Children who show this pattern often are impulsive, overactive, and aggressive and engage in delinquent actions.

Conduct problems in children are best explained by a confluence of causes, or risk factors, operating over time (Burke, 2011; Thio, 2010). These include possible genetic inheritance of a difficult temperament, ineffective parenting, living in a neighborhood where violence is common, and ineffective schools. A recent study revealed that young adolescents' school connectedness served as a protective factor for early adolescent conduct problems (Loukas, Roalson, & Herrera, 2010).

Despite considerable efforts to help children with conduct problems, there is a lack of consensus regarding what works (Mash & Wolfe, 2013). Sometimes recommended is a multisystem treatment carried out with all family members, school personnel, juvenile justice staff, and other individuals in the child's life.

Juvenile Delinquency   What is a juvenile delinquent? What are the antecedents of delinquency? What types of interventions have been used to prevent or reduce delinquency?

What Is Juvenile Delinquency?   The term **juvenile delinquency** refers to a broad range of behaviors, from socially unacceptable behavior (such as acting out in school) to status offenses (such as running away) to criminal acts (such as burglary). For legal purposes, a distinction is made between index offenses and status offenses:

- **Index offenses** are criminal acts regardless of whether they are committed by juveniles or adults. They include acts such as robbery, aggravated assault, rape, and homicide.
- **Status offenses,** such as running away, truancy, underage drinking, sexual promiscuity, and uncontrollability, are less serious acts. They are performed by youth under a specified age, which classifies them as juvenile offenses.

One issue in juvenile justice is whether an adolescent who commits a crime should be tried as an adult. Some psychologists have proposed that individuals 12 and under should not be evaluated under adult criminal laws and that those 17 and older should be (Steinberg, 2009). They also recommend that individuals 13 to 16 years of age be given some type of individualized assessment in terms of whether they ought to be tried in a juvenile court or an adult criminal court. This framework argues strongly against court placement based solely on the nature of an offense and takes into account the offender's developmental maturity. The Society for Adolescent Medicine has argued that the death penalty should not be used with adolescents (Morreale, 2004).

Juvenile court delinquency caseloads in the United States increased dramatically from 1960 to 1996 but have decreased slightly since 1996 (see Figure 13.4) (Puzzanchera & Sickmund, 2008). Note that this figure reflects only adolescents who have been arrested and assigned to juvenile court delinquency caseloads and does not include those who were arrested and not assigned to the delinquency caseloads, nor does the figure include youth who committed offenses but were not apprehended.

Males are more likely to engage in delinquency than are females (Thio, 2010). However, U.S. government statistics revealed that the percentage of delinquency caseloads involving females increased from 19 percent in 1985 to 27 percent in 2005 (Puzzanchera & Sickmund, 2008).

conduct disorder Age-inappropriate actions and attitudes that violate family expectations, society's norms, and the personal or property rights of others.

juvenile delinquency Refers to a great variety of behaviors by an adolescent, ranging from unacceptable behavior to breaking the law.

index offenses Criminal acts, such as robbery, rape, and homicide, whether they are committed by juveniles or adults.

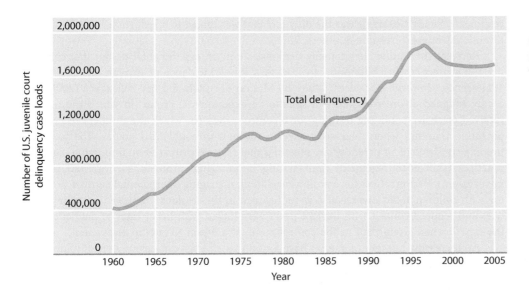

As adolescents reach adulthood, do their rates of delinquency and crime change? Recent analyses indicate that theft, property damage, and physical aggression decrease from 18 to 26 years of age (Schulenberg & Zarrett, 2006). The peak for property damage is 16 to 18 years of age for males, and 15 to 17 years of age for females. However, the peak for violence is 18 to 19 years of age for males and 19 to 21 years of age for females (Farrington, 2009).

A distinction is made between early-onset (before age 11) and late-onset (11 and older) antisocial behavior. Early-onset antisocial behavior is associated with more negative developmental outcomes than late-onset antisocial behavior (Schulenberg & Zarrett, 2006). Early-onset antisocial behavior is more likely to persist into emerging adulthood and is associated with increased problems involving mental health and relationships.

Antecedents of Juvenile Delinquency   Predictors of delinquency include conflict with authority, minor covert acts that are followed by property damage and other more serious acts, minor aggression followed by fighting and violence, identity (negative identity), self-control (low degree), cognitive distortions (egocentric bias), age (early initiation), sex (male), expectations for education (low expectations, little commitment), school achievement (low achievement in early grades), peer influence (heavy influence, low resistance), socioeconomic status (low), parental role (lack of monitoring, low support, and ineffective discipline), siblings (having an older sibling who is a delinquent), and neighborhood quality (urban, high crime, high mobility).

Family support systems are also associated with delinquency (Farrington, 2009; Lansford & others, 2013; Murphy & others, 2013). Parental monitoring of adolescents is especially important in determining whether an adolescent becomes a delinquent (Laird & others, 2008). For example, a study of families living in high-risk neighborhoods revealed that parents' lack of knowledge of their young adolescents' whereabouts was linked to whether the adolescents engaged in delinquency later in adolescence (Lahey & others, 2008). And a recent study found that early parental monitoring in adolescence and ongoing parental support were linked to a lower incidence of criminal behavior in emerging adulthood (Johnson & others, 2011). And a recent study found that for both African American and non-Latino White youth, low parental control predicted delinquency, indirectly through its link to deviant peer affiliation (Deutsch & others, 2012). Further, in a recent study, authoritative parenting increased adolescents' perception of the legitimacy of parental authority, while authoritarian parenting reduced the perception of legitimacy of parental authority (Trinkner & others, 2012). In this study, youths' perception of parental legitimacy was linked to a lower level of future delinquency.

Family discord and inconsistent and inappropriate discipline are also associated with delinquency (Bor, McGee, & Fagan, 2004). Further, recent research indicates that family therapy is often effective in reducing delinquency (Baldwin & others, 2012; Henggeler & Sheidow, 2012). A recent meta-analysis found that of five program types (case management, individual treatment, youth court, restorative justice, and family

status offenses Juvenile offenses, performed by youth under a specified age, that are not as serious as index offenses. These offenses may include acts such as underage drinking, truancy, and sexual promiscuity.

What are some factors that influence whether adolescents will become delinquents?

developmental **connection**

Parenting

A neglectful parenting style is linked with a low level of self-control in children. Chapter 14, p. 401

treatment), family treatment was the only one that was linked to a reduction in recidivism for juvenile offenders (Schwalbe & others, 2012).

Rare are the studies that actually demonstrate in an experimental design that changing parenting practices in childhood can lead to a lower incidence of juvenile delinquency in adolescence. However, one recent study by Marion Forgatch and her colleagues (2009) randomly assigned divorced mothers of sons to an experimental group (in which the mothers received extensive parenting training) or a control group (in which the mothers received no parenting training) when their sons were in the first through third grades. The parenting training consisted of 14 parent group meetings that focused primarily on improving parenting practices (skill encouragement, limit setting, monitoring, problem solving, and positive involvement). Best practices for emotion regulation, managing interparental conflict, and talking with children about divorce also were included in the sessions. Improved parenting practices and reduced contact with deviant peers were linked with lower rates of delinquency in the experimental group than in the control group at a 9-year follow-up assessment.

An increasing number of studies have found that siblings can have a strong influence on delinquency (Bank, Burraston, & Snyder, 2004). In one study, high levels of hostile sibling relationships and older sibling delinquency were linked with younger sibling delinquency in both brother pairs and sister pairs (Slomkowski & others, 2001).

Having delinquent peers increases the risk of becoming delinquent. For example, researchers found that peer rejection and having deviant friends at 7 to 13 years of age were linked with increased delinquency at 14 to 15 years of age (Vitaro, Pedersen, & Brendgen, 2007). Also, another research team found that associating with deviant peers was related to a higher incidence of delinquency in African American adolescents (Bowman, Prelow, & Weaver, 2007).

Although delinquency is less exclusively a lower-SES phenomenon than it was in the past, some characteristics of lower-SES culture can promote delinquency. The norms of many low-SES peer groups and gangs are antisocial, or counterproductive to the goals and norms of society at large. Getting into and staying out of trouble are prominent features of life for some adolescents in low-income neighborhoods. Adolescents from low-income backgrounds may sense that they can gain attention and status by performing antisocial

connecting with careers

Rodney Hammond, Health Psychologist

In describing his college experiences, Rodney Hammond recalls, "When I started as an undergraduate at the University of Illinois at Champaign-Urbana, I hadn't decided on my major. But to help finance my education, I took a part-time job in a child development research program sponsored by the psychology department. There, I observed inner-city children in settings designed to enhance their learning. I saw firsthand the contribution psychology can make, and I knew I wanted to be a psychologist" (American Psychological Association, 2003, p. 26).

Rodney Hammond went on to obtain a doctorate in school and community psychology with a focus on children's development. For a number of years, he trained clinical psychologists at Wright State University in Ohio and directed a program to reduce violence in ethnic minority youth. There, he and his associates taught at-risk youth how to use social skills to effectively manage conflict and to recognize situations that could lead to violence. Today, Hammond is Director of Violence Prevention at the Centers for Disease Control and Prevention in Atlanta. Hammond says that if you are interested in people and problem solving, psychology is a wonderful way to put these together. (Source: American Psychological Association, 2003, pp. 26–27)

Rodney Hammond.

actions. Being "tough" and "masculine" are high-status traits for low-SES boys, and these traits are often measured by the adolescent's success in performing and getting away with delinquent acts. A recent study revealed that engaged parenting and mothers' social network support were linked to a lower level of delinquency in low-income families (Ghazarian & Roche, 2010). And another study found that youth whose families had experienced repeated poverty were more than twice as likely to be delinquent at 14 and 21 years of age (Najman & others, 2010).

The nature of a community can contribute to delinquency (Loeber, Burke, & Pardini, 2009). A community with a high crime rate allows adolescents to observe many models who engage in criminal activities and might be rewarded for their criminal accomplishments. Such communities often are characterized by poverty, unemployment, and feelings of alienation. Poor-quality schools, lack of funding for education, and the absence of organized neighborhood activities are other community factors that might be related to delinquency.

Lack of success in school also is associated with delinquency. A recent study found that poor academic performance and reduced attachment to school at age 15 predicted a higher level of criminal activity at 17 to 19 years of age (Savolainen & others, 2012).

Cognitive factors such as low self-control, low intelligence, and lack of sustained attention also are implicated in delinquency. For example, a recent study revealed that low-IQ habitual delinquents were characterized by low self-control (Koolhof & others, 2007). Another recent study found that at age 16 nondelinquents were more likely to have a higher verbal IQ and engage in sustained attention than delinquents (Loeber & others, 2007). And in a longitudinal study, one of the strongest predictors of reduced likelihood of engaging in serious theft was academic achievement in high school (Loeber & others, 2008).

One individual whose goal is to reduce juvenile delinquency and help adolescents cope more effectively with the challenges in their lives is Rodney Hammond. To read about his work, see *Connecting with Careers* on page 380. Next, read *Connecting Through Research* to find out whether intervening in the lives of children who show early conduct problems can reduce their delinquency risk in adolescence.

connecting through research

Can Intervention in Childhood Reduce Delinquency in Adolescence?

Fast Track is an intervention that attempts to reduce the incidence of juvenile delinquency and other problems (Conduct Problems Prevention Research Group, 2007, 2010a, b, 2011, 2013; Dodge & McCourt, 2010; Jones & others, 2010; Miller & others, 2011). Schools in four areas (Durham, North Carolina; Nashville, Tennessee; Seattle, Washington; and rural central Pennsylvania) were identified as high risk based on neighborhood crime and poverty data. Researchers screened more than 9,000 kindergarten children in the four schools and randomly assigned 891 of the highest-risk and moderate-risk children to intervention or control conditions. The average age of the children when the intervention began was 6.5 years of age. The 10-year intervention consisted of behavior management training of parents, social cognitive skills training of children, reading tutoring, home visitations, mentoring, and a revised classroom curriculum that was designed to increase socioemotional competence and decrease aggression.

The extensive intervention was most successful for children and adolescents who were identified as the highest risk in kindergarten, lowering their incidence of conduct disorder, attention deficit hyperactivity disorder, any externalized disorder, and antisocial behavior. Positive outcomes for the intervention occurred as early as the third grade and continued through the ninth grade. For example, in the ninth grade the intervention reduced the likelihood that the highest-risk kindergarten children would develop conduct disorder by 75 percent, attention deficit hyperactivity disorder by 53 percent, and any externalized disorder by 43 percent. Recently, data have been reported through age 19 (Miller & others, 2011). Findings indicate that the comprehensive Fast Track intervention was successful in reducing youth arrest rates (Conduct Problems Prevention Research Group, 2010b).

LG3 Describe the development of prosocial and antisocial behavior.

Review

- How is altruism defined? How does prosocial behavior develop?
- What is juvenile delinquency? What is conduct disorder? What are key factors in the development of juvenile delinquency?

Connect

- In this section, you learned that being "tough" and "masculine" are high-status traits for low-SES boys and that this can lead to delinquent acts. In Chapter 12, what did researcher Joseph Pleck say about boys who adopt a strong masculine role in adolescence?

Reflect *Your Own Personal Journey of Life*

- Did you commit acts of delinquency as an adolescent? Most adolescents commit one or more acts of juvenile delinquency without becoming habitual juvenile delinquents. Reflect on your experiences of either committing juvenile offenses or not committing them, then review the discussion of factors that are likely causes of juvenile delinquency and apply them to your development.

Religious and Spiritual Development

LG4 Summarize the nature of children's and adolescents' religious and spiritual development.

Childhood

Adolescence

> Religion enlightens, terrifies, subdues; it gives faith, inflicts remorse, inspires resolutions, and inflames devotion.
>
> —**Henry Newman**
> *English Churchman and Writer, 19th Century*

religion An organized set of beliefs, practices, rituals, and symbols that increases an individual's connection to a sacred or transcendent other (God, higher power, or higher truth).

religiousness The degree of affiliation with an organized religion, participation in prescribed rituals and practices, connection with its beliefs, and involvement in a community of believers.

spirituality Experiencing something beyond oneself in a transcendent manner and living in a way that benefits others and society.

Can religion, religiousness, and spirituality be differentiated? A recent analysis by Pamela King and her colleagues (King, Carr, & Boiter, 2011; King, Ramos, & Clardy, 2012) makes the following distinctions:

- **Religion** is an organized set of beliefs, practices, rituals, and symbols that increases an individual's connection to a sacred or transcendent other (God, higher power, or ultimate truth).
- **Religiousness** refers to the degree of affiliation with an organized religion, participation in its prescribed rituals and practices, connection with its beliefs, and involvement in a community of believers.
- **Spirituality** involves experiencing something beyond oneself in a transcendent manner and living in a way that benefits others and society.

CHILDHOOD

How do parents influence children's religious thought and behavior? Societies use many methods—such as Sunday schools, parochial education, and parental teaching—to ensure that people will carry on a religious tradition. In a recent national study, 63 percent of parents with children at home said they pray or read Scripture with their children, and 60 percent reported that they send their children to religious education programs (Pew Research Center, 2008). Does this religious socialization work? In many cases it does, and children usually adopt the religious beliefs of their parents (Paloutzian, 2000). A recent study revealed that parents' religiousness assessed during youths' adolescence was positively related to youths' own religiousness during adolescence, which in turn was linked to their religiousness following the transition to adulthood (Spilman & others, 2012)

ADOLESCENCE

Religious issues are important to many adolescents and emerging adults (Day, 2010; King, Carr, & Boiter, 2011; Lerner & others, 2013; Park & others, 2012a, b; Saroglou, 2013). However, in the twenty-first century, a downtrend in religious interest among college students has occurred. In a national study of American freshmen in 2010, 75 percent said they attended a religious service frequently or occasionally during the past year, down from a high of 85 percent in 1997 (Pryor & others, 2010).

A developmental study revealed that religiousness declined among adolescents between age 14 and age 20 in the United States (Koenig, McGue, & Iacono, 2008) (see Figure 13.5). In this study, religiousness was assessed with items such as frequency of prayer, frequency of discussing religious teachings, frequency of deciding moral actions for religious reasons, and the overall importance of religion in everyday life. As indicated in Figure 13.5, a greater change in religiousness occurred from 14 to 18 years of age than from 20 to 25 years of age. Also, reported frequency of attending religious services was highest at 14 years of age, declining from 14 to 18 years of age and increasing at 20 years of age. More change occurred in attending religious services than in religiousness.

Researchers have found that adolescent girls are more religious than are adolescent boys (King & Roeser, 2009). One study of 13- to 17-year-olds revealed that girls are more likely to attend religious services frequently, perceive that religion shapes their daily lives, participate in religious youth groups, pray more when alone, and feel closer to God (Smith & Denton, 2005).

Analysis of the World Values Survey of 18- to 24-year-olds revealed that emerging adults in less-developed countries were more likely to be religious than their counterparts in more-developed countries (Lippman & Keith, 2006). For example, emerging adults' reports of religion being very important in their lives ranged from a low of 0 percent in Japan to 93 percent in Nigeria, and belief in God ranged from a low of 40 percent in Sweden to a high of 100 percent in Pakistan.

Religion and Cognitive Development   Adolescence and emerging adulthood can be especially important junctures in religious development (Good & Willoughby, 2008; Lerner, Roeser, & Phelps, 2009). Even if children have been indoctrinated into a religion by their parents, because of advances in their cognitive development adolescents and emerging adults may question what their own religious beliefs truly are.

Many of the cognitive changes thought to influence religious development involve Piaget's stages of cognitive development discussed in Chapter 6. More so than in childhood, adolescents think abstractly, idealistically, and logically. The increase in abstract thinking lets adolescents consider various ideas about religious and spiritual concepts. For example, an adolescent might ask how a loving God can possibly exist given the extensive suffering of many people in the world (Good & Willoughby, 2008). Adolescents' increasingly idealistic thinking provides a foundation for questioning whether religion provides the best route to a better, more ideal world. And adolescents' increased logical reasoning gives them the ability to develop hypotheses and systematically sort through different answers to spiritual questions (Good & Willoughby, 2008).

Religion and Identity Development   During adolescence and emerging adulthood, especially emerging adulthood, identity development becomes a central focus (Erikson, 1968; Schwartz & others, 2013). Adolescents and emerging adults are looking for answers to questions such as "Who am I?" "What am I all about as a person?" "What kind of life do I want to lead?" As part of their search for identity, adolescents and emerging adults begin to grapple in more sophisticated, logical ways with questions such as "Why am I on this planet?" "Is there really a God or higher spiritual being, or have I just been believing what my parents and the church imprinted in my mind?" "What are my own religious views?" A recent analysis of the link between identity and spirituality concluded that adolescence and adulthood can serve as gateways to developing a spiritual identity that "transcends, but not necessarily excludes, the assigned religious identity in childhood" (Templeton & Eccles, 2006, p. 261).

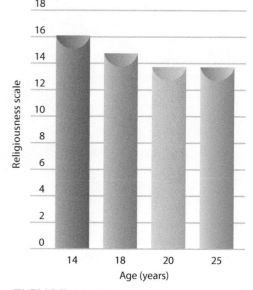

FIGURE **13.5**

DEVELOPMENTAL CHANGES IN RELIGIOUSNESS FROM 14 TO 25 YEARS OF AGE. *Note:* The religiousness scale ranged from 0 to 32, with higher scores indicating stronger religiousness.

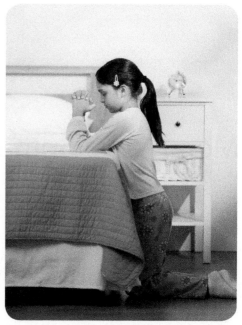

What are some cognitive developmental changes that could influence religious development?

Adolescents participating in a church choir. *What are some positive aspects of religion in adolescents' lives?*

The Positive Role of Religion in Adolescents' Lives

Researchers have found that various aspects of religion are linked with positive outcomes for adolescents (Harakeh & others, 2012; Shek, 2012). A recent study revealed that a higher level of church engagement (based on years of attendance, choice in attending, and participation in activities) was related to higher grades for male adolescents (Kang & Romo, 2011).

Religion also plays a role in adolescents' health and well-being, and whether they engage in problem behaviors (Salas-Wright & others, 2012). In a national random sample of more than 2,000 11- to 18-year-olds, those who were higher in religiosity were less likely to smoke, drink alcohol, use marijuana, be truant from school, engage in delinquent activities, and be depressed than were their low-religiosity counterparts (Sinha, Cnaan, & Gelles, 2007).

A recent meta-analysis found that spirituality/religiosity was positively related to well-being, self-esteem, and three of the Big Five factors of personality (conscientiousness, agreeableness, openness) (Yonker, Schnabelrauch, & DeHaan, 2012). In this meta-analysis, spirituality/religion was negatively associated with risk behavior and depression.

Review Connect Reflect

 LG4 Summarize the nature of children's and adolescents' religious and spiritual development.

Review

• How does religious and spiritual interest and understanding develop in childhood?
• What characterizes religious and spiritual development in adolescence?

Connect

• In this section, you learned that many of the cognitive changes thought to influence adolescents' religious development reflect Piaget's stages of cognitive development. What is the adolescent stage of Piaget's theory called, and what else characterizes it?

Reflect *Your Own Personal Journey of Life*

• Reflect on your religious/spiritual upbringing. How have your religious/spiritual views changed or stayed the same as you developed through childhood and adolescence? Have your religious/spiritual views changed since adolescence? Explain.

reach your **learning goals**

Moral Development

Domains of Moral Development

 LG1 Discuss theory and research on the four domains of moral development.

What Is Moral Development?

Moral Thought

• Moral development involves changes in thoughts, feelings, and behaviors regarding right and wrong. Moral development includes intrapersonal and interpersonal dimensions.

• Piaget distinguished between the heteronomous morality of younger children and the autonomous morality of older children. Kohlberg developed a provocative theory of moral reasoning. He argued that development of moral reasoning consists of three levels—preconventional, conventional, and postconventional—and six stages (two at each level). Kohlberg reasoned that these stages were age related. Influences on the Kohlberg stages include cognitive development, dealing with moral questions and moral conflict, peer relations, and perspective taking. Criticisms of Kohlberg's theory have been made, especially by Gilligan, who advocates a stronger care perspective. Other criticisms focus on the inadequacy of moral reasoning to predict moral behavior, to account for the influences of culture and family, and to assess moral reasoning.

Moral Behavior

- The processes of reinforcement, punishment, and imitation have been used to explain the acquisition of moral behavior, but they provide only a partial explanation. Situational variability is stressed by behaviorists. Social cognitive theory emphasizes a distinction between moral competence and moral performance.

Moral Feeling

- In Freud's theory, the superego is the moral branch of personality. According to Freud, guilt is the foundation of children's moral behavior. Empathy is an important aspect of moral feelings, and it changes developmentally. In the contemporary perspective, both positive and negative feelings contribute to moral development.

Moral Personality

- Recently, there has been a surge of interest in studying moral personality. This interest has focused on moral identity, moral character, and moral exemplars. Moral character involves having strong convictions; persisting; overcoming distractions and obstacles; and having virtues such as honesty, truthfulness, loyalty, and compassion. Moral exemplars have a moral character, identity, personality, and a set of virtues reflecting excellence and commitment; they are honest and dependable.

Social-Cognitive Domain Theory

- Social-cognitive domain theory states that there are different domains of social knowledge and reasoning, including moral, social conventional, and personal domains.

Contexts of Moral Development   Explain how parenting and schools influence moral development.

Parenting

- Warmth and responsibility in mutual obligations of parent-child relationships provide important foundations for the child's positive moral growth. Love withdrawal, power assertion, and induction are discipline techniques. Induction is most likely to be linked with positive moral development. Moral development can be advanced by parenting strategies such as being warm and supportive rather than punitive; using inductive discipline; providing opportunities to learn about others' perspectives and feelings; involving children in family decision making; modeling moral behaviors; and averting misbehavior before it takes place.

Schools

- The hidden curriculum, initially described by Dewey, is the moral atmosphere of each school. Contemporary approaches to moral education include character education, values clarification, cognitive moral education, service learning, and integrative ethical education. Cheating is a moral education concern that can take many forms. Various aspects of the school situation influence whether students will cheat or not.

Prosocial and Antisocial Behavior   Describe the development of prosocial and antisocial behavior.

Prosocial Behavior

- An important aspect of prosocial behavior is altruism, an unselfish interest in helping others. Damon described a sequence by which children develop their understanding of fairness and become willing to share more consistently. Peers play a key role in this development. Forgiveness and gratitude are two additional aspects of prosocial behavior.

Antisocial Behavior

- Conduct disorder is a psychiatric diagnostic category used to describe multiple delinquent-type behaviors occurring over a six-month period. Juvenile delinquency consists of a broad range of behaviors, from socially undesirable behavior to status offenses. For legal purposes, a distinction is made between index and status offenses. Predictors of juvenile delinquency include authority conflict, minor covert acts such as lying, overt acts of aggression, a negative identity, cognitive distortions, low self-control, early initiation of delinquency, being a male, low expectations for education and school grades, low parental monitoring, low parental support and ineffective discipline, having an older delinquent sibling, heavy peer influence and low resistance to peers, low socioeconomic status, and living in a high-crime, urban area. Effective juvenile delinquency prevention and intervention programs have been identified.

Religious and Spiritual Development

 LG4 Summarize the nature of children's and adolescents' religious and spiritual development.

Childhood

Adolescence

- Many children and adolescents show an interest in religion. Many children adopt their parents' religious beliefs.

- The twenty-first century has shown a downturn in adolescents' religious interest. Emerging adults from less-developed countries are more likely to be religious than those from more-developed countries. Cognitive changes in adolescence—such as increases in abstract, idealistic, and logical thinking—increase the likelihood that adolescents will seek a better understanding of religion and spirituality. As part of their search for identity, many adolescents and emerging adults begin to grapple with more complex aspects of religion. Various aspects of religion are linked with positive outcomes in adolescent development.

key terms

moral development 359
heteronomous morality (Piaget) 360
autonomous morality 360
immanent justice 360
preconventional reasoning 361
conventional reasoning 361
postconventional reasoning 362
justice perspective 364

care perspective 364
social cognitive theory of morality 366
empathy 366
moral identity 368
moral exemplars 368
social-cognitive domain theory 368
social conventional reasoning 369

love withdrawal 371
power assertion 371
induction 371
hidden curriculum 372
character education 372
values clarification 373
cognitive moral education 373
service learning 373
altruism 376

forgiveness 377
gratitude 377
conduct disorder 378
juvenile delinquency 378
index offenses 378
status offenses 379
religion 382
religiousness 382
spirituality 382

key people

Jean Piaget 360
Lawrence Kohlberg 360
Carol Gilligan 364
Hugh Hartshorne 366
Mark May 366

Albert Bandura 366
Sigmund Freud 366
Grazyna Kochanska 367
Judith Smetana 369
William Damon 367

Darcia Narváez 368
James Rest 368
Lawrence Walker 369
Ross Thompson 372
John Dewey 373

Gustavo Carlo 377
Marion Forgatch 380
Pamela King 382

section **five**

It is not enough for parents to understand children. They must also accord children the privilege of understanding them.

—**MILTON SAPIRSTEIN**
American Psychiatrist and Writer, 20th Century

Social Contexts of Development

Parents cradle children's lives, but children's growth is also shaped by successive choirs of siblings, peers, friends, and teachers. Children's small worlds widen as they discover new refuges and new people. In the end, there are but two lasting bequests that parents can leave children, one being roots, the other wings. In this section, we will study four chapters: "Families" (Chapter 14), "Peers" (Chapter 15), "Schools and Achievement" (Chapter 16), and "Culture and Diversity" (Chapter 17).

chapter 14

FAMILIES

chapter **outline**

When Shelley Peterman Schwarz (2004) and her husband, David, had been married four years, they decided to have children. They had two children, Jamie and Andrew. When the children were 3 and 5 years old, Shelley was diagnosed with multiple sclerosis. Two years later, she had to quit her job as a teacher of hearing-impaired children because of her worsening condition.

By the time the children were 7 and 9 years old, it was more difficult for Shelley to prepare meals for the family by herself, so David began taking over that responsibility. They also enlisted the children's help in preparing meals.

Despite her multiple sclerosis, Shelley participated in parenting classes and workshops at her children's school. She even initiated a "Mothers of 10-year-olds" support group. But parenting with multiple sclerosis had its frustrations for Shelley. In her words,

Shelley Peterman Schwarz (*left*) with her family.

attending school functions, teacher's conferences, and athletic events often presented problems because the facilities weren't always easily wheelchair accessible. I felt guilty if I didn't at least "try" to attend. I didn't want my children to think I didn't care enough to try. . . .

When Jamie was 19 and Andrew was 17, I started to relax a little. I could see how capable and independent they were becoming. My having a disability hadn't ruined their lives. In fact, in some ways, they are better off because of it. They learned to trust themselves and to face personal challenges head-on. When the time came for them to leave the nest and head off to college, I knew they were ready.

As for me, I now understand that having a disability wasn't the worst thing in the world that could happen to a parent. What would be a tragedy is letting your disability cripple your ability to stay in your children's lives. Parenting is so much more than driving car pools, attending gymnastic meets, or baking cookies for an open house. It's loving, caring, listening, guiding, and supporting your child. It's consoling a child crying because her friends thought her haircut was ugly. It's counseling a child worried because his 12-year-old friend is drinking. It's helping a child understand relationships and what it's like to "be in love." (Schwarz, 2004, p. 5)

preview

This chapter is about the many aspects of children's development in families. We will explore how families work, ways to parent children, relationships among siblings, and the changing family in a changing social world. Along the way, we will examine topics such as child maltreatment, working parents, children in divorced families, stepfamilies, and many others.

Family Processes **LG1** Discuss family processes.

| Interactions in the Family System | Cognition and Emotion in Family Processes | Multiple Developmental Trajectories | Domain-Specific Socialization | Sociocultural and Historical Changes |

As we examine the family and other social contexts of development, it will be helpful to keep in mind Urie Bronfenbrenner's (2000, 2004) ecological theory, which we discussed in Chapter 1. Recall that Bronfenbrenner analyzes the social contexts of development in terms of five environmental systems:

- The *microsystem* or the setting in which the individual lives, such as a family, the world of peers, schools, work, and so on
- The *mesosystem*, which consists of links between microsystems, such as the connection between family processes and peer relations
- The *exosystem,* which consists of influences from another setting that the individual does not experience directly, such as how parents' experiences at work might affect their parenting at home
- The *macrosystem* or the culture in which the individual lives, such as a nation or an ethnic group
- The *chronosystem* or sociohistorical circumstances, such as increased numbers of working mothers, divorced parents, and stepparent families in the United States in the last 30 to 40 years

Let's begin our examination of the family at the level of the microsystem.

INTERACTIONS IN THE FAMILY SYSTEM

Every family is a *system*—a complex whole made up of interrelated and interacting parts. The relationships never go in just one direction. For example, the interaction of mothers and their infants is sometimes symbolized as a dance in which successive actions of the partners are closely coordinated. This coordinated dance can assume the form of *mutual synchrony,* which means that each person's behavior depends on the partner's previous behavior. Or the interaction can be *reciprocal* in a precise sense, which means that the actions of the partners can be matched, as when one partner imitates the other or when there is mutual smiling (Cohn & Tronick, 1988). An important example of early synchronized interaction is mutual gaze or eye contact.

Another example of synchronization occurs in **scaffolding,** which means adjusting the level of guidance to fit the child's performance, as we discussed in Chapter 6 (Melzi, Schick, & Kennedy, 2011). The parent responds to the child's behavior with scaffolding, which in turn affects the child's behavior. Scaffolding can be used to support children's efforts at any age. A study of Hmong families living in the United States revealed that maternal scaffolding, especially in the form of cognitive support, of young children's problem solving the summer before kindergarten predicted the children's reasoning skills in kindergarten (Stright, Herr, & Neitzel, 2009).

developmental **connection**

Theories

An important contribution of Bronfenbrenner's ecological theory is its focus on a range of social contexts that influence the child's development. Chapter 1, p. 27

scaffolding Adjusting the level of parental guidance to fit the child's efforts, allowing children to be more skillful than they would be if they relied only on their own abilities.

reciprocal socialization The bidirectional process by which children socialize parents just as parents socialize them.

The game of peek-a-boo, in which parents initially cover their babies, then remove the covering, and finally register "surprise" at the babies' reappearance, reflects the concept of scaffolding. As infants become more skilled at peek-a-boo, infants gradually do some of the covering and uncovering. Parents try to time their actions in such a way that the infant takes turns with the parent.

In addition to peek-a-boo, patty-cake and so-big are other caregiver games that exemplify scaffolding and turn-taking sequences. In one investigation, infants who had more extensive scaffolding experiences with their parents, especially in the form of turn taking, were more likely to engage in turn taking as they interacted with their peers (Vandell & Wilson, 1988). Engaging in turn taking and games like peek-a-boo reflect the development of joint attention by the caregiver and infant, which we discussed in Chapter 7, "Information Processing" (Tomasello, 2009).

The mutual influence that parents and children exert on each other goes beyond specific interactions in games such as peek-a-boo; it extends to the whole process of socialization (Crouter & Booth, 2013; Shanahan & Sobolewski, 2013). Socialization between parents and children is not a one-way process. Parents do socialize children, but socialization in families is reciprocal (Capaldi, 2013; McHale & Crouter, 2013). **Reciprocal socialization** is socialization that is bidirectional; children socialize parents just as parents socialize children. These reciprocal interchanges and mutual influence processes are sometimes referred to as *transactional* (Sameroff, 2009).

How does the game of peek-a-boo reflect the concept of scaffolding?

Of course, while parents are interacting with their children, they are also interacting with each other. To understand these interactions and relationships, it helps to think of the family as a constellation of subsystems defined in terms of generation, gender, and role. Each family member participates in several subsystems—some *dyadic* (involving two people) and some *polyadic* (involving more than two people). The father and child represent one dyadic subsystem, the mother and father another; the mother-father-child represent one polyadic subsystem, the mother and two siblings another (Parke & others, 2008).

These subsystems interact and influence one another (Carlson & others, 2011). Thus, as Figure 14.1 illustrates, the marital relationship, parenting, and infant/child behavior can have both direct and indirect effects on one another (Belsky, 1981). The link between marital relationships and parenting has received increased attention. The most consistent findings are that compared with unhappily married parents, happily married parents are more sensitive, responsive, warm, and affectionate toward their children (Grych, 2002).

Researchers have found that promoting marital satisfaction often leads to good parenting. The marital relationship provides an important support for parenting (Cowan & others, 2013; Cummings & others, 2012). When parents report more intimacy and better communication in their marriage, they are more affectionate to their children (Grych, 2002). Thus, marriage-enhancement programs may end up improving parenting and helping children. Programs that focus on enhancing parenting skills might also benefit from including attention to the participants' marriages.

Children socialize parents just as parents socialize children.

COGNITION AND EMOTION IN FAMILY PROCESSES

Both cognition and emotion are increasingly thought to be central to understanding how family processes work (Crockenberg & Leerkes, 2013; Thompson, 2013c, d). The role of cognition in family socialization takes many forms, including parents' cognitions, beliefs, and values about their parental role, as well as how parents perceive, organize, and understand their children's behaviors and beliefs. For example, one study found a link between mothers' beliefs and their preschool children's social problem-solving skills (Rubin, Mills, & Rose-Krasnor, 1989). Mothers who placed a higher value on skills such as making friends, sharing with others, and leading or influencing other children had children who were more assertive, prosocial, and competent problem solvers than mothers who valued these skills less.

Children's social competence is also linked to the emotional lives of their parents (Ablow, 2013). For example, one study found that parents who expressed positive emotions had children who were high in competence (Boyum & Parke, 1995). Through interaction with parents, children learn to express their emotions in appropriate ways.

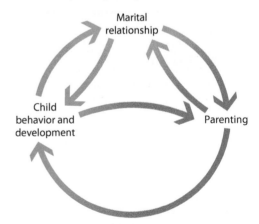

FIGURE **14.1**

INTERACTION BETWEEN CHILDREN AND THEIR PARENTS: DIRECT AND INDIRECT EFFECTS

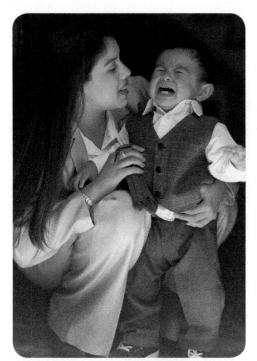

How are cognition and emotion involved in understanding family processes in children's development?

developmental **connection**

Attention

Joint attention can play an important role in interchanges between a caregiver and an infant. Chapter 7, p. 199

developmental **connection**

Parenting

Emotion-coaching parents use more scaffolding and praise when interacting with their children than do emotion-dismissing parents. Chapter 10, p. 289

multiple developmental trajectories Concept that adults follow one trajectory and children and adolescents another one; understanding how these trajectories mesh is important.

Researchers are also finding that parental sensitivity to children's emotions is related to children's ability to manage their emotions in positive ways (Thompson, 2013c, d). Recall from Chapter 10, "Emotional Development," the distinction that was made between emotion-coaching and emotion-dismissing parents (Gottman, 2012). *Emotion-coaching parents* monitor their children's emotions, view their children's negative emotions as opportunities for teaching, assist them in labeling emotions, and coach them in how to deal effectively with emotions. In contrast, *emotion-dismissing parents* view their role as to deny, ignore, or change negative emotions.

MULTIPLE DEVELOPMENTAL TRAJECTORIES

The concept of **multiple developmental trajectories** refers to the fact that adults follow one trajectory and children and adolescents another one (Parke & Buriel, 2006; Parke & Clarke-Stewart, 2011). Tracing how adult and child/adolescent developmental trajectories mesh is important for understanding the timing of entry into various family tasks. Adult developmental trajectories include timing of entry into marriage, cohabitation, or parenthood; child developmental trajectories include timing of child care and entry into middle school. The timing of some family tasks and changes are planned, such as reentry into the workforce or delaying parenthood, whereas others are not, such as job loss or divorce (Parke & Buriel, 2006).

Consider the developmental period of adolescence. Most adolescents' parents either are in middle adulthood or are rapidly approaching this period of life. However, in the last two decades, the timing of parenthood in the United States has undergone some dramatic shifts (Crockett & Beal, 2012). Parenthood is taking place earlier for some, and later for others, than in previous decades. First, the number of adolescent pregnancies in the United States increased considerably in the 1970s and 1980s. Although the adolescent pregnancy rate has decreased since then, the U.S. adolescent pregnancy rate remains one of the highest in the developed world. Second, the number of women who postpone childbearing until their thirties and early forties simultaneously has increased.

What are some advantages of having children early or late? Some of the advantages of having children early (in the twenties) are these: (1) the parents are likely to have more physical energy—for example, they can cope better with such matters as getting up in the middle of the night with infants and waiting up until adolescents come home at night; (2) the mother is likely to have fewer medical problems with pregnancy and childbirth; and (3) the parents may be less likely to build up expectations for their children, as do many couples who have waited many years to have children.

There are also advantages to having children later (in the thirties): (1) the parents will have had more time to consider their goals in life, such as what they want from their family and career roles; (2) the parents will be more mature and will be able to benefit from their experiences to engage in more competent parenting; and (3) the parents will be better established in their careers and have more income for child-rearing expenses.

DOMAIN-SPECIFIC SOCIALIZATION

When discussion turns to how parents socialize children, it has been common to describe the socialization process and child outcomes in general terms, such as "Parents who are warm, sensitive, and involved with their children have children who are socially competent." In such broad descriptions, too often the complexity and specificity of parental socialization and child outcomes are lost.

Recently, interest in the domain specificity of socializing children has increased. Joan Grusec and Marilyn Davidov (2010) proposed a domain-specific view of parenting that emphasizes how parents often operate in different domains characterized by different types of relationships. The five domains are described below:

- *Protection.* Many species, including *homo sapiens,* have evolved so that their young maintain proximity to a caregiver, especially when they are in stressful or dangerous circumstances. In this domain, effective parenting involves responding in such a manner that the child develops a sense of security and perceives being comforted. Child outcomes of appropriate parental protection include the ability to respond appropriately to danger and to engage in self-regulation of distress.

- *Reciprocity.* This domain is not involved when the child is distressed but rather when the parent and child are interacting on an equal basis as partners, as in the context of play. Child outcomes in the reciprocity domain include the development of cooperativeness and a desire to comply with parental requests.
- *Control.* In the control domain, interactions between parents and children typically involve conflict because parents want one thing and children another. The control domain is often activated when children misbehave. In such circumstances, parents can use their power advantage to discourage the misbehavior through various means such as reasoning, social isolation, and physical punishment. Child outcomes in the control domain include the development of moral and principled behavior.
- *Guided Learning.* In this domain, parents guide children's learning of skills through the use of effective strategies and feedback. In the guided learning domain, parents function as teachers and their children as students. Children's outcomes in the guided learning domain include acquiring knowledge and skills.
- *Group Participation.* In this domain, socialization involves increasing children's participation in cultural practices. Child outcomes include conformity to cultural group practices and values that provide the child with a sense of social identity.

Grusec and Davidov (2010) acknowledge that real-life interactions in families often involve overlapping across the domains, but the extent of this overlapping has not yet been identified (Dunn, 2010). Also, how the different domains might play out at different points in children's development has not been adequately researched.

SOCIOCULTURAL AND HISTORICAL CHANGES

Family development does not occur in a social vacuum. Important sociocultural and historical influences affect family processes, reflecting Bronfenbrenner's concepts of the macrosystem and chronosystem (Bronfenbrenner & Morris, 2006). Both great upheavals such as war, famine, or massive immigration and subtle transitions in ways of life may stimulate changes in families (Fuligni, 2012). One example is the effect on U.S. families of the Great Depression of the 1930s. During its height, the Depression produced economic deprivation, adult discontent, and widespread unemployment. It also increased marital conflict, inconsistent child rearing, and unhealthy lifestyles—heavy drinking, demoralized attitudes, and health impairments—especially in fathers (Elder & Shanahan, 2006).

Subtle changes in a culture have significant influences on the family (Mistry, Contreras, & Dutta, 2013). Such changes include increased longevity of older adults, movement to urban and suburban areas, technological advances, and a general dissatisfaction and restlessness (Mead, 1978).

In the first part of the twentieth century, individuals who survived infancy were usually hardy and still closely linked to the family, often helping to maintain the family's existence. Today, individuals live longer, which means that middle-aged children are often pressed into a caregiving role for their parents, or the elderly parents may be placed in a nursing home (Antonucci, Birditt, & Ajrouch, 2013; Fingerman, Secrest, & Birditt, 2013). Older parents may have lost some of their socializing role in the family during the twentieth century as many of their children moved great distances away. However, in the twenty-first century, an increasing number of grandparents are raising their grandchildren (Matzek & Cooney, 2009).

Many of the family moves in the last 75 years have been away from farms and small towns to urban and suburban settings. In the small towns and farms, individuals were surrounded by lifelong neighbors, relatives, and friends. Today, neighborhood and extended-family support systems are not nearly as prevalent. Families now move all over the country, often uprooting children from a school and peer group where they have spent a considerable length of time. And it is not unusual for this type of move to occur every several years as one or both parents are transferred from job to job.

developmental **connection**

Moral Development

The domain view of moral development emphasizes different domains of social knowledge and reasoning, including moral, social conventional, and personal. Chapter 13, p. 369

Two important changes in families are the increased mobility of families and the increase in television viewing. *What are some other changes?*

developmental **connection**

Media

In the twenty-first century, children and adolescents have dramatically increased the amount of time they spend with media and the number of hours they engage in multitasking that involves media. Chapter 17, p. 500

The media and technology also play a major role in the changing family (Jackson & others, 2012; Levinson, 2013; te Velde & others, 2012). Many children who watch television find that parents are too busy working to share this experience with them. Children increasingly experience a world in which their parents are not participants. Instead of interacting in neighborhood peer groups, children come home after school and watch television, play video games, or use the Internet for entertainment and social networking.

Another change in families has been an increase in general dissatisfaction and restlessness. The result of such restlessness and the tendency to divorce and remarry has been a hodgepodge of family structures, with far greater numbers of divorced and remarried families than ever before in history (Lansford, 2009).

Many of the changes we have described in this section apply not only to U.S. families but also to families in many countries around the world. Later in this chapter, we discuss aspects of the changing social world of the child and the family in greater detail.

Review *Connect* Reflect

LG1 Discuss family processes.

Review

- How can the family be viewed as a system? What is reciprocal socialization?
- How are cognition and emotion involved in family processes?
- What characterizes multiple developmental trajectories?
- What are five domain-specific socialization practices?
- What are some sociocultural and historical changes that have influenced the family?

Connect

- In this section, scaffolding was mentioned as an example of synchronization. Which

concept of Vygotsky's is scaffolding also linked to in Chapter 6?

Reflect *Your Own Personal Journey of Life*

- Reflect on your experiences with your own family as you were growing up and give some examples of the family processes discussed in this section as you experienced them in your own family.

Parenting **LG2** Explain how parenting is linked to children's and adolescents' development.

| Parental Roles and the Timing of Parenthood | Adapting Parenting to Developmental Changes in Children | Parents as Managers of Children's Lives | Parenting Styles and Discipline | Parent-Adolescent Relationships | Intergenerational Relationships |

> Parenting is a very important profession, but no test of fitness for it is ever imposed in the interest of children.
>
> —**George Bernard Shaw**
> *Irish Playwright, 20th Century*

Parenting calls on a number of interpersonal skills and makes intense emotional demands, yet there is little in the way of formal education for this task. Most parents learn parenting practices from their own parents. Some of these practices they accept, and others they discard. Husbands and wives may bring different views of parenting to the marriage.

Unfortunately, when parents' methods are passed on from one generation to the next, both desirable and undesirable practices are perpetuated. What have developmentalists learned about parenting? How should parents adapt their practices to developmental changes in their children? How important is it for parents to be effective managers of their children's lives? And how do various parenting styles and methods of discipline influence children's development?

PARENTAL ROLES AND THE TIMING OF PARENTHOOD

Many adults decide when they would like to become parents and consider how parenting will fit with their economic situation. For others, the discovery that they are about to become parents is a startling surprise. In either event, the prospective parents may have mixed emotions and romantic illusions about having a child (Carl, 2012). The needs and expectations of parents have stimulated many myths about parenting.

Currently, there is a tendency to have fewer children. The number of one-child families is increasing. Is there a best time to have children? What are some of the restrictions individuals face when they become parents? These are some of the questions we now consider.

Like the age when people marry for the first time, the age at which individuals have children has been increasing (Lauer & Lauer, 2012). In 2008, the average age at which women gave birth for the first time was 25 years of age, up from 21 years of age in 2001 (U.S. Census Bureau, 2011).

As birth control has become common practice, many individuals choose when they will have children and how many children they will raise. They are not only marrying later but also having children later or not at all. The percentage of 40- to 44-year-old U.S. women who remain childless increased from 10 percent in 1976 to 24 percent in 2006-2010 (Martinez, Daniels, & Chandra, 2012).

ADAPTING PARENTING TO DEVELOPMENTAL CHANGES IN CHILDREN

Children change as they grow from infancy to early childhood and on through middle and late childhood and adolescence. The 5-year-old and the 2-year-old have different needs and abilities. A competent parent adapts to the child's developmental changes (Maccoby, 1984). As we see next, though, considerable adaptation also is required in making the transition to parenting.

The Transition to Parenting   Whether people become parents through pregnancy, adoption, or stepparenting, they face disequilibrium and must adapt (Dew & Wilcox, 2011). Parents want to develop a strong attachment with their infant, but they still want to maintain strong attachments to their spouse and friends, and possibly continue their careers. Parents ask themselves how this new being will change their lives. A baby places new restrictions on partners; no longer will they be able to rush out to a movie on a moment's notice, and money may not be readily available for vacations and other luxuries. Dual-career parents ask, "Will it harm the baby to place her in child care? Will we be able to find responsible babysitters?"

In a longitudinal investigation of couples from late pregnancy until 3½ years after the baby was born, couples enjoyed more positive marital relations before the baby was born than after (Cowan & Cowan, 2000, 2009; Cowan, Cowan, & Barry, 2011; Cowan & others, 2005). Still, almost one-third showed an increase in marital satisfaction. Some couples said that the baby had both brought them closer together and moved them farther apart; being parents enhanced their sense of themselves and gave them a new, more stable identity as a couple. Babies opened men up to a concern with intimate relationships, and the demands of juggling work and family roles stimulated women to manage family tasks more efficiently and pay attention to their own personal growth. A recent study revealed that when new mothers had low marital satisfaction it often was linked to reductions in quality time spent with husbands and perception of unfairness in dividing up household tasks (Dew & Wilcox, 2011).

The Bringing Home Baby project is a workshop that helps new parents strengthen their relationship with their partner, understand and become acquainted with their baby, resolve conflict, and develop parenting skills. Evaluations of the project revealed that parents who participated improved their ability to work together as parents, fathers were more involved with their baby and sensitive to the

> We never know the love of our parents until we have become parents.
>
> —HENRY WARD BEECHER
> *American Clergyman, 19th Century*

What characterizes the transition to parenting?

baby's behavior, mothers had a lower incidence of postpartum depression symptoms, and babies showed better overall development than babies of participants in a control group (Gottman, 2013; Gottman Relationship Institutes, 2009; Gottman, Gottman, & Shapiro, 2009; Shapiro & Gottman, 2005).

Other recent studies have explored the transition to parenthood (Brown, Feinberg, & Kan, 2012). One study found similar negative change in relationship satisfaction for married and cohabiting women during the transition to parenthood (Mortensen & others, 2012). Another study revealed that mothers experienced unmet expectations in the transition to parenting, with fathers doing less than their partners had anticipated (Biehle & Mickelson, 2012).

Infancy   During the first year, parent-child interaction moves from a heavy focus on routine caregiving—feeding, changing diapers, bathing, and soothing—to gradually include more noncaregiving activities, such as play, visual-vocal exchanges, and managing the infant's behavior (Bornstein, 2002).

Early Childhood   Parent-child interactions during early childhood focus on such matters as modesty, bedtime regularities, control of temper, fighting with siblings and peers, eating behavior and manners, autonomy in dressing, and attention seeking (Edwards & Liu, 2002). Although some of these issues—fighting with siblings, for example—are carried forward into the elementary school years, many new issues appear by the age of 7. These include whether children should be made to perform chores and if so, whether they should be paid for them, how to help children learn to entertain themselves rather than relying on parents for everything, and how to monitor children's lives outside the family in school and peer settings.

Middle and Late Childhood   As children move into the middle and late childhood years, parents spend less time with them. In one study, parents spent less than half as much time with their children aged 5 to 12 in caregiving, instruction, reading, talking, and playing as when the children were younger (Hill & Stafford, 1980). Although parents spend less time with their children in middle and late childhood than in early childhood, parents continue to be extremely important in their children's lives. In a recent analysis of the contributions of parents during middle and late childhood, the following conclusion was reached: "Parents serve as gatekeepers and provide scaffolding as children assume more responsibility for themselves and . . . regulate their own lives" (Huston & Ripke, 2006, p. 422).

Parents especially play an important role in supporting and stimulating children's academic achievement in middle and late childhood (Cowan & Heming, 2013; Huston & Ripke, 2006). The value parents place on education can determine whether children do well in school. Parents not only influence children's in-school achievement, but they also make decisions about children's out-of-school activities (Eccles & Roeser, 2013). Whether children participate in sports, music, and other activities is heavily influenced by the extent to which parents sign up children for such activities and encourage their participation (Simpkins & others, 2006).

Elementary school children tend to receive less physical discipline than they did as preschoolers. Instead of spanking or coercive holding, their parents are more likely to use deprivation of privileges, appeals to the child's self-esteem, comments designed to increase the child's sense of guilt, and statements that the child is responsible for his or her actions.

During middle and late childhood, some control is transferred from parent to child. The process is gradual, and it produces *coregulation* rather than control by either the child or the parent alone. Parents continue to exercise general supervision and control, and children are allowed to engage in moment-to-moment self-regulation. The major shift to autonomy does not occur until about the age of 12 or later. A key developmental task as children move toward autonomy is learning to relate to adults outside the family on a regular basis—adults such as teachers who interact with the child much differently from parents.

In sum, considerable adaptation in parenting is required as children develop. Later in the chapter, we will further examine adaptations in parenting when discussing family influences on adolescents' development.

What are some changes in the focus of parent-child relationships in middle and late childhood?

PARENTS AS MANAGERS OF CHILDREN'S LIVES

Parents can play important roles as managers of children's opportunities, as monitors of their lives, and as social initiators and arrangers (Bradley & Corwyn, 2013; Parke & Buriel, 2006; Parke & Clarke-Stewart, 2011). An important developmental task of childhood and adolescence is to develop the ability to make competent decisions in an increasingly independent manner. To help children and adolescents reach their full potential, a parent needs to be an effective manager—one who finds information, makes contacts, helps structure choices, and provides guidance. Parents who fulfill this important managerial role help children and adolescents to avoid pitfalls and to work their way through a myriad of choices and decisions. Mothers are more likely than fathers to engage in a managerial role in parenting.

From infancy through adolescence, parents can play important roles in managing their children's experiences and opportunities. In infancy this might involve taking a child to a doctor and arranging for child care; in early childhood it might involve selecting the preschool that the child will attend; in middle and late childhood it might include directing the child to take a bath, to match their clothes and wear clean clothes, and to put away toys; in adolescence it could involve participating in a parent-teacher conference and subsequently managing the adolescent's homework activity.

Managing and Guiding the Infant's Behavior   In addition to sensitive parenting involving warmth and caring that can result in infants being securely attached to their parents, other important aspects of parenting infants involve managing and guiding their behavior in an attempt to reduce or eliminate undesirable behaviors (Holden, Vittrup, & Rosen, 2011). This management process includes (1) being proactive and childproofing the environment so infants won't encounter potentially dangerous objects or situations, and (2) using corrective methods when infants engage in undesirable behaviors, such as excessive fussing and crying, throwing objects, and so on.

One study assessed results of discipline and corrective methods that parents had used by the time their infants were 12 and 24 months old (Vittrup, Holden, & Buck, 2006) (see Figure 14.2). Notice in Figure 14.2 that the main corrective method parents had used by the time their infant was 12 months old was diverting the infant's attention, followed by reasoning, ignoring, and negotiating. Also note in Figure 14.2 that more than one-third of parents had yelled at their infant, about one-fifth had slapped the infant's hands or threatened the infant, and approximately one-sixth had spanked the infant by their first birthday.

As infants move into the second year of life and become more mobile and capable of exploring a wider range of environments, parental management of the toddler's behavior often involves increased corrective feedback and discipline (Holden, Vittrup, & Rosen, 2011). As indicated in Figure 14.2, in the study just described, yelling increased from 36 percent at 1 year of age to 81 percent by 2 years of age, slapping the infant's hands increased from 21 percent at 1 year to 31 percent by age 2, and spanking increased from 14 percent at age 1 to 45 percent by age 2 (Vittrup, Holden, & Buck, 2006).

A special concern is that such corrective discipline tactics not become abusive. Too often what starts out as mild to moderately intense discipline on the part of parents can move into highly intense anger. Later in this chapter, you will read more extensively about the use of punishment with children and child maltreatment.

Parental Monitoring in Childhood and Adolescence   A key aspect of the managerial role of parenting is effective monitoring, which becomes especially important as children move into the adolescent years (Bradley & Corwyn, 2013). Monitoring includes supervising an adolescent's choices of social settings, activities, and friends. A recent study of more than 36,000 eighth- and tenth-grade students revealed that a higher level of parental monitoring was associated with lower alcohol and marijuana use, with the strongest effects among girls and adolescents who had the highest risk-taking profile (Dever & others, 2013). Further, a research

> There's no vocabulary for love within a family, love that's lived in but not looked at, love within the light of which all else is seen, the love within which all other love finds speech. That love is silent.
>
> —T. S. ELIOT
> *American-Born English Poet, 20th Century*

Method	12 Months	24 Months
Spank with hand	14	45
Slap infant's hand	21	31
Yell in anger	36	81
Threaten	19	63
Withdraw privileges	18	52
Time-out	12	60
Reason	85	100
Divert attention	100	100
Negotiate	50	90
Ignore	64	90

FIGURE **14.2**

PARENTS' METHODS FOR MANAGING AND CORRECTING INFANTS' UNDESIRABLE BEHAVIOR.
Shown here are the percentages of parents who had used various corrective methods by the time their infant was 12 and 24 months old. *Source:* Based on data presented in Table 1 in Vittrup, Holden, & Buck (2006).

connecting with careers

Janis Keyser, Parent Educator

Janis Keyser is a parent educator who also teaches in the Department of Early Childhood Education at Cabrillo College in California. In addition to teaching college classes and conducting parenting workshops, she has coauthored a book with Laura Davis (1997), *Becoming the Parent You Want to Be: A Source-Book of Strategies for the First Five Years.*

Janis also writes as an expert on the iVillage Web site (www.parentsplace.com), and she is a coauthor of a nationally syndicated parenting column, "Growing Up, Growing Together."

Janis Keyser *(right),* conducting a parenting workshop.

What factors are involved in whether adolescents will voluntarily disclose information to their parents?

review of the influence of family functioning on African American students' academic achievement found that when African American parents monitored their son's academic achievement by ensuring that homework was completed, restricted time spent on nonproductive distractions (such as video games and TV), and participated in a consistent, positive dialogue with teachers and school officials, their son's academic achievement benefited (Mandara, 2006).

A current interest involving parental monitoring focuses on adolescents' management of their parents' access to information, especially the extent to which adolescents disclose or conceal strategies about their activities (Amsel & Smetana, 2011; Metzger & others, 2013; Rote & others, 2012). Researchers have found that adolescents' disclosure to parents about their whereabouts, activities, and friends is linked to positive adolescent adjustment and achievement (Laird & Marrero, 2011; Smetana, 2011a, b). For example, a recent study of U.S. and Chinese young adolescents found that adolescents' disclosure to parents was linked to a higher level of academic competence (better learning strategies, autonomous motivation, and better grades) over time (Cheung, Pomerantz, & Dong, 2013).

To read about one individual who helps parents become more effective in managing their children's lives, see *Connecting with Careers*.

Researchers also have found that family management practices are related positively to students' grades and self-responsibility, and negatively to school-related problems (Eccles, 2007; Eccles & Roeser, 2013; Taylor & Lopez, 2005). Among the most important family management practices in this regard are maintaining a structured and organized family environment, such as establishing routines for homework, chores, bedtime, and so on, and effectively monitoring the child's behavior.

PARENTING STYLES AND DISCIPLINE

Good parenting takes time and effort. You can't do it in a minute here and a minute there. You can't do it with DVDs. Of course, it's not just the quantity of time parents spend with children that is important for children's development—the quality of the parenting is clearly important (Grusec, 2013; Grusec & others, 2013). To understand variations in parenting, let's

Calvin and Hobbes   by Bill Watterson

consider the styles parents use when they interact with their children, how they discipline their children, and coparenting.

Baumrind's Parenting Styles   Diana Baumrind (1971, 2012) points out that parents should be neither punitive nor aloof. Rather, they should develop rules for their children and be affectionate with them. She has described four types of parenting styles:

- **Authoritarian parenting** is a restrictive, punitive style in which parents exhort the child to follow their directions and respect their work and effort. The authoritarian parent places firm limits and controls on the child and allows little verbal exchange. For example, an authoritarian parent might say, "You will do it my way or else." Authoritarian parents also might spank the child frequently, enforce rules rigidly but not explain them, and show rage toward the child. Children of authoritarian parents are often unhappy, fearful, and anxious about comparing themselves with others, fail to initiate activity, and have weak communication skills. Sons of authoritarian parents may behave aggressively (Hart & others, 2003).

- **Authoritative parenting** encourages children to be independent but still places limits and controls on their actions. Extensive verbal give-and-take is allowed, and parents are warm and nurturant toward the child. An authoritative parent might put his arm around the child in a comforting way and say, "You know you should not have done that. Let's talk about how you can handle the situation better next time." Authoritative parents show pleasure and support in response to children's constructive behavior. They also expect mature, independent, and age-appropriate behavior by children. Children whose parents are authoritative are often cheerful, self-controlled and self-reliant, and achievement oriented; they tend to maintain friendly relations with peers, cooperate with adults, and cope well with stress.

- **Neglectful parenting** is a style in which the parent is very uninvolved in the child's life. Children whose parents are neglectful develop the sense that other aspects of the parents' lives are more important than they are. These children tend to be socially incompetent. Many have poor self-control and don't handle independence well. They frequently have low self-esteem, are immature, and may be alienated from the family. In adolescence, they may show patterns of truancy and delinquency.

- **Indulgent parenting** is a style in which parents are highly involved with their children but place few demands or controls on them. Such parents let their children do what they want. The result is that the children never learn to control their own behavior and always expect to get their way. Some parents deliberately rear their children in this way because they believe the combination of warm involvement and few restraints will produce a

authoritarian parenting A restrictive, punitive style in which the parent exhorts the child to follow the parent's directions and to respect their work and effort. Firm limits and controls are placed on the child, and little verbal exchange is allowed. This style is associated with children's social incompetence, including a lack of initiative and weak communication skills.

authoritative parenting This style encourages children to be independent but still places limits and controls on their actions. Extensive verbal give-and-take is allowed, and parents are warm and nurturant toward the child. This style is associated with children's social competence, achievement orientation, and self-reliance.

neglectful parenting A style in which the parent is very uninvolved in the child's life. It is associated with children's social incompetence, especially a lack of self-control and poor self-esteem.

indulgent parenting A style in which parents are highly involved with their children but place few demands or controls on them. This is associated with children's social incompetence, especially a lack of self-control and a lack of respect for others.

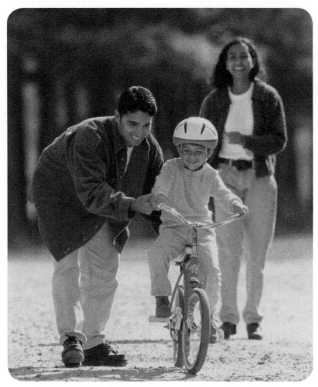

	Accepting, responsive	Rejecting, unresponsive
Demanding, controlling	Authoritative	Authoritarian
Undemanding, uncontrolling	Indulgent	Neglectful

FIGURE 14.3

CLASSIFICATION OF PARENTING STYLES. The four types of parenting styles (authoritative, authoritarian, indulgent, and neglectful) involve the dimensions of acceptance and responsiveness, on the one hand, and demand and control on the other. For example, authoritative parenting involves being both accepting/responsive and demanding/controlling.

According to Ruth Chao, what type of parenting style do many Asian American parents use?

creative, confident child. However, children whose parents are indulgent rarely learn respect for others and have difficulty controlling their behavior. They might be domineering, egocentric, noncompliant, and have difficulties in peer relations.

These four classifications of parenting involve combinations of acceptance and responsiveness on the one hand and demand and control on the other (Maccoby & Martin, 1983). How these dimensions combine to produce authoritarian, authoritative, neglectful, and indulgent parenting is shown in Figure 14.3.

Parenting Styles in Context   Do the benefits of authoritative parenting transcend the boundaries of ethnicity, socioeconomic status (SES), and household composition? Although occasional exceptions have been found, evidence linking authoritative parenting with competence on the part of the child occurs in research across a wide range of ethnic groups, social strata, cultures, and family structures (Low, Snyder, & Shortt, 2012; Milevsky, 2012; Morris, Cui, & Steinberg, 2012; Steinberg & Silk, 2002).

Nonetheless, researchers have found that in some ethnic groups, aspects of the authoritarian style may be associated with more positive child outcomes than Baumrind predicts (Parke & Buriel, 2006). Elements of the authoritarian style may take on different meanings and have different effects depending on the context.

For example, Asian American parents often continue aspects of traditional Asian child-rearing practices that have sometimes been described as authoritarian. The parents exert considerable control over their children's lives. However, Ruth Chao (2001, 2005, 2007; Chao & Otsuki-Clutter, 2011; Chao & Tseng, 2002) argues that the style of parenting used by many Asian American parents is distinct from the domineering control of the authoritarian style. Instead, Chao argues that the control reflects parental concern and involvement in their children's lives and is best conceptualized as a type of training. The high academic achievement of Asian American children may be a consequence of their "training" parents (Stevenson & Zusho, 2002). In recent research involving Chinese American adolescents and their parents, parental control was endorsed as were the Confucian parental goals of perseverance, working hard in school, obedience, and being sensitive to parents' wishes (Russell, Crockett, & Chao, 2010).

An emphasis on requiring respect and obedience is also associated with the authoritarian style, but in Latino child rearing this focus may be positive rather than punitive. Rather than suppressing the child's development, it may encourage the development of a self and an identity that are embedded in the family and require respect and obedience (Harwood & others, 2002).

Even physical punishment, another characteristic of the authoritarian style, may have varying effects in different contexts. African American parents are more likely than non-Latino White parents to use physical punishment (Deater-Deckard & Dodge, 1997). The use of physical punishment has been linked with increased externalized child problems (such as acting out and high levels of aggression) in non-Latino White families but not in African American families. One explanation of this finding points to the need for African American parents to enforce rules in the dangerous environments in which they are more likely to live (Harrison-Hale, McLoyd, & Smedley, 2004). In this context, requiring obedience to parental authority may be an adaptive strategy to keep children from engaging in antisocial behavior that can have serious consequences for their development (McElhaney & Allen, 2012).

Further Thoughts on Parenting Styles   Several caveats about parenting styles are in order. First, the parenting styles do not capture the important themes of reciprocal socialization and synchrony (Crouter & Booth, 2013). Keep in mind that children socialize parents, just as parents socialize children (Capaldi, 2013; Shanahan & Sobolewski, 2013). Second, many parents use a combination of techniques rather than a single technique, although one technique may be dominant. Although consistent parenting is usually recommended, the wise parent may sense the importance of being more permissive in certain situations, more authoritarian under different circumstances, and more authoritative in others. Also, some critics argue that the concept of parenting style is too broad and that more research needs to be conducted to "unpack" parenting styles by studying various components of the styles (Grusec, 2011; Maccoby, 2007). For example, is parental monitoring more important than warmth in predicting child and adolescent outcomes?

Punishment   For centuries, corporal (physical) punishment, such as spanking, has been considered a necessary and even desirable method of disciplining children. Use of corporal punishment is legal in every state in America. A national survey of U.S. parents with 3- and 4-year-old children found that 26 percent of parents reported spanking their children frequently, and 67 percent of the parents reported yelling at their children frequently (Regalado & others, 2004). A cross-cultural comparison found that individuals in the United States and Canada were among those with the most favorable attitudes toward corporal punishment and were the most likely to remember it being used by their parents (Curran & others, 2001) (see Figure 14.4).

An increasing number of studies have examined the outcomes of physically punishing children, although those that have been conducted are correlational. Clearly, it would be highly unethical to randomly assign parents to either spank or not spank their children in an experimental study. Recall that cause and effect cannot be determined in a correlational study. In one correlational study, spanking by parents was linked with children's antisocial behavior, including cheating, telling lies, being mean to others, bullying, getting into fights, and being disobedient (Strauss, Sugarman, & Giles-Sims, 1997).

A research review concluded that corporal punishment by parents is associated with higher levels of immediate compliance and aggression by the children (Gershoff, 2002). The review also found that corporal punishment is linked to lower levels of moral internalization and mental health (Gershoff, 2002). A study in six countries revealed that mothers' use of physical punishment was linked to highest rates of aggression in their children (Gershoff & others, 2010). Another study indicated that a history of harsh physical discipline was related to adolescent depression and externalized problems, such as juvenile delinquency (Bender & others, 2007). And several recent longitudinal studies also have found that physical punishment of young children is associated with higher levels of aggression later in childhood and adolescence (Berlin & others, 2009; Gershoff & others, 2012; Lansford & others, 2011; Taylor & others, 2010).

What are some reasons to avoid spanking or similar punishments? The reasons include the following:

- When adults punish a child by yelling, screaming, or spanking, they are presenting children with out-of-control models for handling stressful situations. Children may imitate this aggressive, out-of-control behavior.

- Punishment can instill fear, rage, or avoidance. For example, spanking the child may cause the child to avoid being around the parent and to fear the parent.

- Punishment tells children what not to do rather than what to do. Children should be given feedback, such as "Why don't you try this?"

- Punishment can be abusive. Parents might unintentionally become so emotional when they are punishing the child that they become abusive (Durrant, 2008; Knox, 2010).

Most child psychologists recommend handling misbehavior by reasoning with the child, especially explaining the consequences of the child's actions for others. *Time out,* in which the child is removed from a setting that offers positive reinforcement, can also be effective. For example, when the child has misbehaved, a parent might take away TV viewing for a specified time.

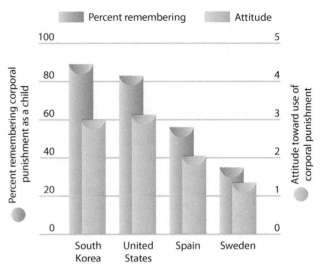

FIGURE 14.4

CORPORAL PUNISHMENT IN DIFFERENT COUNTRIES. A 5-point scale was used to assess attitudes toward corporal punishment, with scores closer to 1 indicating an attitude against its use and scores closer to 5 suggesting an attitude favoring its use. *Why are studies of corporal punishment correlational studies, and how does that affect their interpretation?*

Do Marital Conflict and Individual Hostility Predict the Use of Physical Punishment in Parenting?

A longitudinal study assessed couples across the transition to parenting to investigate possible links between marital conflict, individual adult hostility, and the use of physical punishment with young children (Kanoy & others, 2003). Before the birth of the first child, the level of marital conflict was observed in a marital problem-solving discussion; answers to questionnaires regarding individual characteristics were also obtained. Thus, these characteristics of the couples were not influenced by characteristics of the child. When the children were 2 and 5 years old, the couples were interviewed about the frequency and intensity of their physical punishment of the children. On both occasions, the parents' level of marital conflict was again observed in a marital problem-solving discussion.

The researchers found that both hostility and marital conflict were linked with the use of physical punishment. Individuals with high rates of hostility on the prenatal measures used more frequent and more severe physical punishment with their children. The same was evident for marital conflict—when marital conflict was high, both mothers and fathers were more likely to use physical punishment in disciplining their young children.

A final point about the use of punishment with children is that debate about its effects on children's development continues (Gershoff & others, 2012; Grusec, 2011; Lansford & Deater-Deckard, 2012). Some experts (including Diana Baumrind) argue that much of the evidence for the negative effects of physical punishment has been based on studies in which parents acted in an abusive manner (Baumrind, Larzelere, & Cowan, 2002). She concludes from her research that when parents used punishment in a calm, reasoned manner (which she says characterized most of the authoritative parents in her studies), children's development benefitted. Thus, she emphasizes that physical punishment does not need to present children with an out-of-control adult who is yelling and screaming, as well as spanking. A research review of 26 studies concluded that only severe or predominant use of spanking, not mild spanking, compared unfavorably with alternative practices for disciplining children (Larzelere & Kuhn, 2005).

Indeed, there are few longitudinal studies of punishment and few studies that distinguish adequately between moderate and heavy use of punishment. Thus, in the view of some experts, available research evidence makes it difficult to tell whether the effects of physical punishment are harmful to children's development, even though such a view might be distasteful to some individuals (Grusec, 2009).

In addition to considering whether physical punishment is mild or out of control, another factor in evaluating effects on children's development involves cultural contexts. Recent research has indicated that in countries such as Kenya in which physical punishment is considered normal and necessary for handling children's transgressions, the effects of physical punishment are less harmful than in countries such as Thailand in which physical punishment is perceived as more harmful to children's development (Lansford & others, 2005, 2013).

One thing that is clear regarding research on punishment of children is that if physical punishment is used, it needs to be mild, infrequent, age-appropriate, and used in the context of a positive parent-child relationship (Grusec, 2011). It is also clear that when physical punishment involves abuse, it can be very harmful to children's development (Cicchetti, 2013; Garcia, McKee, & Forehand, 2012).

Earlier in this chapter, we described the family as a system and discussed possible links between marital relationships and parenting practices (Cox & others, 2004). Do marital conflict and individual hostility predict the use of physical punishment in parenting? To find out, read *Connecting Through Research*.

coparenting Support parents provide for each other in jointly raising children.

What characterizes coparenting?

Coparenting The relationship between marital conflict and the use of punishment highlights the importance of **coparenting,** which is the support that parents provide one another in jointly raising a child. Poor coordination between

Darla Botkin, Marriage and Family Therapist

Darla Botkin is a marriage and family therapist who teaches, conducts research, and engages in marriage and family therapy. She is on the faculty of the University of Kentucky. Botkin obtained a bachelor's degree in elementary education with a concentration in special education and then went on to receive a master's degree in early childhood education. She spent the next six years working with children and their families in a variety of settings, including child care, elementary school, and Head Start. These experiences led Botkin to recognize the interdependence of the developmental settings that children and their parents experience (such as home, school, and work). She returned to graduate school and obtained a Ph.D. in family studies from the University of Tennessee. She then became a faculty member in the Family Studies program at the University of Kentucky. Completing further coursework and clinical training in marriage and family therapy, she became certified as a marriage and family therapist.

Botkin's current interests include working with young children in family therapy, addressing gender and ethnic issues in family therapy, and exploring the role of spirituality in family wellness.

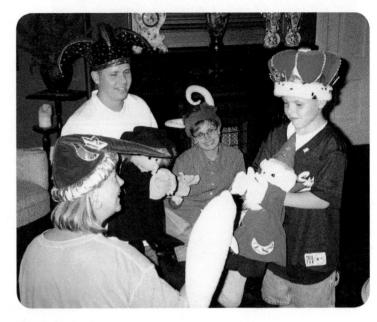

Darla Botkin *(left)*, conducting a family therapy session.

For more information about what marriage and family therapists do, see page 45 in the Careers in Child Development appendix following Chapter 1.

parents, undermining of the other parent, lack of cooperation and warmth, and disconnection by one parent are conditions that place children at risk for problems (Solmeyer & others, 2011; Talbot, Baker, & McHale, 2009). For example, a recent study revealed that coparenting influenced young children's effortful control above and beyond maternal and paternal parenting by themselves (Karreman & others, 2008). And a recent study found that greater father involvement in young children's play was linked to an increase in supportive coparenting (Jia & Schoppe-Sullivan, 2011).

Parents who do not spend enough time with their children or who have problems in child rearing can benefit from counseling and therapy. To read about the work of marriage and family counselor Darla Botkin, see *Connecting with Careers*.

Child Maltreatment Unfortunately, punishment sometimes leads to the abuse of infants and children (Cicchetti, 2011, 2013). In 2009, approximately 702,000 U.S. children were found to be victims of child abuse at least once during that year (U.S. Department of Health and Human Services, 2010). Eighty-one percent of these children were abused by a parent or parents. Laws in many states now require physicians and teachers to report suspected cases of child abuse, yet many cases go unreported, especially those involving battered infants.

Whereas the public and many professionals use the term *child abuse* to refer to both abuse and neglect, developmentalists increasingly use the term *child maltreatment* (Cicchetti, 2011, 2013; Cicchetti & Toth, 2011). This term does not have quite the emotional impact of the term *abuse* and acknowledges that maltreatment includes diverse conditions.

Child maltreatment involves grossly inadequate and destructive aspects of parenting.

—**DANTE CICCHETTI**

Contemporary Developmental Psychologist, University of Minnesota

This family of four children are having dinner in a cramped motel room that's handling shelter overflow. Homeless advocates say many families are being denied shelter. *What are some different types of child abuse?*

Types of Child Maltreatment   The four main types of child maltreatment are physical abuse, child neglect, sexual abuse, and emotional abuse (National Clearinghouse on Child Abuse and Neglect, 2004):

- *Physical abuse* is characterized by the infliction of physical injury as a result of punching, beating, kicking, biting, burning, shaking, or otherwise harming a child. The parent or other person may not have intended to hurt the child; the injury may have resulted from excessive physical punishment (Milot & others, 2010).

- *Child neglect* is characterized by failure to provide for the child's basic needs (Newton & Vandeven, 2010). Neglect can be physical (abandonment, for example), educational (allowing chronic truancy, for example), or emotional (marked inattention to the child's needs, for example). Child neglect is by far the most common form of child maltreatment. In every country where relevant data have been collected, neglect occurs up to three times as often as abuse (Benoit, Coolbear, & Crawford, 2008).

- *Sexual abuse* includes fondling a child's genitals, intercourse, incest, rape, sodomy, exhibitionism, and commercial exploitation through prostitution or the production of pornographic materials (Bahali & others, 2010).

- *Emotional abuse (psychological/verbal abuse/mental injury)* includes acts or omissions by parents or other caregivers that have caused, or could cause, serious behavioral, cognitive, or emotional problems (van Harmelen & others, 2010).

Although any of these forms of child maltreatment may be found separately, they often occur in combination. Emotional abuse is almost always present when other forms are identified.

The Context of Abuse   No single factor causes child maltreatment (Cicchetti, 2011, 2013). A combination of factors, including the culture, family, and developmental characteristics of the child, likely contribute to child maltreatment (Cicchetti & Toth, 2011).

The extensive violence that takes place in the American culture, including TV violence, is reflected in the occurrence of violence in the family (Durrant, 2008). The family itself is obviously a key part of the context of abuse. Among the family and family-associated characteristics that may contribute to child maltreatment are parenting stress, substance abuse, social isolation, single parenting, and socioeconomic difficulties (especially poverty) (Cicchetti, 2013; Laslett & others, 2012; Turner & others, 2012). The interactions of all family members need to be considered, regardless of who performs the violent acts against the child. For example, even though the father may be the one who physically abuses the child, the behavior of the mother, the child, and siblings also should be evaluated.

Were abusive parents abused by their own parents? About one-third of parents who were abused when they were young go on to abuse their own children (Cicchetti & Toth, 2006, 2013). Thus, some, but not a majority, of abusive parents are involved in an intergenerational transmission of abuse.

Developmental Consequences of Abuse   Among the consequences of child maltreatment in childhood and adolescence are poor emotional regulation, attachment problems, problems in peer relations, difficulty in adapting to school, and other psychological problems such as depression and delinquency. A longitudinal study found that early maltreatment was linked to emotional negativity (age 7) that increased poor emotional regulation (age 8), which in turn predicted an increase in internalized symptoms (from age 8 to 9) (Kim-Spoon, Cicchetti, & Rogosch, 2013). As shown in Figure 14.5, maltreated young children in foster care were more likely to show abnormal stress hormone levels than middle-SES young children living with their birth family (Gunnar, Fisher, & The Early Experience, Stress, and Prevention Network, 2006). In this study, the abnormal stress hormone levels were mainly present in the foster children who were neglected, best described as "institutional neglect" (Fisher, 2005). Abuse also may have this effect on young children (Gunnar & others, 2006). Adolescents who experienced abuse or neglect as children are more likely than adolescents who were not maltreated as children to engage in violent romantic relationships,

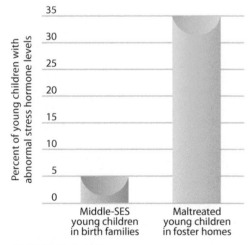

FIGURE **14.5**

ABNORMAL STRESS HORMONE LEVELS IN YOUNG CHILDREN IN DIFFERENT TYPES OF REARING CONDITIONS

delinquency, sexual risk taking, and substance abuse (Shin, Hong, & Hazen, 2010; Wekerle & others, 2009). And a recent study revealed that a significant increase in suicide attempts before age 18 occurred with repeated child maltreatment (Jonson-Reid, Kohl, & Drake, 2012).

Later, during the adult years, individuals who were maltreated as children are more likely to experience problems with physical health, mental health, and sexual function (Lacelle & others, 2012). A 30-year longitudinal study found that middle-aged adults who had experienced child maltreatment had increased risk for diabetes, lung disease, malnutrition, and vision problems (Widom & others, 2012). Another study revealed that child maltreatment was linked to depression in adulthood and to unfavorable outcomes for treatment of depression (Nanni, Uher, & Danese, 2012). Further, adults who were maltreated as children often have difficulty in establishing and maintaining healthy intimate relationships (Dozier, Stovall-McClough, & Albus, 2009). As adults, maltreated children are also at higher risk for violent behavior toward other adults—especially dating partners and marital partners—as well as for substance abuse, anxiety, and depression (Miller-Perrin, Perrin, & Kocur, 2009).

An important agenda is to discover how to prevent child maltreatment or intervene in children's lives when they have been maltreated (Cicchetti & others, 2012; Shapiro, Prinz, & Sanders, 2012). In one study of maltreating mothers and their 1-year-olds, two treatments were effective in reducing child maltreatment: (1) home visitation that emphasized improved parenting, coping with stress, and increasing support for the mother; and (2) parent-infant psychotherapy that focused on improving maternal-infant attachment (Cicchetti, Toth, & Rogosch, 2005).

PARENT-ADOLESCENT RELATIONSHIPS

Even the best parents may find their relationship with their child strained during adolescence. Important aspects of parent-adolescent relationships include autonomy/attachment and conflict.

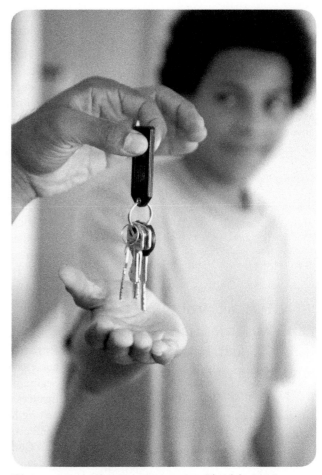

What are strategies that parents can use to guide adolescents in effectively handling their increased motivation for autonomy?

Autonomy and Attachment With most adolescents, parents are likely to find themselves engaged in a delicate balancing act, weighing competing needs for autonomy and control, for independence and connection.

The Push for Autonomy The typical adolescent's push for autonomy and responsibility puzzles and angers many parents. Most parents anticipate that their teenager will have some difficulty adjusting to the changes that adolescence brings, but few parents imagine and predict just how strong an adolescent's desires will be to spend time with peers or how intensely adolescents will want to show that it is they—not their parents—who are responsible for their successes and failures.

Adolescents' ability to attain autonomy and gain control over their behavior is acquired through appropriate adult reactions to their desire for control (Laursen & Collins, 2009; McElhaney & Allen, 2012). At the onset of adolescence, the average individual does not have the knowledge to make appropriate or mature decisions in all areas of life. As the adolescent pushes for autonomy, the wise adult relinquishes control in those areas where the adolescent can make reasonable decisions, but continues to guide the adolescent to make reasonable decisions in areas in which the adolescent's knowledge is more limited. Gradually, adolescents acquire the ability to make mature decisions on their own. In a recent study, young adolescents' perception that their parents promoted more psychological autonomy and less psychological control predicted fewer depressive symptoms two years later (Sher-Censor, Parke, & Coltrane, 2011).

Gender differences characterize autonomy-granting in adolescence. Boys are given more independence than girls. In one study, this was especially true in U.S. families with a traditional gender-role orientation (Bumpus, Crouter, & McHale, 2001). Also, Latino parents protect and monitor their daughters more closely than is the case for non-Latino White parents (McElhaney & Allen, 2012; Updegraff & others, 2010). Although Latino cultures may place a stronger emphasis on parental authority and restrict adolescent autonomy, a recent study revealed that regardless of where

Stacey Christensen, age 16: "I am lucky enough to have open communication with my parents. Whenever I am in need or just need to talk, my parents are there for me. My advice to parents is to let your teens grow at their own pace, be open with them so that you can be there for them. We need guidance; our parents need to help but not be too overwhelming."

developmental **connection**

Attachment

Securely attached infants use the caregiver as a secure base from which to explore the environment. Chapter 10, p. 301

When I was a boy of 14, my father was so ignorant I could hardly stand to have the man around. But when I got to be 21, I was astonished at how much he had learnt in seven years.

—**Mark Twain**
American Writer and Humorist, 19th Century

they were born, Mexican-origin adolescent girls living in the United States had expectations for autonomy at an earlier age than their mothers preferred (Bamaca-Colbert & others, 2012).

The Role of Attachment   Recall from Chapter 1 that one of the most widely discussed aspects of socioemotional development in infancy is secure attachment to caregivers. In the past decade, researchers have explored whether secure attachment also might be an important aspect of adolescents' relationships with their parents (Laursen & Collins, 2009). For example, Joseph Allen and his colleagues (2009) found that adolescents who were securely attached at 14 years of age were more likely to report that they were in an exclusive relationship, comfortable with intimacy in relationships, and achieving increased financial independence at 21 years of age. A recent analysis concluded that the most consistent outcomes of secure attachment in adolescence involve positive peer relations and development of the adolescent's emotion regulation capacities (Allen & Miga, 2010).

Balancing Freedom and Control   We have seen that parents play very important roles in adolescent development (McKinney & Renk, 2011). Although adolescents are moving toward independence, they still need to stay connected with families (McElhaney & Allen, 2012). For example, the National Longitudinal Study on Adolescent Health surveyed more than 12,000 adolescents and found that those who did not eat dinner with a parent five or more days a week had dramatically higher rates of smoking, drinking, marijuana use, getting into fights, and initiation of sexual activity (Council of Economic Advisors, 2000).

Parent-Adolescent Conflict   Although parent-adolescent conflict increases in early adolescence, it does not reach the tumultuous proportions G. Stanley Hall envisioned at the beginning of the twentieth century (Laursen & Collins, 2009). Rather, much of the conflict involves the everyday events of family life, such as keeping a bedroom clean, dressing neatly, getting home by a certain time, and not talking or text messaging for hours at a time. The conflicts rarely involve major issues such as drugs or delinquency.

Conflict with parents often escalates during early adolescence, remains somewhat stable during the high school years, and then lessens as the adolescent reaches 17 to 20 years of age. Parent-adolescent relationships become more positive if adolescents go away to college than if they attend college while living at home (Sullivan & Sullivan, 1980).

The everyday conflicts that characterize parent-adolescent relationships may actually serve a positive developmental function. These minor disputes and negotiations facilitate the adolescent's transition from being dependent on parents to being an autonomous individual. Recognizing that conflict and negotiation can serve a positive developmental function can tone down parental hostility.

The old model of parent-adolescent relationships suggested that as adolescents mature they detach themselves from parents and move into a world of autonomy apart from parents. The old model also suggested that parent-adolescent conflict is intense and stressful throughout adolescence.

The new model emphasizes that parents serve as important attachment figures and support systems while adolescents explore a wider, more complex social world. The new model also emphasizes that, in most families, parent-adolescent conflict is moderate rather than severe and that the everyday negotiations and minor disputes not only are normal but also can serve the positive developmental function of helping the adolescent make the transition from childhood dependency to adult independence (see Figure 14.6).

Still, a high degree of conflict characterizes some parent-adolescent relationships. And this prolonged, intense conflict is associated with various adolescent problems: movement out of the home, juvenile delinquency, school dropout, pregnancy and early marriage, membership in religious cults, and drug abuse (Brook & others, 1990). Further, a recent study revealed that a higher level of parent-adolescent conflict was related to peer-reported aggression and delinquency (Ehrlich, Dykas, & Cassidy, 2012).

Cross-cultural studies reveal that parent-adolescent conflict is lower in some countries than in the United States. Two countries where parent-adolescent conflict is lower than in the United States are Japan and India (Larson, 1999; Rothbaum & others, 2000).

Conflict with parents increases in early adolescence. *What is the nature of this conflict in a majority of American families?*

Old Model	New Model
Autonomy, detachment from parents; parent and peer worlds are isolated	Attachment and autonomy; parents are important support systems and attachment figures; adolescent-parent and adolescent-peer worlds have some important connections
Intense, stressful conflict throughout adolescence; parent-adolescent relationships are filled with storm and stress on virtually a daily basis	Moderate parent-adolescent conflict is common and can serve a positive developmental function; conflict greater in early adolescence

FIGURE **14.6**
OLD AND NEW MODELS OF PARENT-ADOLESCENT RELATIONSHIPS

When families immigrate into another country, children and adolescents typically acculturate more quickly to the norms and values of their new home faster than do their parents (Fuligni, 2012). This likely occurs because of immigrant children's and adolescents' exposure to school and the language of the host country. The norms and values immigrant children and adolescents experience are especially likely to diverge from their parents in areas such as autonomy and romantic relationships. Such divergences are likely to increase parent-adolescent conflict in immigrant families. Andrew Fuligni (2012) argues that these conflicts aren't always expressed in open conflict but are often present in underlying, internal feelings. For example, immigrant adolescents may feel that their parents want them to give up their personal interests for the sake of the family, and the adolescents don't think this is fair. Such acculturation-based conflict focuses on issues related to core cultural values and is likely to occur in immigrant families, such as Latino and Asian American families, who come to the United States to live (Juang & Umana-Taylor, 2012).

INTERGENERATIONAL RELATIONSHIPS

Connections between generations play important roles in development through the life span (Antonucci, Birditt, & Ajrouch, 2013; Fingerman, Cheng, & others, 2012; Fingerman, Pillemer, & others, 2012). With each new generation, personality characteristics, attitudes, and values are replicated or changed (Pratt & others, 2008). As older family members die, their biological, intellectual, emotional, and personal legacies are carried on in the next generation. Their children become the oldest generation and their grandchildren the second generation. In many families, females' relationships across generations are closer and more intimate than are males' relationships (Etaugh & Bridges, 2010).

The following studies provide evidence of the importance of intergenerational relationships in children's development:

- Supportive family environments and parenting in childhood (assessed when the children were 3 to 15 years of age) were linked with more positive relationships (in terms of contact, closeness, conflict, and reciprocal assistance) between the children and their middle-aged parents when the children were 26 years of age (Belsky & others, 2001).

- Children of divorce were disproportionately likely to end their own marriage than were children from intact, never divorced families, although the transmission of divorce across generations has declined in recent years (Wolfinger, 2011).

- Parents who smoked early and often, and persisted in becoming regular smokers, were more likely to have adolescents who became smokers (Chassin & others, 2008).

- Evidence was found for the intergenerational transmission of conduct disorder (multiple delinquent activities) across three generations, with the connection stronger for males than females (D'Onofrio & others, 2007).

The generations of living things pass in a short time, and like runners hand on the torch of life.

—LUCRETIUS
Roman Poet, 1st Century BC

What characterizes intergenerational relatioships?

Review

- What characterizes parental roles and the timing of parenthood?
- In what ways do parents need to adapt their behavior to developmental changes in their children?
- How can parents be effective managers of children's lives?
- What are the main parenting styles and variations in discipline?
- What are some important aspects of parenting adolescents?
- How do intergenerational relationships influence children's development?

Connect

- In this section, we learned about Baumrind's four parenting styles. In Chapter 13, we learned about three types of discipline techniques. Which techniques are more likely to be used by parents from each parenting style?

Reflect *Your Own Personal Journey of Life*

- What was the nature of your relationship with your parents during middle school and high school? Has your relationship with your parents changed since then? Does it involve less conflict today? What do you think are the most important characteristics of a competent parent of adolescents?

Siblings LG3 Identify how siblings influence children's development.

```
Sibling          Birth
Relationships    Order
```

What are sibling relationships like? How extensively does birth order influence behavior?

SIBLING RELATIONSHIPS

Approximately 80 percent of American children have one or more siblings—that is, sisters and brothers (Dunn, 2007). If you grew up with siblings, you probably have a rich memory of aggressive, hostile interchanges. Siblings in the presence of each other when they are 2 to 4 years of age, on average, have a conflict once every 10 minutes. The conflicts go down somewhat from 5 to 7 years of age (Kramer, 2006). One recent study revealed that an increase in sibling conflict was linked to an increase in children's depressive symptoms, whereas an increase in sibling intimacy was related to an increase in children's peer competence (Kim & others, 2007). A research review concluded that sibling relationships in adolescence are not as close, are not as intense, and are more egalitarian than in childhood (East, 2009).

Issues of equality and fairness, as well as invasion of one's personal domain, are common in sibling relationships. A recent study of young adolescents revealed that sibling conflicts involving equality and fairness were associated with an increase in depressed mood one year later, while conflicts associated with invasion of one's personal domain were linked to higher anxiety and lower self-esteem one year later (Campione-Barr, Bassett Greer, & Kruse, 2013).

What do parents do when they encounter siblings in the midst of a verbal or physical confrontation? One study revealed that they do one of three things: (1) intervene and try to help them resolve the conflict, (2) admonish or threaten them, or (3) do nothing at all (Kramer & Perozynski, 1999). Of interest is that in families with two siblings 2 to 5 years of age, the most frequent parental reaction is to do nothing at all.

Laurie Kramer (2006), who has conducted a number of research studies on siblings, says that not intervening and letting sibling conflict escalate is not a good strategy. She developed a program titled "More Fun with Sisters and Brothers" that teaches 4- to 8-year-old siblings social skills for developing positive interactions (Kramer & Radey, 1997). Among the social skills taught in the program are how to appropriately initiate play, how to accept and refuse invitations to play, how to understand another person's perspective, how to deal with angry feelings, and how to manage conflict. A study of 5- to 10-year-old siblings and their parents found that training parents to mediate sibling disputes increased children's understanding of conflicts and reduced sibling conflict (Smith & Ross, 2007).

As intense as it can be, however, conflict is only one of the many dimensions of sibling relations (Dunn, 2013; McHale, Updegraff, & Whiteman, 2011; Milevsky, 2011; Whiteman, Jensen, & Bernard, 2012). Sibling relations include helping, sharing, teaching, fighting, and playing, and siblings can act as emotional supports, rivals, and communication partners (East, 2009).

Judy Dunn (2007), a leading expert on sibling relationships, recently described three important characteristics of sibling relationships:

- *Emotional quality of the relationship.* Both intensive positive and negative emotions are often expressed by siblings toward each other. Many children and adolescents have mixed feelings toward their siblings.

- *Familiarity and intimacy of the relationship.* Siblings typically know each other very well, and this intimacy suggests that they can either provide support or tease and undermine each other, depending on the situation.

- *Variation in sibling relationships.* Some siblings describe their relationships more positively than others. Thus, there is considerable variation in sibling relationships. We previously indicated that many siblings have mixed feelings about each other, but some children and adolescents mainly describe their sibling in warm, affectionate ways, whereas others primarily talk about how irritating and mean a sibling is.

Negative aspects of sibling relationships, such as high conflict, are linked to negative outcomes for adolescents. The negative outcomes can develop not only through conflict but also through direct modeling of a sibling's behavior, as when a younger sibling has an older sibling who has poor study habits and engages in delinquent behavior. By contrast, close and supportive sibling relationships can buffer the negative effects of stressful circumstances in an adolescent's life (East, 2009).

BIRTH ORDER

Whether a child has older or younger siblings has been linked to development of certain personality characteristics. For example, a recent review concluded that "firstborns are the most intelligent, achieving, and conscientious, while later-borns are the most rebellious, liberal, and agreeable" (Paulhus, 2008, p. 210). Compared with later-born children, firstborn children have also been described as more adult oriented, helpful, conforming, and self-controlled. However, when such birth order differences are reported, they often are small.

What accounts for differences related to birth order? Proposed explanations usually point to variations in interactions with parents and siblings associated with being in a particular position in the family. This is especially true in the case of the firstborn child (Teti, 2001). The oldest child is the only one who does not have to share parental love and affection with other siblings—until another sibling comes along. An infant requires more attention than an older child; this means that the firstborn sibling receives less attention after the newborn arrives. Does this result in conflict between parents and the firstborn? In one research study, mothers became more negative,

What are some characteristics of sibling relationships?

The one-child family is becoming much more common in China because of the strong motivation to limit population growth in the People's Republic of China. The effects of this policy have not been fully examined. *In general, what have researchers found the only child to be like?*

coercive, and restraining and played less with the firstborn following the birth of a second child (Dunn & Kendrick, 1982).

What is the only child like? The popular conception is that the only child is a "spoiled brat," with such undesirable characteristics as dependency, lack of self-control, and self-centered behavior. But researchers present a more positive portrayal of the only child. Only children often are achievement oriented and display a desirable personality, especially in comparison with later-borns and children from large families (Falbo & Poston, 1993; Jiao, Ji, & Jing, 1996).

So far, our discussion suggests that birth order might be a strong predictor of behavior. However, an increasing number of family researchers stress that when all of the factors that influence behavior are considered, birth order in itself shows limited ability to predict behavior.

Think about some of the other important factors in children's lives that influence their behavior beyond birth order. They include heredity, models of competency or incompetency that parents present to children on a daily basis, peer influences, school influences, socioeconomic factors, sociohistorical factors, and cultural variations. When someone says firstborns are always like this but last-borns are always like that, the person is making overly simplistic statements that do not adequately take into account the complexity of influences on a child's development.

Review *Connect* Reflect

LG3 Identify how siblings influence children's development.

Review

- How can sibling relationships be characterized?
- What role does birth order play in children's development?

Connect

- In this section, you learned that parents typically respond in one of three ways to sibling conflict. How do these three ways align with Baumrind's parenting styles discussed earlier in this chapter?

Reflect *Your Own Personal Journey of Life*

- If you grew up with a sibling, you likely showed some jealousy of your sibling and vice versa. If you had one or more siblings, how did your parents handle sibling conflict? If and when you become a parent and have two or more children, what strategies will you use to reduce sibling conflict?

The Changing Family in a Changing Social World

LG4 Characterize the changing family in a changing social world.

- Working Parents
- Children in Divorced Families
- Stepfamilies
- Gay and Lesbian Parents
- Cultural, Ethnic, and Socioeconomic Variations in Families

U.S. children are growing up in a greater variety of family contexts than ever before. As we discussed in Chapter 10, "Emotional Development," children are experiencing many sorts of caregiving—not only from stay-at-home mothers but also from stay-at-home fathers, from various types of child-care programs, and from after-school programs. The structure of American families also varies. As shown in Figure 14.7, the United States has a higher percentage of single-parent families than other countries with similar levels of economic and technological development. And many U.S. children are being raised in stepfamilies formed after a divorce and by gay or lesbian parents. How are these and other variations in family life affecting children?

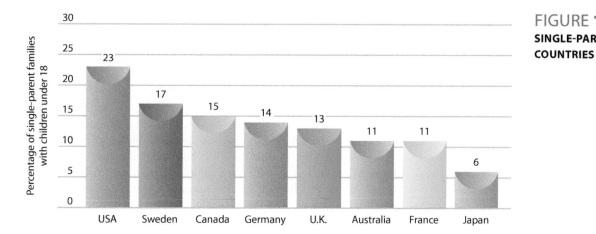

FIGURE **14.7**
SINGLE-PARENT FAMILIES IN DIFFERENT COUNTRIES

WORKING PARENTS

The increased number of mothers in the labor force represents one source of change in families and society in the United States (Goodman & others, 2011; Grzywacz & Demerouti, 2013). Many mothers spend the greatest part of their day away from their children, even their infants. More than one of every two mothers with a child under the age of 5 is in the labor force; more than two of every three mothers with a child from 6 to 17 years of age work outside the home. How have these changes influenced children's development?

Most research on parental work has focused on young children and the mother's employment (Brooks-Gunn, Han, & Waldfogel, 2010). Research on maternal employment and children's development usually reveals few links between the mother's work status and children's cognitive and socioemotional development (Goldberg & Lucas-Thompson, 2008). However, maternal employment may be especially influential in the first several years of the child's life. For example, a recent study of low-income families found that 7-year-old children whose mothers were employed early, especially in the first 8 months, had better socioemotional functioning than their peers whose mothers had remained unemployed (Coley & Lombardi, 2013).

However, it is important to recognize that the effects of working parents involves the father as well as the mother when such matters as work schedules and work-family stress are considered (O'Brien & Moss, 2010; Parke & Clarke-Stewart, 2011; Peeters & others, 2013). Recent research indicates that children's development is affected more strongly by the nature of parents' work than by the employment of one or both parents outside the home (Goodman & others, 2011; Han, 2009; Parke & Clarke-Stewart, 2011).

Ann Crouter (2006) described how parents bring their experiences at work into their homes. She concluded that parents who have poor working conditions, such as long hours, overtime work, stressful work, and lack of autonomy on the job, are likely to be more irritable at home and engage in less effective parenting than their counterparts who enjoy better working conditions. A consistent finding is the children (especially girls) of working mothers engage in less gender stereotyping and have more egalitarian views of gender (Goldberg & Lucas-Thompson, 2008).

CHILDREN IN DIVORCED FAMILIES

Divorce rates changed rather dramatically in the United States and many countries around the world during the late twentieth century (Amato & Dorius, 2010). The U.S. divorce rate increased dramatically in the 1960s and 1970s but has declined since the 1980s. However, the divorce rate in the United States is still much higher than in most other countries.

It is estimated that 40 percent of children born to married parents in the United States will experience their parents' divorce (Hetherington &

developmental **connection**

Family Processes

Research consistently shows that family factors are considerably better at predicting children's developmental outcomes than are child care experiences. Chapter 10, p. 309

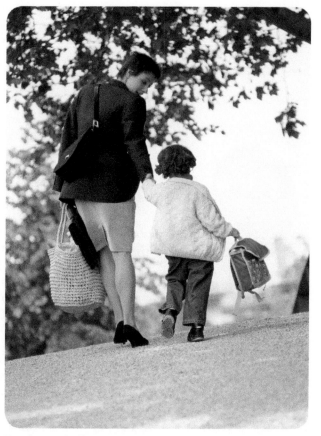

How does work affect parenting?

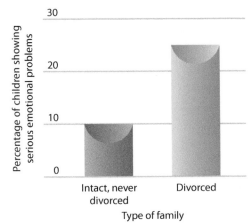

FIGURE **14.8**

DIVORCE AND CHILDREN'S EMOTIONAL PROBLEMS. In Hetherington's research, 25 percent of children from divorced families showed serious emotional problems compared with only 10 percent of children from intact, never-divorced families. However, keep in mind that a substantial majority (75 percent) of the children from divorced families did not show serious emotional problems.

What concerns are involved in whether parents should stay together for the sake of the children or become divorced?

Stanley-Hagan, 2002). Let's examine some important questions about children in divorced families:

• *Are children better adjusted in intact, never-divorced families than in divorced families?* Most researchers agree that children from divorced families show poorer adjustment than their counterparts in nondivorced families (Amato & Dorius, 2010; Hetherington, 2006; Lansford, 2009, 2012; Wallerstein, 2008) (see Figure 14.8). Those who have experienced multiple divorces are at greater risk. Children in divorced families are more likely than children in nondivorced families to have academic problems, to show externalized problems (such as acting out and delinquency) and internalized problems (such as anxiety and depression), to be less socially responsible, to have less competent intimate relationships, to drop out of school, to become sexually active at an early age, to take drugs, to associate with antisocial peers, to have low self-esteem, and to be less securely attached as young adults (Lansford, 2009). A recent study revealed that adolescent girls with divorced parents were especially vulnerable to developing depressive symptoms (Oldehinkel & others, 2008). Another study found that experiencing a divorce in childhood was associated with insecure attachment in early adulthood (Brockmeyer, Treboux, & Crowell, 2005). And a recent study found that adolescent girls from divorced families displayed lower levels of romantic competence (Shulman & others, 2012). However, mothers' ability to provide their daughters with a coherent account of their own adolescent romantic experiences alleviated the negative link of divorce to daughters' romantic behavior. Nonetheless, it is important to remember that most of the children in divorced families do *not* have significant adjustment problems.

• *Should parents stay together for the sake of the children?* Whether parents should stay in an unhappy or conflicted marriage for the sake of their children is one of the most commonly asked questions about divorce (Deutsch & Pruett, 2009; Hetherington, 2006; Ziol-Guest, 2009). If the stresses and disruptions in family relationships associated with an unhappy, conflictual marriage that erode the well-being of children are reduced by the move to a divorced, single-parent family, divorce can be advantageous. However, if the diminished resources and increased risks associated with divorce also are accompanied by inept parenting and sustained or increased conflict, not only between the divorced couple but also among the parents, children, and siblings, the best choice for the children would be for an unhappy marriage to be retained (Hetherington & Stanley-Hagan, 2002). It is difficult to determine how these "ifs" will play out when parents either remain together in an acrimonious marriage or become divorced.

  Note that marital conflict may have negative consequences for children in the context of marriage or divorce (Cummings & Davies, 2010; Kleinsorge & Covitz, 2012). A longitudinal study revealed that conflict in nondivorced families was associated with emotional problems in children (Amato, 2006). Indeed, many of the problems that children from divorced homes experience begin during the predivorce period, a time when parents are often in active conflict with each other. Thus, when children from divorced homes show problems, the problems may be due not only to the divorce but to the marital conflict that led to it (Thompson, 2008).

  E. Mark Cummings and his colleagues (Cummings & Davies, 2010; Cummings, El-Sheikh, & Kouros, 2009; Cummings & Kouros, 2008; Cummings & others, 2012) have proposed emotion security theory, which has its roots in attachment theory and states that children appraise marital conflict in terms of their sense of security and safety in the family. These researchers make a distinction between marital conflict that is negative for children (such as hostile emotional displays and destructive conflict tactics) and marital conflict that can be positive for children (such as marital disagreement that involves a calm discussion of each person's perspective and working together to reach a solution). In a recent study, Cummings and his colleagues (2012) found that parental conflict during the kindergarten year was linked to children's emotional insecurity later in childhood, which in turn was associated with adolescent adjustment, including higher levels of depression and anxiety.

• *How much do family processes matter in divorced families?* In divorced families, family processes matter a great deal (Hetherington, 2006; Lansford, 2009, 2012; Parke &

Clarke-Stewart, 2011; Sigal & others, 2011). When the divorced parents have a harmonious relationship and use authoritative parenting, the adjustment of adolescents is improved (Hetherington, 2006). When the divorced parents can agree on child-rearing strategies and can maintain a cordial relationship with each other, frequent visits by the noncustodial parent usually benefit the child (Fabricius & others, 2010). Following a divorce, father involvement with children drops off more than mother involvement, especially for fathers of girls. Also, a recent study in divorced families revealed that an intervention focused on improving the mother-child relationship was linked to improvements in relationship quality that increased children's coping skills over the short term (6 months) and long term (6 years) (Velez & others, 2011).

- *What factors influence an individual child's vulnerability to suffering negative consequences as a result of living in a divorced family?* Among the factors influencing the child's risk and vulnerability are the child's adjustment prior to the divorce as well as the child's personality and temperament, gender, and custody situation (Hetherington, 2005, 2006). Children whose parents later divorce show poorer adjustment before the breakup (Amato & Booth, 1996; Lansford, 2009). Children who are socially mature and responsible, who show few behavioral problems, and who have an easy temperament are better able to cope with their parents' divorce. Children with a difficult temperament often have problems coping with their parents' divorce (Hetherington, 2005).

  Earlier studies reported gender differences in response to divorce, with divorce being more negative for girls than boys in mother-custody families. However, more recent studies have shown that gender differences are less pronounced and consistent than was previously believed. Some of the inconsistency may be due to the rise in father custody, joint custody, and increased involvement of noncustodial fathers, especially in their sons' lives (Ziol-Guest, 2009). One analysis of studies found that children in joint-custody families were better adjusted than children in sole-custody families (Bauserman, 2002). Joint custody works best for children when the parents can get along with each other (Parke & Clarke-Stewart, 2011). Some studies have shown that boys adjust better in father-custody families, girls in mother-custody families, whereas other studies have not (Maccoby & Mnookin, 1992; Santrock & Warshak, 1979).

- *What role does socioeconomic status play in the lives of children in divorced families?* Custodial mothers experience the loss of about one-fourth to one-half of their predivorce income, in comparison with a loss of only one-tenth by custodial fathers (Emery, 1994). This income loss for divorced mothers is accompanied by increased workloads, high rates of job instability, and residential moves to less desirable neighborhoods with inferior schools (Lansford, 2009).

In sum, many factors are involved in determining how divorce influences a child's development (Amato & Dorius, 2010; Lansford, 2012). To read about some strategies for helping children cope with the divorce of their parents, see *Caring Connections.*

STEPFAMILIES

Not only has divorce become commonplace in the United States, so has getting remarried (Ganong, Coleman, & Jamison, 2011). It takes time for parents to marry, have children, get divorced, and then remarry. Consequently, there are far more elementary and secondary school children than infant or preschool children living in stepfamilies.

The number of remarriages involving children has grown steadily in recent years. Also, divorces occur at a 10 percent higher rate in remarriages than in first marriages (Cherlin & Furstenberg, 1994). About half of all children whose parents divorce will have a stepparent within four years of the separation.

Remarried parents face some unique tasks. The couple must define and strengthen their marriage and at the same time renegotiate the biological parent-child relationships and establish stepparent-stepchild and stepsibling relationships (Ganong, Coleman, & Jamison, 2011). The complex histories and multiple relationships make adjustment difficult in a stepfamily (Goldscheider & Sassler, 2006). Only one-third of stepfamily couples stay remarried. And some remarried individuals are more adult-focused, responding more to the concerns of their

Communicating with Children About Divorce

Ellen Galinsky and Judy David (1988) developed a number of guidelines for communicating with children about divorce.

Explain the Separation

As soon as daily activities in the home make it obvious that one parent is leaving, tell the children. If possible, both parents should be present when children are told about the separation to come. The reasons for the separation are very difficult for young children to understand. No matter what parents tell children, children can find reasons to argue against the separation. It is extremely important for parents to tell the children who will take care of them and to describe the specific arrangements for seeing the other parent.

Explain That the Separation Is Not the Child's Fault

Young children often believe their parents' separation or divorce is their own fault. Therefore, it is important to tell children that they are not the cause of the separation. Parents need to repeat this a number of times.

Explain That It May Take Time to Feel Better

Tell young children that it's normal to not feel good about what is happening and that many other children feel this way when their parents become separated. It is also okay for divorced parents to share some of their emotions with children, by saying something like "I'm having a hard time since the separation just like you, but I know it's going to get better after a while." Such statements are best kept brief and should not criticize the other parent.

Keep the Door Open for Further Discussion

Tell your children to come to you anytime they want to talk about the separation. It is healthy for children to express their pent-up emotions in discussions with their parents and to learn that the parents are willing to listen to their feelings and fears.

Provide as Much Continuity as Possible

The less children's worlds are disrupted by the separation, the easier their transition to a single-parent family will be. This means maintaining the rules already in place as much as possible. Children need parents who care enough to not only give them warmth and nurturance but also set reasonable limits.

Provide Support for Your Children and Yourself

After a divorce or separation, parents are as important to children as before the divorce or separation. Divorced parents need to provide children with as much support as possible. Parents function best when other people are available to give them support as adults and as parents. Divorced parents can find people who provide practical help and with whom they can talk about their problems.

How does the third piece of advice above correspond to what you learned in Chapter 10 about emotion coaching?

partner, while others are more child-focused, responding more to the concerns of the children (Anderson & Greene, 2011).

In some cases, the stepfamily may have been preceded by the death of a spouse. However, by far the largest number of stepfamilies are preceded by divorce rather than death (Pasley & Moorefield, 2004). Three common types of stepfamily structure are (1) stepfather, (2) stepmother, and (3) blended or complex. In stepfather families, the mother typically had custody of the children and remarried, introducing a stepfather into her children's lives. In stepmother families, the father usually had custody and remarried, introducing a stepmother into his children's lives. In a blended or complex stepfamily, both parents bring children from previous marriages to live in the newly formed stepfamily.

In E. Mavis Hetherington's (2006) longitudinal analyses, children and adolescents who had been in a simple stepfamily (stepfather or stepmother) for a number of years were adjusting better than in the early years of the remarried family and were functioning well in comparison with children and adolescents in conflicted nondivorced families and children and adolescents in complex (blended) stepfamilies. More than 75 percent of the adolescents in long-established simple stepfamilies described their relationships with their stepparents as "close" or "very close." Hetherington (2006) concluded that in

How does living in a stepfamily influence a child's development?

long-established simple stepfamilies adolescents seem to eventually benefit from the presence of a stepparent and the resources provided by the stepparent.

Children often have better relationships with their custodial parents (mothers in stepfather families, fathers in stepmother families) than with stepparents (Santrock, Sitterle, & Warshak, 1988). Also, children in simple families (stepmother, stepfather) often show better adjustment than their counterparts in complex (blended) families (Anderson & others, 1999; Hetherington & Kelly, 2002).

As in divorced families, children in stepfamilies show more adjustment problems than children in nondivorced families (Hetherington, 2006). The adjustment problems are similar to those found among children of divorced parents—academic problems and lower self-esteem, for example (Anderson & others, 1999). However, it is important to recognize that a majority of children in stepfamilies do not have problems. In one analysis, 25 percent of children in stepfamilies showed adjustment problems compared with 10 percent in intact, never-divorced families (Hetherington & Kelly, 2002).

Adolescence is an especially difficult time for the formation of a stepfamily (Anderson & others, 1999). Becoming part of a stepfamily may exacerbate normal adolescent concerns about identity, sexuality, and autonomy.

GAY AND LESBIAN PARENTS

Increasingly, gay and lesbian couples are creating families that include children (Patterson & D'Augelli, 2013; Patterson & Farr, 2012) (see Figure 14.9). Approximately 33 percent of lesbian couples and 22 percent of gay couples are parents (Patterson, 2004). There may be more than 1 million gay and lesbian parents in the United States today.

Like heterosexual couples, gay and lesbian parents vary greatly. They may be single or they may have same-gender partners. Many lesbian mothers and gay fathers are noncustodial parents because they lost custody of their children to heterosexual spouses after a divorce. In addition, gays and lesbians are increasingly choosing parenthood through donor insemination or adoption. Researchers have found that the children conceived through new reproductive technologies—such as in vitro fertilization—are as well adjusted as their counterparts conceived by natural means (Golombok, 2011a, b; Golombok & Tasker, 2010).

Researchers have found few differences in children growing up with gay fathers and lesbian mothers in comparison with adolescents growing up with heterosexual parents (Patterson, 2013). For example, children growing up in gay or lesbian families are just as popular with their peers, and there are no differences in the adjustment and mental health of children living in these families in comparison with children in heterosexual families (Hyde & DeLamater, 2011). Also, the overwhelming majority of children growing up in a gay or lesbian family have a heterosexual orientation (Golombok & Tasker, 2010).

CULTURAL, ETHNIC, AND SOCIOECONOMIC VARIATIONS IN FAMILIES

Parenting can be influenced by culture, ethnicity, and socioeconomic status. In Bronfenbrenner's theory (introduced in Chapter 1), these influences are described as part of the macrosystem.

Cross-Cultural Studies Different cultures often give different answers to such basic questions as what the father's role in the family should be, what support systems are available to families, and how children should be disciplined (Conger & others, 2012; Hewlett & McFarlen, 2010; Mistry, Contreras, & Dutta, 2013). There are important cross-cultural variations in parenting (Bornstein & Lansford, 2010). In some countries, authoritarian parenting is widespread. For example, in the Arab world, many families today are very authoritarian, dominated by the father's rule, and children are taught strict codes of conduct and family loyalty (Booth, 2002). In one study, Chinese mothers of preschool children reported that they used more physical coercion, more encouragement of modesty, more shaming and love withdrawal, less warmth, and less democratic participation than U.S. mothers of preschool children (Wu & others, 2002).

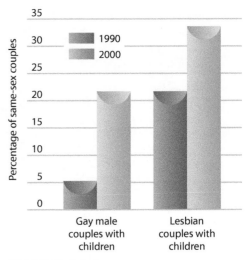

FIGURE 14.9

PERCENTAGE OF GAY MALE AND LESBIAN COUPLES WITH CHILDREN, 1990 AND 2000. *Why do you think more lesbian couples have children than gay male couples?*

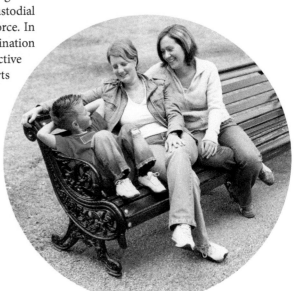

What are the research findings regarding the development and psychological well-being of children raised by gay and lesbian couples?

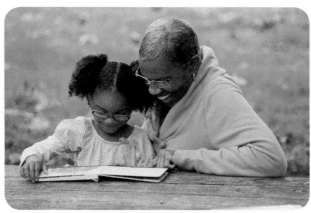

What are some characteristics of families in different ethnic groups?

developmental **connection**

Culture and Ethnicity

Many families that have immigrated to the United States in recent decades, such as Mexican Americans and Asian Americans, come from collectivist cultures in which family obligation is strong. Chapter 17, p. 494

developmental **connection**

Socioeconomic Status

Living in poverty has many psychological effects on both parents and children. Chapter 17, p. 489

What type of parenting is most frequent? In one study of parenting behavior in 186 cultures around the world, the most common pattern was a warm and controlling style, one that was neither permissive nor restrictive (Rohner & Rohner, 1981). The investigators commented that the majority of cultures have discovered, over many centuries, that children's healthy social development is most effectively promoted by love and at least moderate parental control.

Cultural change is coming to families in many countries around the world (Phinney & others, 2013a,b). There are trends toward greater family mobility, migration to urban areas, separation as some family members work in cities or countries far from their homes, smaller families, fewer extended-family households, and increases in maternal employment (Brown & Larson, 2002). These trends can change the resources that are available to children. For example, when several generations no longer live near each other, children may lose support and guidance from grandparents, aunts, and uncles. Also, smaller families may produce more openness and communication between parents and children.

Ethnicity   Families within different ethnic groups in the United States differ in their typical size, structure, composition, reliance on kinship networks, and levels of income and education (Conger & others, 2012; Livas-Dlott & others, 2010). Large and extended families are more common among minority groups than among the non-Latino White majority (Wright & others, 2012). For example, 19 percent of Latino families have three or more children, as compared with 14 percent of African American and 10 percent of non-Latino White families. African American and Latino children interact more with grandparents, aunts, uncles, cousins, and more-distant relatives than do non-Latino White children.

Single-parent families are more common among African Americans and Latinos than among White Americans (Zeiders, Roosa, & Tein, 2011). In comparison with two-parent households, single parents often have more limited resources of time, money, and energy (Wright & others, 2012). Ethnic minority parents also are less educated and more likely to live in low-income circumstances than their non-Latino White counterparts. Still, many impoverished ethnic minority families manage to find ways to raise competent children (McLoyd & others, 2009).

Some aspects of home life can help protect ethnic minority children from injustice. The family can filter out destructive racist messages, and parents can present alternative frames of reference to counter those presented by the majority. For example, TV shows may tell a 10-year-old boy that he will grow up to be either a star athlete or a bum; his parents can show him that his life holds many possibilities other than these. The extended family also can serve as an important buffer to stress (McAdoo, 2006).

Of course, individual families vary, and how ethnic minority families deal with stress depends on many factors (Nieto & Bode, 2012; Schaefer, 2013; Urdan, 2012). Whether the parents are native-born or immigrants, how long the family has been in this country, their socioeconomic status, and their national origin all make a difference (Cooper, 2011). The characteristics of the family's social context also influence its adaptation. What are the attitudes toward the family's ethnic group within its neighborhood or city? Can the family's children attend good schools? Are there community groups that welcome people from the family's ethnic group? Do members of the family's ethnic group form community groups of their own? To read further about ethnic minority parenting, see *Connecting with Diversity*.

Socioeconomic Status   Low-income families have less access to resources than higher-income families do (Duncan, 2012; Duncan & others, 2013). The differential access to resources includes nutrition, health care, protection from danger, and enriching educational and socialization opportunities, such as tutoring and lessons in various activities. These differences are compounded in low-income families characterized by long-term poverty (Santiago & others, 2012).

In America and most Western cultures, differences also have been found in child rearing among different socioeconomic-status (SES) groups (Hoff, Laursen, & Tardif, 2002, p. 246):

- "Lower-SES parents (1) are more concerned that their children conform to society's expectations, (2) create a home atmosphere in which it is clear that parents have authority over children," (3) use physical punishment more in disciplining their children, and (4) are more directive and less conversational with their children.

Acculturation and Ethnic Minority Parenting

Ethnic minority children and their parents "are expected to transcend their own cultural background and to incorporate aspects of the dominant culture" into children's development (Garcia Coll & Pachter, 2002, p. 7). They undergo varying degrees of **acculturation,** which refers to cultural changes that occur when one culture comes in contact with another. Asian American parents, for example, may feel pressed to modify the traditional training style of parental control discussed earlier as they encounter the more permissive parenting typical of the dominant culture.

The level of family acculturation can affect parenting style by influencing expectations for children's development, parent-child interactions, and the role of the extended family (Cooper, 2011; Fuligni, 2012). For example, in one study, the level of acculturation and maternal education were the strongest predictors of maternal-infant interaction patterns in Latino families (Perez-Febles, 1992).

The family's level of acculturation also influences important decisions about child care and early childhood education. For example, "an African American mother might prefer to leave her children with extended family while she is at work because the kinship network is seen as a natural way to cope with maternal absence. This well-intentioned, culturally appropriate decision might, however, put the child at an educational and social disadvantage relative to other children of similar age who have the benefit of important preschool experiences that may ease the transition into early school years" (Garcia Coll & Pachter, 2002, pp. 7–8). Less acculturated and more acculturated family members may disagree about the appropriateness of various caregiving practices, possibly creating conflict or confusion.

The opportunities for acculturation that young children experience depend mainly on their parents and extended family. If parents send the children to a child-care center, school, church, or other community setting, the children are likely to learn about the values and behaviors of the dominant culture, and they may be expected to adapt to that culture's

How is acculturation involved in ethnic minority parenting?

norms. Thus, Latino children raised in a traditional family in which the family's well-being is considered more important than the individual's interests may attend a preschool in which children are rewarded for asserting themselves. Chinese American children, whose traditional parents value behavioral inhibition (as discussed in Chapter 10), may be rewarded outside the home for being active and emotionally expressive. Over time, the differences in the level of acculturation experienced by children and by their parents and extended family may grow (Garcia Coll & Pachter, 2002).

In this interlude you learned that preschools may encourage behavior that is at odds with some ethnic groups' parenting styles. Is this common worldwide? Which type of parenting is most frequently found worldwide?

- "Higher-SES parents (1) are more concerned with developing children's initiative" and delay of gratification, "(2) create a home atmosphere in which children are more nearly equal participants and in which rules are discussed as opposed to being laid down" in an authoritarian manner, (3) are less likely to use physical punishment, and (4) "are less directive and more conversational" with their children.

Parents in different socioeconomic groups also tend to think differently about education (Huston & Ripke, 2006). Middle- and upper-income parents more often think of education as something that should be mutually encouraged by parents and teachers. By contrast, low-income parents are more likely to view education as the teacher's job. Thus, increased school-family linkages especially can benefit students from low-income families. In Chapter 17, "Culture and Diversity," we will have much more to say about socioeconomic variations in families, especially the negative ramifications of poverty for children's development, as well as other aspects of culture and its role in parenting and children's development.

acculturation Cultural changes that occur when one culture comes in contact with another culture.

Review Connect Reflect

 LG4 Characterize the changing family in a changing social world.

Review

- How are children influenced by working parents?
- What characterizes the effects of divorce on children's development?
- How does living in a stepfamily influence children's development?
- How does growing up in a family with same-sex parents influence children's development?
- In what ways is children's development affected by their family's culture, ethnicity, and socioeconomic status?

Connect

- In this section, you learned that low-income families have less access to nutrition, health care, protection from danger, and enriching educational and socialization opportunities. In Chapter 4, what did you learn regarding the specific health outcomes for children living in poverty?

Reflect *Your Own Personal Journey of Life*

- Now that you have studied many aspects of families in this chapter, imagine that you have decided to write a book on some aspect of your own family. What aspect of your family would you focus on? What would be the title of your book? What would be the major theme of the book?

reach your **learning goals**

Families

Family Processes

LG1 Discuss family processes.

Interactions in the Family System

- The family is a system of interrelated and interacting individuals with different subsystems—some dyadic, some polyadic. The subsystems have both direct and indirect effects on one another. Positive marital relations can have a positive influence on parenting. Reciprocal socialization is the bidirectional process in which children socialize parents just as parents socialize them.

Cognition and Emotion in Family Processes

- Cognition and emotion are central to understanding how family processes work. The role of cognition includes parents' cognitions, beliefs, and values about their parental role, as well as the way they perceive, organize, and understand their children's behaviors and beliefs. The role of emotion includes the regulation of emotion in children, understanding emotion in children, and emotion in carrying out the parenting role. Children learn to express and manage emotions appropriately through interaction with emotion-coaching parents and have fewer behavior problems than children of emotion-dismissing parents.

Multiple Developmental Trajectories

- Adults follow one developmental trajectory and children and adolescents another one. Comprehending how these trajectories mesh is important for understanding the effects of timing of entry into various family tasks.

Domain-Specific Socialization

- Increasingly a domain-specific approach to socialization is being emphasized. One recent proposal focuses on five domains, each linked to specific child outcomes. The five domains are protection, reciprocity, control, guided learning, and group participation.

Sociocultural and Historical Changes

- Changes in families may be due to great upheavals, such as war, or more subtle changes, such as technological advances and greater mobility of families. Increased restlessness and dissatisfaction in families has resulted in more divorced and remarried families than at any other point in history.

Parenting

LG2 Explain how parenting is linked to children's and adolescents' development.

Parental Roles and the Timing of Parenthood

Adapting Parenting to Developmental Changes in Children

Parents as Managers of Children's Lives

Parenting Styles and Discipline

Parent-Adolescent Relationships

Intergenerational Relationships

- Currently, there is a trend toward having fewer children and choosing when to have children. Many adults are waiting longer to having children or not having children at all. Differences have been found between the parenting of older and younger parents.

- The transition to parenthood requires considerable adaptation and adjustment on the part of parents. As children grow older, parents increasingly turn to reasoning or withholding privileges in disciplining children. Parents spend less time with children in middle and late childhood, a time when parents play an especially important role in their children's academic achievement. Control is more coregulatory in middle and late childhood.

- A recent trend is to conceptualize parents as managers of children's lives. An important aspect of parenting infants involves managing and guiding infants' behavior. Parents play important roles as managers of children's opportunities, effectively monitoring children's relationships and acting as social initiators and arrangers. Parental monitoring is linked to lower levels of juvenile delinquency, and effective parental management is related to children's higher academic achievement.

- Authoritarian, authoritative, neglectful, and indulgent are the four main parenting styles. Authoritative parenting is associated with socially competent child behavior more than the other styles. However, ethnic variations in parenting styles indicate that in African American and Asian American families, some aspects of authoritarian parenting may benefit children. Latino parents often emphasize connectedness with the family and respect and obedience in their child rearing. There are a number of reasons not to use physical punishment in disciplining children. Intense punishment presents the child with an out-of-control model. Punishment can instill fear, rage, or avoidance in children. Punishment tells children what not to do rather than what to do. Punishment can be abusive. Coparenting has positive outcomes for children. Child maltreatment is a multifaceted problem that involves the cultural context and family influences. Child maltreatment places the child at risk for a number of developmental problems.

- Many parents have a difficult time when their adolescents push for autonomy. Secure attachment to parents increases the likelihood that adolescents will be socially competent. Conflict with parents often increases in early adolescence, but this conflict is generally moderate rather than severe. The increase in conflict probably serves the positive developmental functions of facilitating adolescent autonomy and identity. A subset of adolescents experience high parent-adolescent conflict, and this is linked with negative outcomes for adolescents.

- Connections between parents play important roles in development through the life span. An increasing number of studies indicate that intergenerational relationships influence children's development. Marital interaction, a supportive family environment, divorce, and conduct disorder in the child's family of origin are among the factors that are linked to the child's development.

Siblings

 Identify how siblings influence children's development.

Sibling Relationships

Birth Order

- Three important aspects of sibling relationships involve (1) emotional quality of the relationship, (2) familiarity and intimacy of the relationship, and (3) variation in sibling relationships. Sibling relationships include not only conflict and fighting but also helping, teaching, sharing, and playing—and siblings can function as rivals, emotional supports, and communication partners.

- Birth order is related in certain ways to child characteristics. Firstborn children are more self-controlled, conforming, and argumentative; have more guilt and anxiety; and excel academically and professionally compared with later-born children. However, some critics argue that the influence of birth order has been overestimated as a predictor of child behavior.

The Changing Family in a Changing Social World

 LG4 Characterize the changing family in a changing social world.

Working Parents

- In general, having both parents employed full-time outside the home has not been shown to have negative effects on children. However, depending on the circumstances, work can produce positive or negative effects on parenting. If parents experience poor working conditions, they frequently become inattentive to their children, who show more behavioral problems and do more poorly at school than children whose parents have better working conditions. There is a positive link between participation in extra-curricular activities and academic achievement, psychological adjustment, and positive interaction with parents.

Children in Divorced Families

- Children in divorced families show more adjustment problems than their counterparts in nondivorced families. Whether parents should stay in an unhappy or conflicted marriage for the sake of the children is difficult to determine. Children show better adjustment in divorced families when parents' relationships with each other are harmonious and authoritative parenting is used. Factors to be considered regarding the adjustment of children in divorced families are adjustment prior to the divorce, personality and temperament, developmental status, gender, and custody arrangements. Income loss for divorced mothers may be linked with a number of stresses that can affect the child's adjustment.

Stepfamilies

- As in divorced families, children in stepfamilies have more problems than their counterparts in nondivorced families. Restabilization often takes longer in stepfamilies than in divorced families. Children often have better relationships with their biological parents than with their stepparents and show more problems in complex, blended families than simple ones. Adolescence is an especially difficult time to experience the remarriage of parents.

Gay and Lesbian Parents

- Approximately 33 percent of lesbians and 22 percent of gay men are parents. There is considerable diversity among lesbian mothers, gay fathers, and their children. Researchers have found few differences between children growing up with gay or lesbian parents and children growing up with heterosexual parents.

Cultural, Ethnic, and Socioeconomic Variations in Families

- Cultures vary on a number of issues regarding families. African American and Latino children are more likely than White American children to live in single-parent families, larger families, and families with extended connections. Higher-SES families tend to avoid using physical discipline, strive to create a home atmosphere in which rules are discussed, and are concerned with developing children's initiative and delay of gratification. Lower-SES families are more likely to use physical punishment in disciplining their children, are more directive and less conversational, and want their children to conform to society's expectations.

key terms

scaffolding 392
reciprocal
   socialization 392

multiple developmental
   trajectories 394
authoritarian parenting 401

authoritative
   parenting 401
neglectful parenting 401

indulgent parenting 401
coparenting 404
acculturation 419

key people

Urie Bronfenbrenner 392
Joan Grusec 394
Marilyn Davidov 394

Diana Baumrind 401
Ruth Chao 402
Andrew Fuligni 409

Joseph Allen 408
Laurie Kramer 411
Judy Dunn 411

Ann Crouter 413
E. Mavis
   Hetherington 416

PEERS

chapter **outline**

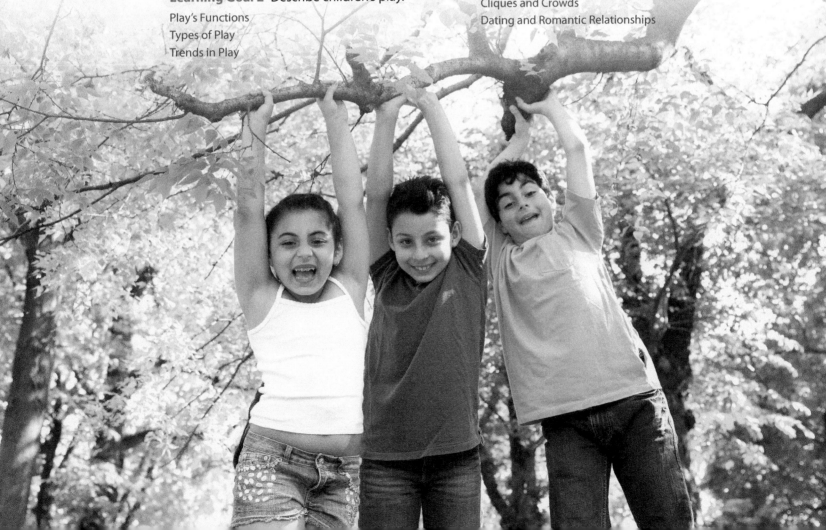

Lynn Brown and Carol Gilligan (1992) conducted in-depth interviews of one hundred 10- to 13-year-old girls who were making the transition to adolescence. They listened to what these girls were saying.

A number of the girls talked about how many girls say nice things to be polite but often don't really mean them. The girls know the benefits of being perceived as the perfect, happy girl. Judy spoke about her interest in romantic relationships. Although she and her girlfriends were only 13, they wanted to be romantic, and she talked about her lengthy private conversations with her girlfriends about boys. Noura said that she learned how very painful it is to be the person everyone doesn't like.

Cliques figured largely in these girls' lives. They provided emotional support for girls who were striving to be perfect but knew they were not. Victoria commented that sometimes girls like her, who weren't very popular, nonetheless were accepted into a "club" with three other girls. Now when she was sad or depressed she could count on the "club" for support. Though they were "leftovers" and did not get into the most popular cliques, these four girls knew they were liked.

Through these interviews, we see the girls' curiosity about the social world they lived in. They kept track of what was happening to their peers and friends. The girls spoke at length about the pleasure they derived from the intimacy and fun of human connection, about the potential for hurt in relationships, and about the importance of friends.

preview

This chapter is about peers, who clearly are very important in the lives of the adolescent girls just described. They also are very important in the lives of children. We begin this chapter by examining a number of ideas about children's peer relations, including their functions and variations. Then we turn to children's play and the roles of friends in children's development. We conclude by discussing peer relationships in adolescence.

Peer Relations — **LG1** Discuss peer relations in childhood.

- Exploring Peer Relations
- The Developmental Course of Peer Relations in Childhood
- The Distinct but Coordinated Worlds of Parent-Child and Peer Relations
- Social Cognition and Emotion
- Peer Statuses
- Bullying

As children grow up, they spend increasing amounts of time with their peers. What are some key aspects of peer relations?

EXPLORING PEER RELATIONS

Peers are children who share the same age or maturity level. They fill a unique role in the child's development. One of their most important functions is to provide a source of information and comparison about the world outside the family. Children receive feedback about their abilities from their peer group. They evaluate what they do in terms of whether it is better than, as good as, or worse than what other children do. It is hard to do this at home because siblings are usually older or younger.

Are Peers Necessary for Development?   Good peer relations may be necessary for normal social development (Brown & Larson, 2009; Bowker, Rubin, & Coplan, 2012; Rubin & others, 2013). Social isolation, or the inability to "plug in" to a social network, is linked with problems and disorders ranging from delinquency and problem drinking to depression (Benner, 2011; Bornstein, Jager, & Steinberg, 2013; Dishion & Tispsord, 2011; Gorrese & Ruggieri, 2012).

Positive and Negative Peer Relations   Peer influences can be both positive and negative (Cillessen & Bellmore, 2011; Rubin & others, 2013; Wentzel, 2013). A recent study found that children who associated with peers who engaged in prosocial behavior at age 9 had a higher level of self-control at age 10 and that those whose peers engaged in deviant behavior at age 9 had a lower level of self-control at age 10 (Meldrum & Hay, 2012). Children and adolescents also explore the principles of fairness and justice by working through disagreements with peers. They also learn to be keen observers of peers' interests and perspectives in order to smoothly integrate themselves into ongoing peer activities. And children and adolescents learn to be skilled and sensitive partners in relationships by forging close friendships with selected peers. They carry these intimacy skills forward to help form the foundation of later dating and marital relationships.

   In contrast, some theorists and researchers have emphasized the negative influences of peers on adolescents' development (Dishion & Tipsord, 2011). Being rejected or overlooked by peers leads some adolescents to feel lonely or hostile. Further, such rejection and neglect by peers are related to an individual's subsequent mental health (Hymel & others, 2011). For some adolescents, the peer culture is a corrupt influence that undermines parental values and control. Further, peer relations are linked to adolescents' patterns of drug use, delinquency, and depression. A recent study found that low parental control was linked to

You are troubled at seeing him spend his early years in doing nothing. What! Is it nothing to be happy? Is it nothing to skip, to play, to run about all day long? Never in his life will he be so busy as now.

—**JEAN-JACQUES ROUSSEAU**
Swiss-Born French Philosopher, 18th Century

peers Children who share the same age or maturity level.

In what ways can peer relations be positive and negative?

higher delinquency in adolescence through its association with deviant peer affiliation (Deutsch & others, 2012).

As you read further about peers, keep in mind that findings about the influence of peers vary according to the way peer experience is measured, the outcomes specified, and the developmental trajectories traversed (Brechwald & Prinstein, 2011; Brown & Larson, 2009; Hartup, 2005). "Peers" and "peer group" are global concepts. A "peer group" of an adolescent might refer to a neighborhood crowd, reference crowd, church crowd, sports team, friendship group, and friend (Brown, 1999).

Peer Contexts   Peer interaction is influenced by contexts, which can include the type of peer the child or adolescent interacts with—such as an acquaintance, a crowd, a clique, a friend, or a romantic partner—and the situation or location—such as a school, neighborhood, community center, dance, religious setting, sporting event, and so on, as well as the culture in which the child or adolescent lives (Brown & Larson, 2009; Dishion & Tipsord, 2011; Rubin & others, 2013). As they interact with peers in these various contexts, children and adolescents are likely to encounter different messages and different opportunities to engage in adaptive and maladaptive behavior that can influence their development (Brechwald & Prinstein, 2011).

In terms of contexts, peers play an important role in the development of individuals in all cultures. However, as indicated in *Connecting with Diversity,* cultures vary in the significance of the socializing role of peers (Way & Silverman, 2012).

Individual Difference Factors   Individual differences among peers also are important to consider in understanding peer relations (Brechwald & Prinstein, 2011). Among the wide range of individual differences that can affect peer relations are personality traits such as how shy or outgoing children are. For example, a very shy child is more likely than a gregarious child to be neglected by peers and have anxiety about introducing himself or herself to new peers. One individual difference factor that impairs peer relations is the trait of negative emotionality, which involves a relatively low threshold for experiencing anger, fear, anxiety, and irritation. For example, one recent study revealed that adolescents characterized by negative emotionality tended to engage in negative interpersonal behavior when interacting with a friend or a romantic partner (Hatton & others, 2008).

THE DEVELOPMENTAL COURSE OF PEER RELATIONS IN CHILDHOOD

Some researchers argue that the quality of peer interaction in infancy provides valuable information about socioemotional development (Hughes & Dunn, 2007; Williams, Ontai, & Mastergeorge, 2010). For example, in one investigation, positive affect in infant peer relations was related to easy access to peer play groups and to peer popularity in early childhood (Howes, 1985). As increasing numbers of children attend child care, peer interaction in infancy takes on a more important developmental role.

Around the age of 3, children already prefer to spend time with same-sex rather than opposite-sex playmates, and this preference increases in early childhood. A recent study of 4-year-olds found that gender was a strong influence on who children selected as playmates (Martin & others, 2013). In this study, young children selected playmates of the same sex with similar levels of gender-typed activities, with the child's sex being a more powerful influence than the child's activities.

During the preschool years the frequency of peer interaction, both positive and negative, picks up considerably (Hartup, 1983; Rubin & others, 2013). Although aggressive interaction and rough-and-tumble play increase, the proportion of aggressive exchanges, compared with friendly exchanges, decreases. Many preschool children spend considerable time in peer interaction just conversing with playmates about such matters as "negotiating roles and rules in play, arguing, and agreeing" (Rubin, Bukowski, & Parker, 2006).

In early childhood, children also distinguish between friends and non-friends (Howes, 2009a). For most young children, a friend is someone to play with. Young preschool children

connecting with diversity

Cross-Cultural Comparisons of Peer Relations

In some countries, adults restrict adolescents' access to peers. For example, in many areas of rural India and in Arab countries, opportunities for peer relations in adolescence are severely restricted, especially for girls (Brown & Larson, 2002). If girls attend school in these regions of the world, it is usually in sex-segregated schools. In these countries, interaction with the other sex or opportunities for romantic relationships are restricted (Booth, 2002).

In a cross-cultural analysis, the peer group was more important to U.S. adolescents than to Japanese adolescents (Rothbaum & others, 2000). Japanese adolescents spend less time outside the home, have less recreational leisure time, and engage in fewer extracurricular activities with peers than U.S. adolescents do (White, 1993). Also, U.S. adolescents are more likely to put pressure on their

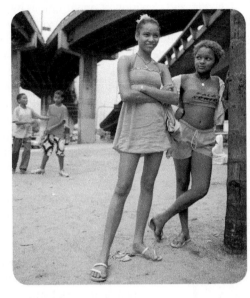

Street youth in Rio de Janeiro.

peers to resist parental influence than Japanese adolescents are (Rothbaum & others, 2000).

In some cultures, children are placed in peer groups for much greater lengths of time at an earlier age than they are in the United States. For example, in the Murian culture of eastern India, both male and female children live in a dormitory from the age of 6 until they get married (Barnouw, 1975). The dormitory is a religious haven where members are devoted to work and spiritual harmony. Children work for their parents, and the parents arrange the children's marriages.

In some cultural settings, peers even assume responsibilities usually handled by parents (Way & Silverman, 2012). For example, street youth in South America rely on networks of peers to help them negotiate survival in urban environments (Welti, 2002).

In Chapter 1, you learned that cross-cultural studies compare aspects of two or more cultures, and the comparison provides information about the degree to which development is similar—or universal—across cultures or is culture-specific. From the results of this cross-cultural study, what can you say about peer pressure?

are more likely than older children to have friends who are of a different gender or ethnicity (Howes, 2009a).

As children enter the elementary school years, reciprocity becomes especially important in peer interchanges. Children play games, function in groups, and cultivate friendships. The amount of time children spend in peer interaction also rises during middle and late childhood and adolescence. Researchers estimate that the percentage of time spent in social interaction with peers increases from approximately 10 percent at 2 years of age to more than 30 percent in middle and late childhood (Rubin, Bukowski, & Parker, 2006). Other changes in peer relations as children move through middle and late childhood involve an increase in the size of their peer group and peer interaction that is supervised less closely by adults (Rubin, Bukowski, & Parker, 2006).

Peer interactions take varied forms—cooperative and competitive, boisterous and quiet, joyous and humiliating. There is increasing evidence that gender plays an important role in these interactions (Bukowski, Buhrmester, & Underwood, 2011). Gender influences not only the composition of children's groups but also their size and the types of interactions within them (Maccoby, 2002). From about 5 years of age onward, boys tend to associate in large clusters more than girls do; girls are more likely than boys to play in groups of two or three. As discussed in Chapter 12, "Gender," boys' groups and girls' groups also tend to favor different types of activities. Boys' groups are more likely to engage in rough-and-tumble play, competition, conflict, ego displays, risk taking, and dominance seeking. By contrast, girls' groups are more likely to engage in collaborative discourse (Leman, Ahmed, & Ozarow, 2005).

What are some developmental changes in peer relations?

THE DISTINCT BUT COORDINATED WORLDS OF PARENT-CHILD AND PEER RELATIONS

Parents may influence their children's peer relations in many ways, both direct and indirect (Updegraff & others, 2010). Parents affect their children's peer relations through their interactions with their children, how they manage their children's lives, and the opportunities they provide their children (Brown & Bakken, 2011). One study revealed that warmth, advice giving, and provision of opportunities by mothers and fathers were linked to children's social competence (high prosocial behavior, low aggression), and subsequently to social acceptance (being well-liked by peers and teachers) one year later (McDowell & Parke, 2009).

Basic lifestyle decisions by parents—their choices of neighborhoods, churches, schools, and their own friends—largely determine the pool from which their children select possible friends. These choices in turn affect which children their children meet, their purpose in interacting, and eventually which children become their friends.

Do these results indicate that children's peer relations always are wedded to parent-child relationships? Although parent-child relationships influence children's subsequent peer relations, children also learn other modes of relating through their relationships with peers. For example, rough-and-tumble play occurs mainly with other children, not in parent-child interaction. In times of stress, children often turn to parents rather than peers for support. In parent-child relationships, children learn how to relate to authority figures. With their peers, children are likely to interact on a much more equal basis and to learn a mode of relating based on mutual influence.

Also remember from Chapter 8 that one of the most consistent findings of attachment research involving adolescents is that secure attachment to parents is linked to positive peer relations (Allen & Miga, 2010). A recent meta-analysis found that the link between mother and peer attachment was much stronger than the relation between father and peer attachment (Gorrese & Ruggieri, 2012).

However, whereas adolescent-parent attachments are correlated with adolescent outcomes, the correlations are moderate, an indication that the success or failure of parent-adolescent attachments does not necessarily guarantee success or failure in peer relationships. Clearly, secure attachment with parents can be an asset for the adolescent, fostering the trust to engage in close relationships with others and lay down the foundation for close relationship skills. Nonetheless, a significant minority of adolescents from strong, supportive families struggle in peer relations for a variety of reasons, such as being physically unattractive, maturing late, and experiencing cultural and socioeconomic-status (SES) discrepancies. On the other hand, some adolescents from troubled families find a positive, fresh start with peer relations that can compensate for their problematic family backgrounds.

What are some links between relationships with parents and relationships with peers?

developmental **connection**

Attachment

Securely attached infants use the caregiver as a secure base from which to explore their environment. Chapter 10, p. 301

developmental **connection**

Social Cognition

Social cognition refers to the processes involved in understanding the world around us, especially how we think and reason about others. Chapter 11, p. 318

SOCIAL COGNITION AND EMOTION

Mariana expects all her playmates to let her play with their toys whenever she asks. When Josh isn't picked for a team on the playground, he thinks his friends have turned against him. These are examples of social cognitions, which involve thoughts about social matters (Dodge, 2011a, b; Lewis & Carpendale, 2011; Peets, Hodges, & Salmivalli, 2011). How might children's social cognitions contribute to their peer relations? Possible influences include children's perspective-taking ability, social information-processing skills, social knowledge, and emotional regulation.

Perspective Taking As children enter the elementary school years, both their peer interaction and their perspective-taking ability increase. As we discussed in Chapter 13, "Moral Development," *perspective taking* involves perceiving another's point of view. Researchers have documented a link between perspective-taking skills and the quality of peer relations, especially in the elementary school years (LeMare & Rubin, 1987).

Perspective taking is important in part because it helps children communicate effectively. In one investigation, the communication exchanges among peers at kindergarten, first-, third-,

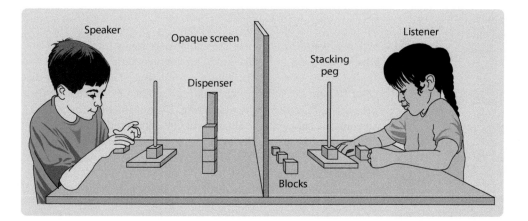

FIGURE **15.1**

THE DEVELOPMENT OF COMMUNICATION

SKILLS. This experimental arrangement of speaker and listener has been used to investigate the development of communication skills.

and fifth-grade levels were evaluated (Krauss & Glucksberg, 1969). Children were asked to instruct a peer in how to stack a set of blocks. The peer sat behind a screen with blocks similar to those the other child was stacking (see Figure 15.1). The kindergarten children made numerous errors in telling the peer how to duplicate the novel block stack. The older children, especially the fifth-graders, were much more efficient in communicating to a peer how to stack the blocks. They were far superior at perspective taking and figuring out how to talk to a peer so that the peer could understand them. During the elementary school years, children also become more efficient at understanding complex messages, so the listening skills of the peer in this experiment probably helped the communicating peer as well.

Social Information-Processing Skills How children process information about peer relationships also influences those relationships (Dodge, 2011a, b; Peets, Hodges, & Salmivalli, 2011; Reijntjes & others; White & Kistner, 2011). For example, suppose Andrew accidentally trips and knocks Alex's soft drink out of his hand. Alex misinterprets the encounter as hostile, which leads him to retaliate aggressively against Andrew. Through repeated encounters of this kind, other peers come to perceive Alex as habitually acting inappropriately.

Peer relations researcher Kenneth Dodge (1993) argues that children go through five steps in processing information about their social world: decoding social cues, interpreting, searching for a response, selecting an optimal response, and enacting it. Dodge has found that aggressive boys are more likely to perceive another child's actions as hostile when the child's intention is ambiguous—and when aggressive boys search for clues to determine a peer's intention, they respond more rapidly, less efficiently, and less reflectively than nonaggressive children.

Social Knowledge As children and adolescents develop, they acquire more social knowledge (also sometimes referred to as social intelligence), and there is considerable individual variation in how much one child or adolescent knows about what it takes to make friends, to get peers to like him or her, and so forth. A recent study of 14- and 15-year-olds examined links between social intelligence and peer popularity (Meijs & others, 2010). In this study, social intelligence was related to peer popularity but not to academic achievement.

Emotional Regulation Not only does cognition play an important role in peer relations, so does emotion (Calkins, 2012). The ability to regulate emotion is linked to successful peer relations (Trommsdorff & Cole, 2011). For example, in a recent study, preschool children who showed high levels of aggressive peer interactions also displayed low levels of self-regulation (Olson & others, 2011). Moody and emotionally negative individuals experience greater rejection by peers, whereas emotionally positive individuals are more popular (Saarni & others, 2006). Children who have effective self-regulatory skills can modulate their emotional expressiveness in contexts that evoke intense emotions, as when a peer says something negative (Denham & others, 2011).

How do aggressive boys process information about their social world?

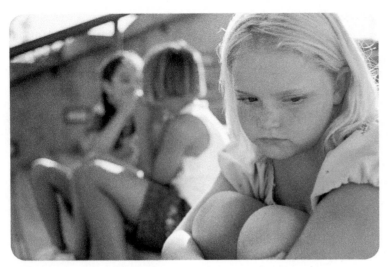

What are some statuses that children have with their peers?

> Peer rejection contributes to subsequent problems of adaptation, including antisocial behavior.
>
> —JOHN COIE
> *Contemporary Psychologist, Duke University*

popular children Children who are frequently identified as a best friend and are rarely disliked by their peers.

average children Children who receive an average number of both positive and negative nominations from their peers.

neglected children Children who are infrequently identified as a best friend but are not disliked by their peers.

rejected children Children who are infrequently identified as a best friend and are actively disliked by their peers.

controversial children Children who are frequently identified both as someone's best friend and as being disliked.

PEER STATUSES

Which types of children are likely to be popular with their peers, and which ones tend to be disliked? Developmentalists address this and similar questions by examining *sociometric status,* a term that describes the extent to which children are liked or disliked by their peer group (Cillessen & van den Berg, 2012; Hymel & others, 2011). Sociometric status is typically assessed by asking children to rate how much they like or dislike each of their classmates. Or it may be assessed by asking children to name the children they like the most and those they like the least.

Developmentalists have distinguished five peer statuses (Wentzel & Asher, 1995):

- **Popular children** are frequently nominated as a best friend and are rarely disliked by their peers.
- **Average children** receive an average number of both positive and negative nominations from their peers.
- **Neglected children** are infrequently nominated as a best friend but are not disliked by their peers.
- **Rejected children** are rarely nominated as someone's best friend and are actively disliked by their peers.
- **Controversial children** are frequently nominated both as someone's best friend and as being disliked.

Popular children have a number of social skills that contribute to their being well liked. Researchers have found that popular children give out reinforcements, listen carefully, maintain open lines of communication with peers, are happy, control their negative emotions, act like themselves, show enthusiasm and concern for others, and are self-confident without being conceited (Hartup, 1983; Rubin, Bukowski, & Parker, 2006). A recent study revealed that the importance of being popular in comparison with other priorities (such as friendship, achievement, and romantic interests) peaked in early adolescence (LaFontana & Cillessen, 2010).

Neglected children engage in low rates of interaction with their peers and are often described as shy by peers. Rejected children often have more serious adjustment problems than those who are neglected (Bukowski, 2012; Reijntjes & others, 2011). One study evaluated 112 boys over a period of seven years from fifth grade until the end of high school (Kupersmidt & Coie, 1990). The best predictor of whether rejected children would engage in delinquent behavior or drop out of school later during adolescence was aggression toward peers in elementary school. One study revealed that over the course of elementary school, during periods of peer rejection children were less likely to engage in classroom participation, but during times when they were not rejected, they participated more in class (Ladd, Herald-Brown, & Reiser, 2008).

Peer Rejection and Aggression The combination of being rejected by peers and being aggressive especially forecasts problems (Bukowski, 2012). For example, one study found that when third-grade boys were highly aggressive and rejected by their peers, they showed markedly higher levels of delinquency as adolescents and young adults than other boys did (Miller-Johnson, Coie, & Malone, 2003).

An analysis by John Coie (2004, pp. 252–253) provided three reasons why aggressive peer-rejected boys have problems in social relationships:

- First, the rejected, aggressive boys are more impulsive and have problems sustaining attention. As a result, they are more likely to be disruptive of ongoing activities in the classroom and in focused group play.
- Second, rejected, aggressive boys are more emotionally reactive. They are aroused to anger more easily and probably have more difficulty calming down once aroused. Because of this they are more prone to become angry at peers and to attack them verbally and physically.

- Third, rejected children have fewer social skills for making friends and maintaining positive relationships with peers.

Not all rejected children are aggressive (Hymel & others, 2011). Although aggression and its related characteristics of impulsiveness and disruptiveness underlie rejection about half the time, approximately 10 to 20 percent of rejected children are shy.

What are the antecedents of peer rejection? According to Gerald Patterson, Tom Dishion, and their colleagues (Patterson, DeBaryshe, & Ramsey, 1989; Patterson, Forgatch, & DeGarmo, 2010; Patterson, Reid, & Dishion, 1992; Shaw & others, 2006), poor parenting skills are at the root of children being rejected by their peers. These researchers especially argue that inadequate monitoring and harsh punishment, in some instances provoked by a child's difficult temperament, produce a child with aggressive, antisocial tendencies. The child carries these tendencies to the world of peers, where the child is rejected by better-adjusted peers who have a more positive temperament (such as "easy" or "effortful control") and have experienced more positive parenting (such as authoritative parenting).

How can rejected children be trained to interact more effectively with their peers? Rejected children may be taught to more accurately assess whether the intentions of their peers are negative. They may be asked to engage in role playing or to discuss hypothetical situations involving negative encounters with peers, such as times when a peer cuts into a line ahead of them. In some programs, children are shown videotapes of appropriate peer interaction and asked to draw lessons from what they have seen (Ladd, Buhs, & Troop, 2004).

Despite the positive outcomes of some programs that attempt to improve the social skills of adolescents, researchers have often found it difficult to improve the social skills of adolescents who are actively disliked and rejected. Many of these adolescents are rejected because they are aggressive or impulsive and lack the self-control to keep these behaviors in check. Still, some intervention programs have been successful in reducing the aggressive and impulsive behaviors of these adolescents (Ladd, Kochendorfer-Ladd, & Rydell, 2011).

Social-skills training programs have generally been more successful with children 10 years of age or younger than with adolescents (Malik & Furman, 1993). Peer reputations become more fixed as cliques and peer groups become more salient in adolescence. Once an adolescent gains a negative reputation among peers as being "mean," "weird," or a "loner," the peer group's attitude is often slow to change, even after the adolescent's problem behavior has been corrected. Thus, researchers have found that skill interventions may need to be supplemented by efforts to change the minds of peers.

BULLYING

Significant numbers of students are victimized by bullies (Espelage & Holt, 2012). In a national survey of more than 15,000 students in grades 6 through 10, nearly one of every three students said that they had experienced occasional or frequent involvement as a victim or perpetrator in bullying (Nansel & others, 2001). In this study, bullying was defined as verbal or physical behavior intended to disturb someone less powerful (see Figure 15.2). Boys are more likely to be bullies than are girls, but gender differences regarding victims of bullying are less clear (Salmivalli & Peets, 2009).

What characterizes bullying? Bullies report that their parents tend to be authoritarian, physically punish them, lack warmth, and show indifference to their children (Espelage & Holt, 2012). Bullies often display anger and hostility, and in many cases are morally disengaged (Obermann, 2011).

Who is likely to be bullied? In the study just described, boys and younger middle school students were most likely to be affected (Nansel & others, 2001). Children who said they were bullied reported more loneliness and difficulty in making friends, while those who did the bullying were more likely to have low grades and to smoke and drink alcohol. Researchers have found that anxious, socially withdrawn, and aggressive children are often the victims of bullying (Hanish & Guerra, 2004). Anxious and socially withdrawn children may be victimized because they are nonthreatening and unlikely to retaliate if bullied, whereas aggressive children may be the targets of bullying because their behavior is irritating to bullies (Rubin & others,

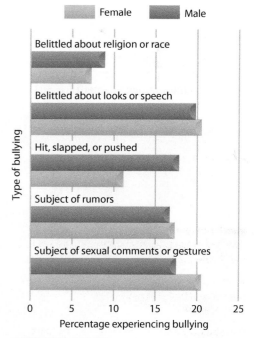

FIGURE **15.2**

BULLYING BEHAVIORS AMONG U.S. YOUTH.
This graph shows the types of bullying most often experienced by U.S. youth (Nansel & others, 2001). The percentages reflect the extent to which bullied students said that they had experienced a particular type of bullying. In terms of gender, note that when they were bullied, boys were more likely than girls to be hit, slapped, or pushed.

2011). A recent study revealed that having supportive friends was linked to a lower level of bullying and victimization (Kendrick, Jutengren, & Stattin, 2012).

Social contexts also influence bullying (Schwartz & others, 2010). Recent research indicates that 70 to 80 percent of victims and their bullies are in the same school classroom (Salmivalli & Peets, 2009). Classmates are often aware of bullying incidents and in many cases witness bullying. The larger social context of the peer group plays an important role in bullying (Salmivalli, Peets, & Hodges, 2011). In many cases, bullies torment victims to gain higher status in the peer group, and bullies need others to witness their power displays. Many bullies are not rejected by the peer group (Peeters, Cillessen, & Scholte, 2010). In one study, bullies were only rejected by peers to whom they were a potential threat (Veenstra & others, 2010). In another study, bullies often affiliated with each other or in some cases maintained their position in the popular peer group (Witvliet & others, 2010).

What are the outcomes of bullying? Researchers have found that children who are bullied are more likely to experience depression, to engage in suicidal ideation, and to attempt suicide than their counterparts who have not been the victims of bullying (Fisher & others, 2012; Lemstra & others, 2012). A recent longitudinal study of more than 6,000 children found that children who were the victims of peer bullying from 4 to 10 years of age were more likely to engage in suicidal ideation at 11½ years of age (Winsper & others, 2012). A recent study also revealed that 11-year-olds who were victims of peer bullying were more likely to have a heightened risk of developing borderline personality disorder symptoms (a pervasive pattern of unstable interpersonal relationships, low self-image, and emotional difficulties) (Wolke & others, 2012). A meta-analysis of 33 studies revealed a small but significant link between peer victimization and lower academic achievement (Nakamoto & Schwartz, 2010). Another study revealed that bullies, victims, or those who were both bullies and victims had more health problems (such as headaches, dizziness, sleep problems, and anxiety) than their counterparts who were not involved in bullying (Srabstein & others, 2006).

A recent study asked 18-year-olds who were former victims of bullying to explain what had actually made the bullying stop (Frisen, Hasselblad, & Holmqvist, 2012). The most common reason given was intervention by school personnel, followed by transitioning to a new school level. A third reason is that they changed the way they coped with the bullying, especially by being more assertive or ignoring the bullying. Researchers have found that many victims cope poorly in bullying situations, reacting by crying and withdrawal in many cases, so teaching them to cope in more effective ways might help to reduce the bullying.

A dramatic increase in *cyberbullying*—bullying on the Internet—has occurred recently (Donnerstein, 2012; Kowalski, Limber, & Agatston, 2012). We will explore the effects of cyberbullying on adolescents in Chapter 17.

What kinds of perspective taking and moral motivation skills do bullies, bully-victims, and prosocial children tend to exhibit? To find out, see *Connecting Through Research*.

Extensive attention is being directed to finding ways to prevent and treat bullying and victimization (Salmivalli, Garandeau, & Veenstra, 2012; Waasdorp, Bradshaw, & Leaf, 2012). A research review yielded mixed results for school-based intervention (Vreeman & Carroll, 2007). School-based interventions vary greatly, ranging from involving the whole school in an antibullying campaign to providing individualized social skills training (Alsaker & Valkanover, 2012; Strohmeier & Noam, 2012). One of the most promising bullying intervention programs has been created by Dan Olweus. This program focuses on 6- to 15-year-olds with the goal of decreasing opportunities and rewards for bullying. School staff are instructed in ways to improve peer relations and make schools safer. When properly implemented, the program reduces bullying by 30 to 70 percent (Olweus, 2003).

To reduce bullying, schools can adopt the following strategies (Cohn & Canter, 2003; Hyman & others, 2006; Limber, 2004):

- Get older peers to serve as monitors for bullying and intervene when they see it taking place.

developmental **connection**

Technology

Recently there has been a substantial increase in youth harassment and cyberbullying on the Internet. Chapter 17, p. 503

What are some strategies to reduce bullying?

connecting through research

What Are the Perspective Taking and Moral Motivation of Bullies, Bully-Victims, Victims, and Prosocial Children?

The following results were obtained in a study exploring the roles that perspective taking and moral motivation play in the lives of bullies, bully-victims, victims, and prosocial children (Gasser & Keller, 2009):

- *Bullies* are highly aggressive toward other children but are not victims of bullying.
- *Bully-victims* not only are highly aggressive toward other children but also are the recipients of other children's bullying.
- *Victims* are passive, non-aggressive respondents to bullying.
- *Prosocial children* engage in such positive behaviors as sharing, helping, comforting, and empathizing.

Teacher and peer ratings in 34 classrooms of 7- and 8-year-old students were used to classify 212 boys and girls into the aforementioned four categories. On a five-point scale (from "never" to "several times a week"), teachers rated (1) how often the child bullied others, and (2) how often the child was bullied. The ratings focused on three types of bullying and being victimized: physical actions, verbal abuse, and excluding others. On a four-point scale (from not applicable to very clearly applicable), teachers also rated children's prosocial behavior on three items: "willingly shares with others," "comforts others if necessary," and "empathizes with others." Peer ratings assessed children's nominations of which children in the classroom acted as bullies, were victimized by bullies, and engaged in prosocial behavior. Combining the teacher and peer ratings after eliminating those that did not agree regarding which children were bullies, victims, or prosocial children, the final sample consisted of 49 bullies, 80 bully-victims, 33 victims, and 50 prosocial children.

Children's perspective-taking skills were assessed using theory of mind tasks, and moral motivation was examined by interviewing children about aspects of right and wrong in stories about children's transgressions. In one theory of mind task, children were tested to see whether they understood that people may have false beliefs about another individual. In another theory of mind task, children were assessed to determine whether they understood that people sometimes hide their emotions by showing emotions that differ from what they really feel. A moral interview also was conducted in which children were told four moral transgression stories (with content about being unwilling to share with a classmate, stealing candy from a classmate, hiding a victim's shoes, and verbally bullying a victim) and then asked to judge whether the acts were right or wrong and how the participants in the stories likely felt.

The results of the study indicated that only bully-victims—but not bullies—were deficient in perspective taking. Further analysis revealed that both aggressive groups of children—bullies and bully-victims—had a deficiency in moral motivation. The analyses were consistent with a portrait of bullies as socially competent and knowledgeable in terms of perspective-taking skills and ability to effectively interact with peers. However, bullies use this social knowledge for their own manipulative purposes. The analysis also confirmed the picture of the bully as being morally insensitive. Another recent study also found that bullying was linked to moral disengagement (Obermann, 2011).

How can researchers ensure that results that might help prevent bullying are properly applied in school settings (and not, for instance, used to label potential bullies or segregate potential victims)?

- Develop school-wide rules and sanctions against bullying and post them throughout the school.
- Form friendship groups for adolescents who are regularly bullied by peers.
- Incorporate the message of the antibullying program into places of worship, schools, and other community activity areas where adolescents are involved.
- Encourage parents to reinforce their adolescent's positive behaviors and model appropriate interpersonal interactions.
- Identify bullies and victims early and use social skills training to improve their behavior.
- Encourage parents to contact the school's psychologist, counselor, or social worker and ask for help with concerns involving bullying or victimization.

Review

- What are some key aspects of peer relations?
- What is the developmental course of peer relations in childhood?
- In what ways are the worlds of parents and peers distinct but coordinated?
- How is social cognition involved in peer relations? How is emotion involved in peer relations?
- What are the five peer statuses of children?
- What is the nature of bullying?

Connect

- Earlier in this chapter and in Chapter 13, you learned that most developmentalists agree that peers play an important role in

children's development of moral reasoning. Of the five peer status groups you learned about in this section, in which group do you think children would have the least opportunity to fully develop their moral reasoning capacities? Why?

Reflect *Your Own Personal Journey of Life*

- Think back to your middle school/junior high and high school years. What kind of relationship did you have with your parents? Were you securely attached or insecurely attached to them? How do you think your relationship with your parents affected your friendships and peer relations?

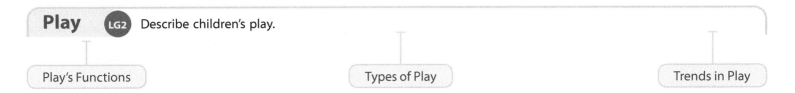

Play (LG2) Describe children's play.

| Play's Functions | Types of Play | Trends in Play |

Much of the time when children, especially young children, are interacting with their peers, they are playing. **Play** is a pleasurable activity that is engaged in for its own sake, and social play is just one type of play.

PLAY'S FUNCTIONS

Play makes important contributions to young children's cognitive and socioemotional development (Bergen & Fromberg, 2009; Coplan & Arbeau, 2009). Theorists have focused on different aspects of play and highlighted a long list of functions.

According to Freud and Erikson, play helps the child master anxieties and conflicts. Play permits children to work off excess physical energy and to release pent-up tensions. Because tensions are relieved in play, the child can cope more effectively with life's problems. Therapists use **play therapy** both to allow the child to work off frustrations and to analyze the child's conflicts and ways of coping with them (Sanders, 2008). Children may feel less threatened and be more likely to express their true feelings in the context of play.

Play also is an important context for cognitive development (Hirsh-Pasek & Golinkoff, 2013). Both Piaget and Vygotsky concluded that play is the child's work. Piaget (1962) maintained that play advances children's cognitive development. At the same time, he said that children's cognitive development *constrains* the way they play. Play permits children to practice their competencies and acquired skills in a relaxed, pleasurable way. Piaget thought that cognitive structures needed to be exercised and that play provided the perfect setting for this exercise.

Vygotsky (1962) also considered play to be an excellent setting for cognitive development. He was especially interested in the symbolic and make-believe aspects of play, as when a child substitutes a stick for a horse and rides the stick as if it were a horse. For young children, the imaginary situation is real. Parents should encourage such imaginary play, because it advances the child's cognitive development, especially creative thought.

play A pleasurable activity that is engaged in for its own sake.

play therapy Therapy that allows the child to work off frustrations and is a medium through which the therapist can analyze the child's conflicts and ways of coping with them. Children may feel less threatened and be more likely to express their true feelings in the context of play.

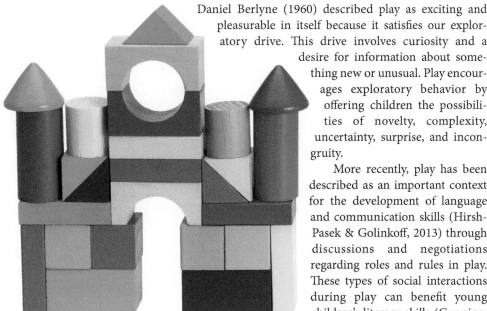

Daniel Berlyne (1960) described play as exciting and pleasurable in itself because it satisfies our exploratory drive. This drive involves curiosity and a desire for information about something new or unusual. Play encourages exploratory behavior by offering children the possibilities of novelty, complexity, uncertainty, surprise, and incongruity.

More recently, play has been described as an important context for the development of language and communication skills (Hirsh-Pasek & Golinkoff, 2013) through discussions and negotiations regarding roles and rules in play. These types of social interactions during play can benefit young children's literacy skills (Gunning, 2013; Morrow, 2012). And as we will discuss in Chapter 16, "Schools and Achievement," play is a central focus of the child-centered kindergarten and thought to be an essential aspect of early childhood education (Feeney, Moravcik, & Nolte, 2013; Henninger, 2013).

An increasing concern is that the large number of hours children spend with electronic media, such as television and computers, takes time away from play (Bergen & Fromberg, 2009). An important priority for parents should be to include ample time for play in their children's lives.

developmental **connection**

Cognitive Theory

Vygotsky emphasized that children mainly develop their ways of thinking and understanding through social interaction. Chapter 6, p. 185

developmental **connection**

Education

The child-centered kindergarten emphasizes the education of the whole child, not just his or her cognitive development, because play is extremely important in the child's development. Chapter 16, p. 453

TYPES OF PLAY

The contemporary perspective on play emphasizes both the cognitive and the social aspects of play (Fung & Cheng, 2012; Vong, 2012). Among the most widely studied types of children's play today are sensorimotor and practice play, pretense/symbolic play, social play, constructive play, and games (Bergen, 1988).

Sensorimotor and Practice Play   **Sensorimotor play** is behavior that allows infants to derive pleasure from exercising their sensorimotor schemes. The development of sensorimotor play follows Piaget's description of sensorimotor thought, which we discussed in Chapter 6. Infants initially engage in exploratory and playful visual and motor transactions during the second quarter of the first year of life. At 9 months of age, infants begin to select novel objects for exploration and play, especially those that are responsive, such as toys that make noise or bounce. At 12 months of age, infants enjoy making things work and exploring cause and effect.

Practice play involves repeating behavior when new skills are being learned or when physical or mental mastery and coordination of skills are required for games or sports. Sensorimotor play, which often involves practice play, is primarily confined to infancy, whereas practice play can be engaged in throughout life. During the preschool years, children often engage in play that involves practicing various skills. Although practice play declines during the elementary school years, practice play activities such as running, jumping, sliding, twirling, and throwing balls or other objects are frequently observed on the playgrounds at elementary schools.

Pretense/Symbolic Play   **Pretense/symbolic play** occurs when the child transforms the physical environment into a symbol. Between 9 and 30 months of age, children increase

sensorimotor play Behavior that allows infants to derive pleasure from exercising their existing sensorimotor schemes.

practice play Play that involves repetition of behavior when new skills are being learned or when physical or mental mastery and coordination of skills are required for games or sports. Practice play can be engaged in throughout life.

pretense/symbolic play Play that occurs when a child transforms the physical environment into a symbol.

What are some different types of play?

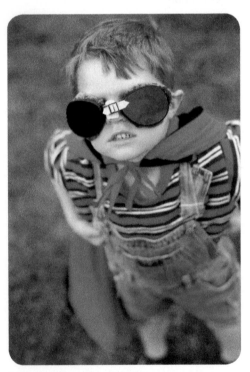
A preschool "superhero" at play.

social play Play that involves interactions with peers.

constructive play Play that combines sensorimotor/practice play with symbolic representation of ideas. Constructive play occurs when children engage in self-regulated creation or construction of a product or a solution.

games Activities engaged in for pleasure that include rules and often competition with one or more individuals.

their use of objects in symbolic play (Lillard, 2007). They learn to transform objects, substituting them for other objects and acting toward them as if they were those other objects (Smith, 2007). For example, a preschool child treats a table as if it were a car and says, "I'm fixing the car," as he grabs a leg of the table.

Many experts on play view the preschool years as the "golden age" of symbolic/pretense play that is dramatic or sociodramatic in nature (Fein, 1986; Rubin, Bukowski, & Parker, 2006). This type of make-believe play often appears at about 18 months of age and reaches a peak at 4 to 5 years of age, then gradually declines. Some child psychologists conclude that pretend play is an important aspect of young children's development and often reflects advances in their cognitive development, especially their capacity for symbolic understanding (Lillard, Pinkham, & Smith, 2011). For example, Catherine Garvey (2000) and Angeline Lillard (2007) emphasize that hidden in young children's pretend play narratives are remarkable capacities for role-taking, balancing of social roles, metacognition (thinking about thinking), testing of the reality-pretense distinction, and numerous nonegocentric capacities that reveal the remarkable cognitive skills of young children. In one recent analysis, a major accomplishment in early childhood is the development of children's ability to share their pretend play with peers (Coplan & Arbeau, 2009).

Social Play   **Social play** is play that involves interaction with peers. Social play increases dramatically during the preschool years and includes varied interchanges such as turn taking, conversations about numerous topics, social games and routines, and physical play (Sumaroka & Bornstein, 2008). Social play often evokes a high degree of pleasure on the part of the participants (Sumaroka & Bornstein, 2008).

Constructive Play   **Constructive play** combines sensorimotor/practice play with symbolic representation of ideas. Constructive play occurs when children engage in the self-regulated creation of a product or a solution. Constructive play increases in the preschool years as symbolic play increases and sensorimotor play decreases. During the preschool years, some practice play is replaced by constructive play. For example, instead of moving their fingers around and around in finger paint (practice play), children are more likely to draw the outline of a house or a person in the paint (constructive play). Constructive play is also a frequent form of play in the elementary school years, both within and outside the classroom. Constructive play is one of the few playlike activities allowed in work-centered classrooms. For example, if children create a skit about a social studies topic, they are engaging in constructive play.

Games   Games are activities that are engaged in for pleasure and are governed by rules. Often they involve competition between two or more individuals. Preschool children may begin to participate in social game play that involves simple rules of reciprocity and turn taking. However, games take on a much more prominent role in the lives of elementary school children. In one study, the highest incidence of game playing occurred between 10 and 12 years of age (Eiferman, 1971). After age 12, games decline in popularity (Bergen, 1988).

In sum, play ranges from an infant's simple exercise of a new sensorimotor talent to a preschool child's riding a tricycle to an older child's participation in organized games. It is also important to note that children's play can involve a combination of the play categories we have described. For example, social play can be sensorimotor (rough-and-tumble), symbolic, and constructive.

TRENDS IN PLAY

Kathy Hirsh-Pasek, Roberta Golinkoff, and Dorothy Singer (Hirsh-Pasek & others, 2009; Singer, Golinkoff, & Hirsh-Pasek, 2006) are concerned about the decline in the amount of free play time that young children have, reporting that it has declined considerably in recent decades. They especially are worried about young children's playtime being restricted at home and school so they can spend more time on academic subjects. They also point out that many schools have eliminated recess. And it is not just the decline in time allotted to free play that bothers them. They underscore that learning in playful contexts captivates children's minds in ways that enhance their cognitive and socioemotional development—Singer, Golinkoff, and Hirsh-Pasek's (2006) first book on play was titled: *Play = Learning.* Among the cognitive benefits of play they described are creative; abstract thinking; imagination; attention, concentration, and persistence; problem-solving; social cognition, empathy, and perspective taking; language; and mastering new concepts. Among the socioemotional experiences and development they believe play promotes are enjoyment, relaxation, and self-expression; cooperation, sharing, and turn-taking; anxiety reduction; and self-confidence. With so many positive cognitive and socioemotional outcomes of play, clearly it is important that we find more time for play in young children's lives.

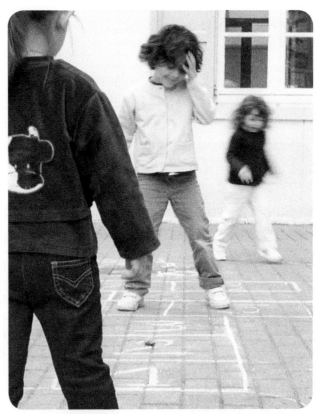

In the elementary school years, children, such as those playing hopscotch here on a school playground, increasingly play games.

Kathy Hirsh-Pasek interacting with a young child in a play context. *What are some of the benefits of play for children, according to Hirsh-Pasek and her colleagues?*

Review Connect Reflect

LG2 Describe children's play.

Review

- What are the functions of play?
- What are the different types of play?
- What are some trends in play?

Connect

- Pretense/symbolic play takes place during what Piaget called the symbolic function substage of the preoperational stage. According to Piaget, what are two

important limitations of children's thought during this substage?

Reflect *Your Own Personal Journey of Life*

- Do you think most young children's lives today are too structured? If and when you become a parent, how will you manage your children's development to provide enough time for play?

Friendship's Functions	Similarity and Intimacy	Gender and Friendship	Mixed Age Friendships	Other-Sex Friendships

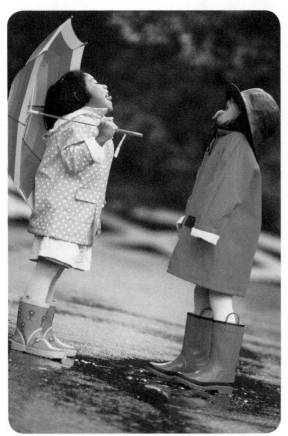

What are some functions of children's friendships?

Children play with varying acquaintances. They interact with some children they barely know, and with others they know well, for hours every day. It is to the latter type—friends—that we now turn.

FRIENDSHIP'S FUNCTIONS

Friendships serve six functions (Gottman & Parker, 1987):

1. *Companionship.* Friendship provides children with a familiar partner, someone who is willing to spend time with them and join in collaborative activities.

2. *Stimulation.* Friendship provides children with interesting information, excitement, and amusement.

3. *Physical support.* Friendship provides resources and assistance.

4. *Ego support.* Friendship provides the expectation of support, encouragement, and feedback that helps children to maintain an impression of themselves as competent, attractive, and worthwhile individuals.

5. *Social comparison.* Friendship provides information about where children stand vis-à-vis others and whether children are doing okay.

6. *Intimacy/affection.* Friendship provides children with a warm, close, trusting relationship with another individual, a relationship that involves self-disclosure.

Although having friends can be a developmental advantage, not all friendships are alike and the quality of friendship is also important to consider (Wentzel, 2013). People differ in the company they keep—that is, who their friends are (Ali & Dwyer, 2011; Wentzel, 2013).

Positive friendship relationships in adolescence are associated with a host of positive outcomes, including lower rates of delinquency, substance abuse, risky sexual behavior, and bullying victimization, and a higher level of academic achievement (Kendrick, Jutengren, & Stattin, 2012; Tucker & others, 2012; Way & Silverman, 2012; Wentzel, 2013). Not having a close relationship with a best friend, having less contact with friends, having friends who are depressed, and experiencing peer rejection all increase depressive tendencies in adolescents (Brendgen & others, 2010; Schwartz-Mette & Rose, 2013). Researchers have found that interacting with delinquent peers and friends greatly increases the risk of becoming delinquent (Deutsch & others, 2012).

Harry Stack Sullivan (1953) was the most influential theorist to discuss the importance of friendships. In contrast with other psychoanalytic theorists' narrow emphasis on the importance of parent-child relationships, Sullivan contended that friends also played important roles in shaping children's and adolescents' well-being and development.

According to Sullivan, all people have a number of basic social needs, including tenderness (secure attachment), playful companionship, social acceptance, intimacy, and sexual relations. Whether or not these needs are fulfilled largely determines our emotional well-being. For example, if the need for playful companionship goes unmet, then we become bored and depressed; if the need for social acceptance is not met, we suffer a lowered sense of self-worth. Sullivan stressed that the need for intimacy intensifies during early adolescence, motivating teenagers to seek out close friends.

Research findings support many of Sullivan's ideas. For example, adolescents report disclosing intimate and personal information to their friends more often

How did Sullivan think friendship changes in adolescence?

than do younger children (Buhrmester, 1990; Buhrmester & Furman, 1987) (see Figure 15.3). Adolescents also say they depend more on friends than on parents to satisfy their needs for companionship, reassurance of worth, and intimacy (Furman & Buhrmester, 1992).

Friendship relationships are often important sources of support (Berndt, 1999; Wentzel, 2013). Sullivan described how adolescent friends support one another's sense of personal worth. When close friends disclose their mutual insecurities and fears about themselves, they discover that they are not "abnormal" and that they have nothing to be ashamed of. Friends also act as important confidants who help children and adolescents work through upsetting problems (such as difficulties with parents or the breakup of romantic relationships) by providing both emotional support and informational advice.

To read about appropriate and inappropriate strategies for making friends, see *Caring Connections*.

SIMILARITY AND INTIMACY

What characteristics do children and adolescents look for in their friends? The answers change somewhat as children grow up, but one characteristic of friends is found throughout the childhood and adolescent years: Friends are generally similar—in terms of age, sex, ethnicity, and many other factors (Giordano, 2009). Similarity is referred to as *homophily*, the tendency to associate with similar others (Brechwald & Prinstein, 2011).

Friends often have similar attitudes toward school, similar educational aspirations, and closely aligned achievement orientations. Friends like the same music, wear the same kinds of clothes, and prefer the same leisure activities (Berndt, 1982). Differences may lead to conflicts that weaken the friendship. For example, if two friends have differing attitudes toward school,

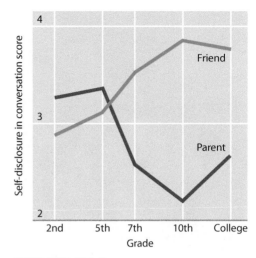

FIGURE **15.3**

DEVELOPMENTAL CHANGES IN SELF-DISCLOSING CONVERSATIONS. Self-disclosing conversations with friends increased dramatically in adolescence while declining in an equally dramatic fashion with parents. However, self-disclosing conversations with parents began to pick up somewhat during the college years. The measure of self-disclosure involved a 5-point rating scale completed by the children and youth, with a higher score representing greater self-disclosure. The data shown represent the means for each age group.

caring *connections*

Making Friends

Here are some strategies that adults can recommend to children and adolescents for making friends (Wentzel, 1997):

- **Initiate interaction.** Learn about a friend: Ask for his or her name, age, favorite activities. Use these prosocial overtures: introduce yourself, start a conversation, and invite him or her to do things.
- **Be nice.** Show kindness, be considerate, and compliment the other person.
- **Engage in prosocial behavior.** Be honest and trustworthy: tell the truth, keep promises. Be generous, share, and be cooperative.
- **Show respect for yourself and others.** Have good manners, be polite and courteous, and listen to what others have to say. Have a positive attitude and personality.
- **Provide social support.** Show you care.

What are some appropriate and inappropriate strategies for making friends?

And here are some inappropriate strategies for making friends that adults can recommend that children and adolescents avoid using (Wentzel, 1997):

- **Be psychologically aggressive.** Show disrespect and have bad manners. Use others, be uncooperative, don't share, ignore others, gossip, and spread rumors.
- **Present yourself negatively.** Be self-centered, snobby, conceited, and jealous; show off, care only about yourself. Be mean, have a bad attitude, be angry, throw temper tantrums, and start trouble.
- **Behave antisocially.** Be physically aggressive, yell at others, pick on them, make fun of them, be dishonest, tell secrets, and break promises.

Based on what you read earlier in this chapter, what might you recommend to an adolescent about approaching someone as a potential friend?

What are some gender differences in peer relations and friendships in adolescence?

one may repeatedly want to play basketball or go to the mall while the other insists on completing homework, and the two may drift apart.

Priorities change as the child reaches adolescence (Brown & Larson, 2009). The most consistent finding in the last two decades of research on adolescent friendships is that intimacy is an important feature of friendship (Berndt & Perry, 1990). In most research studies, **intimacy in friendship** is defined narrowly as self-disclosure or sharing of private thoughts; private or personal knowledge about a friend has been used as an index of intimacy. When young adolescents are asked what they want from a friend or how they can tell someone is their best friend, they frequently say that a best friend will share problems with them, understand them, and listen when they talk about their own thoughts or feelings. When young children talk about their friendships, they rarely comment about intimate self-disclosure or mutual understanding. In one investigation, friendship intimacy was more prominent among 13- to 16-year-olds than among 10- to 13-year-olds (Buhrmester, 1990).

GENDER AND FRIENDSHIP

Are the friendships of girls different from the friendships of boys? An increasing number of studies indicate that they are different (Coyne, Nelson, & Underwood, 2011; Rose & others, 2012). Are the friendships of adolescent girls more intimate than the friendships of adolescent boys? A recent meta-analysis concluded that research indicates girls' friendships are more intimate (Gorrese & Ruggieri, 2012). In this meta-analysis, girls' friendships were deeper, more interdependent, showed more empathy, revealed a greater need for nurturance, and involved a greater desire to sustain intimate relationships. In contrast, boys gave more importance to having a congenial friend with whom they could share their interests in such activities as hobbies and sports, and boys showed more cooperativeness than girls in their friendships. Also in this meta-analysis, adolescent girls showed higher peer attachment, especially related to trust and communication, than did adolescent boys (Gorrese & Ruggieri, 2012). Another analysis concluded that boys' friendships tend to emphasize power and excitement in contrast to girls' interest in intimacy and self-disclosure (Buhrmester & Chong, 2009).

Let's further examine gender differences in the intimacy aspect of friendship. When asked to describe their best friends, girls refer to intimate conversations and faithfulness more than boys do (Rose & others, 2012). For example, girls are more likely to describe their best friend as "sensitive just like me" or "trustworthy just like me" (Duck, 1975). When conflict is present, girls place a higher priority on relationship goals such as being patient until the relationship improves, whereas boys are more likely to seek control over a friend (Rose & Asher, 1999; Blakemore, Berenbaum, & Ruble, 2009). Although girls' friendships in adolescence are more likely to focus on intimacy, boys' friendships tend to emphasize power and excitement (Rose & Smith, 2009). Boys may discourage one another from openly disclosing their problems because self-disclosure is not viewed as masculine (Maccoby, 1996). Boys make themselves vulnerable to being called "wimps" if they can't handle their own problems and insecurities. These gender differences are generally assumed to reflect a greater orientation toward interpersonal relationships among girls than boys.

As indicated in the *Caring Connections* interlude, friendship often provides social support. Recently, though, researchers have found that some aspects of girls' friendships may be linked to adolescent problems (Tompkins & others, 2011). For example, a study of third- through ninth-graders revealed that girls' co-rumination (as reflected in excessively discussing problems) predicted not only an increase in positive friendship quality but also an increase in further co-rumination as well as an increase in depressive and anxiety symptoms (Rose, Carlson, & Waller, 2007). One implication of the research is that some girls who are vulnerable to developing internalized problems may go undetected because they have supportive friendships.

developmental **connection**

Gender

Recent research indicates that relational aggression occurs more often in girls than boys in adolescence but not in childhood. Chapter 12, p. 349

intimacy in friendship Self-disclosure or the sharing of private thoughts.

MIXED-AGE FRIENDSHIPS

Although most adolescents develop friendships with individuals who are close to their own age, some adolescents become best friends with younger or older individuals. A common fear, especially among parents, is that adolescents who have older friends will be encouraged to engage in delinquent behavior or early sexual behavior. Researchers have found that adolescents who interact with older youth do engage in these behaviors more frequently, but it is not known whether the older youth guide younger adolescents toward deviant behavior or whether the younger adolescents were already prone to deviant behavior before they developed the friendship with the older youth (Billy, Rodgers, & Udry, 1984). A recent study also revealed that over time, from the sixth through tenth grades, girls were more likely to have older male friends, which places some girls on a developmental trajectory for engaging in problem behavior (Poulin & Pedersen, 2007). However, a recent study of young adolescents found that mixed-grade friends may protect same-grade friendless girls from feelings of loneliness and same-grade friendless and anxious-withdrawn boys from victimization (Bowker & Spencer, 2010).

OTHER-SEX FRIENDSHIPS

Although adolescents are more likely to have same-sex friends, associations with other-sex friends are more common than is often thought (Brown, 2004). The number of other-sex friendships increases in early adolescence, with girls reporting more other-sex friends than boys, and the number of other-sex friendships increases as adolescence proceeds (Poulin & Pederson, 2007). Other-sex friendships and participation in mixed-sex groups provide a context for adolescents to learn how to communicate with the other sex and reduce anxiety in social and dating heterosexual interactions.

However, researchers have found that other-sex friendships are sometimes linked to negative behaviors such as earlier sexual intercourse, as well as increases in alcohol use and delinquency (Andorfer & Stormshak, 2008; Billari & Mencarini, 2003; Dick & others, 2007; Mrug, Borch, & Cillessen, 2011). Parents likely monitor their daughters' other-sex friendships more closely than their sons' because they perceive boys as having a more negative influence, especially in initiating problem behavior (Poulin & Denault, 2012). A recent study revealed that a higher level of parental monitoring led to fewer other-sex friendships, which in turn was associated with a lower level of subsequent alcohol use (Poulin & Denault, 2012).

Review *Connect* Reflect

 Explain friendship.

Review

- What are six functions of friendship? What is Sullivan's view of friendship?
- What roles do similarity and intimacy play in friendship?
- How does gender influence friendship?
- What is the developmental outcome of mixed-age friendship?
- What characterizes other-sex friendships in adolescence?

Connect

- Relational aggression was discussed here and in Chapter 12. In one of the studies in Chapter 12, what connection was made between parents and the relational aggression of their children?

Reflect *Your Own Personal Journey of Life*

- Examine the list of six functions of friendships at the beginning of this section. Rank the six functions from most (1) to least (6) important to you as you were developing in three different time frames: early childhood, middle and late childhood, and adolescence.

Peer Pressure and Conformity

Cliques and Crowds

Dating and Romantic Relationships

I didn't belong as a kid, and that always bothered me. If only I'd known that one day my differentness would be an asset, then my early life would have been much easier.

—**Bette Midler**
Contemporary American Actress

We already have discussed a number of changes in adolescents' peer relations, including the increasing importance of friendships. Peer relations play such a powerful role in the lives of adolescents that we further consider additional aspects in this section.

Peer relations undergo important changes in adolescence (Bornstein, Jager, & Steinberg, 2013; Wentzel, 2013). In childhood, the focus of peer relations is on being liked by classmates and being included in games or lunchroom conversations. Being overlooked or, worse yet, being rejected can have damaging effects on children's development that sometimes are carried forward to adolescence. Beginning in early adolescence, teenagers typically prefer to have a smaller number of friendships that are more intense and intimate than those of young children. Cliques are formed and shape the social lives of adolescents as they begin to "hang out" together. And romantic relationships become a more central aspect of adolescents' lives.

PEER PRESSURE AND CONFORMITY

Young adolescents conform more to peer standards than children do. Around the eighth and ninth grades, conformity to peers—especially to their antisocial standards—peaks (Berndt, 1979; Brown & Larson, 2009). At this point, adolescents are most likely to go along with a peer to steal hubcaps off a car, draw graffiti on a wall, or steal cosmetics from a store counter. A recent study revealed that 14 to 18 years of age is an especially important time for developing the ability to stand up for what one believes and resist peer pressure to do otherwise (Steinberg & Monahan, 2007). Another study found that U.S. adolescents are more likely than Japanese adolescents to put pressure on their peers to resist parental influence (Rothbaum & others, 2000).

Which adolescents are most likely to conform to peers? Mitchell Prinstein and his colleagues (Brechwald & Prinstein, 2011; Cohen & Prinstein, 2006; Prinstein, 2007; Prinstein & Dodge, 2008) have recently conducted research and analysis addressing this question. They conclude that adolescents who are uncertain about their social identity, which can appear in the form of low self-esteem and high social anxiety, are most likely to conform to peers. This uncertainty often increases during times of transition, such as school and family transitions. Also, peers are more likely to conform when they are in the presence of someone they perceive to have higher status than they do.

What characterizes peer pressure in adolescence?

CLIQUES AND CROWDS

Cliques and crowds assume more important roles in adolescence than in childhood (Brown, 2011; Doornwaard & others, 2012). **Cliques** are small groups that range from 2 to about 12 individuals and average about 5 or 6 individuals. The clique members are usually of the same sex and about the same age. Cliques can form because adolescents engage in similar activities, such as being in a club or on a sports team. Some cliques also form because of friendship. Several adolescents may form a clique because they have spent time with each other and enjoy each other's company. Not necessarily friends, they often develop a friendship if they stay in the clique. What do adolescents do in cliques? They share ideas, hang out together, and often develop an in-group identity in which they believe that their clique is better than other cliques. A recent study indicated that adolescents who identify with some crowds ("populars," for example) have fewer externalizing problem behaviors than their counterparts who identify with other crowds ("metal heads," for example) (Doornwaard & others, 2012). In this study, some crowds had a higher level of internalizing problems ("nonconformists," for example) than others ("jocks," for example).

cliques Small groups that range from 2 to about 12 individuals and average about 5 or 6 individuals. Cliques can form because of friendship or because individuals engage in similar activities, and members usually are of the same sex and about the same age.

crowds The crowd is a larger group structure than a clique. Adolescents usually are members of a crowd based on reputation and may or may not spend much time together. Many crowds are defined by the activities in which adolescents engage.

Dexter Dunphy (1963) documented the increase in mixed-sex groups in a well-known observational study. Figure 15.4 outlines his view of how these mixed-sex groups develop. In late childhood, boys and girls participate in small, same-sex cliques. As they move into the early adolescent years, the same-sex cliques begin to interact with each other. Gradually, the leaders and high-status members form further cliques based on mixed-sex relationships. Eventually, the newly created mixed-sex cliques replace the same-sex cliques. The mixed-sex cliques interact with each other in large crowd activities, too—at dances and athletic events, for example. In late adolescence, the crowd begins to dissolve as couples develop more serious relationships and make long-range plans that may include engagement and marriage.

Crowds are a larger group structure than cliques. Adolescents are usually members of a crowd based on reputation and may or may not spend much time together. Crowds are less personal than cliques. Many crowds are defined by the activities adolescents engage in (such as "jocks" who are good at sports or "druggies" who take drugs) (Brown, 2011).

In one study, crowd membership was associated with adolescent self-esteem (Brown & Lohr, 1987). The crowds included jocks (athletically oriented), populars (well-known students who led social activities), normals (middle-of-the-road students who made up the masses), druggies or toughs (known for illicit drug use or other delinquent activities), and nobodies (low in social skills or intellectual abilities). The self-esteem of the jocks and the populars was highest, whereas that of the nobodies was lowest. One group of adolescents not in a crowd had self-esteem equivalent to that of the jocks and the populars; this group was the independents, who indicated that crowd membership was not important to them. Keep in mind that these data are correlational; self-esteem could increase an adolescent's probability of becoming a crowd member, just as crowd membership could increase the adolescent's self-esteem.

DATING AND ROMANTIC RELATIONSHIPS

Adolescents spend considerable time either dating or thinking about dating (Shulman, Davila, & Shachar-Shapira, 2011). Dating can be a form of recreation, a source of status, or a setting for learning about close relationships, as well as a way of finding a mate.

Types of Dating and Developmental Changes   A number of dating variations and developmental changes characterize dating and romantic relationships. First, we examine heterosexual romantic relationships and then turn to romantic relationships among sexual minority youth (gay and lesbian adolescents).

Heterosexual Romantic Relationships   Three stages characterize the development of romantic relationships in adolescence (Connolly & McIsaac, 2009):

1. *Entry into romantic attractions and affiliations at about 11 to 13 years of age.* This initial stage is triggered by puberty. From 11 to 13, adolescents become intensely interested in romance, and the topic dominates many conversations with same-sex friends. Developing a crush on someone is common, and the crush often is shared with a same-sex friend. Young adolescents may or may not interact with the individual who is the object of their infatuation. When dating occurs, it usually takes place in a group setting.

2. *Exploring romantic relationships at approximately 14 to 16 years of age.* At this point in adolescence, two types of romantic involvement occur: (1) *Casual dating* emerges between individuals who are mutually attracted. These dating experiences are often short-lived, last a few months at best, and usually only endure for a few weeks. (2) *Dating in groups* is common and reflects embeddedness in the peer context. Friends often act as a third-party facilitator of a potential dating relationship by communicating their friend's romantic interest and confirming whether this attraction is reciprocated.

Stage 1: Precrowd stage; isolated same-sex groups

Stage 2: Beginning of the crowd; same-sex groups start group-group interaction

Stage 3: The crowd is in structural transition; same-sex groups are forming heterosexual groups, especially among upper-status members

Stage 4: Fully developed crowd; heterosexual groups are closely associated

Stage 5: Beginning of crowd disintegration; loosely associated groups of couples

☐ Boys   ☐ Girls   ☐ Boys and girls

FIGURE **15.4**

DUNPHY'S PROGRESSION OF PEER GROUP RELATIONS IN ADOLESCENCE

What characterizes adolescents' cliques and crowds?

What are some developmental changes in romantic relationships in adolescence?

3. *Consolidating dyadic romantic bonds at about 17 to 19 years of age.* At the end of the high school years, more serious romantic relationships develop. This is characterized by strong emotional bonds more closely resembling those in adult romantic relationships. These bonds often are more stable and enduring than earlier bonds, typically lasting one year or more.

Two variations on these stages in the development of romantic relationships in adolescence involve early and late bloomers (Connolly & McIsaac, 2009). *Early bloomers* include 15 to 20 percent of 11- to 13-year-olds who say that they currently are in a romantic relationship and 35 percent who indicate that they have had some prior experience in romantic relationships. *Late bloomers* comprise approximately 10 percent of 17- to 19-year-olds who say that they have had no experience with romantic relationships and another 15 percent who report that they have not engaged in any romantic relationships that lasted more than 4 months.

In their early romantic relationships, today's adolescents are not motivated to fulfill attachment or even sexual needs. Rather, early romantic relationships serve as a context for adolescents to explore how attractive they are, how to interact romantically, and how all of these aspects look to the peer group. Only after adolescents acquire some basic competencies in interacting with romantic partners does the fulfillment of attachment and sexual needs become a central function of these relationships (Furman & Wehner, 1998).

Adolescents often find comfort in numbers during their early exploration of romantic relationships (Connolly & McIsaac, 2009). They may begin hanging out together in heterosexual groups. Sometimes they just hang out at someone's house or get organized enough to ask an adult to drive them to a mall or a movie. A special concern in early dating and "going with" someone is the associated risk for adolescent pregnancy and problems at home and school.

Romantic Relationships in Sexual Minority Youth

Most research on romantic relationships in adolescence has focused on heterosexual relationships. Recently, researchers have begun to study romantic relationships in gay, lesbian, and bisexual youth (Diamond, 2013a, b).

The average age of the initial same-sex activity for females ranges from 14 to 18 years of age and for males from 13 to 15 (Diamond, 2013a, b). The most common initial same-sex partner is a close friend. More lesbian adolescent girls have sexual encounters with boys before same-sex activity, whereas gay adolescent boys are more likely to show the opposite sequence (Savin-Williams, 2011, 2013).

Most sexual minority youth have same-sex sexual experience, but relatively few have same-sex romantic relationships because of limited opportunities and the social disapproval such relationships may generate from families or heterosexual peers (Diamond, 2013a, b; Diamond & Savin-Williams, 2011, 2013). The importance of romance to sexual minority youth was underscored in a study that found that they rated the breakup of a current romance as their second most stressful problem, second only to disclosure of their sexual orientation to their parents (D'Augelli, 1991).

The romantic possibilities of sexual minority youth are complex (Diamond, 2013a, b; Diamond & Savin-Williams, 2011, 2013). To adequately address the relational interests of sexual minority youth, we can't generalize from heterosexual youth and simply switch the labels. Instead, we need to consider the full range of variation in sexual minority youths' sexual desires and romantic relationships for same- and other-sex partners.

What characterizes romantic relationships in sexual minority youth?

Romantic Relationships and Adjustment

Researchers have linked dating and romantic relationships with various measures of how well adjusted adolescents are (Furman & Collins, 2009; Vujeva & Furman, 2011). Dating and romantic relationships at an early age can be especially problematic (Connolly & McIsaac, 2009). Researchers have found that early dating and "going with" someone are linked with adolescent pregnancy and problems at home and school (Florsheim, Moore, & Edgington, 2003).

Consider also the following studies that link romantic relationships and adjustment in adolescence:

How are romantic relationships linked to adolescent adjustment?

- The more romantic experiences tenth graders had, the more they reported higher levels of social acceptance, friendship competence, and romantic competence; however, having more romantic experience also was linked to a higher level of substance use, delinquency, and sexual behavior (Furman, Low, & Ho, 2009).

- Adolescent girls who engaged in co-rumination (excessive discussion of problems with friends) were more likely to be involved in a romantic relationship, and together co-rumination and romantic involvement predicted an increase in depressive symptoms (Starr & Davila, 2009). A recent study also found that romantic activity was linked to depression in early adolescent girls (Starr & others, 2013, in press).

- Among adolescent girls, but not adolescent males, having an older romantic partner was linked to an increase in depressive symptoms, largely influenced by an increase in substance use (Haydon & Halpern, 2010).

- Adolescents with a stronger romantic involvement were more likely to engage in delinquency than their counterparts with a lower level of romantic involvement (Cui & others, 2012).

Relationships with Parents and Adolescent Romantic Relationships

Adolescents' relationships with their parents influence their dating and romantic relationships (Ivanova, Veenstra, & Mills, 2012; Nosko & others, 2011; Shulman, Davila, & Shachar-Shapira, 2011; Shulman & others, 2012). Attachment history is linked to couple relationships in adolescence and emerging adulthood (Sroufe & others, 2005; Sroufe, Coffino, & Carlson, 2010). For example, infants who have an anxious attachment with their caregivers in infancy are less likely to develop positive romantic relationships in adolescence than are their securely attached counterparts. It might be that adolescents with a history of secure attachment are better able to control their emotions and more comfortable self-disclosing in romantic relationships. A recent study also found that a positive relationship with parents during adolescence was linked to better-quality romantic relationships in emerging adulthood (Madsen & Collins, 2011). And another recent study revealed that young adolescent girls who had negative relationships with their parents turned to romantic relationships for intimacy and support, which in turn provided the opportunity for early sexual initiation (de Graaf & others, 2012).

Adolescents' observations of their parents' marital relationship also contribute to their own construction of dating relationships. A recent study of 17-year-old Israeli girls and their mothers revealed that mothers who reported a higher level of marital satisfaction had daughters who were more romantically competent (based on multiple dimensions, such as maturity, coherence, and realistic perception of the romantic relationship) (Shulman, Davila, & Shachar-Shapira, 2011).

Marital conflict and divorce also are linked to adolescents' and emerging adults' dating and romantic relationships. One study revealed that parents' marital conflict was linked to increased conflict in an emerging adult's romantic relationships (Cui, Fincham, & Pasley, 2008). Recent research also confirms that parental divorce affects adolescents' romantic relationships. For example, a recent study revealed that an adolescent's first romantic relationship occurred earlier in divorced than non-divorced intact families but only when the divorce occurred in early adolescence (Ivanova, Veenstra, & Mills, 2012).

A longitudinal study examined how youths' personality traits and beliefs about marriage are related to romantic relationships in early adulthood (Masarik & others, 2013). In this study, a higher level of neuroticism in the ninth grade was linked with the belief in late adolescence/

What are some ethnic variations in dating during adolescence?

early adulthood that marriage is not likely to lead to fulfillment in life and happiness as an adult. And less endorsement of the marriage/fulfillment belief, in turn, predicted fewer observed positive interactions with a romantic partner and lower perceived relationship quality in early adulthood.

Sociocultural Contexts and Dating   The sociocultural context exerts a powerful influence on adolescents' dating patterns (Crissey, 2009). This influence may be seen in differences in dating patterns among ethnic groups within the United States. For example, one study found that Asian American adolescents were less likely to have been involved in a romantic relationship in the past 18 months than African American or Latino adolescents (Carver, Joyner, & Udry, 2003).

Values, religious beliefs, and traditions often dictate the age at which dating begins, how much freedom in dating is allowed, whether dates must be chaperoned by adults or parents, and the roles of males and females in dating. For example, Latino and Asian American cultures have more conservative standards regarding adolescent dating than does the Anglo-American culture. Dating may become a source of conflict within a family if the parents have immigrated from cultures in which dating begins at a late age, little freedom in dating is allowed, dates are chaperoned, and dating by adolescent girls is especially restricted. When immigrant adolescents choose to adopt the ways of the dominant U.S. culture (such as unchaperoned dating), they often clash with parents and extended-family members who hold more traditional values.

Review Connect Reflect

 Characterize peer relations in adolescence.

Review

- How are peer pressure and conformity shown in adolescence?
- How are cliques and crowds involved in adolescent development?
- What characterizes adolescents' dating and romantic relationships?

Connect

- In the *Connecting with Diversity* interlude in this chapter, you learned about the Murian culture of eastern India. Based on the information in this last section, how do you think Murian immigrants in the United States might react to their adolescents' dating?

Reflect *Your Own Personal Journey of Life*

- What were your peer relationships like during adolescence? What peer groups were you involved in? How did they influence your development? If you could change anything about the way you experienced peer relations in adolescence, what would it be?

reach your **learning goals**

Peers

Peer Relations

Exploring Peer Relations

 Discuss peer relations in childhood.

- Peers are children who share the same age or maturity level. Peers provide a means of social comparison and a source of information about the world outside the family. Good peer relations may be necessary for normal social development. The inability to "plug in" to a social network is associated with a number of problems. Peer relations can be both positive and negative. Piaget and Sullivan stressed that peer relations provide the context for learning important aspects of relationships, such as observing others' interests and perspectives and exploring fairness and justice by working through disagreements. Peer relations vary according to the way peer experience is measured, the outcomes specified, and the developmental trajectories traversed. Contexts and individual differences influence peer relations.

The Developmental Course of Peer Relations in Childhood

- Some researchers argue that the quality of social interaction with peers in infancy provides valuable information about socioemotional development. As increasing numbers of infants attend child care, infant peer relations have increased. The frequency of peer interaction, both positive and negative, increases during the preschool years. Children spend even more time with peers in the elementary and secondary school years, and their preference for same-sex groups increases. Boys' groups are larger than girls', and they participate in more organized games than girls do. Girls engage in more collaborative discourse in peer groups than boys do.

The Distinct but Coordinated Worlds of Parent-Child and Peer Relations

- Healthy family relations usually promote healthy peer relations. Parents can model or coach their children in ways of relating to peers. Parents' choices of neighborhoods, churches, schools, and their own friends influence the pool from which their children might select possible friends. Rough-and-tumble play occurs mainly in peer relations rather than in parent-child relations. In times of stress, children usually turn to parents rather than peers. Peer relations have a more equal basis than parent-child relations.

Social Cognition and Emotion

- Perspective taking and social information-processing skills are important dimensions of social cognition in peer relations. Perspective taking helps children communicate effectively. Self-regulation of emotion is associated with positive peer relations.

Peer Statuses

- Popular children are frequently identified as a best friend by other children and are rarely disliked by their peers. Average children receive an average number of both positive and negative nominations from their peers. Neglected children are infrequently identified as a best friend but are not disliked by their peers. Rejected children are infrequently identified as a best friend and are disliked by their peers. Rejected children often have more serious adjustment problems than neglected children do. Controversial children are frequently identified both as a best friend and as being disliked by peers.

Bullying

- Bullying is physical or verbal behavior meant to disturb a less powerful individual. Significant numbers of students are bullied, and this is linked to adjustment problems for the victim, the bully, or the individual who is both a bully and a victim.

Play

LG2 Describe children's play.

Play's Functions

- The functions of play include affiliation with peers, tension release, advances in cognitive development, and exploration.

Types of Play

- The contemporary perspective emphasizes both social and cognitive aspects of play. The most widely studied types of play include sensorimotor and practice play, pretense/symbolic play, social play, constructive play, and games.

Trends in Play

- Children's free play time has declined considerably in recent years. Especially important is that children often learn best when they are in playful contexts. Play promotes numerous aspects of socioemotional development.

Friendship

LG3 Explain friendship.

Friendship's Functions

- The functions of friendship include companionship, stimulation, physical support, ego support, social comparison, and intimacy/affection. Sullivan pointed out that whether or not these functions of friendship are fulfilled largely determines our emotional well-being. Sullivan argued that there is a dramatic increase in the psychological importance and intimacy of close friends in early adolescence. Research findings support his view.

Similarity and Intimacy

- Similarity and intimacy are two of the most common characteristics of friendships. Friends often have similar attitudes toward school, similar educational aspirations, and so on. Intimacy in friendship is much more common among adolescents than children.

Gender and Friendship

Mixed-Age Friendships

Other-Sex Friendships

- An increasing number of studies indicate that the friendships of girls differ from the friendships of boys. The influence of friendship, both positive and negative, may be stronger for girls. Intimacy plays a powerful role in girls' friendships, and power, excitement, and control play important roles in boys' friendships.

- Children and adolescents who become friends with older individuals engage in more deviant behaviors than do their counterparts with same-age friends. Girls in grades 6 through 10 who have older male friends may be more likely to engage in problem behavior.

- The number of other-sex friendships increases as adolescence proceeds. Other-sex friendships provide a context for learning how to communicate with the other sex and reduce anxiety in social and dating contexts. However, some aspects of other-sex friendships are linked to negative outcomes, such as earlier sexual intercourse and drug use.

Peer Relations in Adolescence Characterize peer relations in adolescence.

Peer Pressure and Conformity

Cliques and Crowds

Dating and Romantic Relationships

- The pressure to conform to peers is strong during adolescence, especially in eighth and ninth grade, and can have positive or negative effects.

- Cliques and crowds assume more importance in the lives of adolescents than in the lives of children. Cliques become increasingly mixed-sex in adolescence. Membership in certain crowds—especially jocks and populars—is associated with increased self-esteem. Independents also show high self-esteem.

- Three stages characterize the development of romantic relationships in adolescence: (1) entry into romantic attractions and affiliations at about 11 to 13 years of age, (2) exploring romantic relationships at approximately 14 to 16 years of age, and (3) consolidating dyadic romantic bonds at about 17 to 19 years of age. A special concern is early dating, which is associated with a number of problems. Most sexual minority youth have same-sex sexual experience, but relatively few have same-sex romantic relationships. Many sexual minority youth date other-sex peers, which can help them to clarify their sexual orientation or disguise it from others. Adolescents who date have more problems, such as substance abuse, than those who do not date, but they also have more acceptance with peers. Parent-adolescent relationships are linked to adolescents' and emerging adults' dating and romantic relationships. Culture can exert a powerful influence on dating. Many adolescents from immigrant families face conflicts with their parents about dating.

key terms

peers 425
popular children 430
average children 430
neglected children 430
rejected children 430

controversial children 430
play 434
play therapy 434
sensorimotor play 435
practice play 435

pretense/symbolic play 435
social play 436
constructive play 436
games 436
intimacy in friendship 440

cliques 442
crowds 442

key people

Kenneth Dodge 429
Erik Erikson 434
Sigmund Freud 434
Jean Piaget 434

Lev Vygotsky 434
Daniel Berlyne 435
Catherine Garvey 436
Angeline Lillard 436

Kathy Hirsh-Pasek 437
Roberta Golinkoff 437
Dorothy Singer 437

Harry Stack Sullivan 438
Mitchell Prinstein 442
Dexter Dunphy 443

SCHOOLS AND ACHIEVEMENT

chapter outline

The Reggio Emilia approach is an educational program for young children that was developed in the northern Italian city of Reggio Emilia. Children of single parents and children with disabilities have priority in admission; other children are admitted according to a scale of needs. Parents pay on a sliding scale based on income.

The children are encouraged to learn by investigating and exploring topics that interest them. A wide range of stimulating media and materials is available for children to use as they learn—music, movement, drawing, painting, sculpting, collages, puppets and disguises, and photography, for example (Strong-Wilson & Ellis, 2007).

A Reggio Emilia classroom in which young children explore topics that interest them.

In this program, children often explore topics in a group, which fosters a sense of community, respect for diversity, and a collaborative approach to problem solving (Hyson, Copple, & Jones, 2006). Two co-teachers are present to serve as guides for children. The Reggio Emilia teachers view a project as an adventure, which can start from an adult's suggestion, from a child's idea, or from an event, such as a snowfall or something else unexpected. Every project is based on what the children say and do. The teachers allow children enough time to think and to craft a project.

At the core of the Reggio Emilia approach is the image of children who are competent and have rights, especially the right to outstanding care and education. Parent participation is considered essential, and cooperation is a major theme in the schools. Many early childhood education experts believe the Reggio Emilia approach provides a supportive, stimulating context in which children are motivated to explore their world in a competent and confident manner (New, 2005, 2007).

preview

This chapter is about becoming educated and achieving. We will explore topics such as contemporary approaches to student learning, school transitions, the roles that socioeconomic status and ethnicity play in schools, educational issues involving children with disabilities, and motivation to achieve goals.

Exploring Children's Schooling

LG1 Discuss approaches to schooling and development.

| Contemporary Approaches to Student Learning and Assessment | Early Childhood Education | Elementary School | Educating Adolescents | Socioeconomic Status and Ethnicity |

You already have read about many aspects of schools throughout this book, especially in Section 3, "Cognition and Language." Recall our coverage of applications of Piaget's and Vygotsky's theories to education in Chapter 6, strategies for encouraging children's critical thinking in schools in Chapter 7, applications of Gardner's and Sternberg's theories of intelligence to education in Chapter 8, and bilingual education in Chapter 9. Here you will take a closer look at contemporary approaches to student learning in U.S. schools, variations in schooling from early childhood education through high school, and the influence of socioeconomic status and ethnicity on children's education.

For most children, entering the first grade signals new obligations. They form new relationships and develop new standards by which to judge themselves. School provides children with a rich source of new ideas to shape their sense of self. They will spend many years in schools as members of small societies in which there are tasks to be accomplished, people to be socialized and to be socialized by, and rules that define and limit behavior, feelings, and attitudes. By the time students graduate from high school, they will have spent 12,000 hours in the classroom.

CONTEMPORARY APPROACHES TO STUDENT LEARNING AND ASSESSMENT

Controversy surrounds questions about the best ways to teach children and how to hold schools and teachers accountable for whether children are learning (McCombs, 2013; Miller & Reynolds, 2013).

Constructivist and Direct Instruction Approaches The **constructivist approach** is a learner-centered approach to teaching that emphasizes the importance of individuals actively constructing their knowledge and understanding with guidance from the teacher. In the constructivist view, teachers should not attempt to simply pour information into children's minds. Rather, children should be encouraged to explore their world, discover knowledge, reflect, and think critically, with careful monitoring and meaningful guidance from the teacher (Appleton, 2012; O'Donnell, 2012). The constructivists believe that for too long in American education children have been required to sit still, be passive learners, and rotely memorize irrelevant as well as relevant information (Webb, Mehta, & Jordan, 2013).

Today, constructivism may include an emphasis on collaboration—children working together in their efforts to know and understand (Mahn & John-Steiner, 2013). A teacher with

developmental **connection**

Cognitive Theory

Piaget's and Vygotsky's theories can be applied to children's education. Chapter 6, p. 182 and p. 187

> The whole art of teaching is the art of awakening the natural curiosity of young minds.
>
> —**ANATOLE FRANCE**
> *French Novelist, 20th Century*

Is the teaching philosophy in this classroom more likely constructivist or direct instruction? Explain.

constructivist approach A learner-centered approach that emphasizes the importance of individuals actively constructing their knowledge and understanding, with guidance from the teacher.

Education is the transmission
of civilization.

—**Ariel and Will Durant**
American Authors and Philosophers, 20th Century

What characterizes the No Child Left Behind legislation? What are some criticisms of the legislation?

direct instruction approach A teacher-centered approach characterized by teacher direction and control, mastery of academic material, high expectations for students' progress, and maximum time spent on learning tasks.

a constructivist instructional philosophy would not have children memorize information but instead would give them opportunities to meaningfully construct their knowledge and understand the material while guiding their learning (Cruikshank, Jenkins, & Metcalf, 2012).

By contrast, the **direct instruction approach** is a structured, teacher-centered approach that is characterized by teacher direction and control, high teacher expectations for students' progress, maximum time spent by students on academic tasks, and efforts by the teacher to keep negative affect to a minimum. An important goal in the direct instruction approach is maximizing student learning time (Arends, 2012).

Advocates of the constructivist approach argue that the direct instruction approach turns children into passive learners and does not adequately challenge them to think in critical and creative ways (McCombs, 2013). The direct instruction enthusiasts say that the constructivist approaches do not give enough attention to the content of a discipline, such as history or science. They also believe that the constructivist approaches are too relativistic and vague.

Some experts in educational psychology believe that many effective teachers use both a constructivist *and* a direct instruction approach rather than relying exclusively on either one (Bransford & others, 2006; Parkay, 2013). Further, some circumstances may call more for a constructivist approach and others for a direct instruction approach. For example, experts increasingly recommend an explicit, intellectually engaging direct instruction approach when teaching students with a reading or a writing disability (Berninger & O'Malley, 2011).

Accountability   Since the 1990s, the U.S. public and governments at every level have demanded increased accountability from schools. One result was the spread of state-mandated testing to measure what students had or had not learned (Russell & Airasian, 2012). Many states identified objectives for students in their state and created tests to measure whether students were meeting those objectives. This approach became national policy in 2002 when the No Child Left Behind (NCLB) legislation was signed into law.

Advocates argue that statewide standardized testing will have a number of positive effects. These include improved student performance; more time devoted to teaching the subjects that are tested; high expectations for all students; identification of poorly performing schools, teachers, and administrators; and improved confidence in schools as test scores rise.

Critics argue that the NCLB legislation is doing more harm than good (Sadker & Zittleman, 2012). One criticism stresses that using a single test as the sole indicator of students' progress and competence presents a very narrow view of students' skills (Lewis, 2007). This criticism is similar to the one leveled at IQ tests, which we described in Chapter 8. To assess student progress and achievement, many psychologists and educators emphasize that a number of measures should be used, including tests, quizzes, projects, portfolios, classroom observations, and so on. Also, the tests used as part of NCLB don't measure creativity, motivation, persistence, flexible thinking, and social skills (Stiggins, 2008). Critics point out that teachers end up spending far too much class time "teaching to the test" by drilling students and having them memorize isolated facts at the expense of teaching that focuses on thinking skills, which students need for success in life (Pressley, 2007). Also, there is concern that in the era of No Child Left Behind students who are gifted are being neglected in the effort to raise the achievement level of students who are not doing well (Clark, 2008).

Consider also the following: Each state is allowed to have different criteria for what constitutes passing or failing grades on tests designated for NCLB inclusion. An analysis of NCLB data indicated that almost every fourth-grade student in Mississippi knows how to read but only half of Massachusetts' students do (Birman & others, 2007). Clearly, Mississippi's standards for passing the reading test are far below those of Massachusetts. In the recent analysis of state-by-state comparisons, many states have taken the safe route and kept the minimum scores low. Thus, while one of NCLB's goals was to raise standards for achievement in U.S. schools, apparently allowing states to set their own standards has lowered overall achievement.

Despite such criticisms, the U.S. Department of Education is committed to implementing No Child Left Behind, and schools are making accommodations to meet the requirements of this law. Indeed, most educators support the importance of high expectations and high standards of excellence for students and teachers. At issue, however, is whether the tests and procedures mandated by NCLB are the best route for achieving these high standards (Darling-Hammond, 2011; Nitko & Brookhart, 2011; Popham, 2011; Witte, 2012).

Let's now explore what schools are like for different developmental levels of students. We will begin with early childhood education.

EARLY CHILDHOOD EDUCATION

To the teachers in a Reggio Emilia program (described at the beginning of this chapter), preschool children are active learners, exploring the world with their peers, constructing their knowledge of the world in collaboration with their community, aided but not directed by their teachers. In many ways, the Reggio Emilia approach applies ideas consistent with the views of Piaget and Vygotsky discussed in Chapter 6, "Cognitive Developmental Approaches." Our exploration of early childhood education focuses on variations in programs, educational strategies for young children who are disadvantaged, and some controversies in early childhood education.

Variations in Early Childhood Education   Attending preschool is rapidly becoming the norm for U.S. children. There are many variations in the way young children are educated (Feeney, Moravcik, & Nolte, 2013; Henninger, 2013). The foundation of early childhood education has been the child-centered kindergarten.

The Child-Centered Kindergarten   Nurturing is a key aspect of the **child-centered kindergarten,** which emphasizes the education of the whole child and concern for his or her physical, cognitive, and socioemotional development (Segal & others, 2012). Instruction is organized around children's needs, interests, and learning styles. Emphasis is placed on the process of learning, rather than what is learned (Jalongo & Isenberg, 2012). The child-centered kindergarten honors three principles: (1) each child follows a unique developmental pattern; (2) young children learn best through firsthand experiences with people and materials; and (3) play is extremely important in the child's total development. Experimenting, exploring, discovering, trying out, restructuring, speaking, and listening are frequent activities in excellent kindergarten programs. Such programs are closely attuned to the developmental status of 4- and 5-year-old children.

The Montessori Approach   Montessori schools are patterned after the educational philosophy of Maria Montessori (1870–1952), an Italian physician-turned-educator who crafted a revolutionary approach to young children's education at the beginning of the twentieth century. The **Montessori approach** is a philosophy of education in which children are given considerable freedom and spontaneity in choosing activities. They are allowed to move from one activity to another as they desire. The teacher acts as a facilitator rather than a director. The teacher shows the child how to perform intellectual activities, demonstrates interesting ways to explore curriculum materials, and offers help when the child requests it (Drake, 2008; Isaacs, 2012; Lillard, 2008). "By encouraging children to make decisions from an early age, Montessori programs seek to develop self-regulated problem solvers who can make choices and manage their time effectively" (Hyson, Copple, & Jones, 2006, p. 14). The number of Montessori schools in the United States has expanded dramatically in recent years, from one school in 1959 to 355 schools in 1970 to more than 4,000 today.

Some developmentalists favor the Montessori approach, but others conclude that it neglects children's socioemotional development. For example, although Montessori fosters independence and the development of cognitive skills, it deemphasizes verbal interaction between the teacher and child and between the children themselves. Montessori's critics

developmental **connection**

Cognitive Theory

Both Piaget and Vygotsky believed that play is an excellent setting for young children's cognitive development. Chapter 15, p. 434

child-centered kindergarten Education that involves the whole child by considering both the child's physical, cognitive, and socioemotional development and the child's needs, interests, and learning styles.

Montessori approach An educational philosophy in which children are given considerable freedom and spontaneity in choosing activities and are allowed to move from one activity to another as they desire.

Larry Page and Sergey Brin, founders of the highly successful Internet search engine, Google, said that their early years at Montessori schools were a major factor in their success (International Montessori Council, 2006). During an interview with Barbara Walters, they said they learned how to be self-directed learners and self-starters at Montessori (ABC News, 2005). They commented that Montessori experiences encouraged them to think for themselves and allowed them the freedom to develop their own interests.

developmentally appropriate practice Education that focuses on the typical developmental patterns of children (age-appropriateness) and the uniqueness of each child (individual-appropriateness). Such practice contrasts with developmentally inappropriate practice, which relies on abstract paper-and-pencil activities presented to large groups of young children.

Project Head Start Compensatory education designed to provide children from low-income families the opportunity to acquire the skills and experiences important for school success.

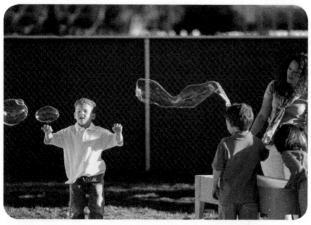

What are some key features of developmentally appropriate education?

also argue that it restricts imaginative play and that its heavy reliance on self-corrective materials may not adequately allow for creativity or accommodate a variety of learning styles.

Developmentally Appropriate and Inappropriate Education

Many educators and psychologists conclude that preschool and young elementary school children learn best through active, hands-on teaching methods such as games and dramatic play. They know that children develop at varying rates and that schools need to allow for these individual differences. They also argue that schools should focus on facilitating children's socioemotional development as well as their cognitive development. Educators refer to this type of schooling as **developmentally appropriate practice (DAP),** which is based on knowledge of the typical development of children within an age span (age-appropriateness), as well as the uniqueness of the child (individual-appropriateness) (Bredekamp, 2011; Squires & others, 2013). In contrast, developmentally inappropriate practice for young children relies on abstract paper-and-pencil activities presented to large groups. Desired outcomes for DAP include thinking critically, working cooperatively, solving problems, developing self-regulatory skills, and enjoying learning. The emphasis in DAP is on the process of learning rather than its content (Ritchie, Maxwell, & Bredekamp, 2009). Figure 16.1 provides recommendations from the National Association for the Education of Young Children (NAEYC) for developmentally appropriate education in a number of areas (NAEYC, 2009).

Many but not all studies show significant positive benefits for developmentally appropriate education (Hyson, 2007). Among the reasons it is difficult to generalize about research on developmentally appropriate education is that individual programs often vary, and developmentally appropriate education is an evolving concept. Recent changes in the concept have focused more attention on sociocultural factors, the teacher's active involvement and implementation of systematic intentions, as well as the degree to which academic skills should be emphasized and how they should be taught.

Education for Young Children Who Are Disadvantaged

For many years, U.S. children from low-income families did not receive any education before entering the first grade. Often, they began first grade already several steps behind their classmates in their readiness to learn. In the summer of 1965, the federal government began an effort to break the cycle of poverty and poor education for young children in the United States through **Project Head Start.** It is a compensatory program designed to provide children from low-income families the opportunity to acquire the skills and experiences important for success in school (Hustedt, Friedman, & Barnett, 2012; Zigler & Styfco, 2010). After almost half a century, Head Start continues to be the largest federally funded program for U.S. children, with almost 1 million children enrolled annually (Hagen & Lamb-Parker, 2008). In 2007, 3 percent of Head Start children were 5 years old, 51 percent were 4 years old, 36 percent were 3 years old, and 10 percent were under 3 years of age (Administration for Children and Families, 2008).

Early Head Start was established in 1995 to serve children from birth to 3 years of age. In 2007, half of all new funds appropriated for Head Start programs were used for the expansion of Early Head Start. Researchers have found positive effects for Early Head Start (Hoffman & Ewen, 2007). For example, a recent study revealed that Early Head Start had a protective effect on risks young children might experience in relation to parenting stress, language development, and self-control (Ayoub, Vallotton, & Mastergeorge, 2011).

Head Start programs are not all created equal. One estimate is that 40 percent of the 1,400 Head Start programs are of questionable quality (Zigler

Core Considerations in Developmentally Appropriate Practice

1 Knowledge to Consider in Making Decisions

In all aspects of working with children, early childhood practitioners need to consider these three areas of knowledge: 1) What is known about child development and learning, especially age-related characteristics; 2) What is known about each child as an individual; and 3) What is known about the social and cultural contexts in which children live.

2 Challenging and Achieveable Goals

Keeping in mind desired goals and what is known about the children as a group and individually, teachers plan experiences to promote children's learning and development.

Principles of Child Development and Learning that Inform Practice

1 All the domains of development and learning—physical, cognitive, emotional, and social—are important, and they are linked.

2 Many aspects of children's learning and development follow well-documented sequences, with later abilities, skills, and knowledge building on those already acquired.

3 Development and learning proceed at varying rates from child to child, and at uneven rates across different areas of a child's individual functioning.

4 Development and learning result from the interaction of biological maturation and experience.

5 Early experiences have strong effects—both cumulative and delayed—on children's development and learning; optimal periods exist for certain types of development and learning.

6 Development proceeds toward greater complexity, self-regulation, and symbolic or representational capacities.

7 Children develop best when they have secure, consistent relationships with responsive adults and opportunities for positive peer relations.

8 Development and learning occur in and are influenced by multiple social and cultural contexts.

9 Always mentally active in seeking to understand the world around them, children learn in a variety of ways; a wide range of teaching strategies can be effective in guiding children's learning.

10 Play is an important context for developing self-regulation and for promoting language, cognition, and social competence.

11 Development and learning advance when children are challenged to achieve at a level just beyond their current mastery and when they are given opportunities to practice newly acquired skills.

12 Children's experiences shape their motivation and approaches to learning, such as persistence, initiative, and flexibility; in turn, these characteristics influence their learning and development.

Selected Guidelines for Developmentally Appropriate Practice

1 Creating a Caring Community of Learners

Each member of the community should be valued by the others; relationships are an important context through which children learn; practitioners ensure that members of the community feel psychologically safe.

2 Teaching to Enhance Development and Learning

The teacher takes responsibility for stimulating, directing, and supporting children's learning by providing the experiences that each child needs.

3 Planning Curriculum to Achieve Important Goals

The curriculum is planned to help children achieve goals that are developmentally appropriate and educationally significant.

4 Assessing Children's Development and Learning

In developmentally appropriate practice, assessments are linked to the program's goals for children.

5 Establishing Reciprocal Relationships with Families

A positive partnership between teachers and families benefits children's learning and development.

FIGURE 16.1

RECOMMENDATIONS BY NAEYC FOR DEVELOPMENTALLY APPROPRIATE PRACTICE IN EARLY CHILDHOOD PROGRAMS SERVING CHILDREN FROM BIRTH THROUGH AGE 8. Source: Adapted from NAEYC (2009). Developmentally appropriate practice in early childhood programs serving children from birth through age 8.

& Styfco, 1994). More attention needs to be given to developing consistently high-quality Head Start programs (Chambers, Cheung, & Slavin, 2006). One individual who is strongly motivated to make Head Start a valuable learning experience for young children from disadvantaged backgrounds is Yolanda Garcia. To read about her work, see *Connecting with Careers*.

Evaluations support the positive influence of quality early childhood programs on both the cognitive and social worlds of disadvantaged young children (Lamy, 2012; Phillips & Lowenstein, 2011). A recent national evaluation of Head Start revealed that the program had a positive influence on the language and cognitive development of the 3- and 4-year-olds who participated (Puma & others, 2010). However, by the end of the first grade, there were few lasting outcomes, except for a larger vocabulary for those who went to Head Start as 4-year-olds and better oral comprehension for those who went to Head Start as 3-year-olds. Another recent study found that when young children initially began Head Start, they were well behind

Yolanda Garcia, Director of Children's Services/Head Start

Yolanda Garcia has been the Director of the Children's Services Department for the Santa Clara, California, County Office of Education since 1980. As director, she is responsible for managing child development programs for 2,500 3- to 5-year-old children in 127 classrooms. Her training includes two master's degrees—one in public policy and child welfare from the University of Chicago and the other in education administration from San Jose State University.

Garcia has served on many national advisory committees that have brought about improvements in the staffing of Head Start programs. Most notably, she served on the Head Start Quality Committee that recommended the development of Early Head Start and revised performance standards for Head Start programs. Garcia currently is a member of the American Academy of Science Committee on the Integration of Science and Early Childhood Education.

Yolanda Garcia, Director of Children's Services/Head Start, working with a Head Start child in Santa Clara, California.

their more academically advantaged peers in literacy and math (Hindman & others, 2010). However, by the end of the first grade, the Head Start children were on par with national averages in literacy and math.

One high-quality early childhood education program (although not a Head Start program) is the Perry Preschool program in Ypsilanti, Michigan, a two-year preschool program that includes weekly home visits from program personnel. In analyses of the long-term effects of the program, adults who had been in the Perry Preschool program were compared with a control group of adults from the same background who had not received the enriched early childhood education (Schweinhart & others, 2005; Weikert, 1993). Those who had been in the Perry Preschool program had fewer teen pregnancies and higher high school graduation rates, and at age 40 they were more likely to be in the workforce, to own their own homes, and to have a savings account, and they were less likely to have been arrested.

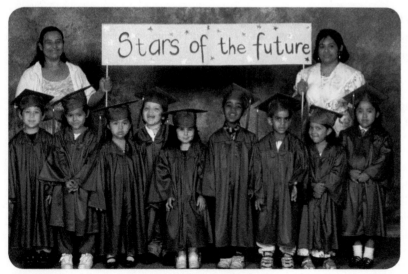

What are two controversies in early childhood education?

Controversies in Early Childhood Education Two current controversies in early childhood education involve (1) what the curriculum for early childhood education should be (Epstein & Barnette, 2012; Moravick, Nolte, & Feeney, 2013), and (2) whether preschool education should be universal in the United States (Zigler, Gilliam, & Jones, 2006).

Curriculum Controversy A current curriculum controversy in early childhood involves on one side those who advocate a child-centered, constructivist approach much like that emphasized by the NAEYC along the lines of developmentally appropriate practice. On the other side are those who endorse an academic, direct instruction approach.

In reality, many high-quality early childhood education programs include both academic and constructivist approaches. Many education experts such as Lilian Katz (1999), though, worry about academic approaches that place too much pressure on young children to achieve and don't provide any opportunities to actively construct knowledge. Competent early childhood programs also should focus on both cognitive development and socioemotional development, not exclusively on cognitive development (Kagan & Scott-Little, 2004).

Universal Preschool Education   Another early childhood education controversy focuses on whether preschool education should be instituted for all 4-year-old children in the United States. Edward Zigler and his colleagues (2006) recently argued that the United States should have universal preschool education. They emphasize that quality preschools prepare children for success in school. Zigler and his colleagues (2006) cite research that shows quality preschool programs increase the likelihood that once children go to elementary and secondary school they will be less likely to be retained in a grade or to drop out of school. They also point to analyses indicating that universal preschool would bring considerable cost savings on the order of billions of dollars because of a diminished need for remedial and justice services (Karoly & Bigelow, 2005).

Critics of universal preschool education argue that the gains attributed to preschool and kindergarten education are often overstated. They especially stress that research has not proven that nondisadvantaged children benefit from attending a preschool. Thus, the critics say it is more important to improve preschool education for young children who are disadvantaged than to mandate preschool education for all 4-year-old children. Some critics, especially homeschooling advocates, emphasize that young children should be educated by their parents, not by schools. Thus, controversy continues to surround the issue of universal preschool education.

In Japan and many developing countries, some of the goals of early childhood education are quite different from those of American programs. To read about the differences, see *Connecting with Diversity*.

ELEMENTARY SCHOOL

For many children, entering the first grade signals a change from being a "home-child" to being a "school-child"—a situation in which new roles and obligations are experienced. Children take up the new role of being a student, interact with peers and teachers, develop new relationships, adopt new reference groups, and discover new standards by which to judge themselves. School provides children with a rich source of new ideas to shape their sense of self.

Too often early schooling proceeds mainly on the basis of negative feedback. For example, children's self-esteem in the latter part of elementary school is lower than it is in the earlier part, and older children rate themselves as less smart, less good, and less hard-working than do younger ones (Blumenfeld & others, 1981; Eccles, 2003).

EDUCATING ADOLESCENTS

What is the transition from elementary to middle or junior high school like? What are the characteristics of effective schools for young adolescents? How can adolescents be encouraged to stay in school?

The Transition to Middle or Junior High School   The first year of middle school or junior high school can be difficult for many students (Anderman, 2012; Anderman, Gray, & Chang, 2013; Eccles & Roeser, 2013). For example, in one study of the transition from sixth grade in an elementary school to seventh grade in a junior high school, adolescents' perceptions of the quality of their school life plunged during the seventh grade (Hirsch & Rapkin, 1987). Compared with their earlier feelings as sixth-graders, the seventh-graders were less satisfied with school, were less committed to school, and liked their teachers less. The drop in school satisfaction occurred regardless of how academically successful the students were. The transition to middle or junior high school is less stressful when students have positive relationships with friends and go through the transition in team-oriented schools in which 20 to 30 students take the same classes together (Hawkins & Berndt, 1985).

As children make the transition to elementary school, they interact and develop relationships with new and significant others. School provides them with a rich source of new ideas to shape their sense of self.

connecting with diversity

Early Childhood Education in Japan and Developing Countries

As in America, there is diversity in Japanese early childhood education. Some Japanese kindergartens have specific aims, such as early musical training or the practice of Montessori strategies. In large cities, some kindergartens are attached to universities that have elementary and secondary schools. In most Japanese preschools, however, little emphasis is put on academic instruction.

In one study, 300 Japanese and 210 American preschool teachers, child development specialists, and parents were asked about various aspects of early childhood education (Tobin, Wu, & Davidson, 1989). Only 2 percent of the Japanese respondents listed "to give children a good start academically" as one of their top three reasons for a society to have preschools. In contrast, over half the American respondents chose this as one of their top three reasons. Japanese preschools do not teach reading, writing, and mathematics but focus on the development of skills like persistence, concentration, and the ability to function as a member of a group. The vast majority of young Japanese children are taught to read at home by their parents.

In the comparison of Japanese and American parents, more than 60 percent of the Japanese parents said that the purpose of preschool is to give children experience being a member of the group, as compared with about 20 percent of the U.S. parents (Tobin, Wu, & Davidson, 1989) (see Figure 16.2). Lessons in living and working together grow naturally out of the Japanese culture. In many Japanese kindergartens, children wear the same uniforms, including caps in different colors to indicate the

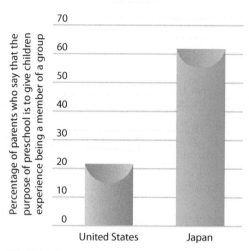

FIGURE 16.2

COMPARISON OF JAPANESE AND U.S. PARENTS' VIEWS ON THE PURPOSE OF PRESCHOOL

classrooms to which they belong. They have identical sets of equipment, kept in identical drawers and shelves. This is not intended to turn the young children into robots, as some Americans have commented, but to impress on them that other people, just like themselves, have needs and desires that are equally important (Hendry, 1995).

Japan is a highly advanced industrialized country. What about developing countries—how do they compare to the United States in educating young children? The wide range of programs and emphasis on the education of the whole child—physically, cognitively, and socioemotionally—that characterize U.S. early childhood education do not exist in many developing countries (Roopnarine & Metindogan, 2006). Economic pressures and parents' belief that education should be academically rigorous have produced teacher-centered rather than child-centered early childhood education programs in most developing countries. Among the countries in which this type of early childhood education has been observed are Jamaica, rural China, Thailand, Kenya, and Turkey. In these countries, young children are usually given few choices and are educated in highly structured settings. Emphasis is on learning academic skills through rote memorization and recitation (Lin, Johnson, & Johnson, 2003). Programs in Mexico, Singapore, Korea, and Hong Kong have been observed to be closer to those in the United States in their emphasis on curriculum flexibility and play-based methods (Cisneros-Cohernour, Moreno, & Cisneros, 2000).

What characterizes early childhood education in Japan?

A kindergarten class in Kingston, Jamaica. *What characterizes kindergarten in many developing countries like Jamaica?*

The transition to middle or junior high school takes place at a time when many changes—in the individual, in the family, and in school—are occurring simultaneously (Anderman, Gray, & Chang, 2013; Eccles & Roeser, 2013). These changes include puberty and related concerns about body image; the emergence of at least some aspects of formal operational thought, including accompanying changes in social cognition; increased responsibility and decreased dependency on parents; change to a larger, more impersonal school structure; change from one teacher to many teachers and from a small, homogeneous set of peers to a larger, more heterogeneous set of peers; and an increased focus on achievement and performance. Moreover, when students make the transition to middle or junior high school, they experience the **top-dog phenomenon** of moving from being the oldest, biggest, and most powerful students in elementary school to being the youngest, smallest, and least powerful students in middle or junior high school.

The transition from elementary to middle or junior high school occurs at the same time as a number of other developmental changes. *What are some of these other developmental changes?*

There can also be positive aspects to the transition to middle or junior high school. Students are more likely to feel grown up, have more subjects from which to select, have more opportunities to spend time with peers and locate compatible friends, and enjoy increased independence from direct parental monitoring. They also may be more challenged intellectually by academic work.

Effective Schools for Young Adolescents   Critics argue that middle and junior high schools should offer activities that reflect a wide range of individual differences in biological and psychological development among young adolescents. In 1989 the Carnegie Corporation issued an extremely negative evaluation of our nation's middle schools. It concluded that most young adolescents attended massive, impersonal schools; were taught from irrelevant curricula; trusted few adults in school; and lacked access to health care and counseling. It recommended that the nation develop smaller "communities" or "houses" to lessen the impersonal nature of large middle schools, have lower student-to-counselor ratios (10 to 1 instead of several hundred to 1), involve parents and community leaders in schools, develop new curricula, have teachers team teach in more flexibly designed curriculum blocks that integrate several disciplines, boost students' health and fitness with more in-school programs, and help students who need public health care to get it. Two decades later, experts are still finding that middle schools throughout the nation need a major redesign if they are to be effective in educating adolescents (Eccles & Roeser, 2011).

High School   Just as there are concerns about U.S. middle school education, so are there concerns about U.S. high school education (Smith, 2009). Critics stress that in many high schools expectations for success and standards for learning are too low. Critics also argue that too often high schools foster passivity and that schools should create a variety of pathways for students to achieve an identity. Many students graduate from high school with inadequate reading, writing, and mathematical skills—including many who go on to college and have to enroll in remediation classes there. Other students drop out of high school and do not have skills that will allow them to obtain decent jobs, much less to be informed citizens (Vaughn & others, 2011).

Robert Crosnoe's (2011) recent book, *Fitting In, Standing Out,* highlighted another major problem with U.S. high schools: How the negative social aspects of adolescents' lives undermine their academic achievement. In his view, adolescents become immersed in complex peer group cultures that demand conformity. High school is supposed to be about getting an education, but the reality for many youth is that high school is as much about navigating the social worlds of peer relations that may or may not value education and academic achievement. The adolescents who fail to fit in, especially those who are obese or gay, become stigmatized.

In the last half of the twentieth century and the first several years of the twenty-first century, U.S. high school dropout rates declined (National Center for Education Statistics, 2012). In the 1940s, more than half of U.S. 16- to 24-year-olds had dropped out of school; by 2011, this figure had decreased to 7.9 percent. The dropout rate of Latino adolescents remains high, although it has been decreasing in the twenty-first century (from 28 percent in 2000 to 16.3 percent in 2010). The lowest dropout rate in 2011 occurred for Asian

top-dog phenomenon The circumstance of moving from the top position in elementary school to the lowest position in middle or junior high school.

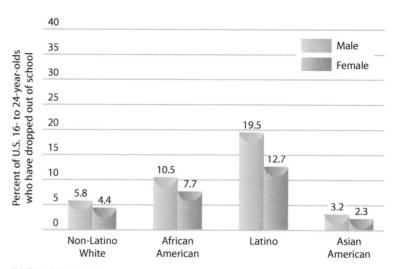

FIGURE 16.3

SCHOOL DROPOUT RATES OF U.S. 16- TO 24-YEAR-OLDS BY GENDER AND ETHNICITY

American adolescents (2.8 percent), followed by non-Latino White adolescents (5.1 percent), African American adolescents (9.1 percent), Native American/Pacific Islander adolescents (14.9), and Latino adolescents (16.3 percent).

Gender differences characterize U.S. dropout rates, with males more likely to drop out than females (9.3 versus 6.5 percent; data for 2010) (National Center for Education Statistics, 2012). The gender gap in dropout rates is especially large for Latino adolescents—19.5 percent for males and 12.7 percent for females. Figure 16.3 shows the dropout rates of 16- to 24-year-olds by ethnicity and gender in 2010.

The average U.S. high school dropout rates just described mask some very high dropout rates in low-income areas of inner cities. For example, in cities such as Detroit, Cleveland, and Chicago, dropout rates are above 50 percent. Also, the percentages cited in Figure 16.3 are for 16- to 24-year-olds. When dropout rates include students who take longer than four years to complete high school, the percentage of students is also much higher than in Figure 16.3. Thus, in considering high school dropout rates, it is important to examine age, the number of years it takes to complete high school, and various contexts including ethnicity, gender, and school location.

Students drop out of school for many reasons. In one study, almost 50 percent of the dropouts cited school-related reasons for leaving school, such as not liking school or being expelled or suspended (Rumberger, 1995). Twenty percent of the dropouts (but 40 percent of the Latino students) cited economic reasons for leaving school. One-third of the female students dropped out for personal reasons such as pregnancy or marriage.

According to one review, the programs that are most effective in discouraging students from dropping out of high school are early reading programs, tutoring, counseling, and mentoring (Lehr & others, 2003). High schools that are effective in reducing dropout rates also emphasize the creation of caring environments and relationships, use block scheduling, and offer community-service opportunities.

Early detection of children's school-related difficulties, and getting children engaged with school in positive ways, are important strategies for reducing the dropout rate. Recently the Bill and Melinda Gates Foundation (2006, 2008) has funded efforts to reduce the dropout rate in schools where dropout rates are high. One strategy that is being emphasized in the Gates' funding is keeping students who are at risk for dropping out of school with the same teachers throughout their high school years. The hope is that the

Students at the Ahfachkee School located on the Seminole Tribe's Big Cypress Reservation in Florida. An important educational goal is to increase the high school graduation rate of Native American adolescents.

"I Have a Dream"

"I Have a Dream" (IHAD) is an innovative, comprehensive, long-term dropout prevention program administered by the national "I Have a Dream" Foundation in New York. Since the national IHAD Foundation was created in 1986, it has grown to comprise more than 180 projects in 64 cities and 27 states, Washington, DC, and New Zealand, serving more than 12,000 children ("I Have a Dream" Foundation, 2013). Local IHAD projects around the country "adopt" entire grades (usually the third or fourth) from public elementary schools, or corresponding age cohorts from public housing developments. These children—"Dreamers"—are then provided with a program of academic, social, cultural, and recreational activities throughout their elementary, middle school, and high school years. An important part of this program is that it is personal rather than institutional: IHAD sponsors and staff develop close, long-term relationships with the children. When participants complete high school, IHAD provides the tuition assistance necessary for them to attend a state or local college or vocational school.

The IHAD program was created in 1981, when philanthropist Eugene Lang made an impromptu offer of college tuition to a class of graduating sixth-graders at P.S. 121 in East Harlem. Evaluations of IHAD programs have found dramatic improvements in grades, test scores, and school attendance, as well as a reduction of behavioral problems among Dreamers. In a recent analysis of the "I Have a Dream" program in Houston, 91 percent of the participants received passing grades in reading/English, 83 percent said they liked school, 98 percent said getting good

These adolescents participate in the "I Have a Dream" (IHAD) program, a comprehensive, long-term dropout prevention program that has been very successful.

grades is important to them, 100 percent said they plan to graduate from high school, and 94 percent reported that they plan to go to college ("I Have a Dream" Foundation, 2008).

---

teachers will get to know these students much better, their relationship with the students will improve, and teachers will be able to monitor and guide the students toward graduating from high school. To read about one program that attempts to reduce the school dropout rate, see *Caring Connections*.

Extracurricular Activities   Adolescents in U.S. schools usually can choose from a wide array of extracurricular activities in addition to their academic courses. These adult-sanctioned activities typically occur in the after-school hours and can be sponsored either by the school or the community. They include such diverse activities as sports, academic clubs, band, drama, and math clubs. Researchers have found that participation in extracurricular activities is linked to higher grades, increased school engagement, reduced likelihood of dropping out of school, improved probability of going to college, higher self-esteem, and lower rates of depression, delinquency, and substance abuse (Eccles & Roeser, 2013). Adolescents benefit from a breadth of extracurricular activities more than focusing on a single extracurricular activity.

Of course, the quality of the extracurricular activities matters (Eccles & Roeser, 2013). High-quality extracurricular activities that are likely to promote positive adolescent development provide competent and supportive adult mentors, opportunities for increasing school connectedness, challenging and meaningful activities, and opportunities for improving skills.

How does participation in extracurricular activities influence development in adolescence and emerging adulthood?

SOCIOECONOMIC STATUS AND ETHNICITY

Children from low-income, ethnic minority backgrounds have more difficulties in school than do their middle-socioeconomic-status, White counterparts (Hutson, 2008). Why? Critics argue that schools are not doing a good job of educating low-income or ethnic minority students (Gollnick & Chinn, 2013; Leong & others, 2013; Spring, 2013). Let's further explore the roles of socioeconomic status and ethnicity in schools.

- - - - - - - - - ->

developmental **connection**

Socioeconomic Status

Socioeconomic differences are a proxy for material, human, and social capital within and beyond the family (Huston & Ripke, 2006). Chapter 17, p. 487

Educating Students from Low-Income Backgrounds Many children living in poverty face problems that present barriers to their learning (Chen & Brooks-Gunn, 2012; Duncan, 2012; Duncan & others, 2013). They might have parents who don't set high educational standards for them, who are incapable of reading to them, or who don't have enough money to pay for educational materials and experiences, such as books and trips to zoos and museums. They might be malnourished or live in areas where crime and violence are a way of life. One study revealed that the longer children experienced poverty, the more detrimental the poverty was to their cognitive development (Najman & others, 2009).

The schools that children from impoverished backgrounds attend often have fewer resources than schools in higher-income neighborhoods (Nelson, Palonsky, & McCarthy, 2013). In low-income areas, schools are more likely to be staffed by young teachers with less experience than are schools in higher-income neighborhoods (Liu & Hernandez, 2008). Schools in low-income areas also are more likely to encourage rote learning, whereas schools in higher-income areas are more likely to work with children to improve their thinking skills (Koppelman & Goodhart, 2011). In sum, far too many schools in low-income neighborhoods provide students with environments that are not conducive to effective learning (McLoyd & others, 2011).

In *The Shame of the Nation,* Jonathan Kozol (2005) criticized the inadequate quality and lack of resources in many U.S. schools, especially those in the poverty areas of inner cities that have high concentrations of ethnic minority children. Kozol praises teachers like Angela Lively (above), who keeps a box of shoes in her Indianapolis classroom for students in need.

Ethnicity in Schools More than one-third of all African American and almost one-third of all Latino students attend schools in the 47 largest city school districts in the United States, compared with only 5 percent of all White and 22 percent of all Asian American students. Many of these inner-city schools are still segregated, are grossly underfunded, and do not provide adequate opportunities for children to learn effectively. Thus, the effects of SES and the effects of ethnicity are often intertwined (Bennett, 2011; Hill & Witherspoon, 2011; Leong & others, 2013).

Even outside of inner-city schools, school segregation remains a factor in U.S. education (Gollnick & Chinn, 2013; Nieto & Bode, 2012). Almost one-third of all African American and Latino students attend schools in which 90 percent or more of the students are from minority groups (Banks, 2008).

The school experiences of students from different ethnic groups vary considerably (Spring, 2013; Urdan, 2012). African American and Latino students are much less likely than non-Latino White or Asian American students to be enrolled in academic, college preparatory programs and are much more likely to be enrolled in remedial and special education programs. Asian American students are far more likely than other ethnic minority groups to take advanced math and science courses in high school. African American students are twice as likely as Latinos, Native Americans, or Whites to be suspended from school.

What are some features of a jigsaw classroom?

Following are some strategies for improving interaction among ethnically diverse students:

- *Turn the class into a jigsaw classroom.* When Elliot Aronson was a professor at the University of Texas at Austin, the school system contacted him for ideas on how to reduce the increasing racial tension in classrooms. Aronson (1986) developed the concept of a "jigsaw classroom" in which students from different cultural backgrounds are placed in a cooperative group where they are required to construct different parts of a project to reach a common goal. Aronson used the term *jigsaw* because he saw the technique as much like a group of students cooperating to put different pieces together to complete a jigsaw puzzle. How might this work? Team sports, drama productions, and music performances are examples of contexts in which students participate cooperatively to reach a common goal; however, the jigsaw technique also lends itself to group science projects, history reports, and other learning experiences involving a variety of subject matter.

- *Encourage students to have positive personal contact with diverse other students.* Mere contact does not do the job of improving relationships with diverse others. For example, busing ethnic minority students to predominantly White schools, or vice versa, has not reduced prejudice or improved interethnic relations. What matters is what happens after children get to school. Especially beneficial in improving interethnic relations is sharing one's worries, successes, failures, coping strategies, interests, and other personal information with people of other ethnicities. When this happens, people tend to look at others as individuals rather than as members of a homogeneous group.

- *Reduce bias.* Teachers can reduce bias by displaying images of children from diverse ethnic and cultural groups, selecting play materials and classroom activities that encourage cultural understanding, helping students resist stereotyping, and working with parents to reduce children's exposure to bias and prejudice at home.

- *Be a competent cultural mediator.* Teachers can play a powerful role as cultural mediators by being sensitive to biased content in curriculum materials and classroom interactions, learning more about different ethnic groups, being sensitive to children's ethnic attitudes, viewing students of color positively, and thinking of positive ways to get parents of color more involved as partners with teachers in educating children (Manning & Baruth, 2009; Taylor & Whittaker, 2009).

- *View the school and community as a team.* James Comer (1988, 2004, 2006, 2010) advocates a community-wide, team-oriented approach as the best way to educate children. Three important aspects of the Comer Project for Change are (1) a governance and management team that develops a comprehensive school plan, assessment strategy, and staff development plan; (2) a mental health or school support team; and (3) a program for parents. Comer believes that the entire school community should have a cooperative rather than an adversarial attitude. The Comer program is currently operating in more than 600 schools in 26 states. Read further about James Comer's work in the *Connecting with Careers* profile.

James Comer, Child Psychiatrist

James Comer grew up in a low-income neighborhood in East Chicago, Indiana, and credits his parents with leaving no doubt about the importance of education. He obtained a bachelor's degree from Indiana University. He went on to obtain a medical degree from Howard University College of Medicine, a Master of Public Health degree from the University of Michigan School of Public Health, and psychiatry training at the Yale University School of Medicine's Child Study Center. He currently is the Maurice Falk professor of Child Psychiatry at the Yale University Child Study Center and an associate dean at the Yale University Medical School. During his years at Yale, Comer has concentrated on promoting a focus on child development as a way of improving schools. His efforts in support of healthy development of young people are known internationally.

Comer is, perhaps, best known for the founding of the School Development Program in 1968, which promotes the collaboration of parents, educators, and the surrounding community to improve social, emotional, and academic outcomes for children.

For more information about what psychiatrists do, see page 43 in the Careers in Child Development appendix following Chapter 1.

James Comer is shown with some of the inner-city children who attend a school that became a better learning environment because of Comer's intervention.

Review Connect Reflect

 LG1 Discuss approaches to schooling and development.

Review

- What are some contemporary approaches to student learning?
- What are some variations in early childhood education?
- What are some characteristics of elementary education?
- How are U.S. adolescents educated, and what are the challenges in educating adolescents?
- How do socioeconomic status and ethnicity affect children's education?

Connect

- In this section, you learned about socioeconomic status (SES) and education.

In Chapter 14, what did you learn about SES and how parents think about education? How does that tie into the importance of programs like IHAD and those sponsored by the Bill and Melinda Gates Foundation?

Reflect *Your Own Personal Journey of Life*

- How would you characterize the approach of the schools that you attended as a child and as an adolescent? Do you think your schools were effective? Explain.

The Scope of
Disabilities

Educational
Issues

What are some of the disabilities that children have? What characterizes the education of children with disabilities?

THE SCOPE OF DISABILITIES

Of all children from 3 to 21 years of age in the United States, 13.1 percent received special education or related services in 2009–2010, an increase of 3 percent since 1980–1981 (Condition of Education, 2012). Figure 16.4 shows the four largest groups of students with a disability who were served by federal programs during the 2009–2010 school year (Condition of Education, 2012).

As indicated in Figure 16.4, students with a learning disability were by far the largest group of students with a disability to be given special education, followed by children with speech or language impairments, intellectual disability, and emotional disturbance. The U.S. government's assessments of the prevalence of students with a disability includes attention deficit hyperactivity disorder (ADHD) in the category of learning disabilities.

Learning Disabilities   The U.S. government created a definition of learning disabilities in 1997 and then reauthorized the definition with a few minor changes in 2004. Following is a description of the government's definition of what determined whether a child should be classified as having a learning disability. A child with a **learning disability** has difficulty in learning that involves understanding or using spoken or written language, and the difficulty can appear in listening, thinking, reading, writing, and spelling. A learning disability also may involve difficulty in doing mathematics (Jittendra & Montague, 2013). To be classified as a learning disability, the learning problem is not primarily the result of visual, hearing, or motor disabilities; intellectual disability; emotional disorders; or due to environmental, cultural, or economic disadvantage.

About three times as many boys as girls are classified as having a learning disability. Among the explanations for this gender difference are a greater biological vulnerability among boys and *referral bias*. That is, boys are more likely to be referred by teachers for treatment because of troublesome behavior.

Approximately 80 percent of children with a learning disability have a reading problem (Shaywitz, Gruen, & Shaywitz, 2007). Three types of learning disabilities are dyslexia, dysgraphia, and dyscalculia:

- **Dyslexia** is a category reserved for individuals who have a severe impairment in their ability to read and spell (Allor & al Otaiba, 2013; Kirk & others, 2012).
- **Dysgraphia** is a learning disability that involves difficulty in handwriting (Mason, Harris, & Graham, 2013). Children with dysgraphia may write very slowly, their writing products may be virtually illegible, and they may make numerous spelling errors because of their inability to match up sounds and letters (Hayes & Berninger, 2013).
- **Dyscalculia,** also known as developmental arithmetic disorder, is a learning disability that involves difficulty in math computation (Fuchs & others, 2013).

The precise causes of learning disabilities have not yet been determined (Hallahan, Kauffman, & Pullen, 2012; Lerner & Johns, 2012; Rosenberg, Westling, & McLeskey, 2011). Researchers have used brain-imaging techniques, such as magnetic resonance imaging, to reveal any regions of the brain that might be involved in learning disabilities (Shaywitz,

Disability	Percentage of All Children in Public Schools
Learning disabilities	4.9
Speech and language impairments	2.9
Intellectual disabilities	1.1
Emotional disturbance	0.8

FIGURE **16.4**

U.S. CHILDREN WITH A DISABILITY WHO RECEIVE SPECIAL EDUCATION SERVICES. Figures are for the 2009–2010 school year and represent the four categories with the highest numbers and percentages of children. Both learning disability and attention deficit hyperactivity disorder are combined in the learning disabilities category (Condition of Education, 2012).

learning disabilities Disabilities involving understanding or using spoken or written language. The difficulty can appear in listening, thinking, reading, writing, spelling, or mathematics. To be classified as a learning disability, the problem must not be primarily the result of visual, hearing, or motor disabilities; intellectual disability; emotional disorders; or environmental, cultural, or economic disadvantage.

dyslexia A category of learning disabilities involving a severe impairment in the ability to read and spell.

dysgraphia A learning disability that involves difficulty in handwriting.

dyscalculia Also known as developmental arithmetic disorder; a learning disability that involves difficulty in math computation.

FIGURE **16.5**

BRAIN SCANS AND LEARNING DISABILITIES.
An increasing number of studies are using MRI brain scans to examine the brain pathways involved in learning disabilities. Shown here is 9-year-old Patrick Price, who has dyslexia. Patrick is going through an MRI scanner disguised by drapes to look like a child-friendly castle. Inside the scanner, children must lie virtually motionless as words and symbols flash on a screen, and they are asked to identify them by clicking different buttons.

developmental **connection**

Attention

Attention, which involves the focusing of mental resources, improves cognitive processing on many tasks. Chapter 7, p. 198

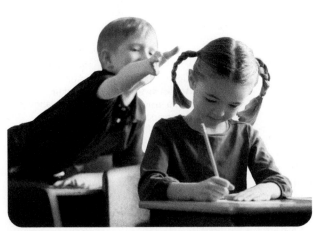

Many children with ADHD show impulsive behavior. *How would you handle this situation if you were a teacher and this were to happen in your classroom?*

attention deficit hyperactivity disorder (ADHD) A disability in which children consistently show one or more of the following characteristics: (1) inattention, (2) hyperactivity, and (3) impulsivity.

Lyon, & Shaywitz, 2006) (see Figure 16.5). This research indicates that it is unlikely learning disabilities reside in a single, specific brain location. More likely, learning disabilities are due to problems in integrating information from multiple brain regions or subtle abnormalities in brain structures and functions.

Interventions with children who have a learning disability often focus on improving reading ability (Lovett, Barron, & Frijters, 2013; Schmitt, Justice, & Pentimonti, 2013). Intensive instruction over a period of time by a competent teacher can help many children (Berninger & Swanson, 2013).

Attention Deficit Hyperactivity Disorder (ADHD) Attention deficit hyperactivity disorder **(ADHD)** is a disability in which children consistently show one or more of the following characteristics over a period of time: (1) inattention, (2) hyperactivity, and (3) impulsivity. Children who are inattentive have so much difficulty focusing on any one thing that they may get bored with a task after only a few minutes—or even seconds. Children who are hyperactive show high levels of physical activity, seeming to be almost constantly in motion. Children who are impulsive have difficulty curbing their reactions; they do not do a good job of thinking before they act. Depending on the characteristics that children with ADHD display, they can be diagnosed as (1) ADHD with predominantly inattention, (2) ADHD with predominantly hyperactivity/impulsivity, or (3) ADHD with both inattention and hyperactivity/impulsivity.

The number of children diagnosed and treated for ADHD has increased substantially in recent decades. The disorder occurs as much as four to nine times more frequently in boys than in girls. There is controversy, however, about the increased diagnosis of ADHD (Friend, 2011). Some experts attribute the increase mainly to heightened awareness of the disorder; others are concerned that many children are being incorrectly diagnosed (Parens & Johnston, 2009).

A recent study examined the possible misdiagnosis of ADHD (Bruchmiller, Margraf, & Schneider, 2012). In this study, child psychologists, psychiatrists, and social workers were given vignettes of children with ADHD (some vignettes matched the diagnostic criteria for the disorder, while others did not). Whether each child was male or female varied. The researchers assessed whether the mental health professionals gave a diagnosis of ADHD to the child described in the vignette. The professionals overdiagnosed ADHD almost 20 percent of the time, and regardless of the symptoms described, boys were twice as likely as girls to be given a diagnosis of ADHD.

Definitive causes of ADHD have not been found. However, a number of causes have been proposed (Faraone & Mick, 2010; Swanson, Harris, & Graham, 2013). Some children likely inherit a tendency to develop ADHD from their parents. Other children likely develop ADHD because of damage to their brain during prenatal or postnatal development (Lindblad & Hjern, 2010). Among early possible contributors to ADHD are cigarette and alcohol exposure during prenatal development, as well as a high level of maternal stress and low birth weight (Choudry & others, 2012; Knopik, 2009). For example, a recent study revealed cigarette smoking during pregnancy was linked to ADHD in elementary-school-aged children (Sciberras, Ukoumunne, & Efron, 2011).

As with learning disabilities, the development of brain-imaging techniques is leading to a better understanding of ADHD (Cubillo & others, 2012). A recent study revealed that peak thickness of the cerebral cortex occurred three years later (10.5 years) in children with ADHD than in children without ADHD (peak at 7.5 years) (Shaw & others, 2007). The delay was more prominent in the prefrontal regions of the brain that are especially important in attention and planning (see Figure 16.6). Another recent study also found delayed development of the brain's frontal lobes in children with ADHD, likely due to delayed or decreased myelination (Nagel & others, 2011). Researchers also are exploring the roles that various neurotransmitters, such as serotonin and dopamine, might play in ADHD (Dalley & Roiser, 2013; Shen, Liao, & Tseng, 2013).

The delays in brain development just described are in areas linked to executive functioning. An increasing focus of interest in the study of children and adolescents with ADHD is their difficulty with executive functioning tasks, such as inhibiting behavior when necessary, use of working memory, and effective planning (Jacobson & others, 2011; Rinsky & Hinshaw, 2011; Van De Voorde & others, 2011). Researchers also have found deficits in theory of mind in children with ADHD (Buhler & others, 2011; Shuai, Chan, & Wang, 2011).

Adjustment and optimal development also are difficult for children who have ADHD, so it is important that the diagnosis be accurate. Children diagnosed with ADHD have an increased risk of school dropout, adolescent pregnancy, substance use problems, and antisocial behavior (Chang, Lichtenstein, & Larsson, 2012; Von Polier, Vioet, & Herpertz-Dahlmann, 2012).

Stimulant medication such as Ritalin or Adderall (which has fewer side effects than Ritalin) is effective in improving the attention of many children with ADHD, but it usually does not improve their attention to the same level as children who do not have ADHD (Sclar & others, 2012). A meta-analysis concluded that behavior management treatments are effective in reducing the severity of ADHD (Fabiano & others, 2009). Researchers have often found that a combination of medication (such as Ritalin) and behavior management tends to improve the behavior of children with ADHD better than medication alone or behavior management alone, although this is not true in all cases (Parens & Johnston, 2009).

Recently, mindfulness training has been given to adolescents with ADHD. In a recent study, 11- to 15-year-old adolescents with ADHD were given 8 weeks of mindfulness training (van de Weijer-Bergsma & others, 2012). Immediately after and 8 weeks following the training, the adolescents' attention improved and they engaged in fewer behavioral problems, although at 16 weeks post-training the effects had waned.

Emotional and Behavioral Disorders
Most children have minor emotional difficulties at some point during their school years. A small percentage have problems so serious and persistent that they are classified as having an emotional or a behavioral disorder (Mash & Wolf, 2013).

Emotional and behavioral disorders consist of serious, persistent problems that involve relationships, aggression, depression, and fears associated with personal or school matters, as well as other inappropriate socioemotional characteristics. Approximately 8 percent of children who have a disability and require an individualized education program (discussed later in this chapter) fall into this classification. Boys are three times as likely as girls to have these disorders.

Autism Spectrum Disorders
Autism spectrum disorders (ASD), also called pervasive developmental disorders, range from the severe disorder labeled autistic disorder to the milder disorder called Asperger syndrome. Autism spectrum disorders are characterized by problems in social interaction, problems in verbal and nonverbal communication, and repetitive behaviors (Hall, 2013). Children with these disorders may also show atypical responses to sensory experiences (National Institute of Mental Health, 2011). Autism spectrum disorders often can be detected in children as young as 1 to 3 years of age.

Recent estimates of autism spectrum disorders indicate that they are increasing in occurrence or are increasingly being detected and labeled (Neal, 2009). Once thought to affect only 1 in 2,500 individuals, autism spectrum disorders were estimated to affect 1 in 88 children in 2008 (Centers for Disease Control & Prevention, 2012). In the most recent survey, autism spectrum disorders were identified five times more often in boys than in girls. Today's estimates suggest that they occur in about 1 in 150 individuals (Centers for Disease Control and Prevention, 2009).

Autistic disorder is a severe developmental autism spectrum disorder that has its onset in the first three years of life and includes deficiencies in social relationships, abnormalities in communication, and restricted, repetitive, and stereotyped patterns of behavior.

Asperger syndrome is a relatively mild autism spectrum disorder in which the child has relatively good verbal ability, milder nonverbal language problems, and a restricted range of interests and relationships (Soares & Patel, 2012). Children with Asperger syndrome often engage in obsessive, repetitive routines and preoccupations with a particular subject. For example, a child may be obsessed with baseball scores or railroad timetables.

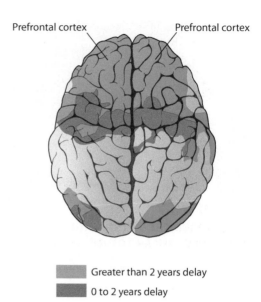

Prefrontal cortex   Prefrontal cortex

Greater than 2 years delay
0 to 2 years delay

FIGURE 16.6
REGIONS OF THE BRAIN IN WHICH CHILDREN WITH ADHD HAD A DELAYED PEAK IN THE THICKNESS OF THE CEREBRAL CORTEX. *Note:* The greatest delays occurred in the prefrontal cortex.

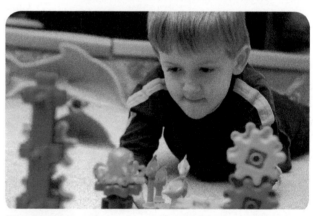

What characterizes autism spectrum disorders?

emotional and behavioral disorders Serious, persistent problems that involve relationships, aggression, depression, fears associated with personal or school matters, as well as other inappropriate socioemotional characteristics.

autism spectrum disorders (ASDs) Also called pervasive developmental disorders, they range from the severe disorder labeled autistic disorder to the milder disorder called Asperger syndrome. Children with these disorders are characterized by problems in social interaction, verbal and nonverbal communication, and repetitive behaviors.

autistic disorder A severe developmental autism spectrum disorder that has its onset in the first three years of life and includes deficiencies in social relationships; abnormalities in communication; and restricted, repetitive, and stereotyped patterns of behavior.

Asperger syndrome A relatively mild autism spectrum disorder in which the child has relatively good verbal skills, milder nonverbal language problems, and a restricted range of interests and relationships.

FIGURE **16.7**

A SCENE FROM THE DVD ANIMATIONS USED IN A STUDY BY BARON-COHEN AND OTHERS (2007). *What did they do to improve autistic children's ability to read facial expressions?*
© Crown copyright MMVI, www.thetransporters.com, courtesy of Changing Media Development.

What causes the autism spectrum disorders? The current consensus is that autism is a brain dysfunction involving abnormalities in brain structure and neurotransmitters (Toma & others, 2012). Recently, interest has focused on a lack of connectivity between brain regions as a key factor in autism (Just & others, 2012; Philip & others, 2012). Genetic factors likely play a role in the development of the autism spectrum disorders (Yates, 2013). One study revealed that mutations—missing or duplicated pieces of DNA—on chromosome 16 can raise a child's risk of developing autism 100-fold (Weiss & others, 2008). There is no evidence that family socialization causes autism. Intellectual disability is present in some children with autism, while others show average or above-average intelligence (Hoekstra & others, 2010).

It is estimated that boys are five times as likely as girls to have autism spectrum disorders (Centers for Disease Control and Prevention, 2012). Expanding on autism's male linkage, Simon Baron-Cohen (2008, 2011) recently argued that autism reflects an extreme male brain, especially indicative of males' lesser ability to show empathy and read facial expressions and gestures. In an attempt to improve these skills in 4- to 8-year-old autistic boys, Baron-Cohen and his colleagues (2007) produced a number of animations on a DVD in which faces showing different emotions are placed on toy trains and tractor characters in a boy's bedroom (see Figure 16.7). (See www.thetransporters.com for a look at a number of the facial expression animations in addition to the one shown in Figure 16.7.) After the autistic children watched the animations 15 minutes every weekday for one month, their ability to recognize real faces in a different context equaled that of children without autism.

Children with autism benefit from a well-structured classroom, individualized instruction, and small-group instruction. Behavior modification techniques are sometimes effective in helping autistic children learn (Iovannone, 2013). A recent research review concluded that when these behavior modifications are intensely provided and used early in the autistic child's life, they are more effective (Howlin, Magiati, & Charman, 2009).

EDUCATIONAL ISSUES

Until the 1970s most U.S. public schools either refused enrollment to children with disabilities or inadequately served them. This changed in 1975, when Public Law 94-142, the Education for All Handicapped Children Act, required that all students with disabilities be given a free, appropriate public education. In 1990, Public Law 94-142 was recast as the Individuals with Disabilities Education Act (IDEA). IDEA was amended in 1997 and then reauthorized in 2004 and renamed the Individuals with Disabilities Education Improvement Act.

IDEA spells out broad mandates for services to children with disabilities of all kinds (Turnbull & others, 2013; Yudof & others, 2012). These services include evaluation and eligibility determination, appropriate education and an individualized education program (IEP), and education in the least restrictive environment (LRE).

An **individualized education program (IEP)** is a written statement that spells out a program that is specifically tailored for the student with a disability. The **least restrictive environment (LRE)** is a setting that is as similar as possible to a classroom in which children who do not have a disability are educated. This provision of the IDEA has given a legal basis to efforts to educate children with a disability in regular classrooms. The term **inclusion** describes educating a child with special educational needs full-time in the regular classroom (Boyle & Provost, 2012; Smith & others, 2012). Figure 16.8 indicates that in a recent school year slightly more than 50 percent of U.S. students with a disability spent more than 80 percent of their school day in a general classroom.

Many legal changes regarding children with disabilities have had extremely positive effects (Friend & Bursuck, 2012; McLeskey, Rosenberg, & Westling, 2013). Compared with several decades ago, far more children today are receiving competent, specialized services. For many children, inclusion in the regular classroom, with modifications or supplemental services, is appropriate. However, some leading experts on special education argue that in some cases the

Increasingly, children with disabilities are being taught in the regular classroom, as is this child with a mild intellectual disability.

individualized education program (IEP) A written statement that spells out a program tailored to the needs of a child with a disability.

least restrictive environment (LRE) The concept that a child with a disability must be educated in a setting that is similar to classrooms in which children without a disability are educated.

inclusion Educating a child with special educational needs full-time in the regular classroom.

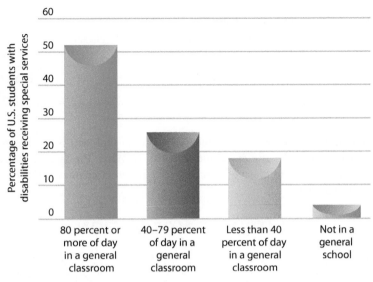

FIGURE **16.8**

PERCENTAGE OF U.S. STUDENTS WITH DISABILITIES 6 TO 21 YEARS OF AGE RECEIVING SPECIAL SERVICES IN THE GENERAL CLASSROOM.
Note: Data for 2004–2005 school year, National Center for Education Statistics, 2007.

effort to educate children with disabilities in the regular classroom has become too extreme. For example, James Kauffman and his colleagues (Kauffman, McGee, & Brigham, 2004) state that inclusion too often has meant making accommodations in the regular classroom that do not always benefit children with disabilities. They advocate a more individualized approach that does not always involve full inclusion but allows options such as special education outside the regular classroom. Kauffman and his colleagues (2004, p. 620) acknowledge that children with disabilities "do need the services of specially trained professionals" and "do sometimes need altered curricula or adaptations to make their learning possible." However, "we sell students with disabilities short when we pretend that they are not different from typical students. We make the same error when we pretend that they must not be expected to put forth extra effort if they are to learn to do some things—or learn to do something in a different way." Like general education, special education should challenge students with disabilities "to become all they can be."

Review *Connect* Reflect

 LG2 Characterize children with disabilities and their education.

Review

- Who are children with disabilities? What characterizes children with learning disabilities? How would you describe children with attention deficit hyperactivity disorder? What are emotional and behavioral disorders? What are autism spectrum disorders, what are they caused by, and how are they characterized?
- What are some issues involved in educating children with disabilities?

Connect

- In this section, you learned that exposure to cigarette smoke during prenatal development may be linked to ADHD. In Chapter 3, what name was used for agents that can potentially cause a birth defect or negatively alter cognitive and behavioral outcomes?

Reflect *Your Own Personal Journey of Life*

- Think about your own schooling and how children with learning disabilities or ADHD either were or were not diagnosed. Were you aware of such individuals in your classes? Were they helped by specialists? You may know one or more individuals with a learning disability or ADHD. Ask them about their educational experiences and whether they think schools could have done a better job of helping them.

| Extrinsic and Intrinsic Motivation | Cognitive Processes | Ethnicity and Culture |

Life is a gift . . . Accept it.

Life is an adventure . . . Dare it.

Life is a mystery . . . Unfold it.

Life is a struggle . . . Face it.

Life is a puzzle . . . Solve it.

Life is an opportunity . . . Take it.

Life is a mission . . . Fulfill it.

Life is a goal . . . Achieve it.

—AUTHOR UNKNOWN

In any classroom, no matter who the teacher is or what approach is used, some children achieve more than others (Schunk & Zimmerman, 2013). Why? The reasons for variations in achievement include motivation, expectations, goals, and other characteristics of the child as well as sociocultural contexts.

EXTRINSIC AND INTRINSIC MOTIVATION

Extrinsic motivation involves external incentives such as rewards and punishments. **Intrinsic motivation** is based on internal factors such as self-determination, curiosity, challenge, and effort. Cognitive approaches stress the importance of intrinsic motivation in achievement. Some students study hard because they want to make good grades or avoid parental disapproval (extrinsic motivation). Other students work hard because they are internally motivated to achieve high standards in their work (intrinsic motivation).

Current evidence strongly favors establishing a classroom climate in which students are intrinsically motivated to learn (Eccles & Roeser, 2011, 2013; Weinstein, Deci, & Ryan, 2011). For example, a study of third- through eighth-grade students found that intrinsic motivation was positively linked with grades and standardized test scores, whereas extrinsic motivation was negatively related to achievement outcomes (Lepper, Corpus, & Iyengar, 2005). A longitudinal study revealed that parental intrinsic/extrinsic motivational practices were linked to children's motivation (Gottfried & others, 2009). In this study, children had higher intrinsic motivation in math and science from 9 to 17 years of age when their parents engaged in task-intrinsic practices (encouraging children's pleasure and engagement in learning) than when their parents engaged in task-extrinsic practices (providing external rewards and consequences contingent on children's performance).

Students are more motivated to learn when they are given choices, become absorbed in challenges that match their skills, and receive rewards that have informational value but are not used for control. Praise also can enhance students' intrinsic motivation. To see why these things are so, let's first explore three perspectives on intrinsic motivation: (1) self-determination and personal choice, (2) interest, and (3) cognitive engagement and self-responsibility. Then we'll discuss how external rewards can either enhance or undermine intrinsic motivation. Finally, we will offer some concluding thoughts about intrinsic and extrinsic motivation.

Self-Determination and Personal Choice
One view of intrinsic motivation emphasizes self-determination (Deci & Ryan, 2000; Ryan & Deci, 2009; Mclellan & Remedios, 2011; Weinstein, Deci, & Ryan, 2011). In this view, students want to believe that they are doing something because of their own will, not because of external success or rewards (Vansteenkiste & others, 2009). The architects of self-determination theory, Richard Ryan and Edward Deci (2009), refer to teachers who create circumstances for students to engage in self-determination as *autonomy-supportive teachers.* A recent study of 34 high school classrooms found that students who perceived their classrooms as allowing and encouraging autonomy in the first several weeks of the semester increased their engagement throughout the course (Hafen & others, 2012).

Researchers have found that students' internal motivation and intrinsic interest in school tasks increase when students have some choice and are given opportunities to take personal responsibility for their learning (Anderman, 2012).

Cognitive Engagement and Self-Responsibility
Another variation on intrinsic motivation emphasizes the importance of creating learning environments that encourage students to become cognitively engaged and to take responsibility for their learning (Appleton, 2012; Blumenfeld, Kempler, & Krajcik, 2006). The goal is to get students to become motivated

These students were given an opportunity to write and perform their own play. These kinds of self-determining opportunities can enhance students' motivation to achieve.

extrinsic motivation Response to external incentives such as rewards and punishments.

intrinsic motivation Internal motivational factors such as self-determination, curiosity, challenge, and effort.

Calvin and Hobbes   by Bill Watterson

to expend the effort to persist and master ideas rather than simply doing enough work to just get by and make passing grades. Especially important in encouraging students to become cognitively engaged and responsible for their learning is to embed subject matter content and skills learning within meaningful contexts, especially real-world situations that mesh with students' interests (Eccles & Roeser, 2011, 2013).

Some Final Thoughts About Intrinsic and Extrinsic Motivation   It is important for parents and teachers to encourage students to become intrinsically motivated and to create learning environments that promote students' cognitive engagement and self-responsibility for learning (Blumenfeld, Marx, & Harris, 2006; Townsend, 2011). That said, the real world is not just one of intrinsic motivation, and too often intrinsic and extrinsic motivation have been pitted against each other as polar opposites. In many aspects of students' lives, both intrinsic and extrinsic motivation are at work (Cameron & Pierce, 2008; Schunk, 2012). Keep in mind, though, that many psychologists recommend that extrinsic motivation by itself is not a good strategy.

COGNITIVE PROCESSES

Our discussion of extrinsic and intrinsic motivation sets the stage for introducing other cognitive processes involved in motivating students to learn. As we explore these additional cognitive processes, notice how intrinsic and extrinsic motivation continue to be important. The processes are (1) sustained attention, effort, and task persistence; (2) mastery motivation and mindset; (3) self-efficacy; (4) expectations; (5) goal setting, planning, and self-monitoring; and (6) purpose.

Sustained Attention, Effort, and Task Persistence   Of course, it is important not only to perceive that effort is an important aspect of achieving, but also to actually engage in sustained attention, effort, and task persistence in school, work, and a career (Padilla-Walker & others, 2013). Recall from Chapter 3 that *sustained attention* is the ability to maintain attention to a selected stimulus for a prolonged period of time. Sustained attention requires effort and as individuals develop through adolescence, school tasks, projects, and work become more complex and require longer periods of sustained attention, effort, and task persistence than in childhood.

Might the extent to which adolescents persist at tasks be linked to how successful they are in a career as an adult? A recent study revealed that task persistence at 13 years of age was related to occupational success in middle age (Andersson & Bergman, 2011).

Mastery Motivation and Mindset   Becoming cognitively engaged and self-motivated to improve are reflected in adolescents with a mastery motivation. These children also have a growth mindset—a belief that they can produce positive outcomes if they put forth the effort.

FIGURE 16.9

BEHAVIORS THAT SUGGEST A HELPLESS ORIENTATION

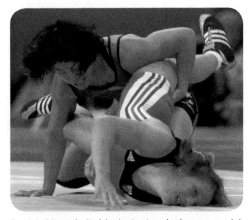

Patricia Miranda (in blue) winning the bronze medal in the 2004 Olympics. *What characterizes her growth mindset and how is it different from someone with a fixed mindset?*

mastery motivation An approach to achievement in which one is task oriented, focusing on learning strategies and the achievement process rather than ability or the outcome.

helpless orientation An orientation in which one seems trapped by the experience of difficulty and attributes one's difficulty to a lack of ability.

performance orientation An orientation in which one focuses on winning rather than achievement outcomes, and happiness is thought to result from winning.

mindset Dweck's concept referring to the cognitive view individuals develop for themselves; individuals have either a fixed or growth mindset.

Mastery Motivation   Developmental psychologists Valanne Henderson and Carol Dweck (1990) have found that children often show two distinct responses to difficult or challenging circumstances. Children who display **mastery motivation** are task oriented; they concentrate on learning strategies and the process of achievement rather than their ability or the outcome. Those with a **helpless orientation** seem trapped by the experience of difficulty, and they attribute their difficulty to lack of ability. They frequently say such things as "I'm not very good at this," even though they might earlier have demonstrated their ability through many successes. And, once they view their behavior as failure, they often feel anxious, and their performance worsens even further. Figure 16.9 describes some behaviors that might reflect helplessness (Stipek, 2002).

In contrast, mastery-oriented children often instruct themselves to pay attention, to think carefully, and to remember strategies that have worked for them in previous situations. They frequently report feeling challenged and excited by difficult tasks, rather than being threatened by them (Anderman, 2012; Dweck, 2013).

Another issue in motivation involves whether to adopt a mastery or a performance orientation. Children with a **performance orientation** are focused on winning, rather than on achievement outcome, and believe that happiness results from winning. Does this mean that mastery-oriented children do not like to win and that performance-oriented children are not motivated to experience the self-efficacy that comes from being able to take credit for one's accomplishments? No. A matter of emphasis or degree is involved, though. For mastery-oriented individuals, winning isn't everything; for performance-oriented individuals, skill development and self-efficacy take a back seat to winning. One recent study of seventh-grade students found that girls were more likely than boys to have mastery rather than performance goals in their approach to math achievement (Kenney-Benson & others, 2006).

A final point needs to be made about mastery and performance goals: They are not always mutually exclusive. Students can be both mastery and performance oriented, and researchers have found that mastery goals combined with performance goals often enhance students' success (Schunk, 2012).

Mindset   Carol Dweck's (2006, 2007, 2013) most recent analysis of motivation for achievement stresses the importance of children developing a **mindset,** which she defines as the cognitive view individuals develop for themselves. She concludes that individuals have one of two mindsets: (1) *fixed mindset,* in which they believe that their qualities are carved in stone and cannot change; or (2) *growth mindset,* in which they believe their qualities can change and improve through their effort. A fixed mindset is similar to a helpless orientation; a growth mindset is much like having mastery motivation (Dweck, 2007, 2013).

In her book *Mindset,* Dweck (2006) argued that individuals' mindsets influence whether they will be optimistic or pessimistic, shape their goals and how hard they will strive to reach those goals, and affect many aspects of their lives, including achievement and success in school and sports. Dweck says that mindsets begin to be shaped as children interact with parents, teachers, and coaches, who themselves have either a fixed mindset or a growth mindset. She described the growth mindset of Patricia Miranda:

> [She] was a chubby, unathletic school kid who wanted to wrestle. After a bad beating on the mat, she was told, "You're a joke." First she cried, then she felt: "That really set my resolve. . . . I had to keep going and had to know if effort and focus and belief and training could somehow legitimize me as a wrestler." Where did she get this resolve?
>
> Miranda was raised in a life devoid of challenge. But when her mother died of an aneurysm at age forty, ten-year-old Miranda . . . [thought] "If you only go through life doing stuff that's easy, shame on you." So when wrestling presented a challenge, she was ready to take it on. Her effort paid off. At twenty-four, Miranda was having the last laugh. She won a spot on the U.S. Olympic team and came home from Athens with a bronze medal. And what was next? Yale Law School. People urged her to stay where she was already on top, but Miranda felt it was more exciting to start at the bottom again and see what she could grow into this time. (Dweck, 2006, pp. 22–23)

Related to her emphasis on encouraging students to develop a growth mindset, Dweck and her colleagues (Blackwell & Dweck, 2008; Blackwell, Trzesniewski, & Dweck, 2007; Dweck, 2013; Dweck & Master, 2009) have recently incorporated information about the brain's plasticity into their effort to improve students' motivation to achieve and succeed. In one study, they assigned two groups of students to eight sessions of either (1) study skills instruction or (2) study skills instruction plus information about the importance of developing a growth mindset (called

www.brainology.us

FIGURE 16.10

DWECK'S BRAINOLOGY PROGRAM. A screen from Carol Dweck's Brainology program, which is designed to cultivate children's growth mindset.

incremental theory in the research) (Blackwell & others, 2007). One of the exercises in the growth mindset group was titled, "You Can Grow Your Brain," which emphasized that the brain is like a muscle that can change and grow as it gets exercise and develops new connections. Students were informed that the more you challenge your brain to learn, the more your brain cells grow. Both groups had a pattern of declining math scores prior to the intervention. Following the intervention, the group who only received the study skills instruction continued to have declining scores, but the group that received the combination of study skills instruction plus the growth mindset information reversed the downward trend and improved their math achievement.

In other work, Dweck has been creating a computer-based workshop, "Brainology," to teach students that their intelligence can change (Blackwell & Dweck, 2008; Dweck, 2012). Students experience six modules about how the brain works and how they can make their brains improve (see Figure 16.10). After the program was tested in 20 New York City schools, students strongly endorsed the value of the computer-based brain modules. Said one student, "I will try harder because I know that the more you try the more your brain knows" (Dweck & Master, 2009, p. 137).

Dweck and her colleagues (Good, Rattan, & Dweck, 2012) also recently have found that a growth mindset can prevent negative stereotypes from undermining achievement. For example, they found that believing math ability can be learned protected women from negative gender stereotyping about math. And other research recently indicated that willpower is a virtually unlimited mindset that predicts how long people will work and resist temptations during stressful circumstances (Dweck, 2012; Job, Dweck, & Walton, 2010; Miller & others, 2012).

Self-Efficacy Like having a growth mindset, **self-efficacy**—the belief that one can master a situation and produce favorable outcomes—is an important cognitive view for children to develop. Albert Bandura (1997, 2000, 2004, 2008, 2009, 2010a, 2012), whose social cognitive theory we described in Chapter 1, argues that self-efficacy is a critical factor in whether or not children achieve. Self-efficacy has much in common with mastery motivation. Self-efficacy is the belief that "I can"; helplessness is the belief that "I cannot" (Stipek, 2002). Children with high self-efficacy agree with statements such as "I know that I will be able to learn the material in this class" and "I expect to be able to do well at this activity."

Dale Schunk (2008, 2012) has applied the concept of self-efficacy to many aspects of students' achievement. In his view, self-efficacy influences a student's choice of activities. Students with low self-efficacy for learning might avoid many learning tasks, especially those that are challenging. In contrast, their high-self-efficacy counterparts eagerly work at learning tasks. High-self-efficacy students are more likely to expend effort and persist longer at a learning task than low-self-efficacy students. High-self-efficacy students are more likely to have confidence in exploring challenging career options (Betz, 2004).

Children's and adolescents' development is influenced by their parents' self-efficacy. A recent study revealed a number of positive developmental outcomes, including more daily opportunities for optimal functioning, better peer relations, and fewer problems, for children and adolescents whose parents had high self-efficacy (Steca & others, 2011).

developmental **connection**

Social Cognitive Theory

Social cognitive theory holds that behavior, environment, and person/cognitive factors are the key influences on development. Chapter 1, pp. 25

They can because they think they can.

—**VIRGIL**

Roman Poet, 1st Century BC

self-efficacy The belief that one can master a situation and produce favorable outcomes.

Expectations   Children's motivation, and likely their performance, are influenced by the expectations that their parents, teachers, and other adults have for their achievement. Children benefit when both parents and teachers have high expectations for them and provide the necessary support for them to meet those expectations. An especially important factor in the lower achievement of students from low-income families is lack of adequate resources, such as an up-to-date computer in the home (or even any computer at all) to support students' learning (Schunk, Pintrich, & Meece, 2008).

Teachers' expectations influence students' motivation and performance (Eccles & Roeser, 2011, 2013; Rubie-Davies, 2011). "When teachers hold high generalized expectations for student achievement and students perceive these expectations, students achieve more, experience a greater sense of self-esteem and competence as learners, and resist involvement in problem behaviors both during childhood and adolescence" (Wigfield & others, 2006, p. 976). In an observational study of 12 classrooms, teachers with high expectations spent more time providing a framework for students' learning, asked higher-level questions, and were more effective in managing students' behavior than teachers with average and low expectations (Rubie-Davies, 2007).

In thinking about teachers' expectations, it also is important to examine these expectations in concert with parents' expectations. For example, a recent study revealed that mothers' and teachers' high expectations had a positive effect on urban youths' achievement outcomes, and further that mothers' high achievement expectations for their youth had a buffering effect in the face of low teacher expectations (Benner & Mistry, 2007). Interestingly, in another recent study, teachers' positive expectations for students' achievement tended to protect students from the negative influence of low parental expectations (Wood, Kaplan, & McLoyd, 2007).

Teachers often have more positive expectations for high-ability than for low-ability students, and these expectations are likely to influence their behavior toward them. For example, teachers require high-ability students to work harder, wait longer for them to respond to questions, respond to them with more information and in a more elaborate fashion, criticize them less often, praise them more often, are more friendly to them, call on them more often, seat them closer to the teacher's desk, and are more likely to give them the benefit of the doubt on close calls in grading than they are for students with low ability (Brophy, 2004). An important strategy for teachers is to monitor their expectations and be sure to have positive expectations for students with low abilities. Fortunately, researchers have found that with support teachers can adapt and raise their expectations for students with low abilities (National Research Council, 2004).

Goal Setting, Planning, and Self-Monitoring

Goal setting, planning, and self-monitoring are important aspects of children's and adolescents' achievement (Anderman, 2012; Eccles & Roeser, 2013; Urdan, 2010). Researchers have found that self-efficacy and achievement improve when individuals set goals that are specific, proximal, and challenging (Bandura, 1997). An example of a nonspecific, fuzzy goal is "I want to be successful." A more concrete, specific goal is "I want to make the honor roll at the end of this semester."

Individuals can set both long-term (distal) and short-term (proximal) goals. It is okay to set some long-term goals, such as "I want to graduate from high school" or "I want to go to college," but it also is important to create short-term goals, which are steps along the way. "Getting an A on the next math test" is an example of a short-term, proximal goal. So is "Doing all of my homework by 4 p.m. Sunday."

Another good strategy is to set challenging goals. A challenging goal is a commitment to self-improvement. Strong interest and involvement in activities is sparked by challenges. Goals that are easy to reach generate little interest or effort. However, goals should be optimally matched to the adolescent's skill level. If goals are unrealistically high, the result will be repeated failures that lower self-efficacy.

Yet another good strategy is to develop personal goals about desired and undesired future circumstances (Wigfield & Cambria, 2010). Personal goals can be a key aspect of an individual's motivation for coping and dealing with life's challenges and opportunities (Maehr & Zusho, 2009).

It is not enough to simply set goals. It also is important to plan how to reach the goals (Wigfield, Klauda, & Cambria, 2011). Being a good planner means managing time effectively, setting priorities, and being organized.

Researchers have found that high-achieving individuals often are self-regulatory learners (Schunk, 2012; Winne, 2011). For example, high-achieving students self-monitor their learning

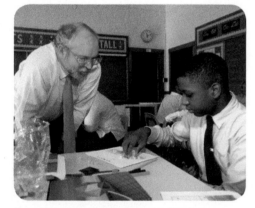

A student and teacher at Langston Hughes Elementary School in Chicago, a school whose teachers have high expectations for students. *How do teachers' expectations influence students' achievement?*

more and systematically evaluate their progress toward a goal more than low-achieving students do. When parents and teachers encourage students to self-monitor their learning, they give them the message that they are responsible for their own behavior and that learning requires their active, dedicated participation (Zimmerman, Bonner, & Kovach, 1996).

One type of self-regulation is *intentional self-regulation,* which involves selecting goals or outcomes, optimizing the means to achieve desired outcomes, and compensating for setbacks along the path to goal achievement (Gestsdottir & others, 2009). A recent study found that intentional self-regulation was especially beneficial to young adolescents from low-income backgrounds (Urban, Lewin-Bizan, & Lerner, 2010). In this study, these high self-regulating adolescents were more likely to seek out extracurricular activities, which resulted in more positive developmental outcomes such as academic achievement. Selecting goals or outcomes was assessed by items such as, "When I decide upon a goal, I stick to it"; optimizing the means to achieve desired outcomes was assessed by items such as, "I think exactly about how I can best realize my plans"; and compensating for setbacks was assessed by items such as, "When things don't work the way they used to, I look for other ways to achieve them."

Barry Zimmerman and his colleagues (Zimmerman, 2002, 2012; Zimmerman & Kitsantas, 1997; Zimmerman & Labuhn, 2012) have developed a model of self-regulation in achievement contexts that has three phrases:

- *Forethought.* Adolescents assess task demands, set goals, and estimate their ability to reach the goals.
- *Performance.* Adolescents create self-regulating strategies such as managing time, attentional focusing, help seeking, and metacognition.
- *Self-Reflection.* Adolescents evaluate their performance, including attributions about factors that affected the outcome and how satisfied they are with their behavior.

In addition to planning and self-regulation/monitoring, delaying gratification is an important aspect of reaching goals—especially long-term goals (Cheng, Shein, & Chiou, 2012; Schlam & others, 2013). Delayed gratification involves postponing immediate rewards in order to attain a larger, more valuable reward at a later point in time. While adolescents may find it more appealing to hang out with friends today than to work on a project that is due for a class assignment later in the week, their decision not to delay gratification can have negative consequences for their academic achievement.

Purpose   In Chapter 11, "The Self and Identity," we discussed William Damon's (2008) ideas on the importance of purpose in identity development. Here we explore how purpose is a missing ingredient in many adolescents' and emerging adults' achievement.

For Damon, *purpose* is an intention to accomplish something meaningful to oneself and to contribute something to the world beyond the self. Finding purpose involves answering questions such as "*Why* am I doing this? *Why* does it matter? *Why* is it important for me and the world beyond me? *Why* do I strive to accomplish this end?" (Damon, 2008, pp. 33–34).

In interviews with 12- to 22-year-olds, Damon found that only about 20 percent had a clear vision of where they wanted to go in life, what they wanted to achieve, and why. The largest percentage—about 60 percent—had engaged in some potentially purposeful activities, such as service learning or fruitful discussions with a career counselor, but they still did not have a real commitment or any reasonable plans for reaching their goals. And slightly more than 20 percent expressed no aspirations and in some instances said they didn't see any reason to have aspirations.

Damon concludes that most teachers and parents communicate the importance of goals such as studying hard and getting good grades, but rarely discuss what the goals might lead to—the purpose for studying

developmental **connection**

Identity

William Damon (2008) concludes that too many of today's youth aren't moving toward any identity resolution. Chapter 11, p. 327

Hari Prabhakar (*in rear*) at a screening camp in India that he created as part of his Tribal India Health Foundation. Hari Prabhakar reflects William Damon's concept of finding a path to purpose. Hari's ambition is to become an international health expert. Hari graduated from Johns Hopkins University in 2006 with a double major in public health and writing. A top student (3.9 GPA), he took the initiative to pursue a number of activities outside the classroom, in the health field. As he made the transition from high school to college, Hari created the Tribal India Health Foundation (www.tihf.org), which provides assistance in bringing low-cost health care to rural areas in India. Juggling his roles as a student and as the foundation's director, Hari spent about 15 hours a week leading Tribal India Health throughout his four undergraduate years.

In describing his work, Hari said (Johns Hopkins University, 2006):

I have found it very challenging to coordinate the international operation. . . . It takes a lot of work, and there's not a lot of free time. But it's worth it when I visit our patients and see how they and the community are getting better.

[*Sources:* Johns Hopkins University (2006); Prabhakar (2007).]

UCLA educational psychologist Sandra Graham is shown talking with adolescent boys about motivation. She has conducted a number of studies which reveal that middle-socioeconomic-status African American students—like their White counterparts—have high achievement expectations and attribute success to internal factors such as effort rather than external factors such as luck.

hard and getting good grades. Damon emphasizes that too often students focus only on short-term goals without exploring the big, long-term picture of what they want to do in life. The following interview questions that Damon (2008, p. 135) has used in his research are good springboards for getting students to reflect on their purpose:

What's most important to you in your life?

Why do you care about those things?

Do you have any long-term goals?

Why are these goals important to you?

What does it mean to have a good life?

What does it mean to be a good person?

If you were looking back on your life now, how would you like to be remembered?

ETHNICITY AND CULTURE

Americans have been especially concerned about two questions related to ethnicity and culture. First, does their ethnicity deter ethnic minority children from high achievement in school? And second, is there something about American culture that accounts for the poor performance of U.S. children in math and science?

Ethnicity   The diversity that exists among ethnic minority children and adolescents is evident in their achievement (Cooper, 2011; Graham, 2011). For example, many Asian American students have a strong academic achievement orientation, but some do not.

Sandra Graham (1986, 1990) has conducted a number of studies that reveal stronger differences in achievement related to socioeconomic status than ethnicity. She is struck by how consistently middle-income African American students, like their White middle-income counterparts, have high achievement expectations and understand that failure is usually due to a lack of effort.

An especially important factor in the lower achievement of students from low-income families is lack of adequate resources, such as an up-to-date computer, or even a computer at all, in the home to support students' learning (Schunk, Pintrich, & Meece, 2008). A recent longitudinal study revealed that African American children or children from low-income families benefited more than children from higher-income families when they did homework more frequently, had Internet access at home, and had a community library card (Xia, 2010).

A special challenge for many ethnic minority students is dealing with negative stereotypes and discrimination. Many ethnic minority students living in poverty must also deal with conflict between the values of their neighborhood and those of the majority culture, a lack of high-achieving role models, and as discussed earlier, poor schools (McLoyd & others, 2009). Even students who are motivated to learn and achieve may find it difficult to perform effectively in such contexts.

Cross-Cultural Comparisons   Since the early 1990s, the poor performance of American children and adolescents in math and science has become well publicized. In a recent large-scale international comparison of 15-year-olds in 65 countries, the top five scores in reading, math, and science were held by Asian countries (China–Shanghai, South Korea, Singapore, China–Hong Kong, and Chinese Taipei), with the exception of 15-year-olds from Finland being third in reading and second in science (OECD, 2010). China–Shanghai 15-year-olds held down first place among the 65 countries in all three academic areas. In this study, U.S. 15-year-olds placed 17th in reading, 32nd in math, and 23rd in science. Figure 16.11 shows international comparisons of reading and math scores in this study.

Why do American students fare so poorly in mathematics? To learn about one researcher's conclusions on the subject, read *Connecting Through Research.*

Reading			Mathematics		
1. China: Shanghai	556		1. China: Shanghai	600	
2. Korea	539		2. Singapore	562	
3. Finland	536		3. China: Hong Kong	555	
4. China: Hong Kong	533		4. Korea	546	
5. Singapore	526		5. Chinese Taipei	543	
6. Canada	524		6. Finland	541	
7. New Zealand	521		7. Liechtenstein	536	
8. Japan	520		8. Switzerland	534	
9. Australia	515		9. Japan	529	
10. Netherlands	508		10. Canada	527	
11. Belgium	506		11. Netherlands	526	
12. Norway	503		12. China: Macao	525	
13. Estonia	501		13. New Zealand	519	
14. Switzerland	501		14. Belgium	515	
15. Iceland	500		15. Australia	514	
16. Poland	500		16. Germany	513	
17. United States	**500**		17. Estonia	512	
18. Liechtenstein	499		18. Iceland	507	
19. Germany	497		19. Denmark	503	
20. Sweden	497		20. Slovenia	501	
21. France	496		21. Norway	498	
22. Ireland	496		22. France	497	
23. Chinese Taipei	495		23. Slovak Republic	497	
24. Denmark	495		24. Austria	496	
25. Hungary	494		25. OECD average	496	
26. United Kingdom	494		26. Poland	495	
27. OECD average	493		27. Sweden	494	
28. Portugal	489		28. Czech Republic	493	
29. China: Macao	487		29. United Kingdom	492	
30. Italy	486		30. Hungary	490	
31. Latvia	484		31. Luxembourg	489	
32. Greece	483		**32. United States**	**487**	

FIGURE **16.11**

INTERNATIONAL COMPARISON OF 15-YEAR-OLDS' READING AND MATH SCORES. Source: OECD (2010). *Strong performers and successful reformers in education: Lessons from PISA for the United States.* Paris, France: OECD.

What Are Some Factors that Influence Children's Math Achievement in Dif[...]

Harold Stevenson conducted research on children's learning for five decades. The research explored the reasons for the poor performance of American students. Stevenson and his colleagues (Stevenson, 1995; Stevenson & others, 1990) completed five cross-cultural comparisons of students in the United States, China, Taiwan, and Japan. In these studies, Asian students consistently outperformed American students. And, the longer the students were in school, the wider the gap became between Asian and American students—the lowest difference was in the first grade, the highest in the eleventh grade (the highest grade studied).

To learn more about the reasons for these large cross-cultural differences, Stevenson and his colleagues spent thousands of hours observing in classrooms, as well as interviewing and surveying teachers, students, and parents. They found that the Asian teachers spent more of their time teaching math than did the American teachers. For example, more than one-fourth of total classroom time in the first grade was spent on math instruction in Japan, compared with only one-tenth of the time in the U.S. first-grade classrooms. Also, the Asian students were in school an average of 240 days a year, compared with 178 days in the United States.

FIGURE [...]

MOTHERS' BELIEFS AB[...] FACTORS RESPONSIBLE FOR CHILDREN'S MATH ACHIEVEMENT IN THREE COUNTRIES. In one study, mothers in Japan and Taiwan were more likely to believe that their children's math achievement was due to effort rather than innate ability, while U.S. mothers were more likely to believe their children's math achievement was due to innate ability (Stevenson, Lee, & Stigler, 1986). If parents believe that their children's math achievement is due to innate ability and their children are not doing well in math, the implication is that they are less likely to think their children will benefit from putting forth more effort.

In addition, differences were found between the Asian and American parents. The American parents had much lower expectations for their children's education and achievement than did the Asian parents. Also, the American parents were more likely to state that their children's math achievement was due to innate ability; the Asian parents were more likely to say that their children's math achievement was the consequence of effort and training (see Figure 16.12). The Asian students were more likely to do math homework than were the American students, and the Asian parents were far more likely to help their children with their math homework than were the American parents (Chen & Stevenson, 1989).

As you'll recall from Chapter 14, Asian and Asian American parenting approaches have been characterized by some as an authoritarian style and by others as a "training" style. Those who endorse the training view note that it reflects the parents' concern and involvement in their children's lives and that the high academic achievement of their children may result from this training.

Other research by Eva Pomerantz and her colleagues (Pomerantz, Cheung, & Qin, 2012; Pomerantz, Kim, & Cheung, 2012) indicates that the more involved parents

Asian grade schools intersperse studying with frequent periods of activities. This approach helps children maintain their attention and likely makes learning more enjoyable. Shown here are Japanese fourth-graders making wearable masks. *What are some differences in the way children in many Asian countries are taught compared with children in the United States?*

(continued)

(continued)

are in children's learning, the higher the level of achievement children will attain. As indicated earlier, East Asian parents spend considerably more time helping their children with homework than do U.S. parents (Chen & Stevenson, 1989). The greater East Asian parental involvement in children's learning is present as early as the preschool years and continues in the elementary school years (Cheung & Pomerantz, 2012; Siegler & Mu, 2008). In East Asia, children's learning is considered to be a far greater responsibility of parents than in the United States (Pomerantz, Kim, & Cheung, 2012). However, a recent study revealed that when U.S. parents are more involved in their children's learning, the children's

achievement benefits (Cheung & Pomerantz, 2012). In this study, for both U.S. and Chinese children, the more parents were involved in their children's learning, the more motivated the children were to achieve in school for parent-oriented reasons, and this increased motivation was linked to enhanced self-regulated learning and higher grades.

What are some differences in the way children in many Asian countries are taught compared with children in the United States?

Review *Connect* Reflect

 LG3 Explain the development of achievement in children.

Review

- What are intrinsic and extrinsic motivation? How are they related to achievement?
- What role do mastery motivation and mindset play in children's achievement?
- What is self-efficacy, and how is it related to achievement? How are expectations involved in children's achievement? Why are goal setting, planning, and self-monitoring important in achievement? What is purpose and how is it involved in achieving?
- How do cultural, ethnic, and socioeconomic variations influence achievement?

Connect

- In this section, you learned about the importance of purpose in adolescents' and emerging adults' achievement. In Chapter 11, what did Damon identify as some of the possible negative outcomes of not having purpose?

Reflect *Your Own Personal Journey of Life*

- Think about several of your own past schoolmates who showed low motivation in school. Why do you think they behaved that way? What teaching strategies might have helped them?

reach your **learning goals**

Schools and Achievement

Exploring Children's Schooling

 LG1 Discuss approaches to schooling and development.

Contemporary Approaches to Student Learning and Assessment

- Contemporary approaches to student learning include direct instruction, which is a teacher-centered approach, and constructivist instruction, which is learner-centered. Some experts recommend that both a constructivist and direct instruction approach be used, depending on circumstances. Increased concern by the public and government in the United States has produced extensive state-mandated testing, which has both strengths and weaknesses and is controversial. The most visible example of the increased state-mandated testing is the No Child Left Behind federal legislation.

Early Childhood Education

- The child-centered kindergarten emphasizes the education of the whole child, paying particular attention to individual variation, the process of learning, and the importance of play in development. The Montessori approach is an increasingly popular early childhood education choice. Developmentally appropriate practice focuses on the typical patterns of children (age-appropriateness) and the uniqueness of each child (individual-appropriateness). Such practice contrasts with developmentally inappropriate practice, which relies on pencil-and-paper activities. The U.S. government has tried to break the poverty cycle with programs such as Head Start. Model programs have been shown to have positive effects on children who live in poverty. Controversy surrounds early childhood education curricula. On the one side are the child-centered, constructivist advocates, on the other are those who advocate an instructivist, academic approach. Another controversy focuses on whether universal preschool education should be implemented.

Elementary School

- Children take up the new role of student, interact, develop new relationships, and discover rich sources of new ideas in elementary school. A special concern is that early elementary school education proceeds too much on the basis of providing negative feedback to children.

Educating Adolescents

- The transition to middle or junior high school coincides with many social, familial, and individual changes in the adolescent's life, and this transition is often stressful. One source of stress is the move from the top-dog to the lowest position in school. Some critics argue that a major redesign of U.S. middle schools is needed. Critics say that U.S. high schools foster passivity and do not develop students' academic skills adequately. A number of strategies have been proposed for improving U.S. high schools, including higher expectations and better support. The overall high school dropout rate declined considerably in the last half of the twentieth century, but the dropout rates of Latino and Native American youth remain very high. Participation in extracurricular activities is associated with positive academic and psychological outcomes. Adolescents benefit from participating in a variety of high-quality extracurricular activities.

Socioeconomic Status and Ethnicity

- Children living in poverty face problems at home and at school that present barriers to learning. Neighborhoods are dangerous, and fear may be a way of life. Many schools' buildings are crumbling with age. Teachers are likely to encourage rote learning, and parents often don't set high educational standards. The school experiences of children from different ethnic groups vary considerably. Teachers often have low expectations for children of color. A number of strategies can be adopted to improve relationships with diverse others.

Children with Disabilities

 Characterize children with disabilities and their education.

The Scope of Disabilities

- Approximately 14 percent of U.S. children from 3 to 21 years of age receive special education or related services. A child with a learning disability has difficulty in learning that involves understanding or using spoken or written language, and the difficulty can appear in listening, thinking, reading, writing, and spelling. A learning disability also may involve difficulty in doing mathematics. To be classified as a learning disability, the learning problem is not primarily the result of visual, hearing, or motor disabilities; intellectual disability; emotional disorders; or due to environmental, cultural, or economic disadvantage. Dyslexia is a category of learning disabilities that involves a severe impairment in the ability to read and spell. Dysgraphia is a learning disability that involves difficulty in expressing thoughts in writing. Dyscalculia is a learning disability that involves difficulties in math computation.

Attention deficit hyperactivity disorder (ADHD) is a disability in which individuals consistently show problems in one or more of these areas: (1) inattention, (2) hyperactivity, and (3) impulsivity. ADHD has been increasingly diagnosed. Emotional and behavioral disorders consist of serious, persistent problems that involve relationships, aggression, depression, fears associated with personal or school matters, as well as other inappropriate socioemotional characteristics. Autism spectrum disorders (ASD), also called pervasive developmental disorders, range from autistic disorder, a severe developmental disorder, to Asperger syndrome, a relatively mild autism spectrum disorder. The current consensus is that autism is a brain dysfunction involving abnormalities in brain structure and neurotransmitters. Children with autism spectrum disorders are characterized by problems in social interaction, verbal and nonverbal communication, and repetitive behaviors.

Educational Issues

- In 1975, Public Law 94-142, the Education for All Handicapped Children Act, required that all children with disabilities be given a free, appropriate public education. This law was renamed the Individuals with Disabilities Education Act (IDEA) in 1990 and updated in 2004. IDEA includes requirements that children with disabilities receive an individualized education program (IEP), which is a written plan that spells out a program tailored to the child, and that children with disabilities be educated in the least restrictive environment (LRE), which is a setting that is as similar as possible to the one in which children without disabilities are educated. Inclusion means educating children with disabilities full-time in the regular classroom.

Achievement

LG3 Explain the development of achievement in children.

Extrinsic and Intrinsic Motivation

- Extrinsic motivation involves external incentives such as rewards and punishment. Intrinsic motivation is based on internal factors such as self-determination, curiosity, challenge, and effort. One view is that giving students some choice and providing opportunities for personal responsibility increase intrinsic motivation. It is important for teachers to create learning environments that encourage students to become cognitively engaged and to develop a responsibility for their learning. Overall, the overwhelming conclusion is that it is a wise strategy to create learning environments that encourage students to become intrinsically motivated. In many real-world situations, both intrinsic and extrinsic motivation are involved, although too often intrinsic and extrinsic motivation have been pitted against each other as polar opposites.

Cognitive Processes

- Children's and adolescents' sustained attention, effort, and task persistence are linked to their achievement. A mastery orientation is preferred over helpless or performance orientations in achievement situations. Mindset is the cognitive view that individuals develop regarding their own potential. Dweck argues that a key aspect of adolescents' development is to guide them in developing a growth mindset. Self-efficacy is the belief that one can master a situation and produce positive outcomes. Bandura points out that self-efficacy is a critical factor in whether students will achieve. Schunk argues that self-efficacy influences a student's choice of tasks, with low-efficacy students avoiding many learning tasks. Students' expectations for success influence their motivation. Children benefit when their parents, teachers, and other adults have high expectations for their achievement. Setting specific, proximal (short-term), and challenging goals benefits students' self-efficacy and achievement. Being a good planner means managing time effectively, setting priorities, and being organized. Self-monitoring is a key aspect of self-regulation that benefits student learning. Recently, Damon has proposed that purpose is an especially important aspect of achievement that has been missing from many adolescents' lives. Purpose is the intention to accomplish something meaningful in one's life and to contribute something to the world beyond oneself. Finding one's purpose involves answering a number of questions.

Ethnicity and Culture

- In most investigations, socioeconomic status predicts achievement better than ethnicity. U.S. children receive lower scores on math and science achievement tests than do children in Asian countries such as China and Japan.

key terms

key people

chapter 17

CULTURE AND DIVERSITY

chapter **outline**

1 Culture and Children's Development

Learning Goal 1 Discuss the role of culture in children's development.

The Relevance of Culture to the Study of Children
Cross-Cultural Comparisons

2 Socioeconomic Status and Poverty

Learning Goal 2 Describe how socioeconomic status and poverty affect children's lives.

What Is Socioeconomic Status?
Socioeconomic Variations in Families, Neighborhoods, and Schools
Poverty

3 Ethnicity

Learning Goal 3 Explain how ethnicity is linked to children's development.

Immigration
Ethnicity and Socioeconomic Status
Differences and Diversity
Prejudice and Discrimination

4 Technology

Learning Goal 4 Summarize the influence of technology on children's development.

Media Use and Screen Time
Television and Electronic Media
Computers and the Internet

Sonya, a 16-year-old Japanese American girl, was upset over her family's reaction to her White American boyfriend. "Her parents refused to meet him and on several occasions threatened to disown her" (Sue & Morishima, 1982, p. 142). Her older brothers reacted angrily to Sonya's dating a White American, warning that they were going to beat him up. Her parents were also disturbed that Sonya's grades, above average in middle school, were beginning to drop.

Generational issues contributed to the conflict between Sonya and her family (Nagata, 1989). Her parents had experienced strong sanctions against dating Whites when they were growing up and were legally prevented from marrying anyone but a Japanese. As Sonya's older brothers were growing up, they valued ethnic pride and solidarity. The brothers saw her dating a White as "selling out" her own ethnic group. Sonya and the other members of her family obviously had different cultural values.

Michael, a 17-year-old Chinese American high school student, was referred to a therapist by the school counselor because he was depressed and had suicidal tendencies (Huang & Ying, 1989). Michael was failing several classes and frequently was absent from school. Michael's parents, successful professionals, expected Michael to excel in school and go on to become a doctor. They were angered by Michael's school failures, especially since he was the firstborn son, who in Chinese families is expected to achieve the highest standards.

The therapist encouraged the parents to put less academic pressure on Michael and to have more realistic expectations for their son (who had no interest in becoming a doctor). Michael's school attendance changed, and his parents noticed his improved attitude toward school. Michael's case illustrates how expectations that Asian American youth will be "whiz kids" can become destructive.

preview

Culture had a strong influence on the conflicts Sonya and Michael experienced within their families and on their behavior outside of the family—in Sonya's case, dating; in Michael's case, school. Of course, a family's cultural background does not always produce conflict between children and other family members, but these two cases underscore the importance of culture in children's development. In this chapter, we will explore many aspects of culture, including cross-cultural comparisons of children's development, the harmful effects of poverty, the role of ethnicity, and the benefits and risks that technology can bring to children's lives.

Culture and Children's Development

LG1 Discuss the role of culture in children's development.

> The Relevance of Culture to the Study of Children

> Cross-Cultural Comparisons

Our most basic common link is that we all inhabit this planet. We all breathe the same air. We all cherish our children's future.

—**JOHN F. KENNEDY**
United States President, 20th Century

developmental **connection**

Theories

In Bronfenbrenner's ecological theory, the macrosystem is the environmental system that involves the influence of culture on children's development. Chapter 1, p. 27

culture The behavior, patterns, beliefs, and all other products of a particular group of people that are passed on from generation to generation.

In Chapter 1, we defined **culture** as the behavior, patterns, beliefs, and all other products of a particular group of people that are passed on from generation to generation. The products result from the interaction between groups of people and their environment over many years. Here we examine the role of culture in children's development.

THE RELEVANCE OF CULTURE TO THE STUDY OF CHILDREN

A key aspect of the relevance of culture to the study of children is that culture is reflected in attitudes that people have and the way they interact with children. For example, culture is manifested in parents' beliefs, values, and goals for their children, and these in turn influence the contexts in which children develop (Mistry, Contreras, & Dutta, 2013; Lessow-Hurley, 2013; Montti-Stefandi & others, 2012).

Despite all the differences among cultures, research by American psychologist Donald Campbell and his colleagues (Brewer & Campbell, 1976) revealed that people in all cultures tend to believe that what happens in their culture is "natural" and "correct" and that what happens in other cultures is "unnatural" and "incorrect"; to perceive their cultural customs as universally valid—that is, they believe that what is good for them is good for everyone; and to behave in ways that favor their cultural group and feel hostile toward other cultural groups. In other words, people in all cultures tend to be *ethnocentric*—favoring their own group over others.

The future will bring extensive contact between people from varied cultural and ethnic backgrounds (Sernau, 2013; Sue & others, 2013; Wright & others, 2012). If the study of child development is to be a relevant discipline in the remainder of the twenty-first century, increased attention will need to be given to culture and ethnicity. Global interdependence is no longer a matter of belief or choice. It is an inescapable reality. Children and their parents are not just citizens of the United States, or Canada, or some other country. They are citizens of the world—a world that, through advances in transportation and technology, has become increasingly interactive. By better understanding the behavior and values of cultures around the world, we may be able to interact more effectively with each other and make this planet a more hospitable, peaceful place in which to live (Kottak & Kozaitis, 2012; Miller & Boyle, 2013; Nolan, 2012).

CROSS-CULTURAL COMPARISONS

As we described in Chapter 1, **cross-cultural studies** compare a culture with one or more other cultures, provide information about other cultures, and examine the role of culture in children's development. This comparison provides information about the degree to which children's development is similar, or universal, across cultures, or the degree to which it is culture-specific (Miller & Boyle, 2013; Mistry, Contreras, & Dutta, 2013). In terms of gender, for example, the experiences of male and female children and adolescents continue to be worlds apart in some cultures (Sernau, 2013). In many countries, males have far greater access to educational opportunities, more freedom to pursue a variety of careers, and fewer restrictions on sexual activity than females (Hyde & Else-Quest, 2013; UNICEF, 2013).

In Chapter 16, "Schools and Achievement," we discussed the higher math and science achievement of Asian children in comparison with U.S. children. A study revealed that from the beginning of the seventh grade through the end of the eighth grade, U.S. adolescents valued academics less and their motivational behavior also decreased (Wang & Pomerantz, 2009). By contrast, the value placed on academics by Chinese adolescents did not change across this time frame, and their motivational behavior was sustained.

In cross-cultural research, the search for basic traits has focused on the dichotomy between individualism and collectivism (Triandis, 2007):

- **Individualism** involves giving priority to personal goals rather than to group goals; it emphasizes values that serve the self, such as feeling good, seeking personal distinction and recognition for achievement, and asserting independence.
- **Collectivism** emphasizes values that serve the group by subordinating personal goals to preserve group integrity, promote interdependence of the members, and foster harmonious relationships.

Figure 17.1 summarizes some of the main characteristics of individualistic and collectivistic cultures. Many Western cultures, such as the United States, Canada, Great Britain, and the Netherlands, are described as individualistic; many Eastern cultures, such as China, Japan, India, and Thailand, are described as collectivistic. Mexican culture also is collectivistic.

Researchers have found that self-conceptions are related to culture. In one study, American and Chinese college students completed 20 sentences beginning with "I am _____" (Trafimow, Triandis, & Goto, 1991). As indicated in Figure 17.2, the American college students were much more likely to describe themselves with personal traits ("I am assertive"), whereas the Chinese students were more likely to identify themselves by their group affiliations ("I am a member of the math club"). A recent study also revealed the lack of a group orientation in the United States (Mejia-Arauz & others, 2007). The study focused on the interaction of 6- to 10-year-old children from three different cultures while they worked on a task. The children were observed in a group of three (triad). Triads of children whose families had immigrated to the United States from indigenous regions of Mexico, and whose mothers averaged only seven years of schooling, were more likely to coordinate their work on the task as an ensemble; in contrast, the triads of European-heritage children who had more extensive schooling more frequently engaged dyadically (in twos) or individually. Mexican-heritage U.S. triads whose mothers had extensive schooling showed an intermediate pattern or more closely resembled the European-heritage children.

Human beings have always lived in groups, whether large or small, and have always needed one another for survival. Critics of the Western notion of psychology argue that the Western emphasis on individualism may undermine the basic need of our species for relatedness (Sernau, 2013). Some social scientists conclude that many problems in Western cultures are intensified by their emphasis on individualism. Compared with collectivist cultures,

Cross-cultural studies involve the comparison of a culture with one or more other cultures. Shown here is a woman from the San tribe (also called Bushmen), an ethnic group in Namibia, southwest Africa.

developmental **connection**

Culture and Ethnicity

In the research of Harold Stevenson and his colleagues, the longer students were in school, the wider the gap was between Asian and U.S. students in math achievement. Chapter 16, p. 477

cross-cultural studies Research that compares a culture with one or more other cultures, provides information about other cultures, and examines the role of culture in children's development.

individualism Giving priority to personal goals rather than to group goals; emphasizing values that serve the self, such as feeling good, striving for personal distinction and recognition for achievement, and asserting independence.

collectivism Emphasizing values that serve the group by subordinating personal goals to preserve group integrity, interdependence of members, and harmonious relationships.

Individualistic	Collectivistic
Focuses on individual	Focuses on groups
Self is determined by personal traits independent of groups; self is stable across contexts	Self is defined by in-group terms; self can change with context
Private self is more important	Public self is most important
Personal achievement, competition, power are important	Achievement is for the benefit of the in-group; cooperation is stressed
Cognitive dissonance is frequent	Cognitive dissonance is infrequent
Emotions (such as anger) are self-focused	Emotions (such as anger) are often relationship based
People who are the most liked are self-assured	People who are the most liked are modest, self-effacing
Values: pleasure, achievement, competition, freedom	Values: security, obedience, in-group harmony, personalized relationships
Many casual relationships	Few, close relationships
Save own face	Save own and other's face
Independent behaviors: swimming, sleeping alone in room, privacy	Interdependent behaviors: co-bathing, co-sleeping
Relatively rare mother-child physical contact	Frequent mother-child physical contact (such as hugging, holding)

FIGURE **17.1**

CHARACTERISTICS OF INDIVIDUALISTIC AND COLLECTIVISTIC CULTURES

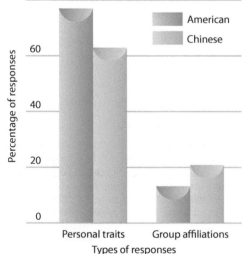

FIGURE **17.2**

AMERICAN AND CHINESE SELF-CONCEPTIONS.
College students from the United States and China completed 20 "I am _____" sentences. Both groups filled in personal traits more than group affiliations. However, the U.S. college students more often filled in the blank with personal traits, the Chinese with group affiliations.

individualistic cultures have higher rates of suicide, drug abuse, crime, teenage pregnancy, divorce, child abuse, and mental disorders.

A recent analysis proposed four values that reflect the beliefs of parents in individualistic cultures about what is required for children's effective development of autonomy: (1) personal choice; (2) intrinsic motivation; (3) self-esteem; and (4) self-maximization, which consists of achieving one's full potential (Tamis-LeMonda & others, 2008). The analysis also proposed that three values reflect the beliefs of parents in collectivistic cultures: (1) connectectness to the family and other close relationships; (2) orientation to the larger group; and (3) respect and obedience.

Critics of the concepts of individualistic and collectivistic cultures argue that these terms are too broad and simplistic, especially in an era of increasing globalization (Greenfield, 2009). Regardless of their cultural background, people need a positive sense of self as well as connectedness to others to develop fully as human beings. The analysis by Catherine Tamis-LeMonda and her colleagues (2008) emphasizes that in many families, children are not reared in environments that uniformly endorse individualistic or collectivistic values, thoughts, and actions. Rather, in many families, children are

> expected to be quiet, assertive, respectful, curious, humble, self-assured, independent, dependent, affectionate, or reserved depending on the situation, people present, children's age, and social-political and economic circles.

Socioeconomic Status and Poverty

LG2 Describe how socioeconomic status and poverty affect children's lives.

```
What Is
Socioeconomic
Status?
```

```
Socioeconomic Variations
in Families, Neighborhoods,
and Schools
```

```
Poverty
```

Many subcultures exist within countries. For example, Sonya's family, discussed in the opening of the chapter, had beliefs and patterns different from those of Michael's family. Some, but not all, subcultures are tied to ethnicity or socioeconomic characteristics or both. For example, the values and attitudes of children growing up in an urban ghetto or rural Appalachia may differ from those of children growing up in a wealthy suburb. In any event, children growing up in these different contexts are likely to have different socioeconomic statuses, and this inequality may influence their development (Duncan & others, 2013; Wright & others, 2012).

WHAT IS SOCIOECONOMIC STATUS?

In Chapter 1, "Introduction," we defined **socioeconomic status (SES)** as the grouping of people with similar occupational, educational, and economic characteristics. Socioeconomic status implies certain inequalities. Generally, members of a society have (1) occupations that vary in prestige, with some individuals having more access than others to higher-status occupations; (2) different levels of educational attainment, with some individuals having more access than others to better education; (3) different economic resources; and (4) different levels of power to influence a community's institutions. These differences in the ability to control resources and to participate in society's rewards produce unequal opportunities (Hurst, 2013; Purtell & McLoyd, 2013). Socioeconomic differences are a "proxy for material, human, and social capital within and beyond the family" (Huston & Ripke, 2006, p. 425).

The number of significantly different socioeconomic statuses depends on the community's size and complexity. Most research on socioeconomic status delineates two categories, low and middle, but some research delineates as many as six categories. Sometimes low socioeconomic status is described as low-income, working class, or blue-collar; sometimes the middle category is described as middle-income, managerial, or white-collar. Examples of low-SES occupations are factory worker, manual laborer, and maintenance worker. Examples of middle-SES occupations include skilled worker, manager, and professional (doctor, lawyer, teacher, accountant, and so on).

developmental **connection**

Socioeconomic Status

Reducing the poverty level and improving the lives of children living in poverty are important goals of U.S. social policy. Chapter 1, p. 10

socioeconomic status (SES) A grouping of people with similar occupational, educational, and economic characteristics.

SOCIOECONOMIC VARIATIONS IN FAMILIES, NEIGHBORHOODS, AND SCHOOLS

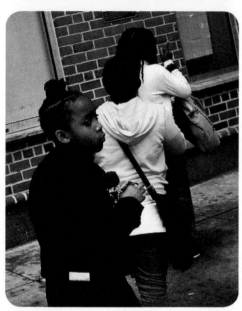

The families, neighborhoods, and schools of children have socioeconomic characteristics. A parent's SES is likely linked to the neighborhoods in which children live and the schools they attend (Hurst, 2013; Wright & others, 2012). Such variations in neighborhood settings can influence children's adjustment (Doob, 2013). For example, one study revealed that neighborhood disadvantage (involving such characteristics as low neighborhood income and high unemployment), was linked to less consistent, less stimulating, and more punitive parenting, and ultimately to negative child outcomes (low verbal ability and behavioral problems) (Kohen & others, 2008). Schools in low-income areas not only have fewer resources than those in higher-income areas but also tend to have more students with lower achievement test scores, lower rates of graduation, and smaller percentages of students going to college (Eccles & Roeser, 2013).

Let's further examine socioeconomic differences in family life. In Chapter 14, "Families," we described socioeconomic differences in child rearing (Hoff, Laursen, & Tardif, 2002). Recall that lower-SES parents are more concerned that their children conform to society's expectations, tend to have an authoritarian parenting style, rely on physical punishment more in disciplining their children, and are more directive and less conversational with their children. By contrast, higher-SES parents tend to be more concerned with developing children's initiative, strive to create a home atmosphere in which children are more nearly equal participants, are less likely to use physical punishment, and are less directive and more conversational with their children.

Like their parents, children from low-SES backgrounds are at high risk for experiencing mental health problems (Hurst, 2013). Problems such as depression, low self-confidence, peer conflict, and juvenile delinquency are more prevalent among children living in low-SES families than among economically advantaged children (Doob, 2013; Duncan, 2012).

Of course, children from low-SES backgrounds vary considerably in intellectual and psychological functioning. For example, a sizable portion of children from low-SES backgrounds perform well in school; some perform better than many middle-SES students. One study found that high educational aspirations among low-income parents were linked to more positive educational outcomes in youth (Schoon, Parsons, & Sacker, 2004). When children from low-SES backgrounds are achieving well in school, it is not unusual to find a parent or parents making special sacrifices to provide the living conditions and support that contribute to school success.

So far we have focused on the challenges faced by many children and adolescents from low-income families. However, research by Souniya Luthar and her colleagues (Ansary & Luthar, 2009; Ansary, McMahon, & Luthar, 2012; Luthar, 2006; Luthar & Goldstein, 2008) suggests that adolescents from affluent families also face challenges. In her research, adolescents from affluent families are vulnerable to high rates of substance abuse. Also, in the affluent families she has studied, males tend to have more adjustment difficulties than females, with affluent female adolescents more likely than male adolescents to attain superior levels of academic success. A recent study, though, found that it was neighborhood wealth rather than family affluence that was linked to adolescent problems (Lund & Dearing, 2013). In this study, boys in affluent neighborhoods had a higher rate of delinquency and girls in affluent neighborhoods had higher levels of anxiety and depression than youth in middle-class neighborhoods. Family influence did not place these adolescents at risk in these domains.

POVERTY

When sixth-graders in a poverty-stricken area of St. Louis were asked to describe a perfect day, one boy said he would erase the world, then he would sit and think (Children's Defense Fund, 1992). Asked if he wouldn't rather go outside and play, the boy responded, "Are you kidding—out *there*?"

Some children are resilient and cope with the challenges of poverty without any major setbacks, but too many struggle unsuccessfully (Duncan & others, 2013; Wadsworth & others, 2013). Each child of poverty who reaches adulthood unhealthy, unskilled, or alienated keeps

(Top) Children playing in Nueva Era, a low-income area on the outskirts of Nuevo Laredo, Mexico. *(Bottom)* Children at an East Harlem public housing complex in New York City. *How might socioeconomic status affect the lives of children like these?*

our nation from being as competent and productive as it can be (Santiago, Kaltman, & Miranda, 2013).

Children and youth who grow up in poverty represent a special concern (Duncan, 2012; Duncan & others, 2013). In 2012, 21.9 percent of U.S. children and adolescents were living in families with incomes below the poverty line (U.S. Census Bureau, 2012). This is an increase from 2001 (16.2 percent) but slightly down from a peak of 22.7 percent in 1993. The U.S. figure of 21.9 percent of youth living in poverty is much higher than the rates in other industrialized nations. For example, Canada has a youth poverty rate of 9 percent and Sweden has a rate of 2 percent.

Poverty in the United States is demarcated along family structure and ethnic lines (U.S. Census Bureau, 2012). In 2008, 36.5 percent of female-headed families lived in poverty compared with only 6.4 percent of married-couple families. Thirty-five percent of African American families and 32 percent of Latino families lived in poverty, compared with only 17 percent of non-Latino White families (U.S. Census Bureau, 2012).

Persistent and long-standing poverty can have especially damaging effects on children (McLoyd & others, 2009, 2011; Williams & Hazell, 2011). One study revealed that the more years children spent in poverty, the more their physiological indices of stress were elevated (Evans & Kim, 2007). And a recent study found that persistent economic hardship as well as very early poverty was linked to lower cognitive functioning in children at 5 years of age (Schoon & others, 2011). Compared with non-Latino White children, ethnic minority children are more likely to experience persistent poverty over many years and to live in isolated poor neighborhoods where social supports are minimal and threats to positive development abundant (Jarrett, 1995) (see Figure 17.3).

Psychological Ramifications of Poverty   Living in poverty has many psychological effects on both adults and children (Duncan & others, 2013; Santiago, Kaltman, & Miranda, 2013). First, the poor are often powerless. In occupations, they rarely are the decision makers. Rules are handed down to them in an authoritarian manner. Second, the poor are often vulnerable to disaster. They are not likely to be given notice before they are laid off from work and usually do not have financial resources to fall back on when problems arise. Third, their range of alternatives is often restricted. Only a limited number of jobs are open to them. Even

What characterizes socioeconomic variations in neighborhoods?

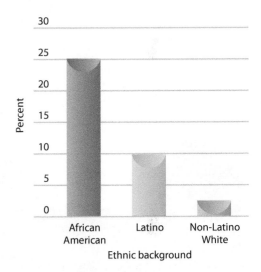

Note: A distressed neighborhood is defined by high levels (at least one standard deviation above the mean) of (1) poverty; (2) female-headed families; (3) high school dropouts; (4) unemployment; and (5) reliance on welfare.

FIGURE **17.3**

PERCENTAGES OF YOUTH UNDER 18 WHO ARE LIVING IN DISTRESSED NEIGHBORHOODS

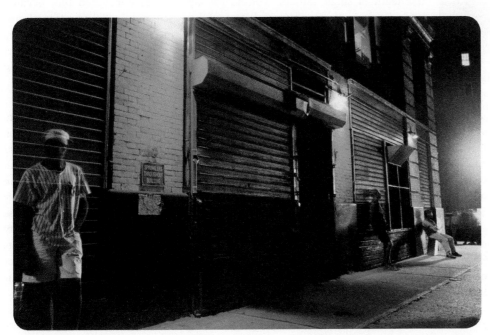

How are the environments that economically more advantaged children and adolescents live in different from the environments that children and adolescents live in that are characterized by poverty?

when alternatives are available, the poor might not know about them or be prepared to make a wise decision, because of inadequate education and inability to read well. Fourth, being poor means having less prestige. This lack of prestige is transmitted to children early in their lives. The child living in poverty observes that many other children wear nicer clothes and live in more attractive houses.

Although positive times occur in the lives of children growing up in poverty, many of their negative experiences are worse than those of their middle-SES counterparts (Doob, 2013; Wadsworth & others, 2013). These adversities involve physical punishment and lack of structure at home, violence in the neighborhood, and domestic violence in their buildings. A research review concluded that compared with their economically more advantaged counterparts, poor children experience widespread environmental inequities that include the following (Evans, 2004, p. 77):

- Exposure "to more family turmoil, violence, separation from their families, instability, and chaotic households" (Emery & Laumann-Billings, 1998)

- "Less social support, and their parents are less responsive and more authoritarian" (Bo, 1994)

- "Read to relatively infrequently, watch more TV, and have less access to books and computers" (Bradley & others, 2001)

- Schools and child-care facilities that are inferior and parents who "are less involved in their children's school activities" (Benveniste, Carnoy, & Rothstein, 2003)

- Air and water that are more polluted and homes that "are more crowded, more noisy, and of lower quality" (Myers, Baer, & Choi, 1996)

- More dangerous and physically deteriorating neighborhoods with less adequate municipal services (Brody & others, 2001)

Do children living in poverty face higher levels of these risks? To find out, see *Connecting Through Research.*

Because of advances in their cognitive growth, adolescents living in poverty likely are more aware of their social disadvantage and the associated stigma than are children (McLoyd & others, 2009). Combined with the increased sensitivity to peers in adolescence, such awareness may cause them to try to hide their poverty status as much as possible from others.

A special concern is the high percentage of single mothers in poverty (Hurst, 2013). More than one-third of single mothers are in poverty, compared with only one-tenth of single fathers. Vonnie McLoyd (1998) concluded that because poor, single mothers are more distressed than their middle-SES counterparts are, they often show low support, nurturance, and involvement with their children. Among the reasons for the high poverty rate of single mothers are women's lower incomes, infrequent awarding of alimony payments, and poorly enforced child support by fathers (Hurst, 2013).

Vonnie McLoyd (*right*) has conducted a number of important investigations of the roles of poverty, ethnicity, and unemployment in children's and adolescents' development. She has found that economic stressors often diminish children's and adolescents' belief in the utility of education and their achievement strivings.

Countering Poverty's Effects   One trend in antipoverty programs is to conduct two-generation interventions (McLoyd, Aikens, & Burton, 2006; Purtell & McLoyd, 2013). That is, the programs provide services for children (such as educational child care or preschool education) as well as services for parents (such as adult education, literacy training, and job-skill training). Evaluations suggest that two-generation programs have more positive effects on parents than they do on children (St. Pierre, Layzer, & Barnes, 1996). Also, when the two-generation programs do show benefits for children, these are more likely to be health benefits than cognitive gains. Some studies have shown that poverty interventions are more effective with young children than with older children and adolescents (Duncan & Magnuson, 2008; McLoyd & others, 2009). However, a downward trajectory is not inevitable for older children and youth living in poverty, and the success of poverty interventions likely depends on the quality and type of intervention (Huston & Bentley, 2010).

In an experimental study, Aletha Huston and her colleagues (2006; Gupta, Thornton, & Huston, 2007) evaluated the effects of New Hope, a program designed to increase parental employment and reduce family poverty, on adolescent development. They randomly assigned families with 6- to 10-year-old children living in poverty to the New Hope program and a control group. New Hope

connecting through research

What Risks Are Experienced by Children Living in Poverty?

In Chapter 1, we briefly described the results of one study that explored multiple risks in the lives of children from poverty and middle-income backgrounds (Evans & English, 2002). Here we provide more details about this study. Six multiple risks were examined in 287 8- to 10-year-old non-Latino White children living in rural areas of upstate New York: family turmoil, child separation (a close family member being away from home often), exposure to violence, crowding, high noise levels, and inferior housing quality. Family turmoil, child separation, and exposure to violence were assessed by maternal reports of the life events their children had experienced. Crowding was determined by the number of people per room, and noise level was measured by the decibel level in the home. Housing quality (based on structural quality, cleanliness, clutter, resources for children, safety hazards, and climatic conditions) was rated by observers who visited the homes. Each of the six factors was defined as presenting a risk or no risk. Thus, the multiple stressor exposure for children could range from 0 to 6. Families were defined as poor if the household lived at or below the federally defined poverty line.

Children in poor families experienced greater risks than their middle-income counterparts. As shown in Figure 17.4, a higher percentage of children in poor families were exposed to each of the six risk factors (family turmoil, child separation, exposure to violence, crowding, excessive noise, and poor quality of housing).

Were there differences in the children's adjustment that might reflect their differing exposure to risk factors? The researchers assessed the children's levels of psychological stress through reports by the children and

Risk factor (stressor)	Poor children exposed (%)	Middle-income children exposed (%)
Family turmoil	45	12
Child separation	45	14
Exposure to violence	73	49
Crowding	16	7
Excessive noise	32	21
Poor housing quality	24	3

FIGURE 17.4

PERCENTAGE OF POOR AND MIDDLE-INCOME CHILDREN EXPOSED TO EACH OF SIX STRESSORS

their mothers. Problems in self-regulation of behavior were determined by whether children chose immediate rather than delayed gratification on a task. Resting blood pressure and overnight neuroendocrine hormones were measured to indicate children's levels of psychophysiological stress.

The researchers found that in comparison with children from middle-income backgrounds, poor children had higher levels of psychological stress, more problems in self-regulation of behavior, and elevated psychophysiological stress. Analysis indicated that cumulative exposure to stressors may contribute to difficulties in socioemotional development for children living in poverty.

---

offered benefits to poor adults who were employed at least 30 hours a week: wage supplements ensuring that net income increased as parents earned more; work supports in the form of subsidized child care (for any child under age 13); and health insurance. Management services were provided to New Hope participants to assist them with job searches and other needs. The New Hope program was available to the experimental group families for three years (until the children were 9 to 13 years old). Five years after the program began and two years after it had ended, the program's effects on the children were examined when they were 11 to 16 years old. Compared with adolescents in the control group, New Hope adolescents were more competent at reading, had better school performance, were less likely to be in special education classes, had more positive social skills, and were more likely to be in formal after-school arrangements. New Hope parents reported better psychological well-being and a greater sense of self-efficacy in managing their adolescents than control parents did. In a further assessment, the influence of the New Hope program on adolescents and emerging adults 9 to 19 years after they left the program was evaluated (McLoyd & others, 2011). Positive outcomes especially occurred for African American males, who were more optimistic about their future employment and career prospects. In the most recent assessment of the New Hope Project, the intervention had positive effects on the youths' future orientation eight years after the program began and five years after the benefits ended (Purtell & McLoyd, 2013). In this study, boys' positive educational expectations were linked to improving the intervention's influence on reducing the boys' pessimism about future employment. To read about another program that benefitted youth living in poverty, see *Caring Connections*.

The Quantum Opportunities Program

A downward trajectory is not inevitable for youth living in poverty (Carnegie Council on Adolescent Development, 1995). One potential positive path out of poverty for such youth is to become involved with a caring mentor. The Quantum Opportunities program, funded by the Ford Foundation, was a four-year, year-round mentoring effort (Carnegie Council on Adolescent Development, 1995). The students involved in this program were entering the ninth grade at a high school with high rates of poverty, were members of ethnic minority groups, and came from families that received public assistance. Each day for four years, mentors provided sustained support, guidance, and concrete assistance to these students.

The Quantum program required students to participate in (1) academic-related activities outside school hours, including reading, writing, math, science, and social studies, peer tutoring, and computer skills training; (2) community service projects, including tutoring elementary school students, cleaning up the neighborhood, and volunteering in hospitals, nursing homes, and libraries; and (3) cultural enrichment and personal development activities, including life skills training, college preparation, and job planning. In exchange for their commitment to the program, students were offered financial incentives that encouraged

Children participating in the Quantum Opportunities program at the Carver Center in Washington, DC.

participation, completion, and long-range planning. A stipend of $1.33 was given to students for each hour they participated in these activities. For every 100 hours of education, service, or development activities they

completed, students received a bonus of $100. The average cost per participant was $10,600 for the four years, which is one-half the cost of one year in prison.

An evaluation of the Quantum project compared the mentored students with a nonmentored control group. Sixty-three percent of the mentored students graduated from high school, but only 42 percent of the control group did; 42 percent of the mentored students were enrolled in college, but only 16 percent of the control group were. Furthermore, control-group students were twice as likely as the mentored students to receive food stamps or welfare, and they had more arrests. Such programs clearly have the potential to overcome the intergenerational transmission of poverty and its negative outcomes. While the original Quantum Opportunities program no longer exists, the Eisenhower Foundation (2013) recently began replicating the Quantum program in Alabama, South Carolina, New Hampshire, Virginia, Mississippi, Oregon, Maryland, and Washington, DC.

These research results confirm what we learned in Chapter 16: the most effective programs to discourage dropping out of high school provide tutoring and mentoring, emphasize the creation of caring environments and relationships, and offer community-service opportunities. This research also reinforces the philosophy that goal-setting (such as planning for college and/or a career) is an integral part of achievement.

Review *Connect* Reflect

 Describe how socioeconomic status and poverty affect children's lives.

Review

- What is socioeconomic status?
- What are some socioeconomic variations in families, neighborhoods, and schools?
- What characterizes children living in poverty?

Connect

- In this section, you learned about antipoverty programs that take a two-generation approach to intervention. How

is this similar to efforts to improve the health of children living in poverty (discussed in Chapter 4)?

Reflect *Your Own Personal Journey of Life*

- How would you label the socioeconomic status of your family as you grew up? In what ways do you think the SES status of your family influenced your development?

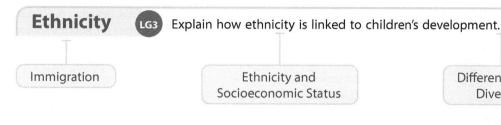

Ethnicity ⓛⓖ3 Explain how ethnicity is linked to children's development.

Immigration | Ethnicity and Socioeconomic Status | Differences and Diversity | Prejudice and Discrimination

Nowhere are cultural changes in the United States more dramatic than in the increasing ethnic diversity of America's children. Recall from Chapter 1 that **ethnicity** refers to characteristics rooted in cultural heritage, including nationality, race, religion, and language. Ninety-three languages are spoken in Los Angeles alone! With increased diversity have come conflict and concerns about the future (Schaefer, 2013).

IMMIGRATION

Relatively high rates of immigration are contributing to the growing proportion of ethnic minority adolescents and emerging adults in the United States (Trejos-Castillo & others, 2013; Yu & Singh, 2012). Immigrant families are those in which at least one of the parents is born outside the country of residence. Variations in immigrant families involve whether one or both parents are foreign-born, whether the child was born in the host country, and the ages at which immigration took place for both the parents and the children (Crosnoe & Fuligni, 2012).

Different models have been proposed to determine whether children and adolescents in immigrant families are more vulnerable or more successful in relation to the general population of children and adolescents (Crosnoe & Fuligni, 2012). Historically, an *immigrant risk model* was emphasized, concluding that youth of immigrants had a lower level of well-being and were at risk for more problems. For example, one study found that the longer immigrant youth from the Dominican Republic lived in the United States, the higher their risk for suicide or suicide attempts (Pena & others, 2012).

More recently, an *immigrant paradox model* has been proposed, emphasizing that despite the many cultural, socioeconomic, language, and other obstacles that immigrant families face, their youth show a high level of well-being and fewer problems than native-born youth (Garcia-Coll & Marks, 2011; Garcia-Coll & others, 2012). Based on current research, some support exists for each model. Robert Crosnoe and Andrew Fuligni reached the following conclusion (2012, p. 1473):

> Some children from immigrant families are doing quite well, some less so, depending on the characteristics of migration itself (including the nation of origin) and their families' circumstances in their new country (including their position in socioeconomic and race-ethnic stratification systems.

Today an increasing proportion of the U.S. population consists of ethnic minorities (Leong & others, 2013), and this growth of ethnic minorities is expected to continue throughout the rest of the twenty-first century. Asian Americans are expected to be the fastest-growing ethnic group of adolescents, with a growth rate of almost 600 percent by 2100. Latino adolescents are projected to increase almost 400 percent by 2100. Figure 17.5 shows the actual numbers of adolescents in different ethnic groups in the year 2000, as well as the numbers projected through 2100. Notice that by 2100, Latino adolescents are expected to outnumber non-Latino White adolescents.

Recently immigrated families may face special problems. Many individuals in immigrant families are dealing with the problems associated with being undocumented. Living in an

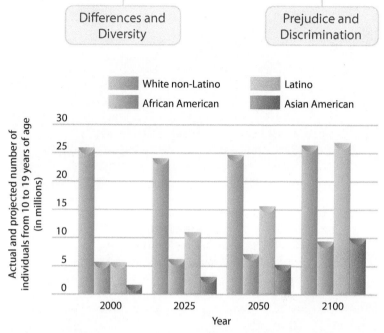

FIGURE **17.5**

ACTUAL AND PROJECTED NUMBER OF U.S. ADOLESCENTS AGED 10 TO 19, 2000 TO 2100. In 2000, there were more than 25 million White non-Latino adolescents 10 to 19 years of age in the United States, whereas the numbers for ethnic minority groups were substantially lower. However, projections for 2025 through 2100 predict dramatic increases in the numbers of Latino and Asian American adolescents, with more Latino than non-Latino White adolescents and more Asian American than African American adolescents expected to be living in the United States by 2100.

ethnicity A dimension of culture based on cultural heritage, nationality, race, religion, and language.

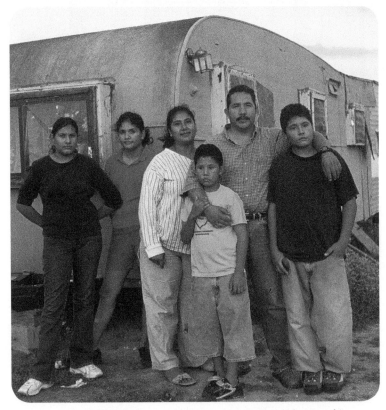

(Top) Immigrant children from 12 countries participating in a U.S. citizenship ceremony in Queens, New York, on June 11, 2009. *(Bottom)* A Latino family who immigrated recently to the Rio Grande Valley in Texas. *What are some characteristics of children and their families who have recently immigrated to the United States?*

undocumented family can affect children's developmental outcomes when parents are unwilling to sign up for services for which they are eligible, parents are limited to low-wage jobs with high stress and low benefits, and there is a lack of cognitive stimulation in the home (Yoshikawa, 2012).

What are some of the circumstances that immigrants face that challenge their adjustment? Immigrants often experience stressors uncommon to or less prominent among longtime residents such as language barriers, dislocations and separations from support networks, the dual struggle to preserve identity and to acculturate, and changes in SES status (Ferguson, Bornstein, & Pottinger, 2012; Gollnick & Chinn, 2013; Lessow-Hurley, 2013). Consequently, when working with adolescents and their immigrant families, counselors need to adapt intervention programs to optimize cultural sensitivity (Suárez-Orozco & Suárez-Orozco, 2010; Sue & others, 2013; Trejos-Castillo & others, 2013).

Recent research indicates that many members of families that have recently immigrated to the United States adopt a bicultural orientation, selecting characteristics of the U.S. culture that help them to survive and advance, while still retaining aspects of their culture of origin (Fuligni, 2012; Kim & others, 2012). Immigration also involves cultural brokering, which has increasingly occurred in the United States as children and adolescents serve as mediators (cultural and linguistic) for their immigrant parents (Villanueva & Buriel, 2010).

Although many ethnic/immigrant families adopt a bicultural orientation, parenting in many ethnic minority families also focuses on issues associated with promoting children's ethnic pride, knowledge of their ethnic group, and awareness of discrimination (Ho & others, 2012; Rogers & others, 2012; Simpkins & others, 2013). In adopting characteristics of the U.S. culture, Latino families are increasingly embracing the importance of education (Cooper, 2011). Although their school dropout rates have remained higher than for other ethnic groups, toward the end of the first decade of the twenty-first century they declined considerably (National Center for Education Statistics, 2010). Ross Parke and his colleagues (2011) have found that Latino families are retaining a strong commitment to family when they immigrate to the United States despite facing challenges advancing economically. For example, divorce rates for Latino families are lower than for non-Latino White families of similar socioeconomic status.

Many of the families that have immigrated in recent decades to the United States, such as Mexican Americans and Asian Americans, come from collectivist cultures that emphasize family obligations and duties (Fuligni & Telzer, 2012). This family obligation and duty may take the form of adolescents assisting parents in their occupations and contributing to the family's welfare (van Geel & Vedder, 2011). This type of support often occurs in service and manual labor jobs, such as those in construction, gardening, cleaning, and restaurants.

However, there are variations in immigrant families' experiences and the degree to which their children and adolescents change as they are exposed to American culture. A recent study found that following their immigration, Mexican American adolescents spent less time with their family and identified less with family values (Updegraff & others, 2012). However, in this study, teens with stronger family values in early adolescence were less likely to engage in risky behavior in late adolescence.

Carola Suárez-Orozco, Immigration Studies Researcher and Professor

Carola Suárez-Orozco currently is Chair and Professor of Applied Psychology and Co-director of Immigration Studies at New York University. She formerly was Co-director of the Harvard University Immigration Projects. Carola obtained her undergraduate degree (in development studies) and doctoral degree (in clinical psychology) at the University of California at Berkeley.

Suárez-Orozco has worked both in clinical and public school settings in California and Massachusetts. While at Harvard, she conducted a five-year longitudinal study of the adaptation of immigrant adolescents (coming from Central America, China, and the Dominican Republic) to schools and society. She especially advocates more research involving the role of cultural and psychological factors in the adaptation of immigrant and ethnic minority youth (Suárez-Orozco, 2007).

Carola Suárez-Orozco, with her husband, Marcelo, who also studies the adaptation of immigrants.

For more information about what researchers and professors do, see page 42 in the Careers in Child Development appendix following Chapter 1.

Individual families vary, and how ethnic minority families deal with stress depends on many factors (Nieto & Bode, 2012; Trejos-Castillo & others, 2013). Whether the parents are native-born or immigrants, how long the family has been in the United States, its socioeconomic status, and its national origin all make a difference (Gonzales & others, 2012). A recent study revealed that parents' education before migrating was strongly linked to their children's academic achievement (Pong & Landale, 2012).

The characteristics of the family's social context also influence its adaptation. What are the attitudes toward the family's ethnic group within its neighborhood or city? Can the family's children attend good schools? Are there community groups that welcome people from the family's ethnic group? Do members of the family's ethnic group form community groups of their own? To read about the work of one individual who studies immigrant adolescents, see *Connecting with Careers*.

ETHNICITY AND SOCIOECONOMIC STATUS

Too often the research on ethnic minority children has failed to tease apart the influences of ethnicity and socioeconomic status (SES). Ethnicity and SES can interact in ways that exaggerate the negative influence of ethnicity because ethnic minority individuals are overrepresented in the lower socioeconomic levels of American society (Hurst, 2013; Wright & others, 2012). Ethnicity has often defined who will enjoy the privileges of citizenship and to what degree and in what ways. In many instances, an individual's ethnic background has determined whether the individual will be alienated or disadvantaged.

In some cases, researchers have given ethnic explanations of child development that were largely based on socioeconomic status rather than ethnicity. For example, decades of research on group differences in self-esteem failed to consider the socioeconomic status

Too often African American male adolescents are negatively stereotyped. As Jason Leonard, age 15 comments, "I want America to know that most of us black teens are not troubled people from broken homes and headed to jail . . . In my relationships with my parents, we show respect for each other and we have values in our house. We have traditions we celebrate together, including Christmas and Kwanzaa.

Consider the flowers of a garden: Though differing in kind, color, form, and shape, yet inasmuch as they are refreshed by the waters of one spring, revived by the breath of one wind, invigorated by the rays of one sun, this diversity increases their charm and adds to their beauty. . . . How unpleasing to the eye if all the flowers and plants, the leaves and blossoms, the fruits, the branches, and the trees of that garden were all of the same shape and color! Diversity of hues, form, and shape enriches and adorns the garden and heightens its effect.

—ABDU'L BAHA
Persian Baha'i Religious Leader, 19th/20th Century

of African American and White American children (Hare & Castenell, 1985). When the self-esteem of African American children from low-income backgrounds is compared with that of White American children from middle-class backgrounds, the differences are often large but not informative because of the confounding of ethnicity and SES (Scott-Jones, 1995).

In a longitudinal study illustrating the importance of separating SES from ethnicity, SES successfully predicted educational and occupational expectations across ethnic groups among 14- to 26-year-olds (Mello, 2009). In this study, after controlling for SES, African American youth reported the highest educational expectations, followed by Latino and Asian American/Pacific Islander, non-Latino White, and American Indian/Alaska Native youth. African American and Asian American/Pacific Islander youth had the highest occupational expectations, followed by Latino, American Indian/Alaska Native, and non-Latino White youth. The ethnic group patterns were consistent across the adolescent and emerging adult years.

Even ethnic minority children from middle-SES backgrounds do not entirely escape the problems of minority status (Cushner, McClelland, & Safford, 2012; Nieto & Bode, 2012). Middle-SES ethnic minority children still encounter much of the prejudice, discrimination, and bias associated with being a member of an ethnic minority group.

Although not all ethnic minority families are poor, poverty contributes to the stressful life experiences of many ethnic minority children (Doob, 2013). Vonnie McLoyd and her colleagues (McLoyd, 1998; McLoyd, Aikens, & Burton, 2006; McLoyd & others, 2009; Purtell & McLloyd, 2013) conclude that ethnic minority children experience a disproportionate share of the adverse effects of poverty and unemployment in America today. Thus, many ethnic minority children experience a double disadvantage: (1) prejudice, discrimination, and bias because of their ethnic minority status; and (2) the stressful effects of poverty.

DIFFERENCES AND DIVERSITY

Historical, economic, and social experiences produce differences between various ethnic minority groups, and between ethnic minority groups and the majority White group (Doob, 2013; Kottak & Kozaitis, 2012; Wright & others, 2012). Individuals living in a particular ethnic or cultural group adapt to the values, attitudes, and stresses of that culture. Recognizing and respecting these differences is an important aspect of getting along with others in a diverse, multicultural world. Children, like all of us, need to take the perspective of individuals from ethnic and cultural groups that are different from their own and think, "If I were in their shoes, what kinds of experiences might I have had?" "How would I feel if I were a member of their ethnic or cultural group?" "How would I think and behave if I had grown up in their world?" Such perspective taking often increases empathy and understanding of individuals from ethnic and cultural groups different from one's own.

For too long, differences between any ethnic minority group and Whites were conceptualized as deficits or inferior characteristics on the part of the ethnic minority group. Indeed, research on ethnic minority groups often focused only on a group's negative, stressful aspects. For example, research on African American adolescent girls invariably examined topics such as poverty, unwed motherhood, and dropping out of school; research on the psychological strengths of African American adolescent girls was sorely needed. The self-esteem, achievement, motivation, and self-control of children from different ethnic minority groups deserve considerable study.

The current, long-overdue emphasis of research on ethnic groups underscores the strengths of various minority groups (Umana-Taylor, 2009). For example, the extended-family support system that characterizes many ethnic minority groups is now recognized as an important factor in coping. And researchers are finding that African American males are better than Anglo-American males at detecting and using nonverbal cues such as body language in communication, at communicating with people from different cultures, and at solving unexpected problems (Evans & Whitfield, 1988).

As we noted in Chapter 1, there is considerable diversity within each ethnic group (Cushner, McClelland, & Safford, 2012). Ethnic minority groups have different social, historical, and economic backgrounds (Spring, 2013). For example, Mexican, Cuban, and Puerto Rican immigrants are Latinos, but they had different reasons for migrating, came from varying socioeconomic backgrounds in their native countries, and experience different rates and types of employment in the United States. The U.S. federal government now recognizes the existence of 511 different Native American tribes, each having a unique ancestral background with differing values and characteristics. Asian Americans include Chinese, Japanese, Filipinos, Koreans, and Southeast Asians, each group having a distinct ancestry and language. The diversity of Asian Americans is reflected in their educational attainment: Some achieve a high level of education; many others have little education (Hurst, 2013). For example, 90 percent of Korean American males graduate from high school, but only 71 percent of Vietnamese American males do.

Diversity also exists within each of these groups (Cushner, McClelland, & Safford, 2012). No group is homogeneous. Sometimes well-meaning individuals fail to recognize the diversity within an ethnic group (Sue, 1990; Sue & others, 2013). For example, a sixth-grade teacher had two Mexican American adolescents in her class. She asked them to be prepared to demonstrate to the class on the following Monday how they danced at home. The first boy got up in front of the class and began dancing in a typical American fashion. The teacher said, "No, I want you to dance like you and your family do at home, like you do when you have Mexican American celebrations." The boy informed the teacher that his family did not dance that way. The second boy demonstrated a Mexican folk dance to the class. Failing to recognize diversity within ethnic groups reinforces stereotypes and encourages prejudice.

developmental **connection**

Identity

Many aspects of sociocultural contexts influence children's and adolescents' ethnic identity. Chapter 11, p. 331

PREJUDICE AND DISCRIMINATION

Prejudice is an unjustified negative attitude toward an individual because of the individual's membership in a group. The group toward which the prejudice is directed can be made up of people of a particular ethnic group, sex, age, religion, or other detectable difference (Biernat & Danahar, 2013). Our concern here is prejudice against members of ethnic minority groups.

Research studies provide insight into the discrimination experienced by ethnic minority children and adolescents (Basanez & others, 2013; Benner & Graham, 2013; Riina & others, 2013). Consider the following three studies:

- Discrimination against seventh- to tenth-grade African American students was related to their lower level of psychological functioning, including perceived stress, symptoms of depression, and lower perceived well-being; more positive attitudes toward African Americans were associated with more positive psychological functioning in adolescents (Sellers & others, 2006). Figure 17.6 shows the percentage of African American adolescents who reported experiencing different types of racial hassles in the past year.

- Chinese American sixth-graders experienced discrimination from their peers that was comparable to discrimination faced by African American sixth-graders (Rivas-Drake, Hughes, & Way, 2009).

- Latino adolescents encountered more discrimination than did Asian American adolescents, and the discrimination was linked to lower grade point averages and self-esteem and to more depressive symptoms and physical complaints (Huynh & Fuligni, 2010).

- African American adolescents' perceived personal racial discrimination was linked to their higher level of delinquency (Martin & others, 2011).

Progress has been made in ethnic minority relations, but discrimination and prejudice still exist, and equality has not been achieved. Much remains to be accomplished (Tobler & others, 2013; Zeiders & others, 2013). To read further about diversity and ethnicity, see *Connecting with Diversity*.

Type of Racial Hassle	Percent of Adolescents Who Reported the Racial Hassle in the Past Year
Being accused of something or treated suspiciously	71.0
Being treated as if you were "stupid," being "talked down to"	70.7
Others reacting to you as if they were afraid or intimidated	70.1
Being observed or followed while in public places	68.1
Being treated rudely or disrespectfully	56.4
Being ignored, overlooked, not given service	56.4
Others expecting your work to be inferior	54.1
Being insulted, called a name, or harassed	52.2

FIGURE 17.6

AFRICAN-AMERICAN ADOLESCENTS' REPORTS OF RACIAL HASSLES IN THE PAST YEAR

prejudice An unjustified negative attitude toward an individual because of her or his membership in a group.

The United States and Canada: Nations with Many Cultures

The United States has been and continues to be a great receiver of ethnic groups. It has embraced new ingredients from many cultures (Fuligni, Hughes, & Way, 2009). The cultures often collide and cross-pollinate, mixing their ideologies and identities. Some of the culture of origin is retained, some of it is lost, and some of it is mixed with the American culture.

Other nations have also experienced the immigration of varied ethnic groups. Possibly we can learn more about the potential benefits, problems, and varied responses by examining their experiences. Canada is a prominent example. Canada comprises a mixture of cultures that are loosely organized along the lines of economic power. The Canadian cultures include the following (Siegel & Wiener, 1993):

- Native peoples, or First Nations, who were Canada's original inhabitants;
- Descendants of French settlers who came to Canada during the seventeenth and eighteenth centuries;
- Descendants of British settlers who came to Canada during and after the seventeenth century, or from the United States after the American Revolution in the latter part of the eighteenth century;

- Descendants of immigrants from Asia, mainly China, who settled on the west coast of Canada in the latter part of the nineteenth and early twentieth centuries;
- Descendants of nineteenth-century immigrants from various European countries, who settled in central Canada and the prairie provinces;
- Twentieth-century and current immigrants from countries in economic and political turmoil (in Latin America, the Caribbean, Asia, Africa, the Indian subcontinent, the former Soviet Union, and the Middle East), who have settled in many parts of Canada

Canada has two official languages: English and French. Primarily French-speaking individuals reside mainly in the province of Quebec; primarily English-speaking individuals reside mainly in other Canadian provinces. In addition to its English- and French-speaking populations, Canada has a large multicultural community. In three large Canadian cities—Toronto, Montreal, and Vancouver—more than 50 percent of the children and adolescents come from homes in which neither English nor French is the native language (Siegel & Wiener, 1993).

(Left) A Canadian Inuit family in Baker Lake, Canada; *(Right)* Chinese girls in Toronto. *What are some characteristics of Canada's Chinese population?*

Canada has two official languages, based on the nation's two largest ethnic populations. If the United States were to base its official languages on the largest ethnic populations they expect to have in 2100, what might they be? (See Figure 17.5.)

Technology

 Summarize the influence of technology on children's development.

```
Media Use and          Television and          Computers and
Screen Time            Electronic Media        the Internet
```

Few developments in society over the last 40 years have had a greater impact on adolescents than television and the Internet (Gross, 2013; Roblyer & Doering, 2013). The persuasion capabilities of television and the Internet are staggering. Many of today's adolescents have spent more time since infancy in front of a television set, and more recently in front of a computer, than with their parents or in the classroom. Although television continues to have a strong influence on adolescents, their increasing use of other media and information/communication devices has led to the creation of the term *screen time,* which encompasses how much time they spend watching/using television, DVDs, computers, video game systems, and mobile media such as smartphones (De Decker & others, 2012).

MEDIA USE AND SCREEN TIME

More than likely, the technology revolution is affecting children and adolescents in both positive and negative ways. Technology can provide expansive knowledge and can be used in a constructive way to enhance children's and adolescents' education (Maloy & others, 2014). However, the possible downside of technology was captured in a recent book, *The Dumbest Generation: How the Digital Age Stupefies Young Americans and Jeopardizes Our Future (Or, Don't Trust Anyone Under 30),* written by Emory University English Professor Mark Bauerlein (2008). Among the book's themes are that many of today's youth are more interested in information retrieval than information formation, don't read books and aren't motivated to read them, can't spell without spellcheck, and have become encapsulated in a world of cell phones, iPods, text messaging, Facebook, YouTube, and other technology contexts. In terms of retaining general information and historical facts, Bauerlein may be correct. And in terms of some skills, such as adolescents' reading and writing, there is considerable cause for concern, with U.S. employers spending 1.3 billion dollars a year to teach writing skills to employees (Begley & Interlandi, 2008). However, in terms of cognitive skills such as thinking and reasoning, Bauerlein likely is wrong given that IQ scores have been rising significantly since the 1930s (Flynn, 2007, 2013). Further, there is no research evidence that being immersed in a technological world of iPods and YouTube impairs thinking skills (Begley & Interlandi, 2008).

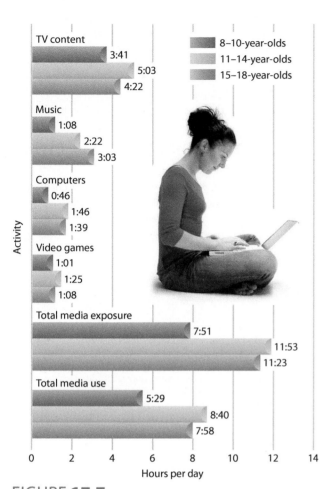

TV content
3:41
5:03
4:22

Music
1:08
2:22
3:03

Computers
0:46
1:46
1:39

Video games
1:01
1:25
1:08

Total media exposure
7:51
11:53
11:23

Total media use
5:29
8:40
7:58

■ 8–10-year-olds
■ 11–14-year-olds
■ 15–18-year-olds

Activity

0   2   4   6   8   10   12   14
Hours per day

FIGURE 17.7

AMOUNT OF TIME U.S. 8- TO 18-YEAR-OLDS SPEND PER DAY IN DIFFERENT ACTIVITIES

If the amount of time spent in an activity is any indication of its importance, there is no doubt that media play important roles in children's and adolescents' lives (Brown & Bobkowski, 2011). To better understand various aspects of media use among U.S. children and adolescents, the Kaiser Family Foundation funded three national surveys in 1999, 2004, and 2009. The 2009 survey interviewed more than 2,000 8- to 18-year-olds and documented that media use among children and adolescents had increased dramatically in the preceding decade (Rideout, Foehr, & Roberts, 2010). Today's youth live in a world in which they are encapsulated by media. In this survey, in 2009, 8- to 11-year-olds used media 5 hours and 29 minutes a day, but 11- to 14-year-olds used media an average of 8 hours and 40 minutes a day, and 15- to 18-year-olds an average of 7 hours and 58 minutes a day (see Figure 17.7). Thus, media use jumps more than 3 hours in early adolescence! The largest increase in media use in early adolescence involves TV and video game use. TV use by youth increasingly has involved watching TV on the Internet, an iPod/MP3 player, and on a cell phone. As indicated in Figure 17.7, time spent listening to music and using computers also increases considerably among 11- to 14-year-old adolescents. Based on the 2009 survey, adding up the daily media use figures to obtain weekly media use leads to the staggering levels of more than 60 hours a week of media use by 11- to 14-year-olds and almost 56 hours a week by 15- to 18-year-olds!

A major trend in the use of technology is the dramatic increase in media multitasking (Brown & Bobkowski, 2011; Levinson, 2013). In the 2009 survey, when the amount of time spent multitasking was included in total media use, 11- to 14-year-olds spent nearly 12 hours a day (compared with almost 9 hours a day when multitasking was not included) exposed to media (Rideout, Foehr, & Roberts, 2010)! In this survey, 39 percent of seventh- to twelfth-graders said "most of the time" they use two or more media concurrently, such as surfing the Web while listening to music. In some cases, media multitasking—such as text messaging, listening to an iPod, and updating a YouTube site—is engaged in at the same time as doing homework. It is hard to imagine that this allows a student to do homework efficiently, although there is little research on media multitasking. A recent study that compared heavy and light media multitaskers revealed that heavy media multitaskers were more susceptible to interference from irrelevant information (Ophir, Nass, & Wagner, 2009). A recent study of 8- to 12-year-old girls also found that a higher level of media multitasking was linked to negative social well-being, while a higher level of face-to-face communication was associated with positive social well-being indicators, such as greater social success, feeling more normal, and having fewer friends whom parents thought were a bad influence (Pea & others, 2012). Mobile media, such as cell phones and iPods, are mainly driving the increased media use by adolescents. For example, in the 2004 survey, only 18 percent of youth owned an iPod or MP3 player; In 2009, 76 percent owned them; in 2004, 39 percent owned a cell phone, a figure that jumped to 66 percent in 2009 (Rideout, Foehr, & Roberts, 2010).

TELEVISION AND ELECTRONIC MEDIA

Few developments during the second half of the twentieth century had a greater impact on children than television (Maloy & others, 2014). And in the last several decades, children increasingly have played video games (De Wall, Anderson, & Bushman, 2013).

Television   Many children spend more time in front of the television set than they do with their parents. Although it is only one of the many mass media that affect children's behavior, television may be the most influential. The persuasive capabilities of television are staggering. The 20,000 hours of television watched by the time the average American adolescent graduates from high school are greater than the number of hours spent in the classroom.

Television can have positive or negative effects on children's and adolescents' development. Television can have a positive influence by presenting motivating educational programs, increasing children's and adolescents' information about the world beyond their immediate environment, and providing models of prosocial behavior (Schmidt & Vandewater, 2008; Wilson, 2008). However, television can have a negative influence on children and adolescents by making them passive learners, distracting them from doing homework, teaching them stereotypes, providing them with violent models of aggression, and presenting them with unrealistic views of the world (Murray & Murray, 2008). Further, researchers have found that a high level of TV viewing is linked to a greater incidence of obesity in children and adolescents (Escobar-Chaves & Anderson, 2008). In a recent study, sleep problems were more common in 3- to 5-year-old children who (1) watched TV after 7 p.m., and (2) watched TV shows with violence (Garrison, Liekweg, & Christakis, 2011). Next, we will further explore the influence of media violence on children's development.

A research review conducted several years ago concluded that children and adolescents who experience a heavy media diet of violence are more likely to perceive the world as a dangerous place and to view aggression as more acceptable than their counterparts who see media violence less frequently (Wilson, 2008). Another research review concluded that there is strong evidence that media violence is a risk factor for aggressive behavior but less evidence linking it to juvenile delinquency and crime (Escobar-Chaves & Anderson, 2008). Much of the media violence described in these two research reviews comes from television, but as we see next, it also includes violent video games.

How might watching aggression on TV and playing violent video games be linked to adolescent aggression?

Video Games   Violent video games, especially those that are highly realistic, also raise concerns about their effects on children and adolescents (DeWall, Anderson, & Bushman, 2013). Correlational studies indicate that children and adolescents who extensively play violent electronic games are more aggressive and more likely to engage in delinquent acts than are their counterparts who spend less time playing the games or do not play them at all (DeWall, Anderson, & Bushman, 2013; Gentile, 2011).

Are there any positive outcomes when adolescents play video games? Far more studies of video game use by adolescents have focused on possible negative outcomes, but an increasing number of studies are examining possible positive outcomes (Adachi & Willoughby, 2013). Researchers found that middle-school students who played prosocial video games subsequently behaved in more prosocial ways (Gentile & others, 2009). In a recent study of university students, violent video game playing by both males and females was linked to lower empathic concern (Fraser & others, 2012). Research also indicates that playing video games can improve adolescents' visuospatial skills (Schmidt & Vandewater, 2008).

Further, researchers have found that video games requiring exercise (exergames) are linked to weight loss in overweight adolescents (Bond, Richards, & Calvert, 2013; Calvert, Bond, & Staiano, 2013). For example, a recent experimental study found that overweight adolescents lost more weight when they participated in a 10-week competitive exergame video condition (video games that require gross motor activity—in this study the Ninendo Wii EA Sports Active video game was used) than their overweight counterparts in a cooperative exergame condition or a no video game play control condition (Staiano, Abraham, & Calvert, 2012). The weight loss in the competitive condition also was linked to improved executive functioning in this study.

Electronic Media, Learning, and Achievement   The effects of electronic media on children depend on the child's age and the type of media. A research review reached the following conclusions about infants and young children (Kirkorian, Wartella, & Anderson, 2008):

- *Infancy:* Learning from electronic media is difficult for infants and toddlers, and they learn much more easily from direct experiences with people.
- *Early childhood:* At about 3 years of age, children can learn from electronic media with educational material if the media use effective strategies, such as repeating concepts a number of times, using images and sounds that

What are some of the ways that researchers are exploring possible positive outcomes of playing some types of video games?

What have researchers found about TV watching by infants?

capture young children's attention, and speaking with the voices of children rather than adults. However, the vast majority of media young children experience is entertainment rather than education oriented.

The American Academy of Pediatrics (2001) has recommended that children under 2 years of age should not watch television because it likely reduces direct interactions with parents. One study found that the more hours 1- and 3-year-olds watched TV per day, the more likely they were to have attention problems at 7 years of age (Christakis & others, 2004), and a recent study also revealed that daily TV exposure at 18 months was linked to increased inattention/hyperactivity at 30 months of age (Cheng & others, 2010). A study of 2- to 48-month-olds indicated that each hour of audible TV was linked to a reduction in child vocalizations (Christakis & others, 2009) and another study revealed that 8- to 16-month-olds who viewed baby DVDs/videos had poor language development (Zimmerman, Christakis, & Meltzoff, 2007).

A recent study revealed that 12 percent of 2- to 4-year-old U.S. children use computers every day and 22 percent of 5- to 8-year-olds use computers daily (Common Sense Media, 2011). A recent recommendation stated that for children 2 to 4 years of age screen time should be limited to no more than 1 hour per day (Tremblay & others, 2012). Many children spend more time with various screen media than they do interacting with their parents and peers.

How does television influence children's attention, creativity, and mental ability? Overall, media use has not been found to cause attention deficit hyperactivity disorder, but a small link has been identified between heavy television viewing and nonclinical reduced attention levels in children (Schmidt & Vandewater, 2008).

Are media use and screen time linked to children's and adolescents' creativity? A recent research review concluded that there is a negative association between children's and adolescents' TV viewing and their creativity (Calvert & Valkenberg, 2011). An exception, though, occurs when they watch educational TV content that is designed to teach creativity through the use of imaginative characters (Calvert & Valkenberg, 2011).

The more children watch TV, the lower their school achievement (Comstock & Scharrer, 2006). Why might TV watching be negatively linked to children's achievement? Three possibilities involve interference, displacement, and self-defeating tastes/preferences (Comstock & Scharrer, 2006). In terms of interference, having a television on while doing homework can distract children while they are doing cognitive tasks. In terms of displacement, television can take away time and attention from engaging in achievement-related tasks, such as homework, reading, writing, and mathematics. Researchers have found that children's reading achievement is negatively linked with the amount of time they watch TV (Comstock & Scharrer, 2006). In terms of self-defeating tastes and preferences, television attracts children to entertainment, sports, commercials, and other activities that capture their interest more than school achievement. Children who are heavy TV watchers tend to view books as dull and boring (Comstock & Scharrer, 2006).

However, some types of television content—such as educational programming for young children—may enhance achievement. In one longitudinal study, viewing educational programs, such as Sesame Street and Mr. Rogers' Neighborhood, as preschoolers was related to a number of positive outcomes through high school, including higher grades, reading of more books, and enhanced creativity (Anderson & others, 2001) (see Figure 17.8). Newer technologies, especially interactive television, hold promise for motivating children to learn and become more exploratory in solving problems.

COMPUTERS AND THE INTERNET

Culture involves change, and nowhere is that change greater than in the technological revolution individuals are experiencing with increased use of computers and the Internet (Jackson & others, 2012; Maloy & others, 2014). Society still relies on some basic nontechnological competencies—for example, good communication skills, positive attitudes, and the ability to solve problems and to think deeply and creatively. But how people pursue these competencies is changing in ways and at a speed that few people had to cope with in previous eras. For youth to be adequately prepared for tomorrow's jobs, technology needs to become an integral part of their lives (Edwards, 2014; Gross, 2013).

The digitally mediated social environment of youth includes e-mail, instant messaging, social networking sites such as Facebook, chat rooms, videosharing and photosharing, multiplayer online computer games, and virtual worlds. The remarkable increase in the popularity of Facebook was reflected in its replacement of Google in 2010 as the most frequently visited Internet site. Most of these digitally mediated social interactions began on computers but more recently have also shifted to cell phones, especially smartphones (Valkenburg & Peter, 2011).

A national survey revealed dramatic increases in adolescents' use of social media and text messaging (Lenhart & others, 2010). In 2009, nearly three-fourths of U.S. 12- to 17-year-olds reported using social networking sites. Eighty-one percent of 18- to 24-year-olds had created a profile on a social networking site and 31 percent of them visited a social networking site at least several times a day. More emerging adult women visited a social networking site several times a day (33 percent) than did their male counterparts (24 percent).

Text messaging has now become the main way that adolescents connect with their friends, surpassing face-to-face contact, e-mail, instant messaging, and voice calling (Lenhart & others, 2010). However, voice mailing is the primary way that most adolescents prefer to connect with parents.

Special concerns have emerged about children's and adolescents' access to information on the Internet, which has been largely unregulated. Youth can access adult sexual material, instructions for making bombs, and other information that is inappropriate for them.

Another concern is peer bullying and harassment on the Internet (called *cyber-bullying*) (Donnerstein, 2012; Sontag & others, 2011). One survey found that peer bullying offline and online were the most frequent threats that children and adolescents encountered (Palfrey & others, 2009). And a recent study of third- to sixth-graders revealed that engaging in cyber aggression was related to increased loneliness, lower self-esteem, fewer mutual friendships, and lower peer popularity (Schoffstall & Cohen, 2011). Information about preventing cyber-bullying can be found at www.stopcyberbullying.org/.

A recent study of college students—mean age 20 years old—found that when the Internet was used for shopping, entertainment, and pornography, negative outcomes included higher levels of drinking and drug use, greater numbers of sexual partners, worse relationships with friends and parents, and lower self-worth; however, when college students used the Internet for schoolwork, positive outcomes included a lower level of drug use and higher self-worth (Padilla-Walker & others, 2010).

Clearly, adolescents' use of the Internet requires parental monitoring and regulation (Jackson & others, 2012; Padilla-Walker & others, 2012). Consider Bonita Williams, who began to worry about how obsessed her 15-year-old daughter, Jade, had become with MySpace (Kornblum, 2006). She became even more concerned when she discovered that Jade was posting suggestive photos of herself and giving her cell phone number to people in different parts of the United States. She grounded her daughter, blocked MySpace at home, and moved Jade's computer from her bedroom to the family room.

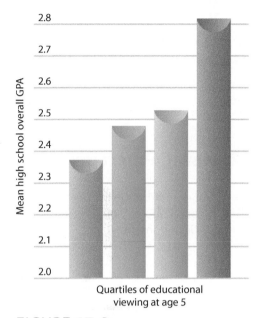

FIGURE **17.8**

EDUCATIONAL TV VIEWING IN EARLY CHILDHOOD AND HIGH SCHOOL GRADE-POINT AVERAGE FOR BOYS. When boys watched more educational television (especially *Sesame Street*) as preschoolers, they had higher grade-point averages in high school. The graph displays the boys' early TV viewing patterns in quartiles and the means of their grade-point averages. The bar on the left is for the lowest 25 percent of boys who viewed educational TV programs, the next bar the next 25 percent, and so on, with the bar on the right for the 25 percent of the boys who watched the most educational TV shows as preschoolers.

What characterizes the online social environment of adolescents?

developmental **connection**

Media Influence

Significant numbers of children are victimized by bullies, and bullying has a number of negative outcomes for children. Chapter 15, p. 431

The following studies explored the role of parents in guiding adolescents' use of the Internet and other media:

- Parents' high estimates of online dangers were not matched by their low rates of setting limits and monitoring their adolescents' online activities (Rosen, Cheever, & Carrier, 2008). Also in this study, adolescents who perceived that their parents had an indulgent parenting style (high warmth and involvement but low levels of strictness and supervision) reported engaging in the most risky online behavior, such as meeting someone in person whom they had initially contacted on the Internet.

- Both maternal and paternal authoritative parenting predicted proactive monitoring of adolescent media use, including restriction of certain media from adolescent use and parent-adolescent discussion of exposure to questionable media content (Padilla-Walker & Coyne, 2011).

- Problematic mother-adolescent (age 13) relationships (such as insecure attachment and autonomy conflicts) predicted emerging adults' preference for online communication and greater probability of forming a relationship of poor quality with someone they met online (Szwedo, Mikami, & Allen, 2011).

Review *Connect* Reflect

LG4 Summarize the influence of technology on children's development.

Review

- What role do mass media play in the lives of children and adolescents?
- How do television and electronic media influence children's development?
- What roles do computers and the Internet play in children's development?

Connect

- In this section, you learned about cyberbullying. In Chapter 15, what did you learn about the outcomes of bullying for those who are bullied?

Reflect *Your Own Personal Journey of Life*

- How much television did you watch as a child? What effect do you believe TV viewing has had on your development?

reach your **learning goals**

Culture and Diversity

Culture and Children's Development   Discuss the role of culture in children's development.

The Relevance of Culture to the Study of Children

Cross-Cultural Comparisons

- Culture refers to the behavior patterns, beliefs, and all other products of a particular group of people that are passed on from generation to generation. If the study of children is to be a relevant discipline in the decades to come, increased attention must be paid to culture. In future years, children will be citizens of the world, and the more we understand the values of other cultures and others' cultural behaviors, the more effectively we will be able to interact.

- Cross-cultural comparisons contrast one culture with one or more other cultures, which provides information about the degree to which characteristics are universal or culture-specific. The social contexts in which children develop—gender, family, and school—display important differences from one culture to another. One analysis of cross-cultural comparisons suggests that children raised in individualistic cultures are taught different values and self-concepts from those raised in collectivistic cultures. However, critics argue that categorization of cultures as individualist or collectivist is too broad and simplistic, and that in many families, parents expect their children to think and act in ways that reflect both individualistic and collectivistic values.

Socioeconomic Status and Poverty

 Describe how socioeconomic status and poverty affect children's lives.

What Is Socioeconomic Status?

- Socioeconomic status (SES) is the grouping of people who share similar occupational, educational, and economic characteristics. SES implies inequalities.

Socioeconomic Variations in Families, Neighborhoods, and Schools

- The families, neighborhoods, and schools of children have SES characteristics that are related to the child's development. Parents from low-SES families are more likely to value conformity and to use physical punishment to a greater extent than their middle-SES counterparts. High-SES children live in more attractive homes and in safer neighborhoods than low-SES children. Low-SES children are more apt to experience problems such as depression, low self-esteem, and delinquency. When low-SES children do well in school, it often is because parents have made sacrifices to improve conditions and provide support that contributes to school success.

Poverty

- Poverty is defined by economic hardship. The poor often face not only economic hardship but also social and psychological difficulties. Poor children are exposed to more family violence, have less access to books and computers, attend inferior child care and schools, and receive less social support. When poverty is persistent and long-lasting, it has particularly adverse effects on children's development.

Ethnicity

 Explain how ethnicity is linked to children's development.

Immigration

- Ethnicity is based on cultural heritage, nationality characteristics, race, religion, and language. The immigration of families to the United States brings about a number of challenges for helping children adapt to their new culture. Immigrant children often experience language barriers, changes in SES, and separation from support networks in addition to struggling to preserve their ethnic identity while adapting to the majority culture. Parents and children may be at different stages of acculturation, leading to intergenerational conflict.

Ethnicity and Socioeconomic Status

- Too often researchers have not distinguished between the influences of ethnicity and socioeconomic status when studying ethnic minority children. Many ethnic minority children experience prejudice and discrimination, along with the difficulties caused by poverty. Although not all ethnic minority families are poor, poverty contributes to the stress of many ethnic minority families and to differences between ethnic minority groups and the White majority.

Differences and Diversity

- Recognizing and respecting differences in ethnicity is an important aspect of getting along with others in a diverse, multicultural world. Too often differences have been described as deficits on the part of ethnic minority individuals. Ethnic minority groups are not homogeneous. Failure to recognize this diversity results in stereotyping.

Prejudice and Discrimination

- Prejudice is an unjustified negative attitude toward an individual because of the individual's membership in a group. Despite progress in the treatment of minority groups, children who are members of these groups often face prejudice and discrimination.

Technology

 Summarize the influence of technology on children's development.

Media Use and Screen Time

- In terms of exposure, a significant increase in media use and screen time has occurred recently, especially among 11- to 14-year-olds. Adolescents are increasing the amount of time they spend in media multitasking. The social environment of adolescents has increasingly become digitally mediated.

Television and Electronic Media

- One negative aspect of television is that it involves passive learning. Watching violence on television is linked to higher levels of aggression in children. There also is concern about adolescents playing violent video games. Recently, researchers have found some positive influences of prosocial and exergame videos. Children's cognitive skills and abilities influence their TV viewing experiences. TV viewing is negatively related to children's mental ability and achievement. However, educational TV programming can enhance achievement.

• Today's children and adolescents are experiencing a technology revolution through the use of computers, the Internet, and sophisticated cell phones. The social environment of children and adolescents has increasingly become digitally mediated. The Internet continues to serve as the main focus of digitally mediated social interaction for adolescents but increasingly involves a variety of digital devices, including cell phones (especially smartphones). Adolescents' online time can have positive or negative outcomes. Large numbers of adolescents engage in social networking on Facebook. A special concern is the difficulty parents face in monitoring the information their children are accessing.

key terms

key people

glossary

A

A-not-B error Also called AB̄ error, this occurs when infants make the mistake of selecting the familiar hiding place (A) to locate an object, rather than looking in the new hiding place (B), as they progress into substage 4 in Piaget's sensorimotor stage.

accommodation Piagetian concept of adjusting schemes to fit new information and experiences.

acculturation Cultural changes that occur when one culture comes in contact with another culture.

active (niche-picking) genotype-environment correlations Correlations that exist when children seek out environments they find compatible and stimulating.

adolescence The developmental period of transition from childhood to early adulthood, entered at approximately 10 to 12 years of age and ending at 18 or 19 years of age.

adolescent egocentrism The heightened self-consciousness of adolescents, which is reflected in adolescents' beliefs that others are as interested in them as they are in themselves, and in adolescents' sense of personal uniqueness and invulnerability.

adoption study A study in which investigators seek to discover whether, in behavior and psychological characteristics, adopted children are more like their adoptive parents, who provided a home environment, or more like their biological parents, who contributed their heredity. Another form of the adoption study is one that compares adoptive and biological siblings.

affordances Opportunities for interaction offered by objects that are necessary to perform activities.

afterbirth The third stage of birth, when the placenta, umbilical cord, and other membranes are detached and expelled.

altruism An unselfish interest in helping another person.

amnion Prenatal life-support system that is a bag or envelope containing a clear fluid in which the developing embryo floats.

amygdala The seat of emotions in the brain.

androgens Hormones, the most important of which is testosterone, that promote the development of male genitals and secondary sex characteristics.

androgyny The presence of masculine and feminine characteristics in the same person.

anger cry A cry similar to the basic cry but with more excess air forced through the vocal cords.

animism A facet of preoperational thought: the belief that inanimate objects have lifelike qualities and are capable of action.

Apgar Scale A widely used method to assess the health of newborns at one and five minutes after birth. The Apgar Scale evaluates infants' heart rate, respiratory effort, muscle tone, body color, and reflex irritability.

aphasia A disorder resulting from brain damage to Broca's area or Wernicke's area that involves a loss or impairment of the ability to use or comprehend words.

Asperger syndrome A relatively mild autism spectrum disorder in which the child has relatively good verbal skills, milder nonverbal language problems, and a restricted range of interests and relationships.

assimilation Piagetian concept of the incorporation of new information into existing knowledge.

attachment A close emotional bond between two people.

attention Concentrating and focusing mental resources.

attention deficit hyperactivity disorder (ADHD) A disability in which children consistently show one or more of the following characteristics: (1) inattention, (2) hyperactivity, and (3) impulsivity.

authoritarian parenting A restrictive, punitive style in which the parent exhorts the child to follow the parent's directions and to respect their work and effort. Firm limits and controls are placed on the child, and little verbal exchange is allowed. This style is associated with children's social incompetence, including a lack of initiative and weak communication skills.

authoritative parenting This style encourages children to be independent but still places limits and controls on their actions. Extensive verbal give-and-take is allowed, and parents are warm and nurturant toward the child. This style is associated with children's social competence, achievement orientation, and self-reliance.

autism spectrum disorders (ASDs) Also called pervasive developmental disorders, they range from the severe disorder labeled autistic disorder to the milder disorder called Asperger syndrome. Children with these disorders are characterized by problems in social interaction, verbal and nonverbal communication, and repetitive behaviors.

autistic disorder A severe developmental autism spectrum disorder that has its onset in the first three years of life and includes deficiencies in

social relationships; abnormalities in communication; and restricted, repetitive, and stereotyped patterns of behavior.

automaticity The ability to process information with little or no effort.

autonomous morality The second stage of moral development in Piaget's theory, displayed by older children (about 10 years of age and older). The child becomes aware that rules and laws are created by people and that, in judging an action, one should consider the actor's intentions as well as the consequences.

average children Children who receive an average number of both positive and negative nominations from their peers.

B

basic cry A rhythmic pattern usually consisting of a cry, a briefer silence, a shorter inspiratory whistle that is higher pitched than the main cry, and then a brief rest before the next cry.

Bayley Scales of Infant Development Initially created by Nancy Bayley, these scales are widely used in assessing infant development. The current version has five scales: cognitive, language, motor, socioemotional, and adaptive.

behavior genetics The field that seeks to discover the influence of heredity and environment on individual differences in human traits and development.

bicultural identity Identity formation that occurs when adolescents identify in some ways with their ethnic group and in other ways with the majority culture.

biological processes Changes in an individual's body.

blastocyst The inner layer of cells that develops during the germinal period. These cells later develop into the embryo.

bonding The formation of a close connection, especially a physical bond, between parents and their newborn in the period shortly after birth.

brainstorming A technique in which children are encouraged to come up with creative ideas in a group, play off one another's ideas, and say practically whatever comes to mind.

Brazelton Neonatal Behavioral Assessment Scale (NBAS) A measure that is used in the first month of life to assess the newborn's neurological development, reflexes, and reactions to people and objects.

breech position The baby's position in the uterus that causes the buttocks to be the first part to emerge from the vagina.

Broca's area   An area of the brain's left frontal lobe that is involved in speech production and grammatical processing.

Bronfenbrenner's ecological theory   An environmental systems theory that focuses on five environmental systems: microsystem, mesosystem, exosystem, macrosystem, and chronosystem.

C

care perspective   The moral perspective of Carol Gilligan, in which people are assessed in terms of their connectedness with others and the quality of their interpersonal communication, relationships with others, and concern for others.

case study   An in-depth look at a single individual.

centration   Focusing attention on one characteristic to the exclusion of all others.

cephalocaudal pattern   The sequence in which the fastest growth occurs at the top of the body—the head—with physical growth in size, weight, and feature differentiation gradually working from top to bottom.

cesarean delivery   Removal of the baby from the mother's uterus through an incision made in her abdomen.

character education   A direct moral education approach that involves teaching students a basic "moral literacy" to prevent them from engaging in immoral behavior or doing harm to themselves or others.

child-centered kindergarten   Education that involves the whole child by considering both the child's physical, cognitive, and socioemotional development and the child's needs, interests, and learning styles.

child-directed speech   Language spoken in a higher pitch than normal, with simple words and sentences.

chromosomes   Threadlike structures that come in 23 pairs, with one member of each pair coming from each parent. Chromosomes contain the genetic substance DNA.

cliques   Small groups that range from 2 to about 12 individuals and average about 5 or 6 individuals. Cliques can form because of friendship or because individuals engage in similar activities, and members usually are of the same sex and about the same age.

cognitive moral education   Education based on the belief that students should learn to value things like democracy and justice as their moral reasoning develops; Kohlberg's theory has been the basis for many of the cognitive moral education approaches.

cognitive processes   Changes in an individual's thinking, intelligence, and language skills.

cohort effects   Effects due to a person's time of birth, era, or generation but not to actual age.

collectivism   Emphasizing values that serve the group by subordinating personal goals to preserve group integrity, interdependence of members, and harmonious relationships.

commitment   Personal investment in identity.

concepts   Cognitive groupings of similar objects, events, people, or ideas.

concrete operational stage   Piaget's third stage, which lasts from approximately 7 to 11 years of age, when children can perform concrete operations, and logical reasoning replaces intuitive reasoning as long as the reasoning can be applied to specific or concrete examples.

conduct disorder   Age-inappropriate actions and attitudes that violate family expectations, society's norms, and the personal or property rights of others.

connectedness   Consists of two dimensions: mutuality, sensitivity to and respect for others' views; and permeability, openness to others' views.

conservation   The realization that altering an object's or substance's appearance does not change its basic properties.

constructive play   Play that combines sensorimotor/practice play with symbolic representation of ideas. Constructive play occurs when children engage in self-regulated creation or construction of a product or a solution.

constructivist approach   A learner-centered approach that emphasizes the importance of individuals actively constructing their knowledge and understanding, with guidance from the teacher.

context   The settings, influenced by historical, economic, social, and cultural factors, in which development occurs.

continuity-discontinuity issue   Question about whether development involves gradual, cumulative change (continuity) or distinct stages (discontinuity).

controversial children   Children who are frequently identified both as someone's best friend and as being disliked.

conventional reasoning   The second, or intermediate, level in Kohlberg's theory of moral development. At this level, individuals abide by certain standards (internal), but they are the standards of others such as parents or the laws of society (external). The conventional level consists of two stages: mutual interpersonal expectations, relationships, and interpersonal conformity (stage 3) and social systems morality (stage 4).

convergent thinking   Thinking that produces one correct answer; characteristic of the kind of thinking required on conventional intelligence tests.

coparenting   Support parents provide for each other in jointly raising children.

core knowledge approach   States that infants are born with domain-specific innate knowledge systems, such as those involving space, number sense, object permanence, and language.

corpus callosum   Brain area where fibers connect the brain's left and right hemispheres.

correlation coefficient   A number based on statistical analysis that is used to describe the degree of association between two variables.

correlational research   Research in which the goal is to describe the strength of the relationship between two or more events or characteristics.

creativity   The ability to think in novel and unusual ways and come up with unique solutions to problems.

crisis   A period of identity development during which the adolescent is choosing among meaningful alternatives.

critical thinking   Thinking reflectively and productively, and evaluating the evidence.

cross-cultural studies   Comparisons of one culture with one or more other cultures. These provide information about the degree to which children's development is similar, or universal, across cultures, and the degree to which it is culture-specific.

cross-sectional approach   A research strategy in which individuals of different ages are compared at the same point in time.

crowds   The crowd is a larger group structure than a clique. Adolescents usually are members of a crowd based on reputation and may or may not spend much time together. Many crowds are defined by the activities in which adolescents engage.

culture   The behavior patterns, beliefs, and all other products of a group that are passed on from generation to generation.

culture-fair tests   Intelligence tests that aim to avoid cultural bias.

D

descriptive research   Research that involves observing and recording behavior.

development   The pattern of movement or change that begins at conception and continues through the life span.

developmental cascade model   Involves connections across domains over time that influence developmental pathways and outcomes.

developmental quotient (DQ)   An overall developmental score that combines subscores on motor, language, adaptive, and personal-social domains in the Gesell assessment of infants.

developmentally appropriate practice Education that focuses on the typical developmental patterns of children (age-appropriateness) and the uniqueness of each child (individual-appropriateness). Such practice contrasts with developmentally inappropriate practice, which relies on abstract paper-and-pencil activities presented to large groups of young children.

dialect   A variety of language that is distinguished by its vocabulary, grammar, or pronunciation.

difficult child   A temperament style in which the child tends to react negatively and cry frequently, engages in irregular daily routines, and is slow to accept new experiences.

direct instruction approach   A teacher-centered approach characterized by teacher direction and control, mastery of academic material, high expectations for students' progress, and maximum time spent on learning tasks.

dishabituation   The recovery of a habituated response after a change in stimulation.

divergent thinking   Thinking that produces many answers to the same question; characteristic of creativity.

divided attention   Concentrating on more than one activity at the same time.

DNA   A complex molecule that contains genetic information.

doula   A caregiver who provides continuous physical, emotional, and educational support for the mother before, during, and after childbirth.

Down syndrome   A chromosomally transmitted form of intellectual disability, caused by the presence of an extra copy of chromosome 21.

dual-process model   States that decision making is influenced by two systems, one analytical and one experiential, that compete with each other. In this model, it is the experiential system—monitoring and managing actual experiences—that benefits adolescent decision making.

dynamic systems theory   A theory, proposed by Esther Thelen, that seeks to explain how motor behaviors are assembled for perceiving and acting.

dyscalculia   Also known as developmental arithmetic disorder; a learning disability that involves difficulty in math computation.

dysgraphia   A learning disability that involves difficulty in handwriting.

dyslexia   A category of learning disabilities involving a severe impairment in the ability to read and spell.

E

early childhood   The developmental period that extends from the end of infancy to about 5 or 6 years of age, sometimes called the preschool years.

early-later experience issue   Controversy regarding the degree to which early experiences (especially during infancy) or later experiences are the key determinants of children's development.

easy child   A temperament style in which the child is generally in a positive mood, quickly establishes regular routines, and adapts easily to new experiences.

eclectic theoretical orientation   An orientation that does not follow any one theoretical approach but rather selects from each theory whatever is considered its best aspects.

ecological view   The view, proposed by the Gibsons, that people directly perceive information in the world around them. Perception brings people in contact with the environment so that they can interact with and adapt to it.

egocentrism   An important feature of preoperational thought: the inability to distinguish between one's own and someone else's perspective.

embryonic period   The period of prenatal development that occurs two to eight weeks after conception. During the embryonic period, the rate of cell differentiation intensifies, support systems for the cells form, and organs appear.

emotion   Feeling, or affect, that occurs when people are engaged in an interaction that is important to them, especially one that influences their well-being.

emotional and behavioral disorders   Serious, persistent problems that involve relationships, aggression, depression, fears associated with personal or school matters, as well as other inappropriate socioemotional characteristics.

emotional intelligence   The ability to perceive and express emotion accurately and adaptively, to understand emotion and emotional knowledge, to use feelings to facilitate thought, and to manage emotions in oneself and others.

empathy   Reacting to another's feelings with an emotional response that is similar to the other's feelings.

encoding   The mechanism by which information gets into memory.

epigenetic view   Theory that development is the result of an ongoing, bidirectional interchange between heredity and environment.

equilibration   A mechanism that Piaget proposed to explain how children shift from one stage of thought to the next. The shift occurs as children experience cognitive conflict, or disequilibrium, in trying to understand the world. Eventually, they resolve the conflict and reach a balance, or equilibrium, of thought.

Erikson's theory   Description of eight stages of human development. Each stage consists of a unique developmental task that confronts individuals with a crisis that must be resolved.

estradiol   An estrogen that is a key hormone in girls' pubertal development.

estrogens   Hormones, the most important of which is estradiol, that influence the development of female physical sex characteristics and help regulate the menstrual cycle.

ethnic gloss   Use of an ethnic label such as *African American* or *Latino* in a superficial way that portrays an ethnic group as being more homogeneous than it really is.

ethnic identity   An enduring aspect of the self that includes a sense of membership in an ethnic group, along with the attitudes and feelings related to that membership.

ethnicity   A dimension of culture based on cultural heritage, nationality, race, religion, and language.

ethology   Stresses that behavior is strongly influenced by biology, is tied to evolution, and is characterized by critical or sensitive periods.

evocative genotype-environment correlations   Correlations that exist when the child's genetically influenced characteristics elicit certain types of environments.

evolutionary psychology   Branch of psychology that emphasizes the importance of adaptation, reproduction, and "survival of the fittest" in shaping behavior.

executive attention   Involves planning actions, allocating attention to goals, detecting and compensating for errors, monitoring progress on tasks, and dealing with novel or difficult circumstances.

executive function   An umbrella-like concept that consists of a number of higher-level cognitive processes linked to the development of the brain's prefrontal cortex. Executive function involves managing one's thoughts to engage in goal-directed behavior and to exercise self-control.

expanding   Restating, in a linguistically sophisticated form, what a child has said.

experiment   A carefully regulated procedure in which one or more of the factors believed to influence the behavior being studied are manipulated while all other factors are held constant.

explicit memory   Conscious memory of facts and experiences.

extrinsic motivation   Response to external incentives such as rewards and punishments.

F

fast mapping   A process that helps to explain how young children learn the connection between a word and its referent so quickly.

fertilization   A stage in reproduction during which an egg and a sperm fuse to create a single cell, called a zygote.

fetal alcohol spectrum disorders (FASD)   A cluster of abnormalities and problems that appear in the offspring of mothers who drink alcohol heavily during pregnancy.

fetal period   The period from two months after conception until birth, lasting about seven months in typical pregnancies.

fine motor skills   Motor skills that involve more finely tuned movements, such as finger dexterity.

forgiveness   An aspect of prosocial behavior that occurs when an injured person releases the injurer from possible behavioral retaliation.

formal operational stage   Piaget's fourth and final stage, which occurs between the ages of 11 and 15, when individuals move beyond concrete experiences and think in more abstract and logical ways.

fragile X syndrome   A genetic disorder involving an abnormality in the X chromosome, which becomes constricted and often breaks.

fuzzy trace theory   States that memory is best understood by considering two types of memory representations: (1) verbatim memory trace; and (2) fuzzy trace, or gist. According to this theory, older children's better memory is attributed to the fuzzy traces created by extracting the gist of information.

G

games   Activities engaged in for pleasure that include rules and often competition with one or more individuals.

gender   The characteristics of people as males and females.

gender identity   The sense of being male or female, which most children acquire by the time they are 3 years old.

gender role   A set of expectations that prescribes how females or males should think, act, and feel.

gender schema theory   According to this theory, gender typing emerges as children gradually develop schemas of what is gender-appropriate and gender-inappropriate in their culture.

gender stereotypes   Broad categories that reflect impressions and widely held beliefs about what behavior is appropriate for females and males.

gender typing   Acquisition of a traditional masculine or feminine role.

gene × environment (G × E) interaction   The interaction of a specific, measured variation in the DNA and a specific, measured aspect of the environment.

genes   Units of hereditary information composed of DNA. Genes help cells to reproduce themselves and manufacture the proteins that maintain life.

genotype   A person's genetic heritage; the actual genetic material present in each cell.

germinal period   The period of prenatal development that takes place in the first two weeks after conception. It includes the creation of the zygote, continued cell division, and the attachment of the zygote to the uterine wall.

gifted   Possession of above-average intelligence (an IQ of 130 or higher) and/or superior talent for something.

goodness of fit   The match between a child's temperament and the environmental demands the child must cope with.

grasping reflex   A neonatal reflex that occurs when something touches the infant's palms. The infant responds by grasping tightly.

gratitude   A feeling of thankfulness and appreciation, especially in response to someone doing something kind or helpful.

gross motor skills   Motor skills that involve large-muscle activities, such as moving one's arms and walking.

H

habituation   Decreased responsiveness to a stimulus after repeated presentations of the stimulus.

helpless orientation   An orientation in which one seems trapped by the experience of difficulty and attributes one's difficulty to a lack of ability.

heritability   The fraction of the variance in a population that is attributed to genetics.

heteronomous morality   The first stage of moral development in Piaget's theory, occurring from 4 to 7 years of age. Justice and rules are conceived of as unchangeable properties of the world, beyond the control of people.

hidden curriculum   The pervasive moral atmosphere that characterizes each school.

horizontal décalage   Piaget's concept that similar abilities do not appear at the same time within a stage of development.

hormones   Powerful chemical substances secreted by the endocrine glands and carried through the body by the bloodstream.

hypotheses   Specific assumptions and predictions that can be tested to determine their accuracy.

hypothetical-deductive reasoning   Piaget's formal operational concept that adolescents have the cognitive ability to develop hypotheses about ways to solve problems and can systematically deduce which is the best path to follow in solving the problem.

I

identity   Who a person is, representing a synthesis and integration of self-understanding.

identity achievement   Marcia's term for the status of individuals who have undergone a crisis and made a commitment.

identity diffusion   Marcia's term for the status of individuals who have not yet experienced a crisis (that is, they have not yet explored meaningful alternatives) or made any commitments.

identity foreclosure   Marcia's term for the status of individuals who have made a commitment but have not experienced a crisis.

identity moratorium   Marcia's term for the status of individuals who are in the midst of a crisis but whose commitments either are absent or are only vaguely defined.

identity versus identity confusion   Erikson's fifth developmental stage, which individuals experience during the adolescent years. At this time, adolescents examine who they are, what they are all about, and where they are going in life.

imaginary audience   The aspect of adolescent egocentrism that involves attention-getting behavior motivated by a desire to be noticed, visible, and "onstage."

immanent justice   Piaget's concept of the childhood expectation that if a rule is broken, punishment will be meted out immediately.

implicit memory   Memory without conscious recollection; memory of skills and routine procedures that are performed automatically.

inclusion   Educating a child with special educational needs full-time in the regular classroom.

index offenses   Criminal acts, such as robbery, rape, and homicide, whether they are committed by juveniles or adults.

individualism   Giving priority to personal goals rather than to group goals; emphasizing values that serve the self, such as feeling good, striving for personal distinction and recognition for achievement, and asserting independence.

individuality   Consists of two dimensions: self-assertion, the ability to have and communicate a point of view; and separateness, the use of communication patterns to express how one is different from others.

individualized education program (IEP)   A written statement that spells out a program tailored to the needs of a child with a disability.

induction   A discipline technique in which a parent uses reasoning and explains how the child's actions are likely to affect others.

indulgent parenting   A style in which parents are highly involved with their children but place few demands or controls on them. This is associated with children's social incompetence, especially a lack of self-control and a lack of respect for others.

infancy   The developmental period that extends from birth to about 18 to 24 months.

infinite generativity   The ability to produce an endless number of meaningful sentences using a finite set of words and rules.

information-processing approach   An approach that focuses on the ways children process information about their world—how they manipulate information, monitor it, and create strategies to deal with it.

information-processing theory   Emphasizes that individuals manipulate information, monitor it, and strategize about it. Central to this theory are the processes of memory and thinking.

insecure avoidant babies   Babies who show insecurity by avoiding the mother.

insecure disorganized babies   Babies who show insecurity by being disorganized and disoriented.

insecure resistant babies   Babies who might cling to the caregiver, then resist her by fighting against the closeness, perhaps by kicking or pushing away.

intellectual disability   A condition of limited mental ability in which the individual (1) has a low IQ, usually below 70 on a traditional intelligence test; (2) has difficulty adapting to everyday life; and (3) has an onset of these characteristics by age 18.

intelligence quotient (IQ)   An individual's mental age divided by chronological age and multiplied by 100; devised in 1912 by William Stern.

intelligence   The ability to solve problems and to adapt to and learn from experiences.

intermodal perception   The ability to relate and integrate information about two or more sensory modalities, such as vision and hearing.

intimacy in friendship   Self-disclosure or the sharing of private thoughts.

intrinsic motivation   Internal motivational factors such as self-determination, curiosity, challenge, and effort.

intuitive thought substage   The second substage of preoperational thought, occurring between approximately 4 and 7 years of age, when children begin to use primitive reasoning.

J

joint attention   Individuals focusing on the same object or event; requires the ability to track another's behavior, one person directing another's attention, and reciprocal interaction.

justice perspective   A moral perspective that focuses on the rights of the individual; individuals independently make moral decisions.

juvenile delinquency   Refers to a great variety of behaviors by an adolescent, ranging from unacceptable behavior to breaking the law.

K

kangaroo care   Treatment for preterm infants that involves skin-to-skin contact.

Klinefelter syndrome   A chromosomal disorder in which males have an extra X chromosome, making them XXY instead of XY.

kwashiorkor   Severe malnutrition caused by a protein-deficient diet, causing the feet and abdomen to swell with water.

L

labeling   Identifying the names of objects.

laboratory   A controlled setting from which many of the complex factors of the "real world" have been removed.

language   A form of communication, whether spoken, written, or signed, that is based on a system of symbols.

language acquisition device (LAD)   Chomsky's term that describes a biological endowment enabling children to detect the features and rules of language, including phonology, syntax, and semantics.

lateralization   Specialization of function in one hemisphere of the cerebral cortex or the other.

learning disabilities   Disabilities involving understanding or using spoken or written language. The difficulty can appear in listening, thinking, reading, writing, spelling, or mathematics. To be classified as a learning disability, the problem must not be primarily the result of visual, hearing, or motor disabilities; intellectual disability; emotional disorders; or environmental, cultural, or economic disadvantage.

least restrictive environment (LRE)   The concept that a child with a disability must be educated in a setting that is similar to classrooms in which children without a disability are educated.

long-term memory   A relatively permanent and unlimited type of memory.

longitudinal approach   A research strategy in which the same individuals are studied over a period of time, usually several years.

love withdrawal   A discipline technique in which a parent withholds attention or love from the child in an effort to control the child's behavior.

low birth weight infant   Infant that weighs less than 5½ pounds at birth.

M

marasmus   Severe malnutrition caused by an insufficient protein-calorie intake, resulting in a shrunken, elderly appearance.

mastery motivation   An approach to achievement in which one is task oriented, focusing on learning strategies and the achievement process rather than ability or the outcome.

meiosis   A specialized form of cell division that forms eggs and sperm (also known as gametes).

memory   Retention of information over time.

menarche   A girl's first menstruation.

mental age (MA)   An individual's level of mental development relative to others.

metacognition   Cognition about cognition, or "knowing about knowing."

metalinguistic awareness   Knowledge about language.

metamemory   Knowledge about memory.

metaphor   An implied comparison between two unlike things.

middle and late childhood   The developmental period that extends from about 6 to 11 years of age, sometimes called the elementary school years.

Millennials   The generation born after 1980, the first to come of age and enter emerging adulthood in the new millennium.

mindfulness   Being alert, mentally present, and cognitively flexible while going through life's everyday activities and tasks.

mindset   Dweck's concept referring to the cognitive view individuals develop for themselves; individuals have either a fixed or growth mindset.

mitosis   Cellular reproduction in which the cell's nucleus duplicates itself with two new cells being formed, each containing the same DNA as the parent cell, arranged in the same 23 pairs of chromosomes.

Montessori approach   An educational philosophy in which children are given considerable freedom and spontaneity in choosing activities and are allowed to move from one activity to another as they desire.

moral development   Changes in thoughts, feelings, and behaviors regarding standards of right and wrong.

moral exemplars   People who have lived extraordinary lives, having developed their personality, identity, character, and virtue to a level that reflects moral excellence and commitment.

moral identity   The aspect of personality that is present when individuals have moral notions and commitments that are central to their lives.

Moro reflex   A neonatal startle response that occurs in reaction to a sudden, intense noise or movement. When startled, the newborn arches its back, throws its head back, and flings out its arms and legs. Then the newborn rapidly closes its arms and legs to the center of the body.

morphology   The rule system that governs how words are formed in a language.

multiple developmental trajectories   Concept that adults follow one trajectory and children and adolescents another one; understanding how these trajectories mesh is important.

myelination   The process of encasing axons with a myelin sheath that increases the speed of processing information.

N

natural childbirth   This method attempts to reduce the mother's pain by decreasing her fear through education about childbirth and relaxation techniques during delivery.

naturalistic observation   Behavioral observation that takes place in real-world settings.

nature-nurture issue   Debate about whether development is primarily influenced by nature or nurture. The "nature" proponents claim biological inheritance is the most important influence on development; the "nurture" proponents claim that environmental experiences are the most influential factors.

neglected children Children who are infrequently identified as a best friend but are not disliked by their peers.

neglectful parenting A style in which the parent is very uninvolved in the child's life. It is associated with children's social incompetence, especially a lack of self-control and poor self-esteem.

neo-Piagetians Developmentalists who have elaborated on Piaget's theory, believing that children's cognitive development is more specific in many respects than Piaget thought and giving more emphasis to how children use memory, attention, and strategies to process information.

Neonatal Intensive Care Unit Network Neurobehavioral Scale (NNNS) An "offspring" of the NBAS, the NNNS provides an assessment of the "at-risk" newborn's behavior, neurological and stress responses, and regulatory capacities.

neuroconstructivist view Theory of brain development emphasizing the following points: (a) biological processes and environmental conditions influence the brain's development, (b) the brain has plasticity and is context dependent, and (c) the development of the brain and the child's cognitive development are closely linked.

neurons Nerve cells, which handle information processing at the cellular level in the brain.

nonshared environmental experiences The child's own unique experiences, both within the family and outside the family, that are not shared by another sibling.

normal distribution A symmetrical distribution with a majority of the cases falling in the middle of the possible range of scores and few scores appearing toward the extremes of the range.

O

object permanence The Piagetian term for one of an infant's most important accomplishments: understanding that objects and events continue to exist even when they cannot directly be seen, heard, or touched.

operations Internalized actions that allow children to do mentally what before they had done only physically. Operations also are reversible mental actions.

organization Piaget's concept of grouping isolated behaviors into a higher-order, more smoothly functioning cognitive system; the grouping or arranging of items into categories.

organogenesis Organ formation that takes place during the first two months of prenatal development.

P

pain cry A sudden appearance of loud crying without preliminary moaning, and a long initial cry followed by an extended period of breath holding.

passive genotype-environment correlations Correlations that exist when the natural parents, who are genetically related to the child, provide a rearing environment for the child.

peers Children who share the same age or maturity level.

perception The interpretation of sensation.

performance orientation An orientation in which one focuses on winning rather than achievement outcomes, and happiness is thought to result from winning.

personal fable The part of adolescent egocentrism that involves an adolescent's sense of uniqueness and invincibility.

perspective taking The social cognitive process involved in assuming the perspective of others and understanding their thoughts and feelings.

phenotype The way an individual's genotype is expressed in observed and measurable characteristics.

phenylketonuria (PKU) A genetic disorder in which an individual cannot properly metabolize an amino acid. PKU is now easily detected but, if left untreated, results in intellectual disability and hyperactivity.

phonics approach An approach emphasizing that reading instruction should focus on teaching the basic rules for translating written symbols into sounds.

phonology The sound system of a language, which includes the sounds used and rules about how they may be combined.

Piaget's theory Theory stating that children actively construct their understanding of the world and go through four stages of cognitive development: sensorimotor, preoperational, concrete operational, and formal operational.

placenta A life-support system that consists of a disk-shaped group of tissues in which small blood vessels from the mother and offspring intertwine.

play A pleasurable activity that is engaged in for its own sake.

play therapy Therapy that allows the child to work off frustrations and is a medium through which the therapist can analyze the child's conflicts and ways of coping with them. Children may feel less threatened and be more likely to express their true feelings in the context of play.

popular children Children who are frequently identified as a best friend and are rarely disliked by their peers.

possible self What an individual might become, would like to become, and is afraid of becoming.

postconventional reasoning The third and highest level in Kohlberg's theory of moral development. At this level, morality is more internal. The postconventional level consists of two stages: social contract or utility and individual rights (stage 5) and universal ethical principles (stage 6).

postpartum depression Characteristic of women who have such strong feelings of sadness, anxiety, or despair that they have trouble coping with daily tasks during the postpartum period.

postpartum period The period after childbirth when the mother adjusts, both physically and psychologically, to the process of childbirth. This period lasts about six weeks or until her body has completed its adjustment and returned to a near prepregnant state.

power assertion A discipline technique in which a parent attempts to gain control over the child or the child's resources.

practice play Play that involves repetition of behavior when new skills are being learned or when physical or mental mastery and coordination of skills are required for games or sports. Practice play can be engaged in throughout life.

pragmatics The appropriate use of language in different contexts.

precocious puberty Very early onset and rapid progression of puberty.

preconventional reasoning The lowest level in Kohlberg's theory. At this level, morality is often focused on reward and punishment. The two stages in preconventional reasoning are punishment and obedience orientation (stage 1) and individualism, instrumental purpose, and exchange (stage 2).

prefrontal cortex The highest level of the frontal lobes that is involved in reasoning, decision making, and self-control.

prejudice An unjustified negative attitude toward an individual because of her or his membership in a group.

prenatal period The time from conception to birth.

preoperational stage The second Piagetian developmental stage, which lasts from about 2 to 7 years of age, when children begin to represent the world with words, images, and drawings.

prepared childbirth Developed by French obstetrician Ferdinand Lamaze, this childbirth strategy is similar to natural childbirth but includes a special breathing technique to control pushing in the final stages of labor and a more detailed anatomy and physiology course.

pretense/symbolic play Play that occurs when a child transforms the physical environment into a symbol.

preterm infants Those born before the completion of 37 weeks of gestation (the time between fertilization and birth).

primary emotions Emotions that are present in humans and other animals, and emerge early in life; examples are joy, anger, sadness, fear, and disgust.

Project Head Start Compensatory education designed to provide children from low-income families the opportunity to acquire the skills and experiences important for school success.

proximodistal pattern   The sequence in which growth starts at the center of the body and moves toward the extremities.

psychoanalytic theories   Theories that describe development as primarily unconscious and heavily colored by emotion. Behavior is merely a surface characteristic, and the symbolic workings of the mind have to be analyzed to understand behavior. Early experiences with parents are emphasized.

psychoanalytic theory of gender   A theory that stems from Freud's view that preschool children develop erotic feelings toward the opposite-sex parent. Eventually these feelings cause anxiety, so that at 5 or 6 years of age, children renounce these feelings and identify with the same-sex parent, unconsciously adopting the same-sex parent's characteristics.

psychosocial moratorium   Erikson's term for the gap between childhood security and adult autonomy that adolescents experience as part of their identity exploration.

puberty   A period of rapid physical maturation involving hormonal and bodily changes that take place primarily in early adolescence.

R

rapport talk   The language of conversation and a way of establishing connections and negotiating relationships; more characteristic of females than of males.

recasting   Rephrasing a statement that a child has said, perhaps turning it into a question, or restating a child's immature utterance in the form of a fully grammatical utterance.

reciprocal socialization   The bidirectional process by which children socialize parents just as parents socialize them.

reflexes   Built-in reactions to stimuli.

reflexive smile   A smile that does not occur in response to external stimuli. It happens during the month after birth, usually during sleep.

rejected children   Children who are infrequently identified as a best friend and are actively disliked by their peers.

religion   An organized set of beliefs, practices, rituals, and symbols that increases an individual's connection to a sacred or transcendent other (God, higher power, or higher truth).

religiousness   The degree of affiliation with an organized religion, participation in prescribed rituals and practices, connection with its beliefs, and involvement in a community of believers.

report talk   Talk that conveys information; more characteristic of males than females.

rooting reflex   A newborn's built-in reaction that occurs when the infant's cheek is stroked or the side of the mouth is touched. In response, the infant turns its head toward the side that was touched, in an apparent effort to find something to suck.

S

satire   The use of irony, derision, or wit to expose folly or wickedness.

scaffolding   Adjusting the level of parental guidance to fit the child's efforts, allowing children to be more skillful than they would be if they relied only on their own abilities.

schema theory   States that when people reconstruct information, they fit it into information that already exists in their minds.

schemas   Mental frameworks that organize concepts and information.

schemes   In Piaget's theory, actions or mental representations that organize knowledge.

scientific method   An approach that can be used to obtain accurate information by carrying out four steps: (1) conceptualize the problem, (2) collect data, (3) draw conclusions, and (4) revise research conclusions and theory.

securely attached babies   Babies who use the caregiver as a secure base from which to explore the environment.

selective attention   Focusing on a specific aspect of experience that is relevant while ignoring others that are irrelevant.

self   All of the characteristics of a person.

self-concept   Domain-specific self-evaluations.

self-conscious emotions   Emotions that require self-awareness, especially consciousness and a sense of "me"; examples include jealousy, empathy, and embarrassment.

self-efficacy   The belief that one can master a situation and produce favorable outcomes.

self-esteem   The global evaluative dimension of the self; also called self-worth or self-image.

self-understanding   A child's cognitive representation of the self—the substance and content of a child's self-conceptions.

semantics   The meaning of words and sentences.

sensation   Reaction that occurs when information contacts sensory receptors—the eyes, ears, tongue, nostrils, and skin.

sensorimotor play   Behavior that allows infants to derive pleasure from exercising their existing sensorimotor schemes.

sensorimotor stage   The first of Piaget's stages, which lasts from birth to about 2 years of age, when infants construct an understanding of the world by coordinating sensory experiences (such as seeing and hearing) with motoric actions.

separation protest   Occurs when infants experience a fear of being separated from a caregiver, which results in crying when the caregiver leaves.

seriation   The concrete operation that involves ordering stimuli along a quantitative dimension (such as length).

service learning   A form of education that promotes social responsibility and service to the community.

shape constancy   Recognition that an object remains the same even though its orientation to the viewer changes.

shared environmental experiences   Siblings' common environmental experiences, such as their parents' personalities and intellectual orientation, the family's socioeconomic status, and the neighborhood in which they live.

short-term memory   Limited-capacity memory system in which information is usually retained for up to 30 seconds, assuming there is no rehearsal of the information. Using rehearsal, individuals can keep the information in short-term memory longer.

sickle-cell anemia   A genetic disorder that affects the red blood cells and occurs most often in people of African descent.

size constancy   Recognition that an object remains the same even though the retinal image of the object changes.

slow-to-warm-up child   A temperament style in which the child has a low activity level, is somewhat negative, and displays a low intensity of mood.

small for date infants   Also called small for gestational age infants, these infants have birth weights that are below normal when the length of pregnancy is considered. Small for date infants may be preterm or full term.

social cognition   The processes involved in understanding the world around us, especially how we think and reason about other people.

social cognitive theory of gender   This theory emphasizes that children's gender development occurs through observation and imitation of gender behavior, and through rewards and punishments they experience for gender-appropriate and gender-inappropriate behavior.

social cognitive theory of morality   The theory that distinguishes between moral competence—the ability to produce moral behaviors—and moral performance—use of those behaviors in specific situations.

social cognitive theory   The view of psychologists who emphasize behavior, environment, and cognition as the key factors in development.

social constructivist approach   An emphasis on the social contexts of learning and the construction of knowledge through social interaction. Vygotsky's theory reflects this approach.

social conventional reasoning   Focuses on conventional rules established by social consensus, as opposed to moral reasoning that stresses ethical issues.

social play   Play that involves interactions with peers.

social policy A government's course of action designed to promote the welfare of its citizens.

social referencing "Reading" emotional cues in others to help determine how to act in a particular situation.

social role theory A theory stating that gender differences result from the contrasting roles of women and men—social hierarchy and division of labor strongly influence gender differences in power, assertiveness, and nurture.

social smile A smile in response to an external stimulus, which, early in development, typically is a face.

social-cognitive domain theory of moral development Theory stating that there are different domains of social knowledge and reasoning, including moral, social conventional, and personal domains. These domains arise from children's and adolescents' attempts to understand and deal with different forms of social experience.

socioeconomic status (SES) A grouping of people with similar occupational, educational, and economic characteristics.

socioemotional processes Changes in an individual's interpersonal relationships, emotions, and personality.

spirituality Experiencing something beyond oneself in a transcendent manner and living in a way that benefits others and society.

standardized test A test with uniform procedures for administration and scoring. Many standardized tests allow a person's performance to be compared with the performance of other individuals.

stereotype threat Anxiety that one's behavior might confirm a stereotype about one's group.

Strange Situation Ainsworth's observational measure of infant attachment to a caregiver, which requires the infant to move through a series of introductions, separations, and reunions with the caregiver and an adult stranger in a prescribed order.

stranger anxiety An infant's fear of and wariness toward strangers; it tends to appear in the second half of the first year of life.

strategy construction Creation of new procedures for processing information.

sucking reflex A newborn's built-in reaction of automatically sucking an object placed in its mouth. The sucking reflex enables the infant to get nourishment before it has associated a nipple with food.

sudden infant death syndrome (SIDS) A condition that occurs when an infant stops breathing, usually during the night, and suddenly dies without an apparent cause.

sustained attention The ability to maintain attention to a selected stimulus for a prolonged period of time. Sustained attention is also called *focused attention* and *vigilance*.

symbolic function substage The first substage of preoperational thought, occurring roughly between the ages of 2 and 4. In this substage, the young child gains the ability to represent mentally an object that is not present.

syntax The ways words are combined to form acceptable phrases and sentences.

T

telegraphic speech The use of short, precise words without grammatical markers such as articles, auxiliary verbs, and other connectives.

temperament Involves individual differences in behavioral styles, emotions, and characteristic ways of responding.

teratogen From the Greek word *tera,* meaning "monster," this term refers to any agent that causes a birth defect. Teratology is the field of study that investigates the causes of birth defects.

testosterone An androgen that is a key hormone in boys' pubertal development.

theory An interrelated, coherent set of ideas that helps to explain and make predictions.

theory of mind Awareness of one's own mental processes and the mental processes of others.

thinking Transforming and manipulating information in memory. Individuals think in order to reason, reflect, evaluate ideas, solve problems, and make decisions.

top-dog phenomenon The circumstance of moving from the top position in elementary school to the lowest position in middle or junior high school.

transitivity Principle that says if a relation holds between a first object and a second object, and holds between the second object and a third object, then it holds between the first object and the third object. Piaget argued that an understanding of transitivity is characteristic of concrete operational thought.

triarchic theory of intelligence Sternberg's theory that intelligence comes in three forms: analytical, creative, and practical.

trophoblast The outer layer of cells that develops in the germinal period. These cells provide nutrition and support for the embryo.

Turner syndrome A chromosome disorder in females in which either an X chromosome is missing, making the person XO instead of XX, or the second X chromosome is partially deleted.

twin study A study in which the behavioral similarity of identical twins is compared with the behavioral similarity of fraternal twins.

U

umbilical cord A life-support system that contains two arteries and one vein and connects the baby to the placenta.

V

values clarification Helping people clarify their sense of their purpose in life and what is worth working for. Students are encouraged to define their own values and understand others' values.

visual preference method A method developed by Fantz to determine whether infants can distinguish one stimulus from another by measuring the length of time they attend to different stimuli.

Vygotsky's theory A sociocultural cognitive theory that emphasizes how culture and social interaction guide cognitive development.

W

Wernicke's area An area of the brain's left hemisphere that is involved in language comprehension.

whole-language approach An approach stressing that reading instruction should parallel children's natural language learning. Reading materials should be whole and meaningful.

working memory A mental "workbench" where individuals manipulate and assemble information when making decisions, solving problems, and comprehending written and spoken language.

X

XYY syndrome A chromosomal disorder in which males have an extra Y chromosome.

Z

zone of proximal development (ZPD) Vygotsky's term for tasks that are too difficult for children to master alone but can be mastered with assistance from adults or more-skilled children.

zygote A single cell formed through fertilization.

references

A

Abasi, M., & others. (2009). The effect of hypnosis on pain relief during labor and childbirth in Iranian pregnant women. *International Journal of Clinical and Experimental Hypnosis, 57,* 174–183.

Abbott, L. C., & Winzer-Serhan, U. H. (2012). Smoking during pregnancy: Lessons learned from epidemiological studies and experimental studies using animals. *Critical Reviews in Toxicology, 42,* 279–303.

ABC News. (2005, December 12). Larry Page and Sergey Brin. Retrieved September 16, 2007, from http://abcnews.go.com?Entertainment/12/8/05

Ablow, J. C. (2013). When parents conflict or disengage: Children's perception of parents' marital distress predicts school adaptation. In P. A. Cowan & others (Eds.), *The family context of parenting in children's adaptation to elementary school.* New York: Routledge.

Accornero, V. H., Anthony, J. C., Morrow, C. E., Xue, L., & Bandstra, E. S. (2006). Prenatal cocaine exposure: An examination of childhood externalizing and internalizing behavior problems at age 7 years. *Epidemiology, Psychiatry, and Society, 15,* 20–29.

Achieve, Inc. (2005). *An action agenda for improving America's high schools.* Washington, DC: Author.

Ackerman, J. P., Riggins, T., & Black, M. M. (2010). A review of the effects of prenatal cocaine exposure among school-aged children. *Pediatrics, 125,* 554–565.

Adachi, P. J. C., & Willoughby, T. (2012, in press). Do video games promote positive youth development? *Journal of Adolescent Research.*

Adams, M. A. (2012). Mass media. In M. Kosut (Ed.), *Encyclopedia of gender in media.* Thousand Oaks, CA: Sage.

Adamson, L., & Frick, J. (2003). The still face: A history of a shared experimental paradigm. *Infancy, 4,* 451–473.

Administration for Children and Families. (2008). *Statistical fact sheet, fiscal year 2008.* Washington, DC: Author.

Adolph, K. E. (1997). Learning in the development of infant locomotion. *Monographs of the Society for Research in Child Development, 62* (3, Serial No. 251).

Adolph, K. E. (2011). Perceptual learning. Retrieved May 5, 2011, from http://www.psych.nyu.edu/adolph/research1.php

Adolph, K. E., & Berger, S. E. (2005). Physical and motor development. In M. H. Bornstein & M. E. Lamb (Eds.), *Developmental psychology* (5th ed.). Mahwah, NJ: Erlbaum.

Adolph, K. E., & Berger, S. E. (2011). Development of the motor system. In H. Pashler & others (Eds.), *Encyclopedia of the mind.* Thousand Oaks, CA: Sage.

Adolph, K. E., & Berger, S. E. (2013, in press). Development of the motor system. In H. Pashler, T. Crane, M. Kinsbourne, F. Ferreira, & R. Zemel (Eds.), *Encyclopedia of the mind.* Thousand Oaks, CA: Sage.

Adolph, K. E., & Joh, A. S. (2009). Multiple learning mechanisms in the development of action. In A. Woodward & A. Needham (Eds.), *Learning and the infant mind.* New York: Oxford University Press.

Adolph, K. E., Joh, A. S., & Eppler, M. A. (2010). Infants' perception of affordances of slopes under low and high friction conditions. *Journal of Experimental Psychology: Human Perception & Performance, 36,* 797–811.

Adolph, K. E., Karasik, L. B., & Tamis-LeMonda, C. S. (2010). Moving between cultures: Cross-cultural research on motor development. In M. Bornstein (Ed.), *Handbook of cross-cultural developmental science, Vol. 1: Domains of development across cultures.* New York: Psychology Press.

Adolph, K. E., & Kretch, K. S. (2012). Infants on the edge: Beyond the visual cliff. In A. Slater & P. Quinn (Eds.), *Developmental psychology: Revisiting the classic studies.* Thousand Oaks, CA: Sage.

Adolph, K. E., & Robinson, S. R. R. (2013). The road to walking: What learning to walk tells us about development. In P. Zelazo (Ed.) *Oxford handbook of developmental psychology.* New York: Oxford University Press.

Adolph, K. E., Vereijken, B., & Shrout, P. E. (2003). What changes in infant walking and why. *Child Development, 74,* 475–497.

Adolph, K. E., & others. (2012, in press). How do you learn to walk? Thousands of steps and dozens of falls per day. *Psychological Science.*

Agency for Healthcare Research and Quality. (2007). *Evidence report/Technology assessment Number 153: Breastfeeding and maternal and health outcomes in developed countries.* Rockville, MD: U.S. Department of Health and Human Services.

Agras, W. S., Hammer, L. D., McNicholas, F., & Kraemer, H. C. (2004). Risk factors for childhood overweight: A prospective study from birth to 9.5 years. *Journal of Pediatrics, 145,* 20–25.

Ahmed, S., & others. (2011). Community kangaroo mother care: Implementation and potential for neonatal survival and health in very low-income settings. *Journal of Perinatology, 31,* 361–367.

Ainsworth, M. D. S. (1979). Infant-mother attachment. *American Psychologist, 34,* 932–937.

Akbari, A., & others. (2011). Parity and breastfeeding are preventive measures against breast cancer in Iranian women. *Breast Cancer, 18,* 51–55.

Akhaven, S., & Lundgren, I. (2012). Midwives' experiences of doula support for immigrant women in Sweden—A qualitative study. *Midwifery, 28,* 80–85.

Akhtar, N., & Herold, K. (2008). Pragmatic development. In M. M. Haith & J. B. Benson (Eds.), *Encyclopedia of infant and early childhood development.* Oxford, UK: Elsevier.

Akolekar, R., Brown, S., Flack, N., Bilardo, C. M., & Nicolaides, K. H. (2011). Prediction of miscarriage and stillbirth at 11–13 weeks and the contribution of chorionic villus sampling. *Prenatal Diagnosis, 31,* 38–45.

Aksglaede, L., & others. (2013). 47, XXY Klinefelter syndrome: Clinical characteristics and age-specific recommendations for medical management. *American Journal of Medical Genetics C: Seminars in Medical Genetics, 163,* 55–63.

Albert, D., & Steinberg, L. (2011a). Judgment and decision making in adolescence. *Journal of Research in Adolescence, 21,* 211–224.

Albert, D., & Steinberg, L. (2011b). Peer influences on adolescent risk behavior. In M. Bardo, D. Fishbein, & R. Milich (Eds.), *Inhibitory control and drug abuse prevention.* New York: Springer.

Alegre, M., & Welsch, D. (2003). *Maxine Hong Kingston after the fire.* Retrieved January 26, 2003, from www.powers.com/authors

Alexander, N., & others. (2012). Interaction of serotonin transporter-linked Polymorphic region and environmental adversity: Increased amygdala-hypothalamus connectivity as a potential mechanism linking neural and endocrine hyperreactivity. *Biological Psychiatry, 72*(1), 49–56.

Ali, M. M., & Dwyer, D. S. (2011). Estimating peer effects in sexual behavior among adolescents. *Journal of Adolescence, 34,* 183–190.

Allen, E. G., & others. (2009). Maternal age and risk for trisomy 21 assessed by the origin of chromosome nondisjunction: A report from the Atlanta and National Down Syndrome Projects. *Human Genetics, 125,* 41–52.

Allen, J. P., & Miga, E. M. (2010). Attachment in adolescence: A move to the level of emotion regulation. *Journal of Social and Personal Relationships, 27,* 181–190.

Allen, J. P., & others. (2009, April). *Portrait of the secure teen as an adult.* Paper presented at the meeting of the Society for Research in Child Development, Denver.

Allor, J., & Al Otaiba, S. A. (2013). In B. G. Cook & M. G. Tankersley (Eds.), *Research-based practices in special education.* Upper Saddle River, NJ: Pearson.

Allstate Foundation. (2005). *Teen driving: Chronic—A report on the state of teen driving.* Northbrook, IL: Author.

Alsaker, F. D., & Valkanover, S. (2012). The Bernese program against victimization in kindergarten and elementary school. *New Directions in Youth Development, 133,* 15–28.

Alvarez, O., & others. (2012, in press). Effect of hydroxyurea on renal function parameters: Results from the multi-center placebo controlled Baby Hug clinical trial for infants with sickle cell anemia. *Pediatric Blood and Cancer.*

Amabile, T. M. (1993). Commentary. In D. Goleman, P. Kaufman, & M. Ray. *The creative spirit.* New York: Plume.

Amabile, T. M., & Hennessey, B. A. (1992). The motivation for creativity in children. In A. K. Boggiano & T. S. Pittman (Eds.), *Achievement and motivation.* New York: Cambridge University Press.

Amato, P. R. (2006). Marital discord, divorce, and children's well-being: Results from a 20-year longitudinal study of two generations. In A. Clarke-Stewart & J. Dunn (Eds.), *Families count*. New York: Cambridge University Press.

Amato, P. R., & Booth, A. (1996). A prospective study of divorce and parent-child relationships. *Journal of Marriage and the Family, 58*, 356–365.

Amato, P. R., & Dorius, C. (2010). Fathers, children, and divorce. In M. E. Lamb (Ed.), *The role of the father in child development* (5th ed.). New York: Wiley.

American Academy of Pediatrics. (2001). Committee on Public Education: Children, adolescents, and television. *Pediatrics, 107*, 423–426.

American Academy of Pediatrics. (2001). Health care supervision for children with Williams syndrome. *Pediatrics, 107*, 1192–1204.

American Academy of Pediatrics Section on Breastfeeding. (2012). Breastfeeding and the use of human milk. *Pediatrics, 129*, e827–e841.

American Academy of Pediatrics Task Force on Infant Positioning and SIDS. (2000). Changing concepts of sudden infant death syndrome. *Pediatrics, 105*, 650–656.

American Pregnancy Association. (2013). *Mercury levels in fish*. Retrieved January 2, 2013, from www.americanpregnancy.org/pregnancyhealth/fishmercury.htm

American Psychological Association. (2003). *Psychology: Scientific problem solvers*. Washington, DC: Author.

Amsel, E., & Smetana, J. G. (Eds.). (2011). *Adolescent vulnerabilities and opportunities: Constructivist and development perspectives*. New York: Cambridge University Press.

Amso, D., & Johnson, S. P. (2010). Building object knowledge form perceptual input. In B. Hood & L. Santos (Eds.), *The origins of object knowledge*. New York: Oxford University Press.

Amsterdam, B. K. (1968). *Mirror behavior in children under two years of age*. Unpublished doctoral dissertation, University of North Carolina, Chapel Hill.

Anderman, E. M. (2012). Adolescence. In K. Harris, S. Graham, & T. Urdan (Eds.), *APA Handbook of Educational Psychology*. Washington, DC: American Psychological Association.

Anderman, E. M., & Anderman, L. H. (2010). *Classroom motivation*. Upper Saddle River, NJ: Prentice Hall.

Anderman, E. M., Gray, D. L., & Chang, Y. (2013). Motivation and classroom learning. In I. B. Weiner & others (Eds.), *Handbook of psychology* (2nd ed., Vol. 7). New York: Wiley.

Anderson, D. R., Huston, A. C., Schmitt, K., Linebarger, D. L., & Wright, J. C. (2001). Early childhood viewing and adolescent behavior: The recontact study. *Monographs of the Society for Research in Child Development, 66*(1), Serial No. 264.

Anderson, D. R., Lorch, E. P., Field, D. E., Collins, P. A., & Nathan, J. G. (1985, April). *Television viewing at home: Age trends in visual attention and time with TV*. Paper presented at the biennial meeting of the Society of Research in Child Development, Toronto.

Anderson, E. R., & Greene, S. M. (2011). "My child and I are a package deal": Balancing adult and child concerns in repartnering after divorce. *Journal of Family Psychology, 25*, 741–750.

Anderson, E., Greene, S. M., Hetherington, E. M., & Clingempeel, W. G. (1999). The dynamics of parental remarriage. In E. M. Hetherington (Ed.), *Coping with divorce, single parenting, and remarriage*. Mahwah, NJ: Erlbaum.

Anderson, P. J., & others. (2011). Attention problems in a representative sample of extremely preterm/extremely low birth weight children. *Developmental Neuropsychology, 36*, 57–73.

Anderson, S. E., Gooze, R. A., Lemeshow, S., & Whitaker, R. C. (2012). Quality of early maternal-child relationship and risk of adolescent obesity. *Pediatrics, 129*, 132–140.

Andersson, H., & Bergman, L. R. (2011). The role of task persistence in young adolescence for successful educational and occupational attainment in middle adulthood. *Developmental Psychology, 47*, 950–960.

Andersson, U. (2010). The contribution of working memory capacity to foreign language comprehension in children. *Memory, 18*, 458–472.

Ang, S., Dyne, L. V., & Tan, M. L. (2011). Cultural intelligence. In R. J. Sternberg & S. B. Kaufman (Eds.), *Cambridge handbook of intelligence*. New York: Cambridge University Press.

Ang, S., Rodgers, J. L., & Wanstrom, L. (2010). The Flynn effect within subgroups in the U.S.: Gender, race, income, education, and urbanization differences in the NYLS-children data. *Intelligence, 38*, 367–384.

Ansary, N. S., & Luthar, S. S. (2009). Distress and academic achievement among adolescents of affluence: A study of externalizing and internalizing problem behaviors and school performance. *Development and Psychopathology, 21*, 319–341.

Ansary, N. S., McMahon, T. J., & Luthar, S. S. (2012). Socioeconomic context and emotional-behavioral achievement links: Concurrent and prospective associations among low- and high-income youth. *Journal of Research on Adolescence, 22*, 14–30.

Anspaugh, D., & Ezell, G. (2013). *Teaching today's health* (10th ed.). Upper Saddle River, NJ: Pearson.

Antonogeorgos, G., & others. (2011). Association of extracurricular sports participation with obesity in Greek children. *Journal of Sports Medicine and Physical Fitness, 51*, 121–127.

Antonopoulos, C., & others. (2011). Maternal smoking during pregnancy and childhood lymphoma: A meta-analysis. *International Journal of Cancer, 129*, 2694–2703.

Antonucci, T. C., Birditt, K., & Ajrouch, K. (2013, in press). Social relationships and aging. In I. B. Weiner & others (Eds.), *Handbook of psychology* (2nd ed., Vol. 6). New York: Wiley.

Apperly, I. A. (2012). EPS prize lecture. "What is theory of mind?": Concepts, cognitive processes, and individual differences. *Quarterly Journal of Experimental Psychology, 65*, 825–839.

Appleton, J. J. (2012). Student engagement in school. In J. R. Levesque (Ed.), *Encyclopedia of adolescence*. New York: Springer.

Aquino, K., McFerran, B., & Laven, M. (2011). Moral identity and the experience of moral elevation in response to acts of uncommon goodness. *Journal of Personality and Social Behavior, 100*, 703–718.

Arbib, M. A. (2012). *How the brain got language*. New York: Oxford University Press.

Arends, R. I. (2012). *Learning to teach* (9th ed.). New York: McGraw-Hill.

Arikan, I., & others. (2012). Cesarean section with relative indications versus spontaneous vaginal delivery: Short-term outcomes of maternofetal health. *Clinical and Experimental Obstetrics and Gynecology, 39*, 288–292.

Arim, R. G., Tramonte, L., Shapka, J. D., Dahinten, V. S., & Willms, J. D. (2011). The family antecedents and the subsequent outcomes of early puberty. *Journal of Youth and Adolescence, 40*, 1423–1435.

Arndorfer, C. L., & Stormshak, E. A. (2007). Longitudinal predictors of antisocial behavior throughout adolescence. *Journal of Youth and Adolescence, 37*, 1059–1070.

Arnett, J. J. (2006). Emerging adulthood: Understanding the new way of coming of age. In J. J. Arnett & J. L. Tanner (Eds.), *Emerging adults in America*. Washington, DC: American Psychological Association.

Arnold, K., & others. (2013). Fetal alcohol spectrum disorders: Knowledge and screening practices of university hospital medical students and residents. *Journal of Population Therapeutics and Clinical Pharmacology, 20*, e18–e25.

Aronson, E. (1986, August). *Teaching students things they think they already know about: The case of prejudice and desegregation*. Paper presented at the meeting of the American Psychological Association, Washington, DC.

Aronson, J. (2002). Stereotype threat: Contending and coping with unnerving expectations. In J. Aronson (Ed.), *Improving academic achievement*. San Diego: Academic Press.

Arseth, A., Kroger, J., Martinussen, M., & Marcia, J. E. (2009). Meta-analytic studies of identity status and the relational issues of attachment and intimacy. *Identity, 9*, 1–32.

Arterberry, M. E. (2008). Perceptual development. In M. E. Haith & J. B. Benson (Eds.), *Encyclopedia of infant and early childhood development*. Oxford, UK: Elsevier.

Asada, K., & Itakura, S. (2012). Social phenotypes of autism spectrum disorders and Williams syndrome: Similarities and differences. *Frontiers in Psychology, 3*, 247.

Asendorph, J. B. (2008). Shyness. In M. M. Haith & J. B. Benson (Eds.), *Encyclopedia of infant and early childhood development*. Oxford, UK: Elsevier.

Ashmead, D. H., & others. (1998). Spatial hearing in children with visual disabilities. *Perception, 27*, 105–122.

Aslin, R. N. (2009). The role of learning in cognitive development. In A. Woodward & A. Needham (Eds.), *Learning and the infant mind*. New York: Oxford University Press.

Aslin, R. N. (2012). Infant eyes: A window on cognitive development. *Infancy, 17*, 126–140.

Aslin, R. N., Jusczyk, P. W., & Pisoni, D. B. (1998). Speech and auditory processing during infancy: Constraints on and precursors to language. In W. Damon (Ed.), *Handbook of child psychology* (5th ed., Vol. 2). New York: Wiley.

Aslin, R. N., & Lathrop, A. L. (2008). Visual perception. In M. M. Haith & J. B. Benson (Eds.), *Encyclopedia of infant and early childhood development*. Oxford, UK: Elsevier.

Asp, F., Eskilsson, G., & Berninger, E. (2011). Horizontal sound localization in children with bilateral cochlear implants: Effects of auditory experience and age at implantation. *Otology and Neurotology, 32*(4), 558–564.

Aspen Institute. (2012). *Two generations, one future.* Washington, DC: Aspen Institute.

Astington, J. W., & Hughes, C. (2013). Theory of mind: Self-reflection and social understanding. In P. D. Zelazo (Ed.), *Oxford handbook of developmental psychology.* New York: Oxford University Press.

Athanasiadis, A. P., & others. (2011). Correlation of second trimester amniotic fluid amino acid profile with gestational age and estimated fetal weight. *Journal of Maternal-Fetal and Neonatal Medicine, 24,* 1033–1038.

Atkinson, J., & Braddick, O. (2013). Visual development. In P. D. Zelazo (Ed.), *Oxford handbook of developmental psychology.* New York: Oxford University Press.

Auyeung, B., & others. (2009). Fetal testosterone predicts sexually differentiated childhood behavior in girls and boys. *Psychological Science, 20,* 144–148.

Avent, N. D. (2012). Refining noninvasive prenatal diagnosis with single-molecule next generation sequencing. *Clinical Chemistry, 58,* 657–658.

Ayoub, C., Vallotton, C. D., & Mastergeorge, A. M. (2011). Developmental pathways to integrated social skills: The role of parenting and early intervention. *Child Development, 82,* 583–600.

B

Babbar, S., Parks-Savage, A. C., & Chauhan, S. P. (2012, in press). Yoga during pregnancy. *American Journal of Perinatology.*

Bacchini, D., & Magliulo, F. (2003). Self-image and perceived self-efficacy during adolescence. *Journal of Youth and Adolescence, 32,* 337–349.

Badaly, D., & Adolph, K. E. (2008). Beyond the average: Walking infants take steps longer than their leg length. *Infant Behavior and Development, 31,* 554–558.

Baddeley, A. D. (1990). *Human memory: Theory and practice.* Boston: Allyn & Bacon.

Baddeley, A. D. (2001). *Is working memory still working?* Paper presented at the meeting of the American Psychological Association, San Francisco.

Baddeley, A. D. (2007). *Working memory, thought, and action.* New York: Oxford University Press.

Baddeley, A. D. (2010). Working memory. *Current Biology, 20,* 136–140.

Baddeley, A. D. (2012). Working memory: Theories, models, and controversies. *Annual Review of Psychology* (Vol. 63). Palo Alto, CA: Annual Reviews.

Baer, J., & Kaufman, J. C. (2013, in press). *Being creative inside and outside the classroom.* The Netherlands: Sense Publishers.

Bagnato, S. J., & Macy, M. (2012). The authentic alternative for assessment in early childhood intervention. In T. Kehle (Ed.), *Oxford handbook of psychological assessment.* New York: Oxford University Press.

Bahali, K., Akcan, R., Tahiroglu, A. Y., & Avci, A. (2010). Child sexual abuse: Seven years into practice. *Journal of Forensic Science, 55*(3), 633–636.

Bahrick, L. E. (2010). Intermodal perception and selective attention to intersensory redundancy: Implications for social development and autism. In J. G. Bremner & T. D. Wachs (Eds.), *Wiley-Blackwell handbook of infant development* (2nd ed.). New York: Wiley.

Bahrick, L. E., & Hollich, G. (2008). Intermodal perception. In M. M. Haith & J. B. Benson (Eds.), *Encyclopedia of infant and early childhood development.* Oxford, UK: Elsevier.

Baillargeon, R. (2008). Innate ideas revisited: For a principle of persistence in infants' physical reasoning. *Perspectives on Psychological Science, 3,* 2–13.

Baillargeon, R. (2014, in press). Cognitive development in infancy. *Annual Review of Psychology* (Vol. 65). Palo Alto, CA: Annual Reviews.

Baillargeon, R., & Carey, S. (2013, in press). Core cognition and beyond: The acquisition of physical and numerical knowledge. In S. Pauen & M. Bornstein (Eds.), *Early childhood development and later achievement.* New York: Cambridge University Press.

Baillargeon, R., & Devoe, S. J. (1991). Object permanence in young children: Further evidence. *Child Development, 62,* 1227–1246.

Baillargeon, R., & others. (2012). Object individuation and physical reasoning in infancy: An integrative account. *Language, Learning, and Development, 8,* 4–46.

Bakeman, R., & Brown, J. V. (1980). Early interaction: Consequences for social and mental development at three years. *Child Development, 51,* 437–447.

Baker, J. K., Fenning, R. M., & Crnic, K. A. (2011). Emotion socialization by mothers and fathers: Coherence among behaviors and associations with parent attitudes and children's competence. *Social Development, 20,* 412–430.

Bakermans-Kranenburg, M. J., & van IJzendoorn, M. H. (2011). Differential susceptibility to rearing environment depending on dopamine-related genes: New evidence and a meta-analysis. *Development and Psychopathology, 23,* 39–52.

Bakermans-Kranenburg, M. J., Breddels-Van Bardewijk, F., Juffer, M. K., Velderman, M. H., & van IJzendoorn, M. H. (2007). Insecure mothers with temperamentally reactive infants. In F. Juffer, M. J. Bakermans-Kranenburg, & M. H. van IJzendoorn (Eds.), *Promoting positive parenting.* Mahwah, NJ: Erlbaum.

Balaji, P., Dhillon, P., & Russell, I. F. (2009). Low-dose epidural top up for emergency cesarean delivery: A randomized comparison of levobpivacaine versus lidocaine/epinephrine/fentanyl. *International Journal of Obstetric Anesthesia, 18,* 335–341.

Baldwin, S. (2011). Growth, development, and behavior: Confronting the issues of international adoption. *Journal of the Arkansas Medical Society, 107,* 183–185.

Baldwin, S. A., Christian, S., Berkeljon, A., & Shadish, W. R. (2012). The effects of family therapies for adolescent delinquency and substance abuse: A meta-analysis. *Journal of Marital and Family Therapy, 38,* 281–304.

Ballard, S. (2011). Blood tests for investigating maternal well-being. 4. When nausea and vomiting in pregnancy becomes pathological: Hyperemesis gravidarum. *Practicing Midwife, 14,* 37–41.

Bamaca-Colbert, M., Umana-Taylor, A. J., Espinosa-Hernandez, G., & Brown, A. M. (2012). Behavioral autonomy expectations among Mexican-origin mother-daughter dyads: An examination of within-group variability. *Journal of Adolescence, 35,* 691–700.

Bandura, A. (1991). Social cognitive theory of moral thought and action. In W. M. Kurtines & J. L. Gewirtz (Eds.), *Handbook of moral behavior and development* (Vol. 1). Hillsdale, NJ: Erlbaum.

Bandura, A. (1997). *Self-efficacy.* New York: W. H. Freeman.

Bandura, A. (1998, August). *Swimming against the mainstream: Accentuating the positive aspects of humanity.* Paper presented at the meeting of the American Psychological Association, San Francisco.

Bandura, A. (2000). Self-efficacy. In A. Kazdin (Ed.), *Encyclopedia of psychology.* Washington, DC, and New York: American Psychological Association and Oxford University Press.

Bandura, A. (2001). Social cognitive theory. *Annual Review of Psychology* (Vol. 52). Palo Alto, CA: Annual Reviews.

Bandura, A. (2002). Selective moral disengagement in the exercise of moral agency. *Journal of Moral Education, 31,* 101–119.

Bandura, A. (2004, May). *Toward a psychology of human agency.* Paper presented at the meeting of the American Psychological Society, Chicago.

Bandura, A. (2007). Social cognitive theory. In W. Donsbach (Ed.), *International encyclopedia of communication.* Thousand Oaks, CA: Sage.

Bandura, A. (2008). Reconstrual of "free will" from the agentic perspective of social cognitive theory. In J. Baer, J. C. Kaufman, & R. F. Baumeister (Eds.), *Are we free? Psychology and free will.* Oxford, UK: Oxford University Press.

Bandura, A. (2009). Social and policy impact of social cognitive theory. In M. Mark, S. Donaldson, & B. Campell (Eds.), *Social psychology and program/policy evaluation.* New York: Guilford.

Bandura, A. (2009). Social and policy impact of social cognitive theory. In M. Mark, S. Donaldson, & B. Campbell (Eds.), *Social psychology and program/policy evaluation.* New York: Guilford.

Bandura, A. (2010a). Self-efficacy. In D. Matsumoto (Ed.), *Cambridge dictionary of psychology.* Cambridge, UK: Cambridge University Press.

Bandura, A. (2010b). Vicarious learning. In D. Matsumoto (Ed.), *Cambridge dictionary of psychology.* Cambridge, UK: Cambridge University Press.

Bandura, A. (2012). Social cognitive theory. *Annual Review of Clinical Psychology* (Vol. 8). Palo Alto, CA: Annual Reviews.

Bank, L., Burraston, B., & Snyder, J. (2004). Sibling conflict and ineffective parenting as predictors of adolescent boys' antisocial behavior and peer difficulties: Additive and interactive effects. *Journal of Research on Adolescence, 14,* 99–125.

Banks, J. A. (2008). *Introduction to multicultural education* (4th ed.). Boston: Allyn & Bacon.

Barabasz, A., & Perez, N. (2007). Salient findings: Hypnotizability as core construct and the clinical utility of hypnosis. *International Journal of Clinical Hypnosis, 55,* 372–379.

Barakat, R., & others. (2011). Exercise during pregnancy improves maternal health perception: A randomized controlled trial. *American Journal of Obstetrics and Gynecology, 204,* 402.

Barbarin, O. A., & Aikens, N. (2009). Supporting parental practices in the language and literacy development of young children. In O. A. Barbarin & H. Wasik (Eds.), *Handbook of child development and early education.* New York: Guilford.

Barnett, S. M., Rindermann, H., Williams, W. M., & Ceci, S. J. (2011). Society and intelligence. In R. J. Sternberg & S. B. Kaufman (Eds.), *Cambridge handbook of intelligence.* New York: Cambridge University Press.

Barnett, W. S., & others. (2006). *Educational effectiveness of the Tools of the Mind curriculum: A randomized trial.* New Brunswick, NJ: National Institute of Early Education Research, Rutgers University.

Barnouw, V. (1975). *An introduction to anthropology: Vol. 2. Ethnology.* Homewood, IL: Dorsey Press.

Baron, I. S., Erickson, K., Ahronovich, M. D., Baker, R., & Litman, F. R. (2011). Neuropsychological and behavioral outcomes of extremely low birth weight at age three. *Developmental Neuropsychology, 36,* 5–21.

Baron, N. S. (1992). *Growing up with language.* Reading, MA: Addison-Wesley.

Baron-Cohen, S. (2008). Autism, hypersystemizing, and truth. *Quarterly Journal of Experimental Psychology, 61,* 64–75.

Baron-Cohen, S. (2009). Autism: The empathizing-systematizing (E-S) theory. *Annals of the New York Academy of Sciences, 1156,* 68–80.

Baron-Cohen, S. (2011). The empathizing-systematizing (E-S) theory of autism: A cognitive developmental account. In U. Goswami (Ed.), *Wiley-Blackwell handbook of childhood cognitive development* (2nd ed.). New York: Wiley.

Baron-Cohen, S., Golan, O., Chapman, E., & Granader, Y. (2007). Transported to a world of emotions. *The Psychologist, 20,* 76–77.

Barr-Anderson, D. J., Adams-Wynn, A. W., Diantis, K. I., & Kumanyika, S. (2012). Family-focused physical activity, diet, and obesity interventions in African-American girls: A systematic review. *Obesity Reviews, 14,* 29–51.

Barrett, D. E., Radke-Yarrow, M., & Klein, R. E. (1982). Chronic malnutrition and child behavior: Effects of calorie supplementation on social and emotional functioning at school age. *Developmental Psychology, 18,* 541–556.

Bartel, M. A., Weinstein, J. R., & Schaffer, D. V. (2012, in press). Directed evolution of novel adeno-associated viruses for therapeutic gene delivery. *Gene Therapy.*

Bartsch, K., & Wellman, H. M. (1995). *Children talk about the mind.* Oxford, UK: Oxford University Press.

Basanez, T., Unger, J. B., Soto, D., Crano, W., & Baezconde-Garbanati, L. (2012, in press). Perceived discrimination as a risk factor for depressive symptoms and substance use among Hispanic students in Los Angeles. *Ethnicity and Health.*

Bascandziev, I., & Harris, P. L. (2011). The role of testimony in young children's solution of a gravity-driven invisible displacement task. *Cognitive Development, 25,* 233–246.

Bassett, H. H., Denham, S. A., Mincic, M. M., & Graling, K. (2012, in press). The structure of preschoolers' relationship knowledge: Model equivalence and validity using an SEM approach. *Early Education and Development.*

Batanova, M. D., & Loukas, A. (2011). Social anxiety and aggression in early adolescents: Examining the moderating roles of empathic concern and perspective taking. *Journal of Youth and Adolescence, 40,* 1534–1543.

Bates, J. E. (2008). Unpublished review of J. W. Santrock's *Children,* 11th ed. (New York: McGraw-Hill).

Bates, J. E. (2012a). Behavioral regulation as a product of temperament and environment. In S. L. Olson & A. J. Sameroff (Eds.), *Biopsychosocial regulatory processes in the development of childhood behavioral problems.* New York: Cambridge University Press.

Bates, J. E. (2012b). Temperament as a tool in promoting early childhood development. In S. L. Odom, E. P. Pungello, & N. Gardner-Neblett (Eds.), *Infants, toddlers, and families in poverty.* New York: Guilford University Press.

Bates, J. E., & Pettit, G. S. (2007). Temperament, parenting, and socialization. In J. E. Grusec & P. D. Hastings (Eds.), *Handbook of socialization.* New York: Guilford.

Battistich, V. A. (2008). The Child Development Project: Creating caring school communities. In L. Nucci & D. Narváez (Eds.), *Handbook of moral and character education.* Clifton, NJ: Psychology Press.

Bauer, P. (2009). Learning and memory: Like a horse and carriage. In A. Needham & A. Woodward (Eds.), *Learning and the infant mind.* New York: Oxford University Press.

Bauer, P. (2013). Memory. In P. D. Zelazo (Ed.), *Oxford handbook of developmental psychology.* New York: Oxford University Press.

Bauer, P. J., & Fivush, R. (Eds.). (2013, in press). *Wiley-Blackwell handbook of children's memory.* New York: Wiley.

Bauer, P. J., Wenner, J. A., Dropik, P. I., & Wewerka, S. S. (2000). Parameters of remembering and forgetting in the transition from infancy to early childhood. *Monographs of the Society for Research in Child Development, 65* (4, Serial No. 263).

Bauer, R. M., & Dunn, C. B. (2013). Research methods in neuropsychology. In I. B. Weiner & others (Eds.), *Handbook of psychology* (2nd ed., Vol. 2). New York: Wiley.

Bauerlein, M. (2008). *The dumbest generation: How the digital age stupefies young Americans and jeopardizes our future (Or, don't trust anyone under 30).* New York: Tarcher.

Bauland, C. G., & others. (2012). Similar risk for hemangiomas after amniocentesis and transabdominal chorionic villus sampling. *Journal of Obstetrics and Gynecology Research, 38,* 371–375.

Baumeister, R. F. (2013, in press). Self-esteem. In E. Anderson (Ed.), *Psychology of classroom learning: An encyclopedia.* Detroit: Macmillan.

Baumeister, R. F., Campbell, J. D., Krueger, J. L., & Vohs, K. D. (2003). Does high self-esteem cause better performance, interpersonal success, happiness, or healthier lifestyles? *Psychological Science in the Public Interest, 4*(1), 1–44.

Baumrind, D. (1971). Current patterns of parental authority. *Developmental Psychology Monographs, 4*(1, Pt. 2).

Baumrind, D. (2012). Authoritative parenting revisited: History and current status. In R. Larzelere, A. S. Morris, & A. W. Harist (Eds.), *Authoritative parenting.* Washington, DC: American Psychological Association.

Baumrind, D., Larzelere, R. E., & Cowan, P. A. (2002). Ordinary physical punishment: Is it harmful? Comment on Gershoff. *Psychological Bulletin, 128,* 590–595.

Bauserman, R. (2002). Child adjustment in joint-custody versus sole-custody arrangements: A meta-analytic review. *Journal of Family Psychology, 16,* 91–102.

Baye, T. M., & others. (2011). Differences in candidate gene association between European ancestry and African American asthmatic children. *PLoS One, 6,* e16522.

Bayley, N. (1969). *Manual for the Bayley Scales of Infant Development.* New York: Psychological Corporation.

Bayley, N. (2006). *Bayley Scales of Infant and Toddler Development* (3rd ed.). San Antonio: Harcourt Assessment.

Beall, S. A., & DeCherney, A. (2012). History and challenges surrounding ovarian stimulation in the treatment of infertility. *Fertility and Sterility, 97,* 795–801.

Beauchamp, G., & Mennella, J. A. (2009). Early flavor learning and its impact on later feeding behavior. *Journal of Pediatric Gastroenterology and Nutrition, 48* (Suppl. 1), S25–S30.

Beauchamp, M. H., & Anderson, V. (2010). SOCIAL: An integrative framework for the development of social skills. *Psychological Bulletin, 136,* 39–64.

Bechtold, A. G., Bushnell, E. W., & Salapatck, P. (1979, April.) *Infants' visual localization of visual and auditory targets.* Paper presented at the meeting of the Society for Research in Child Development, San Francisco.

Beck, D. M., Schaefer, C., Pang, K., & Carlson, S. M. (2011). Executive function in preschool children: Test-retest reliability. *Journal of Cognition and Development, 12,* 169–193.

Bedford, R., & others. (2012). Precursors to social and communication difficulties in infants at-risk for autism: Gaze following and attentional engagement. *Journal of Autism and Developmental Disorders, 42,* 2208–2218.

Beebe, D. W., Rose, D., & Amin, R. (2010). Attention, learning, and arousal of experimentally sleep-restricted adolescents in a simulated classroom. *Journal of Adolescent Health, 47,* 523–525.

Beeghly, M., & others. (2006). Prenatal cocaine exposure and children's language functioning at 6 and 9.5 years: Moderating effects of child age, birthweight, and gender. *Journal of Pediatric Psychology, 31,* 98–115.

Been, J. V., Nurmatov, U., van Schayck, C. P., & Sheikh, A. (2013). The impact of smoke-free legislation on fetal, infant, and child health: A systematic review and meta-analystic approach. *BMJ Open, 3*(2), pii.e002261.

Beets, M. W., & Foley, J. T. (2008). Association of father involvement and neighborhood quality with kindergarteners' physical activity: A multilevel structural equation model. *American Journal of Health Promotion, 22,* 195–203.

Begley, S., & Interlandi, J. (2008, June 2). The dumbest generation? Don't be dumb. *Newsweek*. Retrieved July 22, 2008, from www.newsweek.com/id/138536/

Begus, K., & Southgate, V. (2012). Infant pointing serves an interrogative function. *Developmental Science, 15,* 611–617.

Behrens, H. (2012). Grammatical categories. In E. L. Bavin (Ed.), *Cambridge handbook of child language*. New York: Cambridge University Press.

Belk, C., & Maier, V. B. (2013). *Biology* (4th ed.). Upper Saddle River, NJ: Pearson.

Bell, J. T., & Saffery, R. (2012). The value of twins in epigenetic epidemiology. *International Journal of Epidemiology, 4,* 140–150.

Bell, M. A., & Cuevas, K. (2012). Using EEG to study cognitive development: Issues and practices. *Journal of Cognition and Development, 13,* 281–294.

Bell, M. A., & Cuevas, K. (2013, in press). Psychobiology of executive function in early development. In J. A. Griffin, L. S. Freund, & P. McCardle (Eds.), *Executive function in preschool children*. Washington, DC: American Psychological Association.

Bell, M. A., & Diaz, A. (2012). EEG/ERP measures of emotion/cognition integration during development. In T. A. Dennis & others (Eds.), Physiological measures of emotion from a developmental perspective: State of the science. *Monographs of the Society for Research in Child Development, 77*(2), 8–16.

Bell, S. M., & Ainsworth, M. D. S. (1972). Infant crying and maternal responsiveness. *Child Development, 43,* 1171–1190.

Belsky, J. (1981). Early human experience: A family perspective. *Developmental Psychology, 17,* 3–23.

Belsky, J. (2013). Commentary on perspectives and counter perspectives. In D. Narvaez & others (Eds.), *Evolution, early experience, and development*. New York: Oxford University Press.

Belsky, J., Jaffe, S., Hsieh, K., & Silva, P. (2001). Child-rearing antecedents of intergenerational relations in young adulthood: A prospective study. *Developmental Psychology, 37,* 801–813.

Belsky, J., Steinberg, L., Houts, R. M., Halpern-Felsher, B. L., & The NICHD Child Care Research Network. (2010). The development of reproductive strategy in females: Early maternal harshness → earlier menarche → increased sexual risk. *Developmental Psychology, 46,* 120–128.

Bem, S. L. (1977). On the utility of alternative procedures for assessing psychological androgyny. *Journal of Consulting and Clinical Psychology, 45,* 196–205.

Bender, H. L., & others. (2007). Use of harsh physical discipline and developmental outcomes in adolescence. *Development and Psychopathology, 19,* 227–242.

Bendersky, M., & Sullivan, M. W. (2007). Basic methods in infant research. In A. Slater & M. Lewis (Eds.), *Infant development* (2nd ed.). New York: Oxford University Press.

Bengtsson, H., & Arvidsson, A. (2011). The impact of developing social perspective-taking skills on emotionality in middle and late childhood. *Social Development, 20,* 353–375.

Benner, A. D. (2011). Latino adolescents' loneliness, academic performance, and the buffering nature of friendships. *Journal of Youth and Adolescence, 5,* 556–567.

Benner, A. D., & Graham, S. (2013, in press). The antecedents and consequences of racial/ethnic discrimination during adolescence: Does the source of discrimination matter? *Developmental Psychology*.

Benner, A. D., & Mistry, R. S. (2007). Congruence of mother and teacher educational expectations and low-income youth's academic competence. *Journal of Educational Psychology, 99,* 140–153.

Bennett, C. I. (2010). *Comprehensive multicultural education: Theory and practice* (7th ed.). Boston: Allyn & Bacon.

Bennett, S. A., Bagot, C. N., & Arya, R. (2012). Pregnancy loss and thrombophilia: The elusive link. *British Journal of Hematology, 157,* 529–542.

Benoit, D., Coolbear, J., & Crawford, A. (2008). Abuse, neglect, and maltreatment of infants. In M. M. Haith & J. B. Benson (Eds.), *Encyclopedia of infant and early childhood development*. Oxford, UK: Elsevier.

Benowitz-Fredericks, C. A., Garcia, K., Massey, M., Vassagar, B., & Borzekowski, D. L. (2012). Body image, eating disorders, and the relationship to adolescent media use. P*ediatric Clinics of North America, 59,* 693–704.

Benson, L., Baer, H. J., & Kaelber, D. C. (2009). Trends in the diagnosis of overweight and obesity in children and adolescents: 1999–2007. *Pediatrics, 123,* e153–e158.

Benveniste, L., Carnoy, M., & Rothstein, R. (2003). *All else equal*. New York: Routledge-Farmer.

Berenbaum, S. A., & Bailey, J. M. (2003). Effects on gender identity of prenatal androgens and genital appearance: Evidence from girls with congenital adrenal hyperplasia. *Journal of Clinical Endocrinology and Metabolism, 88,* 1102–1106.

Bergen, D. (1988). Stages of play development. In D. Bergen (Ed.), *Play as a medium for learning and development*. Portsmouth, NH: Heinemann.

Bergen, D., & Fromberg, D. P. (2009). Play and social interaction in middle childhood. *Phi Delta Kappan, 90,* 426–430.

Berk, L. E. (1994). Why children talk to themselves. *Scientific American, 271*(5), 78–83.

Berk, L. E., & Spuhl, S. T. (1995). Maternal interaction, private speech, and task performance in preschool children. *Early Childhood Research Quarterly, 10,* 145–169.

Berko, J. (1958). The child's learning of English morphology. *Word, 14,* 15–177.

Berko Gleason, J. (2003). Unpublished review of J. W. Santrock's *Life-span development,* 9th ed. (New York: McGraw-Hill).

Berko Gleason, J. (2005). The development of language: An overview and a preview. In J. Berko Gleason (Ed.), *The development of language* (6th ed.). Boston: Allyn & Bacon.

Berko Gleason, J. (2009). The development of language. An overview. In J. Berko Gleason & N. B. Ratner (Eds.), *The development of language* (7th ed.). Boston: Allyn & Bacon.

Berko Gleason, J., & Ratner, N. B. (Eds.). (2009). *The development of language* (7th ed.). Boston: Allyn & Bacon.

Berkowitz, M. W. (2012). Moral and character education. In K. R. Harris, S. Graham, & T. Urdan (Eds.), *APA educational psychology handbook* (Vol. 2). New York: American Psychological Association.

Berkowitz, M. W., Battistich, V. A., & Bier, M. (2008). What works in character education: What is known and what needs to be known. In L. Nucci & D. Narvaez (Eds.), *Handbook of moral and character education*. New York: Psychology Press.

Berkowitz, M. W., Sherblom, S., Bier, M., & Battistich, V. (2013). Educating for positive youth development. In M. Killen & J. G. Smetana (Eds.), *Handbook of moral development* (2nd ed.). New York: Routledge.

Berlin, L. J. (2012). Leveraging attachment research to re-vision infant/toddler care for poor families. In S. L. Odom, E. P. Pungello, & N. Gardner-Nesblett (Eds.), *Infants, toddlers, and families in poverty*. New York: Guilford.

Berlin, L. J., & others. (2009). Correlates and consequences of spanking and verbal punishment for low-income, White, African-American, and Mexican American toddlers. *Child Development, 80,* 1403–1420.

Berlyne, D. E. (1960). *Conflict, arousal, and curiosity.* New York: McGraw-Hill.

Berman, R. A. (2010). Developing linguistic knowledge and language use across adolescence. In E. Hoff & M. Shatz (Eds.), *Blackwell handbook of language development*. New York: Wiley.

Berman, S. L., You, Y., Schwartz, S., Teo, G., & Mochizuki, K. (2011). Identity exploration, commitment, and distress: A cross national investigation in China, Taiwan, Japan, and the United States. *Child Youth Care Forum, 40,* 65–75.

Bernard, K., & Dozier, M. (2008). Adoption and foster placement. In M. M. Haith & J. B. Benson (Eds.), *Encyclopedia of infant and early childhood development*. Oxford, UK: Elsevier.

Berndt, T. J. (1979). Developmental changes in conformity to peers and parents. *Developmental Psychology, 15,* 608–616.

Berndt, T. J. (1982). The features and effects of friendships in early adolescence. *Child Development, 53,* 1447–1460.

Berndt, T. J. (1999). Friends' influence on children's adjustment. In W. A. Collins & B. Laursen (Eds.), *Relationships as developmental contexts*. Mahwah, NJ: Erlbaum.

Berndt, T. J., & Perry, T. B. (1990). Distinctive features and effects of early adolescent friendships. In R. Montemayor (Ed.), *Advances in adolescent research*. Greenwich, CT: JAI Press.

Berninger, V. W. (2006). Learning disabilities. In W. Damon & R. Lerner (Eds.), *Handbook of child psychology* (6th ed.). New York: Wiley.

Berninger, V. W., & Abbott, R. (2005, April). *Paths leading to reading comprehension in at-risk and normally developing second-grade readers*. Paper presented at the meeting of the Society for Research in Child Development, Atlanta.

Berninger, V. W., & O'Malley, M. M. (2011). Evidence-based diagnosis and treatment for specific learning disabilities involving impairments in written and/or oral language. *Journal of Learning Disabilities, 44,* 167–183.

Berninger, V., & Swanson, H. L. (2013, in press). Diagnosing and treating specific learning disabilities in reference to the brain's working memory system. In H. L. Swanson & others (Eds.), *Handbook of learning disabilities* (2nd ed.). New York: Guilford.

Berry, D., Deater-Deckard, K., McCartney, K., Wang, Z., & Petrill, S. A. (2012, in press). Gene-environment interaction between DRD4 7-repeat VNTR and early maternal sensitivity predicts inattention trajectories across middle childhood. *Development and Psychopathology.*

Bertenthal, B. I. (2008). Perception and action. In M. M. Haith & J. B. Benson (Eds.), *Infant and early childhood development.* Oxford, UK: Elsevier.

Bertenthal, B. I., Longo, M. R., & Kenny, S. (2007). Phenomenal permanence and the development of predictive tracking in infancy. *Child Development, 78,* 350–363.

Bertoglio, K., & Hendren, R. L. (2009). New developments in autism. *Psychiatric Clinics of North America, 32,* 1–14.

Best, D. L. (2010). Gender. In M. H. Bornstein (Ed.), *Handbook of cultural developmental science.* New York: Psychology Press.

Best, J. R. (2010). Effects of physical activity on children's executive function: Contributions of experimental research on aerobic exercise. *Developmental Review, 30,* 331–351.

Betz, N. E. (2004). Contributions of self-efficacy theory to career counseling: A personal perspective. *Career Development Quarterly, 52,* 340–353.

Bialystok, E. (1997). Effects of bilingualism and biliteracy on children's emerging concepts of print. *Developmental Psychology, 33,* 429–440.

Bialystok, E. (2001). *Bilingualism in development: Language, literacy, and cognition.* New York: Cambridge University Press.

Bialystok, E. (2007). Acquisition of literacy in preschool children: A framework for research. *Language Learning, 57,* 45–77.

Bialystok, E. (2011). *Becoming bilingual: Emergence of cognitive outcomes of bilingualism in immersion education.* Paper presented at the meeting of the Society for Research in Child Development, Montreal.

Bialystok, E., & Craik, F. I. M. (2010). Cognitive and linguistic processing in the bilingual mind. *Current Directions in Psychological Science, 19,* 19–23.

Biehle, S. N., & Mickelson, K. D. (2012). First-time parents' expectations about the division of childcare and play. *Journal of Family Psychology, 26,* 36–45.

Biernat, M., & Danahar, K. (2013). Prejudice. In I. B. Weiner & others (Eds.), *Handbook of psychology* (2nd ed., Vol. 5). New York: Wiley.

Bigelow, A. E., & Power, M. (2012). The effect of mother-infant and skin-to-skin contact on infants' response to the Still Face Task from newborn to three months of age. *Infant Behavior and Development, 35,* 240–251.

Bigelow, A. E., & others. (2010). Maternal sensitivity throughout infancy: Continuity and relation to attachment security. *Infant Behavior and Development, 33,* 50–60.

Bihagi, S. W., & others. (2012). Do epigenetic pathways initiate late onset Alzheimer disease (LOAD): Towards a new paradigm. *Current Alzheimer Research, 9,* 574–588.

Bill and Melinda Gates Foundation. (2006). *The silent epidemic: Perspectives on high school dropouts.* Seattle: Author.

Bill and Melinda Gates Foundation. (2008). *Report gives voice to dropouts.* Retrieved July 5, 2008, from www.gatesfoundation.org/UnitedStates/Education/TransformingHighSchools/Related.

Billari, F., & Mencarini, L. (2003). Gender composition of friendship networks and age at first intercourse: A life-course data analysis. *Statistical Methods and Applications, 12,* 377–390.

Billy, J. O. G., Rodgers, J. L., & Udry, J. R. (1984). Adolescent sexual behavior and friendship choice. *Social Forces, 62,* 653–678.

Birkeland, M. S., Melkevick, O., Holsen, I., & Wold, B. (2012). Trajectories of global self-esteem development during adolescence. *Journal of Adolescence, 35,* 43–54.

Birman, B. F., & others. (2007). *State and local implementation of the "No Child Left Behind Act." Volume II—Teacher quality under "NCLB": Interim report.* Jessup, MD: U. S. Department of Education.

Bishop, K. M., & Wahlsten, D. (1997). Sex differences in the human corpus callosum: Myth or reality? *Neuroscience and Biobehavioral Reviews, 21,* 581–601.

Bjorklund, D. (2012). *Children's thinking* (6th ed.). Belmont, CA: Wadsworth.

Bjorklund, D. F. (2007). *Why youth is not wasted on the young.* Malden, MA: Blackwell.

Bjorklund, D. F. (2012). *Children's thinking* (5th ed.). Boston: Cengage.

Bjorklund, D. F. (2013). Cognitive development: An overview. In P. D. Zelazo (Ed.), *Oxford handbook of developmental psychology.* New York: Oxford University Press.

Bjorklund, D. F., & Pellegrini, A. D. (2002). *The origins of human nature.* New York: Oxford University Press.

Black, M. M., & Hurley, K. M. (2007). Helping children develop healthy eating habits. In R. E. Tremblay, R. G. Barr, C. Peters, & M. Boivin (Eds.), *Encyclopedia on early childhood development* (Rev. Ed.). Retrieved January 21, 2013, from http://www.child-encyclopedia.com/pages/PDF/eating_behaviour.pdf

Black, M. M., & Lozoff, B. (2008). Nutrition and diet. In M. M. Haith & J. B. Benson (Eds.), *Encyclopedia of infant and early childhood development.* Oxford, UK: Elsevier.

Black, M. M., & others. (2009). Participants' comments on changes in the revised special supplemental nutrition program for women, infants, and children food packages: The Maryland food preference study. *Journal of the American Dietetic Association, 109,* 116–123.

Black, M. M., & others. (2012). WIC participation and attenuation of stress-related child health risks of food insecurity and caregiver depressive symptoms. *Archives of Pediatric and Adolescent Medicine, 166,* 444–451.

Blackwell, L. S., & Dweck, C. S. (2008). *The motivational impact of a computer-based program that teaches how the brain changes with learning.* Unpublished manuscript, Department of Psychology, Stanford University, Palo Alto, CA.

Blackwell, L. S., Trzesniewski, K. H., & Dweck, C. S. (2007). Implicit theories of intelligence predict achievement across an adolescent tradition: A longitudinal study and an intervention. *Child Development, 78,* 246–263.

Blaga, O. M., & others. (2009). Structure and continuity of intellectual development in early childhood. *Intelligence, 37,* 106–113.

Blair, C., & Razza, R. P. (2007). Relating effortful control, executive functioning, and false belief understanding to emerging math and literacy ability in kindergarten. *Child Development, 78,* 647–663.

Blakemore, J. E. O., Berenbaum, S. A., & Liben, I. S. (2009). *Gender development.* Clifton, NJ: Psychology Press.

Blakemore, S-J., & Mills, K. (2014, in press). The social brain in adolescence. *Annual Review of Psychology* (Vol. 65). Palo Alto, CA: Annual Reviews.

Blandthorn, J., Forster, D. A., & Love, V. (2011). Neonatal and maternal outcomes following maternal use of buprenophine or methadone during pregnancy: Findings of a retrospective audit. *Women and Birth, 24,* 32–39.

Blass, E. (2008). Suckling. In M. M. Haith & J. B. Benson (Eds.), *Encyclopedia of infant and early childhood development.* Oxford, UK: Elsevier.

Block, J. (1993). Studying personality the long way. In D. Funder, R. D. Parke, C. Tomlinson-Keasey, & K. Widaman (Eds.), *Studying lives through time.* Washington, DC: American Psychological Association.

Bloom, B. (1985). *Developing talent in young people.* New York: Ballantine.

Bloom, L. (1998). Language acquisition in its developmental context. In W. Damon (Ed.), *Handbook of child psychology* (5th ed., Vol. 2). New York: Wiley.

Bloom, L., Lifter, K., & Broughton, J. (1985). The convergence of early cognition and language in the second year of life. Problems in conceptualization and measurement. In M. Barrett (Ed.), *Single word speech.* London: Wiley.

Blumenfeld, P. C., Kempler, T. M., & Krajcik, J. S. (2006). Motivation and cognitive engagement in learning environments. In R. K. Sawyer (Ed.), *The Cambridge handbook of the learning sciences.* New York: Cambridge University Press.

Blumenfeld, P. C., Marx, R. W., & Harris, C. J. (2006). Learning environments. In W. Damon & R. Lerner (Eds.), *Handbook of child psychology* (6th ed.). New York: Wiley.

Blumenfeld, P. C., Pintrich, P. R., Wessles, K., & Meece, J. (1981, April). *Age and sex differences in the impact of classroom experiences on self-perceptions.* Paper presented at the biennial meeting of the Society of Research in Child Development, Boston.

Bo, L. (1994). The sociocultural environment as a source of support. In F. Nestmann & K. Hurrelmann (Eds.), *Social networks and social support in childhood and adolescence.* New York: Walter de Gruyter.

Bodrova, E., & Leong, D. J. (2007). *Tools of the mind* (2nd ed.). Geneva, Switzerland: International Bureau of Education, UNESCO.

Bodrova, E., Leong, D. J., & Akhutina, T.V. (2011). When everything new is well-forgotten old: Vygotsky/Luria insights in the development of executive functions. *New Directions for Child and Adolescent Development, 133,* 11–28.

Bohlin, G., Eninger, L., Brocki, K. C., & Thorell, L. B. (2012). Disorganized attachment and inhibitory capacity: Predicting externalizing problem behaviors. *Journal of Abnormal Child Psychology, 40,* 449–458.

Bohlin, G., & Hagekull, B. (1993). Stranger wariness and sociability in the early years. *Infant Behavior and Development, 16*, 53–67.

Bohlin, G., & Hagekull, B. (2009). Socio-emotional development from infancy to young adulthood. *Scandinavian Journal of Psychology, 50*, 592–601.

Bond, B. J., Richards, M. N., & Calvert, S. L. (2013). Media and pediatric obesity. In D. Lemish (Ed.), *The handbook of children and the media.* New York: Routledge.

Bono, G. (2012, August 5). *Searching for the developmental role of gratitude: A 4-year longitudinal analysis.* Paper presented at the American Psychological Association, Orlando.

Booij, G. E. (2013). Morphological analysis. In B. Eeine & H. Narrog (Eds.), *Oxford handbook of linguistics.* New York: Oxford University Press.

Booth, A. E., & Ware, E. A. (2010). Categories, concepts, and causality: A reply to Samuelson and Perone. *Cognitive Development, 25*, 154–157.

Booth, M. (2002). Arab adolescents facing the future: Enduring ideals and pressures to change. In B. B. Brown, R. W. Larson, & T. S. Saraswathi (Eds.), *The world's youth.* New York: Cambridge University Press.

Bor, W., McGee, T. R., & Fagan, A. A. (2004). Early risk factors for adolescent antisocial behavior: An Australian longitudinal study. *Australian and New Zealand Journal of Psychiatry, 38*, 356–372.

Bornstein, M. H. (1975). Qualities of color vision in infancy. *Journal of Experimental Child Psychology, 19*, 401–409.

Bornstein, M. H. (2002). Parenting infants. In M. H. Bornstein (Ed.), *Handbook of parenting* (2nd ed., Vol. 1). Mahwah, NJ: Erlbaum.

Bornstein, M. H., Jager, J., & Steinberg, L. (2013, in press). Adolescents, parents/friends/peers: A relationship model. In I. B. Weiner & others (Eds.), *Handbook of psychology* (2nd ed., Vol. 6). New York: Wiley.

Bornstein, M. H., & Lansford, J. E. (2010). Parenting. In M. H. Bornstein (Ed.), *Handbook of cultural developmental science.* New York: Psychology Press.

Borup, L., & others. (2009). Acupuncture as pain relief during delivery: A randomized controlled trial. *Birth, 36*, 5–12.

Bosma, H. A., & Kunnen, E. S. (2001). Determinants and mechanisms in ego identity development: A review and synthesis. *Developmental Review, 21*, 39–66.

Bouchard, T. J., Lykken, D. T., McGue, M., Segal, N. L., & Tellegen, A. (1990). Source of human psychological differences: The Minnesota Study of Twins Reared Apart. *Science, 250*, 223–228.

Boucher, J. (2012a). Putting theory of mind in its place: Psychological explanations of the socio—emotional—communicative impairments in autism spectrum disorder. *Autism, 16*, 603–611.

Boucher, J. (2012b). Research review: Structural language in autistic spectrum disorder—characteristics and causes. *Journal of Child Psychology and Psychiatry, 53*, 219–233.

Boucher, J., Mayes, A., & Bigham, S. (2012). Memory in autism spectrum disorder. *Psychological Bulletin, 138*, 458–496.

Boukydis, C. F., & Lester, B. M. (2008). Mother-infant consultation during drug treatment: Research and innovative clinical practice. *Harm Reduction Journal, 5*, 6.

Bower, T. G. R. (1966). Slant perception and shape constancy in infants. *Science, 151*, 832–834.

Bowker, J. C., Rubin, K., & Coplan, R. (2012). Social withdrawal during adolescence. In J. R. Levesque (Ed.), *Encyclopedia of adolescence.* New York: Springer.

Bowker, J. C., & Spencer, S. V. (2010). Friendship and adjustment: A focus on mixed-grade friendships. *Journal of Youth and Adolescence, 39*, 1318–1329.

Bowlby, J. (1969). *Attachment and loss* (Vol. 1). London: Hogarth Press.

Bowlby, J. (1989). *Secure and insecure attachment.* New York: Basic Books.

Bowles, T. (1999). Focusing on time orientation to explain adolescent self concept and academic achievement: Part II. Testing a model. *Journal of Applied Health Behaviour, I*, 1–8.

Bowman, M. A., Prelow, H. M., & Weaver, S. R. (2007). Parenting behaviors, association with deviant peers, and delinquency in African American adolescents: A mediated-moderation model. *Journal of Youth and Adolescence, 36*, 517–527.

Boyer, K., & Diamond, A. (1992). Development of memory for temporal order in infants and young children. In A. Diamond (Ed.), *Development and neural bases of higher cognitive function.* New York Academy of Sciences.

Boyle, J., & Cropley, M. (2004). Children's sleep: Problems and solutions. *Journal of Family Health Care, 14*, 61–63.

Boyle, J. R., & Provost, M. C. (2012). *Strategies for teaching students with disabilities in inclusive classrooms.* Upper Saddle River, NJ: Pearson.

Boynton-Jarrett, R., & others. (2013). Childhood abuse and age at menarche. *Journal of Adolescent Health, 52*, 241–247.

Boyum, L., & Parke, R. D. (1995). Family emotional expressiveness and children's social competence. *Journal of Marriage and the Family, 57*, 593–608.

Bradley, R. H., & Corwyn, R. F. (2008). Infant temperament, parenting, and externalizing behavior in first grade: A test of the differential susceptibility hypothesis. *Journal of Child Psychology and Psychiatry, 49*, 124–131.

Bradley, R. H., & Corwyn, R. F. (2013). From parent to child to parent. . . . Paths in and out of problem behavior. *Journal of Abnormal Child Psychology.*

Bradley, R. H., Corwyn, R. F., McAdoo, H., & Coll, C. (2001). The home environments of children in the United States: Part I. Variations by age, ethnicity, and poverty status. *Child Development, 72*, 1844–1867.

Brainerd, C. J., & Gordon, L. L. (1994). Development of verbatim and gist memory for numbers. *Developmental Psychology, 30*, 163–177.

Brainerd, C. J., & Reyna, V. F. (2004). Fuzzy-trace theory and memory development. *Developmental Review, 24*, 396–439.

Brannon, L. (2012). *Gender* (6th ed.). Upper Saddle River, NJ: Prentice Hall.

Bransford, J., & others. (2006). Learning theories in education. In P. A. Alexander & P. H. Winne (Eds.), *Handbook of educational psychology* (2nd ed.). Mahwah, NJ: Erlbaum.

Brazelton, T. B. (1956). Sucking in infancy. *Pediatrics, 17*, 400–404.

Brazelton, T. B. (2004). Preface: The Neonatal Intensive Care Unit Network Neurobehavioral Scale. *Pediatrics, 113*(Suppl.), S632–S633.

Brechwald, W. A., & Prinstein, M. J. (2011). Beyond homophily: A decade of advances in understanding peer influence processes. *Journal of Research on Adolescence, 21*, 166–179.

Bredekamp, S. (2011). *Effective practices in early childhood education.* Upper Saddle River, NJ: Merrill.

Breedlove, G., & Fryzelka, D. (2011). Depression screening in pregnancy. *Journal of Midwifery and Women's Health, 56*, 18–25.

Bremner, G. (2010). Cognitive development: Knowledge of the physical world. In J. G. Bremner & T. D. Wachs (Eds.), *Wiley-Blackwell handbook of childhood cognitive development* (2nd ed.). New York: Wiley.

Bremner, J. G., & others. (2011). Two- to 8-month-old infants' cross-modal perception of dynamic auditory-visual spatial co-location. *Child Development, 82*, 1210–1223.

Brendgen, M., Lamarche, V., Wanner, B., & Vitaro, F. (2010). Links between friendship relations and early adolescents' trajectories of depressed mood. *Developmental Psychology, 46*(2), 491–501.

Brendgen, R. M. (2009). Aggression, childhood and adolescence. In D. Carr (Ed.), *Encyclopedia of the life course and human development.* Boston: Gale Cengage.

Brent, R. (2011). The pulmonologist's role in caring for pregnant women with regard to reproductive risks of diagnostic radiological studies or radiation therapy. *Clinics in Chest Medicine, 32*(1), 33–42.

Brent, R. L. (2009). Saving lives and changing family histories: Appropriate counseling of pregnant women and men and women of reproductive age concerning the risk of diagnostic radiation exposure during and before pregnancy. *American Journal of Obstetrics and Gynecology, 200*, 4–24.

Brent, R. L., Christian, M. S., & Diener, R. M. (2011). Evaluation of the reproductive and developmental risks of caffeine. *Birth Defects Research, Part B: Developmental and Reproductive Toxicology, 92*, 152–187.

Bretherton, I. (2012). Afterword. In K. H. Brisch, *Treating attachment disorders* (2nd ed.). New York: Guilford.

Bretherton, I., Stolberg, U., & Kreye, M. (1981). Engaging strangers in proximal interaction: Infants' social initiative. *Developmental Psychology, 17*, 746–755.

Brewer, M. B., & Campbell, D. T. (1976). *Ethnocentrism and intergroup attitudes.* New York: Wiley.

Bridgeland, J. M., Dilulio, J. J., & Wulsin, S. C. (2008). *Engaged for success.* Washington, DC: Civic Enterprises.

Bridgett, D. J., & others. (2009). Maternal and contextual influences and the effect of temperament development during infancy on parenting in toddlerhood. *Infant Behavior and Development, 32*, 103–116.

Bril, B. (1999). Dires sur l'enfant selon les cultures. Etat des lieux et perspectives. In B. Bril, P. R. Dasen, C. Sabatier, & B. Krewer (Eds.), *Propos sur l'enfant et l'adolescent. Quels enfants pour quelles cultures?* Paris: L'Harmattan.

Brion, M., & others. (2012, in press). Sarcomeric gene mutations in sudden infant death syndrome (SIDS). *Forensic Science International.*

Brisch, K. H. (2012). *Treating attachment disorders* (2nd ed.). New York: Guilford.

Britton, J. R., Britton, H. L., & Gronwaldt, V. (2006). Breastfeeding, sensitivity, and attachment. *Pediatrics, 118,* e1436–e1443.

Broadbent, K. G., & others. (2012). Brainstem deficiency of the 14-3-3 regulator of serotonin synthesis: A proteomics analysis in the sudden infant death syndrome. *Molecular and Cellular Proteomics, 11,* M111.009530.

Brocardo, P. S., Gil-Mohapel, J., & Christie, B. R. (2011). The role of oxidative stress in fetal alcohol spectrum disorders. *Brain Research Reviews, 67,* 209–225.

Brockmeyer, S., Treboux, D., & Crowell, J. A. (2005, April). *Parental divorce and adult children's attachment status and marital relationships.* Paper presented at the meeting of the Society for Research in Child Development, Atlanta.

Brockmeyer, T., & others. (2012, in press). The thinner the better: Self-esteem and low body weight in anorexia nervosa. *Clinical Psychology and Psychotherapy.*

Brodsky, J. L., Viner-Brown, S., & Handler, A. S. (2009). Change in maternal cigarette smoking among pregnant WIC participants in Rhode Island. *Maternal and Child Health Journal, 13,* 822–831.

Brody, G. H., & others. (2001). The influence of neighborhood disadvantage, collective socialization, and parenting on African American children's affiliation with deviant peers. *Child Development, 72,* 1231–1246.

Brody, N. (2007). Does education influence intelligence? In P. C. Kyllonen, R. D. Roberts, & L. Stankov (Eds.), *Extending intelligence.* Mahwah, NJ: Erlbaum.

Brodzinsky, D. M., & Pinderhughes, E. (2002). Parenting and child development in adoptive families. In M. H. Bornstein (Ed.), *Handbook of parenting* (Vol. 1). Mahwah, NJ: Erlbaum.

Bronfenbrenner, U. (1986). Ecology of the family as a context for human development: Research perspectives. *Developmental Psychology, 22,* 723–742.

Bronfenbrenner, U. (2000). Ecological theory. In A. Kazdin (Ed.), *Encyclopedia of psychology.* Washington, DC, & New York: American Psychological Association and Oxford University Press.

Bronfenbrenner, U. (2004). *Making human beings human.* Thousand Oaks, CA: Sage.

Bronfenbrenner, U., & Morris, P. (1998). The ecology of developmental processes. In W. Damon (Ed.), *Handbook of child psychology* (5th ed., Vol. 1). New York: Wiley.

Bronfenbrenner, U., & Morris, P. A. (2006). The ecology of developmental processes. In W. Damon & R. Lerner (Eds.), *Handbook of child psychology* (6th ed.). New York: Wiley.

Bronstein, P. (2006). The family environment: Where gender role socialization begins. In J. Worell & C. D. Goodheart (Eds.), *Handbook of girls' and women's psychological health.* New York: Oxford University Press.

Brook, J. S., Brook, D. W., Gordon, A. S., Whiteman, M., & Cohen, P. (1990). The psychological etiology of adolescent drug use: A family interactional approach. *Genetic, Social, and General Psychology Monographs, 116,* 110–267.

Brooker, R. J., Widaier, E. P., Graham, L., & Stiling, P. (2014). *Biology* (3rd ed.).

Brooks, J. G., & Brooks, M. G. (1993). *The case for constructivist classrooms.* Alexandria, VA: Association for Supervision and Curriculum.

Brooks, J. G., & Brooks, M. G. (2001). *The case for constructivist classrooms.* (2nd ed.). Upper Saddle River, NJ: Erlbaum.

Brooks. R., & Meltzoff. A. N. (2005). The development of gaze following and its relation to language. *Developmental Science, 8,* 535–543.

Brooks-Gunn, J. (2003). Do you believe in magic?: What we can expect from early childhood programs. *Social Policy Report, Society for Research in Child Development, XVII* (1), 1–13.

Brooks-Gunn, J., Han, W-J., & Waldfogel, J. (2010). First-year maternal employment and child development in the first seven years. *Monographs of the Society for Research in Child Development, 75*(2), 1–147.

Brooks-Gunn, J., & Warren, M. P. (1989). The psychological significance of secondary sexual characteristics in 9- to 11-year-old girls. *Child Development, 59,* 161–169.

Brophy, J. (2004). *Motivating students to learn* (2nd ed.). Mahwah, NJ: Erlbaum.

Brotman, L. M., & others. (2012). Early childhood family intervention and long-term obesity prevention among high-risk minority youth. *Pediatrics, 129,* e621–e628.

Broverman, I., Vogel, S., Broverman, D., Clarkson, F., & Rosenkranz, P. (1972). Sex-role stereotypes: A current appraisal. *Journal of Social Issues, 28,* 59–78.

Brown, A. L., & Day, J. D. (1983). Macrorules for summarizing texts: The development of expertise. *Journal of Verbal Learning and Verbal Behavior, 22,* 1–14.

Brown, B. B. (1999). Measuring the peer environment of American adolescents. In S. L. Friedman & T. D. Wachs (Eds.), *Measuring environment across the life span.* Washington, DC: American Psychological Association.

Brown, B. B. (2004). Adolescents' relationships with peers. In R. M. Lerner & L. Steinberg (Eds.), *Handbook of adolescent psychology* (2nd ed.). New York: Wiley.

Brown, B. B. (2011). Popularity in peer group perspective: The role of status in adolescent peer systems. In A. H. N. Cillessen, D. Schwartz, & L. Mayeux (Eds.), *Popularity in the peer system.* New York: Guilford.

Brown, B. B., & Bakken, J. P. (2011). Parenting and peer relationships: Reinvigorating research on family-peer linkages in adolescence. *Journal of Research on Adolescence, 21,* 153–165.

Brown, B. B., & Larson, J. (2009). Peer relationships in adolescence. In R. L. Lerner & L. Steinberg (Eds.), *Handbook of adolescent psychology* (3rd ed.). New York: Wiley.

Brown, B. B., & Larson, R. W. (2002). The kaleidoscope of adolescence: Experiences of the world's youth at the beginning of the 21st century. In B. B. Brown, R. W. Larson, & T. S. Saraswathi (Eds.), *The world's youth.* New York: Cambridge University Press.

Brown, B. B., & Lohr, M. J. (1987). Peer-group affiliation and adolescent self-esteem: An integration of ego-identity and symbolic-interaction theories. *Journal of Personality and Social Psychology, 52,* 47–55.

Brown, D. (2013, in press). Morphological typology. In J. J. Song (Ed.), *Oxford handbook of linguistic typology.* New York: Oxford University Press.

Brown, H. L., & Graves, C. R. (2013). Smoking and marijuana in pregnancy. *Clinical Obstetrics and Gynecology, 56,* 107–113.

Brown, J. D., & Bobkowski, P. S. (2011). Older and newer media: Patterns of use and effects on adolescents' health and well-being. *Journal of Research on Adolescence, 21,* 95–113.

Brown, L. D., Feinberg, M., & Kan, M. L. (2012). Predicting engagement in a transition to parenthood program for couples. *Evaluation and Program Planning, 35,* 1–8.

Brown, L. M., & Gilligan, C. (1992). *Meeting at the crossroads: Women's and girls' development.* Cambridge, MA: Harvard University Press.

Brown, R. (1958). *Words and things.* Glencoe, IL: Free Press.

Brown, R. (1973). *A first language: The early stage.* Cambridge, MA: Harvard University Press.

Brown, W. H., & others. (2009). Social and environmental factors associated with preschoolers' nonsedentary physical activity. *Child Development, 80,* 45–58.

Brownell, C. (2009). *Brownell – Early social development lab.* Retrieved November 9, 2009, from www.pitt.edu/~toddlers/ESDL/brownell.html

Brownell, C., Nichols, S., Svetlova, M., Zerwas, S., & Ramani, G. (2009). The head bone's connected to the neck bone: When do toddlers represent their own body topography? *Child Development, 81*(3), 797–810.

Brownell, C. A., Ramani, G. B., & Zerwas, S. (2006). Becoming a social partner with peers: Cooperation and social understanding in one- and two-year-olds. *Child Development, 77,* 803–821.

Brownell, C. A., Svetlova, M., Anderson, R., Nichols, S. R., & Drummond, J. (2012, in press). Socialization of early prosocial behavior: Parents' talk about emotions is associated with sharing and helping in toddlers. *Infancy.*

Bruchmiller, K., Margraf, J., & Schneider, S. (2012). Is ADHD diagnosed in accord with diagnostic criteria? Overdiagnosis and influence of client gender on diagnosis. *Journal of Consulting and Clinical Psychology, 80,* 128–138.

Bruck, M., & Ceci, S. J. (1999). The suggestibility of children's memory. *Annual Review of Psychology* (Vol. 50, pp. 419–439). Palo Alto, CA: Annual Reviews.

Bruck, M., & Ceci, S. J. (2012, in press). Forensic developmental psychology in the courtroom. In D. Faust & M. Ziskin (Eds.), *Coping with psychiatric and psychological testimony.* New York: Cambridge University Press.

Brumarui, L. E., & Kerns, K. A. (2010). Mother-child attachment patterns and different types of anxiety symptoms: Is there specificity of relations? *Child Psychiatry and Human Development, 41,* 663–674.

Brumariu, L. E., Kerns, K. A., & Siebert, A. C. (2012, in press). Mother-child attachment, emotion regulation, and anxiety symptoms in middle childhood. *Personal Relationships.*

Bryant, J. B. (2012). Pragmatic development. In E. L. Bavin (Ed.), *Cambridge handbook of child language.* New York: Cambridge University Press.

Bryck, R. L., & Fisher, P. A. (2012). Training the brain: Practical applications of neural plasticity from the intersection of cognitive neuroscience, developmental psychology, and prevention science. *American Psychologist, 67,* 87–100.

Brynes, J. P. (2012). How neuroscience contributes to our understanding of learning and development in typically developing and special needs students. In K. R. Harris, S. Graham, & T. Urdan (Eds.), *APA educational psychology handbook.* Washington, DC: American Psychological Association.

Bryom, S., & Symon, A. (2011). Developing the midwife's role in public health. *Practicing Midwife, 14,* 16–17.

Budd, K. S., Connell, M., & Clark, J. R. (2013). Assessment in a child protection context. In I. B. Wiener & others (Eds.), *Handbook of psychology* (2nd ed., Vol. 11). New York: Wiley.

Buhler, E., & others. (2011). Differential diagnosis of autism spectrum disorder and attention deficit hyperactivity disorder by means of inhibitory control and 'theory of mind.' *Journal of Autism and Developmental Disorders, 41,* 718–726.

Buhrmester, D. (1990). Friendship, interpersonal competence, and adjustment in preadolescence and adolescence. *Child Development, 61,* 1101–1111.

Buhrmester, D., & Chong, C. M. (2009). Friendship in adolescence. In H. Reis & S. Sprecher (Eds.), *Encyclopedia of human relationships.* Thousand Oaks, CA: Sage.

Buhrmester, D., & Furman, W. (1987). The development of companionship and intimacy. *Child Development, 58,* 1101–1113.

Bukowski, R., & others. (2008, January). *Folic acid and preterm birth.* Paper presented at the meeting of the Society for Maternal-Fetal Medicine, Dallas.

Bukowski, W. M. (2012, April). *Gender, culture, and positive and negative experiences with peers.* Paper presented at the Gender Development Research conference, San Francisco.

Bukowski, W. M., Buhrmester, D., & Underwood, M. K. (2011). Peer relations as a developmental context. In M. K. Underwood & L. H. Rosen (Eds.), *Social development.* New York: Guilford.

Bullock, M., & Lutkenhaus, P. (1990). Who am I? Self-understanding in toddlers. *Merrill-Palmer Quarterly, 36,* 217–238.

Bumpus, M. F., Crouter, A. C., & McHale, S. M. (2001). Parental autonomy granting during adolescence: Exploring gender differences in context. *Developmental Psychology, 37,* 161–173.

Burke, J. D. (2011). The relationship between conduct disorder and oppositional defiant disorder and their continuity with antisocial behaviors. In D. Shaffer, E. Leibenluft, & L. A. Rohde (Eds.), *Externalizing disorders of childhood: Refining the research agenda for DSM-V.* Arlington, VA: American Psychiatric Association.

Burke, M. G., & Miller, M. D. (2011). Practical guidelines for evaluating lead exposure in children with mental health conditions: Molecular effects and clinical implications. *Postgraduate Medicine, 123,* 160–168.

Burnham, D., & Mattock, K. (2010). Auditory development. In J. G. Bremner & T. D. Wachs (Eds.), *Wiley-Blackwell handbook of infant development* (2nd ed.). New York: Wiley.

Burns, C., Dunn, A., Brady, M., Starr, N., & Blosser, C. (2013). *Pediatric primary care* (5th ed.). New York: Elsevier.

Burstyn, I., Kuhle, S., Allen, A. C., & Veugelers, P. (2012). The role of maternal smoking in effect of fetal growth restriction on poor scholastic achievement in elementary school. *International Journal of Environmental Research and Public Health, 9,* 408–420.

Burt, S. A., McGue, M., & Iacono, W. G. (2010). Environmental contributions to the stability of antisocial behavior over time: Are they shared or non-shared? *Journal of Abnormal Child Psychology, 38,* 327–337.

Burton, R. V. (1984). A paradox in theories and research in moral development. In W. M. Kurtines & J. L. Gewirtz (Eds.), *Morality, moral behavior, and moral development.* New York: Wiley.

Bushel, P. R., & others. (2012). Population differences in transcript-regulator expression quantitative trait loci. *PLoS One, 7*(3), e34286.

Bushman, B. J., & others. (2009). Looking again, and harder, for a link between low self-esteem and aggression. *Journal of Personality, 77,* 427–446.

Bushnell, I. W. R. (2003). Newborn face recognition. In O. Pascalis & A. Slater (Eds.), *The development of face processing in infancy and early childhood.* New York: NOVA Science.

Buss, D. M. (1995). Psychological sex differences: Origins through sexual selection. *American Psychologist, 50,* 164–168.

Buss, D. M. (2004). *Evolutionary psychology* (2nd ed.). Boston: Allyn & Bacon.

Buss, D. M. (2008). *Evolutionary psychology* (3rd ed.). Boston: Allyn & Bacon.

Buss, D. M. (2012). *Evolutionary psychology* (4th ed.). Boston: Allyn & Bacon.

Buss, K. A. (2011). Which fearful toddlers should we worry about? Context, fear regulation, and anxiety risk. *Developmental Psychology, 47,* 804–819.

Bussey, K., & Bandura, A. (1999). Social cognitive theory of gender development and differentiation. *Psychological Review, 106,* 676–713.

Butcher, K., Sallis, J. F., Mayer, J. A., & Woodruff, S. (2008). Correlates of physical activity guideline compliance for adolescents in 100 cities. *Journal of Adolescent Health, 42,* 360–368.

Byard, R. W. (2012a). Should infants and adults sleep in the same bed together? *Medical Journal of Australia, 196,* 10–11.

Byard, R. W. (2012b). The triple risk model for shared sleeping. *Journal of Pediatric Child Health, 48,* 947–948.

C

Cabrera, N. J., Hofferth, S. L., & Chae, S. (2011). Patterns and predictors of father-infant engagement across race/ethnic groups. *Early Childhood Research Quarterly, 26,* 365–375.

Cabrera, N., Hutchens, R., & Peters, H. E. (Eds.). (2006). *From welfare to childcare.* Mahwah, NJ: Erlbaum.

Caldwell, S. (2013). *Statistics unplugged* (4th ed.). Boston: Cengage.

Cain, M. A., Bornick, P., & Whiteman, V. (2013). The maternal, fetal, and neonatal effects of cocaine exposure in pregnancy. *Clinical Obstetrics and Gynecology, 56,* 124–132.

Calkins, S. D. (2012). Regulatory competence and early disruptive behavior problems: Role of physiological regulation. In S. L. Olson & A. J. Sameroff (Eds.), *Biopsychosocial regulatory processes in the development of childhood behavioral problems.* New York: Cambridge University Press.

Callan, J. E. (2001). Gender development: Psychoanalytic perspectives. In J. Worrel (Ed.), *Encyclopedia of women and gender.* San Diego: Academic Press.

Calvert, S. L., Bond, B. J., & Staiano, A. E. (2013, in press). Electronic game changers for the obesity crisis. In F. Blumberg (Ed.), *Learning by playing: Frontiers of video gaming in education.* New York: Oxford University Press.

Calvert, S. L., & Valkenburg, P. M. (2011). The influence of television, video games, and the Internet on children's creativity. In M. Taylor (Ed.), *Handbook of the development of imagination.* New York: Oxford University Press.

Cameron, J., & Pierce, D. (2008). Intrinsic versus extrinsic motivation. In N. J. Salkind (Ed.), *Encyclopedia of educational psychology.* Thousand Oaks, CA: Sage.

Camos, V., & Barrouillet, P. (2011). Development change in working memory strategies: From passive maintenance to active refreshing. *Developmental Psychology, 47,* 898–904.

Campbell, A. (2010). Oxytocin and human social behavior. *Personality and Social Psychology Review, 14,* 281–295.

Campbell, F. A., Pungello, E. P., Miller-Johnson, S., Burchinal, M., & Ramey, C. T. (2001). The development of cognitive and academic abilities: Growth curves from an early childhood educational experiment. *Developmental Psychology, 37,* 231–243.

Campbell, F. A., & others. (2012). Adult outcomes as a function of an early childhood educational program: An Abcedarian Project follow-up. *Developmental Psychology, 48,* 1033–1043.

Campbell, I. G., Grimm, K. J., de Bie, E., & Feinberg, I. (2012). Sex, puberty, and the timing of sleep EEG measured in adolescent brain maturation. *Proceedings of the National Academy of Sciences U.S.A., 109,* 5740–5743.

Campbell, J. (2012). Self-esteem and the clarity of self-concept. In K. Vohs & R. F. Baumeister (Eds.), *Self and identity.* Thousand Oaks, CA: Sage.

Campbell, L., Campbell, B., & Dickinson, D. (2004). *Teaching and learning through multiple intelligences* (3rd ed.). Boston: Allyn & Bacon.

Campione-Barr, N., Bassett-Greer, K., & Kruse, A. (2013, in press). Differential associations domain of sibling conflict and adolescent emotional development. *Child Development.*

Campos, J. J. (2005). Unpublished review of J. W. Santrock's *Life-span development,* 11th ed. (New York: McGraw-Hill).

Campos, J. J. (2009). Unpublished review of J. W. Santrock's *Life-span development,* 13th ed. (New York: McGraw-Hill).

Campos, J. J., Langer, A., & Krowitz, A. (1970). Cardiac responses on the visual cliff in prelocomotor human infants. *Science, 170,* 196–197.

Camras, L. A., & others. (1998). Production of emotional facial expressions in European American, Japanese, and Chinese infants. *Developmental Psychology, 34,* 616–628.

Capaldi, D. M. (2013). Parental monitoring: A person-environment interaction perspective on this key parenting skill. In A. C. Crouter & A. Booth (Eds.), *Children's influence on family dynamics.* New York: Routledge.

Carbonell, O. A., Alzte, G., Bustamante, M. R., & Quiceno, J. (2002). Maternal caregiving and infant security in two cultures. *Developmental Psychology, 38,* 67–78.

Cardelle-Elawar, M. (1992). Effects of teaching metacognitive skills to students with low mathematics ability. *Teaching and Teacher Education, 8*(2), 109–121.

Carey, S. (1977). The child as word learner. In M. Halle, J. Bresman, & G. Miller (Eds.), *Linguistic theory and psychological reality.* Cambridge, MA: MIT Press.

Carl, J. D. (2012). *Short introduction to the U.S. Census.* Upper Saddle River, NJ: Pearson.

Carlo, G. (2013). Care-based and altruistically based morality. In M. Killen & J. G. Smetana (Eds.), *Handbook of moral development* (2nd ed.). New York: Routledge.

Carlo, G., Knight, G. P., McGinley, M., Zamboanga, B. L., & Jarvis, L. H. (2010). The multidimensionality of prosocial behaviors and evidence of measurement equivalence in Mexican American and European American early adolescents. *Journal of Research on Adolescence, 20,* 334–358.

Carlo, G., Mestre, M. V., Samper, P., Tur, A., & Armenta, B. E. (2011). The longitudinal relations among dimensions of parenting styles, sympathy, prosocial moral reasoning, and prosocial behaviors. *International Journal of Behavioral Development, 35,* 116–124.

Carlson, M. J., Pilkauskas, N. V., McLanahan, S. S., & Brooks-Gunn, J. (2011). Couples as partners and parents over children's early years. *Journal of Marriage and the Family, 73,* 317–334.

Carlson, S. M., Davis, A. C., & Leach, J. G. (2005). Executive function and symbolic representation in preschool children. *Psychological Science, 16,* 609–616.

Carlson, S. M., & White, R. (2011). *Unpublished research on executive function in young children.* Minneapolis: Institute of Child Development, University of Minnesota.

Carlson, S. M., & White, R. (2013, in press). Executive function and imagination. In M. Taylor (Ed.), *Handbook of imagination.* New York: Oxford University Press.

Carlson, S. M., Zelazo, P. D., & Faja, S. (2013). Executive function. In P. D. Zelazo (Ed.), *Oxford handbook of developmental psychology.* New York: Oxford University Press.

Carnegie Council on Adolescent Development. (1995). *Great transitions.* New York: Carnegie Foundation.

Carney, D. P., Brown, J. H., & Henry, L. A. (2013). Executive function in Williams and Down syndromes. *Research in Developmental Disabilities, 34,* 46–55.

Carpendale, J. I., & Chandler, M. J. (1996). On the distinction between false belief understanding and subscribing to an interpretive theory of mind. *Child Development, 67,* 1686–1706.

Carpenter, M. (2011). Social cognition and social motivations in infancy. In U. Goswami (Ed.), *Wiley-Blackwell handbook of childhood cognitive development* (2nd ed.). New York: Wiley.

Carr, P. B., & Dweck, C. (2011). Intelligence and motivation. In R. J. Sternberg & S. B. Kaufman (Eds.), *Cambridge handbook of intelligence.* New York: Cambridge University Press.

Carr, P. B., & Steele, C. M. (2009). Stereotype threat and inflexible perseverance in problem solving. *Journal of Experimental Social Psychology, 45,* 853–859.

Carroll, D. J., & others. (2012, in press). How do alternative ways of responding influence 3- and 4-year-olds' performance on tests of executive function and theory of mind? *Journal of Experimental Child Psychology.*

Carroll, J. (1993). *Human cognitive abilities.* Cambridge: Cambridge University Press.

Carskadon, M. A. (Ed.). (2002). *Adolescent sleep patterns.* New York: Cambridge University Press.

Carskadon, M. A. (2004). Sleep difficulties in young people. *Adolescent Medicine, 158,* 597–598.

Carskadon, M. A. (2005). Sleep and circadian rhythms in children and adolescents: Relevance for athletic performance of young people. *Clinical Sports Medicine, 24,* 319–328.

Carskadon, M. A. (2006, March). *Too little, too late: Sleep bioregulatory across adolescence.* Paper presented at the meeting of the Society for Research on Adolescence, San Francisco.

Carskadon, M. A. (2011). Sleep in adolescents: The perfect storm. *Pediatric Clinics of North America, 58,* 637–647.

Cartwright, R., Agargun, M. Y., Kirkby, J., & Friedman, J. K. (2006). Relation of dreams to waking concerns. *Psychiatry Research, 141,* 261–270.

Carver, K., Joyner, K., & Udry, J. R. (2003). National estimates of romantic relationships. *Annual Review of Psychology* (Vol. 60). Palo Alto, CA: Annual Reviews.

Case, R. (1987). Neo-Piagetian theory: Retrospect and prospect. *International Journal of Psychology, 22,* 773–791.

Case, R. (1999). Conceptual development in the child and the field: A personal view of the Piagetian legacy. In E. K. Skolnick, K. Nelson, S. A. Gelman, & P. H. Miller (Eds.), *Conceptual development.* Mahwah, NJ: Erlbaum.

Case, R., Kurland, D. M., & Goldberg, J. (1982). Operational efficiency and the growth of short-term memory span. *Journal of Experimental Child Psychology, 33,* 386–404.

Casey, B. J., Duhoux, S., & Malter Cohen, M. (2010). Adolescence: What do transmission, transition, and translation have to do with it? *Neuron, 67,* 749–760.

Casey, P. H. (2008). Growth of low birth weight preterm children. *Seminars in Perinatology, 32,* 20–27.

Caspers, K. M., & others. (2009). Association between the serotonin transporter polymorphism (5-HTTLPR) and adult unresolved attachment. *Developmental Psychology, 45,* 64–76.

Caspi, A. (1998). Personality development across the life course. In W. Damon (Ed.), *Handbook of child psychology* (Vol. 3). New York: Wiley.

Caspi, A., & others. (2003). Influence of life stress on depression: Moderation by a polymorphism in the 5-HTT gene. *Science, 301,* 386–389.

Cassidy, J., Woodhouse, S. S., Sherman, L. J., Stupica, B., & Lejuez, C. W. (2011). Enhancing infant attachment security: An examination of treatment efficacy and differential susceptibility. *Development and Psychopathology, 23,* 131–148.

Cassidy, J., & others. (2011). Enhancing infant attachment security: An examination of treatment efficacy and differential susceptibility. *Developmental Psychopathology, 23,* 131–148.

Cassoff, J., Knauper, B., Michaelsen, S., & Gruber, R. (2013, in press). School-based sleep promotion programs: Effectiveness, feasibility, and insights for future research. *Sleep Medicine Reviews.*

Castle, J., & others. (2010). Parents' evaluation of adoption success: A follow-up study of intercountry and domestic adoptions. *American Journal of Orthopsychiatry, 79,* 522–531.

Catalano, R. F., & others (2012). Worldwide application of prevention science in adolescent health. *Lancet, 379,* 1653–1664.

Catani, C., & others. (2010). Tsunami, war, and cumulative risk in the lives of Sri Lankan school children. *Child Development, 81,* 1176–1191.

Caughey, A. B., Hopkins, L. M., & Norton, M. E. (2006). Chorionic villus sampling compared with amniocentesis and the difference in the rate of pregnancy loss. *Obstetrics and Gynecology, 108,* 612–616.

Cavanagh, S. E. (2009). Puberty. In D. Carr (Ed.), *Encyclopedia of the life course and human development.* Boston: Gale Cengage.

Cave, R. K. (2002, August). *Early adolescent language: A content analysis of child development and educational psychology textbooks.* Unpublished doctoral dissertation. University of Nevada–Reno, Reno, NV.

Caylak, E. (2012, in press). Biochemical and genetic analyses of childhood attention deficit/hyperactivity disorder. *American Journal of Medical Genetics B: Neuropsychiatric Genetics.*

Ceci, S. J., & Gilstrap, L. L. (2000). Determinants of intelligence: Schooling and intelligence. In A. Kazdin (Ed.), *Encyclopedia of psychology.* Washington, DC, & New York: American Psychological Association and Oxford University Press.

Ceci, S. J., Papierno, P. B., & Kulkovsky, S. (2007). Representational constraints on children's suggestibility. *Psychological Science, 18,* 503–509.

Center for Science in the Public Interest. (2008, August). *Kids' meals: Obesity on the menu.* Washington, DC: Author.

Centers for Disease Control and Prevention. (2006, December). *Assisted reproductive success rates.* Atlanta: Author.

Centers for Disease Control and Prevention. (2009). *Autism and developmental disabilities monitoring (ADDM) network.* Atlanta: Author.

Centers for Disease Control and Prevention. (2012a). *Birth data.* Atlanta: Author.

Centers for Disease Control and Prevention. (2012b). *Breastfeeding report card United States— Outcome indicators.* Retrieved July 30, 2012, www.cdc.gov/breastfeeding/data/reportcard2.htm

Centers for Disease Control and Prevention. (2012c). CDC estimates 1 in 88 children in the United States has been identified as having an autism spectrum disorder. *CDC Division of News & Electronic Media.* Retrieved January 21, 2013, from http://www.cdc.gov/media/releases/2012/p0329_autism_disorder.html

Centers for Disease Control and Prevention. (2013). *Body mass index for children and teens.* Atlanta: Centers for Disease Control and Prevention.

Chall, J. S. (1979). The great debate: Ten years later with a modest proposal for reading stages. In L. B. Resnick & P. A. Weaver (Eds.), *Theory and practice of early reading.* Hillsdale. NJ: Erlbaum.

Chambers, B., Cheung, A. C. K., & Slavin, R. F. (2006). Effective preschool programs for children at risk of school failure: A best-evidence synthesis. In B. Spodek & O. N. Saracho (Eds.), *Handbook of research on the education of young children.* Mahwah, NJ: Erlbaum.

Chance, P. (2014). *Learning and behavior* (7th ed.). Boston: Cengage.

Chang, Y. K., Liu, S., Yu, H. H., & Lee, Y. H. (2012). Effect of acute exercise on executive function in children with attention deficit hyperactivity disorder. *Archives of Clinical Neuropsychology, 27,* 225–237.

Chang, Z., Lichtenstein, P., & Larsson, H. (2012). The effects of childhood ADHD symptoms on early-onset substance use: A Swedish twin study. *Journal of Abnormal Child Psychology, 40,* 425–435.

Chang, Z., Lichtenstein, P., Asherson, P. J., & Larsson, H. (2013, in press). Developmental twin study of attention problems: High heritabilities throughout development. *JAMA Psychiatry.*

Chao, R. (2001). Extending research on the consequences of parenting style for Chinese Americans and European Americans. *Child Development, 72,* 1832–1843.

Chao, R. K. (2005, April). *The importance of* Guan *in describing control of immigrant Chinese.* Paper presented at a meeting of the Society for Research in Child Development, Atlanta.

Chao, R. K. (2007, March). *Research with Asian Americans: Looking back and moving forward.* Paper presented at a meeting of the Society for Research in Child Development, Boston.

Chao, R. K., & Otsuki-Clutter, M. (2011). Racial and ethnic differences: Sociocultural and contextual explanations. *Journal of Research on Adolescence, 21,* 47–60.

Chao, R., & Tseng, V. (2002). Parenting of Asians. In M. H. Bornstein (Ed.), *Handbook of parenting.* Mahwah, NJ: Erlbaum.

Chaplin, T. M., & Aldao, A. (2013, in press). Gender differences in emotion in children: A meta-analytic review. *Psychological Bulletin.*

Charlet, J., Schnekenburger, M., Brown, K. W., & Diederich, M. (2012). DNA demethylation increases sensitivity of neuroblastoma cells to chemotherapeutic drugs. *Biochemical Pharmacology, 83,* 858–865.

Chase-Lansdale, P. L. (2012, January 12). *Escape from poverty: Two-generation education interventions for low-income parents and children.* Los Angeles: California Center for Population Research.

Chassin, L., & others. (2008). Multiple trajectories of cigarette smoking and the intergenerational transmission of smoking: A multigenerational, longitudinal study of a midwestern community sample. *Health Psychology, 27,* 819–828.

Cheah, C. S. L., & Yeung, C. (2011). The social development of immigrant children: A focus on Asian and Hispanic children in the U.S. In P. K. Smith & C. H. Hart (Eds.), *Wiley-Blackwell handbook of childhood social development* (2nd ed.). New York: Wiley.

Chein, J., Albert, D., O'Brien, L., Uckert, K., & Steinberg, L. (2011). Peers increase adolescent risk taking by enhancing activity in the brain's reward circuitry. *Developmental Science, 14,* F1–F10.

Chemtob, C. M., & others. (2010). Impact of maternal posttraumatic stress disorder and depression following exposure to the September 11 attacks on preschool children's behavior. *Child Development, 81,* 1129–1141.

Chen, C., & Stevenson, H. W. (1989). Homework: A cross-cultural examination. *Child Development, 60,* 551–561.

Chen, J. J., & Brooks-Gunn, J. (2012). Neighborhoods, schools, and achievement. In K. R. Harris, S. Graham, & T. Urdan (Eds.), *APA handbook of educational psychology.* Washington, DC: American Psychological Association.

Chen, X., & others. (1998). Childrearing attitudes and behavioral inhibition in Chinese and Canadian toddlers: A cross-cultural study. *Developmental Psychology, 34,* 677–686.

Chen, X., Chung, J., Lechccier-Kimel, R., & French, D. (2011). Culture and social development. In P. K. Smith & C. H. Hart (Eds.), *Wiley-Blackwell perspectives on childhood social development* (2nd ed.). New York: Wiley.

Chen, X. K., Wen, S. W., Yang, Q., & Walker, M. C. (2007). Adequacy of prenatal care and neonatal mortality in infants born to mothers with and without antenatal high-risk conditions. *Australian and New Zealand Journal of Obstetrics and Gynecology, 47,* 122–127.

Chen, Y., Keen, R., Rosancer, K., & von Hosten, C. (2010). Movement planning reflects skill level and age change in toddlers. *Child Development, 81,* 1846–1858.

Cheng, M., & Berman, S. L. (2013, in press). Globalization and identity development: A Chinese perspective. In S. J. Schwartz (Ed.), *Identity around the world: New directions for child and adolescent development.* San Francisco: Jossey-Bass.

Cheng, S., & others. (2010). Early television exposure and children's behavioral and social outcomes at age 30 months. *Journal of Epidemiology* (Suppl. 2), S482–S489.

Cheng, Y. Y., Shein, P. P., & Chiou, W. B. (2012). Escaping the impulse to immediate gratification: The prospect concept promotes a future-oriented mindset, prompting an inclination towards delayed gratification. *British Journal of Psychology, 103,* 129–141.

Cherlin, A. J., & Furstenberg, F. F. (1994). Stepfamilies in the United States: A reconsideration. In J. Blake & J. Hagen (Eds.), *Annual Review of Sociology.* Palo Alto, CA: Annual Reviews.

Chess, S., & Thomas, A. (1977). Temperamental individuality from childhood to adolescence. *Journal of Child Psychiatry, 16,* 218–226.

Cheung, C. S., Pomerantz, E. M., & Dong, W. (2013). Does adolescents' disclosure to their parents matter for their academic adjustment? *Child Development.*

Cheung, C., & Pomerantz, E. M. (2012, in press). Why does parental involvement in children's learning enhance children's achievement? The role of parent-oriented motivation. *Journal of Educational Psychology, 104,* 820–832.

Chi, M. T. (1978). Knowledge structures and memory development. In R. S. Siegler (Ed.), *Children's thinking: What develops?* Hillsdale, NJ: Erlbaum.

Chick, C. F., & Reyna, V. F. (2012). A fuzzy trace theory of adolescent risk taking: Beyond self-control and sensation seeking. In V. F. Reyna & others (Eds.), *The adolescent brain.* Washington, DC: American Psychological Association.

Childers, J. B., & Tomasello, M. (2002). Two-year-olds learn novel nouns, verbs and conventional actions from massed or distributed exposures. *Developmental Psychology, 38,* 967–978.

Children's Defense Fund. (1992). *The state of America's children, 1992.* Washington, DC: Author.

Chiu, R. W., & Lo, Y. M. (2012). Noninvasive prenatal diagnosis empowered by high-throughput sequencing. *Prenatal Diagnosis, 32,* 401–406.

Chitty, L. S., & others. (2013, in press). Safe, accurate, prenatal diagnosis of thanatophoric dysplasia using ultrasound and free fetal DNA. *Prenatal Diagnosis.*

Choi, N. (2004). Sex role group differences in specific, academic, and general self-efficacy. *Journal of Psychology, 138,* 149–159.

Chomsky, N. (1957). *Syntactic structures.* The Hague: Mouton.

Choudhry, Z., & others. (2012). LPHN3 and attention deficit/hyperactivity disorder: Interaction with maternal stress during pregnancy. *Journal of Child Psychology and Psychiatry, 53,* 892–902.

Christakis, D. A., Zimmerman, F. J., DiGiuseppe, D. L., & McCarty, C. A. (2004). Early television exposure and subsequent attentional problems in children. *Pediatrics, 113,* 708–713.

Christakis, D. A., & others. (2009). Audible television and decreased adult words, infant vocalizations, and conversational turns. *Archives of Pediatrics & Adolescent Medicine, 163,* 554–558.

Christenfeld, N. J. S., & Mandler, G. (2013). Emotion. In I. B. Weiner & others (Eds.), *Handbook of psychology* (2nd ed., Vol. 1). New York: Wiley.

Cicchetti, D. (2011). Pathways to resilient functioning in maltreated children: From single to multilevel investigations. In D. Cicchetti & G. I. Roisman (Eds.), *The origins and organization of adaptation and maladaptation: Minnesota Symposia on Child Psychology* (Vol. 36). New York: Wiley.

Cicchetti, D. (2013). Developmental psychopathology. In P. Zelazo (Ed.), *Oxford handbook of developmental psychology.* New York: Oxford University Press.

Cicchetti, D., & Toth, S. L. (2006). Developmental psychopathology and preventive intervention. In W. Damon & R. Lerner (Eds.), *Handbook of child psychology.* (6th ed.). New York: Wiley.

Cicchetti, D., & Toth, S. L. (2011). Child maltreatment: The research imperative and the exportation of results to clinical contexts. In B. Lester & J. D. Sparrow (Eds.), *Nurturing children and families.* New York: Wiley.

Cicchetti, D., Toth, S. L., Nilsen, W. J., & Manly, J. T. (2013, in press). What do we know and why does it matter? The dissemination of evidence-based interventions for maltreatment. In H. R. Schaffer & K. Durkin (Eds.), *Blackwell handbook of developmental psychology.* Oxford, UK: Blackwell.

Cicchetti, D., Toth, S. L., & Rogosch, F. A. (2005). *A prevention program for child maltreatment.* Unpublished manuscript, University of Rochester, Rochester, NY.

Cillessen, A. H. N., & Bellmore, A. D. (2011). Social skills and social competence in interactions with peers. In P. K. Smith & C. H. Hart (Eds.), *Wiley-Blackwell handbook of childhood social development* (2nd ed.). New York: Wiley.

Cillessen, A. H. N., & van den Berg, Y. H. M. (2012). Popularity and school adjustment. In A. M. Ryan & G. W. Ladd (Eds.), *Peer relationships and adjustment at school.* Charlotte, NC: Information Age Publishing.

Cisneros-Cohernour, E. J., Moreno, R. P., & Cisneros, A. A. (2000). Curriculum reform in Mexico: Kindergarten teachers' challenges and dilemmas. Proceedings of the Lilian Katz Symposium. In D. Rothenberg (Ed.), *Issues in early childhood education: Curriculum reform, teacher education, and dissemination of information.* Urbana-Champaign: University of Illinois.

Citkovitz, C., Schnyer, R. N., & Hoskins, I. A. (2011). Acupuncture during labor: Data are more promising than a recent review suggests. *BJOG, 118,* 101.

Clark, B. (2008). *Growing up gifted* (7th ed.). Upper Saddle River, NJ: Prentice Hall.

Clark, E. (1993). *The lexicon in acquisition.* New York: Cambridge University Press.

Clark, E. V. (2012). Lexical meaning. In E. L. Bavin (Ed.), *Cambridge handbook of child language.* New York: Cambridge University Press.

Clarke-Stewart, A. K., & Miner, J. L. (2008). Effects of child and day care. In M. M. Haith & J. B. Benson (Eds.), *Encyclopedia of infant and early childhood development.* Oxford, UK: Elsevier.

Class, Q. A., Lichtenstein, P., Langstrom, N., & D'Onofrio, B. M. (2011). Timing of prenatal maternal exposure to severe life events and adverse pregnancy outcomes: A population study of 2.6 million pregnancies. *Psychosomatic Medicine, 73,* 234–241.

Clauss, J. A., & Blackford, J. U. (2012). Behavioral inhibition and risk for developing social anxiety disorder: A meta-analytic study. *Journal of the American Academy of Child and Adolescent Psychiatry, 51,* 1066–1075.

Clay, R. (2001, February). Fulfilling an unmet need. *Monitor on Psychology,* No. 2.

Clearfield, M. W., Diedrich, F. J., Smith, L. B., & Thelen, E. (2006). Young infants reach correctly in A-not-B tasks: On the development of stability and perseveration. *Infant Behavior and Development, 29,* 435–444.

Clearfield, M. W., Dineva, E., Smith, L. B., Diedrich, F. J., & Thelen, E. (2009). Cue salience and infant perseverative reaching: Tests of the dynamic field theory. *Developmental Science, 12,* 26–40.

Clifton, R. K., Morrongiello, B. A., Kulig, J. W., & Dowd, J. M. (1981). Developmental changes in auditory localization in infancy. In R. N. Aslin, J. R. Alberts, & M. R. Petersen (Eds.), *Development of perception* (Vol. 1). Orlando, FL: Academic Press.

Clifton, R. K., Muir, D. W., Ashmead, D. H., & Clarkson, M. G. (1993). Is visually guided reaching in early infancy a myth? *Child Development, 64,* 1099–1110.

Clinkinbeard, S. S., Simi, P., Evans, M. K., & Anderson, A. L. (2011). Sleep and delinquency: Does amount of sleep matter? *Journal of Youth and Adolescence, 40,* 916–930.

Cloninger, S. C. (2013). *Theories of personality* (6th ed.). Upper Saddle River, NJ: Pearson.

Clouchoux, C., & Limperopoulos, C. (2012). Novel applications of quantitative MRI for the fetal brain. *Pediatric Radiology, 42,* (Suppl. 1), S24–S32.

Cluett, E. R., & Burns, E. (2009). Immersion in water in labour and birth. *Cochrane Database of Systematic Reviews,* CD000111.

CogMed. (2013). *CogMed: Working memory is the engine of learning.* Upper Saddle River, NJ: Pearson.

Cohen, G. L., & Prinstein, M. J. (2006). Peer contagion of aggression and health-risk behavior among adolescent males: An experimental investigation of effects on public conduct and private attitudes. *Child Development, 77,* 967–983.

Cohen, L. B. (2002, April). *Can infants really add and subtract?* Paper presented at the meeting of the International Conference on Infant Studies, Toronto.

Cohen-Woods, S., Craig, I. W., & McGuffin, P. (2012, in press). The current state of play on the molecular genetics of depression. *Psychological Medicine.*

Cohn, A., & Canter, A. (2003). *Bullying: Facts for schools and parents.* Washington, DC: National Association of School Psychologists Center.

Cohn, J. F., & Tronick, E. Z. (1988). Mother-infant face-to-face interaction. Influence is bidirectional and unrelated to periodic cycles in either partner's behavior. *Developmental Psychology, 24,* 396–397.

Coie, J. (2004). The impact of negative social experiences on the development of antisocial behavior. In J. B. Kupersmidt & K. A. Dodge (Eds.), *Children's peer relations: From development to intervention.* Washington, DC: American Psychological Association.

Colapinto, J. (2000). *As nature made him.* New York: Simon & Schuster.

Colby, A., Kohlberg, L., Gibbs, J., & Lieberman, M. (1983). A longitudinal study of moral judgment. *Monographs of the Society for Research in Child Development, 48* (21, Serial No. 201).

Cole, M., & Packer, M. (2011). Culture in development. In M. H. Bornstein & M. E. Lamb (Eds.), *Cognitive development.* New York: Psychology Press.

Cole, M. W., Yarkoni, T., Repovs, G., Anticevic, A., & Braver, T. S. (2012). Global connectivity of prefrontal cortex predicts cognitive control and intelligence. *Journal of Neuroscience, 32,* 8988–8999.

Cole, P. M., Dennis, T. A., Smith-Simon, K. E., & Cohen, L. H. (2009). Preschoolers' emotion regulation strategy understanding: Relations with emotion socialization and child self-regulation. *Social Development, 18*(2), 324–352.

Cole, P. M., & Tan, P. Z. (2007). Emotion socialization from a cultural perspective. In J. E. Grusec & P. D. Hastings (Eds.), *Handbook of socialization.* New York: Guilford.

Coleman-Phox, Odouli, R., & Li, D. K. (2008). Use of a fan during sleep and the risk of sudden infant death syndrome. *Archives of Pediatric and Adolescent Medicine, 162,* 963–968.

Coley, R. L., & Lombardi, C. M. (2013, in press). Does maternal employment following childbirth support or inhibit low-income children's long-term development? *Child Development.*

Coley, R. L., Votruba-Drzal, E., Miller, P. L., & Koury, A. (2013, in press). Timing, extent, and type of child care and children's functioning in kindergarten. *Developmental Psychology.*

Collett-Solberg, P. F. (2011). Update in growth hormone therapy of children. *Journal of Clinical Endocrinology and Metabolism, 96,* 573–579.

Collins, C. E., & others. (2011). Parent diet modification, child activity, or both in obese children: An RCT. *Pediatrics, 127,* 619–627.

Collins, J. S., Atkinson, K. K., Dean, J. H., Best, R. G., & Stevenson, R. E. (2011). Long-term maintenance of neural tube defects prevention in a high prevalence state. *Journal of Pediatrics, 159,* 143–149.

Colombo, J., Brez, C., & Curtindale, L. (2013, in press). Infant perception and cognition. In I. B. Weiner & others (Eds.), *Handbook of psychology* (2nd ed., Vol. 6). New York: Wiley.

Colombo, J., Shaddy, D. J., Blaga, O. M., Anderson, C. J., & Kannass, K. N. (2009). High cognitive ability in infancy and early childhood. In F. D. Horowitz, R. F. Subotnik, & D. J. Matthews (Eds.), *The development of giftedness and talent across the life span.* Washington, DC: American Psychological Association.

Colombo, J., Shaddy, D. J., Richman, W. A., Maikranz, J. M., & Blaga, O. M. (2004). The developmental course of attention in infancy and preschool cognitive outcome. *Infancy, 4,* 1–38.

Colombo, J., & others. (2009a). Attentional predictors of vocabulary from infancy. In J. Colombo, P. McCardle, & L. Freund (Eds.), *Infant pathways to language.* New York: Psychology Press.

Colombo, J., & others. (2009b). Early attentional predictors of vocabulary in childhood. In J. Colombo, P. McCardle, & L. Freund (Eds.), *Infant pathways to language.* New York: Psychology Press.

Colombo, J., & others. (2010). What habituates in infant visual habituation? A psychophysiological analysis. *Infancy, 15,* 107–124.

Colonnesi, C., Stams, G. J., Koster, I., & Noom, M. J. (2010). The relation between pointing and language development: A meta-analysis. *Developmental Review, 30,* 352–366.

Colvin, C. W., & Abdullatif, H. (2012, in press). Anatomy of female puberty: The clinical relevance of developmental changes in the reproductive system. *Clinical Anatomy.*

Comer, J. (1988). Educating poor minority children. *Scientific American, 259,* 42–48.

Comer, J. (2004). *Leave no child behind.* New Haven, CT: Yale University Press.

Comer, J. (2006). Child development: The under-weighted aspect of intelligence. In P. C. Kyllonen, R. D. Roberts, & L. Stankov (Eds.), *Extending intelligence.* Mahwah, NJ: Erlbaum.

Comer, J. (2010). Comer School Development Program. In J. Meece & J. Eccles (Eds.), *Handbook of research on schools, schooling, and human development.* New York: Routledge.

Common Sense Media. (2011). *Zero to eight: Children's media use in America.* Retrieved June 21, 2012, from www.commonsensemedia.org/research

Commoner, B. (2002). Unraveling the DNA myth: The spurious foundation of genetic engineering. *Harper's Magazine, 304,* 39–47.

Compas, B. E. (2004). Processes of risk and resilience during adolescence: Linking contexts and individuals. In R. Lerner & L. Steinberg (Eds.), *Handbook of adolescent psychology.* New York: Wiley.

Comstock, G., & Scharrer, E. (2006). Media and popular culture. In W. Damon & R. Lerner (Eds.), *Handbook of child psychology* (6th ed.). New York: Wiley.

Conde, C. (2012). Preventing injury. *Texas Medicine, 108,* 35–39.

Conde-Aguedelo, A., Belizan, J. M., & Diaz-Rossello, J. (2011, March 16). Kangaroo care to reduce morbidity and mortality in low birthweight infants. *Cochrane Database of Systematic Reviews,* (3) CD002771.

Condition of Education. (2012). *Participation in education,* Table A-9-1. Washington, DC: National Center for Education Statistics.

Conduct Problems Prevention Research Group. (2007). The Fast Track randomized controlled trial to prevent externalizing psychiatric disorders: Findings from grades 3 to 9. *Journal of the American Academy of Child and Adolescent Psychiatry, 46,* 1250–1262.

Conduct Problems Prevention Research Group. (2010a). The difficulty of maintaining positive intervention effect: A look at disruptive behavior, deviant peer relations, and social skills during the middle school years. *Journal of Early Adolescence, 30,* 593–624.

Conduct Problems Prevention Research Group. (2010b). The effects of the Fast Track preventive intervention on the development of conduct disorder across childhood. *Child Development, 82,* 331–345.

Cong, X., Ludington-Hoe, S. M., & Walsh, S. (2011). Randomized crossover trial of kangaroo care to reduce biobehavioral pain responses in preterm infants: A pilot study. *Biological Research for Nursing, 13,* 204–216.

Conger, R. D., & others. (2012). Resilience and vulnerability of Mexican origin youth and their families: A test of a culturally-informed model of family economic stress. In P. K. Kerig, M. S. Schulz, & S. T. Hauser (Eds.), *Adolescence and beyond.* New York: Oxford University Press.

Conley, M. W. (2008). *Content area literacy: learners in context.* Boston: Allyn & Bacon.

Connolly, J. A., & McIsaac, C. (2009). Romantic relationships in adolescence. In R. M. Lerner & L. Steinberg (Eds.), *Handbook of adolescent psychology* (3rd ed.). New York: Wiley.

Conry-Murray, C., Kim, J. M., & Turiel, E. (2012, April). *U.S. and Korean children's judgments of gender norm violations.* Paper presented at the Gender Development Research conference, San Francisco.

Cook, M., & Birch, R. (1984). Infant perception of the shapes of tilted plane forms. *Infant Behavior and Development, 7,* 389–402.

Cooper, C. R. (2011). *Bridging multiple worlds.* New York: Oxford University Press.

Cooper, C. R., & Grotevant, H. D. (1989, April). *Individuality and connectedness in the family and adolescent's self and relational competence.* Paper presented at the meeting of the Society for Research in Child Development, Kansas City.

Coplan, R. J., & Arbeau, K. A. (2009). Peer interactions and play in early childhood. In K. H. Rubin, W. M. Bukowski, & B. Laursen (Eds.), *Handbook of peer interactions, relationships, and groups.* New York: Guilford.

Cordier, S. (2008). Evidence for a role of paternal exposure in developmental toxicity. *Basic and Clinical Pharmacology and Toxicology, 102,* 176–181.

Cornew, L., & others. (2012, in press). Atypical social referencing in infant siblings of children with autism spectrum disorders. *Journal of Autism and Developmental Disorders.*

Cortes, E., Basra, R., & Kelleher, C. J. (2011). Waterbirth and pelvic floor injury: A retrospective study and postal survey using ICIQ modular long form questionnaires. *European Journal of Obstetrics, Gynecology, and Reproductive Biology, 155,* 27–30.

Cosmides, L. (2013). Evolutionary psychology. *Annual Review of Psychology* (Vol. 64). Palo Alto, CA: Annual Reviews.

Costa, R., & Figueiredo, B. (2011). Infants' psychophysiological profile and temperament at 3 and 12 months. *Infant Behavior and Development, 34,* 270–279.

Costigan, S. A., Barnett, L., Plotnikoff, R. C., & Lubans, D. R. (2013). The health indicators associated with screen-based sedentary behavior among adolescent girls: A systematic review. *Journal of Adolescent Health, 52,* 382–392.

Costley, K. C. (2012). An overview of the life, central concepts, including classroom applications for Lev Vygotsky. *ERIC,* ED529565.

Coté, J. E. (2009). Identity formation and self development in adolescence. In R. M. Lerner & L. Steinberg (Eds.), *Handbook of adolescent psychology* (3rd ed.). New York: Wiley.

Council of Economic Advisors. (2000). *Teens and their parents in the 21st century: An examination of trends in teen behavior and the role of parent involvement.* Washington, DC: Author.

Courage, M. L., Howe, M. L., & Squires, S. E. (2004). Individual differences in 3.5-month-olds' visual attention: What do they predict at 1 year? *Infant Behavior and Development, 127,* 19–30.

Courage, M. L., & Richards, J. E. (2008). Attention. In M. M. Haith & J. B. Benson (Eds.), *Encyclopedia of infant and early childhood development.* Oxford, UK: Elsevier.

Cowan, C. P., Cowan, P. A., & Barry, J. (2011). Couples' groups for parents of preschoolers: Ten-year outcomes of a randomized trial. *Journal of Family Psychology, 25,* 240–250.

Cowan, P. A, & Cowan, C. P. (2000). *When partners become parents: The big life change for couples.* Mahwah, NJ: Erlbaum.

Cowan, P. A., & Cowan, C. P. (2009). How working with couples fosters children's development. In M. S. Schulz, P. K. Kerig, M. K. Pruett, & R. D. Parke (Eds.), *Feathering the nest.* Washington, DC: American Psychological Association.

Cowan, P. A., Cowan, C. P., Ablow, J., Johnson, V. K., & Measelle, J. (2005). *The family context of parenting in children's adaptation to elementary school.* Mahwah, NJ: Erlbaum.

Cowan, P. A., & Heming, G. (2013). How children and parents fare during transition to school. In P. A. Cowan & others (Eds.), *The family context of parenting in children's adaptation to elementary school.* New York: Routledge.

Cowan, P. A., & others. (2013). Family factors in children's adaptation to elementary school: A discussion and integration. In P. A. Cowan & others (Eds.), *The family context of parenting in children's adaptation to elementary school.* New York: Routledge.

Cox, M. J., & others. (2004). The transition to parenting: Continuity and change in early parenting behavior and attitudes. In R. D. Conger, F. O. Lorenz, & K. A. S. Wickrama (Eds.), *Continuity and change in family relations.* Mahwah, NJ: Erlbaum.

Coyne, S. M., Nelson, D. A., & Underwood, M. (2011). Aggression in children. In P. K. Smith & C. H. Hart (Eds.), *Wiley-Blackwell handbook of childhood social development* (2nd ed.). New York: Wiley.

Cozzi, B., & others. (2010). Ontogenesis and migration of metallothionein I/II-containing glial cells in the human telencephalon during the second trimester. *Brain Research, 1327,* 16–23.

Crain, S. (2012). Sentence scope. In E. L. Bavin (Ed.), *Cambridge handbook of child language.* New York: Cambridge University Press.

Crain, S., & Zhou, P. (2012). Semantics and pragmatics: Acquisition of logical connectives and focus. In C. T. J. Huang & R. Sybesma (Eds.), *Encyclopedia of Chinese language and linguistics.* The Netherlands: Brill.

Crespi, B. (2011). The evolutionary biology of child health. *Proceedings of the Royal Society, Biological Sciences, 278,* 1441–1449.

Crespo, C., Kielpikowski, M., Jose, P. E., & Pryor, J. (2010). Relationships between family connectedness and body satisfaction: A longitudinal study of adolescent girls and boys. *Journal of Youth and Adolescence, 39,* 1392–1401.

Creswell, J. W. (2008). *Educational research* (3rd ed.). Upper Saddle River, NJ: Prentice Hall.

Crissey, S. R. (2009). Dating and romantic relationships, childhood and adolescence. In D. Carr (Ed.), *Encyclopedia of the life course and human development*. Boston: Gale Cengage.

Crocetti, E., Jahromi, P., & Meeus, W. (2012). Identity and civic engagement in adolescence. *Journal of Adolescence, 35*, 521–532.

Crockenberg, S. B. (1986). Are temperamental differences in babies associated with predictable differences in caregiving? In J. V. Lerner & R. M. Lerner (Eds.), *Temperament and social interaction during infancy and childhood*. San Francisco: Jossey-Bass.

Crockenberg, S., & Leerkes, E. (2013). Infant negative emotionality, caregiving, and family relationships. In A.C. Crouter & A. Booth (Eds.), *Children's influence on family dynamics*. New York: Routledge.

Crockett, O. J., & Beal, S. J. (2012). The life course in the making: Gender and the development of adolescents' expected timing of adult role transitions. *Developmental Psychology, 48*, 1727–1738.

Cromer, R. (1987). Receptive language in the mentally retarded: Processes and diagnostic distinctions. In R. Schielebusch & L. Lloyd (Eds.), *Language perspectives: Acquisition, retardation, and intervention*. Baltimore: University Park Press.

Crosnoe, R. (2011). *Fitting in, standing out*. New York: Cambridge University Press.

Crosnoe, R., & Fuligni, A. J. (2012). Children from immigrant families: Introduction to the special section. *Child Development, 83*, 1471–1476.

Cross, T. P., Matthews, B., Tommyr, L., Scott, D., & Quimet, C. (2012). Child welfare policy and practice on children's exposure to domestic violence. *Child Abuse and Neglect, 36*, 210–216.

Crouter, A. C. (2006). Mothers and fathers at work. In A. Clarke-Stewart & J. Dunn (Eds.), *Families count*. New York: Cambridge University Press.

Crouter, A. C., & Booth, A. (Eds.). (2013). *Children's influence on family dynamics*. New York: Routledge.

Crowley, K., Callahan, M. A., Tenenbaum, H. R., & Allen, E. (2001). Parents explain more to boys than to girls during shared scientific thinking. *Psychological Science, 12*, 258–261.

Crugnola, C. R., & others. (2013, in press). Maternal attachment influences mother-infant styles of regulation and play with objects at nine months. *Attachment and Human Development*.

Cruikshank, D. R., Jenkins, D. B., & Metcalf, K. K. (2012). *The act of teaching* (6th ed.). New York: McGraw-Hill.

Cubillo, A., Halari, R., Smith, A., Taylor, E., & Rubia, K. (2012). A review of fronto-spatial brain abnormalities in children and adults with Attention Deficit Hyperactivity Disorder (ADHD) and new evidence for dysfunction in adults with ADHD during motivation and attention. *Cortex, 48*, 194–215.

Cuevas, K., Swingler, M. M., Bell, M. A., Maracovitch, S., & Calkins, S. D. (2012). Measures of frontal functioning and the emergence of inhibitory control processes at 10 months of age. *Developmental Cognitive Neuroscience, 2*, 235–243.

Cui, M., Fincham, F. D., & Pasley, B. K. (2008). Young adult romantic relationships: The role of parents' marital problems and relationship efficiency. *Personality and Social Psychology Bulletin, 34*, 1226–1235.

Cui, M., Ueno, K., Fincham, F. D., Donnellan, M. B., & Wickrama, K. A. (2012). The association between romantic relationships and delinquency in adolescence and young adulthood. *Personal Relationships, 19*, 354–366.

Culicover, P. W. (2013). Simpler syntax. In B. Heine & H. Narrog (Eds.), *Oxford handbook of linguistic analysis*. New York: Oxford University Press.

Cummings, E. M., & Davies, P. T. (2010). *Marital conflict and children: An emotional security perspective*. New York: Guilford.

Cummings, E. M., El-Sheikh, M., & Kouros, C. D. (2009). Children and violence: The role of children's regulation in the marital aggression-child adjustment link. *Clinical Child and Family Psychology Review, 12*(1), 3–15.

Cummings, E. M., George, M. R. W., McCoy, K. P., & Davies, P. T. (2012). Interparental conflict in kindergarten and adolescent adjustment: Prospective investigation of emotion security as an explanatory mechanism. *Child Development, 83*, 1703–1715.

Cummings, E. M., & Kouros, C. D. (2008). Stress and coping. In M. M. Haith & J. B. Benson (Eds.), *Encyclopedia of infant and early childhood development, Vol. 3* (pp. 267–281). San Diego: Academic Press.

Cunningham, J. N., Kliewer, W., & Garner, P. W. (2009). Emotion socialization, child emotion understanding and regulation, and adjustment in urban African American families: Differential associations across child gender. *Development and Psychopathology, 21*, 261–283.

Cunningham, P. M. (2013). *Phonics they use: Words for reading and writing* (6th ed.). Boston: Allyn & Bacon.

Curran, K., DuCette, J., Eisenstein, J., & Hyman, I. A. (2001, August). *Statistical analysis of the cross-cultural data: The third year*. Paper presented at the meeting of the American Psychological Association, San Francisco, CA.

Cushner, K. H., McClelland, A., & Safford, P. (2012). *Human diversity in education* (7th ed.). New York: McGraw-Hill.

Cvencek, D., Meltzoff, A. N., & Greenwald, A. G. (2011). Math-gender stereotypes in elementary school children. *Child Development, 82*, 766–779.

D

D'Ardenne, K., & others. (2012). Feature article: Role of the prefrontal cortex and the midbrain dopamine system in working memory updating. *Proceedings of the National Academy of Sciences U.S.A., 109*, 19900-19909.

D'Augelli, A. R. (1991). Gay men in college: Identity processes and adaptations. *Journal of College Student Development, 32*, 140–146.

D'Onofrio, B. M., & others. (2007). Intergenerational transmission of childhood conduct problems: A children of twins study. *Archives of General Psychiatry, 64*, 820–829.

da Fonseca, E. B., Bittar, R. E., Damiao, R., & Zugiab, M. (2009). Prematurity prevention: The role of progesterone. *Current Opinion in Obstetrics and Gynecology, 21*, 142–147.

da Fonseca, E. B., Celik, E., & others. (2007). Progesterone and the risk of preterm birth among women with a short cervix. *New England Journal of Medicine, 357*, 462–469.

Dahl, R. E. (2004). Adolescent brain development: A period of vulnerabilities and opportunities. *Annals of the New York Academy of Sciences, 1021*, 1–22.

Dahlen, H. G., Dowling, H., Tracy, M., Schmied, V., & Tracy, S. (2013, in press). Maternal and perinatal outcomes amongst low risk women giving birth in water compared to six birth positions on land. A descriptive cross sectional study in a birth center over 12 years. *Midwifery*.

Daley, A. J., Macarthur, C., & Winter, H. (2007). The role of exercise in treating postpartum depression: A review of the literature. *Journal of Midwifery & Women's Health, 52*, 56–62.

Daley, C. E., & Onwuegbuzi, A. J. (2011). Race and intelligence. In R. J. Sternberg & S. B. Kaufman (Eds.), *Cambridge handbook of intelligence*. New York: Cambridge University Press.

Dalley, J. W., & Roiser, J. P. (2013, in press). Dopamine, serotonin, and impulsivity. *Neuroscience*.

Damon, W. (1988). *The moral child*. New York: Free Press.

Damon, W. (2008). *The path to purpose* New York: The Free Press.

Daniels, H. (2011). Vygotsky and psychology. In U. Goswami (Ed.), *Wiley-Blackwell handbook of childhood cognitive development* (2nd ed.). New York: Wiley-Blackwell.

Darling-Hammond, N. (2011). Testing, No Child Left Behind, and educational equity. In L. M. Stulberg & S. L. Weinberg (Eds.), *Diversity in higher education*. New York: Routledge.

Darrah. J., & Bartlett, D. J. (2013, in press). Infant rolling abilities—the same or different 20 years after the back to sleep campaign? *Early Human Development*.

Darwin, C. (1859). *On the origin of species*. London: John Murray.

Dasen, P. R. (1977). Are cognitive processes universal? A contribution to cross-cultural Piagetian Psychology. In N. Warran (Ed.), *Studies in cross-cultural psychology* (Vol. 1). London: Academic Press.

Davalos, D. B., Yadon, C. A., & Tregellas, H. C. (2012). Untreated prenatal maternal depression and the potential risks to offspring: A review. *Archives of Women's Mental Health, 15*, 1–14.

Davidson, J. (2000). Giftedness. In A. Kazdin (Ed.), *Encyclopedia of psychology*. Washington, DC, & New York: American Psychological Association and Oxford University Press.

Davidson, J., & Kemp, I. A. (2011). Contemporary models of intelligence. In R. J. Sternberg & S. B. Kaufman (Eds.), *Cambridge handbook of intelligence*. New York: Cambridge University Press.

Davidson, M. R., Davidson, M., London, M. L., & Ladewig, P. W. (2012). *Olds' maternal-newborn nursing & women's health across the lifespan: International Edition* (9th ed.).Upper Saddle River, NJ: Pearson.

Davies, G., & others. (2011). Genome-wide association studies establish that human intelligence is highly heritable and polygenic. *Molecular Psychiatry, 16*, 996–1005.

Davies, J., & Brember, I. (1999). Reading and mathematics attainments and self-esteem in years 2 and 6: An eight-year cross-sectional study. *Educational Studies, 25*, 145–157.

Davis, B. E., Moon, R. Y., Sachs, H. C., & Ottolini, M. C. (1998). Effects of sleep position on infant motor development. *Pediatrics, 102,* 1135–1140.

Davis, C. F., Lazariu, V., & Sekhobo, J. P. (2010). Smoking cessation in the WIC program. *Maternal and Child Health Journal, 14,* 474–477.

Davis, C. L., & Cooper, S. (2011). Fitness, fatness, cognition, behavior, and academic achievement in overweight children: Do cross-sectional associations correspond to exercise trial outcomes? *Preventive Medicine, 52*(Suppl. 1), S65–S69.

Davis, C. L., & others. (2007). Effects of aerobic exercise on overweight children's cognitive functioning: A randomized controlled trial. *Research Quarterly for Exercise and Sport, 78,* 510–519.

Davis, C. L., & others. (2011). Exercise improves executive function and alters neural activation in overweight children. *Health Psychology, 30,* 91–98.

Davis, C. L., & others. (2012). Exercise dose and diabetes risk in overweight and obese children: A randomized controlled trial. *Journal of the American Medical Association, 308,* 1103–1112.

Davis, E. L., & Buss, K. A. (2012). Moderators of the relation between shyness and behavior with peers: Cortisol dysregulation and maternal emotional socialization. *Social Development, 21,* 801–820.

Davis, K., Christodoulou, J., Seider, S., & Gardner, H. (2011). The theory of multiple intelligences. In R. J. Sternberg & S. B. Kaufman (Eds.), *Cambridge handbook of intelligence.* New York: Cambridge University Press.

Davis, S. M., & others. (2013). CHILE: An evidence-based preschool intervention for obesity prevention in Head Start. *Journal of School Health, 83,* 223–229.

Davis, L., & Keyser, J. (1997). *Becoming the parent you want to be.* New York: Broadway Books.

Day, N. L., Goldschmidt, L., & Thomas, C. A. (2006). Prenatal marijuana exposure contributes to the prediction of marijuana use at age 14. *Addiction, 101,* 1313–1322.

Day, R. H., & McKenzie, B. E. (1973). Perceptual shape constancy in early infancy. *Perception, 2,* 315–320.

de Brigard, F., Szpunar, K. K., & Schacter, D. L. (2013, in press). Coming to grips with the past: Effect of repeated stimulation on the perceived plausibility of episodic counterfactual thoughts. *Psychological Science.*

De Decker, E., & others. (2012). Influencing factors of screen time in preschool children: An exploration of parents' perceptions through focus groups in six European countries. *Obesity Reviews, 13*(Suppl. 1), S75–S84.

De Giovanni, N., & Marchetti, D. (2012). Cocaine and its metabolites in the placenta: A systematic review of the literature. *Reproductive Toxicology, 33,* 1–14.

de Graaf, H., van de Schoot, R., Woertman, L., Hawk, S. T., & Meeus, W. (2012). Family cohesion and romantic and sexual initiation: A three wave longitudinal study. *Journal of Youth and Adolescence, 41,* 583–592.

de Haan, M., & Gunnar, M. R. (Eds.). (2009). *Handbook of developmental social neuroscience.* New York: Guilford.

de Haan, M., & Matheson, A. (2009). The development and neural bases of processing emotion in faces and voices. In M. De Haan & M. R. Gunnar (Eds.), *Handbook of developmental social neuroscience.* New York: Guilford.

de Rose, L. M., Shiyko, M. P., Foster, H., & Brooks-Gunn, J. (2011). Associations between menarcheal timing and behavioral developmental trajectories for girls from age 6 to age 15. *Journal of Youth and Adolescence, 40,* 1329–1342.

de Villiers, J., & de Villiers, P. (2013). Syntax acquisition. In P. D. Zelazo (Ed.), *Oxford handbook of developmental psychology.* New York: Oxford University Press.

Deamen, S., & others. (2012). Identity and perceived peer relationship quality in emerging adulthood: The mediating role of attachment-related emotions. *Journal of Adolescence, 35,* 1417–1425.

Deardorff, J., & others. (2011). Father absence, body mass index, and pubertal timing in girls: Differential effects by family income and ethnicity. *Journal of Adolescent Health, 48,* 441–447.

Deary, I. J. (2012). Intelligence. *Annual Review of Psychology* (Vol. 63). Palo Alto, CA: Annual Reviews.

Deary, I. J., & Batty, G. D. (2011). Intelligence as a predictor of health, illness, and death. In R. J. Sternberg & S. B. Kaufman (Eds.), *Cambridge handbook of intelligence.* New York: Cambridge University Press.

Deary, I. J., Penke, L., & Johnson, W. (2010). The neuroscience of human intelligence differences. *Nature Review: Neuroscience, 11,* 201–211.

Deater-Deckard, K. (2013). The social environment and the development of psychopathology. In P. D. Zelazo (Ed.), *Oxford handbook of developmental psychology.* New York: Oxford University Press.

Deater-Deckard, K., & Dodge, K. (1997). Externalizing behavior problems and discipline revisited: Non-linear effects and variation by culture, context and gender. *Psychological Inquiry, 8,* 161–175.

DeCasper, A. J., & Spence, M. J. (1986). Prenatal maternal speech influences newborn's perception of speech sounds. *Infant Behavior and Development, 9,* 133–150.

Deci, E. L., & Ryan, R. M. (2000). The "what" and "why" of goal pursuits: Human needs and the self-determination of behavior. *Psychological Inquiry, 11,* 227–268.

Deeley, Q., & Murphy, D. (2009). Pathophysiology of autism: Evidence from brain imaging. *British Journal of Hospital Medicine, 70,* 138–142.

DeLoache, J. S. (1989). The development of representation in young children. In H. W. Reese (Ed.), *Advances in child development and behavior.* New York: Academic Press.

DeLoache, J. S. (2011). Early development of the understanding and use of symbolic artifacts. In U. Goswami (Ed.), *Wiley-Blackwell handbook of childhood cognitive development* (2nd ed.). New York: Wiley.

DeLoache, J. S., Simcock, G., & Macari, S. (2007). Planes, trains, and automobiles—and tea sets: Extremely intense interests in very young children. *Developmental Psychology, 43,* 1579–1586.

Demetriou, A. (2001, April). *Towards a comprehensive theory of intellectual development: Integrating psychometric and post-Piagetian theories.* Paper presented at the meeting of the Society for Research in Child Development Minneapolis.

Dempster, F. N. (1981). Memory span: Sources of individual and developmental differences. *Psychological Bulletin, 80,* 63–100.

Denham, S. A., Bassett., H. H., & Wyatt, T. (2007). The socialization of emotional competence. In J. E. Grusec & P. D. Hastings (Eds.), *Handbook of socialization.* New York: Guilford.

Denham, S., & others. (2012). Preschoolers' emotion knowledge: Self-regulatory foundations and predictors of school success. *Cognition and Emotion, 26,* 667–679.

Denham, S., Warren, H., von Salisch, M., Benga, O., Chin, J-C., & Geangu, E. (2011). Emotions and social development in childhood. In P. K. Smith & C. H. Hart (Eds.), *Wiley-Blackwell handbook of childhood social development* (2nd ed.). New York: Wiley.

Desai, M., Beall, M., & Ross, M. G. (2013, in press). Developmental origins of obesity: Programmed adipogenesis. *Current Diabetes Reports.*

Deutsch, A. R., Crockett, L. J., Wolf, J. M., & Russell, S. T. (2012). Parent and peer pathways to adolescent delinquency: Variations by ethnicity and neighborhood context. *Journal of Youth and Adolescence, 41,* 1078–1094.

Deutsch, R., & Pruett, M. K. (2009). Child adjustment and high conflict divorce. In R. M. Galatzer-Levy and L. Kraus (Eds.), *The scientific basis of custody decisions* (2nd ed.). New York: Wiley.

Devaney, S. A., Palomaki, G. E., Scott, J. A., & Bianchi, D. W. (2011). Noninvasive fetal sex determination using cell-free DNA: A systematic review and meta-analysis. *Journal of the American Medical Association, 306,* 627–636.

Dever, B. V., & others. (2013, in press). Predicting risk-taking with and without substance use: The effects of parental monitoring, school bonding, and sports participation. *Prevention Science.*

Devers, P. L., & others. (2013, in press). Noninvasive prenatal testing/noninvasive prenatal diagnosis: The position of the National Society of Genetic Counselors. *Journal of Genetic Counseling.*

Devos, T. (2006). Implicit bicultural identity among Mexican American and Asian American college students. *Cultural Diversity and Ethnic Minority Psychology, 12,* 381–402.

Dew, J., & Wilcox, W. B. (2011). "If momma ain't happy": Explaining declines in marital satisfaction among new mothers. *Journal of Marriage and the Family, 73,* 1–12.

DeWall, C. N., Anderson, C. A., & Bushman, B. J. (2013, in press). Aggression. In I. B. Weiner & others (Eds.), *Handbook of psychology* (2nd ed., Vol. 5). New York: Wiley.

Dewey, J. (1933). *How we think.* Lexington, MA: D. C. Heath.

DeZolt, D. M., & Hull, S. H. (2001). Classroom and schools climate. In J. Worell (Ed.), *Encyclopedia of women and gender.* San Diego: Academic Press.

Dhany, A. L., Mitchell, T., & Foy, C. (2012). Aromatherapy and massage intrapartum service impact on use of analgesia and anesthesia in women in labor: A retrospective case note analysis. *Journal of Alternative and Complementary Medicine, 18,* 932–938.

Diamond, A. (2013). Executive functioning. *Annual Review of Psychology* (Vol. 64). Palo Alto, CA: Annual Reviews.

Diamond, A. D. (1985). Development of the ability to use recall to guide action as indicated by infants' performance on AB. *Child Development, 56,* 868–883.

Diamond, A., Barnett, W. S., Thomas, J., & Munro, S. (2007). Preschool program improves cognitive control. *Science, 318,* 1387–1388.

Diamond, A., Casey, B. J., & Munakata, Y. (2011). *Developmental cognitive neuroscience.* New York: Oxford University Press.

Diamond, A., & Lee, K. (2011). Interventions shown to aid executive function development in children 4 to 12 years old. *Science, 333,* 959–964.

Diamond, L. M. (2013a, in press). Gender and same-sex sexuality. In D. T. Tolman & L. M. Diamond (Eds.), *APA handbook on sexuality and psychology.* Washington, DC: American Psychological Association.

Diamond, L. M. (2013b, in press). Sexuality and same-sex sexuality in relationships. In J. Simpson & J. Davidio (Eds.), *Handbook of personality and social psychology.* Washington, DC: American Psychological Association.

Diamond, L. M., & Savin-Williams, R. C. (2013, in press). Same-sex activity in adolescence: Multiple meanings and implications. In R. F. Fassinger & S. L. Morrow (Eds.), *Sex in the margins.* Washington, DC: American Psychological Association.

Diamond, M., & Sigmundson, H. K. (1997). Sex reassignment at birth: Long-term review and clinical implications. *Archives of Pediatric and Adolescent Medicine, 151,* 298–304.

Diaz, A., & Bell, M. A. (2012). Frontal EEG asymmetry and fear reactivity in different contexts at 10 months. *Developmental Psychobiology, 54,* 536–545.

Dick, D. M., & others. (2007). Gender differences in friends' influences on adolescent drinking: A genetic epidemiological study. *Alcoholism: Clinical and Experimental Research, 31,* 2012–2019.

Diego, M. A., Field, T., & Hernandez-Reif, M. (2008). Temperature increases in preterm infants during massage therapy. *Infant Behavior and Development, 31,* 149–152.

Diener, E., & Diener, M. (1995). Cross-cultural correlates of life satisfaction and self-esteem. *Journal of Personality and Social Psychology, 68,* 653–663.

Dietz, L. J., Jennings, K. D., Kelley, S. A., & Marshal, M. (2009). Maternal depression, paternal psychopathology, and toddlers' behavior problems. *Journal of Clinical Child and Adolescent Psychology, 38,* 48–61.

Dietz, P. M., & others. (2010). Infant morbidity and mortality attributable to prenatal smoking in the U.S. *American Journal of Preventive Medicine, 39,* 45–62.

Dimmitt, C., & McCormick, C. B. (2012). Metacognition in education. In K. R. Harris, S. Graham, & T. Urdan (Eds.), *Handbook of educational psychology.* Washington, DC: American Psychological Association.

Dishion, T. J., & Piehler, T. F. (2009). Deviant by design: Peer contagion in development, interventions, and schools. In K. H. Rubin, W. M. Bukowski, & B. Laursen (Eds.), *Handbook of peer interactions, relationships, and groups.* New York: Guilford.

Dishion, T. J., & Tipsord, J. M. (2011). Peer contagion in child and adolescent social and emotional development. *Annual Review of Psychology* (Vol. 62). Palo Alto, CA: Annual Reviews.

Diwadkar, V. A., & others. (2012). Differences in cortico-striatal-cerebellar activation during working memory in syndromal and nonsyndromal children with prenatal exposure to alcohol. *Human Brain Mapping, 69,* 231–242.

Dixon, R. A., McFall, G. P., Whitehead, B. P., & Dolcos, S. (2013, in press). Cognitive development in adulthood and aging. In I. B. Weiner & others (2nd ed., Vol. 6). New York: Wiley.

Dodd, B., & Crosbie, S. (2011). Language and cognition: Evidence from disordered language. In U. Goswami (Ed.), *Wiley-Blackwell handbook of childhood cognitive development.* New York: Wiley.

Dodge, K. A. (1993). Social cognitive mechanisms in the development of conduct disorder and depression. *Annual Review of Psychology* (Vol. 44, pp. 559–584). Palo Alto, CA: Annual Reviews.

Dodge, K. A. (2011a). Context matters in child and family policy. *Child Development, 82,* 433–442.

Dodge, K. A. (2011b). Social information processing models of aggressive behavior. In M. Mikulincer & P. R. Shaver (Eds.), *Understanding and reducing aggression, violence, and their consequences.* Washington, DC: American Psychological Association.

Dodge, K. A., & McCourt, S. N. (2010). Translating models of antisocial behavioral development into efficacious intervention policy to prevent adolescence violence. *Developmental Psychobiology, 52,* 277–285.

Dodge, K. A., & Rutter, M. (Eds.). (2011). *Gene-environment interaction and developmental psychopathology.* New York: Guilford.

Doherty, M. (2009). *Theory of mind.* Philadelphia: Psychology Press.

Dondi, M., Simion, F., & Caltran, G. (1999). Can newborns discriminate between their own cry and the cry of another newborn infant? *Developmental Psychology, 35*(2), 418–426.

Donegan, S., & others. (2010). Two food-assisted maternal and child health nutrition programs help mitigate the impact of economic hardship on child stunting in Haiti. *Journal of Nutrition, 140,* 1139–1145.

Donnerstein, E. (2012). Internet bullying. *Pediatric Clinics of North America, 59,* 623–633.

Doob, C. B. (2013). *Social inequality and social stratification in U.S. Society.* Upper Saddle River, NJ: Pearson.

Doornwaard, S. M., Branje, S., Meeus, W. H. J., & ter Bogt, T. F. M. (2012). Development of adolescents' peer crowd identification in relation to changes in problem behaviors. *Developmental Psychology, 48,* 1366–1380.

Dopp, P. R., Mooney, A. J., Armitage, R., & King, C. (2012). Exercise for adolescents with depressive disorders: A feasibility study. *Depression Research and Treatment.* Article ID: 257472.

Dorn, L. H., & Biro, F. M. (2011). Puberty and its measurement: A decade in review. *Journal of Research on Adolescence, 21,* 180–195.

Doty, R. L., & Shah, M. (2008). Taste and smell. In M. M. Haith & J. B. Benson (Eds.), *Encyclopedia of infant and early childhood development.* Oxford, UK: Elsevier.

Dow, R. S., & Baer, G. T. (2013). *Self-paced phonics* (5th ed.). Boston: Allyn & Bacon.

Dozier, M., Stovall-McClough, K. C., & Albus, K. E. (2009). Attachment and psychopathogy in adulthood. In J. Cassidy & P. R. Shaver (Eds.), *Handbook of attachment* (2nd ed.). New York: Guilford.

Draghi-Lorenz, R., Reddy, V., & Costall, A. (2001). Rethinking the development of "nonbasic" emotions: A critical review of existing theories. *Developmental Review, 21,* 263–304.

Drake, K. M., & others. (2012). Influence of sports, physical education, and active commuting to school on adolescent weight status. *Pediatrics, 130,* e296–e304.

Drake, M. (2008). Developing resilient children after 100 years of Montessori education. *Montessori Life, 20*(2), 28–31.

Dregan, A., & Armstrong, D. (2010). Adolescent sleep disturbances as predictors of adult sleep disturbances—A cohort study. *Journal of Adolescent Health, 46,* 482–487.

Driesen, N. R., & Raz, N. (1995). The influence of sex, age, and handedness on corpus callosum morphology: A meta-analysis. *Psychobiology, 23,* 240–247.

Duck, S. W. (1975). Personality similarity and friendship choices by adolescents. *European Journal of Social Psychology, 5,* 351–365.

Dufour-Rainfray, D., & others. (2011). Fetal exposure to teratogens: Evidence of genes involved in autism. *Neuroscience and Biobehavioral Reviews, 35,* 1254–1265.

Duggan, P. M., Lapsley, D. K., & Norman, K. (2000, April). *Adolescent invulnerability and personal uniqueness: Scale development and initial contact validation.* Paper presented at the biennial meeting of the Society for Research in Child Development, Chicago.

Duncan, A. F., & others. (2011). Elevated systolic blood pressure in preterm very-low-birthweight infants ≤ 3 years of life. *Pediatric Nephrology, 26,* 1115–1121.

Duncan, G. J. (2012). Give us this day our daily breadth. *Child Development, 83,* 6–15.

Duncan, G., & Magnuson, K. (2008). Can society profit from investing in early education programs? In A. Tarlov (Ed.), *Nurturing the national treasure: Childhood education and development before kindergarten.* New York: Palgrave Macmillan.

Duncan, G., Magnuson, K., Kalil, A., & Ziol-Guest, K. (2012). The importance of early childhood poverty. *Social Indicators Research, 108,* 87–98.

Duncan, J. R., & others. (2010). Brainstem serotonergic deficiency in sudden infant death syndrome. *Journal of the American Medical Association, 303,* 430–437.

Duncombe, M. E., Havighurst, S. S., Holland, K. A., & Frankling, E. J. (2012, in press). The contribution of parenting practice and parent emotion factors in children at risk for disruptive behavior disorders. *Child Psychiatry and Human Development, 43,* 715–733.

Dunkel Schetter, C. (2011). Psychological science in the study of pregnancy and birth. *Annual Review of Psychology* (Vol. 62). Palo Alto, CA: Annual Reviews.

Dunn, J. (2007). Siblings and socialization. In J. E. Grusec & P. D. Hastings (Eds.), *Handbook of socialization.* New York: Guilford.

Dunn, J. (2010). Commentary and challenges to Grusec and Davidov's domain-specific approach. *Child Development, 81,* 710–714.

Dunn, J. (2013). Moral development in early childhood and social interaction in the family. In M. Killen & J. G. Smetana (Eds.), *Handbook of moral development* (2nd ed.). New York: Routledge.

Dunn, J., & Kendrick, C. (1982). *Siblings.* Cambridge, MA: Harvard University Press.

Dunphy, D. C. (1963). The social structure of urban adolescent peer groups. *Society, 26,* 230–246.

Dunst, C. J., Simkus, A., & Hamby, D. W. (2012). Relationship between age of onset and frequency of reading and infants' and toddlers' early language and literacy development. *CELLreviews, 5*(3), 1–10.

Durik, A. M., & others. (2006). Ethnicity and stereotypes of emotions. *Sex Roles, 54*(7–8), 429–445.

Durrant, J. E. (2008). Physical punishment, culture, and rights: Current issues for professionals. *Journal of Developmental and Behavioral Pediatrics, 29,* 55–66.

Durrant, R., & Ellis, B. J. (2013, in press). Evolutionary psychology. In I. B. Weiner & others (Eds.), *Handbook of psychology* (2nd ed., Vol. 3). New York: Wiley.

Durston, S., & others. (2006). A shift from diffuse to focal cortical activity with development. *Developmental Science, 9,* 1–8.

Dusek, J. B., & McIntyre, J. G. (2003). Self-concept and self-esteem development. In G. Adams & M. Berzonsky (Eds.), *Blackwell handbook of adolescence.* Malden, MA: Blackwell.

Dvornyk, V., & Waqar-ul-Haq, H. (2012). Genetics of age at menarche: A systematic review. *Human Reproduction Update, 18,* 198–210.

Dweck, C. S. (2006). *Mindset.* New York: Random House.

Dweck, C. S. (2007). Boosting achievement with messages that motivate. *Education Canada, 47,* 6–10.

Dweck, C. S. (2012). Mindsets and human nature: Promoting change in the Middle East, the school yard, the racial divide, and willpower. *American Psychologist, 67,* 614–622.

Dweck, C. S. (2013). Social development. In P. Zelazo (Ed.), *Oxford handbook of developmental psychology.* New York: Oxford University Press.

Dweck, C. S., Mangels, J. A., & Good, C. (2004). Motivational effects on attention, cognition, and performance. In D. Yun Dai & R. J. Sternberg (Eds.), *Motivation, emotion, and cognition.* Mahwah, NJ: Erlbaum.

Dweck, C. S., & Master, A. (2009). Self-theories and motivation: Students' beliefs about intelligence. In K. R. Wentzel & A. Wigfield (Eds.), *Handbook of motivation at school.* New York: Routledge.

Dworkis, D. A., & others. (2011). Severe sickle-cell anemia is associated with increased plasma levels of TNF-R1 and VCAM-1. *American Journal of Hematology, 86,* 220–223.

Dyck, M., & Piek, J. (2010). How to distinguish normal from disordered children with poor language or motor skills. *International Journal of Language and Communication Disorders, 45,* 336–344.

E

Eagly, A. H. (2001). Social role theory of sex differences and similarities. In J. Worrell (Ed.), *Encyclopedia of women and gender.* San Diego: Academic Press.

Eagly, A. H. (2010). Gender roles. In J. Levine & M. Hogg (Eds.), *Encyclopedia of group process and intergroup relations.* Thousand Oaks, CA: Sage.

Eagly, A. H. (2013, in press). Women as leaders: Paths through the labryinth. In M. C. Bligh & R. Riggio (Eds.), *When near is far and far is near: Exploring distance in leader-follower relationships.* New York: Wiley Blackwell.

Eagly, A. H., & Crowley, M. (1986). Gender and helping behavior: A meta-analytic review of the social psychological literature. *Psychological Bulletin, 100,* 283–308.

Eagly, A. H., & Steffen, V. J. (1986). Gender and aggressive behavior: A meta-analytic review of the social psychological literature. *Psychological Bulletin, 100,* 309–330.

Early Growth Genetics (EGG) Consortium & others. (2012). A genome-wide association meta-analysis identifies new childhood obesity loci. *Nature: Genetics, 45,* 526–531.

East, P. (2009). Adolescent relationships with siblings. In R. M. Lerner & L. Steinberg (Eds.), *Handbook of adolescent psychology* (3rd ed.). New York: Wiley.

Easterbrooks, M. A., Bartlett, J. D., Beeghly, M., & Thompson, R. A. (2013, in press). Social and emotional development in infancy. In R. M. Lerner, M. A. Easterbrooks, & J. Mistry (Eds.), *Handbook of psychology* (2nd ed., Vol. 6). New York: Wiley.

Eaton, D. K., & others. (2010). Youth risk behavior surveillance—United States 2009. *MMWR Surveillance Summaries, 59*(5), 1–142.

Eaton, D. K., & others. (2012). Youth risk behavior surveillance—United States, 2011. *MMWR Surveillance Summaries, 8, 61*(4), 1–162.

Eaton, W. O. (2008). Milestones: Physical. In M. M. Haith & J. B. Benson (Eds.), *Encyclopedia of infant and early childhood development.* Oxford, UK: Elsevier.

Ebstein, R. P., Knafo, A., Mankuta, D., Chew, S. H., & Lai, P. S. (2012). The contributions of oxytocin and vasopressin pathway genes to human behavior. *Hormones and Behavior, 61,* 359–379.

Eccles, J. (2003). Education: Junior and high school. In G. Adams & M. Berzonsky (Eds.), *Blackwell handbook of adolescence.* Malden, MA: Blackwell.

Eccles, J. S. (2007). Families, schools, and developing achievement-related motivations and engagement. In J. E. Grusec & P. D. Hastings (Eds.), *Handbook of socialization.* New York: Guilford.

Eccles, J. S., & Roeser, R. W. (2011). Schools as developmental contexts during adolescence. *Journal of Research on Adolescence, 21,* 225–241.

Eccles, J. S., & Roeser, R. W. (2013). Schools as developmental contexts during adolescence. In I. B. Weiner & others (Eds.), *Handbook of psychology* (2nd ed., Vol. 6). New York: Wiley.

Eckerman, C., & Whitehead, H. (1999). How toddler peers generate coordinated action: A cross-cultural exploration. *Early Education & Development, 10,* 241–266.

Eckman, J. R., & Embury, S. H. (2011). Sickle cell anemia pathophysiology: Back to the data. *American Journal of Hematology, 86,* 121–122.

Ednick, M., & others. (2010). Sleep–related respiratory abnormalities and arousal pattern in achondroplasia during early infancy. *Journal of Pediatrics, 155,* 510–515.

Edwards, C. P., & Liu, W. (2002). Parenting toddlers. In M. H. Bornstein (Ed.), *Handbook of parenting* (2nd ed., Vol. 1). Mahwah, NJ: Erlbaum.

Edwards, M. (2014, in press). *Every child, every day: A digital conversion model for student achievement.* Upper Saddle River, NJ: Pearson.

Edwards, R., & Hamilton, M. A. (2004). You need to understand my gender role: An empirical test of Tannen's model of gender and communication. *Sex Roles, 50,* 491–504.

Ehrhardt, A. A., & Baker, S. W. (1974). Fetal androgens, human central nervous system differentiation, and behavior sex differences. In R. C. Friedman, R. M. Richart, & R. L. Vande Wiele (Eds.), *Sex differences in behavior.* New York: Wiley.

Ehrlich, K. B., Dykas, M. J., & Cassidy, J. (2012). Tipping points in adolescent adjustment: Predicting social functioning from adolescents' conflict with parents and friends. *Journal of Family Psychology, 26,* 776–783.

Eiferman, R. R. (1971). Social play in childhood. In R. Herron & B. Sutton-Smith (Eds.), *Child's play.* New York: Wiley.

Eisenberg, N. (2010). Emotion regulation in children. *Annual Review of Clinical Psychology* (Vol. 6). Palo Alto, CA: Annual Reviews.

Eisenberg, N., Morris, A. S., McDaniel, B., & Spinrad, T. L. (2009). Moral cognitions and prosocial responding in adolescence. In R. M. Lerner & L. Steinberg (Eds.), *Handbook of adolescent psychology* (3rd ed.). New York: Wiley.

Eisenberg, N., Spinrad, T. L., & Morris, A. S. (2013). Prosocial development. In P. D. Zelazo (Ed.), *Oxford handbook of developmental psychology.* New York: Oxford University Press.

Eisenberg, N., Spinrad, T., & Sadovsky, A. (2006). Empathy-related responding in children. In M. Killen & J. Smetana (Eds.), *Handbook of moral development.* Mahwah, NJ: Erlbaum.

Eisenberg, N., Spinrad, T., & Sadovsky, A. (2013). Empathy-related responding in children. In M. Killen & J. G. Smetana (Eds.), *Handbook of moral development* (2nd ed.). New York: Routledge.

Eisenberg, N., & Valiente, C. (2002). Parenting and children's prosocial and moral development. In M. H. Bornstein (Ed.), *Handbook of parenting* (2nd ed.). Mahwah, NJ: Erlbaum.

Eisenhower Foundation. (2013). *Quantum Opportunities Program.* Retrieved January 17, 2013, from www.eisenhowerfoundation.org/qop.php

Elbourne, P. (2012). *Meaning.* New York: Oxford University Press.

Elder, G. H., & Shanahan, M. J. (2006). The life course and human development. In W. Damon & R. Lerner (Eds.), *Handbook of child psychology* (6th ed.). New York: Wiley.

El-Hajj, N., & others. (2013, in press). Metabolic programming of MEST DNA methylation by intrauterine exposure to gestational diabetes mellitus. *Diabetes.*

Elkind, D. (1976). *Child development and education. A Piagetian perspective.* New York: Oxford University Press.

Elkind, D. (1978). Understanding the young adolescent. *Adolescence, 13,* 127–134.

Ellis, B. J., Shirtcliff, E. A., Boyce, W. T., Deardorff, J., & Essex, M. J. (2011). Quality of early family relationships and the timing and tempo of puberty: Effects depend on biological sensitivity to context. *Development and Psychopathology, 23,* 85–99.

El-Sheikh, M. (Ed.). (2011). *Sleep and development.* New York: Oxford University Press.

El-Sheikh, M. (2013). *Auburn University Child Sleep, Health, and Development Center.* Auburn, AL: Auburn University.

El-Sheikh, M., & others. (2013, in press). Economic adversity and children's sleep problems: Multiple indicators and moderation of health. *Health Psychology.*

Emery, R. E. (1994). *Renegotiating family relationships.* New York: Guilford Press.

Emery, R. E., & Laumann-Billings, L. (1998). An overview of the nature, causes, and consequences of abusive family relationships. *American Psychologist, 53,* 121–135.

Emes, R. D., & Grant, S. G. N. (2013). Evolution of synapse complexity and diversity. *Annual Review of Neuroscience* (Vol. 35). Palo Alto, CA: Annual Reviews.

Enfield, A., & Collins, D. (2008). The relationship of service-learning, social justice, multicultural competence, and civic engagement. *Journal of College Student Development, 49,* 95–109.

Enright, M. S., Schaefer, L. V., Schaefer, P., & Schaefer, K. A. (2008). Building a just adolescent community. *Montessori Life, 20,* 36–42.

Enright, R. D., Santos, M. J. D., & Al-Mabuk, R. (1989). The adolescent as forgiver. *Journal of Adolescence, 12,* 95–110.

Ensor, R., Spencer, D., & Hughes, C. (2010). "You feel sad?" Emotional understanding mediates effects of verbal ability and mother-child mutuality on prosocial behaviors: Findings from 2 to 4 years. *Social Development, 20,* 93–110.

Epstein, D., & Barnett, W. S. (2012). Early education in the United States: Programs and access. In R. C. Pianta (Ed.), *Handbook of early childhood education.* New York: Guilford.

Ericsson, K. A., Charness, N., Feltovich, P. J., & Hoffman, R. R. (Eds.). (2006). *The Cambridge handbook of expertise and expert performance.* New York: Cambridge University Press.

Ericsson, K. A., Krampe, R., & Tesch-Romer, C. (1993). The role of deliberate practice in the acquisition of expert performance. *Psychological Review, 100,* 363–406.

Erikson, E. H. (1950). *Childhood and society.* New York: W. W. Norton.

Erikson, E. H. (1968). *Identity: Youth and crisis.* New York: W. W. Norton.

Eriksson, U. J. (2009). Congenital malformations in diabetic pregnancy. *Seminar in Fetal and Neonatal Medicine, 14,* 85–93.

Escobar-Chaves, S. L., & Anderson, C. A. (2008). Media and risky behavior. *Future of Children, 18*(1), 147–180.

Espelage, D. L., & Holt, M. K. (2012). Understanding and preventing bullying and sexual harassment in school. In K. R. Harris & others (Eds.), *APA handbook of educational psychology.* Washington, DC: American Psychological Association.

Etaugh, C., & Bridges, J. S. (2010). *Women's lives* (2nd ed.). Boston: Allyn & Bacon.

Evans, B. J., & Whitfield, J. R. (Eds.). (1988). *Black males in the United States: An annotated bibliography from 1967 to 1987.* Washington, DC: American Psychological Association.

Evans, G. W. (2004). The environment of childhood poverty. *American Psychologist, 59,* 77–92.

Evans, G. W., & English, K. (2002). The environment of poverty: Multiple stressor exposure, psychophysiological stress, and socioemotional adjustment. *Child Development, 73,* 1238–1248.

Evans, G. W., & Kim, P. (2007). Childhood poverty and health: Cumulative risk exposure and stress dysregulation. *Psychological Science, 18,* 953–957.

F

Fabiano, G. A., & others. (2009). A meta-analysis of behavioral treatments for attention deficit/hyperactivity disorder. *Clinical Psychology Review, 29*(2), 129–140.

Fabricius, W. V., Braver, S. L., Diaz, P., & Schenck, C. (2010). Custody and parenting time: Links to family relationships and well-being after divorce. In M. E. Lamb (Ed.), *The role of the father in child development* (5th ed.). New York: Wiley.

Fagan, J. F. (1992). Intelligence: A theoretical viewpoint. *Current Directions in Psychological Science, 1,* 82–86.

Fagan, J. F. (2011). Intelligence in infancy. In R. J. Sternberg & S. B. Kaufman (Eds.), *Handbook of intelligence.* New York: Cambridge University Press.

Fagan, J. F., Holland, C. R., & Wheeler, K. (2007). The prediction, from infancy, of adult IQ and achievement. *Intelligence, 35,* 225–231.

Fair, D., & Schlaggar, B. L. (2008). Brain development. In M. M. Haith & J. B. Benson (Eds.), *Encyclopedia of infant and early childhood development.* London, UK: Elsevier.

Fairweather, E., & Cramond, B. (2011). Infusing creative and critical thinking into the classroom. In R. A. Beghetto & J. C. Kaufman (Eds.), *Nurturing creativity in the classroom.* New York: Cambridge University Press.

Falbo, T., & Poston, D. L. (1993). The academic, personality, and physical outcomes of only children in China. *Child Development, 64,* 18–35.

Falck-Ytter, T., & others. (2012, in press). Gaze performance in children with autism spectrum disorder when observing communicative actions. *Journal of Autism and Developmental Disorders.*

Fantz, R. L. (1963). Pattern vision in newborn infants. *Science, 140,* 296–297.

Faraone, S. V., & Mick, E. (2010). Molecular genetics of attention deficit hyperactivity disorder. *Psychiatric Clinics of North America, 33,* 159–180.

Farrington, D. P. (2009). Conduct disorder, aggression, and delinquency. In R. M. Lerner & L. Steinberg (Eds.), *Handbook of adolescent psychology* (3rd ed.). New York: Wiley.

Fasig, L. (2000). Toddlers' understanding of ownership: Implications for self-concept development. *Social Development, 9,* 370–382.

Fearon, R. P., & others. (2010). The significance of insecure attachment and disorganization in the development of children's externalizing behavior: A meta-analytic study. *Child Development, 81,* 435–456.

Feeney, S., Moravcik, E., & Nolte, S. (2013). *Who am I in the lives of children?* (9th ed.). Upper Saddle River, NJ: Pearson.

Feil, R., & Fraga, M. F. (2012). Epigenetics and the environment: Emerging patterns and implications. *Nature Reviews: Genetics, 1,* 97–109.

Fein, G. G. (1986). Pretend play. In D. Görlitz & J. E. Wohlwill (Eds.), *Curiosity, imagination, and play.* Hillsdale, NJ: Erlbaum.

Feldman, H. D., & Morelock, M. J. (Eds.). (2011). *Prodigies and savants.* In R. J. Sternberg & S. B. Kaufman (Eds.), *Handbook of intelligence.* New York: Cambridge University Press.

Feldman, R. (2012). Oxytocin and social affiliation in humans. *Hormones and Behavior, 61,* 380–391.

Ferguson, D. M., Harwood, L. J., & Shannon, F. T. (1987). Breastfeeding and subsequent social adjustment in 6- to 8-year-old children. *Journal of Child Psychology and Psychiatry, 28,* 378–386.

Ferguson, G. M., Bornstein, M. H., & Pottinger, A. M. (2012). Tridimensional acculturation and adaptation among Jamaican adolescent-mother dyads in the United States. *Child Development, 83,* 1486–1493.

Fernandez-Martinez, F .J., & others. (2012). Noninvasive fetal sex determination in maternal plasma: A prospective feasibility study. *Genetics in Medicine, 14,* 101–106.

Field, T. M. (2001). Massage therapy facilitates weight gain in preterm infants. *Current Directions in Psychological Science, 10,* 51–55.

Field, T. M. (2007). *The amazing infant.* Malden, MA: Blackwell.

Field, T. (2010). Postpartum depression effects on early interactions, parenting, and safety practices: A review. *Infant Behavior and Development, 33,* 1–6.

Field, T. M. (2012). Prenatal exercise research. *Infant Behavior and Development, 35,* 397–407.

Field, T. M., Delgado, J., Diego, M., & Medina, L. (2013). Tai chi/yoga reduces prenatal depression, anxiety, and sleep disturbances. *Complementary Therapies in Clinical Practice, 19,* 6–10.

Field, T., Diego, M., & Hernandez-Reif, M. (2008). *International Journal of Neuroscience, 118,* 277–289.

Field, T., Diego, M., & Hernandez-Reif, M. (2010). Preterm infant massage therapy research: A review. *Infant Behavior and Development, 33,* 115–124.

Field, T., Figueiredo, B., Hernandez-Reif, M., Deeds, O., & Ascencio, A. (2008). Massage therapy reduces pain in pregnant women, alleviates prenatal depression in both parents and improves their relationships. *Journal of Bodywork and Movement Therapies, 12,* 146–150.

Field, T. M., Henteleff, T., & others. (1998). Children with asthma have improved pulmonary functions after massage therapy. *Journal of Pediatrics, 132,* 854–858.

Field, T. M., & Hernandez-Reif, M. (2013). Touch and pain perception in infants. In D. Narvaez & others (Eds.), *Evolution, early experience, and development.* New York: Oxford University Press.

Field, T. M., Hernandez-Reif, M., Feije, L., & Freedman, J. (2006). Prenatal, perinatal, and neonatal stimulation. *Infant Behavior & Development, 29,* 24–31.

Field, T. M., Hernandez-Reif, M., Taylor, S., Quintino, O., & Burman, I. (1997). Labor pain is reduced by massage therapy. *Journal of Psychosomatic Obstetrics and Gynecology, 18,* 286–291.

Field, T. M., Lasko, D., & others. (1997). Brief report: Autistic children's attentiveness and responsivity improve after touch therapy. *Journal of Autism and Developmental Disorders, 27,* 333–338.

Field, T. M., Quintino, O., Hernandez-Reif, M., & Koslosky, G. (1998). Adolescents with attention deficit hyperactivity disorder benefit from massage therapy. *Adolescence, 33,* 103–108.

Field, T. M., & others. (2004). Massage therapy by parents improves early growth and development. *Infant Behavior & Development, 27,* 435–442.

Field, T. M., & others. (2012). Yoga and massage therapy reduce prenatal depression and prematurity. *Journal of Bodywork and Movement Therapies, 16,* 204–209.

Finger, B., Hans, S. L., Bernstein, V. J., & Cox, S. M. (2009). Parent relationship quality and infant-mother attachment. *Attachment and Human Development, 11,* 285–306.

Fingerman, K. L., Cheng, Y. P., & others. (2012, in press). Helicopter parents and landing pad kids: Intense parental support of grown children. *Journal of Marriage and the Family.*

Fingerman, K. L., Pillemer, K. A., Silverstein, M., & Suitor, J. J. (2012). The Baby Boomers' intergenerational relationships. *Gerontologist, 52,* 199–209.

Fingerman, K. L., Sechrest, J., & Birditt, K. S. (2013, in press). Intergenerational relationships in a changing world. *Gerontology.*

Fiori, M., & Antonakis, J. (2012). Selective attention to emotional stimuli: What IQ and openness do, and emotional intelligence does not. *Intelligence, 40,* 245–254.

Fischhoff, B., Bruine de Bruin, W., Parker, A. M., Millstein, S. G., & Halpern-Felsher, B. L. (2010). Adolescents' perceived risk of dying. *Journal of Adolescent Health, 46,* 265–269.

Fisher, A., Thiessen, E., Godwin, K., Kloos, H., & Dickerson, J. (2013). Assessing selective sustained attention in 3- to 5-year-old children: Evidence for a new paradigm. *Journal of Experimental Child Psychology, 114,* 275–294.

Fisher, C. B., Busch-Rossnagel, N. A., Jopp, D. S., & Brown, J. L. (2013, in press). Applied developmental science: Contributions and challenges for the 21st century. In I. B. Weiner & others (Eds.), *Handbook of psychology* (2nd ed., Vol. 6). New York: Wiley.

Fisher, H. L. & others. (2012, in press). Bullying victimization and risk of self-harm in early adolescence: Longitudinal cohort study. *British Medical Journal.*

Fisher, P. A. (2005, April). *Translational research on underlying mechanisms of risk among foster children: Implications for prevention science.* Paper presented at the meeting of the Society for Research in Child Development, Washington, DC.

Fitzgerald, A., Fitzgerald, N., & Aherne, C. (2012). Do peers matter? A review of peer and/or friends' influence on physical activity among American adolescents. *Journal of Adolescence, 35,* 941–958.

Fivush, R. (2009). Sociocultural perspectives in autobiographical memory. In M. Courage & N. Cowan (Eds.), *The development of memory in infancy and childhood.* New York: Psychology Press.

Flanagan, C., Beyers, W., & Zukauskiene, R. (2012). Editorial: Political and civic engagement development in adolescence. *Journal of Adolescence, 35,* 471–473.

Flavell, J. H. (1979). Metacognition and cognitive monitoring. A new area of psychological inquiry. *American Psychologist, 34,* 906–911.

Flavell, J. H. (2004). Theory-of-mind development: Retrospect and prospect. *Merrill-Palmer Quarterly, 50,* 274–290.

Flavell, J. H., Friedrichs, A., & Hoyt, J. (1970). Developmental changes in memorization processes. *Cognitive Psychology, 1,* 324–340.

Flavell, J. H., Green, F. L., & Flavell, E. R. (1993). Children's understanding of the stream of consciousness. *Child Development, 64,* 95–120.

Flavell, J. H., Green, F. L., and Flavell, E. R. (1998). The mind has a mind of its own developing knowledge about mental uncontrollability. *Cognitive Development, 13,* 127–138.

Flavell, J. H., & Miller, P. H. (1998). Social cognition. In W. Damon (Ed.), *Handbook of child psychology* (5th ed.). New York: Wiley.

Flavell, J. H., Miller, P. H., & Miller, S. (2002). *Cognitive development* (4th ed.). Upper Saddle River, NJ: Prentice Hall.

Flavell, J., Mumme, D., Green, F., & Flavell, E. (1992). Young children's understanding of different types of beliefs. *Child Development, 63,* 960–977.

Flegal, W. A. (2007). Blood group genotyping in Germany. *Transfusion, 47* (Suppl. I), S47–S53.

Fletcher, B. R., & Rapp, P. R. (2013, in press). Normal neurocognitive aging. In I. B. Weiner & others (Eds.), *Handbook of psychology* (2nd ed., Vol. 3). New York: Wiley.

Flint, M. S., Baum, A., Chambers, W. H., & Jenkins, F. J. (2007). Induction of DNA damage, alteration of DNA repair, and transcriptional activation by stress hormones. *Psychoneuroendocrinology, 32,* 470–479.

Flom, R., & Pick, A. D. (2003). Verbal encouragement and joint attention in 18-month-old infants. *Infant Behavior and Development, 26,* 121–134.

Florin, T., & Ludwig, S. (2011). *Netter's Pediatrics.* New York: Elsevier.

Florsheim, P., Moore, D., & Edgington, C. (2003). Romantic relationships among adolescent parents. In P. C. Florsheim (Ed.), *Adolescent romantic relations and sexual behavior.* Oxford, UK: Routledge.

Flouri, E., & Buchanan, A. (2004). Early father's and mother's involvement and child's later educational outcomes. *British Journal of Educational Psychology, 74,* 141–153.

Flynn, J. R. (1999). Searching for justice: The discovery of IQ gains over time. *American Psychologist, 54,* 5–20.

Flynn, J. R. (2007). The history of the American mind in the 20th century: A scenario to explain gains over time and a case for the irrelevance of *g.* In P. C. Kyllonen, R. D. Roberts, & L. Stankov (Eds.), *Extending intelligence.* Mahwah, NJ: Erlbaum.

Flynn, J. R. (2011). Secular changes in intelligence. In R. J. Sternberg & S. B. Kaufman (Eds.), *Cambridge handbook of intelligence.* New York: Cambridge University Press.

Flynn, J. R. (2013). *Are we getting smarter?* New York: Cambridge University Press.

Flynn, J. R., & Rossi-Case, L. (2012). IQ gains in Argentina between 1964 and 1998. *Intelligence, 40,* 145–150.

Fontenot, H. B. (2007). Transition and adaptation to adoptive motherhood. *Journal of Obstetrics, Gynecologic, and Neonatal Nursing, 36,* 175–182.

Ford, D. Y. (2012). Gifted and talented education: History, issues, and recommendations. In K. R. Harris, S. Graham, & T. Urdan (Eds.), *APA handbook of educational psychology.* Washington, DC: American Psychological Association.

Forgatch, M. S., Patterson, G. R., Degarmo, D. S., & Beldavs, Z. G. (2009). Testing the Oregon delinquency model with 9-year follow-up of the Oregon Divorce Study. *Development and Psychopathology, 21,* 637–660.

Forget-Dubois, N., & others. (2009). Early child language mediates the relation between home environment and school readiness. *Child Development, 80,* 736–749.

Fox, B. J. (2012). *Word identification strategies* (5th ed.). Boston: Allyn & Bacon.

Fox, E., & Alexander, P. A. (2011). Learning to read. In P. A. Alexander & R. E. Mayer (Eds.), *Handbook of research on learning and instruction.* New York: Routledge.

Fox, M. K., Condon, E., Briefel, R. R., Reidy, K. C., & Deming, D. M. (2010). Food consumption patterns of young preschoolers: Are they starting off on the right path? *Journal of the American Dietetic Association, 110*(Suppl. 12), S52–S59.

Fox, M. K., Pac, S., Devaney, B., & Jankowski, L. (2004). Feeding infants and toddlers study: What foods are infants and toddlers eating? *American Journal, 104*(Suppl.), S22–S30.

Fox, S. E., Levitt, P., & Nelson, C. A. (2010). How the timing and quality of early experiences influence the development of brain architecture. *Child Development, 81,* 28–40.

Fraley, R. C., Roisman, G. I., & Haltigan, J. D. (2013). The legacy of early experiences in development: Formalizing alternative models of how early experiences are carried forward over time. *Developmental Psychology.*

Franchak, J. M., & Adolph, K. E. (2010). Visually-guided navigation: Head-mounted eye-tracking of natural locomotion in children and adults. *Vision Research, 50,* 2766–2774.

Franchak, J. M., Kretch, K. S., Soska, K. C., & Adolph, K. E. (2011). Head-mounted eye-tracking: A new method to describe the visual ecology of infants. *Child Development, 82,* 1738–1750.

Frank, M. C., Vul, E., & Johnson, S. P. (2009). Development of infants' attention to faces during the first year. *Cognition, 110,* 160–170.

Franklin, A., Bevis, L., Ling, Y., & Hulbert, A. (2010). Biological components of color preference in infancy. *Developmental Science, 13,* 346–354.

Franz, C. E. (1996). The implications of preschool tempo and motoric activity level for personality decades later. Reported in A. Caspi (1998), Personality development across the life course. In W. Damon (Ed.), *Handbook of child psychology* (Vol. 3, p. 337). New York: Wiley.

Fraser, A. M., Padilla-Walker, L. M., Coyne, S. M., Nelson, L. J., & Stockdale, L. A. (2012). Association between violent video gaming, empathic concern, and prosocial behavior toward strangers, friends, and family members. *Journal of Youth and Adolescence, 41,* 636–649.

Frechette, J. (2012). Beauty and body image: Beauty myths. In M. Kosut (Ed.), *Encyclopedia of gender in media.* Thousand Oaks, CA: Sage.

Frederikse, M., & others. (2000). Sex differences in inferior lobule volume in schizophrenia. *American Journal of Psychiatry, 157,* 422–427.

Freud, S. (1917). *A general introduction to psychoanalysis.* New York: Washington Square Press.

Friedman, S. L., Melhuish, E., & Hill, C. (2010). Childcare research at the dawn of a new millennium: An update. In G. Bremner & T. Wachs (Eds.), *Wiley-Blackwell handbook of infant development* (2nd ed.). Oxford, UK: Wiley-Blackwell.

Friend, M. (2011). *Special education* (3rd ed.). Upper Saddle River, NJ: Merrill.

Friend, M., & Bursuck, W. D. (2012). *Including parents with special needs* (6th ed.). Upper Saddle River, NJ: Pearson.

Frimer, J. A., Walker, L. J., Dunlop, W. L., Lee, B., & Riches, A. (2011). The integration of agency and communion in moral personality: Evidence of enlightened self-interest. *Journal of Personality and Social Psychology, 101,* 149–163.

Frisbie, W. P., Hummer, R. A., & McKinnon, S. (2009). Infant and child mortality. In D. Carr (Ed.), *Encyclopedia of the life course and human development.* Boston: Gale Cengage.

Frisen, A., Hasselblad, T., & Holmqvist, K. (2012). What actually makes bullying stop? Reports from former victims. *Journal of Adolescence, 35,* 981–990.

Froh, J. J., Yurkewicz, C., & Kashdan, T. B. (2009). Gratitude and subjective well-being in early adolescence: Examining gender differences. *Journal of Adolescence, 32*(3), 633–650.

Frost, E. A., Gist, R. S., & Adriano, E. (2011). Drugs, alcohol, pregnancy, and fetal alcohol syndrome. *International Anesthesiology Clinics, 49,* 119–133.

Frye, D. (1999). Development of intention: The relation of executive function to theory of mind. In P. D. Zelazo, J. W. Astington, & D. R. Olson (Eds.), *Developing theories of intention: Social understanding and self-control.* Mahwah, NJ: Erlbaum.

Frye, D. (2004). Unpublished review of J. W. Santrock's *Child development,* 11th ed. (New York: McGraw-Hill).

Fuchs, L. S., & others. (2013). Instructional intervention for students with mathematical learning disabilities. In H. L. Swanson & others (Eds.), *Handbook of learning disabilities* (2nd ed.). New York: Guilford.

Fuligni, A. J. (2012). Gaps, conflicts, and arguments between adolescents and their parents. *New Directions for Child and Adolescent Development, 135,* 105–110.

Fuligni, A. J., Hughes, D. L., & Way, N. (2009). Ethnicity and immigration. In R. M. Lerner & L. Steinberg (Eds.), *Handbook of adolescent psychology* (3rd ed.). New York: Wiley.

Fuligni, A. J., & Telzer, E. H. (2012). The contributions of youth to immigrant families. In A. S. Masten & others (Eds.), *Realizing the potential of immigrant youth.* New York: Cambridge University Press.

Fung, C. K. H., & Cheng, D. P. W. (2012). Consensus or disconsensus? Stakeholders' view on the role of play in learning. *Early years: An International Journal of Research and Development, 32,* 17–33.

Fung, C., & others. (2012). From "best practice" to "next practice": The effectiveness of school-based health promotion in improving healthy eating and physical activity and preventing childhood obesity. *International Journal of Behavioral Nutrition and Physical Activity, 9,* 27.

Fung, H. (2011). Cultural psychological perspectives on social development. In P. K. Smith & C. H. Hart (Eds.), *Wiley-Blackwell handbook of childhood social development* (2nd ed.). New York: Wiley.

Fung, L. K., Quintin, E. M., Haas, B. W., & Reiss, A. L. (2012). Conceptualizing neurodevelopmental disorders through a mechanistic understanding of fragile X syndrome and Williams syndrome. *Current Opinion in Neurology, 25,* 112–124.

Furman, W., & Buhrmester, D. (1992). Age and sex differences in perceptions of networks of personal relationships. *Child Development, 63,* 103–115.

Furman, W., & Collins, W. A. (2009). Adolescent romantic relationships and experiences. In K. H. Rubin, W. M. Bukowksi, & B. Laursen (Eds.), *Handbook of peer interactions, relationships, and groups.* New York: Wiley.

Furman, W., Low, S., & Ho, M. J. (2009). Romantic experience and psychosocial adjustment in middle adolescence. *Journal of Clinical Child and Adolescent Psychology, 38,* 75–90.

Furman, W., & Wehner, E. A. (1998). Adolescent romantic relationships: A developmental perspective. In S. Shulman & W. A. Collins (Eds.), *New directions for child development: Adolescent romantic relationships.* San Francisco: Jossey-Bass.

Furth, H. G. (1973). *Deafness and learning: A psychosocial approach.* Belmont, CA: Wadsworth.

Furth, H. G., & Wachs, H. (1975). *Thinking goes to school.* New York: Oxford University Press.

Fussell, E., & Greene, M. E. (2002). Demographic trends affecting youth around the world. In B. B. Brown, R. W. Larson, & T. S. Saraswathi (Eds.), *The world's youth.* New York: Cambridge University Press.

G

Gabbe, S., & others. (Eds.). (2012). *Obstetrics* (6th ed.). New York: Elsevier.

Gaias, L. M., & others. (2012). Cross-cultural temperamental differences in infants, children, and adults in the United States of America and Finland, *53,* 119–128.

Galambos, N. L., Berenbaum, S. A., & McHale, S. M. (2009). Gender development in adolescence. In R. M. Lerner & L. Steinberg (Eds.), *Handbook of adolescent psychology.* New York: Wiley.

Galbally, M., Lewis, A. J., IJzendoorn, M., & Permezel, M. (2011). The role of oxytocin in mother-infant relations: A systematic review of human studies. *Harvard Review of Psychiatry, 19,* 1–14.

Galinsky, E. (2010). *Mind in the making.* New York: Harper Collins.

Galinsky, E., & David, J. (1988). *The preschool years: Family strategies that work—from experts and parents.* New York: Times Books.

Galland, B. C., Taylor, B. J., Edler, D. E., & Herbison, P. (2012). Normal sleep patterns in infants and children: A systematic review of observational studies. *Sleep Medicine Review, 16,* 213–222.

Galliher, R. V., & Kerpelman, J. L. (2012). The intersection of identity development and peer relationship processes in adolescence and young adulthood: Contributions of the special issue. *Journal of Adolescence, 35,* 1409–1415.

Galloway, J. C., & Thelen, E. (2004). Feet first: Object exploration in young infants. *Infant Behavior & Development, 27,* 107–112.

Ganong, L., Coleman, M., & Jamison, T. (2011). Patterns of stepchild-stepparent relationship development. *Journal of Marriage and the Family, 73,* 396–413.

Garcia Coll, C., & Marks, A. K. (2011). *The immigrant paradox in children and adolescents.* Washington, DC: American Psychological Association.

Garcia Coll, C., & Pachter, L. M. (2002). Ethnic and minority parenting. In M. H. Bornstein (Ed.), *Handbook of parenting* (2nd ed., Vol. 4). Mahwah, NJ: Erlbaum.

Garcia Coll, C., & others. (2012). Understanding the immigrant paradox in youth: Developmental and contextual considerations. In A. S. Masten (Ed.), *Realizing the potential of immigrant youth.* New York: Cambridge University Press.

Garcia, E. P., McKee, L. G., & Forehand, R. (2012). Discipline. In J. R. Levesque (Ed.), *Encyclopedia of adolescence.* New York: Springer.

Gardner, H. (1983). *Frames of mind.* New York: Basic Books.

Gardner, H. (1993). *Multiple intelligences.* New York: Basic Books.

Gardner, H. (2002). Learning from extraordinary minds. In M. Ferrari (Ed.), *The pursuit of excellence through education.* Mahwah, NJ: Erlbaum.

Gardner, M., & Steinberg, L. (2005). Peer influence on risk taking, risk preference, and risky decision making in adolescence and adulthood: An experimental study. *Developmental Psychology, 41,* 625–635.

Garofalo, R. (2010). Cytokines in human milk. *Journal of Pediatrics, 156*(Suppl. 2), S36–S40.

Garrison, M. M., Liekweg, K., & Christakis, D. A. (2011). Media use and child sleep: The impact of content, timing, and environment. *Pediatrics, 128,* 29–35.

Garvey, C. (2000). *Play* (enlarged ed.). Cambridge, MA: Harvard University Press.

Gasser, L., & Keller, M. (2009). Are the competent morally good? Perspective taking and moral motivation of children involved in bullying. *Social Development, 18*(4), 798–816.

Gates, W. (1998, July 20). Charity begins when I'm ready (interview). *Fortune.*

Gathwala, G., Singh, B., & Balhara, B. (2008). KMC facilitates baby attachment in low birth weight infants. *Indian Journal of Pediatrics, 75*, 43–47.

Gaudineau, A., & others. (2010). Factors associated with early menarche: Results from the French Health Behavior in School-Aged Children (HBSC) Study. *BMC Public Health, 10*, 175.

Gauvain, M. (2008). Vygotsky's sociocultural theory. In M. M. Haith & J. B. Benson (Eds.). *Encyclopedia of infant and early childhood development.* Oxford, UK: Elsevier.

Gauvain, M. (2013). Sociocultural contexts of development. In P. D. Zelazo (Ed.), *Oxford handbook of developmental psychology.* New York: Oxford University Press.

Gauvain, M., & Parke, R. D. (2010). Socialization. In M. H. Bornstein (Ed.), *Handbook of cultural developmental science.* New York: Psychology Press.

Gaylord, N., Chyka, D. L., & Lawley, G. (2012). Developmental evaluation of preschool children: A service-learning experience for nursing students. *Journal of Nursing Education, 51*, 710–713.

Geaghan, S. M. (2012). Fetal laboratory medicine: On the frontier of maternal-fetal medicine. *Clinical Chemistry, 58*, 337–352.

Gee, C. L., & Heyman, G. D. (2007). Children's evaluations of other people's self-descriptions. *Social Development, 16*(4), 800–818.

Gelman, R. (1969). Conservation acquisition: A problem of learning to attend to relevant attributes. *Journal of Experimental Child Psychology, 7*, 67–87.

Gelman, R., & Williams, E. M. (1998). Enabling constraints for cognitive development and learning. In W. Damon (Ed.), *Handbook of child psychology* (5th ed., Vol. 4). New York: Wiley.

Gelman, S. A. (2013). Concepts in development. In P. D. Zelazo (Ed.), *Oxford handbook of developmental psychology.* New York: Oxford University Press.

Gelman, S. A., & Kalish, C. W. (2006). Conceptual development. In W. Damon & R. Lerner (Eds.), *Handbook of child psychology* (6th ed.). New York: Wiley.

Gelman, S. A., & Opfer, J. E. (2004). Development of the animate-inanimate distinction. In U. Goswami (Ed.), *Blackwell handbook of childhood cognitive development.* Malden, MA: Blackwell.

Gelman, S. A., Taylor, M. G., & Nguyen, S. P. (2004). Mother-child conversations about gender. *Monographs of the Society for Research in Child Development, 69* (1, Serial No. 275).

Genesee, F., & Lindholm-Leary, K. (2012). The education of English language learners. In K. Harris & others (Eds.), *APA handbook of educational psychology.* Washington, DC: American Psychological Association.

Gennetian, L. A., & Miller, C. (2002). Children and welfare reform: A view from an experimental welfare reform program in Minnesota. *Child Development, 73*, 601–620.

Gentile, D. A. (2011). The multiple dimensions of video game effects. *Child Development Perspectives, 5*, 75–81.

Gentile, D. A., & others. (2009). The effects of prosocial video games on prosocial behaviors: International evidence from correlational, longitudinal, and experimental studies. *Personality and Social Psychology Bulletin, 35*, 752–763.

Georgakilas, A. G. (2011). From chemistry of DNA damage to repair and biological significance. Comprehending the future. *Mutation Research, 711*, 1–202.

Gershkoff-Stowe, L., & Hahn, E. R. (2007). Fast mapping skills in the developing lexicon. *Journal of Speech, Language, and Hearing, 50*, 682–697.

Gershoff, E. T. (2002). Corporal punishment by parents and associated child behaviors and experiences: A meta-analysis and theoretical review. *Psychological Bulletin, 128*, 539–579.

Gershoff, E. T., Lansford, J. E., Sexton, H. R., Davis-Kean, P., & Sameroff, A. (2012). Longitudinal links between spanking and children's externalizing behaviors in a national sample of White, Black, Hispanic, and Asian American families. *Child Development, 83*, 838–843.

Gershoff, E. T., & others. (2010). Parent discipline practices in an international sample: Associations with child behaviors and moderation by perceived normativeness. *Child Development, 81*, 487–502.

Gertner, Y., & Fisher, C. (2012, in press). Predicted errors in children's early sentence comprehension. *Cognition.*

Gesell, A. (1934a). *An atlas of human behavior.* New Haven, CT: Macmillan.

Gesell, A. L. (1934b). *Infancy and human growth.* New York: MacMillan.

Gestsdottir, S., Lewin-Bizan, S., von Eye, A., Lerner, J. V., & Lerner, R. M. (2009). The structure and function of selection, optimization, and compensation in adolescence: Theoretical and applied implications. *Journal of Applied Developmental Psychology, 30*(5), 585–600.

Gewirtz, J. (1977). Maternal responding and the conditioning of infant crying: Directions of influence within the attachment-acquisition process. In B. C. Etzel, J. M. LeBlanc, & D. M. Baer (Eds.), *New developments in behavioral research.* Hillsdale, NJ: Erlbaum.

Ghazarian, S. R., & Roche, K. M. (2010). Social support and low-income, urban mothers: Longitudinal associations with delinquency. *Journal of Youth and Adolescence, 39*, 1097–1108.

Ghetti, S., & Alexander, K. W. (2004). "If it happened, I would remember it": Strategic use of event memorability in the rejection of false autobiographical events. *Child Development, 75*, 542–561.

Ghetti, S., & Bauer, P. J. (Eds.). (2012). *Origins and development of recollection.* New York: Oxford University Press.

Ghosh, S., Feingold, E., Chakaborty, S., & Dey, S. K. (2010). Telomere length is associated with types of chromosome 21 nondisjunction: A new insight into the maternal age effect on Down syndrome birth. *Human Genetics, 127*(4), 403–408.

Gibbons, L., & others. (2013, in press). Inequities in the use of cesarean section deliveries in the world. *American Journal of Obstetrics and Gynecology, 206.*

Gibbs, J. C. (2010). *Moral development and reality* (2nd ed.). Boston: Allyn & Bacon.

Gibbs, J. C., Basinger, K. S., Grime, R. L., & Snarey, J. R. (2007). Moral judgment development across cultures: Revisiting Kohlberg's universality claims. *Developmental Review, 27*, 443–500.

Gibson, E. J. (1969). *Principles of perceptual learning and development.* New York: Appleton-Century-Crofts.

Gibson, E. J. (1989). Exploratory behavior in the development of perceiving, acting, and the acquiring of knowledge. *Annual Review of Psychology* (Vol. 39). Palo Alto, CA: Annual Reviews.

Gibson, E. J. (2001). *Perceiving the affordances.* Mahwah, NJ: Erlbaum.

Gibson, E. J., & Walk, R. D. (1960). The "visual cliff." *Scientific American, 202*, 64–71.

Gibson, J. J. (1966). *The senses considered as perceptual systems.* Boston: Houghton Mifflin.

Gibson, J. J. (1979). *The ecological approach to visual perception.* Boston: Houghton Mifflin.

Giedd, J. N. (2012). The digital revolution and the adolescent brain. *Journal of Adolescent Health, 51*, 101–105.

Giedd, J. N., & others. (2012). Anatomic magnetic resonance imaging of the developing child and adolescent brain. In V. F. Reyna & others (Eds.), *The adolescent brain.* Washington, DC: American Psychological Association.

Gielen, A. C., & others. (2012). Home safety and low-income urban housing quality. *Pediatrics, 130*, 1053–1059.

Gillen-O'Neel, C., Huynh, V. W., & Fuligni, A. J. (2013). To study or to sleep? The academic costs of extra studying at the expense of sleep. *Child Development, 84*, 133–42.

Gillig, P. M., & Sanders, R. D. (2011). Higher cortical functions: Attention and vigilance. *Innovations in Clinical Science, 8*, 43–46.

Gilligan, C. (1982). *In a different voice.* Cambridge, MA: Harvard University Press.

Gilligan, C. (1992, May). *Joining the resistance: Girls' development in adolescence.* Paper presented at the symposium on development and vulnerability in close relationships, Montreal, Quebec.

Gilligan, C. (1996). The centrality of relationships in psychological development: A puzzle, some evidence, and a theory. In G. G. Noam & K. W. Fischer (Eds.), *Development and vulnerability in close relationships.* Hillsdale, NJ: Erlbaum.

Giordano, P. C. (2009). Friendship, childhood and adolescence. In D. Carr (Ed.), *Encyclopedia of the life course and human development.* Boston: Gale Cengage.

Giorgis, C., & Glazer, J. (2013). *Literature for young children: Supporting emergent literacy, ages 0–8* (7th ed.). Upper Saddle River, NJ: Pearson.

Giovannini, M., Verduci, E., Salvatici, E., Paci, S., & Riva, E. (2012, in press). Phenylketonuria: Nutritional advances and challenges. *Nutrition and Metabolism.*

Glessner, J. T., & others. (2009). Autism genome-wide copy number variation reveals ubiquitin and neuronal genes. *Nature, 459*, 569–573.

Gluck, M. E., & others. (2009). Maternal influence, not diabetic intrauterine environment, predicts children's energy intake. *Obesity, 17*, 772–777.

Gobet, F., & Charness, N. (2006). In K. A. Ericsson, N. Charness, P. J. Feltovich, & R. R. Hoffman (Eds.), *The Cambridge handbook of expertise and expert performance.* New York: Cambridge University Press.

Goga, A. E., & others. (2012, in press). Infant feeding practices at routine PMTCT site, South Africa: Results of a prospective observational study amongst HIV exposed and unexposed infants—birth to 9 months. *International Breastfeeding Journal.*

Gogtay, N., & Thompson, P. M. (2010). Mapping gray matter development: Implications for typical development and vulnerability to psychopathology. *Brain and Cognition, 72,* 6–15.

Goldberg, W. A., & Lucas-Thompson, R. (2008). Maternal and paternal employment, effects of. In M. M. Haith & J. B. Benson (Eds.), *Encyclopedia of infant and early childhood development.* Oxford, UK: Elsevier.

Goldenberg, R. L., & Culhane, J. F. (2007). Low birth weight in the United States. *American Journal of Clinical Nutrition, 85*(Suppl.), S584–S590.

Goldenberg, R. L., & Nagahawatte, N. T. (2008). Poverty, mental health, and adverse pregnancy outcomes. *Annals of the New York Academy of Sciences, 1136,* 80–85.

Goldfield, G. S. (2011). Making access to TV contingent on physical activity: Effects on liking and relative reinforcing value of TV and physical activity in overweight and obese children. *Journal of Behavioral Medicine, 35,* 1–7.

Goldfield, G. S., Adamo, K. B., Rutherford, J., & Murray, M. (2012). The effects of aerobic exercise on psychosocial functioning of adolescents who are overweight or obese. *Journal of Pediatric and Adolescent Psychology, 37,* 1136–1147.

Goldfield. B. A., & Snow, C. A. (2009). Individual differences in language development. In J. Berko Gleason & N. Ratner (Eds.), *The development of language* (7th ed.). Boston: Allyn & Bacon.

Goldin-Meadow, S., & Alibali, M. W. A. (2013, in press). Gesture's role in learning and development. In P. Zelazo (Ed.), *Oxford University handbook of developmental psychology.* New York: Oxford University Press.

Goldscheider, F., & Sassler, S. (2006). Creating stepfamilies: Integrating children into the study of union formation. *Journal of Marriage and the Family, 68,* 275–291.

Goldschmidt, L., Richardson, G. A., Willford, J., & Day, N. L. (2008). Prenatal marijuana exposure and intelligence test performance at age 6. *Journal of the American Academy of Child and Adolescent Psychiatry, 47,* 254–263.

Goldstein, M. H., King, A. P., & West, M. J. (2003). Social interaction shapes babbling: Testing parallels between birdsong and speech. *Proceedings of the National Academy of Sciences, 100*(13), 8030–8035.

Goleman, D. (1995). *Emotional intelligence.* New York: Basic Books.

Goleman, D., Kaufman, P., & Ray, M. (1993). *The creative spirit.* New York: Plume.

Gollnick, D. M., & Chinn, P. C. (2013). *Multicultural education in a pluralistic society* (9th ed.). Boston: Allyn & Bacon.

Golombok, S. (2011a). Children in new family forms. In R. Gross (Ed.), *Psychology* (6th ed.). London: Hodder Education.

Golombok, S. (2011b). Why I study lesbian families. In S. Ellis & others (Eds.), *LGBTQ psychologies.* New York: Cambridge University Press.

Golombok, S., MacCallum, F., & Goodman, E. (2001). The "test-tube" generation: Parent-child relationships and the psychological well-being of in vitro fertilization children at adolescence. *Child Development, 72,* 599–608.

Golombok, S., Rust, J., Zervoulis, K., Croudace, T., Golding, J., & Hines, M. (2008). Developmental trajectories of sex-typed behavior in boys and girls: A longitudinal general population study of children aged 2.5–8 years. *Child Development, 79,* 1583–1593.

Golombok, S., & Tasker, F. (2010). Gay fathers. In M. E. Lamb (Ed.), *The role of the father in child development* (5th ed.). New York: Wiley.

Gomes, R. S., & others. (2011). Primary versus secondary hypertension in children followed up at an outpatient tertiary unit. *Pediatric Nephrology, 26,* 441–447.

Goncu, A., & Gauvain, M. (2012). Sociocultural approaches in educational psychology. In K. H. Harris, S. Graham, & T. Urdan (Eds.), *APA educational psychology handbook.* Washington, DC: American Psychological Association.

Gonzales, M., Jones, D. J., Kincaid, C. Y., & Cuellar, J. (2012). Neighborhood context and adjustment in African American youths from single mother homes: The intervening role of hopelessness. *Cultural Diversity and Ethnic Minority Psychology, 18,* 109–117.

Gonzalez, A., Atkinson, L., & Fleming, A. S. (2009). Attachment and the comparative psychobiology of mothering. In M. De Haan & M. R. Gunnar (Eds.), *Handbook of developmental social neuroscience.* New York: Guilford.

González, J. M. (Ed.). (2009). *Encyclopedia of bilingual education.* Thousand Oaks, CA: Sage.

Good, C., Rattan, A., & Dweck, C.S. (2012). Why do women opt out? Sense of belonging and women's representation in mathematics. *Journal of Personality and Social Psychology, 102,* 700–717.

Good, M., & Willoughby, T. (2008). Adolescence as a sensitive period for spiritual development. *Child Development Perspectives, 2,* 32–37.

Goodkind, S. (2013, in press). Single-sex public education for low-income youth of color: A critical theoretical review. *Sex Roles.*

Goodman, W. B., & others. (2011). Parental work stress and latent profiles of father-infant parenting quality. *Journal of Marriage and the Family, 73,* 588–604.

Goodvin, R., Meyer, S., Thompson, R. A., & Hayes, R. (2008). Self-understanding in early childhood: Associations with child attachment security and maternal negative affect. *Attachment and Human Development, 10,* 433–450.

Gopnik, A. (2010). Commentary. In E. Galinsky (2010). *Mind in the making.* New York: Harper Collins.

Gopnik, A., & Meltzoff, A. (1997). *Words, thoughts, and theories.* Cambridge, MA: MIT Press.

Gorgens-Eckermans, G., & Brand, T. (2012). Emotional intelligence as a moderator in the stress-burnout relationship: A questionnaire study on nurses. *Journal of Clinical Nursing, 21,* 2275–2285.

Gorrese, A., & Ruggieri, R. (2012). Peer attachment: A meta-analytic review of gender and age differences and associations with parent attachment. *Journal of Youth and Adolescence, 41,* 650–672.

Gottfried, A. E., Marcoulides, G. A., Gottfried, A. W., & Oliver, P. H. (2009). A latent curve model of motivational practices and developmental decline in math and science academic intrinsic motivation. *Journal of Educational Psychology, 101,* 729–739.

Gottlieb, G. (2007). Probabilistic epigenesis. *Developmental Science, 10,* 1–11.

Gottlieb, G., Wahlsten, D., & Lickliter, R. (2006). The significance of biology for human development: A developmental psychobiological systems view. In W. Damon & R. Lerner (Eds.), *Handbook of child psychology* (6th ed.). New York: Wiley.

Gottman Relationship Institute. (2009). *Research on parenting.* Retrieved December 9, 2009, from www.gottman.com/parenting/research

Gottman, J. M. (2012). *Emotion coaching.* Retrieved July 8, 2012, from www.gottman.com/parenting/

Gottman, J. M. (2013). *Research on parenting.* Retrieved January 10, 2013, from www.gottman.com/parenting/research

Gottman, J. M., & DeClaire, J. (1997). *The heart of parenting: Raising an emotionally intelligent child.* New York: Simon & Schuster.

Gottman, J., Gottman, J., & Shapiro, A. (2009). A new couples approach to interventions for the transition to parenthood. In M. S. Schulz, P. K. Kerig, M. K. Pruett, & R. D. Parke (Eds.), *Feathering the nest.* Washington, DC: American Psychological Association.

Gottman, J. M., & Parker, J. G. (Eds.). (1987). *Conversations of friends.* New York: Cambridge University Press.

Gouin, K., & others. (2011). Effects of cocaine use during pregnancy on low birthweight and preterm birth: Systematic and metanalyses. *American Journal of Obstetrics and Gynecology, 201,* e1–e12.

Gould, S. J. (1981). *The mismeasure of man.* New York: W. W. Norton.

Grabe, S., & Hyde, J. S. (2006). Ethnicity and body dissatisfaction among women in the United States: A meta-analysis. *Psychological Bulletin, 132,* 622–640.

Graber, J. A. (2008). Pubertal and neuroendocrine development and risk for depressive disorders. In N. B. Allen & L. Sheeber (Eds.), *Adolescent emotional development and the emergence of depressive disorders.* New York: Cambridge University Press.

Gradisar, M., Gardner, G., & Dohnt, H. (2011). Recent worldwide sleep patterns and problems during adolescence: A review and meta-analysis of age, region, and sleep. *Sleep Medicine, 12,* 110–118.

Grafenhain, M., Behne, T., Carpenter, M., & Tomasello, M. (2009). Young children's understanding of joint commitments. *Developmental Psychology, 45*(5), 1430–1443.

Graham, G. M., Holt-Hale, S., & Parker, M. A. (2013). *Children moving* (9th ed.). New York: McGraw-Hill.

Graham, S. (1986, August). *Can attribution theory tell us something about motivation in blacks?* Paper presented at the meeting of the American Psychological Association, Washington, DC.

Graham, S. (1990). Motivation in Afro-Americans. In G. L. Berry & J. K. Asamen (Eds.), *Black students: Psychosocial issues and academic achievement.* Newbury Park, CA: Sage.

Graham, S. (2005, February 16). Commentary in *USA TODAY,* p. 2D.

Graham, S. (2011). School racial/ethnic diversity and disparities in mental health and academic outcomes. *Nebraska Symposium on Motivation, 57,* 73–96.

Graham, S., & Perin, D. (2007). A metaanalysis of writing instruction for adolescent students. *Journal of Educational Psychology, 99,* 445–476.

Grammer, J. K., Purtell, K. M., Coffman, J. L., & Ornstein, P. A. (2011). Relations between children's metamemory and strategic performance: Time-varying covariates in early elementary school. *Journal of Experimental Child Psychology, 108,* 139–155.

Grant, A. M., & Gino, F. (2010). A little thanks goes a long way: Explaining why gratitude expressions motivate prosocial behavior. *Journal of Personality and Social Psychology, 98,* 946–955.

Grant, J. P. (1997). *The state of the world's children.* New York: UNICEF and Oxford University Press.

Graven, S. (2006). Sleep and brain development. *Clinical Perinatology, 33,* 693–706.

Gravetter, R. J., & Forzano, L. B. (2012). *Research methods for the behavioral sciences* (4th ed.). Boston: Cengage.

Gray, J. (1992). *Men are from Mars, women are from Venus.* New York: HarperCollins.

Graziano, A. M., & Raulin, M. L. (2013). *Research methods* (8th ed,). Boston: Allyn & Bacon.

Greenfield, P. M. (1966). On culture and conservation. In J. S. Bruner, R. P. Oliver, & P. M. Greenfield (Eds.), *Studies in cognitive growth.* New York: Wiley.

Greenfield, P. M. (2003, February). Commentary. *Monitor on Psychology, 3*(2), 58.

Greenfield, P. M. (2009). Linking social change and developmental change: Shifting pathways of human development. *Developmental Psychology, 43,* 401–418.

Greer, F. R., Sicherer, S. H., Burks, A. W., & Committee on Nutrition and Section on Allergy and Immunology. (2008). Effects of early nutritional interventions on the development of atopic disease in infants and children: The role of maternal dietary restriction, breast feeding, timing of introduction of complementary foods, and hydrolyzed formulas. *Pediatrics, 121,* 183–191.

Gregorson, M., Kaufman, J. C., & Snyder, H. (Eds.). (2013, in press). *Teaching creatively and teaching creativity.* New York: Springer.

Gregory, A. M., Ball, H. A., & Button, T. M. M. (2011). Behavioral genetics. In P. K. Smith & C. H. Hart (Eds.), *Wiley-Blackwell handbook of childhood social development* (2nd ed.). New York: Wiley.

Greif, M. L., & Needham, A. (2012). The development of tool use early in life. In T. McCormack, C. Hoerl, & S. Butterfill (Eds.), *Tool use and causal cognition.* New York: Oxford University Press.

Griffiths, J. D., Marslen-Wilson, W. D., Stamatakis, E. A., & Tyler, L. K. (2013, in press). Functional organization of the neural language system: Dorsal and ventral pathways are critical for syntax. *Cerebral Cortex.*

Grigorenko, E. (2000). Heritability and intelligence. In R. J. Sternberg (Ed.), *Handbook of intelligence.* New York: Cambridge University Press.

Grigorenko, E., Kornilov, S. A., Tan, M., Elliott, J., & Sternberg, R. J. (2012). Gifted identification with Aurora: Widening the spotlight. *Journal of Psychoeducational Assessment, 30,* 117–133.

Grolnick, W. S., Bridges, L. J., & Connell, J. P. (1996). Emotion regulation in two-year-olds: Strategies and emotional expression in four contexts. *Child Development, 67,* 928–941.

Gross, J. J., Fredrickson, B. L., & Levenson, R. W. (1994). The psychophysiology of crying. *Psychophysiology, 31,* 460–468.

Gross, L. S. (2013). *Electronic media* (11th ed.). New York: McGraw-Hill.

Grossman, Z., Silverman, B. G., & Miron, D. (2013). Physician specialty is associated with adherence to treatment guidelines for acute otitis media in children. *Acta Pediatrica, 102,* e29–e33.

Grossmann, K., Grossmann, K. E., Spangler, G., Suess, G., & Unzner, L. (1985). Maternal sensitivity and newborns' orientation responses as related to quality of attachment in northern Germany. In I. Bretherton & E. Waters (Eds.), Growing points of attachment theory and research. *Monographs of the Society for Research in Child Development, 50* (1–2, Serial No. 209).

Grossmann, T., & Johnson, M. H. (2010). Selective prefrontal cortex responses to joint attention in early infancy. *Biological Letters, 6,* 540–543.

Grotevant, H. D., & Cooper, C. R. (1985). Patterns of interaction in family relationships and the development of identity exploration in adolescence. *Child Development, 56,* 415–428.

Grotevant, H. D., & Cooper, C. R. (1998). Individuality and connectedness in adolescent development: Review and prospects for research on identity, relationship, and context. In E. Skoe & A. von der Lippe (Eds.), *Personality development in adolescence: A cross-national and life-span perspective.* London: Routledge.

Grusec, J. E. (2006). The development of moral behavior and conscience from a socialization perspective. In M. Killen & J. G. Smetana (Eds.), *Handbook of moral development.* Mahwah, NJ: Erlbaum.

Grusec, J. E. (2009). Unpublished review of J. W. Santrock's *Child Development,* 13th ed. (New York: McGraw-Hill).

Grusec, J. E. (2011). Human development: Development in the family. *Annual Review of Psychology* (Vol. 62). Palo Alto, CA: Annual Reviews.

Grusec, J. E. (2013). The development of moral behavior and conscience from a socialization perspective. In M. Killen & J. G. Smetana (Eds.), *Handbook of moral development* (2nd ed.). New York: Routledge.

Grusec, J. E., Chaparro, M. P., Johnston, M., & Sherman, A. (2013). Social development and social relationships in middle childhood. In I. B. Weiner & others (Eds.), *Handbook of psychology* (2nd ed., Vol. 6). New York: Wiley.

Grusec, J. E., & Davidov, M. (2010). Integrating different perspectives on socialization theory and research: A domain-specific approach. *Child Development, 81,* 687–709.

Grusec, J. E., Hastings, P., & Almas, A. (2011). Prosocial behavior. In P. K. Smith & C. H. Hart (Eds.), *Wiley-Blackwell handbook of childhood social development* (2nd ed.). New York: Wiley.

Grych, J. H. (2002). Marital relationships and parenting. In M. H. Bornstein (Ed.), *Handbook of parenting.* Mahwah, NJ: Erlbaum.

Gryzwacz, J., & Demerouti, E. (Eds.). (2013). *New frontiers in work and family research.* New York: Routledge.

Guilford, J. P. (1967). *The structure of intellect.* New York: McGraw-Hill.

Gunderson, E. A., Ramirez, G., Levine, S. C., & Beilock, S. L. (2012). The role of parents and teachers in the development of math attitudes. *Sex Roles, 66,* 153–166.

Gunnar, M. R., Fisher, P. A., & The Early Experience, Stress, and Prevention Network. (2006). Bringing basic research on early experience and stress neurobiology to bear on preventive interventions for neglected and maltreated children. *Development and Psychopathology, 18,* 651–677.

Gunnar, M. R., Malone, S., & Fisch, R. O. (1987). The psychobiology of stress and coping in the human neonate: Studies of the adrenocortical activity in response to stress in the first week of life. In T. Field, P. McCabe, & N. Scheiderman (Eds.), *Stress and coping.* Hillsdale, NJ: Erlbaum.

Gunnar, M. R., & Quevado, K. (2007). The neurobiology of stress and development. *Annual Review of Psychology* (Vol. 58). Palo Alto, CA: Annual Reviews.

Gunning, T. G. (2013). *Creating literature instruction for all children in grades pre-K to 4* (2nd ed.). Boston: Allyn & Bacon.

Gupta, A., Thornton, J. W., & Huston, A. C. (2007). Working families should not be poor—the New Hope project. In D. R. Crane & T. B. Heaton (Eds.), *Handbook of families and poverty.* Thousand Oaks, CA: Sage.

Gur, R. C., & others. (1995). Sex differences in regional cerebral glucose metabolism during a resting state. *Science, 267,* 528–531.

Gurwitch, R. H., Silovksy, J. F., Schultz, S., Kees, M., & Burlingame, S. (2001). *Reactions and guidelines for children following trauma/disaster.* Norman, OK: Department of Pediatrics, University of Oklahoma Health Sciences Center.

Gustafsson, J-E. (2007). Schooling and intelligence: Effects of track of study on level and profile of cognitive abilities. In P. C. Kyllonen, R. D. Roberts, & L. Stankov (Eds.), *Extending intelligence.* Mahwah, NJ: Erlbaum.

Guzzetta, A., & others. (2008). Language organization in left perinatal stroke. *Neuropediatrics, 39,* 157–163.

H

Hafen, C. A., & others. (2012). The pivotal role of adolescent autonomy in secondary school classrooms. *Journal of Youth and Adolescence, 41,* 245–255.

Haga, M. (2008). The relationship between physical fitness and motor competence in children. *Child: Child Care and Health Development, 34,* 329–334.

Hagen, J. W., & Lamb-Parker, F. G. (2008). Head Start. In M. M. Haith & J. B. Benson (Eds.), *Encyclopedia of infant and early childhood development.* Oxford, UK: Elsevier.

Haier, R. J. (2011). Biological basis of intelligence. In R. J. Sternberg & S. B. Kaufman (Eds.), *Cambridge handbook of intelligence.* New York: Cambridge University Press.

Hakuta, K. (2001, April 5). *Key policy milestones and directions in the education of English language learners.* Paper prepared for the Rockefeller Foundation Symposium, Leveraging change: An emerging framework for educational equity, Washington, DC.

Hakuta, K. (2005, April). *Bilingualism at the intersection of research and public policy.* Paper presented at the meeting of the Society for Research in Child Development, Atlanta.

Hakuta, K., Butler, Y. G., & Witt, D. (2001). *How long does it take English learners to attain proficiency?* Berkeley, CA: The University of California Linguistic Minority Research Institute Policy Report 2000–1.

Halford, G. S., & Andrews, G. S. (2011). Information processing models of cognitive development. In U. Goswami (Ed.), *Wiley-Blackwell handbook of childhood cognitive development* (2nd ed.). New York: Wiley-Blackwell.

Hall, C. M., & others. (2004). Behavioral and physical masculinization are related to genotype in girls with congenital adrenal hyperplasia. *Journal of Clinical Endocrinology and Metabolism, 89,* 419–424.

Hall, G. N. (2010). *Multicultural psychology* (2nd ed.). Upper Saddle River, NJ: Prentice Hall.

Hall, L. J. (2013). *Autism spectrum disorders* (2nd ed.). Upper Saddle River, NJ: Pearson.

Hallahan, D. P., Kauffman, J. M., & Pullen, P. C. (2012). *Exceptional learners* (12th ed.). Boston: Allyn & Bacon.

Halpern, D. F. (2012). *Sex differences in cognitive abilities* (4th ed.). New York: Psychology Press.

Halpern, D. F., Benbow, C. P., Geary, D. C., Gur, R. C., & Hyde, J. S. (2007). The science of sex differences in science and mathematics. *Psychological Science in the Public Interest, 8,* 1–51.

Halpern, D. F., Beninger, A. S., & Straight, C. A. (2011). Sex differences in intelligence. In R. J. Sternberg & S. B. Kaufman (Eds.), *Handbook of intelligence.* New York: Cambridge University Press.

Halpern, D. F., Eliot, L., & others. (2011). The pseudoscience of single-sex schooling. *Science, 333,* 1706–1717.

Hamilton, B. E., Martin, J. A., & Ventura, S. J. (2012). Births: Preliminary data for 2011. *National Vital Statistics Reports, 61*(5), 1–18.

Han, J. J., Leichtman, M. D., & Wang, Q. (1998). Autobiographical memory in Korean, Chinese, and American children. *Developmental Psychology, 34,* 701–713.

Han, W-J. (2009). Maternal employment. In D. Carr (Ed.). *Encyclopedia of the life course and human development.* Boston: Gale Cengage.

Hanish, L. D., & Guerra, N. G. (2004). Aggressive victims, passive victims, and bullies: Developmental continuity or developmental change? *Merrill-Palmer Quarterly, 50,* 17–38.

Hansen, M. L., Gunn, P. W., & Kaelber, D. C. (2007). Underdiagnosis of hypertension in children and adolescents. *Journal of the American Medical Association, 298,* 874–879.

Hansen, M., Janssen, I., Schiff, A., Zee, P. C., & Dubocovich, M. L. (2005). The impact of school daily schedule on adolescent sleep. *Pediatrics, 115,* 1555–1561.

Harakeh, Z., & others. (2012). Individual and environmental predictors of health risk behaviors among Dutch adolescents: The HBSC study. *Public Health, 126,* 566–573.

Hardy, S. A., Bhattacharjee, A., Reed, A., & Aquino, K. (2010). Moral identity and psychological distance: The case of adolescent socialization. *Journal of Adolescence, 33,* 111–123.

Hare, B. R., & Castenell, L. A. (1985). No place to run, no place to hide: Comparative status and future prospects of Black boys. In M. B. Spencer, G. K. Brookins, & W. R. Allen (Eds.), *Beginnings: The social and affective development of Black children.* Hillsdale, NJ: Erlbaum.

Harkness, S., & Super, B. M. (1995). Culture and parenting. In M. H. Bornstein (Ed.), *Handbook of parenting* (Vol. 3). Hillsdale, NJ: Erlbaum.

Harlow, H. F. (1958). The nature of love. *American Psychologist, 13,* 673–685.

Harris, G., Thomas, A., & Booth, D. A. (1990). Development of salt taste in infancy. *Developmental Psychology, 26,* 534–538.

Harris, J. J., & Attwell, D. (2012). The energetic of CNS white matter. *Journal of Neuroscience, 32,* 356–371.

Harris, J. R. (1998). *The nurture assumption: Why children turn out the way they do: Parents matter less than you think and peers matter more.* New York: Free Press.

Harris, J. R. (2009). *The nurture assumption* (rev. ed.). New York: Free Press.

Harris, J., Golinkoff, R. M., & Hirsh-Pasek, K. (2012). Lessons from the crib for the classroom: How children really learn vocabulary. In S. B. Neuman & D. K. Dickinson (Eds.), *Handbook of early literacy research.* New York: Guilford.

Harris, K. R., Graham, S., Brindle, M., & Sandmel, K. (2009). Metacognition and children's writing. In D. J. Hacker, J. Dunlosky, & A. Graesser (Eds.), *Handbook of metacognition in education.* New York: Elsevier.

Harris, P. L. (2000). *The work of imagination.* New York: Oxford University Press.

Harris, P. L. (2006). Social cognition. In W. Damon & R. Lerner (Eds.), *Handbook of child psychology* (6th ed.). New York: Wiley.

Harris, R. J., Schoen, L. M., & Hensley, D. L. (1992). A cross-cultural study of story memory. *Journal of Cross-Cultural Psychology, 23,* 133–147.

Harrison-Hale, A. O., McLoyd, V. C., & Smedley, B. (2004). Racial and ethnic status: Risk and protective processes among African-American families. In K. L. Maton, C. J. Schellenbach, B. J. Leadbetter, & A. L. Solarz (Eds.), *Investing in children, families, and communities.* Washington, DC: American Psychological Association.

Hart, B., & Risley, T. R. (1995). *Meaningful differences.* Baltimore, MD: Paul Brookes.

Hart, D., Atkins, R., & Donnelly, T. M. (2013). Community service and moral development. In M. Killen & J. G. Smetana (Eds.), *Handbook of moral development* (2nd ed.). New York: Routledge.

Hart, D., Burock, D., London, B., & Atkins, R. (2003). Prosocial development, antisocial development, and moral development. In A. M. Slater & G. Bremner (Eds.), *An introduction to developmental psychology.* Malden, MA: Blackwell.

Hart, D., & Karmel, M. P. (1996). Self-awareness and self-knowledge in humans, great apes, and monkeys. In A. Russon, K. Bard, & S. Parker (Eds.), *Reaching into thought.* New York: Cambridge University Press.

Hart, S., & Carrington, H. (2002). Jealousy in 6-month-old infants. *Infancy, 3,* 395–402.

Harter, S. (1985). *Self-Perception Profile for Children.* Denver: University of Denver. Department of Psychology.

Harter, S. (1986). Processes underlying the construction, maintenance, and enhancement of the self-concept of children. In. J. Suls & A. Greenwald (Eds.), *Psychological perspectives on the self* (Vol. 3). Hillsdale, NJ: Erlbaum.

Harter, S. (1989). *Self-Perception Profile for Adolescents.* Denver: University of Denver. Department of Psychology.

Harter, S. (1998). The development of self-representations. In W. Damon (Ed.), *Handbook of child psychology* (5th ed., Vol. 3). New York: Wiley.

Harter, S. (1999). *The construction of the self.* New York: Guilford.

Harter, S. (2006). The self. In W. Damon & R. Lerner (Eds.), *Handbook of child psychology* (6th ed.), New York: Wiley.

Harter, S. (2012). *The construction of the self* (2nd ed.). New York: Wiley.

Hartshorne, H., & May, M. S. (1928–1930). *Moral studies in the nature of character: Studies in deceit* (Vol. 1); *Studies in self-control* (Vol. 2). *Studies in the organization of character* (Vol. 3). New York: Macmillan.

Hartup, W. W. (1983). The peer system. In P. H. Mussen (Ed.), *Handbook of child psychology* (4th ed., Vol. 4). New York: Wiley.

Hartup, W. W. (2005). Peer interaction: What causes what? *Journal of Abnormal Child Psychology, 33,* 387–394.

Hartup, W. W. (2009). Critical issues and theoretical viewpoints. In K. H. Rubin, W. M. Bukowski, & B. Laursen (Eds.), *Handbook of peer interactions, relationships, and groups .* New York: Guilford.

Harwood, R., Leyendecker, B., Carlson, V., Asencio, M., & Miller, A. (2002). Parenting among Latino families in the U. S. In M. H. Bornstein (Ed.), *Handbook of parenting* (2nd ed.). Mahwah, NJ: Erlbaum.

Hashim, H. A., Freddy, G., & Rosmatunisah, A. (2012). Relationships between negative affect and academic achievement among secondary school students: The mediating effects of habituated exercise. *Journal of Physical Activity and Health, 9,* 1012–1019.

Hashimoto-Torii, K., Kawasawa, Y. I., Kuhn, A., & Rakic, P. (2011). Combined transcriptome analysis of fetal human and mouse cerebral cortex exposed to alcohol. *Proceedings of the National Academy of Sciences U.S.A., 108,* 4212–4217.

Hassepass, F., & others. (2013). Unilateral deafness in children: Audiologic and subjective assessment of hearing ability after cochlear implantation. *Otology and Neurology, 34,* 53–60.

Hastie, A. R., & others. (2013). Rapid genome mapping in nanochannel arrays for highly complete and accurate de novo sequence assembly of the complex aegilops tauschii genome. *PLoS One 8(2),* e55864.

Hatton, H., & others. (2008). Family and individual difference predictors of trait aspects of negative interpersonal behaviors during emerging adulthood. *Journal of Family Psychology, 22,* 448–455.

Hauck, F. R., & others. (2011). Breastfeeding and reduced risk of sudden infant death syndrome : A meta-analysis. *Pediatrics, 128,* 103–110.

Havighurst, S. S., & others. (2013, in press). "Tuning into Kids": Reducing young children's behavior problems using an emotion coaching parenting program. *Child Psychiatry and Human Development.*

Hawkins, J. A., & Berndt, T. J. (1985, April). *Adjustment following the transition to junior high school.* Paper presented at the biennial meeting of the Society for Research in Child Development, Toronto.

Haydon, A., & Halpern, G. T. (2010). Older romantic partners and depressive symptoms during adolescence. *Journal of Youth and Adolescence, 39,* 1240–1251.

Hayes, J. R., & Berninger, V. (2013, in press). Cognitive processes in writing: A framework. In B. Arte, J. Dockrell, & V. Berninger (Eds.), *Writing development and instruction in children with hearing, speech, and language disorders.* New York: Oxford University Press.

Heimann, M., & others. (2006). Exploring the relation between memory, gestural communication, and the emergence of language in infancy: A longitudinal study. *Infant and Child Development, 15,* 233–249.

Hek, K., & others. (2013, in press). A genome-wide association study of depression symptoms. *Biological Psychiatry.*

Helgeson, V. (2009). *Psychology of gender* (3rd ed.). Upper Saddle River, NJ: Prentice Hall.

Helwig, C. C., & Turiel, E. (2011). Children's social and moral reasoning. In P. K. Smith & C. H. Hart (Eds.), *Wiley-Blackwell handbook of childhood social development* (2nd ed.). New York: Wiley.

Henderson, V. L., & Dweck, C. S. (1990). Motivation and achievement. In S. S. Feldman & G. R. Elliott (Eds.), *At the threshold: The developing adolescent.* Cambridge, MA: Harvard University Press.

Hendry, J. (1995). *Understanding Japanese society.* London: Routledge.

Henggeler, S. W., & Sheidow, L. J. (2012). Empirically supported family-based treatments for conduct disorder and delinquency in adolescents. *Journal of Marital and Family Therapy, 38,* 30–58.

Hennessey, B. (2011). Intrinsic motivation and creativity: Have we come full circle? In R. A. Beghetto & J. C. Kaufman (Eds.), *Nurturing creativity in the classroom.* New York: Cambridge University Press.

Henninger, M. L. (2013). *Teaching young children* (5th ed.). Upper Saddle River, NJ: Pearson.

Henriksen, T. B., & others. (2004). Alcohol consumption at the time of conception and spontaneous abortion. *American Journal of Epidemiology, 160,* 661–667.

Hensen, E. F., & others. (2011). High prevalence of founder mutations of the succinate dehydrogenase genes in the Netherlands. *Clinical Genetics, 81,* 284–288.

Herbers, J. E., & others. (2011). Direct and indirect effects of parenting on academic functioning of young homeless children. *Early Education and Development, 22,* 77–104.

Herman-Giddens, M. E. (2007). The decline in the age of menarche in the United States: Should we be concerned? *Journal of Adolescent Health, 40,* 201–203.

Herman-Giddens, M. E., & others. (2012). Secondary sex characteristics in boys: Data from the pediatric research in office settings network. *Pediatrics, 130,* e1058–e1068.

Hernandez-Martinez, C., & others. (2011). Effects of iron deficiency on neonatal behavior at different stages of pregnancy. *Early Human Development, 87,* 165–169.

Hernandez-Reif, M., Diego, M., & Field, T. (2007). Preterm infants show reduced stress behaviors and activity after 5 days of massage therapy. *Infant Behavior and Development, 30,* 557–561.

Herrell, A. L., Jordan, M. L., & Eby, J. W. (2013). *Teaching in elementary school* (6th ed.). Upper Saddle River, NJ: Pearson.

Hertenstein, M. J., & Keltner, D. (2011). Gender and the communication of emotion via touch. *Sex Roles, 64,* 70–80.

Hetherington, E. M. (1993). An overview of the Virginia Longitudinal Study of Divorce and Remarriage with a focus on early adolescence. *Journal of Family Psychology, 7,* 39–56.

Hetherington, E. M. (2005). Divorce and the adjustment of children. *Pediatrics in Review, 26,* 163–169.

Hetherington, E. M. (2006). The influence of conflict, marital problem solving, and parenting on children's adjustment in nondivorced, divorced, and remarried families. In A. Clarke-Stewart & J. Dunn (eds.), *Families count.* New York: Oxford University Press.

Hetherington, E. M., & Kelly, J. (2002). *For better or for worse: Divorce reconsidered.* New York: Norton.

Hetherington, E. M., & Stanley-Hagan, M. (2002). Parenting in divorced and remarried families. In M. H. Bornstein (Ed.), *Handbook of parenting* (2nd ed., Vol. 3). Mahwah, NJ: Erlbaum.

Heuwinkel, M. K. (1996). New ways of learning: Five new ways of teaching. *Childhood Education, 72,* 27–31.

Hewlett, B. S. (1991). *Intimate fathers: The nature and context of Aka Pygmy.* Ann Arbor: University of Michigan Press.

Hewlett, B. S. (2000). Culture, history and sex: Anthropological perspectives on father involvement. *Marriage and Family Review, 29,* 324–340.

Hewlett, B. S., & MacFarlan, S. J. (2010). Fathers' roles in hunter-gatherer and other small-scale cultures. In M. E. Lamb (Ed.), *The role of the father in child development* (5th ed.). New York: Wiley.

Heyman, G. D., & Legare, C. H. (2005). Children's evaluation of source of information about traits. *Developmental Psychology, 41,* 636–647.

Highfield, R. (2008, April 30). *Harvard's baby brain research lab.* Retrieved January 24, 2009, from www.telegraph.co.uk/scienceandtechnology/science/sciencenews/3341166/

Hill, C. R., & Stafford, E. P. (1980). Parental care of children: Time diary estimate of quantity, predictability, and variety. *Journal of Human Resources, 15,* 219–239.

Hill, N. E., & Witherspoon, D. P. (2011). Race, ethnicity, and social class. In M. K. Underwood & L. H. Rosen (Eds.), *Social development.* New York: Guilford.

Hill, P. L., Duggan, P. M., & Lapsley, D. K. (2012). Subjective invulnerability, risk behavior, and adjustment in early adolescence. *Journal of Early Adolescence, 31,* 489–501.

Hilliard, L., & Liben, L. (2012, April). *No boys in ballet: Response to gender bias in mother-child conversations.* Paper presented at the Gender Development Research conference, San Francisco.

Hillier, A., & others. (2012). The impact of WIC food package changes on access to healthful food in two low-income neighborhoods. *Journal of Nutrition Education and Behavior, 44*(3), 210–216.

Hindman, A. H., Skibbek, L. E., Miller, A., & Zimmerman, M. (2010). Ecological contexts and early learning: Contributions of child, family, and classroom factors during Head Start to literacy and mathematics growth through first grade. *Early Childhood Research Quarterly, 25,* 235–250.

Hines, M. (2013). Sex and sex differences. In P. D. Zelazo (Ed.), *Oxford handbook of developmental psychology.* New York: Oxford University Press.

Hirsch, B. J., & Rapkin, B. D. (1987). The transition to junior high school: A longitudinal study of self-esteem, psychological symptomatology, school life, and social support. *Child Development, 58,* 1235–1243.

Hirsh-Pasek, K., & Golinkoff, R. M. (2013, in press). Early language and literacy: Six principles. In S. Gilford (Ed.), *Head Start teacher's guide.* New York: Teacher's College Press.

Hirsh-Pasek, K., Golinkoff, R. M., Singer, D., & Berk, L. (2009). *A mandate for playful learning in preschool: Presenting the evidence.* New York: Oxford University Press.

Ho, J., Yeh, M., McCabe, K., & Lau, A. (2012). Perceptions of the acceptability of parent training among Chinese immigrant parents: Contributions of cultural factors and clinical need. *Behavior Therapy, 43,* 436–449.

Hodapp, R. M., Griffin, M. M., Burke, M. M., & Fisher, M. H. (2011). Intellectual disabilities. In R. J. Sternberg & S. B. Kaufman (Eds.), *Handbook of intelligence.* New York: Cambridge University Press.

Hoefnagels, M. (2013). *Biology: The essentials.* New York: McGraw-Hill.

Hoekstra, R. A., Happe, F., Baron-Cohen, S., & Ronald, A. (2010). Limited genetic covariance between autistic traits and intelligence: Findings from a longitudinal twin study. *American Journal of Medical Genetics, B. Neuropsychiatric Genetics, 153B,* 994–1007.

Hoff, E., Laursen, B., & Tardif, T. (2002). Socioeconomic status and parenting. In M. H. Bornstein (Ed.), *Handbook of parenting* (2nd ed.). Mahwah, NJ: Erlbaum.

Hoffman, E., & Ewen, D. (2007). Supporting families, nurturing young children. *CLASP Policy Brief No. 9,* 1–11.

Hoffman, M. L. (1970). Moral development. In P. H. Mussen (Ed.), *Manual of child psychology* (3rd ed., Vol. 2). New York: Wiley.

Hoffman, M. L. (1988). Moral development. In M. H. Bornstein & E. Lamb (Eds.), *Developmental psychology: An advanced textbook* (2nd ed.). Hillsdale, NJ: Erlbaum.

Holden, G. W., Vittrup, B., & Rosen, L. H. (2011). Families, parenting, and discipline. In M. K. Underwood & L. H. Rosen (Eds.), *Social development.* New York: Guilford.

Holliday, R. E., Brainerd, C. J., & Reyna, V. F. (2011). Developmental reversals in false memory: Now you see them, now you don't! *Developmental Psychology, 47*, 442–449.

Holmes, L. B. (2011). Human teratogens: Update 2010. *Birth Defects Research A: Clinical and Molecular Teratology, 91*, 1–7.

Holsen, I., Carlson Jones, D., & Skogbrott Birkeland, M. (2012). Body image satisfaction among Norwegian adolescents and young adults: A longitudinal study of interpersonal relationships and BMI. *Body Image, 9*, 201–208.

Homae, F., Watanabe, H., Nakano, T., & Taga, G. (2011). Large-scale brain networks underlying language acquisition in early infancy. *Frontiers of Psychology, 2*, 93.

Honzik, M. P., MacFarlane, I. W., & Allen, L. (1948). The stability of mental test performance between two and eighteen years. *Journal of Experimental Education, 17*, 309–324.

Hood, B. M. (1995). Gravity rules for 2- to 4-year-olds? *Cognitive Development, 10*, 577–598.

Hooper, S. R., & others. (2008). Executive functions in young males with fragile X syndrome in comparison to mental age-matched controls: baseline findings from a longitudinal study. *Neuropsychology, 22*, 36–47.

Hopkins, B. (1991). Facilitating early motor development: An intracultural study of West Indian mothers and their infants living in Britain. In J. K. Nugent, B. M. Lester, & T. B. Brazelton (Eds.), *The cultural context of infancy, Vol. 2: Multicultural and interdisciplinary approaches to parent-infant relations.* Norwood, NJ: Ablex.

Hopkins, B., & Westra, T. (1988). Maternal handling and motor development: An intracultural study. *Genetic Psychology Monographs, 14*, 377–420.

Hopkins, B., & Westra, T. (1990). Motor development, maternal expectations, and the role of handling. *Infant Behavior and Development, 13*, 117–122.

Horne, R. S., Franco, P., Adamson, T. M., Groswasser, J., & Kahn, A. (2002). Effects of body position on sleep and arousal characteristics in infants. *Early Human Development, 69*, 25–33.

Horowitz, E. K. (2013). *Becoming a second language teacher* (2nd ed.). Boston: Allyn & Bacon.

Horton, R. (2006). The coming decade for global action on child health. *Lancet, 367*, 3–5.

Houde, O., & others. (2011). Functional magnetic resonance imaging study of Piaget's conservation-of-number task in preschool and school-age children: A neo-Piagetian approach. *Journal of Experimental Child Psychology, 110*, 332–346.

Howe, M. J. A., Davidson, J. W., Moore, D. G., & Sloboda, J. A. (1995). Are there early childhood signs of musical ability? *Psychology of Music, 23*, 162–176.

Howe, M. L., Courage, M. L., & Rooksby, M. (2009). The genesis and development of autobiographical memory. In M. Courage & N. Cowan (Eds.), *The development of memory in infancy and childhood.* New York: Psychology Press.

Howerton, C. L., & Bale, T. L. (2012, in press). Prenatal programming: At the intersection of maternal stress and immune activation. *Hormones and Behavior.*

Howes, C. (1985, April). *Predicting preschool sociometric status from toddler peer interaction.* Paper presented at the meeting of the Society for Research in Child Development, Toronto.

Howes, C. (2009). Friendship in early childhood. In K. H. Rubin, W. M. Bukowski, & B. Laursen (Eds.), *Handbook of peer interactions, relationships, and groups.* New York: Guilford.

Howes, C., & Wishard Guerra, A. G. (2009). Networks of attachment relationships in low-income children of Mexican heritage: Infancy through preschool. *Social Development, 18*(4), 896–914.

Howlin, P., Magiati, I., & Charman, T. (2009). Systematic review of early intensive behavioral interventions with autism. *American Journal on Intellectual and Developmental Disabilities, 114*, 23–41.

Hoyert, D. L. (2012). 75 years of mortality in the United States. *NCHS Data Brief, 88*, 1–8.

Huang, L. N., and Ying, Y. (1989). Chinese American children and adolescents. In J. T. Gibbs and L. N. Huang (Eds.), *Children of color.* San Francisco: Jossey-Bass.

Huebner, A. M., & Garrod, A. C. (1993). Moral reasoning among Tibetan monks: A study of Buddhist adolescents and young adults in Nepal. *Journal of Cross-Cultural Psychology, 24*, 167–185.

Hughes, C., & Dunn, J. (2007). Children's relationships with other children. In C. A. Brownell & C. B. Kopp (Eds.), *Socioemotional development in the toddler years.* New York: Guilford.

Hughes, J. F., & Rozen, S. (2012). Genomics and genetics of human and primate Y chromosomes. *Annual Review of Genomics and Human Genetics* (Vol. 13). Palo Alto, CA: Annual Reviews.

Hunt, E. (2011a). *Human intelligence.* New York: Cambridge University Press.

Hunt, E. (2011b). Where are we? Where are we going? Reflections on the current and future state of research on intelligence. In R. J. Sternberg & S. B. Kaufman (Eds.), *Cambridge handbook of intelligence.* New York: Cambridge University Press.

Hurley, K. M., Black, M. M., Merry, B. C., & Caulfield, L. E. (2013, in press). *Maternal mental health and infant dietary patterns in a statewide sample of Maryland WIC participants. Maternal and Child Nutrition.*

Hurst, C. (2013). *Social inequality* (8th ed.). Upper Saddle River, NJ: Pearson.

Hurt, H., Brodsky, N. L., Roth, H., Malmud, F., & Glannetta, J. M. (2005). School performance of children with gestational cocaine exposure. *Neurotoxicology and Teratology, 27*, 203–211.

Hustedt, J. T., Friedman, A. H., & Barnett, W. S. (2012). Investments in early education: Resources at the federal and state levels. In R. C. Pianta (Ed.), *Handbook of early childhood education.* New York: Guilford.

Huston, A. C., & Bentley, A. C. (2010). Human development in societal context. *Annual Review of Psychology* (Vol. 61). Palo Alto, CA: Annual Reviews.

Huston, A. C., & Ripke, M. N. (2006). Experiences in middle childhood and children's development: A summary and integration of research. In A. C. Huston & M. N. Ripke (Eds.), *Developmental contexts in middle childhood.* New York: Cambridge University Press.

Huston, A. C., & others. (2006). Effects of a family poverty intervention program last from middle childhood to adolescence. In A. C. Huston & M. N. Ripke (Eds.). *Developmental contexts of middle childhood.* New York: Cambridge University Press.

Hutson, J. R., & others. (2013, in press). Adverse placental effect of formic acid on hCG secretion is mitigated by folic acid. *Alcohol and Alcoholism.*

Hutson, R. A. (2008). Poverty. In N. J. Salkind (Ed.), *Encyclopedia of educational psychology.* Thousand Oaks, CA: Sage.

Huttenlocher, J., Haight, W., Bruk, A., Seltzer, M., & Lyons, T. (1991). Early vocabulary growth: Relation to language input and gender. *Developmental Psychology, 27*, 236–248.

Huttenlocher, P. R., & Dabholkar, A. S. (1997). Regional differences in synaptogenesis in human cerebral cortex. *Journal of Comparative Neurology, 37*(2), 167–178.

Huynh, V. W., & Fuligni, A. J. (2010). Discrimination hurts: The academic, psychological, and physical well-being of adolescents. *Journal of Research on Adolescence, 20*, 916–941.

Hwang, S. H., Hwang, J. H., Moon, J. S., & Lee, D. H. (2012). Environmental tobacco smoke and children's health. *Korean Journal of Pediatrics, 55*, 35–41.

Hyde, D. C., & Spelke, E. S. (2009). All numbers are not equal: An electrophysiological investigation of small and large number representations. *Journal of Cognitive Neuroscience, 21*, 1039–1053.

Hyde, D. C., & Spelke, E. S. (2011). Neural signatures of number processing in human infants: Evidence for two core systems underlying numerical cognition. *Developmental Science, 14*, 360–371.

Hyde, D. C., & Spelke, E. S. (2012, in press). Spatio-temporal dynamics of numerical processing: An ERP source localization study. *Human Brain Mapping.*

Hyde, J. S. (2005). The gender similarities hypothesis. *American Psychologist, 60*, 581–592.

Hyde, J. S. (2007). *Half the human experience* (7th ed.). Boston: Houghton Mifflin.

Hyde, J. S., & DeLamater, J. D. (2011). *Understanding human sexuality* (11th ed.). New York: McGraw-Hill.

Hyde, J. S., & Else-Quest, N. (2013). *Half the human experience* (8th ed.). Boston: Cengage.

Hyde, J. S., Lindberg, S. M., Linn, M. C., Ellis, A. B., & Williams, C. C. (2008). Gender similarities characterize math performance. *Science, 321*, 494–495.

Hyde, L. W., Shaw, D. S., & Moilanen, K. L. (2010). Developmental precursors of moral disengagement and the role of moral disengagement in the development of antisocial behavior. *Journal of Abnormal Child Psychology, 38*, 197–209.

Hyman, I., & others. (2006). Bullying: Theory, research, and interventions. In C. M. Evertson & C. S. Weinstein (Eds.), *Handbook of classroom management: Research, practice, and contemporary issues.* Mahwah, NJ: Erlbaum.

Hymel, S., Closson, L. M., Caravita, C. S., & Vaillancourt, T. (2011). Social status among peers: From sociometric attraction to peer acceptance to perceived popularity. In P. K. Smith & C. H. Hart (Eds.), *Wiley-Blackwell handbook of childhood social development* (2nd ed.). New York: Wiley.

Hyoun, S. C., Obican, S. G., & Scialli, A. R. (2012). Teratogen update: Methotrexate. *Birth Defects Research A: Clinical and Molecular Teratology, 94,* 187–204.

Hyson, M. (2007). Curriculum. In R. New & M. Cochran (Eds.), *Early childhood education: An international encyclopedia of early childhood education.* New York: Greenwood.

Hyson, M. C., Copple, C., & Jones, J. (2006). Early childhood development and education. In W. Damon & R. Lerner (Eds.), *Handbook of child psychology* (6th ed.). New York: Wiley.

I

"I Have a Dream" Foundation. (2008). *About us.* Retrieved July 5, 2008, from http://www.ihad.org

"I Have a Dream" Foundation. (2013). *About us.* Retrieved January 13, 2013, from http://www.ihad.org

Ibrahim, R., & Eviatar, Z. (2013, in press). The contribution of two hemispheres to lexical decision in different languages. *Behavioral and Brain Functions.*

Ickovics, J. R., & others. (2011). Effects of group prenatal care on psychosocial risk in pregnancy: Results from a randomized controlled trial. *Psychology and Health, 26,* 235–250.

Ige, F., & Shelton, D. (2004). Reducing risk of sudden infant death syndrome (SIDS) in African-American communities. *Journal of Pediatric Nursing, 19,* 290–292.

Imada, T., & others. (2007). Infant speech perception activates Broca's area: A developmental magnetoencephalography study. *Neuroreport, 17,* 957–962.

Impett, E. A., Schoolder, D., Tolman, L., Sorsoli, L., & Henson, J. M. (2008). Girls' relationship authenticity and self-esteem across adolescence. *Developmental Psychology, 44,* 722–733.

International Montessori Council. (2006). Larry Page and Sergey Brin, founders of Google.com, credit their Montessori education for much of their success on prime-time television. Retrieved June 24, 2010, from www.Montessori.org/enews/barbara_walters.html

Iovannone, R. (2013). Teaching students with autism spectrum disorders. In B. G. Cook & M. G. Tankerslee (Ed.), *Research-based practices in special education.* Upper Saddle River, NJ: Pearson.

Ip, S., Chung, M., Raman, G., Trikalinos, T. A., & Lau, J. (2009). A summary of the Agency for Healthcare Research and Quality's evidence report on breastfeeding in developed countries. *Breastfeeding Medicine, 4*(Suppl. 1), S17–S30.

Iqbal, M., & others. (2012). Placental drug transporters and their role in fetal protection. *Placenta, 33,* 137–142.

Irvin, J. L., Buehl, D. R., & Klemp, R. M. (2007). *Reading and the high school student* (2nd ed.). Boston: Allyn & Bacon.

Irwing, P., Booth, T., Nyborg, H., & Rushton, J. P. (2012). Are *g* and the general factor of personality (GFP) correlated? *Intelligence, 40,* 296–305.

Isaacs, B. (2012). *Understanding the Montessori approach: Early years education practice.* New York: Routledge.

Issel, L. M., & others. (2011). A review of prenatal home-visiting effectiveness for improving birth outcomes. *Journal of Obstetrics, Gynecologic, and Neonatal Nursing, 40,* 157–165.

Ivanova, K., Veenstra, R., & Mills, M. (2012). Who dates? The effects of temperament, puberty, and parenting on early adolescent experiences with dating. *Journal of Early Adolescence, 42,* 340–363.

Izard, C. E. (2009). Emotion theory and research: Highlights, unanswered questions, and emerging issues. *Annual Review of Psychology* (Vol. 60). Palo Alto, CA: Annual Reviews.

J

Jackson, L. A., & others. (2012). The digital divide. In J. R. Levesque (Ed.), *Encyclopedia of adolescence.* New York: Springer.

Jacobson, L. A., & others. (2011). Working memory influences processing speed and reading fluency in ADHD. *Child Neuropsychology, 17*(3), 209–224.

Jaeggi, S. M., Berman, M. G., & Jonides, J. (2009). Training attentional processes. *Trends in Cognitive Science, 37,* 644–654.

Jaffee, S., & Hyde, J. S. (2000). Gender differences in moral orientation: A meta-analysis. *Psychological Bulletin, 126,* 703–726.

Jalongo, M. R., & Isenberg, J. (2012). *Exploring your role in early childhood education* (4th ed.). Upper Saddle River, NJ: Pearson.

James, J., Thomas, P., Cavan, D., & Kerr, D. (2004). Preventing childhood obesity by reducing consumption of carbonated drinks. *British Medical Journal, 328,* 1237.

James, W. (1890/1950). *The principles of psychology.* New York: Dover.

Jan, J. E., & others. (2010). Long-term sleep disturbances in children: A cause of neuronal loss. *European Journal of Pediatric Neurology, 14*(5), 380–390.

Jansen, J., de Weerth, C., & Riksen-Walraven, J. M. (2008). Breastfeeding and the mother-infant relationship—A review. *Developmental Review, 28,* 503–521.

Jardri, R., & others. (2012). Assessing fetal response to maternal speech using a noninvasive functional brain imaging technique. *International Journal of Developmental Neuroscience, 30,* 159–161.

Jarrett, R. L. (1995). Growing up poor: The family experiences of socially mobile youth in low-income African-American neighborhoods. *Journal of Adolescent Research, 10,* 111–135.

Jaswal, V. K., & Fernald, A. (2007). Learning to communicate. In A. Slater & M. Lewis (Eds.), *Introduction to infant development* (2nd ed.). New York: Oxford University Press.

Jencks, C. (1979). *Who gets ahead? The determinants of economic success in America.* New York: Basic Books.

Jenik, A. G., & Vain, N. (2010). The pacifier debate. *Early Human Development, 85* (Suppl. 10), S89–S91.

Jenkins, J. M., & Astington, J. W. (1996). Cognitive factors and family structure associated with theory of mind development in young children. *Developmental Psychology, 32,* 70–78.

Jensen, A. R. (2008). Book review. *Intelligence, 36,* 96–97.

Jentarra, G. M., Rice, S. G., Olfers, S., Safen, D., & Narayanan, V. (2011). Evidence for a population variation in TSC1 and TSC2 gene expression. *BMC Medical Genetics, 12,* 29.

Jesse, D. E., & Kirkpatrick, M. K. (2013). Catching the spirit in cultural care: A midwifery exemplar. *Journal of Midwifery and Women's Health, 58,* 49–56.

Ji, B. T., & others. (1997). Paternal cigarette smoking and the risk of childhood cancer among offspring of nonsmoking mothers. *Journal of the National Cancer Institute, 89,* 238–244.

Jia, M., & others. (2013). HDAM: A resource of human disease associated mutatins from next generation sequencing studies. *BMC Medical Genomics, 6, Suppl 1:* S16.

Jia, R., & Schoppe-Sullivan, S. J. (2011). Relations between coparenting and father involvement in families with preschool-age children. *Developmental Psychology, 47,* 106–118.

Jiao, S., Ji, G., & Jing, Q. (1996). Cognitive development of Chinese urban only children and children with siblings. *Child Development, 67,* 387–395.

Jin, L., & others. (2013). Placental concentrations of mercury, lead, cadmium, and arsenic and the risk of neural tube defects in a Chinese population. *Reproductive Toxicology, 35,* 25–31.

Jin, M. K., Jacobvitz, D., Hagen, N., & Jung, S. H. (2012). Maternal sensitivity and infant attachment security in Korea: Cross-cultural validation of the Strange Situation. *Attachment and Human Development, 14,* 33–44.

Jittendra, A., & Montague, M. (2013). Strategies for improving student outcomes in mathematical reasoning. In B. G. Cook & M. G. Tankersley (Eds.), *Research-based practices in special education.* Upper Saddle River, NJ: Pearson.

Job, V., Dweck, C. S., & Walton, G. M. (2010). Ego-depletion—Is it all in your head? Implicit theories about willpower affect self-regulation. *Psychological Science, 21,* 1686–1693.

Joh, A. S., Jaswal, V. K., & Keen, R. (2011). Imaging a way out of the gravity bias: Preschoolers can visualize the solution to a spatial problem. *Child Development, 82,* 744–750.

Johns Hopkins University. (2006). *Research: Tribal connections.* Retrieved January 31, 2008, from http://www.krieger.jhu.edu/research/spotlight/prabhakar.html

Johnson, A. D., & Brooks-Gunn, J. (2012). Child care and early education for low-income families: Choices and consequences. In V. Maholmes & R. B. King (Eds.), *Oxford handbook of poverty and child development.* New York: Oxford University Press.

Johnson, J. S., & Newport, E. L. (1991). Critical period effects on universal properties of language: The status of subjacency in the acquisition of a second language. *Cognition, 39,* 215–258.

Johnson, L., Giordano, P. C., Manning, W. D., & Longmore, M. A. (2011). Parent-child relations and offending in young adulthood. *Journal of Youth and Adolescence, 40,* 786–799.

Johnson, M. D. (2012). *Human biology* (6th ed.). Upper Saddle River, NJ: Pearson.

Johnson, M. H., & de Haan, M. (2012). *Developmental cognitive neuroscience* (3rd ed.). New York: Wiley-Blackwell.

Johnson, M. H., Grossmann, T., & Cohen-Kadosh, K. (2009), Mapping functional brain development: Building a social brain through Interactive Specialization. *Developmental Psychology, 45,* 151–159.

Johnson, S. B., Dariotis, J. K., & Wang, C. (2012). Adolescent risk taking under stressed and nonstressed conditions: Conservative, calculating, and impulsive types. *Journal of Adolescent Health, 51*(Suppl. 2), S34–S40.

Johnson, S. P. (2004). Development of perceptual completion in infancy. *Psychological Science, 15,* 769–775.

Johnson, S. P. (2010). Perceptual completion in infancy. In S. P. Johnson (Ed.), *Neoconstructivism: The new science of cognitive development.* New York: Oxford University Press.

Johnson, S. P. (2011). A constructivist view of object perception in infancy. In L. M. Oakes, C. H. Cashon, M. Casasola, & D. H. Rakison (Eds.), *Early perceptual and cognitive development.* New York: Oxford University Press.

Johnson, S. P. (2012). Development of the visual system. In P. Rakic & J. Rubenstein (Eds.), *Developmental neuroscience—Basic and clinical mechanisms.* New York: Oxford University Press.

Johnson, S. P. (2013). Object perception. In P. D. Zelazo (Ed.), *Handbook of developmental psychology.* New York: Oxford University Press.

Johnston, M. (2008, April 30). Commentary on R. Highfield, *Harvard's baby brain research lab.* Retrieved January 24, 2008, from www.telegraph.co.uk/scienceandtechnology/science/sciencenews/3341166/

Jones, D., & others. (2010). The impact of the Fast Track prevention trial on health services utilization by youth at risk for conduct problems. *Pediatrics, 125,* 130–136.

Jones, H. W. (2007). Iatrogenic multiple births: A 2003 checkup: *Fertility and Sterility, 87,* 453–455.

Jones, L., & others. (2012). Pain management for women in labor: An overview of systematic reviews. *Cochrane Database of Systematic Reviews, 14*(3), CD009234.

Jones, M. C. (1965). Psychological correlates of somatic development. *Child Development, 36,* 899–911.

Jones, M. D., & Galliher, R. V. (2007). Navajo ethnic identity: Predictors of psychosocial outcomes in Navajo adolescents. *Journal of Research on Adolescence, 17,* 683–696.

Jones, N. A. (2012). Delayed reactive cries demonstrate emotional and physiological dysregulation in newborns of depressed mothers. *Biological Psychiatry, 89,* 374–381.

Jonson-Reid, M., Kohl, P. L., & Drake, B. (2012). Child and adolescent outcomes of chronic child maltreatment. *Pediatrics, 129,* 839–845.

Jordan, S. J., & others. (2008). Serious ovarian, fallopian tube, and primary peritoneal cancers: A comprehensive epidemiological analysis. *International Journal of Cancer, 122,* 1598–1603.

Joseph, J. (2006). *The missing gene.* New York: Algora.

Josephson Institute of Ethics. (2008). *The ethics of American youth 2008.* Los Angeles: Josephson Institute.

Juang, L. P., & Umana-Taylor, A. J. (2012). Family conflict among Chinese- and Mexican-origin adolescents and their parents in the U.S.: An introduction. *New Directions in Child and Adolescent Development, 135,* 1–12.

Juffer, F., & van IJzendoorn, M. H. (2007). Adoptees do not lack self-esteem: A meta-analysis of studies on self-esteem of transracial, international, and domestic adoptees, *Psychological Bulletin, 133,* 1067–1083.

Jusczyk, P. W., & Hohne, E. A. (1997). Infants' memory for spoken words. *Science, 277,* 1984–1986.

Just, M. A., Keller, T. A., Malave, V. L., Kana, R. K., & Varma, S. (2012). Autism as a neural systems disorder: A theory of frontal-posterior underconnectivity. *Neuroscience and Biobehavioral Reviews, 36,* 1292–1313.

K

Kaffashi, F., Scher, M. S., Ludington-Hoe, S. M., & Loparo, K. A. (2013). An analysis of kangaroo care intervention using neonatal EEG complexity: A preliminary study. *Clinical Neurophysiology, 124,* 238–246.

Kagan, J. (1987). Perspectives on infancy. In J. D. Osofsky (Ed.), *Handbook on infant development* (2nd ed.). New York: Wiley.

Kagan, J. (1992). Yesterday's promises, tomorrow's promises. *Developmental Psychology, 28,* 990–997.

Kagan, J. (2000). Temperament. In A. Kazdin (Ed.), *Encyclopedia of psychology.* Washington, DC, & New York: American Psychological Association and Oxford University Press.

Kagan, J. (2002). Behavioral inhibition as a temperamental category. In R. J. Davidson, K. R. Scherer, & H. H. Goldsmith (Eds.), *Handbook of affective sciences.* New York: Oxford University Press.

Kagan, J. (2003). Biology, context, and development. *Annual Review of Psychology* (Vol. 54). Palo Alto, CA: Annual Reviews.

Kagan, J. (2008). Fear and wariness. In M. M. Haith & J. B. Benson (Eds.), *Encyclopedia of infant and early childhood development.* Oxford, UK: Elsevier.

Kagan, J. (2010). Emotions and temperament. In M. H. Bornstein (Ed.), *Handbook of cultural developmental science.* New York: Psychology Press.

Kagan, J. (2013). Temperamental contributions to inhibited and uninhibited profiles. In P. D. Zelazo (Ed.), *Oxford handbook of developmental psychology.* New York: Oxford University Press.

Kagan, J. J., Kearsley, R. B., & Zelazo, P. R. (1978). *Infancy: Its place in human development.* Cambridge, MA: Harvard University Press.

Kagan, J., & Snidman, N. (1991). Infant predictors of inhibited and uninhibited behavioral profiles. *Psychological Science, 2,* 40–44.

Kagan, S. L., & Scott-Little, C. (2004). Early learning standards. *Phi Delta Kappan, 82,* 388–395.

Kail, R. V. (2007). Longitudinal evidence that increases in processing speed and working memory enhance children's reasoning. *Psychological Science, 18,* 312–313.

Kalak, N., & others. (2012). Daily morning running for 3 weeks improved sleep and psychological functioning in health of adolescents compared to controls. *Journal of Adolescent Health, 51,* 615–622.

Kalder, M., Knoblauch, K., Hrgovic, I., & Munstedt, K. (2011). Use of complementary and alternative medicine during pregnancy and delivery. *Archives of Gynecology and Obstetrics, 283*(3), 475–482.

Kamii, C. (1985). *Young children reinvent arithmetic: Implications of Piaget's theory.* New York: Teachers College Press.

Kamii, C. (1989). *Young children continue to reinvent arithmetic.* New York: Teachers College Press.

Kamil, M. L. (2012). Current and historical perspectives on reading research and instruction. In K. R. Harris, S. Graham, & T. Urdan (Eds.), *APA handbook of educational psychology.* Washington, DC: American Psychological Association.

Kang, P. P., & Romo, L. F. (2011). The role of religious involvement on depression, risky behavior, and academic performance among Korean American adolescents. *Journal of Adolescence, 34,* 767–778.

Kanoy, K., Ulku-Steiner, B., Cox, M., & Burchinal, M. (2003). Marital relationship and individual psychological characteristics that predict physical punishment of children. *Journal of Family Psychology, 17,* 20–28.

Kaplan, J. S. (2012). The effects of shared environment on adult intelligence: A critical review of adoption, twin, and MZA studies. *Developmental Psychology, 48,* 1292–1298.

Kar, B. R., Rao, S. L., & Chandramouli, B. A. (2008). Cognitive development in children with chronic energy malnutrition. *Behavioral and Brain Functions, 4,* 31.

Karg, K., & Sen, S. (2012, in press). Gene X environment interaction models in psychiatry. *Current Topics in Behavioral Neuroscience.*

Karoly, L. A., & Bigelow, J. A. (2005). *The economics of investing in universal preschool education in California.* Santa Monica, CA: The RAND Corporation.

Karpov, Y. V. (2006). *The neo-Vygotskian approach to child development.* New York: Cambridge University Press.

Karreman, A., van Tuijl, C., van Aken, M. A. G., & Dekovic, M. (2008). Parenting, coparenting, and effortful control in preschoolers. *Journal of Family Psychology, 22,* 30–40.

Katz, L. (1999). Curriculum disputes in early childhood education. *ERIC Clearinghouse on Elementary and Early Childhood Education,* Document EDO-PS-99-13.

Kauffman, J. M., McGee, K., & Brigham, M. (2004). Enabling or disabling? Observations on changes in special education. *Phi Delta Kappan, 85,* 613–620.

Kaufman, J. C., & Sternberg, R. J. (2012, in press). The creative mind. In C. Jones, M. Lorenzen, & J. Sapsed (Eds.), *Oxford handbook of creative industries.* New York: Oxford University Press.

Kaufman, J. C., & Sternberg, R. J. (2013, in press). The creative mind. In C. Jones, M. Lorenzen, & R. F. Proctor (Eds.), *Handbook of psychology: Experimental psychology,* Vol. 4. New York: Wiley.

Kaur, A., & Phadke, S. R. (2012, in press). Analysis of short stature cases referred for genetic evaluation. *Indian Journal of Pediatrics.*

Kavsek, M. (2009). The perception of subjective contours and neon color spreading figures in young infants. *Attention, Perception, and Psychophysics, 71,* 412–420.

Kavsek, M. (2013, in press). The comparator model of infant visual habituation and dishabituation: Recent insights. *Developmental Psychobiology*.

Kavsek, M., & Granrud, C. E. (2012). Children's and adults' size estimates at near and far distances: A test of the perceptual learning theory of size constancy development. *Iperception, 3,* 459–466.

Kawabata, Y., Tseng, W. L., Murray-Close, D., & Crick, N. R. (2012, in press). Developmental trajectories of Chinese children's relational and physical aggression: Associations with social-psychological adjustment problems. *Journal of Abnormal Child Psychology*.

Keating, D. P. (1990). Adolescent thinking. In S. S. Feldman & G. R. Elliott (Eds.), *At the threshold: The developing adolescent.* Cambridge, MA: Harvard University Press.

Keating, D. P. (2004). Cognitive and brain development. In R. Lerner & L. Steinberg (Ed.), *Handbook of adolescent psychology.* New York: Wiley.

Keating, D. P. (2007). Understanding adolescent development: Implications for driving safety. *Journal of Safety Research, 38,* 147–157.

Keating, D. P. (2009). Developmental science and giftedness: An integrated life-span framework. In F. D. Horowitz, R. F. Subotnik, & D. J. Matthews (Eds.), *The development of giftedness and talent across the life span.* Washington, DC: American Psychological Association.

Keen, R. (2005). Unpublished review of J. W. Santrock's *A topical approach to life-span development,* 3rd ed. (New York: McGraw-Hill).

Keen, R. (2011). The development of problem solving in young children: A critical cognitive skill. *Annual Review of Psychology* (Vol. 62). Palo Alto, CA: Annual Reviews.

Keller, P., & El-Sheikh, M. (2010). Children's emotional security and sleep: Longitudinal relations and directions of effects. *Journal of Child Psychology and Psychiatry, 52*(1), 64–71.

Kellman, P. J., & Arterberry, M. E. (2006). Infant visual perception. In W. Damon & R. Lerner (Eds.), *Handbook of child psychology* (6th ed.). New York: Wiley.

Kellman, P. J., & Banks, M. S. (1998). Infant visual perception. In W. Damon (Eds.), *Handbook of child psychology* (5th ed., Vol. 2). New York: Wiley.

Kellow, J. T., & Jones, B. D. (2008). The effects of stereotypes on the achievement gap: Reexamining the academic performance of African American high school students. *Journal of Black Psychology, 34,* 94–120.

Kelly, D. J., & others. (2007). Cross-race preferences for same-race faces extend beyond the African versus Caucasian contrast in 3-month-old infants. *Infancy, 11,* 87–95.

Kelly, D. J., & others. (2009). Development of the other-race effect in infancy: Evidence toward universality? *Journal of Experimental Child Psychology, 104*(1), 105–114.

Kelly, J. P., Borchert, J., & Teller, D. Y. (1997). The development of chromatic and achromatic sensitivity in infancy as tested with the sweep VEP. *Vision Research, 37,* 2057–2072.

Kelly, K. M., & others. (2013, in press). Children's Oncology Group's 2013 blueprint for research on Hodgkin's lymphoma. *Pediatric and Blood Cancer*.

Kelmanson, I. A. (2010). Sleep disturbances in two-month-old infants sharing the bed with parent(s). *Minerva Pediatrica, 62,* 162–169.

Kendler, K. S., & others. (2012, in press). Genetic and familial environmental influences on the risk for drug abuse: A national Swedish adoption study. *Archives of General Psychiatry*.

Kendrick, K., Jutengren, G., & Stattin, H. (2012). The protective role of supportive friends against bullying perpetration and victimization. *Journal of Adolescence, 35,* 1069–1080.

Kennell, J. H. (2006). Randomized controlled trial of skin-to-skin contact from birth versus conventional incubator for physiological stabilization in 1200 g to 2199 g newborns. *Acta Paediatrica (Sweden), 95,* 15–16.

Kennell, J. H., & McGrath, S. K. (1999). Commentary: Practical and humanistic lessons from the third world for perinatal caregivers everywhere. *Birth, 26,* 9–10.

Kenney-Benson, G. A., Pomerantz, E. M., Ryan, A. M., & Patrick, H. (2006). Sex differences in math performance: The role of children's approach to schoolwork. *Developmental Psychology, 42,* 11–26.

Kerns, K. A., & Siebert, A. C. (2012). Finding your way through the thicket: Promising approaches to assessing attachment in middle childhood. In E. Waters & B. Vaughn (Eds.), *Measuring attachment.* New York: Guilford.

Kerns, K. A., Siener, S., & Brumariu, L. E. (2011). Mother-child relationships, family context, and child characteristics as predictors of anxiety symptoms in middle childhood. *Development and Psychopathology, 23,* 593–604.

Kessen, W., Haith, M. M., & Salapatek, P. (1970). Human infancy. In P. H. Mussen (Ed.), *Manual of child psychology* (3rd ed., Vol. 1). New York: Wiley.

Khodaverdi, M., & others. (2013, in press). Hearing 25 years after surgical treatment of otitis media with effusion in early childhood. *International Journal of Otorhinolaryngology*.

Khuc, K., & others. (2013, in press). Adolescent metabolic syndrome risk is increased with higher infancy weight gain and decreased with longer breast feeding. *Indian Journal of Pediatrics*.

Kidd, C., Piantadosi, S. T., & Aslin, R. N. (2012). The Goldilocks effect: Human infants allocate attention to visual sequences that are neither too simple nor too complex. *PLoS One, 7*(5), e36399.

Kilgore, W. D., & others. (2012). Gray matter correlates of trait and ability models of emotional intelligence. *Neuroreport, 23,* 551–555.

Kilic, S., & others. (2012, in press). Environmental tobacco smoke exposure during intrauterine period promotes granulosa cell apoptosis: A prospective, randomized study. *Journal Maternal-Fetal and Neonatal Medicine*.

Kim, H. K., & others. (2011). Cardiovascular anomalies in Turner syndrome: Spectrum, prevalence, and cardiac MRI findings in a pediatric and young adult population. *AJR American Journal of Roentgenology, 196,* 454–460.

Kim, J., & others. (2006). Trends in overweight from 1980 through 2001 among preschool-aged children enrolled in a health maintenance organization. *Obesity, 14,* 1107–1112.

Kim, J-K., McHale, S. M., Crouter, A. C., & Osgood, D. W. (2007). Longitudinal linkages between sibling relationships and adjustment from middle childhood through adolescence. *Developmental Psychology, 43,* 960–973.

Kim, K. H. (2010, July 10). Interview. *Newsweek,* pp. 42–48.

Kim, S. Y., Chen, Q., Wang, Y., Shen, Y., & Orozco-Lapray, D. (2012, in press). Longitudinal linkages among parent-child acculturation discrepancy, parenting, parent-child sense of alienation, and adolescent adjustment in Chinese immigrant families. *Developmental Psychology*.

Kim-Spoon, J., Cicchetti, D., & Rogosch, F. A. (2013, in press). A longitudinal study of emotion regulation, emotion lability-negativity, and internalizing symptomatology in maltreated and nonmaltreated children. *Child Development*.

King, P. E., Carr, A., & Boiter, C. (2011). Spirituality, religiosity, and youth thriving. In R. M. Lerner, J. V. Lerner, & J. B. Benson (Eds.), *Advances in child development and behavior: Positive youth development.* New York: Elsevier.

King, P. E., Ramos, J. S., & Clardy, C. E. (2012). Searching for the sacred: Religious and spiritual development among adolescents. In K. I. Pargament, J. Exline, & J. Jones (Eds.), *APA handbook of psychology, religion, and spirituality.* Washington, DC: American Psychological Association.

King, P. E., & Roeser, R. W. (2009). Religion and spirituality in adolescent development. In R. M. Lerner & L. Steinberg (Eds.), *Handbook of adolescent psychology* (3rd ed.). New York: Wiley.

Kingsmore, S. F., & others. (2013, in press). Next-generation community genetics for low- and middle-income countries. *Genomic Medicine*.

Kingston, M. H. (1976). *The woman warrior: Memoirs of a girlhood among ghosts.* New York: Vintage Books.

Kini, S., & others. (2010). Lack of impact of semen quality on fertilization in assisted conception. *Scottish Medicine, 55,* 20–23.

Kinzler, K. D., Dupoux, E., & Spelke, E. S. (2012). "Native" objects and collaborators: Infants' object choices and acts of giving reflect favor for native over foreign speakers. *Journal of Cognition and Development, 13,* 67–81.

Kirk, R. E. (2013, in press). Experimental design. In I. B. Weiner & others (Eds.), *Handbook of psychology* (2nd ed., Vol. 2). New York: Wiley.

Kirk, S. A., Gallagher, J. J., Coleman, M. R., & Anastaslow, N. J. (2012). *Educating exceptional children* (13th ed.). Boston: Cengage.

Kirkham, N. Z., Wagner, J. B., Swan, K. A., & Johnson, S. P. (2012). Sound support: Intermodal information facilitates infants' perception of an occluded trajectory. *Infant Behavior and Development, 35,* 174–178.

Kirkorian, H. L., Anderson, D. R., & Keen, R. (2012). Age differences in online processing of video: An eye movement study. *Child Development, 83,* 497–507.

Kirkorian, H. L., Wartella, E. A., & Anderson, D. A. (2008). Media and young children's learning. *Future of Children, 18*(1), 39–61.

Kisilevsky, B. S., & Hains, S. M. J. (2011). Onset and maturation of fetal heart rate response to the mother's voice over late gestation. *Developmental Science, 14*, 214–223.

Kisilevsky, B. S., & others. (2009). Fetal sensitivity to properties of maternal speech and language. *Infant Behavior and Development, 32*, 59–71.

Kisilevsky, S., Hains, S. M., Jacquet, A. Y., Granier-Deferre, C., & Lecanuet, J. P. (2004). Maturation of fetal responses to music. *Developmental Science, 7*, 550–559.

Kitsantas, P., & Gaffney, K. F. (2010). Racial/ethnic disparities in infant mortality. *Journal of Perinatal Medicine, 38*, 87–94.

Kitzinger, S. (2011). Human rights and midwifery. *Birth, 38*, 86–87.

Klahr, A. M., & others. (2011). The relationship between parent-child conflict and adolescent antisocial development: Confirming shared environment mediation. *Journal of Abnormal Child Psychology, 39*, 683–694.

Klaus, M., & Kennell, H. H. (1976). *Maternal-infant bonding.* St. Louis: Mosbv.

Kleiman, E. M., & Riskand, J. H. (2013, in press) Utilized social support and self-esteem mediate the relationship between perceived social support and suicide ideation. *Crisis.*

Klein, S. (2011). *State of public school segregation in the United States, 2007–2010.* Washington, DC: Feminist Majority Foundation.

Kleinsorge, C., & Covitz, L. M. (2012). Impact of divorce on children: Developmental considerations. *Pediatrics in Review, 33*, 147–154.

Klima, C., Norr, K., Conderheld, S., & Handler, A. (2009). Introduction of Centering Pregnancy in a public health clinic. *Journal of Midwifery and Women's Health, 54*, 27–34.

Klimstra, T. A., Hale, W. W., Raaijmakers, Q. A., Branje, S. J. T., & Meeus, W. H. (2010). Identity formation in adolescence: Change or stability? *Journal of Youth and Adolescence, 39*, 150–162.

Knopik, V. S. (2009). Maternal smoking during pregnancy and child outcomes: Real or spurious effect? *Developmental Neuropsychology, 34*, 1–36.

Knox, M. (2010). On hitting children: A review of corporal punishment in the United States. *Journal of Pediatric Health Care, 24*, 103–107.

Kochanska, G., & Aksan, N. (2007). Conscience in childhood: Past, present, and future. *Merrill-Palmer Quarterly, 50*, 299–310.

Kochanska, G., Aksan, N., Prisco, T. R., & Adams, E. E. (2008). Mother-child and father-child mutually responsive orientation in the first two years and children's outcomes at preschool age: Mechanisms of influence. *Child Development, 79*, 30–44.

Kochanska, G., Barry, R. A., Jimenez, N. B., Hollatz, A. L., & Woodard, J. (2009). Guilt and effortful control: Two mechanisms that prevent disruptive developmental trajectories. *Journal of Personality and Social Psychology, 97*, 322–333.

Kochanska, G., Barry, R. A., Stellern, S. A., & O'Bleness, J. J. (2010). Early attachment organization moderates the parent-child mutually coercive pathway to children's antisocial conduct. *Child Development, 80*, 1288–1300.

Kochanska, G., Gross, J. N., Lin, M., & Nichols, K. E. (2002). Guilt in young children: Development, determinants, and relations with a broader set of standards. *Child Development, 73*, 461–482.

Kochanska, G., & Kim, S. (2013, in press). Early attachment organization with both parents and future behavior problems: From infancy to middle childhood. *Child Development.*

Kochanska, G., & others. (2010). Positive socialization mechanisms in secure and insecure parent-child dyads: Two longitudinal studies. *Journal of Child Psychology and Psychiatry, 51*, 998–1009.

Koeblinger, C., & others. (2013, in press). Fetal magnetic resonance imaging of lymphangiomas. *Journal of Perinatal Medicine.*

Koenig, L. B., McGue, M., & Iacono, W. G. (2008). Stability and change in religiousness during emerging adulthood. *Developmental Psychology, 44*, 523–543.

Kohen, D. E., Leventhal, T., Dahinten, V. S., & McIntosh, C. N. (2008). Neighborhood disadvantage: Pathways of effects for young children. *Child Development, 79*, 156–169.

Kohlberg, L. (1958). *The development of modes of moral thinking and choice in the years 10 to 16.* Unpublished doctoral dissertation, University of Chicago.

Kohlberg, L. (1969). Stage and sequence: The cognitive-developmental approach to socialization. In D. A. Goslin (Ed.), *Handbook of socialization theory and research.* Chicago: Rand McNally.

Kohlberg, L. (1986). A current statement on some theoretical issues. In S. Modgil & C. Modgil (Eds.), *Lawrence Kohlberg.* Philadelphia: Falmer.

Kolialexi, A. (2012). Early non-invasive detection of fetal Y chromosome sequences in maternal plasma using multiplex PCR. *European Journal of Obstetrics, Gynecology, and Reproductive Medicine, 161*, 34–37.

Kong, A., & others. (2012). Rate of *de novo* mutations and the importance of father's age to disease risk. *Nature, 488*, 471–475.

Kong, A., & others. (2013). Racial/ethnic differences in dietary intake among WIC families prior to food package revisions. *Journal of Nutrition Education and Behavior, 45*, 39–46.

Koo, Y. J., & others. (2012). Pregnancy outcomes according to increasing maternal age. *Taiwan Journal of Obstetrics and Gynecology, 51*, 60–65.

Koolhof, R., Loeber, R., Wei, E. H., Pardini, D., & D'Escury, A. C. (2007). Inhibition deficits of serious delinquent boys of low intelligence. *Criminal Behavior and Mental Health, 17*, 274–292.

Kopp, C. B. (2011). Socio-emotional development in the early years: Socialization and consciousness. *Annual Review of Psychology* (Vol. 62). Palo Alto, CA: Annual Reviews.

Kopp, C. B., & Neufeld, S. J. (2002). Emotional development in infancy. In R. Davidson & K. Scherer (Eds.), *Handbook of affective sciences.* New York: Oxford University Press.

Kopp, F., & Lindenberger, U. (2012). Effects of joint attention on long-term memory in 9-month-old infants: An event-related potentials study. *Developmental Science, 15*, 540–556.

Koppelman, K., & Goodhart, L. (2011). *Understanding human differences* (3rd ed.). Boston: Allyn & Bacon.

Korat, O. (2009). The effect of maternal teaching talk on children's emergent literacy as a function of type of activity and maternal education level. *Journal of Applied Developmental Psychology, 30*, 34–42.

Koren, G., & Nordeng, H. (2012). Antidepressant use during pregnancy: The benefit-risk ratio. *American Journal of Obstetrics and Gynecology, 207*, 157–163.

Kornblum, J. (2006, March 9). How to monitor the kids? *USA Today, 1D*, p. 1.

Kostovic, I., Judas, M., & Sedmak, G. (2011). Developmental history of the subplate zone, subplate neurons, and interstitial white matter neurons: Relevance for schizophrenia. *International Journal of Developmental Neuroscience, 29*(3), 193–205.

Kotovsky, L., & Baillargeon, R. (1994). Calibration-based reasoning about collision events in 11-month-old infants. *Cognition, 51*, 107–129.

Kottak, C. P., & Kozaitis, K. A. (2012). *On being different* (4th ed.). New York: McGraw-Hill.

Kotte, E. M., Winkler, A. M., & Takken, T. (2013, in press). Fitkids exercise therapy program in the Netherlands. *Pediatric Physical Therapy.*

Kowalski, R. M., Limber, S. P., & Agatston, P. W. (2012). *Cyberbullying* (2nd ed.). New York: Wiley.

Kozol, J. (2005). *The shame of the nation: The restoration of apartheid schooling in America.* New York: Three Rivers Press.

Kramer, L. (2006, July 10). Commentary in "How your siblings make you who you are" by J. Kluger. *Time*, pp. 46–55.

Kramer, L., & Perozynski, L. (1999). Parental beliefs about managing sibling conflict. *Developmental Psychology, 35*, 489–499.

Kramer, L., & Radey, C. (1997). Improving sibling relationships among young children: A social skills training model. *Family Relations, 46*, 237–246.

Krauss, R. A., & Glucksberg, S. (1969). The development of communication: Competence as a function of age. *Child Development, 40*, 255–266.

Kreutzer, L. C., & Flavell, J. H. (1975). An interview study of children's knowledge about memory. *Monographs of the Society for Research in Child Development, 40*(1), Serial No. 159.

Krimer, L. S., & Goldman-Rakic, P. S. (2001). Prefrontal microcircuits. *Journal of Neuroscience, 21*, 3788–3796.

Kring, A. M. (2000). Gender and anger. In A. H. Fischer (Ed.), *Gender and emotion: Social psychological perspectives.* New York: Cambridge University Press.

Kroesbergen, E. H., van 't Noordende, J. E., & Kolkman, M. E. (2013, in press). Training working memory in kindergarten children: Effects on working memory and early numeracy. *Child Neuropsychology.*

Kroger, J., Martinussen, M., & Marcia, J. E. (2010). Identity change during adolescence and young adulthood: A meta-analysis. *Journal of Adolescence, 33*, 683–698.

Kronenberg, G., & others. (2010). Impact of actin filament stabilization on adult hippocampal and olfactory bulb neurogenesis. *Journal of Neuroscience, 30*, 3419–3431.

Kubarych, T. S., & others. (2012). A multivariate twin study of hippocampal volume, self-esteem, and well-being in middle-aged men. *Genes, Brain, and Behavior, 11,* 539–544.

Kuebli, J. (1994, March). Young children's understanding of everyday emotions. *Young Children,* pp. 36–48.

Kuehnle, K., & Connell, M. (2013). Child sexual abuse evaluations. In I. B. Weiner & others (Eds.), *Handbook of psychology* (2nd ed., Vol. 11). New York: Wiley.

Kuhl, P. K. (1993). Infant speech perception: A window on psycholinguistic development. *International Journal of Psycholinguistics, 9,* 33–56.

Kuhl, P. K. (2000). A new view of language acquisition. *Proceedings of the National Academy of Sciences, 97*(22), 11850–11857.

Kuhl, P. K. (2007). Is speech learning 'gated' by the social brain? *Developmental Science, 10,* 110–120.

Kuhl, P. K. (2009). Linking infant speech perception to language acquisition: Phonetic learning predicts language growth. In J. Colombo, P. McCardle, & L. Freund (Eds.), *Infant pathways to language.* New York: Psychology Press.

Kuhl, P. K. (2011). Social mechanisms in early language acquisition: Understanding integrated brain systems and supporting language. In J. Decety & J. Cacioppo (Eds.), *Handbook of social neuroscience.* New York: Oxford University Press.

Kuhl, P. K. (2012, May). Language learning and the developing brain: Cross-cultural studies unravel the effects of biology and culture. *Invited address at the meeting of the Acoustical Society of America, Hong Kong.*

Kuhl, P. K., & Damasio, A. (2012). Language. In E. R. Kandel & others (Eds.), *Principles of neural science* (5th ed.). New York: McGraw-Hill.

Kuhn, D. (1998). Afterword to Volume 2: Cognition, perception, and language. In W. Damon (Ed.), *Handbook of child psychology* (5th ed., Vol. 2). New York: Wiley.

Kuhn, D. (2008). Formal operations from a twenty-first century perspective. *Human Development, 51,* 48–55.

Kuhn, D. (2009). Adolescent thinking. In R. M. Lerner & L. Steinberg (Eds.), *Handbook of adolescent psychology* (3rd ed.). New York: Wiley.

Kuhn, D. (2011). What is scientific thinking and how does it develop? In U. Goswami (Ed.), *Wiley-Blackwell handbook of childhood cognitive development* (2nd ed.). New York: Wiley-Blackwell.

Kuhn, D. (2013). Reasoning. In P. D. Zelazo (Ed.), *Oxford handbook of developmental psychology.* New York: Oxford University Press.

Kuhn, D., & Franklin, S. (2006). The second decade: What develops (and how)? In W. Damon & R. Lerner (Eds.), *Handbook of child psychology* (6th ed.). New York: Wiley.

Kuhn, D., Schauble, L., & Garcia-Mila, M. (1992). Cross-domain development of scientific reasoning. *Cognition and Instruction, 9,* 285–327.

Kuo, L. J., & Anderson, R. C. (2012). Effects of early bilingualism on learning phonological regularities in a new language. *Journal of Experimental Child Psychology, 111,* 455–467.

Kupersmidt, J. B., & Coie, J. D. (1990). Preadolescent peer status, aggression, and school adjustment as predictors of externalizing problems in adolescence. *Child Development, 61,* 1350–1363.

Kwak, H. K., Kim, M., Cho, B. H., & Ham, Y. M. (1999, April). *The relationship between children's temperament, maternal control strategies, and children's compliance.* Paper presented at the meeting of the Society for Research in Child Development, Albuquerque.

L

La Rooy, D. J., Brown. D., & Lamb, M. E. (2013). Suggestibility and witness interviewing. In A. Ridley, F. Gabber, & D. J. La Rooy (Eds.), *Investigative suggestibility.* New York: Wiley.

Lacelle, C., Hebert, M., Lavoie, F., Vitaro, F., & Tremblay, R. E. (2012). Sexual health in women reporting a history of child sexual abuse. *Child Abuse and Neglect, 36,* 247–259.

Ladd, G., Buhs, E., & Troop, W. (2004). School adjustment and social skills training. In P. K. Smith & C. H. Hart (Eds.), *Blackwell handbook of childhood social development.* Malden, MA: Blackwell.

Ladd, G. W., Herald-Brown, S. L., & Reiser, M. (2008). Does chronic peer rejection predict the development of children's classroom participation during the grade school years? *Child Development, 79,* 1001–1015.

Ladd, G. W., Kochenderfer-Ladd, B., & Rydell, A-M. (2011). Children's interpersonal skills and school-based relationships. In P. K. Smith & C. H. Hart (Eds.), *Wiley-Blackwell handbook of social development* (2nd ed.). New York: Wiley.

LaFontana, K. M., & Cillessen, A. H. N. (2010). Developmental changes in the priority of perceived status in childhood and adolescence. *Social Development, 19,* 130–147.

LaFrance, M., Hecht, M. A., & Paluck, E. L. (2003). The contingent smile: A meta-analysis of sex differences in smiling. *Psychological Bulletin, 129,* 305–334.

Lahey, B. B., Van Hulle, C. A., D'Onofrio, B. M., Roders, J. L., & Waldman, I. D. (2008). Is parental knowledge of their offspring's whereabouts and peer associations spuriously associated with offspring delinquency? *Journal of Abnormal Child Psychology, 36,* 807–823.

Laible, D., & Thompson, R. A. (2007). Early socialization: A relationship perspective. In J. E. Grusec & P. D. Hastings (Eds.), *Handbook of socialization.* New York: Oxford University Press.

Laird, R. D., Criss, M. M., Pettit, G. S., Dodge, K. A., & Bates, J. E. (2008). Parents' monitoring knowledge attenuates the link between antisocial friends and adolescent delinquent behavior. *Journal of Abnormal Child Psychology, 36,* 299–310.

Laird, R. D., & Marrero, M. D. (2011). Mothers' knowledge of early adolescents' activities following the middle school transition and pubertal maturation. *Journal of Early Adolescence, 31,* 209–233.

Lamb, M. E. (1994). Infant care practices and the application of knowledge. In C. B. Fisher & R. M. Lerner (Eds.), *Applied developmental psychology.* New York: McGraw-Hill.

Lamb, M. E. (2005). Attachments, social networks, and developmental contexts. *Human Development, 43,* 108–112.

Lamb, M. E. (2013a). Commentary : Early experience, neurobiology, plasticity, vulnerability, and resilience. In D. Narvaez & others (Eds.), *Evolution, early experience, and human development.* New York: Oxford University Press.

Lamb, M. E. (2013b, in press). Non-parental care and emotional development. In S. Pauen & M. Bornstein (Eds.), *Early childhood development and later outcomes.* New York: Cambridge University Press.

Lamb, M. E., Bornstein, M. H., & Teti, D. M. (2002). *Development in infancy* (4th ed.). Mahwah, NJ: Erlbaum.

Lamb, M. E., & Lewis, C. (2013, in press). Father-child relationships. In C. S. Tamis-LeMonda & N. Cabrera (Eds.), *Handbook of father involvement* (2nd ed.). New York: Psychology Press.

Lamb, M. E., & Malloy, L. C. (2013, in press). Child development and the law. In I. B. Weiner & others (Eds.), *Handbook of psychology* (2nd ed., Vol. 6). New York: Wiley.

Lamb, M. E., & Sternberg, K. J. (1992). Sociocultural perspectives in nonparental childcare. In M. E. Lamb, K. J. Sternberg, C. Hwang, & A. G. Broberg (Eds.), *Child care in context.* Hillsdale, NJ: Erlbaum.

Lambert, N. M., Fincham, F. D., & Stillman, T. F. (2012). Gratitude and depressive symptoms: The role of positive reframing and positive emotion. *Cognition and Emotion, 26,* 615–633.

Lambertini, L., & others. (2012). Imprinted gene expression in fetal growth and development. *Placenta, 33,* 480–486.

Lampl, K. M., & others. (2012, in press). Risk of autism spectrum disorders in low birth weight and small for gestational age infants. *Journal of Pediatrics.*

Lampl, M. (2008). Physical growth. In M. M. Hath & J. B. Benson (Eds.), *Encyclopedia of infant and early childhood development.* Oxford, UK: Elsevier.

Lamy, C. (2012). Poverty is a knot, preschool is an untangler. In R. C. Pianta (Ed.), *Handbook of early childhood education.* New York: Guilford.

Landa, S. (2000, Fall). If you can't make waves, make ripples. *Intelligence Connections Newsletter of the ASCD, X*(1), 6–8.

Landau, B., Smith, L., & Jones, S. (1998). Object perception and object naming in early development. *Trends in Cognitive Science, 2,* 19–24.

Lane, H. (1976). *The wild boy of Aveyron.* Cambridge, MA: Harvard University Press.

Langer, E. J. (2005). *On becoming an artist.* New York: Ballantine.

Lansford, J. E. (2009). Parental divorce and children's adjustment. *Perspectives on Psychological Science, 4,* 140–152.

Lansford, J. E. (2012). Divorce. In R. J. R. Levesque (Ed.), *Encyclopedia of adolescence.* New York: Springer.

Lansford, J. E., & Deater-Deckard, K. (2012, in press). Childrearing discipline and violence in developing countries. *Child Development.*

Lansford, J. E., Wager, L. B., Bates, J. E., Pettit, G. S., & Dodge, K. A. (2013, in press). Forms of spanking and children's externalizing problems. *Family Relations.*

Lansford, J. E., & others. (2005). Cultural normativeness as a moderator of the link between physical discipline and children's adjustment: A comparison of China, India, Italy, Kenya, Philippines, and Thailand. *Child Development, 76,* 1234–1246.

Lansford, J. E., & others. (2011). Reciprocal relations between parents' physical discipline and children's externalizing behavior during middle childhood and adolescence. *Development and Psychopathology, 23,* 225–238.

Laopaiboon, M., & others. (2009). Music during caesarean section under regional anaesthesia for improving maternal and infant outcomes. *Cochrane Database of Systematic Reviews,* CD006914.

Lapsley, D. K. (2013). Moral stage theory. In M. Killen & J. Smetana (Eds.), *Handbook of moral development* (2nd ed.). New York: Routledge.

Lapsley, D. K., & Hill, P. L. (2010). Subjective invulnerability, optimism bias, and adjustment in emerging adulthood. *Journal of Youth and Adolescence, 39,* 847–857.

Lapsley, D. K., & Stey, P. (2012). Adolescent narcissism. In R. Levesque (Ed.), *Encyclopedia of adolescence.* New York: Springer.

Lapsley, D. K., & Yeager, D. (2013, in press). Moral-character education. In I. B. Weiner & others (Eds.), *Handbook of psychology* (2nd ed., Vol. 7). New York: Wiley.

Larson, R. W. (1999, September). Unpublished review of J. W. Santrock's *Adolescence,* 8th ed. (New York: McGraw-Hill).

Larson, R. W., Wilson, Z., & Rickman, A. (2009). Globalization, societal change, and adolescence across the world. In R. M. Lerner & L. Steinberg (Eds.), *Handbook of adolescent psychology* (3rd ed.). New York: Wiley.

Larzelere, R. E., & Kuhn, B. R. (2005). Comparing child outcomes of physical punishment and alternative disciplinary tactics: A meta-analysis. *Clinical Child and Family Psychology Review, 8,* 1–37.

Laslett, A. M., Room, R., Dietze, P., & Ferris, J. (2012, in press). Alcohol's involvement in recurrent child abuse and neglect cases. *Addiction.*

Laubjerg, M., & Petersson, B. (2011). Juvenile delinquency and psychiatric contact among adoptees compared to non-adoptees in Denmark: A nationwide register-based comparative study. *Nordic Journal of Psychiatry, 65,* 365–372.

Lauer, R. H., & Lauer, J. C. (2012). *Marriage and family* (8th ed.). New York: McGraw-Hill.

Laursen, B., & Collins, W. A. (2009). Parent-child relationships during adolescence. In R. M. Lerner & L. Steinberg (Eds.), *Handbook of adolescent psychology* (3rd ed.). New York: Wiley.

Lawrence, J. M., Contreras, R., Chen, W., & Sacks, D. A. (2008). Trends in the prevalence of preexisting diabetes and gestational diabetes mellitus among a racially/ethnically diverse population of pregnant women, 1999–2005. *Diabetes Care, 31,* 899–904.

Leach, P. (1990). *Your baby and child: From birth to age five.* New York: Knopf.

Leaper, C. (2013). Gender development during childhood. In P. D. Zelazo (Ed.), *Oxford handbook of developmental psychology.* New York: Oxford University Press.

Leaper, C., & Bigler, R. S. (2004). Commentary. Gender language and sexist thought. *Monographs of the Society for Research in Child Development, 69*(1, Serial No. 275), 128–142.

Leaper, C., & Bigler, R. S. (2011). Gender. In M. K. Underwood & L. S. Rosen (Eds.), *Social development.* New York: Guilford.

Leaper, C., & Friedman, C. K. (2007). The socialization of gender. In J. E. Grusec & P. D. Hastings (Eds.), *Handbook of socialization.* New York: Guilford.

Ledesma, K. (2012). A place to call home. *Adoptive Families.* Retrieved January 19, 2013, from www.adoptivefamilies.com/articles.php?aid-2129

Lee, E., & others. (2009). Reducing low birth weight through home visitation: A randomized controlled trial. *American Journal of Preventive Medicine, 36,* 154–160.

Lee, H. C., El-Sayed, Y. Y., & Gould, J. B. (2008). Population trends in cesarean delivery for breech presentation in the United States, 1997–2003. *American Journal of Obstetrics and Gynecology, 199,* e1–e8.

Lee, K., Cameron, C. A., Doucette, J., & Talwar, V. (2002). Phantoms and fabrications: Young children's detection of implausible lies. *Child Development, 73,* 1688–1702.

Lee, K., Quinn, P. C., Pascalis, O., & Slater, A. (2013). Development of face processing ability in childhood. In P. D. Zelazo (Ed.), *Oxford handbook of developmental psychology.* Oxford, UK: Oxford University Press.

Lee, K. Y., & others. (2011). Effects of combined radiofrequency radiation exposure on the cell cycle and its regulatory proteins. *Bioelectromagnetics, 32,* 169–178.

Lee, T-W, Wu, Y-T., Yu, Y., Wu, H-C., & Chen, T-J. (2012). A smarter brain is associated with stronger neural interaction in healthy young females: A resting EEG coherence study. *Intelligence, 40,* 38–48.

Lee, Y. S., Turkeltaub, P., Granger, R., & Raizada, R. D. (2012). Categorical speech processing in Broca's area: An fMRI study using multivariate pattern-based analysis. *Journal of Neuroscience, 32,* 3942–3948.

Leedy, P. D., & Ormrod, J. E. (2013). *Practical research* (10th ed.). Upper Saddle River, NJ: Pearson.

Leerkes, E. M. (2011). Maternal sensitivity during distressing tasks: A unique predictor of attachment security. *Infant Behavior and Development, 34,* 443–446.

Leerkes, E. M., Parade, S. H., & Gudmundson, J. A. (2011). Mothers' emotional reactions to crying pose risk for subsequent attachment insecurity. *Journal of Family Psychology, 25,* 635–643.

Leger, D., Beck, F., Richard, J. B., & Godeau, E. (2012). Total sleep time severely drops in adolescence. *PLoS One, 7*(10), e45204.

Legerstee, M. (1997). Contingency effects of people and objects on subsequent cognitive functioning in 3-month-old infants. *Social Development, 6,* 307–321.

Lehr, C. A., Hanson, A., Sinclair, M. F., & Christensen, S. I. (2003). Moving beyond dropout prevention towards school completion. *School Psychology Review, 32,* 342–364.

Lehrer, R., & Schauble, L. (2006). Scientific thinking and scientific literacy. In W. Damon & R. Lerner (Eds.), *Handbook of child psychology* (6th ed.). New York: Wiley.

Lemaire, P., & Lecacheur, M. (2011). Age-related changes in children's executive functions and strategy selection: A study in computational estimation. *Cognitive Development, 26,* 282–294.

Leman, P. J., Ahmed, S., & Ozarow, L. (2005). Gender, gender relations, and the social dynamics of children's conversations. *Developmental Psychology, 41,* 64–74.

LeMare, L. J., & Rubin, K. H. (1987). Perspective taking and peer interaction: Structural and developmental analyses. *Child Development, 58,* 306–315.

Lempers, J. D., Flavell, E. R., & Flavell, J. H. (1977). The development in very young children of tacit knowledge concerning visual perception. *Genetic Psychology Monographs, 95,* 3–53.

Lemstra, M. E., Nielsen, G., Rogers, M. R., Thompson, A. T., & Moraros, J. S. (2012). Risk indicators and outcomes associated with bullying in youth aged 9–15 years. *Canadian Journal of Public Health, 103,* 9–13.

Lenhart, A., Purcel, K., Smith, A., & Zickuhr, K. (2010, Feb. 3). *Social media and mobile Internet use among teens and young adults.* Washington, DC: Pew Research Center.

Lenneberg, E. (1967). *The biological foundation of language.* New York: Wiley.

Lennon, E. M., Gardner, J. M., Karmel, B. Z., & Flory, M. J. (2008). Bayley Scales of Infant Development. In M. M. Haith & J. B. Benson (Eds.), *Encyclopedia of infant and early childhood development.* Oxford, UK: Elsevier.

Lenoir, C. P., Mallet, E., & Calenda, E. (2000). Siblings of sudden infant death syndrome and near miss in about 30 families: Is there a genetic link? *Medical Hypotheses, 54,* 408–411.

Lenroot, R. K., & Giedd, J. N. (2011). Annual research review: Developmental considerations of gene by environment interactions. *Journal of Child and Adolescent Psychiatry, 52,* 429–441.

Leonardi-Bee, J. A., Smyth, A. R., Britton, J., & Coleman. T. (2008). Environmental tobacco smoke and fetal health: Systematic review and analysis. *Archives of Disease in Childhood. Fetal and Neonatal Edition, 93,* F351–F361.

Leong, F. T. L., & others. (2013). Ethnic minority psychology. In I. B. Weiner & others (Eds.), *Handbook of psychology* (2nd ed., Vol. 1). New York: Wiley.

Leppanen, J. M., Moulson, M., Vogel-Farley, V. K., & Nelson, C. A. (2007). An ERP study of emotional face processing in the adult and infant brain. *Child Development, 78,* 232–245.

Lepper, M. R., Corpus, J. H., & Iyengar, S. S. (2005). Intrinsic and extrinsic orientations in the classroom: Age differences and academic correlates. *Journal of Educational Psychology, 97,* 184–196.

Lerch, C., Cordes, M., & Baumeister, J. (2011). Effectiveness of prevention programs in female youth soccer: A systematic review. *British Journal of Sports Medicine, 45,* 359.

Lerner, J. V., & others. (2013, in press). Positive youth development: Processes, philosophies, and programs. In I. B. Weiner & others (Eds.), *Handbook of psychology* (2nd ed., Vol. 6). New York: Wiley.

Lerner, J. W., & Johns, B. (2012). *Learning disabilities and related mild disabilities* (12th ed.). Boston: Cengage.

Lerner, R. M., Boyd, M., & Du, D. (2009). Adolescent development. In I. B. Weiner & C. B. Craighead (Eds.), *Encyclopedia of psychology* (4th ed.). Hoboken, NJ: Wiley.

Lerner, R. M., Roeser, R. W., & Phelps, E. (Eds.). (2009). *Positive youth development and spirituality: From theory to research.* West Conshohocken, PA: Templeton Foundation Press.

Lesaux, N. K., & Siegel, L. S. (2003). The development of reading in children who speak English as a second language. *Developmental Psychology, 39,* 1005–1019.

Lessow-Hurley, J. (2013). *Foundations of dual language instruction* (6th ed.). Upper Saddle River, NJ: Pearson.

Lester, B. M., Tronick, E. Z., & Brazelton, T. B. (2004). The Neonatal Intensive Care Unit Network Neurobehavioral Scale procedures. *Pediatrics, 113*(Suppl.), S641–S667.

Lester, B. M., & others. (2002). The maternal lifestyle study: Effects of substance exposure during pregnancy on neurodevelopmental outcome in 1-month-old infants. *Pediatrics, 110,* 1182–1192.

Lester, B. M., & others. (2011). Infant neuro-behavioral development. *Seminars in Perinatology, 35,* 8–19.

Letourneau, N., & others. (2012). Support intervention needs and preferences for fathers affected by postpartum depression. *Journal of Perinatal and Neonatal Nursing, 26,* 69–80.

LeVay, S. (1994). *The sexual brain.* Cambridge, MA: MIT Press.

Levine, M., & O'Connor, A. D. (2012). Obstetric toxicology: An overview. *Emergency Medicine Clinics of North America, 30,* 977–990.

Levine, T. P., & others. (2008). Effects of prenatal cocaine exposure on special education in school-aged children. *Pediatrics, 122,* e83–e91.

Levinson, P. (2013). *New media* (2nd ed.). Upper Saddle River, NJ: Pearson.

Levy, G. D., Sadovsky, A. L., & Troseth, G. L. (2000). Aspects of young children's perceptions of gender-typed occupations. *Sex Roles, 42,* 993–1006.

Levy, Y., & Eilam, A. (2013). Pathways to language: A naturalistic study of children with Williams syndrome and children with Down syndrome. *Journal of Child Language, 40,* 106–138.

Lewald, J. (2012). Exceptional ability of blind humans to hear sound motion: Implications for the emergence of auditory space. *Neuropsychologia, 51,* 181–186.

Lewis, A. C. (2007). Looking beyond NCLB. *Phi Delta Kappan, 88,* 483–484.

Lewis, C., & Carpendale, J. (2011). Social cognition. In P. K. Smith & C. H. Hart (Eds.), *Wiley-Blackwell handbook of childhood social development* (2nd ed.). New York: Wiley.

Lewis, C., Hill, M., Skirton, H., & Chitty, L. S. (2012, in press). Non-invasive prenatal diagnosis for fetal sex determination: Benefits and disadvantages from the service users' perspective. *European Journal of Genetics.*

Lewis, M. (2008). The emergence of human emotions. In M. Lewis, J. M. Haviland Jones, & L. Feldman Barrett (Eds.), *Handbook of emotions* (3rd ed.). New York: Guilford.

Lewis, M. (2010). The emergence of consciousness and its role in human development. In W. F. Overton & R. M. Lerner (Eds.), *Handbook of life-span development.* New York: Wiley.

Lewis, M. D., Todd, R., & Xu, X. (2011). The development of emotion regulation: A neuro-psychological perspective. In R. M. Lerner, W. F. Overton, A. M. Freund, & M. E. Lamb (Eds.), *Handbook of life-span development.* New York: Wiley.

Lewis, M., & Brooks-Gunn, J. (1979). *Social cognition and the acquisition of the self.* New York: Plenum.

Lewis, M., Feiring, C., & Rosenthal, S. (2000). Attachment over time. *Child Development, 71,* 707–720.

Lewis, M., Sullivan, M. W., Sanger, C., & Weiss, M. (1989). Self-development and self-conscious emotions. *Child Development, 60,* 146–156.

Lewis, R. (2012). *Human genetics* (10th ed.). New York: McGraw-Hill.

Lewis, T. L., & Maurer, D. (2005). Multiple sensitive periods in human visual development: Evidence from visually deprived children. *Developmental Psychobiology, 46,* 163–183.

Lewis, T. L., & Maurer, D. (2009). Effects of early pattern deprivation on visual development. *Optometry and Vision Science, 86,* 640–646.

Lhila, A., & Long, S. (2011). What is driving the black-white difference in low birthweight in the U.S.? *Health Economics, 21,* 301–315.

Li, B. J., Jiang, Y. J., Yuan, F., & Ye, H. X. (2010). Exchange transfusion of least incompatible blood for severe hemolytic disease of the newborn due to anti-Rh17. *Transfusion Medicine, 20,* 66–69.

Li, C., Goran, M. I., Kaur, H., Nollen, N., & Ahluwalia, J. S. (2007). Developmental trajectories of overweight during childhood: Role of early life factors. *Obesity, 15,* 760–761.

Li, D., Zhang, W., Li, X., Li, N., & Ye, B. (2012). Gratitude and suicidal ideation and suicide attempts among Chinese adolescents: Direct, mediated, and moderated effects. *Journal of Adolescence, 35,* 55–66.

Li, J., Olsen, J., Vestergaard, M., & Obel, C. (2011). Low Apgar scores and risk of childhood attention deficit hyperactivity disorder. *Journal of Pediatrics, 158,* 775–779.

Li, W., Farkas, G., Duncan, G. J., Burchinal, M. R., & Vandell, D. L. (2013, in press). Timing of high-quality child care and cognitive, language, and preacademic development. *Developmental Psychology.*

Liang, Y. J., Xi, B., Song, A. Q., Liu, J. X., & Mi, J. (2012). Trends in general and abdominal obesity among Chinese children and adolescents, 1993–2009. *Pediatric Obesity, 7,* 355–364.

Liben, L. S. (1995). Psychology meets geography: Exploring the gender gap on the National Geography Bee. *Psychological Science Agenda, 8,* 8–9.

Libertus, K., & Needham, A. (2011). Teach to reach: The effects of active versus passive reaching experiences on action and perception. *Vision Research, 50,* 2750–2757.

Lickliter, R. (2013). Biological development: Theoretical approaches, techniques, and key findings. In P. D. Zelazo (Ed.), *Handbook of developmental psychology.* New York: Oxford University Press.

Lie, E., & Newcombe, N. (1999). Elementary school children's explicit and implicit memory for faces of preschool classmates. *Developmental Psychology, 35,* 102–112.

Liegeois, F., Connelly, A., Baldeweg, T., & Vargha-Khadem, F. (2008). Speaking with a single cerebral hemisphere: IMRI language organization after hemispherectomy in childhood. *Brain and Language, 106,* 195–203.

Liew, J. (2012). Effortful control, executive functions, and education: Bringing self-regulatory and social-emotional competencies to the table. *Child Development Perspectives, 6,* 105–111.

Likis, F. E., & others. (2012). Progestogens for preterm birth prevention: A systematic review and meta-analysis. *Obestetrics and Gynecology, 120,* 897–907.

Lillard, A. (2007). Pretend play in toddlers. In C. A. Brownell & C. B. Kopp (Eds.), *Socioemotional development in the toddler years.* New York: Guilford.

Lillard, A. (2008). How important are Montessori materials? *Montessori Life, 20*(4), 20–25.

Lillard, A., Pinkham, A. M., & Smith, E. (2011). Pretend play and cognitive development. In U. Goswami (Ed.), *Wiley-Blackwell handbook of childhood cognitive development* (2nd ed.). New York: Wiley.

Limber, S. P. (2004). Implementation of the Olweus Bullying Prevention program in American schools: Lessons learned from the field. In D. L. Espelage & S. M. Swearer (Eds.), *Bullying in American schools.* Mahwah, NJ: Erlbaum.

Lin, M., Johnson, J. E., & Johnson, K. M. (2003). *Dramatic play in Montessori kindergartens in Taiwan and Mainland China.* Unpublished manuscript. Department of Curriculum and Instruction, Pennsylvania State University, University Park, PA.

Lincoln, A. J., Searcy, Y. M., Jones, W., & Lord, C. (2007). Social interaction behaviors discriminate young children with autism and Williams syndrome. *Journal of the American Academy of Child and Adolescent Psychiatry, 46,* 323–331.

Lindberg, S. M., Hyde, S. S., Petersen, J. L., & Lin, M. C. (2010). New trends in gender and mathematics performance: A meta-analysis. *Psychological Bulletin, 136,* 1123–1135.

Lindblad, F., & Hjern, A. (2010). ADHD after fetal exposure to maternal smoking. *Nicotine and Tobacco Research, 12,* 408–415.

Lippa, R. A. (2005). *Gender, nature, and nurture* (2nd ed.). Mahwah, NJ: Erlbaum.

Lippman, L. A., & Keith, J. D. (2006). The demographics of spirituality among youth: International perspectives. In E. Roehlkepartain, P. E. King, L. Wagener, & P. L. Benson (Eds.), *The handbook of spirituality in childhood and adolescence.* Thousand Oaks, CA: Sage.

Lipton, J., & Spelke, E. (2004). Discrimination of large and small numerosities by human infants. *Infancy, 5,* 271–290.

Liszkowski, U. (2007, March). *A new look at infant pointing.* Paper presented at the meeting of the Society for Research in Child Development, Boston.

Liu, J., & others. (2010). Neonatal neurobehavior predicts medical and behavioral outcome. *Pediatrics, 125*(1), e90–e98.

Liu, S., & others. (2011). Similarity and difference in the processing of same- and other-race faces as revealed by eye-tracking in 4- to 9-month-old infants. *Journal of Experimental Child Psychology, 108,* 180–189.

Liu, T., Shi, I., Zhang, Q., Zhao, D., & Yang, J. (2007). Neural mechanisms of auditory sensory processing in children with high intelligence. *Neuroreport, 18*(15), 1571–1575.

Liu, W. M., & Hernandez, J. (2008). Social class and classism. In N. J. Salkind (Eds.), *Encyclopedia of educational psychology.* Thousand Oaks, CA: Sage.

Liu, Y. H., Chang, M. Y., & Chen, C. H. (2010). Effects of music therapy on labor pain and anxiety in Taiwanese first-time mothers. *Journal of Clinical Nursing, 19,* 1065–1072.

Livas-Dlott, A., & others. (2010). Commands, competence, and *Carino:* Maternal socialization processes in Mexican American families. *Developmental Psychology, 46,* 566–578.

Livesley, W., & Bromley, D. (1973). *Person perception in childhood and adolescence.* New York: Wiley.

Loeber, R., Burke, J., & Pardini, D. (2009). The etiology and development of antisocial and delinquent behavior. *Annual Review of Psychology* (Vol. 60). Palo Alto, CA: Annual Reviews.

Loeber, R., Farrington, D. P., Stouthamer-Loeber, M., & White, H. R. (2008). *Violence and serious theft: Development and predictions from childhood to adulthood.* New York: Routledge.

Loeber, R., Pardini, D. A., Stouthamer-Loeber, M., & Raine, A. (2007). Do cognitive, physiological, and psychosocial risk and promotive factors predict desistance from delinquency in males? *Development and Psychopathology, 19,* 867–887.

Logsdon, M. C., Wisner, K., & Hanusa, B. H. (2009). Does maternal role functioning improve with antidepressant treatment in women with postpartum depression? *Journal of Women's Health, 18,* 85–90.

Lomas, J., Stough, C., Hansen, K., & Downey, L. A. (2012). Emotional intelligence, victimization, and bullying in adolescents. *Journal of Adolescence, 35,* 207–211.

London, M. L., & others. (2011). *Maternal and child nursing care* (3rd ed.). Upper Saddle River, NJ: Pearson.

Loosli, S. V., Buschkuehl, M., Perrig, W. J., & Jaeggi, S. M. (2012). Working memory training improves reading processes in typically developing children. *Child Neuropsychology, 18,* 62–78.

Loprinzi, P. D., Cardinal, B. J., Loprinzi, K. L., & Lee, H. (2012). Parenting practices as mediators of child physical activity and weight status. *Obesity Facts, 5,* 420–430.

Lorenz, K. Z. (1965). *Evolution and the modification of behavior.* Chicago: University of Chicago Press.

Loukas, A., Roalson, L. A., & Herrera, D. E. (2010). School connectedness buffers the effects of negative family relations and poor effortful control on early adolescent conduct problems. *Journal of Research on Adolescence, 20,* 13–22.

Lovett, M. R., Barron, R. W., & Frijters, J. C. (2013). Word identification difficulties in children and adolescents with learning disabilities: Intervention research findings. In H. L. Swanson & others (Eds.), *Handbook of learning disabilities* (2nd ed.). New York: Guilford.

Low, J., & Simpson, S. (2012). Effects of labeling on preschoolers' explicit false belief performance: Outcomes of cognitive flexibility or inhibitory control? *Child Development, 83,* 1072–1084.

Low, S., Snyder, J., & Shortt, J. W. (2012). The drift toward problem behavior during the transition to adolescence: The contributions of youth disclosure, parenting, and older siblings. *Journal of Research on Adolescence, 22,* 65–79.

Lowe, J. R., & others. (2012). Association of maternal interaction with emotional regulation in 4- and 9-month-old infants during the Still Face Paradigm. *Infant Behavior and Development, 35,* 295–302.

Lubinski, D. (2000). Measures of intelligence: Intelligence tests. In A. Kazdin (Ed.), *Encyclopedia of psychology.* Washington, DC, & New York: American Psychological Association and Oxford University Press.

Lucas, P. J., McIntosh, K., Petticrew, M., Roberts, H., & Shiell, A. (2008). Financial benefits for child health and well-being in low income or socially disadvantaged families in developed world countries. *Cochrane Database of Systematic Reviews, 16.* CD006358.

Luders, E., & others. (2004). Gender differences in cortical complexity. *Nature Neuroscience, 7,* 799–800.

Luders, E., Narr, K. L., Thompson, P. M., & Toga, A. W. (2009). Neuroanatomical correlates of intelligence. *Intelligence, 37,* 156–163.

Luijk, M. P., & others. (2011). Dopaminergic, serotonergic, and oxytonegic candidate genes associated with infant attachment security and disorganization? In search of main and interaction effects. *Journal of Child Psychology and Psychiatry, 52,* 1295–1307.

Luisis, A. J. (2012). Genetics of atherosclerosis. *Trends in Genetics, 28,* 267–275.

Lumeng, J. C., & others. (2012). Observed assertive and intrusive maternal feeding behaviors increase child adiposity. *American Journal of Clinical Nutrition, 95,* 640–647.

Lund, T. J., & Dearing, E. (2013). Is growing up affluent risky for adolescents or is the problem growing up in an affluent neighborhood? *Journal of Research on Adolescence.*

Lunkenheimer, E. S., Shields, A. M., & Cortina, K. S. (2007). Parental coaching and dismissing of children's emotions in family interaction. *Social Development, 16,* 232–248.

Luo, Y., & Baillargeon, R. (2010). Toward a mentalistic account of early psychological reasoning. *Current Directions in Psychological Science, 19,* 301–307.

Luria, A., & Herzog, E. (1985, April). *Gender segregation across and within settings.* Paper presented at the biennial meeting of the Society for Research in Child Development, Toronto.

Luszcz, M. (2013). Executive functioning and cognitive aging. In K. W. Schaie & S. L. Willis (Eds.), *Handbook of the psychology of aging* (8th ed.). New York: Elsevier.

Luthar, S. S. (2006). Resilience in development: A synthesis of research across five decades. In D. Cicchetti & D. J. Cohen (Eds.), *Developmental psychopathology: Vol. 3. Risk, disorder, and adaptation* (2nd ed.). Hoboken, NJ: Wiley.

Luthar. S. S., & Goldstein. A. S. (2008). Substance use and related behaviors among suburban late adolescents: The importance of perceived parent containment. *Development and Psychopathology, 20,* 591–614.

Lyberg, A., Viken, B., Haruna, M., & Severinsson, E. (2012). Diversity and challenges in the management of maternity care for immigrant women. *Journal of Nursing Management, 20,* 287–295.

Lykken, D. (2001). *Happiness: What studies on twins show us about nature, nurture, and the happiness set point.* New York: Golden Books.

Lynn, R. (2009). What caused the Flynn effect? Secular increases in the development quotients of infants. *Intelligence, 37,* 16–24.

Lynn, R. (2012). IQs predict differences in the technological development of nations from 1000 BC through 2000 AD. *Intelligence, 40,* 439–444.

Lyon, G. J., & Wang, K. (2013, in press). Identifying disease mutations in genomic medicine settings: Current challenges and how to accelerate the process. *Genome Medicine.*

Lyon, T. D., & Flavell, J. H. (1993). Young children's understanding of forgetting over time. *Child Development, 64,* 789–800.

Lytle, L. A. (2012). Dealing with the childhood obesity epidemic: A public health approach. *Abdominal Imaging, 37,* 719–724.

M

MacArthur, C. A. (2012). Strategies instruction. In K. R. Harris, S. Graham, & T. Urdan (Eds.), *Handbook of educational psychology.* Washington, DC: American Psychological Association.

Maccoby, E. E. (1984). Middle childhood in the context of the family. In W. A. Collins (Ed.), *Development during middle childhood.* Washington, DC: National Academy Press.

Maccoby, E. E. (1996). Peer conflict and intra-family conflict: Are there conceptual bridges? *Merrill-Palmer Quarterly, 42,* 165–176.

Maccoby, E. E. (2002). Gender and group process: A developmental perspective. *Current Directions in Psychological Science, 11,* 54–57.

Maccoby, E. E. (2007). Historical overview of socialization research and theory. In J. E. Grusec & P. D. Hastings (Eds.), *Handbook of socialization.* New York: Guilford.

Maccoby, E. E., & Martin, J. A. (1983). Socialization in the context of the family: Parent-child interaction. In P. H. Mussen (Ed.), *Handbook of child psychology* (4th ed., Vol. 4). New York: Wiley.

Maccoby, E. E., & Mnookin, R. H. (1992). *Dividing the child: Social and legal dilemmas of custody.* Cambridge, MA: Harvard University Press.

Macdorman, M. F., Declercq, E., & Menacker, F. (2011). Trends and characteristics of home births in the United States by race and ethnicity, 1990–2006. *Birth, 38,* 17–23.

MacFarlane, J. A. (1975). Olfaction in the development of social preferences in the human neonate. In *Parent-infant interaction.* Ciba Foundation Symposium No. 33. Amsterdam: Elsevier.

MacGeorge, E. L. (2004). The myth of gender cultures: Similarities outweigh differences in men's and women's provisions of and responses to supportive communication. *Sex Roles, 50,* 143–175.

MacIntosh, N. J. (2011). History of theories and measurement of intelligence. In R. J. Sternberg & S. B. Kaufman (Eds.), *Cambridge handbook of intelligence.* New York: Cambridge University Press.

Mader, S. S. (2012). *Connect biology* (3rd ed.). New York: McGraw-Hill.

Mader, S. S. (2014). Inquiry into life (14th ed.). New York: McGraw-Hill.

Mader, S. S., & Windelspecht, M. (2013). *Biology* (11th ed.). New York: McGraw-Hill.

Madsen, S. D., & Collins, W. A. (2011). The salience of romantic experiences for romantic relationship qualities in young adulthood. *Journal of Research on Adolescence, 21*(4), 789–801.

Maeda, K. (1999). *The Self-Perception Profile for children administered to a Japanese sample.* Unpublished data, Ibaraki Prefectural University of Health Sciences, Ibaraki, Japan.

Maehr, M. L., & Zusho, A. (2009). Goal-directed behavior in the classroom. In K. Wentzel & A. Wigfield (Eds.), *Handbook of motivation at school.* New York: Routledge.

Magno, C. (2010). The role of metacognitive skills in developing critical thinking. *Metacognition and Learning, 5,* 137–156.

Mahn, H., & John-Steiner, V. (2013). Vygotsky and sociocultural approaches to teaching and learning. In I. B. Weiner & others (Eds.), *Handbook of psychology* (2nd ed., Vol. 7). New York: Wiley.

Mai, X., & others. (2012). Auditory recognition memory in 2-month-old infants as assessed by event-related potentials. *Developmental Neuropsychology, 37,* 400–414.

Major Depressive Disorder Working Group of the Psychiatric GWAS Consortium. (2013, in press). A mega-analysis of genome-wide association studies for major depressive disorder. *Molecular Psychiatry.*

Mak, K. K., Lee, S. L., Ho, S. Y., Lo, W. S., & Lam, T. H. (2012). Sleep and academic performance in Hong Kong adolescents. *Journal of School Health, 82,* 522–527.

Malamitsi-Puchner, A., & Boutsikou, T. (2006). Adolescent pregnancy and perinatal outcome. *Pediatric Endocrinology Reviews, 3*(Suppl. 1), 170–171.

Malatesta-Muncher, R., & Mitsnefes, M. M. (2012). Management of blood pressure in children. *Current Opinion in Nephrology and Hypertension, 21,* 318–322.

Malik, N. M., & Furman, W. (1993). Practitioner review: Problems in children's peer relations: What can the clinician do? *Journal of Child Psychology and Psychiatry, 34,* 1303–1326.

Malizia, B. A., Hacker, M. R., & Penzias, A. S. (2009). Cumulative live-birth rates after in vitro fertilization. *New England Journal of Medicine, 360,* 236–243.

Malloy, L. C., La Rooy, D. J., Lamb, M. A., & Katz, C. (2012). Developmentally sensitive interviewing for legal purposes. In M. E. Lamb, D. J. La Rooy, L. C. Malloy, & C. Katz (Eds.), *Children's testimony* (2nd ed.). New York: Wiley.

Maloy, R. W., & others. (2014, in press). *Transforming learning with new technologies* (2nd ed.). Upper Saddle River, NJ: Pearson.

Malti, T., & Buchmann, M. (2010). Socialization and individual antecedents of adolescents' and young adults' moral motivation. *Journal of Youth and Adolescence, 39,* 138–149.

Mandara, J. (2006). The impact of family functioning on African American males' academic achievement: A review and clarification of the empirical literature. *Teachers College Record, 108,* 206–233.

Mandelman, S. D., & Grigorenko, E. L. (2011). Intelligence: Genes, environment, and their interaction. In R. J. Sternberg & S. B. Kaufman (Eds.), *Handbook of intelligence.* New York: Cambridge University Press.

Mandler, J. (2000). Unpublished review of J. W. Santrock's *Life-span development,* 8th ed. (New York: McGraw-Hill).

Mandler, J. M. (2004). *The foundations of mind.* New York: Oxford University Press.

Mandler, J. M. (2009). Conceptual categorization. In D. H. Rakison & L. M. Oakes (Eds.), *Early category and concept development.* New York: Oxford University Press.

Mandler, J. M. (2010). Jean Mandler. Retrieved May 26, 2010, from http://www.cogsci.ucsd.edu/~jean/

Mandler, J. M., & DeLoache, J. (2013, in press). The beginnings of conceptual development. In S. Pauen & M. Bornstein (Eds.), *Early child development and later outcome.* New York: Cambridge University Press.

Mandler, J. M., & McDonough, L. (1993). Concept formation in infancy. *Cognitive Development, 8,* 291–318.

Mangione, R., & others. (2011). Neurodevelopmental outcome following prenatal diagnosis of an isolated anomaly of the corpus callosum. *Ultrasound in Obstetrics and Gynecology, 37,* 290–295.

Manning, M. L., & Baruth, L. G. (2009). *Multicultural education of children and adolescents* (5th ed.). Boston: Allyn & Bacon.

Marcia, J. E. (1980). Ego identity development. In J. Adelson (Ed.), *Handbook of adolescent psychology.* New York: Wiley.

Marcia, J. E. (1987). The identity status approach to the study of ego identity development. In T. Honess & K. Yardley (Eds.), *Self and identity: Perspectives across the lifespan.* London: Routledge & Kegan Paul.

Marcia, J. E. (1994). The empirical study of ego identity. In H. A. Bosma, T. L. G. Graafsma, H. D. Grotevant, & D. J. DeLevita (Eds.), *Identity and development.* Newbury Park, CA: Sage.

Marcia, J. E. (1996). Unpublished review of J. W. Santrock's *Adolescence,* 7th ed. (Dubuque, IA: Brown & Benchmark).

Marcia, J. E. (2002). Identity and psychosocial development in adulthood. *Identity, 2,* 7–28.

Marengo, L., Farag, N. H., & Canfield, M. (2013, in press). Body mass index and birth defects: Texas, 2005–2008. *Maternal and Child Health Journal.*

Marie, C., & Trainor, L. J. (2012, in press). Development of simultaneous pitch encoding: Infants show a high voice superiority effect. *Cerebral Cortex.*

Markant, J. C., & Thomas, K. M. (2013). Postnatal brain development. In P. D. Zelazo (Ed.), *Handbook of developmental psychology.* New York: Wiley.

Marks, A. K., Patton, F., & Garcia Coll, C. (2011). Being bicultural: A mixed-methods study of adolescents' implicitly and explicitly measured ethnic identities. *Developmental Psychology, 47,* 270–288.

Markus, H. R., & Kitayama, S. (2010). Cultures and selves: A cycle of multiple constitution. *Perspectives on Psychological Science, 5,* 420–430.

Markus, H. R., & Kitayama, S. (2012). Culture and the self. In K. Vohs & R. F. Baumeister (Eds.), *Self and identity.* Thousand Oaks, CA: Sage.

Marshall, C., & others. (2013, in press). WIC participation and breastfeeding among White and Black mothers: Data from Mississippi. *Maternal and Child Health Journal.*

Martin, A., Razza, R., & Brooks-Gunn, J. (2012). Sustained attention at age 5 predicts attention-related problems at age 9. *International Journal of Behavioral Development, 36,* 413–419.

Martin, C. L., & Fabes, R. A. (2001). The stability and consequences of young children's same-sex peer interactions. *Development Psychology, 37,* 431–446.

Martin, C. L., & Ruble, D. N. (2010). Patterns of gender development. *Annual Review of Psychology* (Vol. 61). Palo Alto, CA: Annual Reviews.

Martin, C. L., Ruble, D. N., & Szkrybalo, J. (2002). Cognitive theories of early gender development. *Psychological Bulletin, 128,* 903–933.

Martin, C. L., & others. (2013, in press). The role of sex of peers and gender-typed activities in young children's peer affiliative networks: A longitudinal analysis of selection and influence. *Child Development.*

Martin, J. A., Hamilton, B. E., Menacker, F., Sutton, P. D., & Matthews, T. J. (2005, November 15). Preliminary births for 2004: Infant and maternal health. *Health E-Stats.* Atlanta: National Center for Health Statistics.

Martin, M. J., & others. (2011). The enduring significance of racism: Discrimination, and delinquency among Black American youth. *Journal of Research on Adolescence, 21*(3), 662–676.

Martinez, G., Daniels, K., & Chandra, A. (2012, April). Fertility of men and women aged 15–44 years in the United States: National Survey of Family Growth, 2006–2010. *National Health Statistics Report, 51,* 1–26.

Masarik, A. S., & others. (2013, in press). Romantic relationships in early adulthood: Influences of family, personality, and relationship cognitions. *Personal Relationships.*

Mascolo, M. F., & Fischer, K. (2007). The co-development of self and socio-moral emotions during the toddler years. In C. A. Brownell & C. B. Kopp (Eds.), *Transitions in early development,* New York: Guilford.

Mash, E. J., & Wolfe, D. A. (2007). *Abnormal child psychology* (3rd ed.). Belmont, CA: Wadsworth.

Mash, E. J., & Wolfe, D. A. (2013). Disorders of childhood and adolescence. In I. B. Weiner & others (Eds.), *Handbook of psychology* (2nd ed., Vol. 8). New York: Wiley.

Mashburn, A. J., Justice, L. M., Downer, J. T., & Pianta, R. C. (2009). Peer effects on children's language achievement during pre-kindergarten. *Child Development, 80,* 686–702.

Mason, L., Harris, K. L., & Graham, S. (2013). Strategies for improving student outcomes in written expression. In B. G. Cook & M. G. Tankersley (Eds.), *Research-based practices in special education.* Upper Saddle River, NJ: Pearson.

Masselli, G., & others. (2011). MR imaging in the evaluation of placental abruption: Correlation with sonographic findings. *Radiology*.

Masten, A. S. (2006). Developmental psychopathology: Pathways to the future. *International Journal of Behavioral Development, 31,* 46–53.

Masten, A. S. (2007). Resilience in developing systems: Progress and promise as the fourth wave rises. *Development and Psychopathology, 19,* 921–930.

Masten, A. S. (2009). Ordinary magic: Lessons from research on resilience in human development. *Education Canada, 49*(3), 28–32.

Masten, A. S. (2011). Resilience in children threatened by extreme adversity: Frameworks for research, practice, and translational synergy. *Development and Psychopathology, 23,* 141–153.

Masten, A. S. (2012). Faculty profile: Ann Masten. *The Institute of Child Development further developments.* Minneapolis: School of Education.

Masten, A. S. (2013). Risk and resilience in development. In P. D. Zelazo (Ed.), *Oxford handbook of developmental psychology.* New York: Oxford University Press.

Masten, A. S., & others. (2008). School success in motion: Protective factors for academic achievement in homeless and highly mobile children in Minneapolis. *Center for Urban and Regioinal Affairs Reporter, 38,* 3–12.

Mateus, V., Martins, C., Osorio, A., Martins, E. C., & Soares, I. (2013, in press). Attention at 10 months of age in infant-mother dyads: Contrasting free-toy play with semi-structured toy-play. *Infant Behavior and Development.*

Matlin, M. W. (2012). *The psychology of women* (7th ed.). Boston: Cengage.

Matlow, J. N., Jubetsky, A., Alesksa, K., Berger, H., & Koren, G. (2013, in press). The transfer of ethyl glucuronide across the dually perfused human placenta. *Placenta.*

Matsumoto, D., & Juang, L. (2013). *Culture and psychology* (5th ed.). Boston: Cengage.

Mattson, S., & Smith, J. E. (2011). *Core curriculum for maternal-newborn nursing* (4th ed.). New York: Elsevier.

Matzek, A. E., & Cooney, T. M. (2009). Spousal perceptions of marital stress and support among grandparent caregivers: Variations by life stage. *International Journal of Aging and Human Development, 68,* 109–126.

Maurer, D., & Lewis, T. L. (2013). Sensitive periods in visual development. In P. D. Zelazo (Ed.), *Oxford handbook of developmental psychology.* New York: Oxford University Press.

Maurer, D., Lewis, T. L., Brent, H. P., & Levin, A. V. (1999). Rapid improvement in the acuity of infants after visual input. *Science, 286,* 108–110.

Maurer, D., Mondloch, C. J., & Leis, T. L. (2007). Effects of early visual deprivation on perceptual and cognitive development. In C. von Hofsten & K. Rosander (Eds.), *Progress in Brain Research, 164,* 87–104.

Maxson, S. C. (2013, in press). Behavioral genetics. In I. B. Weiner & others (Eds.), *Handbook of psychology* (2nd ed., Vol. 3). New York: Wiley.

Mayer, K. D., & Zhang, L. (2009). Short- and long-term effects of cocaine abuse during pregnancy on heart development. *Therapeutic Advances in Cardiovascular Disease, 3,* 7–16.

Mayer, R. E. (2008). *Curriculum and instruction* (2nd ed.). Upper Saddle River, NJ: Prentice Hall.

Mayo Clinic. (2013). Pregnancy and fish: *What's safe to eat?* Retrieved January 2, 2013, from www.mayoclinic.com/health/pregnancy-and-fish/PR00158

McAdams, D. P. (2011). Life narratives. In K. L. Fingerman, C. A. Berg, J. Smith, & T. C. Antonucci (Eds.), *Handbook of life-span development.* New York: Springer.

McAdams, D. P. (2012). Personality, modernity, and the storied self. In K. Vohs & R. F. Baumeister (Eds.), *Self and identity.* Thousand Oaks, CA: Sage.

McAdoo, H. P. (2006). *Black families* (4th ed.). Thousand Oaks, CA: Sage.

McBride-Chang, C. (2004). *Children's literacy development* (Texts in Developmental Psychology Series). London: Edward Arnold/Oxford Press.

McBride-Chang, C., & others. (2005). Changing models across cultures: Associations of phonological and morphological awareness to reading in Beijing, Hong Kong, Korea, and America. *Journal of Experimental Child Psychology, 92,* 140–160.

McCabe, K. M., Rodgers, C., Yeh, M., & Hough, R. (2004). Gender differences in childhood onset conduct disorder. *Development and Psychopathology, 16,* 179–192.

McCall, R. B., Appelbaum, M. I., & Hogarty, P. S. (1973). Developmental changes in mental performance. *Monographs of the Society for Research in Child Development, 38* (Serial No. 150).

McCardle, P., Miller, B., Lee, J. R., & Tzeng, O. J. (2011). *Dyslexia across languages.* Baltimore: Paul H. Brookes.

McCartney, K. (2003, July 16). Interview with Kathleen McCartney in A. Bucuvalas, Child care and behavior, *HGSE News,* pp. 1–4. Cambridge, MA: Harvard Graduate School of Education.

McCartney, K., Dearing, E., Taylor, B. A., & Bub, K. L. (2007). Quality child care supports the achievement of low-income children: Direct and indirect pathways through caregiving and the home environment. *Journal of Applied Developmental Psychology, 28,* 411–426.

McClelland, K., Bowles, J., & Koopman, P. (2012). Male sex determination: Insights into molecular mechanisms. *Asian Journal of Andrology, 14,* 164–171.

McCombs, B. L. (2013). Educational psychology and educational transformation. In I. B. Weiner & others (Eds.), *Handbook of psychology* (2nd ed., Vol. 7). New York: Wiley.

McCormack, L. A., & others. (2011). Weight-related teasing in a racially diverse sample of sixth-grade children. *Journal of the American Dietetic Association, 111,* 431–436.

McCormick, C. B., Dimmitt, C., & Sullivan, F. R. (2013, in press). Metacognition, learning, and instruction. In I. B. Weiner & others (Eds.), *Handbook of psychology* (2nd ed., Vol. 7). New York: Wiley.

McCoy, D. C., & Raver, C. C. (2011). Caregiver emotional expressiveness, child emotion regulation, and child behavior problems among Head Start families. *Social Development, 20,* 741–761.

McDermott, B. M., & Cobham, V. E. (2012, in press). Family functioning in the aftermath of a disaster. *BMC Psychiatry, 12,* 55.

McDermott, U., Downing, J. R., & Stratton, M. R. (2011). Genomics and the continuum of cancer care. *New England Journal of Medicine, 364,* 340–350.

McDonald, S. D., & others. (2009). Preterm birth and low birth weight among in vitro fertilization singletons: A systematic review and meta-analyses. *European Journal of Obstetrics, Gynecology, and Reproductive Biology, 146,* 138–148.

McDonald, S. D., & others. (2010). Preterm birth and low birth weight among in vitro fertilization twins: A systematic review and meta-analyses. *European Journal of Obstetrics, Gynecology, and Reproductive Biology, 148,* 105–113.

McDowell, D. J., & Parke, R. D. (2009). Parental correlates of children's peer relations: An empirical test of a tripartite model. *Developmental Psychology, 45,* 224–235.

McElhaney, K. B., & Allen, J. P. (2012). Sociocultural perspectives on adolescent autonomy. In P. K. Kerig, M. S. Schulz, & S. T. Hauser (Eds.), *Adolescence and beyond.* New York: Oxford University Press.

McGarry, J., Kim, H., Sheng, X., Egger, M., & Baksh, L. (2009). Postpartum depression and help-seeking behavior. *Journal of Midwifery and Women's Health, 54,* 50–56.

McGettigan, C., & others. (2012). An application of univariate and multivariate approaches to fMRI to quantifying the hemispheric lateralization of acoustic and linguistic processes. *Journal of Cognitive Neuroscience, 24,* 636–652.

McGuire, W., Dyson, L., & Renfrew, M. (2010). Maternal obesity: Consequences for children, challenges for clinicians and carers. *Seminars in Fetal and Neonatal Medicine, 15,* 108–112.

McHale, S. M., & Crouter, A. C. (2013). How do children exert an impact on family life? In A. C. Crouter & A. Booth (Eds.), *Children's influence on family dynamics.* New York: Routledge.

McHale, S. M., Updegraff, K. A., & Whiteman, S. D. (2011). Sibling relationships. In G. W. Peterson & K. R. Bush (Eds.), *Handbook of marriage and family* (3rd ed.). New York: Springer.

McKinney, C., & Renk, K. (2011). A multivariate model of parent-adolescent relationship variables in early adolescence. *Child Psychiatry and Human Development, 42*(4), 442–462.

McKinney, E., & Murray, S. (2013). *Maternal-child nursing* (4th ed.). New York: Elsevier.

McLean, K. C., Breen, A. V., & Fournier, M. A. (2010). Constructing the self in early, middle, and late adolescent boys: Narrative identity, individuation, and well-being. *Journal of Research on Adolescence, 20,* 166–187.

McLean, K. C., & Jennings, L. E. (2012). Teens telling tales: How maternal and peer audiences support narrative identity development. *Journal of Adolescence, 35,* 1455–1469.

McLean, K. C., & Syed, M. (Eds.). (2013, in press). *Oxford handbook of identity development.* New York: Oxford University Press.

McLellan, R., & Remedios, R. (2011). *Psychology for the classroom: Motivation.* New York: Routledge.

McLeskey, J. M., Rosenberg, M. S., & Westling, D. L. (2013). *Inclusion* (2nd ed.). Upper Saddle River, NJ: Pearson.

McLoyd, V. C. (1998). Children in poverty. In I. E. Siegel & K. A. Renninger (Eds.), *Handbook of child psychology* (5th ed., Vol. 4). New York: Wiley.

McLoyd, V. C., Aikens, N. L., & Burton, L. M. (2006). Childhood poverty, policy, and practice. In W. Damon & R. Lerner (Eds.), *Handbook of child psychology* (6th ed.). New York: Wiley.

McLoyd, V. C., Kaplan, R., Purtell, K. M., Bagley, E., Hardaway, C. R., & Smalls, C. (2009). Poverty and socioeconomic disadvantage in adolescence. In R. M. Lerner & L. Steinberg (Eds.), *Handbook of adolescent psychology* (3rd ed.). New York: Wiley.

McLoyd, V. C., Kaplan, R., Purtell, K. M., & Huston, A. C. (2011). Assessing the effects of a work-based antipoverty program for parents on youth's future orientation and employment experiences. *Child Development, 82,* 113–132.

McMahon, M., & Stryjewski, G. (2011). *Pediatrics.* New York: Elsevier.

McNamara, F., & Sullivan, C. E. (2000). Obstructive sleep apnea in infants. *Journal of Pediatrics, 136,* 318–323.

McNeil, D. A., & others. (2012). Getting more than they realized they needed: A qualitative study of women's experience of group prenatal care. *BMC Pregnancy and Childbirth, 12,* 17.

McNeill, K. L., & Krajcik, J. S. (2013). *Supporting grade 5-8 students in constructing explanations in science.* Upper Saddle River, NJ: Pearson.

Mead, M. (1978, Dec. 30–Jan. 5). The American family: An endangered species. *TV Guide,* pp. 21–24.

Meaney, M. J. (2010). Epigenetics and the biological definition of gene X environment interactions. *Child Development, 81,* 41–79.

Meece, J. L., & Askew, K. S. (2012). Gender, motivation, and educational achievement. In K. R. Harris & others (Eds.), *APA handbook of educational psychology.* Washington, DC: American Psychological Association.

Meerlo, P., Sgoifo, A., & Suchecki, D. (2008). Restricted and disrupted sleep: Effects on autonomic function, neuroendocrine stress systems, and stress responsivity. *Sleep Medicine Review, 12,* 197–210.

Meeus, W. (2011). The study of adolescent identity formation 2000–2010: A review of longitudinal research. *Journal of Research in Adolescence, 21,* 75–84.

Mehari, A., & others. (2012). Mortality in adults with sickle-cell disease and pulmonary hypertension. *Journal of the American Medical Association, 307,* 1254–1256.

Mehta, C. M., & Strough, J. (2010). Gender segregation and gender-typing in adolescence. *Sex Roles, 63,* 251–263.

Meijs, N., Cillessen, A. H. N., Scholte, R. H. J., Segers, E., & Spijkerman, R. (2010). Social intelligence and academic achievement as predictors of adolescent popularity. *Journal of Youth and Adolescence, 39,* 62–72.

Mejia-Arauz, R., Rogoff, B., Dexter, A., & Najafi, B. (2007). Cultural variation in children's social organization. *Child Development, 78,* 1001–1014.

Meldrum, R. C., & Hay, C. (2012). Do peers matter in the development of self-control? Evidence from a longitudinal study of youth. *Journal of Youth and Adolescence, 41,* 691–703.

Mello, Z. R. (2009). Racial/ethnic group and socioeconomic status variation in educational and occupational expectations from adolescence to adulthood. *Journal of Applied Developmental Psychology, 30,* 494–504.

Mellor, J. M., & Freeborn, B. A. (2011). Religious participation and risky health behaviors among adolescents. *Health Economics, 20,* 1226–1240.

Meltzoff, A. N. (2008). Unpublished review of J. W. Santrock's *Life-span development* (12th ed.). New York: McGraw-Hill.

Meltzoff, A. N., & Williamson, R. A. (2013). Imitation: Social, cognitive, and theoretical perspectives. In P. D. Zelazo (Ed.), *Oxford handbook of developmental psychology.* New York: Oxford University Press.

Melzi, G., Schick, A. R., & Kennedy, J. L. (2011). Narrative elaboration and participation: Two dimensions of maternal elicitation style. *Child Development, 82*(4), 1282–1296.

Menezes, V., Malek, A., & Keelan, J. A. (2011). Nanoparticulate drug delivery during pregnancy: Placental passage and fetal exposure. *Current Pharmaceutical Biotechnology, 12,* 731–742.

Menn, L., & Stoel-Gammon, C. (2009). Phonological development: Learning sounds and sound patterns. In J. Berko Gleason & N. B. Ratner (Ed.). *The development of language* (6th ed.). Boston: Allyn & Bacon.

Mennella, J. A. (2009). Taste and smell. In R. A. Shweder & others (Eds.), *The child: An encyclopedic companion.* Chicago: University of Chicago Press.

Menon, R., & others. (2011). Cigarette smoking induces oxidative stress and atopsis in normal fetal membranes. *Placenta, 32,* 317–322.

Menyuk, P., Liebergott, J., & Schultz, M. (1995). *Early language development in full-term and premature infants.* Hillsdale, NJ: Erlbaum.

Mercy, E., & others. (2013, in press). Noninvasive detection of fetal trisomy 21: Systematic review and report of quality and outcomes of diagnostic accuracy studies performed between 1997 and 2012. *Human Reproduction Update.*

Meredith, N. V. (1978). Research between 1960 and 1970 on the standing height of young children in different parts of the world. In H. W. Reece & L. P. Lipsitt (Eds.); *Advances in child development and behavior* (Vol. 12). New York: Academic Press.

Mervis, C. B., & Becerra, A. M. (2007). Language and communicative development in Williams syndrome. *Mental Retardation and Developmental Disabilities Research Review, 13,* 3–15.

Mervis, C. B., & John, A. E. (2010). Cognitive and behavioral characteristics of children with Williams syndrome: Implications for intervention approaches. *American Journal of Medical Genetics. Part C, Seminars in Medical Genetics, 154C,* 229–248.

Mesman, J., van IJzendoorn, M. H., & Bakersman-Kranenburg, M. J. (2009). The many faces of the still-face paradigm: A review and meta-analysis. *Developmental Review, 29,* 120–162.

Messiah, S. E., Miller, T. L., Lipshultz, S. E., & Bandstra, E. S. (2011). Potential latent effects of prenatal cocaine exposure on growth and the risk of cardiovascular and metabolic disease in childhood. *Progress in Pediatric Cardiology, 31,* 59–65.

Messinger, D. (2008). Smiling. In M. M. Haith & J. B. Benson (Eds.), *Encyclopedia of infant and early childhood development.* Oxford, UK: Elsevier.

Metz, E. C., & Youniss, J. (2005). Longitudinal gains in civic development through school-based required service. *Political Psychology, 26,* 413–437.

Metzger, A., & others. (2013, in press). Information management strategies with conversations about cigarette smoking: Parenting correlates and longitudinal associations with teen smoking. *Developmental Psychology.*

Meyer, S. L., Weible, C. M., & Woeber, K. (2010). Perceptions and practice of waterbirth: A survey of Georgia midwives. *Journal of Midwifery and Women's Health, 55,* 55–59.

Mihov, K. M., Denzler, M., & Forster, J. (2010). Hemispheric specialization and creative thinking: A meta-analytic review of lateralization of creativity. *Brain and Cognition, 72,* 442–448.

Milevsky, A. (2011). *Sibling relations in childhood and adolescence.* New York: Columbia University Press.

Milevsky, A. (2012). Parenting styles in adolescence. In J. R. Levesque (Ed.), *Encyclopedia of adolescence.* New York: Springer.

Miller, C. F., & Ruble, D. N. (2005). *Developmental changes in the accessibility of gender stereotypes.* Unpublished manuscript. Department of Psychology, New York University.

Miller, C. F., Lurye, L. E., Zusuls, K. M., & Ruble, D. N. (2009). Accessibility of gender stereotype domains: Developmental and gender differences in children. *Sex Roles, 60,* 870–881.

Miller, C., Martin, C. L., Fabes, R., & Hanish, D. (2013, in press). Bringing the cognitive and social together: How gender detectives and gender enforcers shape children's gender development. In M. Banaji & S. Gelman (Eds.), *Navigating the social world: A developmental perspectives.* New York: Oxford University Press.

Miller, E. M., & others. (2012). Theories of willpower affect sustained learning. *PLoS One, 7*(6), e38680.

Miller, G. E., & Reynolds, W. M. (2013). Future perspectives in developmental psychology. In I. B. Weiner & others (Eds.), *Handbook of psychology* (2nd ed., Vol. 7). New York: Wiley.

Miller, J. (2007). Cultural psychology of moral development. In S. Kitayama & D. Cohen (Eds.), *Handbook of cultural psychology.* New York: Guilford.

Miller, J. (2013). Insights into moral development from cultural psychology. In M. Killen & J. G. Smetana (Eds.), *Handbook of moral development* (2nd ed.). New York: Routledge.

Miller, J. G., & Boyle, J. P. (2013). Culture and social psychology. In I. B. Weiner & others (Eds.), *Handbook of psychology* (2nd ed., Vol. 5). New York: Wiley.

Miller, L. J., & Larusso, E. M. (2011). Preventing postpartum depression. *Psychiatric Clinics of North America, 34,* 53–65.

Miller, P. H. (2011). Piaget's theory: Past, present, and future. In U. Goswami (Ed.), *Wiley-Blackwell handbook of childhood cognitive development* (2nd ed.). New York: Wiley-Blackwell.

Miller, S., & others. (2011). Developmental trajectories of boys' and girls' delinquency: Sex differences and links to later adolescent outcomes. *Journal of Abnormal Child Psychology, 38,* 1021–1032.

Miller-Johnson, S., Coie, J., & Malone, P. S. (2003, April). *Do aggression and peer rejection in childhood predict early adult outcomes?* Paper presented at the biennial meeting of the Society for Research in Child Development, Tampa, FL.

Miller-Jones, D. (1989). Culture and testing. *American Psychologist, 44,* 360–366.

Miller-Perrin, C. L., Perrin, R. D., & Kocur, J. L. (2009). Parental physical and psychological aggression: Psychological symptoms in young adults. *Child Abuse and Neglect, 33,* 1–11.

Mills, C. M. (2013, in press). Knowing when to doubt: Developing a critical stance when learning from others. *Developmental Psychology, 49,* 404–418.

Mills, C. M., Elashi, F. B., & Archacki, M. A. (2011, March). *Evaluating sources of information and misinformation: Developmental and individual differences in the elementary school years.* Paper presented at the biennial meeting of the Society for Research in Child Development, Montreal.

Mills, C. M., & Keil, F. C. (2005). The development of cynicism. *Psychological Science. 16,* 385–390.

Mills, D., & Mills, C. (2000). *Hungarian kindergarten curriculum translation.* London: Mills Production.

Mills-Koonce, W. R., Propper, C. B., & Barnett, M. (2012). Poor infant soothability and later insecure-ambivalent attachment: Developmental change in phenotypic markers of risk or two measures of the same construct? *Infant Behavior and Development, 35,* 215–235.

Milne, E., & others. (2012). Parental prenatal smoking and risk of childhood acute lymphoblastic leukemia. *American Journal of Epidemiology, 175,* 43–53.

Milot, T., Ethier, L. S., St-Laurent, D., & Provost, M. A. (2010). The role of trauma symptoms in the development of behavioral problems in maltreated preschoolers. *Child Abuse and Neglect, 34*(4), 225–234.

Miltenberger, R. G. (2012). *Behavior modification* (5th ed.). Boston: Cengage.

Minde, K., & Zelkowitz, P. (2008). Premature babies. In M. M. Haith & J. B. Benson (Eds.), *Encyclopedia of infancy and early childhood development.* Oxford, UK: Elsevier.

Ming, L., & others. (2012). Synchronization between embryo development and endometrium is a contributing factor for rescue ICSI outcome. *Reproductive Biomedicine Online, 24,* 527–531.

Minnes, S., & others. (2010). The effects of prenatal cocaine exposure on problem behavior in children 4–10 years. *Neurotoxicology and Teratology, 32,* 443–451.

Minnesota Family Investment Program. (2009). *Longitudinal study of early MFIP recipients.* Retrieved January 12, 2009, from www.dhs.state. mn.us/main/

Mischel, W., & Mischel, H. (1975, April). *A cognitive social-learning analysis of moral development.* Paper presented at the meeting of the Society for Research in Child Development, Denver.

Mistry, J., Contreras, M., & Dutta, R. (2013, in press). Culture and development. In I. B. Weiner & others (Eds.), *Handbook of psychology* (2nd ed., Vol. 6). New York: Wiley.

Mitchell, A. B., & Stewart, J. B. (2013, in press). The efficacy of all-male academies: Insights from critical race theory (CRT). *Sex Roles.*

Mitchell, E. A., Stewart, A. W., Crampton, P., & Salarnod, C. (2000). Deprivation and sudden infant death syndrome. *Social Science and Medicine, 51,* 147–150.

Mitchell, G. L., Farrow, C., Haycraft, E., & Meyer, C. (2013). Parental influences on children's eating behavior and characteristics of successful parent-focused interventions. *Appetite, 60,* 85–94.

Mitchell, J. A., Pate, R. R., & Blair, S. N. (2012). Screen-based sedentary behavior and cardiorespiratory fitness from age 11 to 13. *Medical Science and Sports Exercise, 44,* 1302–1309.

Miyake, K., Chen, S., & Campos, J. (1985). Infants' temperament, mothers' mode of interaction and attachment in Japan: An interim report. H. I. Bretherton & F. Waters (Eds.), Growing points of attachment theory and research, *Monographs of the Society for Research in Child Development, 50* (1–2, Serial No. 109), 276–297.

Miyakoshi, K., & others. (2013, in press). Perinatal outcomes: Intravenous patient-controlled fentanyl versus no analgesia in labor. *Journal of Obstetrics and Gynecology Research.*

Mize, K. D., & Jones, N. A. (2012). Infant physiological and behavioral responses to loss of maternal attention to a social-rival. *International Journal of Psychophysiology, 83,* 16–23.

Moffitt, T. E. (2012). *Childhood self-control predicts adult health, wealth, and crime.* Paper presented at the Symposium on Symptom Improvement in well-being, Copenhagen.

Moffitt, T. E., & others. (2011). A gradient of childhood self-control predicts health, wealth, and public safety. *Proceedings of the National Academy of Sciences U.S.A., 108,* 2693–2698.

Moise, K. J., & others. (2013). Circulating cell-free DNA for the detection of RHD status and sex using reflex fetal identifiers. *Prenatal Diagnosis.*

Monette, S., Bigras, M., & Guay, M. C. (2011). The role of executive functions in school achievement at the end of grade 1. *Journal of Experimental Child Psychology, 109,* 158–173.

Money, J. (1975). Ablato penis: Normal male infant sex-reassigned as a girl. *Archives of Sexual Behavior, 4,* 65–71.

Montagna, P., & Chokroverty, S. (2011). *Sleep disorders.* New York: Elsevier.

Montgomery-Downs, H. E., Insana, S. P., Clegg-Kraynok, M. M., & Mancini, L. M. (2010). Normative longitudinal maternal sleep: The first four postpartum months. *American Journal of Obstetrics and Gynecology, 203,* e1–e7.

Monti, J. M., Hillman, C. H., & Cohen, N. J. (2012, in press). Aerobic fitness enhances relational memory in preadolescent children: The FITKids randomized control trial. *Hippocampus.*

Montoya Arizabaleta, A. V., & others. (2010). Aerobic exercise during pregnancy improves health-related quality of life: A randomized trial. *Journal of Physiotherapy, 56,* 253–258.

Montti-Stefandi, F., Berry, J., Chryssochoou, X., Sam, D. L., & Phinney, J. (2012). Positive immigrant youth adaptation in context: Developmental, acculturation, and social psychological perspectives. In A. S. Masten & others (Eds.), *Realizing the potential of immigrant youth.* New York: Cambridge University Press.

Moon, R. Y., & Fu, L. (2012). Sudden infant death syndrome: An update. *Pediatric Reviews, 33,* 314–320.

Moore, D. (2001). *The dependent gene.* New York: W. H. Freeman.

Moore, D. (2013). Behavioral genetics, genetics, and epigenetics. In P. D. Zelazo (Ed.), *Oxford handbook of developmental psychology.* New York: Oxford University Press.

Moore, D. S. (2013). Behavioral genetics, genetics, and epigenetics. In P. D. Zelazo (Ed.), *Handbook of developmental psychology.* New York: Oxford University Press. New York: McGraw-Hill.

Moore, M. (2012). Behavioral sleep problems in children and adolescents. *Journal of Clinical Psychology in Medical Settings, 19,* 77–83.

Moore, M. K., & Meltzoff, A. N. (2008). Factors affecting infants' manual search for occluded objects and the genesis of object permanence. *Infant Behavior and Development, 31,* 168–180.

Morandi, A., & others. (2012). Estimation of newborn risk for child or adolescent obesity: Lessons from longitudinal birth cohorts. *PLoS One, 7*(11). E49919.

Morano, M., & others. (2012). Changes in actual and perceived physical abilities in clinically obese children: A 9-month multi-component intervention study. *PLoS One, 7*(12), e50782.

Morasch, K. C., Raj, V. R., & Bell, M. A. (2013, in press). The development of cognitive control from infancy through childhood. In D. Reisberg (Ed.), *Oxford handbook of cognitive psychology.* New York: Oxford University Press.

Moravcik, E., Nolte, S., & Feeney, S. (2013). *Meaningful curriculum for young children.* Upper Saddle River, NJ: Pearson.

Morgante, J. C., Zolfaghari, R., & Johnson, S. P. (2012). A critical test of temporal and spatial accuracy of the Tobii T60XL eye tracker. *Infancy, 17,* 9–32.

Morra, S., Gobbo, C., Marini, Z., & Sheese, R. (2007). *Cognitive development: Neo-Piagetian perspectives.* Mahwah, NJ: Erlbaum.

Morreale, M. C. (2004). Executing juvenile offenders: A fundamental failure of society. *Journal of Adolescent Health, 35,* 341.

Morris, A. S., Cui, L., & Steinberg, L. (2012). Parenting research and themes: What we have learned and where to go next. In R. E. Larzelere, A. S. Morris, & A. W. Harrist (Eds.), *Authoritative parenting.* Washington, DC: American Psychological Association.

Morris, C. A. (2010). Introduction: Williams syndrome. *American Journal of Medical Genetics. Part C, Seminars in Medical Genetics, 154C,* 203–208.

Morris, R. J., Thompson, K. C., & Morris, Y. P. (2013). Child psychotherapy. In I. B. Weiner & others (Eds.), *Handbook of psychology* (2nd ed., Vol. 8). New York: Wiley.

Morrison, G., Doumas, L. A. A., & Richland, L. E. (2011). A computational account of children's analogical reasoning: Balancing inhibitory control in working memory and relational representation. *Developmental Science, 14,* 516–529.

Morrissey, T. W. (2009). Multiple child-care arrangements and young children's behavioral outcomes. *Child Development, 80,* 59–76.

Morrow, C. E., & others. (2006). Learning disabilities and intellectual functioning in school-aged children with prenatal cocaine exposure. *Developmental Neuropsychology, 30,* 905–931.

Morrow, L. (2012). *Literacy development in the early years* (7th ed.). Boston: Allyn & Bacon.

Mortensen, O., Torsheim, T., Melkevik, O., & Thuen, F. (2012). Adding a baby to the equation. Married and cohabiting women's relationship satisfaction in the transition to parenthood. *Family Process, 51,* 122–139.

Moshman, D. (2011). *Adolescent rationality and development: Cognition, morality, and identity* (3rd ed.). New York: Psychology Press.

Moulson, M. C., & Nelson, C. A. (2008). Neurological development. In M. M. Haith & J. B. Benson (Eds.), *Encyclopedia of infancy and early childhood.* Oxford. UK: Elsevier.

Moya, J., Bearer, C. F., & Etzel, R. A. (2004). Children's behavior and physiology and how it affects exposure to environmental contaminants. *Pediatrics, 113*(Suppl. 4), 996–1006.

Mrug, S., Borch, C., & Cillessen, A. H. N. (2011). Other-sex friendships in late adolescence: Risky associations for substance abuse and sexual debut? *Journal of Youth and Adolescence, 40,* 875–888.

Mrug, S., & McCay, R. (2013, in press). Parental and peer disapproval of alcohol use and its relationship to adolescent drinking: Age, gender, and racial differences. *Psychology of Addictive Behaviors.*

Muller, U., & others. (2012). Knowing minds, controlling actions: The developmental relations between theory of mind and executive function from 2 to 4 years of age. *Journal of Experimental Child Psychology, 111,* 331–348.

Mullola, S., & others. (2012). Gender differences in teachers' perceptions of students' temperament, educational competence, and teachability. *British Journal of Educational Psychology, 82*(Pt 2), 185–206.

Murray, J. P., & Murray, A. D. (2008). Television: Uses and effects. In M. M. Haith & J. B. Benson (Eds.), *Encyclopedia of infant and early childhood development.* Oxford, UK: Elsevier.

Musolino, J., & Landau, B. (2012). Genes, language, and the nature of scientific explanations: The case of Williams syndrome. *Cognitive Neuropsychology, 29,* 123–148.

Myatchin, I., & Lagae, O. (2013, in press). Developmental changes in visuo-spatial working memory in normally developing children: Event-related potentials study. *Brain Development.*

Myer, G. D., & others. (2011). Integrative training for children and adolescents: Techniques and practices for reducing sports-related injuries and enhancing athletic performance. *The Physician and Sports Medicine, 39,* 74–84.

Myers, D. (2008, June 2). Commentary in S. Begley & J. Interlandi, The dumbest generation? Don't be dumb. Retrieved July 22, 2008, from www.newsweek.com/id/138536/

Myers, D. G. (2010). *Psychology* (9th ed.). New York: Worth.

Myers, D., Baer, W., & Choi, S. (1996). The changing problem of overcrowded housing. *Journal of the American Planning Association, 62,* 66–84.

N

Nader, P. R., & others. (2006). Identifying risk for obesity in early childhood. *Pediatrics, 118,* e594–e601.

NAEYC (National Association for the Education of Young Children). (2009). Developmentally appropriate practice in early childhood programs serving children from birth through age 8. Washington, DC: Author.

Nagata, D. K. (1989). Japanese American children and adolescents. In J. T. Gibbs & L. N. Huang (Eds.), *Children of color.* San Francisco: Jossey-Bass.

Nagel, B. J., & others. (2011). Altered white matter microstructure in children with attention-deficit/hyperactivity disorder. *Journal of the American Academy of Child and Adolescent Psychiatry, 50,*283–292.

Najman, J. M., & others. (2009). The impact of episodic and chronic poverty on child cognitive development. *Journal of Pediatrics, 154,* 284–289.

Najman, J. M., & others. (2010). Timing and chronicity of family poverty and development of unhealthy behaviors in children: A longitudinal study. *Journal of Adolescent Health, 46,* 538–544.

Nakamoto, J., & Schwartz, D. (2010). Is peer victimization associated with academic achievement? A meta-analytic review. *Social Development, 19,* 221–242.

Nanni, V., Uher, R., & Danese, A. (2012). Childhood maltreatment predicts unfavorable course of illness and treatment outcome in depression: A meta-analysis. *American Journal of Psychiatry, 169,* 141–151.

Nansel, T. R., & others. (2001). Bullying behaviors among U. S. youth. *Journal of the American Medical Association, 285,* 2094–2100.

Naoi, N., & others. (2012). Cerebral responses to infant-directed speech and the effect of talker familiarity. *Neuroimage, 59,* 1733–1744.

Narváez, D. (2006). Integrative moral education. In M. Killen & J. Smetana (Eds.), *Handbook of moral development.* Mahwah, NJ: Erlbaum.

Narváez, D. (2010a). The embodied dynamism of moral becoming. *Perspectives on Psychological Science, 5*(2), 185–186.

Narváez, D. (2010b). Moral complexity: The fatal attraction of truthiness and the importance of mature moral functioning. *Perspectives on Psychological Science, 5*(2), 163–181.

Narváez, D. (2013). Integrative moral education. In M. Killen & J. G. Smetana (Eds.), *Handbook of moral development* (2nd ed.). New York: Routledge.

Narváez, D., & Hill, P. L. (2010). The relation of multicultural experiences to moral judgment and mindsets. *Journal of Diversity in Higher Education, 3,* 43–55.

Narváez, D., & Lapsley, D. (Eds.). (2009). *Moral personality, identity, and character: An interdisciplinary future.* New York: Cambridge University Press.

Narváez, D., Panksepp, J., Schore, A. N., & Gleason, T. R. (Eds.). (2013). *Evolution, early experience, and development.* New York: Oxford University Press.

NASSPE. (2012). *Single-sex schools/schools with single-sex classrooms/what's the difference?* Retrieved January 21, 2013, from http://www.singlesexschools.org/schools-schools.htm

National Assessment of Educational Progress. (2000). *Reading achievement.* Washington, DC: National Center for Education Statistics.

National Assessment of Educational Progress. (2005). *The nation's report card: 2005.* Washington, DC: U.S. Department of Education.

National Assessment of Educational Progress. (2007). *The nation's report card: 2007.* Washington, DC: U.S. Department of Education.

National Assessment of Educational Progress. (2012). *The nation's report card: 2011.* Washington, DC: U.S. Office of Education.

National Association for Gifted Children. (2009). *State of the states in gifted education: 2008–2009.* Washington, DC: Author.

National Association for Sport and Physical Education. (2002). *Active start: A statement of physical activity guidelines for children birth to five years.* Reston, VA: National Association for Sport and Physical Education.

National Autism Association. (2010). *All about autism.* Retrieved January 5, 2009, from www.nationalautismassociation.org/definitions.php

National Cancer Institute. (2011). *Report to nation finds continued declines in many cancer rates.* Rockville, MD: Author.

National Center for Education Statistics. (2007). *The condition of education, 2007.* Washington, DC: U.S. Department of Education.

National Center for Education Statistics. (2010). *School dropouts.* Washington, DC: U.S. Department of Education.

National Center for Education Statistics. (2011). *The condition of education 2011.* Washington, DC: U.S. Department of Education.

National Center for Education Statistics. (2012). Indicator A-33-3: Status Dropout Rates. *Digest of Education Statistics.* Washington, DC: U.S. Department of Education.

National Center for Health Statistics. (2000). *Health United States, 1999.* Atlanta: Centers for Disease Control and Prevention.

National Center for Health Statistics. (2009, January 7). *Public Release Statement: Preterm births rise 36 percent since early 1980s.* Atlanta: Centers for Disease Control and Prevention.

National Center for Health Statistics. (2011). *Births.* Atlanta: Centers for Disease Control and Prevention.

National Center on Shaken Baby Syndrome. (2011). *Shaken baby syndrome.* Retrieved April 22, 2011, from www.dontshake.org

National Clearinghouse on Child Abuse and Neglect. (2004). *What is child abuse and neglect?* Washington, DC: U.S. Department of Health and Human Services.

National Human Genome Research Institute. (2012). *Genome-wide association method.* Washington, DC: Author.

National Institute of Child Health and Development. (2013). *SIDS.* Rockville, MD: NICHD.

National Institute of Mental Health. (2011). *Autism spectrum disorders (pervasive developmental disorders).* Retrieved July 19, 2008, from http://www.nimh.nih.gov/Publicat/autism.clm

National Institute of Neurological Disorders and Stroke. (2013). *Brain basics: Understanding sleep.* Retrieved January 3, 2013 from www.ninds.nih.gov/disorders/brain_basics/understanding_sleep.htm

National Institutes of Health. (2008). *Clinical trial. gov.* Retrieved April 22, 2008, from http://clinicaltrials.gov/ct2/show/

National Research Council. (2004). *Engaging schools: Fostering high school students' motivation to learn.* Washington, DC: National Academic Press.

National Sleep Foundation. (2006). *Sleep in America poll: Children and sleep.* Washington, DC: National Sleep Foundation.

National Sleep Foundation. (2007). *Sleep in America poll 2007.* Washington, DC: Author.

National Sleep Foundation. (2013). *Children's sleep habits.* Retrieved January 3, 2013, from www.sleepfoundation.org

National Vital Statistics Report. (2004, March 7). Deaths: Leading causes for 2002. Atlantic: Centers for Disease Control and Prevention.

Natsuaki, M. N., & others. (2010). Early pubertal maturation and internalizing problems in adolescence: Sex differences in the role of cortical reactivity to impersonal stress. *Journal of Clinical Child and Adolescent Psychology, 38,* 513–524.

Navab, A., Gillespie-Lynch, K., Johnson, S. P., Sigman, M., & Hutman, T. (2012). Eye tracking as a measure of responsiveness to joint attention in infants at risk for autism. *Infancy, 17,* 416–431.

Neal, A. R. (2009). Autism. In D. Carr (Ed.), *Encyclopedia of the life course and human development.* Boston: Gale Cengage.

Near, C. E. (2013, in press). Selling gender: Associations of box art representation of female characters with sales for teen- and mature-rated video games. *Sex Roles.*

Neblett, E. W., Rivas-Drake, D., & Umana-Taylor, A. J. (2011). The promise of racial and ethnic protective factors in promoting ethnic minority youth development. *Child Development Perspectives, 6,* 295–303.

Needham, A. (2011). Perceptual development: Object perception. In B. Goldstein (Ed.), *Encyclopedia of perception.* Thousand Oaks, CA: Sage.

Needham, A., Barrett, T., & Peterman, K. (2002). A pick-me-up for infants' exploratory skills: Early simulated experiences reaching for objects using "sticky mittens" enhances young infants' object exploration skills. *Infant Behavior and Development, 25,* 279–295.

Needham, A., & Libertus, K. (2011). Neonativism. In M. M. Haith & J. Benson (Eds.), *Encyclopedia of infant and early childhood development* (2nd ed.). New York: Elsevier.

Negriff, S., Susman, E. J., & Trickett, P. K. (2011). The development pathway from pubertal timing to delinquency and sexual activity from early to late adolescence. *Journal of Youth and Adolescence, 40,* 1343–1356.

Neisser, U., & others. (1996). Intelligence: Knowns and unknowns. *American Psychologist, 51,* 77–101.

Nelson, C. A. (2003). Neural development and lifelong plasticity. In R. M. Lerner, F. Jacobs, & D. Wertlieb (Eds.), *Handbook of applied developmental science.* Thousand Oaks, CA: Sage.

Nelson, C. A. (2007). A developmental cognitive neuroscience approach to the study of atypical development: A model system involving infants of diabetic mothers. In D. Coch, G. Dawson, & K. W. Fischer (Eds.), *Human behavior, learning, and the developing brain.* New York: Guilford.

Nelson, C. A. (2012). Brain development and behavior. In A. M. Rudolph, C. Rudolph, L. First, G. Lister, & A. A. Gersohon (Eds.), *Rudolph's pediatrics* (22nd ed.). New York: McGraw-Hill.

Nelson, C. A. (2013a, in press). The effects of early psychosocial deprivation. In M. Woodhead & J. Oates (Es.), *Early childhood in focus 7: Developing brains.* Great Britain: The Open University.

Nelson, C. A. (2013b, in press). Some thoughts on the development and neural bases of face processing. In M. Banaji & S. Gelman (Eds.), *The development of social cognition.* New York: Oxford University Press.

Nelson, J. A., & Eckstein, D. (2008). A service-learning model for at-risk adolescents. *Education and Treatment of Children, 31,* 223–237.

Nelson, J. L., Palonsky, S. B., & McCarthy, M. R. (2013). *Critical issues in education* (8th ed.). New York: McGraw-Hill.

Nelson, K. (1999). Levels and modes of representation: Issues for the theory of conceptual change and development. In E. K. Skolnick, K. Nelson, S. A. Gelman, & P. H. Miller (Eds.), *Conceptual development.* Mahwah, NJ: Erlbaum.

Neukrug, E. S., & Fawcett, R. C. (2010). *Essentials of testing and assessment* (2nd ed.). Boston: Cengage.

Nevarez, M. D., & others. (2010). Associations of early life risk factors with infant sleep duration. *Academic Pediatrics, 10,* 187–193.

Neville, H. J. (2006). Different profiles of plasticity within human cognition. In Y. Munakata & M. H. Johnson (Eds.), *Attention and Performance XXI: Processes of change in brain and cognitive development.* Oxford, UK: Oxford University Press.

Nevo, E., & Breznitz, Z. (2013). The development of working memory from kindergarten to first grade in children with different decoding skills. *Journal of Experimental Child Psychology, 114,* 217–228.

New, R. (2005). The Reggio Emilia approach: Provocations and partnerships with U.S. early childhood educators. In J. I. Roopnarine & J. E. Johnson (Eds.), *Approaches to early childhood education* (4th ed.). Columbus, OH: Merrill/Prentice Hall.

New, R. (2007). Reggio Emilia as cultural activity. *Theory into Practice, 46*(1), 5–13.

Newcombe, N. S. (2007). Developmental psychology meets the mommy wars. *Journal of Applied Developmental Psychology, 28,* 553–555.

Newell, K., Scully, D. M., McDonald, P. V., & Baillargeon, R. (1989). Task constraints and infant grip configurations. *Developmental Psychobiology, 22,* 817–832.

Newton, A. W., & Vandeven, A. M. (2010). Child abuse and neglect: A worldwide concern. *Current Opinion in Pediatrics, 22,* 226–233.

NICHD Early Child Care Research Network. (2000). Factors associated with fathers' caregiving activities and sensitivity with young children. *Developmental Psychology, 14,* 200–219.

NICHD Early Child Care Research Network. (2001). Nonmaternal care and family factors in early development: An overview of the NICHD study of Early Child Care. *Journal of Applied Developmental Psychology, 22,* 457–492.

NICHD Early Child Care Research Network. (2002). Structure→Process→Outcome: Direct and indirect effects of child care quality on young children's development. *Psychological Science, 13,* 199–206.

NICHD Early Child Care Research Network. (2003). Does amount of time spent in child care predict socioemotional adjustment during the transition to kindergarten? *Child Development, 74,* 976–1005.

NICHD Early Child Care Research Network. (2004). Type of child care and children's development at 54 months. *Early Childhood Research Quarterly, 19,* 203–230.

NICHD Early Child Care Research Network. (2005a). *Child care and development.* New York: Guilford.

NICHD Early Child Care Research Network. (2005b). Duration and developmental timing of poverty and children's cognitive and social development from birth through third grade. *Child Development, 76,* 795–810.

NICHD Early Child Care Research Network. (2005c). Predicting individual differences in attention, memory, and planning in first-graders from experiences at home, child care, and school. *Developmental Psychology, 41,* 99–114.

NICHD Early Child Care Research Network. (2006). Infant-mother attachment classification: Risk and protection in relation to changing maternal caregiving quality. *Developmental Psychology, 42,* 38–58.

NICHD Early Child Care Research Network. (2009). Family-peer linkages: The mediational role of attentional processes. *Social Development, 18*(4), 875–895.

NICHD Early Child Care Research Network. (2010). Testing a series of causal propositions relating time spent in child care to children's externalizing behavior. *Developmental Psychology, 46*(1), 1–17.

Nickerson, R. S. (2011). Developing intelligence through instruction. In R. J. Sternberg & S. B. Kaufman (Eds.), *Handbook of intelligence.* New York: Cambridge University Press.

Nieto, S., & Bode, P. (2012). *Affirming diversity* (6th ed.). Boston: Allyn & Bacon.

Nigro, G., & others. (2011). Role of the infections in recurrent spontaneous abortion. *Journal of Maternal-Fetal and Neonatal Medicine, 24,* 983–989.

Nisbett, R. (2003). *The geography of thought.* New York: Free Press.

Nisbett, R. (2009). *Intelligence and how to get it: Why schools and culture count.* New York: Norton.

Nisbett, R. E., & others. (2012). Intelligence: New findings and theoretical developments. *American Psychologist, 67,* 130–159.

Nitko, A. J., & Brookhart, S. M. (2011). *Educational assessment of students* (6th ed.). Boston: Allyn & Bacon.

Noddings, S. N. (2008). Caring and moral education. In L. Nucci & D. Narvaez (Eds.), *Handbook of moral and character education.* Clifton, NJ: Psychology Press.

Nodine, P. M., & Hastings-Tolsma, M. (2012). Maternal obesity: Improving pregnancy outcomes. *MCN American Journal of Maternal Child Nursing, 37,* 110–115.

Nolan, B. (2012). Promoting the well-being of immigrant youth: A framework for comparing outcomes and policies. In A. S. Masten & others (Eds.), *Realizing the potential of immigrant youth*. New York: Cambridge University Press.

Nolen-Hoeksema, S. (2011). *Abnormal psychology* (5th ed.). New York: McGraw-Hill.

Norman, J. E., & others. (2009). Progesterone for the prevention of preterm birth in twin pregnancy (STOPPIT): A randomized, double-blind, placebo-controlled study and meta-analysis. *Lancet, 373,* 2034–2040.

Nosko, A., Tieu, T. T., Lawford, H., & Pratt, M. W. (2011). How do I love thee? Let me count the ways: Parenting during adolescence, attachment styles, and romantic narratives in emerging adulthood. *Developmental Psychology, 47,* 645–657.

Nottleman, E. D., & others. (1987). Gonadal and adrenal hormone correlates of adjustment in early adolescence. In R. M. Lerner & T. T. Foch (Eds.), *Biological-psychological interactions in early adolescence.* Hillsdale, NJ: Erlbaum.

Nucci, L. (2013). Education for moral development. In M. Killen & J. G. Smetana (Eds.), *Handbook of moral development* (2nd ed.). New York: Routledge.

Nucci, L., & Narváez, D. (2008). Introduction and overview. In L. Nucci & D. Narvaez (Eds.), *Handbook of moral and character education.* Clifton, NJ: Psychology Press.

Nyqvist, K. H., & others. (2010). Towards universal Kangaroo Mother Care: Recommendations and report from the First European conference and Seventh International Workshop on Kangaroo Mother Care. *Acta Pediatrica, 99*(6), 820–826.

O

O'Brien, J. M., & Lewis, D. F. (2009). Progestins for the prevention of spontaneous preterm birth: Review and implications of recent studies. *Journal of Reproductive Medicine, 54,* 73–87.

O'Brien, M., & Moss, P. (2010). Fathers, work, and family policies in Europe. In M. E. Lamb (Ed.), *The role of the father in child development* (5th ed.). New York: Wiley.

O'Callaghan, F. V., & others. (2010). The link between sleep problems in infancy and early childhood and attention problems at 5 and 14 years: Evidence from a birth cohort study. *Early Human Development 86,* 419–424.

O'Connor, E., & McCartney, K. (2007). Attachment and cognitive skills: An investigation of mediating mechanisms. *Journal of Applied Developmental Psychology, 28,* 458–476.

O'Donnell, A. M. (2012). Constructivism. In K. R. Harris, S. Graham, & T. Urdan (Eds.), *APA educational psychology handbook.* Washington, DC: American Psychological Association.

O'Grady, W. (2013). An emergent approach to syntax. In B. Heine & H. Narrog (Eds.), *Oxford handbook of linguistic analysis.* New York: Oxford University Press.

O'Hearn, K., & Luna, B. (2009). Mathematical skills in Williams syndrome: Insight into the importance of underlying representations. *Developmental Disabilities Research Reviews, 15,* 11–20.

O'Roak, B. J., & others. (2012). Sporadic autism exomes reveal a highly interconnected protein network of *de novo* mutations. *Nature, 485,* 246–250.

Oakes, L. M. (2012). Advances in eye-tracking in infancy research. *Infancy, 17,* 1–8.

Oates, J., & Abraham, S. (2010). *Llewellyn-Jones fundamentals of obstetrics and gynecology* (9th ed.). New York: Elsevier.

Oates, J., & Grayson, A. (2004). *Cognitive and language development in children.* Malden, MA: Blackwell.

Obermann, M. L. (2011). Moral disengagement in self-reported and peer-nominated school bullying. *Aggressive Behavior, 37,* 133–144.

Ochs, E., & Schieffelin, B. (2008). Language socialization and language acquisition. In P. A. Duff & N. H. Hornberger (Eds.), *Encyclopedia of language and education.* New York: Springer.

OECD. (2010). *Strong performers and successful reformers in education: Lessons from PISA for the United States.* Paris, France: OECD.

Ogden, C. L., Carroll, M. D., Kit, B. K., & Flegal, K. M. (2012, January). Prevalence of obesity in the United States, 2009–2010. *NCHS Data Brief,* 1–9.

Oldehinkel, A. J., Ormel, J., Veenstra, R., De Winter, A., & Verhulst, F. C. (2008). Parental divorce and offspring depressive symptoms: Dutch developmental trends during early adolescence. *Journal of Marriage and the Family, 70,* 284–293.

Olds, D. L., & others. (2004). Effects of home visits by paraprofessionals and nurses: Age four follow-up of a randomized trial. *Pediatrics, 114,* 1560–1568.

Olds, D. L., & others. (2007). Effects of nurse home visiting on maternal and child functioning: Age-9 follow-up of a randomized trial. *Pediatrics, 120,* e832–e845.

Oller, D. K., & Jarmulowicz, L. (2010). Language and literacy in bilingual children in the early school years. In E. Hoff & M. Shatz (Eds.), *Blackwell handbook of language development.* New York:

Olson, B. H., Haider, S. J., Vangjel, L., Bolton, T. A., & Gold, J. G. (2010). A quasi-experimental evaluation of a breastfeeding support program for low-income women in Michigan. *Maternal and Child Health Journal, 14*(1), 86–93.

Olson, B. H., Horodynski, M. A., Brophy-Herb, H., & Iwanski, K. C. (2010). Health professionals' perspectives on the infant feeding practices of low-income mothers. *Maternal and Child Health Journal, 14*(1), 75–85.

Olson, D., & others. (2009). Exercise in pregnancy. *Current Sports Medicine Reports, 8,* 147–153.

Olson, S. L., Lopez-Duran, N., Lunkenheimer, E. S., Chang, H., & Sameroff, A. J. (2011). Individual differences in the development of early peer aggression: Integration contributions of self-regulation, theory of mind, and parenting. *Development and Psychopathology, 23,* 253–266.

Olszewski-Kubilius, P., & Thomson, D. (2013, in press). Gifted education programs and procedures. In I. B. Weiner & others (Eds.), *Handbook of psychology* (2nd ed., Vol. 7). New York: Wiley.

Olweus, D. (2003). Prevalence estimation of school bullying with the Olweus bully/victim questionnaire. *Aggressive Behavior, 29*(3), 239–269.

O'Neill, S., & others. (2013, in press). Cesarean section and subsequent ectopic pregnancy: A systematic review and meta-analysis. *BJOG.*

Opfer, J. E., & Gelman, S. A. (2011). Development of the animate-inanimate distinction. In U. Goswami (Ed.), *Wiley-Blackwell handbook of childhood cognitive development* (2nd ed.). New York: Wiley-Blackwell.

Ophir, E., Nass, C., & Wagner, A. D. (2009). Cognitive control in media multitaskers. *Proceedings of the National Academy of Sciences USA, 106,* 15583–15587.

Ornstein, P., Coffman, J. L., & Grammer, J. K. (2007, April). *Teachers' memory-relevant conversations and children's memory performance.* Paper presented at the biennial meeting of the Society for Research in Child Development, Boston.

Ornstein, P. A., Coffman, J. L., & Grammer, J. K. (2009). Learning to remember. In O. A. Barbarin & B. H. Wasik (Eds.), *Handbook of child development and early education.* New York: Guilford.

Ornstein, P. A., Coffman, J. L., Grammer, J. K., San Souci, P. P., & McCall, L. E. (2010). Linking the classroom context and the development of children's memory skills. In J. Meece & J. Eccles (Eds.), *The handbook of research on schools, schooling, and human development.* New York: Routledge.

Orr, A. J. (2011). Gendered capital: Childhood socialization and the "boy crisis" in education. *Sex Roles, 65,* 271–284.

Orth, U., Robins, R. W., & Roberts. B. W. (2008). Low self-esteem prospectively predicts depression in adolescence and young adulthood. *Journal of Personality and Social Psychology, 95,* 695–708.

Orth, U., Robins, R. W., Trzesniewski, K. H., Maes, J., & Schmitt, M. (2009). Low self-esteem is a risk factor for depressive symptoms from young adulthood to old age. *Journal of Abnormal Psychology, 118*(3), 472–478.

Ortigosa Gomez, S., & others. (2011). Use of illicit drugs over gestation and their neonatal impact. Comparison between periods 1982–1988 and 2002–2008. *Medicina Clinica, 136,* 423–430.

Osborne, J. (2010). Arguing to learn in science: The role of collaborative, critical discourse. *Science, 328,* 463–468.

Ostchega, Y., & others. (2009). Trends of elevated blood pressure among children and adolescents: Data from the National Health and Nutrition Examination Survey 1988–2006. *American Journal of Hypertension, 22,* 59–67.

Owens, J. A., Belon, K., & Moss, P. (2010). Impact of delaying school start time on adolescent sleep, mood, and behavior. *Archives of Pediatric and Adolescent Medicine, 164,* 608–614.

P

Padilla-Walker, L. M., Carlo, G., Christensen, K. J., & Yorgason, J. B. (2012). Bidirectional relations between authoritative parenting and adolescents' prosocial behaviors. *Journal of Research on Adolescence, 22,* 400–408.

Padilla-Walker, L. M., & Coyne, S. M. (2011). "Turn that thing off!" Parent and adolescent predictors of proactive media monitoring. *Journal of Youth and Adolescence, 34*(4), 705–715.

Padilla-Walker, L. M., Coyne, S. M., Fraser, A. M., Dyer, W. J., & Yorgason, J. B. (2012). Parents and adolescents growing up in the digital age: Latent growth curve analysis of proactive media monitoring. *Journal of Adolescence, 35*(5), 1153–1165.

Padilla-Walker, L. M., Day, R. D., Dyer, W. J., & Black, B. (2013). *"Keep on keeping on even when it's hard!": Predictors and outcomes of adolescence persistence.* Unpublished manuscript, Brigham Young University, Provo, Utah.

Padilla-Walker, L. M., Nelson, L. J., Carroll, J. S., & Jensen, A. C. (2010). More than just a game: Video game and Internet use during emerging adulthood. *Journal of Youth and Adolescence, 39*, 103–113.

Paintner, A., Williams, A. D., & Burd, L. (2012). Fetal alcohol spectrum disorders—implications for child neurology, part 1: Prenatal exposure and dosimetry. *Journal of Child Neurology, 27*, 258–263.

Pakzad-Vaezi, K., & Singhal, A. (2012). Trends in pediatric sport- and recreation-related injuries: An injury surveillance study at the British Columbia Children's Hospital (Vancouver, British Columbia) from 1992 to 2005. *Pediatrics & Child Health, 16*, 217–221.

Palfrey, J., Sacco, D., Boyd, D., & DeBonis, L. (2009). *Enhancing child safety and online technologies.* Cambridge, MA: Berkman Center for Internet & Society.

Paloutzian, R. F. (2000). *Invitation to the psychology of religion* (3rd ed.). Needham Heights, MA: Allyn & Bacon.

Pan, B. A., Rowe, M. L., Singer, J. D., & Snow, C. E. (2005). Maternal correlates of growth in toddler vocabulary production in low-income families. *Child Development, 76*, 763–782.

Pan, B. A., & Uccelli, P. (2009). Semantic development. In J. Berko Gleason & N. Ratner (Eds.), *The development of language* (7th ed.). Boston: Allyn & Bacon.

Panigraphy, A., & others. (2012). Neuroimaging biomarkers of preterm brain injury: Toward developing the preterm connectome. *Pediatric Radiology, 42*(Suppl. 1), S33–S61.

Papasavva, T. E. & others. (2013, in press). A minimal set of SNPs for the noninvasive prenatal diagnosis of b-thalassaemia. *Annuals of Human Genetics.*

Parens, E., & Johnston, J. (2009). Facts, values, and attention-deficit hyperactivity disorder (ADHD): An update on the controversies. *Child and Adolescent Psychiatry and Mental Health, 3*, 1.

Parish-Morris, J., Golinkoff, R. M., & Hirsh-Pasek, K. (2013). From coo to code: A brief story of language development. In P. D. Zelazo (Ed.), *Oxford handbook of developmental psychology.* New York: Oxford University Press.

Park, C. J., Yelland, G. W., Taffe, J. R., & Gray, K. M. (2012). Morphological and syntactic skills in language samples of pre-school aged children with autism: Atypical development? *International Journal of Speech and Language Pathology, 14*, 95–108.

Park, C. L. (2012a). Meaning, spirituality, and growth: Protective and resilience factors in health and illness. In A. S. Baum, T. A. Revenson, & J. E. Singer (Eds.), *Handbook of health psychology* (2nd ed.). New York: Sage.

Park, C. L. (2012b, in press). Meaning making in cancer survivorship. In P. T. P. Wong (Ed.), *Handbook of meaning* (2nd ed.). Thousand Oaks, CA: Sage.

Park, W., & Epstein, N. B. (2013, in press). The longitudinal causal directionality between body image distress and self-esteem among Korean adolescents: The moderating effect of relationships with parents. *Journal of Adolescence.*

Parkay, F. W. (2013). *Becoming a teacher* (9th ed.). Upper Saddle River, NJ: Pearson.

Parke, R. D., & Buriel, R. (2006). Socialization in the family: Ethnic and ecological perspectives. In W. Damon & R. Lerner (Eds.), *Handbook of child psychology* (6th ed.). New York: Wiley.

Parke, R. D., & Clarke-Stewart, A. K. (2011). *Social development.* New York: Wiley.

Parke, R. D., Coltrane, S., & Schofield, T. (2011). The bicultural advantage. In J. Marsh, R. Menoza-Denton, & J. A. Smith (Eds.), *Are we born racist?* Boston: Beacon Press.

Parke, R. D., Leidy, M. S., Schofield, T. J., Miller, M. A., & Morris, K. L. (2008). Socialization. In M. M. Haith & J. B. Benson (Eds.), *Encyclopedia of infant and early childhood development.* Oxford, UK: Elsevier.

Parlade, M. V., & others. (2009). Anticipatory smiling: Linking early affective communication and social outcome. *Infant Behavior and Development, 32*, 33–43.

Parrett, A. L., & others. (2011). Adiposity and aerobic fitness are associated with metabolic disease risk in children. *Applied Physiology, Nutrition, and Metabolism, 36*, 72–79.

Pasco Fearon, R. M., & Belsky, J. (2011). Infant-mother attachment and the growth of externalizing problems across the primary-school years. *Journal of Child Psychology and Psychiatary, 52*, 782–791.

Pascual, A., Extebarria, I., Ortega, I., & Ripalda, A. (2012). Gender differences in adolescence in emotional variables relevant to eating disorders. *International Journal of Psychology and Psychological Therapy, 12*, 59–68.

Pasley, K., & Moorefield, B. S. (2004). Stepfamilies. In M. Coleman & L. Ganong (Eds.), *Handbook of contemporary families.* Thousand Oaks, CA: Sage.

Pasterski, V., Golombok, S., & Hines, M. (2011). Sex differences in social behavior. In P. K. Smith & C. H. Hart (Eds.), *Wiley-Blackwell handbook of childhood social development* (2nd ed.). New York: Wiley.

Pate, R. R., Pfeiffer, K. A., Trost, S. G., Ziegler, P., & Dowda, M. (2004). Physical activity among children attending preschools. *Pediatrics, 114*, 1258–1263.

Patel, R., & others. (2011). European guideline for the management of genital herpes, 2010. *International Journal of STD and AIDS, 22*, 1–10.

Patrick, R. B., & Gibbs, J. C. (2012). Inductive discipline, parental expression of disappointed expectations, and moral identity in adolescence. *Journal of Youth and Adolescence, 41*, 973–983.

Patterson, C. J. (2004). What difference does a civil union make? Changing public policies and the experience of same-sex couples. Comment on Solomon, Rothblum, & Balsam (2004). *Journal of Family Psychology, 18*, 287–289.

Patterson, C. J. (2013, in press). Sexual minority youth with sexual minority parents. In A. Ben-Arieh & others (Eds.), *Handbook child research.* Thousand Oaks, CA: Sage.

Patterson, C., &. D'Augelli, A. R. (Eds.). (2013, in press). *The psychology of sexual orientation.* New York: Cambridge University Press.

Patterson, C. J., & Farr, R. H. (2012). Children of lesbian and gay parents: Reflections on the research-policy interface. In H. R. Schaeffer & K. Durkin (Eds.), *Wiley-Blackwell handbook of developmental psychology in action.* New York: Wiley.

Patterson, G. R., DeBaryshe, B. D., & Ramsey, E. (1989). A developmental perspective on antisocial behavior. *American Psychologist, 44*(20), 329–335.

Patterson, G. R., Forgatch, M. S., & DeGarmo, D. S. (2010). Cascading effects following intervention. *Development and Psychopathology, 22*, 949–970.

Patterson, G. R., Reid, J. B., & Dishion, T. J. (1992). *Antisocial boys: Vol. 4. A social interactional approach.* Eugene, OR: Castalia.

Paulhus, D. L. (2008). Birth order. In M. M. Haith & J. B. Benson (Eds.), *Encyclopedia of infant and early childhood development.* Oxford, UK: Elsevier.

Pauli-Pott, U., Friedl, S., Hinney, A., & Hebebrand, J. (2009). Serotonin transporter gene polymorphism (5-HTTLPR), environmental conditions, and development negative emotionality and fear in early childhood. *Journal of Neural Transmission, 116*, 503–512.

Paus, T., & others. (2007). Morphological properties of the action-observation cortical network in adolescents with low and high resistance to peer influence. *Social Neuroscience, 3*, 303–316.

Pavlov, I. P. (1927). In G. V. Anrep (Trans.), *Conditioned reflexes.* London: Oxford University Press.

Pea, R., & others. (2012). Media use, face-to-face communication, media multitasking, and social well-being among 8- to 12-year-old girls. *Developmental Psychology, 48*, 327–336.

Pecot-Hebert, L. (2012). Beauty & body-image: Anorexia/eating disorders. In M. Kosut (Ed.), *Encyclopedia of gender in media.* Thousand Oaks, CA: Sage.

Pederson, D. R., & Moran, G. (1996). Expressions of the attachment relationship outside of the Strange Situation. *Child Development, 67*, 915–927.

Pedroso, F. S. (2008). Reflexes. In M. H. Haith & J. B. Benson (Eds.), *Infant and early childhood development.* Oxford, UK: Elsevier.

Peek, L., & Stough, L. M. (2010). Children with disabilities in the context of disaster: A social vulnerability perspective. *Child Development, 81*, 1260–1270.

Peeters, M., Cillessen, A. H. N., & Scholte, R. H. J. (2010). Clueless or powerful? Identifying subtypes of bullies in adolescence. *Journal of Youth and Adolescence, 39*, 1041–1052.

Peeters, M. C. W., & others. (2013). Consequences of combining work and family roles: A closer look at cross-domain versus within-domain relations. In J. Grzywacz & E. Demerouti (Eds.), *New frontiers in work and family research.* New York: Routledge.

Peets, K., Hodges, E.V., & Salmivalli, C. (2011). Actualization of social cognitions into aggressive behavior toward disliked targets. *Social Development, 20,* 233–250.

Peets, K., Hodges, E. V., & Salmivalli, C. (2013, in press). Forgiveness and its determinants depending on the interpersonal context of hurt. *Journal of Experimental Child Psychology.*

Pelaez, M., Virues-Ortega, J., & Gewirtz, J. L. (2012). Acquisition of social referencing via discrimination training in infants. *Journal of Applied Behavior Analysis, 45,* 23–36.

Pelayo, R., Owens, J., Mindell, J., & Sheldon, S. (2006). Bed sharing with unimpaired parents is not an important risk for sudden infant death syndrome: Letter to the editor. *Pediatrics, 117,* 993–994.

Peltzer-Karpf, A. (2012). The dynamic matching of neural and cognitive growth cycles. *Nonlinear Dynamics, Psychology, and Life Sciences, 16,* 61–78.

Pena, E., & Bedore, J. A. (2009). Bilingualism. In R. G. Schwartz (Ed.), *Handbook of child language disorders.* Clifton, NJ: Psychology Press.

Pena, J. B., Zayas, L. H., Cbrera-Hguyen, P., & Vega, W. A. (2012). U. S. cultural involvement and its association with suicidal behavior among youths in the Dominican Republic. *American Journal of Public Health, 102,* 664–671.

Penela, E. C., & others. (2012). Maternal caregiving moderates the relation between temperamental fear and social behavior with peers. *Infancy, 17,* 715–730.

Penke, L., & others. (2012). Brain white matter tract integrity as a neural foundation for general intelligence. *Molecular Psychiatry, 17,* 1026–1030.

Perez-Febles, A. M. (1992). *Acculturation and interactional styles of Latina mothers and their infants.* Unpublished honors thesis, Brown University, Providence, RI.

Perner, J., Stummer, S., Sprung, M., & Doherty, M. (2002). Theory of mind finds its Piagetian perspective: Why alternative naming comes with understanding belief. *Cognitive Development, 17,* 1451–1472.

Perry, D. G. (2012, April). *The intrapsychics of gender.* Paper presented at the Gender Development Research conference, San Francisco.

Perry, D. G., & Pauletti, R. E. (2011). Gender and adolescent development. *Journal of Research on Adolescence, 21,* 61–74.

Perry, N. B., & others. (2013). The relation between maternal emotional support and child physiological regulation across the preschool years. *Developmental Psychobiology, 55,* 382–394.

Persky, H. R., Dane, M. C., & Jin, Y. (2003). *The nation's report card: Writing 2002.* U.S. Department of Education.

Persson, K. E., Fridlund, B., Kvist, L. J., & Dykes, A. K. (2011). Mothers' sense of security in the first postnatal week: Interview study. *Journal of Advanced Nursing, 67,* 105–116.

Peskin, H. (1967). Pubertal onset and ego functioning. *Journal of Abnormal Psychology, 72,* 1–15.

Peters, H., Whincup, P. H., Cook, D. G., Law, C., & Li, L. (2012). Trends in blood pressure in 9- to 11-year-old children in the United Kingdom, 1980–2008: The impact of obesity. *Journal of Hypertension, 30,* 1708–1717.

Peters, K. F., & Petrill, S. A. (2011). Comparison of the background, needs, and expectations for genetic counseling of adults with experience with Down syndrome, Marfan syndrome, and neurofibromatosis. *American Journal of Medical Genetics A, 155,* 684–696.

Petersen, A. C. (1979, January). Can puberty come any faster? *Psychology Today,* pp. 45–56.

Petersen, I. T., & others. (2012, in press). Interaction between serotonin transporter polymorphism (5-HTTLPR) and stressful life events in adolescents' trajectories of anxious/depressed symptoms. *Developmental Psychology.*

Peterson, C. C. (2005). Mind and body: Concepts of human cognition, physiology and false belief in children with autism or typical development. *Journal of Autism and Developmental Disorders, 35,* 487–497.

Peterson, C. C., Garnett, M., Kelly, A., & Attwood, T. (2009). Everyday social and conversation applications of theory-of-mind understanding by children with autism-spectrum disorders or typical development. *European Child and Adolescent Psychiatry, 18,* 105–115.

Peterson, J. A., McFarland, J. G., Curtis, B. R., & Aster, R. H. (2013, in press). Neonatal alloimmune thrombocytopenia: Pathogenesis, diagnosis, and management. *British Journal of Hematology.*

Petrick-Steward, E. (2012). *Beginning writers in the zone of proximal development.* New York: Psychology Press.

Petrill, S. A., & Deater-Deckard, K. (2004). The heritability of general cognitive ability: A within-family adoption design. *Intelligence, 32,* 403–409.

Pew Research Center. (2008). *Pew forum on religion and public life: U.S. Religious Landscape Survey.* Washington, DC: Author.

Pew Research Center. (2010). *Millennials: Confident, connected, open to change.* Washington, DC: Pew Research Center.

Pfeifer, M., Goldsmith, H. H., Davidson, R. J., & Rickman, M. (2002). Continuity and change in inhibited and uninhibited children. *Child Development, 73,* 1474–1485.

Philip, R. C., & others. (2012). A systematic review and meta-analysis of the fMRI investigation of autism spectrum disorders. *Neuroscience and Biobehavioral Reviews, 36,* 901–942.

Phillips, D. A., & Lowenstein, A. E. (2011). Early child care, education, and development. *Annual Review of Psychology* (Vol. 62). Palo Alto, CA: Annual Reviews.

Phillips, S., & Edwards, S. (2013). Adolescent health. In I. B. Weiner & others (Eds.), *Wiley handbook of psychology,* 2nd ed. (Vol. 9). New York: Wiley.

Phinney, J. S. (2003). Identity and acculturation. In K. M. Chun, P. B. Organista, & G. Marin (Eds.), *Acculturation.* Washington, DC: American Psychological Association.

Phinney, J. S. (2006). Ethnic identity exploration in emerging adulthood. In J. J. Arnett & J. L. Tanner (Eds.), *Emerging adults in America.* Washington, DC: American Psychological Association.

Phinney, J. S. (2008). Bridging identities and disciplines: Advances and challenges in understanding multiple identities. In M. Azmitia, M. Syed, & K. Radmacher (Eds.), *The Intersections of Personal and Social Identities. New Directions for Child and Adolescent Development, 2008*(120), 81–95.

Phinney, J. S., & Alipuria, L. L. (1990). Ethnic identity in college students from four ethnic groups. *Journal of Adolescence, 13,* 171–183.

Phinney, J. S., & Baldelomar, O. A. (2011). Identity development in multiple developmental contexts. In L. Jensen (Ed.), *Bridging cultural and developmental approaches to psychology.* New York: Oxford University Press.

Phinney, J. S., & Ong, A. D. (2007). Conceptualization and measurement of ethnic identity: Current status and future directions. *Journal of Counseling Psychology, 54,* 271–281.

Piaget, J. (1932). *The moral judgment of the child.* New York: Harcourt Brace Jovanovich.

Piaget, J. (1952). *The origins of intelligence in children.* (M. Cook, Trans.). New York International Universities Press.

Piaget, J. (1954). *The construction of reality in the child.* New York: Basic Books.

Piaget, J. (1962). *Play, dreams, and imitation in childhood.* New York: W. W. Norton.

Piaget, J., & Inhelder, B. (1969). *The child's conception of space* (F. J. Langdon & J. L. Lunger, Trans.). New York: W. W. Norton.

Pickrell, J., & Loftus, E. F. (2001). *Creating false memories.* Paper presented at the American Psychological Society, Toronto.

Ping, H., & Hagopian, W. (2006). Environmental factors in the development of type 1 diabetes. *Review in Endocrine and Metabolic Disorders, 7,* 149–162.

Piper, B. J., & others. (2011). Abnormalities in parentally rated executive function in methamphetamine/polysubstance exposed children. *Pharmacology, Biochemistry, and Behavior, 98,* 432–439.

Pipp, S. L., Fischer, K. W., & Jennings, S. L. (1987). The acquisition of self and mother knowledge in infancy. *Developmental Psychology, 23,* 86–96.

Pittman, J. F., Kerpleman, J. L., Soto, J. B., & Adler-Baeder, F. M. (2012). Identity exploration in the dating domain: The role of attachment dimensions and parenting practices. *Journal of Adolescence, 35,* 1485–1499.

Pleck, J. H. (1983). The theory of male sex role identity: Its rise and fall, 1936–present. In M. Levin (Ed.), *In the shadow of the past: Psychology portrays the sexes.* New York: Columbia University Press.

Pleck, J. H. (1995). The gender-role strain paradigm. In R. F. Levant & W. S. Pollack (Eds.), *A new psychology of men.* New York: Basic Books.

Pleh, C. (2012). The history of the nature/nurture issue. *Behavioral and Brain Sciences, 35,* 376–377.

Plomin, R. (2004). Genetics and developmental psychology. *Merrill-Palmer Quarterly, 50,* 341–352.

Plomin, R. (2012). Child development and molecular genetics: 14 years later. *Child Development.*

Plomin, R., DeFries, J. C., & Fulker, D. W. (2007). *Nature and nurture during infancy and early childhood* (2nd ed.). New York: Cambridge University Press.

Plomin, R., DeFries, J. C., McClearn, G. E., & McGuffin, P. (2009). *Behavioral genetics* (5th ed.). New York: W. H. Freeman.

Plucker, J. (2010, July 10). Interview. In P. Bronson & A. Merryman. The creativity crisis. *Newsweek,* pp. 42–48.

Pluess, M., & Belsky, J. (2009). Differential susceptibility to rearing experience: the case of child care. *Journal of Child Psychology and Psychiatry, 50*(4), 396–404.

Poirel, N., & others. (2012). Number conservation is related to children's prefrontal inhibitory control: An fMRI study of a Piagetian task. *PLoS One, 7*(7), e40802.

Polce-Lynch, M., Myers, B. J., Kliewer, W., & Kilmartin, C. (2001). Adolescent self-esteem and gender: Exploring relations to sexual harassment, body image, media influence, and emotional expression. *Journal of Youth and Adolescence, 30,* 225–244.

Pollack, W. (1999). *Real boys.* New York: Owl Books.

Pomerantz, E. M., Cheung, C. S., & Qin, L. (2012). Relatedness between children and parents: Implications for motivation. In R. Ryan (Ed.), *Oxford handbook of motivation.* New York: Oxford University Press.

Pomerantz, E. M., Kim, E. M., & Cheung, C. S. (2012). Parents' involvement in children's learning. In K. R. Harris & others (Eds.), *APA educational psychology handbook.* Washington, DC: American Psychological Association.

Pong, S., & Landale, N. S. (2012). Academic achievement of legal immigrants' children: The roles of parents' pre- and post-immigration characteristics in origin-group differences. *Child Development, 83,* 1543–1559.

Poole, D. A., & Lindsay, D. S. (1996). *Effects of parents' suggestions, interviewing techniques, and age on young children's event reports.* Presented at the NATO Advanced Study Institute, Port de Bourgenay, France.

Popham, W. J. (2011). *Classroom assessment* (6th ed.). Boston: Allyn & Bacon.

Posada, G., & Kaloustian, G. (2010). Parent-infant interaction. In J. G. Bremner & T. D. Wachs (Eds.), *Wiley-Blackwell handbook of infant development* (2nd ed.). New York: Wiley.

Posner, M. I., & Rothbart, M. K. (2007). *Educating the human brain.* Washington, DC: American Psychological Association.

Poston, L., & others. (2011). Obesity in pregnancy: Implications for the mother and lifelong health of the child. A consensus statement. *Pediatric Research, 69,* 175–180.

Poulin, F., & Denault, A-S. (2012). Other-sex friendship as a mediator between parental monitoring and substance use in boys and girls. *Journal of Youth and Adolescence, 41,* 1488–1501.

Poulin, F., & Pedersen, S. (2007). Developmental changes in gender composition of friendship networks in adolescent girls and boys. *Developmental Psychology, 43,* 1484–1496.

Power, F. C., & Higgins-D'Alessandro, A. (2008). The Just Community Approach to moral education and moral atmosphere of the school. In L. Nucci & D. Narvaez (Eds.), *Handbook of moral and character education.* Clifton, NJ: Psychology Press.

Prabhakar, H. (2007). Hopkins Interactive Guest Blog: *The public health experience at Johns Hopkins.* Retrieved January 31, 2008, from http://hopkins.typepad.com/guest/2007/03/the_public_heal.html.

Prameela, K. K. (2011). Breastfeeding—anti-viral potential and relevance to the influenza virus pandemic. *Medical Journal of Malaysia, 66,* 166–169.

Pratt, C., & Bryant, P. E. (1990). Young children understand that looking leads to knowing (so long as they are looking in a single barrel). *Child Development, 61,* 973–982.

Pratt, M. W., Norris, J. E., Hebblethwaite, S., & Arnold, M. L. (2008). Intergenerational transmission of values: Family generativity and adolescents' narratives of parent and grandparent value teaching. *Journal of Personality, 76,* 171–198.

Pressley, M. (2003). Psychology of literacy and literacy instruction. In I. B. Weiner (Ed.). *Handbook of psychology* (Vol. 7). New York: Wiley.

Pressley, M. (2007a). Achieving best practices. In L. B. Gambrell, L. M. Morrow, & M. Pressley (Eds.), *Best practices in literacy instruction.* New York: Guilford.

Pressley, M. (2007b). An interview with Michael Pressley by Terri Flowerday and Michael Shaughnessy. *Educational Psychology Review, 19,* 1–12.

Pressley, M., Allington, R., Wharton-McDonald, R., Block, C. C., & Morrow, L. M. (2001). *Learning to read: Lessons from exemplary first grades.* New York: Guilford.

Pressley, M., & Harris, K. (2006). Cognitive strategies instruction. In P. A. Alexander & P. H. Winne (Eds.), *Handbook of educational psychology* (2nd ed.). Mahwah, NJ: Erlbaum.

Pressley, M., & Hilden, K. (2006). Cognitive strategies. In W. Damon & R. Lerner (Eds.), *Handbook of child psychology* (6th ed.). New York: Wiley.

Pressley, M., Mohan, L., Fingeret, L., Reffitt, K., & Raphael Bogaert, L. R. (2007). Writing instruction in engaging and effective elementary settings. In S. Graham, C. A. MacArthur, & J. Fitzgerald (Eds.), *Best practices in writing instruction.* New York: Guilford.

Pressley, M., Mohan, L., Raphael, L. M., & Fingeret, L. (2007). How does Bennett Woods Elementary School produce such high reading and writing achievement? *Journal of Educational Psychology, 99,* 221–240.

Pressley, M., Raphael, L., Gallagher, D., & Dibella, J. (2004). Providence-St. Mel School: How a school that works for African-American students works. *Journal of Educational Psychology, 96,* 216–235.

Pressley, M., & others. (2003). *Motivating primary-grades teachers.* New York: Guilford.

Prinstein, M. J. (2007). Moderators of peer contagion: A longitudinal examination of depression socialization between adolescents and their best friends. *Journal of Clinical Child and Adolescent Psychology, 36,* 159–170.

Prinstein, M. J., & Dodge, K. A. (2008). Current issues in peer influence. In M. J. Prinstein & K. A. Dodge (Eds.), *Understanding peer influence in children and adolescents.* New York: Guilford.

Prinz, J. (2009). *The emotional construction of morals.* New York: Oxford University Press.

Proulx, M. J., Brown, D. J., Pasqualotto, A., & Meijer, P. (2013, in press). Multisensory perceptual learning and sensory substitution. *Neuroscience and Behavioral Reviews.*

Provenzo, E. F. (2002). *Teaching, learning, and schooling in American culture: A critical perspective.* Boston: Allyn & Bacon.

Pryor, J. H., Hurtado, S., DeAngelo, L., Blake, L. P., & Tran, S. (2010). *The American freshman: National norms for fall 2010.* Los Angeles: Higher Education Institute, UCLA.

Pujol, J., & others. (2004). Delayed myelination in children with developmental delay detected by volumetric MRI. *Neuroimage, 22,* 897–903.

Pulgaron, E. R. (2013). Childhood obesity: A review of increased risk for physical and psychological morbidities. *Clinical Therapeutics, 35,* A18–A32.

Puma, M., & others. (2010). *Head Start impact study. Final report.* Washington, DC: Administration for Children & Families.

Pungello, E. P., Iruka, I. U., Dotterer, A. M., Mills-Koonce, R., & Reznick, J. S. (2009). The effects of socioeconomic status, race, and parenting on language development in early childhood. *Developmental Psychology, 45,* 544–557.

Purtell, K. M., & McLoyd, V. C. (2013, in press). Parents' participation in a work-based anti-poverty program can enhance their children's future orientation: Understanding pathways of influence. *Journal of Youth and Adolescence.*

Putallaz, M., & others. (2007). Overt and relational aggression and victimization: Multiple perspectives within the school setting. *Journal of School Psychology, 45,* 523–547.

Puzzanchera, C., & Sickmund, M. (2008, July). *Juvenile court statistics 2005.* Pittsburgh: National Center for Juvenile Justice.

Q

Quadrelli, R., & others. (2007). Parental decisions to abort or continue a pregnancy following prenatal diagnosis of chromosomal abnormalities in a setting where termination of pregnancy is not legally available. *Prenatal Diagnosis, 27,* 228–232.

Quinn, P. C., & others. (2013, in press). On the developmental origins of differential responding to social category information. In M. R. Banaji & S. A. Gelman (Eds.), *Navigating the social world.* New York: Oxford University Press.

R

Rabbani, B., & others. (2012, in press). Next-generation sequencing: Impact of exome sequencing in Mendelian disorders. *Journal of Human Genetics.*

Radulescu, L., & others. (2013, in press). Multicenter evaluation of Neurelec Digisonic SP cochlear implant reliability. *European Archives of Oto-rhino-laryngology.*

Raffaelli, M., & Ontai, L. L. (2004). Gender socialization in Latino/a families: Results from two retrospective studies. *Sex Roles, 50,* 287–299.

Raikes, H. A., & Thompson, R. A. (2009). Attachment security and parenting quality predict children's problem-solving, attributions, and loneliness with peers. *Attachment and Human Development, 10,* 319–344.

Raikes, H., & others. (2006). Mother-child bookreading in low-income families: Correlates and outcomes during the first three years of life. *Child Development, 77,* 924–953.

Rajaraman, P., & others. (2011). Early life exposure to diagnostic radiation and ultrasound scans and risk of childhood cancer: Case-control study. *British Medical Journal, 342.*

Rajendran, G., & Mitchell, P. (2007). Cognitive theories of autism. *Developmental Review, 27,* 224–260.

Rakison, D. H., & Lawson, C. A. (2013). Categorization. In P. D. Zelazo (Ed.), *Oxford handbook of developmental psychology*. New York: Oxford University Press.

Rakoczy, H. (2012). Do infants have a theory of mind? *British Journal of Developmental Psychology, 30*, 59–74.

Ram, K. T., & others. (2008). Duration of lactation is associated with lower prevalence of the metabolic syndrome in midlife—SWAN, the study of women's health across the nation. *American Journal of Obstetrics and Gynecology, 198*, e1–e6.

Ramchandani, P. G., & others. (2011). Paternal depression: An examination of its links with father, child, and family functioning in the postnatal period. *Depression and Anxiety, 28*, 471–477.

Ramchandani, P. G., & others. (2013). Do early father-infant interactions predict the onset of externalizing behaviors in young children? Findings from a longitudinal cohort study. *Journal of Child Psychology and Psychiatry, 54*, 56–64.

Ramey, C. T., & Campbell, F. A. (1984). Preventive education for high-risk children: Cognitive consequences of the Carolina Abecedarian Project. *American Journal of Mental Deficiency, 88*, 515–523.

Ramey, C. T., & Ramey, S. L. (1998). Early prevention and early experience. *American Psychologist, 53*, 109–120.

Ramey, C. T., Ramey, S. L., & Lanzi, R. G. (2001). Intelligence and experience. In R. J. Sternberg & E. L. Grigorenko (Eds.), *Environmental effects on cognitive abilities*. Mahwah, NJ: Erlbaum.

Ramey, C. T., Ramey, S. L., & Lanzi, R. G. (2006). Children's health and education. In W. Damon & R. Lerner (Eds.), *Handbook of child psychology* (6th ed.). New York: Wiley.

Ramey, S. L. (2005). Human developmental science serving children and families: Contributions of the NICHD study of early child care. In NICHD Early Child Care Network (Eds.), *Child care and development*. New York: Guilford.

Ramphal, C. (1962). *A study of three current problems in education*. Unpublished doctoral dissertation, University of Natal, India.

Ramsdell, H. L., Oller, D. K., Buder, E. H., Ethington, C. A., & Chorna, L. (2012). Identification of prelinguistic phonological categories. *Journal of Speech, Language, and Hearing Research, 55*, 1626–1639.

Rasmussen, S. A. (2012). Human teratogens update 2011: Can we ensure safety during pregnancy? *Birth Defects Research A: Clinical and Molecular Teratology, 94*, 123–128.

Raven, P. H., Johnson, G. B., Mason, K. A., Loscos, J., & Singer, S. (2014). *Biology* (10th ed.). New York: McGraw-Hill.

Raver, C. C., & others. (2011). CSRP's impact on low-income preschoolers preacademic skills: Self-regulation as a mediating mechanism. *Child Development, 82*, 362–378.

Raver, C. C., & others. (2012). Testing models of children's self-regulation within educational contexts: Implications for measurement. *Advances in Child Development and Behavior, 42*, 245–270.

Regalado, M., Sareen, H., Inkelas, M., Wissow, L. S., & Halfon, N. (2004). Parents' discipline of young children: Results from the National Survey of Early Childhood Health. *Pediatrics, 113*, 1952–1958.

Regev, R. H., & others. (2003). Excess mortality and morbidity among small-for-gestational-age premature infants: A population-based study. *Journal of Pediatrics, 143*, 186–191.

Reid, P. T., & Zalk, S. R. (2001). Academic environments: Gender and ethnicity in U.S. higher education. In J. Worell (Ed.), *Encyclopedia of women and gender*. San Diego: Academic Press.

Reijmerink, N. E., & others. (2011). Toll-like receptors and microbial exposure: Gene-gene and gene-environment interaction in the development of atopy. *European Respiratory Journal, 38*, 833–840.

Reijntjes, A., & others. (2011). Explaining the paradoxical rejection-aggression link: The mediating effects of hostile intent attributions, anger, and decreases in state self-esteem on peer rejection-induced aggression in youth. *Personality and Social Psychology Bulletin, 37*, 955–963.

Reindollar, R. H., & Goldman, M. B. (2012). Gonadotropin therapy: A 20th century relic. *Fertility and Sterility, 97*, 813–818.

Reiner, W. G., & Gearhart, J. P. (2004). Discordant sexual identity in some genetic males with cloacal exstrophy assigned to female sex at birth. *New England Journal of Medicine, 350*, 333–341.

Reis, S. M., & Renzulli, J. S. (2011). Intellectual giftedness. In R. J. Sternberg & S. B. Kaufman (Eds.), *Cambridge handbook of intelligence*. New York: Cambridge.

Rende, R. (2013, in press). Behavioral resilience in the post-genomic era: Emerging models linking genes with environment. *Frontiers in Human Neuroscience*.

Renner, P., Grofer Klinger, L., & Klinger, M. R. (2006). Exogenous and endogenous attention orienting in autism spectrum disorders. *Child Neuropsychology, 12*, 361–382.

Repacholi, B. M., & Gopnik, A. (1997). Early reasoning about desires: Evidence from 14- and 18-month-olds. *Developmental Psychology, 33*, 12–21.

Reproductive Endocrinology and Infertility Committee & others. (2012). Advanced reproductive age and fertility. *Journal of Obstetrics and Gynecology Canada*.

Rest, J. R. (1995). *Concern for the social–psychological development of youth and educational strategies: Report for the Kaufmann Foundation*. Minneapolis: University of Minnesota, Department of Educational Psychology.

Reutzel, D. R., & Cooter, R. B. (2012). *Teaching children to read* (6th ed.). Boston: Allyn & Bacon.

Reutzel, D. R., & Cooter, R. B. (2013). *Essentials of teaching children to read* (3rd ed.). Boston: Allyn & Bacon.

Reyna, V. F., & Brainerd, C. J. (1995). Fuzzy-trace theory: An interim synthesis. *Learning and Individual Differences, 7*, 1–75.

Reyna, V. F., & Brainerd, C. J. (2011). Dual processes in decision making and developmental neuroscience: A fuzzy-trace model. *Developmental Review, 31*, 180–206.

Reyna, V., & Farley, F. (2006). Risk and rationality in adolescent decision-making: Implications for theory, practice, and public policy. *Psychological Science in the Public Interest, 7*, 1–44.

Reyna, V. F., & Rivers, S. E. (2008). Current theories of risk and rational decision making. *Developmental Review, 28*, 1–11.

Reyna, V. F., & others. (2010). Gist-based conceptions of risk in adolescent alcohol consumption: A fuzzy trace theory approach. *Annals of Behavioral Medicine, 39*, s196.

Reyna, V. F., & others. (2011). Neurobiological and memory models of risky decision making in adolescents versus young adults. *Journal of Experimental Psychology: Learning, Memory, and Cognition, 37*, 1125–1142.

Reynolds, C. R., & Livingston, R. B. (2012). *Mastering modern psychological testing*. Upper Saddle River, NJ: Pearson.

Reynolds, F. (2010). The effects of maternal labour analgesia on the fetus. *Best Practices & Research. Clinical Obstetrics & Gynaecology, 24*, 289–302.

Reynolds, W. M., & Miller, G. E. (2013). Educational psychology: Contemporary perspectives. In I. B. Weiner & others (Eds.), *Handbook of psychology* (2nd ed., Vol. 7). New York: Wiley.

Reznick, J. S. (2013). Research designs and methods: Toward a cumulative developmental science. In P. D. Zelazo (ed.), *Handbook of developmental psychology*. New York: Oxford University Press.

Richards, J. E. (2009). Attention to the brain in infancy. In S. Johnson (Ed.), *Neuroconstructivism: The new science of cognitive development*. New York: Oxford University Press.

Richards, J. E. (2010). Infant attention, arousal, and the brain. In L. M. Oaks, C. H. Cashon, M. Casaola, & D. H. Rakison (Eds.), *Infant perception and cognition*. New York: Oxford University Press.

Richards, J. E. (2011). Infant attention, arousal, and the brain. In L. Oakes & others (Eds.), *Infant perception and cognition*. New York: Oxford University Press.

Richards, J. E., Reynolds, G. D., & Courage, M. I. (2010). The neural bases of infant attention. *Current Directions in Psychological Science, 19*, 41–46.

Richardson, G. A., Goldschmidt, L., & Willford, J. (2008). The effects of prenatal cocaine use on infant development. *Neurotoxicology and Teratology, 30*, 96–106.

Richardson, G. A., Goldschmidt, L., Leech, S., & Willford, J. (2011). Prenatal cocaine exposure: Effects on mother- and teacher-rated behavior problems and growth in school-aged children. *Neurotoxicology and Teratology, 33*, 69–77.

Rideout, V. J., Foehr, U. G., & Roberts, D. F. (2010). *Generation M2: Media in the lives of 8- to 18-year-olds*. Menlo Park, CA: Kaiser Family Foundation.

Riggins, T. (2012). Building blocks of recollection. In S. Ghetti & P. J. Bauer (Eds.), *Origins of recollection*. New York: Oxford University Press.

Righi, G., & Nelson, C. A. (2013, in press). The neural architecture and developmental course of face processing. In P. Rakic & J. Rubenstein (Eds.), *Comprehensive developmental neuroscience*. New York: Elsevier.

Riina, E. M., Martin, A., Gardner, M., & Brooks-Gunn, J. (2013). Context matters: Links between neighborhood discrimination, neighborhood cohesion, and African American adolescents' adjustment. *Journal of Youth and Adolescence, 42*, 136–146.

Rijlaarsdam, G., & others. (2012). Writing. In K. R. Harris, S. Graham, & T. Urdan (Eds.), *APA handbook of educational psychology*. Washington, DC: American Psychological Association.

Riley, M., & Bluhm, B. (2012). High blood pressure in children and adolescents. *American Family Physician, 85,* 693–700.

Rink, J. E. (2009). *Designing the physical education curriculum.* New York: McGraw-Hill.

Rinsky, J. R., & Hinshaw, S. P. (2011). Linkages between childhood executive functioning and adolescent social functioning and psychopathology in girls with ADHD. *Child Neuropsychology, 17*(4), 368–390.

Rios-Castillo, I., Cerezo, S., Corvalan, C., Martinez, M., & Kain, J. (2013, in press). Risk factors during the prenatal period and the first year of life associated with overweight in 7-year-old low-income Chilean children. *Maternal and Child Nutrition.*

Ritchie, S., Maxwell, K. L., & Bredekamp, S. (2009). Rethinking early schooling: Using developmental science to transform young children's early school experiences. In O. A. Barbarin & B. H. Wasik (Eds.), *Handbook of child development and early education.* New York: Oxford University Press.

Rivas-Drake, D., Hughes, D., & Way, N. (2009). Public ethnic regard and perceived socioeconomic stratification: Associations with well-being among Dominican and Black American youth. *Journal of Early Adolescence, 29,* 122–141.

Rizzo, M. S. (1999, May 8). Genetic counseling combines science with a human touch. *Kansas City Star,* p. 3.

Roberts, R. D., & Lipnevich, A. A. (2012). From general intelligence to multiple intelligences: Meanings, models, and measures. In K. R. Harris, S. Graham, & T. Urdan (Eds.), *APA handbook of educational psychology.* Washington, DC: American Psychological Association.

Robins, R. W., Trzesniewski, K. H., Tracy, J. L., Gosling, S. D., & Potter, J. (2002). Global self-esteem across the life span. *Psychology and Aging, 17,* 423–434.

Robinson-Riegler, B., & Robinson-Riegler, G. L. (2012). *Cognitive psychology* (3rd ed.). Upper Saddle River, NJ: Pearson.

Robledo-Colonia, A. F., & others. (2012). Aerobic exercise training during pregnancy reduces symptoms in nulliparous women: A randomized trial. *Journal of Physiotherapy, 58,* 9–15.

Roblyer, M. D., & Doering, A. H. (2013). *Integrating educational technology into teaching* (6th ed.). Upper Saddle River, NJ: Pearson.

Rochat, P. (2013). Self-conceptualizing in development. In P. D. Zelazo (Ed.), *Oxford handbook of developmental psychology.* New York: Oxford University Press.

Rochlen, A. B., Suizzo, M. A., Scaringi, V., Bredow, A., & McKelley, R. A. (2007, August). *A paper qualitative study of stay-at-home fathers.* Presented at the meeting of the American Psychological Association, San Francisco.

Rode, L., & others. (2009). Systematic review of progesterone for the prevention of preterm birth in singleton pregnancies. *Acta Obstetrica et Gynecologica Scandinavica, 88,* 1180–1189.

Rode, S. S., Chang, P., Fisch, R. O., & Sroufe, L. A. (1981). Attachment patterns of infants separated at birth. *Developmental Psychology, 17,* 188–191.

Rodenburg, G., Kremers, S. P., Oenema, A., & van de Mheen, D. (2012). Associations of children's appetitive traits with weight and dietary behaviors in the context of general parenting. *PLoS One, 7*(12), 50642.

Rodriquez, E. T., & others. (2009). The formative role of home literacy experiences across the first three years of life in children from low-income families. *Journal of Applied Developmental Psychology, 30*(6), 677–694.

Roeser, R. W., & Zelazo, P. D. (2012). Contemplative science, education and child development. *Child Development Perspectives, 6,* 143–145.

Rogers, L. O., & others. (2012). Meaning making in middle childhood: An exploration of the meaning of ethnic identity. *Cultural Diversity and Ethnic Minority Psychology, 18,* 98–108.

Rogoff, B. (1990). *Apprenticeship in thinking.* New York: Oxford University Press.

Rogoff, B. (2003). *The cultural nature of human development.* New York: Oxford University Press.

Rogoff, B., Correa-Chavez, M. & Silva, K. G. (2011). Cultural variation in children's learning and attention. In M. A. Gernsbacher & others (Eds.), *Psychology and the real world.* New York: Worth.

Rogoff, B., Morelli, G. A., & Chavajay, P. (2010). Children's integration in communities and segregation of people of differing ages. *Perspectives on Psychological Science, 5,* 431–440.

Rogoff, B., & others. (2007). Children's development of cultural repertoires through participation in everyday routines and practices. In J. E. Grusec & P. D. Hastings (Eds.), *Handbook of socialization.* New York: Guilford.

Rogoff, B., & others. (2011). *Developing destinies: A Mayan midwife and town.* New York: Oxford University Press.

Rohner, R. P., & Rohner, E. C. (1981). Parental acceptance-rejection and parental control: Cross-cultural codes. *Ethnology, 20,* 245–260.

Roisman, G. I., & Fraley, R. C. (2012). The legacy of early interpersonal experience. *Advances in Child Development and Behavior, 42,* 79–112.

Roisman, G. I., & Groh, A. M. (2011). Attachment theory and research in developmental psychology: An overview and appreciative critique. In M. K. Underwood & L. H. Rosen (Eds.), *Social development.* New York: Guilford.

Roopnarine, J. L., & Metindogan, A. (2006). Early childhood education research in cross-national perspective. In B. Spodek & O. N. Saracho (Eds.). *Handbook of research on the education of young children.* Mahwah, NJ: Erlbaum.

Rose, A. J., & Asher, S. R. (1999). Children's goals and strategies in response to conflicts within a friendship. *Developmental Psychology, 35,* 69–79.

Rose, A. J., Carlson, W., & Waller, E. M. (2007). Prospective associations of co-rumination with friendship and emotional adjustment: Considering the socioemotional trade-offs of co-rumination. *Developmental Psychology, 43,* 1019–1031.

Rose, A. J., & Smith, R. L. (2009). Sex differences in peer relationships. In K. H. Rubin, W. M. Bukowski, & B. Laursen (Eds.), *Handbook of peer interactions, relationships, and groups.* New York: Guilford.

Rose, A. J., & others. (2012). How girls and boys expect disclosure about problems will make them feel: Implications for friendship. *Child Development, 83,* 844–863.

Rose, S. A., Feldman, J. F., & Jankowski, J. J. (2009). A cognitive approach to the development of early language. *Child Development, 80,* 134–150.

Rose, S., Feldman, J. F., Jankowski, J. J., & Van Rossem, R. (2012). Information processing from infancy to 11 years: Continuities and prediction of IQ. *Intelligence, 40,* 445–457.

Rosen, L. D., Cheever, N. A., & Carrier, L. M. (2008). The association of parenting style and child age with parental limit setting and adolescent MySpace behavior. *Journal of Applied Developmental Psychology, 29,* 459–471.

Rosenberg, M. S., Westling, D. L., & McLeskey, J. (2011). *Special education for today's teachers* (2nd ed.). Upper Saddle River, NJ: Merrill.

Rosenblith, J. F. (1992). *In the beginning* (2nd ed.). Newbury Park, CA: Sage.

Rosenkranz, R. R. (2012). Service-learning in higher education relevant to the promotion of physical activity, healthful eating, and prevention of obesity. *International Journal of Preventive Medicine, 3,* 672–681.

Rosenstein, D., & Oster, H. (1988). Differential facial responses to four basic tastes in newborns. *Child Development, 59,* 1555–1568.

Rosnow, R. L., & Rosenthal, R. (1996). *Beginning behavioral research* (2nd ed.). Upper Saddle River, NJ: Prentice Hall.

Rosnow, R. L., & Rosenthal, R. (2013). *Beginning psychological research* (7th ed.). Boston: Cengage.

Ross, J. L., & others. (2012). Behavioral and social phenotypes in boys with 47, XYY syndrome or 47, XXY Klinefelter syndrome. *Pediatrics, 129,* 769–778.

Rossano, F., Carpenter, M., & Tomasello, M. (2012). One-year-old infants follow others' voice direction. *Psychological Science, 23,* 1298–1302.

Rossi, J. S. (2013). Statistical power analysis. In I. B. Weiner & others (Eds.), *Handbook of psychology* (2nd ed.) (Vol. 2). New York: Wiley.

Rote, W. M., Smetana, J. G., Campione-Barr, N., Villalobos, M., & Tasopouos-Chan, M. (2012). Associations between observed mother-adolescent interactions and adolescent information management. *Journal of Research on Adolescence, 22,* 206–214.

Rothbart, M. K. (2004). Temperament and the pursuit of an integrated developmental psychology. *Merrill-Palmer Quarterly, 50,* 492–505.

Rothbart, M. K. (2011). *Becoming who we are.* New York: Guilford.

Rothbart, M. K., & Bates, J. E. (2006). Temperament. In W. Damon & R. Lerner (Eds.), *Handbook of child psychology* (6th ed.). New York: Wiley.

Rothbart, M. K., & Gartstein, M. A. (2008). Temperament. In M. M. Haith & J. B. Benson (Eds.), *Encyclopedia of infant and early childhood development.* Oxford, UK: Elsevier.

Rothbart, M. K., & Sheese, B. E. (2007). Temperament and emotion regulation. In J. J. Gross (Ed.), *Handbook of emotion regulation.* New York: Guilford Press.

Rothbaum, F., Poll, M., Azuma, H., Miyake, K., & Weisz, J. (2000). The development of close relationships in Japan and the United States: Paths of symbiotic harmony and generative tension. *Child Development, 71,* 1121–1142.

Rothbaum, F., & Trommsdorff, G. (2007). Do roots and wings complement or oppose one another?: The socialization of relatedness and autonomy in cultural context. In J. E. Grusec & P. D. Hastings (Eds.), *Handbook of socialization*. New York: Guilford.

Rousssotte, F. F. (2011). Abnormal brain activation during working memory in children with prenatal exposure to drugs of abuse: The effects of methamphetamine, alcohol, and polydrug exposure. *NeuroImage, 54*, 3067–3075.

Rovee-Collier, C. (1987). Learning and memory in children. In J. D. Osofsky (Ed.), *Handbook of infant development* (2nd ed.). New York: Wiley.

Rovee-Collier, C. (2004). Infant learning and memory. In U. Goswami (Ed.), *Blackwell handbook of childhood cognitive development*. Malden, MA: Blackwell.

Rovee-Collier, C. (2007). The development of infant memory. In N. Cowan & M. Courage (Eds.), *The development of memory in childhood*. Philadelphia: Psychology Press.

Rovee-Collier, C., & Barr, R. (2010). Infant learning and memory. In J. G. Bremner & T. D. Wachs (Ed.), *Wiley-Blackwell handbook of infant development* (2nd ed.). New York: Wiley.

Rovers, M. M., de Kok, I. M., & Schilder, A. G. (2006). Risk factors for otitis media: An international perspective. *International Journal of Otorhinolaryngology, 70*, 1251–1256.

Row, C., Burns, S., & Griffin, P. (Eds.). (1998). *Preventing reading difficulties in young children*. Washington, DC: National Academy Press.

Rowe, M. L., & Goldin-Meadow, S. (2009). Differences in early gesture explain SES disparities in child vocabulary size at school entry. *Science, 323*, 951–953.

Royer-Pokora, B. (2012, in press). Genetics of pediatric renal tumors. *Pediatric Nephrology*.

Roza, S. J., & others. (2010). Maternal folic acid supplement use in early pregnancy and child behavioural problems: The Generation R study. *British Journal of Nutrition, 103*, 445–452.

Rubenstein, R. S. (2012). *Adolescent social perspective taking in contexts of social justice: Examining perceptions of social group differences*. Master of Arts Thesis, Department of Human Development and Applied Psychology, Ontario Institute for Studies of Education, University of Toronto, Toronto, CA.

Rubie-Davies, C. M. (2007). Classroom interactions: Exploring the practices of high- and low-expectation teachers. *British Journal of Educational Psychology, 77*, 289–306.

Rubie-Davies, C. M. (Ed.). (2011). *Educational psychology*. New York: Routledge.

Rubin, K. H., Bowker, J. C., McDonald, K. L., & Menzer, M. (2013). Peer relationships in childhood. In P. D. Zelazo (Ed.), *Oxford handbook of developmental psychology*. New York: Oxford University Press.

Rubin, K. H., Bukowski, W., & Parker, J. (2006). Peer interactions, relationships, and groups. In W. Damon & R. Lerner (Eds.), *Handbook of child psychology* (6th ed.). New York: Wiley.

Rubin, K. H., Coplan, R. J., Bowker, J. C., & Menzer, M. (2011). Social withdrawal and shyness. In P. K. Smith & C. H. Hart (Eds.), *Wiley-Blackwell handbook of childhood social development* (2nd ed.). New York: Wiley.

Rubin, K. H., Mills, R. S. L., & Rose-Krasnor, L. (1989). Maternal beliefs and children's competence. In B. Schneider, G. Attili, J. Nadel, & R. Weissberg (Eds.), *Social competence in developmental perspective*. Amsterdam: Kluwer Academic.

Ruchat, S. M., & others. (2012). Nutrition and exercise reduce excessive weight gain in normal-weight pregnant women. *Medicine and Science in Sports and Exercise, 44*, 1419–1426.

Rudang, R., Mellstrom, D., Clark, E., Ohlsson, C., & Lorentzon, M. (2012). Advancing maternal age is associated with lower bone mineral density in young adult male offspring. *Osteoporosis International, 23*, 475–482.

Rueda, M. R., & Posner, M. I. (2013). Development of attentional networks. In P. D. Zelazo (Ed.), *Oxford handbook of developmental psychology*. New York: Oxford University Press.

Rueda, M. R., Posner, M. I., & Rothbart, M. K. (2005). The development of executive attention: Contributions to the emergence of self-regulation. *Developmental Neuropsychology, 28*, 573–594.

Ruffman, T., Slade, L., & Crowe, E. (2002). The relation between children's and mothers' mental state language and theory-of-mind understanding. *Child Development, 73*, 734–751.

Rumberger, R. W. (1995). Dropping out of middle school: The influence of race, sex, and family background. *American Educational Research Journal, 3*, 583–625.

Runquist, J. (2007). Persevering through postpartum fatigue. *Journal of Obstetric, Gynecologic, and Neonatal Nursing, 36*, 28–37.

Russell, A. (2011). Parent-child relationships and influences. In P. K. Smith & C. H. Hart (Eds.), *Wiley-Blackwell handbook of childhood social development* (2nd ed.). New York: Wiley.

Russell, M., & Airasian, P. W. (2012). *Classroom assessment* (7th ed.). New York: McGraw-Hill.

Russell, S. T., Crockett, L. J., & Chao, R. K. (2010). *Asian American parenting and parent-adolescent relationships*. New York: Springer.

Ryan, R. M., & Deci, E. L. (2009). Promoting self-determined school engagement: Motivation, learning, and well-being. In K. Wentzel & A. Wigfield (Eds.), *Handbook of motivation at school*. New York: Routledge.

S

Saarni, C. (1999). *The development of emotional competence*. New York: Guilford.

Saarni, C., Campos, J., Camras, L. A., & Witherington, D. (2006). Emotional development. In W. Damon & R. Lerner (Eds.), *Handbook of child psychology* (6th ed.). New York: Wiley.

Sabbagh, M. A., Xu, F., Carlson, S. M., Moses, L. J., & Lee, K. (2006). The development of executive functioning and theory of mind: A comparison of Chinese and U.S. preschoolers. *Psychological Science, 17*, 74–81.

Sackett, P. R., Hardison, C. M., & Cullen, M. J. (2005). On interpreting research on stereotype threat and test performance. *American Psychologist, 60*, 271–272.

Sadeh, A. (2008). Sleep. In M. M. Haith & J. B. Benson (Eds.), *Encyclopedia of infant and early childhood development*. Oxford, UK: Elsevier.

Sadker, D. M., & Zittleman, K. (2012). *Teachers, schools, and society* (3rd ed.). New York: McGraw-Hill.

Sadker, M. P., & Sadker, D. M. (2005). *Teachers, schools, and society* (7th ed.). New York: McGraw-Hill.

Sagiv, S. K., Epstein, J. N., Bellinger, D. C., & Korrick, S. A. (2013, in press). Pre- and postnatal risk factors for ADHD in a nonclinical pediatric population. *Journal of Attention Disorders*.

Saifer, S. (2007, August 29). *Tools of the Mind—A Vygotskian-inspired early childhood curriculum*. Paper presented at the 17th Annual Conference of the European Early Childhood Education Research Association, Prague.

Salas-Wright, C., Vaughn, M. G., Hodge, D. R., & Perron, B. E. (2012). Religiosity profiles of American youth in relation to substance use, violence, and delinquency. *Journal of Youth and Adolescence, 41*, 1560–1575.

Salley, B., Miller, A., & Bell, M.A. (2013, in press). Associations between temperament and social responsiveness in young children. *Infant and Child Development*.

Salloum, A., & Overstreet, S. (2012). Grief and trauma intervention for children after disaster: Exploring coping skills versus trauma narration. *Behavior Research and Therapy, 50*, 169–179.

Salmivalli, C., Garandeau, C. F., & Veenstra, R. (2012). KiVa Anti-Bullying Program: Implications for school adjustment. In A. M. Ryan & G. W. Ladd (Eds.), *Peer relationships and adjustment at school*. Charlotte, NC: Information Age Publishing.

Salmivalli, C., & Peets, K. (2009). Bullies, victims, and bully-victim relationships in middle childhood and adolescence. In K. H. Rubin, W. M. Bukowski, & B. Laursen (Eds.), *Handbook of peer interactions, relationships, and groups*. New York: Guilford.

Salmivalli, C., Peets, K., & Hodges, E. V. E. (2011). Bullying. In P. K. Smith & C. H. Hart (Eds.), *Wiley-Blackwell handbook of childhood social development* (2nd ed.). New York: Wiley.

Salovey, P., & Mayer, J. D. (1990). Emotional intelligence. *Imagination, Cognition, and Personality, 9*, 185–211.

Sameroff, A. J. (2009). The transactional model. In A. J. Sameroff (Ed.), *The transactional model of development: How children and contexts shape each other*. Washington, DC: American Psychological Association.

Samhan, Y. M., El-Sabae, H. H., Khafagy, H. F., & Maher, M. A. (2013, in press). A pilot study to compare epidural identification and catheterization using a saline-filled syringe versus a continuous hydrostatic pressure system. *Journal of Anesthesia*.

Sanchez, C. E., Richards, J. E., & Almli, C. R. (2012). Neurodevelopmental MRI brain templates from 2 weeks to 4 years of age. *Developmental Psychobiology, 54*, 77–91.

Sanders, E. (2008). Medical art and play therapy with accident survivors. In C. A. Malchiodi (Ed.), *Creative interventions with traumatized children*. New York: Guilford.

Sanson, A., & Rothbart, M. K. (1995). Child temperament and parenting. In M. H. Bornstein (Ed.), *Handbook of parenting* (Vol. 4). Hillsdale, NJ: Erlbaum.

Santiago, C. D., Etter, E. M., Wadsworth, M. E., & Raviv, T. (2012). Predictors of responses to stress among families coping with poverty-related stress. *Anxiety, Stress, and Coping, 25*(3), 239–258.

Santiago, C. D., Kaltman, S., & Miranda, J. (2013). Poverty and mental health: How do low-income adults and children fare in psychotherapy? *Journal of Clinical Psychology, 69*, 115–126.

Santrock, J. W., Sitterle, K. A., & Warshak, R. A. (1988). Parent-child relationships in stepfather families. In P. Bronstein & C. P. Cowan (Eds.), *Fatherhood today: Men's changing roles in the family.* New York: Wiley.

Santrock, J. W., & Warshak, R. A. (1979). Father custody and social development in boys and girls. *Journal of Social Issues, 35*, 112–125.

Saroglou, V. (2013, in press). Religion, spirituality, and altruism. In K. I. Pargament, J. Exline, & J. Jones (Eds.), *Handbook of psychology, religion, and spirituality.* Washington, DC: American Psychological Association.

Sasson, N. J., & Elison, J. T. (2013, in press). Eye tracking in young children with autism. *Journal of Visualized Experiments.*

Saunders, N. R., Liddelow, S. A., & Dziegielewska, K. M. (2012). Barrier mechanisms in the developing brain. *Frontiers in pharmacology, 3*, 46.

Savage, R. S., Abrami, P., Hipps, G., & Dealut, L. (2009). A randomized controlled trial study of the ABRACADABRA reading intervention program in grade 1. *Journal of Educational Psychology, 101*, 590–604.

Savelsbergh, G., van der Kamp, J., & van Wersmerskerken, M. (2013). The development of reaching actions. In P. D. Zelazo (Ed.), *Oxford handbook of developmental psychology.* New York: Oxford University Press.

Savin-Williams, R. (2011). Identity development in sexual-minority youth. In S. Schwartz, K. Luyckx, & V. Vignoles (Eds.), *Handbook of identity theory and research.* New York: Springer.

Savin-Williams, R. C. (2013, in press). The new sexual-minority teenager. In J. S. Kaufman & D. A. Powell (Eds.), *Sexual identities.* Thousand Oaks, CA: Sage.

Savolainen, J., & others. (2012). Antisocial personality, adolescent school outcomes, and the risk of criminal conviction. *Journal of Research on Adolescence, 22*, 54–64.

Scarr, S. (1993). Biological and cultural diversity: The legacy of Darwin for development. *Child Development, 64*, 1333–1353.

Scarr, S., & Weinberg, R. A. (1983). The Minnesota adoption studies: Genetic differences and malleability. *Child Development, 54*, 182–259.

Schaefer, R. T. (2013). *Race and ethnicity in the United States* (7th ed.). Upper Saddle River, NJ: Pearson.

Schaffer, H. R. (1996). *Social development.* Cambridge, MA: Blackwell.

Schaie, K. W. (2012). *Developmental influences on adult intellectual development: The Seattle Longitudinal Study.* New York: Oxford University Press.

Schattschneider, C., Fletcher, J. M., Francis, D. L., Carlson, C. D., & Foorman, B. R. (2004). Kindergarten prediction of reading skills: A longitudinal comparative analysis. *Journal of Educational Psychology, 96*, 265–282.

Scher, A., & Harel, J. (2008). Separation and stranger anxiety. In M. M. Haith & J. B. Benson (Eds.), *Encyclopedia of infant and early childhood development.* Oxford, UK: Elsevier.

Schieffelin, B. (2005). *The give and take of everyday life.* Tucson, AZ: Fenestra.

Schiff, W. J. (2013). *Nutrition for healthy living* (3rd ed.). New York: McGraw-Hill.

Schlam, T. R., Wilson, N. L., Shoda, Y., Mischel, W., & Ayduk, O. (2013, in press). Preschoolers' delay of gratification predicts their body mass 30 years later. *Journal of Pediatrics.*

Schlegel, M. (2000). All work and play. *Monitor on Psychology, 31*(11), 50–51.

Schmidt, J., Shumow, L., & Kackar, H. (2007). Adolescents' participation in service activities and its impact on academic, behavioral, and civic outcomes. *Journal of Youth and Adolescence. 36*, 127–140.

Schmidt, J. A., Shumow, L., & Kackar, H. Z. (2012). Associations of participation in service activities with academic, behavioral, and civic outcomes of adolescents at varying risk levels. *Journal of Youth and Adolescence, 41*, 932–947.

Schmidt, M. E., & Vandewater, E. A. (2008). Media and attention, cognition, and school achievement. *Future of Children, 18*(1), 64–85.

Schmitt, M. B., Justice, L. M., & Pentimonti, J. M. (2013). Language processes: Characterization and prevention of learning disabilities. In H. L. Swanson & others (Eds.), *Handbook of learning disabilities* (2nd ed.). New York: Guilford.

Schmuckler, M. A. (2013). Perceptual-motor relations in obvious and non-obvious domains: A history and review. In P. D. Zelazo (Ed.), *Oxford handbook of developmental psychology.* New York: Oxford University Press.

Schneider, B. H., & others. (2011). Cooperation and competition. In P. K. Smith & C. H. Hart (Eds.), *Wiley-Blackwell handbook of childhood social development* (2nd ed.). New York: Wiley.

Schneider, W. (2004). Memory development in childhood. In P. Smith & C. Han (Eds.), *Blackwell handbook of childhood cognitive development.* Malden, MA: Blackwell.

Schneider, W. (2011). Memory development in childhood. In U. Goswami (Ed.), *Wiley-Blackwell handbook of childhood cognitive development* (2nd ed.). New York: Wiley-Blackwell.

Schneider, W., & Pressley, M. (1997). *Memory development between two and twenty.* Mahwah, NJ: Erlbaum.

Schoffstall, C. L., & Cohen, R. (2011). Cyber aggression: The relation between online offenders and offline social competence. *Social Development, 20*(3), 587–604.

Schoon, I., Jones, E., Cheng, H., & Maughan, B. (2011). Family hardship, family instability, and cognitive development. *Journal of Epidemiology and Community Health, 66*, 718–722.

Schoon, I., Parsons, S., & Sacker, A. (2004). Socioeconomic adversity, educational resilience, and subsequent levels of adult adaptation. *Journal of Adolescent Research, 19*, 383–404.

Schreiber, L. R. (1990). *The parents' guide to kids' sports.* Boston: Little, Brown.

Schulenberg, J. E., & Zarrett, N. R. (2006). Mental health during emerging adulthood: Continuities and discontinuities in course, content, and meaning. In J. J. Arnett & J. Tanner (Eds.), *Advances in emerging adulthood.* Washington, DC: American Psychological Association.

Schunk, D. H. (2008). *Learning theories* (5th ed.). Upper Saddle River, NJ: Prentice Hall.

Schunk, D. H. (2012). *Learning theories: An educational perspective* (6th ed.). Upper Saddle River, NJ: Prentice Hall.

Schunk, D. H., Pintrich, P. R., & Meece, J. L. (2008). *Motivation in education: Theory, research, and applications* (3rd ed.). Upper Saddle River, NJ: Prentice Hall.

Schunk, D. H., & Zimmerman, B. J. (2013). Self-regulation and learning. In I. B. Weiner (Ed.), *Handbook of psychology* (2nd ed.). New York: Wiley.

Schwalbe, C. S., Gearing, R. E., MacKenzie, M. J., Brewer, K. B., & Ibrahim, R. (2012). A meta-analysis of experimental studies of diversion programs for juvenile defenders. *Clinical Psychology Review, 32*, 26–33.

Schwartz, D., Kelly, B. M., Duong, M., & Badaly, D. (2010). Contextual perspective on intervention and prevention efforts for bully/victim problems. In E. M. Vernberg & B. K. Biggs (Eds.), *Preventing and treating bullying and victimization.* New York: Oxford University Press.

Schwartz, S. J., Donnellan, M. B., Ravert, R. D., Luyckx, K., & Zamboanga, B. L. (2013). Identity development, personality, and well-being in adolescence and emerging adulthood: Theory, research, and recent advances. In I. B. Weiner & others (Eds.), *Handbook of psychology* (2nd ed., Vol. 6). New York: Wiley.

Schwartz, S. J., Zamboanga, B. L., Meca, A., & Ritchie, R. A. (2012). Identity around the world: An overview. In S. J. Schwartz (Ed.), *Identity Around the World. New Directions for Child and Adolescent Development, 138*, 1–18.

Schwartz-Mette, R. A., & Rose, A. J. (2013, in press). Co-rumination mediates contagion of internalizing symptoms within youths' friendships. *Developmental Psychology.*

Schwarz, S. P. (2004). A mother's story. Available at http://www.makinglifeeasier.com

Schweinhart, L. J., & others. (2005). *Lifetime effects: The High/Scope Perry Preschool Study Through Age 40.* Ypsilanti, MI: High/Scope Press.

Sciberras, E., Ukoumunne, O. C., & Efron, D. (2011). Predictors of parent-reported attention-deficit/hyperactivity disorder in children aged 6–7 years: A national longitudinal study *Journal of Abnormal Child Psychology, 39*(7), 1025–1034.

Science Daily. (2008, January 15). Human gene count tumbles again (p. 1).

Sclar, D. A., & others. (2012). Attention deficit/hyperactivity disorder among children and adolescents in the United States: Trend in diagnosis and use of pharmacotherapy by gender. *Clinical Pediatrics, 51*, 584–589.

Scott, J. A., Ng, S. Y., & Cobiac, L. (2012). The relationship between breastfeeding and weight status in a national sample of Australian children and adolescents. *BMC Public Health, 12*, 107.

Scott, K. A., Roberts, J. A., & Glennen, S. (2011). How well do children who are internationally adopted acquire language? A meta-analysis. *Journal of Speech, Language, and Hearing Research, 54,* 1153–1169.

Scott, R. M., & Baillargeon, R. (2013, in press). Do infants really expect others to act efficiently? A critical test of the rationality principle. *Psychological Science.*

Scott-Jones, D. (1995, March). *Incorporating ethnicity and socioeconomic status in research with children.* Paper presented at the meeting of the Society for Research in Child Development, Indianapolis.

Scourfield, J., Van den Bree, M., Martin, N., & McGuffin, P. (2004). Conduct problems in children and adolescents: A twin study. *Archives of General Psychiatry, 61,* 489–496.

Seaton, E. K., Caldwell, C. H., Sellers, R. M., & Jackson, J. S. (2010). Developmental characteristics of African American and Caribbean Black adolescents' attributions regarding discrimination. *Journal of Research on Adolescence, 20,* 774–788.

Segal, M., & others. (2012). *All about child care and early education* (2nd ed.). Upper Saddle River, NJ: Pearson.

Sekhobo, J. P., Edmunds, L. S., Reynolds, D. K., & Dalenius, K., & Sharma, A. (2010). Trends in the prevalence of obesity and overweight among children enrolled in the New York State WIC program, 2002–2007. *Public Health Reports, 125,* 218–224.

Sellers, R. M., Linder, N. C., Martin, P. P., & Lewis, R. L. (2006). Racial identity matters: The relationship between racial discrimination and psychological functioning in African American adolescents. *Journal of Research on Adolescence, 16*(2), 187–216.

Selman, R. L. (1980). *The growth of interpersonal understanding.* New York: Academic Press.

Senter, L., Sackoff, J., Landi, K., & Boyd, L. (2010). Studying sudden and unexpected deaths in a time of changing death certification and investigation practices: Evaluating sleep-related risk factors for infant death in New York City. *Maternal and Child Health, 15*(2), 242–248.

Sepulcre, J., & others. (2012). Stepwise connectivity of the model cerebral cortex reveals the multimodal organization of the human brain. *Journal of Neuroscience, 32,* 10649–10661.

Sernau, S. R. (2013). *Global problems* (3rd ed.). Upper Saddle River, NJ: Pearson.

Sethi, V., & others. (2013, in press). Single ventricle anatomy predicts delayed microstructural brain development. *Pediatric Research.*

Sethna, V., Murray, L., & Ramchandani, P. G. (2012, in press). Depressed fathers' speech to their 3-month-old infants: A study of cognitive and mentalizing features in paternal speech. *Psychological Medicine.*

Shah, R., & others. (2012). Prenatal methamphetamine exposure and short-term maternal and infant medical outcomes. *American Journal of Perinatology, 29,* 391–400.

Shanahan, L., & Sobolewski, J. M. (2013). Child effects on family processes. In A. C. Crouter & A. Booth (Eds.), *Children's influence on family dynamics.* New York: Routledge.

Shankaran, S., & others. (2010). Prenatal cocaine exposure and BMI and blood pressure at 9 years of age. *Journal of Hypertension, 28,* 1166–1175.

Shankaran, S., & others. (2011). Risk for obesity in adolescence starts in childhood. *Journal of Perinatology, 31,* 711–716.

Shapiro, A. F., & Gottman, J. M. (2005). Effects on marriage of a psycho-education intervention with couples undergoing the transition to parenthood: Evaluation at 1-year post-intervention. *Journal of Family Communication, 5,* 1–24.

Shapiro, C. J., Prinz, R. J., & Sanders, M. R. (2012). Facilitators and barriers to implementation of an evidence-based parenting intervention to prevent child maltreatment: The Triple P—Positive Parenting Program. *Child Maltreatment, 17,* 86–95.

Sharma, A. R., McGue, M. K., & Benson, P. L. (1996). The emotional and behavioral adjustment of adopted adolescents: Part I: Age at adoption. *Children and Youth Services Review, 18,* 101–114.

Sharma, N., Classen, J., & Cohen, L. G. (2013). Neural plasticity and its contribution to functional recovery. *Handbook of Clinical Psychology, 110,* 3–12.

Shatz, M., & Gelman, R. (1973). The development of communication skills: Modifications in the speech of young children as a function of the listener. *Monographs of the Society for Research in Child Development, 38*(152).

Shaw, D. S. (2013). Commentary: Early father-infant interaction and externalizing behaviors—a response to Ramchandani et al. (2013). *Journal of Child Psychology and Psychiatry, 54,* 65–66.

Shaw, D. S., Dishion, T. J., Supplee, L., & Gardner, F., & Arnds, K. (2006). Randomized trial of family-centered approach to the prevention of early conduct problems: Two-year effects of the family check-up in early childhood. *Journal of Consulting and Clinical Psychology, 74,* 1–9.

Shaw, P., & others. (2007). Attention-deficit/hyperactivity disorder is characterized by a delay in cortical maturation. *Proceedings of the National Academy of Sciences, 104*(49), 19649–19654.

Shayer, M., & Adhami, M. (2010). Realizing the cognitive potential of children 5–7 with a mathematics focus: Post-test and long-term effects of a 2-year intervention. *British Journal of Educational Psychology, 80,* 363–379.

Shaywitz, B. A., Lyon, G. R., & Shaywitz, S. E. (2006). The role of functional magnetic resonance imaging in understanding reading and dyslexia. *Developmental Neuropsychology, 30,* 613–632.

Shaywitz, S. E., Gruen, J. R., & Shaywitz, B. A. (2007). Management of dyslexia, its rationale, and underlying neurobiology. *Pediatric Clinics of North America, 54,* 609–623.

Shehata, F., & others. (2011). Placenta/birthweight ratio and perinatal outcome: A retrospective cohort analysis. *British Journal of Obstetrics & Gynecology, 118,* 741–747.

Shek, D. T. (2012, in press). Spirituality as a positive youth development construct: A conceptual review. *Scientific World Journal.*

Shema, L., Ore, L., Ben-Shachar, M., Haj, M., & Linn, S. (2007). The association between breastfeeding and breast cancer occurrence among Jewish women: A case control study. *Journal of Cancer Research and Clinical Oncology, 133,* 903.

Shen, L. H., Liao, M. H., & Tseng, Y. C. (2013, in press). Recent advances in imaging of dopaminergic neurons for evaluation of neuropsychiatric disorders. *Journal of Biomedicine and Biotechnology.*

Sher-Censor, E., Parke, R. D., & Coltrane, S. (2011). Parents' promotion of psychological autonomy, psychological control, and Mexican-American adolescents' adjustment. *Journal of Youth and Adolescence, 40,* 620–632.

Shibata, Y., & others. (2012). Extrachromosomal microDNAs and chromosomal microdeletions in normal tissues. *Science, 336,* 82–86.

Shields, S. A. (1998, August). *What Jerry Maguire can tell us about gender and emotion.* Paper presented at the meeting of the International Society for Research on Emotions, Wurzburg, Germany.

Shin, S. H., Hong, H. G., & Hazen, A. L. (2010). Childhood sexual abuse and adolescence substance use: A latent class analysis. *Drug and Alcohol Dependence, 109*(1), 226–235.

Shiner, R. L., & DeYoung, C. G. (2013). The structure of temperament and personality: A developmental approach. In P. D. Zelazo (Ed.), *Oxford handbook of developmental psychology.* New York: Oxford University Press.

Shiraev, E., & Levy, D. (2010). *Cross-cultural psychology: Critical thinking and critical applications* (4th ed.). Belmont, CA: Wadsworth.

Short, M. A., Gradisar, M., Lack, L. C., Wright, H. R., & Dohnt, H. (2012, in press). The sleep patterns and well-being of Australian adolescents. *Journal of Adolescence.*

Short, S. J., & others. (2013, in press). Associations between white matter microstructure and infants' working memory. *NeuroImage, 64,* 156–166.

Shuai, L., Chan, R. C., & Wang, Y. (2011). Executive function profile of Chinese boys with attention-deficit hyperactivity disorder: Different subtypes and comorbidity. *Archives of Clinical Neuropsychology, 26,* 120–132.

Shulman, S., Davila, J., & Shachar-Shapira, L. (2011). Assessing romantic competence among older adolescents. *Journal of Adolescence, 34,* 397–406.

Shulman, S., Scharf, M., & Shachar-Shapira, S. (2012). The intergenerational transmission of romantic relationships. In P. K. Kerig, M. S. Schulz, & S. T. Hauser (Eds.), *Adolescence and beyond.* New York: Oxford University Press.

Shulman, S., Zlotnik, A., Shachar-Shapira, L., Connolly, J., & Bohr, Y. (2012). Adolescent daughters' romantic competence: The role of divorce, quality of parenting, and maternal romantic history. *Journal of Youth and Adolescence, 41,* 593–606.

Shwalb, D. W., Shwalb, B. J., & Lamb, M. E. (2013, in press). *Fathers in cultural context.* New York: Routledge.

Shweder, R., Mahapatra, M., & Miller, J. (1987). Culture and moral development. In J. Kagan & S. Lamb (Eds.), *The emergence of morality in young children.* Chicago: University of Chicago Press.

Siegel, L. S., & Wiener, J. (1993, Spring). Canadian special education policies: Children with disabilities in a bilingual and multicultural society. *Social Policy Report, Society for Research in Child Development, 7*, 1–16.

Siegler, R. S. (1976). Three aspects of cognitive development. *Cognitive Psychology, 8*, 481–520.

Siegler, R. S. (1998). *Children's thinking* (3rd ed.). Upper Saddle River, NJ: Prentice Hall.

Siegler, R. S. (2006). Microgenetic analysis of learning. In W. Damon & R. Lerner (Eds.). *Handbook of child psychology* (6th ed.). New York: Wiley.

Siegler, R. S. (2012). From theory to application and back: Following in the giant footsteps of David Klahr. In S. M. Carver & J. Shrager (Eds.), *The journey from child to scientist: Integrating cognitive development and the education sciences.* Thousand Oaks, CA: Sage.

Siegler, R. S. (2013, in press). How do people become experts? In J. Staszewski (Ed.), *Experience and skill acquisition.* New York: Taylor & Francis.

Siegler, R. S., & Mu, Y. (2008). Chinese children excel on novel mathematics problems even before elementary school. *Psychological Science, 19*, 759–763.

Siener, S., & Kerns, K. A. (2012). Emotion regulation and depressive symptoms in preadolescence. *Child Psychiatry and Human Development, 43*, 414–430.

Sigal, A., Sandler, I., Wolchik, S., & Braver, S. (2011). Do parent education programs promote healthy post-divorce parenting? Critical directions and distinctions and a review of the evidence. *Family Court Review, 49*, 120–129.

Silva, C. (2005, October 31). When teen dynamo talks, city listens. *Boston Globe*, pp. 81–84.

Silverman, R. (2012). Stereotypes. In M. Kohut (Ed.), *Encyclopedia of gender in media.* Thousand Oaks, CA: Sage.

Simkin, P., & Bolding, A. (2004). Update on nonpharmacological approaches to relieve labor pain and prevent suffering. *Journal of Midwifery and Women's Health, 49*, 489–504.

Simon, E. J., Dickey, J. L., & Reece, J. B. (2013). *Campbell essential biology* (5th ed.). Upper Saddle River, NJ: Pearson.

Simonetti, G. D., & others. (2011). Determinants of blood pressure in preschool children: The role of parental smoking. *Circulation, 123*, 292–298.

Simpkins, S. D., Delgado, M. Y., Price, C. D., Quach, A., & Starbuck, E. (2013). Socioeconomic status, ethnicity, culture, and immigration: Examining the potential mechanisms underlying Mexican-origin adolescents' organized activity participation. *Developmental Psychology, 49*, 706–721.

Simpkins, S. D., Fredricks, J. A., Davis-Kean, P. E., & Eccles, J. S. (2006). Healthy mind, healthy habits: The influence of activity involvement in middle childhood. In A. C. Huston & M. N. Ripke (Eds.), *Developmental contexts in middle childhood.* Mahwah, NJ: Erlbaum.

Singer, D., Golinkoff, R. M., & Hirsh-Pasek, K. (Eds.). (2006). *Play 5 learning: How play motivates and enhances children's cognitive and social-emotional growth.* New York: Oxford University Press.

Singer, T. (2012, in press). The past, present, and future of social neuroscience: A European perspective. *Neuroimage.*

Sinha, J. W., Cnaan, R. A., & Gelles, R. J. (2007). Adolescent risk behaviors and religion: Findings from a national study. *Journal of Adolescence, 30*, 231–249.

Sisson, S. B., Broyles, S. T., Baker, B. L., & Katzmarzyk, P. T. (2010). Screen time, physical activity, and overweight in U.S. youth: National Survey of Children's Health 2003. *Journal of Adolescent Health, 47*, 309–311.

Siu, A. M., Shek, D. T., & Law, B. (2012). Prosocial norms as a positive youth development construct: A conceptual review. *Scientific World Journal*, 489156.

Sivell, S. & others. (2008). How risk is perceived, constructed, and interpreted by clients in clinical genetics, and the effects on decision making: A review. *Journal of Genetic Counseling, 17*, 30–63.

Skinner, B. F. (1938). *The behavior of organisms: An experimental analysis.* New York: Appleton-Century-Crofts.

Skinner, B. F. (1957). *Verbal behavior.* New York: Appleton-Century-Crofts.

Slater, A. M., Bremner, J. G., Johnson, S. P., & Hayes, R. (2011). The role of perceptual processes in infant addition/subtraction events. In L. M. Oakes, C. H. Cashon, M. Casasola, & D. H. Rakison (Eds.), *Early perceptual and cognitive development.* New York: Oxford University Press.

Slater, A. M., & others. (2010). Visual perception. In G. Bremner & T. Wachs (Eds.), *Blackwell handbook of infant development,* (2nd ed.). Oxford, UK: Blackwell.

Slater, A., Field, T., & Hernandez-Reif, M. (2007). The development of the senses. In A. Slater & M. Lewis (Eds.), *Introduction to infant development* (2nd ed.). New York: Oxford University Press.

Slater, A., Morison, V., & Somers, M. (1988). Orientation discrimination and cortical function in the human newborn. *Perception, 17*, 597–602.

Slavin, R. E. (2011). Instruction based on cooperative learning. In P. A. Alexander & R. E. Mayer (Eds.), *Handbook of research on learning and instruction.* New York: Routledge.

Slobin, D. (1972, July). Children and language: They learn the same way around the world. *Psychology Today*, 71–76.

Slomkowski, C., Rende, R., Conger, K. J., Simmons, R. L., & Conger, R. D. (2001). Sisters, brothers, and delinquency: Social influence during early and middle adolescence. *Child Development, 72*, 271–283.

Smetana, J. G. (2011a). *Adolescents, families, and social development: How adolescents construct their worlds.* New York: Wiley-Blackwell.

Smetana, J. G. (2011b). Adolescents' social reasoning and relationships with parents: Conflicts and coordinations within and across domains. In E. Amsel & J. Smetana (Eds.), *Adolescent vulnerabilities and opportunities: Constructivist and developmental perspectives.* New York: Cambridge University Press.

Smetana, J. G. (2013a). Moral development: The social domain theory view. In P. D. Zelazo (Ed.), *Oxford handbook of developmental psychology.* New York: Oxford University Press.

Smetana, J. G. (2013b, in press). Social-cognitive domain theory: Consistencies and variations in children's moral and social judgments. In M. Killen & J. Smetana (Eds.), *Handbook of moral development* (2nd ed.). New York: Routledge.

Smetana, J. G., & others. (2012). Developmental changes and individual differences in young children's moral judgments. *Child Development, 83*, 683–696.

Smith, C., & Denton, M. L. (2005). *Soul searching: The religious and spiritual lives of American teenagers.* New York: Oxford University Press.

Smith, C. A., Levett, K. M., Collins, C. T., & Jones, L. (2012). Massage, reflexology, and other manual methods for pain management. *Cochrane Database of Systematic Reviews, 15*(2), CD009290.

Smith, J. B. (2009). High school organization. In D. Carr (Ed.), *Encyclopedia of the life course and human development.* Boston: Gale Cengage.

Smith, J., & Ross, H. (2007). Training parents to mediate sibling disputes affects children's negotiation and conflict understanding. *Child Development, 78*, 790–805.

Smith, K. (2002). *Who's minding the kids? Child care arrangements: Spring 1977.* Current Population Reports, P70–86. Washington, DC: U.S. Census Bureau.

Smith, L. E., & Howard, K. S. (2008). Continuity of paternal social support and depressive symptoms among new mothers. *Journal of Family Psychology, 22*, 763–773.

Smith, P. K. (2007). Pretend play and children's cognitive and literacy development: Sources of evidence and some lessons from the past. In K. A. Roskos & J. F. Christie (Eds.), *Play and literacy in early childhood.* Mahwah, NJ: Erlbaum.

Smith, R. A., & Davis, S. F. (2013). *The psychologist as detective* (6th ed.). Upper Saddle River, NJ: Prentice Hall.

Smith, R. L. (2009). *Social perspective-taking in the friendships of adolescents: Implications for friendship quality and emotional adjustment.* Thesis, U. of Missouri–Columbia.

Smith, R. L., & Rose, A. J. (2011). The "cost of caring" in youths' friendships: Considering associations among social perspective taking, co-rumination, and empathetic distress. *Developmental Psychology, 47*, 1792–1803.

Smith, R. L., Rose, A. J., & Schwartz-Mette, R. A. (2010). Relational and overt aggression in childhood and adolescence: Clarifying mean-level gender differences and associations with peer acceptance. *Social Development, 19*, 243–269.

Smith, T. E., Polloway, E. A., Patton, J. R., & Dowdy, C. A. (2012). *Teaching students with special needs in inclusive settings* (6th ed.). Upper Saddle River, NJ: Pearson.

Snarey, J. (1987, June). A question of morality. *Psychology Today*, pp. 6–8.

Snijders, B. E., & others. (2007). Breast-feeding duration and infant atopic manifestations, by maternal allergic status, in the first two years of life (KOALA study). *Journal of Pediatrics, 151*, 347–351.

Snow, C. E., & Kang, J. Y. (2006). Becoming bilingual, biliterate, and bicultural. In W. Damon & R. Lerner (Eds.), *Handbook of child psychology* (6th ed.). New York: Wiley.

Snowdon, A. W., & others. (2008). The effectiveness of a multimedia intervention on parents' knowledge and use of vehicle safety systems for children. *Journal of Pediatric Nursing, 23*, 126–139.

So, H. K., Li, A. M., Choi, K. C., Sung, R. Y., & Nelson, E. A. (2013, in press). Regular exercise and a healthy dietary pattern are associated with lower resting blood pressure in non-obese adolescents: A population-based study. *Journal of Human Hypertension.*

Soares, N. S., & Patel, D. R. (2012). Office screening and early identification of children with autism. *Pediatric Clinics of North America, 59*, 89–102.

Sokol, B. W., Snjezana, H., & Muller, U. (2010). Social understanding and self-regulation: From perspective-taking to theory of mind. In B. Sokol, U. Muller, J. Carpendale, A. Young, & G. Larocci (Eds.), *Self-and social cognition*. New York: Oxford University Press.

Solheim, K. N., & others. (2011). The effect of cesarean delivery rates on the future incidence of placenta previa, placenta accrete, and maternal mortality. *Journal of Maternal-Fetal and Neonatal Medicine, 24*, 1341–1346.

Solmeyer, A. R., McHale, S. M., Killoren, S. E., & Updegraff, K. A. (2011). Coparenting around siblings' differential treatment in Mexican-origin families. *Developmental Psychology, 25*, 251–260.

Solomon, D., Watson, M. S., & Battistich, V. A. (2002). Teaching and school effects on moral/prosocial development. In V. Richardson (Ed.), *Handbook for research on teaching*. Washington, DC: American Educational Research Association.

Song, L. J., & others. (2010). The differential effects of general mental ability and emotional intelligence on academic performance and social interactions. *Intelligence, 38*, 137–143.

Sontag, L. M., Clemans, K. H., Graber, J. A., & Lyndon, S. T. (2011). Traditional and cyber aggressors and victims: A comparison of social characteristics. *Journal of Youth and Adolescence, 40*(4), 392–404.

Sontag-Padilla, L. M., & others. (2012). Executive functioning, cortisol reactivity, and symptoms of psychopathology in girls with premature adrenarche. *Development and Psychopathology, 24*, 211–223.

Sophian, C. (1985). Perseveration and infants' search: A comparison of two- and three-location tasks. *Developmental Psychology, 21*, 187–194.

Sorensen, A., & others. (2013, in press). Changes in human placental oxygenation during maternal hyperoxia as estimated by BOLD MRI. *Ultrasound in Obstetrics and Gynecology*.

Soter, A. O. (2013). *Grammar, usage, and punctuation*. Boston: Allyn & Bacon.

Spangler, G., Johann, M., Ronai, Z., & Zimmermann, P. (2009). Genetic and environmental influence on attachment disorganization. *Journal of Child Psychology and Psychiatry, 50*, 952–961.

Spector, L. G., & others. (2013, in press). Children's Oncology Group's 2013 blueprint for research: Epidemiology. *Pediatric and Blood Cancer*.

Spelke, E. S. (1979). Perceiving bimodally specified events in infancy. *Developmental Psychology, 5*, 626–636.

Spelke, E. S. (1991). Physical knowledge in infancy: Reflections on Piaget's theory. In S. Carey & R. Gelman (Eds.), *The epigenesis of mind: Essays on biology and cognition*. Hillsdale, NJ: Erlbaum.

Spelke, E. S. (2000). Core knowledge. *American Psychologist, 55*, 1233–1243.

Spelke, E. S. (2011). Natural number and natural geometry. In E. Brannon & S. Dehaene (Eds.), *Space, time, and number in the brain*. New York: Oxford University Press.

Spelke, E. S., Bernier, E. P., & Snedeker, J. (2013, in press). Core social cognition. In M. R. Banaji & S.A. Gelman (Eds.), *Navigating the social world: What infants, children, and other species can teach us*. New York: Oxford University Press.

Spelke, E. S., Breinlinger, K., Macomber, J., & Jacobson, K. (1992). Origins of knowledge. *Psychological Review, 99*, 605–632.

Spelke, E. S., & Hespos, S. J. (2001). Continuity, competence, and the object concept. In E. Dupoux (Ed.), *Language, brain, and behavior*. Cambridge, MA: Bradford/MIT Press.

Spelke, E. S., & Kinzler, K. D. (2007). Core knowledge. *Development Science, 10*, 89–96.

Spelke, E. S., & Kinzler, K. D. (2009). Innateness, learning and rationality. *Cognitive Development Perspectives, 3*(2), 96–98.

Spelke, E. S., & Owsley, C. J. (1979). Intermodal exploration and knowledge in infancy. *Infant Behavior and Development, 2*, 13–28.

Spence, J. T., & Buckner, C. E. (2000). Instrumental and expressive traits, trait stereotypes, and sexist attitudes: What do they signify? *Psychology of Women Quarterly, 24*, 44–62.

Spence, J. T., & Helmreich, R. (1978). *Masculinity and femininity: Their psychological dimensions*. Austin: University of Texas Press.

Spencer, J. P., & others. (2009). Short arms and talking eggs: Why we should no longer abide the nativist-empiricist debate. *Child Development Perspectives, 3*, 79–87.

Spencer, J. R., & Lamb, M. E. (Eds.). (2013, in press). Children and cross-examination: Time to change the rules. Oxford, UK: Hart.

Spilman, S. K., Neppl, T. K., Donnellan, M. B., Schofield, T. J., & Conger, R. D. (2012, in press). Incorporating religiosity into a developmental model of positive family functioning across generations. *Developmental Psychology*.

Spring, J. (2013). *Deculturalization and the struggle for equality* (7th ed.). New York: McGraw-Hill.

Squires, J., Pribble, L., Chen, C-I., & Pomes, M. (2013, in press). Early childhood education: Improving outcomes for young children and families. In I. B. Weiner & others (Eds.), *Handbook of psychology* (2nd ed., Vol. 7). New York: Wiley.

Srabstein, J. C., McCarter, R. J., Shao, C., & Huang, Z. J. (2006). Morbidities associated with bullying behaviors in adolescents: School-based study of American adolescents. *International Journal of Adolescent Medicine and Health, 18*, 587–596.

Sroufe, L. A., Coffino, B., & Carlson, E. A. (2010). Conceptualizing the role of early experience: Lessons from the Minnesota longitudinal study. *Developmental Review, 30*, 36–51.

Sroufe, L. A., Egeland, B., Carlson, E., & Collins, W. (2005a). *The development of the person: The Minnesota Study of Risk and Adaptation from birth to maturity*. New York: Guilford.

Sroufe, L. A., Egeland, B., Carlson, E., & Collins, W. A. (2005b). The place of early attachment in developmental context. In K. E. Grossman, K. Grossman, & E. Waters (Eds.), *The power of longitudinal attachment research: From infancy and childhood to adulthood*. New York: Guilford.

Sroufe, L. A., Waters, E., & Matas, L. (1974). Contextual determinants of infant affectional response. In M. Lewis & L. Rosenblum (Eds.), *Origins of fear*. New York: Wiley.

St. Pierre, R., Layzer, J., & Barnes, H. (1996). *Regenerating two-generation programs*. Cambridge, MA: Abt Associates.

Staiano, A. E., Abraham, A. A., & Calvert, S. L. (2012). Competitive versus cooperative exergame play for African American adolescents' executive functioning skills. *Developmental Psychology, 48*, 337–342.

Stanovich, K. E. (2013). *How to think straight about psychology* (10th ed.). Upper Saddle River, NJ: Pearson.

Stanovich, K. E., West, R. F., & Toplak, M. E. (2012). Judgment and decision making in adolescence: Separating intelligence from rationality. In V. F. Reyna (Ed.), *The adolescent brain*. Washington, DC: American Psychological Association.

Starr, C., Taggart, R., Evers, C., & Starr, L. (2013). *Evolution of life* (13th ed.). Boston: Cengage.

Starr, L. R., & Davila, J. (2009). Clarifying co-rumination: Associations with internalizing symptoms and romantic involvement among adolescent girls. *Journal of Adolescence, 32*, 19–37.

Starr, L. R., & others. (2013). Love hurts (in more ways than one): Specificity of psychological symptoms as predictors and consequences of romantic activity among early adolescent girls. *Journal of Clinical Psychology*.

Staszewski, J. (Ed.). (2013, in press). *Expertise and skill acquisition: The impact of William C. Chase*. New York: Taylor & Francis.

Steca, P., Bassi, M., Caprara, G. V., & Fave, A. D. (2011). Parents' self-efficacy beliefs and their children's psychosocial adaptation during adolescence. *Journal of Youth and Adolescence, 40*(3), 320–331.

Steel, A. J., & Sutcliffe, A. (2010). Long-term health implications for children conceived by IVF/ICSI. *Human Fertility, 12*, 21–27.

Steinberg, L. (2009). Adolescent development and juvenile justice. *Annual Review of Clinical Psychology* (Vol. 5). Palo Alto, CA: Annual Reviews.

Steinberg, L. (2012). Adolescent risk-taking: A social neuroscience perspective. In E. Amsel & J. Smetana (Eds.), *Adolescent vulnerabilities and opportunities: Constructivist developmental perspectives*. New York: Cambridge University Press.

Steinberg, L. (2013, in press). How should the science of adolescent brain development inform legal policy? In J. Bhabha (Ed.),*Coming of age: A new framework for adolescent rights*. Philadelphia: University of Pennsylvania Press.

Steinberg, L. D., & Silk, J. S. (2002). Parenting adolescents. In M. Bornstein (Ed.), *Handbook of parenting* (2nd ed., Vol. 1). Mahwah, NJ: Erlbaum.

Steinberg, L., & Monahan, K. (2007). Age differences in resistance to peer influence. *Developmental Psychology, 43*, 1531–1543.

Steiner, J. E. (1979). Human facial expressions in response to taste and smell stimulation. In H. Reese & L. Lipsitt (Eds.), *Advances in child development and behavior* (Vol. 13). New York: Academic Press.

Steiner, N. J., Sheldrick, R. C., Gotthelf, D., & Perrin, E. C. (2011). Computer-based attention training in schools for children with attention deficit hyperactivity disorder: A preliminary trial. *Clinical Pediatrics, 50*, 615–622.

Steming, C. (2008). Centering Pregnancy: Group prenatal care. *Creative Nursing, 14,* 182–183.

Stephens, J. M. (2008). Cheating. In N. J. Salkind (Ed.), *Encyclopedia of educational psychology.* Thousand Oaks, CA: Sage.

Stern, S. J., Matok, I., Kapur, B., & Koren, G. (2011). A comparison of folic acid pharmacokinetics in obese and nonobese women of childbearing age. *Therapeutic Drug Monitoring, 33,* 336–340.

Sternberg, R. J. (1986). *Intelligence applied.* Fort Worth, TX: Harcourt Brace.

Sternberg, R. J. (2004). Individual differences in cognitive development. In P. Smith & C. Hart (Eds.), *Blackwell handbook of cognitive development.* Malden, MA: Blackwell.

Sternberg, R. J. (2010). Intelligence. In B. McGaw, P. Peterson, & E. Baker (Eds.), *International encyclopedia of education* (3rd ed.). New York: Elsevier.

Sternberg, R. J. (2012a). Intelligence. *Dialogues in Clinical Neuroscience, 14,* 19–27.

Sternberg, R. J. (2012b). Intelligence in its cultural context. In M. Gelfand, C-Y Chiu, & Y-Y Hong (Eds.), *Advances in cultures and psychology* (Vol. 2). New York: Oxford University Press.

Sternberg, R. J. (2013a). Contemporary theories of intelligence. In I. B. Weiner & others (Eds.), *Handbook of psychology* (2nd ed., Vol. 7). New York: Wiley.

Sternberg, R. J. (2013b, in press). Personal wisdom in balance. In M. Ferrari & N. Westrate (Eds.), *Personal wisdom.* New York: Springer.

Sternberg, R. J. (2013c). The triarchic theory of successful intelligence. In D. P. Flanagan & P. L. Harrison (Eds.), *Contemporary intellectual assessment* (3rd ed.). New York: Guilford.

Sternberg, R. J., & Sternberg, K. (2013, in press). Teaching cognitive science. In D. Dunn (Ed.), *Teaching psychology education.* New York: Oxford University Press.

Sternberg, R. J., & Williams. W. M. (1996). *How to develop student creativity.* Alexandria, VA: ASCD.

Sternberg, R. J., & Sternberg, K. (2012). *Cognitive psychology* (7th ed.). Boston: Cengage.

Stevens, C., & Bavelier, D. (2012). The role of selective attention on academic foundations: A cognitive neuroscience perspective. *Developmental Cognitive Neuroscience, 15*(Suppl. 1), S30–S48.

Stevenson, H. W. (1995). Mathematics achievement of American students: First in the world by the year 2000? In C. A. Nelson (Ed.), *Basic and applied perspectives on learning, cognition, and development.* Minneapolis: University of Minnesota Press.

Stevenson, H. W., Lee, S., Chen, C., Stigler, J. W., Hsu, C., & Kitamura, S. (1990). Contexts of achievement. *Monograph of the Society for Research in Child Development, 55* (Serial No. 221).

Stevenson, H. W., Lee, S., & Stigler, J. W. (1986). Mathematics achievement of Chinese, Japanese, and American children. *Science, 231,* 693–699.

Stevenson, H. W., & Zusho, A. (2002). Adolescence in China and Japan: Adapting to a changing environment. In B. B. Brown, R. W. Larson, & T. S. Saraswathi (Eds.), *The world's youth.* New York: Cambridge University Press.

Stiggins, R. (2008). *Introduction to student-involved assessment for learning* (5th ed.). Upper Saddle River. NJ: Prentice Hall.

Stipek, D. (2005, February 16). Commentary in *USA TODAY,* p. 1D.

Stipek, D. J. (2002). *Motivation to learn* (4th ed.). Boston: Allyn & Bacon.

Stochholm, K., Juul, S., & Grayholt, C. H. (2012). Socio-economic factors affecting mortality in 47, XYY syndrome—A comparison with background population and Klinefelter syndrome. *American Journal of Medical Genetics A, 158A,* 2421–2429.

Stocker, C., & Dunn, J. (1990). Sibling relationships in childhood: Links with friendships and peer relationships. *British Journal of Developmental Psychology, 8,* 227–244.

Stoll, C., Dott, B., Alembik, Y., & Roth, M. P. (2011). Associated malformations among infants with neural tube defects. *American Journal of Medical Genetics A, 155A,* 565–568.

Strathearn, L. (2007). Exploring the neurobiology of attachment. In L. C. Mayes, P. Fonagy, & M. Target (Eds.), *Developmental science and psychoanalysis.* London: Karnac Press.

Strathearn, L. (2011). Maternal neglect: Oxytocin, dopamine, and the neurobiology of attachment. *Journal of Neuroendocrinology, 23,* 1054–1065.

Strathearn, L., Iyenger, U., Fonagy, P., Kim, S. (2012). Maternal oxytocin response during mother-infant interaction: Associations with adult temperament. *Hormones and Behavior, 61,* 429–435.

Strauss, M. A., Sugarman, D. B., & Giles-Sims, J. (1997). Spanking by parents and subsequent anti-social behavior in children. *Archives of Pediatrics and Adolescent Medicine, 151,* 761–767.

Strenze, T. (2007). Intelligence and socioeconomic success: A meta-analytic review of longitudinal research. *Intelligence, 35,* 401–426.

Streri, A. (1993). *Seeing, reaching, touching: The relations between vision and touch in infancy.* London: Harvester Wheatshaft.

Stright, A. D., Herr, M. Y., & Neitzel, C. (2009). Maternal scaffolding of children's problem solving and children's adjustment in kindergarten: Hmong families in the United States. *Journal of Educational Psychology, 101,* 207–218.

Strohmeier, D., & Noam, G. G. (2012). Bullying in schools: What is the problem and how can educators solve it? *New Directions in Youth Development, 133,* 7–13.

Strong-Wilson, T., & Ellis, J. (2007). Children and place: Reggio Emilia's environment as a third teacher. *Theory Into Practice, 46,* 5–13.

Stuart, S. (2012). Interpersonal psychotherapy for postpartum depression. *Clinical Psychology and Psychotherapy, 19,* 134–140.

Stuebe, A. M., & Schwartz, E. G. (2010). The risks and benefits of infant feeding practices for women and their children. *Journal of Perinatology, 30,* 155–162.

Su, M. W., & others. (2012). Gene-gene and gene-environmental interactions of childhood asthma: A multifactor dimension reduction approach. *PLoS One, 7*(2), e30694.

Su, R., Rounds, J., & Armstrong, P. I. (2009). Men and things, women and people: A meta-analysis of sex differences in interests. *Psychological Bulletin, 135,* 859–884.

Suárez-Orozco, C. (2007, March). *Immigrant family educational advantages and challenges.* Paper presented at the meeting of the Society for Research in Child Development, Boston.

Suárez-Orozco, M., & Suárez-Orozco, C. (2010). Globalization, immigration, and schooling. In J. A. Banks (Ed.), *The Routledge international companion to multicultural education.* New York: Psychology Press.

Sue, D., Sue, D. W., Sue, S., & Sue, D. M. (2013). *Understanding abnormal behavior* (10th ed.). Boston: Cengage.

Sue, S. (1990, August). *Ethnicity and culture in psychological research and practice.* Paper presented at the meeting of the American Psychological Association, Boston.

Sue, S., & Morishima, J. K. (1982). *The mental health of Asian Americans: Contemporary issues in identifying and treating mental problems.* San Francisco: Jossey-Bass.

Sugita, Y. (2004). Experience in early infancy is indispensable for color perception. *Current Biology, 14,* 1267–1271.

Sullivan, H. S. (1953). *The interpersonal theory of psychiatry.* New York: W. W. Norton.

Sullivan, K., & Sullivan, A. (1980). Adolescent-parent separation. *Developmental Psychology, 16,* 93–99.

Sultan, C., Gaspari, L., Kaifa, N., & Paris, F. (2012). Clinical expression of precocious puberty in girls. *Endocrine Development, 22,* 84–100.

Sumaroka, M., & Bornstein, M. H. (2008). Play. In M. M. Haith & J. B. Benson (Eds.), *Encyclopedia of infant and early childhood development.* Oxford, UK: Elsevier.

Summerbell, C. D., & others. (2012). Evidence-based recommendations for the development of obesity prevention programs targeted at preschool children. *Obesity Reviews, 13*(Suppl. 1), S129–S132.

Sung, L., & others. (2013, in press). Children's oncology group's 2012 blueprint for research: Cancer control and supportive care. *Pediatric and Blood Cancer.*

Super, C. M., & Harkness, S. (2010). Culture and infancy. In J. G. Bremner & T. D. Wachs (Eds.), *Wiley-Blackwell handbook of infant development* (2nd ed.). New York: Wiley.

Susman, E. J., & Dorn, L. D. (2013). Puberty: Its role in development. In I. B. Weiner & others (Eds.), *Handbook of psychology* (2nd ed., Vol. 6). New York: Wiley.

Susman, E. J., & others. (2010). Longitudinal development of secondary sexual characteristics in girls and boys between 9½ and 15½ years. *Archives of Pediatric and Adolescent Medicine, 164,* 166–173.

Sutcliffe, K., & others. (2012). Comparing midwife-led and doctor-led maternity care: A systematic review of reviews. *Journal of Advanced Nursing, 68,* 2376–2386.

Suzuki, L. A., Short, E. L., & Lee, C. S. (2011). Racial and ethnic group differences in intelligence in the United States. In R. J. Sternberg & S. B. Kaufman (Eds.), *Cambridge handbook of intelligence.* New York: Cambridge University Press.

Swaab, D. F., Chung, W. C., Kruijver, F. P., Hofman, M. A., & Ishunina, T. A. (2001). Structural and functional sex differences in the human hypothalamus. *Hormones and Behavior, 40,* 93–98.

Swaiman, K., Ashwal, S., Ferriero, D., & Schor, N. (2012). *Swaiman's pediatric neurology.* New York: Elsevier.

Swamy, G. K., Ostbye, T., & Skjaerven, R. (2008). Association of preterm birth with long-term survival, reproduction, and next generation preterm birth. *Journal of the American Medical Association, 299,* 1429–1436.

Swanson, H. L. (1999). What develops in working memory: A life-span perspective. *Developmental Psychology, 35,* 985–1000.

Swanson, H. L., Harris, K. R., & Graham, S. (2013). Overview of foundations, causes, instruction, and methodology in the field of learning disabilities. In H. L. Swanson, K. R. Harris, & S. Graham (Eds.), *Handbook of learning disabilities* (2nd ed.). New York: Guilford.

Sweeting, H. N. (2008). Gendered dimensions of obesity in childhood and adolescence. *Nutrition Journal, 14,* 1.

Swing, E. L., Gentile, D. A., Anderson, C.A., & Walsh, D. A. (2010). Television and video game exposure and the development of attention problems. *Pediatrics, 126,* 214–221.

Syed, M. (2010). Memorable everyday events in college: Narratives of the intersection of ethnicity and academia. *Journal of Diversity in Higher Education, 3,* 56–69.

Syed, M. (2011). Developing an integrated self: Academic and ethnic identities among ethnically-diverse college students. *Developmental Psychology, 46,* 1590–1604.

Syed, M. (2013, in press). Assessment of ethnic identity and acculturation. In K. Geisinger (Ed.), *APA handbook of testing and assessment in psychology.* Washington, DC: American Psychological Association.

Syed, M., & Azmitia, M. (2010). Narrative and ethnic identity exploration: A longitudinal account of emerging adults' ethnicity-related experiences. *Developmental Psychology, 46,* 208–219.

Sykes, C. J. (1995). *Dumbing down our kids: Why America's children feel good about themselves but can't read, write, or add.* New York: St. Martin's Press.

Szwedo, D. E., Mikami, A. Y., & Allen, J. P. (2011). Qualities of peer relations on social networking websites: Predictions from negative mother-teen interactions. *Journal of Research on Adolescence, 21,* 595–607.

T

Tabara, Y., Kohara, K., & Miki, T. (2012). Hunting for genes for hypertension: The Millenium Genome Project for Hypertension. *Hypertension Research, 35,* 567–573.

Taddio, A. (2008). Circumcision. In M. M. Haith & J. B. Benson (Eds.), *Encyclopedia of infant and early childhood development.* Oxford, UK: Elsevier.

Taige, N. M., & others. (2007). Antenatal maternal stress and long-term effects on child neurodevelopment: How and why? *Journal of Child Psychology and Psychiatry, 48,* 245–261.

Talbot, J., Baker, J. K., & McHale, J. P. (2009). Sharing the love: Prebirth adult attachment status and coparenting adjustment during infancy. The transition to parenthood. *Parenting: Science & Practice, 9,* 56–77.

Tamis-Lemonda, C. S., & McFadden, K. E. (2010). The United States of America. In M. H. Bornstein (Ed.), *Handbook of cultural developmental science.* New York: Psychology Press.

Tamis-LeMonda, C. S., & Song, L. (2013, in press). Parent-infant communicative interactions in cultural context. In R. M. Lerner (Ed.), *Handbook of psychology* (Vol. 6). New York: Wiley.

Tamis-LeMonda, C. S., & others. (2008). Parents' goals for children: The dynamic coexistence of individualism and collectivism in cultures and individuals. *Social Development, 17,* 183–209.

Tang, Y., & Posner, M. I. (2009). Attention training and attention state training. *Trends in Cognitive Science, 13,* 222–227.

Tannen, D. (1990). *You just don't understand!* New York: Ballantine.

Tappan, M. B. (1998). Sociocultural psychology and caring psychology: Exploring Vygotsky's "hidden curriculum." *Educational Psychologist, 33,* 23–33.

Tappan, M. B. (2013). Mediated moralities: Sociocultural approaches to moral development. In M. Killen & J. G. Smetana (Eds.), *Handbook of moral development* (2nd ed.). New York: Routledge.

Taylor, C. A., Manganello, J. A., Lee, S. J., & Rice, J. C. (2010). Mothers' spanking of 3-year-old children and subsequent risk of children's aggressive behavior. *Pediatrics, 125,* e1057–e1065.

Taylor, L. S., & Whittaker, C. R. (2009). *Bridging multiple worlds* (2nd ed.). Boston: Allyn & Bacon.

Taylor, R. D., & Lopez, E. I. (2005). Family management practice, school achievement, and problem behavior in African American adolescents: Mediating processes. *Applied Developmental Psychology, 26,* 39–49.

Taylor, S. E. (2002). *The tending instinct.* New York: Times Books.

te Velde, S. J., & others. (2012). Energy balance-related behaviors associated with overweight and obesity in preschool children: A systematic review of prospective studies. *Obesity Reviews, 13*(Suppl. 1), S56–S74.

Teenage Research Unlimited. (2004, November 10). *Diversity in word and deed: Most teens claim multicultural friends.* Northbrook, IL: Teenage Research Unlimited.

Teery-McElrath, Y. M., O'Malley, P. M., & Johnston, L. D. (2012). Factors affecting sugar-sweetened beverage availability in competitive venues of U.S. secondary schools. *Journal of School Health, 82,* 44–55.

Telzer, E. H., Fuligni, A. J., Liberman, M. D., & Galvan, A. (2013, in press). Meaningful family relationships: Neurocognitive buffers of adolescent risk taking. *Journal of Cognitive Neuroscience.*

Temple, C. A., Nathan, R., & Temple, C. (2013). *Beginnings of writing* (4th ed.). Boston: Allyn & Bacon.

Temple, C., Nathan, R., Temple, F., & Burris, N. A. (1993). *The beginnings of writing* (3rd ed.). Boston: Allyn & Bacon.

Templeton, J. L., & Eccles, J. S. (2006). The relation between spiritual development and identity processes. In E. Roehlkepartain, P. E. King, L. Wagener, & P. L. Benson (Eds.), *The handbook of spirituality in childhood and adolescence.* Thousand Oaks, CA: Sage.

Tenenbaum, H. R., Callahan, M., Alba-Speyer, C., & Sandoval, L. (2002). Parent-child science conversations in Mexican-descent families: Educational background, activity, and past experience as moderators. *Hispanic Journal of Behavioral Sciences, 24,* 225–248.

Terman, L. (1925). *Genetic studies of genius. Vol. 1: Mental and physical traits of a thousand gifted children.* Stanford, CA: Stanford University Press.

Teti, D. (2001). Retrospect and prospect in the psychological study of sibling relationships. In J. P. McHale & W. S. Grolnick (Eds.), *Retrospect and prospect in the psychological study of families.* Mahwah, NJ: Erlbaum.

Teti, D. M., Kim, B. R., Mayer G., & Countermine, M. (2010). Maternal emotional availability at bedtime predicts infant sleep quality. *Journal of Family Psychology, 24,* 307–315.

Thabet, A. A., Ibraheem, A. N., Shivram, R., Winter, E. A., & Vostanis, P. (2009). Parenting support and PTSD in children of a war zone. *International Journal of Social Psychiatry, 55,* 225–227.

Tharp, R. G. (1994). Intergroup differences among Native Americans in socialization and child cognition: An erthogenetic analysis. In P. M. Greenfield & R. Cocking (Eds.), *Cross-cultural roots of minority child development.* Mahwah, NJ: Erlbaum.

Tharp, R. G., & Gallimore, R. (1988). *Rousing minds to life: Teaching, learning, and schooling in social context.* New York: Cambridge University Press.

The Hospital for Sick Children & others. (2010). *The Hospital for Sick Children's handbook of pediatrics* (11th ed.). London: Elsevier.

Thelen, E. (2000). Perception and motor development. In A. Kazdin (Ed.), *Encyclopedia of psychology.* Washington, DC, & New York: American Psychological Association and Oxford University Press.

Thelen, E., & Smith, L. B. (1998). Dynamic systems theory. In W. Damon (Ed.), *Handbook of child psychology* (5th ed., Vol. 1.). New York: Wiley.

Thelen, E., & Smith, L. B. (2006). Dynamic development of action and thought. In W. Damon & R. Lerner (Eds.), *Handbook of child psychology* (6th ed.). New York: Wiley.

Thelen, E., & others. (1993). The transition to reaching: Mapping intention and intrinsic dynamics. *Child Development, 64,* 1058–1098.

Theokas, C. (2009). Youth sports participation—A view of the issues: Introduction to the special section. *Developmental Psychology, 45,* 303–306.

Therrell, B. L., & others. (2010). Newborn Screening System Performance Evaluation Assessment (PEAS). *Seminars in Perinatology, 34,* 105–120.

Thio, A. (2010). *Deviant behavior* (10th ed.). Boston: Allyn & Bacon.

Thomas, A., & Chess, S. (1991). Temperament in adolescence and its functional significance. In R. M. Lerner, A. C. Petersen, & J. Brooks-Gunn (Eds.), *Encyclopedia of adolescence* (Vol. 2). New York: Garland.

Thomas, M. S. C., & Johnson, M. H. (2008). New advances in understanding sensitive periods in brain development. *Current Directions in Psychological Science, 17,* 1–5.

Thompson, D. R., & others. (2007). Childhood overweight and cardiovascular disease risk factors: The National Heart, Lung, and Blood Institute Growth and Health Study. *Journal of Pediatrics, 150,* 18–25.

Thompson, J., Manore, M., & Vaughan, L. (2013). *Science of nutrition* (3rd ed.). Upper Saddle River, NJ: Pearson.

Thompson, P. M., & others. (2000). Growth patterns in the developing brain detected by using continuum mechanical tensor maps. *Nature, 404,* 190–193.

Thompson, R. (2006). The development of the person. In W. Damon & R. Lerner (Eds.), *Handbook of child psychology* (6th ed.). New York: Wiley.

Thompson, R. A. (1994). Emotion regulation: A theme in search of a definition. *Monographs of the Society for Research in Child Development, 59*(Serial No. 240), 2–3.

Thompson, R. A. (2006). The development of the person. In W. Damon & R. Lerner (Eds.), *Handbook of child psychology* (6th ed.). New York: Wiley.

Thompson, R. A. (2008). Unpublished review of J. W. Santrock's *Life-span development,* 2nd ed. (New York: McGraw-Hill).

Thompson, R. A. (2009). Early foundations: Conscience and the development of moral character. In D. Narváez & D. Lapsley (Eds.), *Moral personality, identity, and character: Prospects for a new field of study.* New York: Cambridge University Press.

Thompson, R. A. (2010). Feeling and understanding through the prism of relationships. In S. D. Calkins & M. A. Bell (Eds.), *Child development at the intersection of emotion and cognition.* Washington, DC: American Psychological Association.

Thompson, R. A. (2011). The emotionate child. In D. Cicchetti & G.I. Roisman (Eds.), *The origins and organization of adaptation and maladaptation. Minnesota Symposium on Child Psychology* (Vol. 36). New York: Wiley.

Thompson, R. A. (2012). Whither the preoperational child? Toward a life-span moral development theory. *Child Development Perspectives, 6,* 423–429.

Thompson, R. A. (2013a, in press). Attachment development: Precis and prospect. In P. Zelazo (Ed.), *Oxford handbook of developmental psychology.* New York: Oxford University Press.

Thompson, R. A. (2013b, in press). Interpersonal relations. In A. Ben-Arieh, I. Frones, F. Cases, & J. Korbin (Eds.), *Handbook of child well-being.* New York: Springer.

Thompson, R. A. (2013c, in press). Relationships, regulation, and development. In R. M. Lerner (Ed.), *Handbook of child psychology* (7th ed.). New York: Wiley.

Thompson, R. A. (2013d, in press). Socialization of emotion regulation in the family. In J. Gross (Ed.), *Handbook of emotion regulation* (2nd ed.). New York: Guilford.

Thompson, R. A., Meyer, M., & McGinley, M. (2013). Understanding values in relationships: The development of conscience. In M. Killen & J. G. Smetana (Eds.), *Handbook of moral development* (2nd ed.). New York: Routledge.

Thompson, R. A., Winer, A. C., & Goodvin, R. (2011). The individual child: Temperament, emotion, self, and personality. In M. Bornstein & M. E. Lamb (Eds.), *Developmental science: An advanced textbook* (6th ed.). New York: Psychology Press / Taylor & Francis.

Thompson, R. A., & others. (2009, April). *Parent-child relationships, conversation, and developing emotion regulation.* Paper presented at the meeting of the Society for Research in Child Development, Denver.

Thorisdottir, A., Gunnarsdottir, I., & Thorisdottir, I. (2013, in press). Revised infant dietary recommendations: The impact of maternal education and other parental factors on adherence rates in Iceland. *Acta Pediatrica.*

Tikotzky, L., Sadeh, A., & Glickman-Gavrieli, T. (2010). Infant sleep and paternal involvement in infant caregiving during the first 6 months of life. *Journal of Pediatric Psychology, 36*(1), 36–46.

Tikotzky, L., & Shaashua, L. (2012). Infant sleep and early parental sleep-related cognitions predict sleep in pre-school children. *Sleep Medicine, 13,* 185–192.

Tincoff, R., & Jusczyk, P. W. (2012, in press). Six-month-olds comprehend words that refer to parts of the body. *Infancy.*

To, W. W. (2012). Prenatal diagnosis and assessment of facial clefts: Where are we now? *Hong Kong Medical Journal, 18,* 146–152.

Tobin, J. J., Wu, D. Y. H., & Davidson, D. H. (1989). *Preschool in three cultures.* New Haven, CT: Yale University Press.

Tobler, A. L., & others. (2013, in press). Perceived racial/ethnic discrimination, problem behaviors, and mental health among minority urban youth. *Ethnicity and Health.*

Tolani, N., & Brooks-Gunn, J. (2008). Family support, international trends. In M. M. Haith & J. B. Benson (Eds.), *Encyclopedia of infant and early childhood development.* Oxford, UK: Elsevier.

Toma, C., & others. (2012, in press). Neurotransmitter systems and neurotrophic factors in autism: Association study of 37 genes suggests involvement of DDC. *World Journal of Biology.*

Tomasello, M. (2008). *Origins of human communication.* Cambridge, MA: MIT Press.

Tomasello, M. (2009). *Why we cooperate.* Cambridge, MA: MIT Press.

Tomasello, M. (2011a). *Human culture in evolutionary perspective.* New York: Oxford University Press.

Tomasello, M. (2011b). Language development. In U. Goswami (Ed.), *Wiley-Blackwell handbook of childhood cognitive development* (2nd ed.). New York: Wiley.

Tomasello, M., & Hamann, K. (2012). Collaboration in young children. *Quarterly Journal of Experimental Psychology, 65,* 1–12.

Tomasello, M., & Vaish, A. (2013, in press). Origins of human cooperation and morality. *Annual Review of Psychology.* Palo Alto, CA: Annual Reviews.

Tompkins, G. E. (2013). *Language arts* (8th ed.). Boston: Allyn & Bacon.

Tompkins, T. L., Hockett, A. R., Abraibes, N., & Witt, J. L. (2011). A closer look at co-rumination: Gender, coping, peer functioning, and internalizing/externalizing problems. *Journal of Adolescence, 34*(5), 801–811.

Torres, J. M. (2013, in press). Breast milk and labor support: Lactation consultants' and doulas' strategies for navigating the medical context of maternity care. *Sociology of Health and Illness.*

Tortora, G. J., Funke, B. R., & Case, C. L. (2013). *Microbiology* (11th ed.). Upper Saddle River, NJ: Pearson.

Townsend, M. (2011). Motivation, learning, and instruction. In C. M. Rubie-Davies (Ed.), *Educational psychology.* New York: Routledge.

Trafimow, D., Triandis, H. C., & Goto, S. G. (1991). Some tests of the distinction between the private and collective self. *Journal of Personality and Social Psychology, 60,* 649–655.

Trautner, H. M., & others. (2005). Rigidity and flexibility of gender stereotypes in children: Developmental or differential? *Infant and Child Development, 14,* 365–381.

Trehub, S. E., Schneider, B. A., Thorpe, L. A., & Judge, P. (1991). Observational measures of auditory sensitivity in early infancy. *Developmental Psychology, 27,* 40–49.

Trejos-Castillo, E., Bedore, S., & Trevino Schafer, N. (2013, in press). Human capital development among immigrant youth. In E. Trejos-Castillo (Ed.), *Youth: Practices, perspectives, and challenges.* Hauppage, NY: Nova Science Publishers.

Tremblay, M. S., & others. (2012). Canadian sedentary behavior guidelines for the early years (0–4 years). *Applied Physiology, Nutrition, and Metabolism, 37,* 370–380.

Trentacosta, C. J., & Fine, S. E. (2009). Emotion knowledge, social competence, and behavior problems in childhood and adolescence: A meta-analytic review. *Social Development, 19*(1), 1–29.

Triandis, H. C. (2007). Culture and psychology: A history of their relationship. In S. Kitayama & D. Cohen (Eds.), *Handbook of cultural psychology.* New York: Guilford.

Triche, E. W., & Hossain, N. (2007). Environmental factors implicated in the causation of adverse pregnancy outcome. *Seminars in Perinatology, 31,* 240–242.

Trimble, J. E. (1988, August). *The enculturation of contemporary psychology.* Paper presented at the meeting of the American Psychological Association, New Orleans.

Trinkner, R., Cohn, E. S., Rebellon, C. J., & Van Gundy, K. (2012). Don't trust anyone over 30: Parental legitimacy as a mediator between parenting style and changes in delinquent behavior over time. *Journal of Adolescence, 35,* 119–132.

Trommsdorff, G., & Cole, P. M. (2011). Emotion, self-regulation, and social behavior in cultural contexts. In X. Chen & K. Rubin (Eds.), *Socioemotional development in cultural context.* New York: Guilford.

Trost, S. G., Fees, B., & Dzewaltowski, D. (2008). Feasibility and efficacy of "move and learn" physical activity curriculum in preschool children. *Journal of Physical Activity and Health, 5,* 88–103.

Tucker, J. S., & others. (2012). Resisting smoking when a best friend smokes: Do intrapersonal and contextual factors matter? *Journal of Research on Adolescence, 22,* 113–122.

Turnbull, A., Rutherford-Turnbull, H., Wehmeyer, M. L., & Shogren, K. A. (2013). *Exceptional lives* (7th ed.). Upper Saddle River, NJ: Pearson.

Turner, H. A., & others. (2012). Family context, victimization, and child trauma symptoms: Variations in safe, stable, and nurturing relationships during early and middle childhood. *American Journal of Orthopsychiatry, 82,* 209–219.

U

Udry, J. R., & others. (1985). Serum androgenic hormones motivate sexual behavior in adolescent boys. *Fertility and Sterility, 43,* 90–94.

Ueno, K., & McWilliams, S. (2010). Gender-typed behaviors and school adjustment. *Sex Roles, 63,* 580–591.

Umana-Taylor, A. J. (2009). Research with Latino early adolescents. *Journal of Early Adolescence, 29,* 5–15.

Umana-Taylor, A. J., Gonzales-Backen, M. A., & Guimond, A. B. (2009). Latino adolescents' ethnic identity: Is there a developmental progression and does growth in ethnic identity predict growth in self-esteem? *Child Development, 80,* 391–405.

Umana-Taylor, A. J., Wong, J. J., Gonzalez, N. A., & Dumka, L. E. (2012, in press). Ethnic identity and gender as moderators of the association between discrimination and academic adjustment among Mexican-origin adolescents. *Journal of Adolescence.*

Underwood, M. K. (2011). Aggression. In M. K. Underwood & L. Rosen (Eds.), *Social development.* New York: Guilford.

UNICEF. (2003). *The state of the world's children: 2003.* Geneva, Switzerland: Author.

UNICEF. (2004). *The state of the world's children: 2004.* Geneva, Switzerland: Author.

UNICEF. (2006). *The state of the world's children: 2006.* Geneva, Switzerland: Author.

UNICEF. (2007). *The state of the world's children: 2007.* Geneva, Switzerland: Author.

UNICEF. (2011). *The state of the world's children: 2011.* Geneva, Switzerland: Author.

UNICEF. (2012). *The state of the world's children: 2012.* Geneva, Switzerland: Author.

UNICEF. (2013). *The state of the world's children, 2013.* Geneva, Switzerland: Author.

United Nations. (2002). *Improving the quality of life of girls.* Geneva: UNICEF.

Updegraff, K. A., Kim, J-Y, Killoren, S. E., & Thayer, S. M. (2010). Mexican American parents' involvement in adolescents' peer relationships: Exploring the role of culture and adolescents' peer experiences. *Journal of Research on Adolescence, 20,* 65–87.

Updegraff, K. A., Umana-Taylor, A. J., McHale, S. M., Wheeler, L. A., & Perez-Brena, J. (2012). Mexican-origin youths' cultural orientations and adjustment: Changes from early to late adolescence. *Child Development, 83,* 1655–1671.

Urban, J. B., Lewin-Bizan, S., & Lerner, R. M. (2010). The role of intentional self-regulation, lower neighborhood ecological assets, and activity involvement in youth developmental outcomes. *Journal of Youth and Adolescence, 39,* 783–800.

Urbina, S. (2011). Tests of intelligence. In R. J. Sternberg & S. B. Kaufman (Eds.), *Cambridge handbook of intelligence.* New York: Cambridge University Press.

Urdan, T. (2009, April). *Motivation, achievement, and acculturation.* Paper presented at the annual meeting of the American Educational Research Association, San Diego.

Urdan, T. (2010). Classroom goal structures, motivation, and learning. In J. Meece & J. Eccles (Eds.), *Handbook of research on schools, schooling, and motivation.* New York: Routledge.

Urdan, T. (2012). Factors affecting the motivation and achievement of immigrant students. In K. R. Harris, S. Graham, & T. Urdan (Eds.), *APA educational psychology handbook.* Washington, DC: American Psychological Association.

Ursache, A., Blair, C., & Raver, C. C. (2012). The promotion of self-regulation as a means of enhancing school readiness and early achievement in children at risk for school failure. *Child Development Perspectives, 6,* 122–128.

Ursache, A., Blair, C., Stifter, C., & Voegtline, K. (2013, in press). Emotional reactivity and regulation in infancy interact to predict executive functioning in early childhood. *Developmental Psychology.*

U.S. Census Bureau. (2011, May 8). *Mother's day:* Retrieved August 28, 2011, from www.census/gov/newsroom/releases/archives/facts_for_features_special_editions/cb

U.S. Census Bureau. (2012). *People: Poverty.* Washington, DC: U.S. Department of Labor.

U.S. Department of Energy. (2001). *The human genome project.* Washington, DC: U.S. Department of Energy.

U.S. Department of Health and Human Services. (2009). *Folic acid.* Retrieved January 19, 2009, from http://www.cdc.gov/ncbddd/folicacid

U.S. Department of Health and Human Services. (2010). *Child maltreatment 2009.* Washington, DC: Author.

USA Today. (2000, October 10). All-USA first teacher team. Retrieved November 15, 2004, from http://www.usatoday.com/life/teacher/teach/htm

V

Vacca, J. A., & others. (2012). *Reading and learning to read* (8th ed.). Boston: Allyn & Bacon.

Vaish, A., Carpenter, M., & Tomasello, M. (2010). Young children selectively avoid helping people with harmful intentions. *Child Development, 81,* 1661–1669.

Valenzuela, C. F., Morton, R. A., Diaz, M. R., & Topper, L. (2012, in press). Does moderate drinking harm the fetal brain? Insights from animal models. *Trends in Neuroscience.*

Valkenburg, P. M., & Peter, J. (2011). Online communication among adolescents: An integrated model of its attraction, opportunities, and risks. *Journal of Adolescent Health, 48,* 121–127.

van Bers, B., & others. (2011). The dynamics of development on the dimensional change card sort task. *Developmental Science, 14,* 960–971.

Van De Voorde, S., Roeyers, H., Verte, S., & Wiersema, J. R. (2011). The influence of working memory load on response inhibition in children with attention-deficit/hyperactivity disorder or reading disorder. *Journal of Clinical Neuropsychology, 33*(7), 753–764.

van de Weijer-Bergsma, E., Formsma, A. R., de Bruin, E. I., & Bogels, S. M. (2012). The effectiveness of mindfulness training on behavioral problems and attentional functioning in adolescents with ADHD. *Journal of Child and Family Studies, 21,* 775–787.

van den Boom, D. C. (1989). Neonatal irritability and the development of attachment. In G. A. Kohnstamm, J. E. Bates, & M. K. Rothbart (Eds.), *Temperament in childhood.* New York: Wiley.

van der Stel, M., & Veenman, M. V. J. (2010). Development of metacognitive skillfulness: A longitudinal study. *Learning and Individual Differences, 20,* 220–224.

Van Dyck, P. C. (2007). Final commentary on the special volume of articles from the National Survey of Children's Health. *Pediatrics, 119*(Suppl.), S122–S123.

van Geel, M., & Vedder, P. (2011). The role of family obligations and school adjustment in explaining the immigrant paradox. *Journal of Youth and Adolescence, 40*(2), 187–196.

van Goethem, A. A. J., & others. (2012). The role of adolescents' morality and identity in volunteering. Age and gender differences in the process model. *Journal of Adolescence, 35,* 509–520.

van Harmelen, A. L., & others. (2010). Child abuse and negative explicit and automatic self-associations: The cognitive scars of emotional maltreatment. *Behavior Research and Therapy, 48*(6), 486–494.

Van Hecke, V., & others (2012). Infant responding to joint attention, executive processes, and self-regulation in preschool children. *Infant Development and Behavior, 35,* 303–311.

van IJzendoorn, M. H., & Kroonenberg, P. M. (1988). Cross-cultural patterns of attachment: A meta-analysis of the Strange Situation. *Child Development, 59,* 147–156.

van IJzendoorn, M. H., Kranenburg, M. J., Pannebakker, F., & Out, D. (2010). In defense of situational morality: Genetic, dispositional, and situational determinants of children's donating to charity. *Journal of Moral Education, 39,* 1–20.

Van Norstrand, D. W., & others. (2012). Connexin43 mutation causes heterogeneous gap junction loss and sudden infant death. *Circulation, 125,* 474–481.

Van Ryzin, M. J., Carlson, E. A., & Sroufe, L. A. (2011). Attachment discontinuity in a high-risk sample. *Attachment and Human Development, 13,* 381–401.

Vandehey, M., Diekhoff, G., & LaBeff, E. (2007). College cheating: A 20-year follow-up and the addition of an honor code. *Journal of College Development, 48,* 468–480.

Vandell, D. L., & Wilson, K. S. (1988). Infants' interactions with mother, sibling, and peer: Contrasts and relations between interaction systems. *Child Development, 48,* 176–186.

Vandell, D. L., & others. (2010). Do effects of early childcare extend to age 15 years? From the NICHD Study of Early Child Care and Youth Development. *Child Development, 81,* 737–756.

Vansteenkiste, M., Sierens, E., Soenens, B., Luyckx, K., & Lens, W. (2009). Motivational profiles from a self-determination perspective: The quality of motivation matters. *Journal of Educational Psychology, 101*(3), 671–688.

Vasquez, M. J., & Berg, O. R. (2012). The Baby-Friendly journey in a U.S. public hospital. *Journal of Perinatal and Neonatal Nursing, 26,* 37–46.

Vaughn, M. G., Beaver, K. M., Wexler, J., DeLisi, M., & Roberts, G. J. (2011). The effect of school dropout on verbal ability in adulthood: A propensity score matching approach. *Journal of Youth and Adolescence, 40,* 197–206.

Veenstra, R., Lindenberg, S., Munniksma, A., & Dijkstra, J. K. (2010). The complex relationship between bullying, victimization, acceptance, and rejection: Giving special attention to status, affection, and sex differences. *Child Development, 81*(2), 480–486.

Velez, C. E., Wolchik, S. A., Tein, J. Y., & Sandler, I. (2011). Protecting children from the consequences of divorce: A longitudinal study of the effects of parenting on children's coping responses. *Child Development, 82,* 244–257.

Venners, S. A., & others. (2004). Paternal smoking and pregnancy loss: A prospective study using a biomarker of pregnancy. *American Journal of Epidemiology, 159,* 993–1001.

Verma, S., & Saraswathi, T. S. (2002). Adolescence in India: Street urchins or Silicon Valley millionaires? In B. B. Brown, R. W. Larson, & T. S. Saraswathi (Eds.), *The world's youth.* New York: Cambridge University Press.

Vermeersch, H., T'Sjoen, G., Kaufman, J. M., & Vincke, J. (2008). The role of testosterone in aggressive and non-aggressive risk-taking in boys. *Hormones and Behavior, 53,* 463–471.

Vesco, K. K., & others. (2012). Healthy Moms, a randomized trial to promote and evaluate weight maintenance among obese pregnant women: Study design and rationale. *Contemporary Clinical Trials, 33,* 777–785.

Vida, M., & Maurer, D. (2012). The development of fine-grained sensitivity to eye contact after 6 years of age. *Journal of Experimental Child Psychology, 112,* 243–256.

Villanueva, C. M., & Buriel, R. (2010). Speaking on behalf of others: A qualitative study of the perceptions and feelings of adolescent Latina language brokers. *Journal of Social Issues, 66,* 197–210.

Villegas, R., & others. (2008). Duration of breast-feeding and the incidence of type 2 diabetes mellitus in the Shanghai Women's Health Study. *Diabetologia, 51,* 258–266.

Vinik, J., Almas, A., & Grusec, J. (2011). Mothers' knowledge of what distresses and comforts their children predicts children's coping, empathy, and prosocial behavior. *Parenting: Science and Practice, 11,* 56–71.

Vitaro, F., Pedersen, S., & Brendgen, M. (2007). Children's disruptiveness, peer rejection, friends' deviancy, and delinquent behaviors: A process-oriented approach. *Development and Psychopathology, 19,* 433–453.

Vittrup, B., Holden, G. W., & Buck, M. (2006). Attitudes predict the use of physical punishment: A prospective study of the emergence of disciplinary practices. *Pediatrics,117,* 2055–2064.

Vivier, P. M., & others. (2011). The important health impact of where a child lives: Neighborhood characteristics and the burden of lead poisoning. *Maternal and Child Health Journal, 15,* 1195–1202.

Vladutiu, C. J., Evenson, K. R., & Marshall, S. W. (2010). Physical activity and injuries during pregnancy. *Journal of Physical Activity and Health, 7,* 761–769.

Vohs, K., & Baumeister, R. F. (Eds.). (2012). *Self and identity.* Thousand Oaks, CA: Sage.

Volbrecht, M. M., & Goldsmith, H. H. (2010). Early temperamental and family predictors of shyness and anxiety. *Developmental Psychology, 46,* 1192–1205.

Von Hofsten, C. (2008). Motor and physical development manual. In M. M. Haith & J. B. Benson (Eds.), *Encyclopedia of infant and early childhood development.* Oxford, UK: Elsevier.

Von Korff, L., & Grotevant, H. D. (2011). Contact in adoption and adoptive family identity formation: The mediating role of family conversation. *Journal of Family Psychology, 25,* 393–401.

Von Polier, G. G., Vioet, T. D., & Herpertz-Dahlmann, B. (2012). ADHD and delinquency—A developmental perspective. *Behavioral Sciences and the Law, 30,* 121–139.

Vong, K-I. (2012). Play—A multimodal manifestation in kindergarten education in China. *Early Years: An International Journal of Research and Development, 32, 1,* 35–48.

Votavova, H., & others. (2012). Deregulation of gene expression induced by environmental tobacco smoke exposure in pregnancy. *Nicotine and Tobacco Research, 14,* 1073–1082.

Votruba-Drzal, E., Coley, R. L., & Chase-Lansdale, P. L. (2004). Child care and low-income children's development: Direct and moderated effects. *Child Development, 75,* 296–312.

Vreeman, R. C., & Carroll, A. E. (2007). A systematic review of school-based interventions to prevent bullying. *Archives of Pediatric and Adolescent Medicine, 161,* 78–88.

Vujeva, H. M., & Furman, W. (2011). Depressive symptoms and romantic relationship qualities from adolescence through emerging adulthood: A longitudinal examination of influences. *Journal of Clinical Child and Adolescent Psychology, 40,* 123–135.

Vukelich, C., Christie, J., & Enz, B. J. (2008). *Helping children learn language and literacy.* Boston: Allyn & Bacon.

Vygotsky, L. S. (1962). *Thought and language.* Cambridge, MA: MIT Press.

W

Waasdorp, T. E., Bradshaw, C. P., & Leaf, P. J. (2012). The impact of schoolwide positive behavioral interventions and supports on bullying and peer rejection: A randomized controlled effectiveness trial. *Archives of Pediatric and Adolescent Medicine, 166,* 149–156.

Wachs, T. D. (1994). Fit, context and the transition between temperament and personality. In C. Halverson, G. Kohnstamm, & R. Martin (Eds.), *The developing structure of personality from infancy to adulthood.* Hillsdale, NJ: Erlbaum.

Wachs, T. D. (2000). *Necessary but not sufficient.* Washington, DC: American Psychological Association.

Wachs, T. D., & Bates, J. E. (2010). Temperament. In J. G. Bremner & T. D. Wachs (Eds.), *Wiley-Blackwell handbook of infant development* (2nd ed.). New York: Wiley.

Waddell, L. (2012). The power of vitamins. *Journal of Family Health Care, 22,* 16–20, 22–25.

Wadsworth, M. E., & others. (2013, in press). A longitudinal examination of the adaptation to poverty-related stress model: Predicting child and adolescent adjustment over time. *Journal of Clinical Child and Adolescent Psychology.*

Wadsworth, S. J., Olson, R. K., & Defries, J. C. (2010). Differential genetic etiology of reading difficulties as a function of IQ: An update. *Behavior Genetics, 40,* 751–758.

Wagner, L., & Hoff, E. (2013, in press). Language development. In I. B. Weiner & others (Eds.), *Handbook of psychology* (2nd ed.). New York: Wiley.

Wagner, R. K., & Sternberg, R. J. (1986). Tacit knowledge and intelligent functioning in the everyday world. In R. J. Sternberg & R. K. Wagner (Eds.), *Practical intelligence.* New York: Cambridge University Press.

Wainryb, C. (2013). Moral development in culture: Diversity, tolerance, and justice. In M. Killen & J. G. Smetana (Eds.), *Handbook of moral development* (2nd ed.). New York: Routledge.

Waiter, G. D., & others. (2009). Exploring possible neural mechanisms of intelligence differences using processing speed and working memory tasks. *Intelligence, 37,* 199–206.

Wald, E. R. (2011). Acute otitis media and acute bacterial sinusitis. *Clinical Infectious Diseases, 52* (Suppl. 4), S277–S283.

Walden, T. (1991). Infant social referencing. In J. Garber & K. Dodge (Eds.), *The development of emotional regulation and dysregulation.* New York: Cambridge University Press.

Walker, L. (1982). The sequentiality of Kohlberg's stages of moral development. *Child Development, 53,* 1130–1136.

Walker, L. J. (2002). Moral exemplarity. In W. Damon (Ed.), *Bringing in a new era of character education.* Stanford, CA: Hoover Press.

Walker, L. J. (2004). Progress and prospects in the psychology of moral development. *Merrill-Palmer Quarterly, 50,* 546–557.

Walker, L. (2006). Gender and morality. In M. Killen & J. G. Smetana (Eds.), *Handbook of moral development.* Mahwah, NJ: Erlbaum.

Walker, L. J. (2013, in press). Moral personality, motivation, and identity. In M. Killen & J. G. Smetana (Eds.), *Handbook of moral development* (2nd ed.). New York: Routledge.

Walker, L. J., & Hennig, K. H. (2004). Differing conceptions of moral exemplars: Just, brave, and caring. *Journal of Personality and Social Psychology, 86,* 629–647.

Walker, L. J., Hennig, K. H., & Krettenauer, T. (2000). Parent and peer contexts for children's moral development. *Child Development, 71,* 1033–1048.

Walker, L. J., & Pitts, R. C. (1998). Naturalistic conceptions of moral maturity. *Developmental Psychology, 34,* 403–419.

Wallerstein, J. S. (2008). Divorce. In M. M. Haith & J. B. Benson (Eds.), *Encyclopedia of infant and early childhood development*. Oxford, UK: Elsevier.

Wallis, C. (2011). Performing gender: A content analysis of gender display in music videos. *Sex Roles, 64,* 160–172.

Walsh, R. (2011). Lifestyle and mental health. *American Psychologist, 66,* 579–592.

Wang, M. L., & others. (2013). Dietary and physical activity factors related to eating disorder symptoms among middle school youth. *Journal of School Health, 83,* 14–20.

Wang, Q., & Pomerantz, E. M. (2009). The motivational landscape of early adolescence in the United States and China: A longitudinal study. *Child Development, 80*(4), 1272–1287.

Wang, Z., Deater-Deckard, K., Petrill, S. A., & Thompson, L. (2012). Externalizing problems, attention regulation, and household chaos: A longitudinal behavioral genetic study. *Development and Psychopathology, 24,* 755–769.

Ward, L. M. (2004). Wading through stereotypes: Positive and negative associations between media use and black adolescents' conceptions of self. *Developmental Psychology, 40,* 284–294.

Wariki, W. M., & others. (2013). Risk factors associated with outcomes of very low birthweight infants in four Asian countries. *Journal of Pediatrics and Child Health, 49,* E23–E27.

Warshak, R. A. (2007, January). Personal communication, Department of Psychology, University of Texas at Dallas, Richardson.

Watamura, S. E., Phillips, D. A., Morrissey, D. A., McCartney, T. W., & Bub, K. (2011). Double jeopardy: Poorer social-emotional outcomes for children in the NICHD SECCYD who experience home and child-care environments that convey risk. *Child Development, 82,* 48–65.

Waterman, A. S. (1985). Identity in the context of adolescent psychology. In A. S. Waterman (Ed.), *Identity in adolescence: Processes and contents*. San Francisco: Jossey-Bass.

Waterman, A. S. (1992). Identity as an aspect of optimal psychological functioning. In G. R. Adams, T. P. Gullotta, & R. Montemayor (Eds.), *Adolescent identity formation*. Newbury Park, CA: Sage.

Watson, D. (2012). Objective tests as instruments of psychological theory and research. In H. Cooper (Ed.), *APA handbook of research methods in psychology*. Washington, DC: American Psychological Association.

Watson, J. B. (1928). *Psychological care of infant and child*. New York: W. W. Norton.

Watson, J. B., & Rayner, R. (1920). Conditioned emotional reactions. *Journal of Experimental Psychology, 3,* 1–14.

Watt, H. M. G. (2008). Gender and occupational outcomes: An introduction. In H. M. G. Watt & J. S. Eccles (Eds.), *Gender and occupational outcomes*. Washington, DC: American Psychological Association.

Watt, H. M. G., & Eccles, J. S. (Eds.). (2008). *Gender and occupational outcomes*. Washington, DC: American Psychological Association.

Way, N., & Silverman, L. R. (2012). The quality of friendships during adolescence: Patterns across context, culture, and age. In P. K. Kerig, M. S. Shulz, & S. T. Hauser (Eds.), *Adolescence and beyond*. New York: Oxford University Press.

Wayne, A. (2011). Commentary in interview: Childhood cancers in transition. Retrieved April 12, 2011, from http://home.ccr.cancer.gov/connections/2010/Vol4_No2/clinic2.asp

Webb, L. D., Metha, A., & Jordan, K. F. (2013). *Foundations of American education* (7th ed.). Upper Saddle River, NJ: Pearson.

Weber, M. A., Risdon, R. S., Ashworth, M. T., Malone, M. T., & Sebire, N. J. (2012). Autopsy findings of co-sleeping-associated sudden unexpected death in infancy: Relationship between pathological features and asphyxial mode of death. *Journal of Pediatric and Child Health, 48,* 335–341.

Webster, N. S., & Worrell, F. C. (2008). Academically-talented adolescents' attitudes toward service in the community. *Gifted Child Quarterly, 52,* 170–179.

Wei, R., & others. (2013, in press). Dynamic expression of microRNAs during the differentiation of human embryonic stem cells into insulin-producing cells. *Gene.*

Weikert, D. P. (1993). *Long-term positive effects in the Perry Preschool Head Start Program*. Unpublished data, High Scope Foundation, Ypsilanti, MI.

Weinraub, M., & others. (2012, in press). Patterns of developmental change in infants' nighttime sleep awakenings from 6 through 36 months of age. *Developmental Psychology.*

Weinstein, N., Deci, E. L., & Ryan, R. M. (2011). Motivational determinants of integrating positive and negative past identities. *Journal of Personality and Social Psychology, 100,* 527–544.

Weinstein, R. S. (2004). *Reaching higher: The power of expectations in schooling*. Cambridge, MA: Harvard University Press.

Weiss, L. A., & others. (2008). Association between microdeletion and microduplication at 16p 11.2 and autism. *New England Journal of Medicine, 358,* 667–675.

Wekerle, C., & others. (2009). The contribution of childhood emotional abuse to teen dating violence among child protective services-involved youth. *Child Abuse and Neglect, 33*(1), 45–58.

Weller, D., & Lagattuta, K. H. (2013, in press). Helping the in-group feels better: Children's judgments and emotion attributions in response to prosocial dilemmas. *Child Development.*

Wellman, H. M. (2011). Developing a theory of mind. In U. Goswami (Ed.), *The Blackwell handbook of childhood cognitive development* (2nd ed.). New York: Wiley.

Wellman, H. M., Cross, D., & Watson, J. (2001). Meta-analysis of theory-of-mind development: The truth about false belief. *Child Development, 72,* 655–684.

Wellman, H. M., & Woolley, J. D. (1990). From simple desires to ordinary beliefs: The early development of everyday psychology. *Cognition, 35,* 245–275.

Wells, E. M., & others. (2011). Body burdens of mercury, lead, selenium, and copper among Baltimore newborns. *Environmental Research, 111,* 411–417.

Welsh, J. A., Nix, R. L., Blair, C., Bierman, K. L., & Nelson, K. E. (2010). The development of cognitive skills and gains in academic school readiness for children from low-income families. *Journal of Educational Psychology, 102,* 43–53.

Welti, C. (2002). Adolescents in Latin America: Facing the future with skepticism. In B. B. Brown, R. W. Larson, & T. S. Saraswathi (Eds.), *The world's youth*. New York: Cambridge University Press.

Wendelken, C., Baym, C. L., Gazzaley, A., & Bunge, S. A. (2011). Neural indices of improved attentional modulation over middle childhood. *Developmental Cognitive Neuroscience, 1,* 175–186.

Wentzel, K. (1997). Student motivation in middle school: The role of perceived pedagogical caring. *Journal of Educational Psychology, 89,* 411–419.

Wentzel, K. R. (2013). School adjustment. In I. B. Weiner & others (Eds.), *Handbook of psychology* (2nd ed., Vol. 7). New York: Wiley.

Wentzel, K. R., & Asher, S. R. (1995). The academic lives of neglected, rejected, popular, and controversial children. *Child Development, 66,* 754–763.

Wertsch, J. V. (2007). Mediation. In H. Daniels, J. Wertsch, & M. Cole (Eds.), *The Cambridge companion to Vygotsky*. New York: Cambridge University Press.

Westerman, G., Thomas, M. S. C., & Karmiloff-Smith, A. (2011). Neuroconstructivism. In U. Goswami (Ed.), *Wiley-Blackwell handbook of childhood cognitive development* (2nd ed.). New York: Wiley.

Whaley, L. (2013, in press). Syntactic typology. In J. J. Song (Ed.), *Oxford handbook of linguistic typology*. New York: Oxford University Press.

Whaley, S. E., Jiang, L., Gomez, J., & Jenks, E. (2011). Literacy promotion for families participating in the Women, Infants, and Children program. *Pediatrics, 127,* 454–461.

Whaley, S. E., Ritchie, L. D., Spector, P., & Gomez, J. (2012). Revised WIC food package improves diets of WIC families. *Journal of Nutrition and Education Behavior, 44,* 204–209.

White, B. A., & Kistner, J. A. (2011). Biased self-perceptions, peer rejection, and aggression in children. *Journal of Abnormal Child Psychology, 39,* 645–656.

White, M. (1993). *The material child: Coming of age in Japan and America*. New York: Free Press.

Whitehurst, G., & Lonigan, C. (1998). Child development and emergent literacy. *Child Development, 69*(3), 848–872.

Whiteman, S. D., Jensen, A., & Bernard, J. M. (2012). Sibling influences. In J. R. Levesque (Ed.), *Encyclopedia of adolescence*. New York: Springer.

Whittle, S., & others. (2008). Prefrontal and amygdala volumes are related to adolescents' affective behaviors during parent-adolescent interactions. *Proceedings of the National Academy of Sciences USA, 105,* 3652–3657.

WIC New York. (2010). *WIC program: Women, infants, and children*. Retrieved August 12, 2010, from www.health.state.ny.us/prevention/nutrition/wic/

WIC New York. (2011). *The new look of the women, infants, and children (WIC) program*. Retrieved March 26, 2011, from www.health.state.ny.us/prevention/nutrition/wic/the_new_look_of_wic.htm

Wichers, M., & others. (2013, in press). Genetic innovation and stability in externalizing problem behavior across development: A multi-informant twin study. *Behavioral Genetics.*

Widom, C. S., Czaja, S. J., Bentley, T., & Johnson, M. S. (2012). A prospective investigation of physical health outcomes in abused and neglected children: New findings from a 30-year follow-up. *American Journal of Public Health, 102,* 1135–1144.

Wiesel, A., Spix, C., Mergenthaler, A., & Queisser-Luft, A. (2011). Maternal occupational exposure to ionizing radiation and birth defects. *Radiation and Environmental Biophysics, 50,* 325–328.

Wigfield, A., & Cambria, J. (2010). Students' achievement values, goal orientations, and interest: Definitions, development, and relations to achievement outcomes. *Developmental Review, 30,* 1–35.

Wigfield, A., Eccles, J. S., Schiefele, U., Roeser, R., & Davis-Kean, P. (2006). Development of achievement motivation. In W. Damon & R. Lerner (Eds.), *Handbook of child psychology* (6th ed.). New York: Wiley.

Wigfield, A., Klauda, S. L., & Cambria, J. (2011). Motivational sources and outcomes of self-regulated learning and performance. In B. J. Zimmerman & D. H. Schunk (Eds.), *Handbook of self-regulation of learning and performance.* New York: Routledge.

Wilcox, J. (2009–2010). The easiest birth yet. *Midwifery Today with International Midwife, 23,* 63–64.

Williams, D. D., Yancher, S. C., Jensen, L. C., & Lewis, C. (2003). Character education in a public high school: A multi-year inquiry into unified studies. *Journal of Moral Education, 32,* 3–33.

Williams, E. P., Wyatt, S. B., & Winters, K. (2013, in press). Framing body size among African American women and girls. *Journal of Child Health Care.*

Williams, J. E., & Best, D. L. (1982). *Measuring sex stereotypes: A thirty-nation study.* Newbury Park, CA: Sage.

Williams, J. E., & Best, D. L. (1989). *Sex and psyche: Self-concept viewed cross-culturally.* Newbury Park, CA: Sage.

Williams, R., & Hazell, P. (2011). Austerity, poverty, resilience, and the future of mental health services for children and adolescents. *Current Opinion in Psychiatry, 24,* 263–266.

Williams, S. T., Ontai, L. L., & Mastergeorge, A. M. (2010). The development of peer interaction in infancy: Exploring the dyadic process. *Social Development, 19,* 348–368.

Williamson, R. A., Jaswal, V. K., & Meltzoff, A. N. (2010). Learning the rules: Observation and imitation as a sorting strategy by 36-month-old children. *Developmental Psychology, 46,* 57–65.

Wilson, B. J. (2008). Media and children's aggression, fear, and altruism. *Future of Children, 18*(1), 87–118.

Winn, I. J. (2004). The high cost of uncritical teaching. *Phi Delta Kappan, 85,* 496–497.

Winne, P. H. (2011). Cognitive and metacognitive factors in self-regulated learning. In B. J. Zimmerman & D. H. Schunk (Eds.), *Handbook of self-regulation of learning and performance.* New York: Routledge.

Winner, E. (1986, August). Where pelicans kiss seals. *Psychology Today,* pp. 24–35.

Winner, E. (1996). *Gifted children: Myths and realities.* New York: Basic Books.

Winner, E. (2000). The origins and ends of giftedness. *American Psychologist, 55,* 159–169.

Winner, E. (2006). Development in the arts: Drawing and music. In W. Damon & R. Lerner (Eds.), *Handbook of child psychology* (6th ed.), New York: Wiley.

Winsler, A., Carlton, M. P., & Barry, M. J. (2000). Age-related changes in preschool children's systematic use of private speech in a natural setting. *Journal of Child Language, 27,* 665–687.

Winsper, C., Lereya, T., Zanarini, M., & Wolke, D. (2012). Involvement in bullying and suicide-related behavior at 11 years: A prospective birth cohort study. *Journal of the Academy of Child and Adolescent Psychiatry, 51,* 271–282.

Wit, J. M., Kiess, W., & Mullis, P. (2011). Genetic evaluation of short stature. *Best Practices & Research: Clinical Endocrinology and Metabolism, 25,* 1–17.

Witelson, S. F., Kigar, D. L., & Harvey, T. (1999). The exceptional brain of Albert Einstein. *The Lancet, 353,* 2149–2153.

Witherington, D. C., Campos, J. J., Harriger, J. A., Bryan, C., & Margett, T. E. (2010). Emotion and its development in infancy. In J. G. Bremner & T. D. Wachs (Eds.), *Wiley-Blackwell handbook of infant development* (2nd ed.). New York: Wiley.

Witkin, H. A., & others. (1976). Criminality in XYY and XXY men. *Science, 193,* 547–555.

Witte, R. (2012). *Classroom assessment for teachers.* New York: McGraw-Hill.

Wittig, S. L., & Spatz, D. L. (2008). Induced lactation: Gaining a better understanding. *MCN. The Journal of Maternal Child Nursing, 33,* 76–81.

Wittmeier, K. D., Mollard, R. C., & Kriellaars, D. J. (2008). Physical activity intensity and risk of overweight and adiposity in children. *Obesity, 16,* 415–420.

Witvliet, M., & others. (2010). Peer group affiliation in children: The role of perceived popularity, likeability, and behavioral similarity in bullying. *Social Development, 19,* 285–303.

Wolfinger, N. H. (2011). More evidence for trends in the intergenerational transmission of divorce: A completed cohort approach using data from the general social survey. *Demography, 48,* 581–592.

Wolke, D., Schreier, A., Zanarini, M. C., & Winsper, C. (2012). Bullied by peers in childhood and borderline personality symptoms at 11 years of age: A prospective study. *Journal of Child Psychology and Psychiatry, 53,* 846–855.

Women in Academia. (2011). *A historical summary of gender differences in college enrollment rates.* Retrieved June 12, 2011, from www.wiareport.com

Women's Sports Foundation. (2001). *The 10 commandments for parents and coaches in youth sports.* Eisenhower Park, NY: Women's Sports Foundation.

Wong Briggs, T. W. (2004, October 14). *USA Today's* 2004 all-USA team. *USA Today,* p. 6D.

Wong Briggs, T. (2005, October 13). *USA Today's* 2005 all-USA teacher team. *USA Today,* p. 6D.

Wong Briggs, T. (2007, October 18). An early start for learning. *USA Today,* p. 6D.

Wong, M. M., Brower, K. J., Nigg, J. T., & Zucker, R. A. (2010). Childhood sleep problems, response inhibition, and alcohol and drug outcomes in adolescence and young adulthood. *Alcoholism, Clinical and Experimental Research, 34,* 10033–10044.

Wood, D., Kaplan, R., & McLoyd, V. C. (2007). Gender differences in educational expectations of urban, low-income African American youth: The role of parents and school. *Journal of Youth and Adolescence, 36,* 417–427.

Woodhill, B. M., & Samuels, C. A. (2004). Desirable and undesirable androgyny: A prescription for the twenty-first century. *Journal of Gender Studies, 13,* 15–28.

Woodward, A. L., & Markman, E. M. (1998). Early word learning. In D. Kuhn & R. S. Siegler (Eds.), *Handbook of child psychology* (5th ed., Vol. 2). New York: Wiley.

Woodward, A., Markman, E., & Fitzsimmons, C. (1994). Rapid word learning in 13- and 18-month-olds. *Developmental Psychology, 30,* 553–566.

Woolett, L. A. (2011). Review: Transport of maternal cholesterol to the fetal circulation. *Placenta, 32*(Suppl. 2), S18–S21.

Wright, R. H., Mindel, C. H., Tran, T. V., & Habenstein, R. W. (2012). *Ethnic families in America* (5th ed.). Upper Saddle River, NJ: Pearson.

Wu, P., & others. (2002). Similarities and differences in mothers' parenting of preschoolers in China and the United States. *International Journal of Behavioural Development, 6,* 481–491.

Wu, Z. C., Yu, J. T., Li, Y., & Tan, L. (2012). Clustering in Alzheimer's disease. *Advances in Clinical Chemistry, 56,* 155–173.

Wuest, D. A., & Fisette, J. L. (2012). *Foundations of physical education, exercise science, and sport* (17th Ed.). New York: McGraw-Hill.

Wynn, K. (1992). Addition and subtraction by human infants. *Nature, 358,* 749–570.

X

Xia, N. (2010). *Family factors and student outcomes.* Unpublished doctoral dissertation, RAND Corporation, Pardee RAND Graduate School, Pittsburgh.

Xia, Q., & Grant, S. F. (2013, in press). The genetics of human aging. *Annals of the New York Academy of Sciences.*

Xiao, Y., & others. (2012, in press). Systematic identification of functional modules related to heart failure with different etiologies. *Gene.*

Xie, Q., & Young, M. E. (1999). Integrated child development in rural China. *Education: The World Bank.* Washington, DC: The World Bank.

Xu, F., Spelke, E., & Goddard, S. (2005). Number sense in human infants. *Developmental Science, 8,* 88–101.

Xu, L., & others. (2011). Parental overweight/obesity, social factors, and child overweight/obesity at 7 years of age. *Pediatric International, 53,* 826–831.

Y

Yang, S., & Sternberg, R. J. (1997). Taiwanese Chinese people's conceptions of intelligence. *Intelligence, 25,* 21–36.

Yates, D. (2013, in press). Neurogenetics: Unraveling the genetics of autism. *Nature Reviews: Neuroscience.*

Yeung, W. J. (2012). Explaining the black-white achievement gap: An international stratification and developmental perspective. In K. R. Harris, S. Graham, & T. Urdan (Eds.), *APA handbook of educational psychology.* Washington, DC: American Psychological Association.

Yi, O., & others. (2012). Association between environmental tobacco smoke exposure of children and parental socioeconomic status: A cross-sectional study in Korea. *Nicotine and Tobacco Research, 14,* 607–615.

Yin, R. K. (2012). Case study methods. In H. Cooper (Ed.), *APA handbook of research methods in psychology.* Washington, DC: American Psychological Association.

Yolton, K., & others. (2010). Associations between secondhand smoke exposure and sleep patterns in children. *Pediatrics, 125,* e261–e268.

Yonker, J. E., Schnabelrauch, C. A., & DeHaan, L. G. (2012). The relationship between spirituality and religiosity on psychological outcomes in adolescents and emerging adults: A meta-analytic review. *Journal of Adolescence, 35,* 299–314.

Yoshikawa, H. (2012). *Immigrants raising citizens: Undocumented parents and their young children.* New York: Russell Sage.

Young, K. T. (1990). American conceptions of infant development from 1955 to 1984: What the experts are telling parents. *Child Development, 61,* 17–28.

Yu, S. M., & Singh, G. K. (2012). High parenting aggravation among U.S. immigrant families. *American Journal of Public Health, 102,* 2102–2108.

Yu, T., Pettit, G. S., Lansford, J. E., Dodge, K., & Bates, J. E. (2010). The interactive effects of marital conflict and divorce on parent-adult children's relationships. *Journal of Marriage and the Family, 72,* 282–292.

Yu, B., & others. (2013, in press). Association of genome-wide variation with highly sensitive cardiac tropin-T (hs-cTnT) levels in European- and African-Americans: A meta-analysis from the Atherosclerosis Risk in Communities and the Cardiovascular Health studies. *Circulation: Cardiovascular Genetics.*

Yudof, M. G., Levin, B., Moran, R., & Ryan, J. M. (2012). *Educational policy and the law* (5th ed.). Boston: Cengage.

Yuen, R., Chen, B., Blair, J. D., Robinson, W. P., & Nelson, D. M. (2013, in press). Hypoxia alters the epigenetic profile in cultured human placental trophoblasts, *Epigenetics.*

Z

Zaccaro, A., & Freda, M. F. (2013, in press). Making sense of risk diagnosis in case of prenatal and reproductive genetic counseling for neuromuscular diseases. *Journal of Health Psychology.*

Zannas, A. S., & others. (2012). Stressful life events, perceived stress, and 12-month course of geriatric depression: Direct effects and moderation by the 5-HTTLPR and COMT Val158Met polymorphisms. *Stress, 15,* 425–434.

Zask, A., Adams, J. K., Brooks, L. O., & Hughes, D. F. (2012). Tooty Fruity Vegie: An obesity prevention intervention evaluation in Australian preschools. *Health Promotion Journal of Australia, 23,* 10–15.

Zeanah, C. H., Fox, N. A., & Nelson, C. A. (2012). Case study in ethical issues in research: The Bucharest Early Intervention Project. *Journal of Nervous and Mental Disease, 200,* 243–247.

Zeiders, K. H., Roosa, M. W., & Tein, J. Y. (2011). Family structure and family processes in Mexican-American families. *Family Process, 50,* 77–91.

Zeiders, K. H., Umana-Taylor, A. J., & Derlan, C. L. (2013, in press). Trajectories of depressive symptoms and self-esteem in Latino youths: Examining the role of gender and perceived discrimination. *Developmental Psychology.*

Zelazo, P. D. (2013). Developmental psychology: A new synthesis. In P. D. Zelazo (Ed.), *Oxford handbook of developmental psychology.* New York: Oxford University Press.

Zelazo, P. D. (2013). Developmental psychology: A new synthesis. In P. D. Zelazo (Ed.), *Handbook of developmental psychology.* New York: Wiley.

Zelazo, P. D., & Lyons, K. E. (2012). The potential benefits of mindfulness training in early childhood: A developmental social cognitive perspective. *Child Development Perspectives, 6,* 154–160.

Zelazo, P. D., & Muller, U. (2011). Executive function in typical and atypical development. In U. Goswami (Ed.), *Wiley-Blackwell handbook of childhood cognitive development.* New York: Wiley.

Zeller, M. H., Reiter-Purtell, J., & Ramey, C. (2008). Negative peer perceptions of obese children in the classroom environment. *Obesity, 16,* 755–762.

Zembal-Saul, C. L., McNeill, K. L., & Hershberger, K. (2013). *What's your evidence?* Upper Saddle River, NJ: Pearson.

Zeskind, P. S., Klein, L., & Marshall, T. R. (1992). Adults' perceptions of experimental modifications of durations of pauses and expiratory sounds in infant crying. *Developmental Psychology, 28,* 1153–1162.

Zhai, F., Raver, C. C., & Jones, S. (2012). Quality of subsequent schools and impacts of early interventions: Evidence from a randomized controlled trial in Head Start settings. *Children and Youth Services Review, 34,* 946–954.

Zhang, L., Zhang, X. H., Liang, M. Y., & Ren, M. H. (2010). Prenatal cytogenetic diagnosis study of 2782 cases of high-risk pregnant women. *China Medicine (English), 123,* 423–430.

Zhang, L-F., & Sternberg, R. J. (2013, in press). Learning in cross-cultural perspective. In T. Husen & T. N. Postlethwaite (Eds.), *International encyclopedia of education* (3rd ed.). New York: Elsevier.

Zhou, Q., Chen, S. H., & Main, A. (2012). Commonalities and differences in the research on children's effortful control and executive function: A call for an integrated model of self-regulation. *Child Development Perspectives, 6,* 112–121.

Zhou, Q., Lengua, L. J., & Wang, Y. (2009). The relations of temperament reactivity and effortful control to children's adjustment problems in the United States and China. *Developmental Psychology, 45,* 724–739.

Zielinksi, D. S., Eckenrode, J., & Olds, D. L. (2009). Nurse home visitation and the prevention of child maltreatment: Impact on the timing of official reports. *Development and Psychopathology, 21,* 441–453.

Ziemer, C. J., Plumert, J. M., & Pick, A. D. (2012). To grasp or not to grasp: Infants' actions toward objects and pictures. *Infancy, 17,* 479–497.

Zigler, E., Gilliam, W. S., & Jones, S. M. (2006). *A vision for universal preschool education.* New York: Cambridge University Press.

Zigler, E. F., & Styfco, S. J. (1994). Head Start: Criticisms in a constructive context. *American Psychologist, 49,* 127–132.

Zigler, E. F., & Styfco, S. J. (2010). *The hidden history of Head Start.* New York: Oxford University Press.

Zimmerman, B. J. (2002). Becoming a self-regulated learner: An overview. *Theory into Practice, 41,* 64–70.

Zimmerman, B. J. (2012). Motivational sources and outcomes of self-regulated learning and performance. In B. J. Zimmerman & D. H. Schunk (Eds.), *Handbook of self-regulation of learning and performance.* New York: Routledge.

Zimmerman, B. J., Bonner, S., & Kovach, R. (1996). *Developing self-regulated learners.* Washington, DC: American Psychological Association.

Zimmerman, B. J., & Kitsantas, A. (1997). Developmental phases in self-regulation: Shifting from process goals to outcome goals. *Journal of Educational Psychology, 89,* 29–36.

Zimmerman, B. J., & Labuhn, A. S. (2012). Self-regulation of learning: Process approaches to personal development. In K. R. Harris & others (Eds.), *APA handbook of educational psychology.* Washington, DC: American Psychological Association.

Zimmerman, F. J., Christakis, D. A., & Meltzoff, A. N. (2007). Associations between media viewing and language development in children under age 2 years. *Journal of Pediatrics, 151,* 364–368.

Ziol-Guest, K. M. (2009). Child custody and support. In D. Carr (Ed.), *Encyclopedia of the life course and human development.* Boston: Cengage.

Zitzer-Comfort, C., Doyle, T. F., Masataka, N., Korenberg, J., & Bellugi, U. (2007). Nature and nurture: Williams syndrome across cultures. *Developmental Science, 10,* 755–762.

Zosuls, K. M., & others. (2009). The acquisition of gender labels in infancy: Implications for gender-typed play. *Developmental Psychology, 45,* 688–701.

Zotter, H., & Pichler, G. (2012). Breast feeding is associated with decreased risk of sudden infant death syndrome. *Evidence Based Medicine, 17,* 126–127.

Zugazaga Cortazar, A., & Martin Martinez, C. (2012). Usefulness of magnetic resonance imaging in the prenatal study of malformations in the face and neck. *Radiologia, 54,* 387–400.

credits

PHOTO CREDITS

Front Matter

Page vi(top): © Ariel Skelley/Corbis; p. vi(bottom): © MedicalRF.com/Getty Images RF; p. viii: © Beau Lark/Fancy/PhotoLibrary RF; p. ix: © Ariel Skelley/Blend Images/Getty Images RF; p. x: © Monkey Business Images/PhotoLibrary RF; p. xvi: Image courtesy of Dr. Karen E. Adolph; p. xviii(top): © Tom Grill/Corbis RF; p. xviii(bottom): © Ocean/Corbis RF; p. xix: Courtesy of Helen Hadani.

Chapter 1

Opener: © Ariel Skelley/Blend Images LLC RF; p. 2–3: © Ariel Skelley/Corbis; p. 4: © Ariel Skelley/Corbis; p. 5(Kaczynski adult): © Seanna O'Sullivan; p. 5(Kaczynski teen): © WBBM-TV/AFP/Getty Images; p. 5(Walker adult): © AP Wide World Photos; p. 5(Walker child): Courtesy of Alice Walker; p. 7(top): Courtesy of Luis Vargas; p. 7 (bottom): National Association for the Education of Young Children, © Robert Maust/Photo Agora; p. 8(top): © Nancy Agostini; p. 8(bottom): © Photo by Debbie Egan-Chin/NY Daily News Archive via Getty Images; p. 9: © Naser Siddique/UNICEF Bangladesh; p. 11: Courtesy of the Children's Defense Fund; 1.5a(left to right): © Brand X Pictures/PunchStock RF; Courtesy of Dr. John Santrock; © Laurence Mouton/Photoalto/PictureQuest RF; © McGraw-Hill Companies Inc./Ken Karp, photographer; © Getty Images/SW Productions RF; p. 15: © Marian Stanca/Alamy; p. 17: © Rubberball/PictureQuest RF; p. 18: © Zuma Wire Service/Alamy; p. 19: © Bettmann/Corbis; p. 20: © Sarah Putman; p. 21(left to right): © BananaStock/PunchStock RF; © Tomas Rodriguez/Corbis RF; © Corbis RF; © PunchStock/Image Source RF; 1.9 (left to right): © Stockbyte/Getty Images RF; © BananaStock/PunchStock RF; © image100/Corbis RF; © RF/Corbis; p. 23(top): © Yves de Braine/Black Star/Stock Photo; p. 23(bottom): Courtesy of A.R. Lauria/Dr. Michael Cole, Laboratory of Human Cognition, University of California, San Diego; p. 24: © Creatas Images/Jupiter Images RF; p. 25(top left): Courtesy of Professor Benjamin Harris; p. 25(top right): © AP Wide World Photos; p. 25 (bottom): © Linda A. Cicero/Stanford News Service; p. 26: © Nina Leen/Time Life Pictures/Getty Images; p. 28: Courtesy of Urie Bronfenbrenner; p. 29: © Charles Fox/MCT/ Newscom; p. 31: © Bettmann/Corbis; 1.14: Dr. Susan Tapert, University of California at San Diego; 1.15: © Digital Vision/PunchStock RF; p. 35: © The McGraw-Hill Companies, Inc./Mark Dierker, photographer; p. 37: Courtesy of Dr. Pam Reid, University of Saint Joseph; p. 38(left): © Olaf Doering/Alamy; p. 38(right): © Stretch Photography/Blend Images LLC; p. 44: Courtesy of Katherine Duchen Smith.

Chapter 2

Opener: © MedicalRF.com/Getty Images RF; p. 48: © Image Source/Getty Images RF; p. 49: © The Denver Post/Getty Images; p. 51: © Frans Lemmens/Corbis; 2.1: © Photodisc/Getty Images RF; p. 52: © David Wilkie; p. 54(left): © AP Photo/Chris Martinez; p. 54(right): © Rick Rickman; p. 55(2.3): © Science Source/Photo Researchers; (2.4a): © Biophoto Associates/Science Source/Getty Images; (2.4b): © Biophoto Associates/Science Source/Getty Images; p. 57: © James Shaffer/PhotoEdit; p. 58: From R. Simensen and R. Curtis Rogers, "Fragile X Syndrome" in *American Family Physician,* 39(5): 186, May 1989 © American Academy of Family Physicians; p. 59: © Andrew Eccles/August Images; p. 60: Courtesy of Holly Ishmael; p. 61: © Jacques Pavlovsky/Sygma/Corbis; 2.7: © Larry Berman; p. 62: © Frank Peters/ZumaPress/Newscom; p. 64: © Jackson Lee/Tom Meinelt/Splash News/Newscom; p. 65: © Photodisc/Getty Images RF; p. 67: © Myrleen Pearson/PhotoEdit; p. 68: © Cuomo/Corbis; p. 70: © iStockphoto.com/Francisco Romero.

Chapter 3

Opener: © Lennart Nilsson/Scanpix Sweden AB; p. 74: Courtesy of Dr. John Santrock; 3.3(top to bottom): © Lennart Nilsson/Scanpix Sweden AB; © Lennart Nilsson/Scanpix Sweden AB; © Brand X Pictures/PunchStock RF; p. 79: © AP Wide World Photos; 3.4: © Lennart Nilsson/Scanpix Sweden AB; p. 81: Courtesy of Dr. Ann Streissguth; p. 82(top): © Anthony West/Corbis; p. 82(bottom): © Ted Thai/The LIFE Picture Collection/Getty Images; p. 83: © R.I.A. Novosti/Gamma/H.P.P./Eyedea; p. 84(top): © Wendy Stone/Corbis/Getty Images; p. 84(bottom): © iStockphoto.com; p. 85(top): © Barbara Penoyar/Getty Images RF; p. 85(middle): © Rafal Strzechowski/agefotostock; p. 85(bottom): © David Butow/Corbis Saba/Corbis; p. 86(top): © Tracy Frankel/The Image Bank/Getty Images; p. 86(bottom): © Stephen Maturen; p. 88(top): © Jonathan Nourok/Getty Images; p. 88(bottom): © Viviane Moos/Corbis; p. 89(top): © RF/Corbis; p. 89(bottom): © Barros & Barros/Stockbyte/Getty Images RF; p. 90: Courtesy of Linda Pugh; p. 91(left): Dr. Holly Beckwith; p. 91(right): © Comstock/PunchStock RF; 3.6: © Stephen Marks/The Image Bank/Getty Images; p. 93: © AP Wide World Photos; p. 95(top): © Marc Asnin/Corbis Saba/Corbis; p. 95(bottom): Courtesy of Dr. Tiffany Field; p. 98(top): Courtesy of Diane Sanford, Photograph: © Tony Schanuel; p. 98(bottom): © Howard Grey/Getty Images RF; p. 99: © Kaz Mori/The Image Bank/Getty Images.

Chapter 4

Opener: © Christopher Futcher/The Agency Collection/Getty Images RF; p. 105: © Robert Glenn/DK Stock/Corbis; p. 106: © Chris Windsor/Digital Vision/Getty Images RF; p. 109(left): © Ingram Publishing/Alamy RF; p. 109(right): © image100/Corbis RF; p. 110: © Value RF/Corbis; 4.5: © A. Glauberman/Photo Researchers; 4.6: © ER Productions/Getty Images RF; 4.8: © Benjamin Benschneider/The Seattle Times; 4.9: Courtesy of Dr. Harry T. Chugani, Children's Hospital of Michigan; 4.10(a): © David Grugin Productions, Inc. Reprinted by permission; 4.10(b): Image courtesy of Dana Boatman, Ph.D., Department of Neurology, John Hopkins University, reprinted with permission from *The Secret Life of the Brain,* Joseph Henry Press; 4.11: © Photo Researchers; p. 119: © Marla Teljeiro/Cultura/Getty Images RF; p. 120: © Tom Grill/Getty Images; p. 121: © Jim LoScalzo; p. 123: © AP Wide World Photos; p. 124: © The McGraw-Hill Companies, Inc./Mark Steinmetz, photographer; p. 125: © Blend Images/Getty Images RF; p. 126: © Peter Charlesworth/LightRocket/Getty Images; p. 127(top): © Wendy Stone/Corbis; p. 127(bottom): © Dave Bartruff/Corbis; p. 128: © USDA Food and Nutrition Service, Supplemental Nutrition Assistance Program; p. 129: Courtesy Brazelton Touchpoints Center; p. 130: © Jules Frazier/Getty Images RF; p. 131(top): Courtesy of Barbara Deloin; p. 131(bottom): © Image Source/PunchStock RF; p. 132–133: © RubberBall Productions/Getty Images RF; p. 134: Dallas Morning News, photographer Vernon Bryant.

Chapter 5

Opener: © Image Source/Getty Images RF; p. 139(left): © Reuters New Media Inc./Corbis; p. 139(right): © Reuters/Corbis; p. 140: Courtesy of Esther Thelen; p. 141(top): © Camille

Tokerud/Taxi/Getty Images; p. 141(bottom): © Petit Format/Photo Researchers; p. 142: © Laurence Mouton/PhotoAlto/Getty Images RF; p. 143: © Fabio Cardosa/zefa/Corbis; 5.2: © Dr. Karen Adolph, New York University; 5.3(left to right): © Barbara Penoyar/Getty Images RF; © Digital Vision/Getty Images RF; © Image Source/Getty Images RF; © Titus/Getty Images RF; © Digital Vision RF; © BananaStock/Getty Images RF; © Corbis/PictureQuest RF; © BrandX/PunchStock RF; p. 145: © Charlie Edwards/Getty Images RF; p. 146(top left): © Michael Greenlar/The Image Works; p. 146(top right): © Frank Baily Studios; p. 146(bottom): © Photodisc/Getty Images RF; p. 147: © Getty Images RF; p. 148: © Newstockimages/SuperStock; 5.4: Courtesy Amy Needham, Duke University; 5.5: Reprinted from Keen, R. (2011) The development of problem solving in young children: a critical cognitive skill. In *Annual Review of Psychology, 62, pp 1.1–1.21.* Copyright © 2011 by Annual Reviews. Reprinted with permission. p. 150: © Dorling Kindersley/Getty Images; 5.6(b): © David Linton; 5.8: Image courtesy of Dr. Karen E. Adolph; 5.9: © Kevin Peterson/Getty Images/Simulation by Vischeck RF; 5.11: © Mark Richards/PhotoEdit; 5.12: Courtesy of Dr. Bruce Hood; 5.13(a): © McGraw-Hill Companies, Inc./Jill Braaten, photographer; 5.13(b): Dr. Melanie Spence, University of Texas, Dallas; 5.14: © Jean Guichard/Corbis; 5.15: Rosenstein, D & Oster, H (1988) Differential facial responses to four basic tastes in newborns. *Child Development,* 59, p. 1561; p. 159: © Dorling Kindersley/Getty Images; p. 160: © altrendo images/Getty Images; p. 161: © Philip Kaake.

Chapter 6

Opener: © Beau Lark/Fancy/PhotoLibrary RF; p. 166: © Lifesize/Getty Images RF; p. 168: © Maya Kovacheva Photography/Getty Images; p. 169: © Plush Studios/Brand X Pictures/JupiterImages RF; 6.1(left to right): © Stockbyte/Getty Images RF; © BananaStock/PunchStock RF; © image100/Corbis RF; © RF/Corbis; p. 171: © PunchStock RF; 6.3: © Doug Goodman/Photo Researchers; p. 174: © Joe McNally; p. 175: © baobao ou/Flickr/Getty Images RF; 6.8: © Paul Fusco/Magnum Photos; p. 180: © Jim West/Alamy; p. 181: © Image Source/JupiterImages RF; p. 183(top): © RF/Corbis; p. 183(bottom): © Bill Anderson/Science Source/Getty Images; p. 184: © Olivier Asselin/Alamy; p. 185(6.11): © Ariel Skelley/Blend Images; p. 186: Courtesy Barbara Rogoff; p. 187(top): © James Wertsch/Washington University, St. Louis; p. 187(bottom): © BananaStock/PunchStock RF; 6.12: Images courtesy of E. Bodrova and D.J Leong, from *Tools of the Mind,* 2007; 6.13(Vygotsky): Courtesy of

A.R. Lauria/Dr. Michael Cole, Laboratory of Human Cognition, University of California, San Diego; 6.13(Piaget): © Bettmann/Corbis.

Chapter 7

Opener: © Peter Dazeley/Getty Images; p. 194: Courtesy of Laura Bickford; p. 196(top): © BananaStock/agefotostock RF; p. 196(bottom): © Digital Vision/Getty Images RF; p. 198: © Photodisc Collection/Getty Images RF; p. 199: © Myrleen Pearson/PhotoEdit; 7.1: © XiXinXing/age fotostock; p. 200(top): © Ocean/Corbis RF; p. 200(bottom): © BananaStock/PunchStock RF; p. 201: © Yellow Dog Productions/Getty Images; p. 204: © Tetra Images/Alamy RF; p. 205: © Pascal Deloche/Godong/Corbis; 7.5: Courtesy of Dr. Carolyn Rovee-Collier; p. 208: © Stretch Photography/Blend Images/Getty Images RF; p. 209(top): © Travel Pictures/Alamy; p. 209(middle): © Carlo Allegri/Getty Images; p. 209(bottom): © 2013 www.polychromemedia/jameskamp; 7.10: From Jean Mandler, University of California, San Diego. Reprinted by permission of Oxford University Press, Inc.; p. 211: Courtesy of Dr. John Santrock; p. 212: © Anthony Harvel/Getty Images RF; 7.11: © vwPix/Shutterstock; p. 213: © Simon Jarratt/Corbis; p. 214: Courtesy of Helen Hadani; p. 215: © Dale Sparks; p. 216: Courtesy of Judy DeLoache; p. 217: © BananaStock/PunchStock RF; p. 218: © Jutta Klee/Corbis; p. 219: © Scott Houston/Corbis; p. 220: © John Flavell; p. 221: © Joe Baker, Images.com/Corbis; p. 223: © Robin Nelson/PhotoEdit; p. 224: © Thinkstock/Comstock Images/Getty Images RF.

Chapter 8

Opener: © Ocean/Corbis RF; p. 231: © Bettmann/Corbis; p. 233: Courtesy of Robert Sternberg; p. 234(top): © Alistair Berg/Digital Vision/Getty Images RF; p. 234(bottom): © Jetta Productions/Walter Hodges/Getty Images RF; 8.4: © ER Productions/Getty Images RF; p. 237: © Owen Franken/Corbis; p. 238(left): © Voluntary Service Overseas/Robert Harding/Alamy Stock Photo; p. 238(right): © Ben Simmons Photography; p. 240: © McGraw-Hill Education; p. 241: Courtesy of Dr. John Santrock; p. 242: Bayley Scales of Infant and Toddler Development-Third Edition (Bayley-III). Copyright © 2006 by NCS Pearson, Inc. Reproduced with permission. All rights reserved; p. 244(top): © Stockbyte/Veer RF; p. 244(bottom): © Koichi Kamoshida/Newsmakers/Getty Images; p. 245: © Deborah Feingold/Corbis/Getty Images; p. 246(top): Courtesy of Sterling C. Jones; p. 246(bottom): © Scott Buschman; p. 247: © Purestock/Getty Images RF.

Chapter 9

Opener: © Jack Hollingsworth/Getty Images RF; p. 252: Library of Congress, Prints and

Photographs Division, LC-USZ61-326; p. 253: © Vanessa Davies/Dorling Kindersley/Getty Images; p. 256: © Don Hammond/Design Pics/Corbis RF; 9.2: © 2003 University of Washington, Institute for Learning and Brain Sciences (I-LABS); p. 257: © Niki Mareschal/Photographer's Choice/Getty Images; p. 258(top): © Yang Liu/Corbis; p. 258(bottom): © Nicole Duplaix/Photolibrary/Getty Images; p. 260: Courtesy of Sharla Peltier; p. 261(top): © Vetta/Getty Images; p. 261(bottom): © Hill Street Studios/Blend Images/agefotostock RF; p. 263: © Deepak Budhraja/Asia Images/Corbis; p. 264: © Gideon Mendel/Corbis; p. 265: © Comstock/PunchStock RF; p. 267(top): © Blend Images - KidStock/Getty Images; p. 267(bottom): Courtesy of Salvador Tamayo; p. 268: © Elizabeth Crews; p. 269: © PunchStock/Digital Vision RF; p. 270: © Nigel Pavitt/AWL Images/Getty Images; p. 271: © AFP/Getty Images; 9.10: © Michael Goldstein, Cornell University; p. 272(top): © Elyse Lewin/Brand X Pictures/Getty Images RF; p. 272(bottom): © RF/Corbis; p. 273: © John Carter/Photo Researchers; p. 274: Courtesy of James Verougstraete, Father.

Chapter 10

Opener: © Ariel Skelley Blend Images/Getty Images RF; p. 280: © Meg Takamura/Getty Images RF; p. 281: © Rick Gomez/Corbis; p. 283: © Digital Archive Japan/Alamy Stock Photo; 10.2(joy): © BananaStock/PictureQuest RF;(sadness): © The McGraw-Hill Companies, Inc./Jill Braaten, photographer; (fear): © David Sacks/Getty Images; (surprise): © Getty Images RF; 10.3: Photo by Kenny Braun and courtesy of Dr. Sybil L. Hart, Texas Tech University; p. 286: © Andy Cox/Stone/Getty Images; 10.4: © Dr. Daniel Messinger, University of Miami, FL; p. 288(top): © Photodisc Collection/Getty Images RF; p. 288(bottom): © James Woodson/Digital Vision/Getty Images RF; p. 289: © LWA-Dann Tardif/Corbis; p. 290: © MacGregor & Gordon/Getty Images; p. 291:© Justin Lane/epa/Corbis; p. 292–293: © Tom Merton/Getty Images RF; p. 293(top): © Girl Ray/Getty Images; p. 295: © MIXA/Getty Images RF; p. 296: © RF/Corbis; p. 298: © Britt Erlanson/Getty Images; 10.7: Courtesy of Celia A. Brownell, University of Pittsburgh; p.300 (10.8): © Martin Rogers/Getty Images; p. 301(top): © Camille Tokerud/Getty Images RF; p. 301(bottom): © George Doyle/Stockbyte/Getty Images RF; p. 303: © Penny Tweedie/Stone/Getty Images; 10.10: © ER Productions/Getty Images RF; p. 305: Courtesy of Dr. Barry Hewlett; p. 306: © Lawrence Schwartzwald; p. 307: Courtesy of Wanda Mitchell; p. 308: © Christopher Futcher/Getty Images.

CREDIT LIST

Chapter 1

p. 1 From the book 100 Ways to Build Self-Esteem and Teach Values. Copyright © 1994, 2003 by Diana Loomans. Reprinted with permission of HJ Kramer/New World Library, Novato CA. www.newworldlibrary.com. **Fig. 1.1,** p. 13 From The State of the World's Children, 2004, Geneva, Switzerland: UNICEF, Fig. 5, p. 27. Reprinted by permission of UNICEF. **Fig. 1.3,** p. 16 From Santrock, Life-Span Development, 11th ed., Fig. 1.4. Copyright © 2008. Reprinted by permission of The McGraw-Hill Companies, Inc. TA1.10, p. 19 Peanuts: © United Feature Syndicate TA1.11, p. 21 © Robert Weber/The New Yorker Collection/ www.cartoonbank.com **Fig.1.11,** p. 48 From "Bronfenbrenner's Ecological Theory of Development," C.B. Kopp & J.B. Krakow, 1982, Child Development in the Social Context, p. 648. Reprinted by permission of Pearson Education, Inc. **Fig.1.12,** p. 49 From Santrock, Children, 8th ed., Fig. 2.9. Copyright © 2005. Reprinted by permission of The McGraw-Hill Companies, Inc. **Fig. 1.13,** p. 51 Crowley et al., PSYCHOLOGICAL SCIENCE, Vol. 12, Issue 3, Copyright 2001 by Sage. Reproduced with permission of Sage Publications. **Fig.1.15,** p. 55 From Adolescence, 12ed, by John Santrock. Copyright © 2008. Reprinted by permission of The McGraw-Hill Companies, Inc. **Fig.1.16,** p. 57 From Santrock, Children, 7th ed., Fig. 2.11. Copyright © 2003. Reprinted by permission of The McGraw-Hill Companies, Inc.

Chapter 2

Fig. 2.1, p. 101 Bonner, John T., THE EVOLUTION OF CULTURE IN ANIMALS. © 1980 Princeton University Press. Reprinted by permission of Princeton University Press. **Fig. 2.2,** p. 105 "CELLS, CHROMOSOMES, DNA, AND GENES" from p. 58 of Santrock Life-Span Development 13e. Reprinted by permission of McGraw-Hill Companies, Inc. TA2.6, p. 106 CALVIN AND HOBBES © 1991, 1993 Watterson. Dist by UNIVERSAL UCLICK. Reprinted with permission. All rights reserved. **Fig. 2.5,** p. 111 From Santrock, Life-Span Development, 11th ed., Fig. 3.7. Copyright © 2008. Reprinted by permission of The McGraw-Hill Companies, Inc. **Fig. 2.9,** p. 123 From Golombok et al., 2001, "The 'Test-Tube' Generation," Child Development, 72, 599–608. Reprinted with permission of the Society for Research in Child Development. **Fig. 2.10,** p. 130 From Santrock, Children, 7th ed., Fig. 3.14. Copyright © 2003. Reprinted by permission of The McGraw-Hill Companies, Inc. **Fig. 2.11,** p. 133 From Santrock, Life-Span Development, 12ed. Copyright © 2009. Reprinted by permission of The McGraw-Hill Companies, Inc.

Chapter 3

Fig. 3.1, p. 151 From Charles Carroll and Dean Miller, Health: The Science of Human Adaptation, 5th ed. Copyright © 1991. Reprinted by permission of The McGraw-Hill Companies, Inc. **Fig. 3.6,** p. 180 Virginia Apgar, "The Apgar Scale" from "A Proposal for a New Method of Evaluation of a Newborn Infant," Anesthesia and Analgesia (32), pp. 260–267. © 1975. Reprinted by permission. **Fig. 3.9,** p. 186 Reprinted from Infant Behavior and Development, 30, "Preterm Infants Show Reduced Stress Behaviors and Activity After Five Days of Massage Therapy," pp. 557–561. Copyright © 2007 with permission from Elsevier.

Chapter 4

Fig. 4.1, p. 203 From Santrock, Children, 7th ed., Fig. 3. 14. Copyright © 2003. Reprinted by permission of The McGraw-Hill Companies, Inc. TA4.4, p. 207 Reprinted by permission of ICM Partners Copyright © [1985] by Breathed, Berkeley. **Fig. 4.2,** p. 209 From Santrock, Adolescence, 8th ed., Fig. 3.4. Copyright © 2001. Reprinted with permission of The McGraw-Hill Companies, Inc. **Fig.4.3,** p. 210 Reproduced from "Standards from Birth to Maturity for Height, Weight, Height Velocity: British Children" by J.M. Tanner, R.H. Whitehouse, and M. Takaishi, Archives of Diseases in Childhood, vol. 41, issue 220. Copyright © 1966 with permission from BMJ Publishing Group Ltd. **Fig. 4.4,** p. 211 Originally appeared in J.M. Tanner, "Growing Up," Scientific American, September 1973. Reprinted by permission of Nelson H. Prentiss. **Fig.4.6,** p. 216 From Santrock, Children, 9th ed., Fig. 6.6. Copyright © 2003. Reprinted by permission of The McGraw-Hill Companies, Inc. **Fig. 4.7,** p. 217 From Santrock, Child Development, 9th ed. Copyright © 2001. Reprinted by permission of The McGraw-Hill Companies, Inc. **Fig. 4.12** p. 114 From The Postnatal Development of the Human Cerebral Cortex, Volumes I–VIII, by Jesse LeRoy Conel, Cambridge, Mass.: Harvard University Press, Copyright © 1939, 1941, 1947, 1951, 1955, 1959, 1963, 1967 by the President and Fellows of Harvard College. Copyright © renewed 1967, 1969, 1975, 1979, 1983, 1987, 1991. **Fig. 4.13,** p. 223 From Santrock, Psychology, 7th ed., p. 128. Copyright © 2003. Reprinted by permission of The McGraw-Hill Companies, Inc. **Fig. 4.15,** p. 227 From Santrock, Essentials of Life-Span Development, Fig 9.3. Copyright © 2008. Reprinted by permission of The McGraw-Hill Companies, Inc. **Fig.4. 16,** p. 231 From Santrock, Children, 10th ed., Fig. 5.10. Copyright © 2008. Reprinted by permission of The McGraw-Hill Companies, Inc. **Fig. 4.17,** p. 238 Data from National Center for Health Statistics and Center for Disease Control & Prevention, Atlanta. **Fig. 4.18,** p. 243 From Santrock, Children, 10th ed., Fig. 5.11. Copyright © 2008. Reprinted by permission of The McGraw-Hill Companies, Inc. **Fig. 4.21,** p. 260 From Santrock, Children, 10th ed., Fig. 14.10. Copyright © 2008. Reprinted by permission of The McGraw-Hill Companies, Inc.

Chapter 5

Fig. 5.5, p. 280 Reprinted from Journal of Pediatrics, 71, W.K. Frankenburg & J.B. Dodds, "The Denver Development Screening Test," vol 71, issue 2, pp. 181–191, © 1967, with permission from Elsevier. p. 286–287 Reprinted with the permission of the Women's Sports Foundation. **Fig. 5.6,** p. 296 Adapted from Alexander Semenoick, in R.L. Fantz, "The Origin of Form Perception," Scientific American, 1961. **Fig. 5.7,** p. 297 From Slater, et al., 1988, "Orientation Discrimination and Cortical Function in the Human Newborn," Perception, 17, 597–602 (Figure 1 and Table 1). Reprinted with permission of Pion Limited, London. **Fig. 5.10,** p. 303 Bennett I. Bertenthal, Matthew R. Longo, and Sarah Kenny, "Phenomenal Permanence and the Development of Predictive Tracking in Infancy" from Child Development, 78, p. 354, © 2007 by John Wiley & Sons. Reprinted with permission.

Chapter 6

p. 325–326 Reprinted from The Origins of Intelligence by J. Piaget by permission of International Universities Press, Inc. Copyright 1952 by International Universities Press Inc. and Taylor & Francis Books UK. **Fig. 6.1,** p. 330 From Santrock, Topical Life-Span, 2ed., Fig. 6.1. Copyright © 2005. Reprinted by permission of The McGraw-Hill Companies, Inc. **Fig. 6.2,** p. 331 From Santrock, Life-Span Development, 11ed., Fig. 6.1. Copyright © 2008. Reprinted by permission of The McGraw-Hill Companies, Inc. **Fig. 6.4,** p. 335 From R. Baillargeon & J. Devoe, "Object Permanence in Young Children: Further Evidence," Child Development, 62, pp. 1227–1246. Reprinted with permission of the Society for Research in Child Development. **Fig. 6.6,** p. 344 From Santrock, Children, 7ed., Fig. 10.1. Copyright © 2003. Reprinted by permission of The McGraw-Hill Companies, Inc. **Fig. 6.7,** p. 344 Reprinted courtesy of D. Wolf and J. Nove. TA 6.7, p. 345 © Lee Lorenz/The New Yorker Collection/www.cartoonbank.com **Fig. 6.8,** p. 346 From Santrock, Children, 7ed., Fig. 10.4. Copyright © 2003. Reprinted by permission of The McGraw-Hill Companies, Inc. **Fig. 6.9,** p. 346 From Santrock, Children, 7ed., Fig. 10.5. Copyright © 2003. Reprinted by permission of The McGraw-Hill Companies, Inc. **Fig. 6.10,** p. 349 From Santrock, Children, 7ed., Fig. 13.1. Copyright © 2003. Reprinted by

Inc. **Fig 12.6**, p. 716 Reproduced by special permission of the Publisher, MIND GARDEN, Inc., www.mindgarden.com from the BEM SEX ROLE INVENTORY by Sandra Bem. Copyright 1978, 1981 by Consulting Psychologists Press, Inc. Further reproduction is prohibited without the Publisher's written consent.

Chapter 13

Fig. 13.1, p. 735 From R.S. Selman, "Social-Cognitive Understanding," in Thomas Lickona (Ed.) *Moral Development and Behavior*, 1976. Reprinted by permission of Thomas Lickona. **Fig. 13.2**, p. 737 From Colby, et al., 1983, "A Longitudinal Study of Moral Judgment," *Monographs for the Society for Research in Child Development*, Serial #201. Reprinted with permission of the Society for Research in Child Development. **Fig 13.4**, p. 772 From *Adolescence*, 13ed, by John Santrock.Copyright © 2010. Reprinted by permission of The McGraw-Hill Companies, Inc.

Chapter 14

TA 14.10, p. 818 CALVIN AND HOBBES © 1991, 1993 Watterson.Dist by UNIVERSAL UCLICK. Reprinted with permission. All rights reserved. **Fig. 14.3**, p. 822 From Santrock, *Life-Span Development*, 11th ed, Fig. 9.6. Copyright © 2008. Reprinted by permission of The McGraw-Hill Companies, Inc. **Fig. 14.4**, p. 830 From p. 666 of "Bringing basic research on early experience and stress neurobiology to bear on preventative interventions for neglected and maltreated children" by M.R. Gunnar and P.A. Fisher, and the Early Experience, Stress, and Prevention Network (2006). From *Development and Psychopathology*, 18, pp. 651–677. Reprinted with the permission of Cambridge University Press. **Fig. 14.5**,

p. 835 From Santrock, *Child Development*, 9th ed. Copyright © 2001. Reprinted by permission of The McGraw-Hill Companies, Inc. **Fig. 14.8**, p. 851 From Santrock, *Life-Span Development*, 11th ed, Fig. 15.9. Copyright © 2008. Reprinted by permission of The McGraw-Hill Companies, Inc. p. 799–800 Reprinted by permission of Shelley Peterman Schwarz. Ch. 14, p. 855–856 *Handbook of Parenting*, 2ed by Garcia Coll and Patcher. Copyright 2002 by Taylor & Francis Group LLC - Books. Reproduced with permission of Taylor & Francis Group LLC - Books via Copyright Clearance Center.

Chapter 15

p. 883–884 Coie, J. "Children's peer relations: From development to intervention." *The impact of negative social experiences on the development of antisocial behavior*. Published by the American Psychological Association. **Fig. 15.2**, p. 885 From Nansel, et al., 2001, "Bullying Behaviors Among U.S. Youth," *Journal of the American Medical Association*, Vol. 285, pp. 2094–2100. **Fig. 15.4**, p. 907 From Dexter C. Dunphy, "The Social Structure of Urban Adolescent Peer Groups," *Sociometry*, Vol. 26, 1963.American Sociological Association, Washington, DC.

Chapter 16

Fig. 16.1, p. 932 NAEYC. 2009. "Developmentally Appropriate Practice in Early Childhood Programs Serving Children from Birth through Age 8." Position statement. Washington, DC: Author. www.naeyc.org/files/naeyc/file/positions/PSDAP.pdf **Fig. 16.2**, p. 938 From Santrock, *Life-Span Development*, 11th ed, Fig. 18.9. Copyright © 2008. Reprinted by permission of The McGraw-Hill Companies, Inc. **Fig. 16.3**, p. 942 "SCHOOL DROPOUT RATES OF U.S. 16-24-YEAR OLDS BY GENDER AND

ETHNICITY." from p. 531 of Santrock A Topical Approach to Life-Span Development. Reprinted by permission of The McGraw-Hill Companies, Inc. **Fig. 16.4**, p. 951 From Santrock, *Life-Span Development*, 11th ed, Fig. 10.3. Copyright © 2008. Reprinted by permission of The McGraw-Hill Companies, Inc. **Fig. 16.6**, p. 955 From Shaw et al. (2007). "Attention deficit/hyperactivity disorders is characterized by a delay in cortical maturation," PNAS, Dec. 4, 2007, Vol. 104. P. 19650 gif 2. Copyright © 2007 National Academy of Sciences, USA. Reprinted by permission. TA 16.25, p. 964 CALVIN AND HOBBES © 1991, 1993 Watterson. Dist by UNIVERSAL UCLICK. Reprinted with permission. All rights reserved. **Fig. 16.9**, p. 965 From Santrock, *Adolescence*, 12th ed, Fig. 16.6. Copyright © 2008. Reprinted by permission of The McGraw-Hill Companies, Inc. **Fig. 16.11**, p. 975 OECD (2011), Lessons from PISA for the United States, Strong Performers and Successful Reformers in Education, OECD Publishing. http://dx.doi.org/10.1787/9789264096660-en

Chapter 17

Fig. 17.1, p. 994 From Harry C. Triandis, *Making Basic Texts in Psychology More Culture-Inclusive and Culture-Sensitive*. Used by permission of the author. **Fig. 17.5**, p. 1010 From Santrock, *Topical Life-Span Development*, 4th ed, Fig. 15.2. Copyright © 2008. Reprinted by permission of The McGraw-Hill Companies, Inc. **Fig. 17.6**, p. 1018 From Santrock, *Adolescence*, 12th ed, Fig. 12.3. Copyright © 2008. Reprinted by permission of The McGraw-Hill Companies, Inc. **Fig. 17.8**, p. 1023 From Santrock, *Topical Life-Span Development*, 4th ed, Fig. 15.8. Copyright © 2008. Reprinted by permission of The McGraw-Hill Companies, Inc. TA 17.14, p. 1028 © Tribune Media Services, Inc. All Rights Reserved. Reprinted with permission.

name index

Bartel, M. A., 56
Bartlett, D. J., 119
Bartlett, J. D., 17, 282, 287, 294, 298, 316
Bartsch, K., 221
Baruth, L. G., 463
Basanez, T., 497
Bascandziev, I., 156
Basinger, K. S., 363, 364
Basra, R., 91
Bassett, H. H., 288, 289
Bassett-Greer, K., 410
Bassi, M., 473
Batanova, M. D., 320
Bates, J. E., 293–297, 311, 379, 404
Battistich, V., 372, 373
Battistich, V. A., 373, 375
Batty, G. D., 232
Bauer, P., 175, 183, 203, 206–208, 211
Bauer, P. J., 205–207
Bauer, R. M., 31
Bauerlein, M., 201, 499
Bauland, C. G., 61
Baum, A., 54
Baumeister, J., 147
Baumeister, R. F., 321, 322, 324–325
Baumrind, D., 401, 402, 404, 412
Bauserman, R., 415
Bavelier, D., 198, 200
Baye, T. M., 57
Bayley, N., 241
Baym, C. L., 201
Beal, S. J., 394
Beall, M., 84
Beall, S. A., 62
Bearer, C. F., 122
Beauchamp, G., 158
Beaver, K. M., 459
Becerra, A. M., 274
Bechtold, A. G., 159
Beck, D. M., 212
Beck, F., 120
Bedford, R., 153
Bedore, J. A., 267
Bedore, S., 8, 37, 493–495
Beebe, D. W., 120
Beecher, H. W., 397
Beeghly, M., 17, 82, 282, 287, 294, 298, 316
Beets, M. W., 132
Begley, S., 201, 499
Begus, K., 256
Behne, T., 319
Behrens, H., 264
Beilock, S. L., 348
Beldavs, Z. G., 380
Belizan, J. M., 95
Belk, C., 53
Belksy, J., 393
Bell, A. G., 252
Bell, J. T., 66
Bell, K., 373
Bell, M. A., 13, 112, 115, 116, 175, 200, 212, 282, 294
Bell, S. M., 288
Bellinger, D. C., 82
Bellmore, A. D., 425
Bellugi, U., 274

Belon, K., 121
Belsky, J., 51, 107, 292, 409
Bem, S. L., 352
Benbow, C. P., 348
Bender, H. L., 403
Bendersky, M., 151, 153
Benga, O., 429
Bengtsson, H., 319–320
Beninger, A. S., 240
Benner, A. D., 8, 37, 425, 474, 497
Bennett, S. A., 81
Benoit, D., 406
Ben-Shachar, M., 125
Benson, L., 130
Benson, P. L., 64
Bentley, A. C., 490
Bentley, T., 407
Benveniste, L., 490
Berenbaum, S. A., 107, 305, 339, 341, 345–347, 349, 350
Berg, O. R., 124–125
Bergen, D., 434, 435, 437
Berger, S. E., 140–143, 145, 151, 161, 299
Bergman, L.R ., 471
Berk, L., 437
Berk, L. E., 187
Berkeljon, A., 379
Berko, J., 259, 260
Berko Gleason, J., 253, 257, 259, 263, 264, 269, 270
Berkowitz, M. W., 372–373
Berlin, L. J., 304, 306, 403
Berlyne, D., 435
Berman, M. G., 200
Berman, R. A., 268
Berman, S. L., 331
Bernard, J. M., 411
Bernard, K., 64
Berndt, T. J., 439, 440, 442, 457
Berninger, E., 158
Berninger, V., 465, 466
Berninger, V. W., 260, 264, 452
Bernstein, V. J., 303
Berry, D., 69
Berry, J., 484
Bertenthal, B. I., 155
Bertoglio, K., 223
Best, D. L., 132, 345–346, 353
Betti, U., 315
Betz, N. E., 473
Bevis, L., 155
Beyers, W., 374
Bhattacharjee, A., 371
Bialystok, E., 267
Bianchi, D. W., 62
Bickford, L., 194
Biehle, S. N., 398
Bier, M., 372–373
Bierman, K. L., 203
Biernat, M., 497
Bigelow, A. E., 298, 303
Bigelow, J. A., 457
Bigham, S., 223
Bigler, R. S., 342, 344, 346
Bigras, M., 203
Bihagi, S. W., 69
Bilardo, C. M., 61

Bill and Melinda Gates Foundation, 460, 464
Billari, F., 441
Billy, J.O.G., 441
Binet, A., 231, 249
Birch, R., 155
Birditt, K., 14, 395, 409
Birditt, K. S., 395
Birkeland, M. S., 325
Birman, B. F., 452
Biro, F. M., 106
Bishop, K. M., 347
Bittar, R. E., 93
Bjorklund, D. F., 24, 51, 195, 196, 201, 207, 216, 224
Black, B., 471
Black, M. M., 82, 124, 128, 129
Blackford, J. U., 292
Blackwell, L. S., 472–473
Blaga, O. M., 242, 245
Blair, C., 203, 212, 283, 287
Blair, S. N., 130, 134
Blake, L. P., 383
Blake, W., 286
Blakemore, J. E. O ., 440
Blakemore, J.E.O., 107, 305, 345–347, 350
Blakemore, S. J., 13, 304
Blandthorn, J., 83
Blass, E., 142
Block, C. C., 217
Block, J., 295
Bloom, B., 245
Bloom, L., 256, 258, 272
Blosser, C., 6, 105, 106
Bluhm, B., 130
Blumenfeld, P. C., 457, 470, 471
Bo, L., 490
Bobkowski, P. S., 500
Bocelli, A., 139
Bode, P., 418, 463, 495, 496
Bodrova, E., 189, 212
Bogels, S. M., 467
Bohlin, G., 287, 295, 304
Boiter, C., 382, 383
Bolding, A., 91
Bond, B. J., 501
Bonner, S., 475
Bono, G., 377
Booij, G. E., 254
Booth, A., 393, 402, 415
Booth, A. E., 211
Booth, D. A., 158
Booth, M., 417, 427
Booth, T., 234
Bor, W., 379
Borch, C., 441
Borchert, J., 154–155
Bornstein, M. H., 155, 168, 398, 417, 436, 442, 494
Borup, L., 91
Bosma, H. A., 331
Botkin, D., 405
Bouchard, T. J., 49
Boucher, J., 223
Boukydis, C. F., 93
Boutsikou, T., 94
Bower, T.G.R., 155

Bowker, J. C., 318, 425, 426, 431–432, 441
Bowlby, J., 26, 287, 300, 301, 303, 311
Bowles, J., 56
Bowles, T., 324
Bowman, M. A., 380
Boyce, W. T., 107
Boyd, D., 503
Boyd, Dorothy, 337
Boyd, L., 119
Boyd, M., 117
Boyer, K., 207
Boyle, J., 120
Boyle, J. P., 484–485
Boyle, J. R., 468
Boynton-Jarrett, R., 107
Boyum, L., 393
Braddick, O., 154
Bradley, R. H., 297, 399, 490
Bradshaw, C. P., 432
Brady, M., 6, 105, 106
Brainerd, C. J., 204, 219
Brand, T., 234
Branje, S., 442
Branje, S.J.T., 328
Brannon, L., 340
Bransford, J., 452
Braver, S., 414–415
Braver, S. L., 415
Braver, T. S., 235
Brazelton, T. B., 93, 128, 129, 142
Brechwald, W. A., 426, 439, 442
Breddels-Van Bardewijk, F., 303
Bredekamp, S., 454
Bredow, A., 305
Breedlove, G., 85
Breen, A. V., 328
Breinlinger, K., 174
Brember, I., 324
Bremner, G., 174
Bremner, J. G., 155, 159, 160
Brendgen, M., 380, 438
Brendgen, R. M., 348
Brent, H. P., 160
Brent, R., 83
Brent, R. L., 81, 83
Bretherton, I., 287, 300–304
Brewer, K. B., 379–380
Brewer, M. B., 484
Brez, C., 151, 198, 199
Breznitz, Z., 203
Bridgeland, J. M., 374
Bridges, J. S., 409
Bridges, L. J., 287
Bridgett, D. J., 285
Brigham, M., 469
Bril, B., 144
Brin, S., 454
Brindle, M., 266
Brion, M., 119
Brisch, K. H., 302
Britton, H. L., 126
Britton, J., 82
Britton, J. R., 126
Broadbent, K. G., 119
Brocardo, P. S., 81
Brocki, K. C., 304
Brockmeyer, S., 414

Brockmeyer, T., 325
Brodsky, J. L., 128
Brodsky, N. L., 82
Brody, G. H., 490
Brody, N., 232, 234–235
Brodzinsky, D. M., 64–65
Bromley, D., 317
Bronfenbrenner, U., 27, 28, 40, 392, 395, 484
Bronstein, P., 341, 342
Brook, D. W., 408
Brook, J. S., 408
Brookhart, S. M., 453
Brooks, J. G., 213
Brooks, L. O., 131
Brooks, M. G., 213
Brooks, R., 199
Brooks-Gunn, J., 108, 110, 198, 237, 238, 306, 316, 393, 413, 462, 497
Brophy, J., 474
Broughton, J., 258
Broverman, D., 345
Broverman, I., 345
Brower, K. J., 120
Brown, A. L., 217
Brown, A. M., 408
Brown, B. B., 354, 418, 425–428, 440–443
Brown, D., 209, 254
Brown, D. J., 139
Brown, J. D., 500
Brown, J. H., 275
Brown, J. V., 99
Brown, K. W., 80
Brown, L. D., 398
Brown, L. M., 424
Brown, R., 270, 271
Brown, S., 61
Brown, W. H., 132
Brownell, C., 316
Brownell, C. A., 285, 298, 299
Broyles, S. T., 134
Bruchmiller, K., 466
Bruck, M., 209
Bruine de Bruin, W., 181
Bruk, A., 114, 262
Brumariu, L. E., 304
Bruner, 277
Bryan, C., 282, 286
Bryant, J. B., 255, 261, 264
Bryant, P. E., 221
Brynes, J. P., 183
Bryom, S., 88
Bryson, L., 218
Bub, K., 309
Bub, K. L., 307
Buchanan, A., 305
Buchmann, M., 371
Buck, M ., 399
Buckner, C. E., 352
Budd, K. S., 209
Buder, E. H., 256
Buehl, D. R., 266
Buhler, E., 467
Buhrmester, D., 427, 439, 440
Buhs, E., 431
Bukowski, R., 84

Bukowski, W., 426, 427, 430, 436
Bukowski, W. M., 427, 430
Bullock, M., 316
Bumpus, M. F., 407
Bunge, S. A., 201
Burchinal, M., 238, 404
Burchinal, M. R., 309
Burd, L., 81
Buriel, R., 305, 394, 399, 402, 494
Burke, J., 381
Burke, J. D., 378
Burke, M. G., 122
Burke, M. M., 243
Burks, A. W., 125
Burlingame, S., 291
Burman, I., 96
Burnham, D., 157
Burns, C., 6, 105, 106
Burns, E., 91
Burns, S., 262
Burock, D., 401
Burraston, B., 380
Burris, N. A., 265
Burstyn, I., 81–82
Bursuck, W. D., 468
Burt, S. A., 68
Burton, L. M., 490, 496
Burton, R., 46
Burton, R. V., 366
Buschkuehl, M., 203
Bushel, P. R., 57
Bushman, B. J., 324, 500, 501
Bushnell, E. W., 159
Bushnell, I.W.R., 154
Buss, D. M., 16, 51, 340, 350
Buss, K. A., 295
Bussey, K., 341
Bustamante, M. R., 303
Butcher, K., 133
Butler, Y. G., 268
Button, T.M.M., 70
Byard, R. W., 118, 119

C

Cabrera, N., 307
Cabrera, N. J., 305
Cagle, M., 246
Caldwell, S., 33
Calenda, E., 119
Calkins, S. D., 282, 287, 429
Callahan, M., 30
Callahan, M. A., 30
Callan, J. E., 341
Caltran, G., 286
Calvert, S. L., 501, 502
Cambria, J., 474
Cameron, C. A., 319
Cameron, J., 471
Camos, V., 203
Campbell, B., 233
Campbell, D. T., 484
Campbell, F. A., 114, 238
Campbell, J., 321, 322
Campbell, J. D., 324–325
Campbell, L., 233
Campione-Barr, N., 400, 410
Campos, J., 283, 285, 290, 301, 429

Campos, J. J., 156, 282, 285, 286, 291, 303
Camras, L. A., 283, 285, 290, 429
Canter, A., 432
Capaldi, D. M., 393, 402–403
Caprara, G. V., 473
Caravita, C. S., 425, 430, 431
Carbonell, O. A., 303
Cardelle-Elawar, M., 220
Cardinal, B. J., 134
Carey, S., 174, 175, 183, 259
Carl, J. D., 397
Carlo, G., 376, 377
Carlson, C. D., 263
Carlson, E. A., 302, 303, 445
Carlson, M. J., 393
Carlson, S. M., 116, 212, 222, 288–289
Carlson, V., 402
Carlson, W., 440
Carlson Jones, D., 109
Carlton, M. P., 187
Carnegie Corporation, 459
Carnegie Council on Adolescent Development, 492
Carney, D. P., 275
Carnoy, M., 490
Carpendale, J., 319, 428
Carpendale, J. I., 222
Carpenter, M., 199, 200, 271, 319, 361
Carr, A., 382, 383
Carr, P. B., 240
Carrier, L. M., 504
Carrington, H., 285
Carroll, A. E., 432
Carroll, D. J., 222
Carroll, J., 235
Carroll, J. S., 503
Carroll, L., 326
Carroll, M. D., 130
Carskadon, M. A., 120, 121
Cartwright, R., 118
Carver, K., 446
Case, C. L., 53
Case, R., 184, 207
Casey, B. J., 116, 181
Casey, P. H., 94
Cash, J., 373, 376
Cash, J. E., 358
Caspers, K. M., 69
Caspi, A., 69, 295
Cassidy, J., 17, 408
Cassoff, J., 121
Castenell, L. A., 495–496
Castle, J., 64–65
Catalano, R. F., 122
Catani, C., 290
Caughey, A. B., 62
Caulfield, L. E., 128, 129
Cavan, D., 131
Cavanaugh S. E., 110
Cave, R. K., 269
Caylak, E., 53
Cbrera-Hguyen, P., 493
Ceci, S. J., 209, 236, 237, 239
Celik, E., 93
Center for Academic Integrity, 375
Center for Science in the Public Interest, 129

CenteringPregnancy, 86
Centering Pregnancy, 87
CenteringPregnancy Plus, 86
Centers for Disease Control and Prevention, 63, 94, 124, 125, 467, 468
Cerezo, S., 124
Chae, S., 305
Chakaborty, S., 85
Chall, J. S., 264
Chambers, B., 455
Chambers, W. H., 54
Chan, R. C., 467
Chandler, M. J., 222
Chandra, A., 397
Chandramouli, B. A., 128
Chang, H., 429
Chang, M. Y., 91
Chang, P., 99
Chang, Y., 457, 459
Chang, Y. K., 212
Chang, Z., 467
Chao, R., 402
Chao, R. K., 402
Chaparro, M. P., 7, 16, 17, 70, 303, 400
Chaplin, T. M., 350
Chapman, E., 468
Charlet, J., 80
Charman, T., 468
Charness, N., 204
Chase-Lansdale, P. L., 10, 307
Chassin, L., 409
Chauhan, S. P., 91
Chavajay, P., 185
Cheah, C.S.L., 354
Cheever, N. A., 504
Chein, J., 116
Chemtob, C. M., 290
Chen, C., 477, 478
Chen, C. H., 91
Chen, C-I., 237, 454
Chen, J. J., 462
Chen, Q., 494
Chen, S., 301
Chen, S. H., 212
Chen, W., 84
Chen, X., 295
Chen, X. K., 94
Chen, Y., 149, 502
Cheng, D.P.W., 435
Cheng, H., 489
Cheng, M., 331
Cheng, Y. P., 409
Cheng, Y. Y., 475
Cherlin, A. J., 415
Chess, S., 31, 292–295, 311
Cheung, A.C.K., 455
Cheung, C., 478
Cheung, C. S., 400, 477–478
Chew, S. H., 304
Chi, M. T., 204
Chick, C. F., 220
Child Development Project, 375
Childers, J. B., 260
Children's Defense Fund, 11, 488
Chin, J-C., 429
Chinn, M., 331

Chinn, P. C., 462, 463, 494
Chiou, W. B., 475
Chitty, L. S., 62
Chiu, R. W., 62
Cho, B. H., 297
Choi, K. C., 133
Choi, N., 352
Choi, S., 490
Chokroverty, S., 119
Chomsky, N., 270, 271, 277
Chong, C. M., 440
Chorna, L., 256
Choudhry, Z., 466
Christakis, D. A., 501, 502
Christenfeld, N.J.S., 282
Christensen, S., 407
Christensen, S. I., 460
Christian, M. S., 81
Christian, S., 379
Christie, B. R., 81
Christie, J., 263
Chryssochoou, X., 484
Chung, J., 295
Chung, M., 125, 126
Chung, W. C., 347
Chyka, D. L., 374
Cicchetti, D., 34, 303, 304, 404–407
Cillessen, A.H.N., 425, 429, 430, 432, 441
Cisneros, A. A., 458
Cisneros-Cohernour, E. J., 458
Citkovitz, C., 91
Clardy, C. E., 382
Clark, B., 452
Clark, E., 85, 259–260
Clark, E. V., 263
Clark, J. R., 209
Clarke-Stewart, A. K., 68, 305–307, 394, 399, 413, 414–415
Clarkson, F., 345
Clarkson, M. G., 148
Class, Q. A., 85
Clauss, J. A., 292
Clay, R., 98
Clearfield, M. W., 140, 172
Clegg-Kraynok, M. M., 97
Clemans, K. H., 503
Clifton, R. K., 148, 159
Clingempeel, W. G., 417
Clinkinbeard, S. S., 120
Cloninger, S. C., 353
Closson, L. M., 425, 430, 431
Clouchoux, C., 61
Cluett, E. R., 91
Cnaan, R. A., 384
Cobham, V. E., 290
Cobiac, L., 125
Coffino, B., 302, 303, 445
Coffman, J. L., 208
CogMed, 212
Cohen, G. L., 442
Cohen, L. B., 174
Cohen, L. H., 288, 289
Cohen, N. J., 132–133
Cohen, P., 408
Cohen, R., 503
Cohen-Kadosh, K., 116
Cohen-Woods, S., 53

Cohn, A., 432
Cohn, E. S., 379
Cohn, J. F., 392
Coie, J., 430
Coie, J. D., 430
Colapinto, J., 340
Colby, A., 363
Cole, M., 205
Cole, M. W., 235
Cole, P. M., 283, 288, 289, 429
Coleman, M., 415
Coleman, M. R., 465
Coleman. T., 82
Coleman-Phox, 119
Coleridge, S. T., 75
Coley, R. L., 306, 307, 413
Coll, C., 490
Collett-Solberg, P. F., 105
Collins, C. E., 79, 131
Collins, D., 374
Collins, P. A., 200
Collins, W. A., 407, 408, 444–445
Colombo, J., 151, 198, 199, 245, 275
Colonnesi, C., 256
Coltrane, S., 407, 494
Colvin, C. W., 107
Comer, J., 463, 464
Committee on Nutrition and Section on Allergy and Immunology, 125
Commoner, B., 54
Common Sense Media, 502
Compas, B. E., 325
Comstock, G., 502
Conde, C., 122
Conde-Aguedelo, A., 95
Conderheld, S., 86
Condition of Education, 465
Conduct Problems Prevention Research Group, 381
Conel, J. L., 114
Cong, X., 95
Conger, K. J., 380
Conger, R. D., 380, 382, 417, 418
Conley, M. W., 266
Connell, J. P., 287
Connell, M., 209
Connelly, A., 112
Connolly, J. A., 443–445
Conry-Murray, C., 344
Contreras, M., 8, 9, 27, 70, 395, 417, 484, 485
Contreras, R., 84
Cook, D. G., 123
Cook, M., 155
Coolbear, J., 406
Cooney, T. M., 395
Cooper, 418
Cooper, C. R., 330, 331, 419, 476, 494
Cooper, S., 132–133
Cooter, R. B., 265
Coplan, R., 425
Coplan, R. J., 431–432, 434, 436
Copple, C., 133, 189, 450, 453
Cordes, M., 147
Cordier, S., 85
Cornew, L., 299
Corporation for National and Community Service, 373–374

Corpus, J. H., 470
Correa-Chavez, 185, 186
Cortes, E., 91
Cortina, K. S., 289
Corvalan, C., 124
Corwyn, R. F., 297, 399, 490
Cosmides, L., 50
Costa, R., 92
Costall, A., 285
Costigan, S. A., 130, 134
Costley, K. C., 187
Coté, J. E., 327, 329
Council of Economic Advisors, 408
Countermine, M., 118
Courage, M. I., 112
Courage, M. L., 199, 204, 206–207
Covitz, L. M., 414
Cowan, C. P., 397
Cowan, P. A., 393, 397, 398, 404
Cox, M., 404
Cox, M. J., 404
Cox, S. M., 303
Coyne, S. M., 440, 501, 504
Cozzi, B., 79
Craig, I. W., 53
Craik, F.I.M., 267
Crain, S., 259, 264
Cramond, B., 247
Crampton, P., 119
Crawford, A., 406
Crespi, B., 122
Crespo, C., 109
Creswell, J. W., 30
Crick, N. R., 349
Criss, M. M., 379
Crissey, S. R., 446
Crnic, K. A., 289
Crocetti, E., 374
Crockenberg, S., 393
Crockenberg, S. B., 295
Crockett, L. J., 379, 402, 425–426, 438
Crockett, O. J., 394
Cromer, R., 275
Cropley, M., 120
Crosbie, S., 275
Crosnoe, R., 38, 459, 493
Cross, D., 221
Cross, T. P., 10
Croudace, T., 338
Crouter, A. C., 393, 402, 407, 410, 413
Crowe, E., 222
Crowell, J. A., 414
Crowley, K., 30
Crowley, M., 353
Crugnola, C. R., 303
Cruikshank, D. R., 452
Cubillo, A., 466
Cuellar, J., 495
Cuevas, K., 112, 115, 200, 212, 282
Cui, L., 402
Cui, M., 445
Culhane, J. F., 93
Culicover, P. W., 254
Cullen, M. J., 240
Cummings, E. M., 414
Cunningham, J. N., 289
Cunningham, P. M., 265
Curran, K., 403

Curtindale, L., 151, 198, 199
Cushner, K. H., 496, 497
Cvencek, D., 347
Czaja, S. J., 407

D

Dabholkar, A. S., 114, 115
da Fonseca, E. B., 93
Dahinten, V. S., 107, 488
Dahl, R. E., 116–117
Dalenius, K., 128
Daley, A. J., 98
Daley, C. E., 236
Dalley, J. W., 466
Damasio, A., 253
Damiao, R., 93
Damon, W., 327, 365, 367, 368, 374, 376, 385, 475–476, 478, 480
Danahar, K., 497
Dane, M. C., 266
Danese, A., 407
Daniels, H., 185, 187
Daniels, K., 397
D'Ardenne, K., 112
Dariotis, J. K., 219
Darling-Hammond, N., 453
Darrah. J., 119
Darwin, C., 50, 53, 71
Dasen, P. R., 184
D'Augelli, A. R., 417, 444
Davalos, D. B., 85
David, J., 416
Davidov, M., 394, 395
Davidson, D. H., 458
Davidson, J., 234, 244
Davidson, J. W., 245
Davidson, M., 86, 89
Davidson, M. R., 86, 89
Davidson, R. J., 293
Davies, G., 236
Davies, J., 324
Davies, P. T., 414
Davila, J., 443, 445
Davis, B. E., 144
Davis, C. F., 128
Davis, C. L., 131, 132–133, 146, 236
Davis, E. L., 295
Davis, L., 400
Davis, S. F., 18
Davis- Kean, P., 403, 404
Davis-Kean, P., 474
Davis-Kean, P. E., 398
Day, J. D., 217
Day, N. L., 82–83
Day, R. D., 471
Day, R. H., 155
Dealut, L., 265
Deamen, S., 331
DeAngelo, L., 383
Deardorff, J., 107
Dearing, E., 307, 488
Deary, I. J., 230, 232, 235, 236, 238
Deater-Deckard, K., 66, 69, 188, 236, 402, 404
DeBaryshe, B. D., 431
DeBonis, L., 503
De Brigard, F., 203

de Bruin, E. I., 467
DeCasper, A. J., 157
DeCherney, A., 62
Deci, E. L., 470
DeClaire, J., 289
Declercq, E., 88
De Decker, E., 499
Deeds, O., 91
Deeley, Q., 223
DeFries, J. C., 294
Degarmo, D. S., 380
DeGarmo, D. S., 431
De Giovanni, N., 82
de Graaf, H., 445
DeHaan, L. G., 384
de Haan, M., 13, 282, 287, 304
de Kok, I. M., 125
Dekovic, M., 405
DeLamater, J. D., 417
Delgado, M. Y., 494
DeLisi, M., 459
DeLoache, J., 176
DeLoache, J. S., 211, 216
Deloin, B., 131
Demerouti, E., 413
Demetriou, A., 184
Dempster, F. N., 207
Denault, A-S., 441
Denham, S., 288, 289, 429
Denham, S. A., 288, 289
Dennis, T. A., 288, 289
Denton, M. L., 383
Denzler, M., 112
Derlan, C. L., 497
de Rose, L. M., 110
Desai, M., 84
D'Escury, A. C., 381
Deutsch, A. R., 379, 425–426, 438
Deutsch, R., 414
Devaney, B., 124
Devaney, S. A., 62
Dever, B. V., 399
de Villiers, J., 253, 254, 259
de Villiers, P., 253, 254, 259
DeVoe, S. J., 173
Devos, T., 331, 332
Dew, J., 397
DeWall, C. N., 500, 501
de Weerth, C., 126
Dewey, J., 373, 385
De Winter, A., 414
Dexter, A., 485
Dey, S. K., 85
DeYoung, C. G., 295
DeZolt, D. M., 342, 348
Dhillon, P., 89
Diamond, A., 13, 111–113, 115, 116,
    172, 175, 181, 189, 201, 207, 211,
    212, 298
Diamond, L. M., 444
Diamond, M., 340
Diaz, A., 13, 112, 294
Diaz, M. R., 81
Diaz, P., 415
Diaz-Rossello, J., 95
Dibella, J., 217
Dick, D. M., 441
Dickey, J. L., 50

Dickinson, D., 233
Diederich, M., 80
Diedrich, F. J., 140, 172
Diego, M., 95, 96
Diego, M. A., 95
Diekhoff, G., 375
Diener, E., 324
Diener, M., 324
Diener, R. M., 81
Dietz, L. J., 99
Dietz, P. M., 119
Dietze, P., 406
DiGiuseppe, D. L., 502
Dijkstra, J. K., 432
Dilulio, J. J., 374
Dimmitt, C., 197, 207, 216, 220, 265,
    266, 320
Dineva, E., 140
Dishion, T. J., 349, 425, 426, 431
Diwadkar, V. A., 81
Dixon, R. A., 14, 17
Dodd, B., 275
Dodge, K., 402
Dodge, K. A., 70, 379, 381, 404, 428,
    429, 442
Doering, A. H., 15, 499
Doherty, M., 215, 221, 222
Dohnt, H., 120
Dolcos, S., 14, 17
Dondi, M., 286
Donegan, S., 128
Dong, W., 400
Donnellan, M. B., 382, 445
Donnelly, T. M., 374
Donnerstein, E., 432, 503
D'Onofrio, B. M., 85, 379, 409
Doob, C. B., 8, 10, 488, 490, 496
Doornwaard, S. M., 442
Dopp, P. R., 133
Dorius, C., 413–415
Dorn, L. D., 31, 107, 108, 110
Dorn, L. H., 106
Dott, B., 79
Dotterer, A. M., 262
Doty, R. L., 158
Doucette, J., 319
Doumas, L.A.A., 216
Dow, R. S., 265
Dowd, J. M., 159
Dowda, M., 133
Downer, J. T., 272
Downey, L. A., 234
Downing, J. R., 59
Doyle, T. F., 274
Dozier, M., 64, 407
Draghi-Lorenz, R., 285
Drake, B., 407
Drake, K. M., 146
Drake, M., 453
Dregan, A., 120
Driesen, N. R., 347
Dropik, P. I., 206
Drummond, J., 285
Du, D., 117
Dubocovich, M. L., 120
DuCette, J., 403
Duck, S.W., 440
Dufour-Rainfray, D., 80

Duggan, P. M., 181, 182
Duhoux, S., 116
Dumka, L. E., 332
Duncan, A. F., 94
Duncan, G., 10, 12, 418, 462, 487–490
Duncan, G. J., 10, 309, 418, 462,
    488, 489
Duncan, J. R., 119
Duncombe, M. E., 282
Dunkel Schetter, C., 85
Dunlop, W. L., 368, 369
Dunn, A., 6, 105, 106
Dunn, C. B., 31
Dunn, J., 289, 364, 395, 410,
    411–412, 426
Dunphy, D. C., 443
Dunst, C. J., 271
Duong, M., 432
Dupoux, E., 174
Durant, A., 452
Durant, W., 452
Durik, A. M., 346
Durrant, J. E., 403, 406
Durrant, R., 16, 17, 50
Durston, S., 116
Dusek, J. B., 322
Dutta, R., 8, 9, 27, 70, 395, 417,
    484, 485
Dvornyk, V., 107
Dweck, C., 240, 480
Dweck, C. S., 16, 148, 472–473
Dworkis, D. A., 58
Dwyer, D. S., 438
Dyck, M., 203
Dyer, W. J., 471
Dykas, M. J., 408
Dykes, A. K., 99
Dyne, L.V., 239
Dyson, L., 79
Dzewaltowski, D., 132
Dziegielewska, K. M., 76

E

Eagly, A., 340
Eagly, A. H., 8, 340, 348–350, 353
The Early Experience, Stress, and
    Prevention Network, 406
Early Growth Genetics Consortium
    (EGG), 53
Early Head Start, 454, 456
East, P., 410, 411
Easterbrooks, M. A., 17, 282, 287, 294,
    298, 316
Eaton, D. K., 133, 134
Eaton, W. O., 144
Ebstein, R. P., 304
Eby, J. W., 215
Eccles, J., 457
Eccles, J. S., 8, 348, 383, 398, 400, 457,
    459, 461, 470, 471, 474, 488
Eckenrode, J., 87
Eckerman, C., 298
Eckman, J. R., 58
Eckstein, D., 374
Edelman, M. W., 11
Edgington, C., 445
Edler, D. E., 117–118

Edmunds, L. S., 128
Ednick, M., 119
Edwards, C. P., 398
Edwards, M., 503
Edwards, R., 349
Edwards, S., 122
Efron, D., 466
Egger, M., 98
Ehrhardt, A. A., 339
Ehrlich, K. B., 408
Eiferman, R. R., 437
Eilam, A., 275
Einstein, A., 18, 235
Eisenberg, N., 288, 350, 367, 368, 371,
    372, 374, 376–377
Eisenhower Foundation, 492
Eisenstein, J., 403
Elashi, F. B., 320
Elbourne, P., 255
Elder, G. H., 395
El Hajj, N, 84
Eliot, T. S., 399
Elison, J. T., 153
Elkind, D., 177, 181, 182, 191
Elliott, J., 244, 245
Ellis, A. B., 347
Ellis, B. J., 16, 17, 50, 107
Ellis, J., 450
El-Sayed, Y. Y., 90
Else-Quest, N., 8, 37, 52, 323, 340, 343,
    348, 350, 485
El-Sheikh, M., 119, 120, 414
Embury, S. H., 58
Emerson, R. W., 253
Emery, R. E., 415, 490
Emes, R. D., 111
Enfield, A., 374
English, K., 10, 11, 491
Eninger, L., 304
Enright, M. S., 373
Enright, R. D., 377
Ensor, R., 288
Enz, B. J., 263
Eppler, M. A., 151
Epstein, D., 456
Epstein, J. N., 82
Erickson, K., 94
Ericsson, K. A., 204, 245
Erikson, E. H., 19–21, 31, 40, 278, 300,
    327–331, 334, 335, 383
Erikson, J., 20
Eriksson, U. J., 84
Escobar-Chaves, S. L., 501
Eskilsson, G., 158
Espelage, D. L., 431
Espinosa-Hernandez, G., 408
Essex, M. J., 107
Etaugh, C., 409
Ethier, L. S., 406
Ethington, C. A., 256
Etter, E. M., 418
Etzel, R. A., 122
European Union, 306
Evans, B. J., 496
Evans, G. W., 10, 11, 489–491
Evans, M. K., 120
Evenson, K. R., 86
Evers, C., 55, 56

Hernandez-Martinez, C., 92
Hernandez-Reif, M., 95, 96, 155, 174, 199
Herold, K., 261
Herpertz- Dahlmann, B., 467
Herr, M. Y., 392
Herrell, A. L., 215
Herrera, D. E., 378
Hershberger, K., 215
Hertenstein, M. J., 350
Herzog, E., 342
Hespos, S. J., 174
Hetherington, E. M., 27, 413–417
Heuwinkel, M. K., 182
Hewlett, B. S., 305, 417
Heyman, G. D., 319, 320
Higgins-D'Alessandro, A., 373
Highfield, R., 175
Hilden, K., 217
Hill, C., 309
Hill, C. R., 398
Hill, M., 62
Hill, N. E., 463
Hill, P. L., 181, 182, 364
Hilliard, L., 341
Hillier, A., 128
Hillman, C. H., 132–133
Hindman, A. H., 455–456
Hines, M., 338–340, 342
Hinney, A., 294
Hinshaw, S. P., 467
Hipps, G., 265
Hirsch, B. J., 457
Hirsh-Pasek, K., 256, 257, 260, 271, 274, 434, 435, 437
Hitchens, D., 345
Hjern, A., 466
Ho, J., 494
Ho, M. J., 445
Ho, S. Y., 120
Hockett, A. R., 440
Hodapp, R. M., 243
Hodge, D. R., 384
Hodges, E. V., 377, 428, 429
Hodges, E.V.E., 432
Hoefnagels, M., 50
Hoekstra, R. A., 468
Hoff, E., 257, 273, 418, 488
Hofferth, S. L., 305
Hoffman, E., 454
Hoffman, M. L., 371
Hoffman, R. R., 204
Hofman, M. A., 347
Hogarty, P. S., 242
Hohne, E. A., 257
Holden, G. W., 399
Holland, C. R., 242
Holland, K. A., 282
Hollatz, A. L., 367
Hollich, G., 159
Holliday, R. E., 204
Holmes, L. B., 80
Holmqvist, K., 432
Holsen, I., 325
Holsen, L., 109
Holt, M. K., 431
Holt-Hale, S., 6
Homae, F., 112

Hong, H. G., 406–407
Honzik, M. P., 242
Hood, B. M., 156
Hooper, S. R., 58
Hopkins, B., 146
Hopkins, L. M., 62
Horne, R. S., 119
Horowitz, E. K., 268
Horton, R., 123
Hoskins, I. A., 91
Hossain, N., 85
Houde, O., 178
Hough, R., 378
Houts, R. M., 107
Howard, K. S., 99
Howe, M. L., 204, 206–207
Howe, M.J.A., 245
Howerton, C. L., 85
Howes, C., 289, 307, 426–427
Howlin, P., 468
Hoyert, D. L., 94
Hoyt, J., 223
Hrgovic, I., 91
Hsieh, K., 409
Hsu, C., 477
Huang, L. N., 483
Huang, Z. J., 432
Hubbard, J., 59
Hubbard, S., 59
Huebner, A. M., 364
Hughes, C., 288, 318, 426
Hughes, D., 497
Hughes, D. F., 131
Hughes, D. L., 498
Hughes, J. F., 53
Hulbert, A., 155
Hull, S. H., 342, 348
Human Genome Project, 53, 54
Hummer, R. A., 122
Hunt, E., 236
Hurley, K. M., 128, 129
Hurst, C., 487, 488, 490, 495, 497
Hurt, H., 82
Hurtado, S., 383
Hustedt, J. T., 454
Huston, A. C., 343, 398, 419, 462, 487, 489–491, 502
Hutchens, R., 307
Hutman, T., 153
Hutson, R. A., 462
Huttenlocher, J., 114, 262
Huttenlocher, P. R., 114, 115
Huynh, V. W., 120, 497
Hwang, J. H., 122
Hwang, S. H., 122
Hyde, D. C., 174
Hyde, J. S., 8, 37, 52, 109, 323, 340, 343, 344, 347–348, 350, 355, 365, 417, 485
Hyde, L. W., 379
Hyde, S. S., 347
Hyman, I., 432
Hyman, I. A., 403
Hymel, S., 425, 430, 431
Hyoun, S. C., 80
Hyson, M., 454
Hyson, M. C., 133, 189, 450, 453

I
Iacono, W. G., 68, 383
Ibraheem, A. N., 290
Ibrahim, R., 112, 379–380
Ickovics, J. R., 87
Ige, F., 119
"I Have a Dream" Foundation (IHAD), 461, 464
IJzendoorn, M., 304
Imada, T., 115
Impett, E. A., 323
Inhelder, B., 176
Inkelas, M., 403
Insana, S. P., 97
Interlandi, J., 201, 499
International Association of Infant Formula Manufacturers, 127
International Montessori Council, 454
Iovannone, R., 468
Ip, S., 125, 126
Iqbal, M., 76
Iruka, I. U., 262
Irvin, J. L., 266
Irwing, P., 234
Isaacs, B., 453
Isenberg, J., 453
Ishmael, H., 60
Ishunina, T. A., 347
Issel, L. M., 87
Itakura, S., 274
Ivanova, K., 445
Iyengar, S. S., 470
Iyenger, U., 304
Izard, C. E., 282

J
Jackson, L. A., 396, 502, 503
Jacobson, K., 174
Jacobson, L. A., 196, 467
Jacobvitz, D., 303
Jacquet, A. Y., 157
Jaeggi, S. M., 200, 203
Jaffe, S., 409
Jaffee, S., 365
Jager, J., 442
Jahromi, P., 374
Jalongo, M. R., 453
James, J., 131
James, W., 154
Jamison, T., 415
Jan, J. E., 120
Jankowski, J. J., 275
Jankowski, L., 124
Jansen, J., 126
Janssen, I., 120
Jardri, R., 157
Jarmulowicz, L., 267
Jarrett, R. L., 489
Jarvis, L. H., 377
Jaswal, V. K., 156, 215, 271
Jencks, C., 232
Jenik, A. G., 119
Jenkins, D. B., 452
Jenkins, F. J., 54
Jenkins, J. M., 221
Jenks, E., 128
Jennings, K. D., 99

Jennings, L. E., 331
Jennings, S. L., 315
Jensen, A., 411
Jensen, A. C., 503
Jensen, A. R., 234
Jensen, L. C., 373
Jentarra, G. M., 59
Ji, B. T., 86
Ji, G., 412
Jiang, L., 128
Jiang, Y. J., 83
Jiao, S., 412
Jimenez, N. B., 367
Jin, M. K., 303
Jin, Y., 266
Jing, Q., 412
Jittendra, A., 465
Job, V., 473
Joh, A. S., 144, 151, 156
Johann, M., 303
John, A. E., 274
Johns, B ., 465
Johns Hopkins University, 475
Johnson, A. D., 237
Johnson, J. E., 458
Johnson, J. S., 266
Johnson, K. M., 458
Johnson, L., 379
Johnson, M. D., 55, 58, 155, 159, 160, 172
Johnson, M. H., 13, 116, 200, 266–267
Johnson, M. S., 407
Johnson, S. B., 219
Johnson, S. P., 153–155, 159, 160, 172, 175
Johnson, V. K., 397
Johnson, W., 235, 238
John-Steiner, V., 23, 185, 187, 188, 451
Johnston, J., 466, 467
Johnston, M., 7, 16, 17, 70, 175, 303, 400
Jolie, A., 64
Jones, B. D., 240
Jones, D., 381
Jones, D. J., 495
Jones, E., 489
Jones, H. W., 63
Jones, J., 133, 189, 450, 453
Jones, L., 91
Jones, M. C., 109
Jones, M. D., 332
Jones, N. A., 286, 294
Jones, S., 211, 246, 289
Jones, S. M., 456, 457
Jones, W., 274
Jonides, J., 200
Jonson-Reid, M., 407
Jordan, K. F., 451
Jordan, M. L., 215
Jordan, S. J., 125
Jose, P. E., 109
Joseph, J., 49
Josephson Institute of Ethics, 374–375
Joyner, K., 446
Juang, L., 353
Juang, L. P., 409
Judas, M., 79

Judge, P., 157
Juffer, F., 65
Juffer, M. K., 303
Jung, C., 6
Jung, S. H., 303
Jusczyk, P. W., 157, 257
Just, M. A., 468
Justice, L. M., 272, 466
Jutengren, G., 432, 438
Juul, S., 58

K

Kackar, H., 374
Kaczynski, T., 5, 10, 15
Kaelber, D. C., 123, 130
Kagan, J., 16, 17, 282, 285, 287, 292–295, 303, 311
Kagan, J. J., 287
Kagan, S. L., 456–457
Kahn, A., 119
Kaifa, N., 107
Kail, R. V., 196
Kain, J., 124
Kaiser Family Foundation, 500
Kalak, N., 133
Kalder, M., 91
Kalil, A., 10, 12, 418, 462, 487–489
Kalish, C. W., 259
Kaloustian, G., 303
Kaltman, S., 488–489
Kamehameha Elementary Education Program (KEEP), 187–188
Kamii, C., 183
Kamil, M. L., 265
Kan, M. L., 398
Kana, R. K., 468
Kang, J. Y., 268
Kang, P. P., 384
Kannass, K. N., 245
Kanoy, K., 404
Kaplan, J. S., 66
Kaplan, R., 418, 462, 474, 476, 489–491, 496
Kapur, B., 84
Kar, B. R., 128
Karasik, L. B., 146
Karg, K., 69
Karmel, B. Z., 241
Karmel, M. P., 316
Karmiloff-Smith, A., 111
Karoly, L. A., 457
Karpov, Y. V., 190
Karpyk, P., 215
Karreman, A., 405
Kashdan, T. B., 377
Katz, C., 209
Katz, L., 456
Katzmarzyk, P. T., 134
Kauffman, J. M., 243, 465, 469
Kaufman, J. C., 247
Kaufman, J. M., 108
Kaufman, P., 234
Kaur, A., 58
Kaur, H., 124
Kavsek, M., 155, 199
Kawabata, Y., 349

Kawasawa, Y. I., 76–77
Kearsley, R. B., 287
Keating, D. P., 218, 245
Keelan, J. A., 76
Keen, R., 145–146, 148, 149, 153, 156, 161
Kees, M., 291
Keil, F. C., 320
Keith, J. D., 383
Kelleher, C. J., 91
Keller, H., 252, 253, 255
Keller, M., 433
Keller, P., 120
Keller, T. A., 468
Kelley, S. A., 99
Kellman, P. J., 150, 154, 155
Kellow, J. T., 240
Kelly, A., 223
Kelly, B. M., 432
Kelly, D. J., 154
Kelly, J., 417
Kelly, J. P., 154–155
Kelly, K. M., 123
Kelmanson, I. A., 119
Keltner, D., 350
Kemp, I. A., 234
Kempler, T. M., 470
Kendler, K. S., 67
Kendrick, C., 411–412
Kendrick, K., 432, 438
Kenko, Y., 282
Kennedy, J. F., 484
Kennedy, J. L., 392
Kennell, H. H., 99
Kennell, J. H., 99
Kenney-Benson, G. A., 472
Kenny, S., 155
Kerns, K. A., 304
Kerpelman, J. L., 330–331
Kerr, D., 131
Kessen, W., 142
Key School, 234, 249
Keyser, J., 400
Khodaverdi, M., 158
Khuc, K., 125
Kidd, C., 198
Kielpikowski, M., 109
Kiess, W., 105
Kigar, D. L., 235
Kilgore, W. D., 234
Kilic, S., 82
Killoren, S. E., 404–405, 407, 428
Kilmartin, C., 343
Kim, B. R., 118
Kim, E. M., 477–478
Kim, H., 98
Kim, H. K., 58
Kim, J., 124
Kim, J. M., 344
Kim, J-K., 410
Kim, J-Y, 407, 428
Kim, K. H., 247
Kim, M., 297
Kim, P., 10, 489
Kim, S., 302, 304
Kim, S. Y., 494
Kim-Spoon, J., 406
Kincaid, C. Y., 495

King, A. P., 271
King, C., 133
King, P. E., 382–383
Kingsmore, S. F., 60
Kingston, M. H., 314, 315, 332
Kini, S., 63
Kinzler, K. D., 174
Kirk, R. E., 33
Kirk, S. A., 465
Kirkby, J., 118
Kirkham, N. Z., 159
Kirkorian, H. L., 153, 501
Kisilevsky, B. S., 156
Kisilevsky, S., 157
Kistner, J. A., 429
Kit, B. K., 130
Kitamura, S., 477
Kitayama, S., 318
Kitsantas, A., 475
Kitsantas, P., 119
Kitzinger, S., 88
Klahr, A. M., 68
Klauda, S. L., 474
Klaus, M., 99
Kleiman, E. M., 325
Klein, L., 286
Klein, R. E., 128
Klein, S., 343
Kleinsorge, C., 414
Klemp, R. M., 266
Kliewer, W., 289, 343
Klima, C., 87
Klimstra, T. A., 328
Klinger, M. R., 223
Knafo, A., 304
Knauper, B., 121
Knight, G. P., 377
Knoblauch, K., 91
Knopik, V. S., 466
Knox, M., 403
Kochanska, G., 302, 367, 371
Kochenderfer-Ladd, B., 431
Kocur, J. L., 407
Koenig, L. B., 383
Kohara, K., 59
Kohen, D. E., 488
Kohl, P. L., 407
Kohlberg, L., 360–365, 370, 371, 373, 375, 384–385
Kolialexi, A., 62
Kolkman, M. E., 203
Kong, A., 85
Koo, Y. J., 85
Koolhof, R., 381
Koopman, P., 56
Kopp, C. B., 287
Kopp, F., 200
Koppelman, K., 462
Korat, O., 262
Koren, G., 81, 84
Korenberg, J., 274
Kornblum, J., 503
Kornilov, S. A., 244, 245
Korrick, S. A., 82
Koslosky, G., 96
Koster, I., 256
Kostovic, I., 79
Kotovsky, L., 173

Kottak, C. P., 484–485, 496
Kotte, E. M., 131
Kouros, C. D., 414
Koury, A., 306
Kovach, R., 475
Kowalski, R. M., 432
Kozaitis, K. A., 484–485, 496
Kozol, J., 462
Kraemer, H. C., 130
Krajcik, J. S., 215, 470
Kramer, L., 410, 411
Krampe, R., 245
Kranenburg, M. J., 366
Krauss, R. A., 428–429
Kremers, S. P., 130
Kretch, K. S., 153, 156
Krettenauer, T., 371
Kreutzer, L. C., 223
Kreye, M., 287
Kriellaars, D. J., 132
Krimer, L. S., 112
Kring, A. M., 350
Kroesbergen, E. H., 203
Kroger, J., 330
Kronenberg, G., 79
Kroonenberg, P. M., 301–302
Krowitz, A., 156
Krueger, J. L., 324–325
Kruijver, F. P., 347
Kruse, A., 410
Kubarych, T. S., 66
Kuebli, J., 289
Kuehnle, K., 209
Kuhl, P. K., 253, 257, 271
Kuhle, S., 81–82
Kuhn, A., 76–77
Kuhn, B. R., 404
Kuhn, D., 116, 175, 181, 184, 195–197, 214, 218, 220, 224
Kulig, J. W., 159
Kulkovsky, S., 209
Kunnen, E. S., 331
Kuo, L. J., 267
Kupersmidt, J. B., 430
Kurland, D. M., 207
Kvist, L. J., 99
Kwak, H. K., 297

L

LaBeff, E., 375
Labuhn, A. S., 475
Lacelle, C., 407
Lack, L. C., 120
Ladd, G., 431
Ladd, G. W., 430, 431
Ladewig, P. W., 86, 89
LaFontana, K. M., 430
LaFrance, M., 350
Lagae, O., 203
Lagattuta, K. H., 377
Lahey, B. B., 379
Lai, P. S., 304
Laible, D., 299, 316, 371
Laird, R. D., 379, 400
Lam, T. H., 120
Lamarche, V., 438
Lamb, M. A., 209

Lamb, M. E., 17, 99, 113, 168, 209, 281, 299, 305, 306
Lambert, N. M., 377
Lambertini, L., 56
Lamb-Parker, F. G., 454
Lampl, K. M., 94
Lampl, M., 105
Lamy, C., 455
Landa, S., 229, 230
Landale, N. S., 495
Landau, B., 211, 274
Landi, K., 119
Lane, H., 253
Lang, E., 461
Langer, A., 156
Langer, E. J., 213
Langston Hughes Elementary School, 474
Langstrom, N., 85
Lansford, J. E., 396, 403, 404, 414–415, 417
Lanzi, R. G., 238
Laopaiboon, M., 91
Lapsley, D., 372, 373
Lapsley, D. K., 181, 182, 363
La Rooy, D. J., 209
Larson, J., 425, 426, 440, 442
Larson, R. W., 354, 418, 427
Larson, R.W., 408
Larsson, H ., 467
Larusso, E. M., 98
Larzelere, R. E., 404
Lasko, D., 96
Laslett, A. M., 406
Lathrop, A. L., 154
Lau, A., 494
Lau, J., 125, 126
Laubjerg, M., 64
Lauer, J. C., 397
Lauer, R. H., 397
Laumann-Billings, L., 490
Laursen, B., 407, 408, 418, 488
Laven, M., 368
Lavoie, F., 407
Law, B., 377
Law, C., 123
Lawford, H., 445
Lawley, G., 374
Lawrence, D. H., 316
Lawrence, J. M., 84
Lawson, C. A., 175, 183, 197, 210
Layzer, J., 490
Lazariu, V., 128
Leach, P., 204
Leaf, P. J., 432
Leaper, C., 8, 338, 342, 344–346, 350
Lecacheur, M., 216
Lecanuet, J. P., 157
Lechccier-Kimel, R., 295
Ledesma, K., 64
Lee, B., 368, 369
Lee, C. S., 239, 240
Lee, D. H., 122
Lee, E., 87
Lee, H., 134
Lee, H. C., 90
Lee, J. R., 263

Lee, K., 154, 212, 222, 298, 319
Lee, K. Y., 54, 156
Lee, S., 477
Lee, S. J., 403
Lee, S. L., 120
Lee, T-W., 235, 270
Leech, S., 82
Leedy, P. D., 30, 32, 33
Leerkes, E., 393
Leerkes, E. M., 288, 303
Legare, C. H., 320
Leger, D., 120
Legerstee, M., 298
LEGO, 214
Lehr, C. A., 460
Lehrer, R., 215
Leichtman, M. D., 205
Leidy, M. S., 393
Leis, T. L., 160
Lejuez, C. W., 17
Lemaire, P., 216
Leman, P. J., 427
LeMare, L. J., 428
Lemeshow, S., 128
Lempers, J. D., 221
Lemstra, M. E., 432
Lengua, L. J., 293
Lenhart, A., 503
Lenneberg, E., 275
Lennon, E. M., 241
Lenoir, C. P., 119
Lenroot, R. K., 116
Lens, W., 470
Leonard, J., 496
Leonardi-Bee, J. A., 82
Leong, D. J., 189, 212
Leong, F.T.L., 8, 462, 463, 493
Leppanen, J. M., 298
Lepper, M. R., 470
Lerch, C., 147
Lereya, T., 432
Lerner, J. V., 12, 383, 475
Lerner, J. W., 465
Lerner, R. M., 117, 383, 475
Lesaux, N. K., 268
Lessow-Hurley, J., 484, 494
Lester, B. M., 82, 93
Letourneau, N., 98
LeVay, S., 347
Levenson, R. W., 350
Leventhal, T., 488
Levin, A. V., 160
Levin, B., 468
Levine, M., 80
Levine, S. C., 348
Levine, T. P., 82
Levinson, P., 396, 500
Levitt, P., 129
Levy, D., 365
Levy, G. D., 344
Levy, Y., 275
Lewald, J., 139
Lewin-Bizan, S., 475
Lewis, A. C., 452
Lewis, A. J., 304
Lewis, C., 62, 281, 299, 305, 319, 373, 428
Lewis, D. F., 93

Lewis, J., 49, 50
Lewis, M., 285, 288, 302, 316
Lewis, M. D., 288
Lewis, R., 56
Lewis, R. L., 497
Lewis, T. L., 159, 160
Leyendecker, B., 402
Lhila, A., 93
Li, A. M., 133
Li, B. J., 83
Li, C., 124
Li, D., 377
Li, D. K., 119
Li, J., 92
Li, L., 123
Li, N., 377
Li, W., 309
Li, X., 377
Li, Y., 59
Liang, Y. J., 130
Liao, M. H., 466
Liben, I. S., 107, 305, 345–347, 350
Liben, L., 341
Liben, L. S., 348
Liberman, M. D., 117
Libertus, K., 148
Lichtenstein, P., 85, 467
Lickliter, R., 54
Liddelow, S. A., 76
Lie, E., 207
Liebergott, J., 257
Lieberman, M., 363
Liegeois, F., 112
Liekweg, K., 501
Liew, J., 212
Lifter, K., 258
Lillard, A., 435–436, 453
Limber, S. P., 432
Limperopoulos, C., 61
Lin, M., 367, 458
Lin, M. C., 347
Lincoln, A. J., 274
Lindberg, S. M., 347
Lindblad, F., 466
Lindenberg, S., 432
Lindenberger, U., 200
Linder, N. C., 497
Lindholm-Leary, K., 267, 268
Lindsay, D. S., 209
Linebarger, D. L., 343, 502
Ling, Y., 155
Linn, M. C., 347
Linn, S., 125
Lipnevich, A. A., 235
Lippa, R. A., 339
Lippman, L. A., 383
Lipshultz, S. E., 82
Lipton, J., 174
Liszkowski, U., 199
Litman, F. R., 94
Liu, J., 93
Liu, J. X., 130
Liu, S., 154
Liu, T., 235
Liu, W., 398
Liu, W. M., 462
Liu, Y. H., 91
Livas-Dlott, A., 418

Lively, A., 462
Livesly, W., 317
Livingston, R. B., 230, 232
Lo, W. S., 120
Lo, Y. M., 62
Loeber, R., 381
Loftus, E. F., 209
Logsdon, M. C., 98
Lohr, M. J., 443
Lomas, J., 234
Lombardi, C. M., 413
London, B., 401
London, M. L., 86, 89
Long, S., 93
Longfellow, H. W., 10
Longmore, M. A., 379
Longo, M. R., 155
Lonigan, C., 271
Loomans, D., 1
Loosli, S. V., 203
Lopez, E. I., 400
Lopez-Duran, N., 429
Loprinzi, K. L., 134
Loprinzi, P. D., 134
Lorch, E. P., 200
Lord, C., 274
Lorentzon, M., 85
Lorenz, K. Z., 26, 99
Loukas, A., 320, 378
Love, V., 83
Lovett, M. R., 466
Low, J., 221
Low, S., 402, 445
Lowe, J. R., 298
Lowenstein, A. E., 237, 455
Lozoff, B., 128, 129
Lubans, D. R., 130, 134
Lubinski, D., 232, 235
Lucas, P. J., 307
Lucas-Thompson, R., 413
Lucretius, 409
Luders, E., 235, 347
Ludington-Hoe, S. M., 95
Ludwig, S., 105
Luijk, M. P., 303
Luisis, A. J., 53
Lumeng, J. C., 128
Luna, B., 274
Lund, T. J., 488
Lundgren, I., 89
Lunkenheimer, E. S., 289, 429
Luo, Y., 173
Luria, A., 342
Lurye, L. E., 346
Luszcz, M., 213
Luthar, S. S., 488
Lutkenhaus, P., 316
Luyckx, K., 470
Lyberg, A., 86
Lykken, D. T., 49
Lyndon, S. T., 503
Lynn, R., 234, 237
Lyon, G. S., 53
Lyon, G. R., 465–466
Lyon, T. D., 222
Lyons, K. E., 213
Lyons, T., 114, 262
Lytle, L. A., 130

Pruett, M. K., 414
Pryor, J., 109
Pryor, J. H., 383
Pugh, L., 90
Pujol, J., 115
Pullen, P. C., 243, 465
Puma, M., 455
Pungello, E. P., 238, 262
Purcel, K., 503
Purtell, K. M., 8, 10, 12, 418, 462, 476, 487, 489–491, 496
Putallaz, M., 349
Puzzanchera, C., 378

Q

Qin, L., 477–478
Quach, A., 494
Quadrelli, R., 62
Quantum Opportunities program, 492
Queisser-Luft, A., 83
Quevado, K., 158, 283
Quiceno, J., 303
Quimet, C., 10
Quinn, P. C., 154, 210, 211, 298
Quintino, O., 96

R

Raaijmakers, Q. A., 328
Rabbani, B., 53
Radey, C., 411
Radke-Yarrow, M., 128
Radulescu, L., 158
Raffaelli, M., 354
Raikes, H., 271
Raikes, H. A., 302
Raine, A., 381
Raj, V. R., 112, 175
Rajaramank, P., 83
Rajendran, G., 223
Rakic, P., 76–77
Rakison, D. H., 175, 183, 197, 210
Rakoczy, H., 221
Ram, K. T., 126
Raman, G., 125, 126
Ramani, G., 316
Ramani, G. B., 298, 299
Ramchandani, P. G., 98, 305
Ramey, C., 130, 237
Ramey, C. T., 238
Ramey, S. L., 238, 309
Ramirez, G., 348
Ramos, J. S., 382
Ramphal, C., 237
Ramsdell, H. L., 256
Ramsey, E., 431
Rao, S. L., 128
Raphael, L., 217
Rapkin, B. D., 457
Rapp, P. R., 31
Rasmussen, S. A., 83
Ratner, N. B., 270
Rattan, A., 473
Raulin, M. L., 30, 32, 36
Raver, C. C., 212, 289
Raviv, T., 418
Ray, J., 261
Ray, M., 234

Rayner, R., 24, 25
Raz, N., 347
Razza, R., 198
Razza, R. P., 212
Rebellon, C. J., 379
Reddy, V., 285
Reece, J. B., 50
Reed, A., 371
Regalado, M., 403
Regev, R. H., 93
Rehbein, M., 31, 113, 114
Reid, J. B., 431
Reid, P. T., 37
Reijmerink, N. E., 57
Reijntjes, A., 429, 430
Reimer, B., 340
Reindollar, R. H., 62
Reiner, W. G., 339
Reis, S. M., 244
Reiser, M., 430
Reiter-Purtill, J., 130
Remedios, R., 470
Rende, R., 56, 380
Renfrew, M., 79
Renk, K., 408
Renner, P., 223
Renzulli, J. S., 244
Repacholi, B. M., 221
Repovs, G., 235
Reproductive Endocrinology and Infertility Committee, 85
Rest, J. R., 368
Reutzel, D. R., 265
Reyna, V. F., 181, 204, 219, 220
Reynolds, C. R., 230, 232
Reynolds, D. K., 128
Reynolds, F., 92
Reynolds, G. D., 112
Reynolds, W. M., 8, 451
Reznick, J. S., 262
Rice, J. C., 403
Rice, S. G., 59
Richard, J. B., 120
Richards, J. E., 112, 198, 199
Richards, M. N., 501
Richardson, G. A., 82
Riches, A., 368, 369
Richland, L. E., 216
Richman, W. A., 245
Rickman, A., 418
Rickman, M., 293
Rideout, V. J., 201, 500
Riesman, D., 253
Riggins, T., 82, 206
Righi, G., 112
Riina, E. M., 497
Rijlaarsdam, G., 266
Riksen-Walraven, J. M., 126
Riley, M., 130
Rindermann, H., 236, 237, 239
Rinsky, J. R., 467
Rios-Castillo, I., 124
Ripalda, A., 350
Ripke, M. N., 398, 419, 462, 487
Risdon, R. S., 118
Riskand, J. H., 325
Risley, T. R., 262
Ritchie, L. D., 128

Ritchie, S., 454
Riva, E., 58
Rivas-Drake, D., 332, 497
Rivers, S. E., 181, 204, 219
Rizzo, M. S., 60
Roalson, L. A., 378
Roberts, B. W., 325
Roberts, D. F., 201, 500
Roberts, G. J., 459
Roberts, H., 307
Roberts, J. A., 64
Roberts, R. D., 235
Robins, R. W., 323, 325
Robinson, S.R.R., 140, 142, 143, 151, 161, 299
Robinson-Riegler, B., 196
Robinson-Riegler, G. L., 196
Robledo-Colonia, A. F., 86
Roblyer, M. D., 15, 499
Rochat, P., 315
Roche, K. M., 381
Rochlen, A. B., 305
Rode, L., 93
Rode, S. S., 99
Rodenburg, G., 130
Roders, J. L., 379
Rodgers, C., 378
Rodgers, J. L., 237, 441
Rodriquez, E. T., 262–263
Roeser, R., 474
Roeser, R. W., 8, 213, 383, 398, 400, 457, 459, 461, 470, 471, 474, 488
Roeyers, H., 467
Rogers, L. O., 494
Rogers, M. R., 432
Rogoff, B., 185, 186, 485
Rogosch, F. A., 406, 407
Rohner, E. C., 418
Rohner, R. P., 418
Roiser, J. P., 466
Roisman, G. I., 300–303
Romo, L. F., 384
Ronai, Z., 303
Ronald, A., 468
Ronquillo, A., 332, 333
Rooksby, M., 206–207
Room, R., 406
Roopnarine, J. L., 458
Roosa, M. W., 418
Rosancer, K., 149
Rose, A. J., 242, 320, 349, 438, 440
Rose, D., 120
Rose, S. A., 275
Rose-Krasnor, L., 393
Rosen, L. D., 504
Rosen, L. H., 399
Rosenberg, M. S., 465, 468
Rosenblatt, R., 20
Rosenblith, J. F., 199
Rosenkranz, P., 345
Rosenkranz, R. R., 374
Rosenstein, D., 158
Rosenthal, R., 29, 232
Rosenthal, S., 302
Rosmatunisah, A., 134
Rosnow, R. L., 29, 232
Ross, H., 411
Ross, J. L., 58

Ross, M. G., 84
Rossano, F., 199
Rossi, J. S., 32
Rossi-Case, L., 237
Rote, W. M., 400
Roth, H., 82
Roth, M.P., 79
Rothbart, M. K., 200, 201, 286, 293, 294, 296, 297, 311
Rothbaum, F., 303, 408, 427, 442
Rothstein, R., 490
Rounds, J., 349
Rousseau, J-J., 169, 425
Roussotte, F. F., 82
Rovee-Collier, C., 151, 205–206
Rovers, M. M., 125
Row, C., 262
Rowe, M. L., 256, 262
Royal, J., 209
Royer-Pokora, B., 56
Roza, S. J., 84
Rozen, S., 53
Rubenstein, R. S., 320
Rubia, K., 466
Rubie-Davies, C. M., 474
Rubin, K., 425
Rubin, K. H., 318, 393, 425–428, 430, 431–432, 436
Ruble, D. N., 344, 346
Ruchat, S. M., 86
Rudang, R., 85
Rueda, M. R., 112, 198, 200
Ruffman, T., 222
Ruggieri, R., 425, 428, 440
Rumberger, R. W., 460
Runquist, J., 97
Rushton, J. P., 234
Russell, A., 68
Russell, I. F., 89
Russell, M., 452
Russell, S. T., 379, 402, 425–426, 438
Rust, J., 338
Rutherford, J., 133
Rutherford-Turnbull, H., 468
Rutter, M., 70
Ryan, A. M., 472
Ryan, J. M., 468
Ryan, R. M., 470
Rydell, A-M., 431

S

Saarni, C., 283–285, 290, 429
Sabbagh, M. A., 222
Sacco, D., 503
Sachs, H. C., 144
Sacker, A., 488
Sackett, P. R., 240
Sackoff, J., 119
Sacks, D. A., 84
Sadeh, A., 118
Sadker, D. M., 342, 452
Sadker, M. P., 342
Sadovsky, A., 367, 376–377
Sadovsky, A. L., 344
Safen, D., 59
Saffery, R., 66
Safford, P., 496, 497

subject index

brainstorming, 247
Brazelton Neonatal Behavioral
    Assessment Scale (NBAS), 92–93
breast feeding
    in Africa, 127
    bottle feeding vs., 124–126
    trends in, 126
breech position, 90
Bringing Home Baby project, 397–398
Broca's area, 270
Bronfenbrenner's ecological
    theory, 27–28
bullying
    cyberbullying, 432, 503
    nature of, 431–432
    strategies to prevent, 432–433

C

caffeine, 81
Canada, 498
cancer
    breast feeding and incidence of, 125
    in children, 122–123
cardiovascular disease, 13
careers, 344. See also child development
    careers
caregiving
    attachment and, 26–27, 303–305
    fathers as, 281, 305
    of infants, 287
    mothers as, 305
care perspective, 364–365
case studies, 31
cataracts, 160
causality, 173
causation, 33
Centering Pregnancy program, 86
centration
    explanation of, 176
    preoperational thought and, 177–178
cephalographic pattern, 104
cesarean delivery, 90
character education, 372, 373
cheating, 374–375
childbirth
    methods of, 89–92
    natural, 89
    prepared, 89–90
    setting and attendants for, 88–89, 91
    stages of, 88
child care
    effects of, 308–309
    international policies for, 306
    overview of, 305–306
    parental leave and, 306
    strategies regarding, 308
    variations in, 306–308
child-care directors, 307
child-care health consultants, 44
child-centered kindergarten, 453–454
child development
    biological, cognitive and
        socioemotional processes
        and, 12–13
    cohort effects and, 14–15
    gender and, 8–10
    issues in, 15–18

parenting and, 7
periods of, 14, 15
punishment and, 404
research in, 18
child development careers. See also
    specific careers
    clinical and counseling, 43–44
    dealing with education and research,
        42–43
    dealing with families and
        relationships, 45
    medical, nursing, and physical
        development, 44–45
Child Development Project, 375
child development theories. See also
    specific theories
    behavioral, 24–25
    comparison of, 28
    eclectic theoretical orientation to,
        28–29
    ecological, 27–28
    ethological, 26–27
    overview of, 18–19
    psychoanalytic, 19–20
    social cognitive, 25–26
child-directed speech, 271
childhood amnesia, 206–207
child life specialists, 45
child maltreatment, 405–407
child neglect, 406
child psychiatrists, 464
children. See also adolescents; early
        childhood; infants; middle and
        late childhood
    adopted, 64–66
    attention in, 200–201
    brain development in, 115–116
    in divorced families, 413–416
    education for, 8
    ethnic minority, 419
    gender development and, 9–10
    health and well-being of, 6
    involved in disasters and terrorist
        attacks, 291
    from low-income families, 454–456
    masculinity and, 352–353
    metacognition in, 222–224
    motor development in, 145–149
    nutrition in, 129–131
    overweight in, 103, 128–131
    parenting practices and, 7, 399–400
    participation in sports, 146–147
    peer relations for, 426–427
    peer statuses for, 430
    religious and spiritual development
        in, 382
    resilience in, 10, 11
    sleep in, 119–120
    social policy and, 10–12
    sociocultural contexts and diversity
        of, 8
children with disabilities
    attention deficit hyperactivity
        disorder, 466–467
    autism spectrum, 467–468
    educational issues related to,
        468–469
    emotional and behavioral, 467

intellectual, 243–244
    learning, 465–466
    poverty and, 291
    statistics related to, 465, 469
child welfare workers, 45
chorionic villus sampling (CVS), 61, 62
chromosomal abnormalities, 57–58,
    274–275
chromosomes, 53, 55
chronosystem, 27–28, 392
circular reactions, 170, 171
classical conditioning theory, 24
classification, 179–180
clinical psychologists, 7, 43
cliques, 442–443
cocaine, prenatal exposure to, 82
cochlear implants, 158
Code of Ethics (American
    Psychological Association), 36
cognition
    family processes and, 393–394
    language and, 274–275
cognitive development
    malnutrition and, 126, 128
    mechanisms of change and, 196–197
    media use and, 499
    play as context of, 434–435, 437
    religion and, 383
    timing of, 183–184
cognitive development theories. See
    also specific theories
    child development issues and, 28
    evaluation of, 24
    information-processing approach to,
        23–24, 195–197
    overview of, 20
    Piaget's, 22–23, 168–184
    Vygotsky's, 23, 185–190
cognitive engagement, 470–471
cognitive moral education, 373
cognitive processes
    achievement and, 471–476
    explanation of, 13
    gender and, 344–345
cognitive resources, 195–196, 218
cohort effects, 14
collectivism, 485
collectivistic cultures, 485, 486
college/university professors, 42
color vision, 154–155
Comer program, 463
commitment, identity, 328
communication
    about divorce, 416
    gender differences in, 349–350
computers, 502–504
conception, 75
concepts, 210
concrete operational stage
    classification in, 179–180
    conservation in, 179
    description of, 22–23, 170, 178
conduct disorder, 378
confidentiality, in research, 36
conformity, 442
congenital adrenal hyperplasia
    (CAH), 339
connectedness, 330

conservation
    explanation of, 176
    preoperational thought and, 177–179
conservation-of-liquid task, 178, 179
constructive play, 436–437
constructivist approach, 160, 188,
    451–452
context, 8. See also sociocultural
    contexts
continuity, 16
continuity-discontinuity issue, 16
control domain, 395
control groups, 33
controversial children, 430
conventional reasoning, 361
convergent thinking, 247
cooing, 256
cooperation, 299
coparenting, 404–405
coregulation, 398
core knowledge approach, 174–175
corporal punishment. See punishment
corpus callosum, 116, 347
correlational research, 32–33, 324
correlation coefficient, 32
counseling psychologists, 43
crawling, 143, 150–151
creative intelligence, 233
creativity
    intelligence and, 246–247
    media use and, 502
    teaching strategies for encouraging,
        247–248
crisis, identity, 328
critical thinking, 213, 218
cross-cultural studies, 8, 485–486. See
    also culture/cultural diversity
cross-sectional approach to research,
    33–34
crowds, 442, 443
crying, 256, 286–288
cultural bias, 37–38
cultural-familial intellectual
    disability, 244
cultural-specific hypothesis, 205
culture/cultural diversity. See also
    ethnicity/ethnic groups
    achievement and, 476–478
    adoption and, 64
    attachment and, 303
    in childbirth practices, 88–89
    child care and, 306
    cognitive development and, 184
    cross-cultural studies of, 8, 485–486
    emotions and, 283
    explanation of, 8, 484
    family variations and, 417–419
    gender roles and, 354
    gender stereotypes and, 345–346
    guided participation and, 186
    identity development and, 331–332
    as influence on families, 395–396
    intelligence and, 239–240
    language development and, 258,
        271–272
    low birth weight infants and, 94
    memory and, 205
    moral reasoning and, 363–365

motor development and, 146
parent-adolescent conflict and,
    408–409
peer relations and, 427
physical growth and, 105
relevance of, 484–485
second-language learning and, 267
temperament and, 295
trends in tolerance of, 14–15
culture-fair tests, 239
curriculum, in early childhood
    education, 456–457
cyberbullying, 432, 503

D

danger invulnerability, 181
data collection methods
    case studies as, 31
    observation as, 29–30
    physiological measures as, 31
    standardized tests as, 30–31
    surveys and interviews as, 30
dating
    adjustment and, 444–445
    heterosexual relationships and,
        443–444
    patents and adolescent, 445–446
    same-sex relationships and, 444
    sociocultural contexts and, 446
death, of children, 122, 124
debriefing, 36
deception, in research, 36
decision making, in adolescents,
    218–220
dendrites, 114
dependent variables, 33
depression
    maternal, 85
    postpartum, 97–98
    self-esteem and, 324
depth perception, 156
descriptive research, 32
developing countries, early childhood
    education in, 458
development. See also child
    development
    evolutionary psychology and,
        51–52
    explanation of, 6
    key processes in, 14, 15
    periods of, 14
developmental cascade model, 303
developmental cognitive neuroscience,
    13, 175
developmentally appropriate practice
    (DAP), 454, 455
developmental psychologists, 214
developmental quotient (DQ), 241
developmental social neuroscience, 13,
    116, 304
diabetes, 84, 125
dialect, 268, 269
diet
    overweight and, 130–131
    during pregnancy, 84–85
difficult child, 292, 293
direct instruction approach, 452

disabilities. See also children with
    disabilities
    attention deficit hyperactivity
        disorder, 466–467
    autism spectrum, 467–468
    emotional and behavioral, 467
    intellectual, 243–244
    learning, 465–466
discipline. See also punishment
    juvenile delinquency and, 379
    moral development and, 371
discontinuity, 16. See also continuity-
    discontinuity issue
discrimination, 497
disease
    breast vs. bottle feeding and, 125
    in children, 122–123
    overweight and, 130
    poverty and, 123–124
dishabituation, 151–153, 199
distortion, 209
divergent thinking, 247
diversity. See culture/cultural diversity
divided attention, 198
divorce
    communicating with children
        about, 416
    effects on children, 414–415
    sociocultural change and, 396
    statistics related to, 413
DNA (deoxyribonucleic acid), 53, 56.
    See also genes; genetics
domain-specific socialization, 395–396
dominant-recessive genes principle, 56
doulas, 89
Down syndrome, 57, 275
drug counselors, 44
drugs
    during childbirth, 89, 99
    during prenatal period, 81
    psychoactive, 81–83
dual-process model, 219–220
dynamic systems theory, 140–141
dyscalculia, 465
dysgraphia, 465
dyslexia, 465

E

early bloomers, 444
early childhood. See also children
    adopted children and, 65
    brain development in, 115–116
    education in, 453–457
    electronic media and, 501–502
    emotional development in, 288–289
    empathy development in, 367
    explanation of, 14
    fine motor skills in, 149
    gender stereotyping in, 346
    illness and injuries in, 122
    language development in, 258–263
    nutrition in, 129–131
    parent-child interaction in, 398
    peer relations in, 426–427
    physical activity in, 132
    physical growth in, 105
    preoperational stage in, 22, 176–178

self-understanding in, 316–317
social cognition in, 318–319
early childhood education. See also
    education
    child-centered kindergarten and, 453
    for children who are disadvantaged,
        454–456
    controversies in, 456–457
    developmentally appropriate practice
        in, 454, 455
    in Japan and developing countries, 458
    Montessori approach to, 453–454
early childhood educators, 43
early-later experience issue, 16–17
easy child, 292, 293
eating behavior
    in children, 129–131
    in infants, 124–128
eclectic theoretical orientation, 28–29
ecological theory, 27–28
ecological view, 150–151
education. See also achievement; early
    childhood education; schools
    of adolescents, 457, 459–461
    character, 372, 373
    for children who are disadvantaged,
        454–455
    of children with disabilities, 468–469
    cognitive development and, 184
    cognitive processes and, 471–476
    constructivist approach to, 451–452
    developmentally appropriate, 454, 455
    direct instruction approach to, 452
    for disadvantaged children, 454–456
    early childhood, 453–458
    ethnicity and, 462–463, 476–478
    extracurricular activities and, 461
    issues for children, 8
    moral, 372–375
    motivation and, 470–471
    Piaget's theory and, 182–183
    poverty and, 454–456, 462
    socioeconomic status and, 419, 462
    universal preschool, 457
educational and developmental
    psychologists, 37
educational psychologists, 43
effortful control, 293
egocentrism
    adolescent, 181–182
    explanation of, 176
eight frames of mind (Gardner), 233–234
elaboration, as memory strategy, 208
electronic media, 501–502
elementary schools, 457. See also
    schools
elementary school teachers, 42, 188
embryo, 75
embryonic period, 75–77
emotional abuse, 406
emotional and behavioral disorders, 467
emotional competence, 283–284
emotional development
    in early childhood, 288–289
    in infants, 284–288
    in middle and late childhood, 289–291
    parenting and, 289
emotional expression, 285–287

emotional intelligence, 234
emotional regulation
    in early childhood, 288–289
    gender differences in, 350
    in infants, 287–288
    peer relations and, 429
    temperament and, 295
emotion-coaching parents, 394
emotion-dismissing parents, 394
emotions. See also temperament
    attachment and, 300–305
    biological foundations of, 282
    cultural variations in, 283
    explanation of, 282
    family processes and, 393–394
    functionalist view of, 283
    gender and, 337, 350
    during pregnancy, 85
    primary, 285
    self-conscious, 285
    social orientation and, 298–299
emotion security theory, 414
empathy, 367–368
empiricists, 159, 160
encoding, 196, 197, 202
endoderm, 75
environmental hazards, prenatal
    exposure to, 83
environmental influences. See also
    nature-nurture issue
    child development and, 16
    heredity-environment correlations
        and, 67–70
    on intelligence, 236–238
    on language development, 270–272
    overweight children and, 130
    physical growth and, 105
    shared and nonshared, 68
epigenetic view, 69
equality, 376
equilibration, 169
Erikson's psychosocial theory
    explanation of, 19–20
    identity development and, 327
    life-span stages in, 19–20
    strategies based on, 21
estradiol, 107–108
estrogens, 107–108, 339
ethical issues, related to research, 36
ethnic bias, 37–38
ethnic gloss, 38
ethnic identity, 330–333
ethnicity/ethnic groups. See also
    culture/cultural diversity
    achievement and, 476
    child care and, 307
    differences and diversity within,
        496–497
    education and, 462–463
    explanation of, 8, 493
    family variations and, 418
    identity development and, 331–333
    immigration and, 493–495
    poverty and, 489
    prejudice toward, 497
    research on, 38
    school dropout rate and, 459–461
    socioeconomic status and, 495–496

nutrition
  in children, 128–131
  in infants, 124–128
  in low-income families, 124, 128
  prenatal, 84–85

prenatal diagnostic tests, 61–62
prenatal nurses, 90
preoperational stage
    centration and, 177–178
    description of, 22, 170
    intuitive thought substage of, 177
    symbolic function substage of,
        176–177
preoperational thought
    centration and, 177–178
    explanation of, 176
prepared childbirth, 90
preschool children. *See also* children
    attention in, 201
    executive functioning in, 212
    literacy development for, 261–263
    memory in, 223–224
    motor development in, 145–146
    peer relations in, 426
    perception in, 221
    physical activity in, 132, 133
    play by, 436
    sex-typed behavior in, 338
    universal education for, 457
preschool teachers, 43
pretense/symbolic play, 435–436
preterm infants
    explanation of, 93
    issues affecting, 93–94
    methods to nurture, 94–95
    tobacco use during pregnancy and,
        81–82
primary circular reactions, 170
primary emotions, 285
private speech, 186
problem solving
    explanation of, 215
    strategies for, 215–217
professional journals, 35
progestin, 93
Project Head Start, 454–455
prosocial behavior, 376–377
proximodistal pattern, 105
psychiatrists, 43
psychoactive drugs, during prenatal
        development, 81–83
psychoanalytic theories
    child development issues and, 28
    Erikson's psychosocial, 19–20
    evaluation of, 20
    explanation of, 19
    Freud's, 19
    of gender, 341
    moral feeling and, 366–367
psychological invulnerability, 181
psychology, evolutionary, 50–52
psychosocial moratorium, 327
psychosocial theory. *See* Erikson's
        psychosocial theory
puberty. *See also* adolescents
    body image and, 109
    determinants of, 106–108
    early and late maturation in,
        109–110
    explanation of, 106
    growth spurt in, 108
    precocious, 107
    sexual maturation in, 108–109

punishment. *See also* discipline
    developmental change and, 398
    ethnicity and, 402
    juvenile delinquency and, 379
    moral development and, 371
    overview of, 403
    perspectives on use of, 403–404
purpose, achievement and, 475–476

Q

Quantum Opportunities program, 492

R

rapport talk, 349
reaction-time tasks, 196
reading
    developmental stages in, 264–265
    gender differences in, 348
    to infants and, 271–272
recasting, 271
reciprocal socialization, 392, 393
reciprocity domain, 395
reconstructive memory, 209
reflexes, 140–142
reflexive smile, 286
Reggio Emilia approach, 450
rejected children, 430, 431
relational aggression, 349
religious development, 382–384
REM sleep, 118
report talk, 349
reproductive technology, 62–63
research
    bias in, 37–38
    correlational, 32–33, 324
    data collection methods for, 29–31
    descriptive, 32
    ethical issues related to, 36–38
    experimental, 33, 324
    importance of, 18
    journal publication of, 35
    scientific method in, 18
    time span of, 33–34
researchers, 42
resilience, 10, 11
respiratory tract infections, 125
retrieval, information, 202
risk taking, 219
romantic relationships
    adjustment in, 444–445
    heterosexual, 443–444
    identity and, 331
    parents and adolescent, 445–446
    same-sex, 444
    sociocultural contexts and, 446
rooting reflex, 140, 141
Rubella, 83
rules, problem solving using, 215–216

S

satire, 268
scaffolding, 185–186, 392, 393
schemas
    explanation of, 168, 202–204
    internalization of, 171–172

schema theory, 202–204
school counselors, 43
school dropout rate, 348, 459–461, 494
school psychologists, 43
schools. *See also* achievement; education
    accountability from, 452–453
    children with disabilities in, 465–469
    elementary, 457, 458
    ethnicity in, 462–463
    exercise habits and, 134
    extracurricular activities in, 461
    gender development and, 342–343
    hidden curriculum in, 372, 373
    high, 459–461
    issues related to, 8
    middle or junior high, 457, 459
    moral development and, 372–375
    sleep patterns and early start of, 121
    socioeconomic variations in, 488
scientific method, 18. *See also* research
scientific thinking, 214–215
scripts, 205
secondary circular reactions, 171
second-language learning, 266–268
securely attached babies, 301
selective attention, 198
self, 315
self-concept
    assessment of, 322–323
    explanation of, 321–322
self-conceptions, 485
self-conscious emotions, 285
self-consciousness, 317
self-control, 212, 366
self-determination, 470
self-efficacy, 473
self-esteem
    assessment of, 322–323
    ethnicity and socioeconomic status
        and, 495–496
    explanation of, 321–322
    methods to increase, 325
    variations in, 323–326
self-integration, 318
self-modification, 197
self-monitoring, 474–475
Self-Perception Profile for
        Adolescents, 322
Self-Perception Profile for
        Children, 322
self-regulation, 293, 474–475
self-responsibility, 470–471
self-understanding
    in adolescents, 317–318
    in early childhood, 316–317
    explanation of, 315
    in infants, 315–316
    in middle and late childhood, 317
semantics, 254–255, 259–261
sensation, 150
sensorimotor play, 435
sensorimotor stage
    A-not-B error and, 172
    description of, 22, 169, 170
    evaluation of, 172, 174
    nature-nurture issue and, 174–175
    object permanence in, 172, 173
    substages of, 169–172

sensory development
    ecological view of, 150–151
    hearing and, 156–158
    in infants, 105, 151–153
    smell and, 158
    taste and, 158
    touch and pain and, 158
    visual perception and, 154156
separation protest, 287
seriation, 180
service learning, 373–374
sex-linked chromosomal abnormalities,
        57–58
sex-linked genes, 56
sexual abuse, 406
sexual maturation, 108–109
sexual minority youth, 444
shaken baby syndrome, 112
shape constancy, 155
shared environmental experiences, 68
shared sleeping, 118–119
sharing, 376
short-term memory, 202, 203
siblings
    juvenile delinquency and, 380
    relationships between, 410–411
sickle-cell anemia, 58–59
simple reflexes, 170
Single mothers, 489, 490
size constancy, 155
sleep
    in adolescents, 120–121
    in children, 119–120
    function of, 117
    in infants, 117–119
    REM, 118
sleep deprivation, 97
slow-to-warm-up child, 292, 293
small for date infants, 93
smell, 158
smiling, 286
social cognition
    in adolescents, 320–321
    in early childhood, 318–319
    explanation of, 318
    in middle and late childhood,
        319–320
    peer relations and, 428–429
social-cognitive domain theory,
        369–370
social cognitive theory
    child development issues and, 28
    evaluation of, 26
    explanation of, 24
    of gender, 341, 344
    of morality, 366
    overview of, 25–26
social constructivist approach, 188
social conventional reasoning, 369–370
social information-processing skills, 429
socialization
    domain-specific, 395–396
    gender and, 341
    peer relations and, 425
social knowledge, 429
social media, 499, 503
social orientation, in infants, 298–299
social play, 436

social policy, 10–12
social referencing, 299
social relationships
  communication in, 349–350
  emotional expression and,
    285–287
social role theory, 340
social smile, 286
social workers, 43
sociocultural cognitive theory. See
  Vygotsky's theory
sociocultural contexts. See also culture/
  cultural diversity; ethnicity/ethnic
  groups
  dating and, 446
  diversity and, 8–9
  explanation of, 8
  family development and, 395–396
socioeconomic status (SES). See also
  poverty
  children in divorced families
    and, 415
  educational issues and, 462
  ethnicity and, 495–496
  explanation of, 8, 487
  families and, 418–419, 488
  juvenile delinquency and, 380–381
  poverty and, 488–492 (See also
    poverty)
  schools and, 488
  variations in, 487
socioemotional development
  gender and, 348–350
  play and, 437
socioemotional processes, 13
sounds, recognition of, 257
spatial intelligence, 233
special education teachers, 42–43
specificity of learning, 144
speech pathologists, 260
speech therapists, 45
spina bifida, 79
spiritual development, 382–384
sports, 146–147
stages of development (Piaget),
  168–184
standardized tests, 30–31
Stanford-Binet test, 231
status offenses, 378, 379
stepfamilies, 415–417
stereotypes, 344–350. See also bias;
  gender stereotypes
stereotype threat, 240
storage, information, 202
stranger anxiety, 286–287
Strange Situation, 301–302
strategies, problem solving, 216–217
strategy construction, 197
stress
  coping with, 290–291
  poverty and, 10, 11
  during pregnancy, 85
substance abuse, during pregnancy,
  81–83

sucking, 151–153
sucking reflex, 140, 141
sudden infant death syndrome (SIDS),
  119, 125
supervisors of gifted and talented
  education, 246
surveys, as data collection method, 30
sustained attention, 198–201, 471
symbolic function substage, 176–177
syntax, 254, 259–261
syphilis, 83
systems, 392

T

taste, 158
teachers
  automony-supportive, 470
  elementary school, 42, 188
  of exceptional children, 42–43
  expectations of, 474
  gender development and, 342–343
teaching. See education; schools
teaching strategies
  based on Vygotsky's theory,
    187–188
  for children who are gifted,
    245–246
  for English language learners, 268
  for memory, 208
  for problem solving, 217
technology
  computers and Internet and,
    502–504
  learning and achievement and,
    501–502
  media use and screen time and,
    499–500
  television, 343, 500–501
  trends in, 499
  video games, 501
telegraphic speech, 258
television
  effects of, 500–501
  gender development and, 343
  learning and achievement and, 502
temperament
  biological influences on, 294–296
  classification of, 292–294
  developmental connections to, 295
  developmental contexts of,
    295–296
  explanation of, 291
  gender, culture and, 294–295
  goodness of fit and, 296–297
  parenting and, 296–297
temporal lobes, 111
teratogens
  explanation of, 78
  exposure to, 80–81
  medications as, 81
  prenatal development and, 80
  psychoactive drugs as, 81–83
teratology, 80–81

tertiary circular reactions, 171
testosterone, 107
tests
  culture-fair, 239
  intelligence, 231–232, 239
  prenatal diagnostic, 61–62
  standardized, 30–31
text messaging, 503
theories
  connecting research methods to, 34
  explanation of, 18
theory of mind, child's, 221–223, 319
thinking
  in adolescents, 218–220
  in children, 211–217
  convergent, 247
  critical, 213, 218
  decision making and, 218–220
  divergent, 247
  explanation of, 210
  in infants, 210–211
  language and, 186–187
  problem solving and, 215–217
  scientific, 214–215
  teaching strategies to
    encourage, 194
Thousand Genomes Project, 53–54
three-mountains task, 176–177
time out, 403
time span of research, 33–34
tobacco use
  exposure to smoke from, 122
  during pregnancy, 81–82
toddlers. See also infants; preschool
  children
  attention in, 200
  fine motor skills in, 148–149
  gross motor skills in, 145
  language development and, 258,
    271, 273
  media use and, 501, 502
  perception in, 221
  problem-solving skills of, 215
  self-awareness in, 316
Tools of the Mind curriculum, 189
top-dog phenomenon, 459
touch, in newborns, 158
transitivity, 180
triarchic theory of intelligence,
  232–233
trimesters, 78
trophoblast, 75
trust vs. mistrust stage, 19
Turner syndrome, 57, 58
twins, 55
twin studies, 63, 66

U

ultrasound sonography, 61
umbilical cord, 76, 77
undocumented immigrants,
  493–494
university professors, 42

V

values clarification, 373
verbal intelligence, 233
verbatim memory trace, 204
victimization, bullying, 431–433
video games, 501
violence. See aggression
visual acuity, 154
visual perception
  in children, 156
  in infants, 151–156
visual preference method, 151
vocabulary development
  in early childhood, 259–261
  in infants, 257–259
  in middle and late childhood,
    263–264
  reading comprehension and,
    264–265
Vygotsky's theory
  evaluation of, 188, 190
  explanation of, 23, 185
  language and thought in, 186–187
  overview of, 23
  Piaget's theory compared to, 190
  scaffolding in, 185–186
  teaching strategies based on,
    187–188
  Tools of the Mind curriculum
    and, 189
  zone of proximal development
    in, 185

W

walking, in infants, 143–144, 150–151
waterbirth, 91
Wechsler scales, 232
Wernicke's area, 270
whole-language approach, 265
WIC program, 128
Williams syndrome, 274–275
words, first, 257–258
working memory, 202, 203, 212
working parents, 413
writing development, 265–266, 348

X

X-ray radiation, prenatal exposure
  to, 83
XYY syndrome, 57, 58

Y

yoga, 91

Z

zone of proximal development
  (ZPD), 185, 187
zygote, 55, 75